Cheshire and North's
Private International Law

Cheshire and North's
Private International Law

Twelfth edition

P. M. North CBE, MA, DCL, FBA
*Principal of Jesus College, Oxford; Vice Chancellor Elect, University
of Oxford; Honorary Bencher of the Inner Temple; Honorary Fellow of
Keble College, Oxford and of the University College of North Wales,
Bangor; Associé de l'Institut de Droit International*

and

J. J. Fawcett LLB, PHD
Solicitor, Professor of Law, University of Leicester

Butterworths
London, Dublin, Edinburgh
1992

United Kingdom   Butterworth & Co (Publishers) Ltd, Halsbury House, 35 Chancery Lane, LONDON WC2A 1EL and 4 Hill Street, EDINBURGH EH2 3JZ

Australia   Butterworths, SYDNEY, MELBOURNE, BRISBANE, ADELAIDE, PERTH, CANBERRA and HOBART

Canada   Butterworths Canada Ltd, TORONTO and VANCOUVER

Ireland   Butterworth (Ireland) Ltd, DUBLIN

Malaysia   Malayan Law Journal Sdn Bhd, KUALA LUMPUR

New Zealand   Butterworths of New Zealand Ltd, WELLINGTON and AUCKLAND

Puerto Rico   Butterworth of Puerto Rico, Inc, SAN JUAN

Singapore   Butterworths Asia, SINGAPORE

South Africa   Butterworths Publishers (Pty) Ltd, DURBAN

USA   Butterworth Legal Publishers, CARLSBAD, California and SALEM, New Hampshire

Reprinted 1994

A CIP Catalogue record for this book is available from the British Library

ISBN 0 406 53081 5

Filmset in Times New Roman by
Selwood Systems, Midsomer Norton
Printed and bound in Great Britain by
Redwood Books, Trowbridge, Wiltshire

∞   This text paper meets the requirements of ISO 9706/1994. Information and Documentation — paper for documents — requirements for permanence.

Preface to the twelfth edition

Although this new edition does not witness major structural changes in the book of a kind or extent introduced in the previous edition, the need for substantial rewriting continues unabated. Once more these changes are necessitated by a combination of pressures: judicial activity, academic writing, law reform proposals and legislation, not least that engendered by activity within the European Community.

The work of the Law Commission has necessitated discussion of their Reports on Choice of Law in Torts, on Choice of Law in Marriage and on Domicil. This last is worthy of particular note given the Government's acceptance of its proposals. Law reform activity which has resulted in legislation includes the private international law aspects of the Family Law Reform Act 1987 as well as the Foreign Marriage (Amendment) Act 1988 which statutes have necessitated rewriting in the chapters on Marriage, Declarations, and Legitimacy, Legitimation and Adoption. The most substantial need for rewriting as a result of legislative change is to be found, however, in the Contracts chapter which is essentially a new chapter to take account of the Contracts (Applicable Law) Act 1990 implementing, after a ten-year delay, the 1980 European Community Rome Convention on the law applicable to contractual obligations. Major rewriting is also to be found in the Trusts chapter, recast in the light of the Recognition of Trusts Act 1987 which is the fruit of a Convention (1986) of the Hague Conference on Private International Law. Regard has also to be had to that same body's 1988 Convention on Succession.

Once again, a considerable degree of rewriting is evident in the chapters on the jurisdiction of the courts and the recognition of foreign judgments as a result of a substantial body of case law both from our courts and from the European Court of Justice, as well as that resulting from the activities of legislators within the European Community and elsewhere. So, for example, these chapters are written on the assumption that the amendments to the Brussels Convention on jurisdiction and the enforcement of judgments in civil and commercial matters consequent upon the accession of Spain and Portugal (the San Sebastian Convention) are in force throughout the European Community. The Civil Jurisdiction and Judgments Act 1991 implementing the similar rules, contained in the Lugano Convention, between the European Community and EFTA States has also been brought into force. Other areas where the judicial development and exposition of the law have been seen to be particularly significant are the rules relating to jurisdiction of the courts in matrimonial causes and the rules for the recognition of foreign custody rights and orders under the Child Abduction and Custody Act 1985. Indeed, the domestic jurisdictional rules in this latter field have been altered, most significantly as to terminology, by the Children Act 1989. Despite, however, the recognition of significant judicial law-making both in this country and abroad, the brunt of reform and development has, once more, been borne by legislative activity.

We have relied on the help and guidance of friends and colleagues in preparing this edition and we would like particularly to thank the Attorneys-General of Guernsey and Jersey, Professor David Hayton, Lesley Hitchins, Nicholas Hodgson, Professor Judith Masson, Oliver Parker, Professor Mark Thompson, Professor Dick Webb and Professor Robin White. Our wives have provided us with continued support and encouragement for which we are most grateful.

Our publishers have prepared all the various tables and the index and we thank them for this and for all their other help and co-operation.

We have endeavoured to state the law as on 1 March 1992, though it has been possible to include some more recent material. As mentioned above, we have assumed that the amendments to the Brussels Convention on jurisdiction and the enforcement of judgments brought about by the San Sebastian Convention are in force throughout the European Community. It has been assumed that the Modified Convention contained in Schedule 4 of the Civil Jurisdiction and Judgments Act 1982 has been amended in the light of the San Sebastian and Lugano Conventions.

Oxford   P.M.N.
and Leicester   J.J.F.
15 May 1992

Preface to the first edition

Convention demands that in the preface to a new book the author should excuse his temerity in adding to the literature on the subject and should also state the objects he hopes to attain. My excuse is the fascination, perhaps my readers will say the fatal fascination, of the subject. Of all the departments of English law, Private International Law offers the freest scope to the mere jurist. It is the perfect antithesis of such a topic as real property law. It is not overloaded with detailed rules; it has been only lightly touched by the paralysing hand of the Parliamentary draftsman; it is perhaps the one considerable department in which the formation of a coherent body of law is in course of process; it is, at the moment, fluid not static, elusive not obvious; it repels any tendency to dogmatism; and, above all, the possible permutations of the questions that it raises are so numerous that the diligent investigator can seldom rest content with the solution that he proposes. Despite its value as a subject of academic study it is curiously neglected in the legal education of this country, a fact which is remarkable if regard is had to the number of different legal systems that the British Empire comprises. On the Continent and in the United States of America, Private International Law is one of the major subjects of study at the Universities but in England it cannot claim a professorship of its own and it forms only an insignificant part of the chief law examinations.

The purpose of this book, however, is not merely to indulge my own fancy, but to provide students with a shorter account of the subject than most of those already published. Further, my object has been, not to remain satisfied with mere exposition but to approach the more controversial topics in a spirit of constructive criticism. There are many instances in which I have found it impossible to agree with the views of such great masters as Dicey and Westlake, and in which I have ventured, perhaps rashly, to suggest that the relevant authorities indicate a somewhat different principle, but in all such cases I have been careful to present the reader with what may be called the generally accepted textbook view of each matter. Some of the mild strictures contained in this book may not be well founded, but even so they can do little harm, for there is no doubt that the subject in general sorely needs criticism. It may be doubted, indeed, whether all is well with the English system of Private International Law. Instances are numerous in the last thirty years in which the Courts have adopted some plausible principle, without serious investigation of its merits and without considering what the effect will be if it is applied to a case with slightly different facts. There are other cases in which it is difficult to extract the *ratio decidendi*, or indeed any clear principle, from the judgments. Private International Law, in fact, presents a golden opportunity, perhaps the last opportunity, for the judiciary to show that a homogeneous and scientifically constructed body of law, suitable to the changing needs of society, can be evolved without the aid of the legislature, and, though the task must necessarily be performed by the judges, there seems no reason why the jurist should stand aside in cloistered inactivity.

The book contains no account of the law relating to British nationality. This is a subject which should be dealt with solely in works on Constitutional Law, for it clearly has little, if any, connexion with Private International Law. Whether a person is a national of a particular country is relevant neither to the question of choice of law, nor, it is submitted, for purposes of jurisdiction.

Oxford　　　　　　　　　　　　　　　　　　　　　　　　　　　G.C.C.
1 January 1935

Contents

Selected bibliography

Anton   *Private International Law; A treatise from the standpoint of Scots law*, by A. E. Anton, 2nd ed (1990)

Anton: Jurisdiction   *Civil Jurisdiction in Scotland*, by A. E. Anton (1984)

Audit   *La Fraude à la Loi*, by Bernard Audit (1974)

Batiffol and Lagarde   *Droit International Privé*, by Henri Batiffol and Paul Lagarde, 7th ed (1981–1983)

Beale   *The Conflict of Laws*, by J. H. Beale (1935)

Binchy   *Irish Conflicts of Law*, by William Binchy (1988)

Castel   *Canadian Conflict of Laws*, by J-G. Castel, 2nd ed (1986)

Cavers   *The Choice-of-Law Process*, by D. F. Cavers (1965)

Cavers: Essays   *The Choice of Law: Selected Essays 1933–1983*, by D. F. Cavers (1985)

Collier   *Conflict of Laws*, by J. G. Collier (1987)

Collins   *The Civil Jurisdiction and Judgments Act 1982*, by L. A. Collins (1983)

Cook   *Logical and Legal Bases of the Conflict of Laws*, by W. W. Cook (1942)

Currie   *Selected Essays on the Conflict of Laws*, by Brainerd Currie (1963)

De Boer   *Beyond Lex Loci Delicti*, by Th. M. De Boer (1987)

Dicey and Morris   *The Conflict of Laws*, by Lawrence Collins and others, 11th ed (1987)

Droz   *Compétence Judiciaire et Effects des Jugements dans le Marché Commun*, by George A. L. Droz (1972)

Ehrenzweig   *Private International Law* vols I–III, by A. A. Ehrenzweig and E. Jayme (1967–1977)

Ehrenzweig: Treatise   *A treatise on the Conflict of Laws* by A. A. Ehrenzweig (1962)

Falconbridge   *Essays on the Conflict of Laws*, by J. D. Falconbridge, 2nd ed (1954)

Fletcher   *Conflict of Laws and European Community Law*, by I. F. Fletcher (1982)

Francescakis   *La Théorie du Renvoi*, by Ph. Francescakis (1958)

Graveson   *Conflict of Law: Private International Law*, by R. H. Graveson, 7th ed (1974)

Hancock   *Torts in the Conflict of Laws*, by M. Hancock (1942)

Hartley   *Civil Jurisdiction and Judgments*, by T. C. Hartley (1984)

Jackson   *The 'Conflicts' Process*, by David C. Jackson (1975)

Jaffey   *Introduction to the Conflict of Laws*, by A. J. E. Jaffey (1988)

Kahn-Freund   *The Growth of Internationalism in English Private International Law*, by O. Kahn-Freund (1960)

Kaye   *Civil Jurisdiction and Enforcement of Foreign Judgments*, by Peter Kaye (1987)

Kegel   *Internationales Privatrecht*, by G. Kegel, 6th ed (1987)

Lalive   *The Transfer of Chattels in the Conflict of Laws*, by Pierre A. Lalive (1955)

Lasok and Stone   *Conflict of Laws in the European Community*, by D. Lasok and P. A. Stone (1987)

Leflar   *American Conflicts Law*, by Robert A. Leflar, 4th ed (1986)

Lorenzen   *Selected Articles on the Conflict of Laws*, by Ernest G. Lorenzen (1947)

Mann   *Foreign Affairs in English Courts*, by F. A. Mann (1986)

Mann: Money   *The Legal Aspect of Money*, by F. A. Mann, 5th ed (1992)

McClean   *Recognition of Family Judgments in the Commonwealth*, by J. D. McClean (1983)

McLeod   *The Conflict of Laws*, by James G. McLeod (1983)

Mendelssohn-Bartholdy   *Renvoi in Modern English Law*, by A. Mendelssohn-Bartholdy (1937)

Morris   *The Conflict of Laws*, by J. H. C. Morris, 3rd ed (1984)

Morris: Essays   *Contemporary Problems in the Conflict of Laws*, essays in honour of J. H. C. Morris (1978)

Morris and North   *Cases and Materials on Private International Law*, by J. H. C. Morris and P. M. North (1984)

Morse   *Torts in Private International Law*, by C. G. J. Morse (1978)

North   *The Private International Law of Matrimonial Causes in the British Isles and the Republic of Ireland*, by P. M. North (1977)

North: Contract   *Contract Conflicts*, ed by P. M. North (1982)

Nygh   *Conflict of Laws in Australia*, by P. E. Nygh, 5th ed (1991)

O'Malley and Layton   *European Civil Practice*, by Stephen O'Malley and Alexander Layton (1989)

Palsson   *Marriage and Divorce in Comparative Conflict of Laws*, by Lennart Palsson (1974)

Palsson: Marriage   *Marriage in Comparative Conflict of Laws: Substantive Conditions*, by Lennart Palsson (1981)

Patchett   *Recognition of Commercial Judgments and Awards in the Commonwealth*, by K. W. Patchett (1984)

Plender   *The European Contracts Convention*, by Richard Plender (1992)

Rabel   *The Conflict of Laws: A Comparative Study*, by Ernst Rabel, 2nd ed (1958–1964)

Read   *Recognition and Enforcement of Foreign Judgments*, by H. E. Read (1938)

Reese, Rosenberg and Hay   *Cases and Materials on Conflict of Laws*, by Willis L. M. Reese, Maurice Rosenberg and Peter Hay, 9th ed (1990)

Restatement 2d   *American Law Institute Restatement of the Law 2d: Conflict of Laws* (1971)

Robertson   *Characterization in the Conflict of Laws*, by A. H. Robertson (1940)

Savigny   *A Treatise on the Conflict of Laws*, by Friedrich Carl von Savigny, translated into English by W. Guthrie (all references are to the first edition, published in 1869)

Scoles and Hay   *Conflict of Laws*, by E. F. Scoles and P. Hay (1982)

Shapira   *The Interest Approach to Choice of Law*, by Amos Shapira (1970)

Story   *Commentaries on the Conflict of Laws*, by Joseph Story, 8th ed by G. Melville Bigelow (1883)

Sykes and Pryles   *Australian Private International Law*, by E. I. Sykes and M. C. Pryles, 3rd ed (1991)

Sykes and Pryles: Casebook   *Conflict of Laws Commentary and Materials*, by E. I. Sykes and M. C. Pryles, 3rd ed (1988)

Von Mehren and Trautman   *The Law of Multistate Problems: Cases and Materials on Conflict of Laws*, by A. T. Von Mehren and D. T. Trautman (1965)

Weintraub   *Commentary on the Conflict of Laws*, by Russell J. Weintraub, 3rd ed (1986)

Westlake   *A Treatise on Private International Law*, by John Westlake, 7th ed by Norman Bentwich (1925)

Wolff   *Private International Law*, by M. Wolff, 2nd ed (1950)

Zaphiriou   *The Transfer of Chattels in Private International Law*, by G. A. Zaphiriou (1956)

Table of statutes

References in this table to *Statutes* are to Halsbury's Statutes of England (Fourth Edition) showing the volume and page at which the annotated text of the Act may be found. Page references printed in **bold** type indicate where the section of an Act is set out in part or in full.

Table of cases

Page references printed in **bold** type indicate where the facts of a case are set out.

Decisions of the European Court of Justice are listed both alphabetically and numerically. The numerical Table follows the alphabetical.

PAGE

H

X

Part I

Introduction

SUMMARY

Chapter 1

Definition, nature and scope of private international law

SUMMARY

1. INTRODUCTION

That part of English law known as private international law comes into operation whenever the court is faced with a claim that contains a foreign element. It functions only when this element is present, and its objects are threefold.

First, to prescribe the conditions under which the court is competent to entertain such a claim.

Secondly, to determine for each class of case the particular municipal system of law by reference to which the rights of the parties must be ascertained.

Thirdly, to specify the circumstances in which (a) a foreign judgment can be recognised as decisive of the question in dispute; and (b) the right vested in the judgment creditor by a foreign judgment can be enforced by action in England.

The *raison d'être* of private international law is the existence in the world of a number of separate municipal systems of law—a number of separate legal units—that differ greatly from each other in the rules by which they regulate the various legal relations arising in daily life. The occasions are frequent when the courts in one country must take account of some rule of law that exists in another. A sovereign is supreme within his own territory and, according to the universal maxim of jurisprudence, he has exclusive jurisdiction over everybody and everything within that territory and over every

3

transaction that is there effected. He can, if he chooses, refuse to consider any law but his own. The adoption, however, of this policy of indifference, though common enough in other ages, is impracticable in the modern civilised world, and nations have long found that they cannot, by sheltering behind the principle of territorial sovereignty, afford to disregard foreign rules of law merely because they happen to be at variance with their own territorial or internal system of law. Moreover, as will be shown later, it is no derogation of sovereignty to take account of foreign law.

The recognition of a foreign law in a case containing a foreign element may be necessary for at least two reasons. In the first place, the invariable application of the law of the forum, ie the local law of the place where the court is situated, would often lead to gross injustice. Suppose that a person engaged in English litigation is required to prove that she is the lawful widow of a man who has just died, the marriage having taken place abroad many years ago. The marriage ceremony, though regular according to the law of the place where it was performed, did not perhaps satisfy the formal requirements of English law, but nevertheless to apply the English Marriage Act 1949 to such a union, and thereby to deny that the couple were man and wife, would be nothing but a travesty of justice.

Secondly, if the court is to carry out in a rational manner the policy to which it is now committed—that of entertaining actions in respect of foreign claims—it must in the nature of things take account of the relevant foreign law or laws. A plaintiff, for instance, claims damages for breach of a contract that was made and was to be performed in France. Under the existing practice the court is prepared to create and to enforce in his favour, if he substantiates his case, an English right corresponding as nearly as possible to that which he claims, but obviously neither the nature nor the extent of the relief to which he is rightly entitled, nor, indeed, whether he is entitled to any relief, can be determined if the law of France is disregarded. To consider only English law might well be to reverse the legal obligations of the parties as fixed by the law to which their transaction, both in fact and by intention, was originally subjected. A promise, for instance, made by an Englishman in Italy and to be performed there, if valid and enforceable by Italian law, would not be held void by an English court merely because it was unsupported by consideration.[1]

In justifying this reference to a foreign law, judges and textbook writers have frequently used[2] the term *comity of nations*, "a phrase which is grating to the ear, when it proceeds from a court of justice."[3] The term is, indeed, frequently found in English writings and judgments, but on analysis it will be found to be either meaningless or misleading. The word itself is incompatible with the judicial function, for comity is a matter for sovereigns, not for judges required to decide a case according to the rights of the parties.[4] Again, if the word is given its normal meaning of courtesy it is scarcely consistent with the readiness of English courts to apply enemy law in time

1 *Re Bonacina* [1912] 2 Ch 394; and see now the Contracts (Applicable Law) Act 1990.
2 Eg *Amin Rasheed Shipping Corp v Kuwait Insurance* Co [1984] AC 50 at 65; *Spiliada Maritime Corp v Cansulex Ltd* [1987] AC 460 at 477; *Société Nationale Industrielle Aerospatiale v Lee Kui Jak* [1987] AC 871 at 895.
3 De Nova (1964) 8 Am JLH 136, 141, citing the early American author, Livermore.
4 Nadelmann, *Conflict of Laws: International and Interstate*, p 8; for further discussion see Wolff, pp 14–15; Yntema (1966) 65 Mich LR 1; Kahn-Freund (1974) III Hague Recueil 147, 164.

of war. Moreover, if courtesy formed the basis of private international law a judge might feel compelled to ignore the law of Utopia on proof that Utopian courts apply no law but their own. If, on the other hand, comity means that no foreign law is applicable in England except with the permission of the sovereign, it is nothing more than a truism. The fact is, of course, that the application of a foreign law implies no act of courtesy, no sacrifice of sovereignty. It merely derives from a desire to do justice.

Private international law, then, is that part of law which comes into play when the issue before the court affects some fact, event or transaction that is so closely connected with a foreign system of law as to necessitate recourse to that system. It has, accordingly, been described as meaning "the rules voluntarily chosen by a given State for the decision of cases which have a foreign complexion".[5] The legal systems of the world consist of a variety of territorial systems, each dealing with the same phenomena of life—birth, death, marriage, divorce, bankruptcy, contracts, wills and so on—but in most cases dealing with them differently. The moment that a case is seen to be affected by a foreign element, the court must look beyond its own internal law, lest the relevant rule of the internal system to which the case most appropriately belongs should happen to be in conflict with that of the forum. The forms in which this foreign element may appear are numerous. One of the parties may be foreign by nationality or domicil; a trader may be declared bankrupt in England, having numerous creditors abroad; the action may concern property situated abroad or a disposition made abroad of property situated in England; if the action is on a bill of exchange, the foreign element may consist in the fact that the drawing or acceptance or endorsement was made abroad; a contract may have been made in one country to be performed in another; two persons may resort to the courts of a foreign country where the means of contracting or of dissolving a marriage are more convenient than in the country of their domicil. It is the existence of such foreign elements as these that has caused the courts to frame a number of different *rules for the choice of law* which demonstrate the most appropriate legal system to govern the issue that has arisen.

2. SPACE AND TIME

(a) SPACE

It is frequently stressed that the function of private international law is to indicate the area over which a rule of law extends—that it "deals primarily with the application of laws in space".[6] The essence of this is that a rule of substantive law, eg the English rule that every simple contract must be supported by consideration, is generally expressed in universal terms and seems to have no dimension in space, for according to its wording it applies to all contracts wherever made. But its dimension in space, ie its sphere of authority, is the very thing that is fixed by private international law, for a sovereign is free to provide, if he chooses, that the area over which a rule of substantive law, whether domestic or foreign, is to prevail shall be wider than the territorial jurisdiction in which it originated. If, for instance, an English court decides that the goods situated in England belonging to a man who died intestate and domiciled in France shall be distributed according to the

5 Baty, *Polarized Law*, p 148.
6 Beale, p 1; see especially, Unger (1957) 43 Transactions of the Grotius Society, 87, 94 et seq.

provisions of the Code Napoléon, what it decides in effect is that the rule of
the French internal law relating to intestacy is, in the case of persons domiciled
in France, to be given effect outside the territorial limits of the French law-
maker, provided of course that French laws so permits. In the words of
Savigny:

> It is this diversity of positive laws which makes it necessary to mark off for each,
> in sharp outline, the area of its authority, to fix the limits of different positive laws
> in respect to one another.[7]

This method of expressing the function of the subject does not mean that the
sphere of application of each rule of law is, or can be, determined once and
for all for every situation to which it may be relevant.[8] The area over which
any given rule of law extends will vary with the particular circumstances in
which its operation is under consideration. The English rules governing
contractual capacity will apply to certain transactions effected by domiciled
Englishmen abroad, but not to others.

(b) TIME

There are certain circumstances in which the factor of time as well as that of
space may require consideration.[9] In the dimension of space, for instance,
the rights of a husband and wife to each other's property are usually governed,
in the absence of a marriage settlement, by the law of the domicil. But does
this rule of selection refer to domicil at the time of the marriage or to domicil
as it may change from time to time?[10] Again, whether a will has been effectively
revoked by the execution of a later will or by its destruction is determinable
by the law of the testator's domicil, but if his domicil does not remain
constant this selective rule will produce no decision until it has been decided
whether the reference is to the law of the domicil at the time of the execution
or of the act of destruction, or at the time of the testator's death.[11]

Another type of case in which the factor of time is relevant arises where,
subsequently to the transaction in issue, there has been a change in the foreign
law selected to govern the rights of the parties. Here, it is essential to ascertain
whether the English court must apply the foreign law as it stood at the time
of the transaction or as it now exists after the change.[12] Speaking generally,
the latter is the solution that is preferred by the courts.[13]

A variety of situations in which the factor of time is pertinent will be
considered at later stages in this book.

---

7 *Private International Law*, Guthrie's translation, p 6.
8 Cook, *Logical and Legal Bases of Conflict of Laws*, p 7.
9 On this topic, see, F.A. Mann (1954) 31 BYBIL 317; Grodecki (1959) 35 BYBIL 58; Spiro
   (1960) 9 ICLQ 357; Kahn-Freund (1974) III Hague Receuil 147, 441–446; Fassberg (1990)
   38 ICLQ 956; Grodecki, 3 *International Encyclopedia of Comparative Law*, Chapter 8; Dicey
   and Morris, pp 59–72; Morris, Chapter 32.
10 See infra, pp 869–872.
11 See infra, pp 848–849.
12 See for instance, infra, pp 573–574.
13 *Re Chesterman's Trusts* [1923] 2 Ch 466 at 478.

3. SCOPE OF PRIVATE INTERNATIONAL LAW

Private international law is not a separate branch of law in the same sense as, say, the law of contract or of tort. It is all-pervading.

> It starts up unexpectedly in any court and in the midst of any process. It may be sprung like a mine in a plain common law action, in an administrative proceeding in equity, or in a divorce case, or a bankruptcy case, in a shipping case or a matter of criminal procedure. ... The most trivial action of debt, the most complex case of equitable claims, may be suddenly interrupted by the appearance of a knot to be untied only by Private International Law.[14]

Nevertheless, private international law is a separate and distinct unit in the English legal system just as much as the law of tort or of contract, but it possesses this unity, not because it deals with one particular topic, but because it is always concerned with one or more of three questions, namely:

    (a) Jurisdiction of the English court.
    (b) Recognition and enforcement of foreign judgments.
    (c) The choice of law.

We must be prepared to consider almost every branch of private law, but only in connection with these three matters.

(a) JURISDICTION

The basic rule at common law is that the English court has no jurisdiction to entertain an action *in personam* unless the defendant has been personally served with a writ of summons in England or Wales. This rule, which cannot be satisfied while the defendant is abroad, applies, of course, whether the case has a foreign complexion or not, but there are three reasons which require the question of jurisdiction to be separately treated in a book on private international law. First, there are certain circumstances in which the court is empowered by statute to assume jurisdiction over absent defendants, a power which naturally is of greater significance in foreign than in domestic cases.[15] Secondly, there are certain types of action, such as a petition for divorce, where the mere presence of the defendant in the country does not render the court jurisdictionally competent.[16] Thirdly, there is a separate regime of jurisdictional rules in the case of a defendant domiciled (in a special sense) in a Member State of the European Community.[17]

(b) RECOGNITION

It may be that there has been litigation abroad, but that the defendant has most of his assets in this country. It is then a matter of importance whether English law will give recognition or effect to the judgment from the courts of the foreign country. The basic rule is that, provided the foreign court had jurisdiction to adjudicate on the case, according to principles of English private international law, the English court will recognise the foreign judgment as if it is one of its own and it can be enforced accordingly.[18] Again, our membership of the European Community has led to the introduction of

14 Frederic Harrison, *Jurisprudence and the Conflict of Laws*, pp 101–102.
15 Infra, pp 190 et seq.
16 Infra, pp 630 et seq.
17 See the Civil Jurisdiction and Judgments Act 1982, infra, pp 279 et seq.
18 Infra, pp 345 et seq.

important specific rules for the recognition of judgments from courts of the Member States.[19]

(c) CHOICE OF LAW

If the English court decides that it possesses jurisdiction, then a further question, as to the choice of law, must be considered; ie which system of law, English or foreign, must govern the case?[20] The action before the English court, for instance, may concern a contract made or a tort committed abroad or the validity of a will made by a person who died domiciled abroad. In each case that part of English law which consists of private international law directs what legal system shall apply to the case, ie, to use a convenient expression, what system of internal law shall constitute the applicable law. English private international law, for instance, requires that the movable property of a British subject who dies intestate domiciled in Italy shall be distributed according to Italian law. These rules for the choice of law, then, indicate the particular legal system by reference to which a solution of the dispute must be reached. This does not necessarily mean that only one legal system is applicable, for different aspects of a case may be governed by different laws, as is the case with marriage where formal and essential validity are governed by different laws.[21]

It must be observed that the function of private international law is complete when it has chosen the appropriate system of law. Its rules do not furnish a direct solution of the dispute, and it has been said that this department of law resembles the inquiry office at a railway station where a passenger may learn the platform at which his train starts. If, for instance, the defence to an action for breach of contract made in France is that the formalities required by French law have not been observed, private international law ordains that the formal validity of the contract shall be determined by French law. But it says no more. The relevant French law must then be proved by a witness expert in the subject.

It is generally said that the judge at the forum "applies" or "enforces" the chosen law, or alternatively that the case is "governed" by the foreign law. These expressions are convenient to describe loosely what happens, but they are not accurate. Neither is it strictly accurate to say that the judge enforces not the foreign law, but a right acquired under the foreign law.[22] The only law applied by the judge is the law of the forum, the only rights enforced by him are those created by the law of the forum. But owing to the foreign element in the case the foreign law is a fact that must be taken into consideration, and what the judge attempts to do is to create and to enforce a right as nearly as possible similar to that which would have been created by the foreign court had it been seised of a similar case which was purely domestic in character.[1]

19 Infra, pp 411 et seq.
20 For the view that this question is becoming less significant in comparison with jurisdictional issues, see Briggs (1989) 9 OJLS 251, 252–257; Fawcett [1991] Current Legal Problems 39.
21 Infra, pp 572 et seq.
22 *Re Askew* [1930] 2 Ch 259 at 267.
 1 Infra, pp 30–31, and see Lorenzen (1920) 20 Col LR 247, 259.

4. MEANING OF "FOREIGN LAW"

For the purposes of private international law the expression "foreign system of law" means a distinctive legal system prevailing in a territory other than that in which the court functions. It therefore includes, not merely the law existing in a state under a foreign political sovereignty, but also the law prevailing in a subdivision of the political state of which the forum is part. Thus, for the purpose of private international law and so far as English courts are concerned, the law of Scotland, of the Channel Islands, of Northern Ireland, or of one of the member countries of the Commonwealth or European Community is just as much a foreign law as the law of Japan or Brazil.

5. INTERNATIONAL VARIETY OF PRIVATE INTERNATIONAL LAW RULES

Private international law is not the same in all countries. There is no one system that can claim universal recognition, though there has been a significant movement in recent years towards the harmonisation of private international law rules between groups of countries. This book is concerned solely with the English rules, that is to say, with the rules that guide an English court whenever it is seised of a case that contains some foreign element. A writer on public international law may perhaps claim with some justification that the doctrines which he propounds are entitled to universal recognition. Thus, in theory at any rate, a German and a French jurist should agree as to what constitutes an effective blockade. But the writer on private international law can make no such claim. This branch of law as found, for instance, in Japan shows many striking contrasts with its English counterpart, and though the English and American rules show considerable similarity they are fundamentally different on a number of points. The many questions relating to the personal status of a party depend in England on the law of his domicil, but in France, Italy, Spain and most other Continental European countries on the law of his nationality. Again, the principles applied by various legal systems to divorce jurisdiction may so conflict that the same two persons are deemed married in one jurisdiction but unmarried in another. On the other hand, though Scottish internal law differs substantially from that of England, yet the principles of private international law are so similar in both countries that an English decision is usually, though not invariably, followed in Scotland and vice versa.

6. AVOIDING CONFLICTS

There are two possible ways in which this lack of unanimity among the various systems of private international law may be ameliorated.[2]

---

2 For an excellent account of the various methods of seeking unanimity, and an assessment of their success, see David, 2 *International Encyclopedia of Comparative Law*, Chapter 5.

(a) UNIFICATION OF INTERNAL LAWS

The first is to secure by international conventions the unification of the *internal* laws of the various countries on as many legal topics as possible. When attention is paid to the fundamental and basic differences in principle that distinguish one legal system from another, especially in the common law systems as contrasted with their civil law counterparts, it is obvious that this form of unification holds out no great prospect of success. Nevertheless, a certain amount of progress has been made in the few departments of law where this unity is imperative and possible.

An important example of unification is the Warsaw Convention of 1929 as amended at The Hague, 1955, and supplemented by the Guadalajara Convention, 1961,[3] which makes the international carriage of persons or goods by aircraft for reward subject to uniform rules as regards both jurisdiction and the law to be applied, and provides that any agreement by the parties purporting to alter the rules on these matters shall be null and void. The Convention has been made binding in England by the Carriage by Air Act 1961. Further examples of the unification of internal laws are the Carriage of Goods by Sea Act 1924,[4] the Carriage of Goods by Road Act 1965, the Carriage of Passengers by Road Act 1974, the Merchant Shipping Act 1979 and the International Transport Conventions Act 1983, all of which give effect to conventions made at international conferences. Mention may also be made of the Berne Convention of 1886, since amended several times, by which an international union for the protection of the rights of authors over their literary and artistic works was formed. The Council of the League of Nations entrusted to the Institute for the Unification of Private Laws—UNIDROIT, established by the Italian Government in Rome, the task of indicating the lines along which further unification might be attained.[5] An important result of its labours, in conjunction with those of the Hague Conference,[6] was the conclusion at The Hague in 1964 of a convention which establishes a uniform set of rules on international sales of goods and also on the formation of contracts for such sales. These conventions were accepted by the United Kingdom and incorporated in the Uniform Laws on International Sales Act 1967 which, when its provisions apply, excludes the rules of private international law.[7] There is now a successor to the 1964 convention, the United Nations Convention on Contracts for the International Sale of Goods (1980),[8] prepared under the auspices of another body concerned with the unification of law, the United Nations Committee on International Trade Law—UNCITRAL. The United Kingdom is not yet a party to the 1980 Convention. On a smaller scale, the Scandinavian countries[9] and a number of Latin-American countries[10] have adopted conventions unifying various areas of their laws.

3 This was made part of the law of the United Kingdom by the Carriage by Air (Supplementary Provisions) Act 1962.
4 The Hague Rules which are contained in the Act were amended by a Brussels Protocol of 1968 which is embodied in the Carriage of Goods by Sea Act 1971 which came into force in 1977.
5 See David, op cit, pp 133–141.
6 Infra, p 11.
7 Graveson, Cohn and Graveson, *Uniform Laws on International Sales Act 1967*.
8 See Honnold, *Uniform Law for International Sales Act under the 1980 United Nations Convention* (2nd edn, 1989).
9 David, op cit, pp 181–188.
10 Ibid, pp 148–150; and see Parra–Aranguren (1979) III Hague Recueil 55; Maekelt (1982) IV Hague Recueil 193.

(b) UNIFICATION OF PRIVATE INTERNATIONAL LAW

The second method by which the inconvenience that results from conflicting national rules may be diminished is to unify the rules of private international law, so as to ensure that a case containing a foreign element shall result in the same decision irrespective of the country of its trial.[11] So desirable is it to have a code of private international law common to the civilised world that several attempts have been made in the Hague Conference on Private International Law to reduce the number of topics on which the rules for the choice of law obtaining in different countries are in conflict. Prior to the seventh session in 1951 the sessions were confined to the Continental states of Europe, for, owing to the fundamental differences between the common law and the civil law which forms the basis of most European systems, there seemed little prospect of agreement being reached between the two groups. The British delegates, however, attended the seventh and subsequent sessions, no longer as mere observers but as full members of the conference[12] and they have since been joined by delegations from other common law jurisdictions, including Australia, Canada and the USA.[13]

A step of great significance taken in 1951 was the drafting of a charter designed to place the Hague Conference on a lasting footing by the establishment of a permanent bureau. This charter has been accepted by many countries, including the United Kingdom, and the Bureau, consisting of a Secretary-General and two Assistant Secretaries belonging to different countries, has been set up with its seat at The Hague. Its chief functions are to examine and prepare proposals for the unification of private international law and to keep in touch with the Council of Europe and with governmental and non-governmental organisations, such as the International Law Association.[14] The Bureau works under the general direction of the Standing Government Commission of the Netherlands, which was established by Royal Decree in 1897, with the object of promoting the codification of private international law. Fairly recent English statutes relating to private international law problems which owe their existence, at least in part, to acceptance by the United Kingdom of Hague Conventions,[15] include the Wills Act 1963,[16] the Adoption Act 1968,[17] the Evidence (Proceedings in Other Jurisdictions) Act 1975,[18] the Child Abduction and Custody Act 1985,[19] Part II of the Family Law Act 1986,[20] and the Recognition of Trusts Act 1987.[21]

In addition to the conventions mentioned above, many similar arrangements have been made between individual countries, as for example the bilateral conventions on civil procedure concluded by the United Kingdom

11 Vitta (1969) I Hague Recueil 111–232; van Loon, in *Forty Years On: The Evolution of Postwar Private International Law in Europe* (1990), pp 101–122.
12 Van Hoogstraten (1963) 12 ICLQ 148.
13 Nadelmann (1965) 30 Law & Contemporary Problems 291; Pfund (1985) 19 Int Lawyer 505; Reese (1985) 19 Int Lawyer 881.
14 See Nadelmann (1972) 20 AJCL 323; David, op cit, pp 141–148; Droz (1980) III Hague Recueil 123.
15 See North (1981) 6 Dal LJ 417.
16 Infra, pp 839–843.
17 Substantially replaced by the Adoption Act 1976, infra pp 759 et seq.
18 Infra, p 83.
19 Infra, pp 733–737.
20 Infra, pp 655 et seq.
21 Infra, pp 880 et seq.

with a large number of foreign states. An example of a limited multilateral convention is that concluded in 1969[1] between the Benelux states—Belgium, the Netherlands and Luxembourg—which unified the rules of private international law on the more important matters, such as capacity and status, succession to property on death and the essential validity of contracts.[2]

Finally, the European Community is proving to be a major force not only for the creation of uniform Community law, but also for the unification of private international law between the Member States,[3] and, indeed, a Convention on contractual obligations was agreed in 1980,[4] which has now been implemented here in the Contracts (Applicable Law) Act 1990.[5] There are also directives and regulations containing private international law provisions. Equally importantly, there is now in force between Member States of the European Community a Convention governing jurisdiction and the recognition and enforcement of foreign judgments.[6] A major effect of this is to make judgments given in one Contracting State in the European Community effective and enforceable throughout the other Contracting States. An even broader "full faith and credit" area has been created with the implementation of the Lugano Convention (1988)[7] extending a similar regime to include also the EFTA countries.

7. THE NAME OF THE SUBJECT

Though the matter may seem to be of little importance, a word must be said about the name or title of the subject. No name commands universal approval. The expression "Private International Law", coined by Story in 1834,[8] has been adopted by the earlier English authors, such as Westlake and Foote, and is used in most civil law countries. The chief criticism directed against its use is its tendency to confuse private international law with the law of nations or public international law, as it is usually called. There are obvious differences between the two. The latter primarily governs the relations between sovereign states and it may perhaps be regarded as the common law of mankind in an early state of development;[9] the former is designed to regulate disputes of a private nature, notwithstanding that one of the parties may be a sovereign state.[10] There is, at any rate in theory, one common system of public international law, consisting of the "customary and treaty rules which are considered legally binding by States in their

1 Replacing a convention of 1951 which is summarised by the Dutch delegate, E. M. Meijers (1953) 2 AJCL 1.
2 For discussion of the activities of the Fourth Inter-American Specialised Conference on Private International Law (1989), see Parra-Aranguren, in *Conflicts and Harmonisation* (1990) 155–175.
3 *Harmonisation of Private International Law by the EEC* (ed Lipstein); Fletcher, *Conflict of Laws and European Community Law* (1982); Lasok and Stone, *Conflict of Laws in the European Community* (1987); North, in *Forty Years On: The Evolution of Postwar Private International Law in Europe* (1990), pp 29–48; Duintjer Tebbens, ibid, pp 49–69.
4 See OJ No L 266, 9 October 1980; North, *Contract Conflicts* (1982).
5 Infra, pp 459 et seq.
6 Civil Jurisdiction and Judgments Act 1982, infra pp 279 et seq, 411 et seq.
7 OJ L319, November 25 1988. See the Civil Jurisdiction and Judgments Act 1991, discussed infra, pp 340 et seq, 442 et seq.
8 *Commentaries on the Conflict of Laws* (1st edn), S 9.
9 C. W. Jenks, *The Common Law of Mankind*; Jessup, *Transnational Law*.
10 See, eg *Re Maldonado's Estate* [1954] P 223, [1953] 2 All ER 300; infra, pp 50–52.

intercourse with each other",[11] but, as we have seen, there are as many systems of private international law as there are systems of municipal law. Moreover, as often as not a question of private international law arises between two persons of the same nationality, as, for instance, where the issue is the validity of a divorce between two English persons in a foreign country.

It would, of course, be a fallacy to regard public and private international law as totally unrelated. Some principles of law, such as requirements of natural justice are common to both; some rules of private international law, as for example the traditional common law doctrine of the "proper law" of a contract, have been adopted by a court in the settlement of a dispute between sovereign states, equally, some rules of public international law are applied by a municipal court when hearing a case containing a foreign element.[12]

An equally common title to describe the subject is "The Conflict of Laws", a title generally used in the USA. This is innocuous if it is taken as referring to a difference between the internal laws of two countries on the same matter. When, for instance, a question arises whether the assignment in France of a debt due from a person resident in England ought to be governed by English or by French internal law, it may be said that these two legal systems are in conflict with each other in the sense that they can each put forward claims to govern the validity of the assignment. But the title is misleading if it is used to suggest that two systems of law are struggling to govern a case. If an English court decides that the assignment must be governed by French law, it does not do so because English law has been worsted in a conflict with the law of France, but because it is held by the law of England, albeit another part of the law of England, ie private international law, that in the particular circumstances it is expedient to refer to French law. In fact, the very purpose of private international law is to avoid conflicts of law, and the one case where a genuine conflict arises is where two territorial systems, differing in themselves, both seek to regulate the same matter, as, for example, where the bequest of a Greek citizen dying domiciled in England is governed by the law of his domicil according to the English doctrine, but by the national law according to the Greek view.

The fact is that no title can be found that is accurate and comprehensive,[13] and the two titles "Private International Law" and "The Conflict of Laws" are so well known to, and understood by, lawyers that no possible harm can ensue from the adoption of either of them. It might be argued that the latter title is preferable, because it is a little unrealistic to speak in terms of international law if the facts of the case are concerned with England and some other part of the British Isles. However, the former is the title most widely used throughout the world and, significantly for this country, it is the description used in the European Community and most other international bodies of which the United Kingdom is a member.

11 Oppenheim, *International Law* (1967) 8th edn, Vol I, pp 4–5.
12 Eg the doctrine of sovereign immunity, infra, p 265 et seq. The interaction of public and private international law has been fully canvassed by Wortley (1954) I Hague Recueil 245; Hambro (1962) I Hague Recueil 1–68. See also Vallindas (1959) 8 ICLQ 620–624; Lipstein (1972) I Hague Recueil 104, 167–194; Kahn-Freund (1974) III Hague Recueil 147, 165–196; Lowenfeld (1979) II Hague Recueil 311; Mann, *Foreign Affairs in English Courts* (1986).
13 Other terms which have been used to describe the subject are "International Private Law", "Intermunicipal Law", "Comity", and the "Extra-territorial Recognition of Rights".

Chapter 2

Historical development and current theories

SUMMARY

Although private international law as found in this country is a substantive part of English law and is almost entirely the result of judicial decisions, its growth has been influenced to a considerable extent by the writings of jurists in other countries, and especially by the doctrines that have found acceptance on the Continent. More recent influence is found in the twentieth century analyses, in the United States, of the basis of the subject, of which it has been said that "Nothing like it has been seen in any other country or in any other period of the centuries-long history of our subject."[1] It is difficult to study the subject without at any rate a slight acquaintance with the historical development of the earlier and current trends of thought. It is therefore proposed to start by giving a short sketch of the historical development of this branch of law both generally and in England,[2] before moving on to look briefly at the varied twentieth century approaches to the subject.

---

1 Morris, p 504.
2 The only separate work in English of an historical nature is Sack, *Conflicts of Laws in the*

1. GENERAL HISTORICAL DEVELOPMENT

(a) THE ROMAN EMPIRE

The state of things which necessitates a system of private international law, namely a number of conflicting territorial laws, certainly existed in the Roman Empire, but the texts do not throw a great deal of light on the way in which the law of Rome resolved the conflicts.

The existence of conflicting territorial laws was due to the fact that after the close of the Republic the Empire was broken up into a number of urban communities, each of which had its own magistrates, its own jurisdiction and to a certain extent its own system of internal law. Italy, with the exception of Rome, consisted of a large number of towns, generally called municipia, while the rest of the Empire was divided into separate provinces, the constitutions of which gradually approximated to the municipal system of Italy.[3]

Every inhabitant was necessarily connected either with Rome or with one or more of these urban communities. The bond of connection was either citizenship or domicil. Citizenship resulted from *origo*, adoption, manumission or election, so that it was possible for one person to be a citizen of several urban communities at the same time.[4] A person had his *origo* in the place to which his father, or if he was illegitimate to which his mother, belonged.[5] Domicil meant the relation between a man and that urban community which he had chosen for his permanent abode, and therefore for the centre of his legal relations and his business. It was constituted by residence in a place, accompanied by an intention to make the stay permanent.[6]

Clearly, then, a person could be connected with more than one urban community at the same time, as, for instance, when he was born in one place, adopted in another and domiciled in another. The result in such a case was that he became subject to several jurisdictions, since the rule was that he might be sued before the magistrates of any urban community of which he was a citizen or in which he had his domicil. An action against a man possessing this multiple connection would immediately raise a question of the choice of the applicable law, for though a defendant might be sued in one of several places he obviously could not be subject to different and perhaps contradictory rules of law. It is probable that as a general rule a defendant was subject to his personal law,[7] but the question is—which system of personal law? The law of his *origo* or of his domicil?

Savigny had no hesitation in affirming that when a person had citizenship and domicil in two different places he was subject to the system of law that obtained in the place where he was a citizen and not to the law of his domicil. If he was a citizen of more places than one, the law of the place of his birth applied. If he was a citizen of no place, he was subject to the law of his domicil.[8]

History of the English Law, in *Law: A Century of Progress 1835–1935*, Vol 3, pp 342–454. Beale gives a full and valuable outline of the general history of the subject in *Conflict of Laws*, pp 1881–1975. See also Wolff, pp 19–51; Westlake, pp 1–22; Yntema (1953) 2 AJCL 297; de Nova (1966) II Hague Recueil 441–477; Lipstein (1972) I Hague Recueil 104–166; and see Kegel (1964) II Hague Recueil 103–111; Juenger (1985) IV Hague Recueil 123, 136–169.

3 Savigny, *The Conflict of Laws*, Guthrie's translation, sec 351, p 45.
4 Ibid, pp 46–48.
5 Wolff, p 101.
6 Savigny, op cit, p 54.
7 Westlake, p 11.
8 Savigny, op cit, p 76.

It is clear, however, that all cases where a choice of law issue arose could not be determined by the simple method of applying the personal law of the defendant. If, for instance, the dispute concerned a contract or a disposition of property in which two persons belonging to different provinces were concerned, some other rule must have existed to show what law was applicable. The texts of the *Corpus Juris* are not particularly helpful, but certain isolated rules on the subject can be discovered.[9] For instance, questions concerning contracts appear to have been decided according to the law of the place where the contract was made, and transactions relating to property were governed by the law of the situs.

(b) FALL OF THE ROMAN EMPIRE, SIXTH TO TENTH CENTURIES

After the barbarians overthrew the Roman Empire and settled tribe after tribe in the territories where hitherto Roman law had prevailed, there arose what is called the system of personal laws. There ceased to be a territorial law applicable to all persons living within a certain defined space. Instead, each tribe, Visigoth, Lombard, Burgundian and so on, retained its own tribal law, in much the same way as nowadays Hindus and Muslims in India have their own family and religious laws.[10] There were, of course, exceptions to this system of personal or tribal laws. Criminal law and the canon law were of universal application, and there seem to have been certain matters such as the tutelage of women, dowry and the extent of a husband's authority, that were subject to rules of general application. For the most part, however, it was necessary to discover the racial law of each party to a dispute and then to choose which of these laws was applicable.

It is obvious that under this system questions must frequently have arisen bearing a close analogy to those which nowadays fall within the sphere of private international law, but the manner in which they were resolved cannot now be completely and exactly stated.[11] Certain rules, however, are reasonably clear. Thus the general principle was that the system of law to which the defendant was subject must prevail in every suit. Capacity to contract was governed by the personal law of each party; succession was regulated by the personal law of the deceased; a transfer of property had to comply with the formalities required by the law of the transferor; in an action of tort the law of the wrongdoer prevailed; and marriage was solemnised according to the law of the husband.

(c) THE PERIOD OF TERRITORIALITY, ELEVENTH AND TWELFTH CENTURIES

The state of society in this period was, broadly speaking, the direct antithesis of that which had existed for the previous three or four hundred years, for the system of personal laws, which lasted until about the end of the tenth century, gradually gave way to a system of separate territorial laws. The cause of this change was not the same everywhere.

The cause north of the Alps was the gradual transformation of society into a number of feudal units. Feudalism is the negation of personality. A Frank

9 Coleman Phillipson, *The International Law and Custom of Ancient Greece and Rome*, i, 285 *et seq*; Beale, *Conflict of Laws*, pp 1881–1885.
10 Westlake, p 12; see also Savigny, Vol i, c 3. Cathcart's translation; and see Gibbon, *Decline and Fall of the Roman Empire*, c xxxviii.
11 See *Étude sur le principe de la personnalité des lois depuis les invasions barbares jusqu'au XII*ᵉ *siècle*, by L. Stouff; Gutermann (1961) 7 *New York Law Forum* 131.

or a Burgundian who found himself in the position of vassal to a feudal overlord could not invoke the personal law of his race but would be obliged to recognise that he was merely the man of his lord, and as such subject to the law of his lord. This was essentially territorial, applicable without exception to all persons and to all transactions within the fief. The policy of a feudal superior was rigorously to disregard all laws save his own and to refuse protection to rights that had been acquired under an extraneous legal system. Thus, for instance, strangers were rightless. A person who passed from one fief to another was in danger of losing his property and even his freedom, and, though the treatment that he received varied infinitely in different fiefs, an almost universal burden was that he could not transmit his property on death. In a world which is organised on a feudal basis it is clear that there is no room for what we now know as private international law. That branch of law presupposes inter-state or international relations and the readiness of courts to apply foreign laws when necessary in the interests of justice, but feudalism recognised nothing except the local law of the land. All laws were "real" in the sense that they were effective only within the territory of the legislator.

South of the Alps the substitution of territoriality for personality was due, not to feudalism, but to the growth of the Italian cities. The bond of union between men in Italy came to be neither race nor subjection to a common feudal overlord, but residence in the same city. There gradually emerged a large number of prosperous cities, such as Florence, Bologna, Milan, Pisa and Padua, which had succeeded in winning their independence, and which not only had their own territories but also possessed laws that showed many individual variations from the generally prevailing Roman law. It was this diversity of municipal laws, combined with commerce between city and city, that demanded that some respect be paid to alien laws and that ultimately gave rise to the science of private international law.

(d) THE ERA OF THE STATUTISTS, THIRTEENTH TO EIGHTEENTH CENTURIES

In the thirteenth century the stage on which determined efforts were made to formulate rules for fixing the proper field of law was thus set in Italy. The feudal doctrine of the reality of laws became unworkable in a country like Italy, where commercial intercourse between the inhabitants of the various cities was a matter of daily occurrence. If that doctrine were to prevail, a Florentine who set foot in Bologna would be compelled to recognise the exclusive authority of the Bolognese law, since a contract made, a right acquired, or a judgment delivered in Florence could have no effect in Bologna or in any other city.

The post-glossators

It is to the credit of the jurists of those days that a search for some reasonable principle on which these daily clashes could be composed was seriously instituted. This was the period of the renaissance of Roman law. The Italian universities were frequented by the learned from other parts of Europe and their jurists commanded considerable respect. Already the glossators of the eleventh century had done much for the revival of Roman law by the explanatory notes or *glossae* that they had added to the text of the *Corpus Juris*, but it was the post-glossators or commentators of the thirteenth century, the jurists attached to the law schools of Bologna, Padua, Perugia and Pavia, who made the first serious attempt to apply a scientific mode of reasoning to the reconciliation of conflicting laws. The method of the post-glossators was not merely to add explanatory notes to the text of the *Corpus Juris*, but to write elaborate and reasoned disquisitions on the doctrines that were dealt with in the text. The relevance of the texts is not always apparent. Thus the post-glossators who wrote on what we should now term private international law connected their disquisitions to the first law of the *Corpus Juris*. This was the law *De summa Trinitate et fide Catholica*, by which the Emperors Gratian, Valentinian and Theodosius had sought to compel all Roman citizens to observe the Christian faith. It began as follows:

> Cunctos populos quos clementiae nostrae regit temperamentum in tali volumus religione versari, quam divum Petrum apostolum tradidisse Romanis religio usque adhuc ab ipso insinuata declarat.

There is no obvious connection between an abstruse religious dogma and a solution of the legal problems arising from a variety of laws. Presumably the argument for connecting the two is this: since the enactment *Cunctos populos* is confined in terms to persons subject to the imperial rule and does not extend to other persons, it shows that Roman law, and therefore other laws, have a limited application. Therefore it is appropriate that any discussion as to which law applies to a dispute between two persons subject to different legal systems should be appended to this particular enactment. The fact, of course, as Wolff has said, is that though the Italian jurists broke entirely new ground, "they pretended that they only developed rules latent in the *Corpus Juris*".[12] As an example of the method adopted we may cite the following gloss appended to this law of the Code by Accursius as early as 1228.[13]

> Quod si Bononiensis Mutinae conveniatur non debet indicari secundum statuta Mutinae quibus non subest cum dicat: quos nostrae clementiae regit temperamentum.
>
> If a citizen of Bologna is sued at Modena he ought not to be judged according to the statutes of Modena to which he is not subject, since it says [in the law *Cunctos populos*] "quos nostrae clementiae regit temperamentum".

This gloss of Accursius set the fashion, and thereafter the post-glossators always treated their remarks on private international law as a commentary on the law *Cunctos populos* of the Code.[14] Pre-eminent among these jurists was Bartolus (1314–57), successively professor of law at Bologna, Pisa and Perugia, who may aptly be described as the father of private international law.[15] He was the first man to deal with the subject on principle, and his method was to determine the province of each rule of law. His preoccupation was—"What groups of relationship fall under a given rule of law?"[16]

Statute theory

The post-glossators originated the statute theory which became the centre of interest in this department of law for many succeeding centuries. In the Middle Ages the word "statute" was used to indicate any local law, whether legislative or customary, in an Italian city that was peculiar to the city and

---

12 *Private International Law*, p 26.
13 Pillet, *Manuel de droit international privé*, ii, 338.
14 Weiss, *Manuel de droit international privé* (1920 edn), p 344.
15 See Woolf, *Bartolus of Sassoferrato*; Beale, *Bartolus on the Conflict of Laws*; though see Ehrenzweig (1963) 12 AJCL 384.
16 Wolff, *Private International Law* (2nd edn), p 24.

contrary to the general law prevailing in Italy, ie contrary to the Roman law and to the Lombardic law. In its origin the object of the statute theory was to settle conflicts which arose, first, between the local laws of the numerous cities in Italy and, secondly, between the local laws and what may be called the "common law", ie the legislation that affected all the subjects of the Emperor of Germany and the King of Lombardy.[17]

The post-glossators interpreted each statute in order to ascertain its object and thus to fix its rightful sphere of application. To this end they classified each law according as it concerned a person or a thing, and in the result evolved the following doctrine:

First, all statutes are either real, personal or mixed. A real statute is one whose principal object is to regulate things; a personal statute is one that chiefly concerns persons; while a mixed statute is one that concerns acts, such as the formation of a contract, rather than a person or a thing.[18]

Secondly, these three categories of statute differ in their field of application. Real statutes are essentially territorial. Their application is restricted to the territory of the enacting sovereign.[19] Personal statutes, on the other hand, apply only to persons domiciled within the territorial jurisdiction of the enacting sovereign, but they remain so applicable even within the jurisdiction of another territorial sovereign. A personal statute of Florence overrides a Bolognese personal statute if a Florentine does business in Bologna, provided that the business does not relate to something that falls within the scope of a real or a mixed statute. Mixed statutes apply to all acts done in the country of the enacting sovereign, even though they raise litigation in another country.

At first sight this classification of laws appears to afford a simple and effective solution, but any attempt to discover from the post-glossators what statutes are real and what personal meets with the utmost confusion. The truth is, of course, that the problem is insoluble. Is, for instance, a law which regulates one's capacity to transfer land to be classified as personal because it concerns persons, or as real because it affects land? Some jurists in dealing with the subject of capacity distinguished between favourable and onerous statutes. The incapacity of minority, for instance, which might be regarded as favourable, was to follow the person affected no matter where he went; but a law which made a person incapable of succeeding to property, being onerous, must cease to apply outside the territory of the legislator. Bartolus seems to have made the distinction between real and personal laws turn on the grammatical construction of the enactment. A statute is real if things are mentioned first, eg *Bona decedentium veniant in primogenitum*; personal, if persons occupy the first place, eg *Primogenitus succedat in omnibus rebus.*[20]

---

17 Pillet, *Manuel de droit international privé*, ii, 339.

18 Some jurists defined a mixed statute as one which affected both persons and things.

19 Statutes relating to movables were personal, *mobilia sequuntur personam*; Wolff, p 24.

20 According to Beale, *Conflict of Laws*, pp 1891–1891, this was merely "an unfortunate illustration of a distinction which was one of the most original and ingenious discoveries of the great master; a discovery which his contemporaries could not make, and his successors for 500 years failed to understand. Yet the distinction is a necessary one; a statute might well be interpreted either as determining personal status or as affecting the inheritance of property."

Developments in France

In the sixteenth century the statute theory was carried into France, where it was developed and refined by several jurists, the most notable of whom were Dumoulin (1501–1566), D'Argentré (1519–1590), and Gui Coquille (1523–1603). The political organisation of France rendered a study of private international law imperative. The different provinces, though politically parts of the same country as the States of the USA now are, each had a separate system of law, called *coutume* or custom. These customs varied in each province and therefore, owing to inter-provincial trade, were in constant conflict with each other. The jurists who wrote on the subject used the old term *statuta* to describe the customs.

The French jurists of the sixteenth century elaborated the statute theory and made it applicable to every legal relation. Dumoulin, described by Westlake as "one of the greatest legal geniuses" in the sphere of private international law,[1] was the first exponent of the doctrine that the law to govern a contract is the law intended by the parties,[2] a doctrine that, as we shall see, has been propounded in England for many years. D'Argentré, on the other hand, was essentially territorially-minded. He supported, not the autonomy of the parties, but the autonomy of the provinces.[3] He placed exaggerated emphasis on the real statute, and although he admitted the existence of a third class, the mixed statute, ie one concerning both persons and things, he affirmed that it must be regarded as real. After saying that a law obtaining in the country of the domicil and relating to the condition or quality of a person is a personal statute and must therefore be recognised in other countries (eg a rule which fixes the age of majority), he pointed out that some laws, although their operation appears to be confined to persons, have in reality a close connection with property. He gave as an example a law that permits a child to be legitimated. At first sight the object of this is to confer family rights on the child, but in truth it is something more than a personal law, since it carries the right of succession to the paternal property.

Developments in the Netherlands

In the seventeenth century the Dutch jurists were chiefly responsible for the further development of the statute theory. Their fundamental principle was the exclusive sovereignty of the state. The United Netherlands consisted of a number of provinces, each with its own system of law, so that the same need arose for some body of doctrine that would enable conflicts between opposing laws to be resolved. The chief writers were Burgundus (1586–1649), Rodenburg (1618–1668), Paul Voet (1619–1677), Huber (1636–1694), and John Voet (1647–1714).

Huber deserves particular notice if only for the influence that he has exercised on the development of private international law both in England and in North America.[4] This eminent jurist laid down the following three maxims, from which he considered a sufficiently comprehensive system for the reconciliation of conflicting laws could be evolved.

---

1 7th edn, p 17.
2 Kuhn, *Comparative Commentaries on Private International Law*, pp 9–10; Beale, pp 1894–1895.
3 Kuhn, op cit, p 10. For a fuller account of him see Beale, pp 1895–1898.
4 See Lipstein (1972) I Hague Recueil 97, 121–131.

(a) The laws of a state have absolute force within, but only within, the territorial limits of its sovereignty.
(b) All persons who, whether permanently or temporarily, are found within the territory of a sovereign are deemed to be his subjects and as such are bound by his laws.
(c) By reason of comity, however, every sovereign admits that a law which has already operated in the country of its origin shall retain its force everywhere, provided that this will not prejudice the subjects of the sovereign by whom its recognition is sought.[5]

After pointing out in justification of the third maxim that nothing can be more destructive of international commerce than to neutralise rights validly acquired in one place merely because they are void according to a conflicting law elsewhere, Huber affirms the principle that all acts and transactions validly effected according to the law of a particular place are to be recognised as valid even in a country whose law would regard them as void, but that acts and transactions effected in a place contrary to the local law, being void ab initio, are void everywhere.[6] In other words, although each state is free by virtue of its sovereignty to construct its own system of private international law, it does not in fact act arbitrarily but, on the supposed principle of comity, allows the operation within its own territory of a right that has already been validly acquired within another territorial sovereignty. Comity and the pressure of international commerce require that acts duly performed in one jurisdiction shall be sustained in other jurisdictions.[7] These views of Huber made a deep impression on the earlier common law writers, especially on Dicey who, while rejecting the doctrine of comity, adopted as his general theme the theory of vested or acquired rights.[8]

Its limited importance

In the eighteenth century the statute theory continued to receive attention from the French jurists, some of whom favoured the Dutch doctrine that the application of laws was limited to the territory of the legislator, while others, such as Bouhier (1673–1746), increased the scope of personal statutes and so favoured the extra-territorial operation of laws. It is needless to discuss the theory further. It has played a great part in breaking down the doctrine of territoriality, and it has found disciples even in modern times,[9] but it lacks a scientific basis and affords no solid ground on which a sound and logical system can be erected.

(e) SAVIGNY

The great German jurist, Savigny, made a decisive break with all former approaches to the subject in his book on the Conflict of Laws published in

5 For translations of the title *De Conflictu Legum*, and for accounts of Huber's influence, see Lorenzen, *Selected Articles on the Conflict of Laws*, Chapter 6; Llewelfryn Davies (1937) 18 BYBIL 49.
6 Beale, iii, pp 1903–1904.
7 Yntema (1953) 2 AJCL, 297, 307.
8 Infra, pp 27–30.
9 Eg Vareilles-Sommières, *La Synthèse du droit international privé*. Lipstein (1972) I Hague Recueil 143–144, discusses the "Sociological Neo-Statutists" of the nineteenth and twentieth centuries.

1849,[10] in which he maintained that it was possible to construct a system of private international law common to all civilised nations. Savigny derived little satisfaction from what had already been done. He dismissed the statute theory as being both incomplete and ambiguous and he denied the inference drawn by Huber from territorial sovereignty that a judge must apply his own law exclusively except in the case of rights already vested under some foreign law.

> This principle [he said] leads into a complete circle; for we can only know what are vested rights, if we know beforehand by what local law we are to decide as to their complete acquisition.[11]

Savigny advocated a more scientific method. The problem, in his view, is not to classify laws according to their object, but to discover for every legal relation that local law to which in its proper nature it belongs. Each legal relation has its natural seat in a particular local law, and it is that law which must be applied when it differs from the law of the forum.[12] The principal determinants of this natural seat are:

> The domicil of a person affected by the legal relation.
> The place where a thing, which is the object of a legal relation, is situated.
> The place where a juridical act is done.
> The place where a tribunal sits.[13]

The search for the appropriate local law must, however, be influenced by the free will of the person interested, for in some cases, such as obligations, a party may freely submit himself to the authority of a particular legal system, while in others his submission results from his voluntary acquisition of a right. If, for example, he acquires land in a foreign country, an act which he is free to do or not to do, he must be taken to have accepted the authority of the law of the situs.[14]

The criticism that has been levelled against Savigny's theory in modern times is that it assumes the uniformity of legal relations in all systems of law.[15] This, as we shall see,[16] is a false assumption. A person, for instance, who breaks a promise to marry another, commits a breach of contract according to some legal systems, but a tort according to some and no wrong according to others. If, therefore, the same set of facts may create a contractual, delictual or no legal relationship according to the system of law to which reference is made it is scarcely possible to determine the one natural seat of any resulting legal relation. Perhaps a more apposite criticism in English eyes is that the system of private international law envisaged by Savigny is a will-o'-the-wisp, a goal easier longed for than found. Just as 500 years of argument produced no agreement on what statutes were real and what personal, so now there are wide differences of opinion as to the most appropriate law to govern each legal relation. These juristic approaches to

10 This was the final volume of his *System of Modern Roman Law*. It was translated into English by William Guthrie in 1869, and it is this translation that will be referred to in the following pages. For discussions of Savigny's views, see De Nova (1966) II Hague Recueil 456–464; Lipstein (1972) I Hague Recueil 131–135.
11 Savigny, Guthrie's translation, pp 102–103.
12 Savigny, op cit, p 89.
13 Ibid, p 96.
14 Ibid, pp 89–90.
15 Yntema (1953) 2 AJCL 297, 312.
16 Infra, pp 43 et seq.

the subject are, in fact, incomprehensible to an English lawyer, or at any rate alien to his upbringing and traditions.

Nevertheless, although it is true that the basis of the common law is not logic but experience, it is submitted that the method adopted in practice by English courts corresponds in general with that suggested by Savigny. In the light of all the relevant circumstances, they attempt to decide each case according to the legal system to which it seems most naturally to belong.[17]

2. DEVELOPMENT OF ENGLISH PRIVATE INTERNATIONAL LAW

(a) EARLY HISTORY

When the mind dwells on the vigour and the duration of the Continental discussions, it is at first sight surprising to learn that English lawyers did not find it necessary to deal with choice of law problems until a couple of centuries ago. Yet such is the case. There was not even an awareness of the problem in this country until the eighteenth century; it was not mentioned by Blackstone, and the middle of the nineteenth century had been reached before a connected treatise on private international law was written by an Englishman.[18] Professor Sack has rendered a valuable service in tracing this tardiness of development to the special features of the common law and to the English system of administration of justice.[19] His explanation in brief is as follows.

The intra-national conflicts, that had long been inevitable on the Continent owing to the existence of different legal systems within the territory of a single nation, could not arise in England after the whole country had been brought under the sway of a single common law. International conflicts were precluded by the rule, established at an early date, that the common law courts were unable to entertain foreign causes. This rule was the necessary result of the practice by which the members of the jury were summoned from the place where the operative facts had occurred, since their function was to decide according to their knowledge of the facts. The sheriff could scarcely summon a jury from a foreign country in which the dispute between the parties had arisen. It is true that special courts were set up to deal with cases that might contain foreign elements. The King established courts to consider complaints made by foreigners whom he had invited to England and who were therefore entitled to his protection. The staple courts and the pie-powder courts decided mercantile disputes. But in each of these cases the law administered was the law merchant which, at any rate in theory, was regarded as a universally binding system. There was no question of applying a foreign law at variance with the law of England.

When English traders began to extend their commercial activities beyond the seas, it was inevitable that they should occasionally suffer from this inability to obtain redress in respect of transactions effected abroad. A remedy ultimately became available to them in the Court of Admiralty, which extended its jurisdiction to foreign causes as early as the middle of the

---

17 For the view that a *droit international commun* is in course of emergence between certain groups of States, see Goldie (1962) 38 BYBIL 216, 240–254.

18 Westlake, 1858.

19 See Sack, *Conflicts of Laws in the History of English Law*, in *Law: A Century of Progress, 1835–1935* Vol III, pp 342–454; and see Anton (1956) 5 ICLQ 534; Nygh (1961) 1U Tas LR 555; (1964) 2 U Tas LR 28.

fourteenth century. By the middle of the sixteenth century it was competent to try disputes arising out of mercantile dealings abroad.[1] Again, however, there was no question of choice of law, for the court dispensed the general law maritime or, in cases of purely commercial matters, the general law merchant.[2]

By the end of the sixteenth century the common law courts had begun to compete for this jurisdiction. The technical difficulty that formerly stood in their way had disappeared, for the jury relied no longer on its own knowledge but on the testimony of witnesses. The initial step was to deal with "mixed" cases, ie those in which some of the operative facts occurred in England, others abroad, as, for example, where the defendant failed to perform in Spain a charter-party that had been made in England.[3] The final step, that of trying cases connected solely with a foreign country, was facilitated by the new division of actions into local and transitory. In transitory actions, ie where the cause of action might have arisen anywhere, there was no necessity to summon the jury from one particular neighbourhood. The plaintiff could sue the defendant where he was to be found, and could lay the *venue* (ie the place from which the jury was summoned) where he liked. By Coke's time it was settled that the courts at Westminster could entertain all actions that were of a transitory nature, such as actions for breach of contract or on bills of exchange, notwithstanding that the relevant facts were connected with a foreign country.[4]

Thus the stage was reached at which it should have been necessary to deal with the familiar problem of choice of law. But in the case of mercantile disputes, which must have formed the bulk of those brought to court, the problem was avoided for many generations, since they were decided according to the general law merchant common to European nations. By the nineteenth century, when the international nature of this law had ceased and it had been incorporated as one of the municipal branches of English law, the modern doctrines of private international law had already taken root in England.[5] Moreover, although the common law courts had expressed their willingness to take cognisance of foreign law, they were reluctant to entertain actions in which this would be necessary.[6] When the necessity became pressing, their first reaction was to require foreign cases to be tried by the appropriate court abroad, and to accompany this with a readiness to enforce the foreign judgment in England. This recognition of foreign judgments, which dates at least from 1607,[7] has never involved a reference to the foreign municipal law. All the English courts have ever done in this connection is to inquire whether the foreign court had jurisdiction in the international sense and whether its judgment was final.[8]

1 Sack, op cit, pp 353–355.
2 Ibid, p 355.
3 Ibid, pp 359–360.
4 Ibid, pp 370–371.
5 Ibid, pp 375–377.
6 Ibid, p 381.
7 *Wier's Case* (1607) 1 Roll Abr 530 K 12.
8 The cases such as *Penn v Baltimore* (1750) 1 Ves Sen 444, in which equity exercises personal jurisdiction in respect of acts occurring abroad, do not involve the application of foreign law; infra, pp 255–264.

(b) LATER DEVELOPMENT

The growth of the British Empire inevitably led to greater intercourse between British subjects owing obedience to a variety of laws, and consequently to an increase in the number of disputes that required, if justice were to be done, a reference to something more than the common law of England. Yet the emergence of anything approaching a connected system of private international law proved to be a slow and laborious process.

First hesitant steps are to be seen in *Robinson v Bland*[9] in 1790. Here the question whether a contract valid by the law of France where it was made, though void by English law, could be sued on in England was discussed but not decided.

> The plaintiff had lent £300 to X in Paris, which X immediately lost to the plaintiff by gaming, together with an additional £372. X gave the plaintiff a bill of exchange payable in England for the whole amount. It was found that in France "money lost at play between gentlemen may be recovered as a debt of honour before the Marshals of France, who can enforce obedience to their sentences by imprisonment".[10] After the death of X the plaintiff brought assumpsit against his administrator on three counts: on the bill of exchange, for money lent, and for money had and received. It was held that the bill of exchange was void and that no action lay for the recovery of the money won at play. The plaintiff, however, was held entitled to recover on the loan.

The reason for the decision given by two of the three judges was that the laws of France and of England were the same on all these points, and that therefore it was unnecessary to consider which law would apply had there been a difference between them. The judges, however, expressed their opinions on the question. WILMOT J considered it "a great question", but inclined to the belief that a claim contrary to public policy could not be pursued in England. DENISON J felt that English law would govern, since the plaintiff had chosen an English forum. It was left to Lord MANSFIELD to give a more modern flavour to the discussion.

> The general rule, established *ex comitate et jure gentium*, is that the place where the contract is made, and not where the action is brought, is to be considered in expounding and enforcing the contract. But this rule admits of an exception when the parties at the time of making the contract had a view to a different kingdom.[11]

He amplified his remark as to the exception in these words:

> The law of the place can never be the rule, where the transaction is entered into with an express view to the law of another country, as the rule by which it is to be governed.[12]

This was the first mention of the doctrine that the law to govern a contract is the law intended by the parties. But what is noteworthy about the decision is that as late as 1760 the rules on so important a matter were completely unsettled.

In 1775 in *Mostyn v Fabrigas*[13] Lord MANSFIELD also adumbrated part of

---

9 (1760) 1 Wm Bl 234, 2 Burr 1077.
10 WILMOT J described it as "this wild, illegal, fantastical Court of Honour"! 2 Burr at p 1083.
11 1 Wm Bl 234 at 258–259.
12 2 Burr 1077 at 1078.
13 (1774) 1 Cowp 161.

the rule that now governs liability in tort, though it was not finally settled until 1869.[14] He laid down that what was a justification by the law of the place of the tort could be pleaded as a defence to an action in England. Other principles suggested or established in the eighteenth century were that the law of the place of celebration governs the formal validity of a marriage,[15] that movables are subject to the law of the domicil of the owner for the purpose of succession[16] and bankruptcy distribution,[17] and that actions relating to foreign immovables are not sustainable in England.[18] It was not, however, until nearly the close of the century that a clear acknowledgment was made of the duty of English courts to give effect to foreign laws. It was made, once again, by Lord MANSFIELD.

> Every action here must be tried by the law of England, but the law of England says that in a variety of circumstances, with regard to contracts legally made abroad, the laws of the country where the cause of action arose shall govern.[19]

Thus the eighteenth century represents the embryonic period of private international law, a period which extended to at least the middle of the next century. As late as 1825 BEST CJ felt justified in remarking that "these questions of international law do not often occur",[20] and though the era of development was at hand, a considerable time had yet to pass before the main rules were determined. Thus, although rules to govern contracts, torts and legitimation were laid down in 1865, 1869 and 1881 respectively, it was not until 1895 that the dependence of divorce jurisdiction on domicil was established. Such matters as capacity to marry, choice of law in nullity and legitimacy are still unsettled. The formative period is not yet at an end. There are still transactions and events common in daily life that are governed by comparatively ancient decisions, and there are others on which the decisions are so hesitating and vacillating that it is difficult to extract with assurance the governing principle. Moreover, the number of decisions on choice of laws issues is still relatively small[21] in comparison with the case law that surrounds such topics as contracts and torts. Indeed, this general state of the authorities, coupled with the movement in favour of unification by conventions,[22] and the establishment of the Law Commissions,[23] has led in recent years to increasing legislative intervention in the field of private international law.[24]

(c) DOUBTFUL VALUE OF OLD DECISIONS

An important fact, and one that should never be overlooked either by the student or the practitioner, is that many of the older decisions are faulty and dangerous guides, and especially so when the point at issue has been the

14 *Phillips v Eyre* (1870) LR 6 QB 1.
15 *Scrimshire v Scrimshire* (1752) 2 Hag Con 395.
16 *Pipon v Pipon* (1744) Amb 25.
17 *Solomons v Ross* (1764) 1 Hy Bl 131 n.
18 *Shelling v Farmer* (1726) 1 Stra 646.
19 *Holman v Johnson* (1775) 1 Cowp 341. Lord STOWELL spoke to the same effect in *Dalrymple v Dalrymple* (1811) 2 Hag Con 54.
20 *Arnott v Redfern* (1825) 2 C & P 88 at 90.
21 One area where there is a substantial number of reported decisions is that relating to jurisdictional disputes, infra, pp 182 et seq.
22 Supra, pp 10–12; and see particularly the Civil Jurisdiction and Judgments Act 1982; Contracts (Applicable Law) Act 1990; Civil Jurisdiction and Judgments Act 1991.
23 See, eg Domicile and Matrimonial Proceedings Act 1973; Matrimonial and Family Proceedings Act 1984, Part III; Foreign Limitation Periods Act 1984; Family Law Act 1986.
24 See North (1982) 46 RabelsZ 490,500 et seq; Reese (1987) 35 AJCL 395.

subject of more recent adjudication. This is one sphere in which the wisdom of our elders is less sacrosanct than usual. We can affirm without exaggeration that to cite a decision on private international law of 200 years ago is little more helpful than to search for the law of landlord and tenant in the medieval reports of the Common Pleas. In fact we can go further and say that a decision given in the middle of the last century is often suspect. The reason is that the time during which the courts have addressed themselves seriously to the construction of a connected series of principles is all too short for anything like a complete and comprehensive system to have yet emerged, especially when it is remembered that private international law touches every branch of private law. The early judges worked on virgin soil, and their decisions were necessarily hesitating and tentative. Circumstances have necessitated a process of trial and error, and unless it is realised that the early decisions frequently represent the halting steps of pioneers it will be long before this branch of law attains a state of elegant cohesion.

3. MODERN THEORIES AND DEVELOPMENTS[1]

The theoretical interest in and development of private international law did not end with the nineteenth century and more recent developments must now briefly be surveyed. We have seen that the earlier theoretical development of the subject was very much a task undertaken by civil lawyers. In recent years, much of the civil and socialist lawyers' energies in this field has been directed to the formulation of new or replacement Codes,[2] whilst the mantle of theoretical analysis has passed to the common lawyers and, in particular, to theorists in the USA.

(a) THEORY OF ACQUIRED RIGHTS

The theory of vested or acquired rights[3] originated with Huber but it was elaborated earlier this century by common lawyers, by Dicey[4] in England and by Beale[5] in the USA. This theory is based on the principle of territoriality. A judge cannot directly recognise or sanction foreign laws nor can he directly enforce foreign judgments, for it is his own territorial law which must exclusively govern all cases that require his decision. The administration of private international law, however, raises no exception to the principle of territoriality, for what the judge does is to protect rights that have already been acquired by a claimant under a foreign law or a foreign judgment. Extra-

1 The diverse theories are conveniently summarised and analysed by Anton, pp 18–43; Nygh, Chapter 3; Morris, Chapter 34.
2 Samuel (1988) 37 ICLQ 681; Simeonides (1989) 37 AJCL 187 (Switzerland); Palmer (1980) 28 AJCL 197 (Austria); Gabor (1980) 55 Tul LR 63 (Hungary); (1983) 72 Rev. Crit. d. i. p. 141 (Turkey); ibid, p 353 (Yugoslavia); Dickson (1985) 34 ICLQ 231 (Federal Republic of Germany); Sarcevic (1985) 33 AJCL 283 (Yugoslavia); Lisbonne (1986) 75 Rev. Crit. d. i. p 192 (Peru); Bruch (1987) 35 AJCL 255; Simeonides, ibid, 259 (Louisiana), and generally on codification: Jayme (1982) IV Hague Recueil 9, and a symposium in (1990) 38 AJCL 423 et seq.
3 See Morris, pp 507–511; Nygh, pp 18–19.
4 *Conflict of Laws* (5th edn), pp 17, 43; see Nadelmann, *Conflict of Laws: International and Interstate*, pp 14–18; Lipstein [1972B] CLJ 67–71.
5 *Conflict of Laws*, pp 1967–1969.

territorial effect is thus given, not to the foreign law itself, but merely to the rights that it has created.[6]

Support for this theory is claimed from the judgment of Sir William SCOTT in *Dalrymple v Dalrymple*,[7] where the question at issue was whether Miss Gordon was the wife of Mr Dalrymple. Sir William SCOTT said:

> The cause being entertained in an English court it must be adjudicated according to the principles of English law applicable to such a case. But the only principle applicable to such a case by the law of England is that the validity of Miss Gordon's marriage rights must be tried by reference to the law of the country where, if they exist at all, they had their origin.[8]

This theory of acquired rights receives scant support at the present day and it has, indeed, been devastatingly criticised.[9] It no doubt stresses one of the principal objects of private international law, for, as we have already seen, one of the elementary duties of a civilised court is impartially to protect existing rights even though they originated abroad. Nevertheless it must be observed that to protect a right is to give effect to the legal system to which it owes its origin, for a right is not a self-evident fact, but a conclusion of law.[10]

The theory is open to several objections. First, it is advanced in explanation of an imaginary difficulty, namely, that of reconciling the recognition of a foreign law with the general principle that the laws of a sovereign state have force only within its own territorial jurisdiction. But this is to ascribe too narrow a meaning to the expression "territorial law", which is not confined to the positive rules that regulate acts and events occurring within the jurisdiction, but includes also rules for the choice of the applicable law.[11] English choice of law rules are part of the law of England and when a court, for instance, tests the substantial validity of a contract made by two foreigners in Paris by reference to French law, it applies a rule imposed by the English sovereign and it may accurately be described as putting into force part of the territorial law of England.

Secondly, the theory is futile if its supposed objective is to indicate what legal system governs each legal relation. As Savigny has insisted, it begs the question and produces a vicious circle. A judge who is merely directed to protect a foreign acquired right is not far advanced on his journey, for he still needs to identify the particular legal system, out of perhaps several possible choices, which is entitled to determine whether acquisition is complete—a search which is not facilitated by the bald statement that a right once vested is inviolable. Once the appropriate law to govern a case has been determined, the rights that it has vested in the litigant ought certainly to be recognised as far as possible, but that fact can scarcely be called "the foundation of judicial decisions" on private international law.[12] As Cook has

6 Holland, *Jurisprudence* (9th edn), pp 398–399; *Re Askew* [1930] 2 Ch 259 at 267.
7 (1811) 2 Hag Con 54.
8 Ibid, at p 58.
9 P Arminjon (1933) I Hague Recueil 1–105; Cook, *Logical and Legal Bases of the Conflict of Laws*, passim; Carswell (1959) 8 ICLQ 268; Kahn-Freund (1974) III Hague Recueil 147, 464–465.
10 Carswell (1959) 8 ICLQ 268, 285.
11 Arminjon, op cit, p 27; see also Lord MANSFIELD in *Holman v Johnson* (1775) 1 Cowp 341 at 343.
12 Dicey, *Conflict of Laws* (5th edn), p 18.

shown, there are no fundamental and logical principles which infallibly indicate in any given situation what court has jurisdiction and what law is applicable.[13]

Thirdly, the theory is untrue in fact, since the choice of law rules current in much of the common law world can require the enforcement of a right that is unrecognised, or even repudiated, by the chosen law.[14]

A French widow, for instance, claims a share of her husband's English land. This claim raises a question either of succession or of the mutual property rights of husband and wife. If the English judge classifies the issue as one concerned with the mutual property rights of spouses he must enforce whatever right is granted to a widow by that particular part of French law. But if French law would have classified the case as one of succession, it may well be that the English judge will enforce a right that would not have been admitted in France.

The theory as advocated by Beale is open to a difficulty of a different nature. He insisted that the municipal law of the country under which a right has been acquired must be followed *to the exclusion of its choice of law rules*. This no doubt is correct as a general principle;[15] but if so, the result will frequently be that the right enforced by the court of the forum will not correspond with that recognised by the relevant foreign law. The logic of the vested rights theory requires that the court of the forum shall apply, not merely the domestic rules, but also the choice of law rules, of the legal system under which the right is said to have been acquired. If, for instance, an American citizen were to die intestate domiciled in Italy, some American courts would apply the law of his domicil and would grant to the relatives such rights to the movable property of the deceased as would have been granted to them by the relevant provisions of the Italian Civil Code had the deceased been an Italian with no foreign connexions. But Italian private international law, in its insistence that intestacy is governed by the law of the patriality, would deny that the relatives possess any such rights.

Again it was said by Dicey in his lifetime that

the incidents of a right of a type recognised by English law acquired under the law of any civilised country must be determined in accordance with the law under which the right is acquired.[16]

This is not completely true, for the incidents and consequences attached to a foreign right when enforced in England may differ from those recognised in its country of origin. An English court, for instance, may exact maintenance from a husband living in England, although he and his wife are domiciled in a country where no such obligation is recognised.

The theory of vested rights is analytically defective and is inadequate as an explanation of the pattern of rules of private international law. On the other hand it may have performed a useful role in the development of the subject. As has already been pointed out, the theory stresses one of the primary objectives of private international law. It serves to emphasise the need to find solutions with an international flavour. The notion that a foreign right is vested and as such requires respect, although analytically a fiction, tends to induce the correct psychological background for the formulation of

13 *Logical and Legal Bases of the Conflict of Laws*, pp 18–19.
14 Arminjon, op cit, pp 32–33, 47–48.
15 Infra, pp 58–59, 71–72.
16 Dicey, *Conflict of Laws*, (5th edn) p 43, General Principle No V.

choice of law rules. The fiction of vested rights is a fiction inimicable to insular prejudices.

(b) LOCAL LAW THEORY

A second theory is that which is generally called the *local law theory*.[17] This was expounded by Walter Wheeler Cook, who differed from earlier jurists with regard to the value of so-called fundamental principles. His method, congenial to English lawyers, was to derive the governing rules, not from the logical reasoning of philosophers and jurists, but by observing what the courts have actually done in dealing with cases involving private international law issues. He stressed that what lawyers investigate in practice is how judges have acted in the past, in order that it may be prophesied how they will probably act in the future. A statement of law is "true", not because it conforms to an alleged "inherent principle", but because it represents the past, and therefore the probable future, judicial attitude.

The gist of the local law theory as formulated by Cook is that the court of the forum recognises and enforces a local right, ie one created by its own law. This court applies its own rules to the total exclusion of all foreign rules. But, since it is confronted with a foreign-element case, it does not necessarily apply the rule of the forum that would govern an analogous case purely domestic in character, but, for reasons of social expedience and practical convenience, takes into account the laws of the foreign country in question. It creates its own local right, but fashions it as nearly as possible on the law of the country in which the decisive facts have occurred.

Since the court of the forum adopts the view that the chosen law would have taken not of the actual case, but of an equivalent domestic case, it does not necessarily recognise the right that would have been vested in the plaintiff according to that law. If the court of the chosen law had tried the actual case, it would not have regarded it as a domestic case. Owing to the presence of foreign elements, it would have been guided by its own choice of law rules, and therefore it might well have applied some law other than its own domestic system. Cook sums up the theory in these words:

> The forum, when confronted by a case involving foreign elements, always applies its own law to the case, but in doing so adopts and enforces as its own law a rule of decision identical, or at least highly similar though not identical, in scope with a rule of decision found in the system of law in force in another state or country with which some or all of the foreign elements are connected, the rule so selected being in many groups of cases, and subject to the exceptions to be noted later, the rule of decision which the given foreign state or country would apply, not to the very group of facts now before the court of the forum, but to *a similar but purely domestic group of facts involving for the foreign court no foreign element*. ... The forum thus enforces, not a foreign right, but a right created by its own law.[18]

It is scarcely deniable, however, that this local law theory is little more than what one writer has stigmatised as a sterile truism—sterile because it affords no basis for the systematic development of private international law.[19] To remind an English judge, about to try a case containing a foreign element, that whatever decision he gives he must enforce only the law of the forum is

17   Cook, especially Chapter I; Lorenzen, *Selected Articles on the Conflict of Laws*, I; de Sloovère (1927) 41 HLR 421; Cheatham (1945) 58 HLR 561; Falconbridge (1937) 53 LQR 556; Falconbridge, *Conflict of Laws* (2nd edn), pp 30–37; Morris, pp 511–512; Nygh, pp 19–20.
18   Cook, pp 20–21.
19   Yntema (1953) 2 AJCL 297, 317.

a technical quibble that explains nothing and solves nothing. It provides no guidance whatever as to the limits within which he must have regard to the foreign law. The theory, indeed, marks a retrogression from the more scientific and more satisfying thesis of Savigny.[20]

(c) THE AMERICAN REVOLUTION[1]

The major theoretical developments of private international law over the last few decades have taken place in the USA. Indeed they have been described as a new American revolution.[2] Whilst a variety of new ways of tackling choice of law problems has been put forward in the USA, they tend to have a similar basic characteristic—an analysis of the issues arising in a particular case with a concern to devise the appropriate rule for this more narrowly formulated problem as compared with the far more broadly based conventional choice of law rules. This analysis of issues in individual cases requires the court to examine the particular substantive rules of law in conflict in the case, to identify the policies at issue and to resolve any conflict so identified by choice of law rules appropriate to that narrowly defined conflict.

In order to examine briefly these new developments, we shall have to look first at two general approaches common to most of the "revolutionaries" before looking at the main theoretical approaches put forward.

(i) Two general approaches

Rule selection or jurisdiction selection? English choice of law rules cover a wide variety of matters—such as the rule that the formal validity of a marriage is governed by the law of the place of celebration, that the essential validity of a contract is governed by the law chosen by the parties or (in the absence of choice) by the law of the country with which the contract is most closely connected, or that succession to movables is governed by the law of the testator's domicil. All these rules, however, have one thing in common. They are, in the terminology of the American writers, "jurisdiction-selecting" rules. They require the court to apply the law of the country chosen by the choice of law rule irrespective of the content of the particular rule of law thereby selected. This is to be compared with the technique of "rule-selection" favoured in the USA which emphasises a choice between different substantive rules of law which in turn leads to a balancing of the respective "interests" involved in the application of a particular substantive rule of one legal system rather than a different substantive rule of another legal system.

The choice between a jurisdiction-selecting or a rule-selecting approach has been put thus:

> Should a court in dealing with a claim that a foreign law is applicable to the case before it or to an issue in that case choose between its own and the foreign legal system or, instead, choose between its own rule and the foreign rule?[3]

Rule-selection is preferred by the American writers and in some fields by the courts, but such an approach can take a variety of forms. Before attempting to outline some of these forms, it is necessary to examine a further general

20 Supra, pp 21–23.
1 See De Boer, *Beyond Lex Loci Delicti* (1987).
2 See Kegel (1964) II Hague Recueil 95.
3 Cavers (1970) III Hague Recueil 75, 122.

issue which may eradicate the need for any choice at all, namely the question whether there is a true or false conflict.

True and false conflicts.[4] A jurisdiction-selecting approach to choice of law leads to the application of the rules of law of the chosen jurisdiction irrespective of which of the rules of substantive law of two or more apparently involved legal systems is to be applied. There is a basic assumption here that rules from two or more legal systems do have a claim to be applied. If they do not, and on analysis only one has such a claim, there is no choice to be made. This latter situation has been described as a "false conflict";[5] the former case where more than one set of rules has a legitimate claim to application, thereby necessitating the development of rules for choosing between them, is a "true conflict". There is a third possibility,[6] which has been described as a "no-interest" case,[7] where a conflict of decision may result from the application of the laws of the different states, but where neither state has an interest in its law being applied.[8]

> The classic "no interest" case is one in which the plaintiff's state has a law favourable to the defendant and the defendant's state has a law favourable to the plaintiff. ... The plaintiff's state has no interest in protecting the defendant who comes from another state and the defendant's state has no reason to give the plaintiff more compensation than he would get under the law of his own state.[9]

It will be apparent that in this whole area a two-stage analysis is involved. First, does the case concern a true or a false conflict? This question is to be answered by a proper interpretation of the rules in issue in the light of their respective purposes and the facts of the case.[10] Indeed, it is said that if, after such a test has been applied, a true conflict is seen to exist, the test should be applied more carefully again in the hopes that on truer analysis the conflict will prove to be false and the need for choice of law rules that much the less.[11]

If, despite re-analysis, the choice of law problem still remains in the form of a "true" conflict, the next stage of analysis is reached, ie the selection between the various rules which have a legitimate claim to application. On this, American writers have put forward a variety of rule-selection techniques, which we must now examine.

(ii) Rule-selection techniques

Governmental interest analysis. Currie, described as the father[12] of the governmental interest analysis approach, proposed[13] that the court should examine the policies expressed in the rules of substantive law in apparent conflict and assess the interests of the respective states in having the policies embodied in

---

4 Pryles (1987) 10 Sydney LR 284.
5 This term covers the case where the laws of the two states are the same or would produce the same result, eg *Scheer v Rockne Motors Corpn* 68 F 2d 942 (1934) and where the laws are different but only one has an interest in being applied; eg *Babcock v Jackson* 12 NY 2d 473 (1963), 191 NE 2d 279 (1963); *Williams v Rawlings Truck Line Inc* 357 F 2d 581 (1965).
6 For a range of seven possibilities, see Westen (1967) 55 Calif LR 74.
7 Eg Currie, *Selected Essays on the Conflict of Laws* (1963) pp 152–156.
8 *Hurtado v Superior Court* 522 P 2d 666 (1974).
9 Weintraub (1977) 41 Law & Contemporary Problems 146, 153.
10 Cavers (1970) III Hague Recueil 75, 129.
11 Currie (1963) 63 Col LR 1233, 1241–1242.
12 *Bernhard v Harrah's Club* 546 P 2d 719 at 722 (1976).
13 Currie, *Selected Essays on the Conflict of Laws* (1963) especially Chapters 4 and 12; (1963) 63 Col LR 1233.

their rules applied in a fact situation not restricted to the one state. If, on careful assessment, the rules, policies and interests are found to be in conflict, a "true" conflict, then the law of the forum is to be applied. This is so notwithstanding the fact that the other state has an interest in the application of its own contrary policy.

The main role of interest analysis is to determine whether the conflict is true or false and application of the law of the forum, without more, to a true conflict is, in truth, an abandonment of the internationalism of private international law. Furthermore, the technique of interest analysis, particularly in a country like England where choice of law problems are more likely to be international than inter-state,[14] suffers from major defects.[15] The weighing of interests is limited to the identification of whether the conflict is true or false; it plays no part at the crucial stage of determining the applicable law. The latter is as important as the former. Furthermore, any weighing of interests is limited to state interests. This may be thought legitimate in the field of public international law; but in the context of private international law, the court should seek "conflicts justice"[16] and this requires due regard to be paid to the interests of the parties in the individual case.

Another disadvantage of governmental interest analysis is that it assumes a willingness and ability on the part of judges to identify and to evaluate the policies and interests expressed in the substantive laws under review. There are real difficulties here. How is the court to determine the policy underpinning a statutory rule;[17] and is the policy evident at the time the statute was passed still one that justifies its retention? There are similar problems caused by the passage of time in relation to judge-made law and the policies justifying the rule may never have been articulated clearly. The problems are compounded when the policy assessment has to be made in relation to the law of a foreign country whose legal system and law-making processes are very different from ours.[18] It is no answer to these difficulties to say that American courts have, mainly in the areas of tort and contract, applied interest analysis for three decades or so. Most of the relevant cases have involved inter-state rather than international conflicts[19] and, more often than not, no real attempt has been made to discover the policy basis of the rules in conflict. There tends to be merely a statement, without evidence, as to what the policies of the rules must be—very much a forum oriented assessment.

There are further difficulties with this approach. Not only is it inherently uncertain, it normally requires a judicial determination of where the balance of interests lies. This inhibits lawyers from giving advice and it suggests (as has proved to be the case) that the approach may best be used in cases such as torts where "the function of the law is substantially pathological and the view of the court is essentially retrospective".[20] It has been little used in family law and in property matters where the law's function may more often be

14 See Shapira, *The Interest Approach to Choice of Law* (1970), pp 34–44.
15 For criticism of Currie's views, see Kegel (1964) II Hague Recueil 95, 180–207; Reese (1965) 16 UTLJ 228; Shapira, op cit, pp 175–185; Cavers (1970) III Hague Recueil 75, 147–148; Kahn-Freund (1974) III Hague Recueil 147, 413–415; Reese (1976) II Hague Recueil 1, 44–62, 181–191; Hancock (1977) 26 ICLQ 799; North (1980) I Hague Recueil 9, 33–38; Juenger (1984) 32 AJCL 1, 25–50; cf Kay (1989) III Hague Recueil 9.
16 Kegel (1964) II Hague Recueil 95, 181–189.
17 See Brilmayer (1980) 78 Mich LR 392.
18 Fawcett (1982) 31 ICLQ 189.
19 See Kegel (1979) 27 AJCL 615.
20 North (1980) I Hague Recueil 9, 37.

prospective, involving advice as to the future. A final disadvantage concerns what Currie has described as "the disinterested third State".[21] This is the case where the interests of three states have to be assessed, where the forum has no interest in its law being applied but where there is a true conflict between the interests of the two other states. The Currie analysis breaks down; there is no merit in applying the law of the forum and no rule for deciding which other law to apply.

Comparative impairment. There is a body of opinion in the USA which, though prepared to go much of the way with Currie's interest analysis and the identification, and thus elimination, of false conflicts, is not willing to accept that the law of the forum automatically be applied in cases of true conflicts. Courts are able to and ought to weigh the conflicting interests. The criterion for such evaluation is suggested as that of "comparative impairment". This approach, first propounded in 1963 by Baxter[1] and since supported by the Supreme Court of California,[2] requires the court to determine which of the conflicting states' interests would be more impaired if its policy were subordinated to the policy of the other state. Though this approach is open to all the objections that may be made against any rule-selection approach, with its underlying premise that the identification of governmental interests or state policies implicit in the conflicting rules is easy to accomplish, it does meet some of the criticisms of Currie's mechanistic forum oriented approach and of his failure to solve the problem of the disinterested third state. The essence of the comparative impairment approach has been summed up thus:

> the comparative impairment approach to the resolution of true conflicts attempts to determine the relative commitment of the respective states to the laws involved. The approach incorporates several factors for consideration: the history and current status of the states' laws: the function and purpose of those laws.[3]

Principles of preference. As long ago as 1933 Cavers advocated[4] the abandonment of a jurisdiction-selecting approach in favour of rule-selection. Later, he developed[5] his choice of law rules as "principles of preference". He and Currie have much in common. They are both supporters of rule-selection: both would utilise this analysis to identify cases of true and false conflict. Resolution of false conflicts is easy—there is no conflict. The parting of the ways comes with true conflicts. Cavers does not accept "Currie's stern rejection of all choice-of-law rules".[6] Instead, he seeks to develop choice of law rules for the resolution of true conflicts. Accepting that the detailed development of rule-selection rules may be a long process, he suggests that the courts should develop broad principles of preference:

> The court is to seek a rule for choice of law or a principle of preference which would either reflect relevant multistate policies or provide the basis for a reasonable

21 (1963) 28 Law and Contemporary Problems 754.
1 (1963) 16 Stan LR 1; and see Horowitz (1974) 21 UCLALR 719, 748–758.
2 *Bernhard v Harrah's Club* 546 P 2d 719 (1976); *Offshore Rental Co Inc v Continental Oil Co* 583 P 2d 721 (1978); and see *Liew v Official Receiver* 685 F 2d 1192 (1982).
3 *Offshore Rental Co Inc v Continental Oil Co*, supra at 727. For criticisms of this approach, see Bradley (1976) 29 Stan LR 127, 146; Weintraub (1977) 41 Law and Contemporary Problems 146, 158; North (1980) I Hague Recueil 9, 38–40; Kay (1980) 68 Calif LR 577.
4 (1933) 47 Harv LR 173.
5 *The Choice-of-law Process* (1965); (1970) III Hague Recueil 75; (1977) 26 ICLQ 703; *The Choice of Law, Selected Essays* (1985).
6 *The Choice-of-law Process* (1965), p 94.

accommodation of the laws' conflicting purposes. A principle of preference would be applicable to all cases having the same general pattern of law and fact and would identify a preferred result on choice-of-law grounds. If the case could not thus be generalised, the court should state the reasons leading it to prefer one result to the other on choice-of-law grounds. In either case it should apply the law leading to the preferred result.[7]

This is the gradualist approach. It involves the introduction of broad principles of preference, worked out by Cavers in some fields, namely torts, contracts and conveyances, but not developed at all in others. The main objective is to do justice between the parties and, from these just principles, it is envisaged that more specific detailed rules will emerge as a result of judicial development.[8]

The main appeal of Cavers' approach is that it attempts a solution to the true conflict, but in the process it attracts all the criticisms of any rule selection approach.[9] It is still necessary to identify and evaluate state policies or interests. Uncertainty and unpredictability remain, even with principles of preference. This is because their evolution is seen in terms of judicial development and choice of law rules based on principles of such detail as is necessary to accommodate so many varied policies will take a very long time to develop. This may be easier in a federal state, as Cavers himself admits,[10] than with the type of international conflicts with which English courts tend to be faced.

Interpretation of forum policy. Criticism of both the traditional jurisdiction selecting approaches and more recent governmental interests analysis is found in the writings of Ehrenzweig.[11] In his view, a court, in searching for the appropriate choice of law rule, should give pre-eminence to the law of the forum—an approach described as "interpretation of forum policy".[12] He maintained that, in practice, the courts have applied the law of the forum as the general rule, and suggested that foreign law was not to be regarded as "applicable" to govern a case, merely that it should be "tolerated".[13] Reference to a foreign law was only to be made in exceptional circumstances where application of the law of the forum would be unfair to the parties or contrary to their intentions. Application of the law of the forum has the obvious advantages for all concerned in litigation that it is easy and cheap to apply; but it depends on knowing what the forum is going to be. Ehrenzweig's approach is a recipe for "forum-shopping", for the plaintiff seeking to sue in the country with the law most favourable to him. It is hardly satisfactory that the merits of his approach to choice of law issues depend on the availability of controls over jurisdictional rules. Furthermore, a forum oriented approach cannot provide choice of law decisions in the absence of litigation.[14]

7 Ibid, p 64.
8 The courts have, in some cases, attempted to develop such detailed rules; see *Neumeier v Kuehner* 286 NE 2d 454 (1972); *First National Bank in Fort Collins v Rostek* 514 P 2d 314 (1973); *Bader v Purdom* 841 F 2d 38 (1988).
9 For criticisms, see de Nova (1966) II Hague Recueil 597–603; Lipstein (1972) I Hague Recueil 157–161.
10 (1933) 47 Harv LR 173, 203.
11 *A Treatise on the Conflict of Laws* (1962); *Private International Law*, Vols I–III (1967–1977); (1960) 58 Mich LR 637; (1961) 49 Cal LR 240; (1968) II Hague Recueil 178.
12 Cavers (1970) III Hague Recueil 75, 150.
13 *A Treatise on the Conflict of Laws* (1962), p 311.
14 For other criticisms, see Shapira, *The Interest Approach to Choice of Law* (1970), pp 205–208; Kegel (1964) II Hague Recueil 95, 224–236; Lipstein (1972) I Hague Recueil 144–147.

Choice of law factors. There are two, fairly similar, American approaches to choice of law problems under which the applicable law is determined by reference to a variety of choice of law factors. The first of these is the American Law Institute's Restatement of the Conflict of Laws, Second, which adopts as its basic criterion for choice of law the application of the law of the state which has the most significant relationship to the particular issue under principles laid down in para 6 of the Restatement. This requires the court to follow a statutory directive of its own state on choice of law but, in the absence of such a directive, the factors relevant to the choice of the applicable law include:

    (a) the needs of the interstate and international systems.
    (b) the relevant policies of the forum.
    (c) the relevant policies of other interested states and the relative interests of those states in the determination of the particular issue.
    (d) the protection of justified expectations.
    (e) the basic policies underlying the particular field of law.
    (f) certainty, predictability and uniformity of result, and
    (g) ease in the determination and application of the law to be applied.

The most significant relationship test, with these choice influencing factors, is applied to a whole variety of conflicts issues, ranging from contract and tort to marriage and property.

Reese, the Reporter of the Second Restatement and architect of this approach,[15] would describe the test provided in the Restatement as an "approach" to choice of law and not as providing in itself rules for the solution of specific choice of law problems.[16] Nevertheless, it is perceived as a means to the end of development of clear, precise rules:

> I believe that one ultimate goal, be it ever so distant, should be the development of hard-and-fast rules of choice of law. I believe that in many instances these rules should be directed, at least initially, at a particular issue. And I believe that in the development of these rules consideration should be given to the basic objectives of choice of law, to the relevant local law rules of the potentially interested states and, of course, to the contacts of the parties and of the occurrence with these states.[17]

The attraction of this approach is that, in reality, it attempts to have the best of all worlds. It provides specific choice of law rules, unlike the forum oriented approach of Currie and Ehrenzweig. It does not require an analysis into true and false conflicts with its difficulties of determining in detail the interests of the states whose laws are competing, or the policies underlying the creation or retention of such rules; yet it provides some consolation, in the reference to "the relevant policies of other interested states and the relative interests of those states in the determination of the particular issue", to those who are supporters of interest analysis. It acknowledges the desirability of certainty and ease of application of the law, surely very necessary elements in the formulation of new rules of law. It requires a new look at the old choice of law rules, and encourages that new look to be issue-oriented rather than aimed at whole areas of the law such as "contract", "tort" or "marriage". Indeed, it is both jurisdiction-selecting and rule-selecting at the same time.[18] The purpose of indicating that regard should be had to the policies of

15 Cheetham and Reese (1952) 52 Col LR 959.
16 Reese (1976) II Hague Recueil 1, 44–65.
17 Ibid, p 180.
18 See Shapira, *The Interest Approach to Choice of Law* (1970), p 214.

the interested states and their relative interests in the determination of the particular issue must be in order to aid the selection of the more appropriately applicable rule—a form of interest analysis or rule-selection. In giving consideration, as Reese does in the passage just quoted, to the contacts of the parties and of the occurrence with the interested states, Reese relies on a "grouping of contacts" approach which is predominantly jurisdiction selecting.

Although the Restatement Second has had a significant impact on the decision of tort cases in the USA involving choice of law issues,[19] it does not escape criticisms, which are of two main kinds. The first is that "the factors often point in different directions and carry in themselves no measure of their significance".[20] You cannot point in rule selection and jurisdiction selection directions at one and the same time. Secondly, it is hard to be certain as to the purpose of the Restatement's choice influencing factors. They read like an exhortation to a law reformer, as criteria to be weighed in formulating new rules. Their effectiveness depends both on litigation and on judicial creativity, on a willingness of judges to cast aside old rules in a search for better ones, despite any uncertainty that may bring. It is not surprising that their main impact has been in the field of choice of law in tort, where the role of the law is far more retrospective than prospective.

The second approach involving choice of law factors is that of Leflar who has advocated that courts resolve choice of law issues by reference to five "choice-influencing considerations". In no particular order of priority, he lists them[1] as:

(A) Predictability of result;
(B) Maintenance of interstate and international order;
(C) Simplification of the judicial task;
(D) Advancement of the forum's governmental interests;
(E) Application of the better rule of law.

All but the last of these essentially mirror factors to be found in the list in the Restatement Second. They have the same attractions and are subject to the same criticisms; but the fifth factor, that of "the better rule of law," calls for separate comment. It is a factor which has proved attractive to the judiciary, though one which is more likely to lead to a court concluding that its own, the forum's, rule of law is the better rule.[2] Nevertheless, it is a dangerous factor to use in the choice of law process because it confuses the issue of the reform of the substantive law of one country with that of choosing the most appropriate law to govern a dispute with links with two or more countries. It is certainly not the task of a judge in one country to try to reform the law in another.[3]

Impact of the revolution. Whilst the direct influence of these American developments of private international law theory is essentially limited to

---

19 Eg *Babcock v Jackson* 191 NE 2d 279 (1963); *Pancotto v Sociedade de Safaris de Mocambique SARL* 422 F Supp 405 (1976).
20 Cavers (1970) III Hague Recueil 75, 145.
1 Leflar, *American Conflicts Law* (1986) 4th edn, pp 277–279. For an assessment of Leflar's work, see the symposium in (1980) 34 Ark LR 199.
2 Eg *Clark v Clark* 222 A 2d 205 (1966); *Turcotte v Ford Motor Co* 494 F 2d 173 (1974); *Wille v Farm Bureau Mutual Insurance Co* 432 NW 2d 784 (1988); cf *Boucher v Boucher* 553 A 2d 313 (1988).
3 Cavers (1971) 49 Texas LR 211, 215; but contrast Juenger (1985) IV Hague Recueil 123, 253–318.

the USA,[4] writers from, for example, France,[5] Italy[6] and Germany[7] have welcomed the developments as, at least, providing an impetus for reappraisal of the civil lawyer's[8] approach to choice of law problems. At the same time, however, the voices of American critics[9] of interest analysis and the like are growing ever stronger, concerned with many of the criticisms of the "revolution" which have been mentioned earlier. Few, however, are as robust as this:

> Conflicts of law has become a veritable playpen for judicial policymakers. . . . [The] courts are saddled with a cumbersome and unwieldy body of conflicts law that creates confusion, uncertainty and inconsistency, as well as complication of the judicial task. The approach has been like that of the misguided physician who treated a case of dandruff with nitric acid, only to discover that the malady would have been remedied with medicated shampoo. Neither the doctor nor the patient need have lost his head.[10]

In truth, the impact of the new ideas has been limited. Whilst its effects on choice of law have been substantial in the area of tort law,[11] and have been significant in the context of contract rules, interest analysis and its progeny have been little discussed in the context of family law[12] or property matters and have had little impact on judicial decisions in those fields.

(d)   THE ENGLISH APPROACH[13]

What, in the light of the theories and approaches discussed above, is the theoretical or doctrinal basis of English private international law? In considering its nature do we find ourselves perplexed by the enigma that apparently it subordinates the sovereignty of the law of the forum to that of a foreign power? To answer this last question first, the position surely is that for the forum of its own volition to give effect to a foreign law or to enforce a right that is the creature of that law involves no abdication of sovereignty. To describe a foreign right as vested may perhaps be misleading in so far as it implies that it *cannot* be disregarded. For this danger to be dispelled, however, it is only necessary to realise that the forum's recognition of the

---

4 Though some direct influence in England can be seen on our choice of law rules in tort in
  Boys v Chaplin [1971] AC 356, infra, pp 534–536. For a survey of the different approaches
  taken throughout the USA, see Smith (1987) 38 Hastings LJ 1941.
5 Audit (1979) 27 AJCL 589.
6 Vitta (1982) 30 AJCL 1.
7 Kegel (1979) 27 AJCL 618.
8 See further the symposium papers collected in (1982) 30 AJCL 1–146; Jayme, in *Forty Years
  On: The Evolution of Postwar Private International Law in Europe* (1990) pp 15–27.
9 Eg Juenger (1984) 32 AJCL 1; (1985) 46 Ohio State LJ 509; (1985) IV Hague Recueil 123,
  227–252; (1988) 21 UC Davis LR 515; Rosenberg (1981) 81 Col LR 946; Korn (1983) 83 Col
  LR 772; Brilmayer (1985) 46 Ohio State LJ 459; (1984) 35 Mercer LR 555; (1989) 98 Yale
  LJ 1277; Dane (1987) 96 Yale LJ 1191; and see Baxter (1987) 36 ICLQ 92; cf Weintraub
  (1984) 35 Mercer LR 629; Posnak (1988) 36 AJCL 681; Kay (1989) III Hague Recueil 9.
10 *Paul v National Life* 352 NE 2d 550 at 551, 553 (1986).
11 It is often the case that a court may be influenced by more than one approach, as in *Mitchell
  v Craft* 211 So 2d 509 (1968). For a striking example of a federal court applying a variety of
  approaches to different claims arising from one accident, see *Re Air Crash Disaster Near
  Chicago Illinois on May 25, 1979* 644 F 2d 594 (1981).
12 North (1980) I Hague Recueil 9.
13 The English approach is, through our membership of the European Community, becoming
  an increasingly European approach, seen most clearly in the context of the jurisdiction of
  the courts and recognition of foreign judgments (infra, pp 279 et seq, 411 et seq) and choice
  of law in contract (infra, pp 459 et seq).

foreign right is not based on an admission that it has any force in itself, but on the forum's realisation that its own positive rules of law, though in its view best suited for matters solely connected with its own country, are not always the right and proper rules for the regulation of matters that contain some foreign element. It therefore provides its own special rules for dealing with such cases—rules which specify when its courts shall be competent to try a foreign-element case, and which indicate the particular legal system that shall guide the courts in their exercise of this jurisdiction. These rules are as much part of its own territorial law as those that regulate the conveyance of land in its own country.

But on what principle are the rules constructed? Is there one overriding principle from which they can all be deduced? Must they conform to a single doctrine? Are there certain maxims or axioms by reference to which the correct solution of all the diverse cases that arise in practice can be discovered? Do our difficulties disappear if we are reminded that all laws are personal, or that they are all real, or that every right duly established under the law of a civilised country must in general be sanctioned by an English judge? Clearly, such theoretical analyses are unsupported in English private international law. They are alien to the common law tradition and if offered in argument would be a matter of surprise to an English judge. The instinct of the English lawyer is to test a proposed rule by its practical bearing on normal human activities and expectations. It is by this method that in his opinion the purpose of law, which at bottom is to promote justice and convenience, can best be furthered. He is nothing if not an empiricist and a pragmatist. This is the spirit in which our choice of law rules have been conceived until the stage has been reached at which it is possible to extract a general principle from the existing stream of authority. In so doing, regard will be had to the policy objectives of choice of law rules. This task is undertaken not, as in the USA,[14] to provide individual choice of law solutions for each case that arises, but in order to develop clear rules properly applicable to the generality of cases in a particular field.

There is no sacred principle that pervades all decisions, but when the circumstances indicate that the internal law of a foreign country will provide a solution more just, more convenient and more in accord with the expectations of the parties than the internal law of England, the English judge does not hesitate to give effect to the foreign rules. What particular foreign law shall be chosen depends on different considerations in each legal category. Neither justice nor convenience is promoted by rigid adherence to any one principle; it is preferable that the various principles should fit the needs of the different legal relations, and should harmonise with the social, legal and economic traditions of England. Thus, for instance, the law to govern capacity will vary according as the matter under consideration is a commercial contract, a contract of marriage or a disposition of property. Again, the law to govern the essential validity of a contract is, in the absence of choice, the law of the country with which the contract is most closely connected, but the ascertainment of this will necessitate the consideration of a variety of presumptions and other factors, such as the residence or place of central administration of the parties, the situs of any immovable property involved, the place of performance and the legal form of any contractual documents. The presumptions are rebuttable and weight is given to all the factors. None

14 Supra, pp 31–38.

is exclusive. Private international law is no more an exact science than is any other part of the law of England; it is not scientifically founded on the reasoning of jurists, but it is beaten out on the anvil of experience.

Part II

Preliminary topics

SUMMARY

Chapter 3

Classification[1]

SUMMARY

	PAGE
1 Introduction	43
2 Classification of the cause of action	44
(a) Meaning of classification	44
(b) Difficulties	44
(c) Basis on which classification is made	45
3 Classification of a rule of law	47
(a) The problem described	47
(b) Basis on which classification is made	47
(i) Classification of an English rule	47
(ii) Classification of a foreign rule	49

1. INTRODUCTION

In a case containing a foreign element, the English court will have to examine various matters in sequence. First, it will have to be determined that the English court has jurisdiction both over the parties and the cause of action. The detailed rules on jurisdiction are discussed later.[2] Then, having satisfied itself that it possesses jurisdiction, the court must next determine the juridical nature of the question that requires decision. Is it, for instance, a question of breach of contract or the commission of a tort? Until this is determined, it is obviously impossible to apply the appropriate rule for the choice of law and thus to ascertain the applicable law. This is the first issue of classification to be discussed in this chapter—classification of the cause of action. The court, having done this, must next select the legal system that governs the matter. This selection will be conditioned by what has aptly been called a connecting factor,[3] ie some outstanding fact which establishes a natural connection between the factual situation before the court and a particular system of law. The connecting factor varies with the circumstances. If, for

---

1 "An alternative English word for classification is 'characterization'. In French it is called *qualification*. The problems that it raises, since their discovery by Kahn in 1891 and Bartin in 1897, have been widely discussed both in England and abroad. The following are the chief contributions in English: Beckett (1934) 15 BYBIL 46; Robertson, *Characterization in the Conflict of Laws* (1940); Falconbridge, pp 51–123; Cook, pp 211 et seq; Lorenzen (1920) 20 Col LR 247; Unger (1937) 19 Bell Yard 3; Lederman (1951) 29 Can BR 3, 168; Inglis (1958) 74 LQR 493, 503 et seq; Lipstein, [1972B] CLJ 67, 77–83; Ehrenzweig, *XXth Century Comparative and Conflicts Law*, pp 395 et seq; Kahn-Freund (1974) III Hague Recueil 147, 367 et seq; Dine [1983] Jur Rev 73; Jackson, *The "Conflicts" Process*, Chapters 5 & 6; Levontin, *Choice of Law and Conflict of Laws*, Chapter 5; Anton, pp 65–75; Wolff, pp 146–167; Morris, pp 481–488; Dicey & Morris, pp 34–38; Nygh, pp 190–204.

2 Infra, p 179 et seq.

3 Falconbridge (1937) 53 LQR 235, 236, adopted by Robertson, *Characterization in the Conflict of Laws*, p 92.

instance, a British subject dies intestate, domiciled in France, leaving movables in England and land in Scotland, his movables will be distributed according to the law of France because of his domicil in that country; but Scots law, as being the law of the situs, will determine the succession to the land. This raises the second issue of classification to be examined here—classification of a rule of law. This is the identification of the department of law under which a particular legal rule falls, in order to ascertain whether it falls within the department with regard to which the chosen law is paramount.

2. CLASSIFICATION OF THE CAUSE OF ACTION

(a)   MEANING OF CLASSIFICATION

What is meant by the "classification of the cause of action" is the allocation of the question raised by the factual situation before the court to its correct legal category, and its object is to reveal the relevant rule for the choice of law. The rules of any given system of law are arranged under different categories, some being concerned with status, others with succession, procedure, contract, tort and so on, and until a judge, faced with a case involving a foreign element, has determined the particular category into which the question before him falls, he can make no progress, for he will not know what choice of law rule to apply. He must discover the true basis of the plaintiff's claim.[4] He must decide, for instance, whether the question relates to the administration of assets or to succession, for in the case of movables left by a deceased person, the former is governed by the law of the forum, the latter by the law of the domicil. This process of classification, which consciously or unconsciously must always be performed, is usually accomplished automatically and without difficulty. If, for instance, the defendant is sued for the negligent damaging in France of the plaintiff's goods, the factual situation before the court clearly raises a question of tort.

(b)   DIFFICULTIES

Occasionally, however, the matter is far from simple. In the first place, it may be a case near the line in which it is difficult to determine whether the question falls naturally within this or that judicial category. Secondly, it may be a case where English law and the relevant foreign law hold diametrically opposed views on the correct classification. There may, in other words, be a conflict of classification, as, for instance, where the question whether a will is revoked by marriage may be regarded by the forum as a question of matrimonial law, but by the foreign legal system as a testamentary matter.[5]

These two difficulties are well illustrated by the historic *Maltese Marriage Case*,[6] decided by the Court of Appeal at Algiers in 1889, which made the problem of classification a fashionable subject of study.

A husband and wife, who were domiciled in Malta at the time of their marriage, acquired a French domicil. The husband bought land in France. After his death his widow brought an action in France claiming a usufruct

4 *Re Musurus's Estate* [1936] 2 All ER 1666 at 1667.
5 Cf *Re Martin, Loustalan v Loustalan* [1900] P 211.
6 *Anton v Bartolo* Clunet (1891) 1171. For a fuller and more detailed account see Robertson, *Characterization in the Conflict of Laws*, pp 158–62; Beckett (1934), 15 BYBIL 46, 50, note 1; Wolff, p 149.

in one quarter of this land. There was uniformity in the rules for the choice of law of both countries: succession to land was governed by the law of the situs, but matrimonial rights were dependent on the law of the domicil at the time of the marriage.

The first essential, therefore, was to decide whether the facts raised a question of succession to land or of matrimonial rights. At this point, however, a conflict of classification emerged. In the French view the facts raised a question of succession; in the Maltese view a question of matrimonial rights. When a conflict of this nature arises it is apparent that *if a court applies its own rule of classification*, the ultimate decision on the merits will vary with the country in which the action is brought. On this hypothesis, the widow would have failed in France but have succeeded in Malta.[7]

The crucial question, therefore, is—on what principles do English judges classify the cause of action? Or, to put it in another way—according to what system of law must the classification be made? Must it be made according to the internal law of England, on the ground that the internal rules and the rules of private international law in any country are based on the same legal conceptions?[8] It is arguable, for instance, that when English private international law submits intestate succession to movables to the law of the deceased's domicil, the expression "intestate succession" must be given the meaning that it bears in English internal law and not a more extensive meaning than may be attributed to it in the foreign domicil. In opposition to this view, which had wide support, it has been suggested that classification must be based on the "essential general principles of professedly universal application" of analytical jurisprudence and comparative law.[9] But to solve the problem in this scientific manner, desirable though it certainly may be, is scarcely practicable so long as agreement is lacking on general jurisprudential principles.

(c) BASIS ON WHICH CLASSIFICATION IS MADE

There can be little doubt that classification of the cause of action is in practice effected on the basis of the law of the forum; ie an English judge, by an application of the principles of English law, makes his own analysis of the question before him, and after determining its juridical nature in accordance with those principles assigns it to a particular legal category. But, since the classification is required for a case containing a foreign element, it should not necessarily be identical with that which would be appropriate in a purely domestic case. Its object in this context is to serve the purposes of private international law and, since one of the functions of this department of law is to formulate rules applicable to a case that impinges on foreign laws, it is obviously incumbent on the judge to take into account the accepted rules and institutions of foreign legal systems. It follows, therefore, that the judge must not rigidly confine himself to the concepts or categories of English internal law, for if he were to adopt this parochial attitude, he might be compelled to disregard some foreign concept merely because it was unknown to his own law. The concepts of private international law, such as "contract", "tort", "corporation", "bill of exchange",[10] must be given a wide meaning

7 In fact the French court applied the matrimonial law of Malta.
8 Cf Jackson, *The "Conflicts" Process*, pp 72–82.
9 Beckett (1934) 15 BYBIL 46, 59.
10 *G & H Montage GmbH v Irvani* [1990] 1 WLR 667 at 678.

in order to embrace "analogous legal relations of foreign type".[11] In the words of one author:

> The various legal categories, into one of which the judge must decide that the question falls before he can select his conflicts rule, must be wider than the categories of the internal law, because otherwise the judge in a conflicts question will be unable to make provision for any rule or institution of foreign law which does not find its counterpart in his own internal law, and thus one of the reasons for the existence of the science of conflict of laws will be defeated.[12]

Two examples will show that English judges have been prepared to solve the problem of classification in this broad spirit. In *De Nicols v Curlier*:[13]

> A husband and wife, French both by nationality and by domicil, were married in Paris without making an express contract as to their proprietary rights. Their property, both present and future, thus became subject by French law to the system of community of property. The husband died domiciled in England and left a will which disregarded his widow's rights under this French doctrine of community. The widow took proceedings in England to recover her community share.

The rule of English private international law is that the proprietary rights of a spouse to movables are governed primarily by any contract, express or implied, that the parties may have made before marriage. Failing a contract, the rights are determined by the law of the matrimonial domicil of the parties. Thus the problem of classification was whether the right claimed by the widow was to be treated as contractual or testamentary, for only after that had been decided would it be possible to choose between the French law governing the contract and the English law governing testamentary questions. It was clear that in the eyes of English internal law no contract had been made, but the House of Lords held that according to French law a husband and wife are bound by an implied contract to adopt the system of community, despite the absence of an express agreement to that effect. Thus the court, by its readiness to recognise a foreign concept, widened the category of contracts as understood by English internal law.

A second illustration of the international spirit in which English judges fulfil the task of classification is that, when required to determine whether or not the property in dispute is to be regarded as land and thus subject to the law of the situs, they abandon the distinction between realty and personalty in favour of the more universal distinction between movables and immovables.[14] Thus land in England, subject to a trust for sale but not yet sold, is regarded under the domestic doctrine of conversion as already possessing the character of personalty. If, therefore, the owner dies intestate domiciled abroad, it is arguable that he has died entitled not to land, but to pure personalty, and that the relevant intestacy rules are those of the law of his domicil, not of the law of the situs. It is held, however, that his right must be classified as a right to an immovable to be governed by the law of the situs.[15]

There is, however, one type of case in which the English judge will probably not make the classification on the basis of English law as the law of the forum. This is where the only possible applicable law is either the law of

11 Nussbaum (1940) 40 Col LR 1461, 1470.
12 Robertson, op cit, p 33.
13 [1900] AC 21; cf *Tezcan v Tezcan* (1990) 68 DLR (4th) 277.
14 Discussed, infra, pp 780–782.
15 *Re Berchtold* [1923] 1 Ch 192.

country X or the law of country Y and both these laws classify the question in the same manner, though in a manner different from that usual in English law.[16]

3. CLASSIFICATION OF A RULE OF LAW

(a) THE PROBLEM DESCRIBED

Once the main legal category has been determined the next step is to apply the correct choice of law rule in order that the governing law may be ascertained. As we have seen, the correct rule will depend on some connecting factor, such as domicil or the situation of immovables, which relates the question to a definite legal system.

X, for instance, dies intestate domiciled in France, leaving movables in England. Since, therefore, he has been connected by domicil with France, the operative rule for the choice of law is that the question of intestate succession must be governed by French law.

However, at this stage the second process of classification has to be gone through. It may be necessary to identify the legal category into which some particular rule falls, in order to discover whether it falls within a category with regard to which the law selected by our choice of law rules is paramount. That law has a certain sphere of control, ie it governs some, but not all, aspects of the juridical question as classified by the English court in the sense already indicated. Thus, for instance, in an action brought in England for breach of a contract made and performable in France, French law governs matters of formal and essential validity, but all questions of procedure are subject to English law. A French procedural rule is outside the sphere of control of the chosen French law relating to matters of substance. If, therefore, a particular French rule is pleaded and if it is doubtful whether it relates to procedure or to substance, its true nature must obviously be determined. It must be ignored if it is procedural in character, otherwise it must be applied. Likewise, an English domestic rule is excluded if it relates to form or substance, but is applicable if it is procedural in nature.

(b) BASIS ON WHICH CLASSIFICATION IS MADE

The critical and controversial question is the basis on which the classification should be made, and illustrations from the authorities will now be given to show how the English judges have dealt with the matter. It is, however, essential to appreciate that a rule either of the foreign chosen law or of English law itself may require to be classified and that the line of reasoning is not necessarily the same in each of these situations.

(i) Classification of an English rule

Leroux v Brown[17] illustrates the process applied to an English rule.

An oral agreement had been made in France by which the defendant, resident in England, undertook to employ the plaintiff in France for a period longer than a year. The substantive validity of the contract was

---

16 Robertson, op cit, pp 76–78; Lorenzen (1920) 20 Col LR 247, 281; Beckett (1934) 15 BYBIL 46, 62.

17 (1852) 12 CB 801; and see *Mahadervan v Mahadervan* [1964] P 233, [1962] 3 All ER 1108.

governed by French law and by this law the contract was valid as to substance. The defendant pleaded, however, that a claim by the plaintiff to recover damages was unenforceable in England, since the Statute of Frauds provided that "no action shall lie upon a contract not to be performed within the space of one year from the making thereof" unless the agreement or some note or memorandum thereof is in writing signed by the defendant.

This plea required the court to decide whether the statutory rule was of a procedural character.[18] If so it was fatal to the plaintiff, for being a rule of English procedure it was necessarily binding in an English action. Unfortunately, the members of the court took the line of least resistance and, ignoring the larger issues involved, confined their attention to the literal wording of the statute. The reasoning of MAULE J, for instance, lacked nothing in simplicity: the statute provides that no action shall be brought on an agreement not to be performed within a year, unless it is evidenced by a written memorandum; the present agreement is of this nature and there is no memorandum; "the case, therefore, plainly falls within the distinct words of the statute".[19]

The defect of this reasoning lay in basing classification on English internal law instead of on private international law. The court failed to appreciate that the classification of the statutory rule was required for an international case, not for a purely domestic one. The issues are different. The fact that a rule has been classified, or that it ought properly to be classified, in a particular way for a domestic transaction containing no foreign element, does not preclude an entirely different approach when a question of private international law is involved. In this latter type of case, a condition precedent to the classification of an English rule is to ascertain the policy that the rule is designed to serve. Was it, for instance, the policy of the Statute of Frauds that no oral contract of guarantee should be actionable in England, irrespective of the law by which it was governed or of the country in which it was performable? Unless this was clearly the policy of the Act, it was an unfortunate application of mechanical jurisprudence to read the words—*no action shall be brought*—in a rigid and literal sense and thus to deprive the plaintiff of a right recognised as valid and enforceable by the law with which it was alone connected. To do this is to strike at the roots of private international law and to defeat one of its fundamental objects. At the present day, when the principles of this part of the law are more mature and its purpose better understood, it is believed that a court, if required to classify a rule of English law, would have regard to the foreign features of the case and would solve the problem more realistically than the Court of Common Pleas did in *Leroux v Brown*.[20]

---

18 For the present law, see infra, pp 75–77.
19 (1852) 12 CB 801.
20 Cf *Bernkrant v Fowler* 55 Cal 2d 558, 360 P 2d 906 (1961). Among other examples of the classification of an English rule see *Anderson v Equitable Assurance Society of the United States* (1926) 134 LT 557, at 566; *Re Cohn* [1945] Ch 5 (the Law of Property Act 1925, s 184, dealing with commorientes classified as part of the substantive, not procedural, law, infra, p 52); *Re Priest* [1944] Ch 58, [1944] 1 All ER 51 (rule that a gift to an attesting witness to a will renders the gift void goes to essential validity, not to form); *Re Maldonado's Estate* [1954] P 223, [1953] 2 All ER 300, infra, pp 50–51; *Re Fuld's Estate (No 3)* [1968] P 675 at 697–698 (rule as to knowledge and approval in the proof of wills is evidential and thus procedural).

(ii) Classification of a foreign rule

Parental consent to marry The classification of a foreign rule, several examples of which are to be found in the law reports, is best introduced by reference to the controversial decision given by the Court of Appeal in *Ogden v Ogden*.[1]

A domiciled Frenchman, aged nineteen, married a domiciled English-woman in England without first obtaining the consent of his only surviving parent as required by Article 148 of the French code. This article amounted to an express prohibition against the marriage of a minor without consent. The husband obtained an annulment of this marriage in a French court on the ground of want of consent. The wife subsequently went through a ceremony of marriage in England with a domiciled Englishman. In the present action, the latter petitioned for a decree of nullity on the ground that at the time of the ceremony the respondent was still married to the Frenchman.

The factual situation, therefore, raised the question of the validity of the French marriage. There were two connecting factors: the husband was domiciled in France; the marriage was solemnised in England. Guided by these factors, English private international law indicated two rules:

First, the essential validity of the marriage, including the capacity of the husband, must be governed by French law.

Secondly, the formal validity of the marriage ceremony must be tested by English law.

The sphere of control of French law was confined to the essential validity of the union. It followed, therefore, that if the purpose of Article 148 was to incapacitate the husband from matrimony unless he complied with its provisions, it affected the essential validity of any marriage that he might contract and should be granted extraterritorial recognition.

So far all is straightforward. Moreover, there is no difficulty if both English and French law agree on the juridical nature of the consent rule and therefore on its sphere of application. Complications arise, however, when the true nature of the rule is doubtful. The difficulty then is to discover the reasoning by which a solution must be reached. Is, for instance, the French classification to be followed blindly? Again, is the English view of an analogous rule in the internal law of England, presuming that one exists, to be adopted? Neither alternative is satisfactory. The rational method is for the English judge to examine the rule in its foreign setting, in order to ascertain its intended scope, the policy by which it has been dictated and the part that it is designed to play by the French legislature.

Only by this process can full and proper effect be given to the English choice of law rule. French law, having been chosen to govern essential validity, must be allowed within reason to determine which of its domestic rules are essential rather than formal. To take the opposite course and to uphold a marriage essentially void under the personal law of the parties by attributing a merely ceremonial character to a rule regarded as essential by that law would not only be the negation of so-called comity, but would incongruously debilitate the English choice of law rule. The only reservation

1 [1908] P 46.

is that a foreign classification must be repudiated, if to adopt it will contravene the English doctrine of public policy or be repugnant to some fundamental principle of English law.

In *Simonin v Mallac*,[2] decided forty-eight years before *Ogden v Ogden*, the court was confronted with a different French provision that was obviously not intended to affect capacity in the strict sense of the word.

Two domiciled French persons came to this country and went through a ceremony of marriage in the English form, returning to Paris two or three days later. The wife subsequently petitioned the English court for a decree of nullity on the ground of want of parental consent. By French law, the parties were capable of inter-marriage, but they were required to ask advice of their parents, and this request had to be repeated each month for three months if the parents were adverse to the marriage. At the end of the fourth month the marriage might take place despite parental disapproval.

It was clear that absence of the consent required by this rule did not render the parties incapable of inter-marriage. The obtaining of consent was in essence an additional formality and, since the form of the ceremony is a matter solely for the law of the place of celebration, the marriage was rightly adjudged to be valid.[3]

In *Ogden v Ogden*, however, the relevant French rule was to this effect:

The son who has not reached the age of twenty-five cannot contract marriage without the consent of his father and mother.

Although it seems almost unarguable that the object of this provision was to impose a total incapacity on the parties unless they obtained parental consent, the Court of Appeal held the marriage to be valid, since the ceremony had been performed in accordance with the requirements of English law, the law of the place of celebration. The later marriage between the respondent and the Englishman was therefore bigamous. It is submitted that this case was not on the same footing as *Simonin v Mallac*, and that it is opposed to established principles. For the English court to classify the rule as formal was in effect to infringe the principle that the essential validity of a marriage falls to be determined by the law of the domicil.[4] The most unfortunate feature of *Ogden v Ogden* is its suggestion that every rule requiring parental consent to a marriage must be classified as formal.[5]

Bona vacantia An outstanding example of a foreign rule being construed in its context, with a view to deciding whether it fell within the sphere of control of the foreign governing law, is afforded by *Re Maldonado's Estate*,[6] where the facts were these:

A person died intestate domiciled in Spain leaving assets to the extent of some £26,000 in England. By Spanish law those assets passed to the Spanish

2 (1860) 2 Sw & Tr 67.
3 *Infra*, pp 572–573.
4 The Court of Appeal in *Ogden v Ogden* refused to recognise the French annulment of the marriage, with the result that the parties possessed the status of married persons in England, but of unmarried persons in France. Under Part II of the Family Law Act 1986, however, the French decree of nullity would be recognised as valid, *infra*, pp 657 et seq.
5 In *Lodge v Lodge* (1963) 107 Sol Jo 437, Hewson J, after hearing expert evidence, held that a contravention of Art 148 of the French Code rendered the marriage voidable, and he followed *Ogden v Ogden*. The Law Commission has left any reform to judicial development: Law Com No 165 (1987).
6 [1954] P 223, [1953] 2 All ER 300; Lipstein [1954] CLJ 22.

State, since the deceased left no relatives entitled to take them by way of succession.

The English choice of law rule applicable to this factual situation is that intestate succession to movables must be determined according to Spanish law as being the law of the domicil. Therefore, the sphere of control of Spanish law in the instant case was confined to matters of succession, and the problem was whether the Spanish rule under which the assets passed to the State was to be classified as a rule of succession.

At this point it is pertinent to notice that, though the movables of a deceased owner who dies intestate without leaving recognised successors pass to the State in the great majority of countries, yet the capacity in which the State takes is not uniform throughout the world. In some countries, such as Italy and Germany, it has been regarded as an heir taking by way of succession; in others, such as Turkey, Austria and formerly England, the State has been held to act in its capacity as the paramount sovereign authority and confiscates the movables as being bona vacantia, ownerless goods.[7] If, for example, the deceased dies domiciled in Turkey, the Turkish law, since it governs only questions of succession and since it does not regard the State as a successor, has been considered to have no say in the matter and movables found in England pass to the Crown.[8]

The exact words of the Spanish code applicable to the facts of the *Maldonado Case* are "The State shall inherit" movables. Moreover, the expert evidence accepted by the court showed that in the Spanish view this was a true case of taking by way of succession, not a case of seizing ownerless goods. Thus the rule under which movables, failing relatives, pass to the State is classified as a rule of succession in Spain but as a confiscatory rule in England, and the short question was whether in an English action this foreign conception of the relationship between the State and the deceased was to prevail with regard to movables found in England. Could the law of the domicil dictate to the English court what meaning should be attributed to heirship?

It was argued for the Crown that the English rules of private international law are dominant so far as property in England is concerned, and that no one can be described as a "successor" in the eyes of English law unless he has a personal nexus with the deceased, a connection which certainly cannot be claimed by a sovereign State to which the property passes. This argument, however, did not prevail. It was held, both by BARNARD J and by the Court of Appeal, that the Spanish law of the domicil, which admittedly governed all questions of intestate succession, must be allowed to determine the sense and scope of the term "succession". Further, the alleged requirement of a personal nexus between the deceased and the heir was dismissed as a fallacy, for in the words of JENKINS LJ:

> The heir or successor is surely the person, whether related to the deceased or not, who under the relevant law is entitled to inherit or to succeed.[9]

7 See Wolff, p 157. Under s 46(1)(vi) of the Administration of Estates Act 1925 it is arguable that the Crown takes by succession and not by virtue of a prerogative right to ownerless property; *Re Mitchell, Hatton v Jones* [1954] Ch 525, [1954] 2 All ER 246; cf *Re Hanley's Estate* [1942] P 33, [1941] 3 All ER 301; but see Ing, *Bona Vacantia*, pp 57–62.

8 *Re Musurus's Estate* [1936] 2 All ER 1666 (Turkey); *Re Barnett's Trust* [1902] 1 Ch 847 (Austria).

9 [1954] P 223 at 249, [1953] 2 All ER 1579 at 1586.

Finally, there was nothing contrary to public policy or repugnant to English law in allowing a sovereign State to take property in the capacity of an heir.

Other examples In an earlier case, UTHWATT J, when required to decide in a case of commorientes whether the relevant rule of the German law of the domicil was to be applied as affecting substance or rejected as being procedural in nature, followed the same process of construing the rule in its foreign setting and in the result accepted the German classification.[10] In the later case of *Adams v National Bank of Greece and Athens*,[11] DIPLOCK J found it necessary to decide whether a certain Greek decree related to status or to the discharge of contractual liabilities, and he was insistent that for this purpose he was bound "to look at the substance of the law, not merely at its form".[12] There is no need at this stage to discuss other cases in which English courts have classified foreign rules, since examples will appear from time to time in the course of the following pages.[13]

10 *Re Cohn* [1945] Ch 5.
11 [1958] 2 QB 59, [1958] 2 All ER 3.
12 [1958] 2 QB 59 at 75. For the later history of this case, see infra, pp 898–899.
13 *General Steam Navigation Co v Guillou* (1843) 11 M & W 877, infra, p 88 (whether a French rule affected procedure or the substantive law of tort); *Re Doetsch* [1896] 2 Ch 836 and other similar cases, infra, p 88 (whether a rule regulating the order in which parties must be sued affected procedure or substance); *Huntington v Attrill* [1893] AC 150, infra, p 119 (whether a New York statutory rule was penal or remedial); *Re Martin, Loustalan v Loustalan* [1900] P 211, infra, p 850 (whether revocation of a will by marriage was a testamentary or matrimonial question); *Re Wilks* [1935] Ch 645 (whether the time at which shares forming part of an estate must be sold was a question of succession or administration); *Re Korvine's Trusts, Levashoff v Block* [1921] 1 Ch 343 (whether a gift in the event of death is to be classed as a bequest or a gift inter vivos); and see *Metal Industries (Salvage) Ltd v ST Harle (Owners)* 1962 SLT 114.

Chapter 4

The incidental question

SUMMARY

1. WHAT IS AN INCIDENTAL QUESTION?

It may be that in a case involving private international law, there is not only a main question before the court but also some further subsidiary issue. After the law to govern the main question has been ascertained by the application of the relevant rule for the choice of law, a further choice of law rule may be required to answer the subsidiary question affecting the main issue.

This problem may be illustrated as follows. Suppose that W claims rights of intestate succession to H's immovables in Italy. According to English rules of private international law, this falls to be determined by Italian law as the law of the situs.[1] Assume further that under English conflict rules, W is recognised as H's widow, but not under Italian rules, because, for instance, Italian law does not recognise H's divorce from his first wife. The main problem, whether W can succeed to H's estate, is clearly determinable by Italian law, but must the subsidiary problem of the validity of the marriage also be referred to that law? A question of this nature has been aptly termed by Wolff, the "incidental question",[2] though the less satisfactory expression "the preliminary question" is widely used.[3]

2. THE ELEMENTS OF AN INCIDENTAL QUESTION

An incidental question properly so-called presumes the existence of three facts.[4] The main issue should, under the English rules of private international law, be governed by a foreign law. There should be a subsidiary question involving a foreign element which could have arisen separately and which

---

1 Infra, pp 851–852.
2 Op cit, p 206. The problem has been described by Ehrenzweig, p 340, as "another miscreant of a conceptualism gone rampant".
3 For discussion of this problem, see Robertson, Chapter 6; Dicey & Morris, Chapter 3; Levontin, *Choice of Law and Conflict of Laws*, Chapter 4; Gotlieb (1955) Can BR 523; de Nova (1966) II Hague Recueil 443, 557–569; Kahn-Freund (1974) III Hague Recueil 147, 437–440; Gotlieb (1977) 26 ICLQ 734; Juenger (1985) IV Hague Recueil 123, 195–197; Wengler, Vol III *International Encyclopedia of Comparative Law*, Chapter 7.
4 See Dicey & Morris, pp 49–50.

has its own independent choice of law rule. This latter choice of law rule should lead to a conclusion different from that which would have been reached had the law governing the main question been applied. Without these pre-requisites there is no "incidental question",[5] and in most of the cases where a true problem has arisen the court has not appreciated that a determination of the law to govern the incidental question is required. This is an issue on which support of jurists may be found for a variety of solutions. Some support the law governing the main issue,[6] others the choice of law rules of the forum[7] and others consider that the determination of the problem will depend on the nature of the individual case and the policy of the forum thereto.[8]

3. THE PROBLEM ILLUSTRATED

The way in which an incidental question arises may be illustrated by two decisions, one English, the other Canadian, on the inter-relation of the choice of law rules for divorce recognition and for capacity to marry.[9] The English case is *Lawrence v Lawrence*:[10]

> The first husband and his wife married in Brazil and lived there until 1970. In that year the wife obtained a divorce in Nevada, USA, which was not recognised in Brazil; but the next day she married the second husband in Nevada. Later the second husband petitioned for a declaration as to the validity of this second marriage. An incidental question arose from the fact that, under Brazilian law, being that of the wife's domicil to which English choice of law rules referred capacity to marry, she lacked capacity to marry the second husband. On the other hand, the Nevada divorce was recognised in England under our divorce recognition rules.[11]

The Court of Appeal, by a variety of reasoning, upheld the validity of the second marriage.[12] The effect of this was to give primacy to the divorce recognition issue at the expense of that of capacity to marry.[13]

The Canadian decision in *Schwebel v Ungar*[14] provides a converse example of the incidental question, where the capacity rule prevailed over that of divorce recognition. The facts were these:

> A Jewish husband and wife, domiciled in Hungary, decided to settle in Israel. When they were in Italy, en route to Israel, the husband divorced

5 See the discussion of *Shaw v Gould* (1868) LR 3 HL 55, infra, pp 747–750, by Webb & Davis, *Casebook on the Conflict of Laws in New Zealand*, pp 86–87; cf Gotlieb (1955) 33 Can BR 523, 535–537. In the context of legitimacy, contrast *Motala v A-G* [1990] 2 FLR 261, [1990] Fam Law 340, infra, pp 751–752.
6 Wolff, p 206; Robertson, p 141; Lipstein [1972B] CLJ 67, 90–96.
7 Breslauer, pp 18–21; Nussbaum, pp 104–109; Falconbridge (1939) 17 Can BR 369, 377–378.
8 Dicey & Morris, p 50; Anton, pp 88–89; Nygh, p 216; and see Gotlieb (1955) 33 Can BR 523, 555.
9 Infra, pp 603–605.
10 Infra, pp 603–604.
11 Recognition of Divorces and Legal Separations Act 1971; see now Family Law Act 1986, Part II, infra, pp 655 et seq.
12 For a converse approach, see *R v Brentwood Superintendent Registrar of Marriages, ex p Arias* [1968] 2 QB 956, [1968] 3 All ER 279.
13 This result would now be reached by statute under the Family Law Act 1986, s 50.
14 (1963) 42 DLR (2d) 622, affd (1964) 48 DLR (2d) 644; Lysyk (1965) 43 Can BR 363; Webb (1965) 14 ICLQ 659.

his wife by "gett". Under Hungarian law, the law of their domicil, and under Italian law this divorce was invalid, but it was effective according to Israeli law. They then acquired an Israeli domicil and whilst so domicileb the wife later visited Ontario and married a second husband who ultimately petitioned the Ontario court for a decree of nullity on the ground of his "wife's" bigamy.

The Canadian court had not only to consider the question of the wife's capacity to marry, governed under Ontario choice of law rules by Israeli law, but also the question of the validity of the wife's divorce by gett. Under the Ontario rules of private international law the divorce would not be recognised, but it would under the Israeli rules. The Supreme Court of Canada upheld the validity of the second marriage. It was valid by the law of Israel, the law governing capacity to marry and this prevailed over the Ontario rule denying recognition to the divorce.[15] Here, capacity was regarded as the main question, to which divorce recognition was incidental.

The majority of the decisions in which an incidental question has arisen have applied the law applicable to the main issue, though often without an apparent realisation that an incidental question was involved.[16] So unthinking and mechanical an approach cannot be justified and the determination of this issue must vary according to the class of case under review. If it is one, such as succession to movables, in which the doctrine of total renvoi requires the whole law of the foreign country to be followed then both the main and incidental questions should, probably, be referred to that law.[17] Where, on the other hand, it is one in which the court is referred to the internal law of the foreign country, as perhaps in the case of a question of torts,[18] then there should be a greater likelihood of the court's separating the incidental from the main question and applying the appropriate English choice of law rule to each. However, as *Schwebel v Ungar*[19] illustrates, even in this type of case the court may still apply the law governing the main question on the grounds that "to hold otherwise would be to determine the personal status of a person not domiciled in Ontario by the law of Ontario instead of by the law of that person's country of domicile".[20] However, if one turns the issue round and asks why, in a question of status, should the law of the forum subordinate its own choice of law rules to those of some other jurisdiction, then any real justification for the decision in that case is harder to find.[1]

15 This approach is approved in *Padolecchia v Padolecchia* [1968] P 314 at 338–340, though on the facts as found no true incidental question arose.
16 Eg *Re Johnston* [1903] 1 Ch 821; *Baindail v Baindail* [1946] P 122 at 127; *Haque v Haque* (1962) 108 CLR 230; *Schwebel v Ungar*, supra; *R v Brentwood Superintendent Registrar of Marriages, ex p Arias*, supra; and see *Breen v Breen* [1964] P 144, [1961] 3 All ER 225; Gotlieb (1977) 26 ICLQ 734 at 771 et seq.
17 Infra, p 72; eg, *Re Johnson*, supra; *Baindail v Baindail*, supra; *Haque v Haque*, supra; Gotlieb (1955) Can BR 523, 545, 547; and see the interesting problem posed by Webb & Davis, *Casebook on the Conflict of Laws in New Zealand*, p 88.
18 Cf *Re Degaramo's Estate* 33 NYS 502 (1895); and see *Meisenhelder v Chicago and North Western Rly Co* 170 Minn 317 (1927); Webb & Davis, op cit, pp 84–85; cf de Nova (1966) II Hague Recueil 443, 566–567.
19 Supra, p 54; and see *Padolecchia v Padolecchia*, supra.
20 (1963) 42 DLR (2d) 622 at 633.
1 Lysyk (1965) 43 Can BR 363 at 379; though cf *Breen v Breen* [1964] P 144, [1961] 3 All ER 225.

4. DÉPEÇAGE

A problem related to that of the incidental question is that of "picking and choosing"[2] or "dépeçage". A case involving foreign elements may give rise to issues which involve different choice of law rules. To take the simplest example,[3] if a husband and wife, both domiciled in England, marry in France, then any dispute as to the validity of their marriage may have to be referred to English or French law. In fact, if the dispute is as to the formal validity of the marriage, reference will be made to French law as the law of the place of celebration and if the issue is one of capacity it will be determined according to English law as the ante-nuptial domiciliary law of the parties.[4] Here it is clear that the one general issue of the validity of the marriage has to be analysed into two separate sub-issues referable to different laws. The court will pick and choose between these two sub-issues. A similar example is provided in the law of contract where the parties are free to choose different laws to govern different parts of their contract.[5]

In other cases the question whether there are two issues referable to different laws or but one single issue is less easy to determine. Although a failure to distinguish separate issues may produce an unjust and distorted result, it might also be said that the decision to pick and choose may be motivated by a desire to avoid the application of a rule that is regarded as undesirable. The most commonly cited example relates to interspousal immunity in tort.[6] If a husband and wife, both domiciled in a foreign country, are involved in a motor accident in England in which the husband negligently injures the wife, this would be classified as a tort problem to which the appropriate choice of law rules would be applied, pointing towards the application of English law.[7] Let us assume, however, that although an action will lie between husband and wife under English law, it will not so lie under the law of their domicil. Are we to say that the question of interspousal immunity arising in a tort claim is a tort issue,[8] or should we adopt a more subtle categorisation and suggest that the interspousal immunity issue is a matter of status to be segregated from the tort context in which it arose and to be referred to the law of the domicil?[9] The latter is the better approach.

The problem can become more complex, as where the law of the domicil would permit the spouses to sue but its substantive tort rules would deny the wife recovery, eg, because she was guilty of contributory negligence, whilst under the law governing liability in tort a wife cannot sue her husband but, apart from that, she has a good claim in tort.[10] If one picks and chooses, then the law governing the tort issue may only be applied to the tort elements of the wife's claim, whilst the law of the domicil is applied to the question of

2 Cavers (1970) III Hague Recueil 137–140; Morris, pp 529–530; Ehrenzweig, *Private International Law*, pp 119–121; Reese (1973) 73 Col LR 58.
3 Lipstein (1972) I Hague Recueil 214.
4 Infra, pp 586 et seq.
5 Contracts (Applicable Law) Act 1990, Sch 1, Art 3 (1), infra, pp 476–477; but see Mclachlan (1990) 61 BYBIL 311.
6 Cavers (1970) III Hague Recueil 138; Morris, pp 529–530.
7 Infra, pp 533 et seq.
8 Eg *Schmidt v Government Insurance Office of New South Wales* [1973] 1 NSWLR 59; *Corcoran v Corcoran* [1974] VR 164, infra pp 560–561.
9 Eg *Warren v Warren* [1972] Qd R 386.
10 Cavers (1970) III Hague Recueil 138.

interspousal immunity. The result is that the wife can recover by picking and choosing different laws to govern different issues, though had any one law been applied to all issues, she would have failed.

The *mechanical operation* 57

interspousal immunity. The result is that the wife can recover. Had the
choosing different laws to govern different issues, though had any of the
been applied to the same, the would have failed.

Chapter 5

Renvoi[1]

SUMMARY

1. THE PROBLEM STATED

Once it is decided that a court has jurisdiction, how the issue before it is to
be characterised in terms of private international law and what choice of law
rules are applicable, it might be thought that the judge's task was reaching
its conclusion. Nothing remains for him to do but apply the chosen law. If
this is English law there is no doubt that what he is required to do is to give
effect to English internal law. Thus, where a person dies intestate domiciled
in England leaving movables here the rules of distribution contained in the

---

1 The literature on the subject is immense; among the contributions in English see: Bate, *Notes
on the Doctrine of Renvoi*; Mendelssohn-Bartholdy, *Renvoi in Modern English Law*; Rabel,
i, 75 et seq; Lorenzen (1910) 10 Col LR 190, 327; Abbot (1908) 24 LQR 133; Falconbridge,
pp 137–263; Lorenzen (1917) 27 YLJ 509; Schreiber (1917) 31 HLR 523; Griswold (1938)
51 HLR 1165; Morris (1937) 18 BYBIL 32; Cowan (1938) 87 U of Pa Law Rev 34; Griswold,
ibid 257; Falconbridge (1953) 6 Vanderbilt Law Review 708; Inglis (1958) 74 LQR 493; Von
Mehren, *XXth Century Comparative and Conflicts Law*, 360; de Nova (1966) II Hague Recueil
443, 478–577; Kahn-Freund (1974) III Hague Recueil 147, 392–397, 431–437; Levontin,
Choice of Law and Conflict of Laws, Chapter 3; Dicey & Morris, pp 73–91; Anton, pp 75–
84, Morris, pp 469–480; Nygh, pp 205–214; Scoles and Hay, pp 67–72.

Administration of Estates Act 1925 must be applied. There can be no question of paying any further regard to the private international law of England. The function of that department of the law is purely selective and its selection of English law as the applicable law must perforce refer to English internal law, ie to the rules applicable to a purely domestic situation having no foreign complexion.

If, however, the applicable law is that of a foreign country the situation may be more complex. The difficulty is to determine the sense in which the applicable "law" must be understood. If, for example, the English rule for the choice of law refers to the law of Italy, what meaning must be attributed to "the law of Italy"? The difficulty is not obvious at first sight, but it can be demonstrated by a simple illustration.

X, a British subject, dies intestate, domiciled in Italy, and an English court is required to decide how his movables in England are to be distributed.

It is clearly desirable that the mode of distribution should be the same everywhere, in the sense that no matter what national court deals with the matter there ought to be universal agreement as to what particular legal system shall indicate the actual beneficiaries. The fact, however, that there are different systems of private international law militates against this ideal solution. Thus, according to the English rules for the choice of law the question of intestate succession to movables is governed by Italian law as being the law of X's domicil at the time of death, but according to the Italian rules it must be referred to the law of England as being the law of his nationality. In the above example, for instance, an English court has no option but to refer the question of succession to Italian law; while an Italian judge if faced with this issue is under an equal necessity to apply the national law. The English judge, of course, is exclusively governed by his own system of private international law, and must therefore decide that X's goods shall be distributed according to Italian law. Despite this obvious conclusion, however, we are still confronted with the question—what is meant by Italian law? Does it mean Italian internal law, ie the rules enacted by the Italian Code analogous to section 46 of the Administration of Estates Act 1925 which regulate the distribution of an intestate's property? Or does it mean the whole of Italian law, including in particular the rules of private international law as recognised in Italy? If the latter is the correct meaning, a further difficulty is caused by the difference between the English and Italian rules for the choice of law; for on referring to Italian private international law we find ourselves referred back to English law. This being so, the question is whether we are to ignore the divergent Italian rule or to accept the reference back that it makes. If we accept the reference back, are we to stop finally at that point and to distribute X's goods according to the Administration of Estates Act?

2. POSSIBLE SOLUTIONS

When a case is complicated in this fashion, owing to a difference in the private international law of two countries, there are three possible solutions. These are as follows:

The judge who is faced with this issue and who is referred by English private international law to, say, the law of Italy, may

(i)   take "the law of Italy" to mean the internal law of Italy; *or*
(ii) decide the case on the assumption that the doctrine of single renvoi is recognised by English law; *or*
(iii) take "the law of Italy" to mean the law which an Italian judge would administer if he were seised of the matter, ie the doctrine of double renvoi.

These possible courses will now be discussed with the view of showing that, at least in certain types of case, the third solution has rightly or wrongly been frequently adopted by the judges.

(a) APPLY INTERNAL LAW ONLY

The first solution, and the one which is in general correct and desirable, is to read the expression "the law of a country" as meaning only the internal rules of that law. The following words of an eminent jurist would seem to represent the sensible view:

> If England chooses the law of a person's domicil as the best one to apply to a certain relationship, does she mean the ordinary law for ordinary people, his friends and neighbours, in that domicil? Or does she include that country's rules for the choice of law? Common sense could answer that the last alternative is absurd and otiose: a rule for the choice of an appropriate law has already been applied, namely our own. To proceed to adopt a foreign rule is to decide the same question twice over.[2]

This would seem to be in accord with the intention of the propositus. If, for instance, a man voluntarily abandons England and acquires a domicil in Italy where he permanently resides until his death many years later, the natural inference is that he willingly submits himself to the internal law of that country. This seems also to be the obvious answer in those cases, such as contract,[3] where the parties are allowed expressly to choose the law to govern their relationship. Few businessmen would voluntarily choose the doctrine of renvoi. This approach has been definitely adopted in at least two early English decisions, one by a court of first instance,[4] the other by the Privy Council.[5] It is, and always has been, unconsciously adopted in a multitude of decisions.[6]

(b) DOCTRINE OF SINGLE RENVOI

The second solution is to apply the doctrine of renvoi, in the form of single renvoi. Such doctrine is to this effect: if a judge in country A is referred by his own rule for the choice of a law to the "law" of country B, but the rule for the choice of law in B refers such a case to the "law" of A, then the judge in A must apply the internal law of his own country. The operation of this famous but regrettable doctrine, which demands that a reference to the law of a country shall mean a reference to the whole of its law, including its private international law, is best explained by the example already given:

2 Baty, *Polarised Law* (1914), p 116.
3 Infra, pp 475 et seq.
4 *Hamilton v Dallas* (1875) 1 Ch D 257.
5 *Bremer v Freeman* (1857) 10 Moo PCC 306; see also *Re Annesley* [1926] Ch 692 at 709; *Re Askew* [1930] 2 Ch 259 at 278; cf *Re Ross* [1930] 1 Ch 377 at 402.
6 Infra, pp 72–73.

X, a British subject, dies intestate, domiciled in Italy, and an English court is required to decide how his movables in England are to be distributed.

The English court is directed by its own private international law to refer this question of distribution to Italian law as being the law of the deceased's domicil. When, however, it examines the provisions relating to the choice of the applicable law contained in the Italian Code, it finds that in the case of succession to movables they prefer the law of the deceased's nationality to that of his domicil, and that if an Italian court had been hearing this matter in the first instance it would have resorted to the law of England. Thus, the English court finds itself referred back to English law as being the law of X's nationality. There is a renvoi or remission to English law.

If the court accepts this remission and distributes the property according to the Administration of Estates Act 1925, it is true to say that the doctrine of renvoi is part of English law. Italian law has been allowed, not to give a direct solution of the problem under consideration, but to indicate what legal system shall furnish the final solution. Where the court that is hearing the matter accepts the remission and applies its own municipal law it recognises the doctrine in its simplest form. Renvoi, properly so called, is best exemplified by the well-known decision of the French Cour de Cassation in *Forgo's Case*.[7]

Forgo, a Bavarian national, died intestate in France, where he had lived since the age of five. The question before the French court was whether his movables in France should be distributed according to the internal law of France or of Bavaria. Collateral relatives were entitled to succeed by Bavarian law, but under French law the property passed to the French Government to the exclusion of collaterals. French private international law referred the matter of succession to Bavarian law, but Bavarian private international law referred it to French law. The Cour de Cassation in France accepted the remission and applied the succession provisions of French law.

Where, as in *Forgo's Case*, there are only two legal systems concerned— where the reference is merely from country A to country B and back from B to A—the doctrine of renvoi appears in its simplest form. It can best be described as *remission*. A case may occur, however, where the reference is from A to B, and from B to C. Suppose, for instance, that an Italian testator dies domiciled in France leaving movables in England, English law will refer the question of succession to movables to the law of his domicil, French law. If, however, France were to refer the same question to the law of his nationality, Italian law, this would be a case of reference from B to C, best described as *transmission*.

This particular doctrine of renvoi, whether in the form of remission or transmission, which is now generally called *partial* or *single* renvoi,[8] is not part of English law.[9] That is to say, if English law refers a matter to the law of the domicil and if the latter remits the question to English law, the judge does not automatically accept the remission and apply English internal law.

---

7 (1883) 10 Clunet 64; and see Juenger (1985) IV Hague Recueil 123, 197–199.
8 Dicey and Morris, p 75.
9 *Re Askew* [1930] 2 Ch 259 at 268: "An English court can never have anything to do with it [renvoi], except so far as foreign experts may expound the doctrine as being part of the *lex domicilii*", per MAUGHAM J.

He does not act as the French court did in *Forgo's Case*. It seems unnecessary, therefore, to elaborate the objections to which the doctrine is open.

(c) DOCTRINE OF TOTAL RENVOI

(i) The doctrine stated

The third possible solution is to adopt what may be called the *foreign court theory* or the doctrine of double renvoi[10] or total renvoi,[11] or "the English doctrine of renvoi". This demands that an English judge, who is referred by his own law to the legal system of a foreign country, must apply whatever law a court in that foreign country would apply if it were hearing the case. Let us assume, for example, a question concerning the testamentary dispositions of a British subject who dies domiciled in Belgium, leaving assets in England. A Belgian judge dealing with this matter would be referred by his rules of private international law to English law, but he would then find that the case was remitted to him by English law. Evidence must therefore be adduced in the English proceedings to show what the Belgian judge would in fact do. He might accept the remission and apply his own internal law, and this would be his course if renvoi in the *Forgo* sense (single renvoi) is recognised in Belgium, or he might reject the remission and apply English internal law. Whatever he would do inexorably determines the decision of the English judge.[12] If this third solution is adopted, it is vital to realise that the decision given by the English judge will depend on whether the doctrine of single renvoi is recognised by the particular foreign law to which he is referred. The doctrine, for instance, is repudiated in Italy but recognised in France. Therefore, if the issue in England is the intrinsic validity of a will made by a British subject domiciled in Italy, the judge, if he is to make an imaginary judicial journey to Italy, will reason as follows:

An Italian judge would refer the matter to English law, as being the national law of the propositus. English law remits the question to Italian law as being the law of his domicil.

Italian law does not accept this remission, since it repudiates the single renvoi doctrine.

Therefore an Italian judge would apply English internal law.[13]

A French domicil, however, would produce the opposite result, since a court sitting in France would accept the remission from England and would ultimately apply French internal law.[14]

(ii) Objections to the doctrine

This third solution does not lack support in England and North America. Certain English decisions, which will be discussed later, may be cited in its favour; throughout his life Dicey maintained its truth; the editor of his fifth

10 Rabel, i, 81.
11 Dicey and Morris, p 76; Falconbridge, p 170.
12 The doctrine is ambiguous in the sense that the grounds on which the English judge must arrive at the Belgian decision are far from clear. Must he reason on the basis of the actual circumstances of the case, especially the presence of the assets in England? Or, must he reason on a false assumption, namely, that the assets are in Belgium? There is judicial authority for both views. See Dobrin (1934) 15 BYBIL 36, 37–45.
13 *Re Ross* [1930] 1 Ch 377, infra, pp 68–69.
14 *Re Annesley* [1926] Ch 692, infra, p 68.

edition was equally strong in advocating its merits;[15] and an American jurist sums up his conclusions in these words:

> When a court is referred by its own conflicts rule to a foreign law, it should, as a matter of course, look to the entire foreign law as the foreign court would administer it.[16]

Before estimating the value of the English decisions, therefore, it is appropriate to consider a few of the objections that may be raised to this total renvoi doctrine. The burden of the following pages is that it is objectionable in principle, is based on unconvincing authority and cannot be said to represent the general rule of English law. It is submitted that, subject to certain well-defined exceptions, an English judge, when referred by a rule for the choice of law to the legal system of a foreign country, is not required to consider whether the renvoi doctrine is recognised by the private international law of either country, but must administer the internal law of the legal system to which he has been referred.

The following objections, amongst others, may be directed against the doctrine:[17]

The total renvoi doctrine does not necessarily ensure uniform decisions. The laudable objective of those who favour the doctrine either of single or of total renvoi is to ensure that the same decision shall be given on the same disputed facts, irrespective of the country in which the case is heard. In truth, however, the doctrine of renvoi, in whatever form it is expressed, will produce this uniformity only if it is recognised in one of the countries concerned and rejected in the other—not if it is recognised in both. If, for example, the law of the domicil, to which the English judge is referred, ordains that the case is to be decided exactly as the national (English) court would decide it, what is the judge to do on finding that by English law his decision is to be exactly what it would be in the country of the domicil?[18] Where is a halt to be called to the process of passing the ball from one judge to another? There is no apparent way in which this inextricable circle can be broken—this international game of tennis be terminated.

Uniformity will, indeed, be attained if the law of the domicil repudiates the doctrine of total renvoi, ie if, instead of seeking guidance from a foreign judge, it categorically provides that the national (English) law shall govern the matter, for in this case English internal law will apply and harmony will prevail. It is true that the total renvoi doctrine is apparently unrecognised in countries outside the Commonwealth, but none the less it is difficult "to approve a doctrine which is workable only if the other country rejects it".[19] The fact is, of course, that uniformity of decisions is unattainable on any consistent principle with regard to matters that are determined in some countries by the law of the nationality, in others by the law of the domicil.

A second obstacle to uniformity of decisions is that the foreign court doctrine does not require, in fact does not allow, the English judge to don the mantle of his foreign colleague without any reservations. Matters that are classified as procedural in England must be submitted to English internal

---

15 Dicey, *Conflict of Laws* (5th edn), pp 863 et seq; Keith (1942) 24 JCL 69.
16 Griswold (1938) 51 HLR 1165, 1183.
17 See also Morris, pp 478–480; Nygh, pp 212–214.
18 Morris (1937) 18 BYBIL 32, 37; and see Schreiber (1917) 31 HLR 523; cf Anton, pp 78–79.
19 Lorenzen (1941) 50 YLJ 743, 753.

law, even though the foreign judge might have regarded them as substantive.[1]
This may well lead to a discrepancy of result. Moreover, the application of
a rule of foreign law will sometimes be excluded on grounds of public policy
or because it is considered to be a penal, revenue or other public law matter.[2]

*The total renvoi doctrine signifies the virtual capitulation of the English rules
for choice of law.* Stripped of its verbiage, the doctrine involves nothing less
than a substitution of the foreign for the English choice-of-law rules. In the
case, for instance, of the British subject who dies intestate domiciled in Italy,
the English rule selects the law of Italy as the governing law, but the equivalent
Italian rule selects the law of England. When, therefore, the English judge
defers to the decision that an Italian judge would have given, he applies the
internal law of England and thus shows a preference for the Italian selective
rule. The English rule is jettisoned, since it does not meet with the approval of
the law-maker in Italy. This, indeed, is the apotheosis of comity.[3] Moreover, a
rule for the choice of the applicable law is essentially selective in nature,[4] and
that it should have no other effect than to select another and contradictory
rule of selection savours of incompatibility and paradox. Furthermore, the
application of the law selected by the foreign country's choice of law rules
may be unacceptable in public policy terms.[5]

One acute critic, however, finds nothing strange in this surrender to a
foreign rule for the choice of law.[6] He denies that there is any logical reason
why an English rule of this nature should not be taken to indicate the private
international law of a foreign country rather than its internal law. To regard
a reference to the law of the domicil as a reference to the internal law is, he
says, merely to beg the question. This argument, it is submitted, ignores both
the nature and genesis of a rule for the choice of the applicable law. The
truth is that such a rule is based on substantial grounds of national policy.
It represents what appears to the enacting authority to be right and proper,
having regard to the sociological and practical considerations involved. The
English principle, for instance, that an intestate's movables shall be distributed according to the law of his last domicil is founded on the reasoning
that rights of succession should depend on the law of the country where the
deceased established his permanent home. Having voluntarily become an
inhabitant of the country, it is the view of English law that in this matter he
should be on the same footing as other inhabitants. Moreover, the natural
inference is that he submits himself to the law which binds his friends and
neighbours. This would seem to be his presumed intention. Thus, if the
reference to the law of his domicil is regarded as a reference to whatever
internal system the private international law of the domicil may choose, then
not only is the deliberate policy of English law reversed, but the probable
intention of the propositus is ignored. Indeed, his expectations may be
flouted. He may, for instance, have refrained from making a will, having

1 Infra, pp 74–79.
2 Infra, Chapter 8.
3 See the dissenting judgment of TASCHEREAU J in the Canadian case of *Ross v Ross* (1894) 25
  SCR 307; and see Schreiber (1917) 31 HLR 523, 561–564.
4 Schreiber, op cit, p 533.
5 In such circumstances a Canadian court has applied the internal law of the country chosen
  by the forum's choice of law rules, ie ignored the doctrine of renvoi on public policy grounds:
  Vladi v Vladi (1987) 39 DLR (4th) 563.
6 Griswold (1938) 51 HLR 1165, 1176–1178.

been content with the local rules governing intestacy, the substance of which it will have been a simple matter for him to ascertain. A quite different set of rules, however, may operate if the private international law of his domicil is to have effect.

The total renvoi doctrine is difficult to apply. The doctrine obliges the English judge to ascertain as a fact the precise decision that the foreign court would give. This confronts him with two difficulties. First, he must ascertain what view prevails in the foreign country with regard to the doctrine of single renvoi. Secondly, where the foreign rule for the choice of law selects the national law of the propositus, the judge must ascertain what is meant by national law.

As we have already seen, the chosen law that emerges from an application of the doctrine depends inter alia on whether the doctrine of single renvoi is recognised by the law of the domicil.[7] If the court of the domicil would accept the remission made to it by English law, it would determine the case according to its own internal law; otherwise it would apply the internal law of England. This dependence of the rights of the parties on the attitude of the law of the domicil to the renvoi doctrine is a cause of acute embarrassment. There are few matters on which it is more difficult to obtain reliable information. Often, an undue influence is possessed by the expert witness. Alternatively, the English judge may be confronted with a somewhat arduous and invidious task, as witness the following remarks of WYNN-PARRY J:

> It would be difficult to imagine a harder task than that which faces me, namely, of expounding for the first time either to this country or to Spain the relevant law of Spain as it would be expounded by the Supreme Court of Spain, which up to the present time has made no prouncement on the subject, and having to base that exposition on evidence which satisfies me that on this subject there exists a profound cleavage of legal opinion in Spain and two conflicting decisions of courts of inferior jurisdiction.[8]

The second difficulty that may arise is to ascribe a definite meaning to the expression "national law". When the private international law rules of the country in which the English judge is presumed to sit select the nationality of a person as the connecting factor, it becomes necessary to correlate the national law with some precise system of internal law by which the issue before the court may be determined. This is a simple matter when the person is a national of some country, such as Sweden, which has a unitary system of territorial law.[9] There is a single body of internal law applicable throughout the territory known as Sweden. The position is far different where the country of nationality comprises several systems of territorial law, as is true for example of the United Kingdom and the USA. What, for instance, is the national law of a British subject? For an English court, the question is really pointless, because the law that governs a British subject in personal matters varies according to the territory of the foreign country in which he is domiciled. It is one system in England, another in Scotland, and so on. The case of *Re O'Keefe*[10] will serve to illustrate both the nature of the difficulty and the speciousness of the total renvoi doctrine. The facts were these:

7 Supra, p 62.
8 *Re Duke of Wellington* [1947] Ch 506 at 515, [1947] 2 All ER 854 at 858, 859; infra, p 70.
9 For a stimulating *exposé* of the present difficulty see Falconbridge, pp 202–216. See also Anton p 84; Morris (1940) 56 LQR 144.
10 [1940] Ch 124, [1940] 1 All ER 216. See Nadelmann (1969) 17 AJCL 418, 443–448.

The question before the English court was the way in which the movables of X, a spinster who died intestate, were to be distributed. X's father was born in 1835 in Ireland, but at the age of 22 he went to India, and except for various stays in Europe lived there throughout his life and died in Calcutta in 1885. X was born in India in 1860; from 1867 to 1890 she lived in various places in England, France and Spain; but in 1890 she settled down in Naples and resided there until her death 47 years later in 1937. About the year 1878 she had made a short tour in Ireland with her father. She never lost her British nationality, but it was held that she had acquired a domicil in Italy.

The law selected by English private international law to govern the question of distribution was, therefore, the law of her domicil. An Italian judge, however, had he been hearing the case, would have been referred by the Italian Civil Code to her national law. He would have rejected any remission made to him by the national law, since the single renvoi doctrine was not adopted in Italy. The Civil Code used the general expression "national law" and fails to define what this means when the country of nationality contains more than one legal system. Which system of internal law, then, out of those having some relation to X, would be regarded by an Italian court as applicable? The issue raised in the case was whether it was the law of England, of Ireland or of India. Which of these systems would be selected by a court in Italy? The expert witnesses agreed that it would be the law of the country to which X "belonged" at the time of her death. She certainly did not "belong", whatever that may mean, to England in the sense of attracting to herself English internal law, for she had spent no appreciable time in the country. She might perhaps, by reason of her birth in Calcutta, be regarded as belonging to India, though she had not been there for seventy years. The reasonable man might even be excused for thinking that she most properly belonged to Italy, the country where she had continuously spent the last forty-seven years of her life.[11] CROSSMAN J, however, would have none of these. He reverted to X's domicil of origin, and held that she belonged to Ireland because that was the country where her father was domiciled at the time of her birth. In the result, therefore, the succession to her property was governed by the law of a country which she had never entered except during one short visit some sixty years before her death; which was not even a separate political unit until sixty-two years after her birth; of whose succession laws she was no doubt profoundly and happily ignorant; and under the law of which it was impossible in the circumstances for her to claim citizenship. The convolutions by which such a remarkable result is reached are interesting. First, the judge is referred by the English rule to the law of the domicil, which in the instant case means the law of the domicil of choice; then he bows to the superior wisdom of a foreign legislator and allows the law of the domicil to be supplanted by the law of the nationality; then, upon discovering that the law of the nationality is meaningless, he throws himself back on the domicil of origin; and thus determines the rights of the parties by a legal system which is neither the national law nor the law of the domicil as envisaged by the English rule for choice of law.[12] Comment is surely superfluous.

---

11 Morris points out (56 LQR 144, 146) that the originating summons did not suggest Italian law as a possible choice, and he assumes that the decision is no authority against the view that the internal law of the domicil should have been applied.

12 The difficulty of identifying the law to which a British national is subject was ignored in *Re Ross* [1930] 1 Ch 377, infra, pp 68–69; *Re Askew* [1930] 2 Ch 259, infra, pp 69–70; and *Re*

(iii) Analysis of decisions supporting the doctrine

A number of cases are often cited in support of the total renvoi doctrine. They are, however, far from satisfactory as decisions, as we shall see. The first of these is *Collier v Rivaz*,[13] where the facts were as follows:

A British subject, who according to English law was domiciled in Belgium at the time of his death, had executed seven testamentary instruments, a will and six codicils. The will and two of the codicils had been executed in accordance with the formalities required by Belgian internal law. The remaining four codicils, though formally valid according to the Wills Act 1837, were not made in the form required by Belgian internal law. According to the law of Belgium the testator had never acquired a domicil in that country, since he had not obtained the necessary authorisation from the government. The question was whether the instruments could be admitted to probate in England.

Sir Herbert JENNER, after propounding the theory that he must sit as a Belgian judge, admitted the will and two codicils to probate because they satisfied the formalities of the internal law of the country in which the testator was domiciled in the English sense; and he extended the same indulgence to the remaining codicils on the ground that, since the testator had not acquired a domicil in Belgium in the Belgian sense, a judge in Brussels would apply Belgian private international law, under which the formal validity of the instruments would be tested by English internal law.

This decision is open to many criticisms.[14] It is obvious that, when a choice of law rule selects a particular legal system as the one to govern a given question, it is necessary to decide whether this means the internal law or the private international law of the selected system. It cannot mean both, for the private international law rules may indicate some other legal system, the internal law of which differs from the internal law of the selected system. If the question in *Collier v Rivaz* had been, not the formal, but the essential, validity of the testamentary instruments, and if, for instance, some of them had been lawful by English internal law but unlawful by Belgian internal law, while others had been lawful in Belgium but unlawful in England, it would have been impossible to uphold them in their totality. Sir Herbert JENNER, however, had it both ways. He held that the formal validity of a will cannot be denied if it satisfies either the internal law or the private international law of the selected legal system. There is much to be said for this benevolent rule in the one case of formal validity, since it is obviously desirable that the intention of a testator, clearly expressed and not intrinsically objectionable, should be respected if reasonably possible.[15] What is impossible is that the rule should be allowed a general operation.[16]

Duke of Wellington [1947] Ch 506, [1947] 2 All ER 854, infra, p 70. In these cases English law was chosen without argument.

13 (1841) 2 Curt 855; see also *Frere v Frere* (1847) 5 Notes of Cases 593; cf *Bremer v Freeman* (1857) 10 Moo PCC 306, infra, p 839.

14 See especially: Abbot (1908) 24 LQR 133, 143; Falconbridge, pp 143–145, 151–152; Morris (1937) BYBIL 32, 43–44; Mendelssohn-Bartholdy, *Renvoi in English Law*, pp 58–64; Nygh, pp 208–209.

15 Choice of law rules relating to wills are discussed infra, pp 837–851, 852–859.

16 *Re Lacroix Goods* (1877) 2 PD 94, was another case where the English judge seems to have applied both the private international law rules and the internal law of the domicil; see Morris (1937) 18 BYBIL 32, 42. The operation of any renvoi doctrine in matters concerning the formal validity of wills has now been virtually excluded by the Wills Act 1963 which governs wills of testators dying after 1963, and under which there is a variety of systems of internal law by which the formal validity of a will may be tested; infra, p 840.

Re Annesley[1] was concerned with the essential validity of a will.

An Englishwoman was domiciled at the time of her death in France according to the principles of English law, but was domiciled in England in the eyes of French law, since she had never obtained the authorisation of the government which, before 1927, was necessary for the acquisition of domicil. Her testamentary dispositions were valid by English internal law, but invalid by French internal law, since she had failed to leave two-thirds of her property to her children.

RUSSELL J held that the validity of the dispositions must be determined by French law. His actual decision, therefore, was in accordance with the view that a reference to the law of a given country is a reference to its internal law,[2] but he did not reach his conclusion in this simple fashion. He preferred the total renvoi theory. The judge's reasoning is not altogether clear, but it seems that he ultimately reached the haven of French internal law by the following route:

> English private international law refers the matter to French law as being the law of the domicil.
> A French judge would be referred by his own rules to English law.
> He would, however, find himself referred back by English private international law to French law.
> Single renvoi is recognised in France.
> Therefore, a French court would accept the remission, and in the result would apply French internal law.

It is to be noted, however, that there was an alternative and simpler ground on which the judge would have preferred to base his decision had he not thought himself bound by previous authorities. This, the direct antithesis of the approach that we have just considered, was that the natural meaning of the expression "the law of a country" is the internal law of the country in question.

> When we say that French law applies to the administration of the personal estate of an Englishman who dies domiciled in France, we mean that French municipal law which France applies in the case of Frenchmen.[3]

Another case concerned with the essential validity of a will is *Re Ross*.[4]

The testatrix, a British subject, who was domiciled in Italy, both in the English and the Italian sense, disposed of her property by a will which excluded her son from the list of beneficiaries. This exclusion was justifiable by English internal law, but contrary to Italian internal law which required that one-half of the property should go to the son as his *legitima portio*. She left land in Italy and movable property both in England and Italy.

LUXMOORE J held with regard to the movables that in accordance with the English rule for the choice of law the claim of the son to his *legitima portio* must be determined by Italian law as being the law of the testatrix's domicil. He then put the question—What is meant by the law of the domicil? Does it

---

1 [1926] Ch 692.
2 Supra, p 60.
3 [1926] Ch 692 at 709. This view was rejected by LUXMOORE J in *Re Ross* [1930] 1 Ch 377 at 402; in a later case, *Re Askew* [1930] 2 Ch 259 at 278, MAUGHAM J considered that there was "much to be said for it".
4 [1930] 1 Ch 377.

refer merely to the municipal law of the domicil or does it include its rules of private international law?[5]

In the result the judge applied English internal law and disallowed the claim of the son. This was the conclusion which an Italian judge would have reached. He would have referred the matter to the law of the nationality and would have rejected the remission made to him by English law. As regards the land, the English rule for the choice of law referred the judge to Italian law as being the law of the situs. The expert evidence showed that an Italian court would again turn to the law of the nationality and would adopt the rule of English internal law applicable to land situated in England and belonging to an English testator. It was held once more, therefore, that the claim of the son failed. In this way Mrs Ross was allowed to evade one of the cardinal rules of the legal system, the protection of which she had enjoyed for the last fifty-one years of her life.

The next case, *Re Askew*,[6] raised an issue of legitimacy.

By an English marriage settlement made on the marriage of X, a British subject domiciled in England, to his first wife, Y, it was provided that X, if he married again, might revoke in part the settled trusts and make a new appointment to the children of *such subsequent marriage*. Some time before 1911, X, who had long been separated from Y, acquired a German domicil. In 1911, having obtained a divorce from a competent German court, he married Z, in Berlin. Some time *before the divorce* a daughter had been born to X and Z in Switzerland. In 1913 X exercised his power of revocation and made an appointment in favour of his daughter.

The question before the English court was the validity of this appointment. A short answer to this question, and one that would have involved no reference to private international law, was that the daughter of Z was in no sense a child of the "subsequent marriage", for the only marriage subsisting at the time of her birth was that between X and Y. She might be legitimate, but she could not possibly be the child of a non-existing marriage.[7] This fact, however, was not brought to the notice of MAUGHAM J, who insisted that the validity of the appointment depended on whether the daughter was legitimate. She could not claim legitimacy under the Legitimacy Act 1926[8] since at the time of her birth her father was married to someone other than her mother.[9] By English private international law, however, her legitimacy depended on whether German law, being that of her father's domicil both at the time of her birth and also at the time of his marriage to Z, recognised legitimation by subsequent marriage. In such a case, however, German private international law referred the matter to the law of the father's nationality. Moreover, the doctrine of single renvoi was generally accepted in Germany. If, therefore, a German court were required to pronounce on the legitimacy of Z's daughter, it would first refer to English law, and then, on finding a remission made by English law to the law of the domicil, would

---

5 Ibid, at 388, 389.
6 [1930] 2 Ch 259; followed in *Collins v A-G* (1931) 145 LT 551.
7 *Re Wicks' Marriage Settlement* [1940] Ch 475; cf *Colquitt v Colquitt* [1948] P 19 at 25 where it was suggested that no difference should be drawn between phrases such as a "legitimate child" and a "child of a subsisting marriage".
8 Now replaced by the Legitimacy Act 1976.
9 Section 1 (2) of the 1926 Act. This rule was abrogated by the Legitimacy Act 1959, s 1; see now the Legitimacy Act 1976, infra, pp 757–758.

accept this and apply German internal law. In other words, if the English reference to the law of the domicil was a reference to the private international law rules of the domicil, the daughter would be legitimate. MAUGHAM J felt that both on principle and on the authorities he was obliged to consider the private international law of Germany. He therefore decided in favour of the legitimacy of the daughter and the validity of the appointment.

The facts of *Re Duke of Wellington*[10] were as follows:

> The Duke of Wellington, a British subject domiciled in England, left two wills, one dealing with his Spanish, the other with his English, property. By the former he left his land in Spain to the person who would succeed both to his English dukedom and to his Spanish dukedom of Ciudad Rodrigo.[11] He died a bachelor, with the result that by the internal law of England his English dukedom passed to his uncle, while by the internal law of Spain his sister succeeded to the Spanish dukedom. Therefore, the Spanish land remained undisposed of, since there was no one person qualified to take both dukedoms.

The problem, therefore, was to identify the person to whom the Spanish land passed, and this depended on whether the solution was to be found in the internal law of Spain or of England. By the former, the testator was entitled to devise only half of his land, the other half passing as on intestacy;[12] by English internal law, the land would pass to the next Duke of Wellington under the residuary gift contained in the English will.

WYNN-PARRY J decided in favour of English internal law for the following reasons: the English choice of law rule referred him in the first instance to Spanish law, which, having regard to such cases as *Re Ross*,[13] included the private international law of Spain; the Spanish code provided that testate and intestate succession shall be determined by the national law of the deceased, whatever be the country in which the property is situated; therefore, the question was whether a Spanish court, having thus been referred to the national (English) law, would accept the remission made by that law to the law of the situs. In short, was the doctrine of single renvoi recognised in Spain? After considering the conflicting evidence of the expert witnesses and the conflicting decisions of two Spanish courts of first instance, the judge reached the conclusion that a court in Spain would not accept the remission made by the national law. Therefore, the Duke of Wellington was entitled to the land under the English will.

The final case to be considered is *Re Fuld's Estate (No 3)*[14] where the facts were as follows:

> The testator, a German by origin, had acquired Canadian nationality when resident in Ontario, but he died domiciled in Germany. His will and its second codicil were executed in England and were considered formally valid in England.[15] The three other codicils to his will were executed in Germany and, thus, according to English private international law, German law, as the law of his domicil, governed their formal validity. The

10 [1947] Ch 506, [1947] 2 All ER 854.
11 This will also disposed of his movables in Spain.
12 This difference is not brought out in the report, see Morris (1948) 64 LQR 264, 266.
13 Supra, pp 68–69.
14 [1968] P 675, [1965] 3 All ER 776; Graveson (1966) 15 ICLQ 937, 941–944.
15 Under the Wills Act 1861, s 2.

last two of these codicils were invalid as to form under German domestic law, but valid under English and Ontario domestic law.

What had to be determined was whether reference to German law was to German internal law or the whole of German law, including its rules of private international law. This involved a difficult problem of the interpretation of the German Civil Code which allowed reference in such cases to either the law governing validity or that of the place of execution. SCARMAN J construed this latter reference as a reference to the internal law of Germany. However, the reference under German law to the law governing validity was to the law of Ontario as the law of the nationality. This was considered to be a reference to the whole of Ontario law, including its rules of private international law. These led to a reference back to German law, as the law of the domicil, and this reference back was accepted by German law under the Civil Code. German internal law was applied and the codicils were invalid.

3. SCOPE OF THE APPLICATION OF RENVOI

(a) RENVOI INAPPLICABLE IN MANY CASES

This review of the principal decisions[16] discloses that the total renvoi doctrine is not of general application. Its scope appears to be limited to certain matters concerning either status or the disposition of property on death. In countless cases dealing with such matter as torts,[17] insurance, sale of movables, gifts *inter vivos* or *mortis causa*, mortgages, negotiable instruments, partnerships, dissolution of foreign companies and so on, the English courts, when referred to "the law" of a foreign country, have never had the slightest hesitation in applying the internal law of that country. One of the clearest rejections of any renvoi doctrine is to be found in the field of contract, it being thought that no sane businessman or his lawyers would choose the application of renvoi. Not only was the rejection made clear at common law,[1] but this position has been confirmed by Article 15 of the (1980) Rome Convention on the law applicable to contractual obligations to which effect is given by the Contracts (Applicable Law) Act 1990.[2] The clear terms of Article 15 are that:

> The application of the law of any country specified by this Convention means the application of the rules of law in force in that country other than its rules of private international law.[3]

There are, however, as we have seen, decisions which do apply renvoi in certain limited areas. These cases perhaps show that the judges, in considering whether the reference may not be to the private international law of the chosen country, have taken the view that "the various categories of cases

---

16 It is thought that *Armitage v A-G* [1906] P 135 was not a case on renvoi, but rather a decision on the jurisdiction of the courts: Falconbridge, p 745; Lipstein [1972 B] CLJ 66, 84–86; cf Nygh, pp 211–212.

17 *M'Elroy v M'Allister* 1949 SC 110 at 126, infra, pp 542–543; and see *Pfau v Trent Aluminum Co* 263 A 2d 129 at 136–137 (1970); Law Com No 193 (1990), para 3.56.

1 *Re United Railways of the Havana and Regla Warehouses Ltd* [1960] Ch 52 at 97; *The Evia Luck (No 2)* [1990] 1 Lloyd's Rep 319 at 327, affd sub nom *Dimskal Shipping Co SA v International Transport Workers Federation* [1991] 3 WLR 875, HL; *Amin Rasheed Shipping Corpn v Kuwait Insurance Co* [1984] AC 50 at 61–62; and see *Kutchera v Buckingham International Holdings Ltd* [1988] IR 61 at 68; cf Briggs (1989) 9 OJLS 251, 254–256.

2 Infra, pp 459 et seq.

3 For a possible application of renvoi concepts to the interrelation of contract and tort, see infra, p 563, n19.

merit individual consideration in the light of expediency"[4] and that the entire problem is not to be decided on a priori reasoning. One writer, who has done much to illuminate the subject, suggests that the renvoi doctrine cannot be rejected in toto, since it has proved to be a useful and justifiable expedient for the solution of at least certain special questions.[5] The conclusion, in fact, is that in general a reference made by an English rule for choice of law to a foreign legal system is to the internal law, not to the private international law, of the chosen system, but that this general principle is subject to a number of exceptions.[6]

(b) ISSUES TO WHICH RENVOI MAY APPLY

(i) **Validity of bequests**

Where the essential validity of a will[7] or intestate succession to movables[8] is determinable by the law of a foreign country, the view that would be taken of the matter by the foreign judge, if he were hearing the case, must be adopted. Also, in cases in which the testator died before 1964 and in cases in which, although he died after 1963, the formal validity of his will is considered under the old common law rule of reference to the law of the domicil, a grant of probate will not be denied on the ground of formal invalidity if the will is formally valid according to the private international law, though not according to the internal law, of the governing legal system.[9]

(ii) **Claims to foreign immovables**

Where a question arises of the right to foreign immovables, as in *Re Ross*,[10] the English court will apply the private international law rules of the country where the immovables are situated, if they would be applied by a court of the situs hearing the same question.[11] This may be justified on the ground that it promotes the security of title.[12]

(iii) **Some cases of movables**

If the English choice of law rule refers a disputed title to movables to the law of their situs at the time when the alleged title was said to have been acquired, it is probable that the court will apply the internal system of law that a court of the situs would apply in the particular circumstances of the case.[13]

---

4 Rabel, i, 77.

5 Falconbridge (1953) 6 Vanderbilt Law Review 708.

6 The Hague Convention of 1951, designed to reconcile the clash between the law of the domicil and the law of the nationality—the most usual situation to raise a question of renvoi—has not been accepted by the United Kingdom. For the text see (1954) Cmnd 9068, App. B.

7 *Re Annesley* [1926] Ch 692, supra, pp 68–69; *Re Ross* [1930] 1 Ch 377, supra, pp 68–69; *Re Adams* [1967] IR 424.

8 *Re O'Keefe* [1940] Ch 124, [1940] 1 All ER 216, supra, pp 65–66; cf *Re Thom* (1987) 40 DLR (4th) 184.

9 *Collier v Rivaz* (1841) 2 Curt 855, supra, p 67; *Frere v Frere* (1847) 5 Notes of Cases 593; and see Wills Act 1963, infra, pp 839–843.

10 [1930] 1 Ch 377, supra, p 68.

11 *Re Ross*, supra, p 68; *Re Duke of Wellington* [1947] Ch 506, supra, p 68; *Re Bailey* [1985] 2 NZLR 656; *Re Schneider's Estate* 96 NYS 2d 652 (Surr Ct 1950), discussed by Morris (1951) 4 ILQ 268; Falconbridge (1953) 6 Vanderbilt Law Review 708, 725–731.

12 Yntema (1957) 35 Can BR 721, 740.

13 See *Winkworth v Christie Manson and Woods Ltd* [1980] Ch 496 at 514; and see infra, pp 799–800.

(iv) Family law issues

The one area of family law where there is clear authority for the application of renvoi is that of the recognition, at common law, of legitimation by subsequent marriage.[14] There is also some authority for the application of the doctrine of renvoi to matrimonial property issues[15] and to both formal[16] and essential[17] validity of marriage.[18] What is not wholly clear is whether renvoi allows the validity of a marriage to be upheld if it is valid either under the internal law of the country to which our choice of law rules refer or under that country's private international law rules—a rule of alternative reference.[19]

---

14 *Re Askew* [1930] 2 Ch 259, supra, p 69. It is doubtful whether the doctrine of renvoi applies to recognition of a foreign legitimation under the Legitimacy Act 1976, s 3, infra, pp 757–758.

15 *Vladi v Vladi* (1987) 39 DLR (4th) 563.

16 *Taczanowska v Taczanowski* [1957] P 301, [1957] 2 All ER 563; see also *Hooper v Hooper* [1959] 2 All ER 575, infra, pp 576–577.

17 *R v Brentwood Superintendent Registrar of Marriages, ex p Arias* [1968] 2 QB 956, infra, p 600. The actual decision in this case would now be different by reason of the Family Law Act 1986, s 50, infra, pp 603–605.

18 This view was provisionally supported in Law Commission Working Paper No 89 (1985), paras 2.39, 3.39; but not all commentators agreed, see Law Com No 165 (1987), paras 2.5–2.6.

19 Infra, p 602.

Chapter 6

Substance and procedure

SUMMARY

1. DIFFERENCE BETWEEN SUBSTANCE AND PROCEDURE

(a) PROCEDURE GOVERNED BY THE LAW OF THE FORUM

One of the eternal truths of every system of private international law is that a distinction must be made between substance and procedure, between right

74

and remedy.[1] The substantive rights of the parties to an action may be governed by a foreign law, but all matters appertaining to procedure are governed exclusively by the law of the forum.[2]

At first sight the principle seems almost self-evident. A person who resorts to an English court for the purpose of enforcing a foreign claim cannot expect to occupy a different procedural position from that of a domestic litigant. The field of procedure constitutes perhaps the most technical part of any legal system, and it comprises many rules that would be unintelligible to a foreign judge and certainly unworkable by a machinery designed on different lines. A party to litigation in England must take the law of procedure as he finds it. He cannot by virtue of some rule in his own country enjoy greater advantages than other parties here; neither must he be deprived of any advantages that English law may confer upon a litigant in the particular form of action.[3] To take an old example, an English creditor who sued his debtor in Scotland could not insist on trial by jury, nor, in the converse case, could a Scottish creditor suing in England refuse the intervention of a jury, on the ground that in Scotland, where the debt arose, the case would have been tried by a judge alone.[4]

(b) IMPORTANCE OF DISTINCTION BETWEEN SUBSTANCE AND PROCEDURE

Certain and universal though the principle is, however, its application is frequently one of considerable difficulty, for by what test is a procedural rule to be distinguished from one of substantive law? Unless the distinction is made with a clear regard to the underlying purpose of private international law, the inevitable result will be to defeat that purpose. So intimate is the connection between substance and procedure, that to treat an English rule as procedural may defeat the policy which demands the application of a foreign substantive law. A glaring example of this is afforded by section 4 of the Statute of Frauds which formerly provided that no action should be brought on certain contracts unless they were evidenced by a note or memorandum signed by the party to be charged or by his lawfully authorised agent. In *Leroux v Brown*:[5]

An oral agreement was made in France by which the defendant, resident in England, agreed to employ the plaintiff, resident in France, for a period that was longer than a year. The contract was valid and enforceable by French law, which was the law by which it was to be governed, but had it been an English domestic contract it would, though valid, nevertheless have been unenforceable under the Statute of Frauds. An action brought

---

1 Cf Szaszy (1966) 15 ICLQ 436, 455–456; and see Spiro (1969) 18 ICLQ 949. This distinction is, in principle, drawn by the Contracts (Applicable Law) Act 1990, infra, pp 459 et seq, which excludes (in Sch 1, Art 1(2) (h)) from its rules for determining the law applicable to a contract matters of evidence and procedure, subject to a number of limited exceptions, discussed infra, pp 473–474.
2 *British Linen Co v Drummond* (1830) 10 B & C 903; *De la Vega v Vianna* (1830) 1 B & Ad 284; *Huber v Steiner* (1835) 2 Bing NC 202; *Don v Lippmann* (1837) 5 Cl & Fin 1 at 13; *Boys v Chaplin* [1971] AC 356, at 378–379, 381–382, 392–393, 394.
3 *De la Vega v Vianna* (1830) 1 B & Ad 284 at 288; *Boys v Chaplin* [1971] AC 356 at 394.
4 *Don v Lippmann* (1837) 5 Cl & Fin 1 at 14.
5 (1852) 12 CB 801; and see *Morris v Baron & Co* [1918] AC 1 at 15. The statute now just applies to a contract of guarantee: Law Reform (Enforcement of Contracts) Act 1954, s 1. In the case of contracts concerning land they need to be made by signed writing. If not, the contract is invalid: Law of Property (Miscellaneous Provisions) Act 1989, s 2.

in England for its breach failed on the ground that the statute imposed a rule of procedure which was binding on all litigants suing in England.

A moment's reflection will show that this decision, though possibly based on an intelligible principle of domestic law, is repugnant to the principles on which English private international law is founded. That law exists to fulfil foreign rights, not to destroy them. The law governing the contract in *Leroux v Brown* undoubtedly entitled the plaintiff to recover damages for the breach of the undertaking, and had he obtained judgment in France in an action to which the defendant voluntarily appeared, nothing would have prevented him from succeeding in an action brought on the judgment in England. Moreover, he would have succeeded had he done something in furtherance of the contract that constituted an act of part performance in the eyes of English law.[6] To refuse him a right of action in England on the contract was tantamount to denying that the contract, admittedly governed as to substance by French law, conferred a right on him. It is a stultification of private international law to refuse recognition to a foreign right substantively valid under its governing law, unless its recognition will conflict with some rule of public policy so insistent as to override all other considerations. WILLES J attacked the decision in two later cases, and evidently thought that in the circumstances the statutory rule should not have been treated as procedural.[7]

The Court of Appeal took a somewhat different approach in *Monterosso Shipping Co Ltd v International Transport Workers' Federation*:[8]

The plaintiffs, a Maltese company, owned a ship which was managed by a Norwegian company with Norwegian officers and a Spanish crew. The defendants were an international federation of trade unions with whom the plaintiffs had purported to enter into a collective agreement in 1980. However, the defendants "blacked" the ship when it started a regular run between Swedish ports, because the Swedish seamen's union objected to the use of a Spanish and not a Swedish crew. The plaintiffs claimed damages for breach of the 1980 collective agreement, and the issue was raised whether the law governing the agreement was English or Spanish. The Court of Appeal held that it was Spanish; but the court also had to consider whether to give effect to section 18 of the Trade Union and Labour Relations Act 1974, which declares that a collective agreement "shall be conclusively presumed not to have been intended by the parties to be a legally enforceable contract unless the agreement . . . states that the parties intend that the agreement shall be a legally enforceable contract". It was argued by the defendants that this section was procedural in effect so that an English court should apply the section irrespective of the law governing the contract.

6   *Mahadervan v Mahadervan* [1964] P 233 at 242, [1962] 3 All ER 1108 at 1115.
7   *Williams v Wheeler* (1860) 8 CBNS 299 at 316; *Gibson v Holland* (1865) LR 1 CP 1 at 8. This view has been adopted in the USA: *Bernkrant v Fowler* 55 Cal 2d 588, 360 P 2d 906 (1961). However, in *G & H Montage GmbH v Irvani* [1990] 2 All ER 225, [1990] 1 WLR 667 it was suggested that the reasoning in *Leroux v Brown* was "unassailable" and that only the House of Lords could overrule the decision: [1990] 1 WLR 667 at 684, and see at p 690. On the other hand, in considering the Contracts (Applicable Law) Act 1990 and the Rome Convention on the law applicable to contractual obligations (infra, pp 507–508) it should be borne in mind that it has been suggested that whether a contract has to be in writing may be regarded as a matter of the substantive formal validity of a contract: Giuliano and Lagarde Report OJ C282/31, 31 October 1980.
8   [1982] 3 All ER 841.

The Court of Appeal held that section 18 was to be classed as substantive and not procedural. In so doing dissatisfaction was expressed[9] with the reasoning in *Leroux v Brown*[10] and, in holding section 18 of the 1974 Act to be substantive, Lord DENNING MR had this to say:

> It seems to me that the true distinction is between the existence of a contract (which is substantive law) and the remedies for breach of it (which is procedural law). The right course is to analyse the statute and see whether it negatives the existence of a contract or not. If there is no contract, then there is nothing to enforce. That is substantive law. If there is a contract, but the statute says it cannot be enforced (except in writing or within a stated period) that is procedural law. It is governed by the *lex fori*.
>
> In this present case, as I construe s. 18 of the 1974 Act, it negatives the existence of any contract at all.[11]

(c) HOW IS THE DISTINCTION TO BE MADE?

It remains to consider further how the line between substance and procedure is to be drawn for the purposes of private international law. Only the most general definitions of "the law of procedure" have been given by the English judges. Perhaps the best known is that of LUSH LJ:

> The mode of proceeding by which a legal right is enforced, as distinguished from the law which gives or defines the right, and which by means of the proceeding the court is to administer the machinery as distinguished from its product.[12]

This substitution of "mode of proceeding" for "procedure" does not carry us far. Nor does the definition ensure a just and convenient solution. It implies that, since the owner has chosen to fashion his foreign-acquired right into a new form through the instrumentality of English machinery, he must rest content with the design and movement of that machine. This sounds sensible but if, as in *Leroux v Brown*, the machinery refuses to move, one part of private international law is nullified by another. Nor shall we arrive at a solution if we change the metaphor and concentrate on the contrast between right and remedy. They do not always admit of contrast in law. Historically they are inseparably connected. As GOULDING J has said:[13]

> Within the municipal confines of a single legal system, right and remedy are indissolubly connected and correlated, each contributing in historical dialogue to the development of the other, and, save in very special circumstances, it is as idle to ask whether the court vindicates the suitor's substantive right or gives the suitor a procedural remedy as to ask whether thought is a mental or cerebral process. In fact the court does both things by one and the same act.

The truth is that substance and procedure cannot be relegated to clear-cut categories. There is no preordained dividing line between the two, having some kind of objective existence discoverable by logic. What is procedural, what substantive, cannot be determined in the abstract. A line between the two must, of course, be drawn, but in deciding where to draw it we must have regard to the relativity of legal terms and must realise the exact purpose for which we are making the distinction.

9 Ibid, at 846.
10 And with the leading cases on limitation of actions, see infra, p 80.
11 [1982] 3 All ER 841 at 846; and see at 848–849, per May LJ.
12 *Poyser v Minors* (1881) 7 QBD 329 at 333; adopted in *Re Shoesmith* [1938] 2 KB 637, [1938] 3 All ER 186.
13 *Chase Manhatten Bank N A v Israel-British Bank (London) Ltd* [1981] Ch 105 at 124.

This problem was faced, clearly, by SCARMAN J in *Re Fuld's Estate (No 3)*[14] when he asked:

> When is a question one of substantive law? When is a question merely one of evidence or procedure? I attempt no general answer to these questions; for answer can only be made after an analysis of the specific questions calling for decision, its legal background and factual context.

This shows that the line should not be drawn in the same place for all purposes. It should be drawn in the light of the relevant circumstances, one of which is that the purposes of private international law as distinct from municipal law require fulfilment. Thus it is at least arguable that whether section 4 of the Statute of Frauds is of a procedural or substantive nature should be decided differently according as a foreign or purely English transaction is involved. The crux of the matter is—Why is the distinction between substance and procedure made in private international law? The answer presumably is—For the convenience of the court. The court, when faced with a conflict of laws problem, though bound to apply the law selected by the choice of law rules, cannot be expected to import all the relevant rules of the foreign law. To apply, for instance, the foreign rules concerned with such matters as service of process, evidence and methods of enforcing judgments would be not only inconvenient but impracticable. Nevertheless, the overriding policy is to apply the foreign substantive law, and if this will be defeated by a slavish adherence to the domestic distinction between substance and procedure, the court should consider whether in the circumstances such adherence is necessary. For:

> It is not everything that appears in a treatise on the law of evidence that is to be classified internationally as adjective law, but only provisions of a technical or procedural character—for example rules as to the admissibility of hearsay evidence or what matters may be noticed judicially.[15]

"If we admit", says Cook, "that the 'substantive' shades off by imperceptible degrees into the 'procedural', and that the 'line' between them does not 'exist', to be discovered merely by logic and analysis, but is rather to be drawn so as best to carry out our purpose, we see that our problem resolves itself substantially into this: How far can the court of the forum go in applying the rules taken from the foreign system of law without unduly hindering or inconveniencing itself?"[16] One critic has replied, "Not much farther than we have already gone";[17] but at least it would be possible to go far enough to avoid such decisions as *Leroux v Brown*[1] and a Canadian court has suggested that legislation should be categorised as procedural only if the question is beyond doubt.[2]

14 [1968] P 675 at 695.
15 *Mahadervan v Mahadervan* [1964] P 233 at 243, [1962] 3 All ER 1108 at 1115.
16 Cook, *Logical and Legal Bases of the Conflict of Laws*, 166. A more radical solution has been suggested by Cavers, *The Choice-of-Law Process*, p. 289, that "Before trial each party could move...for the use of one or more specifically identified procedural rules, to be drawn from the law of the state supplying the substantive law of the case relevant to the issue or issues to which the procedural rules related and to be used for specified purposes in the trial or other proceedings in the case. If the motions were granted, the rules thereby allowed to be used would take the place of the rules of the forum that would otherwise be applied for the same purposes."
17 Ailes (1941) 39 Mich LR 392, 418.
1 Supra, p 75.
2 *Block Bros Realty Ltd v Mollard* (1981) 122 DLR (3d) 323 at 328.

It should be borne in mind that the issue whether a rule is one of substance or procedure may arise in more than one context. The most common context, as illustrated by *Leroux v Brown*, is the determination of the nature of a rule of English law in circumstances where the governing law is foreign. If the English rule is procedural, it is applied notwithstanding the foreign governing law. If the English rule is substantive, it is ignored and the foreign law applied. The problem can, however, arise in circumstances where there is no doubt that the applicable law is foreign but where there is doubt as to whether rules of that country's law are procedural (and to be ignored here) or substantive (and to be applied here). In *Chase Manhatten Bank NA v Israel-British Bank (London) Ltd:*[3]

The plaintiff, a New York bank, sought to trace and recover in equity £2 million paid by mistake to the account of the defendant bank. The issue was whether the plaintiff bank was entitled to trace the proceeds. Although the court held that there was no significant difference between the two relevant laws, English and New York law, on the right to trace, Goulding J asked the question "whether the equitable right of a person who pays money by mistake to trace and claim such money under the law of New York is conferred by substantive law or is of a merely procedural character."[4] He concluded[5] that, viewed by an English court, the plaintiff New York bank had, under New York law, an equitable interest as a cestui que trust which was substantive in nature.

Why did the judge ask the question as to the nature of the equitable right to trace? Presumably, because if he had found the New York rule to be procedural, he would have been unwilling to apply it in England.

2. PARTICULAR ISSUES

Authority is scarcely needed for the proposition that all routine matters arising in the successive stages of litigation must be governed exclusively by English law as being the law of the forum. It is generally said that these include: service of process; the form that the action must take and whether any special procedure is permissible; the title of the action, eg by what persons and against what persons it should be brought; the competency of witnesses and questions as to the admissibility of evidence; the respective functions of judge and jury; the right of appeal, and, according to some writers, the burden of proof.[6]

It is necessary to consider separately certain issues whose classification as substantive or procedural raises difficulties.

(a) THE TIME WITHIN WHICH AN ACTION MUST BE BROUGHT

Until 1984, English law was committed to the view that statutes of limitation, if they merely specified a certain time after which rights could not be enforced

---

3 [1981] Ch 105.
4 Ibid, at 122.
5 Ibid, at 127.
6 Lord REID has said in *Carl Zeiss Stiftung v Rayner and Keeler Ltd (No 2)* [1967] 1 AC 853 at 919 that "estoppel is a matter for the lex fori but the lex fori ought to be developed in a manner consistent with good sense," see infra, p 374.

by action, affected procedure and not substance.[7] This meant that limitation was governed by English law, as the law of the forum, and any limitation provision of the applicable law was ignored.[8] Where, however, it could be shown that the effect of a statute of limitation of the foreign applicable law was not just to bar the plaintiff's remedy, but also to extinguish his cause of action,[9] then the English courts would be prepared to regard the foreign rule as substantive and to be applied here.[10]

The common law rule tends to have no counterpart in civil law countries which usually treat statutes of limitation as substantive,[11] and has been criticised in a number of common law jurisdictions.[12] Furthermore, the Contracts (Applicable Law) Act 1990, implementing the European Community Convention on the Law Applicable to Contractual Obligations (1980),[1] provides that the law which governs the essential validity of a contract is to govern "the various ways of extinguishing obligations, and prescription and limitation of actions".[2] In 1982 the Law Commission concluded that "there is a clear case for the reform of the present English rule"[3] and their recommendations formed the basis of the Foreign Limitation Periods Act 1984.[4]

The general principle of the 1984 Act abandons the common law approach which favoured the application of the domestic law of limitation.[5] Instead, the English court is to apply the law which governs the substantive issue according to our choice of law rules, and this new approach is applied to both actions[6] and arbitrations[7] in England. In tort claims, however, English law, as the law of the forum, will still be relevant[8] because of the choice of law rule which requires actionability both by the law of the forum and by the law of the place of the tort.[9] The corollary of the main rule is that English law is no longer automatically to be applied. There is, of course, a significant difference between a rule under which a claim is to be held to be statute barred here if statute barred under the governing law, a reform which seems widely to be welcomed, and a further rule that, if the claim is not statute barred abroad, it must be allowed to proceed here. This is more controversial and the question whether any, and if so what, restriction should be placed

---

7 *Black-Clawson International Ltd v Papierwerke Waldhof-Aschaffenburg AG* [1975] AC 591 at 630.

8 *British Linen Co v Drummond* (1830) 10B & C 903; *Huber v Steiner* (1835) 2 Bing NC 202; *Don v Lippmann* (1837) 5 Cl & Fin 1; *Harris v Quine* (1869) LR4 QB 653.

9 Examples in English law are provided by acquisitive prescription under the Prescription Act 1832 or express extinction of the former owner's title under the Limitation Act 1980, ss 3 and 17.

10 *Harris v Quine* (1869) LR 4 QB 653 at 656.

11 See Law Commission Working Paper No 75 (1980), paras 25–26.

12 Law Com No 114 (1982), paras 3.3–3.8.

1 Infra, p 517.

2 Sch 1, Art 10(1)(d); and see North, *Contract Conflicts* (1982), p 16.

3 Law Com No 114 (1982), para 3.10.

4 Carter (1985) 101 LQR 68; Stone [1985] LMCLQ 497.

5 S 1(5); but the doctrine of *renvoi* may be relevant in determining, under s 1(1), the relevant foreign substantive law; see Law Com No 114 (1983), para 4.33; Stone [1985] LMCLQ 497, 506–507.

6 S 1(1)(a).

7 S 5.

8 See s 1(2).

9 *Metall und Rohstoff AG v Donaldson Lufkin & Jenrette Inc* [1990] 1 QB 391 at 438; and see infra, pp 533 et seq.

on the application of the foreign rule was examined at length by the Law Commission.[10] At the end of the day, they decided not to adopt, for example, any "long-stop" provision such as that an action could not proceed after, say, 50 years;[11] but concluded that the courts had adequate power under the doctrine of public policy to disapply either an extremely long or a very short foreign limitation period. Such a public policy exception to the general rule is to be found in section 2(1) of the 1984 Act; but it is worth noting that it is reinforced by a provision,[12] not found in the Law Commission's draft Bill, to the effect that the causing of undue hardship to a party by the application of the foreign period would be contrary to public policy. Such hardship has been held to arise where the defendants had agreed to an extension of time which proved to be ineffective under what the court held to be the governing law, given that the parties were unaware that that law would apply.[13]

There are some practical limits to the application of a foreign limitation rule. For example, it is for English law to determine the time at which the limitation period stops running against the plaintiff, eg the commencement of the litigation[14]—to do otherwise might involve the English court in detailed matters of foreign procedure; also foreign rules as to the interruption of the running of the period because of the absence of a party from the jurisdiction are to be ignored.[15] On the other hand, if there is a discretion under the foreign law, for example to suspend the running of the period, the English court must attempt to exercise it in the same way as it would be exercised in the foreign courts.[16] Furthermore, although the English rule is preserved whereby equitable relief may be refused, apart from any statute of limitation, if for example the plaintiff has been guilty of delay, the English court is instructed where there is a foreign applicable law to have regard, in exercising its discretion, to the relevant rules of that legal system.[17]

(b) EVIDENCE

(i) Evidence a matter for the law of the forum

Every system of law has its own principles for deciding the way in which the truth of facts, acts and documents shall be ascertained, and it is obvious that whether the question at issue is domestic or foreign in origin those principles must usually apply. If another system of evidence were admissible it would be equally reasonable to permit another mode of trial.[18]

> Whether a witness is competent or not [said LORD BROUGHAM], whether a certain matter requires to be proved by writing or not, whether certain evidence proves a

---

10 Law Com No 114 (1982), paras 4.35–4.50.
11 It might be noted that the Scottish Law Commission, having toyed with a similar idea, rejected it as inappropriate and undesirable: Scot Law Com No 74 (1983), para 7.8; cf Carter (1985) 101 LQR 68, 70.
12 S 2(2).
13 *The Komninos S* [1990] 1 Lloyd's Rep 541.
14 S 1(3).
15 S 2(3); and see Law Com No 114 (1982), paras 4.26–4.32.
16 S 1(4).
17 S 4(3). Section 3 of the 1984 Act which deals with foreign judgments on limitation points is discussed infra, pp 403–404.
18 *Yates v Thompson* (1835) 3 Cl & Fin 544 at 587.

certain fact or not, that is to be determined by the law of the country where the question arises.[19]

Leroux v Brown[20] is an outstanding example of the rule that the law of the forum determines whether written evidence is required.

There is, however, in the case of contracts an important statutory exception to the rule that proof of facts is for the law of the forum. Under the Contracts (Applicable Law) Act 1990,[21] a contract or an act intended to have legal effect may be proved in any way allowed by the law of the forum or by reference to any law governing the formal validity of the contract or act,[22] provided that the mode of proof under such law can be administered in the courts of the forum.

(ii) Distinction between interpretation and proof of document

With regard to the evidence necessary to prove a certain fact, an important distinction exists where a document is in issue. The interpretation of the document must be distinguished from its proof. The foreign document must be interpreted according to the system of law by which it is governed, but it must be proved in accordance with the requirements of the law of the forum. The English court that is hearing the matter must investigate the governing law as a fact and must take such expert evidence as shows what the construction would be in the foreign country, but at that point the reference to the foreign law must stop. What evidence that law admits, what it rejects, is irrelevant.[23] Thus, for example, the meaning of technical expressions used in a charter-party must be ascertained by reference to the governing law, but the existence of the charter-party itself must be proved in the manner required by English law. Thus in *Brown v Thornton*:[1]

> An action was brought in England to recover freight due under a charter-party that had been made in Batavia. It was found that charter-parties were made in Batavia by the instrument being written in the book of a notary, and then signed by the parties. Each party received a copy signed and sealed by the notary and counter-signed by the principal officer of the Government of Java. A charter-party was sufficiently proved in a Javanese court by production of the notary's book, but, since such books were not allowed to be removed from Java, courts in other parts of the Dutch dominions admitted the copies as evidence.

The plaintiff was nonsuited owing to his failure to prove the charter-party in the manner required by English law. The original contract contained in the notary's book was not produced. Secondary evidence would have been admissible had it been given in the form either of a copy made by the public officer of a court or of a copy made by some person authorised by each party to give a binding copy, but neither of these ways was available.

The Crown, however, has power under the Evidence (Foreign Dominion

---

19 *Bain v Whitehaven Rly Co* (1850) 3 HLCas 1 at 19; and see *Mahadervan v Mahadervan* [1964] P 233 at 243; *Re Fuld's Estate (No 3)* [1968] P 675 at 697–698.
20 (1852) 12 CB 801, supra, p 75. See now the Contracts (Applicable Law) Act 1990 and the Giuliano and Lagarde Report OJ C282/31, 31 October 1980, infra, pp 507–508.
21 Sch1, Art 14(2).
22 Art 9.
23 *Yates v Thompson* (1835) 3 Cl & Fin 544 at 586.
 1 (1837) 6 Ad & El 185.

and Colonial Documents) Act 1933[2] to issue Orders in Council providing that entries contained in the public registries of other countries, whether part of the Commonwealth or not, shall be admissible evidence in English proceedings, and that they shall be proved by means of duly authenticated official certificates.[3]

(iii) Evidence (Proceedings in Other Jurisdictions) Act 1975; Protection of Trading Interests Act 1980

The Evidence (Proceedings in Other Jurisdictions) Act 1975[4] gives effect to the Hague Convention on the Taking of Evidence Abroad in Civil and Commercial Matters (1970).[5] It empowers the High Court to order the taking of evidence (including its video recording)[6] in England when requested to do so by a foreign court, if the evidence is to be obtained for the purpose of actual or contemplated proceedings in any civil or commercial matter[7] or actual criminal proceedings.[8] In general, the court has a discretion whether or not to order such taking of evidence and it will refuse permission where the request amounts to a "fishing expedition";[9] but under the Protection of Trading Interests Act 1980 it must refuse to make an order if the request by the foreign court infringes the jurisdiction of the United Kingdom or is otherwise prejudicial to the United Kingdom.[10] The 1980 Act was passed because of concern over the effect of American anti-trust litigation involving British companies[11] and it also permits[12] the Secretary of State to give directions prohibiting compliance with an order of a foreign court requiring a person in the United Kingdom to produce commercial documents, not within the territorial jurisdiction of the foreign court, or to provide commercial

---

2 As amended by the Oaths and Evidence (Overseas Authorities and Countries) Act 1963, s 5. For existing orders, see the *Supreme Court Practice*, annotations to Order 38, r 10. Evidence of documents may also be admitted under s 1 of the Evidence Act 1938: *Henaff v Henaff* [1966] 1 WLR 598; Dicey & Morris, p 616.
3 See *North v North* (1936) 52 TLR 380; *Motture v Motture* [1955] 3 All ER 242n, [1955] 1 WLR 1066 and the *Practice Direction* in [1955] 2 All ER 465, [1955] 1 WLR 668.
4 See Sutherland (1982) 31 ICLQ 784; Collins (1986) 35 ICLQ 765.
5 The English courts regard their jurisdiction hereunder as wholly statutory: *Boeing Co v PPG Industries Inc* [1988] 3 All ER 839. However the US Supreme Court has held that the procedures of the Hague Convention are optional, not mandatory: *Société Nationale Industrielle Aerospatiale v United States District Court for the Southern District of Iowa* 107 S Ct 2542 (1987); Slomanson (1988) 37 ICLQ 391; Minch (1988) 22 Int Lawyer 511; Prescott and Alley, ibid, 939; Born and Hoing (1990) 24 Int Lawyer 393; Griffin and Bravin (1991) 25 Int Lawyer 331; Black (1991) 40 ICLQ 901. For a comparative analysis, see Morse in *Legal History and Comparative Law: Essays in Honour of Albert Kiralfy* (ed Plender) (1990) 159.
6 *Barber & Sons v Lloyd's Underwriters* [1987] QB 103, [1986] 2 All ER 845.
7 *Re State of Norway's Application (Nos 1 & 2)* [1990] 1 AC 723, [1989] 1 All ER 745; Carter [1989] BYBIL 494; Lipstein (1990) 39 ICLQ 120. The House of Lords held that the proceedings had to be so classified under the law of both the requesting and requested states and, on this basis, included fiscal proceedings. A Special Commission (1989) of the Hague Conference on Private International Law has preferred an autonomous interpretation of the phrase; see F.A. Mann (1990) 106 LQR 354.
8 *Re Westinghouse Electric Corpn Uranium Contract* [1978] AC 547, [1978] 1 All ER 434; *Re Asbestos Insurance Coverage Cases* [1985] 1 All ER 716, [1985] 1 WLR 331, HL; *R v Rathbone, ex p Dikko* [1985] QB 630; and see Sutherland (1982) 31 ICLQ 784.
9 *Re State of Norway's Application (Nos 1 & 2)* [1990] 1 AC 723 at 766–767, 810.
10 S 4.
11 Huntley (1981) 30 ICLQ 213; for rather different American perspectives see Batista (1983) 17 Int Lawyer 61; Blythe (1983) 31 AJCL 99.
12 S 2. For the effect of the 1980 Act on the recognition and enforcement of foreign judgments, see infra, pp 473–474.

information from such documents if it appears to the Secretary of State that the request infringes United Kingdom jurisdiction, or is otherwise prejudicial to the United Kingdom, or if compliance would be prejudicial to the security of the United Kingdom or its relations with other governments.[13]

(iv) Interpretation distinguished from evidence

Evidence must be distinguished from interpretation. The rule of English law, for instance, that if a contract is written, "the writing is the grand criterion of what terms are intended to be contractual and what not"[14] and that therefore oral evidence is inadmissible to add to, vary or contradict the writing, is a rule of evidence properly so called that must be applied in every English action.[15] But, despite its deceptive similarity, the rule which admits oral evidence to show that the parties intended to incorporate a certain condition customarily included in a contract of a particular kind is a rule of interpretation that is not necessarily applicable merely because the action is in England. It concerns interpretation, not proof.[16] Owing to the imperfect manner in which the contract has been drafted, the intention of the parties is not clear and the object of the particular rule is to explain what they meant.

A distinction must also be made between facts that are relevant and the evidence by which such facts are proved, for the former fall to be decided according to the law governing the transaction, while the latter is a matter of procedure for the law of the forum. This was considered in *The Gaetano and Maria*.[17]

> An action was brought in England on a bottomry bond given at the Azores by the master of a ship flying the Italian flag, without any communication with his owners. By Italian law the bond was valid; by English law its validity depended on proof that at the time it was given the ship was in distress and in need of repair and that the circumstances were such as to render it impossible for the master to communicate with the cargo-owners. It was accordingly argued that, since proof of the necessity of immediate repairs is a matter of evidence, the question of the validity of the bond must be determined by English law as being the law of the forum. The flaw in this argument was exposed by the Court of Appeal.

The sole fact in issue was one of substance, namely whether the master had authority to give a valid bond, a question that fell to be determined by Italian law as being the law of the flag. The equivalent English rule on this question no doubt differed from that under Italian law, but since it affected substance, not procedure, it was not to be invoked merely because the action was brought in England.

(v) Presumptions and burden of proof

A controversial question is whether presumptions and burden of proof are matters that affect procedure or substance.[18] The classification of pre-

---

13 See *British Airways Board v Laker Airways Ltd* [1984] QB 142 at 195–198; affd on this issue [1985] AC 58 at 87–92.
14 *Korner v Witkowitzer* [1950] 2 KB 128 at 162, [1950] 1 All ER 558 at 575.
15 [1950] 2 KB 128 at 162–163, [1950] 1 All ER 558 at 576.
16 [1950] 2 KB 128 at 163, [1950] 1 All ER 558 at 576.
17 (1882) 7 PD 137.
18 See Wolff, pp 234–236.

sumptions will depend on their nature and effect.[19] Presumptions of fact pose no problem for they raise no legal issue. Presumptions of law may be either irrebuttable or rebuttable. The former would appear to be substantive in effect,[20] but it is not clear how rebuttable presumptions should be classified. It has been suggested[21] that those which apply to a restricted class of case should be treated as substantive, but that it is uncertain how presumptions of general application, such as the presumptions of death or validity of marriage, should be classified. There is authority for treating the presumption as to the validity of a marriage as substantive so that a marriage may be upheld under the presumption of the foreign governing law.[1] But if the English law presumption favoured the validity of the marriage whilst the foreign one did not, it is tempting to conclude that the public policy of the forum in favour of validity would prevail.[2]

Whilst there may be much to be said for the view that the burden of proof is regulated by the law governing matters of substance,[3] the contrary view has been voiced.[4] Indeed, in *Re Fuld's Estate (No 3)*[5] SCARMAN J concluded that the English Probate Court "must in all matters of burden of proof follow scrupulously its own lex fori".[6]

The question whether a rule distributing the burden of proof affects substance or procedure has arisen in the United States of America on a plea of contributory negligence. There is authority for the view that the burden of proving contributory negligence is a question of substantive law, to be determined by the law governing such substantive issues.[7]

Again, in the case of contracts there is a special statutory rule. The Contracts (Applicable Law) Act 1990 provides[8] that the rules of the law governing the substance of the contract which "raise presumptions of law or determine the burden of proof" shall be applied. It is only if these rules are to be classified as ones of substance that they are to be applied in place of the law of the forum. If they are merely procedural, they are inapplicable.[9]

(c) PARTIES

Two questions need to be considered in connection with the identity of the parties to the action. The first is the determination of the appropriate person to sue, and the second concerns the identity of the person to be sued.[10]

---

19 Dicey & Morris, pp 183–184.
20 *Re Cohn* [1945] Ch 5; see *Monterosso Shipping Co Ltd v International Transport Workers Federation* [1982] 3 All ER 841.
21 Dicey & Morris, pp 183–184; and see Morse, *Torts in Private International Law*, pp 178–179.
 1 *De Thoren v AG* (1876) 1 App Cas 686; *Mahadervan v Mahadervan* [1964] P 233.
 2 Cf Nygh, pp 229–230.
 3 Dicey & Morris, p 183.
 4 *The Roberta* (1937) 58 L1 L Rep 159.
 5 [1968] P 675.
 6 Ibid, at 697; and see at 698–699.
 7 See *Fitzpatrick v International Railway* 252 NY 127 (1929); Hancock, *Torts in the Conflict of Laws*, 159 et seq; Webb & Brownlie (1962) 50 Can BR 79, 87–89; Morse, *Torts in Private International Law*, pp 174–178.
 8 Sch 1, Art 14(1).
 9 Indeed they fall outside the legislation altogether: Art 1(2)(h), infra, pp 473–474.
10 See Prott (1989) V Hague Recueil 215, 245–254.

(i) The proper plaintiff

The first question is whether the name in which an action may be brought falls to be determined exclusively by the law of the forum on the ground that it is a mere matter of procedure. It is a question that arises principally where the plaintiff is not the original owner of the subject-matter of the dispute, but has acquired it derivatively from the original owner, as, for instance, in the case of the assignment of a debt or other intangible movable. In those cases where English law requires the assignee to sue in the name of the assignor, it has been said,[11] and indeed on one occasion held,[12] that the requirement must be observed in an action in this country, even though it is not necessary by the law governing the transaction.

But on principle it is doubtful whether every rule that regulates the name in which an action must be brought is merely procedural in character. It would seem to be an unwarranted extension of the province of procedure, at any rate in cases falling within the sphere of private international law, to regard a rule as procedural if the effect is to deprive the plaintiff of a right which he has definitely acquired under the governing legal system.[13] If, for instance, English law still regarded a contractual right as so essentially personal as to be actionable only at the suit of the original contracting party, it would surely be the negation of principle, and indeed of justice, to enforce such a rule indiscriminately as being one of procedure, and thus to defeat a plaintiff who had acquired a contractual right derivatively under some legal system that regarded the transaction as valid. To adopt this attitude would be to mistake substance for procedure. There is little authority on the matter, but the early case of *O'Callaghan v Thomond*[14] at least shows that the English courts have not always adopted this attitude:

> The assignee of an Irish judgment brought an action of debt in his own name in England to recover the amount of the judgment. He was entitled so to sue by Irish law.

The argument of counsel for the defendant was instructive. Though admitting the general principle that the law of one country would recognise and enforce obligations raised by the law of another country, he contended that the principle applied only to the substance of the contract, and could neither affect the form of enforcing an obligation in another country nor be allowed to contravene the general rule of English law that intangible movables were unassignable. He therefore argued that no action could be maintained in the present circumstances except in the name of the person who recovered the judgment. The court, however, was unanimous that the rule was a matter of substance, not of procedure.

One problem which can arise in determining who is a proper plaintiff is whether a person will be permitted to sue here in a representative capacity, relying on an appointment made under a foreign law. In *Kamouh v Associated*

---

11 *Wolff v Oxholm* (1817) 6 M & S 92 at 99.

12 *Jeffery v M'Taggart* (1817) 6 M & S 126.

13 In *Bumper Development Corpn v Metropolitan Police Comr* [1991] 4 All ER 638, [1991] 1 WLR 1362, the Court of Appeal, whilst accepting that the issue whether a foreigner (here a ruined Indian Hindu temple recognised in India as a juristic person) could sue in England was a matter for English law as the law of the forum, took the broad view that it would not be contrary to public policy so to permit it.

14 (1810) 3 Taunt 82. See also *Innes v Dunlop* (1800) 8 Term Rep 595; *Trimbey v Vignier* (1834) 1 Bing NC 151 at 160; cf *Regas Ltd v Plotkins* (1961) 29 DLR (2d) 282.

Electrical Industries International Ltd[15] the plaintiff was Lebanese and, because his brother had disappeared, he caused himself to be appointed by a court in Beirut as his brother's "judicial administrator" and, in that capacity, sought to bring an action in England on a contract made between his brother and the defendants. Parker J refused to recognise his title to sue, observing[16] that, in such cases, there are two conflicting principles to be examined:

first, that these courts should as a matter of comity give effect to the curator's or tuteur's right under foreign law to sue in his own name; second that municipal procedure should be applied.

The first principle prevails in the case of bankruptcy,[17] receivership[18] and the curatorship of the mentally ill;[19] whilst the second holds sway in respect of an administrator of the property of a deceased[20] or absent[21] person.

(ii) The appropriate defendant

The second question relates to the party sued. To decide whether a foreign rule determining the identity of the party to be sued, or prescribing the order in which parties must be sued, is one of substance or of procedure, it is necessary to classify the exact nature and effect of the rule according to the legal system of which it forms a part.

The question is of especial importance in partnership cases.[22] The doctrine, for instance, of English law that any one partner may be sued alone for the totality of the partnership debts is in sharp contrast with the rule, obtaining in many other jurisdictions, that a creditor cannot sue an individual partner until he has first sued the partners jointly and the assets of the firm have been exhausted. A rule of this nature, if pleaded as a bar to an English action, must be classified in its foreign context. It must not be dismissed as procedural, if the result will be to impose a liability that does not exist by the law governing the transaction; but if it merely requires the enforcement in a particular manner of an admitted liability, it must be dismissed as a rule affecting only the mode of process. The principle applied by the courts appears to be as follows:

If the law governing matters of substance regards the defendant's liability as undoubted, though it makes it a condition precedent to an action that other parties be sued first, this is a rule of procedure that, unless it obtains in England, is ignored in English proceedings. If, on the other hand, the governing law regards the defendant as being under no liability whatever

15 [1980] QB 199.
16 Ibid, at 206.
17 *Macaulay v Guarantee Trust Co of New York* (1927) 44 TLR 99.
18 *Schemmer v Property Resources Ltd* [1975] Ch 273, [1974] 3 All ER 45, where it is emphasised, at 287, that recognition will depend on there being sufficient connection between the defendant and the country in which the receiver was appointed; and see *Thorne, Ernst & Whinney Inc v Sulpetro Ltd* (1987) 47 DLR (4th) 315; *White v Verkouille* [1990] 2Qd R 191.
19 *Didisheim v London and Westminster Bank* [1900] 2 Ch 15, infra, pp 774–775.
20 *New York Breweries Co v A-G* [1899] AC 62.
21 *Kamouh v Associated Electrical Industries International Ltd* [1980] QB 199.
22 It may also arise in cases where, under the foreign law, a creditor must sue the principal debtor before he can sue a surety. This rule has been held to be procedural: *Waung v Subbotovsky* [1968] 3 NSWR 499, affd on other grounds (1969) 121 CLR 337.

unless other parties are sued first, it imposes a rule of substance that must be observed in English proceedings.[23]

Thus in an action brought against the executors of a deceased member of a Spanish firm, a claim that according to Spanish law creditors could not institute a suit against the separate estate of a deceased partner until they had had recourse to and had exhausted the property of the firm was not upheld because the rule in question determined merely the mode of procedure.[1]

The distinction was neatly raised in the leading case of *General Steam Navigation Co v Guillou*,[2] where the facts were as follows:

The plaintiffs brought an action in England to recover damages for injury caused to one of their ships by the negligent navigation of a French ship which at the time of the accident was under the direction and management of the defendant's servants. The offending ship belonged to a French company of which the defendant was a shareholder and acting director.

The third plea to the action stated that:

By the law of France the defendant ... was not ... responsible for or liable to be sued or impleaded individually, or in his own name or person, in any manner whatsoever, in respect of the said causes of action, ... but by the law of France the said company alone, by their said style or title, or the master in command for the time being of the said ship, was ... responsible for, and liable to be sued or impleaded for, the said causes of action.

The one question, therefore, that fell to be decided here was whether the French law, as disclosed in the plea, absolved the defendant from all liability in any circumstances, or whether it imposed on him an undoubted, though a joint, liability. Although the court unanimously took this distinction,[3] the judges of the Court of Exchequer were equally divided on the question on the facts, although the plea clearly alleged a denial of liability by French law. Lord ABINGER and ALDERSON B held that French law merely required the defendant to be sued jointly with his co-owners in the name of the company; while Barons PARKE and GURNEY considered that according to the plea the defendant incurred no responsibility whatsoever, joint or several, for the acts of the master. This judicial difference of opinion on the question of fact is of no great moment, for the importance of the decision lies in the clearness with which the general principle is stated.

(d) PRIORITIES

It has consistently been held that the order in which property in the possession of the court is distributable among creditors must be governed by English law. The priority of creditors in such a case is a procedural matter that is determinable by the law of forum;[4] though it does not necessarily follow that the forum's rule as to priorities should be the same in an international claim

23 *General Steam Navigation Co v Guillou* (1843) 11 M & W 877; *Bank of Australasia v Harding* (1850) 9 CB 661; *Bullock v Caird* (1875) LR 10 QB 276; *Re Doetsch* [1896] 2 Ch 836. The suggested principle is criticised by Wolff, p 240.
1 *Re Doetsch*, supra.
2 Supra.
3 (1843) 11 M & W 877 at 895.
4 *Pardo v Bingham* (1868) LR 6 Eq 485; *Re Melbourn* (1870) 6 Ch App 64; *The Colorado* [1923] P 102; *The Halcyon Isle* [1981] AC 221; dist. priority of assignees of intangible movables, infra, pp 816–818.

as in a purely domestic case.[5] The law of the forum governs because the issue of priority forms no part of the transaction under which a creditor has acquired his right. It is extrinsic and comprises in effect a privilege dependent on the law of the country where the remedy is sought.[6] Thus priorities of creditors claiming in bankruptcy or in the administration of a deceased insolvent's estate are governed exclusively by the law of forum. It is the same in the case of liens. Where, for instance, two or more persons prosecute claims against a ship that has been arrested in England, the order in which they are entitled to be paid is governed exclusively by English law.[7]

In the case of a right in rem such as a lien, however, this principle must not be allowed to obscure the rule that the substantive right of the creditor depends on the governing law. The validity and nature of the right must be distinguished from the order in which it ranks in relation to other claims. Before it can determine the order of payment, the court should examine the law governing the transaction upon which the claimant relies in order to verify the validity of the right and to establish its precise nature. When the nature of the right is thus ascertained the principle of procedure then ought to come into play and ordain that the order of payment prescribed by English law for a right of that particular kind shall govern.

Whilst this is the basis on which courts ought to proceed, decisions in relation to maritime liens have not consistently followed this line.[8] A clear and, it is suggested, correct illustration of the approach to be adopted is provided by *The Colorado*:[9]

> The two claimants to a ship were A, who held a French mortgage, and B, who had executed necessary repairs to her at Cardiff. The transaction under which A claimed did not constitute a mortgage as understood by English law, but its effect by French law was to give the mortgagee a right equivalent in nature and extent to the maritime lien as recognised in England. With regard to priorities the English rule is that the claim of a necessaries man is postponed to that of a lienor, while by French law the claim of a mortgagee is postponed to that of a necessaries man.

On these facts it was accordingly held by the Court of Appeal that A was entitled to rank first. French law determined the substance of A's right; English law determined whether a right of that nature ranked before or after an opposing claim.[10]

At least one earlier decision[11] had failed[12] to draw the crucial distinction between the substance of the right, an issue for the governing law, and the question of priorities, a remedial matter for the law of the forum. A similar

---

5 Carter (1983) 54 BYBIL 207, 211–212.

6 *Harrison v Sterry* (1809) 5 Cranch 289 at 298; approved in *The Colorado* [1923] P 102 at 107.

7 *The Milford* (1858) Sw 362 at 366; *The Tagus* [1903] P 44; *American Surety Co of New York v Wrightson* (1910) 16 Com Cas 37; *The Colorado* [1923] P 102; *The Halcyon Isle* [1981] AC 221.

8 Carter (1983) 54 BYBIL 207.

9 [1923] P 102; and see *The Acrux* [1965] P 391 at 404.

10 In *The Zigurds* [1932] P 113, German claimants failed to gain priority over other English claimants because, although they enjoyed such priority under German law, that was as a matter of German procedural (and not substantive) law; and it was for English procedural law to determine priorities.

11 *The Tagus* [1903] P 44.

12 As is pointed out by the Supreme Court of Canada in *Todd Shipyards Corpn v Altema Compania Maritima SA* (1972) 32 DLR (3d) 571 at 575–576.

failure is evident in the decision of the majority in the Privy Council in *The Halcyon Isle*:[13]

> The *Halcyon Isle* was a British registered ship. An English bank had a mortgage on the ship which was repaired in the USA by American ship repairers. The repair bill was unpaid and the ship was arrested in Singapore and ordered by the court to be sold, but the proceeds were insufficient to satisfy the claims of both the bank and the repairers. So a question of priorities arose. Under Singapore law (which was the same as English law), the mortgagees had priority because the ship repairers were not regarded as having a maritime lien. Under United States law, the repairers were regarded as having such a lien as would give them priority.

The Singapore Court of Appeal held in favour of the repairers,[14] but they were reversed by a majority in the Privy Council who gave priority to the English bank as mortgagees. Whilst both majority and dissenting minority in the Privy Council agreed that matters of priority are procedural and to be governed by the law of the forum, they disagreed as to the analysis of the claims to be ranked in order of priority. Lord Diplock, for the majority, concluded that the issue of priority depended

> upon whether or not if the repairs to the ship had been done in Singapore, the repairers would have been entitled under the law of Singapore to a maritime lien on the *Halcyon Isle* for the price of them. The answer to that question is that they are not. The mortgagees are entitled to priority.[15]

This approach fails to give due consideration to the law of the United States. It is for that law, as the governing law, to consider both whether the claim by the repairers was valid and whether it would lead to the creation, *under United States law*, of a maritime lien. The basis of the majority judgment seems to be that whether the repairers are entitled to a lien is solely a procedural matter, and Lord Diplock claimed that such analysis is consistent with the decision in *The Colorado*.[16]

Much to be preferred is the analysis of the minority,[17] who found in favour of the ship repairers, and the essence of whose approach is succinctly expressed thus:

> The question is—does English law, in circumstances such as these, recognise the maritime lien created by the law of the United States of America, ie the lex contractus where no such lien exists by its own internal law? In our view the balance of authorities, the comity of nations, private international law and natural justice all answer this question in the affirmative. If this be correct then English law (the lex fori) gives the maritime lien created by the lex loci contractus precedence over the mortgagees' mortgage. If it were otherwise, injustice would prevail. The ship-repairers would be deprived of their maritime lien, valid as it appeared to be throughout the world, and without which they would obviously never have allowed the ship to sail away without paying a dollar for the important repairs.[18]

---

13 [1981] AC 221.
14 Following the decision of the Supreme Court of Canada in *Todd Shipyards Corpn v Altema Compania Maritima SA* (1972) 32 DLR (3d) 571.
15 [1981] AC 221 at 241.
16 Supra. See [1981] AC 221 at 238. He also, thereby, disapproved of the Supreme Court of Canada's decision in *Todd Shipyards Corpn v Altema Compania Maritima SA*, supra: [1981] AC 221 at 241–242.
17 Lord Salmon and Lord Scarman.
18 [1981] AC 221 at 246–247.

(e) THE NATURE AND EXTENT OF THE REMEDY

It is obvious that a plaintiff who seeks to enforce a foreign claim in England can demand only those remedies recognised by English law, and cannot demand even them unless they harmonise with the right according to its nature and extent as fixed by the foreign law.[19] "Put in another way", to quote Lord PARKER CJ, in *Phrantzes v Argenti*,[20]

> if the machinery by way of remedies here is so different from that in Greece as to make the right sought to be enforced a different right, that right would not, in my judgment, be enforced in this country.

That particular case[1] was concerned with the Greek law relating to the obligation of a man to provide a dowry for his son-in-law. By that law, a father was obliged to establish a dowry for his daughter on her marriage, the amount of which depended inter alia on his finances, the number of his children and the social position of himself and his son-in-law. If a father failed to fulfil this obligation, his daughter, and she alone, had a cause of action to compel him to enter into a dowry contract not with herself, but with her husband. If the father was abroad, he could be directed by the Greek court to conclude the contract wherever he might happen to be, in the presence either of a public notary or the Greek consul.

It was against this background that Mrs Phrantzes brought an action in England against her father, claiming a declaration that she was entitled to be provided with a dowry and petitioning that the amount properly due to her should be assessed.

All parties were Greek nationals, and it was assumed that the father was domiciled in Greece.

Lord PARKER was satisfied that the obligation of a man to establish a dowry in favour of his son-in-law was one that on general principles was enforceable in England. It could not be excluded on the ground that the right of the beneficiary was unknown to English law.[2] Nevertheless, he held that for at least two reasons the action must fail.

First, there was no remedy at common law appropriate to enforce the exact right vested in the plaintiff by Greek law, namely, "a right to obtain an order condemning someone to enter into a contract in a particular form with a person not even a party to the proceedings".[3]

Secondly, the daughter did not come to the English court possessed of a right to a definite sum of money. What she was entitled to was such sum as, failing agreement, a court in its discretion might assess, and this assessment depended on a wide variety of factors such as the social position of the parties in a Greek environment.

All these enquiries and decisions [said Lord PARKER] are essentially matters for the

---

19 *Boys v Chaplin* [1971] AC 356 at 381–382, 394; and see *Baschet v London Illustrated Standard* [1900] 1 Ch 73.
20 [1960] 2 QB 19 at 35–36, [1960] 1 All ER 778 at 784.
1 For an American example, see *Slater v Mexican National Rly Co* 194 US 120 (1904).
2 Distinguishing in this respect such decisions as *Re Macartney [1921] 1 Ch 522, and De Brimont v Penniman* (1873) 10 Blatch 436, where a New York court refused to enforce the duty, recognised by French law, of a father-in-law to support his son-in-law, infra, p 381.
3 [1960] 2 QB 19 at 35, [1960] 1 All ER 778 at 784.

domestic courts, and matters largely for the discretion of those courts and not our courts.[4]

It is established that a claim to set-off affects procedure, not substance, since the issue that it raises is whether the relief claimed by the defendant shall be granted in the plaintiff's action or whether it is obtainable only by a counter-action.[5] If the court, in accordance with its own procedural code, refuses the privilege of set-off, it makes no attack on the substance of the defendant's claim, but, without adjudging the merits of the claim, merely rules that it must be put in suit in separate proceedings.[6]

(f) DAMAGES

The subject of damages raises a problem of some difficulty in private international law, not because the principles are obscure but because the English authorities are scanty.

Various different questions must be segregated. In brief, remoteness of damage and heads of damage must be distinguished from measure of damages. The rules relating to remoteness indicate what kind of loss actually resulting from the commission of a tort or from a breach of contract is actionable; the rules for the measure of damages show the method by which compensation for an actionable loss is calculated. There is one principle of remoteness in tort, another in contract with similar variations between the two causes of action as to the heads of damage or loss for which recovery may be made. But the rule that regulates the measure of damages is the same for contracts as it is for torts. It requires *restitutio in integrum*.

(i) Remoteness of damage

There can be no doubt, at least on principle, that remoteness of damage must be governed by the law governing the obligation that rests on the defendant. Not only the existence, but also the extent, of an obligation, whether it springs from a breach of contract or the commission of a wrong, must be determined by the system of law from which it derives its source.[7] The governing law admittedly determines the nature and content of the right created by a contract, and it is clear that the kind of loss for which damages are recoverable on breach forms part of that content. Both the nature and the content of a contractual right depend in part on the question whether certain consequential loss that may ensue if the contract is unperformed will be too remote in the eye of the law. If the governing law determines what constitutes a breach, it is also to determine the consequences of a breach.[8]

> Suppose, for the sake of argument, that by French law a purchaser who sues a seller for non-delivery of goods is entitled to recover for the loss that he has suffered through failure to carry out any sub-contracts he may have made.

A purchaser under a French contract for the sale of goods acquires, on this

---

4 Ibid; cf *Khalij Commercial Bank Ltd v Woods* (1985) 17 DLR (4th) 358.
5 *Meyer v Dresser* (1864) 16 CBNS 646; and see Wood, *English and International Set-off* (1989) ch 23.
6 But see Wolff, pp 233, 234, where it is shown that under Continental laws set-off is extrajudicial and is regarded as a matter of substance; and see Wood, op cit, ch 24.
7 *Slater v Mexican National Rly Co* 194 US 120 (1904).
8 Contracts (Applicable Law) Act 1990, Sch 1, Art 10 (1) (c), infra, pp 516–517; and see *Drew Brown v The Orient Trader* (1972) 34 DLR (3d) 339.

hypothesis, a right of a perfectly definite extent, and the principles of private international law as embodied in the Contracts (Applicable Law) Act 1990[9] require that his position in this respect shall be neither improved nor prejudiced by the fact that he happens to bring his action in England. If the court applies the rule of internal English law, that compensation cannot be recovered for sub-contract losses, the result is to diminish the content of the right as fixed by the governing law. Of course, an exception must be made when the type of loss for which recovery may be had in the foreign country is contrary to the distinctive policy of the law of the forum.[10]

In *D'Almeida Araujo Lda v Becker & Co Ltd*, a case of breach of contract, PILCHER J based his decision on the distinction between remoteness of damage and measure of damages.[11] The facts were these:

> By a contract, made on 20 March and governed as to substantial validity by Portuguese law, the plaintiffs, merchants in Lisbon, agreed to sell 500 tons of palm oil to the defendants, a British company carrying on business in London.
>
> With a view to the fulfilment of their undertaking, the plaintiffs agreed to buy 500 tons of palm oil from one Mourao, a Portuguese dealer. This contract provided that, in the event of its breach, the party in default should indemnify the other to the extent of 5 per cent of the total value of the contract, a sum that in fact amounted to the equivalent of £3,500. The plaintiffs were forced into the payment of this sum, since the defendants broke the contract of 20 March.

In the present action, the plaintiffs claimed to recover by way of damages the £3,500 which they had been obliged to pay under the indemnity. It was admitted that according to English law the loss suffered by reason of this payment would found no claim to damages, since it was not the kind of loss that ensued in the usual course of things from such a breach of contract. The judge, however, held that English law was irrelevant. He said:

> I conclude that the question whether the plaintiffs are entitled to claim from the defendants the £3,500 which they have paid to Mourao, depends on whether such damage is or is not too remote. In my view, the question here is one of remoteness, and therefore falls to be determined in accordance with Portuguese law.[12]

It should logically follow from the *D'Almeida Case* that remoteness of damage in tort is also a matter of substance to be determined by the governing law.[13] To rule otherwise would permit a plaintiff to exact compensation for what was no ground of liability under that law.

(ii) Heads of damage

A further issue in which the distinction between substance and procedure has arisen is that of deciding whether a particular head of damage is recoverable, ie whether this is a matter of the quantification of the measure of damages and thus procedural, or whether it raises a substantive issue. Whilst there seems little doubt that, in the field of contract, this is a substantive issue for

9 Ibid.
10 1990 Act, Sch 1, Art 16.
11 [1953] 2 QB 329, [1953] 2 All ER 288.
12 [1953] 2 QB 329 at 338, [1953] 2 All ER 288 at 293. The case would be decided the same way under the Contracts (Applicable Law) Act 1990.
13 See Morse, *Torts in Private International Law*, pp 197–200.

the law governing the contract, tort claims can cause more difficulty because of the basic choice of law rule that the claim must be actionable both by English law as the law of the forum and by the law of the place of the tort.[14] There are some circumstances where the court may be justified in not applying the law of the foreign place of the tort, with the result that the governing law is English law. In such a case the question whether a particular head of damage affects procedure or substance is, of course, merely academic. Such was the position of *Boys v Chaplin*[15] which concerned a motor accident involving two British servicement in Malta. Maltese law, the law of the place of the tort gave the plaintiff a right of action to recover pecuniary loss but not damages for the pain and suffering incurred in his motor cycle accident. English law, the law of the forum, would permit recovery for both heads of damage. Whilst all five judges in the House of Lords concurred that English law should be applied, their reasons for so doing were far from unanimous. Two, Lord GUEST[16] and Lord DONOVAN,[17] concluded that compensation for pain and suffering was "merely an element in the quantification of the total compensation"[18] and fell to be determined by English law as the law of the forum governing procedural matters. It is quite clear that Lord HODSON was "persuaded that questions such as whether loss of earning capacity or pain and suffering are admissible heads of damage must be questions of substantive law",[19] a view with which Lord PEARSON agreed.[20] Both their Lordships decided, for reasons that will be considered more fully later,[21] that English law alone was to be applied in that case to issues of substance. Lord WILBERFORCE also accepted this conclusion and referred only briefly to the "quasi-mechanical"[1] solution to the case based on the substance/procedure dichotomy. However, he pointed to the artificiality of classifying the right to recover damages for pain and suffering as a matter of procedure. He, also, avoided the application of Maltese law by deciding that English law was the governing law and that determination of the heads of damage was a substantive issue.

We can conclude from the majority approach in *Boys v Chaplin* that so far, for example, as a claim for solatium is concerned, not only will the separate right of action given for instance by Scots law to the near relatives of an injured party be classed as substantive,[2] but so also will a claim by the injured party himself for damages for pain and suffering.[3] Similarly, the question whether recovery may be had in a tort action for heads of economic

---

14 Infra, pp 533 et seq.
15 [1971] AC 356, infra, pp 534–536; and see *Kohnke v Karger* [1951] 2 KB 670 at 677, [1951] 2 All ER 179 at 182.
16 Ibid at 381–383.
17 Ibid at 383; and see Lord UPJOHN in the Court of Appeal [1968] 2 QB 1 at 32–33.
18 Ibid at 382.
19 [1971] AC 356 at 379.
20 Ibid at 394–395.
21 Infra, pp 545–546.
 1 [1971] AC 356 at 392–393.
 2 Eg *Naftalin v London, Midland and Scottish Rly Co* 1933 SC 259; *McElroy v McAllister* 1949 SC 110; and see *Mackinnon v Iberia Shipping Co Ltd* 1955 SC 20; but cf Walker, *The Law of Delict in Scotland*, 2nd edn, pp 67–68.
 3 Cf Lord GUEST [1971] AC 356 at 382–383; but see Lord WILBERFORCE, at pp 392–393. It should be pointed out that, in Scots law, the concept of solatium constitutes an independent right of action for grief suffered through the death of a near relative and is also an element in a claim for damages by an injured plaintiff representing compensation for pain and suffering: Walker *The Law of Delict in Scotland*, 2nd edn, pp 66–68.

loss is a matter of substance and not of procedure,[4] as is a claim for exemplary damages.[5] It must be borne in mind, however, that, in the usual tort case where actionability is required by both the law of the place of the tort and by English law as the law of the forum, the substantive law determining liability or non-liability is a combination of the law of the forum and the law of the place of the tort.[6] It would appear, therefore, that both laws must agree on the question whether recovery may be had by the plaintiff against the defendant for a particular head of damage.[7]

(iii) Measure of damages

The next question is—By what law is the measure of damages governed? A rule as to the measure of damages in the narrow sense is a mere rule of calculation. Its function is to quantify in terms of money the sum payable by the defendant in respect of the injury, whether it be a tort or breach of contract, for which his liability has already been determined by the governing law. A plaintiff who seeks to recover compensation in England in respect of an obligation that is governed as to substance by a foreign law has already acquired a right the nature and extent of which have been fully determined. His object is that his right as established shall be converted by the English court into a right to receive a definite sum of money. He is entitled to be paid in full for the injury suffered and he takes advantage of the English process and machinery in order to exact this payment.

It would seem, therefore, that all questions that arise in the course of this quantification of the amount payable should be governed by English law as the law of the forum. Although PILCHER J has said that

> the quantification of damage, which according to the proper law is not too remote, should be governed by the lex fori[8]

Some opposition has been expressed. Indeed McNAIR J has found

> the greatest possible difficulty in appreciating the distinction ... between remoteness of damage and measure of damage.[9]

Nevertheless it is suggested, with the support of the House of Lords,[10] that the distinction is both valid and valuable. Reference of the issue of measure of damages to the law of the forum will mean that if, for instance, the defendant pleads a tender of the amount due, he must prove that the tender is in accordance with English law, for if the task of the court is to fix the amount payable it must also be competent to decide whether in its view payment has in effect already been made.[11] Furthermore, the question whether

---

4 *Mitchell v McCulloch* 1976 SC 1; *Breavington v Godleman* (1988) 169 CLR 41.
5 *Waterhouse v Australian Broadcasting Corpn* (1989) 86 ACTR 1.
6 [1971] AC 356 at 398.
7 Eg *Mitchell v McCulloch* 1976 SC 1, infra, p 102 and see *Li Lian Tan v Durham and General Accident Fire and Life Assurance Corpn Ltd* [1966] SASR 143. *Boys v Chaplin* itself was held to be a case falling outside the general double-barrelled rule in that the majority held English law alone to be the applicable law; cf *Kemp v Piper* [1971] SASR 25.
8 The *D'Almeida Case* [1953] 2 QB 329 at 336.
9 *N V Handel Maatschappij J Smits Import-Export v English Exporters Ltd* [1955] 2 Lloyd's Rep 69 at 72. This is a view with which Lord UPJOHN has sympathised, in *Boys v Chaplin* [1968] 2 QB 1 at 31; and see *Livesley v Horst* [1925] 1 DLR 159 at 164.
10 *Boys v Chaplin* [1971] AC 356 at 378–379, 382–383, 392–393, 394.
11 *The Baarn* [1933] P 251.

the damages should be paid in a lump sum or by means of periodic payments is a procedural matter for the law of the forum.[12]

Special statutory provision is once more made in the case of contracts. Under the Contracts (Applicable Law) Act 1990 the law governing the substance of the contract is also to govern "the consequences of breach, including the assessment of damages in so far as it is governed by rules of law", provided that this is within the powers conferred on the court of the forum by its procedural law.[13] This is intended only to apply rules of law for the assessment of damages to be found in the governing law; "questions of fact will always be for the court hearing the action."[14]

(iv) Payment of interest

The issue as to whether interest is payable necessitates consideration of whether interest is claimed by virtue of a term in a contract or as damages and whether what is in issue is the right to interest or the rate at which it is payable. It was well established at common law that whether interest is payable on a contractual debt, and if so at what rate, is a matter to be determined by the law governing the essential validity of the contract,[15] and this would appear still clearly to be the case under the Contracts (Applicable Law) Act 1990.[16] This rule has been applied in the case of dishonour of a bill of exchange. So, whether interest is recoverable on dishonour depends on the law governing the contract under which the defendant rendered himself liable.[17] Where there is a claim, not for a debt but for damages for breach of contract, the right to interest on the damages is governed by the law applicable to the contract.[18] There is some authority for the conclusion that the right to interest on damages in tort is governed by the law, or laws, governing the substantive tort issues.[19] Turning now to the rate at which interest is to be paid, or whether the interest is to be compound or simple, there seems little doubt again that, in the case of a contractual claim for interest, these matters are governed by the law applicable to the contract.[20] There is less certainty as to the law to determine the rate of interest payable on damages. In an action for damages for breach of contract, it was decided in *Miliangos v George Frank (Textiles) Ltd (No 2)*[21] that the question of the rate of interest is a matter relating to measure of damages, and thus a matter of procedure

12 McGregor (1970) 33 MLR 1, 21 et seq.
13 Sch 1, Art 10(1)(c).
14 Giuliano and Lagarde Report, OJ 1980, C282/33.
15 *Montreal Trust Co v Stanrock Uranium Mines Ltd* (1965) 53 DLR (2d) 594; and see *Shrichand & Co v Lacon* (1906) 22 TLR 245; *Mount Albert Borough Council v Australasian Temperance and General Mutual Life Assurance Society* [1938] AC 224, [1937] 4 All ER 206; Law Com No 124 (1983), para 2.29.
16 Sch 1, Art 10(1)(c).
17 *Allen v Kemble* (1848) 6 Moo PCC 314; *Gibbs v Fremont* (1853) 9 Exch 25.
18 See, at common law, *Miliangos v George Frank (Textiles) Ltd (No 2)* [1977] QB 489, [1976] 3 All ER 599; *cf Midland International Trade Services Ltd v Sudairy* (1990) Financial Times, 2 May. Similarly, in a claim for restitutionary relief based on frustration, the law governing the frustrated contract has been applied to determine a claim to interest: *BP Exploration Co (Libya) Ltd v Hunt (No 2)* [1979] 1 WLR 783 at 845–850, affd [1983] 2 AC 352.
19 *Ekins v East India Co* (1717) 1 P Wms 395; Dicey & Morris, p 1334.
20 This was clearly the position at common law: *Fergusson v Fyffe* (1841) C1 & Fin 121 at 140 (compound interest); *Mount Albert Borough Council v Australasian Temperance and General Mutual Life Assurance Society* [1938] AC 224, [1937] 4 All ER 206 (rate of interest.)
21 [1977] QB 489; and see *The Funabashi* [1972] 1 WLR 666 at 671.

governed by the law of the forum.[22] This has been dissented from by KERR J:

> Both the right to interest and its amount should be determined by the proper law. ... The proper law results from the express or implied choice of both parties or from the nature of the transaction. The lex fori, if it differs, merely results from the choice of the plaintiff and may even be more or less fortuitous according to where it happens to be convenient to institute proceedings. The difference between them may be important.[23]

There are no clear answers to be discerned from the Contracts (Applicable Law) Act 1990 which simply excludes matters of procedure from its scope, without defining them.[24] So we are thrown both on the common law decisions for guidance. There are difficulties with KERR J's approach. The argument in relation to the governing law is not apposite to tort and there one must choose between the rate according to the law of the place of the tort or according to the law of the forum. There are also difficulties in the case of contractual claims for damages in foreign currency. The currency of the law governing the contract may be different from the currency of account, the currency of the loss and the currency of the forum.[25] The rates of interest relevant to each may well reflect the strength and weaknesses of the various currencies. If the rate of interest is governed by the law of the forum, this means that, in England, the court has a discretion as to the rate[26] and it has been made clear by the Court of Appeal that, prima facie, interest should be awarded at the rate applicable to the currency of the judgment.[1] This might not be possible if the governing law of the contract determined the rate. The Law Commission has considered this issue and concluded, though without proposing legislation on the matter, that the practical arguments in favour of the application of the law of the forum should prevail.[2]

(g) JUDGMENTS IN FOREIGN CURRENCY[3]

(i) Old rule: judgment must be in sterling

It was accepted in England for many years that an English court could not order payment of debts or damages except in English currency.[4] The amount due to the plaintiff in foreign currency had to be converted into sterling and

---

22 See now Contracts (Applicable Law) Act 1990, Sch 1, Art 10(1)(c).
23 *Helmsing Schiffahrts GmbH & Co KG v Malta Drydocks Corpn* [1977] 2 Lloyd's Rep 444 at 450.
24 Sch 1, Art 1 (2)(h).
25 Infra, pp 102 et seq.
26 Supreme Court Act 1981, s 35A (added by the Administration of Justice Act 1982, s 15 and Sch 1).
1 *Shell Tankers (UK) Ltd v Astro Comino Armadora SA* [1981] 2 Lloyd's Rep 40 at 45–47; and see *Miliangos v George Frank (Textiles) Ltd (No 2)* [1977] QB 489, [1976] 3 All ER 599. The prima facie rule was displaced in *Helmsing Schiffahrts GmbH & Co KG v Malta Drydocks Corpn*, supra.
2 Working Paper No 80 (1981), paras 4.23–4.27; Law Com No 124 (1983), paras 3.55–3.56.
3 Mann, *The Legal Aspect of Money*, 5th edn (1992), Part II; Goode, *Payment Obligations and Financial Transactions* (1983), Chapter V; Bowles, *Law and the Economy* (1982), Chapter 9. The whole question of foreign money liabilities has been considered by the Law Commission in Law Com No 124 (1983).
4 *Manners v Pearson & Son* [1898] 1 Ch 581

the appropriate exchange rate was that at the date the cause of action arose, eg the date of the breach of a contract[5] or the commission of a tort.[6]

(ii) *Miliangos v George Frank (Textiles) Ltd*

The rule that judgment must be in sterling came under increasing attack culminating in the decision of the House of Lords in *Miliangos v George Frank (Textiles) Ltd*:[7]

> The plaintiff, a Swiss national, agreed to sell a quantity of polyester yarn to the English defendants. The yarn was delivered in 1971. The law governing the contract was Swiss. The money of account and of payment was Swiss francs. The defendant failed to pay and the plaintiff claimed the sum due under the contract. More particularly, he claimed the sterling equivalent of the sum due in Swiss francs at the date when payment should have been made. However, after a decision of the Court of Appeal allowing judgment to be given in a foreign currency,[8] the plaintiff in this case was given leave to amend his claim so as to claim the amount due to him in Swiss francs.

The problem facing the House of Lords was a fairly simple one. Were they to act on the Practice Direction of 1966[9] and reverse an earlier but fairly recent decision of their own[10] and accept the line already taken by the Court of Appeal, or were they to confirm the well-established rule that judgment could only be given in sterling with a conversion date as of the date of breach? The significance of the decision to the plaintiff, in an era of rapidly fluctuating interest rates, and especially when the Swiss franc was strong and sterling weak was very considerable. Judgment in Swiss francs, converted into sterling as at the date of judgment, would give him almost 50 per cent more in sterling than conversion as at the date of the breach. Their Lordships decided to abandon the old rule and allow judgment to be given in foreign currency, here Swiss francs.[11] This was a decision of major commercial and financial significance but it left a whole range of further issues undecided, many of which have since been resolved by judicial decision, and which we must now examine. The most important of them are: how far beyond judgments for debts expressed in foreign currency does the *Miliangos* decision go? And in what currency may a court give judgment?

---

5 Eg *Re United Railways of the Havana and Regla Warehouses Ltd* [1961] AC 1007, [1960] 2 All ER 332.

6 Eg *SS Celia v SS Volturno* [1921] 2 AC 544.

7 [1976] AC 443, [1975] 3 All ER 801. It had already been decided that an arbitral award (*Jugoslavenska Oceanska Plovidba v Castle Investment Co Inc* [1974] QB 292, [1973] 3 All ER 498) and a judgment for a debt (*Schorsch Meier GmbH v Hennin* [1975] QB 416, [1975] 1 All ER 152) could be made in foreign currency.

8 *Schorsch Meier GmbH v Hennin* [1975] QB 416, [1975] 1 All ER 152.

9 [1966] 1 WLR 395.

10 *Re United Railways of the Havana and Regla Warehouses Ltd* [1961] AC 1007, [1960] 2 All ER 332.

11 Lord SIMON of Glaisdale dissented, believing that such a revolutionary change should only be made by Parliament: [1976] AC 443 at 470. However, the Law Commission has since examined the whole question of foreign money liabilities and has concluded that "the principle underlying the decision in *Miliangos* and the consequences which flow from it are greatly to be preferred to the rules which that decision superseded": Law Com No 124 (1983), para 3.8; cf Bowles and Whelan (1982) 45 MLR 434.

(iii) Claims to which the *Miliangos* rule applies

The first issue to be considered is the scope of the *Miliangos* decision. Their Lordships were very careful to limit their new principle to the type of case before them, leaving it to future decisions to work out the further implications of it. Indeed, Lord WILBERFORCE said:

> I would confine my approval at the present time of a change in the breach-date rule to claims such as those with which we are concerned, ie, to foreign money obligations, sc obligations of a money character to pay foreign currency arising under a contract whose proper law is that of a foreign country and where the money of account and payment is that of that country, or possibly of some other country, but not of the United Kingdom.[12] ... In my opinion it should be open for future discussion whether the rule applying to money obligations, which can be a simple rule, should apply as regards claims for damages for breach of contract or for tort.[13]

Development has come very rapidly. It started with cases of debt, then extended to liquidated damages for breach of contract and eventually to claims for unliquidated damages.[14] The result is that it is now established that the court can give judgment for a sum in foreign currency as damages for breach of contract[15] and as damages in tort.[16] Furthermore, the new principle applies in contractual claims whether the law governing the contract is English law[1] or foreign law.[2] It extends also to restitutionary claims,[3] winding up orders[4] and voluntary liquidations;[5] and it also seems clear that it will apply to salvage claims.[6]

In all these cases it has been the plaintiff who has been seeking payment in a currency other than sterling because of the depreciation of sterling. Indeed there is now much greater variation in exchange rates. "Sterling is no longer a stable currency, nor are US dollars, nor French francs. No currency is stable. They all swing about with every gust that blows."[7] So what happens if sterling appreciates? In the case of an action for a debt it seems clear that

---

12 But see Mann (1976) 92 LQR 165, 166. A Scottish court has since refused to give judgment in foreign currency where the money of account and of payment were sterling: *L/F Foroya Fiskasola v Charles Mauritzen Ltd* 1978 SLT (Sh Ct) 27.

13 [1976] AC 443 at 467–468; and see 497–498, 503; see *Owners of Eleftheratria v Despina R, The Despina R* [1979] AC 685 at 695.

14 For discharge of foreign currency obligations, especially debts, other than where there is a judgment, see Dicey & Morris, pp 1453–1457.

15 *Services Europe Atlantique Sud v Stockholms Rederiaktiebolag SVEA, The Folias* [1979] AC 685; and see *Kraut AG v Albany Fabrics Ltd* [1977] QB 182; *Federal Commerce and Navigation Co Ltd v Tradax Export SA* [1977] QB 324 at 341–342; revsd on other grounds [1978] AC 1, [1977] 2 All ER 849.

16 *Owners of Eleftheratria v Despina R, The Despina R* [1979] AC 685; *Hoffman v Sofaer* [1982] 1 WLR 1350.

1 Eg *Services Europe Atlantique Sud v Stockholms Rederiaktiebolag SVEA, The Folias,* supra; *Barclays Bank International Ltd v Levin Bros (Bradford) Ltd* [1977] QB 270; *Federal Commerce and Navigation Co Ltd v Tradax Export SA,* supra, at pp 341–342.

2 *Miliangos v George Frank (Textiles) Ltd* [1976] AC 443.

3 *BP Exploration Co (Libya) Ltd v Hunt (No 2)* [1982] 1 All ER 925, [1979] 1 WLR 783, affd [1983] 2 AC 352.

4 *Re Dynamics Corpn of America* [1976] 2 All ER 669, [1976] 1 WLR 757.

5 *Re Lines Bros Ltd* [1983] Ch 1, [1982] 2 All ER 183; *Re Lines Bros Ltd (No 2)* [1984] Ch 438.

6 *Services Europe Atlantique Sud v Stockholms Rederiaktiebolag SVEA, The Folias,* [1979] QB 491 at 516; affd [1979] AC 685; and see *Miliangos v George Frank (Textiles) Ltd* [1976] AC 443 at 468.

7 [1979] QB 491 at 513.

the plaintiff ought to be entitled to judgment in the currency of the debt, converted into sterling as at the date of payment, and not judgment in sterling converted from the currency of the debt as at the date of breach. As was said in *Miliangos*, "the creditor has no concern with pounds sterling: for him what matters is that a Swiss franc for good or ill should remain a Swiss franc".[8] A similar rule ought to apply to claims for damages in foreign currency. The plaintiff should be entitled to judgment in the currency of his loss[9] and not in sterling calculated as at the date the cause of action arose. In this way the plaintiff is protected against changes in the value of his currency as against sterling but is not, and should not be, protected against changes in the internal value of his own currency.[10]

(iv) Interest

Interest may be allowed in an action for payment of a debt or damages in foreign currency at a rate which may be different from the English rate for sterling.[11] Interest on any judgment given in a foreign currency has, however to be paid at the appropriate English statutory rate for judgment debts.[12] This can cause injustice because the English rate is fixed in relation to the strength of sterling, which may be much stronger or weaker than the foreign currency of the judgment. To remedy this, the Law Commission has recommended[13] that, in the case of judgments in a foreign currency, the rate of interest payable on the judgment should be in the discretion of the court and not the fixed statutory rate for judgments in sterling.

(v) Procedural nature of the *Miliangos* rule

The rule propounded in the *Miliangos* decision is a rule of procedure and not of substance;[14] thus English law is applied as the law of forum. This can be seen from the fact that the rule has been applied where the law governing the substance of the contract in question was foreign[15] and without reference, in tort, to the law of the place of the tort.[16]

(vi) Date for conversion of currency

Although judgment may be given in foreign currency, a question of conversion into sterling may still arise. The judgment may be satisfied by payment of the sum in foreign currency[17] but, failing such satisfaction, the plaintiff will seek to enforce the judgment and this will necessitate conversion of the

---

8 [1976] AC 443 at 466.
9 Discussed, infra, pp 103–105.
10 *Owners of Eleftheratria v Despina R, The Despina R* [1979] AC 685 at 697.
11 *Miliangos v George Frank (Textiles) Ltd (No 2)* [1977] QB 489, [1976] 3 All ER 599; *Helmsing Schiffahrts GmbH & Co KG v Malta Drydocks Corpn* [1977] 2 Lloyd's Rep 444; *Shell Tankers (UK) Ltd v Astro Comino Armadora SA* [1981] 2 Lloyd's Rep 40; *Maschinenfabrik v Altikar Pty Ltd* [1984] 3 NSWLR 152; *The Kefalonia Wind* [1986] 1 Lloyd's Rep 292n; and see Bowles and Phillips (1976) 39 MLR 196.
12 *Practice Direction* [1976] 1 All ER 669, [1976] 1 WLR 83, as amended by *Practice Direction* [1977] 1 All ER 544, [1977] 1 WLR 197.
13 Law Com No 124 (1983), para 4.15.
14 *Owners of Eleftheratria v Despina R, The Despina R* [1979] AC 685 at 704.
15 Eg *Miliangos v George Frank (Textiles) Ltd* [1976] AC 443, [1976] 3 All ER 599.
16 *Owners of Eleftheratria v Despina R, The Despina R* [1979] AC 685.
17 See *Practice Direction* [1976] 1 All ER 669, [1976] 1 WLR 83, as amended by *Practice Direction* [1977] 1 All ER 544, [1977] 1 WLR 197.

judgment into sterling.[18] In fact in *Miliangos* itself, the House of Lords considered that the claim could be in the alternative, either for the foreign currency or the sterling equivalent at "the date of payment". What then is the "date of payment" at which conversion must be made? In normal cases this will be the date at which the court authorises enforcement of the judgment in terms of sterling,[19] and this also applies to the case of an arbitrator's award.[20] In the case of the winding up of a company (both compulsory and voluntary), the appropriate date will be the date of the winding-up order.[1]

There are various cases where it has been provided by statute that the conversion into sterling shall be made according to the rate of exchange prevailing at the time of judgment and, of course, these are unaffected by the *Miliangos* decision. The judgment-date rule applies to carriage by air[2] but not to carriage of goods by road.[3] In the case of foreign judgments expressed in foreign currency and registered in England under the Foreign Judgments (Reciprocal Enforcement) Act 1933[4] for the purposes of recognition and enforcement, they are to be registered in the foreign currency with conversion at the date of payment[5] just as if the plaintiff had sued on the original cause of action or, it is assumed, as if there was an action on the judgment at common law.[6] There is no provision in the Civil Jurisdiction and Judgments Act 1982,[7] which governs the recognition and enforcement of judgments given in the European Community States,[8] indicating the date for converting into sterling the currency in which the foreign judgment was given, but it is assumed[9] that the same principles will apply. The rules are different for the enforcement of foreign maintenance orders,[10] where the conversion date is

18 *Miliangos v George Frank (Textiles) Ltd* [1976] AC 443 at 497, 501.
19 Ibid, at 468–469, 497–498, 501–502; and see *Practice Direction* [1976] 1 All ER 669, [1976] 1 WLR 83, as amended by *Practice Direction* [1977] 1 All ER 544, [1977] 1 WLR 197; *The Halcyon Skies (No 2)* [1977] 1 Lloyd's Rep 22; *George Veflings Rederi A/S v President of India* [1979] 1 All ER 380, [1979] 1 WLR 59. The Law Commission has reexamined this rule and supports its retention, but has also made a number of detailed proposals for changes to the relevant procedural rules: Law Com No 124 (1983) Part V. On garnishee orders against foreign currency bank accounts, see *Choice Investments Ltd v Jeromnimon* [1981] QB 149, [1981] 1 All ER 225. In the case of set-off, see *The Transoceanica Francesca and Nicos V* [1987] 2 Lloyd's Rep 155 (tort); *Smit Tak International Zeesleepen Berginsbedrijk B V v Selco Salvage Ltd* [1988] 2 Lloyd's Rep 398 (contract).
20 Ibid, at 469; Law Com No 124 (1983), para 2.43; cf *Jugoslovenska Oceanska Plovidba v Castle Investment Co Inc* [1974] QB 292, [1973] 3 All ER 498.
1 *Re Dynamics Corpn of America* [1976] 2 All ER 669, [1976] 1 WLR 757; cf *Miliangos v George Frank (Textiles) Ltd* [1976] AC 443 at 469, 498 (compulsory); *Re Lines Bros Ltd* [1983] Ch 1, [1982] 2 All ER 183; *Re Lines Bros (No 2)* [1984] Ch 438 (voluntary); and see *Re Gresham Corpn Pty Ltd* [1990] 1 Qd R 306.
2 Carriage by Air Act 1961, Sch I, Art 22 (5), and see s 4 (4).
3 Carriage of Goods by Road Act 1965, Sch, Art 27 (2).
4 S 2 (3), for the main provisions see infra, pp 397 et seq.
5 Administration of Justice Act 1977, ss 4, 32 (4), Sch 5, which also repeals the Bills of Exchange Act 1882, s 72 (4).
6 *East India Trading Co Inc v Carmel Exporters and Importers Ltd* [1952] 2 QB 439, [1952] 1 All ER 1053 would, it is suggested, be decided differently after *Miliangos*, see *Batavia Times Publishing Co v Davis* (1978) 88 DLR (3d) 144 esp at 151–154; and see Law Com No 124 (1983), para 2.38.
7 Except in the case of maintenance orders, infra.
8 Infra, pp 411 et seq.
9 Collins, *The Civil Jurisdiction and Judgments Act 1982* (1983), p 116; Law Com No 124 (1983), paras 2.39–2.42, 3.45–3.46.
10 Infra, pp 714 et seq.

not that, under the *Miliangos* rule, of actual payment or when enforcement is authorised but rather the earlier date of the registration of the order.[11] This difference of approach can be justified on grounds of convenience.[12] It is quite impracticable for the sums due under a foreign maintenance order, often payable weekly, to vary from week to week in the light of currency fluctuations.[13] In the case of claims for damages falling within section 14 of the Merchant Shipping Act 1979[14] the rate of exchange is either that at the date of judgment or at the date agreed by the parties.[15]

(vii) In what currency should the court give judgment?

A further major question arising from the *Miliangos* decision is that of identifying the currency, other than sterling, in which a court may give judgment. This is but part of a problem which existed before the *Miliangos* decision. For example, in a tort claim, although damages were awarded in sterling, converted as at the date the cause of action arose, it was in theory necessary to know from what currency conversion was to be made into sterling. This issue has, however, become far more significant now that judgment may be given in the foreign currency.

We have seen that the question whether damages can be given in a foreign currency is a procedural issue. This leads to a further issue of classification. Given that an English court can award damages in a foreign currency, is it for English law as the procedural law of the forum to provide the legal rules for deciding in which currency this is to be done, or is the question of the identification of the currency a matter of substantive law? For example, if the governing law of a contract is French, and the English court is prepared to give damages in a foreign currency, does the court use the English or the French rules for deciding which is the appropriate currency? This issue would appear to be a matter of substance. In the field of contract, the currency in which damages are to be calculated has been held to be a matter for the law governing substantive issues,[16] as in *Kraut AG v Albany Fabrics Ltd*.[17]

> The plaintiffs, a Swiss company, sold cloth to the English defendants. The law governing the contract was Swiss law. The defendants failed to pay and the plaintiffs claimed various sums owing to them and damages for breach of contract. The issue before the court was whether judgment could be given in Swiss francs.

This was the first case after *Miliangos v George Frank (Textiles) Ltd*[18] where the court had to consider whether the principle of that decision extended to a claim for damages for breach of contract, rather than a claim for the

---

11 Maintenance Orders (Reciprocal Enforcement) Act 1972, s 16; Civil Jurisdiction and Judgments Act 1982, s 8; Civil Jurisdiction and Judgments Act 1991, Sch 2, para 2; cf *Re May's Marriage* (1987) 90 FLR 134.
12 Law Com No 124 (1983), paras 2.48–2.51, 3.47–3.49.
13 English maintenance orders may be made in foreign currency (eg *R v Cambridge County Court, ex p Ireland* [1985] Fam Law 23) but in such cases conversion is effected at the date the enforcement procedure is initiated: see Law Com No 124 (1983), para 2.52.
14 Giving effect to the Athens Convention on the Carriage of Passengers by Sea, contained in Sch 3, Part I of the 1979 Act.
15 1979 Act, Sch 3, Part I, Art 9 (2).
16 *Services Europe Atlantique Sud v Stockholms Rederiaktiebolag SVEA, The Folias* [1979] AC 685 at 700; and see *Miliangos v George Frank (Textiles) Ltd* [1976] AC 443 at 465.
17 [1977] QB 182, [1977] 2 All ER 116.
18 [1976] AC 443, [1975] 3 All ER 801.

payment of a debt. In allowing the claim in Swiss francs, EVELEIGH J relied on Swiss law, the law governing the contract, under which law the defendants were treated as if they were debtors. This justified the application of the *Miliangos* principle that judgment may be given in a foreign currency, but also indicated that the currency in which the loss is to be calculated should be determined by the governing law. The questions whether, in a contract action, judgment should be given in a foreign currency and, in a case where there is more than one possible currency, in which currency, have been held to depend on general principles of the law of contract and on rules of private international law:

> The former require application, as nearly as possible of the principle of restitutio in integrum, regard being had to what was in the reasonable contemplation of the parties. The latter involve ascertainment of the proper law of the contract, and application of that law. If the proper law is English, the first step must be to see whether, expressly or by implication, the contract provides an answer to the currency question.[19]

It ought logically to follow that, if the determination of the currency in which damages for breach of contract are to be calculated is a matter of substance for the law governing the contract, it should also be a matter of substance so far as claims in tort are concerned. The tort position is less clear because in the one relevant decision, *The Despina R*,[20] English law was applied without reference to the fact that the tort in issue was committed in China. One can argue that, where foreign law is not pleaded, it is deemed to be the same as English law.[21] But where foreign law is pleaded, reference cannot be made to the currencies applicable under both the law of the place where the tort was committed and the law of the forum. This would appear to be a situation where the former law must yield to the law of the forum with the result that, as in *The Despina R*, the English rule will be applied.

Turning now to the English rules for determining the currency in which damages should be assessed, the House of Lords has taken the view[1] that, once the obligation to give judgment in sterling has been abandoned, any rule[2] that, where damages consisted of loss incurred directly in a foreign currency, they must be assessed in that currency, should also be abandoned. Instead the court must identify the currency of the plaintiff's loss for:

> a plaintiff, who normally conducts his business through a particular currency, and who, when other currencies are immediately involved, uses his own currency to obtain those currencies, can reasonably say that the loss he sustains is to be measured not by the immediate currencies in which the loss first emerges but by the amount of his own currency, which in the normal course of operation, he uses to obtain those currencies. This is the currency in which his loss is felt, and is the currency which it is reasonably foreseeable he will have to spend.[3]

---

19 *Services Europe Atlantique Sud v Stockholms Rederiaktiebolag SVEA, The Folias* [1979] AC 685 at 700.
20 [1979] AC 685, infra p 104. In *Hoffman v Sofaer* [1982] 1 WLR 1350, another tort case, both the law of the place where the tort was committed and the law of the forum was English.
21 Infra, pp 107–108.
 1 *Services Europe Atlantique Sud v Stockholms Rederiaktiebolag SVEA, The Folias* [1979] AC 685.
 2 Eg *Di Ferdinando v Simon, Smits & Co Ltd* [1920] 3 KB 409; *SS Celia v SS Volturno* [1921] 2 AC 544; *The Canadian Transport* (1932) 43 L1 L Rep 409.
 3 [1979] AC 685 at 697.

Guidance in determining the currency of loss in claims for damages is provided by two decisions, which were consolidated on appeal to the House of Lords, one in contract, the other in tort. In *Services Europe Atlantique Sud v Stockholms Rederiaktiebolag SVEA, The Folias*[4] the facts were as follows:

> The plaintiffs, a French company, chartered a Swedish ship from the defendants. The law governing the contract was English law. The ship was used to carry cargo to Brazil and the cargo was damaged on arrival owing to defective refrigeration. The plaintiffs settled a claim by the receiver of the cargo, paying him in Brazilian currency. To obtain this currency, the plaintiffs had used French francs, being a French company. In arbitration proceedings, the defendants admitted liability, but maintained that they should reimburse the plaintiffs in Brazilian currency, which was the currency the plaintiffs had used to settle the claim and not in French francs, the currency used by the plaintiffs to buy the Brazilian cruzeiros.

Judgment was given in French francs as the currency most truly expressing the plaintiffs' loss. Again, the significance of the decision lies in inflation, because the Brazilian currency had weakened greatly against the French franc between the date of settling the claim and the date of judgment and the decision protected the plaintiff from the effects of this fluctuation.

Where a contract is governed by English law, the determination of the currency in which payment is to be made is ascertained in the first instance by reference to the terms of the contract. If it provides expressly or impliedly for the currency in which damages are to be calculated[5] then judgment should be given in that currency. In the absence of such provision in the contract, where the plaintiff incurs expenditure as a consequence of the defendant's breach of contract, judgment for damages should be in the currency most truly expressing the plaintiff's loss,[6] provided the parties can be taken reasonably to have this in contemplation.[7] This will not necessarily be the currency of the expenditure which may[8] or may not[9] be the currency of the contract.

The other House of Lords decision is in the tort field: *The Despina R*.[10]

> The plaintiffs' ship and the defendants' ship were in collision in Shanghai harbour. Both were Greek ships. The plaintiffs' ship received temporary repairs in Shanghai and then went to Japan and eventually to the USA for further repairs. The plaintiffs expended sums on repairs and other expenses in Chinese and Japanese currencies, in US dollars and in sterling. The plaintiffs sought payment of these sums as damages for the harm neg-

---

4 [1979] AC 685; Bowles and Whelan (1979) 42 MLR 452; and see *Ozalid Group (Export) Ltd v African Continental Bank Ltd* [1979] 2 Lloyd's Rep 231; *The Food Corpn of India v Carras (Hellas) Ltd* [1980] 2 Lloyd's Rep 577; *Societe Francaise Bunge SA v Belcan NV* [1985] 3 All ER 378.
5 Ibid, at p 700; and see *Jugoslavenska Oceanska Plovidba v Castle Investment Co Inc* [1974] QB 292 at 298.
6 [1979] AC 685, 701–703, 705.
7 Ibid at p 701; see *Metaalhandel JA Magnus BV v Ardfields Transport Ltd* [1988] 1 Lloyd's Rep 197.
8 *Federal Commerce and Navigation Co Ltd v Tradax Export SA* [1977] QB 324 at 341–342; revsd on other grounds [1978] AC 1, [1977] 2 All ER 849.
9 [1979] AC 685 at 702.
10 [1979] AC 685; Knott (1980) 43 MLR 18; and see *The Lash Atlantico* [1987] 2 Lloyd's Rep 114.

ligently done to their ship and argued that they should be expressed in US dollars, that being the currency in which they carried on their business.

Their Lordships held that damages in tort, as in contract, are payable in the currency of the plaintiffs' loss, here US dollars; though Lord WILBERFORCE added:

> I wish to make it clear that I would not approve of a hard and fast rule that in all cases where a plaintiff suffers a loss or damage in a foreign currency the right currency to take for the purpose of his claim is "the plaintiff's currency." I should ... emphasise that it does not suggest the use of a personal currency attached, like nationality, to a plaintiff, but a currency which he is able to show is that in which he normally conducts trading operations.[11]

Reference to the currency of the plaintiff's loss must be qualified, for if the plaintiff has exacerbated his loss by use of his own currency, he runs the risk that the use of his own currency may be too remote a consequence of the defendant's conduct as to justify quantifying his loss by reference to it.[12] Although the decision in *The Despina R* concerns only the tort of negligence and damage to property,[13] the principle laid down in that case is one of general application, whatever the basis of the tort claim. In *Hoffman v Sofaer*[14] the court was prepared to award the plaintiff, an American, damages in dollars for loss of earnings stemming from negligent medical treatment suffered in England. Damages for pain, suffering and loss of amenity were given in sterling, however, on the ground that it would be impossible to assess them in dollars.[15]

We have seen that judgments, other than for unliquidated damages, may be given in foreign currency. In the case of a debt or claim for liquidated damages, the contract may provide for the currency in which the debt is to be paid; and judgment should be given in that currency.[16] In other cases, where the money of account (the currency in which the obligation is measured) is different from the money of payment (the currency in which the obligation is discharged) judgment should normally be given in the former.[17] If, however, the contract provides an agreed rate of exchange between the two, judgment should be given in the money of payment.[18] In the case of a restitutionary claim,[19] the award should be related not to the plaintiff's loss but to the currency of the defendant's benefit. Where the benefit is money, the award should normally be for repayment by the defendant in the same currency as that in which he received payment. If the benefit is other than money, then the award should be in the currency in which the benefit can be "most fairly and appropriately valued".[20]

11 Ibid at 698.
12 See the Court of Appeal, [1978] QB 396 at 437; and see [1979] AC 685 at 697–699.
13 Cf *North Scottish Helicopters Ltd v United Technologies Corpn Inc (No 2)* 1988 SLT 778n.
14 [1982] 1 WLR 1350; and see *Kraut AG v Albany Fabrics Ltd* [1977] QB 182 at 189.
15 Ibid at 1357.
16 *Services Europe Atlantique Sud (SEAS) v Stockholms Rederiaktiebolag SVEA, The Folias* [1979] QB 491 at 514.
17 *George Veflings Rederi A/S v President of India* [1978] 3 All ER 838, [1978] 1 WLR 982, affd [1979] 1 All ER 380, [1979] 1 WLR 59; cf *BP Exploration Co (Libya) Ltd v Hunt (No 2)* [1979] 1 WLR 783 at 840–841.
18 *President of India v Taygetos Shipping Co SA* [1985] 1 Lloyd's Rep 155.
19 *BP Exploration Co (Libya) Ltd v Hunt (No 2)* [1979] 1 WLR 783 at 837–845 (affd [1983] 2 AC 352).
20 Ibid at 840.

(h) EXECUTION

Judgments and the execution of judgments, being integral parts of the process which the plaintiff has elected to adopt, are necessarily subject to the law of the forum. The particular mode of execution admitted by that law, whether more or less favourable to the plaintiff than that recognised by the law governing the transaction, has exclusive application. This principle covers such matters as whether the judgment may be satisfied out of land or goods;[21] whether debts in the hands of third parties can be attached by garnishment; whether a receiver may be appointed; whether a writ *ne exeat regno* is procurable; or whether personal constraint is permissible.

Thus, where a Portuguese, who had been arrested in the course of English proceedings for non-payment of a debt which was due to a Spaniard under a Portuguese contract, applied to be discharged from custody on the ground that he was not liable to arrest by the law governing the contract, the application was refused.[22]

---

21 But where, in the case of a mortgage, the governing law provides that both the property mortgaged and other property of the debtor are liable for the debt, this amounts to a substantive rule, applicable even though the law of the forum restricts the claim to the property mortgaged: *Sigurdson v Farrow* (1981) 121 DLR (3d) 183; and see *243930 Alberta Ltd v Wickham* (1990) 73 DLR (4th) 474.
22 *De la Vega v Vianna* (1830) 1 B & Ad 284.

Chapter 7

The proof of foreign law[1]

SUMMARY

		PAGE
1	Foreign law: a question of fact	107
2	How foreign law is proved	108
3	Witnesses who can prove foreign law	109
4	The role of the court	111

1. FOREIGN LAW: A QUESTION OF FACT

The established rule is that knowledge of foreign law, even of the law obtaining in some other part of the common law world, is not to be imputed to an English judge.[1a] Unless the foreign law with which a case may be connected is pleaded by the party relying thereon, then it is assumed that it is the same as English law.[2] The onus of proving that it is different, and of proving what it is, lies on the party who pleads the difference.[3] If there is no such plea, or if the difference is not satisfactorily proved, the court must give a decision according to English law, even though the case may be connected solely with some foreign country.[4] Foreign law is, therefore, treated as a question of fact but it is "a question of fact of a peculiar kind".[5] To describe it as one of fact is no doubt apposite, in the sense that the applicable law must be ascertained according to the evidence of witnesses, yet there can be no doubt that what is involved is at bottom a question of law. This has been recognised by the courts. The rule, for instance, in a purely domestic case is

---

1 Fentiman (1992) 108 LQR 142.
1a *Nelson v Bridport* (1846) 8 Beav 547; though cf *Saxby v Fulton* [1909] 2 KB 208 at 211; *Harold Meyers Travel Service Ltd v Magid* (1975) 60 DLR (3d) 42 at 44. Judicial notice is taken of European Community law, which, of course, is not technically foreign law, see the European Communities Act 1972, s 3.
2 This presumption may not be applied where the plaintiff asks for summary judgment: *National Shipping Corpn v Arab* [1971] 2 Lloyd's Rep 363. It should be pointed out that there are one or two anomalous cases where an English court has not assumed the foreign law to be the same as English statute law: *R v Brixton Prison Governor, ex p Coldough* [1961] 1 All ER 606; *Osterreichische Länderbank v S'Elite Ltd* [1981] QB 565 at 569; and see *Purdom v Pavey & Co* (1896) 26 SCR 412; *BP Exploration Co (Libya) Ltd v Hunt* (1980) 47 FLR 317; *The Mercury Bell v Amosin* (1986) 27 DLR (4th) 641; cf *De Reneville v De Reneville* [1948] P 100, [1948] 1 All ER 56.
3 *The King of Spain v Machado* (1827) 4 Russ 225 at 239; *Ascherberg Hopwood and Crew v Casa Musicale Sonzogno* [1971] 1 WLR 173, affd ibid at 1128; *Kutchera v Buckingham International Holdings Ltd* [1988] IR 61 at 68.
4 *Warner Bros v Nelson* [1937] 1 KB 209; *Cressington Court (Owners) v Marinero (Owners), The Marinero* [1955] 1 All ER 676; *Mount Cook (Northland) Ltd v Swedish Motors Ltd* [1986] 1 NZLR 720; cf *Guépratte v Young* (1851) 4 De G & Sm 217 at 224–225. As to the alternatives open to a court when a party fails to prove foreign law, see Kahn-Freund (1974) III Hague Recueil 139, 422–426.
5 *Parkasho v Singh* [1968] P 233 at 250.

that an appellate court will disturb a finding of fact by the trial judge only with the greatest reluctance, but this is not so when the "fact" that has been found in the court below is the relevant rule of a foreign legal system. In such a case the role of the appellate court has been described as follows:

> I think it is our duty ... to examine the evidence of foreign law which was before the justices and to decide for ourselves whether that evidence justifies the conclusion to which they came.[6]

Nevertheless, the courts have concluded that a mistake as to foreign law is to be regarded as a mistake of fact.[7]

2. HOW FOREIGN LAW IS PROVED

It is clear that the relevant foreign law on some particular matter must be proved, like other matters of which no knowledge is imputed to the judge, "by appropriate evidence, ie by properly qualified witnesses",[8] unless both parties agree to leave the investigation to the judge and to dispense with the aid of witnesses.[9] Subject to section 4(2) of the Civil Evidence Act 1972,[10] it cannot be proved, for instance, by citing a previous decision of an English court in which the same foreign rule was in issue,[11] or by merely presenting the judge with the text of the foreign law and leaving him to draw his own conclusions,[12] or by referring to a decision in which a court of the foreign country has stated the meaning and effect of the law in question.[13] A fortiori, it cannot be proved by referring to a decision as to the law of the foreign country in question given in the courts of some other foreign country.[14] Nor can it be proved by the assertion of an opinion as to the effect of the foreign law without reference to the relevant authorities.[15] Those parts of the United Kingdom, however, for which the House of Lords is the ultimate appellate tribunal in civil matters form an exception to these rules. Thus Scottish law must be proved by evidence in the courts inferior to the House of Lords, but in the House of Lords itself, which is the common forum of both England and

6 Ibid; *Dalmia Dairy Industries Ltd v National Bank of Pakistan* [1978] 2 Lloyd's Rep 223 at 286; and see Webb (1967) 16 ICLQ 1152, 1155–1156.
7 *The Amazonia* [1990] 1 Lloyd's Rep 236, CA; and see *Andre & Cie SA v Ets Michel Blanc & Fils* [1979] 2 Lloyd's Rep 427, CA.
8 *Nelson v Bridport* (1845) 8 Beav 527 at 536; *Beatty v Beatty* [1924] 1 KB 807 at 814; *Lazard Bros & Co v Midland Bank* [1933] AC 289. This is by no means a universal law. By German law, for instance, foreign law requires proof only to the extent to which it is unknown to the judge. The judge is not confined to material put before him by the parties, but may use his own sources of information; cf *Lear v Lear* (1973) 51 DLR (3d) 56.
9 *Jabbour (F & K) v Custodian of Israeli Absentee Property* [1954] 1 All ER 145 at 153, [1954] 1 WLR 139 at 147–148; *Dalmia Dairy Industries Ltd v National Bank of Pakistan* [1978] 2 Lloyd's Rep 223 at 236.
10 Infra.
11 *Lazard Brothers & Co v Midland Bank Ltd*, supra; *McCormick v Garnett* (1854) 23 LJ Ch 777; *Re Marseilles Extension Rly and Land Co* (1885) 30 Ch D 598 at 602. But in *Re Sebba* [1959] Ch 166, [1958] 3 All ER 393, DANCKWERTS J considered that in the circumstances he was justified in departing from this rule.
12 *Buerger v New York Life Assurance Co* (1927) 96 LJKB 930 at 940.
13 *Beatty v Beatty* [1924] 1 KB 807 at 814–815; *Guaranty Trust Co of New York v Hannay & Co* [1918] 2 KB 623 at 638, 667.
14 *Callwood v Callwood* [1960] AC 659, [1960] 2 All ER 1; Webb (1960) 23 MLR 556; Carter (1960) 36 BYBIL 408.
15 *Mount Cook (Northland) Ltd v Swedish Motors Ltd* [1986] 1 NZLR 720.

Scotland, it is a matter of which their Lordships have judicial knowledge.[16]

However, proof of foreign law, including Scots and Northern Irish law, is rendered easier by section 4(2) of the Civil Evidence Act 1972. It provides that, when any question of foreign law has been determined in civil or criminal proceedings in the High Court, the Crown Court, certain other courts or in appeals therefrom, or in proceedings before the Judicial Committee of the Privy Council on appeal from courts abroad,[17] any finding made or decision given in such proceedings shall, if reported in citable form,[18] be admissible in later civil proceedings as evidence of the foreign law. Indeed, the foreign law shall be taken to be in accordance with such finding or decision unless the contrary is proved, provided it does not conflict with another finding of foreign law adduced in the same proceedings.[19]

The English courts have not adopted the practice in civil law systems according to which a Government may be requested to give an official statement of the law on some particular matter. By the British Law Ascertainment Act 1859, however, a court within Her Majesty's Dominions, which is of the opinion that it is necessary or expedient for the disposal of a case to ascertain the law of some part of Her Majesty's Dominions, may remit to a superior court in the latter place the question of law on which a ruling is required.[20] The provisions of this Act may be extended by Order in Council to other British territories.[21]

Foreign law had formerly to be proved to the satisfaction of the jury, but the Supreme Court Act 1981[22] has now provided as follows:

> Where ... it is necessary to ascertain the law of any other country which is applicable to the facts of the case, any question as to the effect of the evidence given with respect to that law shall, instead of being submitted to the jury, be decided by the judge alone.

3. WITNESSES WHO CAN PROVE FOREIGN LAW

It is obvious that no witness can speak to a question of law as a fact and that all he can do is to express his opinion. The rule is, therefore, that he must be an expert. The question as to who is a sufficient expert in this matter has not been satisfactorily resolved by the English decisions.[1] Though no doubt the court has a discretion in the matter, the general principle has been that no person is a competent witness unless he is a practising lawyer in the particular legal system in question, or unless he occupies a position or follows a calling in which he must necessarily acquire a practical working knowledge of the

---

16 *Elliott v Joicey* [1935] AC 209 at 236. This rule is unaffected by the Civil Evidence Act 1972, s 4(2), infra.
17 S 4(4).
18 S 4(5).
19 Findings or decisions as to foreign law in earlier proceedings may only be adduced if notice is given to all other parties: s 4(3).
20 S 1. The European Convention on Information on Foreign Law, Treaty Series No 117 (1969) (Cmnd 4229) sets out to achieve the same aims as the 1859 Act in respect of foreign countries generally. The Convention has been ratified by the UK, but not yet implemented. See Dicey and Morris, pp 226–227.
21 Foreign Jurisdiction Act 1890, s 5, Sch 1.
22 S 69(5), replacing Administration of Justice Act 1920, s 15 and Supreme Court of Judicature (Consolidation) Act 1925, s 102. The Act applies to criminal trials: *R v Hammer* [1923] 2 KB 786.
1 Falconbridge, op cit, pp 833–838.

foreign law. In other words, practical experience is a sufficient qualification. Thus, in accordance with this principle:

A Roman Catholic bishop was allowed to testify to the matrimonial law of Rome, since a knowledge of its provisions was essential to the performance of his official duties.[2]

A hotel-keeper in London, a native of Belgium, who had formerly been a commissioner of stocks in Brussels, was admitted to prove the Belgian law of promissory notes, on the ground that his business had made him conversant with commercial law.[3]

An ex-Governor of Hong Kong was held competent to prove the marriage law of that colony.[4]

A secretary to the Persian Embassy was allowed to depose to the law of Persia, on it being shown that there were then no professional lawyers in that country, but that all diplomatic officials had to be thoroughly versed in the law.[5]

Where it was necessary to ascertain the meaning of a bill of exchange given in Chile, the evidence of a London bank director with long experience of banking in South America was preferred to that of a young man who had been at the Chilean Bar for four years.[6]

An experienced police officer from Quebec was able to prove the road traffic law of that Province before an Ontario court.[7]

The view taken by the courts was that a mere academic knowledge of foreign law scarcely qualified a man as an expert witness. Thus in *Bristow v Sequeville*[8] where it was necessary to prove the law in force at Cologne, a witness was called who stated that he was a jurist and legal adviser to the Prussian consul in England, and that having studied law at Leipzig University he knew from his studies there that the Code Napoléon applied in Cologne. It was held that he was not a competent witness, ALDERSON B saying:

If a man who has studied law in Saxony, and never practised in Prussia, is a competent witness to prove the law of Prussia, why may not a Frenchman, who has read books relating to Chinese law, prove what the law of China is?[9]

But although it has been said that study alone is not sufficient qualification,[10] the courts did not consistently observe the requirement of practical experience. Thus the Reader in Roman-Dutch Law to the Council of Legal Education, who had made a special study of that law for the purpose of his lectures, was admitted to testify to Rhodesian law;[11] an English barrister, who in the course of his profession had made researches into the marriage

2 *The Sussex Peerage Case* (1844) 11 Cl & Fin 85; distinguish *R v Savage* (1876) 13 Cox CC 178; see also *R v Ilich* [1935] NZLR 90.
3 *Vander Donckt v Thellusson* (1849) 8 CB 812; distinguish *Perlak Petroleum Maatschappij v Deen* [1924] 1 KB 111.
4 *Cooper-King v Cooper-King* [1900] P 65. The only lawyer who could be found to give such expert evidence had demanded "a prohibitive fee of fifteen guineas".
5 *Re Dhost Aly Khan's Goods* (1880) 6 PD 6.
6 *De Beéche v South American Stores* [1935] AC 148. The evidence of a bank manager was also accepted in *Said Ajami v Customs Comptroller* [1954] 1 WLR 1405; distinguished in *Clyne v Federal Commissioner of Taxation (No 2)* (1981) 57 FLR 198.
7 *Guerin v Proulx* (1982) 37 OR (2d) 558.
8 (1850) 5 Exch 275; *Re Bonelli's Goods* (1875) 1 PD 69.
9 Ibid, at pp 276–277.
10 *Re Turner* [1906] WN 27.
11 *Brailey v Rhodesia Consolidated Ltd* [1910] 2 Ch 95; and see *Barford v Barford* [1918] P 140.

laws of Malta, was held competent to prove the validity of a marriage that had been solemnised at Valetta;[12] evidence as to the law of Chile was admitted from an English solicitor who, though never a practitioner in that country, stated that he had considerable experience of its laws;[13] and, in another case,[14] evidence as to Egyptian law was admitted from an English barrister who had practised before the mixed courts and British consular courts in Egypt until they ceased to function, thirteen years earlier. Since then he had had no right of audience in Egyptian courts, though he had done his best to keep his knowledge of Egyptian law up to date. It has now been made clear, by section 4(1) of the Civil Evidence Act 1972, that evidence as to foreign law may be given by a person who is qualified to do so on account of his knowledge and experience "irrespective of whether he has acted or is entitled to act as a legal practitioner there".[15]

4. THE ROLE OF THE COURT

The evidence of the expert may exceptionally be given by affidavit, but it is usually given orally, and he is of course open to cross-examination. Although he must state his opinion as based on his knowledge or practical experience of the foreign law, he may refer to codes, decisions or treatises for the purpose of refreshing his memory, but in such an event the court is at liberty to examine the law or passage in question in order to arrive at its correct meaning.[16] Even if the expert witness is uncontradicted by other expert testimony, the court may examine the texts in order to reach its own conclusions on the foreign law, though where the expert evidence is uncontradicted, the court should be reluctant to reject it,[17] unless it is absurd.[18] The court should not examine texts which have not been relied on by the expert or by counsel.[19] Again, if there is a conflict of testimony between the expert witnesses on either side, the court must place its own interpretation on the foreign law in the light of all the evidence given.[20] In all cases, in fact, it is the right and duty of the court to examine and criticise the evidence.[21]

---

12 *Wilson v Wilson* [1903] P 157.
13 *Re Whitelegg's Goods* [1899] P 267.
14 *Rossano v Manufacturers' Life Insurance Co Ltd* [1963] 2 QB 352.
15 See *Practice Direction (Foreign Law Affidavit)* [1972] 3 All ER 912, [1972] 1 WLR 1433.
16 *Concha v Murietta* (1889) 40 Ch D 543; *Russian Commercial and Industrial Bank v Comptoir d'Escompte de Mulhouse* [1923] 2 KB 630 at 643; *Re Cohn* [1945] Ch 5; see 61 LQR 340; *De Beéche v South American Stores Ltd and Chilian Stores Ltd* [1935] AC 148 at 158–159; *Parkasho v Singh* [1968] P 233 at 250–252, 254.
17 *Sharif v Azad* [1967] 1 QB 605 at 616.
18 Contrast the view of expert evidence taken in *Re Russian Bank for Foreign Trade* [1933] Ch 745 with the view taken of the same expert's evidence in *Re Banque des Marchands de Moscou (Koupetschesky)* [1958] Ch 182, [1957] 3 All ER 182 and see Civil Evidence Act 1972, s 4(2), supra, pp 108–109.
19 *Bumper Development Corpn Ltd v Metropolitan Police Comr* [1991] 4 All ER 638, [1991] 1 WLR 1362.
20 *Trimbey v Vignier* (1834) 1 Bing NC 151; *Di Sora v Phillips* (1863) 10 HL Cas 624 at 636–642; *Lazard Brothers & Co v Midland Bank Ltd* [1933] AC 289 at 298; *Sinfra Akt v Sinfra Ltd* [1939] 2 All ER 675; *Parkasho v Singh* [1968] P 233.
21 *Tallina Laevaushisus (A/S) v Estonian State SS Line* (1947) 80 Ll L Rep 99 at 108; *Rouyer Guillet et Cie v Rouyer Guillet & Co Ltd* [1949] 1 All ER 244n; *Re Fuld's Estate (No 3), Hartley v Fuld* [1968] P 675 at 700–703; as to the question of the court examining the constitutionality of foreign legislation, see Mann (1943) 59 LQR 155; Lipstein (1967) 42 BYBIL 265; Kahn-Freund (1974) III Hague Recueil 139, 449–452; Kahn-Freund, *Festschrift für F.A. Mann*, p 207.

The question of proof of foreign law in an appellate court has been examined by Sir Jocelyn SIMON P who said:

> Foreign law is, it is true, regarded in English courts as a question of fact; and appellate courts are slow to interfere with trial courts on questions of fact; but that only applies with particular force as regards the assessment of relative veracity and the judgment of matters of degree. Where the inference of fact depends on the consideration of written material, an appellate court is at no particular disadvantage compared to a trial court and will regard itself as freer to review the decision of the trial court.[1]

1 *Parkasho v Singh*, supra, at 254.

Chapter 8

Exclusion of foreign law

SUMMARY

It is obvious that circumstances will occasionally arise in which the law of the forum must be preferred to the foreign law that would normally be applicable to the case. An outstanding example of this is the civil law doctrine of *ordre public* under which any domestic rule designed to protect the public welfare must prevail over an inconsistent foreign rule. The danger of a doctrine so vague as this is that it may be interpreted to embrace such a multitude of domestic rules as to provide a fatally easy excuse for the application of the law of the forum and thus to defeat the underlying purpose of private international law. The analogous English doctrine, though less unruly, is indeed not above suspicion in this respect. Summarily stated, it withholds all recognition from any foreign law or judgment which is repugnant to the distinctive policy of English law, and it refuses to enforce any foreign law which is of a penal, revenue or other public law nature.[1] Furthermore, foreign expropriatory laws will, in some circumstances, not be recognised, and, in other circumstances, although recognised, will not be enforced. Finally, the mandatory rules of the forum may be applied, with the result that, to that extent, a foreign law is excluded.

We will now deal separately with these four[2] cases.

1. FOREIGN REVENUE, PENAL AND OTHER PUBLIC LAWS

Dicey and Morris[3] employs a three-fold classification of foreign laws which will not be enforced by English courts, ie revenue laws, penal laws and other

---

1 Holder (1968) 17 ICLQ 926; Smart (1986) 35 ICLQ 704; Carter (1989) 48 CLJ 417; Lipstein at 38 and Forsyth at 94 in *United Kingdom Law in the 1980s* (ed Banakas).
2 There is also the doctrine of foreign Act of State, which is beyond the scope of this book, *see Buttes Gas and Oil Co v Hammer (No 3)* [1982] AC 888; Dicey and Morris, pp 109–112.
3 Dicey and Morris, pp 101–109.

public laws. This classification, which was first adopted by Lord Denning in *A-G of New Zealand v Ortiz*,[4] has been endorsed by the Court of Appeal on a number of occasions,[5] and has finally been given the support of the House of Lords in *Re State of Norway's Applications (Nos 1 and 2).*[6] The same classification has also been adopted by the High Court of Australia[7] and the Court of Appeal in New Zealand.[8] "Public laws" is, seemingly, the umbrella concept which encompasses both revenue and penal laws, but also allows for a category of "other public laws."[9] The common thread running through the exclusionary rule in relation to revenue, penal and other public laws is that laws will not be enforced if they involve an assertion of sovereign authority by one state within the territory of another.[10] If the exclusionary rule applies it has been said that, in conceptual terms, what the court is doing is declining to exercise its jurisdiction.[11] Whether the claim sought to be enforced in the English courts is one which involves a penal, revenue or other public law is an issue to be determined according to the criteria of English law.[12] The three related concepts of revenue, penal and other public laws will now be examined.

(a) FOREIGN REVENUE LAWS[13]

(i) **The prohibition on enforcement**

Although it has been generally accepted, at any rate since the time of Lord MANSFIELD,[14] that no action lies in England for the enforcement of a foreign revenue law, authority for the proposition long remained a little nebulous, since until fairly recently the issue had been raised clearly on only one or two occasions.[15] All doubts were, however, stilled in 1955 by the decision of the House of Lords in *Government of India v Taylor*,[16] where the facts were as follows:

4 [1984] AC 1 at 20 et seq. Cf Ackner LJ at 34 and O'Connor LJ at 35. The House of Lords decided the case on a narrow point of construction: infra, pp 118–119.
5 See *Williams & Humbert Ltd v W & H Trade Marks (Jersey) Ltd* [1986] AC 368 at 394, 401; see also in the House of Lords the judgment of Lord Mackay at 437, cf Lord Templeman at 428; *Re State of Norway's Application* [1987] QB 433 at 477–478; *United States of America v Inkley* [1989] QB 255 at 264–265.
6 [1990] 1 AC 723, [1989] 1 All ER 745. If the Law Commissions' Report on choice of law in tort and delict is implemented the three-fold exclusionary rule will become enshrined in statutory form for that area: Law Com No 193 (1990), para 3.55.
7 *A-G (UK) v Heinemann Publishers Australia Pty Ltd (No 2)* (1988) 165 CLR 30.
8 *A-G for the United Kingdom v Wellington Newspapers Ltd* [1988] 1 NZLR 129.
9 *US v Inkley*, op cit, at 264–265.
10 *Re State of Norway's Applications (Nos 1 and 2)*, op cit, at 807–808.
11 Ibid.
12 *US v Inkley*, op cit, at 265.
13 See especially M Mann (1954) 3 ICLQ 465, and the judgment of KINGSMILL MOORE J in the Irish case of *Peter Buchanan Ltd and Macharg v McVey* [1955] AC 516 n, [1954] IR 89. See also Albrecht (1950) 30 BYBIL 454, 459–465; Castel (1964) 42 Can BR 277; Stoel (1967) 16 ICLQ 663, 671 et seq; F.A. Mann (1971) I Hague Recueil 115, 172–181; Carter (1984) 55 BYBIL 111.
14 *Holman v Johnson* (1775) 1 Cowp 341 at 343.
15 See eg *Sydney Municipal Council v Bull* [1909] 1 KB 7; *Re Visser* [1928] Ch 877. See also *The Eva* [1921] P 454; *King of the Hellenes v Brostrom* (1923) 16 L1 L Rep 167 and 190; *Metal Industries (Salvage) v Owners of the S T Harle* 1962 SLT 114; cf *The Acrux* [1965] P 391, [1965] 2 All ER 323; Webb (1965) 28 MLR 591.
16 [1955] AC 491, [1955] 1 All ER 292; see also *Williams and Humbert Ltd v W and H Trade Marks (Jersey) Ltd* [1986] AC 368 at 428, discussed infra pp 124–125; *USA v Harden* (1963) 41 DLR (2d) 721.

The Delhi Electric Supply and Traction Co Ltd, which was a company registered in England but carrying on business in India, sold its business to the Indian Government for a sum of money which it remitted to England as soon as received. After the company had gone into voluntary liquidation, a demand was made on it by the Indian Commissioner of Income Tax for the payment of a large sum of income tax in respect of the capital gain derived from the sale of the business. The Commissioner claimed to prove for this debt in the liquidation, but his claim was rejected by the liquidator and by the lower courts.

It was argued for the appellants in the House of Lords that the alleged rule excluding the recognition of foreign revenue laws did not extend to taxes similar to those imposed in England, but was confined to penal laws, and that in any event it demanded modification in the case of a foreign country belonging to the Commonwealth. Further, it was said that the rule, even if accepted in toto, did not apply to liquidation proceedings, for a liquidator is under a statutory duty to discharge all the "liabilities" of the company, which is a word of wide import not confined to debts directly enforceable by action.

These arguments were rejected. Their Lordships were unanimous in holding that the rule expressed by Lord MANSFIELD rested on a solid basis of authority and convenience.[17] They also held, with one dissentient,[18] that the duty of a liquidator in the winding up of a company is confined to the discharge of such liabilities as are legally enforceable.

(ii) Indirect enforcement

The rule that no action lies to recover foreign taxes is not affected by the identity of the plaintiff or by the form in which the action is brought.

> In every case the substance of the claim must be scrutinised, and if it then appears that it is really a suit brought for the purpose of collecting the debts of a foreign revenue it must be rejected.[19]

That an indirect evasion of the rule will not be tolerated is well illustrated by *Rossano v Manufacturers' Life Insurance Co Ltd.*[20]

The plaintiff was an Egyptian national resident in Alexandria; the defendants were an insurance company with a head office in Toronto and branches in many other countries. The action was to recover money due under three policies of life insurance issued by the defendants. The first two policies

---

17 But the rule will only operate if the English court classifies the claim as a tax or revenue claim, eg, *Weir v Lohr* (1967) 65 DLR (2d) 717; *Connor v Connor* [1974] 1 NZLR 632; the former case also indicates that the rule may well not operate between the States of a Federal country; see also *Permanent Trustee Co (Canberra) Ltd v Finlayson* (1967) 9 FLR 424, revsd on another point (1968) 122 CLR 338.
18 Lord KEITH.
19 *Peter Buchanan Ltd and Macharg v McVey* [1955] AC 516 n at 529, [1954] IR 89 at 107; approved by the House of Lords in *Government of India v Taylor supra;* but see on these cases *Williams and Humbert Ltd v W and H Trade Marks (Jersey) Ltd* [1986] AC 368 at 440; see also *Re Lord Cable* [1977] 1 WLR 7 at 13. It is suggested in this last case that proceedings in England by a foreign government for direct enforcement of that government's currency control regulations, even against a citizen of that country, would be contrary to the principle of non-enforcement of foreign revenue laws; but cf *Kahler v Midland Bank Ltd* [1950] AC 24 at 46–47, 57; see also *A-G of New Zealand v Ortiz* [1984] AC 1 at 24 (per Lord DENNING MR in the Court of Appeal).
20 [1963] 2 QB 352, [1962] 2 All ER 214.

required payment in London in pounds sterling; the third directed payment at New York in dollars.

One defence raised by the defendants was that two garnishee orders[21] had been served on three of their branches in Cairo which would render them responsible for the payment of certain taxes alleged to be due from the plaintiff to the Egyptian government if they paid him before he had satisfied this fiscal liability. The defence failed, for to allow the garnishee orders, which related solely to taxation debts, to defeat the plaintiff's cause of action would constitute an indirect enforcement of a foreign revenue law. The obvious result of dismissing the action would be the recovery of the taxes by the Egyptian government.[22]

However, the prohibition on indirect enforcement of foreign revenue laws does not prevent an English court from assisting a foreign State to obtain evidence against one of that State's taxpayers. Thus an English court will accede to a request by a foreign State that witnesses in England give oral evidence pursuant to the Evidence (Proceedings in Other Jurisdictions) Act 1975,[23] even though this is in connection with proceedings in the foreign State against one of its taxpayers.[24] Seemingly, this is the case regardless of whether the taxpayer supports the request.

It is questionable whether the general ban on indirect enforcement is not too rigid. If, for instance, in the *Rossano Case*, the defendants had in fact paid the taxes due to the government, would not an action based upon the unjust enrichment of the plaintiff have succeeded? It may even be questioned whether such a decision as that reached in *Municipal Council of Sydney v Bull*,[25] where the plaintiff failed in its bid to recover a contribution imposed by a local statute in respect of certain street improvements effected in the area where the defendant owned property, accords with the growing practice of States and their subordinate bodies to furnish services in return for payment. The distinction is not obvious between, say, a claim for unpaid water rates and a claim by a State owned railway to recover the charge due for goods carried.

The narrow dividing line is illustrated by *Brokaw v Seatrain UK Ltd.*[26]

Goods were shipped from the USA to England in an American ship. Whilst the ship was at sea, the US Treasury served a notice of levy, in respect of taxes unpaid by the owners of the goods, on the shipowners demanding that the goods should be surrendered. When the ship arrived at Southampton, the shipowners refused to deliver the goods to the consignee, who claimed delivery or their value.

By reason of interpleader proceedings, the court had to consider the claim of the US Treasury, which was rejected on the basis that to allow it amounted to indirect enforcement of a foreign revenue law by seizure of goods.

---

21 As to garnishment, see infra, pp 818–819.
22 See, for example, *Peter Buchanan Ltd and Macharg v McVey* [1955] AC 516 n, [1954] IR 89; *Williams and Humbert Ltd v W and H Trade Marks (Jersey) Ltd* [1986] AC 368 at 437–441; cf *Ayres v Evans* (1981) 39 ALR 129.
23 Supra, pp 83–84.
24 *Re State of Norway's Applications (Nos 1 and 2)* [1990] 1 AC 723, [1989] 1 All ER 745.
25 [1909] 1 KB 7.
26 [1971] 2 QB 476, [1971] 2 All ER 98; see *A-G of New Zealand v Ortiz* [1984] AC 1 at 31–32 (per ACKNER LJ in the Court of Appeal). See also *Re Van de Mark and Toronto–Dominion Bank* (1989) 68 OR (2d) 379.

However, had the notice of levy been effective to reduce the goods into the possession of the US Treasury, their claim would have been upheld, for the court would then have been enforcing a possessory title rather than a revenue law.

(iii) Recognition of a foreign revenue law

This rule that no action will lie at the instance of a foreign State to enforce a revenue law does not mean, despite what Lord MANSFIELD said in *Holman v Johnson*,[1] that such a law is to be totally ignored.[2] Refusal to enforce it implies no disclaimer of its lawful existence, and circumstances may require that its existence be recognised. Thus, on the ground that public policy demands the maintenance of harmonious relations with other nations, the courts will not countenance any transaction, such as a fraudulent tax-evasion scheme, which is knowingly designed to violate a revenue law of a foreign and friendly State.[3] If personal representatives have had personally to pay taxes on a foreign estate under foreign revenue laws, those foreign laws will be recognised here so as to enable the personal representatives to be indemnified from assets of the estate situated here.[4] Furthermore, in such cases the personal representatives should be given leave to remit the assets to the foreign country for payment of the taxes.[5]

(b) FOREIGN PENAL LAWS[6]

It is well settled that an English court will not lend its aid to the enforcement, either directly or indirectly, of a foreign penal law.[7] The imposition of a penalty normally reflects the exercise by a State of its sovereign power, and it is an obvious principle that an act of sovereignty can have no effect in the territory of another State.

(i) The meaning of a penalty

The word "penalty" is equivocal, and if understood without qualification it comprises penalties to the enforcement of which there can be no objection as for example one incorporated in a commercial contract with the object of inducing the prompt performance of his contract by one of the parties.[8] What, therefore, is the meaning of the word in the present context? The

---

1 (1775) 1 Cowp 341 at 343: "No country takes notice of the revenue laws of another."
2 *Regazzoni v KC Sethia (1944) Ltd* [1956] 2 QB 490 at 515, [1956] 2 All ER 487 at 490; affd [1958] AC 301 at 319, [1957] 3 All ER 286 at 291; *X Y and Z v The Bank* [1983] 2 Lloyd's Rep 535 at 546–547; cf *Sharif v Azad* [1967] 1 QB 605 at 617; *Mackender v Feldia AG* [1967] 2 QB 590 at 601.
3 *Re Emery's Investment Trusts* [1959] Ch 410; *Pye Ltd v B G Transport Service Ltd* [1966] 2 Lloyd's Rep 300 at 308–309. See also *Euro-Diam Ltd v Bathurst* [1990] 1 QB 1 at 39–40.
4 *Re Lord Cable* [1976] 3 All ER 417, [1977] 1 WLR 7; and see *Re Reid* (1970) 17 DLR (3d) 199.
5 *Re Lord Cable* [1977] 1 WLR 7 at 25–26; and see *Scottish National Orchestra Ltd v Thomson's Executor* 1969 SLT 325.
6 See especially F A Mann (1954) 40 Grotius Society 25; M Mann (1956) 42 Grotius Society 133, and see Stoel (1967) 16 ICLQ 663.
7 *Folliott v Ogden* (1789) 3 Term Rep 726; *Wolff v Oxholm* (1817) 6 M & S 92; *Huntington v Attrill* [1893] AC 150; *Frankfurther v W L Exner Ltd* [1947] Ch 629; *Empresa Exportadora De Azucar v Industria Azucarera Nacional S A (The Playa Larga)* [1983] 2 Lloyd's Rep 171; *X Y and Z v The Bank* [1983] 2 Lloyd's Rep 535; *A-G of New Zealand v Ortiz* [1984] AC 1; *Williams and Humbert Ltd v W and H Trade Marks (Jersey) Ltd* [1986] AC 368.
8 *Huntington v Attrill* [1893] AC 150 at 156.

answer given by the Privy Council in *Huntington v Attrill*,[9] the leading English authority on the subject, is that it is limited to a fine or other exaction imposed by the State for some violation of public order of a criminal complexion.[10] Lord DENNING MR has indicated[11] that, in the context of recognition of foreign judgments, a judgment for exemplary damages is not to be denied recognition as being in respect of "a penalty".[12] It may well be, therefore, that a foreign law as to exemplary damages will be applied here and will not be castigated as a penal law. On the other hand, there is a statutory prohibition on the enforcement of foreign judgments for multiple damages,[13] such as treble damages under the USA anti-trust laws. These laws have been described as penal.[14]

(ii) Examples of the prohibition on indirect enforcement of a penal law

A modern example of an attempt to enforce a foreign penalty indirectly is *Banco de Vizcaya v Don Alfonso de Borbón y Austria*[15] where the facts were these:

> The former King of Spain had bought certain securities with his own money and had instructed that they should be held by a London bank to the order of his agents, the Banco de Vizcaya, a Spanish concern. The Spanish Republican Government later decreed that all his property, wherever situated, should be confiscated and that anything deposited with Spanish banks should be delivered to the Treasury. The plaintiffs claimed delivery of the securities from the London bank on the ground that they had a contractual right of recovery by virtue of the instructions given by King Alfonso at the time of the original deposit.

LAWRENCE J held that the plaintiffs were not in reality asserting their own contractual rights as they originally existed, but the rights of the Spanish Republic. Therefore their claim failed, since to countenance it would in effect be to enforce an admittedly penal law of the Republic.

A more recent case to discuss the question of enforcement of a foreign penal law is *A-G of New Zealand v Ortiz*,[16] the facts of which were as follows:

> A Maori carved door was removed from New Zealand without permission of the appropriate authorities and was eventually offered for sale by the first defendant by auction in London. The Attorney-General of New Zealand (the plaintiff) alleged that the State was the owner of the door and sought an injunction in the English courts restraining the sale and an order for delivery up of the door. The basis of this claim was a New Zealand statute which, in certain circumstances, provided for the forfeiture, without compensation, of historic articles.

---

9 [1893] AC 150.
10 See *Schemmer v Property Resources Ltd* [1975] Ch 273, [1974] 3 All ER 451.
11 *S A Consortium General Textiles v Sun and Sand Agencies Ltd* [1978] QB 279 at 299–300.
12 Infra, pp 381–382.
13 Protection of Trading Interests Act 1980, s 5; infra, pp 382–384. Under the 1980 Act the Secretary of State can make orders prohibiting persons in the UK from complying with foreign extra-territorial measures which are damaging to UK trading interests; see ss 1–3.
14 *British Airways Board v Laker Airways Ltd* [1984] QB 142 at 163 (PARKER J), and in the Court of Appeal at 201; see also Law Commission Working Paper No 87 (1984), paras 5.62–5.63.
15 [1935]1 KB 140. A similar case is *Frankfurther v W L Exner Ltd* [1947] Ch 629. For an early example see *Ogden v Folliott* (1790) 3 Term Rep 726.
16 [1984] AC 1; Nott (1984) 33 ICLQ 203.

STAUGHTON J, at first instance, gave judgment for the plaintiff. The Court of Appeal allowed an appeal on the basis of a point of construction of the New Zealand statute.[17] It was held that the statute only provided for the forfeiture of historic articles when the goods had been seized by the appropriate New Zealand authorities, and this had not happened in the present case. However, the Court of Appeal went on to discuss the wider point of the nature of the New Zealand statute. Lord Justices ACKNER and O'CONNOR held, obiter, that the New Zealand statute was a penal law and, therefore, would not be enforced in England.[18] The claim was made by the Attorney-General on behalf of the State, the cause of action concerned a public right—the preservation of historic articles within New Zealand, and vindication of the right was sought through forfeiture of the property without compensation.[19] Lord DENNING expressed himself in different terms; he regarded the New Zealand statute as coming within the category of a public law[1] rather than a penal law.[2]

(iii) Characterisation of the foreign law/right of action

It is undeniable that the English court must itself characterise the alleged penal, revenue or other public law, but regard will be had to the attitude adopted in the courts in the foreign jurisdiction.[3] According to the Privy Council in *Huntington v Attrill*[4] nothing can be regarded as a penalty unless it is "recoverable at the instance of the State or of an official duly authorised to prosecute on its behalf, or of a public informer".[5] The facts of the case were as follows:

> A New York statute, designed inter alia to protect the public against company promoters, provided that the directors of a corporation should be personally liable for its debts on proof that false reports of its financial condition had been published. Sums recoverable under this provision were payable to creditors in satisfaction pro tanto of their claims. A creditor instituted a suit under the statute in a New York court and obtained judgment for a large sum. He later brought an action on the judgment in Ontario. The New York courts had decided that actions brought under the statute were of a penal character.

The Privy Council held, first, that it was for the Ontario court to put its own interpretation on the statutory provision; and, secondly, that the statute was remedial, not penal, since it permitted a subject to enforce a liability in his own interests and for the protection of his own private rights.[6]

---

17 [1984] AC 1 at 17–18, 29, 35.
18 At 31–34, 35.
19 At 33–34 (per ACKNER LJ).
 1 At 20–24; see infra, pp 121–122.
 2 On appeal to the House of Lords, the decision of the Court of Appeal was upheld solely on the narrow point of construction of the New Zealand statute. The Law Lords, at 45–49 (per Lord BRIGHTMAN), having heard no argument on the point relating to the enforcement of a penal law, declined to express any opinion on the correctness of the obiter dicta on this matter in the Court of Appeal.
 3 *United States of America v Inkley* [1989] QB 255 at 265.
 4 [1893] AC 150; and see *Metal Industries (Salvage) Ltd v Owners of S T Harle* 1962 SLT 114 at 116.
 5 At 157, 158. See *A-G of New Zealand v Ortiz* [1984] AC 1 at 32 (per Ackner LJ).
 6 The Supreme Court of the US reached the same conclusion: (1892) 146 US 657.

In *United States of America v Inkley*,[7] the Court of Appeal was faced with a more complex case involving an action by a foreign state, but which was clothed in civil form.

An action was brought by the United States government for enforcement of a judgment for the amount of an appearance bond plus interest obtained in a federal court in Florida, sitting as a civil court, against the defendant who had been released on bail but had subsequently failed to appear to answer criminal charges.

The Court of Appeal refused to enforce the judgment on the basis that this was an action by a foreign state to enforce the execution of its own public/penal law. Dicey and Morris' three-fold classification of the exclusionary rule was adopted. "Public laws" was seen as the wide overall exclusionary category, and a foreign penal law will necessarily also be a foreign public law. Whether the right of action which it is sought to have enforced in England is public or private was said to depend on three considerations: the party in whose favour the right is created; the purpose of the law on which the right is based; the general context of the case as a whole. The Court of Appeal held[8] that the action was concerned with the right of the United States government to ensure the due observance of its criminal law; the purpose of the action was part of a public law process aimed to ensure the attendance of persons accused of crime before the criminal courts; the general context was criminal or penal. The essentially public/penal law nature of the action was not affected by the fact that it was dressed up in civil form. Applying these considerations to the facts of the case it was concluded that "Notwithstanding its civil clothing, the purpose of the action initiated by the writ issued in this case was the due execution by the United States of America of a public law process aimed to ensure the attendance of persons accused of crime before the criminal courts".[9]

(iv) Recognition of foreign penal laws

The enforcement of a foreign penal law must be distinguished from its application or recognition.[10] Although enforcement will not be allowed, it is going too far to assert that "the penal laws of one country cannot be taken notice of in another".[11] This is scarcely true for, subject to the possible intervention of the doctrine of public policy,[12] such a law must be regarded as operative even in English proceedings if it is part of the foreign legal system which, according to the relevant rule for the choice of law, governs the transaction that is sub judice.[13] If, for example, a Ruritanian statute makes the export of certain raw materials a crime punishable by fine and confiscation of property, in no circumstances will the fine be recoverable by an action in England. Nevertheless, if a Ruritanian businessman, by a contract that falls to be governed by the law of that country, agrees to sell the prohibited materials to an Englishman, an action brought against him in England for non-delivery must necessarily fail. The illegality of the contract

7 [1989] QB 255, [1988] 3 All ER 144; Carter (1988) BYBIL 347.
8 At 265–266.
9 At 266.
10 M Mann (1956) 42 Grotius Society 133, 135–136.
11 *Folliott v Ogden* (1789) 3 Term Rep 726 at 733.
12 Infra, pp 128–137.
13 See *A-G of New Zealand v Ortiz* [1984] AC 1 at 31 (per ACKNER LJ in the Court of Appeal).

according to its governing law, though springing from a crime and from a penal law devoid of extra-territorial effect, cannot be ignored.[14]

(c) OTHER FOREIGN PUBLIC LAWS

Judicial adoption[15] of Dicey and Morris's three-fold classification of foreign laws which will not be enforced means that this third category is now firmly established. What we are concerned with are public laws which are not revenue or penal ones. It is not difficult to find examples of "other public laws". Dicey and Morris[16] give the following as illustrations: import and export regulations; trading with the enemy legislation; price control regulations; and anti-trust legislation.[17] However, it is much more difficult to give a precise definition to the concept of "public laws", since the common law does not as yet recognise any clear distinction between public and private laws.[18] In *A-G of New Zealand v Ortiz*[19] Lord DENNING admitted that the concept of "other public laws" was very uncertain, but went on to explain that they are laws which are eiusdem generis with penal or revenue laws.[20] He found a common thread underlying these three categories in the principles applied in international law; in particular, in the principle that laws will not be enforced if they involve an exercise by a government of its sovereign authority over property beyond its territory. He concluded that legislation providing for the automatic forfeiture to the State of works of art should they be exported would come within this principle, and, accordingly, within the category of other public laws.

The exclusion of other public laws has been accepted by the High Court of Australia and the Court of Appeal in New Zealand in the *Spycatcher Cases*,[1] which involved the important issues of confidentiality and state security.

The Attorney-General of the United Kingdom sought, inter alia, injunctions in Australia and New Zealand to prevent publication in those respective countries of the whole or parts of *Spycatcher*, the memoirs of Peter Wright—a former intelligence officer of the British Security Services. The Attorney-General's argument, that Wright was acting in breach of duties of confidence (fiduciary and contractual) owed to the United Kingdom Government, was assumed to be correct. One of the defences in both cases was that the Australian and New Zealand courts will not enforce a foreign penal or other public law.

Both the Australian and New Zealand courts refused to grant the relief

14 The same principle affects a foreign revenue law, supra, p 117.
15 Supra, pp 113–114.
16 Dicey and Morris p 108.
17 Anti-trust laws may be penal, see supra, p 118.
18 *Re State of Norway's Application* [1987] QB 433 at 475, affd by HL without discussion of this specific point [1990] 1 AC 723, 458. The problem of identifying public laws also arises in the context of jurisdiction under the Brussels and Lugano Conventions, see infra, pp 286–288.
19 [1984] AC 1.
20 At 20.
1 In Australia: *A-G (UK) v Heinemann Publishers Australia Pty Ltd* (1988) 165 CLR 30; see also *Trade Practices Commission v Australia Meat Holdings Pty Ltd* (1988) 83 ALR 299 at 360–363. In New Zealand: *A-G for the United Kingdom v Wellington Newspapers Ltd* [1988] 1 NZLR 129. Criticised by Mann (1988) 104 LQR 497; Collier [1989] CLJ 33; see also Lord Keith in *A-G v Guardian Newspapers Ltd (No 2)* [1990] 1 AC 109, 264–265. The exclusion of "other public laws" has also been accepted in Hong Kong in a different context: *Nonus Asia Inc v Standard Chartered Bank* [1990] 1 HKLR 396.

sought, albeit on different grounds. The High Court of Australia regarded the action as one whereby the United Kingdom Government sought to protect the efficiency of its Security Services as part of the defence of the country; as such, it fell within the exclusion of "other public laws". The New Zealand Court of Appeal, however, took a different view. The duty of confidentiality was said to arise from the relationship between the parties as employer and employee. An action for damages (an injunction having earlier been refused on the basis that the contents of the book were already in the public domain) was therefore not barred by the exclusionary rule in relation to foreign penal or other public laws. None the less, this was not thought to be a proper case for protecting the United Kingdom's security secrets since there had been prior publication abroad of the information in *Spycatcher*; moreover, the New Zealand public interest justified publication.

2. FOREIGN EXPROPRIATORY LEGISLATION

A somewhat troublesome question is the extent to which foreign expropriatory legislation is recognised in England when it is directed, not against a particular person as in *Don Alfonso's Case*[2] or a particular item as in the *Ortiz Case*,[3] but against national property generally. It would seem that legislation of this nature may take four forms.[4]

First, *requisition*, which term is generally confined to the seizure of property in the public interest for a limited period, usually until the end of some emergency, and in return for compensation.

Secondly, *nationalisation*, which is the permanent absorption of property into public ownership in furtherance of some political aim and in return for compensation.

Thirdly, *compulsory acquisition*, which is the permanent seizure of property in fulfilment of some economic or social aim, and in exchange for compensation.

Fourthly, *confiscation*, which is the permanent seizure of private property without payment of compensation.[5]

The main question of private international law in this connection is the extent to which, in the eyes of English law, a decree of a foreign State implementing one of these forms of expropriation affects property belonging either to nationals of that State or to aliens.

The general principles that have a bearing on the question defy simple harmonisation, for against the principles that neither foreign legislation nor foreign penal laws have extra-territorial effect, stands the equally fundamental doctrine that a foreign sovereign cannot normally be impleaded.[6] If, for instance, the Ruritanian Government obtains possession of jewellery held by a London bank on the ground that it falls within the scope of a Ruritanian decree of confiscation and if the decree is not regarded by English law as

2 Supra, p 118.
3 Supra, pp 118–119.
4 See *I Congreso del Partido* [1983] 1 All ER 1092 at 1103, CA, revsd on a different point [1983] AC 244; *Williams and Humbert Ltd v W and H Trade Marks (Jersey) Ltd* [1986] AC 368; infra, pp 124–126.
5 Foreign confiscation orders may be enforced under the Drug Trafficking Offences Act 1986.
6 Infra, pp 265–271.

applicable to property in England, how can this view be rendered effective against a sovereign power that is immune from the jurisdiction?

Another obstacle to a simple generalisation of the law is the doubt whether all forms of property stand on the same footing for the purpose of determining the effect of expropriation. The suggestion, for instance, by no means unsupported by authority, has been made that a merchant ship stands in a category of its own, since it has a permanent situs in the country to which it belongs.[7] If this is correct a State which requisitions or confiscates its national ships exercises a quasi-territorial, not an extra-territorial, act of authority.

If an English judge is required to determine the effect of foreign expropriatory legislation, his decision will depend on three main factors, namely the interpretation of the foreign legislation; the situs of the property at the time of the legislative decree; and the question whether the foreign sovereign was in actual possession or control of the property outside his territory at the time when the facts giving rise to the litigation occurred. The present law appears to be as follows.

(a) PROPERTY WITHIN THE FOREIGN JURISDICTION AT TIME OF DECREE

The English courts recognise without hesitation that the ownership of property is conclusively and finally determined by the terms of the foreign decree of expropriation, if the property is situated within the jurisdiction of the sovereign at the time of the decree, notwithstanding that it is later brought to England and is still there at the time of the action. For instance, in *Luther v Sagor*:[8]

Timber, situated in Russia and belonging to the plaintiffs, a private company incorporated according to the law of Russia, was seized by the Soviet authorities under a decree that had nationalised all profits belonging to industrial and commercial establishments. Part of the timber was later brought to England and there sold to the defendants by a Soviet agent. The plaintiffs sued for damages in trover on the ground that the ownership of the timber was still vested in them.

The Court of Appeal, on grounds which were not identical, found for the defendants.

In the view of WARRINGTON LJ, no sovereign State must sit in judgment upon the acts of another foreign State affecting property within its own territory.[9] BANKES LJ found it impossible to ignore the law of Russia, the law of the situs at the time of the decree, under which the seller had acquired a good title to the goods.[10] SCRUTTON LJ, following perhaps a more doubtful line of reasoning, argued that, since the doctrine of immunity would have prevented any investigation of the Russian sovereign's title had the timber been found in England in the possession of a Russian official, it followed that no such investigation was possible where possession had been given

7 McNair (1946) 31 Grotius Society 30.
8 [1921] 3 KB 532 at 548. Followed in *Princess Olga Paley v Weisz* [1929] 1 KB 718; and see *Oppenheimer v Cattermole* [1976] AC 249 at 282–283; *Buttes Gas and Oil Co v Hammer (No 3)* [1982] AC 888 at 931; *Williams and Humbert Ltd v W and H Trade Marks (Jersey) Ltd* [1986] AC 368; infra, pp 124–125. Cf *Carl Zeiss Stiftung v Rayner and Keeler Ltd* [1967] 1 AC 853. *Quaere* whether the decision would be the same if the owner escaped with his property from the country after the decree but before he had been deprived of possession by the local authorities.
9 [1921] 3 KB 532 at 548–549.
10 Ibid, at 545.

to a private purchaser. "What the court cannot do directly, it cannot do indirectly."[11]

But surely the simple and decisive justification of the decision is the rule that a title to movables, valid according to the law of the situs at the time of its acquisition, is recognised by English law.[12] The law of the situs must prevail in such circumstances unless the rule of that law under which the title has been acquired is so immoral or so alien to the principles of justice as understood in England that it must be disregarded as being contrary to public policy. The Court of Appeal considered this objection, but found it impossible to regard the nationalisation decree as anything else but the expression of a policy, designed, whether mistakenly or not, to promote the best interests of Russians.

The principle of *Luther v Sagor* was followed recently by the House of Lords in *Williams and Humbert Ltd v W and H Trade Marks (Jersey) Ltd*.[13] One point that should be noted from the outset about this case is that at first instance and in the Court of Appeal the case was regarded as one of con-fiscation of property, ie expropriation *without* payment, whereas the House of Lords treated it as a case of compulsory acquisition, ie expropriation *with* payment. Nonetheless, the principle in *Luther v Sagor* was still applied in all three courts. The facts of the case, according to the House of Lords, were as follows:

> The Spanish government compulsorily acquired all the shares of a company incorporated in Spain, Rumasa, and of the subsidiary companies of Rumasa incorporated in Spain, including two banks—"Jerez" and "Norte". Rumasa also held all the shares in an English company, Williams and Humbert; this company was now, therefore, indirectly controlled by the Spanish government. The plaintiffs, the English company and the three above-named Spanish companies, at the instigation of the Spanish government, brought actions in England against the defendants, the orig-inal owners of the Spanish companies, the Mateos family, and a Jersey company, for the return of property (in the form of trademarks and money), which it was alleged had been improperly diverted from the English company and one of the Spanish companies, and for damages. The defendants argued that the proceedings were an attempt to enforce a foreign penal law and/or it would be contrary to public policy to grant the relief sought. NOURSE J ordered that the defence be struck out, as disclosing no reasonable defence, and this was upheld by a majority of the Court of Appeal. There were appeals to the House of Lords.

The House of Lords unanimously dismissed the appeals. Lord TEMPLEMAN, with whom the other Law Lords concurred, examined the decision in *Luther v Sagor* and then stated the principle that "an English court will recognise the compulsory acquisition law of a foreign state and will recognise the change of title to property which has come under the control of the foreign state and will recognise the consequences of that change of title".[14] Here, the property was the shares in the Spanish companies and this property was

---

11　Ibid, at 555–556.
12　See the remarks of DEVLIN J in *Bank voor Handel en Scheepvaart NV v Slatford* [1953] 1 QB 248 at 260.
13　[1986] AC 368; F A Mann (1986) 102 LQR 191; (1987) 103 LQR 26; (1988) 104 LQR 346; (1985) BYBIL 316; Carter (1986) BYBIL 439.
14　At 431.

situated in Spain, the companies being incorporated there. The change in ownership of the shares was, accordingly, recognised. The Spanish government would have no right to confiscate the English property, ie the shares in Williams and Humbert; but, according to Lord TEMPLEMAN, it did not purport to do so, since this property would remain in the ownership of Rumasa, one of the Spanish companies.[15] In reality though, the Spanish government would control Williams and Humbert. The Spanish government would, therefore, be able to achieve by indirect means (confiscation of Rumasa) what it could not achieve by direct confiscation.

When it came to the specific allegation that what was involved was enforcement of a foreign penal law, Lord TEMPLEMAN doubted if the Spanish law could be regarded as penal.[16] Even if it was accepted that it was a penal law there was no attempt directly to enforce this law in England,[17] since the objective of the law, to acquire and control various companies, had already been achieved in Spain. Nor was there an attempt indirectly to enforce the Spanish law, since the actions were brought by the companies, and under well established principles of company law these were distinct entities from the Spanish government which owned the companies.[1] If the argument that it was a penal law were to be accepted, it would produce the anarchic result that none of the companies could pursue actions outside Spain and wrongdoers vis à vis the companies would be released from liability.[2]

The *Williams and Humbert Case* is also interesting for its discussion at first instance[3] and in the Court of Appeal[4] of foreign confiscatory laws. The Court of Appeal[5] agreed with NOURSE J, at first instance, that confiscatory laws should be classified as follows:

Class 1 laws, which the English courts will not recognise:
A. Foreign confiscatory laws which, by reason of their being discriminatory on grounds of race, religion or the like, constitute so grave an infringement of human rights that they ought not to be recognised as laws at all.
B. Foreign laws which discriminate against nationals of this country in time of war by purporting to confiscate their moveable property situated in the foreign state.

Class 2 laws, which will be recognised, but to which effect will not be given:
A. Foreign laws confiscating property situated in the foreign state, if they are penal.
B. Foreign laws which purport to confiscate property situated in this country.

Class 3 laws, to which effect will be given provided they do not fall within Class 1:
Foreign laws which confiscate property in the foreign state and where title has been perfected there.[6]

It was argued, at first instance, by counsel for the defence that there was a further category within Class 1 of foreign confiscatory laws which are aimed

15 At 428, 433.
16 At 428; see also 437 (per Lord MACKAY).
17 At 428–429; see also 437–441 (per Lord MACKAY).
 1 At 429.
 2 At 429–430. Lord TEMPLEMAN rejected the suggestion that a receiver should be appointed to deal with English assets and to recover debts; cf F A Mann (1962) 11 ICLQ 471; (1986) 102 LQR 191.
 3 [1986] 1 AC 375 at 379.
 4 [1986] 1 AC 389; Forsyth [1985] CLJ 376.
 5 At pp 392, 414.
 6 This quotation is from *Settebello Ltd v Banco Totta* [1985] 1 WLR 1050 at 1056 where the Court of Appeal adopted the classification of NOURSE J in the *Williams and Humbert Case*.

at confiscating the property of particular individuals or classes of individuals,[7] but NOURSE J denied the existence of any such category. It was at this point that it was argued, unsuccessfully,[8] that on the facts of the case there was an attempt to enforce a foreign confiscatory law which was penal or a public law (Class 2A).

One final point to note about the *Williams and Humbert Case* is that, seemingly, it introduces a principle that, for reasons of comity, a party cannot plead in a case of compulsory acquisition that the foreign government has acted in an oppressive way.[9] Neither will the English courts consider the merits of the compulsory acquisition or the motives of the foreign government.[10] What is new is the suggestion that such matters cannot even be pleaded by a party.

The last question which has to be asked is whether the principle of *Luther v Sagor* applies where the confiscated property, though situated within the jurisdiction of the confiscating State, belongs to aliens. This was the main issue raised in *Anglo-Iranian Oil Co v Jaffrate* better known as *The Rose Mary*[11] where the court took the view that *Luther v Sagor* does not condone the confiscation of movables belonging to an owner who is not a national of the confiscating State unless adequate compensation is paid to him in return. It has subsequently been held by UPJOHN J, however, that neither the nationality of the dispossessed owner nor the payment of compensation to him affects the general principle laid down in *Luther v Sagor* and other cases.[12] The principle is that English law recognises the extra-territorial effectiveness of confiscatory legislation passed by a foreign State in respect of movables situated within its territory or of contracts governed by its law, unless the object is to confiscate the property of individual persons or classes of persons.

(b) PROPERTY OUTSIDE THE FOREIGN JURISDICTION AT TIME OF DECREE

If the property was outside the territory of the confiscating or requisitioning sovereign at the time of the decree, whether in England, in a foreign country or on the high seas, the first task of the judge is to construe the decree in order to ascertain whether it is in terms confined to property within the jurisdiction or whether it purports to affect property outside the territory. It is for the judge to form his own opinion on this question after hearing the evidence of expert witnesses.

If he comes to the conclusion that the decree was neither expressly nor implicitly directed against property in other countries or on the high seas, then the question is no longer significant. This was the substantial basis of the House of Lords decision in *Lecouturier v Rey*.[13] Under a French statute, the Carthusian monks had been expelled from France and deprived of their

---

7 [1986] 1 AC 375 at 381.
8 See the judgment of NOURSE J at pp 382–386; the argument was also rejected in the Court of Appeal, LLOYD LJ dissenting; for the House of Lords see supra, pp 124–125.
9 [1986] 1 AC 368 at 431, 434, 436.
10 See also *Settebello Ltd v Banco Totta and Acores* [1985] 1 WLR 1050—a case involving the issue of letters of request.
11 [1953] 1 WLR 246.
12 *Re Helbert Wagg & Co Ltd* [1956] Ch 323, [1956] 1 All ER 129. However, see O'Connell (1955) 4 ICLQ 270; Wortley, *Expropriation in Public International Law*, 33–36, 95; F A Mann (1954) 70 LQR 181, 188–190.
13 [1910] AC 262; *The Jupiter (No 3)* [1927] P 122.

property. They continued, but now in Spain, to manufacture the liqueur known as Chartreuse, according to its original secret formula. Their Lordships held that the monks, rather than the French liquidator, were still free to exploit in England the reputation which Chartreuse had obtained there. The statute neither expressly nor by implication affected property outside France.

If, on the other hand, the judge comes to the conclusion that the foreign legislation is intended to have extra-territorial operation, the first general principle to be considered is that legislation has no extra-territorial effect. Broadly speaking, jurisdiction is coincident with power, and how can power be exerted within the territory of another sovereign?[14]

The clear implication of the territorial principle is that property situated, say, in England cannot be affected by a foreign decree of expropriation and that the rights of the owner remain unimpaired. The only doubt is whether the decree is effective against a national of the foreign State, since historical authority is not lacking for the view that the right to expropriate property may be based on the allegiance of its owner as well as upon its situs.[1] Whether this view is justifiable or not, it has found few adherents.[2] Thus in one case MAUGHAM J held that a Soviet confiscatory decree was ineffective with regard to property in England although the owner was a Russian subject at the time of the decree.[3] The application of the principle, however, that the legislative power of a State is only territorial, may be frustrated by the impact of the equally well established principle[4] that a foreign State or sovereign cannot normally be impleaded, for if the sovereign is in possession or control of the expropriated property, even though it may be in England, the owner is unable to enforce his rights.[5]

If property is not in the possession or control of the foreign State at the time of the proceedings and if it was outside the territorial jurisdiction of that State at the time of the expropriatory decree, it is now established that the rights of the owner are unaffected.[6] A contrary rule would conflict not only with the principle that legislative power is territorial, but also in the particular case of confiscation with the doctrine that the penal laws of another country will not be indirectly enforced in England.[7] Since the foreign State is not in possession at the time of the proceedings, the principle that the State is immune from the jurisdiction of the court has no application, for if the foreign State commences the proceedings this amounts to submission and there is no immunity.[8]

---

14 *Jabbour (F & K) v Custodian of Israeli Absentee Property* [1954] 1 WLR 139 at 150, and authorities there cited; *Williams and Humbert Ltd v W and H Trade Marks (Jersey) Ltd* [1986] AC 368 at 427–428; and see Dicey & Morris, pp 969–970.
1 McNair (1946) 31 Grotius Society 30, 35 et seq.
2 But see *Lorentzen v Lydden & Co* [1942] 2 KB 202, infra.
3 *Re Russian Bank for Foreign Trade* [1933] Ch 745.
4 Governed now by the State Immunity Act 1978, infra, pp 265–271.
5 Eg *Compania Naviera Vascongado v SS Cristina* [1938] AC 485, though there would now not appear to be immunity in such a case involving a ship used for commercial purposes, by reason of the State Immunity Act 1978, s 10 (2).
6 *Tallina Laevauhisus (A/S) v Estonian State S S Line* (1947) 80 LI L Rep 99; *Novello & Co Ltd v Hinrichsen Edition Ltd* [1951] Ch 595; *Bank voor Handel en Scheepvaart NV v Slatford* [1953] 1 QB 248, [1952] 2 All ER 956.
7 *Frankfurther v W L Exner Ltd* [1947] Ch 629 at 636–637.
8 State Immunity Act 1978, s 2 (3).

(c) REQUISITION OF PROPERTY

Owing to the decision of ATKINSON J in *Lorentzen v Lydden & Co,*[9] it was for some time doubtful whether an extra-territorial effect should not be attributed to the requisition, as distinct from the confiscation, of property by a foreign State. In that case, the Norwegian Government, on the eve of their escape to England in 1940, issued a decree whose effect, inter alia, was to requisition, in return for compensation, all Norwegian ships lying in harbours of the United Kingdom. Since England and Norway were engaged together in a war against Germany for their very existence, the judge took the view that the enforcement of the decree was demanded by public policy.[10]

The position may now be regarded as settled by *Bank voor Handel en Scheepvaart NV v Slatford,*[11] where DEVLIN J followed an earlier Scots decision[12] in preference to that of ATKINSON J.

In that case the Dutch Government, at the time when it was exercising sovereign powers in England with the consent of the British Government, issued a decree which entitled it to assume control of any property belonging to persons resident in the Netherlands.

It was held that the rights thus vested in the Dutch Government were not exercisable in respect of a quantity of gold that had been deposited in London in 1939 by a Dutch bank. DEVLIN J favoured "the simple rule that generally property in England is subject to English law and to none other."[13]

3. FOREIGN LAWS REPUGNANT TO ENGLISH PUBLIC POLICY[1]

(a) GENERAL PRINCIPLES

It is a well-established principle that any action brought in this country is subject to the English doctrine of public policy. Certain heads of the domestic doctrine of public policy command such respect, and certain foreign laws and institutions seem so repugnant to English notions and ideals, that the English view must prevail in proceedings in this country, for SCARMAN J has said that "an English court will refuse to apply a law which outrages its sense of justice and decency".[2] However, he also struck a note of caution in suggesting that "before it exercises such power it must consider the relevant foreign law as a whole".[3]

The occasional exclusion of a foreign law on the grounds of public policy is no doubt inevitable, but the English domestic doctrine of public policy covers a multitude of sins varying in their degree of turpitude, and it is

9 [1942] 2 KB 202.
10 This is an unusual application of the doctrine of public policy. "The judge invokes it, not in order to exclude foreign law which would normally be applicable", (see infra) "but to allow foreign law to impose itself although it would normally not be applicable"; Wolff, p 528. See also the observations of DEVLIN J in *Bank voor Handel en Scheepvaart NV v Slatford* [1953] 1 QB 248 at 263–264, [1951] 2 All ER 779 at 790–791.
11 [1953] 1 QB 248, [1951] 2 All ER 779 (on appeal, [1952] 2 All ER 956).
12 *The El Condado* (1939) 63 LIL Rep 330, 1939 SC 413.
13 [1953] 1 QB 248 at 260, [1951] 2 All ER 779 at 788.
1 On this subject see Kahn-Freund (1953) 39 Grotius Society 39; Nygh (1964) 13 ICLQ 39; Kahn-Freund (1974) III Hague Recueil 139, 426–431; F A Mann, *Foreign Affairs in English Courts* (1986) ch 8.
2 *Re Fuld's Estate (No 3)* [1968] P 675 at 698.
3 Ibid.

essential to resist the suggestion that an action concerning a transaction governed by a foreign law must necessarily fail because it would have failed had the governing law been English. Judges in the past have now and then expressed somewhat extravagant views on the matter. Thus, for instance, in a restraint of trade case,[4] FRY J seemed to suggest that every limb of the domestic doctrine must apply in every action in England. This can scarcely be so. The conception of public policy is, and should be, narrower and more limited in private international law than in internal law.[5] A transaction that is valid by its foreign governing law should not be nullified on this ground unless its enforcement would offend some moral, social or economic principle so sacrosanct in English eyes as to require its maintenance at all costs and without exception. In the words of CARDOZO J in a New York case:

> We are not so provincial as to say that every solution of a problem is wrong because we deal with it otherwise at home ... The courts are not free to refuse to enforce a foreign right at the pleasure of the judges, to suit the individual notion of expediency or fairness. They do not close their doors unless help would violate some fundamental principle of justice, some prevalent conception of good morals, some deep-rooted tradition of the common weal.[6]

The particular rule of public policy that the defendant invokes may be of this overriding nature and therefore enforceable in all actions. Or it may be local in the sense that it represents some feature of internal policy. If so it must be confined to cases where the governing law is English.[7] The mere fact that, for example, a contract, governed by a foreign law, infringes some rule of English domestic law such as the need for consideration to support a simple contract will not prevent its enforcement in England.[8]

To ascertain whether it is all-pervading or merely local, it must be examined "in the light of its history, the purpose of its adoption, the object to be accomplished by it, and the local conditions".[9] Perhaps the most important question to ask in each case is—what is the rule designed to prevent?[10] Presumably, for instance, the policy underlying the rule which invalidates a promise by an employee not to compete against his employer in the future is to further the economic well-being of the country by enabling every person freely to exploit in England the trade that he has learnt. If so, only a rigid doctrinaire would claim that this particular rule is of universal application, designed to control relations between employers and employees in other countries. The English prohibition of contracts in restraint of trade is only concerned with freedom of trade in *England*.[11] Similarly, the English attitude towards marriage brockage contracts and towards conditions in restraint of marriage would appear to reflect a merely local policy.

If the court decides that, having regard to the particular circumstances, the distinctive policy of English law is in truth affected, then the incompatible

---

4 *Rousillon v Rousillon* (1880) 14 ChD 351 at 369. Actually the governing law in the circumstances of the case was English law. Therefore, of course, the domestic doctrine applied; cf *Timms v Nicol* 1968 (1) SA 299.
5 *Vervaeke v Smith* [1983] 1 AC 145 at 164 (per Lord SIMON).
6 *Loucks v Standard Oil Co of New York* 224 NY 99 at 111 (1918).
7 Cf *Mackender v Feldia AG* [1967] 2 QB 590 at 601.
8 *Re Bonacina, Le Brasseur v Bonacina* [1912] 2 Ch 394. See now the Rome Convention, discussed infra, pp 505–506.
9 Wharton, *Conflict of Laws* (3rd edn), i, 16.
10 See eg, *Block Bros Realty Ltd v Mollard* (1981) 122 DLR (3d) 323.
11 *Warner Bros v Nelson* [1937] 1 KB 209, [1936] 3 All ER 160.

foreign rule must, indeed, be totally excluded. Some of the older decisions, however, have perhaps tended to invoke the domestic doctrine of public policy in all its ramifications with remorseless determination.

Kaufman v Gerson[12] provides a striking example of insularity.

The husband of the defendant had misappropriated money entrusted to him by the plaintiff. By a contract made and to be performed in France the defendant agreed to pay to the plaintiff by instalments out of her own money the full amount misappropriated, in consideration that the plaintiff would refrain from prosecuting the husband for what was a crime by French law. Both the plaintiff and defendant were French nationals domiciled in France; the misappropriation had occurred in France; the contract was valid by French law.

This contract could scarcely be regarded as offensive to some fundamental principle of justice, for there is nothing particularly reprehensible in allowing a person to escape criminal proceedings at the price of paying full compensation to the sufferer. Nevertheless, an action for the recovery of instalments still due was dismissed on the ground that "to enforce a contract so procured would be to contravene what by the law of this country is deemed an essential moral interest".[13] In *Addison v Brown*,[14] however, a more recent case on the subject, a less insular interpretation was put on the reservation of public policy.

A wife sued her husband to recover arrears of maintenance due under a contract that was governed by Californian law. It was expressly agreed that neither party would apply to any court for the variation of the contract and that if in fact it were varied by any court in subsequent divorce proceedings it should nevertheless remain in force as written. Ten years later the husband obtained a divorce in California, and the contract, far from being varied, was incorporated in the judgment.

The contract, since it contained an agreement by the parties to oust the jurisdiction of the court, was contrary to the doctrine of public policy as understood in England, and it was therefore pleaded that the action was not maintainable. STREATFIELD J, however, refused to treat this particular segment of the doctrine as being of universal application. He said that there could be no objection in England to an agreement that purports to oust the jurisdiction of a foreign court.[15]

The principle that emerges in *Addison v Brown* is that, in order to apply the English domestic rules on public policy to an agreement, it must be shown that the agreement relates to England, in some important way. The same principle was applied, in a different context, in *Trendtex Trading Corpn v Credit Suisse*.[16] There, the House of Lords held that, since an assignment of a cause of action savoured of champerty, it was contrary to public policy and therefore void. A crucial point in the case was that the assignment related to an *English* cause of action.

12 [1904] 1 KB 591, CA reversing WRIGHT J [1903] 2 KB 114. The decision was not followed in the Canadian case of *National Surety Co v Larsen* [1929] 4 DLR 918.
13 [1904] 1 KB 591 at 599–600.
14 [1954] 2 All ER 213, [1954] 1 WLR 779.
15 [1954] 1 WLR 779 at 784.
16 [1982] AC 679; Thornley [1982] 41 CLJ 29. See also *Sigurdson v Farrow* (1981) 121 DLR (3d) 183.

Before turning to a summary of cases where domestic policy is affected, one final general point has to be made, namely that most of these cases arise in the context of contract choice of law. This area has recently been put largely on a statutory footing.[17] However, the substance of the public policy exception would not appear to be affected.[18]

(b) SUMMARY OF CASES WHERE DISTINCTIVE POLICY IS AFFECTED

It is no easy matter to classify those cases in which the English court will refuse to enforce a foreign acquired right, on the ground that its enforcement would affront some moral principle the maintenance of which admits of no possible compromise. However, the following is suggested as the probable classification.

(i) **Where the fundamental conceptions of English justice are disregarded** The established rule, which will be stated later,[19] that a foreign judgment cannot be recognised in England if it offends the principles of natural justice, as, for example, if the defendant was denied the opportunity of presenting his case to the foreign court, exemplifies this aspect of English public policy. Another example is the rule that a contract obtained by what the judge regards as coercion is unenforceable in England.[20] Consistent with this, a foreign judgment granted in respect of a contract entered into under undue influence, duress or coercion may be refused enforcement in England on the ground of public policy.[1]

(ii) **Where the English conceptions of morality are infringed** It cannot be doubted that a contract or other transaction which is objectionable in English eyes on the ground that it tends to promote sexual immorality,[2] such as a contract for prostitution, will receive no judicial recognition in England, though it may be innocuous according to its foreign governing law.[3] Similarly, an agreement to be performed abroad involving payment for the use of personal influence in securing a contract will not be enforced in England, at least not in the situation where the foreign place of performance applies the same public policy.[4] Neither, in this age of commercial fraud, will a contract drafted to deceive third parties be enforced.[5]

(iii) **Where a transaction prejudices the interests of the United Kingdom or its good relations with foreign powers** An example of the first part of the state-

17 See the Contracts (Applicable Law) Act 1990; infra, pp 459–521.
18 But see the problems raised in relation to the comity of nations/public policy cases like *Foster v Driscoll* [1929] 1 KB 470; infra pp 503–504.
19 Infra pp 384–387.
20 *Kaufman v Gerson* [1904] 1 KB 591, supra, p 130. See Dicey & Morris, p 1232; *Société des Hôtels Réunis SA v Hawker* (1913) 29 TLR 578; *Kahler v Midland Bank Ltd* [1950] AC 24 at 44–45; cf *A. M. Luther v James Sagor & Co* [1921] 3 KB 532 at 558–559.
1 *Israel Discount Bank of New York v Hadjipateras* [1984] 1 WLR 137; infra, p 371. For public policy as a defence to recognition and enforcement of foreign judgments see *Vervaeke v Smith* [1983] 1 AC 145; generally infra, pp 380–381.
2 See, for example: *Pearce v Brooks* (1866) LR 1 Exch 213; *Ayerst v Jenkins* (1873) LR 16 Eq 275; *Taylor v Chester* (1869) LR 4 QB 309.
3 *Robinson v Bland* (1760) 2 Burr 1077 at 1084.
4 *Lemenda Trading Co Ltd v African Middle East Petroleum Co Ltd* [1988] QB 448, [1988] 1 All ER 513; Carter (1988) BYBIL 356. The law governing the agreement was English, but no doubt the result would have been the same if it had been a foreign one, under which the agreement was not objectionable.
5 *Mitsubishi Corpn v Aristidis I Alafouzos* [1988] 1 Lloyd's Rep 191.

ment is the prohibition of business with an alien enemy.[6] In one case, for instance, an English company, owning mines in Spain, made a contract in 1910 for the delivery by instalments spread over a number of years of minerals to a German company.[7] The contract contained a suspensory clause which provided that in the event of war the obligations of the parties should be suspended during hostilities. The English company brought an action in 1916 claiming a declaration that the contract was not merely suspended but was abrogated by the existence of a state of war between Great Britain and Germany. The objection was taken that this was a German contract and that therefore it fell to be governed by German law. It was argued that illegality according to English law was irrelevant. What had to be shown was that the contract was illegal by German law. It was held, however, that the German character of the contract had no bearing on the question. "It is illegal for a British subject to become bound in a manner which sins against the public policy of the King's realm",[8] and it has long been established that the prohibition of trading with an alien enemy rests on public policy.

Support for the second part of our statement may be derived from the rule that it is contrary to public policy as understood in all civilised nations for persons in England to enter into an engagement with the avowed object of causing injury to a friendly Government,[9] as, for example, by raising a loan to further a revolt,[10] by an agreement to import liquor contrary to a prohibition law,[11] to defraud its revenue[12] or to export a prohibited commodity.[13] Such conduct is a breach of international comity and tends to injure the relations of the British Government with friendly powers.[14] It is not, however, contrary to public policy to enforce a contract, judgment or arbitral award between nationals of two foreign countries, both friendly to the United Kingdom, even though the two foreign states are enemies of each other.[1] A court in this country cannot set itself up as a judge of the rights and wrongs of a controversy between two countries friendly to us.[2]

(iv) Where a foreign law or status offends the English conceptions of human liberty and freedom of action The history of the world affords many instances of legal disabilities firmly established in some countries but unknown and even execrated in others. Obvious examples are disqualifications arising from slavery, excommunication, heresy, infamy, civil death, popish recusancy and nonconformity. Happily most of these illustrate the intolerance of a past age, but analogies are not wanting even in the modern world, as is evident from

6　*Robson v Premier Oil and Pipe Line Co* [1915] 2 Ch 124 at 136.
7　*Dynamit Actien-Gesellschaft v Rio Tinto Co Ltd* [1918] AC 260.
8　Ibid, at p 294.
9　*British Nylon Spinners Ltd v ICI Ltd* [1955] Ch 37 at 52, [1954] 3 All ER 88 at 91; *Bodley Head Ltd v Flegon* [1972] 1 WLR 680 at 687–688.
10　*De Wutz v Hendricks* (1824) 2 Bing 314.
11　*Foster v Driscoll* [1929] 1 KB 470; cf *Toprak v Finagrain* [1979] 2 Lloyd's Rep 98.
12　*Re Emery's Investments Trusts* [1959] Ch 410, [1959] 1 All ER 577; *Pye Ltd v BG Transport Service Ltd* [1966] 2 Lloyd's Rep 300 at 308–309.
13　*Regazzoni v K. C. Sethia (1944) Ltd* [1958] AC 301, [1957] 3 All ER 286. For a critical study of this decision, see F A Mann (1958) 21 MLR 130 et seq. Cf *Trinidad Shipping Co v Alston* [1920] AC 888; *Dalmia Dairy Industries Ltd v National Bank of Pakistan* [1978] 2 Lloyd's Rep 223 at 267–268.
14　This sort of case now will have to come within the new statutory public policy exception introduced by the Contracts (Applicable Law) Act 1990, see infra, p 504.
1　*Dalmia Dairy Industries Ltd v National Bank of Pakistan, supra,* at 299–301.
2　*Empresa Exportadora De Azucar v Industria Azucarera Nacional SA, The Playa Larga* [1983] 2 Lloyd's Rep 171; Carter (1983) 54 BYBIL 297.

the history of the Nazi régime in Germany.[3] It may be said without hesitation that all disqualifications of this description, which restrict human freedom by penalising certain classes of the population to the profit of others, have only intra-territorial effect,[4] for, in the eloquent words of Wharton: "To stretch international law further would be to engraft on free countries the paralysing restrictions of despotisms."[5]

(c) CASES INVOLVING A FOREIGN STATUS

Any attempt to classify the foreign laws that are offensive to the English concept of public policy is not easy to reconcile with decisions on the measure of recognition to be given to a foreign status. The short answer, no doubt, is that, though the court must recognise the existence of a person's status as fixed by the law of his foreign domicil, it need not necessarily give effect to the results or incidents attributed to it by that law including the capacities and incapacities of the person affected.[6] The problem, however, is to determine what incidents may be accepted, what must be repudiated. Obviously an incident must be repudiated if it is contrary to a positive rule of English internal law. Again, a remedy permitted by the foreign law of the status will not be granted if English law is not adapted to its enforcement. Thus, the parties to a polygamous marriage, valid according to their personal law, possess the status of married persons in the eyes of English law;[7] but, until the Matrimonial Proceedings (Polygamous Marriages) Act 1972,[8] the remedy of divorce, based on the principle of monogamy, was not open to them.[9] Again, an English court was quite prepared to recognise that under Greek law a father should provide his daughter with a dowry, though the nature of the daughter's right was such that it should not be enforced here.[10] Finally, a foreign status or incident of status will be disregarded if it offends the English doctrine of public policy. So far as English internal law is concerned, it has long been settled that a judge is no longer free to invent new heads of public policy. He may expound, but must not expand this branch of the law.[11] In the field of private international law, however, exposition has gradually blossomed into expansion to such an extent that apparently the judges now feel free to exclude the law of the domicil whenever[12] they feel it proper to do so in the circumstances.

The ancestry of this extreme view may be traced back to *Worms v De Valdor*[13] in 1880. That case was concerned with the French status of prodi-

3 Contrast *Re Meyer* [1971] P 298, [1971] 1 All ER 378 with *Igra v Igra* [1951] P 404.
4 *Sommersett's Case* (1772) 20 State Tr 1; *Forbes v Cochrane* (1824) 2 B & C 448 at 467; *Regazzoni v K. C. Sethia (1944) Ltd* [1956] 2 QB 490 at 524; cf *Santos v Illidge* (1860) 8 CBNS 861 (slavery).
5 *Conflict of Laws* (3rd edn), s 104.
6 Allen (1930) 46 LQR 277, 293 et seq.; Inglis (1957) 6 ICLQ 202, 220–224; Falconbridge, p 751.
7 *Baindail v Baindail* [1946] P 122, [1946] 1 All ER 342.
8 See now the Matrimonial Causes Act 1973, s 47, infra, pp 628–629.
9 *Hyde v Hyde* (1866) LR 1P & D 130; infra, pp 608–609.
10 *Phrantzes v Argenti* [1960] 2 QB 19; supra, pp 91–92; Webb (1960) 23 MLR 446; Carter (1960) 36 BYBIL 412; and see *Shahnaz v Rizwan* [1965] 1 QB 390 (recognition of deferred dower); cf *Re Macartney* [1921] 1 Ch 522; *Khalij Commercial Bank Ltd v Woods* (1985) 17 DLR (4th) 358.
11 *Fender v St John-Mildmay* [1938] AC 1 at 40, [1937] 3 All ER 402 at 414; *Vervaeke v Smith* [1983] 1 AC 145 at 164—existing principles can be applied to new circumstances.
12 *Russ v Russ* [1964] P 315, [1962] 3 All ER 193.
13 (1880) 49 LJ Ch 261.

gality which arises when a court appoints an adviser, a *conseil judicaire,* to safeguard the interests of an adult person of extravagant habits. The court may prohibit him from compromising claims, borrowing or receiving money, alienating or mortgaging property and bringing or defending actions without the collaboration of his adviser. The question in *Worms v De Valdor* was whether an action for the cancellation of certain bills of exchange, brought by a prodigal in his own name and without the assistance of his *conseil judiciaire,* could succeed. FRY J, unaided by expert evidence, made his own researches into French law and concluded that the appointment of a *conseil judiciaire* neither changed the status of a prodigal nor subjected him to a personal disqualification. Had it done so, the judge intimated that he would have disregarded the disqualification as being penal in nature. He did in fact allow the action to proceed, but on the ground, it would seem, that whether the prodigal could sue in England in his own name was a procedural question determinable by English law as that of the forum.

In the case of *Re Selot's Trusts,*[14] the question was whether the status of prodigality, imposed on the plaintiff by the French law of his domicil, precluded his recovery of a legacy bequeathed to him by an English will. FARWELL J, affecting to follow *Worms v De Valdor,* held that the disability of the prodigal to bring an action without the assistance of his legal adviser was a penal restriction that had no effect in English proceedings. What the judge overlooked was that this was not the ratio decidendi of FRY J in the earlier case.[15]

A later case concerned with a status of incompetence is *Re Langley's Settlement Trusts.*[16] The Court of Appeal held that the joint exercise of a power to withdraw part of settled funds by the settlor and his wife was effective, even though the settlor was disqualified as incompetent by the law of his residence and domicil, California. The exercise complied with English law which governed the settlement that created the power, since the document had been signed by a man who was not incompetent in the eyes of English internal law. It also complied with the law that governed the man's status, for the wife in signing the document had obeyed the express directions of the Californian court.

What, however, is more pertinent to the present discussion is that the Court of Appeal gave an alternative reason for the decision. The principle, it was said, is that it is a matter of judicial discretion whether a foreign status shall be recognised.[17] Had the only facet of the Californian law requiring investigation in the present case been the ban placed on the settlor's right to withdraw the settled funds, the court would have exercised its discretion against the recognition of his status of incompetence. But in order that the law may be reasonably certain and predictable it has long been established that judicial discretion must be exercised in accordance with settled rules, not in an arbitrary or capricious manner. It is not an unfettered discretion,

14 [1902] 1 Ch 488.
15 The two decisions have sometimes been said to support the proposition that a foreign status unknown to English law will not be recognised in England. See, eg *Republica de Guatemala v Nunez* [1927] 1 KB 669 at 701. The proposition is unfounded. For example, the married status of the parties to a polygamous marriage is recognised and, indeed, English courts will now grant matrimonial relief to the parties to such a marriage. So also was the status arising from a foreign adoption or a foreign legitimation *per subsequens matrimonium* recognised before those institutions were accepted by English internal law.
16 [1961] 1 All ER 78, [1961] 1 WLR 41; affd [1962] Ch 541, [1961] 3 All ER 803; Grodecki (1962) 11 ICLQ 578.
17 See *De Reneville v De Reneville* [1948] P 100 at 109, [1948] 1 All ER 56 at 57.

but one, as Lord ELDON said in a specific performance case, that "must be regulated upon grounds that will make it judicial".[18] What, therefore, was the particular head of public policy that justified the rejection of the Californian status? The Court of Appeal, affirming BUCKLEY J in the court below, classified the status as penal since it deprived the settlor of his power to deal with a valuable interest. The word "penal", said BUCKLEY J, "means law of a kind which deprives the person affected of his rights or property in a way which adversely affects his interests".[19] But this is to attribute to the word a meaning that is warranted neither by the dictionary nor by the nature of the particular status. The object of the Californian order was not to penalise the invalid, but to protect him against the machinations of "artful or designing persons".[20] Similarly, the subjection of a spendthrift to the status of prodigality is designed to protect him against his own extravagance. It would seem, therefore, that to stigmatise as penal any law which deprives him of a valuable interest is to invent a new head of public policy that is supported by no authority except the doubtful decision of FARWELL J in *Re Selot's Trusts*. It is a proposition that scarcely accords with the views expressed in *Luther v Sagor*.[1]

Moreover, the proposition that a judge has a free discretion to exclude a foreign status or its incidents if he considers that in the particular circumstances it will adversely affect a person's right to deal with his property cannot be accepted with any degree of complacency. Its impact on the doctrine of public policy would, at first sight, be disastrous, for what has been laboriously shaped into a reasonably ordered form would become once more amorphous and indeterminate. It is difficult to disagree with the criticism that it is "a revolutionary innovation in our private international law",[2] and that "the courts might just as well abandon any attempt to formulate and apply defined rules of law if these can be overridden by an undefinable discretion".[3]

However, this whole problem of a free discretion is perhaps more apparent than real. The most common situation where the recognition of a foreign status arises is in cases involving the effect of a foreign divorce, annulment or legal separation. But, as will be seen below, the whole area of recognition of foreign divorces, etc is now put on a statutory basis and it is clear that recognition cannot be refused on the ground of a lack of substantial justice.

(d) RECOGNITION OF FOREIGN DIVORCES, ETC[4]

Until recently, the discretion to refuse to recognise a foreign status applied in the context of recognition of foreign divorces, annulments and legal separations. It was said that there was a power to refuse to recognise a foreign divorce "which offends against English ideas of substantial justice".[5] The

18 *White v Damon* (1802) 7 Ves 30 at 35.
19 [1961] 1 All ER 78 at 81, [1961] 1 WLR 41 at 46.
20 Californian Probate Code, s 1466.
 1 [1921] 3 KB 532, supra, pp 123–124.
 2 Nygh (1964) 13 ICLQ 39, 50; and see Dicey & Morris, pp 98–99.
 3 Ibid, p51; and see *Boys v Chaplin* [1971] AC 356 at 378.
 4 Public policy as a defence in cases of recognition of foreign divorces, etc is dealt with more fully infra, pp 680–685.
 5 *Middleton v Middleton* [1967] P 62 at 69; see also *Gray (otherwise Formosa) v Formosa* [1963] P 259; *Lepre v Lepre* [1965] P 52, [1963] 2 All ER 49. For the reintroduction of this concept, but now in the area of enforcement of foreign commercial judgments, see *Adams v Cape Industries Plc* [1990] Ch 433 at 557 et seq; discussed infra, p 386.

inherent difficulty in defining this concept was a cause for concern, as was the width of the doctrine.[6] In *Gray v Formosa*,[7] for example, the Court of Appeal went into the merits of a foreign nullity decree and found that a Maltese law which allowed the annulment of a marriage on the ground that a Roman Catholic had not married in a Roman Catholic Church was against English ideas of substantial justice. However, the recognition of foreign divorces, annulments and legal separations is now put on a statutory basis and under the relevant statute[8] recognition has to be given to foreign divorces, etc unless the court exercises its discretion on a limited listed number of grounds to deny recognition. These grounds do not contain any provision allowing the courts to refuse recognition on the basis of want of substantial justice.[9] It is possible, though, to refuse recognition in cases where there has been, in effect, a denial of natural justice,[10] and in cases where recognition would be "manifestly contrary to public policy".[11] It is not entirely clear whether the use of the common law concept of public policy as one of the statutory grounds of non-recognition and the exclusion of the concept of substantial justice represents a shift in substance or merely one of terminology.[12] However, it is clear that, in recent years, the courts have been willing to use public policy as a ground for non recognition of foreign divorces in circumstances where one might have expected a reluctance to do so. Thus in *Joyce v Joyce*[13] public policy was used as a ground[14] for non-recognition of a Quebec divorce, even though this involved criticism of the laws and procedure of a foreign and friendly country as being unfair to the respondent. More recently, in *Vervaeke v Smith*[15] a foreign nullity decree was refused recognition in the House of Lords on the basis of public policy, where there was no unfairness to the respondent. No criticism was made of the foreign law.[16] Rather, their Lordships were concerned to uphold the English policy of maintaining the validity of sham marriages, which was to be preferred to the Belgian policy, and that this policy should not be avoided by petitioners going abroad to obtain a nullity decree,[17] especially when the petitioner had

6 See Carter (1962) 38 BYBIL 497; Lewis (1963) 12 ICLQ 298; Blom-Cooper (1963) 26 MLR 94; Carter (1965–1966) 41 BYBIL 445; Unger (1966) 29 MLR 327. See also *Varanand v Varanand* (1964) 108 Sol Jo 693, cited in *Qureshi v Qureshi* [1972] Fam 173 at 201.
7 [1963] P 259.
8 The Family Law Act 1986; see s 51.
9 Furthermore, a declaration as to status under Part III of the 1986 Act is to be granted as of right, and not by discretion (s 58 (1)).
10 Family Law Act 1986, s 51 (3) (a).
11 Family Law Act 1986, s 51 (3) (c). There are a number of other circumstances in which public policy issues arise, in the context of family law. A foreign law of domicil governing capacity to marry may not be recognised if it is repugnant to English public policy: *Cheni v Cheni* [1965] P 85 at 98–99, infra, p 599. Restraint on remarriage after a foreign divorce may be regarded as penal, so that the restriction will be regarded as inoperative outside the jurisdiction in which it was imposed, see infra, pp 605–606.
12 See *Vervaeke v Smith* [1983] 1 AC 145 at 164 (per Lord SIMON, who seems to regard the two concepts as being, in substance, the same). The Law Commission regards the courts' treatment of the two concepts as involving the same approach, Law Com No 137 (1984), para 2.26.
13 [1979] Fam 93; infra, p 683; cf *Igra v Igra* [1951] P 404 at 412. The public policy defence did not succeed in *Sabbagh v Sabbagh* [1985] FLR 29.
14 It was also decided that there had been a denial of the opportunity to take part in the proceedings under s 8 (2) (a) (ii) of the Recognition of Divorces and Legal Separations Act 1971; now s 51 (3) (a) (ii) of the Family Law Act 1986.
15 [1983] 1 AC 145; Smart (1983) 99 LQR 24; Jaffey (1983) 32 ICLQ 500; infra, p 681.
16 See at 156 (per Lord HAILSHAM).
17 At 156–157, 163–167.

previously put forward a bogus case in England which had failed. A policy of upholding sham marriages is odd enough, but to give this policy overriding force in an international context is even stranger.

4. MANDATORY RULES

The concept of mandatory rules has only recently been introduced into English law. Mandatory rules of the forum have been described by the Law Commissions as domestic rules which "are regarded as so important that as a matter of construction or policy they must apply in any action before a court of the forum, even where the issues are in principle governed by a foreign law selected by a choice of law rule."[18] The statutory rules on choice of law in respect of trusts[19] and contracts [20] both have rules providing for the application of the mandatory rules of the forum, and, if the Law Commissions' proposals for tort choice of law are implemented, there will be a similar provision in that area.[1] An example of English mandatory rules is provided by the controls on exemption clauses contained in the Unfair Contract Terms Act 1977; the Act itself stipulates[2] that, in certain circumstances, these controls shall apply despite the parties' choice of a foreign law to govern the contract. The concept of mandatory rules is a positive one; the concern is to apply a particular domestic rule. This contrasts with the exclusionary rules previously examined in this chapter where the concern is that a foreign rule should not be applied, ie they are negative concepts. However, the effect of the application of a mandatory rule is that a foreign domestic law, which would otherwise govern under choice of law rules, is not applied. To that extent application of mandatory rules can be regarded as an exclusionary concept. At the same time, and this brings out the essentially different nature of mandatory rules, there can be circumstances where the concern is to apply the mandatory rules of a foreign country, rather than those of the forum. The statutory rules on choice of law for trusts and contracts[3] provide for the application of foreign mandatory rules. Naturally, under these particular provisions it is not a case of the exclusion of a foreign law, but of its application.

---

18 Law Com Working Paper No 87 (1984), Scot Law Com Consultative Memorandums No 62 (1984), para 4.5.
19 Infra, pp 890–891.
20 Infra, pp 499–503.
 1 Law Com No 193 (1990), Scot Law Com No 129 (1990), para 3.55.
 2 S 27 (2).
 3 Infra, pp 891, 503.

Chapter 9

Domicil[1]

SUMMARY

1. INTRODUCTION

It has been universally recognised that questions affecting the personal status of a human being should be governed constantly by one and the same law, irrespective of where he may happen to be or of where the facts giving rise to the question may have occurred.[2] But unanimity goes no further. There is disagreement on two matters. What is the scope of this "personal law", as it is called, and should its criterion be domicil or nationality?[3] In England, however, it has long been settled that questions affecting status are determined

1 Kahn, *South African Law of Domicil of Natural Persons* (1972); North (1990) I Hague Recueil 13, 26–48.
2 Rabel, i, 109; and see Kahn-Freund (1974) III Hague Recueil 139, 334–335, 391–392.
3 On the respective merits of nationality and domicil see infra, pp 165–167.

by the law of the domicil of the *propositus* and that, broadly speaking, such questions are those affecting family relations and family property.[4] To be more precise, the following matters are to a greater or lesser extent governed by the personal law: the essential validity of a marriage; the effect of marriage on the proprietary rights of husband and wife; jurisdiction in divorce and nullity of marriage, though only to a limited degree; legitimacy, legitimation and adoption; wills of movables and intestate succession to movables.

When it comes to a definition of domicil, this is no easy matter. The concept of domicil is not uniform throughout the world. To a civil lawyer it means habitual residence, but at common law it is regarded as the equivalent of a person's permanent home.[5] Such a definition gives a misleading air of simplicity to the English concept of domicil. It fails to mention, for example, that there are two main classes of domicil: the *domicil of origin* that is communicated by operation of law to each person at birth, ie the domicil of his father or of his mother, according as he is legitimate or illegitimate;[6] and the *domicil of choice* which every person of full age is free to acquire in substitution for that which he at present possesses. This distinction relates merely to the acquisition and loss of domicil, not to its effects. It also fails to point out that the acquisition of a domicil of choice requires not only residence in a territory subject to a distinctive legal system,[7] but also an intention by the *propositus* to remain there permanently. "There must be the act and there must be the intention."[8] But, as will be seen,[9] both the concept of permanency and the ascertainment of a person's intentions are fraught with difficulty.

The English concept of domicil is bedevilled by rules; these are complex, often impossible to justify in policy terms, and lead to uncertainty of outcome. Before looking at these rules in detail, one preliminary matter should be considered. This is the question of whether the same test for domicil applies, regardless of the context in which the matter is raised.

According to what W W Cook called the "single conception theory", English law takes the view that the test which determines the place of a man's domicil must remain constant no matter what the nature of the issue may be before the court. Cook,[10] however, denied that this was true in practice. He regarded "domicil" as a relative term which varies in meaning according to the different situations (for example, taxation, divorce, intestate succession) to which it is applicable. A judge, he said, must inevitably focus his attention on the concrete problem before him, otherwise he will neglect the "social and economic" requirements of the situation. Although there appears to be a growing tendency in the United States of America to adopt this view,[11] the conventional approach in England has been to reject it.[12] However, it should

---

4 It will be seen, infra pp 284–285, that domicil is an important basis of jurisdiction in the very different context of jurisdiction in civil and commercial matters, where domicil is given a different meaning, see the Civil Jurisdiction and Judgments Act 1982, ss 41–46, as amended by Sch 2, paras 16–21, of the Civil Jurisdiction and Judgments Act 1991.
5 *Whicker v Hume* (1858) 7 HL Cas 124 at 160.
6 Infra, p 159.
7 *Henderson v Henderson* [1967] P 77 at 79.
8 *Munro v Munro* (1840) 7 Cl & Fin 842.
9 Infra, pp 144 et seq.
10 *Logical and Legal Bases of the Conflict of Laws*, pp 194 et seq; Kahn-Freund (1974) III Hague Recueil 139, 404–405.
11 Reese (1955) 55 Col LR 589; Restatement 2d, section 11(2).
12 Eg 7th Report of the Private International Law Committee, 1963 (Cmnd 1955) para 12.

be noted that under the Inheritance Tax Act 1984[13] there is a special definition whereby, for certain purposes, persons are treated as domiciled in the United Kingdom. Also it is hard to believe that judges in this country have not been influenced by an awareness of the consequences of the finding as to domicil in the particular case before them.[14] There is evidence[15] that the courts wish to achieve a number of policy objectives: in particular, to validate wills and to take jurisdiction to grant a divorce whenever possible. It is easy for courts to achieve the right result by manipulating the process of ascertaining the domicil, and this is a likely explanation of many cases which are otherwise hard to reconcile on their facts.

2. GENERAL RULES

There are five general rules that may be briefly discussed.

It is a settled principle that nobody shall be without a domicil, and in order to make this effective the law assigns what is called a domicil of origin to every person at his birth, namely, to a legitimate child the domicil of the father, to an illegitimate child the domicil of the mother,[16] and to a foundling the place where he is found.[17] This prevails until a new domicil has been acquired,[18] so that if a person leaves the country of his origin with an undoubted intention of never returning to it again, nevertheless his domicil of origin adheres to him until he actually settles with the requisite intention in some other country.[19]

Second, a person cannot have two domicils.[1] Since the object of the law in insisting that no person shall be without a domicil is to establish a definite legal system by which certain of his rights and obligations may be governed, and since the facts and events of his life frequently impinge upon several countries, it is necessary on practical grounds to hold that he cannot possess more than one domicil at the same time, at least for the same purpose.[2]

Domicil signifies connection with what has conveniently been called a "law district",[3] ie a territory subject to a single system of law. In the case of a federation, where the legislative authority is distributed between the State and federal legislatures, this law district is generally represented by the particular State in which the *propositus* has established his home.[4] A resident in the USA, for instance, is not normally domiciled in the USA as such, but in one of its States. Nevertheless, the doctrine of unity of domicil—one man, one domicil—may be modified by federal legislation. Thus the Family Law Act 1975, which has force throughout the Commonwealth of Australia,

---

13 S 267; see the Finance Act 1986, s 100(1)(a); Booth, *Residence, Domicile and UK Taxation* (1986), para 7.17.
14 See Fawcett (1985) 5 OJLS 378.
15 Fawcett, ibid.
16 *Udny v Udny* (1869) LR 1 Sc & Div 441 at 457.
17 Westlake, s 248; Dicey and Morris, p 126; Castel, *Canadian Conflict of Laws*, 2nd edn (1986), para 27. See also *Re McKenzie* (1951) 51 SRNSW 293.
18 *Munro v Munro* (1840) 7 Cl & Fin 842 at 876.
19 Infra, pp 156–157.
 1 *IRC v Bullock* [1976] 1 WLR 1178 at 1184; *Lawrence v Lawrence* [1985] Fam 106 at 132.
 2 Cf supra, pp 139–140, and see Restatement 2d, section 11(2).
 3 Dicey & Morris, pp 118–119.
 4 Cf Nigeria: *Odiase v Odiase* [1965] NMLR 196.

provides inter alia that proceedings for a decree of dissolution of marriage may be instituted if either party to the marriage is "domiciled in Australia".[5] Thus, the effect within a limited field is to create an Australian, as distinct from a State, domicil and, indeed, one that, because of statutory amendments in this limited context,[6] is different from domicil in a State for other purposes, eg succession.[7]

Third, the fact that domicil signifies connection with a single system of territorial law does not necessarily connote a system that prescribes identical rules for all classes of persons. It may well be that in a unit such as India different legal rules apply to different classes of the population according to their religion, race or caste, but none the less it is the territorial law of India that governs each person domiciled there, notwithstanding that Hindu law may apply to one case, Moslem to another.

Fourth, there is a presumption in favour of the continuance of an existing domicil. Therefore the burden of proving a change lies in all cases on those who allege that a change has occurred.[8] This presumption may have a decisive effect, for if the evidence is so conflicting or indeterminate that it is impossible to elicit with certainty what the resident's intention is, the court will decide in favour of the existing domicil.[9]

The standard of proof necessary to rebut the presumption is that adopted in civil actions, which requires the intention of the *propositus* to be proved on a balance of probabilities, not beyond reasonable doubt as is the case in criminal proceedings.[10] It has been said that there is a heavy burden of proof of loss of a domicil of origin[11] and SIR JOCELYN SIMON P has gone further and suggested that, when the displacement of a domicil of origin by a domicil of choice is alleged, "the standard of proof goes beyond a mere balance of probabilities".[12] This observation no doubt stems from such cases as *Winans v A-G*[13] which appear to regard the intention in favour of retaining the domicil of origin as an almost irrebuttable presumption. SCARMAN J, however, after observing that the language used in such cases emphasises as much the nature and quality of the intention to be proved as the standard of proof required, observed that "Two things are clear—first that unless the judicial conscience is satisfied by evidence of change, the domicil of origin persists; and secondly, that the acquisition of a domicil of choice is a serious matter not to be lightly inferred from slight indications or casual words."[14] The Court of Appeal

5 Family Law Act 1975, s 39(3)(b).
6 Ibid, s 4(3); see Nygh (1976) 25 ICLQ 674.
7 *Lloyd v Lloyd* [1961] 2 FLR 349; and see *Re Benko* [1968] SASR 243 (both decisions on the earlier Matrimonial Causes Act 1959); but now see the Domicile Act 1982, s 11 (adopted uniformly in Australia), and in New Zealand the Domicile Act 1976, s 10. The Canadian Divorce Act 1968 provided similarly that divorce jurisdiction could be exercised over a petitioner "domiciled in Canada": s 5(1); however, domicil is no longer used as a connecting factor in cases of divorce jurisdiction: Divorce and Corollary Relief Act 1985.
8 *Winans v A-G* [1904] AC 287 at 289; *Re Lloyd Evans* [1947] Ch 695; *Messina v Smith* [1971] P 322 at 330; *Puttick v A-G* [1980] Fam 1 at 17.
9 See, for example, *Winans v A-G*, supra, Lord HALSBURY's speech.
10 *Re Fuld's Estate (No 3)* [1968] P 675 at 685–686; *Re Flynn* [1968] 1 WLR 103 at 115; *Re Edwards, Edwards v Edwards* (1969) 113 Sol Jo 108; *Buswell v IRC* [1974] 1 WLR 1631 at 1637; but see *Lawrence v Lawrence* [1985] Fam 106 at 110, 111, where the matter was left open by LINCOLN J; affd by the Court of Appeal, ibid at 120, without discussion of this point.
11 *Holden v Holden* [1968] NI 7.
12 *Henderson v Henderson* [1967] P 77 at 80; *Steadman v Steadman* [1976] AC 536 at 563.
13 [1904] AC 287, infra, pp 145–146.
14 *Re Fuld's Estate (No 3)* [1968] P 675 at 686; see also *Re Clore (No 2)* [1984] STC 609 at 614.

when endorsing this approach, has actually disapproved of the use of the phrase "heavy burden".[15]

The fifth and final[16] rule is that, subject to certain statutory exceptions,[17] the domicil of a person is to be determined according to the English and not the foreign concept of domicil.[1]

3. THE ACQUISITION OF A DOMICIL OF CHOICE[2]

The two requisites for the acquisition of a fresh domicil are residence and intention. It must be proved that the person in question established his residence in a certain country with the intention of remaining there permanently. Such an intention, however unequivocal it may be, does not per se suffice.[3] These two elements of residence and intention must concur, but this is not to say that there need be unity of time in their concurrence. The intention may either precede or succeed the establishment of the residence. The emigrant forms his intention before he leaves England for Australia; the émigré who flees from persecution may not form it until years later.

(a) RESIDENCE

Residence and intention are separate but interrelated concepts. "Residence in a country for the purposes of the law of domicile is physical presence in that country as an inhabitant of it."[4] In one case[5] a taxpayer who spent ten to twelve weeks each year in Quebec for the purpose of maintaining her links with that Province with a view ultimately to returning to live was held not to be a resident of Quebec during her presence there since she was not there as an inhabitant. Normally, though, the requirement of residence is easy to establish.

Residence and intention are interrelated in that, strictly speaking, residence is a fact, though a necessary one, from which intention may be inferred.[6] Older cases adopted a presumption in favour of domicil which grew in strength with the length of the residence and was hard to rebut.[7] However, more recent cases,[8] including House of Lords authorities,[9] have attached less weight to the length of residence, and have taken the view that, although a material consideration, it is rarely decisive.

Whatever weight is given to the length of residence it is undeniable that

---

15 *Brown v Brown* (1982) 3 FLR 212 at 218, 220.
16 See infra, p 163.
17 Family Law Act 1986 s46(5), infra pp 658–659.
1 For recent authorities see *Lawrence v Lawrence* [1985] Fam 106 at 132; *Rowan v Rowan* [1988] ILRM 65 at 67
2 The question of capacity to acquire a fresh domicil is discussed infra p 163.
3 *Harrison v Harrison* [1953] 1 WLR 865.
4 *IRC v Duchess of Portland* [1982] Ch 314 at 318–319.
5 Ibid.
6 *Munro v Munro* (1840) 7 Cl & Fin 842 at 877.
7 *Stanley v Bernes* (1830) 3 Hag Ecc 373; *Re Marrett, Chalmers v Wingfield* (1887) 36 Ch D 400; *Hodgson v De Beauchesne* (1858) 12 Moo PCC 285 at 329; *Udny v Udny* (1869) LR 1 Sc & Div 441 at 455; *Re Liddell-Grainger's Will Trusts, Dormer v Liddell-Grainger* [1936] 3 All ER 173.
8 Eg *Puttick v A-G* [1980] Fam 1 at 17.
9 *Winans v A-G* [1904] AC 287 at 297–298; *Bowie (or Ramsay) v Liverpool Royal Infirmary* [1930] AC 588; both cases are discussed infra, pp 145–147.

time is not the sole criterion of domicil.[10] Long residence does not constitute nor does brief residence negative domicil. Everything depends on the attendant circumstances, for they alone disclose the nature of the person's presence in a country. In short, the residence must answer "a qualitative as well as a quantitative test".[11] Thus in *Jopp v Wood*[12] it was held that a residence of twenty-five years in India did not suffice to give a certain John Smith an Indian domicil because of his alleged intention ultimately to return to Scotland, the land of his birth. Again, in *IRC v Bullock*[13] a Canadian who had a domicil of origin in Nova Scotia was held not to have become domiciled in England, despite the fact that he had either served in the RAF or lived in England for over forty years. He retained his domicil in Nova Scotia because he intended to return there should his wife predecease him.

Conversely, brevity of residence is no obstacle to the acquisition of a domicil if the necessary intention exists. If a man clearly intends to live in another country permanently, as, for example, where an emigrant, having wound up his affairs in the country of his origin, flies off with his wife and family to Australia, his mere arrival there will satisfy the element of residence.[14]

A striking example of this truth occurred in America:[15]

A man abandoned his home in State X and took his family to a house in State Y, about half a mile from X, intending to live there permanently. Having deposited his belongings there, he and his family returned to X, in order to spend the night with a relative. He fell ill and died there. It was held that his domicil at death was in Y.

It is possible for a person to be resident in several countries at the same time. In such a case of dual or multiple residence a domicil of choice can only be acquired in a country if this can be shown to be the chief residence. This was established in *Plummer v IRC*.[16]

The taxpayer had an English domicil of origin. She spent the majority of each year in England, where she was being educated. However, she spent more than three months of each year in Guernsey, which had become her family home.

HOFFMANN J held that, despite the taxpayer's retention of a residence in England, her domicil of origin, she could acquire a domicil of choice in Guernsey if she could show that this was her chief residence. This she was unable to do. She had not yet settled in Guernsey. Accordingly she retained her English domicil. The case could, though, have been decided on the much simpler ground that she lacked the requisite intention for acquisition of a Guernsey domicil of choice.[17]

10 *Hodgson v De Beauchesne* (1858)12 Moo PCC 285 at 329, 330.
11 *Bowie (or Ramsay) v Liverpool Royal Infirmary* [1930] AC 588 at 598.
12 (1865) 4 De GJ & Sm 616; and see *A-G v Yule* (1931)145 LT 9.
13 [1976] 3 All ER 353, [1976] 1 WLR 1178.
14 *Hodgson v De Beauchesne* (1858)12 Moo PCC 285 at 330; *Bell v Kennedy* (1868) LR 1 Sc & Div 307at 319.
15 *White v Tennant* 31 W Va 790, 8 SE 596 (1888).
16 [1988] 1 All ER 97, [1988] 1 WLR 292; Kunzlik [1988] CLJ 187; Carter (1988) 59 BYBIL 350; Smart (1990) 10 OJLS 572. However, dual residence can lead to a dual domicil for the purposes of the Civil Jurisdiction and Judgments Act 1982: *Daniel v Foster* 1989 SLT 90.
17 But see Fentiman [1991] CLJ 445, who argues that the case is evidence of a shift in the law away from intention and towards factual connection.

Problems in relation to residence will disappear if the Law Commissions' proposal,[18] that residence be replaced by the simpler concept of presence, is adopted.

(b) THE REQUISITE INTENTION

(i) The nature of the intention

An intention to reside permanently As has already been mentioned,[19] the acquisition of a domicil of choice requires an intention by the *propositus* to remain permanently in the territory in which he resides. This is not difficult to understand if the word permanent is used in its correct sense as signifying the opposite of "temporary". According to the *Shorter Oxford English Dictionary* it means "lasting or designed to last indefinitely without change", and this indeed is the definition that most of the judges have recognised when required to consider the nature of the intention necessary for a change of domicil. In *Udny v Udny*[20], for instance, Lord WESTBURY described the intention as being one to reside "for an unlimited time". A more modern statement to the same effect is that of SCARMAN J [21] who referred to an intention to reside "indefinitely".

The essence, therefore, of these and many other similar statements is that the intended residence must not be for a limited period, whether the limitation is expressed in terms of time or made dependent on the occurrence of a contingency, such as the accomplishment of a definite task, that will occur if at all during the life of the *propositus*.

It is also clear that a conditional intention will not suffice. Thus in *Cramer v Cramer*[22] a woman with a French domicil of origin who came to England intending to remain here and marry an Englishman, who was already married, did not acquire an English domicil of choice. Her intention to remain was conditional on both herself and her proposed husband obtaining divorces and on their relationship continuing. It would, no doubt, have been different if she had intended to remain here come what may, but this was not her intention.

Unlikely contingencies In cases where the termination of residence is dependent on the occurrence of a contingency this will not prevent the acquisition of a domicil unless the contingency is itself unambiguous and realistic. In the words of SCARMAN J:

> If a man intends to return to the land of his birth upon a clearly foreseen and reasonably anticipated contingency, eg the end of his job, the intention required by law is lacking; but, if he has in mind only a vague possibility, such as making a fortune (a modern example might be winning a football pool) ... such a state of mind is consistent with the intention required by law.[1]

Subsequently, a distinction has been drawn between the question of whether

---

18 Law Com No 168 (1987), Scot Law Com No 107 (1987), para 5.7.
19 Supra, p 142.
20 (1869) LR 1 Sc & Div 441 at 458.
21 *Re Fuld's Estate (No 3)* [1968] P 675 at 684; and see *Re Edwards, Edwards v Edwards* (1969) 113 Sol Jo 108; *Cramer v Cramer* [1987] 1 FLR 116. For Australia see Domicile Acts 1982, s 10. For New Zealand see Domicile Act 1976, s 9.
22 [1987] 1 FLR 116.
 1 *Re Fuld's Estate (No 3)*, supra, at 684–685; and see *Henderson v Henderson* [1967] P 77 at 80–81; *Buswell v IRC* [1974] 1 WLR 1631 at 1637; *IRC v Bullock* [1976] 1 WLR 1178 at 1186; *Re Furse* [1980] 3 All ER 838; *Gould v Gould* 1968 SLT 98.

a contingency itself is clear and the question of whether a contingency which is clear will happen.[2]

If a contingency is not sufficiently clear to be identified then it cannot operate to prevent the acquisition of a domicil of choice. Thus in *Re Furse*[3] evidence that the *propositus*, who had a Rhode Island domicil of origin, would leave England, where he had lived for nearly forty years, if he was no longer able to live an active physical life on his farm was not fatal to a change of domicil, and it was held that the *propositus* had acquired an English domicil of choice.

On the other hand, if the contingency can be identified, it has to be asked whether there is a substantial possibility of the contingency happening; if there is, this will prevent the acquisition of a domicil of choice. Thus in *IRC v Bullock*,[4] where a husband intended to return to Canada to live permanently if his wife predeceased him, it was held that the husband did not acquire an English domicil of choice, since there was a real possibility, in view of their ages, of this happening. Of course, if there is no substantial possibility of a contingency happening the evidence evincing a desire to leave the residence will not prevent the acquisition of a domicil of choice.[5]

The former attitude towards contingencies: *Winans v A-G, Ramsay v Liverpool Royal Infirmary* That a contingency must be something more than a vague possibility if it is to prevent the acquisition of a domicil in the country of residence has not been invariably accepted by the courts. It has several times been affirmed, and more than once by the House of Lords, that the present residence of a man is not to be equated with domicil if he contemplates some remote or uncertain event, whose occurrence at some indeterminate time in the future might cause him to leave his country of residence. If this possibility is present to his mind, even an intention to reside indefinitely in the country is said to be ineffective.[6] This view appears to equate the word "permanent" with "perpetual", and to require for a change of domicil an irrevocable intention never to abandon the present place of domicil. Yet it is no part of the law that the intention to maintain the residence should be irrevocable,[7] for such a requirement would virtually exclude the acquisition of a domicil of choice.[8] Nevertheless, in *Winans v A-G*[9] and in *Ramsay v Liverpool Royal Infirmary*,[10] the House of Lords came very near to regarding a vague possibility as if it were, to cite the words of SCARMAN J again, "a clearly foreseen

2 *IRC v Bullock* [1976] 1 WLR 1178 at 1186.
3 [1980] 3 All ER 838. See also *Doucet v Geoghegan* (1878) 9 Ch D 441; *Lawrence v Lawrence* [1985] Fam 106 at 111–111; affd by the Court of Appeal without discussion on this point.
4 [1976] 1 WLR 1178; Carter (1976–77) 48 BYBIL 362; *Cramer v Cramer* [1987] 1 FLR 116; see also *Qureshi v Qureshi* [1972] Fam 173, [1971] 1 All ER 325.
5 *Pletinka v Pletinka* (1965) 109 Sol Jo 72; see also *Osvath-Latkoczy v Osvath-Latkoczy* (1959) 19 DLR (2d) 495.
6 *Moorhouse v Lord* (1863) 10 HL Cas 272 at 285–286; *Jopp v Wood* (1865) 4 De GJ & Sm 616; *Goulder v Goulder* [1892] P 240; *Winans v A-G* [1904] AC 287; *Bowie (or Ramsay) v Liverpool Royal Infirmary* [1930] AC 588; *A-G v Yule* (1931) 145 LT 9; *Wahl v A-G* (1932) 147 LT 382. The rigorous theory adopted in these decisions has been rejected in South Africa: *Eilon v Eilon* 1965 1 SA 703 at 708–709.
7 *Gulbenkian v Gulbenkian* [1937] 4 All ER 618 at 627; *IRC v Bullock* [1976] 1 WLR 1178 at 1184; *Lawrence v Lawrence* [1985] Fam 106 at 111–111; affd by the Court of Appeal, without discussion of this point.
8 See *A-G v Pottinger* (1861) 30 LJ Ex 284 at 292.
9 [1904] AC 287.
10 [1930] AC 588.

and reasonably anticipated contingency".[11] The facts of the former case were these:

> Winans was born in 1823 in the United States, where he was continuously engaged in his father's business until 1850. From 1850 to 1859 he resided in Russia. He married a British subject and appears never to have set foot again in the U.S.A. In 1859 he showed signs of consumption, and, being advised by the doctors to winter in Brighton in England, he reluctantly took rooms at a hotel there, and in 1860 leased two adjoining houses. He still held these houses at the time of his death. From 1860 to 1893 he spent time each year in England but also time in Scotland, Germany or Russia. From 1893 until he died in 1897 he lived entirely in England. Estate duty was paid on his English fortune of over two million pounds, but the Crown now claimed legacy duty on a comparatively small amount of property abroad. Such duty was payable only if he had acquired an English domicil at the time of his death.

The fact that he had resided principally in England for the last thirty-seven years of his life raised a very strong presumption in favour of an English domicil, but there was no direct evidence as to what his intention was. LORD MACNAGHTEN analysed with some particularity the hopes, projects and daily habits of Mr Winans. He found that, in addition to the care of his health, Mr Winans had two objects in life. The first was the construction in Baltimore of a large fleet of spindle-shaped vessels, which would give America superiority at sea over Britain. The second object was to develop a large property of about 200 acres in Baltimore. On this, wharves and docks were to be constructed for the spindle-shaped vessels, and a large house built in which Mr Winans intended to live in order that he might take personal command of the whole undertaking. He succeeded in getting control of the property only at the very end of his life, and at the time of his death he was working day and night on the scheme.

LORD MACNAGHTEN reached the conclusion that the domicil of origin in New Jersey had not been lost. He said that "up to the very last he had an expectation or hope of returning to America and seeing his grand schemes inaugurated."[12] Lord HALSBURY found it impossible to infer from the evidence what Mr Winans' intention was, and he held therefore that the Crown had not discharged its duty of proving a change of domicil. Lord LINDLEY vigorously dissented. In his view Winans had given up all serious idea of returning to America.[13]

Bowie (or Ramsay) v Liverpool Royal Infirmary[14] concerned one George Bowie, who had left a will that was formally valid if his domicil at death was Scottish but invalid if it was English. The story of his life was uneventful.

> He was born in Glasgow in 1845 with a Scottish domicil of origin. He gave up his employment as a commercial traveller at the age of thirty-seven and refused to do any more work during the remaining forty-five years of his life. But even the idle must be fed, and after residing with his mother and

11 Supra, p 144.
12 [1904] AC 287 at 298.
13 [1904] AC 287 at 300. The decision against the acquisition of an English domicil was virtually that of Lord MACNAGHTEN alone. In the courts below, KENNEDY J, PHILLIMORE J (83 LT 634), COLLINS MR, STIRLING LJ and MATHEW LJ (85 LT 508), reached the opposite conclusion without any hesitation.
14 [1930] AC 588.

sisters in Glasgow, he moved his residence to Liverpool in 1892 in order to live on the bounty of his brother. At first he lived in lodgings, but moved to his brother's house when the latter died twenty-one years later, and resided there with his sole surviving sister until she died in 1920. He remained there until his own death in 1927.

Thus George lived in England for the last thirty-six years of his life. During that time he left the country only twice, once on a short visit to the USA, on the second occasion to take a holiday in the Isle of Man. Though he often said he was proud to be a Glasgow man, he resolutely refused on several occasions to return to Scotland, even for the purpose of attending his mother's funeral. On the contrary, he had expressed his determination never to set foot in Glasgow again and had arranged for his own burial in Liverpool.

Thus evidence was completely lacking of any inclination, either by words or actions, to disturb a long and practically uninterrupted residence in England. Nevertheless the House of Lords held unanimously that George died domiciled in Scotland. Their Lordships denied that his prolonged residence disclosed an intention to choose England as his permanent home. Rather, they inferred that had his English source of supply failed he would have retreated to Glasgow.

Evaluation of judicial statements and decisions It would, however, be a mistake to exaggerate the importance of judicial pronouncements or decisions which on the surface appear to distort the character of the intention that is necessary for the acquisition of a domicil. SCARMAN J has stressed that the difficulty of reconciling the numerous statements arises not from lack of clarity of judicial thought, but from the nature of the subject. The cases involve a detailed examination of the facts and it is not surprising that different judicial minds concerned with different factual situations have chosen different language to describe the law.[15] SCARMAN J would regard the difference between the statements of judges in earlier cases as showing a difference of emphasis and therefore as being of no great moment.[16]

It may well be, then, that to construct a formula which describes the precise intention required by English law for the acquisition of a domicil of choice is an impossibility, but perhaps the most satisfactory definition was that offered over a hundred years ago by KINDERSLEY V–C:

That place is properly the domicil of a person in which he has voluntarily fixed the habitation of himself and his family, not for a mere special and temporary purpose, but with a present intention of making it his permanent home, unless and until something (which is unexpected or the happening of which is uncertain) shall occur to induce him to adopt some other permanent home.[17]

Time at which intention is relevant The traditional statement that there must be a *present* intention of permanent residence merely means that so far as the mind of the person at the relevant time was concerned he possessed the requisite intention. The relevant time varies with the nature of the inquiry. It may be past or present. If, for example, the inquiry relates to the domicil of a deceased person, it must be ascertained whether at some period in his life he had formed and retained a fixed and settled intention of residence in a given country. Once this is established, evidence of his subsequent fluc-

15 *Re Fuld's Estate (No 3)* [1968] P 675 at 682–683.
16 Ibid, at 684.
17 *Lord v Colvin* (1859) 4 Drew 366 at 376.

tuations of opinion as to whether he would or would not move elsewhere will be ignored.[18] If, on the other hand, the essential validity of a proposed marriage depends on the law of X's domicil and if the identity of this law is in doubt, what must be examined is his immediate intention.

(ii) Evidence of intention

It is impossible to lay down any positive rule with respect to the evidence necessary to prove intention. All that can be said is that every conceivable event and incident in a man's life is a relevant and an admissible indication of his state of mind. It may be necessary to examine the history of his life with the most scrupulous care, and to resort even to hearsay evidence where the question concerns the domicil that a person, now deceased, possessed in his lifetime.[19] Nothing must be overlooked that might possibly show the place which he regarded as his permanent home at the relevant time.[20] No fact is too trifling to merit consideration.[1] Indeed, one of the defects of English law is that the evidence adduced in a disputed case of domicil is often both voluminous and difficult to assess. This is due to the over-scrupulous manner in which the courts attempt to discover a man's exact intention. The tendency is to investigate his actual state of mind, rather than to rest content with the natural inference of his long-continued residence in a given country. This, indeed, is to set sail on an uncharted sea. Nothing must be neglected that can possibly indicate the bent of the resident's mind. His aspirations, whims, *amours*, prejudices, health, religion, financial expectations—all are taken into account.[2]

Having regard, therefore, to the roving commission imposed on the courts, it is not surprising that their decisions exhibit a multiplicity of different factors that have been regarded as *indicia* of intention. Without attempting to give an exhaustive list, it may be useful to observe that at one time or another the following have been regarded as relevant criteria of intention: naturalisation,[3] retention of citizenship,[4] purchase of a house[5] or of a burial ground,[6] the exercise of political rights,[7] the establishment of children in business,[8] the statutory declaration made by a candidate for naturalisation that he intends to reside permanently in the United Kingdom,[9] the place where a man's wife and family reside,[10] departure from a country owing to

---

18 *Re Marrett, Chalmers v Wingfield* (1887) 36 Ch D 400.
19 *Scappaticci v A-G* [1955] P 47, [1955] 1 All ER 193n.
20 See, for example, the voluminous evidence considered by CHITTY J in *Re Craignish* [1892] 3 Ch 180.
 1 *Drevon v Drevon* (1864) 34 LJ Ch 129 at 133; and see *Re Flynn, Flynn v Flynn* [1968] 1 WLR 103 at 107.
 2 *Casdagli v Casdagli* [1919] AC 145 at 178.
 3 *D'Etchegoyen v D'Etchegoyen* (1888) 13 PD 132; *Qureshi v Qureshi* [1972] Fam 173 at 190–191.
 4 *IRC v Bullock* [1976] 3 All ER 353, [1976] 1 WLR 1178.
 5 *D'Etchegoyen v D'Etchegoyen*, supra; *Moorhouse v Lord* (1863) 10 HL Cas 272; for the history of this case see Thompson and Mackie [1979] Jur Rev 138; *Stevenson v Masson* (1873) LR 17 Eq 78; *Re Craignish* [1892] 3 Ch 180.
 6 *Stevenson v Masson*, supra; *Haldane v Eckford* (1869) LR 8 Eq 631.
 7 *Drevon v Drevon* (1864) 34 LJ Ch 129 at 137.
 8 *Stevenson v Masson* (1873) LR 17 Eq 78.
 9 *Gulbenkian v Gulbenkian* [1937] 4 All ER 618; distinguish *Wahl v A-G* (1932) 147 LT 382 and see *Steiner v IRC* (1973) 49 TC 13.
10 *Forbes v Forbes* (1854) Kay 341; *Aitchison v Dixon* (1870) LR 10 Eq 589; cf *IRC v Bullock* [1976] 1 WLR 1178 at 1185.

compulsion of war,[11] the refusal of a foreign *fiancée* to leave her own country,[12] statements as to his domiciliary intentions made by a deceased person in his lifetime,[13] the effect of racial intolerance on domiciliary intention,[14] and the fact that a family is split between England and abroad.[15]

Undue stress must not be laid on any single fact, however impressive it may appear when viewed out of its context, for its importance as a determining factor may well be minimised when considered in the light of other qualifying events. Again, no one fact is of constant value, for every case varies in its circumstances, and what is of decisive importance in one may be of little weight in another.[16]

It is for this reason that it is impossible to formulate a rule specifying the weight to be given to particular evidence. All that can be gathered from the authorities in this respect is that more reliance is placed on conduct than on declarations of intention, especially if they are oral.[17] Nevertheless, the common law rule, that expressions of intention by a living person cannot be received in evidence unless against his own interest, is not applicable to an issue of domicil,[18] and it is common enough for witnesses to testify to parol declarations made during his life by the person whose domicil is in question. This kind of evidence, however, especially when given long after the conversation occurred, is suspect, for witnesses may lie or forget.[19] Declarations should contain "a real expression of intention",[20] for it only too frequently happens that they cannot be taken at their face value. They may be interested statements designed to flatter or to deceive the hearer; they may represent nothing more than vain expectations unlikely to be fulfilled; and the very facility with which they can be made requires their sincerity to be manifested by some active step taken in furtherance of the expressed intention. The circumstances in which the statement is made need to be considered, and any declaration must be backed up by conduct consistent with the declared intention.[1]

Even lower in the scale of values is evidence given in the course of the trial by the person himself not of his past declarations, but of his past intention. This must be accepted with very considerable reserve, for on such a personal issue as his own place of domicil he is under a bias that is likely to influence his mind, perhaps even his veracity.[2]

11 *Re Lloyd Evans* [1947] Ch 695.
12 *Donaldson v Donaldson* [1949] P 363.
13 *Scappaticci v A-G* [1955] P 47, [1955] 1 All ER 193n.
14 *Qureshi v Qureshi* [1972] Fam 173 at 193.
15 *Begum v Entry Clearance Officer, Dacca* [1983] Imm AR 163.
16 *Hodgson v De Beauchesne* (1858) 12 Moo PCC 285 at 330; *Doucet v Geoghegan* (1878) 9 Ch D 441 at 445; *Wahl v A-G* (1932) 147 LT 382.
17 *McMullen v Wadsworth* (1889) 14 App Cas 631 at 636, PC.
18 *Bryce v Bryce* [1933] P 83; Civil Evidence Act 1968, s 2(1).
19 *Hodgson v De Beauchesne* (1858) 12 Moo PCC 285; *Re Liddell-Grainger's Will Trusts* [1936] 3 All ER 173; *Re Fuld's Estate (No 3)* [1968] P 675 at 691–692.
20 *Hodgson v De Beauchesne*, op cit, at 325.
 1 *Ross v Ross* [1930] AC 1 at 6; and see *Qureshi v Qureshi* [1972] Fam 173 at 192–193. In several cases even written declarations have been disregarded: *Re Martin* [1900] P 211 (declaration in mortgage deed); *Re Liddell-Grainger's Will Trusts* [1936] 3 All ER 173 (declaration in a will); *Wahl v A-G* (1932) 147 LT 382 (declaration in naturalisation papers); *Buswell v IRC* [1974] 2 All ER 520, [1974] 1 WLR 1631 (declaration on an Inland Revenue form).
 2 *Bell v Kennedy* (1868) LR 1 Sc & Div 307 at 313; *Re Craignish* [1892] 3 Ch 180 at 190; *Chaudhary v Chaudhary* [1985] Fam 19 at 26, affd by CA, ibid at 33; but see *Brown v Brown* (1982) 3 FLR 212 at 214–215 where the declaration was consistent with conduct.

In at least two respects, motive in the sense of the antecedent desire that determines the will to act is one of the indicia of the intention requisite for the acquisition of a domicil of choice. First, it may throw light on the question whether the removal to another country was intended to be permanent. It will serve, for instance, to contrast the case of a man who flees to England to escape political persecution in his own country with that of a retired officer who goes to Jersey to avoid heavy taxation. Secondly, it may provide a means of testing the sincerity of a declaration of intention. Thus, if a widower testifies that at the time of his wife's death he and she regarded Scotland as their permanent home, the fact that by Scots law he is entitled to one-half of his wife's property may make his testimony a little suspect.[3]

It is important to realise that the only intention relevant to a change of domicil is an intention to settle permanently in a country. This will effect a change of domicil even if the *propositus* intended to retain his former personal law.[4] One of the legal consequences of an intention to settle in country X is that the person in question becomes subject to the law of X whether this is his wish or not. It is the inevitable effect of his residence in that country coupled with his intention to remain there without any limit of time.[5] Thus in one case:

> An Englishman, having taken up his residence in Hamburg with the intention of settling there for good, remained there until his death some fifty years later. On one occasion, when he came to England for a temporary purpose, he made a will in which he declared that though he intended to return to Hamburg it was not his intention to renounce his English domicil of origin.

It was held that this declaration, which suggested a desire to have two simultaneous domicils, could not nullify the consequences of having in fact acquired a German domicil.[6]

(iii) The Law Commissions' proposals

The English and Scottish Law Commissions, in a joint Report,[7] have made proposals for the introduction of a statutory statement of the major rules on domicil. This would contain much, although not all, of the law on domicil. One important aspect examined was that of acquisition of a new domicil. The Law Commissions started off on the basis that the greater mobility in the world should be reflected in the rules on domicil, and that it should be a little easier to acquire a new domicil.[8] To achieve this, it is proposed that the standard of proof in all acquisition cases should be the normal civil standard,[9] and that it should be sufficient to show that a person intended to settle in the country in question for an indefinite period.[10] In their view a person who

3 Cf *Re Craignish* [1892] 3 Ch 180.
4 *Douglas v Douglas* (1871) LR 12 Eq 617 at 644, 645.
5 *Re Craignish* [1892] 3 Ch 180 at 188, 189.
6 *Re Steer* (1858) 3 H & N 594. To the same effect, *Re Liddell-Grainger's Will Trusts* [1936] 3 All ER 173.
7 Law Com No 168 (1987), Scot Law Com No 107 (1987); Kaye (1988) NLJ 773.
8 Para 5.3.
9 Para 5.6.
10 Paras 5.8–5.14. For the use of an intention to reside *indefinitely* under the present law see *Re Fuld's Estate (No 3)* [1968] P 675, supra, p 144. See also *In Estate of Slavinsky* (1989) 53 SASR 221; *M(C) v M(T)* [1988] ILRM 456.

makes his home in country A, and has no present intention to return to a country of an earlier domicil or to establish a home in another country should be regarded as domiciled in country A. This would overrule older cases like *Ramsay* but would not appear to involve a significantly different test from that adopted in more modern cases. The major criticism of this proposal is not in relation to the ease of change of domicil but in relation to the uncertainty created by the use of the words "indefinitely" and "settle". The Law Commissions' Working Paper sought to get over the difficulties of ascertaining the requisite intention by having a presumption as to the intention necessary to acquire a domicil; this was based on a notion of seven years' habitual residence in a country.[11] However, this controversial idea was dropped in the Report because of fears of injustice to individuals who would be put to the expense of having to rebut the presumption, particularly for tax reasons.[12] The dropping of the presumption has been criticised. The proposal in the Working Paper sought to walk a tightrope between certainty and flexibility, but now the tightrope walker is deprived of his balancing pole—the presumption.[13] Nonetheless, the dropping of the presumption does avoid the criticism that the proposals make a change of domicil too easy. In particular, what is proposed is unlikely to have any significant impact on the incidence of taxation,[14] which has always been a stumbling block to reform in the past. The Government has accepted the recommendations in the Law Commissions' Report and will introduce legislation when a suitable opportunity arises.[15]

(c) VOLUNTARY RESIDENCE

It is a commonplace that to constitute domicil a residence must be voluntary—a matter of free choice,[16] not of constraint. In several cases, the circumstances may raise a doubt whether such freedom exists.

(i) Prisoners

A clear example of constraint preclusive of this freedom is imprisonment in a foreign country, and there is no doubt that a prisoner, except perhaps one transported or exiled for life, retains the domicil that he possessed before his confinement.[17]

(ii) Refugees

It cannot be predicated that refugees, such as those who fled from Hitler's Germany, necessarily retain their former domicil. The motive that induced the flight no doubt militates against the inference that there was an intention of permanent residence in the chosen asylum. There is a presumption against a change of domicil, but "what is dictated by necessity in the first instance

---

11 Law Com Working Paper No 88 (1985), Scot Law Com Consultative Memorandum No 63 (1985), paras 5.11–5.16.
12 Paras 5.15–5.22.
13 North (1990) I Hague Recueil 13 at 44.
14 Law Com No 168 (1987), Scot Law Com No 107 (1987), para 9.16.
15 Attorney-General, Hansard (HC) 17 Oct 1991, vol 196 col 177.
16 It may perhaps be more accurate to say that in all cases physical presence in a country satisfies the requirement of residence, and that constraint is relevant only to the question of intention; see McClean (1962) 11 ICLQ 1156–1160.
17 *Burton v Fisher* (1828) Milw 183; *Burton v Dolben* (1756) 2 Lee 312 at 318; *Re the late Emperor Napoleon Bonaparte* (1853) 2 Rob Eccl 606.

may afterwards become a matter of choice",[18] and the presumption may well be reversed by subsequent circumstances, as, for example, by the continued retention of the residence after a return to the original country has become safe and practicable.[19]

(iii) Fugitives from justice

Another example of involuntary residence in a new country is that of the fugitive from justice. Nevertheless, if a man leaves his domicil in order to escape the consequences of a crime, the natural inference is that he has left it for ever and that a presumption arises in favour of the acquisition of a fresh domicil in the country of refuge. His departure has, indeed, been forced upon him, yet this does not necessarily mean that he intends it to be temporary. In *Re Martin, Loustalan v Loustalan*,[20] however, LINDLEY LJ suggested that the "all-important" factor is whether there is a definite period after which a wrongdoer may return home in safety. In other words, if the crime ceases to be punishable or the sentence to be enforceable after a given number of years, residence in another country, unless fortified by other facts, does not effect a change of domicil; but if the fugitive remains perpetually liable to proceedings, then the new place of residence becomes the new domicil.[21] This view was not adopted by the other members of the court, RIGBY LJ remarking that to suggest that the fugitive in question intended at the time of his escape from France to return as soon as he could safely do so (twenty years in the particular case) was "so irrational that, in default of the strongest evidence, it ought not to be imputed to him".[22] It is, indeed, difficult to agree with LINDLEY LJ, except possibly where the offence is trifling and the term of prescription short.

Re Martin was concerned with the possibility of a fugitive from justice being free to return to his domicil abroad; more recently, the entirely different problem has arisen of the possibility of a fugitive being forced to return to face justice abroad under an extradition treaty. If the fugitive never set up a home and has no affection for England, merely seeing it as a place of refuge, and is ready to move on if detection and arrest is imminent, a domicil of choice will not be acquired.[23]

(iv) Fugitive debtors

Freedom of choice is also affected when a man finds it desirable to flee the country to avoid his creditors. Whether this raises a presumption against an intention to return to his own country must obviously depend on a variety of circumstances, such as the amount of the debts, the possibility of meeting them, the imminence of legal proceedings, the activities of the debtor in his new residence and so on. It certainly cannot be said that the adoption of the new residence per se effects a change of domicil.[24]

---

18 *Winans v A-G* (1901) 85 LT 508 at 510.
19 *De Bonneval v De Bonneval* (1838) 1 Curt 856; *May v May* [1943] 2 All ER 146; cf *Re Evans* [1947] Ch 695.
20 [1900] P 211.
21 Ibid, at 232.
22 Ibid, at 235.
23 *Puttick v A-G* [1980] Fam 1 at 18.
24 For example, see *Pitt v Pitt* (1864) 4 Macq 627; *Udny v Udny* (1869) LR 1 Sc & Div 441; *Briggs v Briggs* (1880) 5 PD 163; *Re Robertson* (1885) 2 TLR 178; *Re Wright's Trusts* (1856) 25 LJ Ch 621 at 624.

(v) Invalids

The case of an invalid who settles in a foreign country for the sake of his health, not merely for the purpose of convalescence, should on principle cause no difficulty. The principle is that unless a man is a free agent his adoption of a new residence does not effect a change of domicil. He must have an alternative—either to stay or to go. But it would seem that an alternative is open to every invalid. To take even the extreme case, if a man, being assured by his doctors that he has only a few months to live, decides to spend the short remainder of his life in a country where the climate may alleviate his suffering, it would seem clear, if all sentiment of pity is dismissed, that of his own volition he has chosen a new and permanent home, since he intends to continue his new residence until death. The residence and intention essential for a change of domicil are present. Yet, this suggestion has been stigmatised by LORD KINGSDOWN as "revolting to common sense and the common feelings of humanity".[25] No doubt it is, and no doubt a court would in fact declare against a change of domicil in such circumstances, but nevertheless the decision would be difficult to reconcile with strict principle unless, perhaps, it could be buttressed by the argument that the invalid contemplated a return to his former home if the medical verdict should prove to be unfounded.

The case just put, however, is an extreme one. Where the necessity of selecting a different climate is of a less compelling nature, where there is no immediate danger,[26] the normal principle is consistently applied and the fact that the invalid's sole reason for departure is a desire to enjoy better health or to retard the progress of a disease cannot per se be regarded as excluding an intention to remain permanently in the chosen place. Otherwise a most artificial meaning would be attached to intention. We should be forced to hold, for example, that an Englishman who settles in France in order to escape income-tax retains his English domicil, since he will probably return if the cost of living falls. The exact point arose in *Hoskins v Matthews*.[27]

In that case a testator with an English domicil of origin went to Florence at the age of 60, and, except for three or four months in each year, lived in a villa that he had bought there until he died twelve years later. He was suffering from an injury of the spine and there is no doubt that he left England solely because he thought the warmer climate of Italy might benefit his health or might even cure him. His housekeeper deposed that his wish was to return to England if his state of health would allow him to do so, and in her view he would have done so had he been restored to health.

It was contended, therefore, that since the residence in Florence was a matter of necessity, not of choice, it did not suffice to cause a change of domicil. In the result it was held that the English domicil had been lost. TURNER J said that in settling in Italy "*he was exercising a preference, and not acting upon a necessity*, and I cannot venture to hold that in such a case the domicil cannot be changed."[28]

25 *Moorhouse v Lord* (1863) 10 HL Cas 272; see also *Johnstone v Beattie* (1843) 10 Cl & Fin 42 at 139.
26 *Hoskins v Matthews* (1856) 8 De GM & G 13 at 28.
27 (1856) 8 De GM & G 13; *Philippi v IRC* [1971] 3 All ER 61, [1971] 1 WLR 684; cf *Re James* (1908) 98 LT 438.
28 (1856) 8 De GM & G 13 at 28–29, italics added. See also *Re Adams* [1967] IR 424 at 443–445, 447, 449.

(vi) Miscellaneous cases

There are various other cases, somewhat analogous to those just discussed, in which the reason to which a change of residence is due has a rather more decisive effect on the question of intention. Thus, if a person resides abroad in pursuance of his duties as a public servant of his own Government, as, for example, an ambassador, a military or naval officer or a consul, or if he is an employee under contract to go where sent, the inference to be drawn from the cause of the residence is that it is not intended to be permanent.[1]

In such cases the existing domicil is retained unless there are additional circumstances from which a contrary intention can be collected.[2] Thus, to take an extreme case, it has been held that even a member of the armed forces may acquire a domicil in a foreign country where he is compulsorily resident and whence he is liable to be removed at any moment by higher authority, if there is sufficient evidence of his intention to settle there permanently as soon as he once more becomes a free agent.[3] The fact that the area of his new home coincides with his area of service does not per se preclude him from acquiring a new domicil. It has also been held that, if the requisite residence and intention are satisfactorily proved, he may acquire a domicil in a country other than that in which he is compulsorily serving.[4] It would seem that a person who enters the armed forces of a foreign power, in such circumstances as to necessitate his indefinite residence in the foreign country, acquires a new domicil there.[5]

(d)   THE BURDEN OF PROOF

The burden of proof that lies on those who allege a change of domicil varies with the circumstances. In this connection there are two observations that may be made. First, English judges have taken the view that it requires far stronger evidence to establish the abandonment of a domicil of origin in favour of a fresh domicil than to establish a change from one domicil of choice to another.[6] Secondly, and by way of contrast, there is authority for the view that a change of domicil from one country to another under the same sovereign, as from Jersey or Scotland to England, is more easily proved than a change to a foreign country.[7] It is not lightly to be inferred that a man intends to settle permanently in a country where he will possess the status of an alien, with all the difficulties and conflict of duties that such a status involves.

---

1 *Re Patten's Goods* (1860) 6 Jur NS 151 (naval); *A-G v Lady Rowe* (1862) 1 H & C 31 (Chief Justice of Ceylon); *Firebrace v Firebrace* (1878) 4 PD 63 (army officer); *Re Mitchell, ex p Cunningham* (1884) 13 QBD 418 (army officer); *Re Macreight, Paxton v Macreight* (1885) 30 Ch D 165 (Jerseyman serving in British Army); *A-G v Kent* (1862) 31 LJ Ex 391 at 397 (attaché to Portuguese Embassy); *Sharpe v Crispin* (1869) LR 1 P & D 611 (consul).
2 *Re Smith's Goods* (1850) 2 Rob Eccl 332; and see *McEwan v McEwan* 1969 SLT 342.
3 *Donaldson v Donaldson* [1949] P 363; *Cruickshanks v Cruickshanks* [1957] 1 All ER 889, [1957] 1 WLR 564. So held also in Scotland, *Sellars v Sellars* 1942 SC 206.
4 *Stone v Stone* [1959] 1 All ER 194, [1958] 1 WLR 1287.
5 *Re Mitchell, ex p Cunningham* (1884) 13 QBD 418 at 421, as qualified by the earlier remarks of PAGE WOOD V–C in *Forbes v Forbes* (1854) Kay 341 at 356.
6 Infra, pp 155–156.
7 *Lord v Colvin* (1859) 4 Drew 366 at 422–423; *Whicker v Hume* (1858) 7 HL Cas 124 at 159; *Moorhouse v Lord* (1863) 10 HL Cas 272 at 287.

(e) CHANGE OF DOMICIL AND CHANGE OF NATIONALITY

It is important to emphasise that nationality and domicil are two different conceptions and that a man may change the latter without divesting himself of his nationality.[8] An Englishman may remain an Englishman in the sense that his allegiance renders him subject to certain duties to the Crown, and yet he may so change his residence that many of his legal rights and obligations will be determinable by a foreign system of law, as being the law of his domicil.[9] The mere fact that an alien living in England under a certificate of registration is liable to deportation for misbehaviour or has even been recommended for deportation does not prevent him from acquiring an English domicil of choice,[10] or deprive him of a domicil already acquired.[11] Indeed, a domicil of choice may even continue after deportation if re-entry is lawful.[12] Neither the permissive nor the precarious character of his residence nullifies his intention to settle in England.[13] Although it has been held, in Canada, that an illegal immigrant may acquire a domicil of choice in the country which he has entered illegally,[14] the predominant view[15] which has been accepted in England[16] is that no domicil of choice can be acquired in defiance of the laws of the country entered.

4. DOMICIL OF ORIGIN AND DOMICIL OF CHOICE CONTRASTED

As compared with the views held in civil law countries, in the USA, in New Zealand and Australia,[17] the domicil of origin is regarded by the present English law[18] as fundamentally different from a domicil of choice. It differs in its character, in the conditions necessary for its abandonment and in its capacity for revival.

(a) TENACITY OF THE DOMICIL OF ORIGIN

There is the strongest possible presumption in favour of the continuance of a domicil of origin. As contrasted with a domicil of choice, it has been said by LORD MACNAGHTEN that "its character is more enduring, its hold stronger

---

8 *Boldrini v Boldrini* [1932] P 9 at 15; *Bradfield v Swanton* [1931] IR 446; *Re Adams* [1967] IR 424 at 447–448. For the converse case of a change of nationality without a change of domicil, see *Wahl v A-G* (1932) 147 LT 382. See the discussion by Westlake, *Private International Law* (7th edn), pp 348–354.
9 *Udny v Udny* (1869) LR 1 Sc & Div 441 at 452.
10 *Boldrini v Boldrini* [1932] P 9; *May v May* (1943) 169 LT 42; *Zanelli v Zanelli* (1948) 64 TLR 556; *Szechter v Szechter* [1971] P 286, [1970] 3 All ER 905; and see *Lim v Lim* [1973] VR 370.
11 *Cruh v Cruh* [1945] 2 All ER 545.
12 *Thiele v Thiele* (1920) 150 LT Jo 387; and see Dicey & Morris, p 142.
13 *Zanelli v Zanelli*, supra. But no domicil of choice is required if the intention is primarily to avoid detection; see *Puttick v A-G* [1980] Fam 1 at 18, supra, p 152.
14 *Jablonowski v Jablonowski* (1972) 28 DLR (3d) 440.
15 *Solomon v Solomon* (1912) 29 WN NSW 68; *Smith v Smith* 1962 (3) SA 930; discussed by Spiro (1963) 12 ICLQ 680; Kahn, op cit, pp 62–64.
16 *Puttick v A-G* [1980] Fam 1; Pilkington (1984) 33 ICLQ 885.
17 See the New Zealand Domicile Act 1976 and the Australian Domicile Acts 1982; Nygh, pp 177–178.
18 For proposals for reform see infra, pp 158–159.

and less easily shaken off".[19] In fact, decisions such as *Winans v A-G*[20] and *Ramsay v Liverpool Royal Infirmary*[1] warrant the conclusion that almost overwhelming evidence is required to shake it off. In the latter of these cases evidence was completely lacking of the slightest indication, either by words or actions, that George Bowie intended to live anywhere else than in England. Yet it was held that the tenacity of his Scottish domicil of origin had not yielded. Much more recently, in *Cramer v Cramer* Stephen BROWN and BALCOMBE LJJ held that the burden of proving a change of domicil from one of origin to one of choice was a heavy one.[2]

(b) ABANDONMENT OF AN EXISTING DOMICIL

Since a domicil of choice is voluntarily acquired if there is the requisite intention and residence, so it is extinguishable in the same manner, ie merely by a removal from the country with an intention not to return and even without acquiring a fresh domicil.[3] In cases of dual or multiple residence what is necessary is that the country ceases to be the chief residence[4] with, presumably, an intention not to reside there as the chief residence. The only distinction between acquisition and abandonment is that the latter requires less evidence than the former.[5] There cannot be abandonment by intention alone.[6]

But it has been objected by MEGARRY J, obiter, that to require proof of an intention not to return is too rigorous a test, since it denies effect to a departure from a country without an intention of returning. In his view, it is unnecessary to prove a positive intention not to return, since the "merely negative absence of any intention"[7] to resume the residence will suffice to effect an abandonment of the domicil.

It is submitted that this suggested distinction between an intention not to return and the absence of an intention to return is fallacious. The difference between the two variants of intention is not obvious, but presumably the absence of an intention not to return can only mean that at the time of departure the person in question has not decided whether to return or not. If this is the state of his mind, the result in law is that his domicil is unchanged. In other words, it would seem clear on the authorities that there must always be a positive intention not to return before it can be said that a domicil of choice has been lost. Irresolution effects nothing. But the identification of a person's domicil is always inferred from his conduct together with his declarations, if any, and at the time when the question falls to be determined

---

19 *Winans v A-G* [1904] AC 287 at 290; and see *A-G v Yule and Mercantile Bank of India* (1931) 145 LT 9; *Wahl v A-G* (1932) 147 LT 382; *Hyland v Hyland* (1971) 18 FLR 461.
20 Supra, pp 145–146.
  1 [1930] AC 588, supra, pp 146–147.
  2 [1987] 1 FLR 116; cf the attitude towards the domicil of origin shown in *Brown v Brown* (1982) 3 FLR 212; infra, p 157.
  3 *Udny v Udny* (1869) LR 1 Sc & Div 441 at 450; *Fielden v IRC* (1965) 42 TC 501 at 507; *Tee v Tee* [1974] 1 WLR 213 at 215.
  4 *Plummer v IRC* [1988] 1 WLR 292 at 295.
  5 *Re Evans* [1947] Ch 695.
  6 *In re Raffenel's Goods* (1863) 3 Sw & Tr 49; *Faye v IRC* (1961) 40 TC 103; *Re Adams* [1967] IR 424 at 452; *IRC v Duchess of Portland* [1982] Ch 314 discussed infra, pp 163–165; *Rowan v Rowan* [1988] ILRM 65.
  7 *In re Flynn* [1968] 1 WLR 103 at 113; approved in *Qureshi v Qureshi* [1972] Fam 173 at 191; a negative test was used in *IRC v Duchess of Portland* [1982] Ch 314 at 318.

the inference from the evidence may well be that what began as indecision has been gradually transformed into a definite resolve not to return.

But the domicil of origin, which in its inception is not a matter of free will but is communicated to a person by operation of law, is not extinguished by mere removal with an intention not to return. It cannot be lost by mere abandonment. It endures until supplanted by a fresh domicil of choice. *Bell v Kennedy*[8] is the leading authority for this rule.

The domicil of origin of Bell was in Jamaica, where he had been born of Scottish parents domiciled in that island. He was educated in Scotland but returned to Jamaica after reaching his majority. Some fourteen years later, in 1837, he left the island without any intention of returning, resided with his mother-in-law in Scotland, and occupied himself in looking for an estate in that country on which to settle down. He had not been successful in this when his wife died in 1838, but after her death he bought an estate and it was admitted that at the time of the trial he had acquired a Scottish domicil. The question for decision, however, was—what was his domicil at the time of his wife's death?

It was held that his domicil at that moment was in Jamaica. Although he had abandoned the island for good in 1837 and was resident in Scotland, he had not at that time decided to make his permanent residence there. The evidence showed that in 1838 his mind was vacillating with regard to his future home. Therefore, since he had not acquired a Scottish domicil of choice, he retained his domicil of origin.

A modern instance of removal from the domicil of origin with an intention not to return is *Brown v Brown*.[9] In this case there was evidence of a willingness by the court to infer the intention necessary for the acquisition of a domicil of choice, on the basis that the person in question, who worked for a multinational oil company, had severed his links with his domicil of origin in the United States, and the nature of his work meant that he had opportunities for the acquisition of a new domicil abroad.[10]

(c) REVIVAL OF THE DOMICIL OF ORIGIN

If the domicil of origin is displaced as a result of the acquisition of a domicil of choice, the rule of English law is that it is merely placed in abeyance for the time being. It remains in the background ever ready to revive and to fasten upon the *propositus* immediately he abandons his domicil of choice.[11] The position may be illustrated by an example, based on the hypothesis that the George Bowie, whose case was decided in *Ramsay v Liverpool Royal Infirmary*,[12] had married after his arrival in England and that a son, X, had been born to him. In these circumstances X's domicil of origin would have been Scottish, since at his birth his father was domiciled in Scotland. Let us now suppose the following:

At the age of 22, X, who has developed a strong dislike for the United Kingdom, leaves the country determined never to set foot here again. He

8 (1868) LR 1 Sc & Div 307.
9 (1982) 3 FLR 212. Cf *Vien Estate v Vien Estate* (1988) 49 DLR (4th) 558.
10 Ibid, at 215, 217.
11 *Udny v Udny* (1869) LR 1 Sc & Div 441; *Tee v Tee* [1974] 1 WLR 213, at 215–216; see also Wade (1983) 32 ICLQ 1 at 12 et seq.
12 Supra, pp 146–147.

acquires a domicil of choice in Peru. After residing there for forty years, in the course of which he has amassed a fortune, he leaves the country for good and takes up his temporary residence in New York, being undecided whether to settle permanently in Virginia or California.

The result is that immediately on his departure from Peru his Peruvian domicil ceases abruptly, but his Scots domicil of origin revives and remains attached to him until he has in fact acquired a domicil of choice in some other country. It is clear, of course, that during his period of indecision in New York there must be some personal law applicable to him. This might be either Peruvian or Scottish law. In the United States of America, where the doctrine of revival is not accepted,[13] it would be the law of Peru. According to Lord Chancellor HATHERLEY, however, to admit this is to be driven to the absurdity of asserting a person to be domiciled in a country which he has resolutely forsaken and cast off, simply because he may (perhaps for years) be deliberating before he settles himself elsewhere.[14]

Yet certain doubts suggest themselves. Is it so absurd to prefer the law under which the man has recently been living, perhaps for a prolonged period? Are the claims of the law which is imposed on him at birth, independently of his volition, superior to that which he has voluntarily chosen and long retained? At any rate the advantages of preferring the domicil of origin in the case of our hypothetical X are not particularly conspicuous. The country that determines his personal law is one that he has never visited and for which he feels a repugnance. Nevertheless, if he wishes to marry, his capacity will be determined by reference to the law of Scotland. If he dies intestate leaving movables in England, they will be distributed according to Scots law and United Kingdom inheritance tax will be payable. These illustrations, which could be multiplied, provoke the thought that the virtues of the doctrine of revival are not so obvious as appeared to the mid-Victorian judges. The doctrine of revival has in fact been rejected in New Zealand[15] and in Australia,[16] and its rejection in the United Kingdom has been proposed by the Law Commissions.

(d) THE LAW COMMISSIONS' PROPOSALS

The Law Commissions, in their Report on the reform of the law of domicil, have sought to simplify the existing law, and have taken a bold line in recommending that the domicil of origin should be abolished.[17] There would be just one set of rules for determining the domicil of children, which would apply to ascertaining the domicil at birth as well as during the rest of childhood. The domicil taken at birth would not have the special characteristics of the domicil of origin.[18] Thus, no special tenacity would be given to the domicil received at birth and the doctrine of revival would be replaced by a rule that an adult's domicil would continue until he obtains another domicil. A continuance rule would not only be simpler to operate but would

---

13 *Re Jones' Estate* (1921) 192 Iowa 78, 182 NW 227.
14 *Udny v Udny* (1869) LR 1 Sc & Div 441 at 450.
15 Domicile Act 1976, s 11; see Webb (1977) 26 ICLQ 194; but see generally for the position in Commonwealth countries, McClean, *Recognition of Family Judgments in the Commonwealth* (1983), ch 1.
16 Domicile Acts 1982, s 7; Nygh, pp 173–174.
17 Law Com No 168 (1987), Scot Law Com No 107 (1987), paras 4.21–4.24.
18 Paras 5.6, 5.23–5.25.

also ensure that a person is domiciled in a country with which he has or has had some real connection.

5. DOMICIL OF DEPENDENT PERSONS

There are two classes of dependent persons—children[19] and mentally disordered persons.

(a) CHILDREN

(i) A child's domicil of origin

A child acquires at birth a domicil of origin by operation of law, namely, if legitimate and born in his father's lifetime, the domicil of his father;[20] if illegitimate[1] or born after his father's death,[2] the domicil of his mother.[3] A foundling is domiciled in the country where he is found.[4] If a child is born illegitimate, but is later legitimated, his father's domicil will be communicated to him from the date of legitimation, but it is probable that his domicil of origin remains that of his mother, presuming that at his birth his parents were domiciled in different countries.[5] It is important to note that a domicil of origin once acquired remains constant throughout life.[6]

(ii) When an independent domicil can be acquired

Before reaching the age of 16, an unmarried child is utterly incapable of acquiring by his own act an independent domicil of choice.[7] He is powerless to alter his civil status. Once that age is reached, then a child, whether male or female, is fully capable of having an independent domicil.[8] Furthermore, any child below that age who is validly married can acquire an independent domicil. Although this will not affect the status of English domiciled children, who are incapable of marriage until the age of 16, it does mean that any child

19 Palmer (1974) 4 Fam Law 35; Binchy (1979) 11 Ottowa LR 279; Blaikie [1984] Jur Rev 1.
20 *Forbes v Forbes* (1854) Kay 341 at 353; *Udny v Udny* (1869) LR 1 Sc & Div 441 at 457. Does an adopted child acquire a new domicil of origin on adoption based on the domicil of his adoptive father (or mother, if unmarried) as at the date of adoption? See Adoption Act 1976, s 39 (1), (5).
1 *Udny v Udny*, supra; *Re Wright's Trusts* (1856) 2 K & J 595; *Urquhart v Butterfield* (1887) 37 ChD 357; *Carmona v White* (1980) 25 SASR 525. But see for proposals for reform, infra p 162; for New Zealand, see the Domicile Act 1976, s6; for Australia the Domicile Acts 1982, s 9.
2 There appears to be no English authority for this.
3 Though see discussion of legitimacy, infra, pp 746–756. Although the Family Law Reform Act 1987 very largely assimilates the rights of children, regardless of whether they are legitimate or illegitimate, the concept of legitimacy is still relevant for domicil purposes.
4 Westlake, s 248; Dicey and Morris, p 126; Castel, *Canadian Conflict of Laws*, 2nd edn (1986), para 27.
5 Wolff, pp 118–119.
6 Except perhaps in the case of adoption, supra.
7 *Forbes v Forbes* (1854) Kay 341 at 353.
8 Domicile and Matrimonial Proceedings Act 1973, s 3(1). A child who was over 16 or was married but was incapable of having an independent domicil before 1 January 1974 is regarded as capable from that date. Sections 3 and 4 of the 1973 Act are not retrospective, and, therefore, in considering the domicil of a child as at any time before 1 January 1974, the old law is still applicable. Under such rules a child is incapable of acquiring an independent domicil until reaching full age whether or not married: *Harrison v Harrison* [1953] 1 WLR 865. A female married child takes the domicil of her husband but if widowed reverts to that of her father until majority: *Shekleton v Shekleton* [1972] 2 NSWR 675.

below that age whose foreign marriage is recognised here[9] will be regarded as capable of having an independent domicil.

(iii) The effect of a change in the parent's domicil

Although an unmarried child under 16[10] is unable to acquire a domicil of choice by his own act there is nothing to prevent the acquisition of a domicil of choice *for* him by the act of one of his parents. This may be effected either by the father or by the mother. The primary rule is that the domicil of a legitimate child[11] automatically changes with any change that occurs in the domicil of the father.[12] As between a living father and his legitimate child there is a necessary unity of domicil, even though they may reside in different countries. This unity is not destructible at the will of the father. It is not terminated if he purports to create a separate domicil for his son, for instance, by setting him up in business abroad.[13] This doctrine, that a change in the father's domicil is necessarily communicated to the child, is generally laid down in absolute terms, but it has been altered by the Domicile and Matrimonial Proceedings Act 1973[14] in the one case where both parents[15] are alive but are living apart. In such a case the child's domicil is that of the mother, if the child has his home with her and no home with his father,[16] or if he has acquired his mother's domicil in this way and has not since then had a home with his father.[17] This latter provision means that a child who has his home with his mother keeps her domicil, though he ceases to live with her, provided he does not later have a home with his father. Furthermore, a child who has his mother's domicil by reason of these provisions continues to retain it after her death unless and until he has a home with his father.[18]

Two points should be stressed in relation to these statutory provisions. They apply only to the determination of a child's dependent domicil and do not appear to affect the determination of his domicil of origin. Thus, a child born of parents who are married but living apart at the time of his birth would appear to acquire his father's domicil as his domicil of origin[19] but, immediately thereafter, a domicil of dependence with his mother, where his home is. Secondly, these provisions apply only to the case where both parents are alive and are living apart, and provided the child is legitimate[20] or adopted.[1] It is unfortunate that other cases giving rise to problems relating

9 Eg *Alhaji Mohamed v Knott* [1969] 1 QB 1, [1968] 2 All ER 563.
10 Hereafter described as a "child".
11 The position of an adopted child is equated to that of a child born in wedlock: Adoption Act 1976, s 39.
12 *D'Etchegoyen v D'Etchegoyen* (1888) 13 PD 132. As to whether a change in a guardian's domicil is communicated to his ward, see Spiro (1956) 5 ICLQ 196 et seq.
13 Wolff, p 117.
14 S 4(1); see *Williams, Petr* 1977 SLT (Notes) 2. The equivalent in Australia is the Domicile Acts 1982, s 9; in New Zealand the Domicile Act 1976, s 6.
15 Including adoptive parents: Adoption Act 1976, s 39. Section 4(5) of the Domicile and Matrimonial Proceedings Act 1973 was repealed in its application to adopted children by the Children Act 1975, Sch 4, Pt I.
16 S 4(2)(a). On the meaning of "home", see *Re P (GE) (An Infant)* [1965] Ch 568 at 585–586; *Re Y (Minors) (Adoption: Jurisdiction)* [1985] Fam 136.
17 S 4(2)(b).
18 S 4(3).
19 See Palmer (1974) 4 Fam Law 35, 36; cf Dicey & Morris, p 126, where it is suggested that a child, born to parents who have been divorced, takes his mother's domicil at birth.
20 S 4(4).
1 Adoption Act 1976, ss 38, 39.

to a child's dependent domicil are left to be dealt with by the common law.[2] If a father, on the death of his wife, abandons his children and acquires a fresh domicil elsewhere, and the children are left to be cared for by grand parents, their domicil is still decided by obscure common law rules. However, it seems most unlikely that a court would affirm the inevitability of the application of the father's domicil. This was the view at common law, taken by Lord MACDERMOTT LCJ in the Northern Ireland case of *Hope v Hope*,[3] of the situation where the mother was alive, where he characterised the capacity of a father to change the domicil of his minor child as "a manifestation of parental authority and responsibility". Therefore he asked: "why should it apply to tie the domicil of the child to the will of a father who has abjured his responsibility by walking out of his child's life?"[4] It is suggested that this view is still valid in those cases unaffected by the Domicile and Matrimonial Proceedings Act 1973.

The domicil that a child acquires by reason of his father or mother moving to another country is a domicil of choice, or better perhaps of quasi-choice,[5] and his domicil of origin continues to be that imposed upon him at birth.[6] This rule may become important at a later stage in his life. For instance, a father, domiciled in England at the time of his son's birth, acquires a domicil of choice in France and retains it until after his son reaches the age of 16. At the age of twenty-five, the son acquires a domicil of choice in Italy, but later abandons that country for good and dies without having acquired another permanent home. In these circumstances, the English domicil will revive on the loss of his Italian domicil and English law will govern testamentary or intestate succession to his movables.

A child acquires, on the death of his father, the domicil of his mother.[7] The question that has arisen here is whether such a child's domicil continues to follow that of the mother, or whether there are any circumstances in which it will remain unaffected by her acts. The general doctrine is that if after the death of the father the child continues to live with the mother, then any new domicil acquired by the mother is prima facie to be regarded as communicated to the child.[8] But this is not necessarily so. It is recognised that the mother is empowered to change her children's domicil either by taking them to a new domicil acquired by her, or by leaving them where their father was domiciled at the time of his death[9] or even, it would seem, by placing them in another country under the care of a competent person. But this power must be exercised bona fide and with the sole object of promoting the welfare of the children. Thus, even the prima facie rule, that a new domicil acquired by the mother is communicated to her children, is displaced if this is disadvantageous to them or if the change of domicil is due to some fraudulent

---

2 See Palmer (1974) 4 Fam Law 35, 36–38.

3 [1968] NI 1; not following the Scottish decision in *Shanks v Shanks* 1965 SLT 330; cf *Re B (S) (An Infant)* [1968] Ch 204 at 208.

4 [1968] NI 1 at 5; and see Carter (1968–69) 43 BYBIL 239.

5 *Harrison v Harrison* [1953] 1 WLR 865, suggested by counsel at 866.

6 *Henderson v Henderson* [1967] P 77, [1965] 1 All ER 179.

7 *Potinger v Wightman* (1817) 3 Mer 67. The domicil of a child whose father is dead, or of an illegitimate child, is unaffected by s 4 of the Domicile and Matrimonial Proceedings Act 1973: s 4(4). For Australia see the Domicile Acts 1982, s 9; for New Zealand the Domicile Act 1976, s 6.

8 *Johnstone v Beattie* (1843) 10 Cl & Fin 42 at 138.

9 *Re Beaumont* [1893] 3 Ch 490; *Re G* [1966] NZLR 1028; Blaikie [1984] Jur Rev 1 at 4 et seq. This power would go under the Law Commissions' proposals, see infra, p 162.

design on her part, as, for example, where her motive is to take advantage of a law of succession more beneficial to herself.[10]

(iv) The Law Commissions' proposals[11]

The Law Commissions have criticised the present rules governing the domicil of children on the basis that they "discriminate between legitimate and illegitimate children and between their fathers and mothers. They also fail to deal adequately with the cases where a child is abandoned, his parents die, the child is fostered or is taken into the care of a local authority."[12] They have recommended that, instead of a dependency rule, the basic rule should be that a child is domiciled in the country with which he is for the time being most closely connected.[13] In order to provide certainty there would be rebuttable presumptions for determining the country of closest connection. Thus, for example, in cases "where the child's parents are domiciled in the same country and he has his home with either or both of them, it is to be presumed unless the contrary is shown, that the child is most closely connected with that country".[14] There is a separate presumption to deal with cases where the child's parents are not domiciled in the same country. According to this, if the child has its home with one of the parents it is presumed to be most closely connected with the country in which that parent is domiciled.

(b) MENTAL DISORDER

Although there is no direct authority, it is generally agreed that the domicil of a mentally disordered person cannot be changed either by himself, since he is incapable of forming an intention, or by the person to whose care he has been entrusted.[15] Of course, in accordance with the general principle applicable to children, the domicil of the father will be communicated to a child of unsound mind during the childhood of the latter, but a somewhat irrational distinction has been suggested as regards an adult who is mentally disordered. If he has been continuously disordered both during childhood and after the age of 16, it is said that his domicil will continue to change with that of his father; but that if he first becomes disordered after reaching the age of 16, his then domicil becomes indelible, for if the power of changing it were vested in the father great danger might be done to "the interests of others".[16] There are two possible solutions, though neither is yet supported by authority in England. First, as the paramount consideration is the interest of the mentally disordered person, not of others, it might be advisable that the Court of Protection should be entitled to change his domicil if this appears to be for his benefit. The Law Commissions have recommended an alternative approach which is that an adult who is mentally disordered should be

---

10 *Potinger v Wightman* (1817) 3 Mer 67 at 79, 80.
11 Law Com No 168 (1987), Scot Law Com No 107 (1987), part IV.
12 Para 3(2) (d).
13 Cf Law Com Working Paper No 88 (1985), Scot Law Com Consultative Memorandum No 63 (1985), Part IV.
14 Para 4.15.
15 *Urquhart v Butterfield* (1887) 37 ChD 357 at 382; and see *Bempde v Johnstone* (1796) 3 Ves 198; *Sharpe v Crispin* (1869) LR 1 P & D 611; Dicey & Morris, pp 161–162; Westlake, p 251; cf *Re G* [1966] NZLR 1028.
16 *Sharpe v Crispin* (1869) LR 1 P & D 611 at 618.

domiciled in the country with which he is for the time being most closely connected.[17]

(c) CAPACITY TO ACQUIRE A DOMICIL

It has been suggested that the capacity of a dependent person to acquire a fresh domicil is not always governed by English law, the law of the forum. Such a possibility was adumbrated obiter in an English case in 1887,[18] and more recently it has been canvassed by Graveson.[19] It is submitted, however, that this thesis is based upon a fundamental misconception, since it overlooks the fact that domicil is no more than a connecting factor. Its acquisition is not *itself* a problem for the solution of which a rule for the choice of law is required. For the connecting factor in any English choice of law rule must logically always be interpreted according to English notions.[20]

6. DOMICIL OF MARRIED WOMEN[21]

(a) THE ABOLITION OF DEPENDENCY

Until 1974, the rule was that the domicil of a husband was communicated to his wife immediately on marriage and it was necessarily and inevitably retained by her for the duration of the marriage. This rule was much criticised as "the last barbarous relic of a wife's servitude"[22] and was abolished by section 1 of the Domicile and Matrimonial Proceedings Act 1973.[23] The domicil of a married woman as at any time on or after 1st January 1974 "shall, instead of being the same as her husband's by virtue only of marriage, be ascertained by reference to the same factors as in the case of any other individual capable of having an independent domicile".

This means that for all purposes[24] a married woman is to be treated as capable of acquiring a separate domicil; though in the vast majority of cases she and her husband will, independently, acquire the same domicil. It is, however, quite possible for happily married spouses to have separate domicils as where, for example, a student at an English university who is domiciled in New York marries a fellow student domiciled in England, both intending at the end of their studies to go to live in New York.[1]

(b) TRANSITIONAL PROBLEMS

The 1973 Act deals also with the transitional problem of the domicil of dependence of a wife acquired before 1974. A woman, married before 1974, who, therefore, acquired her husband's domicil on marriage, is to be treated

---

17 Law Com No 168 (1987), Scot Law Com No 107 (1987), Part IV.
18 *Urquhart v Butterfield* (1887) 37 Ch D 357 at 384.
19 (1950) 3 ILQ 149; and see Mendes da Costa, *Studies in Canadian Family Law* (1972), Vol II, pp 914–916; cf Nygh, pp 184–185; New Zealand Domicile Act 1976, s 5(2).
20 *Re Martin* [1900] P 211 at 227; *Re Annesley* [1926] Ch 692 at 705.
21 Palmer (1974) 124 NLJ 49, 73, 95.
22 *Gray v Formosa* [1963] P 259 at 267; and see *Adams v Adams* [1971] P 188 at 216.
23 S 1.
24 Earlier proposals for reform had been more limited and proposed a separate domicil for limited purposes, mainly matrimonial jurisdiction; see eg the Royal Commission on Marriage & Divorce (1956), Cmnd 9678, para 825; the Domicile Bill (1959); Law Com No 48 (1972) paras 27–34.
1 See *Puttick v A-G* [1980] Fam 1 at 17; *IRC v Duchess of Portland* [1982] Ch 314 at 319–320.

as retaining that domicil as a domicil of choice if it was not the wife's own domicil of origin, until it is changed by acquisition of a new domicil of choice or revival of the domicil of origin on or after 1st January 1974.[2] This means that, after that date, the wife's domicil is to be treated not as dependent on her husband but as her own domicil of origin, or of choice, until she acquires a new domicil of choice or until her domicil of origin revives.[3] The operation of these transitional provisions is shown in *IRC v Duchess of Portland*:[4]

> The taxpayer, who had a domicil of origin in Canada, married her husband, an English domiciliary, in 1948, thereby acquiring an English domicil of dependency. The couple set up home in England. However, the taxpayer, throughout her marriage, maintained close links with Canada, including retaining a bank account, owning a house and returning for visits for ten to twelve weeks each year. It was agreed that when her husband retired they would both live permanently in Canada. The taxpayer was assessed to income tax for the years 1973–1978 on the basis that she was domiciled in England throughout that period. She appealed against this decision to the special commissioners who held that during the period in question the taxpayer had been domiciled in Quebec, since her domicil of origin had revived after the coming into force of the Domicile and Matrimonial Proceedings Act 1973. The Crown appealed.

NOURSE J, allowing the appeal, held that the taxpayer had not reacquired her domicil of origin in Canada and retained her domicil of choice in England during the period in question. He reasoned as follows: the 1973 Act turned the taxpayer's domicil of dependency into one of choice; she had not abandoned this English domicil of choice, notwithstanding her intention to return to Canada, since she had not ceased to reside in England.[5] The judge regarded the language of the transitional provisions as clear and said that the above construction "does not . . . lead to any result which is unjust and anomalous or absurd".[6]

These transitional provisions may give rise to a problem similar to one found at common law when the husband died. Let us take the following hypothetical case:

> H domiciled in France marries W domiciled in Scotland. They live in England. In 1972, H leaves W in England and returns to live in France. Where is W domiciled in 1974?

After 1973[7] W retains H's domicil in France as if it were a domicil of choice

---

2 Domicile and Matrimonial Proceedings Act 1973, s 1(2).
3 For a different interpretation of s 1(2) of the 1973 Act, see Wade (1983) 32 ICLQ 1, particularly at 6 et seq.
4 [1982] Ch 314; Wade, op cit, at 3 et seq; Thompson (1983) 32 ICLQ 237; Carter (1982) 53 BYBIL 295.
5 The same approach was applied earlier in *Oundjian v Oundjian* (1979) 1 FLR 198 at 202.
6 Op cit at p 320. However, the New Zealand Domicile Act 1976, ss 4 and 5 and the Australian Domicile Acts 1982, s 5(1) and (2) give a different solution. The English and Scottish Law Commissions in Law Com No 168 (1987) and Scot Law Com No 107 (1987) Part VIII, favour the Australian and New Zealand solution, and the reversal of *IRC v Duchess of Portland*. It is proposed that the new rules apply to times before the legislation comes into force but only for the purpose of determining where at a time after the legislation comes into force an individual is domiciled.
7 In considering the domicil of a married woman as at any time before 1 January 1974, the old law will apply, so that she will be regarded as incapable of acquiring a domicil independent from that of her husband.

and this will continue until she utilises her new capacity to acquire a domicil of choice in England, where she wishes to remain living. Does she acquire such an English domicil merely by continuing, and intending, to live permanently in England? On the analogy of common law decisions involving acquisition of a domicil of choice after the death of a husband,[8] W immediately acquires an English domicil and no further act on her part is necessary. Authority for this view can be found in obiter dicta in *IRC v Duchess of Portland*.[9]

7. DOMICIL, NATIONALITY AND RESIDENCE[10]

(a) NATIONALITY AND DOMICIL CONTRASTED

Nationality is a possible alternative to domicil as the criterion of the personal law. These are two different conceptions. Nationality represents a man's political status, by virtue of which he owes allegiance to some particular country; domicil indicates his civil status and it provides the law by which his personal rights and obligations are determined.[11] Nationality depends, apart from naturalisation, on the place of birth or on parentage; domicil, as we have seen, is constituted by residence in a particular country with the intention of residing there permanently. It follows that a man may be a national of one country but domiciled in another.

If one looks at the historical development, it will appear that, over the last two centuries, the ascertainment of the personal law, which ought to be governed by legal and practical considerations, has in fact been influenced by varying political and economic factors. The French revolution, the struggles of Italy to win independence, the wave of nationalism that swept Europe in the nineteenth century, the desire of the poorer countries to share in the prosperity of their emigrants—these and other similar circumstances have led to a widespread idolatry of the principle of nationality. At present many countries in Europe and South America adopt nationality as the criterion of personal law, whilst the common law jurisdictions of the Commonwealth and the USA, among others, still stand by the test of domicil.[12] As immigration has increased in western Europe since the second world war domicil has gained ground at the expense of nationality.[13]

It may be asked, what are the respective merits of domicil and nationality as a determinant of the law to govern status and personal rights generally? Each has its merits and demerits.[14]

---

8 *Re Cooke's Trusts* (1887) 56 LJ Ch 637; *Re Scullard, Smith v Brock* [1957] Ch 107, [1956] 3 All ER 898.

9 [1982] Ch 314 at 319.

10 de Winter (1969) III Hague Recueil 357–503; Nadelmann (1969) 17 AJCL 418; and see Palsson, *Marriage and Divorce in Comparative Conflict of Laws*, ch 3; North, *Private International Law of Matrimonial Causes*, pp 5–15.

11 *Udny v Udny* (1869) LR 1 Sc & Div 441 at 457.

12 In 1968 it was estimated that about 1450 million persons were subject to the law of the domicil, 1600 million to the law of the nationality, and about 350 million were citizens of countries which applied the principle of nationality to their own subjects and that of domicil to foreigners residing there: de Winter (1969) II Hague Recueil 357 at 358.

13 Pålsson (1986) IV Hague Recueil 316, 332 et seq.

14 See de Winter, op cit, pp 400–418; Kahn-Freund (1974) III Hague Recueil 139, 314, 389–391, 467–468.

(i) The merits and demerits of domicil

The English preference for domicil is based on two main grounds. First, domicil means the country in which a man has established his permanent home, and what can be more natural or more appropriate than to subject him to his home law? It is difficult to agree that he should be excommunicated from that law merely because technically he is a citizen of some State that he may have abandoned years ago.[15] Secondly, domicil furnishes the only practicable test in the case of such political units as the United Kingdom, Canada, Australia and the USA where the same nationality embraces a number of, sometimes diverse, legal systems. The expression "national law" when applied to a British subject is meaningless. It is one system in England, another in Scotland; similarly for a Canadian, there is one system in Ontario and a quite different one in Quebec.

In the course of its development in England, however, the law relating to domicil has acquired certain vices. A short mention of these will suffice here, as they have already been discussed in this chapter. First, it will not infrequently happen that the legal domicil of a man is out of touch with reality, for the exaggerated importance attributed to the domicil of origin, coupled with the technical doctrine of its revival, may well ascribe to a man a domicil in a country which by no stretch of the imagination can be called his home.[16] Secondly, an equally irrational result may ensue from the view, sometimes accepted by the English courts, that long residence is not equivalent to domicil if accompanied by the contemplation of some uncertain event the occurrence of which will cause a termination of the residence.[17] Thirdly, the ascertainment of a man's domicil depends to such an extent on proof of his intention, the most elusive of all factors, that only too often it will be impossible to identify it with certainty without recourse to the courts.[18]

(ii) The merits and demerits of nationality

Nationality, as compared with domicil, enjoys the advantages that it is relatively easy to understand as a concept and normally it is easily ascertainable.[19] Nevertheless, it is objectionable as a criterion of the personal law on at least three grounds.[20]

First, it may be a country with which the person in question has lost all connection, or with which perhaps he has never been connected. It is a strange notion, for instance, that a Neapolitan, who has emigrated to California in his youth without becoming naturalised in the USA, should throughout his life remain subject to Italian law with regard to such matters as marital and testamentary capacity. Secondly, nationality is sometimes a more fallible criterion than domicil. In the eyes of English law no man can be without a

---

15 Of course, if a country which adopts the principle of nationality also accepts the doctrine of *renvoi*, the practical result may be the substitution of the law of the domicil for the law of nationality, supra, pp 58–73.
16 Supra, pp 155 et seq.
17 Supra, pp 144 et seq.
18 Supra, pp 148 et seq.
19 See generally Law Com No 168 (1987), Scot Law Com No 107 (1987), para 3.9. It is ascertained by reference to the law of the state of the nationality concerned; eg *Oppenheimer v Cattermole* [1976] AC 249, [1975] 1 All ER 538; see also *R v Secretary of State for the Home Department, ex p Bibi* [1985] Imm AR 134.
20 North, *Private International Law of Matrimonial Causes*, pp 9–10. See also Law Com No 168 (1987), Scot Law Com No 107 (1987), paras 3.10–3.11.

domicil, no man can have more than one domicil at the same time. On the other hand, he may be stateless or may simultaneously be a citizen of two or more countries.[1] Thirdly, nationality cannot always determine the internal law to which a man is subject. This is the case, as we have seen, when one political unit such as the USA comprises a variety of legal systems. Similarly, nationality breaks down as a connecting factor in the case of the United Kingdom where, for many purposes, there is no such thing as United Kingdom law. The application of the concept of nationality in such circumstances will lead to eccentric decisions such as that given in *Re O'Keefe*.[2]

Perhaps a fair conclusion, speaking very generally, is to say that, as determinants of the personal law, nationality yields a predictable but frequently an inappropriate law; domicil yields an appropriate but frequently an unpredictable law.

This division of the world into those countries that adopt the principle of nationality and those that prefer the test of domicil is unfortunate, since it obstructs the movement for the unification of rules of private international law. The reconciliation of the opposing views is highly desirable. Moreover, whilst there has been a tendency on the Continent to substitute domicil for nationality as the test of personal law, there has been a natural reluctance to absorb the English principles in toto.[3] This has led to international efforts to reach agreement on the meaning of both domicil and also residence as connecting factors.[4] However, the gap between English and Continental law will lessen when legislation is introduced giving effect to the Law Commissions' proposals for reform of the law of domicil.[5] This will produce a new definition of "domicil", simpler and more workable and more in accord with the civil law conception of habitual home.

(b) CONCEPTS OF RESIDENCE

Dissatisfaction with nationality as a connecting factor has led to a realisation of the defects of domicil also. This has had several consequences. One has been attempts in England to reform the concept of domicil,[6] but, so far, these have been successful only in relation to the dependent domicil of children and married women.[7] Problems in the basic definition of domicil remain. However, the Law Commissions have made proposals which tackle these problems.[8] These proposals have been accepted by the Government, although legislation has not yet been introduced. None the less, the failure, over many years, to reform domicil has led, in its turn, to a tendency to reject it as a connecting factor in favour of residence.[9] One of the main forces in this direction has been the fact that the Hague Conventions have relied on "habitual residence" as a connecting factor.[10] The Rome Convention on

1 Eg *Torok v Torok* [1973] 3 All ER 101, [1973] 1 WLR 1066.
2 [1940] Ch 124, [1940] 1 All ER 216, discussed supra, pp 65–66, and *Re Johnson* [1903] 1 Ch 821.
3 Folke Schmidt (1951) 4 ILQ, pp 39–52; Cheshire, ibid, 52–59; de Winter (1969) III Hague Recueil 357, 419–423.
4 Eg Council of Europe Resolution (72) 1 on the Standardisation of the Legal Concepts of "Domicile" and of "Residence".
5 Infra, p 75.
6 Ibid.
7 Domicile and Matrimonial Proceedings Act 1973, ss 1, 3, 4, supra, pp 159–165.
8 See infra, p 75.
9 North, *Private International Law of Matrimonial Causes*, pp 10–15.
10 de Winter (1969) III Hague Recueil 357, 419–454; Cavers (1972) 21 Am ULR 475.

contract choice of law[11] also utilises this concept, but now in the commercial sphere. This has resulted in the concept being introduced into English law as legislation is passed to implement these conventions.[12] The wheel has then turned full circle as purely domestic legislation has also adopted "habitual residence" as a major connecting factor in matrimonial jurisdiction.[13] The Law Commissions, whilst acknowledging the increasing use of habitual residence as an alternative connecting factor, were firmly against any general substitution of habitual residence for domicil.[14] They were concerned that the connection between a person and a country provided by habitual residence was not sufficiently strong to justify that person's affairs always being determined by the law of that country. They were thinking in particular of the example of English expatriates working abroad, in countries such as Saudi Arabia, on long term contracts. Their personal affairs, such as their capacity to enter a marriage, should be determined by the law of England, their domicil, not by the law of Saudi Arabia, their habitual residence.

(i) Ordinary residence[15]

"Ordinary residence" has been known as a connecting factor in English law for some time. It used to form a basis for service of a writ out of the jurisdiction;[16] it used to be a basis of jurisdiction in matrimonial causes in the case of a petitioning wife;[17] it is a significant connecting factor for the purposes of immigration[18] and social security law;[19] it is an important connecting factor in taxation statutes;[20] it is the criterion used for determining eligibility for a mandatory student award from the local authority;[21] and it is the basis for determining whether a student is a home or overseas student for the purpose of payment of university fees.[22]

There is some authority on the meaning of "ordinary residence", though

---

11 See Arts 4(2) and 5, infra, pp 492–493, 495.

12 Eg Wills Act 1963, infra, pp 839 et seq; Adoption Act 1976, infra, pp 763–770; Child Abduction and Custody Act 1985, infra, pp 733–734; Family Law Act 1986, Pt II, infra, p 659 et seq; Contracts (Applicable Law) Act 1990, infra, pp 460–461.

13 Domicile and Matrimonial Proceedings Act 1973, ss 5, 6, infra, pp 631–633; Family Law Act 1986, Parts I and III, infra, pp 694–698, 722–725.

14 Law Com No 168 (1987), Scot Law Com No 107 (1987), paras 3.5–3.8. Cf Irish Law Reform Commission's Report on Domicile and Habitual Residence as Connecting Factors in the Conflict of Laws of 1983; Binchy, *Irish Conflicts of Law* pp 98–100.

15 Smart (1989) 38 ICLQ 175.

16 Ord 11, r 1(1)(*c*), of the old Rules of the Supreme Court, replaced by Ord 11, r 1(1)(a) of the new Rules; see infra, p 192.

17 Matrimonial Causes Act 1973, s 46(1)(b), repealed by the Domicile and Matrimonial Proceedings Act 1973, s 17(2), Sch 6.

18 Immigration Act 1971, s 2(1)(c); Evans, *Immigration Law*, pp 44–46; *Man Chiu Yu v Secretary of State for the Home Department* [1981] Imm AR 161; it must be questionable whether the case would now be decided the same way in the light of the decisions in *R v Barnet London Borough, ex p Shah* [1983] 2 AC 309, [1983] 1 All ER 226; *R v Secretary of State for the Home Department, ex p Margueritte* [1983] QB 180, [1982] 3 All ER 909 (acquisition of UK citizenship); *Britto v Secretary of State for the Home Department* [1984] Imm AR 93.

19 Eg National Insurance Decision No R (P) 1/72; Calvert, *Social Security Law*, (2nd edn), pp 49–50; Ogus and Barendt, *The Law of Social Security*, (3rd edn), p 364.

20 See *Levene v Inland Revenue Comrs* [1928] AC 217; *Inland Revenue Comrs v Lysaght* [1928] AC 234; *Reed v Clark* [1986] Ch 1.

21 Education Act 1962, s 1(1)(a), as amended by the Education Act 1980, s 19 and Sch 5; *R v Barnet London Borough, ex p Shah* [1983] 2 AC 309, [1983] 1 All ER 226; *R v Lancashire County Council, ex p Huddleston* [1986] 2 All ER 941.

22 See *Orphanos v Queen Mary College* [1985] AC 761, [1985] 2 All ER 233.

its precise meaning has caused difficulty.[23] One judge went so far as to say that the adjective adds nothing to the noun.[24] However, Lord SCARMAN in giving the judgment of the House of Lords in *R v Barnet London Borough, ex p Shah*,[1] said that this adjective brings out two important features of ordinary residence, namely residence must be adopted voluntarily, ie not by virtue of kidnapping or imprisonment, and for settled purposes, which can include for the purposes of "education, business or profession, employment, health, family or merely love of the place".[2] The words "ordinary residence" should be given their natural and ordinary meaning, which will be the same regardless of the context, unless it can be shown that the statutory framework requires a different meaning.[3] Ordinary residence does not connote continuous physical presence, but physical presence with some degree of continuity, notwithstanding occasional temporary absences.[4] There must, however, be some physical presence. Intention to reside is not, alone, sufficient.[5] A person cannot rely on his unlawful presence, eg in breach of the immigration laws, to constitute *ordinary* residence.[6]

Each case must, of course, depend on its own peculiar facts, but the authorities show that even absence for a considerable time will not terminate a person's ordinary residence if it is due to some specific and unusual cause, as for instance when a wife accompanies her husband during his employment in a foreign country.[7] Again, the significance of a comparatively prolonged absence will be weakened if, during the relevant period, the *propositus* has maintained a house or flat in England ready for immediate occupation.[8]

(ii) Habitual residence[9]

There is now some authority on the meaning of "habitual residence". One decision where the meaning of the concept and its inter-relation with domicil was considered is *Cruse v Chittum*.[10] The court had to determine whether a spouse had been habitually resident in Mississippi for the purposes of deciding whether to recognise a divorce obtained in that State.[11] Habitual residence could be summed up as "a regular physical presence which must endure for some time".[12] It does not require continual physical presence and can continue

23 McClean (1962) 11 ICLQ 1153, 1161–1166.
24 *Hopkins v Hopkins* [1951] P 116 at 121–122.
1 [1983] 2 AC 309 at 342. Lord SCARMAN was referring to the adverb "habitually" but he equated this with "ordinarily".
2 Ibid, at 344; *Britto v Secretary of State for the Home Department* [1984] Imm AR 93.
3 Ibid, at pp 341–343.
4 *Levene v Inland Revenue Comrs* [1928] AC 217 at 232; *R v Barnet London Borough, ex p Shah* [1983] 2 AC 309, at 341–342; *R v Immigration Appeal Tribunal, ex p Siggins* [1985] Imm AR 14; *Re Vassis* (1986) 64 ALR 407.
5 National Insurance Decision No R(P) 1/72.
6 *R v Barnet London Borough, ex p Shah* [1983] 2 AC 309, at 343–344, 349. See also *R v Secretary of State for the Home Department, ex p Marguerrite* [1983] QB 180, [1982] 3 All ER 909; s 50(5) British Nationality Act 1981; *Immigration Appeal Tribunal v Chelliah* [1985] Imm AR 192. On the lawfulness of a person's residence and the qualification to vote see *Hipperson v Newbury District Electoral Registration Officer* [1985] QB 1060, [1985] 2 All ER 456.
7 *Stransky v Stransky* [1954] P 428, [1954] 2 All ER 536; *Lewis v Lewis* [1956] 1 All ER 375, [1956] 1 WLR 200; *R v Barnet London Borough, ex p Shah*, op cit, at 343.
8 Ibid, and see *Casey v Casey* 1968 SLT 56.
9 de Winter (1969) III Hague Recueil 357; Hall (1975) 24 ICLQ 1; and see Council of Europe Resolution 72(1): Standardisation of the Legal Concepts of "Domicile" and "Residence".
10 [1974] 2 All ER 940.
11 See now the Family Law Act 1986, s 46, infra, p 659.
12 [1974] 2 All ER 940 at 943.

despite considerable periods of absence.[13] Habitual residence appears to be different from domicil in that the element of "animus" required is weaker. Indeed, it ought to be a requirement of present intention to reside unlike the intention required in domicil which is concerned with whether there is a future intention to live elsewhere. No more than a present intention to reside should be necessary for habitual residence and this ought to be assumed from the fact of continuous residence. It is impossible to say in the abstract how long this period of residence must be. It will all depend on the circumstances. In *V v B (A Minor) (Abduction)*[14] an habitual residence was acquired after less than three months residence in Australia, the parties, according to the plaintiff, having decided to settle there. Whilst in another case the Court of Appeal of Alberta[15] held that two short periods of a few months each were not sufficient to establish an habitual residence in Hawaii. The House of Lords in *Re J (A Minor) (Abduction: Custody Rights)*[16] held that residence for an "appreciable period of time and a settled intention"[17] to reside on a long-term basis are needed for acquisition of a new habitual residence. On the other hand, a person can cease to be habitually resident in a country in a single day if he or she leaves it with a settled intention not to return but to take up long-term residence elsewhere. It follows that a person may, for a time, not be habitually resident in any country. Domicil is a legal concept, whereas habitual residence is far more a question of fact[18] and one without the various legal artificialities of domicil,[19] such as the doctrine of revival.[20]

What is questionable is whether there is any difference between habitual residence and ordinary residence. In *Cruse v Chittum* LANE J said that the two concepts were different, with habitual residence being more akin to the residence required for the acquisition of a domicil of choice.[21] However, this must now be regarded as wrong in the light of the House of Lords decision in *R v Barnet London Borough, ex p Shah*, in which, seemingly, habitual residence was equated with ordinary residence.[22] This was certainly the view of BUSH J in *Kapur v Kapur*.[23] In this case it was held that an Indian domiciliary who had been ordinarily resident in England for one year for educational purposes, under the House of Lords definition of ordinary residence, was therefore, necessarily, habitually resident in England for the same period when it came to the question of jurisdiction to entertain proceedings for divorce. Similarly in *V v B (A Minor) (Abduction)*[24] it was held that habitual residence for the purposes of the Hague Convention on the Civil Aspects of International Child Abduction was to be equated with ordinary residence. If this view of habitual residence is correct, and it is hard to deny, one conse-

---

13 *Oundjian v Oundjian* (1979) 1 FLR 198, where over one third of the period was spent abroad.
14 [1991] FCR 451, [1991] 1 FLR 266.
15 *Adderson v Adderson* (1987) 36 DLR (4th) 631. Cf *Pershadsingh v Pershadsingh* (1987) 60 OR (2d) 437, which involved purchasing a house and living in Ontario for two years.
16 [1990] 2 AC 562.
17 Ibid, at 578–579.
18 *In Re J (A Minor) (Abduction: Custody Rights)* [1990] 2 AC 562 at 578; de Winter, op cit, p 428; and see Law Com No 34 (1970), p 15.
19 See *Re S (A Minor) (Abduction)* [1991] 2 FLR 1 at 20.
20 Supra, pp 157–158.
21 [1974] 2 All ER 940 at 943. Cf *R v Secretary of State for the Home Department, ex p Margueritte* [1982] 3 All ER 909 at 913.
22 [1983] 2 AC 309 at 340, 342, 349; cf *Adderson v Adderson*, op cit, at 197.
23 [1984] FLR 920, infra pp 631–632.
24 [1991] 1 FLR 266 at 271–272.

quence of this is that a man may have an habitual residence in more than one country,[25] since it is well established that it is possible to be ordinarily resident in more than one country.[26]

8. THE POSITION OF CORPORATIONS[1]

A connection with a particular country must be assigned to a corporation in order that the different rights and obligations by which it is affected may be determinable by the appropriate system of law. The subject is not free from difficulty, for the facts, such as nationality, domicil and residence, which connect the individual with a country are at first sight a little incongruous with the nature of an artificial person. Reasoning based on the analogy of a human being is apt to appear somewhat forced and strained. Nevertheless, the analogy has in general been followed by the courts, and the result of their decisions is that in the eyes of the law a corporation may be connected with a particular country by reason of any one of the following factors: presence, residence, domicil, nationality. Each of these requires separate treatment, since the country whose law governs the various matters concerning a corporation varies with the character of the questions requiring a decision.

(i) Presence

The determination of whether a corporation is present in England will be examined later in the context of the jurisdiction of the English court.[2]

(ii) Residence

The determination of the residence of a company is of major significance in the field of taxation.[3] A company is regarded by the law as resident in the country where the centre of control exists, ie where the seat and directing power of the affairs of the company are located. The place of incorporation is only one of the evidentiary facts to be considered in the course of ascertaining where the control resides. This test of control was laid down by the Exchequer Division in *Cesena Sulphur Co v Nicholson*,[4] a decision which has been repeatedly approved and followed,[5] and which, it has been said, cannot now be overruled.[6]

The Cesena company was incorporated in England under the Companies Acts 1862 and 1867 for the purpose of taking over and working sulphur mines at Cesena in Italy. The practical business of manufacturing and selling the sulphur was administered by an Italian delegation, including the managing director, who was permanently resident at Cesena. No

---

25 Cf Blom (1973) 22 ICLQ 109, 136.
26 Eg *IRC v Lysaght* [1928] AC 234; *Hopkins v Hopkins* [1951] P 116, [1950] 2 All ER 1035; *R v Barnet London Borough, ex p Shah* [1983] 2 AC 309, at 342; *Britto v Secretary of State for the Home Department* [1984] Imm AR 93.
1 Farnsworth, *The Residence and Domicil of Corporations.* For other literature see Young (1908) 22 HLR 1; Schuster (1917) 2 Grotius Society 57; Vaughan Williams and Chrussachi (1933) 49 LQR 334; Drucker (1968) 17 ICLQ 28.
2 Infra, pp 185 et seq.
3 See Tiley, *Revenue Law* (3rd edn), paras 36.15 et seq.
4 (1876) 1 Ex D 428.
5 *San Paulo (Brazilian) Rail Co Ltd v Carter* [1896] AC 31; *Goerz v Bell* [1904] 2 KB 136; *De Beers Consolidated Mines v Howe* [1906] AC 455; *American Thread Co v Joyce* (1913) 108 LT 353.
6 *Egyptian Delta Land and Investment Co v Todd* [1929] AC 1 at 19.

products were ever sent to England, the books of account were kept in Italy, the company was registered in Italy and two-thirds of the shareholders were resident Italians. Taken by themselves, these facts went to show that the centre of business was in Italy. As against them, however, the memorandum of association set up a Board of Directors in London which controlled the "sale, order, direction, and management" of "the working of the company's mines, the mode of the disposal thereof, and the general business of the company". The shareholders' meetings were held in London, and it was there that dividends were declared.

In the result it was held that, since almost every act of the company connected with its management was done in London, the main place of business was in London, and that therefore the company was resident in England. By reason of this residence it was liable to pay income tax on the whole of its profits, wherever earned.

Thirty years later any doubt that might have lingered as to whether central control was the correct test of residence for tax purposes was dispelled by the House of Lords in the leading case of *De Beers Consolidated Mines Ltd v Howe.*[7] This company, unlike the Cesena company, was incorporated not in England but in South Africa, where the whole of its profits were made from the mining and disposal of diamonds. The directors met both in South Africa and in London, but the majority of them resided and met in London, and it was found as a fact that the chief control of the company's affairs resided in the hands of the London board. Thus, the profits, though arising entirely from the raising and sale of diamonds in South Africa, were subject to income tax. Lord LOREBURN, in a well-known passage, said that the analogy of an individual should be applied. "We ought therefore to see where it really keeps house and does business ... the real business is carried on where the central management and control actually abide."[8]

One result of these decisions is to fix the residence of a corporation in the country where it is in fact controlled, not necessarily where, according to its constitution, it ought to be controlled.[9] Thus, if a subsidiary company, with its own board of directors, is registered abroad but is in fact controlled by its owners, a company resident in England, it is itself resident in England, notwithstanding that such external control may be unauthorised by its memorandum or articles of association.[10]

The natural inference from the above decisions is that for taxation purposes it is impossible for a company to have simultaneous residences in two or more countries since a company cannot, according to the ordinary use of language, have a central control and management in more than one place.[11] Nevertheless, the matter cannot be dismissed in this summary though sensible fashion without considering two more leading cases, *Swedish Central Rail Co Ltd v Thompson*[12] and *Egyptian Delta Land and Investment Co v Todd.*[13]

---

7 [1906] AC 455. The residence of a company for the purposes of service of a writ is a different matter, see *Kwok Chi Leung Karl v Com of Estate Duty* [1988] 1 WLR 1035 at 1041.
8 Op cit at 458.
9 *Unit Construction Co Ltd v Bullock (Inspector of Taxes)* [1960] AC 351, [1959] 3 All ER 831.
10 Ibid.
11 *Swedish Central Rail Co Ltd v Thompson* [1925] AC 495 at 508; see also ATKIN LJ in the court below [1924] 2 KB 255 at 274.
12 Supra.
13 [1929] AC 1.

In each of these cases the company was an investment company, ie of a passive or static nature, not engaged in active trading operation, but interested solely in the receipt of money arising abroad. In each, the question was whether the company was liable, as being resident in England, for income tax on such money. There were certain similarities in the facts of each case.[14] In the *Swedish Case*:

The company was incorporated in England in 1870 with the object of constructing and running a railway in Sweden. Its registered office was in London. In 1900 it leased the railway to a traffic company for 50 years at an annual rent of £33,500 payable in England. In the same year the articles of association were altered so as to remove the control and management to Sweden, and after that time the general meetings of shareholders (most of whom were Swedish) and the meetings of the directors were held at Stockholm. Dividends were declared there and no profits were transmitted to England except in the shape of dividends due to the English shareholders. On the other hand, a committee which met regularly was established in London to deal with share transfers, to draft and attach the seal to share certificates and to sign cheques on the London banking account. The secretary resided in London and it was there that the annual accounts were made up and audited.

In the *Egyptian Case*:

The company was incorporated in England in 1904 for the purpose of acquiring and disposing of any land served by the Egyptian Delta Railways Ltd. Since 1907 the business had been controlled, managed and directed entirely in Cairo. The secretary-general, all the directors, the seal, share register, books and bank account were in Cairo.

In order to satisfy the requirements of the 1908 Companies Act, there was a registered office in London where the necessary lists and registers were kept. This office did not consist of a separate room. All that the company did was to employ a Mr Horne, who carried on the business of secretary of public companies, to keep the necessary documents and to post the name of the company on the door of his office.

The Crown claimed income tax in respect of interest accruing from mortgages and leases of land made in Egypt.

It was held by the House of Lords in the *Swedish Case* that the company was resident both in England and in Sweden; in the *Egyptian Case* that the company was resident only in Egypt.

These two decisions confuse rather than enlighten the law. It is clear, of course, that the business done in England was of a far more substantial character in the *Swedish* than in the *Egyptian Case*. It is also clear that the contention of the Crown in the *Egyptian Case*, that a company is inevitably resident in the country where it has been incorporated and where its registered office is situated, was untenable, for if this were so the decisions in the Cesena type of case would have been put on that short and simple ground. Nevertheless, how is the decision in the *Swedish Case* to be reconciled with the rule, established by the House of Lords, that a company resides where its real business is carried on and that the real business is carried on where the central control and management abide? It can scarcely be said, as

14 For an analysis of them in parallel columns see Farnsworth, op cit, p 107.

POLLOCK MR said, that this is not the only test.[15] If words mean anything, there is a natural reluctance to accept the statement of Lord CAVE that "the *central* control and management of a company may be divided".[16] Again, it is difficult to resist the conclusion that Lord SUMNER, in explaining away the *Swedish* decision by the remark that the business done in London was little less important than that transacted in Sweden, virtually repudiated the principle of central control. Nevertheless, the joint effect of the Swedish and Egyptian decisions seems to be that, if the control is so evenly divided between two or more countries as to preclude the possibility of identifying one place of central control, then the company must be regarded as resident in each country in which to a substantial degree control is in fact exercised.[17]

(iii) Domicil[18]

Questions concerning the status of a body of persons associated together for some enterprise, including the fundamental question whether it possesses the attribute of legal personality, must on principle be governed by the same law that governs the status of the individual, ie by the law of the domicil. What this law is admits of no doubt if we reason on the analogy of the individual. Every person, natural and artificial, acquires at birth a domicil of origin by operation of law. In the case of the legitimate natural person it is the domicil of his father; in the case of the juristic person it is the country in which it is born, ie in which it is incorporated.[19] If it is a corporation, it can be so only by virtue of the law by which it was incorporated. It is to this law alone that all questions concerning the creation and dissolution of the corporate status are referred.[20]

Thus the tests of domicil and of residence are different. A company is resident where its control and management abide; it is domiciled where it is incorporated.[1] But the domicil of a corporation has this peculiarity, that it cannot be changed. It cannot be converted into a domicil of choice. "The domicil of origin, or the domicil of birth, using with respect to a company a familiar metaphor, clings to it throughout its existence."[2] However, it has been suggested that, although a corporation cannot of its own volition change its domicil, the law of the domicil, if its internal rules so admit, may refer the particular issue to another system of law.[3]

It must finally be mentioned that the domicil is an important basis of jurisdiction in civil and commercial matters and in this context when it comes to companies, the seat of a corporation is treated as its domicil. As will be

---

15 *Swedish Central Rly Co Ltd v Thompson* [1924] 2 KB 255 at 265. For a different way of reconciling the cases see Lipstein [1989] Lloyd's MCLQ 385 at 386.
16 Ibid, [1925] AC 495 at 501.
17 See the remarks of Lord SIMONDS and Lord RADCLIFFE in *Unit Construction Co Ltd v Bullock (Inspector of Taxes)* [1960] AC 351 at 360–361, 367–369, [1959] 3 All ER 831 at 833, 834, 836–838.
18 See generally Farnsworth, op cit, pp 201 et seq; Smart [1990] JBL 126—for the problem of multiple incorporation.
19 *Gasque v IRC* [1940] 2 KB 80.
20 *Lazard Brothers & Co v Midland Bank Ltd* [1933] AC 289 at 297.
 1 *A-G v Jewish Colonisation Association* [1990] 2 QB 556.
 2 *Gasque v IRC* [1940] 2 KB 80 at 84, applying the statement of SARGANT LJ in *Todd v Egyptian Land and Investment Co* [1928] 1 KB 152 at 173; *Kuenigl v Donnersmarck* [1955] 1 QB 515 at 535.
 3 *Carl Zeiss Stiftung v Rayner and Keeler Ltd (No 3)* [1970] Ch 506 at 544; and see Nygh (1976) 12 UWALR 467.

seen,[4] the seat of a corporation is a technical concept which is defined by statute.[5] It must be stressed, however, that this statutory definition only applies for the purpose of the statute in question.

(iv) Nationality

The test of the nationality of a corporation according to English law is the country of its incorporation,[6] but according to most Continental laws the country where its centre of management exists.[7] It is seldom, however, that its nationality will be relevant to a question of the English conflict of laws.

9. REFORM[8]

Previous attempts at the wholesale reform of the law of domicil[9] have been unsuccessful because they were thought to be too radical. However, the English and Scottish Law Commissions[10] have recently put forward in a joint Report a set of proposals for reform of the major rules which, at least as regards the ease of change of a domicil, are more conservative. The Law Commissions' recommendations, which have already been examined,[11] have been accepted by the Government, and legislation will be introduced when a suitable opportunity arises.[12] These proposals have been strongly influenced by the reform of this area of law in New Zealand,[13] Australia[14] and Canada.[15]

When it comes to domicil issues other than that of ease of change of domicil, a bolder line has been taken, leading to major improvements in the law. The abolition of the domicils of origin,[16] choice and dependency, and their replacement by a domicil for children and a domicil for adults willl greatly simplify the position. The recommended rules on the domicil of children[17] will ensure that a child will have a domicil in a state in which it has a close conection. All in all, the Law Commissions' proposals represent "a further important step in the process of improving the structure, effectiveness and fairness of the rules of domicile".[18]

---

4 Infra, p 285.
5 Civil Jurisdiction and Judgments Act 1982, s 42; as amended by para 17, Sch 2 of the Civil Jurisdiction and Judgments Act 1991.
6 *Janson v Driefontein Consolidated Mines Ltd* [1902] AC 484 at 497, 498, 501, 505; *A-G v Jewish Colonisation Association* [1901] 1 KB 123 at 135. See the dicta collected and set out by Farnsworth, op cit, pp 302, 303; *Kuenigl v Donnersmarck* [1955] 1 QB 515 at 535, 536, [1955] 1 All ER 46 at 52, 53.
7 Wolff, p 308.
8 See Carter (1987) 36 ICLQ 713; North (1990) I Hague Recueil 13, 34–48.
9 See the Private International Law Committee's first report (Cmnd 9068 of 1954) and its seventh report (Cmnd 1955 of 1963); M Mann (1963) 12 ICLQ 1326.
10 Law Com No 168; Scot Law Com No 107 (1987). This follows Law Com Working Paper No 88 (1985), Scot Law Com Consultative Memorandum No 63; on which see Fawcett (1986) 49 MLR 225; Fentiman (1986) 6 OLJS 353.
11 Supra, pp 150–151, 158–159, 162.
12 Attorney-General, Hansard (HC) 17 Oct 1991, vol 196 col 177.
13 Domicile Act 1976.
14 Domicile Acts 1982.
15 The Domicile and Habitual Residence Act 1983 of Manitoba.
16 Supra, p 158.
17 Supra, p 162.
18 North, op cit, p 45.

Part III

Jurisdiction, foreign judgments and awards

SUMMARY

Chapter 10

Jurisdiction of the English courts—an introduction

SUMMARY

"Jurisdiction" is a word susceptible of several different meanings, but in the present account it is used in its widest sense to refer to the question of whether an English court will hear and determine an issue upon which its decision is sought. The position is complicated by the fact that there are now four separate sets of rules determining the jurisdiction of English courts. First, there are the traditional rules. Second, there are the rules under the European Community Convention on Jurisdiction and the Enforcement of Judgments in Civil and Commercial Matters (the Brussels Convention). Third, there are the rules contained in a modified version of the Brussels Convention (the Modified Convention). Fourth, there are the rules under the EC/EFTA Convention (the Lugano Convention).

1. JURISDICTION UNDER THE TRADITIONAL RULES

The traditional rules on jurisdiction are still applicable in cases falling outside the Brussels and Lugano Conventions and the Modified Convention. Before the implementation of the Brussels and Lugano Conventions by the Civil Jurisdiction and Judgments Acts 1982 and 1991 these rules were applied in all cases, and their historical roots make it appropriate to refer to them as the traditional rules.

Jurisdiction under the traditional rules involves three major issues:

(i) Whether the English courts have power to hear the case As will be seen in the next chapter, the competence of the courts to hear a case is a procedural matter and is dependent on the service of a writ on the defendant. A writ can be served on the defendant if he is present within the jurisdiction, if he submits to the jurisdiction of the English courts, or if the courts authorise service of a writ out of the jurisdiction under Order 11 of the Rules of the Supreme Court.

(ii) Whether the court will decline jurisdiction or stay the proceedings Notwithstanding that it is competent to hear the case, the court can decline jurisdiction or stay the proceedings in cases where the doctrine of *forum non conveniens* applies or where a decision to proceed with the case would be contrary to an exclusive jurisdiction clause or an arbitration clause. The courts' discretionary powers to refuse to take jurisdiction will be discussed in Chapter 12.

(iii) Whether there is a limitation upon the exercise of jurisdiction. Even though there has been service of process, the jurisdiction of the courts is subject to certain limitations, the effect of which is to render the court incompetent to determine the issue. These limitations relate to the subject matter of the issue (eg the case involves foreign land); the kind of relief sought (eg the case involves granting a divorce); and the persons between whom the issue is joined (eg the defendant is a foreign sovereign State). There are also certain statutory limitations on jurisdiction which derive from international conventions (eg the case involves international carriage by air). These limitations will be discussed in Chapter 13.

2. JURISDICTION UNDER THE BRUSSELS CONVENTION

In broad terms, the rules on jurisdiction contained in the Brussels Convention apply where:

(a) the matter is within the scope of the Convention (a civil and commercial matter), and
(b) the defendant is domiciled in a European Community State (ie in France, Belgium, Luxembourg, the Netherlands, Germany, Italy, Denmark, the United Kingdom, Ireland, Greece, Spain or Portugal). Even if he is not, certain provisions in the Convention will still apply, eg where the case involves title to land in a Contracting State or where there is an agreement conferring jurisdiction on the courts of a Contracting State.

Jurisdiction under the Convention does not depend on the service of a writ on the defendant, but rather on a specified connection with the forum, eg that the defendant is domiciled there. Furthermore, if a Contracting State is allocated jurisdiction under the Convention, the courts in that State have no discretion to decline to take jurisdiction, at least not in cases where the alternative forum is another Contracting State. The Brussels Convention is discussed in detail in Chapter 14.

3. JURISDICTION UNDER THE MODIFIED CONVENTION

The Civil Jurisdiction and Judgments Act 1982 applies a modified version of the Brussels Convention in cases where:

(a) the matter is within the scope of the Convention (a civil and commercial matter) and
(b) the defendant is domiciled in the United Kingdom or the proceedings are of a kind where jurisdiction is allocated regardless of domicil, eg the case involves title to land in part of the United Kingdom.

Because of its close links with the Brussels Convention, the Modified Convention is also discussed in detail in Chapter 14.

4. JURISDICTION UNDER THE LUGANO CONVENTION

In broad terms, the rules on jurisdiction contained in the Lugano Convention are applied in the United Kingdom and in other EC Contracting States[1] where:

(a) the matter is within the scope of the Convention (a civil and commercial matter), and

(b) the defendant is domiciled in an EFTA Contracting State.[2] Even if he is not, certain provisions in the Convention will still apply, eg where the case involves title to land in an EFTA Contracting State or where there is an agreement conferring jurisdiction on the courts of an EFTA Contracting State.

The Lugano Convention is a parallel Convention to the Brussels Convention and is accordingly also discussed in detail in Chapter 14.

---

1 The Convention has been ratified by the following EC States: France, the United Kingdom, Luxembourg, the Netherlands.
2 Switzerland is the only EFTA Contracting State at the moment. Austria, Finland, Iceland, Norway and Sweden have still to ratify the Convention. It is possible for non-EFTA/EC States to become parties to the Convention.

Chapter 11

The competence of the English courts under the traditional rules

SUMMARY

1. ACTIONS IN PERSONAM

An action in personam, better called an action *inter partes*, is designed to settle the rights of the parties as between themselves,[1] eg an action for damages for breach of contract, an action for an injunction in a tort case, or an action for possession of tangible property. The most striking feature of the English common law rules relating to competence in actions in personam is their purely procedural character. Anyone may invoke or become amenable to the jurisdiction, provided only that the defendant has been served with a writ of summons, or its equivalent, eg an originating summons.

This procedural approach has meant that, apart from cases where matrimonial relief is sought,[2] the courts have not been concerned with the connection that the parties to the dispute have with England. Two important consequences stem from this. First, the mere service of a writ will give the English courts power to try actions which may be inappropriate for trial in England; for example, the defendant may be a foreigner who is only in the course of passage through England and the cause of action may have no factual connection with England. The development of a wide, flexible discretion to stay actions on the basis of *forum non conveniens* is an effective solution to this problem. This allows courts, although competent to try the case, to refuse to do so where trial here would be inappropriate. As will be seen,[3] the English doctrine of *forum non conveniens* has now reached the stage of development when it can perform this role.

The second consequence of this procedural approach is the converse of the first. If the defendant is not present within the jurisdiction, the English courts

---

1 *Tyler v Judges of the Court of Registration* (1900) 175 Mass 71.
2 Infra, pp 627 et seq.
3 Infra, pp 221–234.

are denied power to try actions in many cases in which it would be appropriate for trial to be held here, such as when a tort has been committed in England or when the defendant is domiciled, but not physically present, in England. This defect was recognised many years ago and was remedied by statute so as to give a discretionary power to the courts (now contained in Order 11 of the Rules of the Supreme Court) to authorise service of a writ on a defendant abroad in certain cases. Another exception to the normal principle that the courts have no power to entertain an action against a defendant who is outside the jurisdiction was found to be necessary to deal with cases where the defendant submitted to the English courts' jurisdiction.

The result of these developments is that the English courts are now competent to try an action in personam in three situations:

(a) where there has been service of a writ on a defendant present within the jurisdiction;
(b) where the defendant has submitted to the English court's jurisdiction;
(c) where there has been service of a writ out of the jurisdiction under Order 11 of the Rules of the Supreme Court.

(a) SERVICE OF A WRIT ON A DEFENDANT PRESENT WITHIN THE JURIDICTION

(i) **Individuals**

As has already been seen, at common law "whoever is served with the King's writ and can be compelled consequently to submit to the decree made is a person over whom the courts have jurisdiction".[4] Service must be made personally on the defendant, or by post, or by inserting a copy of the writ through the defendant's letterbox.[5] Jurisdiction accordingly depends on the presence of the defendant in England. To this extent, therefore, it is possible to agree with HOLMES J that "the foundation of jurisdiction is physical power".[6] Once the court has asserted its power by service of process on the defendant it is not rendered incompetent by his subsequent departure from the country.[7] The corollary to this is that if a defendant escapes service, by reason of his absence abroad, no proceedings can be brought against him.[8]

Even the mere transient presence of a person in England suffices to render him amenable to the jurisdiction of the courts. If a writ is served, for example, on a Japanese during a visit of a few hours to London, an action may then be brought against him in his absence concerning a matter totally unrelated to anything that has occurred in England.[9] Not only is the justice of this exercise of power suspect, but in many cases it will be ineffective, for, in this

4 *John Russell & Co Ltd v Cayzer, Irvine & Co Ltd* [1916] 2 AC 298 at 302, HL.
5 RSC Ord 10, r 1. In certain circumstances service can be made on an agent in England acting on behalf of a foreign principal, Ord 10, r 2. For problems in relation to letterbox service, see *Barclays Bank of Swaziland Ltd v Hahn* [1989] 2 All ER 398, [1989] 1 WLR 506, HL (date of service deemed to be when the defendant first knew about the writ); Beck (1990) 106 LQR 47. See also *India Videogram Association Ltd v Patel* [1991] 1 All ER 214, [1991] 1 WLR 173.
6 *McDonald v Mabee* 243 US 90 at 91 (1917).
7 *Razelos v Razelos (No 2)* [1970] 1 All ER 386 n, [1970] 1 WLR 392; cf the American case of *Michigan Trust Co v Ferry* 228 US 346 (1913).
8 *Laurie v Carroll* (1958) 98 CLR 310; *Myerson v Martin* [1979] 3 All ER 667, [1979] 1 WLR 1390, CA; *Mondial Trading Pty Ltd v Interocean Marine Transport Inc* (1985) ALR 155; cf *Porter v Freudenberg* [1915] 1 KB 857 at 887–888. If he leaves after issue but before service then there may be special circumstances justifying substituted service: *Jay v Budd* [1898] 1 QB 12, CA; *Porter v Freudenberg*, supra. See generally *The Vrontados* [1982] 2 Lloyd's Rep 241, CA.
9 Cf *Carrick v Hancock* (1895) 12 TLR 59; infra, p 349.

example a judgment given in the action will be of no use to the plaintiff unless followed by proceedings in Japan for its enforcement, and a Japanese court can scarcely be expected to recognise a jurisdiction based on such flimsy grounds. This English doctrine is inevitable in domestic law because of the procedural significance of the writ of summons, but it is unfortunate from the point of view of private international law that no jurisdictional distinction is drawn between presence and residence.[10] Nevertheless, it has been twice confirmed by the Court of Appeal, holding that the court had jurisdiction over a defendant who was served whilst visiting England for a few days unconnected with the litigation,[11] or even whilst visiting England for Ascot races.[12] Similarly service on a defendant who has been brought within the jurisdiction in police custody or who has come in answer to a subpoena has been held to be good and to confer jurisdiction on the court.[13] If, however, a defendant is enticed within the jurisdiction fraudulently or improperly, then service of the writ may be set aside.[14]

(ii) Partnerships

In the case of a partnership, the plaintiff may serve the writ on an individual partner who is present in England, or on the partnership firm under Order 81 of the Rules of the Supreme Court. This Order, after providing that co-partners carrying on business in England may be sued in the name of the firm,[15] permits the writ to be served on one or more of the partners, or on the person having control of the business at the principal place of business in England, or by post to the firm at the principal place of business within the jurisdiction, whether or not any member of the firm is out of the jurisdiction.[16] Therefore, service which is effected on the person in control of the English business operates as a valid service on all the partners, even in the case of a foreign firm all the members of which are resident abroad.[17] Again, service on one partner present in England is effective against the co-partners out of the jurisdiction,[18] and service effected with the leave of the court under Order 11, rule 1 (1)[19] on one partner out of the jurisdiction is a good service on all the other partners out of the jurisdiction.[20] Service on the partnership in

10 The Foreign Judgments (Reciprocal Enforcement) Act 1933, whose object it is to facilitate the enforcement in England of judgments obtained abroad, specifies the residence, not the mere presence, of the defendant in the country as one of the circumstances sufficient to found the jurisdiction of a court of that country, infra, p 399.
11 *Colt Industries Inc v Sarlie* [1966] 1 All ER 673, [1966] 1 WLR 440, following *Carrick v Hancock* (1895) 12 TLR 59 at 60.
12 *HRH Maharanee Seethaderi Gaekwar of Baroda v Wildenstein* [1972] 2 QB 283, [1972] 2 All ER 689, CA. The presence rule has been accepted by the US Supreme Court in *Burnham v Superior Court of California* 109 L Ed 2d (1990); Collins (1991) 107 LQR 10.
13 *Doyle v Doyle* (1974) 52 DLR (3d) 143; *John Sanderson & Co (NSW) Pty Ltd v Giddings* [1976] VR 421; *Baldry v Jackson* [1976] 1 NSWLR 19, affd without discussion of this issue [1976] 2 NSWLR 415.
14 *Watkins v North American Land and Timber Co Ltd* (1904) 20 TLR 534, HL; *Colt Industries Inc v Sarlie*, supra, at 443–444.
15 Ord 81, r 1. Ord 81 applies to an individual foreigner carrying on a business here in a name other than his own name: Ord 81, r 9. Valid service can be effected on a person acting on a partner's instructions to accept service: *Kenneth Allison Ltd v A E Limehouse & Co* [1991] 4 All ER 500, [1991] 3 WLR 671, HL.
16 Ord 81, r3.
17 *Worcester City and County Banking Co v Firbank, Pauling & Co* [1894] 1 QB 784, CA.
18 *Lysaght Ltd v Clark & Co* [1891] 1 QB 552.
19 Discussed, infra, pp 190 et seq.
20 *Hobbs v Australian Press Association* [1933] 1 KB 1, CA.

England will allow the plaintiff to seek leave to serve a partner abroad, under Order 11, rule 1(1)(c) as a "proper party to the action".[21]

(iii) Companies

The same principle applies for corporate defendants as for individual defendants: the defendant is subject to the jurisdiction of the English court if he is present in England. Of course, a company cannot literally be present in England. It is therefore necessary to give an artificial presence to a corporate defendant, according to which a foreign company can be present in England by virtue of the transaction of business. Originally, jurisdiction was determined by the application of common law rules, and the courts laid down a series of requirements that had to be satisfied before the inference could be drawn that the company was present in England.[1] If it was so regarded, process had to be served on a person such as the chairman or secretary of the company under Order 65, rule 3 of the Rules of the Supreme Court. But it is to the Companies Act 1985 that a plaintiff has now to turn if jurisdiction is to be taken against a foreign company by service of a writ within the jurisdiction.

The Companies Act 1985 A company registered in England under the Companies Act 1985 is regarded as present in England and service of a writ can be effected by sending it to the registered office of the company.[2] A company registered in Scotland which carries on business in England can be served with a writ by sending it to the principal place of business in England with a copy to its registered office.[3] The position of a foreign corporation is less straightforward. In order to facilitate the service of a writ on an "oversea company",[4] section 691 of the Companies Act 1985 obliges it to file with the registrar of companies the names and addresses of some one or more persons authorised to accept service of process on its behalf.[5] So long as the name of such a person remains on the file, service of a writ on him renders the company subject to the jurisdiction of the court even though the company no longer carries on business in England.[6] It can be said in favour of this approach that it prevents foreign companies from running up debts in England and then shutting up shop. However, it can sometimes involve unfairness to the defendant company. In such circumstances it is always possible for the defendant to seek a stay of proceedings on the basis of *forum non conveniens*.[7] A more radical solution, advocated in the Court of Appeal in *Rome v Punjab National Bank (No 2)*[8] would be to amend the Companies Act so that a company which had ceased to carry on business and had removed itself would only be subject to jurisdiction in relation to matters which arose during the period in which the company carried on business in

---

21 *West of England SS Owners Protection and Indemnity Association Ltd v John Holman & Sons* [1957] 3 All ER 421 n, [1957] 1 WLR 1164; infra, pp 193–195.
1 *Okura & Co Ltd v Forsbacka Jernverks Aktiebolag* [1914] 1 KB 715 at 718, CA; *The Theodohos* [1977] 2 Lloyd's Rep 428; the requirements are set out in the 11th edn at p 190.
2 Companies Act 1985, s 725 (1).
3 Ibid, s 725 (2), (3).
4 See Companies Act 1985, s 744; discussed infra, p 186.
5 Companies Act 1985, s 691 (1) (b) (ii).
6 *Rome v Punjab National Bank (No 2)* [1990] 1 All ER 58, [1989] 1 WLR 1211; *Sabatier v Trading Co* [1927] 1 Ch 495.
7 *Rome v Punjab National Bank (No 2)* [1989] 1 WLR 1211 at 1220 (per Sir John May).
8 Ibid, at 1221 (per Parker L J and Sir Roualeyn Cumming-Bruce).

England. If a company fails to comply with its statutory obligations, or if the persons on the register are dead or no longer resident here, or if they refuse to accept service, the writ may be served on the company by leaving it at or posting it to "any place of business established by the company in Great Britain".[9] These last words have been interpreted to mean a place of business that is still established at the time of service.[10] Service is not adequate if effected at a former place of business that has ceased to function.

In 1977, BRANDON J held in *The Theodohos*[11] that the procedure for service laid down in the Companies Act 1948 (consolidated now in the Companies Act 1985) was the only procedure available in the case of an oversea company with a place of business here. In other words, service on the company had to be by leaving the writ at, or posting it to, the place of business established in Great Britain. It was not sufficient to serve the writ in England, under Order 65, rule 3, personally on the president of the defendant corporation; though in fact the judge also found that the defendant corporation was not carrying on business in England at the material time. This principle has been endorsed subsequently by the Court of Appeal.[12]

The decision in *The Theodohos* tells us *which procedure* is to be used. This is important at the practical level of deciding how the writ is to be served against a corporate defendant, ie whether it is to be served on a person or at the place of business. This is also important at the conceptual level, since it must follow that the basis for taking jurisdiction against foreign companies following service of a writ within the jurisdiction is to be found in the provisions of the Companies Act, and not in the common law concept of corporate presence. However, *The Theodohos* does not tell us *when* the Companies Act procedure can be used. The answer to this is when the foreign company is an "oversea company".

Section 744 of the Companies Act 1985 states that an "oversea company" means—

  (a) a company incorporated elsewhere than in Great Britain which, after the commencement of this Act, establishes a place of business in Great Britain, and
  (b) a company so incorporated which has, before that commencement, established a place of business and continues to have an established place of business in Great Britain at that commencement.

This definition inevitably leads on to the question of when a foreign company "establishes a place of business in Great Britain".

Establishment of a place of business   There is no rigid list of requirements for this.[13] Instead, it is a question of examining the activities of the corporate defendant in England.[14] This is clear from the Court of Appeal decision in

  9 Companies Act 1985, s 695.
 10 *Deverall v Grant Advertising Inc* [1955] Ch 111, [1954] 3 All ER 389, CA; and see *Bethlehem Steel Corpn v Universal Gas and Oil Co Inc* (1978) Times, 3 August, HL.
 11 [1977] 2 Lloyd's Rep 428: cf *Bethlehem Steel Corpn v Universal Gas and Oil Co Inc* (1978) Times, 3 August, per Lord SCARMAN.
 12 *The Vrontados* [1982] 2 Lloyd's Rep 241 at 244 (Lord DENNING); *South India Shipping Corpn Ltd v Export-Import Bank of Korea* [1985] 1 WLR 585 at 588, CA.
 13 Common law decisions on corporate presence are only of limited relevance: *Adams v Cape Industries Plc* [1990] Ch 433 at 528
 14 *Rome v Punjab National Bank (No 2)* [1989] 2 Lloyd's Rep 354 at 361 (HIRST J), which concerned activities in connection with winding down a business, affd [1989] 1 WLR 1211 at 1220, CA.

South India Shipping Corpn Ltd v Export-Import Bank of Korea.[15]

The defendant bank was incorporated in Korea and conducted their main business there. However, the bank rented an office in London, the functions of which were gathering and providing information and liaising with other banks. The plaintiff company, incorporated in India, sent a writ by post to the defendant's office in London.

The Court of Appeal held that the writ had been duly served on the defendant since the defendant had established a place of business here under the Companies Act.[16] ACKNER LJ, who gave the judgment of the court, treated this question as being one simply of fact, without any rigid list of requirements to be satisfied.[17] He pointed out that the defendant had both premises and staff within the jurisdiction and then detailed the activities carried on by the defendant here. It was not necessary to show that these activities constituted a substantial part of the foreign company's business; and no objection was made to the fact that the activities in London were merely incidental to the defendant's main objects.[18] ACKNER LJ said that "Parliament has placed no express qualification or limitation on the words 'a place of business' and there seems no good reason why we should imply one".[19] It is worthy of note that the Court of Appeal showed little concern as to whether contracts were concluded in London on behalf of the defendant bank, despite the fact that, seemingly, no banking business was conducted here. In a branch office case like this a company uses its own employees to conduct business in England and there can be no question but that the employee is acting on behalf of the company. However, if a foreign company uses an independent "agent" to carry on its business in England the question necessarily arises of whether this person is carrying on business on his own behalf or on behalf of the foreign company. In answering this question, the "agent's" power to bind the corporation contractually is of particular importance. If the "agent" never makes contracts which bind the foreign company this is a powerful factor pointing against the presence of the foreign company in England.[20]

In the *South India Shipping Case* the foreign company unquestionably carried on business from a fixed and definite place in England and there was, accordingly, no discussion of this particular point. However, this point was raised subsequently in *Re Oriel Ltd.*[1] In this case, the Court of Appeal held that a specific location for the business is necessary in order to come within the terms of what is now section 691 of the Companies Act 1985. The establishment of a place of business was said to imply some degree of continuity and a location recognisable to outsiders. It is also not enough for the company merely to own land in England; it has to be shown that the business of the foreign company is habitually carried on from that land.[2]

---

15 [1985] 1 WLR 585, [1985] 2 All ER 219, CA.
16 The case was decided under the Companies Act 1948, ss 407 and 412; now the relevant provisions are contained in the Companies Act 1985, ss 691 and 695.
17 See [1985] 1 WLR 585 at 592.
18 ACKNER LJ followed a case decided under the common law: *Hercules Aktieselskabet Dampskib v Grand Trunk Pacific Rly Co* [1912] 1 KB 222, CA.
19 [1985] 1 WLR 585 at 591.
20 *Adams v Cape Industries Plc* [1990] Ch 433 at 530–531; discussed infra, pp 350–351. See also *BHP Petroleum Pty Ltd v Oil Basins Ltd* [1985] VR 725 at 731–734.
1 [1985] 3 All ER 216, [1986] 1 WLR 180, CA, a case under s 106 of the Companies Act 1948, which discusses ss 407 and 412 of that Act (now ss 691 and 695 of the Companies Act 1985).
2 Ibid, at 223.

However, a private residence of one of the directors of the company can constitute a place of business if the company transacts business from there.[3] Moreover the business premises do not have to be owned or leased by the company.[4] If the foreign company carries on business in England by means of an independent "agent", the latter will doubtless own or lease the business premises. Nonetheless, the foreign company may have established a place of business in England.[5] The lack of some external manifestation of the defendant company, such as a nameplate, at the premises, although a relevant factor, is not a decisive one.

The above principles are probably equally applicable to cases where a foreign company carries on business in England by means of a wholly-owned subsidiary company rather than by means of a branch office or an independent "agent".[6] Under principles of company law the foreign parent and English subsidiary are separate legal entities. In most cases the English subsidiary will carry on its own business and not that of the parent. The result is that the foreign parent company will not be present/resident in England. In the rare situation where a subsidiary does operate on behalf of the parent[7] (and the ability of the former to bind the latter contractually will be an important factor in determining this) it is possible to regard the parent as being present/resident in England. The current law still places undue reliance on traditional notions of agency. It would be better, as United States courts have done, to look at the economic realities of the situation; if the parent and subsidiary form one economic unit it should be possible to found jurisdiction against the foreign parent on the basis of the presence of its subsidiary in England, or indeed against a foreign subsidiary on the basis of the presence of the parent in England.[8] More generally, the whole of the law on jurisdiction against corporate defendants would make more sense if instead of applying a misleading analogy with individuals it was recognised that corporate defendants are very different and that jurisdiction should be based on the notion of their economic presence within the jurisdiction rather than on the establishment of a place of business.[9]

(b) SUBMISSION TO THE JURISDICTION

Despite the fundamental principle that the court cannot entertain an action against a defendant who is absent from England, it has long been recognised that an absent defendant may confer jurisdiction on the court by submitting to it. This may be done in a variety of ways, such as by the defendant acknowledging service before actual service of the writ,[10] or instructing a

---

3 Ibid, at 222.
4 Ibid, at 220.
5 *Cleveland Museum of Art v Capricorn Art International SA* [1990] 2 Lloyd's Rep 166. The English proceedings were, however, stayed, see infra, p 232.
6 See *Adams v Cape Industries Plc* [1990] Ch 433, [1991] 1 All ER 929; a case on enforcement of a foreign judgment discussed infra, pp 350–351.
7 See eg Case 218/86 *Sar Schotte GmbH v Parfums Rothschild* [1987] ECR 4905, a case concerned with jurisdiction under Article 5 (5) of the Brussels Convention; *Amalgamated Wireless (Australasia) Ltd v McDonnell Douglas Corpn* (1988) 77 ALR 537 at 540.
8 See *Bulova Watch Co Inc v Hattori and Co Ltd* 508 F Supp 1322 at 1342 (1981); Fawcett (1988) 37 ICLQ 645 at 663 et seq. Such an approach was rejected in *Adams v Cape Industries Plc* [1990] Ch 433 at 532 et seq, CA.
9 Fawcett, op cit. Cf *Ets Soules et Cie v Handgate Co Ltd SA, The Handgate* [1987] 1 Lloyd's Rep 142.
10 RSC Ord 10, r 1(5).

solicitor to accept service on his behalf.[11] Commencing an action as a plaintiff will give the court jurisdiction over a counterclaim.[12] Although a defendant who appears and contests the case on its merits will be held to have submitted to the jurisdiction,[13] an appearance merely to protest that the court does not have jurisdiction will not constitute submission,[14] even if the defendant also seeks a stay of proceedings pending the outcome of proceedings abroad.[15]

Furthermore, any person may contract, either expressly or impliedly, to submit to the jurisdiction of a court to which he would not otherwise be subject.[16] Thus, in the case of an international contract it is common practice for the parties, one or even both of whom are resident abroad, to agree that any dispute arising between them shall be settled by the English court or by an arbitrator in England.[1] A party to such a contract, having consented to the jurisdiction, cannot afterwards contest the binding effect of the judgment.[2] Such an agreement is recognised and made procedurally effective by a rule of court which permits the parties to prescribe, in the event of an action, the method by which the writ shall be served on the defendant, whether in England or elsewhere.[3] For example, the defendant out of the jurisdiction may be deemed to have been served by service on his agent within the jurisdiction.[4] However, this rule is only dealing with the method of service, and a writ which has been served out of the jurisdiction in accordance with a contract shall not be deemed to have been duly served unless leave has been granted under Order 11, rule 1 (1) or service of the writ is permitted without leave under Order 11, rule 1 (2).[5] If no method of service is prescribed by the parties, Order 11 will have to be resorted to in respect of a foreign defendant.[6]

It must be noted that the parties cannot by submission confer jurisdiction on the court to entertain proceedings beyond its authority.[7] Submission will

11 RSC Ord 10, r 1(4). See also *Manta Line Inc v Sofianites and Midland Bank plc* [1984] 1 Lloyd's Rep 14, CA; *Sphere Drake Insurance plc v Gunes Sigorta Anonim Sirketi* [1987] 1 Lloyd's Rep 139.

12 RSC Ord 15, r 2.

13 *Boyle v Sacker* (1888) 39 ChD 249, CA; cf *Redhead v Redhead and Crothers* [1926] NZLR 131. See also *Obikoya v Silvernorth Ltd* (1983) Times, 6 July.

14 RSC Ord 12, r 8(6); *Re Dulles' Settlement (No 2), Dulles v Vidler* [1951] Ch 842, [1951] 2 All ER 69, CA; and see *Tallack v Tallack and Broekma* [1927] P 211; *Razelos v Razelos (No 2)* [1970] 1 WLR 392 at 403. The principle is the same when it comes to enforcement of foreign judgments: Civil Jurisdiction and Judgments Act 1982, s 33, as amended by the Civil Jurisdiction and Judgments Act 1991, Sch 2, para 15 discussed infra, pp 354–357.

15 *Williams and Glyns Bank Plc v Astro Dinamico Cia Naviera SA* [1984] 1 All ER 760, [1984] 1 WLR 438, HL; cf *The Messiniaki Tolmi* [1984] 1 Lloyd's Rep 266, CA; *Finnish Marine Insurance Co Ltd v Protective National Insurance Co* [1990] 1 QB 1078, [1989] 2 All ER 929.

16 *Feyerick v Hubbard* (1902) 71 LJKB 509; *Copin v Adamson* (1875) 1 ExD 17, CA, infra, p 352; Pryles (1976) 25 ICLQ 543; Kahn-Freund (1977) 26 ICLQ 825; Anton, *Civil Jurisdiction in Scotland*, paras 10.72–10.77.

1 Infra, p 484. It is most unlikely that English courts would accept an implied agreement to submit; cf *Adams v Cape Industries Plc* [1990] Ch 433, infra, p 353.

2 A choice of the law to govern a contract does not, of itself, amount to agreement to submit to that jurisdiction; *Dunbee Ltd v Gilman & Co (Australia) Pty Ltd* [1968] 2 Lloyd's Rep 394; cf *Acrow (Automation) Ltd v Rex Chainbelt Inc* [1971] 1 WLR 1676 at 1683, CA.

3 RSC Ord 10, r 3.

4 *Tharsis Sulphur and Copper Co Ltd v Société Industrielle et Commerciale des Métaux* (1889) 58 LJQB 435.

5 Ord 10, r 3(2).

6 Where the court's leave is required Ord 11, r 1(1)(d)(iv) allows the court to grant this, infra, p 198.

7 *In re Paramount Airways Ltd (in administration)* [1992] Ch 160 at 171.

not, for example, confer jurisdiction in divorce or nullity proceedings,[8] or over proceedings principally concerned with a question of title to foreign land.[9]

(c) SERVICE OF A WRIT ON A DEFENDANT OUT OF THE JURISDICTION[10]

The rule at common law, that no action in personam will lie against a defendant unless he has been served with a writ while present in England, often precludes a plaintiff from enforcing a claim in the most appropriate forum. As we have seen, the fact that a tort has been committed or that a contract has been made and broken in England does not of itself render the English court competent, even though the defendant is domiciled and ordinarily resident in the country. Again, if before the issue of a writ an English debtor escapes abroad or if a foreigner returns home after entering into a contract here, the judicial machinery of England cannot be put in motion.[11] Under the common law rule the only remedy of the aggrieved party in such cases is to follow the wrongdoer to his place of residence. The one exception is that in the case of a matrimonial cause, such as a petition for divorce, the petitioner has an absolute right to serve process on the respondent abroad without obtaining the leave of the court.[12]

Owing to considerations of this nature an entirely different kind of jurisdiction, generally called "assumed" jurisdiction, was introduced many years ago by the Common Law Procedure Act 1852, which gave the courts a discretionary power to summon absent defendants, whether English or foreign. The exercise of this jurisdiction is now governed by Order 11 of the Rules of the Supreme Court. This Order has been altered over the years, and following the Civil Jurisdiction and Judgments Act 1982 substantial amendments were made to it.[13] Some of the changes were necessitated by the changes in the law on jurisdiction brought about by the 1982 Act, others were the result of case law exposing problems in the original wording.

Order 11 permits service of a writ on a defendant who is out of the jurisdiction (ie not to be found in England or Wales) in the circumstances that will be considered below. In some cases service is only permissible with the leave of the court; in others, it is permissible without the leave of the court. The new Rules of the Supreme Court have greatly increased the number of cases where service out of the jurisdiction is permissible without the leave of the court;[14] nonetheless, in England leave is still required in many cases, whereas some common law jurisdictions have dispensed with the requirement altogether.[15]

---

8 Infra, pp 630–633.
9 Civil Jurisdiction and Judgments Act 1982, s 30, as amended by the Civil Jurisdiction and Judgments Act 1991, Sch 2, para 13; infra, p 262.
10 Collins (1972) 21 ICLQ 656.
11 Eg *Wilding v Bean* [1891] 1 QB 100, CA.
12 Matrimonial Causes Rules 1977, r 117(1). See *Wyler v Lyons* [1963] P 274 at 281, [1963] 1 All ER 821 at 825.
13 RSC (Amendment No 2) 1983 (SI 1983/1181). The new Rules came into force on 1 January 1987 when the Brussels Convention came into force. The rules will need to be further amended to take account of the implementation of the Lugano Convention by the Civil Jurisdiction and Judgments Act 1991.
14 Infra, p 210.
15 For Canada, see Castel, *Canadian Conflict of Laws* (2nd edn, 1986), para 122; for New Zealand, see NZ High Court Rule 219; *Kuwait Asia Bank EC v National Mutual Life Nominees Ltd* [1991] 1 AC 187, [1990] 3 All ER 404 (service can nonetheless be set aside on the application of the defendant).

(i) Service of a writ out of the jurisdiction with leave of the court

Order 11, rule 1 (1) empowers the court, upon an application being made to it, to permit service of a writ[16] on a defendant who is abroad. However, permission will only be given if the case is a proper one for service out of the jurisdiction.[17] The court has to be satisfied: first that the plaintiff has a good arguable case on the merits; second, that one of the heads of Order 11, rule 1 (1) applies; and third, that the discretion should be exercised to allow service of a writ out of the jurisdiction. The onus is on the plaintiff to satisfy these three points.[18] Although there are three stages to the grant of leave, cases should be looked at in the round and not over-analysed.[19]

A good arguable case on the merits. The plaintiff must show a good arguable case on the merits, ie that the action has a good chance of succeeding if brought in England.[20] This can raise choice of law questions at the jurisdictional stage of the action. Thus in *Metall und Rohstoff AG v Donaldson Lufkin and Jenrette Inc*[21] the Court of Appeal applied the English tort choice of law rules to determine whether the plaintiff had a good arguable case on the merits. For the plaintiff to succeed, actionability by English law had to be shown, which there was in respect of the plaintiff's claim for inducement of a breach of contract, but not in respect of his claim, as pleaded, for conspiracy.

The heads of Order 11, rule 1 (1). The following are the cases where the service of a writ out of the jurisdiction is permissible with the leave of the court. The plaintiff must show a strong probability that one of these heads of Order 11 is satisfied.[22]

General

(a) Where "relief is sought against a person domiciled within the jurisdiction."[23] This head is an extensive departure from common law principles. It renders jurisdiction possible over practically any kind of action[24] against an absent person (including a corporation), provided that he is domiciled in England. In this context, domicil is now determined in accordance with the definition contained in the Civil Jurisdiction and Judgments Act 1982, as

16 See *Afro Continental Nigeria Ltd v Meridian Shipping Co SA, The Vrontados* [1982] 2 Lloyd's Rep 241.
17 Ord 11, r 4(2).
18 *Metall und Rohstoff AG v Donaldson Lufkin & Jenrette Inc* [1990] 1 QB 391 at 434.
19 In *re* ERAS EIL Actions (1991) Times, 28 November, CA.
20 *Metall Und Rohstoff v Donaldson Lufkin and Jenrette Inc* [1990] 1 QB 391 at 434, overruled on a different point in *Lonhro plc v Fayed* [1991] 3 All ER 303, [1991] 3 WLR 188, HL; Fentiman [1989] CLJ 191; Fawcett [1991] Current Legal Problems 39 at 42–43; In *re* ERAS EIL Actions (1991) Times 28 November, CA; *Overseas Union Insurance Ltd v Incorporated General Insurance Ltd* (1991) Times, 11 December.
21 [1990] 1 QB 391.
22 *Metall und Rohstoff AG v Donaldson Lufkin and Jenrette Inc* [1990] 1 QB 391 at 434; *Overseas Union Insurance Ltd v Incorporated General Insurance Ltd* (1991) Times, 11 December; *EI Du Pont de Nemours & Co v IC Agnew and K W Kerr* [1987] 2 Lloyd's Rep 585 at 595; *Contender 1 Ltd v LEP International Pty Ltd* (1988) 82 ALR 394, HC of Australia. Cf *Attock Cement Co Ltd v Romanian Bank for Foreign Trade* [1989] 1 All ER 1189, [1989] 1 WLR 1147: "a good arguable case" must be shown.
23 Ord 11, r 1(1) (a); formerly Ord 11 r 1(1) (c), which provided for ordinary residence as an alternative to domicil.
24 *Re Liddell's Settlement Trusts* [1936] Ch 365, [1936] 1 All ER 239, CA; Dicey & Morris, p 309.

amended by the Civil Jurisdiction and Judgments Act 1991.[25] This definition is used primarily in cases arising within the Brussels Convention or Lugano Convention,[1] and is a very complex one. In broad terms, it provides that an individual is domiciled in a state if: (a) he is resident in that state; and (b) the nature and circumstances of his residence indicate that he has a substantial connection with it. Of course, the jurisdiction rules contained in the Brussels Convention and/or the Modified Convention will apply in a case where the defendant is domiciled in England provided that it is a civil and commercial matter. This head is therefore concerned with cases which do not involve such a matter.

(b) Where "an injunction is sought ordering the defendant to do or refrain from doing anything within the jurisdiction (whether or not damages are also claimed in respect of a failure to do or the doing of that thing)."[2] The courts refuse to grant permission under this head unless the substantial and genuine dispute between the parties is whether an injunction against some act in England ought to be granted. The plaintiff cannot found the jurisdiction of the English court by claiming an injunction that is only incidental to the relief that he in fact desires.[3] This head is wide enough to cover a permanent injunction restraining threatened breaches of contract and torts within the jurisdiction.[4] However, it does not cover the issue of a "Mareva"[5] injunction, ie an *interlocutory* injunction[6] to restrain a defendant from removing his assets from the jurisdiction or from dissipating them pending the trial of an action against him. There is no power to order the issue of a writ out of the jurisdiction under this head of Order 11 merely because a "Mareva" injunction is sought.[7]

At one time a "Mareva" injunction could only be granted where the court had jurisdiction over the main action.[8] This rule operated as a very real limitation on the power to issue "Mareva" injunctions, given that Order 11, rule 1(1)(b) does not operate to give jurisdiction over the main action merely because a "Mareva" injunction is sought. However, this restriction on the issue of "Mareva" injunctions no longer operates in many cases, following United Kingdom accession to the Brussels Convention and more recent Lugano Convention. Section 25[9] of the Civil Jurisdiction and Judgments Act 1982 allows an English court to grant "interim relief"[10] such as a "Mareva"

---

25 Ord 11, r 1(4). The definition is contained in ss 41–46 of the 1982 Act, which have been amended by the 1991 Act, Sch 2, paras 16–21; discussed infra, pp 284–285. Previously under Ord 11 domicil was given the traditional meaning in English conflict of laws, discussed supra, pp 138–175.
1 Infra, pp 279–344.
2 Ord 11, r 1(1)(b); formerly Ord 11, r 1(1)(i).
3 *Rosler v Hilbery* [1925] Ch 250, CA.
4 *James North & Sons Ltd v North Cape Textiles Ltd* [1984] 1 WLR 1428, CA.
5 *Mareva Cia Naviera SA v International Bulk Carriers SA* [1980] 1 All ER 213 n, CA.
6 Under s 37 of the Supreme Court Act 1981.
7 *Siskina (Cargo Owners) v Distos Cia Naviera SA, The Siskina* [1979] AC 210, [1977] 3 All ER 803, HL; and see *Perry v Zissis* [1977] 1 Lloyd's Rep 607 at 616–617, CA; *Serge Caudron v Air Zaire* [1986] ILRM 10, SC of Ireland.
8 *The Siskina*, op cit, at 255. For the position in respect of an *Anton Piller* order (sometimes referred to as a "search warrant for civil proceedings"), see *Altertext Inc v Advanced Data Communications Ltd* [1985] 1 WLR 457 at 463. The general question of jurisdiction over movables is discussed infra, pp 212–213.
9 As amended by Sch 2, para 12, Civil Jurisdiction and Judgments Act 1991 to reflect the implementation of the Lugano Convention; discussed infra, pp 330–331.
10 It has been doubted whether this includes security for costs, see *Bank Mellat v Helliniki Techniki SA* [1984] QB 291.

injunction, in respect of proceedings which have been or are to be commenced in another Contracting State to the Brussels Convention[11] or Lugano Convention or in another part of the United Kingdom. This means, for example, that a plaintiff who is going to sue a defendant in France in respect of a civil and commercial matter can obtain a "Mareva" injunction in England preventing the defendant from dissipating or removing his English and overseas assets.[12] The result of granting the injunction is to preserve, for example, the defendant's assets in England so that a subsequent French judgment, which is enforceable here under the Brussels Convention, can be satisfied. However, section 25 will not apply in respect of proceedings in a non-Contracting State, such as the United States, unless section 25 has been extended to that State by an Order in Council.[13] Section 25 does not require that the defendant be domiciled in a Contracting State to the Brussels Convention or Lugano Convention. Nonetheless, the domicil of the defendant is relevant when it comes to the question of the service of the writ abroad. This is possible without the leave of the court in cases where the defendant is domiciled in a Contracting State to the Brussels Convention or the Lugano Convention.[14] In cases where the defendant is not so domiciled the plaintiff can seek the leave of the court for service abroad under Ord 11 r 1(1)(b).[15] Section 24 of the 1982 Act provides that the English courts can grant a "Mareva" injunction pending trial in England where the issue to be tried is whether the court has jurisdiction to entertain the proceedings.

(c) Where "the claim is brought against a person duly served within or out of the jurisdiction and a person out of the jurisdiction is a necessary or proper party thereto."[16] Leave to serve a person abroad may be obtained under this head of the Rule in circumstances that are not covered by any of the other heads, for instance, when a tort has been committed in a foreign country by two persons jointly, only one of whom is subject to the court's jurisdiction.[17] This provision is concerned with the situation where there are two defendants:[18] a first defendant, who has actually been served; and a second defendant whom the plaintiff now wishes to serve out of the jurisdiction. There are separate requirements in respect of each defendant.

It must be shown that the first defendant was "duly served". It is thus necessary for the writ to have been properly issued and served, ie "in accordance with law, particularly the Rules of the Supreme Court".[19] The service can be within the jurisdiction or, now,[20] out of the jurisdiction under Order 11. It must also be shown that the claim is brought against the defendant

---

11 This includes proceedings in, for example, the Netherlands commenced prior to the 1978 Accession Convention coming into effect there: *Alltrans Inc v Interdom Holdings Ltd* [1991] 4 All ER 458.
12 *Republic of Haiti v Duvalier* [1990] 1 QB 202, [1989] 1 All ER 456, CA.
13 S 25(3). So far, no such Order in Council has been made.
14 Ord 11 r 1(2); infra, pp 210–211.
15 *X v Y* [1990] 1 QB 220, [1989] 3 All ER 689.
16 Ord 11, r 1(1)(c); formerly Ord 11, r 1(1)(j).
17 *Croft v King* [1893] 1 QB 419.
18 They do not need to be joint or even alternative defendants: *Bank of New South Wales v Commonwealth Steel Co Ltd* [1983] 1 NSWLR 69; *Westpac Banking Corpn v Commonwealth Steel Co Ltd* [1983] 1 NSWLR 735. The provision now applies to third party proceedings: Ord 16, r 3(4); Collins, *The Civil Jurisdiction and Judgments Act 1982*, p 150.
19 *Derby and Co Ltd v Larsson* [1976] 1 All ER 401 at 413 (per Lord SIMON), [1976] 1 WLR 202, HL.
20 Cf the predecessor to the present provision, Ord 11, r 1(1)(j).

who has been duly served. However, it need no longer be shown that the claim is "properly brought" against this person. Whilst getting rid of a large number of cases, the ending of the requirement that the action be "properly brought" does not diminish the very real problems that this concept was used to solve. In essence, it allowed the courts to scrutinise the claim against the first defendant and thereby to protect the second defendant who is out of the jurisdiction.[21] It was held that the action was not "properly brought" against the first defendant in the following three situations. First, where the action was not a bona fide one against the first defendant, ie he was joined with the sole object of making the second defendant answerable to the English court's jurisdiction.[22] Second, where the action against the first defendant was bound to fail.[23] Third, where there was some procedural irregularity in relation to jurisdiction, but this was waived by the first defendant by a voluntary appearance before the court; in such a case, the policy was that the second defendant should not be prejudiced by the actions of the first defendant.[24] There is, at first glance, some uncertainty as to how these situations will be dealt with under the new Rules of the Supreme Court. It is arguable that the omission of the words "properly brought" from Order 11, rule 1(1)(c) shows a change of policy and that these situations should now be allowed to come within this head. However, it is doubtful if this was what was intended, since there is a separate requirement under Order 11, rule 4(1)(d) that the plaintiff's application for service out of the jurisdiction under rule 1(1)(c) must be supported by an affidavit stating the grounds for his belief that there is a real issue between himself and the first defendant. There is, however, no express requirement in the wording of rule 1(1)(c) that there must be a real issue between the parties, although it would be possible for it to be regarded as an implied requirement, and certainly it is a matter which could be considered by the courts when deciding whether to exercise their discretion to allow service out of the jurisdiction. Moreover, as will be seen,[1] it is possible for the courts to use the requirement under rule 1(1)(c) that the second defendant must be "a necessary or proper party" in order to deny service of the writ out of the jurisdiction in the situation where there is no real issue between the plaintiff and the first defendant and in any other situation where it used to be held that the action was not "properly brought".

It must be shown that the second defendant, whom the plaintiff wishes to serve out of the jurisdiction, is "a necessary or proper party"[2] to the action against the first defendant. This will not be the case if the second defendant

---

21 *Tyne Improvement Commissioners v Armement Anversois SA (The Brabo)* [1949] AC 326 at 351, [1949] 1 All ER 294.
22 *Multinational Gas and Petrochemical Co v Multinational Gas and Petrochemical Services Ltd* [1983] Ch 258 at 284–285; Fawcett (1984) 100 LQR 17; *Goldenglow Nut Food Co Ltd v Commodin (Produce) Ltd and Societe Generale De Surveillance SA and New Hampshire Insurance Co Ltd* [1987] 2 Lloyd's Rep 569 at 578.
23 *Tyne Improvement Commissioners v Armement Anversois S/A (The Brabo),* op cit; *Multinational Gas and Petrochemical Co v Multinational Gas and Petrochemical Services Ltd,* op cit.
24 *John Russell and Co Ltd v Cayzer Irvine and Co Ltd* [1916] 2 AC 298, HL; *Derby and Co Ltd v Larsson* [1976] 1 All ER 401; *R A Lister and Co Ltd v E G Thomson (Shipping) Ltd and P T Djkarta Lloyd, The Benarty* [1983] 1 Lloyd's Rep 361, CA; *Amanuel v Alexandros Shipping Co (The Alexandros P)* [1986] QB 464, [1986] 1 All ER 278.
1 *Infra,* p 195.
2 See generally, *Massey v Heynes and Co* (1888) 21 QBD 330; *Qatar Petroleum v Shell International Petroleum* [1983] 2 Lloyd's Rep 35; *International Commercial Bank plc v Insurance Corp of Ireland plc* [1989] IR 466.

has a good defence in law to the plaintiff's claim and therefore the claim is bound to fail;[3] nor will it be the case if the plaintiff's rights are predominantly against the first defendant.[4] More surprisingly, it has been held that this requirement is not met if the plaintiff's claim should have been principally brought against the *second defendant*.[5] It is, therefore, possible for the courts to protect the first defendant in cases where the action brought against the first defendant was not a bona fide one, by holding that the second defendant is not a necessary or proper party to that action.[6]

There has, for many years, been a particular reluctance to exercise the discretion to allow service out of the jurisdiction under this head[7], even though a refusal may require more than one action in more than one country.[8] The reason for this was given in *Multinational Gas and Petrochemical Co v Multinational Gas and Petrochemical Services Ltd*[9] where MAY LJ said of the predecessor of rule 1(1)(c) that:

> It is anomalous in that, different from the other sub-paragraphs, it is not founded upon any territorial connection between the claim, the subject of the relevant action and the jurisdiction of the English courts. This requires one to look particularly closely at any application founded upon this sub-paragraph.[10]

The lack of connection under this head is equally apparent in its newly worded form; indeed, it may be even greater than under the old head since the first defendant can now be a foreigner who is served out of the jurisdiction, whereas, in the past, he had to be served in England. It is, therefore, likely that the courts will continue to be very reluctant to use this head of Order 11.

This normal reluctance will no doubt be increased in cases where the action against the first defendant is not a bona fide one, or where it is bound to fail, or where the conduct of the first defendant prejudices the position of the second defendant. In the past, the first two of these factors have been regarded as relevant ones to be taken into account against exercising the discretion to allow service out of the jurisdiction.[11] Leave will also not be granted where there are substantial defendants in England and there is no real advantage to the plaintiff in joining the persons who are abroad.[12]

---

3 *Multinational Gas and Petrochemical Co v Multinational Gas and Petrochemical Services Ltd* [1983] Ch 258 at 273, 287, CA.
4 *Re Schintz* [1926] Ch 710.
5 *Rosler v Hilbery* [1925] Ch 250, CA.
6 On the close relationship between "properly brought" and "a necessary and proper party", see *Multinational Gas and Petrochemical Co v Multinational Gas and Petrochemical Services Ltd*, op cit, at p 279.
7 See *Tyne Improvement Commissioners v Armement Anversois S/A (The Brabo)*, op cit; *Qatar Petroleum v Shell International Petroleum* [1983] 2 Lloyd's Rep 35; *Goldenglow Nut Food Co Ltd v Commodin (Produce) Ltd and Societe Generale De Surveillance SA and New Hampshire Insurance Co Ltd* [1987] 2 Lloyd's Rep 569 at 576.
8 *Golden Ocean Assurance Ltd and World Mariner Shipping SA v Christopher Julian Martin, The Goldean Mariner* [1990] 2 Lloyd's Rep 215 at 222. Cf *Virgo SS Co SA v Skaarup Shipping Corpn, The Kapetan Georgis* [1988] 1 Lloyd's Rep 352.
9 Op cit.
10 At 271.
11 *Rosler v Hilbery*, op cit; *Tyne Improvement Commissioners v Armement Anversois (The Brabo)*, op cit, at 349–350; *The Manchester Courage* [1973] 1 Lloyd's Rep 386, 391; *Multinational Gas and Petroleum Co v Multinational Gas and Petroleum Services Ltd*, op cit, at 279.
12 *Chaney v Murphy* [1948] WN 130, 64 TLR 489.

Contract

(d) *Where "the claim is brought to enforce, rescind, dissolve, annul or otherwise affect a contract,*[13] *or to recover damages or obtain other relief in respect of the breach of a contract"*[14] *in the following cases:*[15] (i) *Where the contract "was made within the jurisdiction."*[16]

It is sufficient for this provision if the contract was substantially made within the jurisdiction.[17] If quasi-contractual liability arises from something that has occurred in England, then the "quasi-contract" is deemed to have been made in England.[18] The principle of English law is that in the case of a contract of employment the employer may be sued either in tort or for breach of contract if he neglects his implied duty to take reasonable care for the safety of the employee. If, therefore, the contract is made in England for employment abroad, or, indeed, if the contract is governed by English law,[19] the servant may invoke this part of the rule without being driven to rely on rule (f) given below which is confined to a tort where the damage was sustained, or resulted from an act committed, in England.[20]

(ii) *Where the contract "was made by or through an agent trading or residing within the jurisdiction on behalf of a principal trading or residing out of the jurisdiction."*[21]

This part of the rule is applicable even though the agent has no authority to effect a completed contract. Thus in *National Mortgage and Agency Co of New Zealand Ltd v Gosselin*[1] the London agent of a Belgian firm, who was employed merely for the purpose of obtaining orders, sent the firm's price list to the plaintiff. The plaintiff gave an order which was forwarded by the agent and accepted through the post by the Belgian firm. It was held that the contract had been made "through" the agent, for, though the final acceptance

---

13 *EF Hutton and Co (London) Ltd v Mofarij* [1989] 1 WLR 488. The issue may be whether there was a contract between the parties; see *Chevron International Oil Co Ltd v A/S Sea Team (The T. S. Havprins)* [1983] 2 Lloyd's Rep 356, which held that for jurisdictional purposes this is a matter for English law. However, this must now be looked at in the light of Art 8 of the Rome Convention, infra, pp 505–507. If the plaintiff seeks a declaration which denies the existence of a contract with the defendant the case does not come within this head: *Finnish Marine Insurance Co Ltd v Protective National Insurance Co* [1990] 1 QB 1078, [1989] 2 All ER 929; Carter (1990) 61 BYBIL 395; cf *The Olib* [1991] 2 Lloyd's Rep 108. This head does include proceedings for a declaration that a contract has been frustrated or for a claim for relief under the Law Reform (Frustrated Contracts) Act 1943; *BP Exploration Co (Libya) Ltd v Hunt* [1976] 3 All ER 879, [1976] 1 WLR 788.
14 *Official Solicitor v Stype Investments* [1983] 1 All ER 629—relief in respect of a breach of contract included an action involving a trustee's contractual obligations under a declaration of trust. See also *South Adelaide Football Club v Fitzroy Football Club* (1988) 92 FLR 117.
15 Ord 11, r 1(1)(d); formerly Ord 11, r 1(1)(f) and Ord 11, r 2.
16 Eg *Mackender v Feldia AG* [1967] 2 QB 590, [1966] 3 All ER 847; *Aaronson Brothers Ltd v Maderera del Tropico SA* [1967] 2 Lloyd's Rep 159; *Howard Houlder and Partners Ltd v Marine General Transporters Corpn, The Panaghia P* [1983] 2 Lloyd's Rep 653. As to where a contract is deemed to have been made, see infra, pp 505–507.
17 *BP Exploration Co (Libya) Ltd v Hunt* [1976] 1 WLR 788 at 797–798.
18 *Bowling v Cox* [1926] AC 751; *Re Intended Action Rousou's Trustee v Rousou* [1955] 2 All ER 169, [1955] 1 WLR 545; see also *BP Exploration Co (Libya) Ltd v Hunt* [1976] 1 WLR 788 at 797; *In re Jogia (a bankrupt)* [1988] 2 All ER 328, [1988] 1 WLR 484; *Newtherapeutics Ltd v Katz* [1991] Ch 226, [1991] 2 All ER 151.
19 See (iii) infra, p 197.
20 *Matthews v Kuwait Bechtel Corporation* [1959] 2 QB 57, [1959] 2 All ER 345.
21 Eg *Gibbon v Commerz und Creditbank Aktiengesellschaft* [1958] 2 Lloyd's Rep 113.
 1 (1922) 38 TLR 832, CA. See also *Citadel Insurance Co v Atlantic Union Insurance Co SA* [1982] 2 Lloyd's Rep 543, CA.

did not lie with him, he had negotiated its terms. However, the agent must be acting on behalf of the defendant principal, and not as a broker on behalf of the plaintiff.[2]

(iii) *Where the contract "is by its terms, or by implication, governed by English law."*

This has traditionally meant that what is called the *proper law*[3] of the contract must be English law. However, the proper law doctrine has been largely replaced by the European Community rules contained in the Rome Convention of 1980.[4] Ascertainment of the governing law is presumably now a matter for the uniform rules contained in that Convention. Admittedly, there is an argument that, for the purpose of this head of Order 11, the old proper law doctrine should continue to be applied. This is on the basis that the Rome Convention excludes procedural matters from its scope,[5] and Order 11 jurisdiction is a procedural matter. But against this, it has to be pointed out that there is nothing to stop any Contracting State from applying the rules contained in the Rome Convention as part of its own private international law. The United Kingdom could, if it so wished, amend the wording of rule 1 (1) (d) (iii) so as expressly to provide that the governing law is to be ascertained according to the Rome Convention. As presently worded, it does not, of course, expressly so provide but impliedly it does so. For the only sensible way to interpret this provision is to say that it is referring to the English choice of law rules as they alter from time to time. Rule 1 (1) (d) (iii) presupposes that one law governs the whole of the contract.[6] Yet under the Rome Convention it is possible for different laws to govern different parts of the contract.[7] If the dispute only relates to part of the contract it should be enough that this part of the contract is governed by English law.

The court normally has only to reach a tentative or provisional conclusion that English law governs,[8] but this presupposes that there is room for further investigation of facts or law later on.[9] If the facts are before the court and not in dispute a definite conclusion as to the applicable law should be reached at this jurisdictional stage of the action.[10]

Whilst at one time the courts showed a considerable reluctance to exercise

2 *Gill and Duffus Landauer Ltd v London Export Corpn GmbH* [1982] 2 Lloyd's Rep 627. See also *Union International Insurance Co Ltd v Jubilee Insurance Co Ltd* [1991] 1 All ER 740, [1991] 1 WLR 415.
3 See, e g, *Amin Rasheed Shipping Corpn v Kuwait Insurance Co* [1984] AC 50, [1983] 2 All ER 884.
4 Infra, pp 459–521.
5 Infra, pp 473–474.
6 See *Armar Shipping Co Ltd v Caisse Algerienne d'Assurance et de Reassurance, The Armar* [1980] 2 Lloyd's Rep 450 at 456.
7 Infra, pp 476–477.
8 *Compania Naviera Micro SA v Shipley International Inc, The Parouth* [1982] 2 Lloyd's Rep 351 at 354; *Mitsubishi Corpn v Aristidis Alafouzos* [1988] 1 Lloyd's Rep 191, at 193; *Attock Cement Co Ltd v Romanian Bank for Foreign Trade* [1989] 1 WLR 1147 at 1152–1156, CA; Collier [1990] CLJ 39; *Finnish Marine Insurance Co Ltd v Protective National Insurance Co* [1990] 1 QB 1078 at 1084.
9 *E F Hutton & Co (London) Ltd v Mofarrij* [1989] 1 WLR 488 at 495, CA; *Islamic Arab Insurance Co v Saudi Egyptian American Reinsurance Co* [1987] 1 Lloyd's Rep 315 at 317, CA
10 *Ilyssia Cia Naviera SA v Ahmed Abdul Qawi Bamaodah, The Elli 2* [1985] 1 Lloyd's Rep 107 at 114, CA; *Enichem Anic Spa v Ampelos Shipping Co Ltd, The Delfini* [1988] 2 Lloyd's Rep 599 at 602–603; appeal on other grounds dismissed [1990] 1 Lloyd's Rep 252.

their discretion under this particular head,[11] this has been replaced by a neutral attitude.[12] The exercise of the discretion depends on the individual circumstances of the case.[13]

(iv) *Where the contract "contains a term to the effect that the High Court shall have jurisdiction to hear and determine any action in respect of the contract."*[14]

The idea here is that the parties should be bound by the jurisdiction clause to which they have agreed unless there is some strong reason to the contrary.[15]

(e) Where "the claim is brought in respect of[16] *a breach committed within the jurisdiction*[17] *of a contract made within or out of the jurisdiction, and irrespective of the fact, if such be the case, that the breach was preceded or accompanied by a breach committed out of the jurisdiction that rendered impossible the performance of so much of the contract as ought to have been performed within the jurisdiction."*[18] The latter part of the rule meets such a case as *Johnson v Taylor Bros & Co Ltd*[19] where Swedish sellers failed to ship goods that they had sold to English buyers under a contact c.i.f. Leeds. Under the rule as it then stood,[20] leave for service out of the jurisdiction was refused, for, though the failure to deliver the shipping documents represented a breach in England, the substantial breach was the non-shipment of the goods at Stockholm. Under the present rule, however, leave could be granted in such a case. It will be noticed that leave cannot be granted under this rule unless three conditions are fulfilled: the alleged contract must in fact have been made; it must have been broken; and the breach must have occurred in England. If the breach involves a failure to perform, it is necessary to look at where the

---

11 *Amin Rasheed Shipping Corpn v Kuwait Insurance Co*, op cit, at 68 (per Lord DIPLOCK).
12 *Spiliada Maritime Corpn v Cansulex Ltd* [1987] AC 460, [1986] 3 All ER 843; following Lord WILBERFORCE in the *Amin Rasheed Case* at 72.
13 *Spiliada Maritime Corpn v Cansulex Ltd*, op cit, at 481–482; see infra, pp 204–210.
14 Ord 11, r 1(1)(d)(iv); formerly Ord 11, r 2. English law was applied in order to determine whether the contract contained such a term in *Chevron Oil Co Ltd v A/S Sea Team (The T S Havprins)* [1983] 2 Lloyd's Rep 356. But see now Art 8 of the Rome Convention, discussed infra, pp 505–507.
15 *Unterweser Reederei GmbH v Zapata Off-Shore Co, The Chaparral* [1968] 2 Lloyd's Rep 158. When proceedings were brought before the US courts an injunction was, originally, granted enjoining the parties from proceeding in England, but the US Supreme Court ruled that the English jurisdiction clause should be enforced unless such enforcement would be unreasonable or unjust: *The Chaparral* [1972] 2 Lloyd's Rep 315; *The Vikfrost* [1980] 1 Lloyd's Rep 560, CA; *Chevron International Oil Co Ltd v A/S Sea Team (The T.S. Havprins)* [1983] 2 Lloyd's Rep 356; *Kutchera v Buckingham International Holdings Ltd* (1988) 9 ILRM 501, SC of Ireland; cf *The Eleftheria* [1970] P 94, esp at pp 103–104, infra, pp 235–236. See Collins (1973) 22 ICLQ 332. The English courts are unlikely to grant a stay of the proceedings under the doctrine of *forum non conveniens* where there is an English choice of jurisdiction clause, see *The Hida Maru* [1981] 2 Lloyd's Rep 510; *Commercial Bank of the Near East Plc v A, B, C and D* [1989] 2 Lloyd's Rep 319; infra, p 225.
16 See *GAF Corporation v Amchem Products Inc* [1975] 1 Lloyd's Rep 601 at 605–606. It encompasses a claim in quasi-contract: *McFee Engineering Pty Ltd v CBS Construction Pty Ltd* (1980) 44 FLR 340.
17 *Citadel Insurance Co v Atlantic Union Insurance Co SA* [1982] 2 Lloyd's Rep 543; *Cantieri Navali Riuniti SpA v NV Omne Justitia and Others (The Stolt Marmaro)* [1985] 2 Lloyd's Rep 428.
18 Ord 11, r 1(1)(e); formerly Ord 11, r 1(1)(g); see generally *Oppenheimer v Louis Rosenthal & Co A-G* [1937] 1 All ER 23.
19 [1920] AC 144.
20 "The action is founded on any breach within the jurisdiction of any contract wherever made, which, according to the terms thereof, ought to be performed within the jurisdiction."

performance was to take place.[21] It has been held that the court in its discretion may grant leave where the plaintiff claims an account against a person abroad, despite the fact that usually the foreign forum is the most convenient place for the production of the relevant books and documents.[22]

Tort

(f) When "the claim is founded on a tort and the damage was sustained, or resulted from an act committed, within the jurisdiction."[23] The wording of this head has been substantially altered when compared with that of its predecessor. This required that the action be founded on "a tort committed within the jurisdiction". A difficult definitional problem was created in cases, for example, where a product was defectively manufactured in New York and subsequently caused injury in England; the question was then whether the tort was committed in New York, where the negligent act took place, or in England, where the subsequent injury occurred. The solution adopted was to look for where the wrongful act was done or, as it was put more recently, to ask where in substance the cause of action arose.[24] Order 11, rule 1(1)(f) avoids this definitional problem by making it clear that jurisdiction can be taken in England if *either* the damage was sustained *or* the act (from which the damage resulted) was committed in England. The result is to make the tort head a very wide one, and to bring tort cases under Order 11 into line with tort cases under the jurisdiction rules contained in the Brussels Convention (and now contained in the Lugano Convention as well).[25] By using the tort provision under the Brussels Convention as the model for rule 1(1)(f), not only are the virtues of the former (its width and clarity) incorporated into Order 11, but also its weaknesses. These are examined more fully when the Brussels and Lugano Conventions are considered in detail;[26] suffice it to say that the relevant provision in the Brussels and Lugano Conventions and, therefore, Rule 1(1)(f), does not cover injunctions to restrain threatened wrongs;[1] nor is it appropriately worded to deal with cases of libel, since these do not require proof of *damage* to be actionable; nor does it solve all the definitional problems that can arise.

For example there can be problems over whether the damage is sustained in England. If the act and injury take place in State A, but the plaintiff is hospitalised in State B, is damage sustained there?[2] Moreover, the damage to

21 See *Brinkibon Ltd v Stahag Stahl und Stahlwarenhandelsgesellschaft GmbH* [1983] 2 AC 34, 49–50, HL; *Gill and Duffus Landauer Ltd v London Export Corpn GmbH* [1982] 2 Lloyd's Rep 627, 630.
22 *International Corporation Ltd v Besser Manufacturing Co* [1950] 1 KB 488, [1950] 1 All ER 355.
23 Ord 11, r 1(1)(f); formerly Ord 11, r 1(1)(h). Claims founded on a constructive trust do not come within this head: *Metall Und Rohstoff A G v Donaldson Lufkin and Jenrette Inc* [1990] 1 QB 391 at 474; overruled on a different point in *Lonrho Plc v Fayed* [1991] 3 All ER 303, [1991] 3 WLR 188, HL.
24 See *Distillers Co (Biochemicals) Ltd v Thompson* [1971] AC 458. The problem of where a tort is committed can still arise in the context of jurisdiction (supra, p 191 and infra, p 200), as well as that of choice of law (infra pp 551–557).
25 See Art 5(3) of the Conventions; Case 21/76 *Bier v Mines de Potasse* [1976] ECR 1735, [1978] QB 708, [1977] 1 CMLR 284, infra, p 301.
26 Infra, pp 300–302.
1 Ord 11, r 1(1)(b) (formerly Ord 11, r 1(1)(i)) may however be applicable; see *James North and Sons Ltd v North Cape Textiles Ltd* [1984] 1 WLR 1428 at 1431; supra, pp 192–193.
2 See *Vile v Von Wendt Zurich Insurance Co* (1980) 103 DLR (3d) 356, where it was held that it was. Cf *Thomas v Penna* [1985] 2 NSWLR 171, but now see *Flaherty v Girgis* (1988) 71 ALR 1, H C of Australia.

the plaintiff might have been suffered in more than one country, particularly in a case involving an economic tort. The Court of Appeal in *Metall Und Rohstoff AG v Donaldson Lufkin and Jenrette Inc*[3] held that it is not necessary that all the damage has been sustained within the jurisdiction; it is "enough if some significant damage has been sustained in England".[4] The same problem arises in relation to the tortious act from which the damage resulted. The act may have been committed partly within the jurisdiction and partly without. Again, it is not necessary that all of the acts have been committed within the jurisdiction. It is enough if "substantial and efficacious acts"[5] have been committed within the jurisdiction, even if substantial and efficacious acts have also been committed outside the jurisdiction.

The courts showed a distinct willingness to exercise their discretion to allow service out of the jurisdiction under the predecessor to rule 1(1)(f). In *Cordoba Shipping Co Ltd v National State Bank, Elizabeth, New Jersey, The Albaforth*[6] it was said that "the jurisdiction in which a tort has been committed is prima facie the natural forum for the determination of the dispute".[7] A presumption in terms of the state in which a tort is committed looks singularly unsuitable now that the tort head of Order 11 is no longer concerned with whether a tort has been committed within the jurisdiction. Nonetheless, this presumption has continued to be applied. In the *Metall Und Rohstoff Case*[8] the new tort head of Order 11 was satisfied in that significant damage was sustained in England. Yet, when it came to the exercise of the discretion, the Court of Appeal followed the *Cordoba Shipping Case*. The substance of the tort of inducement of breach of contract was committed in London; this had been determined earlier on when the issue of where the tort was committed had to be decided in the context of applying the tort choice of law rules.[9] The presumption was therefore that England was the appropriate forum for trial.[10] Whilst the use of presumptions is very questionable when a discretion is being exercised,[11] it has to be admitted that the results achieved by their use in tort-cases is a good one. If a tort has been committed in England, an English court will apply English law, which suggests that an English court should also try the case.[12] There is a strong case for continuing to show a willingness to exercise the discretion in favour of allowing service out of the jurisdiction in cases coming under the tort head of Order 11. One further consideration justifying this is the fact that the equivalent provision under the Brussels and Lugano Conventions gives jurisdiction to a State, without any discretion in the Conventions to refuse to take jurisdiction.[13] The assimilation of the jurisdiction rules in tort cases under the Brussels and Lugano

3 [1990] 1 QB 391, [1988] 3 All ER 116; overruled on a different point in *Lonrho plc v Fayed* [1991] 3 All ER 303, [1991] 3 WLR 188, HL; Carter (1989) 60 BYBIL 485.
4 Ibid, at 437.
5 Ibid.
6 [1984] 2 Lloyd's Rep 91; Fawcett [1985] Lloyd's MCLQ 6; Carter (1984) 55 BYBIL 347.
7 At 94.
8 Op cit.
9 Infra, pp 553–554, where the facts of the case are considered in more detail. The tort choice of law rules were relevant to the question of whether the plaintiff had a good arguable case on the merits: supra, p 191.
10 [1990] 1 QB 391 at 484.
11 Infra, p 209.
12 See *Voth v Manildra Flour Mills Pty Ltd* (1990) 171 CLR 538 at 566 et seq, HC of Australia.
13 On the question of when an English court can use the traditional English doctrine of *forum non conveniens*, see infra, pp 331–334.

Conventions and under Order 11[14] would be helped by a willingness to use the discretion to allow service out of the jurisdiction under Order 11, rule 1(1)(f).

Property

(g) Where *"the whole subject-matter of the action is land situate within the jurisdiction (with or without rents or profits) or the perpetuation of testimony relating to land so situate."*[15] The most obvious example of this is an action for the recovery of land.[16]

(h) When *"the claim is brought to construe, rectify, set aside or enforce an act, deed, will, contract, obligation or liability affecting land situate within the jurisdiction."*[17] The matters included in this head are not altogether clear,[18] but from the few relevant decisions it appears that what is complained of by the plaintiff must be something that directly affects the land itself, not something that merely affects its value.[19] It has been held that the rule includes an action against the assignee of a lease for breach of covenant to repair,[20] a claim by a tenant of a farm to recover compensation for improvements,[21] and an action to enforce obligations under a declaration of trust in respect of land which had been sold at the time of the action,[22] but not an action for the recovery of rent,[23] and not an action concerning royalties in respect of the production of oil.[24]

(i) Where *"the claim is made for a debt secured on immovable property or is made to assert, declare or determine proprietary or possessory rights, or rights of security, in or over movable property, or to obtain authority to dispose of movable property situate within the jurisdiction."*[25] This head is wider than its predecessor in that it now covers a claim for a debt secured on *immovable* property, for example an action for non-payment of a bank loan secured by a mortgage of a house. As regards *movable* property it would cover, for example, an action in relation to a life policy assigned to a lender as security for a loan.[26]

(j) Where *"the claim is brought to execute the trusts of a written instrument being trusts that ought to be executed according to English law and of which the person to be served with the writ is a trustee, or for any relief or remedy*

---

14 On the relevance of this in relation to the exercise of the discretion see *James North and Sons Ltd v North Cape Textiles Ltd*, op cit, at 1433–1434.
15 Ord 11, r 1(1)(g); formerly Ord 11, r 1(1)(a).
16 *Agnew v Usher* (1884) 14 QBD 78; affd (1884) 51 LT 752.
17 Ord 11, r 1(1)(h); formerly Ord 11, r 1(1)(b).
18 Dicey & Morris, pp 918–922; and see *State of Victoria v Hansen* [1960] VR 582; *Muusers v State Government Insurance Office* (1980) 2 NSWLR 73.
19 *Casey v Arnott* (1876) 2 CPD 24.
20 *Tassell v Hallen* [1892] 1 QB 321.
21 *Kaye v Sutherland* (1887) 20 QBD 147.
22 *Official Solicitor v Stype Investments (Jersey) Ltd* [1983] 1 All ER 629.
23 *Agnew v Usher* (1884) 14 QBD 78; cf Morris, p 75.
24 *BHP Petroleum Pty Ltd v Oil Basins Ltd* [1985] VR 725.
25 Ord 11, r 1(1)(i); formerly Ord 11, r 1(1)(k). It is modelled on Art 5(8) of the Modified Convention allocating jurisdiction within the UK, contained in the Civil Jurisdiction and Judgments Act 1982, Sch 4 discussed infra, p 338.
26 See *Deutsche National Bank v Paul* [1898] 1 Ch 283, which held that such a claim did not fall within one of the contract heads, what is now Ord 11, r 1(1)(e), (formerly Ord 11, r 1(1)(g)), hence the introduction of a new head of Ord 11 (formerly Ord 11, r 1(1)(k)) to deal with this.

which might be obtained in any such action.''[1] The major limitation on the operation of the former trusts head was that the property subject to the trusts had to be situated in England. This meant, for example, that if a defendant trustee had sold the entire trust funds and had departed abroad with the proceeds the trusts head was not applicable.[2] This limitation has now been removed and there is no need for the property subject to the trusts to be situated in England.

(k) Where "the claim is made for the administration of the estate of a person who died domiciled[3] *within the jurisdiction or for any relief or remedy which might be obtained in any such action.''*[4]

(l) Where "the claim is brought in a probate action within the meaning of Order 76.''[5] This head applies to an action for the grant of probate, or letters of administration of an estate, or for the revocation of such a grant, or for a decree pronouncing against the validity of a will, provided the action is not non-contentious or common form probate business.

Enforcement of Judgments or Arbitral Awards

(m) Where "the claim is brought to enforce any judgment or arbitral award.''[6] This is an entirely new head of Order 11, rule 1(1). The background to it is the rule that any action in England to enforce a foreign judgment at common law requires the English rules as to jurisdiction and service of writs to be satisfied.[7] If the plaintiff was unable to satisfy this requirement, he was always left with the option of bringing a new action on the original cause of action, with the possibility of using Order 11 as the basis of jurisdiction. Section 34 of the Civil Jurisdiction and Judgments Act 1982 now prevents the plaintiff from doing this,[8] hence the need for some basis for serving a writ on a defendant in order to enforce the foreign judgment. Rule 1(1)(m) provides the means for satisfying this requirement. This new rule also applies in respect of arbitral awards.[9]

Taxes

(n) Where "the claim is brought against a defendant not domiciled[10] *in Scotland or Northern Ireland in respect of a claim by the Commissioners of Inland Revenue for or in relation to any of the duties or taxes which have been, or are for the time being, placed under their care and management.''*[11]

1 Ord 11, r 1(1)(j); formerly Ord 11, r 1(1)(e).
2 *Winter v Winter* [1894] 1 Ch 421. See also *Official Solicitor v Stype Investments (Jersey) Ltd* [1983] 1 All ER 629.
3 As defined in accordance with ss 41–46 of the Civil Jurisdiction and Judgments Act 1982, which have been amended by Sch 2, paras 16–21 of the Civil Jurisdiction and Judgments Act 1991, infra, pp 584–586, see Ord 11, r 1(4).
4 Ord 11, r 1(1)(k); formerly Ord 11, r 1(1)(d). It is very debatable whether the discretion would be exercised in the case of foreign immovables; see Davis (1966) 2 NZULR 243 at 244–245.
5 Ord 11, r 1(1)(l); formerly Ord 11, r 1(1)(m).
6 Ord 11, r 1(1)(m).
7 *Perry v Zissis* [1977] 1 Lloyd's Rep 607, see infra, pp 348–349.
8 Infra, p 347.
9 However, it has been doubted whether committal proceedings to enforce a "Mareva" injunction come within this head: *Mansour v Mansour* [1990] FCR 17, [1989] 1 FLR 418.
10 Ord 11, r 1(4) provides that domicil is defined under ss 41–46 of the Civil Jurisdiction and Judgments Act 1982, which have been amended by Sch 2, paras 16–21, of the Civil Jurisdiction and Judgments Act 1991; discussed supra, pp 191–192 and infra, pp 584–586.
11 Ord 11, r 1(1)(n); formerly Ord 11, r 1(1)(o); *IRC v Stype Investments Ltd* [1982] Ch 456.

Miscellaneous

(o) Where "the claim is brought under the Nuclear Installations Act 1965 or in respect of contributions under the Social Security Act 1975." [12]

(p) Where "the claim is made for a sum to which the Directive of the Council of the European Communities dated 15 March 1976 No 76/308/EEC applies, and service is to be effected in a country which is a member State of the European Economic Community." [13] The Directive in question deals with claims for an agricultural levy or other sum.

(q) Where "the claim is made under the Drug Trafficking Offences Act 1986." [14] This is concerned with claims relating to the proceeds of drug trafficking.

(r) Where "the claim is made under the Financial Services Act 1986 or the Banking Act 1987." [15]

(s) Where "the claim is made under Part VI of the Criminal Justice Act 1988." [16] This is concerned with claims relating to the confiscation of the proceeds of crime.

(t) Where "the claim is brought for money had and received or for an account or other relief against the defendant as constructive trustee, and the defendant's alleged liability arises out of acts committed, whether by him or otherwise, within the jurisdiction." [17]

The interaction of the different heads of Order 11, rule 1(1) It should be pointed out that an overlap between the various provisions of Order 11, rule 1(1) is possible, and one case may come within several heads. At the same time the "rules under Order 11 are to be read disjunctively and each subsection is complete in itself and independent of the others".[18] This means, for example, that an employee, who has suffered personal injury abroad (following a negligent act there) during the course of his employment and who can sue his employer for damages either for breach of contract or in tort, can elect to frame his action in contract rather than in tort, thereby bringing his case within one of the heads of Order 11, rule 1(1).[19] However, if service abroad has been allowed under one of the heads, the plaintiff is not allowed later to add to his statement of claim a claim for another cause of action for which leave to serve a writ out of the jurisdiction would not have been given.[20]

The exercise of the discretion under Order 11, rule 1(1) The courts *may*, rather than *must*, allow service of a writ out of the jurisdiction. Where the case falls within one of the heads of Order 11, rule 1(1) the exercise of assumed

---

12 Ord 11, r 1(1)(o); formerly, Ord 11, r 1(1)(l).
13 Ord 11, r 1(1)(p); formerly, Ord 11, r 1(1)(p).
14 Ord 11, r 1(1)(q).
15 Ord 11, r 1(1)(r).
16 Ord 11, r 1(1)(s).
17 Ord 11, r 1(1)(t).
18 *Matthews v Kuwait Bechtel Corporation* [1959] 2 QB 57 at 62; and see *Tassell v Hallen* [1892] 1 QB 321.
19 *Matthews v Kuwait Bechtel Corporation*, op cit.
20 *Waterhouse v Reid* [1938] 1 KB 743, [1938] 1 All ER 235; *The Siskina* [1979] AC 210 at 254–255.

jurisdiction in any given case lies within the discretion of the court.[21] The criterion for exercise of the Order 11 discretion is that of *forum conveniens*,[1] ie service out of the jurisdiction will only be allowed where England is clearly the most appropriate forum in the interests of the parties and the ends of justice. The law in this area has been exhaustively re-examined and restated by the House of Lords in *Spiliada Maritime Corpn v Cansulex Ltd*[2] where Lord GOFF, with whom the other Law Lords concurred, set out the relevant principles for the exercise of the discretion.

The basic principle　Lord GOFF said that the underlying fundamental principle was "to identify the forum in which the case can be suitably tried for the interests of all the parties and for the ends of justice".[3] The same principle underlies the discretion to stay actions on the basis of *forum non conveniens* after the service of a writ.[4] Lord GOFF then went on to state a number of other principles which help to explain the basic principle. These principles relate to the following: the appropriate forum; other considerations; the exorbitant nature of Order 11 jurisdiction; and the particular head of Order 11 being employed.

The appropriate forum　The burden of proof is on the plaintiff to show that England is the appropriate forum for trial, and that this is clearly so.[5] Appropriateness, in this context,[6] comprises a wide range of considerations. "The court must take into account the nature of the dispute, the legal and practical issues involved, such questions as local knowledge, availability of witnesses and their evidence and expense."[7] It also involves looking at the expense and inconvenience to a foreign defendant in having trial in England.[8] As well as these matters of litigational convenience, the courts have considered the connections that the parties and the cause of action have with the alternative fora.[9] Beyond this, the circumstances of an individual case may raise other considerations. The fact that English law is applicable to the dispute in question may point towards England as being the appropriate

---

21 RSC Ord 11, r 4(2). For an appeal court's powers to review the discretion vested in a judge see *Hadmor Productions Ltd v Hamilton* [1983] 1 AC 191; *Spiliada Maritime Corpn v Cansulex Ltd* [1987] AC 460 [1986] 3 All ER 843, HL. If the application is for leave to serve a writ in Scotland or Northern Ireland and it appears that there is a concurrent remedy there, the courts in deciding whether to grant leave should have regard to the comparative cost and convenience of proceeding thereon in England: RSC Ord 11, r 4(3).
1 This presupposes that there is an obvious alternative forum abroad; if there is not it is proper to allow service out of the jurisdiction: *Ets Soules et Cie v Handgate Co Ltd SA, The Handgate* [1987] 1 Lloyd's Rep 142.
2 [1987] 1 AC 460.
3 Ibid, at 480.
4 Infra, pp 221–234. See also *Voth v Manildra Flour Mills Pty Ltd* (1990) 171 CLR 538 at 563–564, HC of Australia. The Australian test for service out of the jurisdiction is, however, easier for the plaintiff to satisfy than the English one, only being concerned with whether the forum is clearly inappropriate, see Collins (1991) 107 LQR 182.
5 *Spiliada Maritime Corpn v Cansulex Ltd* [1987] AC 460 at 481.
6 The cases on appropriateness in respect of stays of action on the basis of a foreign choice of jurisdiction clause (discussed infra, pp 234–236) are not of much assistance in this context, see per Lord WILBERFORCE in *Amin Rasheed Corpn v Kuwait Insurance Co* [1984] AC 50 at 172. But cases on stays of action on the basis of *forum non conveniens* are of assistance; see *Spiliada Maritime Corpn v Cansulex Ltd* [1987] 1 AC 460 infra, pp 221–234.
7 Per Lord WILBERFORCE in *Amin Rasheed Corpn v Kuwait Insurance Co*, op cit.
8 *Société Generale de Paris v Dreyfus Brothers* (1885) 29 ChD 239 at 242; *George Monro Ltd v American Cyanamid and Chemical Corporation* [1944] KB 432, [1944] 1 All ER 386; *Cordova Land Co Ltd v Victor Brothers Inc* [1966] 1 WLR 793 at 801–802.
9 *Kroch v Rossell et Cie* [1937] 1 All ER 725; *Amanuel v Alexandros Shipping Co (The Alexandros P)* [1986] 1 QB 464; *Spiliada Maritime Corpn v Cansulex Ltd* [1987] AC 460.

forum for trial.[10] On the other hand, if trial in England would lead to a multiplicity of proceedings, with concurrent actions, involving the same parties and the same issues, taking place in England and abroad, this would be a ground for exercising the discretion against allowing service out of the jurisdiction.[11]

Where the parties have agreed to submit their disputes under a contract to the jurisdiction of a foreign court, then an English court will need very strong reasons to allow one of them to go back on his word.[12] A distinction has been drawn between foreign jurisdiction clauses which are "exclusive" and those which are not, with the corollary that the court is even less likely to allow service out in the former case.[13] It seems that it is for the governing law (in principle, this should be that of the jurisdiction agreement) to determine whether the clause is "exclusive".[14] However, the fact that this rule is not an inexorable and inflexible one may be illustrated by *Evans Marshall & Co Ltd v Bertola SA*.[15]

The plaintiffs, an English firm of wine merchants, agreed with the first defendants, Spanish producers and shippers of wine, that the plaintiffs should be the first defendants' sole agents in England for the sale of the latter's sherry. The agreement provided that any dispute should be submitted to the Spanish courts. The first defendants later purported to appoint another English firm, the second defendants, as their agents.

When the plaintiffs sought an injunction and damages against both defendants, and sought leave to serve the first defendants out of the jurisdiction under RSC, Order 11, rule 1, the Court of Appeal had to consider the effect of the express clause submitting disputes to the Spanish courts.

In granting leave under Order 11, rule 1, both KERR J and the Court of Appeal considered this case exceptional in that various factors connected the proceedings closely with England. The substance of the claim related to the marketing of sherry in England; the essential witnesses were English; the second defendants were English and one of the claims was of conspiracy between the two defendants; and Spanish procedure was very slow compared with that before the English courts and the Spanish courts would not grant interlocutory relief.

Other considerations Identification of "the forum in which the case can be suitably tried for the interests of all the parties and for the ends of

10 *Cordoba Shipping Co Ltd v National State Bank, Elizabeth, New Jersey (The Albaforth)* [1984] 2 Lloyd's Rep 91 at 93–94, CA (involving tort); *Spiliada Maritime Corpn v Cansulex Ltd* [1987] AC 460, HL (contract), discussed infra, p 210; see also *Voth v Manildra Flour Mills Pty Ltd* (1990) 171 CLR 538 at 566 et seq, H C of Australia.
11 *The Hagen* [1908] P 189; *El Du Pont de Nemours & Co v I C Agnew and K W Kerr* [1987] 2 Lloyd's Rep 585. See also *Spiliada Maritime Corpn v Cansulex Ltd*, op cit—a case involving third party proceedings.
12 *Mackender v Feldia AG* [1967] 2 QB 590 at 604; *Unterweser Reederei GmbH v Zapata Off-Shore Co, The Chaparral* [1968] 2 Lloyd's Rep 158 at 163–164. For the position where the contract provides for arbitration abroad see *A and B v C and D* [1982] 1 Lloyd's Rep 166, affd sub nom *Qatar Petroleum v Shell International Petroleum* [1983] 2 Lloyd's Rep 35, CA. Cf *Evans Marshall & Co Ltd v Bertola SA* [1973] 1 All ER 992, [1973] 1 WLR 349, infra.
13 *Evans Marshall & Co Ltd v Bertola SA* [1973] 1 WLR 349 at 360–362.
14 Ibid, at 361; *The Sindh* [1975] 1 Lloyd's Rep 372; cf *The Makefjell* [1976] 2 Lloyd's Rep 29; Knight (1977) 26 ICLQ 664. For rules on when foreign jurisdiction clauses can be escaped from, see infra, pp 237–239.
15 [1973] 1 All ER 992, [1973] 1 WLR 349. In cases involving Spanish defendants see now the Brussels Convention, infra pp 279–334.

justice" involves looking not only at factors of appropriateness but at other considerations as well.[16] Guidance on the range of considerations to be taken into account when exercising the Order 11 discretion can be found in cases on the discretion to stay actions on the basis of *forum non conveniens* after the service of a writ within the jurisdiction.[17] This follows from the fact that the same basic principle underlies the exercise of the discretion in both areas, although there are differences between the burdens of proof and in respect of the fact that Order 11 is regarded as an exorbitant form of jurisdiction.[18] Two particular considerations, which have not been mentioned so far, need to be examined.

First, there is the question, which was asked even before the *Spiliada Case*, of whether justice will be obtained in the foreign court.[19] If it appears probable that the plaintiff, owing to political or other reasons, will not receive a fair trial abroad, the court may well exercise its discretion in favour of the application for service out of the jurisdiction, even though both parties to the suit are foreigners and even though their rights fall to be governed by foreign law.[20] The Court of Appeal has been prepared to take this idea further and has held[21] that, where the foreign jurisdiction is "compelled to apply a law which is contrary to the general understanding of commercial men,"[1] this is a good reason for the exercise of the discretion, notwithstanding the inconvenience to the defendant. A recent example of injustice abroad includes the fact that Saudi Arabia lacks a specialist court and lawyers concerned with insurance matters, whereas England has this.[2] However, this involves making the sort of comparison which English courts are not supposed to make.[3]

Second, there is the question of whether the plaintiff will obtain a legitimate personal or juridical advantage from trial in England. This has traditionally been one of the factors to be considered when exercising the discretion to stay on the basis of *forum non conveniens*. The effect of the *Spiliada Case* is to introduce this factor as a consideration when exercising the discretion to allow service out of the jurisdiction in Order 11 cases. Lord GOFF said[4] that the court should not be deterred from refusing leave in Order 11 cases simply because the plaintiff will be deprived of an advantage, such as higher damages

---

16 *Metall Und Rohstoff AG v Donaldson Lufkin and Jenrette Inc* [1990] 1 QB 391; overruled on a different point in *Lonrho plc v Fayed* [1991] 3 All ER 303, [1991] 3 WLR 188, HL.

17 Infra, pp 221–234.

18 *Spiliada Maritime Corpn v Cansulex Ltd* [1987] AC 460 at 481. See generally Edinger (1986) 64 Can BR 283. If a case involves some defendants outside the jurisdiction, and others within the jurisdiction, the case is looked at in the round: *El Du Pont de Nemours & Co v IC Agnew and K W Kerr* [1987] 2 Lloyd's Rep 585 at 593.

19 *Aaronson Brothers Ltd v Maderera del Tropico SA* [1967] 2 Lloyd's Rep 159 at 162; and *Unterweser Reederei GmbH v Zapata Off-Shore Co, The Chaparral* [1968] 2 Lloyd's Rep 158.

20 *Oppenheimer v Louis Rosenthal and Co AG* [1937] 1 All ER 23.

21 *Coast Lines v Hudig and Veder Chartering NV* [1972] 2 QB 34. See also *Seashell Shipping Corpn v Mutualidad de Seguros Del Instituto Nacional De Industria, The Magnum Ex Tarraco Augusta* [1989] 1 Lloyd's Rep 47 at 53 (the foreign court might not apply the law agreed by the parties); Carter (1989) 60 BYBIL 482; *Kloeckner & Co AG v Gatoil Overseas Inc* [1990] 1 Lloyd's Rep 177 at 207.

1 *Coast Lines v Hudig and Veder Chartering NV*, op cit at 45; see also *Britannia Steamship Insurance Association Ltd v Ausonia Assicurazioni SpA* [1984] 2 Lloyd's Rep 98 at 102.

2 *Islamic Arab Insurance Co v Saudi Egyptian American Reinsurance Co* [1987] 1 Lloyd's Rep 315 at 319–320.

3 Infra, pp 228–229.

4 [1987] 1 AC 460 at 482–484.

or a more generous limitation period,[5] provided that the court is satisfied that substantial justice will be done in the available appropriate forum abroad. It is envisaged that the sort of advantage mentioned above, which is to the benefit of the plaintiff and to the detriment of the defendant, will not be decisive. However, the position may be different in the situation where the advantage to the plaintiff is not to the disadvantage of the defendant. Thus, on the facts of the *Spiliada Case* one crucial point was that the plaintiffs obtained an advantage from trial in England in that similar proceedings involving the same defendant company, lawyers, expert witnesses and insurers had been commenced and eventually settled in England.[6] The advantage that this gave to the plaintiffs in terms of "efficiency, expedition and economy" did not involve a countervailing disadvantage to the defendants. Indeed, it was in the objective interests of justice that trial should take place in England. The result was that the House of Lords allowed service out of the jurisdiction. The advantage that the plaintiff obtains from the award of costs in English proceedings has been taken into account on the basis that substantial justice would not be done in the foreign proceedings if the plaintiff would have to pay costs there.[7]

On the other hand, it seems that certain considerations cannot be taken into account when exercising the discretion. The courts are not "to embark upon a comparison of the procedures, or methods, or reputation or standing of the courts of one country as compared with those of another".[8] More controversially, the question of the difficulties that may be encountered in enforcing an English judgment abroad after jurisdiction has been taken under Order 11, rule 1(1) is, seemingly, irrelevant to the exercise of the discretion.[9]

An exorbitant basis of jurisdiction   Order 11, rule 1 (1) is regarded as being an "exorbitant" or "extraordinary" basis of jurisdiction,[10] it is a wider jurisdiction than we recognise in others, in that if a foreign court took jurisdiction in similar circumstances English courts would not be prepared to recognise that court's judgment.[11] Assumed jurisdiction is seen as conflicting with the general principles of comity between civilised nations, and, because of this, it has been said that the power to allow service of a writ out of the jurisdiction should be exercised with extreme caution.[12]

This reluctance to allow service out of the jurisdiction manifests itself in a

---

5 If the English proceedings are set aside this may be on condition that the defendant should waive its right to rely on the time bar in the foreign proceedings, per Lord GOFF at 487–488. See on time-bars *Metall und Rohstoff AG v Donaldson Lufkin and Jenrette Inc* [1990] 1 QB 391 at 488; overruled on a different point in *Lonrho plc v Fayed* [1991] 3 All ER 303, [1991] 3 WLR 188, HL.
6 At 484–486.
7 *Roneleigh Ltd v MII Exports Inc* [1989] 1 WLR 619 at 623; cf *Pride Shipping Corpn v Chung Hwa Pulp Corpn* [1991] 1 Lloyd's Rep 126 at 135.
8 *Amin Rasheed Corpn v Kuwait Insurance Co* [1984] AC 50 at 72 (per Lord WILBERFORCE), at 67 (per Lord DIPLOCK). For further discussion of this point see infra, pp 228–229.
9 *Coast Lines v Hudig and Veder Chartering NV* [1972] 2 QB 34 at 45, [1972] 1 All ER 451 at 456, CA; Bissett-Johnson (1972) 21 ICLQ 53; compare Collins (1972) 21 ICLQ 656; Graupner (1963) 12 ICLQ 357. See also *Kutchera v Buckingham International Holdings Ltd* (1988) 9 ILRM 501 at 505–506, SC of Ireland.
10 *Spiliada Maritime Corpn v Cansulex Ltd* [1987] 1 AC 460 at 481. See generally De Winter (1968) 17 ICLQ 706; Collins (1991) 107 LQR10.
11 See infra, pp 360–362. For the position under the Brussels and Lugano Conventions, see infra, p 413.
12 *Cordova Land Co Ltd v Victor Brothers Inc* [1966] 1 WLR 793 at 796; *Mackender v Feldia AG* [1967] 2 QB 590 at 599; *Amin Rasheed Corpn v Kuwait Insurance*, op cit, at 65.

number of general principles, all of which operate against the exercise of assumed jurisdiction. The power conferred by Order 11 is only exercisable by the court in cases "which seem to it to fall within the spirit as well as the letter of the various classes of case provided for".[13] As has been seen,[14] the plaintiff must show a good arguable case on the merits. If, in the circumstances, the construction of the Order is at all doubtful it should be resolved in favour of the defendant.[15] The plaintiff must also show that England is *clearly* the appropriate forum.[16] Moreover, since the application for leave is made ex parte, full and fair disclosure of all the facts is necessary.[17] Any unreasonable delay by the plaintiff in seeking leave militates against leave being given.[18] Strict compliance with the procedural requirements under Order 11 is usually required and irregularities cannot normally be cured at a later stage of the action.[19]

Whilst a reluctance to exercise jurisdiction under Order 11 is understandable, it should perhaps be tempered by a realisation: first, that other countries have exorbitant bases of jurisdiction;[20] and second, that the Brussels and Lugano Conventions require jurisdiction to be taken in England, without any discretion in either Convention to decline to do so,[1] in cases where, if the traditional rules on jurisdiction had to be used, one of the heads of Order 11, rule 1(1) would be applicable.[2] Now that we have a *forum non conveniens* discretion to stay actions once a writ has been served it would rationalise the English law on jurisdiction if service out of the jurisdiction was automatically available without the leave of the court. The *forum non conveniens* discretion could then come into play once the writ had been served. After all, this discretion is based on the same fundamental principle as the Order 11 discretion. However, it is the notion that Order 11 is an exorbitant form of jurisdiction with the consequential placing of the burden of proof on the plaintiff that makes this rationalisation impossible.

The significance of the particular head of Order 11   Whilst accepting that Order 11 is an exorbitant form of jurisdiction, Lord GOFF has pointed out that the circumstances specified under the different heads vary greatly, and that this affects the court's willingness to exercise the discretion in favour of allowing service out of the jurisdiction.[3] In cases coming under what is now

13 *Johnson v Taylor Brothers* [1920] AC 144 at 153.
14 Supra, p 191.
15 *The Hagen* [1908] P 189 at 201; *The Siskina* [1979] AC 210 at 254–255; cf *Buttes Gas and Oil Co v Hammer* [1971] 3 All ER 1025 (for later proceedings, see [1975] QB 557).
16 *Spiliada Maritime Corpn v Cansulex Ltd* [1987] 1 AC 460 at 481; *Islamic Arab Insurance Co v Saudi Egyptian American Reinsurance Co* [1987] 1 Lloyd's Rep 315 at 318–319.
17 *Kuwait Oil Co (KSC) v Idemitsu Tankers KK (The Hida Maru)* [1981] 2 Lloyd's Rep 510; *Trafalgar Tours Ltd v Alan James Henry* [1990] 2 Lloyd's Rep 298; *Newtherapeutics Ltd v Katz* [1991] Ch 226, [1991] 2 All ER 151.
18 *The Nimrod* [1973] 2 Lloyd's Rep 91.
19 *Camera Care Ltd v Victor Hasselblad AB* (1986) Times, 6 January, [1986] ECC 373; *Leal v Dunlop Bio Processes Ltd* [1984] 2 All ER 207. Cf *Midland International Trade Services Ltd v Sudairy* (1990) Financial Times, 2 May.
20 See De Winter (1968) 17 ICLQ 706; Art 3 of the Brussels and Lugano Conventions, discussed infra, p 290.
 1 On the question of when an English court can use the traditional English doctrine of *forum non conveniens*, see infra, pp 331–334.
 2 See *James North and Sons Ltd v North Cape Textiles Ltd* [1984] 1 WLR 1428 at 1433–1434, on the importance of harmonising English law with that in other European Community countries as a factor in favour of exercising the discretion to allow service abroad.
 3 *Spiliada Maritime Corpn v Cansulex Ltd* [1987] AC 460 at 481.

Order 11, rule 1(1)(c),[4] the judgment of the Court of Appeal in *Multinational Gas and Petrochemical Co v Multinational Gas and Petrochemical Services Ltd*[5] shows that, because of the lack of connection, under this head, between the claim and an English forum, there has been an even greater reluctance to use the discretion than is normal. In contrast to this, if the parties have agreed on trial in England by putting an English jurisdiction clause in their contract, the courts have been very willing to allow service out of the jurisdiction under Order 11, rule 1(1)(d)(iv),[6] unless there was a strong reason to the contrary, since the parties should abide by their agreement.[7] In tort cases the starting point for the operation of the discretion has been a willingness to allow service out of the jurisdiction. As has already been mentioned,[8] ACKNER LJ in *Cordoba Shipping Co Ltd v National State Bank, Elizabeth, New Jersey, The Albaforth*[9] introduced a presumption that "the jurisdiction in which a tort has been committed is prima facie the natural forum for the determination of the dispute".[10]

However, the real question is always whether it is appropriate *in the circumstances of the particular case* for a writ to be served out of the jurisdiction. It is certainly important to look at the relevant ground of Order 11 invoked by the plaintiff, to ask whether there is a close connection with England on the facts of the case, whether English law will apply and whether the parties have agreed on trial in England, but generalisations or presumptions about particular heads of Order 11 do not help. Lord GOFF in the *Spiliada Case* said that the importance to be attached to any particular head of Order 11 may vary from case to case.[11] The fact that English law is the law governing the contract would, in some cases, be of very great importance, and, in others, of little importance, depending on the circumstances. On the facts of the case the head of Order 11 in question was what is now rule 1(1)(d)(iii)[12]—the law governing the contract is English law. It was said to be a relevant factor in the exercise of the discretion that the litigation was being fought under a contract, the governing law of which was English law.[13] Indeed, this was said to be by no means an insignificant factor since the dispute was, inter alia, as to the nature of the obligation under the contract. The fact that English law governs a contract is of very great importance in cases raising an issue of English public policy.[14] It is highly desirable that such an issue should be determined by an English court.

4 Previously Ord 11, r1(1)(j).
5 [1983] Ch 258, 271–272, CA, supra, p 195. See also *Goldenglow Nut Food Co Ltd v Commodin (Produce) Ltd and Societe Generale De Surveillance SA and New Hampshire Insurance Co Ltd* [1987] 2 Lloyd's Rep 569 at 576; *Golden Ocean Assurance Ltd and World Mariner Shipping SA v Christopher Julian Martin, The Golden Mariner* [1990] 2 Lloyd's Rep 215 at 222.
6 Formerly Ord 11, r2, supra, p 198.
7 See *Unterweser Reederei GmbH v Zapata Off-shore Co, The Chaparral* [1968] 2 Lloyd's Rep 158; *The Vikfrost* [1980] 1 Lloyd's Rep 560, CA; *Chevron International Oil Co Ltd v A/S Sea Team (The T. S. Havprins)* [1983] 2 Lloyd's Rep 356.
8 Supra, pp 200–201.
9 [1984] 2 Lloyd's Rep 91.
10 At 94; at 96 (per Robert GOFF LJ). Applied in *Metall und Rohstoff AG v Donaldson Lufkin and Jenrette Inc* [1990] 1 QB 391, [1989] 3 All ER 14; overruled on a different point in *Lonrho plc v Fayed* [1991] 3 All ER 303, [1991] 3 WLR 188, HL; cf *Voth v Manildra Flour Mills Pty Ltd* (1990) 171 CLR 538 at 566, HC of Australia.
11 [1987] AC 460 at 481.
12 Formerly Ord 11, r1(1)(f)(iii).
13 At 486.
14 *Mitsubishi Corpn v Aristidis I Alafouzos* [1988] 1 Lloyd's Rep 191 at 196; *E I Du Pont de Nemours and Co v I C Agnew* [1987] 2 Lloyd's Rep 585 at 594–595.

The operation of the principles   This can be best illustrated by examining the *Spiliada Case*[15] itself.

The plaintiff shipowners, a Liberian company, alleged that the *Spiliada* had been damaged by wet sulphur being loaded on it by order of the defendant shippers, a British Columbia company, and sought damages for breach of contract. A similar action had previously been started by different plaintiffs against, inter alia, the defendants, following damage to the ship *Cambridgeshire*. In the *Spiliada* action it was held at first instance that there was a contract governed by English law. Although one of the heads of Order 11 was satisfied, the Court of Appeal held that it was not a proper case for exercising the discretion to allow service out of the jurisdiction and set aside the writ.

The House of Lords allowed the appeal. Lord GOFF stated the principles to be applied in relation to the exercise of the Order 11 discretion, as set out above.[16] The availability of witnesses and the risk of a multiplicity of proceedings were examined. However, the crucial point was the *Cambridgeshire* factor. If the *Spiliada* action also took place in England there would be teams of lawyers and experts available who had prepared for the *Cambridgeshire* action. This would contribute to the efficient administration of justice.[17] The court would be assisted in reaching a just decision, and the possibility of a settlement of the proceedings (as happened in the *Cambridgeshire* action) would be enhanced. Trial in England was not merely a matter of financial advantage to the plaintiff (without being to the disadvantage of the defendant) but was "in the objective interests of justice". Moreover, it was a relevant factor that the litigation was being fought under a contract governed by English law, and on the facts this was by no means an insignificant factor.[18]

(ii) Service of a writ out of the jurisdiction with the leave of the court in admiralty proceedings

RSC Order 75, rule 4[19] empowers the court, in certain curcumstances, to allow service of a writ in personam out of the jurisdiction in admiralty proceedings, for example where there is a claim arising out of a collision between two ships or a claim arising from oil pollution.

(iii) Service of a writ out of the jurisdiction without the leave of the court

Order 11, rule 1(2) allows service of a writ out of the jurisdiction *without* the leave of the court in two situations. The first[20] is where the court has jurisdiction by virtue of the Civil Jurisdiction and Judgments Act 1982. This statute, as amended by the Civil Jurisdiction and Judgments Act 1991, is concerned with cases coming within the Brussels and Lugano Conventions and the Modified Convention; the question of service of the writ in such cases will be discussed when jurisdiction under these Conventions is examined

---

15   *Spiliada Maritime Corpn v Cansulex Ltd* [1987] AC 460.
16   Supra, pp 204 et seq.
17   [1987] AC 460 at 485–486.
18   Supra.
19   *The Aegean Captain* [1980] 1 Lloyd's Rep 617; Jackson, *Enforcement of Maritime Claims* (1985) pp 63–64.
20   Ord 11, r 1(2)(a). For safeguards in respect of issue of the writ, see Ord 6, r 7, and in respect of default judgments, Ord 13, r7 B; Collins, *Civil Jurisdiction and Judgments Act 1982*, p 148.

in detail.[21] Rule 1(2) is wide enough to cover the situation where interim relief, such as a "Mareva" injunction, is sought in England in support of proceedings in another Brussels or Lugano Contracting State or in another part of the United Kingdom by virtue of section 25 of the Civil Jurisdiction and Judgments Act 1982.[22] However, rule 1(2) does require that the defendant is domiciled in a Contracting State to the Brussels Convention or Lugano Convention.[23] The second[24] is where the court has power to hear and determine the claim by virtue of any other enactment, even though the defendant is not within the jurisdiction or the wrongful act, neglect or default giving rise to the claim did not take place within the jurisdiction. An example of such an enactment is the Protection of Trading Interests Act 1980.[25] Order 11, rule 1(2) will also apply to actions brought under certain statutes passed as the result of international conventions which give a party the right to sue in England, ie the Carriage by Air Act 1961, the Carriage by Air (Supplementary Provisions) Act 1962, the Carriage of Goods by Road Act 1965, the Merchant Shipping (Oil Pollution) Act 1971 and the Civil Aviation Act 1982.

(iv) Service of the writ

Where service of a writ out of the jurisdiction is allowed, there is the practical problem of how this is to be effected on a defendant who is abroad. Actions that contain a foreign element must frequently require the assistance of judicial and administrative officers in other countries, and the United Kingdom has therefore concluded conventions with a number of States in order to facilitate the conduct of legal proceedings in civil and commercial matters, and is a party to the Hague Convention[1] on the service abroad of judicial and extra-judicial documents in civil or commercial matters, which came into effect in 1969. These conventions regulate such matters as the service of judicial and extra-judicial documents, the taking of evidence, security for costs, the right of access to courts, and the right of free legal assistance.[2]

(d) ARE THERE OTHER BASES OF COMPETENCE?

(i) Will the presence of the defendant's movable assets in England found jurisdiction?

When answering this question it is important to distinguish between the situation where the claim is *unrelated* to the movable assets situated in England and the situation where the claim is *related* to the movable assets.

Where the claim is unrelated to the movables A doctrine of arrestment *ad fundandam jurisdictionem* obtains in Scotland[3] and in certain civil law

---

21 Infra, p 324.
22 *Republic of Haiti v Duvalier* [1990] 1 QB 202, [1989] 1 All ER 456. S 25 is discussed supra, pp 192–193.
23 Or that the case comes within Arts 16 or 17. For the situation where he is not so domiciled and Arts 16 or 17 do not apply, see Ord 11, r 1(1)(b) supra, pp 192–193.
24 Ord 11, r 1(2)(b). See *Re Harrods (Buenos Aires) Ltd* [1992] Ch 72 at 115–116.
25 See infra, pp 382–384.
 1 (1964) Cmnd 1613; see (1965) 14 ICLQ 564–572.
 2 Ord 11, rr 5, 6.
 3 It does not apply where the defendant is domiciled in the United Kingdom: Civil Jurisdiction and Judgments Act 1982, Sch 8, r 2(8). Nor does it apply where the case is within the scope of the Brussels or Lugano Conventions and the defendant is domiciled in a Contracting State to either Convention, Art 3 of the Conventions; discussed, infra, p 290.

countries[4] under which an action may be brought against a person absent from the forum if movables[5] situated there and belonging to him have been taken into the custody of the law at the instance of the plaintiff.[6] The court can deal with a claim unconnected with the movables and deliver a personal judgment against the owner that will be wholly or partially satisfied by their sale. Another instance is the jurisdiction *quasi in rem* that is recognised in the USA, which enables a personal claim against a defendant living abroad to be satisfied out of chattels owned by him but situated in the forum. Attachment of the chattels confers jurisdiction on the court of the situs, but any judgment that may be given is limited in its effect to the value of the property attached.[7]

English law stands aloof from this doctrine. It insists that no action in personam will lie against a defendant unless he has been served with a writ while present in England or unless by virtue of some statutory power notice of the writ has been served on him abroad. To take an example: if an American takes a lease of a London house and furnishes it but then remains abroad, the landlord cannot maintain an action for arrears of rent under English law unless he is able to serve a writ out of the jurisdiction under Order 11. The landlord might be able to use one of the contract heads of Order 11,[8] but there is no head of Order 11 which allows service out of the jurisdiction simply on the basis that the defendant has movable property in England. At least, there is no such head in cases where the claim is unrelated to the movables.[9] There was an unsuccessful attempt in *The Siskina*[10] to introduce indirectly a head based on the presence of assets in the forum. The Court of Appeal was prepared to recognise a "Mareva" injunction, which can be granted when the defendant has assets in England and there is a danger of their removal, as coming within what is now Order 11, rule 1 (1)(b),[11] thereby allowing a writ to be served out of the jurisdiction in respect of the main dispute between the parties. The effect of this would have been to allow service out of the jurisdiction on the basis of the defendant's assets in England, even if the main action between the parties was unrelated to these assets. However, as has already been mentioned,[12] the House of Lords overruled this decision and held that a "Mareva" injunction was outside the scope of what is now Order 11, rule 1 (1)(b) and a foreign defendant could not be brought within the head by adding a claim for a "Mareva" injunction to the main action.

Where the claim is related to the movables If the plaintiff claims some interest in or right to movables the position is very different. Although there is no

4 A Contracting State to the Brussels or Lugano Conventions cannot use this form of jurisdiction in the situation where the case is within the scope of either Convention and the defendant is domiciled in a Contracting State to either Convention: Art 3 of the Conventions, discussed infra, p 290.
5 Jurisdiction over immovables is discussed, infra, pp 253–263.
6 For Scots law see Civil Jurisdiction and Judgments Act 1982, Sch 8, r2(8); Anton, *Civil Jurisdiction in Scotland*, paras 10.36–10.38; Anton, *Private International Law*, pp 188–193.
7 Restatement 2d, Conflict of Laws, s 66; Hay (1986) 35 ICLQ 32; *Shaffer v Heitner* 433 US 186 at 210 (1977); *Rush v Savchuck* 444 US 320 (1980).
8 Supra, pp 196–199.
9 For the position where the claim is related to the movables see infra.
10 *Siskina (owners of cargo lately laden on board) v Distos Cia Naviera SA, The Siskina* [1979] AC 210.
11 Formerly, Ord 11, r 1 (1)(i).
12 Supra, p 192.

separate basis of jurisdiction founded on the presence of movables in England, in practice, in cases where the defendant has assets here and the claim relates to those assets, it is often possible for the plaintiff either to serve a writ out of the jurisdiction under Order 11 or to find a suitable English defendant upon whom a writ can be served within the jurisdiction.

(i) Service of a writ out of the jurisdiction
Order 11 allows a writ to be served out of the jurisdiction with the leave of the court where the claim is made inter alia to determine proprietary rights over movable property situate within the jurisdiction.[13]

(ii) Service of a writ within the jurisdiction
Where the action is in respect of movables in England, it may be possible to find a suitable English defendant upon whom a writ can be served, even in order to make a foreign defendant a party to this action. For example, a plaintiff who alleges that he has bought from a foreign seller (Y) goods stored in England, can bring an action against the English warehouseman. The latter, can apply for an interpleader summons with a view to making Y a party to the action. If he is successful and if further he obtains the leave of the court to serve notice of the summons on Y abroad,[14] the position as regards jurisidiction is the same as if Y had been served with a writ while present in England. In this indirect manner, therefore, a claim against movables in England will normally be sustainable even against a person abroad under whose control they happen to be.

(ii) Can new bases of competence be introduced?

It is not open to the courts to introduce new additional bases of competence. In *The Siskina*,[1] Lord DIPLOCK, the other Law Lords concurring, said that any extension of the jurisdiction of the courts over foreign defendants requires subordinate legislation by the rules committee if not primary legislation by Parliament itself.[2]

2. ACTIONS IN REM[3]

(a) AN ACTION AGAINST A SHIP AS DEFENDANT

In Roman law an action in rem was one brought in order to vindicate a jus in rem, ie a right such as ownership available against all persons, but the only action in rem known to English law is that which lies in an Admiralty court against a particular res, namely a ship or some other res, such as cargo, associated with the ship.[4]

The Supreme Court Act 1981 lists the claims that lie within the Admiralty

---

13 Ord 11, r 1 (1)(i); supra, p 201.
14 RSC Ord 16, r 1; cf *Dubout & Co v Macpherson* (1889) 23 QBD 340.
1 *Siskina (owners of cargo lately laden on board) v Distos Cia Naviera SA, The Siskina* [1979] AC 210. See also *Serge Caudron v Air Zaire* [1986] ILRM 10, SC of Ireland.
2 At 260; see also at 262–263 (Lord HAILSHAM).
3 Jackson, *Enforcement of Maritime Claims* (1985), pp 71–85. For a recent examination of this whole subject in Australia, see ALRC 33 (1986); Davenport [1987] Lloyd's MCLQ 317.
4 The owner and other persons interested are also made defendants. The action also lies against an aircraft, Supreme Court Act 1981, s 21(3), or hovercraft, Hovercraft Act 1968, s 2(1).

Court[5] and goes on to make detailed provision as to when an action in rem may be brought.[6] To take one instance, the rule has long been that a maritime lien attaches to and remains enforceable against a ship that collides with and damages another.[7] Such a lien "is a privileged claim upon a vessel in respect of service done to it or injury caused by it, to be carried into effect by legal process. It is a right acquired by one over a thing belonging to another—a *jus in re aliena*".[8]

That the ship is the defendant in an action brought to enforce the lien is underlined by the legal process available to the plaintiff. After obtaining the issue of a summons in rem, he may procure a warrant for the arrest of the ship which is then affixed by the Admiralty Marshal for a short time on any mast of the ship or on the outside of any suitable part of the ship's superstructure, being later replaced by a true copy.[9] There is no alternative method.[10]

The person is the ship, and therefore it is essential that it should be "so situated as to be within the lawful control of the State under the authority of which the court sits".[11] In short, the court is competent to entertain the action if the ship lies within the territorial waters of England. However, the Court of Appeal in *The Vasso (formerly Andria)*[12] held that the exercise of the power to arrest a ship is a discretionary one, as is the power to release a ship under arrest.[13] In exercising this discretion it is relevant to consider the purpose for which the plaintiff wishes to obtain the arrest. The power to arrest is designed to provide security in respect of the action in rem, and it should not be exercised for the purpose of providing security for an award which may be made in arbitration proceedings.[14] The specific question of providing security for the satisfaction of arbitration awards has, however, been changed by section 26 of the Civil Jurisdiction and Judgments Act 1982. This provides that, where a court stays Admiralty proceedings on the ground that the dispute should be submitted to arbitration or to court proceedings outside England, the court may order that the property which has previously been arrested be retained as security for the satisfaction of any award or judgment. It would be very odd, when there is now a power to retain as security for an award in arbitration proceedings property which has already been arrested, if the courts did not exercise their power to arrest the property for this purpose in the first place.[15]

5 See Supreme Court Act 1981, s 20. This includes, eg a claim "arising out of any agreement relating to the carriage of goods in a ship or to the use or hire of a ship," s 20(2) (h), on which see *The Antonis P Lemos* [1985] AC 711, [1985] 1 All ER 695; see also *Gatoil International Inc v Arkwright-Boston Manufacturers Mutual Insurance Co* [1985] AC 255, [1985] 1 All ER 129, HL. It also includes a claim "in respect of goods . . . supplied to a ship for her operation," s 20 (2) (m), on which see *The River Rima* [1988] 2 All ER 641, [1988] 1 WLR 758, HL; Jackson [1988] Lloyd's MCLQ 423.

6 S 21.

7 S 21 (3).

8 *The Ripon City* [1897] P 226 at 242.

9 RSC Ord 75, r 11.

10 *The Prins Bernhard* [1964] P 117, [1963] 3 All ER 735.

11 *Castrique v Imrie* (1870) LR 4 HL 414 at 429; *General Motors-Holdens Ltd v The Ship Northern Highway* (1982) 29 SASR 138.

12 [1984] 1 Lloyd's Rep 235.

13 Release can be made subject to conditions, see eg *The Vannessa Ann* [1985] 1 Lloyd's Rep 549.

14 *The Vasso (formerly Andria)* [1984] 1 Lloyd's Rep 235 at 241–242; distinguished in *The Tuyuti* [1984] QB 838, [1984] 2 All ER 545.

15 See *The Vasso (formerly Andria)* [1984] 1 Lloyd's Rep 235 at 242; *The Jalamatsya* [1987] 2 Lloyd's Rep 164.

The granting of security aspect of the action in rem is underlined by the fact that the ship or other chattel can be sold under the authority of the court and the proceeds adjudged to the plaintiff in satisfaction of his claim.[16] If a sale is ordered, the judgment operates in rem in the sense that it divests the property in the ship from the owners and confers an absolute title on the purchaser, good against all persons.[17]

(b) AN ACTION AGAINST A SHIP OTHER THAN THE PRIMARY SHIP

Normally the action lies only against the primary ship (eg the offending ship in a collision case)[18] but in the case of certain claims that arise in connection with a ship for which "the relevant person" (ie the owner, charterer, person in possession or control of the ship) would be liable in an action in personam,[1] the Supreme Court Act 1981, section 21(4) allows an action in rem to be brought against either (i) that ship (the primary ship) or (ii) another ship owned by "the relevant person,"[2] but not both.[3] However, it does not allow an action to be brought against a ship owned by a sister company of the owners of the primary ship.[4]

In cases where the action is brought against the primary ship "the relevant person" must be, at the time when the action is brought, either the beneficial owner of that ship or the charterer of it under a charter by demise,[5] under which he would have full possession and control but not ownership.

In cases where the action is brought against another ship it must be shown that "the relevant person" is the beneficial owner of that ship. It is clear from the wording of section 21 (4)[6] that it is not enough to show that "the relevant person" is a charterer under a charter by demise. However, if "the relevant person" does own another ship the ambit of section 21(4) is very wide. Since "the relevant person" can include a mere charterer, whether under a charter by demise or under some other type of charter,[7] of the primary ship, it follows that an action can be brought against another ship owned by a charterer of the primary ship[8] although this is not a sister ship.

---

16 *The Henrich Björn* (1886) 11 App Cas 270 at 276–277.
17 *Minna Craig SS Co v Chartered Mercantile Bank of India, London and China* [1897] 1 QB 460.
18 Eg *The Beldis* [1936] P 51; *The Atlantic Star* [1974] AC 436.
1 See *The Gulf Venture* [1984] 2 Lloyd's Rep 445.
2 Eg *The Soya Margareta* [1960] 2 All ER 756, [1961] 1 WLR 709; *The Span Terza* [1982] 1 Lloyd's Rep 225; *The Mawan* [1988] 2 Lloyd's Rep 459.
3 *The Banco* [1971] P 137, [1971] 1 All ER 524; *The Stephan J* [1985] 2 Lloyd's Rep 344. It is, however, possible to have writs issued against several ships and then to serve one of these writs on the ship which comes conveniently within the jurisdiction, see *The Berny* [1979] QB 80, [1978] 1 All ER 1065; Supreme Court Act 1981, s 21(8); see also *The Helene Roth* [1980] QB 273, [1980] 1 All ER 1078; *The Freccia Del Nord* [1989] 1 Lloyd's Rep 388.
4 *The Evpo Agnic* [1988] 3 All ER 810, [1988] 1 WLR 1090.
5 S 21 (4).
6 Compare s 21 (4)(i) with s 21 (4)(ii).
7 *The Span Terza* [1982] 1 Lloyd's Rep 225, CA (involving a time charterer); *The Sextum* [1982] 2 Lloyd's Rep 532 (Hong Kong Supreme Court).
8 *The Span Terza* [1982] 1 Lloyd's Rep 225, CA; *The Sextum* [1982] 2 Lloyd's Rep 532 (Hong Kong Supreme Court). Cf the *obiter dicta* by Lord DIPLOCK in *The Jade*, sub nom *The Eschersheim* [1976] 1 All ER 920 at 925; *The Maritime Trader* [1981] 2 Lloyd's Rep 153.

(c) A STAY OF PROCEEDINGS WHICH IS SUBJECT TO CONDITIONS

A problem may arise, once an action in rem against a ship has been brought and the ship arrested or security for it given, if the defendant seeks to have the proceedings stayed. The court has a discretion to order the stay of the proceedings if the parties have agreed to submit their dispute to a foreign court,[9] if a foreign court would be a more appropriate forum[10] or under section 4(1) of the Arbitration Act 1950.[11] If the case falls under section 1 of the Arbitration Act 1975,[12] a stay is mandatory. If the action in rem is stayed, section 26 of the Civil Jurisdiction and Judgments Act 1982 provides that the arrested ship or other security can now be retained as a security for the other proceedings, such as for payment of an arbitration award;[13] alternatively, the court can make the staying of the action conditional on the defendant giving some other security. It is irrelevant whether or not the other proceedings have actually started.[14] However, it seems that section 26 cannot apply if the proceedings are outside the jurisdiction of the Admiralty Court.[15]

(d) ACTIONS IN REM AND JUDGMENTS IN REM

Although this Admiralty proceeding is the only action in rem known to English law, it should be observed that the judgment in rem in which it results may equally well result from certain other actions in personam. In the Admiralty action, the court decrees what the status of the ship shall be after its sale, and this decree is binding on all persons. The title to the res is now vested in the purchaser. But a ship is not the only res whose status may be changed against all persons. A marriage, for instance, is not strictly a res, but, as Lord DUNEDIN remarked, it has always been treated as savouring of a res.[16] If, therefore, in matrimonial proceedings, the court adjudges that a marriage shall be dissolved or annulled, its judgment amounts to a declaration that the status of the parties, ie their legal position in or with regard to the rest of a community,[17] rather than just inter se, is now changed.[18]

Among other judgments in rem may be mentioned the judgment of a court of probate establishing a will,[1] an adjudication order or an order of discharge made in the course of bankruptcy proceedings, and an order for the dissolution of a company.

---

9 Infra, pp 234–236; see *The Athenee* (1922) 11 Ll L Rep 6; *The Fehmarn* [1957] 2 All ER 707, [1957] 1 WLR 815; *The Eleftheria* [1970] P 94, [1969] 2 All ER 641.
10 Infra, pp 221–234; see *The Cap Bon* [1967] 1 Lloyd's Rep 543; *The Atlantic Star* [1974] AC 436, [1973] 2 All ER 175.
11 Infra, pp 240–241.
12 Infra, pp 239–240, see *The Golden Trader* [1975] QB 348, [1974] 2 All ER 686; *Marazura Navegacion SA v Oceanus Mutual Underwriting Association (Bermuda) Ltd* [1977] 1 Lloyd's Rep 283 at 287–288; *The Rena K* [1979] QB 377, [1979] 1 All ER 397.
13 See *The Vasso* [1984] 1 Lloyd's Rep 235 at 243; *Spiliada Maritime Corpn v Cansulex Ltd* [1987] AC 460, HL; *The World Star* [1986] 2 Lloyd's Rep 274; *The Silver Athens (No 2)* [1986] 2 Lloyd's Rep 583; *The Emre II* [1989] 2 Lloyd's Rep 182.
14 *The Jalamatsya* [1987] 2 Lloyd's Rep 164; *The Nordglimt* [1988] QB 183 at 204.
15 *The Nordglimt*, ibid.
16 *Salvesen v Administrator of Austrian Property* [1927] AC 641 at 662.
17 *Niboyet v Niboyet* (1878) 4 PD 1 at 11; Tolstoy (1968) 84 LQR 245.
18 *Thynne v Thynne* [1955] P 272 at 294, [1955] 3 All ER 129 at 133.
1 *Re Langton's Estate* [1964] P 163 at 178, 179, [1964] 1 All ER 749 at 758, 759.

(e) THE EFFECT OF THE BRUSSELS[2] AND LUGANO CONVENTIONS

(i) The basis of jurisdiction

The Convention on Jurisdiction and the Enforcement of Judgments in Civil and Commercial Matters of 1968 (the Brussels Convention) normally applies in cases where the defendant is domiciled in a European Community State and the matter in question is a civil and commercial matter.[3] The Lugano Convention normally applies in cases where the defendant is domiciled in an EFTA Contracting State and it is a civil and commercial matter. However, Article 57 of the Brussels and Lugano Conventions preserves other conventions relating to jurisdiction previously entered into by the United Kingdom, eg the Convention Relating to the Arrest of Sea-Going Ships of 1952 (the Arrest Convention[4]). It follows that English courts are still able to take jurisdiction under the provisions of the Supreme Court Act 1981, in so far as these provisions are derived from the Arrest Convention,[5] even if the defendant is domiciled in a Contracting State to the Brussels or Lugano Conventions, and even if that state is not a party to the Arrest Convention.[6] To take an example, it is still possible to bring an action in rem against a ship, owned by a Frenchman, which is arrested in English waters following a collision at sea. On the other hand, in cases coming within the Brussels or Lugano Conventions, jurisdiction has to be taken under that Convention, and cannot be taken under any provision in the Supreme Court Act 1981, if that provision is not derived from the Arrest Convention. The Arrest Convention requires a ship actually to be arrested. In *The Deichland*[7] a writ in rem was served on a ship in England, but then, as is commonly the case, the demise charterers (Deich) gave undertakings as to security in consideration of the ship not being arrested. There was jurisdiction under the 1981 Act (ignoring for the moment the Brussels Convention) but this was not based on the Arrest Convention, since the ship had not been arrested. Deich was domiciled in Germany and under Article 2 of the Brussels Convention had to be sued there. The Court of Appeal granted a declaration that the English courts lacked jurisdiction. Although this was an action in rem, Deich was treated as the defendant for the purposes of Article 2 of the Brussels Convention.

Moreover, in cases coming within the Brussels or Lugano Conventions, it will no longer be possible to take jurisdiction in rem against aircraft, hovercraft or against property connected with a ship, ie the cargo or freight, since the Arrest Convention only provides for jurisdiction against ships. Instead, jurisdiction will have to be taken under the Brussels or Lugano Conventions.[8]

---

2 Jackson, *Civil Jurisdiction and Judgments—Maritime Claims* (1987); Brice [1987] Lloyd's MCLQ 281; Blackburn [1988] Lloyd's MCLQ 91.

3 Discussed infra, pp 286–292.

4 Also, rather confusingly, often referred to as the Brussels Convention.

5 On the complex question of the extent to which the 1981 Act is based on the Arrest Convention, see Jackson *The Enforcement of Maritime Claims* (1985), pp 71–83; *Gatoil International Inc v Arkwright-Boston Manufacturers Mutual Insurance Co* [1985] AC 255, [1985] 1 All ER 129, HL; *The Deichland* [1990] 1 QB 361, [1989] 2 All ER 1066.

6 Art 57 of the Brussels Convention, as substituted by the 1989 Accession Convention of Spain and Portugal; Art 57 of the Lugano Convention, infra, pp 286, 415, 443–444. However, the Arrest Convention must, of course, apply in respect of that particular defendant, see Jackson, *Enforcement of Maritime Claims*, pp 159–160.

7 [1990] 1 QB 361; Carter (1989) BYBIL 489. Cf *The Po* [1991] 2 Lloyd's Rep 206.

8 See, in particular, Art 5(7) of the Brussels and Lugano Conventions; discussed infra, pp 305–306.

Article 57 also preserves the 1952 International Convention on Certain Rules Concerning Civil Jurisdiction in Matters of Collision (the Collision Convention).[9] What matters is that the United Kingdom legislation, which was designed to implement the Collision Convention, is in accordance with that Convention. It does not matter that that Convention has not been directly implemented in the United Kingdom.[10]

(ii) Stays of action

From what has been said so far the effect of the Brussels and Lugano Conventions can be seen to be slight. However, of more significance is the fact that in cases coming within the Brussels and Lugano Conventions English courts cannot stay or dismiss the proceedings if the alternative forum is a European Community or EFTA Contracting State.[11] It is submitted that this principle applies even where it is a case of jurisdiction in rem under, for example, the Arrest Convention or Collision Convention as preserved by Article 57 of the Brussels and Lugano Conventions. The power to stay an action in rem, unlike the action in rem itself, does not derive from an international convention. It is part of the English courts' inherent jurisdiction and cannot be used where to grant a stay would be inconsistent with the Brussels or Lugano Conventions,[12] ie in cases where the alternative forum is a Contracting State to the Brussels or Lugano Conventions. On the other hand, it is clear that an action in rem can be stayed or dismissed in the situation where the alternative forum is a non-Contracting State to the Brussels or Lugano Conventions. In *The Po*[13] the Court of Appeal applied the doctrine of *forum non conveniens* to a case involving jurisdiction under the Collision Convention, despite the fact that the defendants were domiciled in Italy, which brought the case within the Brussels Convention. It is important to note that the case was argued on the basis that the alternative forum for trial was Brazil. However, on the particular facts the first instance decision refusing a stay was upheld, the defendants having failed to show that Brazil was a clearly more appropriate forum.

Whatever the position may be in relation to *forum non conveniens* it is clear that Articles 21 (lis alibi pendens) and 22 (related actions) of the Brussels and Lugano Conventions[14] can apply in cases where jurisdiction has been brought under the Arrest Convention. Whilst Article 57 of the Brussels and Lugano Conventions preserves the Arrest Convention, the latter says nothing about concurrent proceedings in two different jurisdictions.[15] Article 21 is concerned with the situation where "proceedings involving the same cause of action and between the same parties are brought in the courts of different Contracting States". The court first seised of the action takes priority and any other court must decline jurisdiction once the jurisdiction of the court first seised has been established. There is no requirement that either party be domiciled in a Contracting State (ie in a European Community or EFTA State). Article 21 requires that the two sets of proceedings involve the same

9 See *The Po* [1991] 2 Lloyd's Rep 206; Hartley [1991] Lloyd's MCLQ 446.
10 Ibid, at 211.
11 *Re Harrods (Buenos Aires) Ltd* [1992] Ch 72; infra, pp 332–334.
12 Civil Jurisdiction and Judgments Act 1982 s 49; amended by the Civil Jurisdiction and Judgments Act 1991, Sch 2, para 24.
13 [1991] 2 Lloyd's Rep 206. See also *The Nordglimt* [1988] QB 183 at 205.
14 Infra, pp 326–330.
15 See *The Linda* [1988] 1 Lloyd's Rep 175 at 178.

parties. If one action is in personam (against a person) and the other in rem (against a ship) it has been held that the parties are not the same and Article 21 will not apply.[16] Nonetheless, the actions may be related ones and the court seised second may stay its proceedings under Article 22 of the Brussels or Lugano Conventions.[17] An action in rem will cease to be one in rem and will become one in personam if the defendant, as frequently happens, provides security so that the ship is released from arrest.[18] At this stage, there will be two actions in personam and Article 21 will apply. On the other hand, if the defendant merely appears in the action and defends it, the proceedings whilst continuing in personam do not lose their in rem character and Article 22 should be used rather than Article 21.[19] It has been held, perhaps surprisingly, that with an action in rem an English court is seised of the proceedings from the moment of service of a writ or arrest of a ship (whichever is earlier) rather than from the more obvious time of the issue of the writ.[20] It is possible to use section 26 of the Civil Jurisdiction and Judgments Act 1982 in cases where an English court has declined jurisdiction under Article 21. The arrested ship can thus be retained as security and made available to meet a judgment in the foreign action in the court first seised of the proceedings.[21]

16 *The Nordglimt* [1988] QB 183. There must be doubts now over the correctness of this, in the light of the Court of Appeal's decision in *The Deichland* [1990] 1 QB 361, a case on Art 2 of the Brussels Convention; infra, p 293; see *The Sylt* [1991] 1 Lloyd's Rep 240.
17 *The Nordglimt* at 201; *The Linda* [1988] 1 Lloyd's Rep 175 at 179.
18 *The Linda* [1988] 1 Lloyd's Rep 175 at 179; cf *The Nordglimt* [1988] QB 183 at 201. See also *The Deichland* [1990] 1 QB 361 at 383–385.
19 *The Nordglimt*, op cit, at 201–202.
20 *The Freccia del Nord* [1989] 1 Lloyd's Rep 388. The same rule has been adopted for actions in personam: *Dresser UK Ltd v Falcongate Freight Management Ltd* [1992] 2 WLR 319, CA.
21 *The Nordglimt* [1988] QB 183 at 203–204. The position is more problematical if security has been given to prevent arrest; Hartley (1989) 105 LQR 640 argues that Art 22 has to be used in such a case.

Chapter 12

Stays of English proceedings and restraining foreign proceedings

SUMMARY

1. STAYS OF ENGLISH PROCEEDINGS

Even though an English court has power to try a case, ie a writ has been served on the defendant in accordance with the rules set out in the previous chapter, it can, nonetheless, refuse to take jurisdiction and stay the English proceedings.[1] Although the English court is technically only regulating its own jurisdiction, the effect of a stay is to force a plaintiff to go abroad to sue or, in some cases, to go to arbitration.[2] The court is therefore, in reality, choosing between alternative fora for trial, or between trial and arbitration.[3] The power to stay English proceedings is derived from the court's inherent jurisdiction, which is preserved by statute,[4] and from certain statutes dealing with arbitration.[5] The power is exercised in three situations:

(a) Where the doctrine of *forum non conveniens* applies.

(b) Where there is a foreign choice of jurisdiction clause.

---

1 The stay should be sought at the time when the proceedings are commenced; any delay may be used as a reason for not exercising the discretion to stay, see *Coupland v Arabian Gulf Oil Co* [1983] 2 All ER 434, [1983] 1 WLR 1136.
2 The arbitration may be in England or abroad, see infra, pp 239–241.
3 In some cases where there is an arbitration agreement, a stay of proceedings will be mandatory; infra, pp 239–240.
4 See s 49 (3) of the Supreme Court Act 1981; *European Asian Bank AG v Punjab and Sind Bank* [1982] 2 Lloyd's Rep 356, at 360–361; *The Abidin Daver* [1984] AC 398 at 417 (per Lord BRANDON). See also s 49 of the Civil Jurisdiction and Judgments Act 1982, as amended by the Civil Jurisdiction and Judgments Act 1991, Sch 2 para 24; discussed infra, pp 331–334. A court has power to stay an action in which its own jurisdiction is in issue: *Williams and Glyn's Bank plc v Astro Dinamico Compania Naviera SA* [1984] 1 All ER 760, [1984] 1 WLR 438.
5 The Arbitration Act 1975, s 1 and the Arbitration Act 1950, s 4; discussed infra, pp 239–241.

(c) Where there is an agreement on arbitration.

Each of these three situations will be examined in turn.

(a) FORUM NON CONVENIENS[6]

(i) Development of the doctrine of forum non conveniens in English law

It has already been seen that the discretionary power to allow service of a writ out of the jurisdiction is exercised on the basis of *forum conveniens*.[7] There is also a discretion to stay actions on the basis of *forum non conveniens* (ie where England is not the appropriate forum for trial) in certain specific situations. These are as follows: cases involving the administration of estates and trusts;[8] and cases where there are concurrent proceedings in respect of a marriage, for instance for divorce, taking place both in England and outside the jurisdiction.[9] What we are concerned with in this chapter, however, is a *general power* to stay actions on the basis of *forum non conveniens*. Whilst there has been such a power in Scotland[10] and the United States[11] for a number of years, it is only recently that a general doctrine of *forum non conveniens* has been accepted in England.

Until the House of Lords decision in *The Atlantic Star*,[12] in the absence of *lis alibi pendens*,[13] a stay of proceedings would only be granted in the narrow situation where the plaintiff set out deliberately to harass the defendant by seeking trial in England. In *The Atlantic Star* a majority of their Lordships accepted that the traditional English rule, which confined the granting of a stay to cases of vexation and oppression,[14] should be interpreted more liberally and flexibly,[15] and a stay was granted even though the plaintiff had not acted in bad faith. The liberalisation process continued with the later House of Lords decision in *MacShannon v Rockware Glass Ltd*,[16] even though their Lordships declined to equate English law with Scots law and did not accept a general doctrine of *forum non conveniens*.[17] A stay was granted however

6 Briggs (1983) 3 LS 74; Briggs [1984] 2 Lloyd's MCLQ 227; Briggs [1985] 3 Lloyd's MCLQ 360; Barma and Elvin (1985) 101 LQR 48; Schuz (1986) 35 ICLQ 374; (for a comparison with Dutch law) Verheul (1986) 35 ICLQ 413; Robertson (1987) 103 LQR 398; Slater (1988) 104 LQR 554; Fawcett (1989) 9 OJLS 205.
7 Supra, pp 204–210.
8 *Ewing v Orr-Ewing* (1885) 10 App Cas 453; *Chellaram v Chellaram* [1985] Ch 409, [1985] 1 All ER 1043; Evans (1986) 102 LQR 28. There may also be a discretion to stay in tort cases which involve forum shopping, see *Boys v Chaplin* [1971] AC 356 at 406; and see *Maharanee of Baroda v Wildenstein* [1972] 2 QB 283 at 292, 297.
9 Domicile and Matrimonial Proceedings Act 1973, s 5 (6) and Sch I, para 9; *Gadd v Gadd* [1985] 1 All ER 58, [1984] 1 WLR 1435; *Thyssen-Bornemisza v Thyssen-Bornemisza* [1986] Fam 1, [1985] 1 All ER 328; *De Dampierre v De Dampierre* [1988] AC 92, HL; infra, pp 637–638. There is also a power to stay proceedings on the basis of appropriateness in cases involving children: s 5 (2) (b) of the Family Law Act 1986, as amended by the Children Act 1989 Sch 13, infra, pp 726–729; *quaere* the meaning of "appropriate" in this context.
10 Anton, *Private International Law* (2nd edn, 1990), pp 212–218; *Credit Chimique v James Scott Engineering Group Ltd* 1979 SC 406, 1982 SLT 131.
11 Leflar, *American Conflicts Law*, (4th edn 1986) pp 152–156; *Gulf Oil Corp v Gilbert* 330 US 501 (1946); *Piper Aircraft Co v Reyno* 454 US 235 (1981).
12 [1974] AC 436 at 453–454, 462, 464, 473, 475–477, [1973] 2 All ER 175.
13 Ie concurrent proceedings in England and abroad involving the same parties and the same matter, see infra, pp 231–234.
14 See *Logan v Bank of Scotland (No 2)* [1906] 1 KB 141; *Egbert v Short* [1907] 2 Ch 205; *Re Norton's Settlement* [1908] 1 Ch 471.
15 [1974] AC 436, at 454, 468.
16 [1978] AC 795, [1978] 1 All ER 625
17 [1978] AC 795 at 817, 822, 825.

and the criteria of oppression and vexation abandoned in favour of a less stringent approach, hard to distinguish from one of *forum non conveniens*. Final acceptance by the House of Lords that a doctrine of *forum non conveniens* is applied when exercising the discretion to stay English proceedings came in *The Abidin Daver*.[18] Lord DIPLOCK explained that "judicial chauvinism has been replaced by judicial comity" to the extent that it was now time to acknowledge that the English discretion to stay was indistinguishable from the Scottish doctrine of *forum non conveniens*.[19] This view has been endorsed by the House of Lords in the leading case on stays of action, *Spiliada Maritime Corpn v Cansulex Ltd*.[20] It is clear from this case that the same basic criterion applies in cases involving stays of action as in cases involving the exercise of the discretion to serve a writ out of the jurisdiction.[21] The *Spiliada Case* set off a chain reaction in a number of common law jurisdictions, and has been followed[1] in New Zealand,[2] Canada,[3] Hong Kong,[4] Brunei,[5] Singapore,[6] and Gibraltar,[7] but not in Australia,[8] where a majority of the High Court, in a very unclear and much criticised decision, required there to be vexation or oppression for the grant of a stay, but could not agree on what this meant. However, it has been established subsequently that this can be shown by the fact that the forum is a clearly inappropriate one for trial[9] (a formula loaded in favour of trial in the forum).

(ii) The principles on which the discretion to stay is exercised

As the law has developed, a number of different formulations of the principles to be applied in this area have been laid down by the House of Lords. Lord DIPLOCK in *MacShannon v Rockware Glass Ltd*[10] adopted a rigid formulation

---

18 [1984] AC 398, [1984] 1 All ER 470. Lords EDMUND-DAVIES, KEITH and TEMPLEMAN concurred with Lord DIPLOCK.

19 Op cit, at 411.

20 [1987] AC 460; Briggs [1987] Lloyd's MCLQ 1; Collier [1987] CLJ 33; Carter (1986) 57 BYBIL 429.

21 Supra, pp 204–210.

1 For Scots reaction see *Sokha v Secretary of State for the Home Department* (1991) Times, 15 August.

2 *McConnell Dowell Constructors Ltd v Lloyd's Syndicate 396* [1988] 2 NZLR 257, CA; *Club Mediterranee NZ v Wendell* [1989] 1 NZLR 216, CA; *Crane Accessories Ltd v Lim Swee Hee* [1989] 1 NZLR 221; Paterson (1989) 13 NZULR 337.

3 *United Oilseed Products v Royal Bank of Canada* [1988] 5 WWR 181 (Alberta); *Burt v Clarkson Gordon* (1989) 62 DLR (4th) 676 (Manitoba); *ECCO Heating Prod Ltd v J K Campbell & Assoc Ltd* [1990] 5 WWR 687 (British Columbia). There was some authority for a *forum non conveniens* discretion in Canada even before the *Spiliada Case*, see McLeod, *The Conflict of Laws*, pp 132–134; Castel, *Canadian Conflict of Laws* (2nd edn 1986), paras 132–133.

4 *The Adhiguna Meranti* [1988] 1 Lloyd's Rep 384, Hong Kong CA.

5 *Syarikat Bumiputra Kimanis v Tan Kok Voon* [1988] 3 MLJ 315.

6 *J H Rayner (Mincing Lane) Ltd v Teck Hock and Co (Pte) Ltd* [1990] 2 MLJ 142—an Ord 11 case.

7 *Aldington Shipping Ltd v Bradstock Shipping Corpn and Mabanaft GmbH, The Waylink and Brady Maria* [1988] 1 Lloyd's Rep 475, Gibraltar CA.

8 *Oceanic Sun-Line Special Shipping Co Inc v Fay* (1988) 165 CLR 197, HC of Australia. See Pryles (1988) 62 ALJ 774; Reynolds (1989) 105 LQR 40; Briggs (1989) 105 LQR 200; Briggs [1989] Lloyd's MCLQ 216; Collins (1989) 105 LQR 364; Garner (1989) 38 ICLQ 361; McLachlan [1990] CLJ 37.

9 *Voth v Manildra Flour Mills Pty Ltd* (1990) 171 CLR 538, HC of Australia; following Deane J in the *Oceanic Case*, op cit, at 247–248. See Collins (1991) 107 LQR 182; Pryles (1991) 65 ALJ 442; Brereton (1991) 40 ICLQ 895.

10 [1978] AC 795, [1978] 1 All ER 625. Lord FRASER concurred. Lords KEITH and SALMON were more flexible in their approaches.

which set out two pre-conditions necessary for the grant of a stay:[11] one was concerned with the appropriate forum; the other with the plaintiff's advantage in obtaining trial in England. However, in *Castanho v Brown and Root (UK) Ltd*[12] Lord SCARMAN warned against these two pre-conditions being construed as a statute.[13] Lord BRANDON in *The Abidin Daver*[14] was in favour of a weighing process. He said that "the exercise of the court's discretion in any particular case necessarily involves the balancing of all the relevant factors on either side, those favouring the grant of a stay on the one hand, and those militating against it on the other".[15] This accords with the very flexible approach towards the discretion which is currently adopted by the courts. The law was exhaustively considered and restated by the House of Lords in *Spiliada Maritime Corpn v Cansulex Ltd*,[16] where Lord GOFF, giving the unanimous judgment of the Law Lords, set out a number of principles on which the discretion should be exercised. Before turning to examine these principles, one general point needs to be made. The decision on the exercise of the discretion is essentially one for the judge at first instance, and an appellate court should not interfere merely because it would give different weight to the factors involved.[17]

(a) The basic principle

The basic principle is that a stay will only be granted on the ground of forum non conveniens where the court is satisfied that there is some other available forum, having jurisdiction, which is the appropriate forum for trial of the action, ie in which the case may be tried more suitably for the interests of all the parties and the ends of justice.[18]

This is the most important of the principles and sums up the whole basis of the *forum non conveniens* discretion. In a number of subsequent cases[19] the courts have not looked beyond this basic principle. Lord GOFF, however, did lay down a number of other subordinate principles.[20]

(b) A clearly more appropriate forum abroad

The burden of proof is on the defendant to show that there is another available forum which is clearly or distinctly more appropriate than the English forum.[1] It is not enough just to show that England is not the natural

---

11 Ibid, at 82.
12 [1981] AC 557, [1981] 1 All ER 143.
13 Ibid, at 575.
14 [1984] AC 398, [1984] 1 All ER 470.
15 Ibid, at 419.
16 [1987] AC 460, [1986] 3 All ER 843. The facts of the case are discussed supra, p 210.
17 Ibid, at 486.
18 Ibid, at 476. For a case where there was no alternative forum see *Evers v Firth* (1987) 10 NSWLR 22.
19 See *Banco Atlantico SA v The British Bank of the Middle East* [1990] 2 Lloyd's Rep 504, discussed infra, p 231; *Irish Shipping Ltd v Commercial Union Assurance Co plc* [1991] 2 QB 206, [1989] 3 All ER 853; *Cleveland Museum of Art v Capricorn Art International SA* [1990] 2 Lloyd's Rep 166.
20 For cases which refer to all or many of the subordinate principles see *Charm Maritime Inc v Minas Xenophon Kyriakou and David John Mathias* [1987] 1 Lloyd's Rep 433, discussed infra, pp 230–231; *E I Du Pont De Nemours & Co v Agnew and Kerr* [1987] 2 Lloyd's Rep 585; *Meadows Indemnity Co Ltd v Insurance Corpn of Ireland Ltd and International Commercial Bank plc* [1989] 1 Lloyd's Rep 181; affd [1989] 2 Lloyd's Rep 298, CA; *Re Harrods (Buenos Aires) Ltd* [1992] Ch 72 at 126.
1 Op cit, at 474.

or appropriate forum for trial. Neither is it enough to establish a mere balance of convenience in favour of the foreign forum.[2] This principle is designed to reflect the fact that, in cases where a stay is sought on the basis of *forum non conveniens*, jurisdiction will have been founded as of right, ie a writ will have been served within the jurisdiction.

In ascertaining whether there is a clearly more appropriate forum abroad, the search is for the country with which the action has the most real and substantial connection.[3] The court will look for connecting factors "and these will include not only factors affecting convenience or expense (such as availability of witnesses), but also other factors such as the law governing the relevant transaction . . . ,and the place where the parties respectively reside or carry on business".[4]

Thus in *MacShannon v Rockware Glass Ltd:*[5]

Four appeals were consolidated. They all involved Scotsmen living and working in Scotland who suffered industrial injuries in Scotland. All the defendants were English companies with registered offices in England. All the witnesses, medical and otherwise, lived in Scotland. The plaintiffs served writs on the defendants at their English registered offices, the English courts thus having jurisdiction. The defendants sought to have the English proceedings stayed, leaving the plaintiffs to bring the claims in Scotland.

The House of Lords held that the appropriate or "natural" forum for trial was in Scotland[6] on the basis that every significant factor pointed towards there, and, since there was no justification for the plaintiffs coming to England for trial,[7] a stay of proceedings was granted.

The term "natural forum" has frequently been employed since *Mac-Shannon*. Lord KEITH in that case said that it referred to the country with which the action has the most real and substantial connection.[8] Although in theory this raises the question of whether the issue of litigational convenience is given as much emphasis under the notion of the "natural forum" as it is given under the notion of appropriateness, it appears, in practice, that the terms "natural forum" and "appropriate forum" are used synonymously.[9] Indeed, Lord GOFF in *Spiliada Maritime Corpn v Cansulex Ltd* used Lord KEITH's definition of the natural forum as the basis of his explanation as to what the court must look for when deciding whether there is clearly a more appropriate forum abroad.[10]

An agreement by the parties to trial in a foreign country, in the form of a foreign choice of jurisdiction clause in their contract, is a strong indication

2 Ibid; *Banco Atlantico SA v The British Bank of the Middle East*, op cit, at 508.
3 *Spiliada Maritime Corpn v Cansulex Ltd* [1987] AC 460 at 477–478.
4 At 478. See also *Trendtex Trading Corpn v Credit Suisse* [1980] 3 All ER 721 at 734; affd by the House of Lords [1982] AC 679, [1981] 3 All ER 520; *Muduroglu Ltd v TC Ziraat Bankasi* [1986] QB 1225 at 1234–1245, 1262–1263. Sheen J in *The Sidi Bishr* [1987] 1 Lloyd's Rep 42 also took into account whether the defendants genuinely desired trial abroad or only sought a procedural advantage.
5 [1978] AC 795.
6 Ibid, at 812, 816, 822, 831.
7 Ibid, at 814–816, 820, 822, 823, 831; see infra, p 228.
8 [1978] AC 795 at 829. See also *The Abidin Daver* [1984] AC 398 at 415 (Lord KEITH); *The Forum Craftsman* [1984] 2 Lloyd's Rep 102 at 108 (SHEEN J); affd by the Court of Appeal [1985] 1 Lloyd's Rep 291.
9 See *MacShannon v Rockware Glass Ltd* [1978] AC 795 at 812 (per Lord DIPLOCK); see also *Trendtex Trading Corpn v Credit Suisse* [1980] 3 All ER 721 at 734; *European Asian Bank AG v Punjab and Sind Bank* [1982] 2 Lloyd's Rep 356 at 364.
10 [1987] AC 460 at 477–478.

that the appropriate forum is abroad and operates as a weighty factor in favour of a stay of the English proceedings being granted under the *forum non conveniens* doctrine.[11] Conversely, where the parties have agreed, in the event of a dispute arising, on trial in England, and particularly where they have also agreed that English law will govern the contract, this is a weighty factor against a stay of the proceedings.[12]

(c) Cases where there is no clearly more appropriate forum abroad

In cases where there is no clearly more appropriate forum abroad, ie where either there is no country which is the natural forum or England is the natural forum, the courts will ordinarily refuse a stay of proceedings.[13] Thus in *European Asian Bank AG v Punjab and Sind Bank*:[14]

> The plaintiff West German bank brought an action in England against an Indian bank by serving a writ on a branch office for payment under a letter of credit following a series of events that took place in India and Singapore. The defendant bank sought a stay of the English proceedings.

The Court of Appeal upheld the first instance decision to refuse a stay of proceedings. Neither India nor Singapore was clearly more appropriate for trial of the action than England. An English court was an appropriate court to try a claim involving the letter of credit, on the basis that the contract created by the issue of a letter of credit is independent of any contract between buyer and seller and must be performed by prompt payment against documents. There was no natural forum for trial and a stay was refused. When an action arises out of a collision on the high seas there is also no natural forum for trial and a stay will be refused.[15] A stay will likewise be refused in cases where it is possible to identify the natural forum and this is England.[16] In cases where the court has exercised its discretion to allow service out of the jurisdiction under Order 11 of the Rules of the Supreme Court, the court has already decided that England is the most appropriate forum for trial.[17] It follows that a stay of proceedings will not be granted subsequently on the basis of *forum non conveniens*. In practice therefore stays are sought in cases where a writ has been served within the jurisdiction, rather

11 See *Trendtex Trading Corpn v Credit Suisse* [1980] 3 All ER 721 at 737 and in the Court of Appeal, at 758, affd by the House of Lords, [1982] AC 679, [1981] 3 All ER 520. A stay may alternatively be granted on the basis of the foreign choice of jurisdiction clause, see infra, pp 234–236.

12 *Kuwait Oil Co (KSC) v Idemitsu Tankers KK, The Hida Maru* [1981] 2 Lloyd's Rep 510 at 514, CA; *Dimskal Shipping Co SA v International Transport Workers Federation, The Evia Luck* [1986] 2 Lloyd's Rep 165 at 179; *Saipem SpA v Dredging VO 2 BV and Geosite Surveys Ltd, The Volvox Hollandia* [1987] 2 Lloyd's Rep 520 at 529, appeal on a separate narrow point allowed [1988] 2 Lloyd's Rep 361; *S and W Berisford plc v New Hampshire Insurance Co* [1990] 1 Lloyd's Rep 454 at 463.

13 *Spiliada Maritime Corpn v Cansulex Ltd* [1987] AC 460 at 478. See also *Metal Scrap Trade Corpn v Kate Shipping Co Ltd* [1990] 1 WLR 115 at 133 (per Lord GOFF) HL; *The Maciej Rataj* [1991] 2 Lloyd's Rep 458 at 467.

14 [1982] 2 Lloyd's Rep 356.

15 *Spiliada Maritime Corpn v Cansulex Ltd*, op cit, at 477; *The Vishva Abha* [1990] 2 Lloyd's Rep 312 at 314. The position may be the same after a collision in territorial waters, see *The Po* [1990] 1 Lloyd's Rep 418; affd by the Court of Appeal [1991] 2 Lloyd's Rep 206. But cf *The Wellamo* [1980] 2 Lloyd's Rep 229; *The Abidin Daver* [1984] AC 398, [1984] 1 All ER 470.

16 *OTM Ltd v Hydronautics* [1981] 2 Lloyd's Rep 211.

17 Supra, pp 204–210.

than in cases where a writ has been served out of the jurisdiction under Order 11.

In the *European Asian Bank Case*, having decided that there was no natural forum for trial, the court did not find it necessary to go on to examine considerations aside from those involving connections and matters of litigational convenience.[18] This was a pre-*Spiliada Case* but one which was used by Lord GOFF to illustrate his third principle. Since the *Spiliada Case*, numerous cases have been decided on the basis that there was no clearly more appropriate forum abroad. But what is noticeable about these cases is that in virtually all of them the courts have considered all the circumstances of the case, including considerations going beyond those of appropriateness. This has often been on the basis that the ultimate question is what justice demands and all the factors for and against a stay have to be considered together.[19] As will be seen under the next principle, in cases where there is a clearly more appropriate forum abroad the courts will necessarily go on to consider the other relevant circumstances in the case.

(d) Cases where there is a clearly more appropriate forum abroad: the requirements of justice

Lord GOFF has said that

> if there is some other available forum which prima facie is clearly more appropriate for the trial of the action, it [the court] will ordinarily grant a stay unless there are circumstances by reason of which justice requires that a stay should nevertheless not be granted.[20]

Once it has been shown that there is a clearly more appropriate forum for trial abroad the burden of proof shifts to the plaintiff to justify coming to England.[1] Relatively little attention has been paid in subsequent cases to this aspect of the discretion. Questions of burden of proof, whilst very important when operating a rule, are much less important when operating what are a series of broad guidelines to be taken into account when exercising a discretion.[2] The court is concerned with the question of whether justice requires that a stay should not be granted.[3] All the circumstances of the case will be taken into account. The court will consider the fact that a plaintiff may not obtain justice abroad because, for example, the judiciary is not independent.[4] It has also been held that it is not conducive to justice to require a plaintiff, who had an arguable claim under what we would regard as the governing

---

18 [1982] 2 Lloyd's Rep 356 at 366, 369. Cf *The Wladyslaw Lokotiek* [1978] 2 Lloyd's Rep 520 at 540; Carter (1979) 50 BYBIL 245.

19 See, eg, *Charm Maritime Inc v Minas Xenophon Kyriakou and David John Mathias* [1987] 1 Lloyd's Rep 433 at 447. See also *The Po* [1990] 1 Lloyd's Rep 418 at 424; affd by the Court of Appeal [1991] 2 Lloyd's Rep 206; *Arkwright Mutual Insurance Co v Bryanston Insurance Co Ltd* [1990] 2 Lloyd's Rep 70 at 83; cf *Meadows Indemnity Co Ltd v Insurance Corpn of Ireland Ltd and International Commercial Bank plc* [1989] 1 Lloyd's Rep 181 at 190; affd [1989] 2 Lloyd's Rep 298.

20 *Spiliada Maritime Corpn v Cansulex Ltd*, op cit, at 478.

1 [1987] AC 460 at 476. This has been described as an evidential burden: *Charm Maritime Inc v Minas Xenophon Kyriakou and David John Mathias* [1987] 1 Lloyd's Rep 433 at 448.

2 See *Muduroglu Ltd v TC Ziraat Bankasi* [1986] QB 1225, [1986] 3 All ER 682.

3 *Spiliada Maritime Corpn v Cansulex Ltd* [1987] AC 460 at 478, HL.

4 *The Abidin Daver* [1984] AC 398 at 411. See also *Muduroglu Ltd v TC Ziraat Bankasi* [1986] QB 1225, [1986] 3 All ER 682, CA. See also *Middle East Banking Co SAL v Al-Haddad* (1990) 70 OR (2d) 97 (complete break down of the administration of justice because of civil war).

law, to litigate abroad in a country which would summarily reject the plaintiff's claims.[5] Inordinate delay of the order of magnitude of ten years before an action comes to trial abroad has also been held to be a denial of justice;[6] as has a derisorily low limit on damages imposed by the foreign court.[7] In another case, doubts were expressed as to whether any foreign judge "could conscientiously resolve with any confidence that he was reaching a correct answer" a question as to the effect of a contract as a matter of English public policy.[8] Neither is it just to stay proceedings in England when the plaintiff would be liable to imprisonment if he were to return to the alternative forum abroad.[9] Much more commonly, though, what is considered is whether, by staying the proceedings, the plaintiff will be deprived of some advantage that he would have obtained from trial in England.

(e) Treatment of the advantage to the plaintiff

The mere fact that the plaintiff obtains a legitimate personal or juridical advantage cannot be decisive.[10]

(i) The meaning of an advantage to the plaintiff[11] The advantage to the plaintiff can be a personal or a juridical one. There is a personal advantage in trial in England if the plaintiff is an English resident.[12] A juridical advantage can relate to a substantive matter, ie the existence in English law of some more favourable substantive rule than would apply elsewhere.[13] For example, in *Power Curber International Ltd v National Bank of Kuwait SAK*[14] the fact that an English court would apply choice of law rules which would result in a summary judgment for the plaintiff was said to be a legitimate juridical advantage. More commonly, though, the advantage to the plaintiff in trial in England has been a procedural one, eg the plaintiff obtains security for the full amount of his claim,[15] or a cheaper and quicker trial,[16] or higher damages,[17] or an award of interest,[18] or costs[19] or a more generous limitation period.[20]

Not every advantage to the plaintiff can be considered when exercising the

---

5 *Banco Atlantico SA v The British Bank of the Middle East* [1990] 2 Lloyd's Rep 504 at 509.
6 *The Vishva Ajay* [1989] 2 Lloyd's Rep 558 at 560.
7 *The Adhiguna Meranti* [1988] 1 Lloyd's Rep 384 at 395–396, Hong Kong CA. For an English case on limitation of liability see *The Falstria* [1988] 1 Lloyd's Rep 495.
8 *EI Du Pont de Nemours & Co v Agnew and Kerr* [1987] 2 Lloyd's Rep 585 at 595; see also *Mitsubishi Corpn v Aristidis I Alafouzos* [1988] 1 Lloyd's Rep 191 at 196.
9 *Purcell v Khayan* (1987) Times, 23 November.
10 *Spiliada Maritime Corpn v Cansulex Ltd* [1987] AC 460 at 482. See also *De Dampierre v De Dampierre* [1988] AC 92 at 109–110.
11 Briggs [1984] Lloyd's MCLQ 227 at 234–239; Schuz (1986) 35 ICLQ 374 at 386–395.
12 *MacShannon v Rockware Glass Ltd* [1978] AC 795 at 819; *The Wladyslaw Lokotiek* [1978] 2 Lloyd's Rep 520 at 540.
13 *The Atlantic Star* [1974] AC 436 at 468 (per Lord WILBERFORCE).
14 [1981] 1 WLR 1233 at 1240. See also *The Hida Maru* [1981] 2 Lloyd's Rep 510 at 513; *The Iran Vojdan* [1984] 2 Lloyd's Rep 380 at 387; *Irish Shipping Ltd v Commercial Union Assurance Co plc* [1991] 2 QB 206 at 221. See also in the context of RSC Ord 11, *Britannia SS Insurance Association Ltd v Ausonia Assicurazioni SpA* [1984] 2 Lloyd's Rep 98.
15 *The Atlantic Star* [1984] AC 436 at 454 (Lord REID); *The Wladyslaw Lokoteik* [1978] 2 Lloyd's Rep 520 at 540; *The El Amria* [1981] 2 Lloyd's Rep 539 at 542.
16 *MacShannon v Rockware Glass Ltd* [1978] AC 795 at 814–815.
17 *The Atlantic Star* [1974] AC 436 at 469; *Spiliada Maritime Corpn v Cansulex Ltd* [1987] AC 460 at 482.
18 *Spiliada Maritime Corpn v Cansulex Ltd*, op cit, at 482.
19 *The Vishva Ajay* [1989] 2 Lloyd's Rep 558.
20 *Spiliada Maritime Corpn v Cansulex Ltd*, op cit, at 482.

forum non conveniens discretion. There are three clear limitations in respect of the advantage to the plaintiff. First, the advantage must be *real*, ie objectively demonstrated. This was established in *MacShannon v Rockware Glass Ltd*,[1] where the plaintiffs' mere honest belief, after legal advice, that they would obtain certain advantages from trial in England was held to be insufficient. In the absence of such objective evidence, it was held that the plaintiffs would gain no advantage from trial in England. Second, what must be shown is an advantage to the plaintiff when trial in England is compared with trial in the alternative forum abroad. For example, there is no advantage in being able to obtain security for a claim which is available in an action in rem in England when there has been an undertaking to put up security in the alternative forum abroad.[2] Third, the advantage must be a *legitimate* one.[3] This would obviously exclude any benefit to the plaintiff which he seeks to obtain by harassing the defendant. Beyond this, in the different context of restraining foreign proceedings it has been held that the benefit that a party would derive from the contingency fee system in the United States was not a legitimate juridical advantage in respect of obtaining trial in that country.[4]

(ii) Comparing the quality of justice The House of Lords has held that the courts should not engage in the invidious task of comparing the quality of justice obtained under the English common law system of procedure with that obtained under a civil law system.[5] The fact that trial in England would take place before the Commercial Court or the Admiralty Court, with their great experience and international standing, should no longer be taken into account as an advantage to the plaintiff.[6] When it comes to other forms of procedural advantage, the effect of this prohibition on making comparisons between different legal systems is less clear. In *The Traugutt*[7] SHEEN J held that having the benefit of the English process of pre-trial discovery could not be considered as an advantage to the plaintiff since it was not open to him to make comparisons between English and Belgian processes of justice. On the other hand, the same factor was said by GOFF LJ in *Bank of Tokyo Ltd v Karoon* to be a most valuable juridical advantage.[8] The House of Lords in *Spiliada Maritime Corpn v Cansulex Ltd* was prepared to regard a more complete procedure for discovery as an advantage to the plaintiff, along with

1 [1978] AC 795 at 812, 820, 830. See also *Spiliada Maritime Corpn v Cansulex Ltd* [1987] AC 460 at 478; *Avenue Properties Ltd v First City Development Corpn Ltd* (1987) 32 DLR (4th) 40 at 46–47.
2 *The Abidin Daver* [1984] AC 398 at 410.
3 *MacShannon v Rockware Glass Ltd* [1978] AC 795 at 812. Lord SCARMAN in *Castanho v Brown and Root (UK) Ltd* [1981] AC 557 at 575 said that time should not be spent in speculating about the meaning of "legitimate advantage".
4 *Smith Kline and French Laboratories Ltd v Bloch* [1983] 1 WLR 730 at 738, 747.
5 *Amin Rasheed Shipping Corpn v Kuwait Insurance Co* [1984] AC 50 at 67; *The Abidin Daver* [1984] AC 398 at 410. See also *Aratra Potato Co Ltd v Egyptian Navigation Co, The El Amria* [1981] 2 Lloyd's Rep 119 at 127, CA.
6 *The Abidin Daver* [1984] AC 398 at 424–425; *Hawke Bay Shipping Co Ltd v The First National Bank of Chicago, The Efthimis* [1986] 1 Lloyd's Rep 244 at 260. But see *Islamic Arab Insurance Co v Saudi Egyptian American Reinsurance Co* [1987] 1 Lloyd's Rep 315 at 319, 320; Slater (1988) 104 LQR 554. The earlier case of *The Wladyslaw Lokotiek* [1978] 2 Lloyd's Rep 520 at 540 must now be regarded as wrong on this point.
7 [1985] 1 Lloyd's Rep 76 at 79.
8 [1987] AC 45 at 62–63, CA. See also *Trendtex Trading Corpn v Credit Suisse* [1980] 3 All ER 721 at 737 (decided before the House of Lords cases forbidding the making of comparisons); *Metall Und Rohstoff AG v ACLI Metals (London) Ltd* [1984] 1 Lloyd's Rep 598—a case on restraining foreign proceedings.

other juridical advantages, but was not prepared to give decisive weight to such advantages when operating the discretion.[9] Certainly, when faced with *undisputed evidence* of a specific substantial procedural advantage to the plaintiff of trial in England, the courts have been willing to take this into account.[10] Similarly if there is positive and cogent evidence that the plaintiff, if forced to litigate abroad, would not obtain justice, for example because the judiciary is not independent, then this will be considered.[11] English courts are concerned that a minimum standard of justice is available in the alternative forum and the Court of Appeal has warned that "the court must not be too unworldly in its approach" and that "there are other parts of the world where things are badly wrong".[12] The courts are, however, not going to be easily convinced of the existence of such injustice, particularly when it is alleged that it arises in a country which is one with which the United Kingdom has close ties, such as a fellow European Community State.[13]

(iii) The weight to be attached to the advantage to the plaintiff At one time great weight was attached to this factor, and if the plaintiff obtained a substantial advantage from trial in England the courts were unlikely to grant a stay of the English proceedings. The House of Lords in the *Spiliada Case* sought to reduce the weight given to the advantage to the plaintiff when exercising the discretion to stay. Hence the principle that the mere fact that the plaintiff has a legitimate personal or juridical advantage in proceedings in England cannot be decisive. Lord GOFF gave an example:[14] an English court would not, in ordinary circumstances, hesitate to stay English proceedings merely because the plaintiff would be deprived of a higher award of damages here. Nonetheless, he was concerned to pay regard to the interests of all the parties and of the ends of justice. All the circumstances of the case have to be considered. Circumstances can arise which lead to a different conclusion and to the refusal of the grant of a stay. He said that, in the situation where the plaintiff is time-barred from proceeding abroad but comes within the English limitation period, it would not be just to deprive him of the benefit of trial in England if he acted reasonably in commencing proceedings here and did not act unreasonably in failing to commence proceedings in the foreign jurisdiction.[15] Seemingly, if the plaintiff obtains an advantage from trial in England, which does not involve a corresponding disadvantage to the defendant (eg there is a similar action before the English courts involving the same defendant, expert witnesses, lawyers and insurers), there may be injustice to the plaintiff in depriving him of this advantage by staying the English action.[16] If by trial in England the plaintiff is able to

9 [1987] AC 460 at 482–483.
10 *The El Amria* [1981] 2 Lloyd's Rep 119 at 127; *The Jalakrishna* [1983] 2 Lloyd's Rep 628 at 630–631; *The Po* [1991] 2 Lloyd's Rep 206 at 213.
11 *The Abidin Daver* [1984] AC 398 at 411. See also *Muduroglu Ltd v TC Ziraat Bankasi* [1986] QB 1225, [1986] 3 All ER 682; *Aldington Shipping Ltd v Bradstock Shipping Corpn and Mabanaft GmbH, The Waylink and Brady Maira* [1988] 1 Lloyd's Rep 475 at 482, Gibraltar CA.
12 *Muduroglu Ltd v TC Ziraat Bankasi* [1986] QB 1225 at 1248.
13 *Dubai Electricity Co v Islamic Republic of Iran Shipping Lines, The Iran Vojdan* [1984] 2 Lloyd's Rep 380 at 388.
14 Op cit, at 482.
15 Op cit, at 483–484. See also *The Blue Wave* [1982] 1 Lloyd's Rep 151; *Metall Und Rohstoff AG v Donaldson Lufkin & Jenrette Inc* [1990] 1 QB 391 at 486–488; overruled on a different point in *Lonrho plc v Fayed* [1991] 3 All ER 303, [1991] 3 WLR 188, HL.
16 Op cit, at 485–486; see also supra, p 207.

continue proceedings against two separate defendants in the same action, this is a significant advantage to the plaintiff yet not to the detriment of the defendant.[17] The fact that an English court can award costs to a successful litigant can be an important advantage and one that operates for the benefit of both parties.[18]

The concern to reduce the weight to be attached to the advantage to the plaintiff is a development to be welcomed. Although there has been considerable judicial condemnation of the practice of forum shopping,[19] it appears in the past that the more that the plaintiff had to gain from this practice the more likely he was to be allowed to continue his action in England.[20] This may seem curious, but it has to be borne in mind that there is a public interest in allowing trial in England of what are, in essence, foreign actions.[1] When foreigners litigate in England this forms a valuable invisible export,[2] and confirms judicial pride in the English legal system. The emphasis in the House of Lords is now very much on chauvinism being replaced by judicial comity.[3] However, the extent to which this new spirit has filtered down to lower courts is questionable. The *Spiliada Case* does not appear to have led to a dramatic increase in the number of stays granted. In many cases the courts have concluded that the interests of justice demand that a stay be refused, even though the clearly most appropriate forum is abroad. As has been seen, there are numerous recent examples of cases where English courts have held that there would be positive injustice in trial abroad or an important advantage to the plaintiff in trial in England.

(iii) The operation of the principles

The operation of the above principles can be seen by looking at two recent decisions of the Court of Appeal. The first is *Charm Maritime Inc v Minas Xenophon Kyriakou and David John Mathias*:[4]

> The plaintiff, a Liberian company, began proceedings in England against the first defendant, a Greek shipowner, and the second defendant to enforce alleged rights in certain shares as assignee of rights of the second defendant under a trust deed. The first defendant applied for a stay of proceedings on the basis that Greece was the more appropriate forum. This was refused at first instance.

The Court of Appeal dismissed an appeal against this decision. SLADE LJ set out the principles contained in the *Spiliada Case*. He said that the questions of the appropriate forum and the advantage to the plaintiff should be considered

---

17 *Charm Maritime Inc v Minas Xenophon Kyriakou and David John Mathias* [1987] 1 Lloyd's Rep 433.

18 *The Vishva Ajay* [1989] 2 Lloyd's Rep 558; see also *Roneleigh Ltd v MII Exports Inc* [1989] 1 WLR 619.

19 *Boys v Chaplin* [1971] AC 356 at 406, 380, 383; *The Atlantic Star* [1974] AC 436 at 454; see Fawcett (1984) 35 NILQ 141; Schuz (1986) 35 ICLQ 374.

20 Cf GOFF LJ in *Bank of Tokyo Ltd v Karoon* [1987] AC 45 at 62–63, CA.

1 Compare the position in the United States where the public interest is against the trial of such actions, see *Gulf Oil Corpn v Gilbert* 330 US 501 (1946); *Piper Aircraft Co v Reyno* 454 US 235 (1981).

2 Kerr (1978) 41 MLR 1; Lord DEVLIN, *Samples of Lawmaking* (1962), at pp 29–30. See also *Camilla Cotton Oil Co v Granadex SA* [1976] 2 Lloyd's Rep 10 at 14.

3 See *The Abidin Daver* [1984] AC 398 at 411 (per Lord DIPLOCK). See also *Owens Bank Ltd v Bracco* [1991] 4 All ER 833 at 858, CA in relation to litigation within the European Community in cases outside the Brussels Convention.

4 [1987] 1 Lloyd's Rep 433.

together, rather than separately under a two stage process.[5] There were factors pointing towards trial in Greece, including an estoppel point arising out of the fact that an earlier action between the parties commenced in Greece had been dismissed on procedural grounds. On the other hand, there were two key factors that pointed towards trial in England: the trust was governed by English law; there was also a clear and legitimate advantage to the plaintiff in being able to proceed against both defendants in the same action in England (the second defendant could probably not have been sued in Greece). Accordingly, the defendant could not show that Greece was a clearly more appropriate forum for trial than England or that justice required a trial in Greece rather than in England.

The second case is *Banco Atlantico SA v The British Bank of the Middle East*:[6]

> The plaintiffs, a bank incorporated in Spain, commenced proceedings in England against the defendants, a bank incorporated in England, as indorsers or guarantors of certain bills of exchange, which were in Spanish but provided for payment to be made in the United Arab Emirates. The defendants sought a stay of proceedings on the ground that the appropriate forum was the United Arab Emirates. This was granted at first instance.

The Court of Appeal allowed an appeal against this decision. BINGHAM LJ (STOCKER and NOURSE LJJ concurring) placed reliance on Lord GOFF's basic principle in the *Spiliada Case*; the other principles enunciated by the House of Lords were not referred to. The defendants failed to show that the United Arab Emirates was a clearly more appropriate forum having regard to the interests of all the parties and the achievement of justice. Two factors were regarded as being of great importance in reaching this decision. First, the defendants' very solid connection with England, being incorporated there. It was said that rarely would the English courts refuse jurisdiction in such a case; very clear and weighty grounds would be needed before it did so. Second, it would not be conducive to justice to require the plaintiffs to litigate in the courts of the United Arab Emirates, which would not apply the law governing the contract but, instead, would apply their own law under which the plaintiffs would lose their action.

(iv) Multiplicity of proceedings

If litigation involving the same parties and the same issues is continuing simultaneously in two different countries, this is referred to as a case of *lis alibi pendens*.[1] In such cases the issue facing the English court is not simply that of deciding to which of the alternative fora the plaintiff should have to go to bring his action. Instead, the choice is between, on the one hand, trial in England *plus* trial abroad (if a stay is refused) and, on the other hand, trial abroad (if a stay is granted). It is very undesirable to have concurrent actions in England and abroad: this involves more expense and inconvenience to the parties than if trial were held in merely one country; it can also lead to two conflicting judgments, with an unseemly race by the parties to be the first to

5 Ibid, at 447; cf *The Adhiguna Meranti* [1988] 1 Lloyd's Rep 384 at 385, Hong Kong CA.
6 [1990] 2 Lloyd's Rep 504.
1 On the significance of a multiplicity of proceedings in RSC, Ord 11 cases see supra, p 205.

obtain a judgment and to subsequent problems of estoppel.[2] The objection to concurrent proceedings is said to be even stronger if this involves in one of the two states proceedings for a negative declaration (a declaration that a person is not liable in an existing action).[3] If there is a multiplicity of proceedings in England and abroad, but the parties or the issues are different in each of the actions, this is technically not a case of *lis alibi pendens*; nonetheless, it is undesirable to have this multiplicity of proceedings and some, if not all, of the objections inherent in cases of *lis alibi pendens* will still be applicable.[4]

In cases where the concurrent proceedings are in the United Kingdom and in another European Community State or in an EFTA State which has ratified the Lugano Convention the *lis alibi pendens* provision contained in Article 21[5] of the Brussels Convention or Lugano Convention may be applicable. However, what we are concerned with in this chapter are cases which do not fall within Article 21, for example, where there are concurrent proceedings in England and New York.

The fact that the refusal of a stay of English proceedings will lead to a multiplicity of proceedings in England and abroad is an important additional element to be taken into account under the doctrine of *forum non conveniens*.[6] Lord GOFF in the *Spiliada Case* did not explain how the new restated principles in relation to *forum non conveniens* would operate in cases involving a multiplicity of proceedings. However, in *De Dampierre v De Dampierre*[7] he said that the "same principle is applicable whether or not there are other relevant proceedings already pending in the alternative forum".[8] The defendant[9] has to show that there is a clearly more appropriate forum abroad, ie *the* natural forum must be abroad.[10] This will be determined in the light of the fact that the case involves a multiplicity of proceedings.

The new approach towards a multiplicity of proceedings can be illustrated by looking at two recent decisions in this area. In *Cleveland Museum of Art v Capricorn Art International SA*[11] there were concurrent proceedings in Ohio and England between the same parties involving the same issues. HIRST J applied the basic principle in the *Spiliada Case*. He examined the factors in favour of trial in Ohio and England, took into account the fact that the

---

2 *The Abidin Daver* [1984] AC 398 at 412 (per Lord DIPLOCK), 423–424 (per Lord BRANDON). See also *The Messiniaki Tolmi* [1983] 1 Lloyd's Rep 666 at 672. On estoppel see infra, pp 372–376.

3 *First National Bank of Boston v Union Bank of Switzerland* [1990] 1 Lloyd's Rep 32 at 38–39. See also *Saipem Spa v Dredging V02 BV and Geosite Surveys Ltd, The Volvox Hollandia* [1988] 2 Lloyd's Rep 361 at 371 CA; *Sohio Supply Co v Gatoil (USA) Inc* [1989] 1 Lloyd's Rep 588 at 593.

4 See *Metall Und Rohstoff AG v ACLI Metals (London) Ltd* [1984] 1 Lloyd's Rep 598, CA; *Hawke Bay Shipping Co Ltd v The First National Bank of Chicago, The Efthimis* [1986] 1 Lloyd's Rep 244, CA.

5 Infra, pp 326–329.

6 For the effect of the risk of a multiplicity of proceedings in RSC Ord 11 cases, see supra, p 205.

7 [1988] AC 92, [1987] 2 All ER 1.

8 Ibid, at 108.

9 For cases involving the plaintiff seeking a stay of English proceedings see *A-G v Arthur Andersen & Co (United Kingdom)* [1989] ECC 224; *Australian Commercial Research and Development Ltd v ANZ McCaughan Merchant Bank Ltd* [1989] 3 All ER 65.

10 Cf Lord DIPLOCK's formulation in the earlier case of *The Abidin Daver* [1984] AC 398. It is inappropriate now to use Lord DIPLOCK's formulation, see *Arkwright Mutual Insurance Co v Bryanston Insurance Co Ltd* [1990] 2 QB 649 at 665.

11 [1990] 2 Lloyd's Rep 166.

action was now ready for trial in Ohio and the undesirable consequences of concurrent litigation, both in terms of expense and inconvenience to the parties and in terms of the possibility of conflicting judgments, and concluded that the Ohio court was clearly the more appropriate forum for trial of the action, in the sense of being the one in which the case may be tried more suitably for the interests of all the parties and the ends of justice. A stay of the English proceedings was accordingly granted.

In contrast to this, the operation of the same approach by the Court of Appeal in *E I Du Pont de Nemours & Co v Agnew and Kerr*[12] led to the refusal of a stay, despite the undesirability of having concurrent proceedings. This was on the basis that the defendants had not shown that Illinois was a clearly more appropriate forum for trial than England. The case involved a claim for an indemnity under a contract of insurance. A key factor that influenced the Court of Appeal in reaching its decision was the fact that the contract was governed by English law; questions of English public policy would arise and doubts were expressed as to whether any foreign court could fairly resolve them. A stay will also be refused if there is no country which is a natural forum for trial, even if this will mean a multiplicity of proceedings. Thus a stay was refused in *The Coral Isis*,[13] where a collision occurred in international waters between two ships of different nationalities.

The weight to be attached to the factor of multiplicity of proceedings will depend on the circumstances of the case. It is not a decisive factor in the sense of automatically making a foreign forum clearly more appropriate and shifting the burden of proof to the plaintiff to justify trial in England.[14] It does not matter, in principle, whether the action was commenced first in England or abroad; this is merely an accident of timing.[15] However, it is seemingly relevant whether it is a case of the same plaintiff starting proceedings in two different jurisdictions or a case where the plaintiff in one jurisdiction is the defendant in another jurisdiction and vice versa. In the former case the plaintiff will generally be forced to elect the country in which he wants trial.[16] If he elects for trial abroad the court will then dismiss the English proceedings. It is also relevant to look at the motivation behind the commencement of the foreign proceedings and the progress made in them. If an action is commenced abroad not because of a genuine desire for trial in that country but merely to avoid being time-barred and to demonstrate the possibility of trial in that country, the factor of multiplicity of proceedings will be given no weight.[17] Likewise, if no substantial progress has been made in the foreign proceedings, for example there has been no discovery,[18] the

12 [1987] 2 Lloyd's Rep 585. See also *Hawke Bay Shipping Co Ltd v The First National Bank of Chicago, The Efthimis* [1986] 1 Lloyd's Rep 244.

13 [1986] 1 Lloyd's Rep 413.

14 *Meadows Indemnity Co Ltd v Insurance Corp of Ireland Ltd and International Commercial Bank plc* [1989] 1 Lloyd's Rep 181 at 189; affd [1989] 2 Lloyd's Rep 298, CA.

15 *The Coral Isis* [1986] 1 Lloyd's Rep 413; *E I Du Pont de Nemours & Co v Agnew and Kerr* [1987] 2 Lloyd's Rep 585 at 593. Cf Art 21 of the Brussels Convention, infra, pp 326–329. See also *McConnell Dowell Constructors Ltd v Lloyd's Syndicate 396* [1988] 2 NZLR 257 at 273.

16 See *Australian Commercial Research and Development Ltd v ANZ McCaughan Merchant Bank Ltd* [1989] 3 All ER 65 at 70. See also *Manufacturers Life Insurance Co v Guarantee Co of North America* (1988) 62 OR (2d) 147. Cf *A-G v Arthur Anderson & Co* [1989] ECC 224. See generally Smart [1990] Lloyd's MCLQ 326.

17 *De Dampierre v De Dampierre*, op cit, at 108. See also *Irish Shipping Ltd v Commercial Union Assurance Co plc* [1991] 2 QB 206 at 232, 245.

18 *Arkwright Mutual Insurance Co v Bryanston Insurance Co Ltd* [1990] 2 Lloyd's Rep 70 at 80.

multiplicity of proceedings will be given little weight. On the other hand, if genuine proceedings have developed abroad to the stage where they have some impact upon the dispute, especially if this is likely to be of continuing effect then this may be relevant.[19] In one case,[20] the fact that the dispute might come to trial abroad during the year made the multiplicity of proceedings a relevant factor. In *The Abidin Daver* one of the factors pointing towards Turkey as the natural forum for trial was the fact that proceedings were promptly started there soon after a collision in Turkish waters between a Cuban-owned vessel and a Turkish-owned vessel, and were proceeding with dispatch; indeed, the Turkish court had appointed a surveyor who had already interviewed relevant witnesses and prepared a report for the court.[21]

(b) FOREIGN JURISDICTION CLAUSES[22]

If parties have agreed on trial in a European Community State, or in an EFTA State which has ratified the Lugano Convention, Article 17 of the Brussels Convention or Lugano Convention may be applicable,[23] according to which the European Community or EFTA Contracting State on which jurisdiction has been conferred by the parties is given exclusive jurisdiction. What we are concerned with here, however, are cases where Article 17 is not applicable, for example where the parties have agreed on trial in New York.

(i) The exercise of the discretion to stay

As has been seen,[24] an English court will be most reluctant to permit service out of the jurisdiction in the face of an agreement by the parties to submit their disputes to the exclusive jurisdiction of a foreign court.[25] In the situation where the English court has undoubted jurisdiction over actions properly instituted here, there is an inherent discretion in the court to disregard an express foreign jurisdiction clause. This differs from the previous situation insofar as there is a heavier burden in the Order 11 cases on the plaintiff to persuade the court not to give effect to the express clause.[26] Nonetheless, in accordance with the principle that a contractual undertaking should be honoured, there is a *prima facie* rule that an action brought in England in defiance of an agreement to submit to a foreign jurisdiction will be stayed.[1] However, the court does have a discretion in the matter, and where the parties are amenable to the jurisdiction, as, for example, where the defendant is

---

19 *De Dampierre v De Dampierre*, op cit. See also *The Coral Isis*, op cit.
20 *Meadows Indemnity Co Ltd v Insurance Corp of Ireland Ltd and International Commercial Bank plc* [1989] 1 Lloyd's Rep 181 at 189, affd [1989] 2 Lloyd's Rep 298, CA.
21 [1984] AC 398 at 410, 421.
22 Pryles (1976) 25 ICLQ 543; Kahn-Freund (1977) 26 ICLQ 825; Robertson (1982) 20 Alberta LR 296; Briggs [1984] Lloyd's MCLQ 227 at 241–248; Barma and Elvin (1985) 101 LQR 48 at 65–67.
23 Infra, pp 314–322.
24 Supra, p 205.
25 *Mackender v Feldia AG* [1967] 2 QB 590 at 604. The courts have adopted a similar approach when considering, under Ord 11, r 1(1)(d)(iv), supra, p 198, 209, English, rather than foreign, jurisdiction clauses: *Unterweser Reederei GmbH v Zapata Off-shore Co, The Chaparral* [1968] 2 Lloyd's Rep 158.
26 *Evans Marshall & Co Ltd v Bertola SA* [1973] 1 WLR 349 at 362; though see *The Makefjell* [1976] 2 Lloyd's Rep 29 at 34–35, 38.
 1 *The Eleftheria* [1970] P 94, [1969] 2 All ER 641; *The Sindh* [1975] 1 Lloyd's Rep 372; *The Makefjell* [1976] 2 Lloyd's Rep 29; *The Biskra* [1983] 2 Lloyd's Rep 59; *The Indian Fortune* [1985] 1 Lloyd's Rep 344; *The Ruben Martinez Villena (No 2)* [1988] 1 Lloyd's Rep 435.

present in England, it will allow the English action to continue if it considers that the ends of justice will be better served by a trial in this country.[2]

There is a very clear statement by BRANDON J in *The Eleftheria*,[3] which the same judge repeated in *The El Amria*,[4] of the principles on which the decision whether or not to stay an action should be based:

The principles established by the authorities can, I think, be summarised as follows: (1) Where plaintiffs sue in England in breach of an agreement to refer disputes to a foreign court, and the defendants apply for a stay, the English court, assuming the claim to be otherwise within its jurisdiction, is not bound to grant a stay but has a discretion whether to do so or not. (2) The discretion should be exercised by granting a stay unless strong cause for not doing so is shown. (3) The burden of proving such strong cause is on the plaintiffs. (4) In exercising its discretion the court should take into account all the circumstances of the particular case. (5) In particular, but without prejudice to (4), the following matters, where they arise, may properly be regarded: (a) In what country the evidence on the issues of fact is situated, or more readily available, and the effect of that on the relative convenience and expense of trial as between the English and foreign courts.[5] (b) Whether the law of the foreign court applies and, if so, whether it differs from English law in any material respects.[6] (c) With what country either party is connected, and how closely.[7] (d) Whether the defendants genuinely desire trial in the foreign country, or are only seeking procedural advantages.[8] (e) Whether the plaintiffs would be prejudiced by having to sue in the foreign court because they would: (i) be deprived of security for their claim; (ii) be unable to enforce any judgment obtained; (iii) be faced with a time bar not applicable in England;[9] or (iv) for political, racial, religious or other reasons be unlikely to get a fair trial.[10]

This list is not intended to be exhaustive.[11] Thus the inconvenience to the plaintiff of having to bring two sets of proceedings in different venues if the English proceedings were stayed has been taken into account as a decisive

---

2 *The Athenee* (1922) 11 Ll L Rep 6; *The Fehmarn* [1958] 1 All ER 333, [1958] 1 WLR 159; *The Adolf Warski* [1976] 2 Lloyd's Rep 241; *Carvalho v Hull Blyth (Angola) Ltd* [1979] 3 All ER 280, [1979] 1 WLR 1228; *Aratra Potato Co Ltd v Egyptian Navigation Co, The El Amria* [1981] 2 Lloyd's Rep 119, CA; *Kutchera v Buckingham International Holdings Ltd* (1988) 9 ILRM 501, SC; *Apple Computer Inc v Apple Corpn SA* [1990] 2 NZLR 598.

3 [1970] P 94 at 110.

4 *Aratra Potato Co Ltd v Egyptian Navigation Co, The El Amria* [1981] 2 Lloyd's Rep 119, CA. These principles have been confirmed by the House of Lords in *The Sennar (No 2)* [1985] 1 WLR 490 at 500; see also *Trendtex Trading Corpn v Crédit Suisse* [1980] 3 All ER 721; affd by the House of Lords [1982] AC 679.

5 *The Panseptos* [1981] 1 Lloyd's Rep 152.

6 *Trendtex Trading Corpn v Crédit Suisse* [1980] 3 All ER 721 at 735, affd by the House of Lords [1982] AC 679; *The Panseptos* [1981] 1 Lloyd's Rep 152.

7 The courts have also looked more generally at the connections that the facts of the case have with the alternative fora. If there is no connection with England it has been said that only a perverse exercise of the discretion would lead to refusal of a stay: *The Sennar (No 2)* [1985] 1 WLR 490, HL at 501 (per Lord BRANDON); see also *The Star of Luxor* [1981] 1 Lloyd's Rep 139.

8 *The Vishva Prabha* [1979] 2 Lloyd's Rep 286; *The Atlantic Song* [1983] 2 Lloyd's Rep 394; *The Pia Vesta* [1984] 1 Lloyd's Rep 169; *The Iran Vojdan* [1984] 2 Lloyd's Rep 380; *The Frank Pais* [1986] 1 Lloyd's Rep 529.

9 See *The Adolf Warski* [1976] 2 Lloyd's Rep 241; *The El Amria and El Minia* [1981] 2 Lloyd's Rep 539; *The Blue Wave* [1982] 1 Lloyd's Rep 151; *The Sennar (No 2)* [1984] 2 Lloyd's Rep 142, CA; affd [1985] 2 All ER 104, [1985] 1 WLR 490, HL; *The Indian Fortune* [1985] 1 Lloyd's Rep 344. See also *Spiliada Maritime Corpn v Cansulex Ltd* [1987] AC 460, HL.

10 See *Carvalho v Hull, Blyth (Angola) Ltd* [1979] 3 All ER 280, [1979] 1 WLR 1228.

11 Ibid, at 1238.

factor, in refusing a stay[12] although not fitting easily within any of the above considerations. In *The El Amria*[13] BRANDON LJ added that judges should not be drawn into making comparisons between the two different systems of administering justice used by English courts on the one hand and foreign courts on the other.[14] It has been said in other cases that it ill-behoves a party who has agreed to trial in a particular foreign country subsequently to argue that he would suffer some procedural disadvantage from trial there,[15] or to argue that the substantive law which would be applied by the foreign court would be disadvantageous to him.[16]

Although the criteria listed in *The El Amria* encompass the same factors of appropriateness which are considered under the doctrine of *forum non conveniens*,[17] the law has not yet reached the stage where the two forms of discretion can be assimilated.[18] The principle that the parties should abide by their agreement is of great importance in cases involving an exclusive jurisdiction clause. The starting point is that the English proceedings should be stayed if there is such a clause providing for the exclusive jurisdiction of a foreign court, whereas under the *forum non conveniens* discretion the starting point is that an action properly commenced in England should be allowed to continue. This means that the burden of proof is different under each discretion.[19] In cases involving foreign exclusive jurisdiction clauses the burden is on the plaintiff to show why a stay should not be granted.[20] In cases of *forum non conveniens* the burden is on the defendant, at least as regards showing that the natural forum is abroad.[21] Moreover, a plaintiff cannot complain of the procedure of the foreign court if that court has been chosen by the parties.[1]

(ii) Reliance on, escape from, exclusive jurisdiction clauses

The impact of a foreign exclusive jurisdiction clause on service out of the jurisdiction under Order 11 of the Rules of the Supreme Court and on stays of action is such that a defendant who does not wish to face trial in England will seek to rely on such a clause wherever possible, whereas a plaintiff who wishes to bring his action in England will seek to escape from such a clause.

When can a defendant rely on an exclusive jurisdiction clause? The impact of a foreign choice of jurisdiction clause will be lessened if it does not provide for *exclusive* jurisdiction, since the courts will require stronger grounds for allowing the action to continue here if there is an exclusive jurisdiction clause

12 *The Rewia* [1991] 1 Lloyd's Rep 69 at 75; overruled on a different point [1991] 2 Lloyd's Rep 325, CA.
13 [1981] 2 Lloyd's Rep 119.
14 Ibid, at 127. See also *The Abidin Daver* [1984] AC 398, discussed supra, pp 228–229.
15 *Trendtex Trading Corpn v Crédit Suisse* [1980] 3 All ER 721 at 736–737; affd by the House of Lords [1982] AC 679; *The Kislovodsk* [1980] 1 Lloyd's Rep 183 at 186.
16 *The Benarty* [1984] 2 Lloyd's Rep 244 at 251, CA.
17 See *The Frank Pais* [1986] 1 Lloyd's Rep 529 at 535.
18 Cf Briggs [1984] Lloyd's MCLQ 227 at 241–248; Barma and Elvin (1985) 101 LQR 48 at 65–67.
19 *Trendtex Trading Corpn v Crédit Suisse* [1980] 3 All ER 721 at 734–735; affd by the House of Lords [1982] AC 679.
20 If the plaintiff discharges this burden a stay will not be granted to the defendant on the basis of *forum non conveniens*, see *The Frank Pais* [1986] 1 Lloyd's Rep 529 at 535.
21 Supra, p 223.
 1 *Trendtex Trading Corpn v Crédit Suiss* [1980] 3 All ER 721 at 734–735; affd by the House of Lords [1982] AC 679.

than if there is a non-exclusive clause.[2] Seemingly, it is for the governing law to determine whether the clause is, as a matter of construction,[3] "exclusive".[4] In principle, this should be the law governing the agreement on jurisdiction[5] rather than the contract as a whole. The burden of proving that the clause is exclusive is said to rest on the person who relies on it.[6] Moreover, a defendant who is not a party to a contract containing an exclusive jurisdiction clause will not be able to rely on it, unless he can show that under the governing law he has an enforceable right to invoke the clause.[7]

When can a plaintiff escape from an exclusive jurisdiction clause? A plaintiff cannot avoid a foreign exclusive jurisdiction clause by simply framing his action in tort, since it is for the law governing (presumably) the agreement on jurisdiction, and not for English law as the law of the forum, to determine whether the claim lies in contract or in tort.[8] Furthermore, if a foreign court has given a judgment deciding that the exclusive jurisdiction clause applies to the plaintiff's claim, this may create an issue estoppel preventing the plaintiff from denying this.[9]

However, a plaintiff can escape from a foreign exclusive jurisdiction clause by showing that it is void and therefore of no effect.[10] It will only be in rare cases that the plaintiff will succeed in establishing this. It is not enough to show that part of the agreement between the parties is void, if the foreign choice of jurisdiction clause is still left intact. Thus in *Trendtex Trading Corpn v Crédit Suisse*[11] the House of Lords held that, although the assignment of a cause of action in England was void as being against English public policy,[12] this did not have the effect of automatically striking out the other clauses in the parties' agreement, including an exclusive jurisdiction clause providing for trial in Switzerland.[13] Moreover, there were other issues to be tried between the parties. A stay of English proceedings was therefore granted, in accordance with the usual principle that the parties should abide by their agreement. The plaintiff will have to show either that the *whole* agreement is void or that the choice of jurisdiction clause itself is void.

As regards the validity of the whole agreement, it has been held that, if this question arises at the jurisdictional stage of the proceedings, it is to be decided according to English domestic law and not according to the governing

---

2 *Evans Marshall and Co Ltd v Bertola SA* [1973] 1 WLR 349 at 361, supra, p 205; *Green v Australian Industrial Investment Ltd* (1990) 90 ALR 500.
3 *Sohio Supply Co v Gatoil (USA) Inc* [1989] 1 Lloyd's Rep 588 at 591; *S & W Berisford plc v New Hampshire Insurance Co* [1990] 2 All ER 321 at 326.
4 *Evans Marshall and Co Ltd v Bertola SA*, op cit.
5 This will be determined under traditional common law rules; the Rome Convention excludes agreements on jurisdiction from its scope, infra pp 471–472.
6 *Evans Marshall and Co Ltd v Bertola SA*, op cit, at 361.
7 *The Forum Craftsman* [1985] 1 Lloyd's Rep 291. Quaere whether this is the law governing the agreement on jurisdiction or of the contract as a whole.
8 *The Sindh* [1975] 1 Lloyd's Rep 372, CA; cf *The Makefjell* [1976] 2 Lloyd's Rep 29; Knight (1977) 26 ICLQ 664. See also *The Sennar (No 2)* [1984] 2 Lloyd's Rep 142 at 148–149, CA; although this decision was affd by the House of Lords [1985] 1 WLR 490, it was thought unnecessary to express any view on this particular matter, per Lord BRANDON at 500.
9 *The Sennar (No 2)* [1985] 1 WLR 490, discussed infra, pp 375–376.
10 It is not clear on which party the burden of proof lies in respect of the validity of the exclusive jurisdiction clause.
11 [1982] AC 679, [1981] 3 All ER 520.
12 [1982] AC 679 at 695.
13 It is for the Swiss governing law to decide on the effect on the agreement as a whole of the assignment being void, ibid at 695, 696, 704.

law.[14] However, this is now subject to the new contract choice of law rules contained in the Rome Convention, according to which the validity of a contract is governed by the rules on the applicable law set out in the Convention.[15] When it comes to the question of the validity of just the exclusive jurisdiction clause it has been held that this is to be decided by applying the governing law, and the clause will be struck down if it is void according to this law.[16] In principle, this should be the law governing the agreement on jurisdiction,[17] not the contract as a whole.

An exclusive jurisdiction clause may also be void because of the terms of an English statute implementing an international convention. *The Hollandia*[18] provides an example of a situation in which the plaintiff was able to have an exclusive jurisdiction clause struck down for this reason:

> The plaintiff shippers brought an action in rem in England and claimed damages for breach of contract against the defendant carriers, despite the presence in the bill of lading of an exclusive jurisdiction clause providing for trial in the Netherlands. The defendant carriers sought a stay of the English proceedings, relying on this clause.

The House of Lords held that the exclusive jurisdiction clause was rendered null and void and of no effect by virtue of the Hague-Visby Rules, which are part of English law.[19] The Rules provide, inter alia, that any clause lessening the liability of the carrier otherwise than as provided for under the Rules shall be null and void.[20] The Dutch exclusive jurisdiction clause had the effect, albeit indirectly, of lessening the carrier's liability, since, if trial was held in Holland, the Dutch courts would apply Dutch law which set a lower maximum limit on the carrier's liability than that provided for under the Rules.[21] In the absence of an exclusive jurisdiction clause and of any other basis for the granting of a stay the shipper's action was allowed to proceed.[22]

In *The Hollandia* the continuance of the plaintiff's action depended ultimately on the wording of the Hague-Visby Rules. The same is true of the later case of *The Benarty*.[23] In that case the Court of Appeal held that an exclusive jurisdiction clause providing that actions should be brought in the Indonesian courts was not rendered void under the Hague-Visby Rules, since the case concerned a tonnage limitation (ie one calculated on the tonnage of

14 *Mackender v Feldia AG* [1967] 2 QB 590 at 598–599, 602–603, CA. See also *Chevron International Oil Co Ltd v A/S Sea Team, The TS Havprins* [1983] 2 Lloyd's Rep 356 on the question of whether a valid contract has been made for the purposes of RSC Ord 11. Cf Dicey and Morris, p 405; Hartley, in *Current Issues in European and International Law* (eds White and Smythe), p 156.
15 Art 8 (1), infra, pp 505–506.
16 *The Iran Vojdan* [1984] 2 Lloyd's Rep 380; *The Frank Pais* [1986] 1 Lloyd's Rep 529 at 530. The position is the same in relation to whether the clause has been incorporated into the contract; cf *Oceanic Sun-Line Special Shipping Co Inc v Fay* (1988) 165 CLR 197, HC of Australia.
17 To be determined under traditional common law rules; the Rome Convention excludes agreements on jurisdiction from its scope, infra, pp 471–472.
18 [1983] 1 AC 565, [1982] 3 All ER 1141; sub nom *The Morviken* [1983 1 Lloyd's Rep 1; Mann (1983) 99 LQR 376 at 400–406. *The Hollandia* is unaffected by the Rome Convention, see infra, p 521.
19 See the Carriage of Goods by Sea Act 1971.
20 See the Schedule to the Carriage of Goods by Sea Act 1971, Art III, para 8.
21 [1983] 1 AC 565 at 574–575.
22 Ibid, at 576–577.
23 [1984] 2 Lloyd's Rep 244; Reynolds [1984] Lloyd's MCLQ 545.

the ship carrying the goods), and not a package limitation[1] as in *The Hollandia* (ie one calculated on the number of packages or on their weight). In consequence, the principle that the parties should abide by their agreement was applied and a stay of the English[2] proceedings was granted.

(c) ARBITRATION AGREEMENTS[3]

(i) **Non-domestic arbitration agreements**

Section 1 of the Arbitration Act 1975 substantially gives effect to Article II of the New York Convention on the Recognition and Enforcement of Arbitral Awards (1958).[4] It applies to all written arbitration agreements[5] which are not "domestic arbitration agreements".[6] These latter are defined[7] as arbitration agreements which do not provide, expressly or by implication, for arbitration outside the United Kingdom. Furthermore, no party to the agreement must, at the time of commencement of the proceedings,[8] be either a national of or habitually resident in any country other than the United Kingdom, or a corporation incorporated in, or whose management and control is exercised in, any country other than the United Kingdom. This very narrow definition of domestic arbitration agreements means that agreements with no real foreign element fall within section 1 of the 1975 Act. Furthermore, it is not confined to awards whose enforcement is governed by the 1958 Convention and applies to arbitrations which are to take place either in England[9] or abroad[10] and whether the arbitration agreement is governed by English or foreign law.[11]

In the case of all agreements that are not domestic arbitration agreements, the court must order a stay of any court proceedings brought by one party to the arbitration agreement against another party thereto in respect of any matter which they have agreed to refer to arbitration.[12] The application for a stay may be made at any time after appearance, but must be before the delivery of pleadings or any other steps being taken in the court proceedings.[13]

1 Ibid, at 250–251, 253–254.
2 Ibid, at 251, 255.
3 Mustill and Boyd, *Commercial Arbitration* 2nd edn (1989), pp 462–483.
4 And replaces s 4(2) of the Arbitration Act 1950; see 1975 Act, s 8(2)(a).
5 1975 Act, s 7(1); *Excomm Ltd v Ahmed Abdul-Qawi Bamardah, The St Raphael* [1985] 1 Lloyd's Rep 403; *Zambia Steel v Clark and Eaton* [1986] 2 Lloyd's Rep 225.
6 1975 Act, s 1(2).
7 Ibid, s 1(4).
8 The commencement of proceedings may be before the arbitration agreement has been made, *The Tuyuti* [1984] QB 838 at 852–853.
9 Eg *The Rena K* [1979] QB 377.
10 Eg *Nova (Jersey) Knit Ltd v Kammgarn Spinnerei GmbH* [1977] 2 All ER 463, [1977] 1 WLR 713.
11 Ibid.
12 1975 Act, s 1(1); *Ellerine Bros (Pty) Ltd v Klinger* [1982] 2 All ER 737; *Hayter v Nelson and Home Insurance Co* [1990] 2 Lloyd's Rep 265. There need have been no actual submission to arbitration. See *Republic of Liberia v Gulf Oceanic Inc* [1985] 1 Lloyd's Rep 539. For the question of who is entitled to the benefit of the arbitration clause see *The Leage* [1984] 2 Lloyd's Rep 259. If the facts are within the contemplation of the statute the court cannot use its inherent jurisdiction to stay the proceedings: *Etri Fans Ltd v NMB (UK) Ltd* [1987] 1 WLR 1110.
13 1975 Act, s 1 (1); and see *The Maria Gorthon* [1976] 2 Lloyd's Rep 720 at 725, 727–728. Leave for service out of the jurisdiction under Ord 11 RSC will not be granted if the proceedings would be stayed under s 1(1) of the 1975 Act, see *Qatar Petroleum Producing Authority v Shell Internationale Petroleum Maatschappij NV* [1983] 2 Lloyd's Rep 35 at 42.

The staying of the proceedings is mandatory[14] unless the court is satisfied that the arbitration agreement is null and void,[15] inoperative,[16] or incapable of being performed, or that there is not in fact any dispute between the parties with regard to the matter agreed to be referred to arbitration.[17] The burden of proof is on the party alleging this.[18] No choice of law is provided for these issues.

The question whether an arbitration agreement is null and void is a matter for the law governing the arbitration agreement.[19] The same law governs the question whether a contract contains an arbitration clause.[20] The determination of the scope of an arbitration clause and whether it covers the matter in dispute between the parties is likewise an issue for the law governing the arbitration agreement.[21] The question whether the arbitration agreement is incapable of being performed relates not to whether one of the parties can satisfy any award that may be made but rather to whether the agreement can be performed up to the stage of an award being made.[1]

(ii) Domestic arbitration agreements

The power to stay proceedings in the case of a domestic arbitration agreement[2] is still governed by section 4(1) of the Arbitration Act 1950.[3] The court has a discretion to stay English proceedings brought in breach of a written[4] agreement, whether or not the agreement is subject to English law[5] or the arbitration is to take place in England or abroad. The application for a stay

14 And must be unconditional: *The Rena K* [1979] QB 377 at 400, supra, p 216; *The Vasso formerly Andria* [1984] 1 Lloyd's Rep 235 at 242. However, security available in an action in rem can be retained: *The Tuyuti* [1984] QB 838.

15 On the position where the Hague-Visby Rules apply see *The Hollandia* [1983] 1 AC 565 at 575–576, HL, supra, pp 238–239.

16 See *The Merak* [1965] P 223 at 239, decided under s 4(2) of the Arbitration Act 1950; *Astro Valiente Compania Naviera SA v Pakistan Ministry of Food and Agriculture (No 2)* [1982] 1 All ER 823, [1982] 1 WLR 1096.

17 1975 Act, s 1(1). See *First Steamship Co Ltd v CTS Commodity Transport Shipping Schiffahrtsgesellschaft mbh, The Ever Splendor* [1988] 1 Lloyd's Rep 245. If part of a claim can be identified as indisputably due, as where summary judgment for it might be given under RSC Ord 14, then there is no dispute with regard to that part and a stay will be refused; but this is not possible if there is no separate quantified sum: *Associated Bulk Carriers Ltd v Koch Shipping Inc* [1978] 2 All ER 254. See also *Sethia (SL) Liners v State Trading Corpn of India Ltd* [1986] 1 Lloyd's Rep 31; *Comdel v Siponex* [1987] 1 Lloyd's Rep 325.

18 *Overseas Union Insurance Ltd v AA Mutual International Insurance Co Ltd* [1988] 2 Lloyd's Rep 63 at 70.

19 See *Astro Venturoso Compania Naviera v Hellenic Shipyards SA, The Mariannina* [1983] 1 Lloyd's Rep 12. This will be determined according to traditional common law rules; the Rome Convention excludes arbitration agreements from its scope, infra, pp 471–472.

20 *Marc Rich & Co AG v Societa Italiana Impianti PA, The Atlantic Emperor* [1989] 1 Lloyd's Rep 548; the case was referred to the European Court of Justice on a different point, see infra, p 289. See also *O T M Ltd v Hydronautics* [1981] 2 Lloyd's Rep 211. Cf *The Rena K* [1979] QB 377. Where a foreign court gives a judgment on the question of incorporation this may create an estoppel, see *Tracomin SA v Sudan Oil Seeds Co Ltd (Nos 1 and 2)* [1983] 1 WLR 1026, discussed infra, p 391.

21 *Nova (Jersey) Knit Ltd v Kammgarn Spinnerei GmbH* [1977] 1 WLR 713 at 718–719, 730.

1 *The Rena K* [1979] 1 QB 377 at 393.

2 Defined by the 1975 Act, s 1(4), supra, p 239.

3 If a non-domestic arbitration agreement fails to satisfy the requirements for a mandatory stay under s 1(1) of the 1975 Act, there is no power to grant a discretionary stay under the 1950 Act; see 1975 Act, s 1(2).

4 Arbitration Act 1950, s 32.

5 It may be subject to the *lex mercatoria*: *Home and Overseas Insurance Co (UK) Ltd (in liq)* [1989] 3 All ER 74, [1990] 1 WLR 153.

may be made at any time after appearance, but must be before the delivery of pleadings or any other steps being taken in the proceedings.[6] The matter has to be one that has been agreed to be referred to arbitration, and the validity and scope of the arbitration agreement are determined by its governing law.[7] The discretion conferred by section 4(1) is exercised not just on a balance of convenience,[8] but rather[9] on the same principles as those on which a court decides whether to uphold an agreement to submit disputes to the courts of a foreign jurisdiction.[10]

2. RESTRAINING FOREIGN PROCEEDINGS

An English court cannot prohibit a foreign court from trying an action. However, it does have a discretionary power, in certain circumstances, to grant an injunction restraining a party from commencing or continuing as plaintiff with foreign proceedings.[11] The injunction operates in personam[12] and if it is disobeyed the person against whom it is directed can be punished for contempt of court. Unlike the situation in which a court grants a stay of English proceedings, a court when restraining foreign proceedings is not regulating its own jurisdiction. The consequences of this are twofold. First, a court must have jurisdiction to grant an injunction restraining the plaintiff from continuing with the foreign proceedings.[13] There is no difficulty in a case where the person against whom the injunction is directed is an English resident. The position is more complicated in a case where he is a foreign resident. There is jurisdiction to grant the injunction if the person against whom it is directed is a party to proceedings in England,[14] or if he has sufficient connection with England to justify this,[15] eg where he has brought an action abroad in breach of an agreement providing for arbitration in England.[16] Furthermore, if a writ has been served out of the jurisdiction on the defendant under Order 11 of the Rules of the Supreme Court, the courts will thereby have power to grant an injunction, restraining foreign proceedings.[17] If there is jurisdiction to grant the injunction the courts will

---

6 Ibid, s 4(1); see *Turner & Goudy v McConnell* [1985] 2 All ER 34, [1985] 1 WLR 898.
7 *The Elizabeth H* [1962] 1 Lloyd's Rep 172.
8 *Brazendale & Co Ltd v Saint Freres SA* [1970] 2 Lloyd's Rep 34.
9 *Bulk Oil (Zug) AG v Trans Asiatic Oil Ltd SA* [1973] 1 Lloyd's Rep 129.
10 *The Eleftheria* [1970] P 94 at 100, supra, pp 235–236.
11 See generally Hartley (1987) 35 Am J Comp Law 487. This power to restrain foreign proceedings is also referred to as enjoining foreign proceedings. For the powers of the High Court in respect of injunctions see the Supreme Court Act 1981, s 37.
12 *Ellerman Lines Ltd v Read* [1928] 2 KB 144, CA; *Settlement Corpn v Hochschild* [1966] Ch 10 at 15.
13 *Castanho v Brown and Root (UK) Ltd* [1981] AC 557, [1981] 1 All ER 143, HL; *Midland Bank plc v Laker Airways Ltd* [1986] QB 689; *Bank of Tokyo Ltd v Karoon* [1987] AC 45 at 59, CA; *Société Nationale Industrielle Aerospatiale v Lee Kui Jak* [1987] AC 871 at 892; Thomas [1983] Lloyd's MCLQ 692.
14 *Royal Exchange Assurance Co Ltd v Compania Naviera Santi SA, The Tropaioforos* [1962] 1 Lloyd's Rep 410; *Castanho v Brown and Root (UK) Ltd,* op cit.
15 Ibid.
16 *Tracomin SA v Sudan Oil Seeds Co Ltd (Nos 1 and 2)* [1983] 1 WLR 1026, an agreement to arbitrate in England can alternatively be regarded as a submission to jurisdiction for these purposes.
17 *Royal Exchange Assurance v Compania Naviera Santi SA, The Tropaioforos,* op cit.

not consider the possibility that a foreign defendant will not obey this order.[18] Second, although the writ is directed at a person there is, nonetheless, an implicit interference with the jurisdiction of a foreign court whenever an English court grants an injunction restraining foreign proceedings. There are obvious comity problems inherent in the exercise of the power to restrain foreign proceedings; for this reason it has often been said that the power must be exercised with caution.[19]

It is possible to identify three categories where the discretion has been exercised in favour of granting the injunction:[20]

(a) Where there are two or more available forums for trial (one of which is England).
(b) Where one party, by bringing, or threatening to bring, proceedings abroad, has invaded, or threatens to invade, a legal or equitable right of the other party not to be sued abroad.
(c) Where the bringing of the proceedings abroad would be unconscionable.

Before turning to look at each of these categories, it must be asked whether this is an exhaustive list; in other words, can the courts grant an injunction even though the instant case does not fall into any of these categories? In *Castanho v Brown and Root (UK) Ltd*[21] Lord SCARMAN, with whom the other Law Lords concurred, was firmly of the opinion that "the width and flexibility of equity are not to be undermined by categorisation".[1] On this view, an injunction is available whenever justice so demands.[2] This approach was affirmed by the House of Lords in *British Airways Board v Laker Airways Ltd*.[3] However, more recently, a differently constituted House of Lords in *South Carolina Insurance Co v Assurantie NV*[4] held, by a majority of three to two, that the effect of earlier decisions was that the power of the High Court to grant injunctions is limited to the three categories listed above.[5] The facts of the case were as follows:

The plaintiffs, an American insurance company, brought an action in England against the defendants, a Dutch company and two Middle or Far Eastern companies, under a contract of reinsurance. The defendants commenced proceedings in the United States for pre-trial discovery of documents relevant to the claim against persons resident there who were not parties to the English action. The plaintiffs sought an injunction restraining the defendants from taking any further steps in the American

18 *Castanho v Brown and Root (UK) Ltd*, op cit.
19 See, eg, *Castanho v Brown and Root (UK) Ltd*, op cit; *British Airways Board v Laker Airways Ltd* [1985] AC 58 at 95 (per Lord SCARMAN), [1984] 3 All ER 39, HL; *South Carolina Insurance Co v Assurantie NV* [1987] AC 24 at 40, HL (per Lord BRANDON); *Société Nationale Industrielle Aerospatiale v Lee Kui Jak*, op cit at 892.
20 See *South Carolina Insurance Co v Assurantie NV* [1987] AC 24 at 39–41, HL; Carter (1986) 57 BYBIL 434; note, (1987) 103 LQR 157; Forsyth [1988] CLJ 177.
21 [1981] AC 557, [1981] 1 All ER 143, HL.
 1 Ibid, at 573.
 2 Ibid; *Bank of Tokyo Ltd v Karoon* [1987] AC 45 at 59, CA; *Société Nationale Industrielle Aerospatiale v Lee Kui Jak*, op cit at 892.
 3 [1985] AC 58 at 81.
 4 [1987] AC 24.
 5 Ibid at 39–41 (per Lord BRANDON—Lords BRIDGE and BRIGHTMAN concurring); followed in *Amchem Products Inc v British Columbia (Workers' Compensation Board)* (1991) 75 DLR (4 th) 1 at 23–24.

proceedings. This was granted by the judge at first instance, and, on appeal, the Court of Appeal dismissed the appeal on the basis that once the parties had accepted trial in England they must abide by the procedure of that country and the court must be master of its own procedure.

The House of Lords unanimously held that the injunction must be discharged. However, the same reasoning was not adopted by all the Law Lords. Lord BRANDON, who gave the speech for which there was majority support, held that the facts of the case did not come within any of the three categories listed above, which were the only categories in respect of which a power to grant an injunction existed. In contrast to this, Lord GOFF (Lord MACKAY concurring) held that the power to grant injunctions is not restricted, and should not be restricted, to certain limited categories. Nonetheless, the grant of an injunction was not necessary to protect the English jurisdiction on the facts of the case. Lord GOFF repeated this view when delivering the unanimous judgment of the Privy Council in the subsequent case of *Société Nationale Industrielle Aerospatiale v Lee Kui Jak*.[6]

It is to be regretted that the House of Lords should depart from two of its own recent decisions in this way, particularly when it merely purports to be stating the effect of these earlier decisions. It is submitted that Lord GOFF's view is to be preferred and that the power to grant an injunction should not be restricted to the three well established existing categories. New categories should be capable of introduction where justice so demands. We now turn to examine the established categories.

(a) THERE ARE TWO OR MORE AVAILABLE FORUMS FOR TRIAL (ONE OF WHICH IS ENGLAND)[7]

In this situation the courts are deciding whether trial should take place in England or abroad, for the effect of granting an injunction restraining foreign proceedings is to force the plaintiff to sue in England. For many years the courts exercised the power to restrain foreign proceedings on the basis of vexation or oppression.[8] The widening of the principles to be applied in respect of the stay of English proceedings in *The Atlantic Star*[9] and *Mac-Shannon v Rockware Glass Ltd*[10] soon filtered through to cases on restraining foreign proceedings. In *Castanho v Brown and Root (UK) Ltd*[11] Lord SCARMAN, giving the judgment of the House of Lords, said that

The principle is the same whether the remedy sought is a stay of English proceedings or a restraint on foreign proceedings.[12]

He went on to transpose the conditions for the grant of a stay of English proceedings as stated in *MacShannon v Rockware Glass Ltd*[13] into the present context. This meant that the court was concerned with (a) the appropriate forum for trial, and (b) the question of the advantage to the plaintiff in trial

6 [1987] AC 871 at 892.
7 This situation has been described as an exception to the normal principles in respect of which an injunction is granted, see *South Carolina Co v Assurantie NV*, op cit, at 40.
8 See *Cohen v Rothfield* [1919] 1 KB 410.
9 [1974] AC 436, discussed supra, pp 221–222.
10 [1978] AC 795, discussed supra, pp 221–222.
11 [1981] AC 557, [1981] 1 All ER 143.
12 At 574.
13 [1978] AC 795 at 812.

abroad.[14] The same approach was accepted in obiter dicta in the *South Carolina Case*.[15]

However, as has already been seen,[16] the issues raised in this context are different from those raised when a court is asked to stay English proceedings, and, accordingly, there was from the outset a strong argument for using different principles when exercising the discretion in these two different contexts.[17] The argument became even stronger once the principles to be applied in respect of a stay of English proceedings were restated by the House of Lords in *Spiliada Maritime Corporation v Cansulex Ltd*,[18] in particular now that the advantage to the plaintiff is to be given less weight. Lord GOFF in the *Spiliada Case*[1] was careful to state the principles on *forum non conveniens* without reference to injunctions restraining foreign proceedings. Nonetheless, the danger, after *Spiliada*, was that, in practice, injunctions restraining foreign proceedings would simply be granted on the basis that England was the natural forum for trial. This was recognised by the Privy Council in *Société Nationale Industrielle Aerospatiale v Lee Kui Jak*,[2] which held that it was no longer right, in the light of the *Spiliada Case*, to apply the same criteria to restraining foreign proceedings as those applied when granting a stay of English proceedings. To do so would be against comity and would disregard the fundamental requirement that an injunction will only be granted where the ends of justice so require. The basic approach adopted in *Castanho* was therefore wrong. When it comes to the criteria to be applied for determining whether to grant an injunction, Lord GOFF resurrected the old language of vexation and oppression:

> in a case such as the present where a remedy for a particular wrong is available both in the English ... court and in a foreign court, the English ... court will, generally speaking, only restrain the plaintiff from pursuing proceedings in the foreign court if such pursuit would be vexatious or oppressive.[3]

This old terminology was then combined with the modern terminology of the natural forum. According to Lord GOFF the vexation or oppression test that is now being adopted generally presupposes that the English court has first concluded that it provides the natural forum for trial.[4] But vexation or oppression requires more than this (and hence is a more stringent test than that used in the *Castanho Case*). It has to be shown that there would be injustice to the defendant if the plaintiff is allowed to pursue the foreign proceedings. Since the court is ultimately concerned with the ends of justice, account must also be taken of the plaintiff's position; "the court will not grant an injunction if, by doing so, it will deprive the plaintiff of advantages in the foreign forum of which it would be unjust to deprive him".[5]

14 [1981] AC 557 at 575.
15 [1987] AC 24 at 40.
16 Supra, pp 241–242.
17 Briggs (1982) 31 ICLQ 189; Barma and Elvin (1985) 101 LQR 48 at 63–65; Schuz (1986) 35 ICLQ 374 at 409. See also the US position, *Laker Airways Ltd v Sabena Belgian World Airlines* (1984) 731 F 2d 909; *Bank of Tokyo Ltd v Karoon*, op cit at 63.
18 [1987] AC 460, supra, pp 221 et seq.
1 Op cit, at 480. See also *Société Nationale Industrielle Aerospatiale v Lee Kui Jak* [1987] AC 871 at 896.
2 [1987] AC 871; Kunzlik [1987] CLJ 406; Briggs [1987] Lloyd's MCLQ 391; Carter (1988) 59 BYBIL 342.
3 At 896.
4 See *Kornberg v Kornberg* (1991) 76 DLR (4th) 379.
5 The *Société Aerospatiale Case*, op cit, at 896.

The application of these principles to particular facts can be seen by looking at the *Société Aerospatiale Case*:

The plaintiffs were the widow and administrators of the estate of a business-man, resident in Brunei, who was killed when the helicopter on which he was a passenger crashed in Brunei. The helicopter was manufactured by the defendant S, a French company, and operated by the defendant BM, a Malaysian company. The plaintiffs instituted proceedings against S and BM both in Brunei and Texas (where S carried on business). S sought an injunction in Brunei restraining the plaintiffs from continuing with the Texas action. This was refused by the Court of Appeal of Brunei.

On appeal to the Privy Council it was held that an injunction should be granted. The natural forum for trial of the plaintiffs' action against S was held to be Brunei. This was on the basis of the strong connections with Brunei, including the fact that the accident happened there, Brunei law was applicable, the deceased was resident there and carried on his principal business there. However, this in itself was not enough to justify the grant of an injunction restraining the foreign proceedings.[6] Generally speaking, what has to be shown is vexation or oppression. Trial in Texas would involve serious injustice to S amounting to oppression in that the company might be unable to claim a contribution from BM in the Texas proceedings. Instead, S might have to bring a separate action in Brunei against BM with attendant difficulties. At the same time, there was no injustice in depriving the plaintiffs of trial in Texas. Any advantages that the plaintiffs obtained from trial in Texas (such as superior means of gathering evidence to mount a case against S, availability of expert counsel, the contingency fee system, prospects of an early trial) were effectively neutralised by undertakings given by S that, for example, evidence already obtained in the Texas proceedings would be available in Brunei proceedings.

A number of problems arise out of this decision. The first is that we now have a clash between the decisions of the House of Lords in the *Castanho* and *South Carolina Cases* and that of the Privy Council in the *Société Aerospatiale Case*. The Privy Council seemingly regarded the *Castanho Case* as not only wrong in policy terms but also as no longer authoritative, being based on an outmoded view of the law on the discretion to stay English proceedings.[7] No doubt the obiter dicta in the *South Carolina Case* supporting *Castanho* would be regarded in the same way. Significantly, the Court of Appeal in subsequent cases[8] has accepted that the law in this area is as laid down by the Privy Council and has applied the approach and principles set out in the *Société Aerospatiale Case*.

Secondly, what is meant by vexation or oppression? Despite what was said in the Privy Council,[9] older cases can be of little value in ascertaining this. The problem faced by the courts nowadays is that of plaintiffs forum shopping in countries, such as the United States, where a very wide jurisdiction is taken, a very different sort of problem from that faced by courts in the 19th

---

6 Cf *Amchem Products Inc v British Columbia (Workers' Compensation Board)* (1991) 75 DLR (4th) 1 which purports to follow the *Société Aerospatiale Case*.
7 At 895–896.
8 *EI du Pont de Nemours & Co and Endo Laboratories Inc v Agnew (No 2)* [1988] 2 Lloyd's Rep 240; *Hemain v Hemain* [1988] 2 FLR 388. See also *National Mutual Holdings Pty Ltd v Sentry Corp* (1989) 87 ALR 539.
9 At 896.

century.[10] The use of language from the 19th century only serves to obscure the basic considerations that should be taken into account in this area: the interests of the parties; the connections with the alternative fora; the dictates of comity and the need for caution before restraining foreign proceedings.[11] A modern example of oppression is provided by a British Columbia court,[12] which held that the defendants' conduct in obtaining a counter injunction in Texas (designed to prevent the plaintiffs from obtaining an injunction in British Columbia restraining the Texas proceedings) was oppressive. In *Sohio Supply Co v Gatoil (USA) Inc*[13] it was said that continuance of foreign proceedings brought in breach of a contractual clause providing for the exclusive jurisdiction of the English courts may well in itself be vexatious and oppressive. In refusing to interfere with the grant of an injunction at first instance, the Court of Appeal was also influenced by the undesirability of having concurrent proceedings in two different jurisdictions involving the same subject matter, and the need to discourage parties from seeking negative declarations when they were apprehensive that proceedings would be commenced against them in England. On the other hand, there is no oppression in suing a defendant abroad in a state with which the proceedings have very real connections, such as part of the property in dispute being situated there and the defendant being permanently resident there.[14]

Thirdly, what is meant in the present context by an advantage to the plaintiff? It is doubtful whether this would encompass the higher damages, for example punitive damages, available in the United States. Indeed, it seems to be suggested[15] that the fact that the plaintiffs sought this advantage in Texas might have had some relevance as evidence of oppression if this point had not been neutralised by undertakings given by the plaintiffs. This contrasts with the treatment of the advantage to the plaintiff in the *Castanho Case*[16] where the plaintiff had the prospect of receiving much higher damages in Texas, and this was considered to be a legitimate advantage. However, since then the House of Lords in the *Spiliada Case* has, of course, greatly reduced the significance to be attached to this type of advantage.

Fourthly, *Société Aerospatiale* was a case where the plaintiffs had started proceedings in two different fora. Nonetheless, the principles set out by the Privy Council are seemingly equally applicable in cases where the roles of the parties are reversed, ie the plaintiff in the foreign proceedings is the defendant in the English proceedings and vice versa.[17] Thus, in *E I Du Pont & Co v I C Agnew*,[18] the Court of Appeal refused to grant an injunction

10 At 894.
11 See *Metall und Rohstoff AG v ACLI Metals (London) Ltd* [1984] 1 Lloyd's Rep 598, where considerable weight was attached to the need for caution.
12 *Amchem Products Inc v British Columbia (Workers' Compensation Board)* (1990) 65 DLR (4th) 567; affd (1991) 75 DLR (4th) 1. The British Columbia Court of Appeal would, however, have allowed the injunction on the much wider basis of the tenuous connection with Texas and the absence there of a power to stay the proceedings.
13 [1989] 1 Lloyd's Rep 588.
14 *Kornberg v Kornberg* (1991) 76 DLR (4th) 379. See also *Pan American World Airways v Andrews* (1991) Times, 29 October.
15 [1987] 1 AC 871 at 899.
16 [1981] AC 557 at 575–576; see also *Thyssen-Bornemisza v Thyssen-Bornemisza* [1986] Fam 1 at 9; *Bank of Tokyo Ltd v Karoon* [1987] AC 45 at 55, CA; *Smith Kline and French Laboratories Ltd v Bloch* [1983] 1 WLR 730 at 736–737.
17 Cf the position in relation to stays of English proceedings in cases involving a multiplicity of proceedings.
18 [1988] 2 Lloyd's Rep 240.

restraining insurers from continuing an action against the insured in Illinois when all that could be shown was that England was the natural forum for trial of the action brought by the insured against the insurers; the Illinois court considered that it was the appropriate forum for trial, and to grant an injunction in such circumstances would mean that the English court was taking upon itself the power to resolve the dispute between the Illinois and English courts as to which was the natural forum. In *Hemain v Hemain*[19] the application of the principles in the *Société Aerospatiale Case* led to the grant of an injunction. The husband sought a stay of the wife's English divorce proceedings, but was not prepared in the meantime to halt the proceedings he had instituted in France. His application for a stay was held to be vexatious, oppressive and an abuse of the process of the court, and an injunction was granted restraining his prosecution of the French divorce proceedings pending the hearing of the application for a stay of the English proceedings. There was a suggestion in this case[20] that the courts should be even more cautious about granting an injunction in reversed role cases than in cases where a plaintiff has instituted proceedings in two different jurisdictions, on the ground that in the former case the plaintiff in the foreign proceedings has been compelled to appear in the English proceedings. However, this was balanced by the fact that the injunction sought was only one for a limited period and purpose, and the court should be more willing to grant such an injunction.

Moreover, it is probably the case that an English court can grant an injunction enjoining foreign proceedings, even if proceedings in respect of the main cause of action have not yet been commenced here. The only concern is that England is available as a forum. In the situation where this is not the case, it is necessary to turn to the following two categories which may apply even though the foreign country is the only available forum for trial.

(b) THE BRINGING OF PROCEEDINGS ABROAD IS AN INVASION OF A LEGAL OR EQUITABLE RIGHT NOT TO BE SUED THERE[21]

A right not to be sued abroad may be contractual in origin.[22] Where there is an agreement valid under its governing law to arbitrate in England and foreign proceedings are pending, the court has an inherent power to restrain the parties from bringing or continuing the foreign proceedings, for that would constitute a breach of contract.[23] However, the court's discretion is exercised on the balance of convenience in the particular case,[24] and the jurisdiction to restrain foreign proceedings in this category, as in cases in the

---

19 [1988] 2 FLR 388. See infra, p 639, for the significance of the case in relation to matrimonial causes.
20 At 390, quoting from *Cohen v Rothfield* [1919] 1 KB 410 at 414. The latter case was cited with approval in the *Société Aerospatiale Case* at 892.
21 See *South Carolina Co v Assurantie NV* [1987] AC 24 at 40, HL. The facts of the case did not come within this category, see pp 40–41. See also *Beecham (Australia) Pty Ltd v Roque Pty Ltd* (1987) 11 NSWLR 1.
22 *British Airways Board v Laker Airways Ltd* [1985] AC 58 at 81.
23 *Pena Copper Mines Ltd v Rio Tinto Co Ltd* (1911) 105 LT 846; *Tracomin SA v Sudan Oil Seeds Co Ltd (Nos 1 and 2)* [1983] 1 WLR 1026; *Canadian Home Assurance Co v Cooper* (1986) 29 DLR (4th) 419; Mustill and Boyd, *Commercial Arbitration* 2nd edn (1989) p 460.
24 *The Maria Gorthon* [1976] 2 Lloyd's Rep 720; *Marazura Navegacion SA v Oceanus Mutual Underwriting Association (Bermuda) Ltd* [1977] 1 Lloyd's Rep 283.

other categories, is to be used sparingly.[25] It is important to consider whether the failure to restrain the foreign proceedings will result in inconsistent judgments in England and abroad, and the effect that a foreign judgment may have on the arbitration in England.[1] In lieu of the injunction, the court may award damages against the party bringing the proceedings abroad for acting in breach of the clause.[2] The position is the same where proceedings are brought abroad in breach of an exclusive jurisdiction clause providing for trial before the English courts.[3]

(c) THE BRINGING OF THE PROCEEDINGS ABROAD WOULD BE UNCONSCIONABLE

In *British Airways Board v Laker Airways Ltd*[4] the House of Lords stressed that relief by way of an injunction restraining foreign proceedings is not confined to cases coming within the preceding two categories.

> The power of the English court to grant the injunction exists, if the bringing of the suit in the foreign court is in the circumstances so unconscionable that in accordance with our principles of a "wide and flexible" equity it can be seen to be an infringement of an equitable right of the applicant.[5]

There is a judicial reluctance to define what is meant by "unconscionable" conduct.[6] However, the House of Lords in *South Carolina Insurance Co v Assurantie NV*[7] did hold that it included "conduct which is oppressive or vexatious or which interferes with the due process of the court". Guidance on the meaning of unconscionable conduct can also be found in *British Airways Board v Laker Airways Ltd*[8] where Lord DIPLOCK said that unconscionable conduct encompasses the bringing of an action against a person who has a right not to be sued because a defence, such as estoppel in pais, promissory estoppel, election, waiver, standing by and laches, is available to him under English law.[9]

It may not be easy to satisfy the court that there has been unconscionable conduct. In the *South Carolina Case* a party to an English action sought to obtain in the United States discovery of documents from a third party. United States pre-trial procedure allows this evidence to be obtained, whereas English procedure does not. The House of Lords held that there was no unconscionable conduct. There was no interference with the due process of the English courts. The English courts still controlled their own procedure, since

25 *Tracomin SA v Sudan Oil Seeds Co Ltd (Nos 1 and 2)* [1983] 1 WLR 1026 at 1035. See also *Mike Trading and Transport Ltd v R Pagnan and Fratelli (The Lisboa)* [1980] 2 Lloyd's Rep 546 at 549, 551.

 1 *Tracomin SA v Sudan Oil Seeds Co Ltd (Nos 1 and 2)*, op cit at 1036; distinguished in *World Pride Shipping Ltd v Daiichi Chuo Kisen Kaisha (The Golden Anne)* [1984] 2 Lloyd's Rep 489.

 2 *Mantovani v Carapelli SpA* [1980] 1 Lloyd's Rep 375 at 383, CA; *Mike Trading and Transport Ltd v R Pagnan and Fratelli (The Lisboa)* [1980] 2 Lloyd's Rep 546 at 549, CA; Mustill and Boyd, *Commercial Arbitration* 2nd edn (1989) p 461.

 3 *Mike Trading and Transport Ltd v R Pagnan and Fratelli (The Lisboa)* [1980] 2 Lloyd's Rep 546, CA; *British Airways Board v Laker Airways Ltd* [1985] AC 58 at 81. See also *Ellerman Lines Ltd v Read* [1928] 2 KB 144.

 4 [1985] AC 58, [1984] 3 All ER 39, HL; Collier [1984] CLJ 253; Carter (1984) 44 BYBIL 358.

 5 Ibid, at 95 (per Lord SCARMAN); see also p 81 (per Lord DIPLOCK); *Midland Bank plc v Laker Airways Ltd* [1986] QB 689 at 701, 711–712.

 6 See *South Carolina Insurance Co v Assurantie NV* [1987] AC 24 at 41, HL.

 7 Ibid.

 8 [1985] AC 58.

 9 Ibid, at 81.

it is up to the parties to obtain, either in England or abroad, the relevant evidence.[10] Moreover, mere extra cost and inconvenience to the parties cannot be characterised as interference with the court's control of its own process.[11]

Similarly, in *British Airways Board v Laker Airways Ltd* the House of Lords unanimously allowed an appeal against the grant of an injunction restraining an action in the United States by Laker Airways Ltd (Laker), a Jersey company with its principal office in London, against British Airways and another British airline. The action was for multiple damages for breach of United States anti-trust laws by conspiring to eliminate Laker as a competitor by fixing "predatory" air fare tariffs. There was no cause of action under English law, and the only country in which Laker could obtain a remedy was the United States. For this reason the case was distinguishable from cases where a choice is being made between alternative fora; those cases were of no assistance here.[12] Caution was said to be very necessary in these single forum cases.[13] It was not unconscionable to allow the proceedings in the United States to continue, seemingly, because no complaint could be made about Laker's conduct. It had been argued that, since Laker was admitted to the scheduled airlines' club and submitted to the regulations required by the club, it could not complain about the conduct of fellow members of the club that was permitted by the club's rules in relation to fares. This argument was rejected on the basis that Laker's action was founded not on the actual fares charged but on the fact that the other airlines were allegedly in breach of United States law.[14] It is to be noted that in exercising their discretion their Lordships did not give weight to the fact that it would be impossible to enforce in England an American judgment for multiple damages in an anti-trust case.[15]

On the other hand, in *Midland Bank plc v Laker Airways Ltd*[16] the Court of Appeal held it to be unconscionable conduct for Laker to bring an anti-trust suit in the United States against the Midland Bank and an injunction was allowed restraining those threatened proceedings. The alleged liability of the Bank arose out of banking acts done in England and intended to be governed by English law; the Bank had never submitted to United States anti-trust law or United States jurisdiction; and there was no claim against it in England.[17] It was also relevant that the evidence of conspiracy under United States law was weak, although the court was reluctant to examine the question of the weight of the evidence too closely. However, in rare cases where it is clear that the action abroad is bound to fail, this will make the plaintiff's foreign action frivolous and vexatious and therefore unconscionable.[18] On the other hand, the fact that a party will be exposed to pretrial discovery in the United States proceedings is not a source *per se* of injustice.[19]

In principle, there is even more need for caution in restraining foreign

10 Op cit, at 41–44.
11 At 42–43.
12 [1985] AC 58, at 80, 85.
13 Ibid, at 95.
14 Ibid, at 84–85.
15 See the Protection of Trading Interests Act 1980, s 5, discussed infra, pp 382–384. See also the judgment of PARKER J at first instance [1984] 1 QB 142 at 162–163.
16 [1986] QB 689, CA.
17 Ibid, at 699–700, 704–705, 712–713.
18 Ibid, at 700, 702, 710, 712–713. See also *British Airways Board v Laker Airways Ltd* [1985] AC 58 at 86.
19 Ibid, at 714.

proceedings in cases where the plaintiff has only a single forum in which he can sue than there is in cases when there are alternative fora for trial, since the effect of granting the stay is to decide the substantive issue against the plaintiff. It is questionable whether this need for extra caution was either fully appreciated or met under the criteria for exercise of the discretion laid down in the two *Laker Cases.*

The need for caution is even stronger if a judgment has actually been obtained in the forum abroad and a worldwide injunction is sought to restrain a party from relying on this judgment. Even if that party is acting unconscionably the court may exercise its discretion and refuse to grant the injunction.[20]

3. STAYS OF ENGLISH PROCEEDINGS AND RESTRAINING FOREIGN PROCEEDINGS IN CASES WHERE THE BRUSSELS CONVENTION OR LUGANO CONVENTION APPLIES

The discussion in this chapter has been conducted so far on the assumption that jurisdiction has been taken under the traditional rules.[21] It must, however, be asked whether the courts can exercise their powers to stay English proceedings or restrain foreign proceedings in cases coming within the Brussels Convention or Lugano Convention.[1]

Section 49 of the Civil Jurisdiction and Judgments Act 1982, in effect, provides that an English court cannot stay any proceedings before it "on the ground of *forum non conveniens* or otherwise" where this is inconsistent with the Brussels Convention or Lugano Convention.[2] The wording of section 49 is wide enough to cover the granting of stays not only on the basis of *forum non conveniens* but also on the basis that there is a foreign choice of jurisdiction clause or an agreement on arbitration. If either Convention applies, the question of whether the grant of a stay on any of these bases is inconsistent with the Convention is one of considerable complexity and is examined later[3] when the rules under each Convention are looked at in detail. It suffices to say at this point, that the position appears to be the same in relation to both Conventions. In broad terms the grant of a stay will be inconsistent with the Brussels or Lugano Convention whenever the Convention in question applies, ie where the matter is within the scope of the Convention (a civil and commercial matter) and the defendant is domiciled in a Contracting State, unless, seemingly, the alternative forum is a non-Contracting State to the Brussels or Lugano Convention. The grant of a stay may also be inconsistent with the Brussels or Lugano Convention even where the defendant is not domiciled in a Contracting State to that Convention if the *lis pendens* rule contained in each Convention[4] applies. This rule only applies in the situation where proceedings are brought in two Contracting States to the Convention in question. There is an additional complication in cases involving the trial of a dispute in respect of which there has been an

---

20 *E D & F Man (Sugar) Ltd v Yani Haryanto (No 2)* [1991] 1 Lloyd's Rep 161 at 167–168.
21 Supra, pp 182–219.
  1 For when the Brussels and Lugano Conventions apply see infra, pp 286–292, 341.
  2 See *The Sennar (No 2)* [1984] 2 Lloyd's Rep 142 at 154, CA.
  3 Infra, pp 331–334. For when a stay of proceedings in England is inconsistent with the Modified Convention see infra, pp 339–340.
  4 Art 21 of both Conventions, discussed infra, pp 326–329.

agreement to go to arbitration, since it is not clear whether such cases are within the scope of the Brussels or Lugano Conventions in the first place.[5]

Section 49 only deals with a court staying its own proceedings; it does not explain what the position is in respect of restraining foreign proceedings in cases coming within the Brussels Convention or Lugano Convention. In many cases where trial takes place in another Contracting State to either of the Conventions[6] the English courts will lack jurisdiction to grant an injunction to restrain those proceedings under the criteria set out above.[7] In general, under both Conventions trial will take place in the Contracting State in which the defendant is domiciled; if this is in a Contracting State other than the United Kingdom, it is very unlikely that the defendant will also be resident in England. However, in cases where jurisdiction is given to another Contracting State on the basis, for example, of an injury sustained there, the English court may have jurisdiction to grant an injunction, since the defendant may be resident in England. It is submitted that the discretion should be exercised against the grant of an injunction restraining proceedings in another Contracting State where that State has jurisdiction under either of the Conventions. To grant an injunction restraining the foreign proceedings in such circumstances raises problems going beyond the normal ones of comity.[8] As will be seen,[9] both Conventions allocate jurisdiction to the courts of a particular Contracting State, and it would be contrary to the spirit of each Convention for a court in another Contracting State to that Convention to interfere, albeit indirectly, with this.[10]

5 Infra, p 289. If such cases are within the Brussels Convention or the Lugano Convention, this would pose the problem for English lawyers that s 49 directs the court not to stay proceedings when this is inconsistent with the Brussels Convention or the Lugano Convention, whereas s 1 the Arbitration Act 1975 directs the court to stay the proceedings.
6 Infra, pp 279–280, 340.
7 Supra, pp 241–250.
8 Discussed supra, pp 241–243.
9 Infra, pp 292–324, 342–344.
10 In cases of "exclusive" jurisdiction under either Convention, infra, pp 309–313, the effect of restraining the proceedings would be to deprive the plaintiff of a forum in which to sue!

Chapter 13

Limitations on jurisdiction

SUMMARY

1. INTRODUCTION

Jurisdiction under the traditional rules is subject to certain limitations, the effect of which is to render the court incompetent to determine the issue notwithstanding that the defendant has been properly served with a writ. These limitations have been judicially classified into the following three types.[1]

(i) *Limitations that affect the subject matter of the issue.* Broadly stated, these limitations preclude a right of action if the issue relates to foreign immovables,[2] foreign intellectual property rights,[3] foreign taxes,[4] the rights and liabilities arising under a foreign penal or other public law,[5] or discovery of documents outside the jurisdiction.[6]

(ii) *Limitations that affect the kind of relief sought.* These restrict the power of the court to grant relief affecting the matrimonial status of the parties. In this type of case it is not enough that the respondent has been served with process. As will be seen in the chapter on matrimonial causes, the competence of the court to proceed with the trial is conditioned by such factors as the domicil or habitual residence of the parties.[7]

(iii) *Limitations relating to persons between whom the issue is joined.* There are certain persons against whom the jurisdiction cannot be enforced, and others by whom it cannot be invoked.[8]

---

1 *Garthwaite v Garthwaite* [1964] P 356 at 387, [1964] 2 All ER 233 at 243.
2 Infra, p 253 et seq.
3 Infra, pp 263–264.
4 Supra, p 114 et seq.
5 Supra, p 117 et seq.
6 *Mackinnon v Donaldson Lufkin and Jenrette Securities Corpn* [1986] Ch 482, [1986] 1 All ER 563.
7 Infra, pp 630–633.
8 Infra, pp 264–277.

(iv) *Limitations on jurisdiction imposed by certain statutes*[9] It is intended in this chapter to deal with limitations in respect of foreign immovables and foreign intellectual property rights, limitations relating to the parties, and limitations imposed by certain statutes. The other limitations mentioned above, are more appropriately dealt with elsewhere in the book.

2. JURISDICTION IN RESPECT OF FOREIGN PROPERTY

(a) FOREIGN IMMOVABLES[10]

The limitations on jurisdiction in relation to foreign immovables are derived from two sources: first, certain common law rules; second, the Brussels and Lugano Conventions as implemented by the Civil Jurisdiction and Judgments Acts 1982 and 1991. Each of these limitations will be examined in turn.

(i) The common law limitation

(a) The exclusionary rule

An English court has no jurisdiction to adjudicate upon the right of property in, or the right to possession of, foreign immovables, even though the parties may be resident or domiciled in England.[11] This general rule is based on the practical consideration that only the court of the situs can make an effective decree with regard to land.

It was at one time thought, however, that as regards this country the rule was not based on substantial grounds, but was due to the technicalities of the English law of procedure. A distinction was made between local and transitory actions. If a cause of action was one that might have arisen anywhere, it was *transitory*; if it was one that could have arisen only in one place, it was *local*. In local matters, such as claims to the ownership of land,[12] the *venue* had to be laid with accuracy, but in transitory matters the plaintiff was allowed to lay the *venue* where he pleased. However, local *venues* were abolished by the Judicature Act 1873. This removed the technical objection to the possibility of bringing an action in respect of foreign immovables before an English court, and it was not long before it was suggested, and indeed decided, that such actions could now be entertained. This argument was strongly pressed in *British South Africa Co v Companhia de Moçambique*:[13]

> This was an action of trespass brought against the defendants for having broken into and taken possession of large tracts of lands and mines in South Africa.

The Court of Appeal held that, local *venues* having been abolished, such an action could properly be brought here.[14] The House of Lords, however, reversed this decision and held that an English court has no jurisdiction to

9 Infra, pp 277–278.
10 On the distinction between movables and immovables see infra, pp 779–783.
11 *British South Africa Co v Companhia de Moçambique* [1893] AC 602; *Deschamps v Miller* [1908] 1 Ch 856; *Hesperides Hotels Ltd v Aegean Turkish Holidays Ltd* [1979] AC 508, [1978] 2 All ER 1168; Merills (1979) 28 ICLQ 523; Carter (1978) 49 BYBIL 286. For a Canadian authority on this point see *Jeske v Jeske* (1982) 29 RFL (2d) 348.
12 The place from which the jury was summoned.
13 [1893] AC 602.
14 [1892] 2 QB 358.

entertain a suit with respect to foreign immovables, and moreover, it finally dispelled the idea that this principle ever rested on a technical rule of procedure.[15] Stated more explicitly, what this decision now signifies is that the jurisdiction of the court is barred where the action raises the issue of the title to, or right to possession of, land abroad.

This exclusion of jurisdiction is justified on the basis that any judgment in rem that might be given would be totally ineffective unless it were accepted and implemented by the authorities in the situs.[16] However, this issue must be raised directly, for

> it is the action *founded on* a disputed claim of title to foreign lands over which an English court has no jurisdiction, and ... where no question of title arises, or only arises as a collateral incident of the trial of other issues, there is nothing to exclude the jurisdiction.[17]

Examples of a refusal of jurisdiction on this ground are:

proceedings for the partition of land in Ireland;[18]
an action to test the validity of a devise of land situated in Pennsylvania;[19]
an action[20] or a petition of right[21] to recover possession of Colonial land;
a claim to obtain inspection of documents, possessed by the defendant in England, in aid of an action for the recovery of land that was pending in India;[1] an action for a declaration of title to fishery rights.[2]

A question that has arisen at least once is whether an action to recover arrears of rent charged on land abroad is maintainable in England. In *Whitaker v Forbes*:[3]

> An English testator devised land in Australia to the defendant, but charged it with the payment of an annuity of £500 to the plaintiff.

An action to recover arrears of this rentcharge inevitably failed, for it had been commenced before the abolition of the rules of *venue* by the Judicature Act and thus the court had no option but to enforce the technical rule that the action was local and therefore not maintainable. Lord CAIRNS, however, remarked that it might possibly be maintainable in the future.[4] In this particular case, of course, the defendant, having assumed no contractual obligation, was liable solely on the ground of privity of estate arising from his possession of the land, and there can be no doubt that a liability which

15 [1893] AC 602 at 629.
16 It is unlikely that foreign judgments relating to title to English land will be recognised in this country, see p 363, below.
17 *St Pierre v South American Stores (Gath and Chaves) Ltd* [1936] 1 KB 382 at 397, interpreting the speech of Lord HERSCHELL in the *Moçambique Case* [1893] AC 602 at 626; and see *Tito v Waddell (No 2)* [1977] Ch 106 at 262–264, 310. The rule in the *Moçambique Case* will not apply where what is involved is more than a mere dispute between private individuals, see *Buttes Gas and Oil Co v Hammer (No 3)* [1982] AC 888, [1981] 3 All ER 616.
18 *Cartwright v Pettus* (1676) 2 Cas in Ch 214.
19 *Pike v Hoare* (1763) Amb 428.
20 *Roberdeau v Rous* (1738) 1 Atk 543.
21 *Re Holmes* (1861) 2 John & H 527.
 1 *Reiner v Marquis of Salisbury* (1876) 2 ChD 378.
 2 *Toome Eel Fishery (Northern Ireland) v Jangaard and Butler* [1960] CLY 1297.
 3 (1875) 1 CPD 51.
 4 Ibid, at 52.

rests on privity of contract, as where a borrower charges his land with the repayment of the loan, will be enforceable in English proceedings.

(b) Exceptions to the exclusionary rule

There are two exceptions to the exclusion of jurisdiction under the rule in the *Moçambique Case*.

(i) Action founded on a personal obligation

If the conscience of the defendant is affected in the sense that he has become bound by a personal obligation to the plaintiff, the court, in the exercise of its jurisdiction in personam, will not shrink from ordering him to convey or otherwise deal with foreign land. For the argument that a court cannot, by its judgments or decrees, directly bind or affect land that lies within the confines of another State has no force where the issue before the court is not a right in rem relating to foreign immovables, but an obligation enforceable in personam against the defendant.[5]

The primary essential is that the defendant should be subject to the general jurisdiction of the court.[6] This jurisdiction, as we have seen, is founded on his presence in England, but as regards the power to pronounce a decree in personam against him it is equally well founded by service of a writ under Order 11.[7] Once the court is thus empowered to take cognizance of the matter, the doctrine that equity acts in personam may be freely and effectively applied. A decree may be issued which, though personal in form, will indirectly affect land abroad. The operation of this rule may readily be illustrated by recent decisions on the making of *Anton Piller* orders, ie ex parte orders for the inspection of property, in relation to property abroad. If the defendant has been properly served in England, the court has power to, and may well make, the order. It is, however, a discretionary order and though an order has been granted for the inspection of premises in Paris,[8] an order has been refused in relation to premises in Scotland.[9] Furthermore if the jurisdiction of the court is based on service of the writ out of the jurisdiction following an ex parte application under Order 11, execution of the *Anton Piller* order abroad may be suspended until the defendant has had an opportunity to seek to set aside the service of the writ.[10]

If, for instance, a mortgagee of land in Ireland refuses to reconvey on receipt of principal, interest and costs, there is no way by which a direct transfer of the property to the mortgagor can be effected at the instance of the English court. But the court can indirectly produce the desired result by saying to the recalcitrant mortgagee, "You are subject to our jurisdiction by reason of your presence in England, and if you refuse to take the steps required by the law of the situs for a reconveyance of the property to the mortgagor, we shall imprison you or sequestrate your English property until you comply." The distinction is that the court cannot act upon the land directly, but acts on the conscience of the defendant.[11]

5 *Ewing v Orr-Ewing* (1883) 9 App Cas 34 at 40.
6 *Razelos v Razelos (No 2)* [1970] 1 WLR 392 at 403.
7 *Re Liddell's Settlement Trusts* [1936] Ch 365 at 374, [1936] 1 All ER 239 at 248. For Ord 11 see supra, pp 191–211.
8 *Cook Industries Inc v Galliher* [1979] Ch 439, [1978] 3 All ER 945.
9 *Protector Alarms Ltd v Maxim Alarms Ltd* [1978] FSR 442.
10 *Altertext Inc v Advanced Data Communications Ltd* [1985] 1 All ER 395, [1985] 1 WLR 457.
11 *Cranstown v Johnston* (1796) 3 Ves 170 at 182; *Companhia de Moçambique v British South Africa Co* [1892] 2 QB 358 at 364.

This right to affect foreign land was finally established by the decision in *Penn v Baltimore*[12] in 1750. In that case:

A contract had been made in England between the plaintiff and the defendant, by which a scheme was arranged for fixing the boundaries of Pennsylvania and Maryland. To a claim for specific performance brought in this country the defendant objected that the court had no jurisdiction, since it could neither make an effectual decree nor execute its own judgment. Lord HARDWICKE, while admitting that he could not make a decree in rem, granted specific performance, on the ground that the strict primary decree in a court of Equity was in personam.

The exercise of this jurisdiction, of course, is not confined to questions concerning foreign land. It extends to any case where the defendant has been guilty of conduct that in the eyes of the court is contrary to equity and good conscience. An important example of the general jurisdiction occurs where a person who is amenable to the jurisdiction commences legal proceedings abroad, the institution of which is inequitable. In such circumstances the court has a power to issue an injunction in restraint of the foreign proceedings, for a decree of this nature is not directed against the authority of the foreign court but merely commands a person within the English jurisdiction what he is to do.

Even where a person has actually obtained judgment abroad, an injunction may be issued restraining him from reaping its fruits, if he has obtained it in breach of some contractual or fiduciary duty or in a manner contrary to the principles of equity and conscience.[13]

We must now, however, confine the discussion to the manner in which the exercise of this personal jurisdiction may affect foreign land. The fundamental requirement is that the defendant should be subject to some personal obligation arising from his own act, for it is only when his conscience is affected that the court is entitled to interfere. This personal obligation can arise "out of contract or implied contract, fiduciary relationship, or fraud, or other conduct which, in the view of the Court of Equity in this country, would be unconscionable, and do not depend for their existence on the law of the *locus* of the immovable property".[14] It will lead, perhaps, to a better appreciation of the subject if we attempt to tabulate the various circumstances that have been considered sufficient to raise the necessary personal equity. It should, however, be stressed that the courts may decide that a personal equity exists without going on to categorise the situation before them. Thus the Court of Appeal has held[15] that there is jurisdiction to grant a wife an order restraining her husband from disposing of a villa in Spain, since the right to financial relief arising from divorce proceedings is concerned with a personal equity and this is enough to give jurisdiction.

Contracts relating to foreign land It is clear that a party to a contract concerning foreign land is subject to a personal obligation which affects his conscience and which can be enforced by the personal process of a court of

---

12 (1750) 1 Ves Sen 444.
13 *Ellerman Lines Ltd v Read* [1928] 2 KB 144.
14 *Deschamps v Miller* [1908] 1 Ch 856 at 863. See also Westlake, S 172; Foote, p 224; Dicey and Morris, pp 923–924; *Companhia de Moçambique v British South Africa Co* [1892] 2 QB 358 at 364.
15 *Hamlin v Hamlin* [1986] Fam 11.

equity,[16] even if his contractual right can only be pursued by an uncontested assertion of his title to foreign land.[1] The existence of a contractual obligation was the ground of the decision in *Penn v Baltimore*.[2] In the very early case of *Archer v Preston*[3] the defendant, who refused to perform a contract for the sale of land in Ireland, was successfully sued for specific performance while on a casual visit to England. Again, a decree for specific performance was made against the English executors of a testator who had agreed for valuable consideration to execute a legal mortgage of land in the island of Dominica;[4] and an action has lain in England for recovery of rent due under a lease of land in Chile.[5] More recently, specific performance of a contract for the sale of land in Scotland has been decreed against an English purchaser, notwithstanding the argument that there was considerable difference between Scots and English land law.[6] In Canada, specific performance has been granted by a New Brunswick court against a vendor who attempted to repudiate a contract for the sale of land in Quebec.[7]

Fraud and other unconscionable conduct The objection was raised as long ago as 1682, in the case of *Arglasse v Muschamp*,[8] that the English court has no jurisdiction to determine a claim founded on fraud if the fraud is concerned solely with foreign land. In overruling the objection, the Lord Chancellor stigmatised it as "only a jest put upon the jurisdiction of this court by the common lawyers".[9] Fraud is an extrinsic, collateral act, violating all proceedings, even those of courts of justice,[10] and it always creates a right in the injured party to sue the defendant in personam wherever he can find him, no matter where the cause of action has arisen or where the subject-matter of the action is situated. The leading case is *Cranstown v Johnston*.[11]

The plaintiff was liable under an arbitrator's award to pay to the defendant at Lloyd's Coffee House in London the sum of £2,521 10s 9d but owing to absence abroad he was unable to make the payment at the required time. He was entitled to a plantation of great value in the island of St Christopher. The law of that island allowed a creditor to proceed against an absent debtor after leaving a summons at the freehold of the debtor and nailing another on the court-house door. The defendant availed himself of this procedure and, after judgment had been obtained without any actual notice to the plaintiff, the plantation was seized by the Provost-Marshal and the plaintiff's interest therein sold to the defendant for £2,000,

---

16 *Cood v Cood* (1863) 33 LJ Ch 273; *British South Africa Co v De Beers Consolidated Mines Ltd* [1910] 2 Ch 502 at 523, 524; *St Pierre v South American Stores (Gath and Chaves) Ltd* [1936] 1 KB 382.
1 *Tito v Waddell (No 2)* [1977] Ch 106 at 264, 310; infra, p 258.
2 (1750) 1 Ves Sen 444.
3 Undated, but cited in *Arglasse v Muschamp* (1682) 1 Vern 76 at 77.
4 *Re Smith, Lawrence v Kitson* [1916] 2 Ch 206.
5 *St Pierre v South American Stores (Gath and Chaves) Ltd* [1936] 1 KB 382.
6 *Richard West & Partners (Inverness) Ltd v Dick* [1969] 2 Ch 424; affirmed, ibid p 435. In view of the general requirement of jurisdiction over the defendant, discussed supra pp 183 et seq, it is hard to see why HARMAN LJ [1969] 2 Ch 424 at 436 was unwilling to commit himself if the defendant was not domiciled in England.
7 *Ward v Coffin* (1972) 27 DLR (3d) 58.
8 (1682) 1 Vern 76.
9 Ibid, at 77.
10 *Duchess of Kingston's Case* (1776) 20 State Tr 355 at 544; *White v Hall* (1806) 12 Ves 321.
11 (1796) 3 Ves 170. For a more recent example, see *Cook Industries Inc v Galliher* [1979] Ch 439, [1978] 3 All ER 945.

which was far less than its true value. The plaintiff filed a bill for relief in the English Court of Equity.

The Master of the Rolls decreed that on receipt of what was due for principal, interest and costs the defendant should reconvey the plantation to the plaintiff. He did not deny that what had been done was in accordance with the law of the situs, but he pointed out that the defendant had used the local law not to satisfy the debt, but to obtain an estate at an inadequate price. This was a "gross injustice" sufficient to justify the court in acting on the conscience of the defendant.

Fiduciary relationship A trust attached to foreign land may be enforced by the English court, provided that the trustee is present in this country.[12] This is so, even though the author of the trust is not subject to the English jurisdiction.[13] However, two different types of problem may arise in relation to a trust or other equitable obligation concerning foreign land. The first is where the dispute before the court concerns the enforcement of the trust. It may be that a beneficiary can only establish his right to benefit under the trust by asserting evidence of his title to foreign land. In that event, the question of title to the land, though relevant to the plaintiff's claim, is only incidental to the dispute before the court, namely the enforcement of the trust, such as a trust of royalties from the mining of land.[14] If, on the other hand, there are rival claimants to the land, then the plaintiff's assertion of title is part of the subject matter of the dispute and would come within the *Moçambique* rule, whether the claim related to a trust[15] or to a contractual obligation[16] concerning the foreign land.

Again, a personal equity arising from a mortgage of foreign land may justify an action in this country. Thus, where the mortgagor of land in Jamaica had obtained a decree from the English court which directed certain accounts to be taken with a view to redemption, the court granted an injunction restraining the mortgagees, who were present in England, from instituting foreclosure proceedings in Jamaica.[17] The mortgagor had a clear equity to be protected from a double account. The same principle applies to foreclosure proceedings. In English proceedings a decree in a foreclosure action is merely a decree in personam since it destroys the right of redemption given by equity to the mortgagor, and it can therefore be made by an English court against a mortgagor who is within the jurisdiction, although the subject of the mortgage may be immovables situated abroad.[18]

Whether a personal obligation is such as to affect the defendant's conscience is a matter to be determined solely by English law. According to *Re Courtney*,[19] the court does not refuse to exercise its equitable jurisdiction

---

12 *Kildare v Eustace* (1686) 1 Vern 437; see also *Razelos v Razelos (No 2)* [1970] 1 WLR 392. It is not clear, in the latter case, whether jurisdiction was assumed on the basis of fraud or of a fiduciary relationship: Chesterman (1970) 33 MLR 209, 212–213.

13 *Ewing v Orr-Ewing* (1883) 9 App Cas 34; and see *Chellaram v Chellaram* [1985] Ch 409 at 426–427.

14 *Tito v Waddell (No 2)* [1977] Ch 106 at 262–264, 272, 310.

15 Ibid, at 263, 310.

16 Supra, pp 256–257.

17 *Beckford v Kemble* (1822) 1 Sim & St 7; cf *Inglis v Commonwealth Trading Bank of Australia* (1972) 20 FLR 30; Pryles (1973) 22 ICLQ 756.

18 *Toller v Carteret* (1705) 2 Vern 494; *Paget v Ede* (1874) LR 18 Eq 118.

19 (1840) Mont & Ch 239 at 251; *Re The Anchor Line (Henderson Brothers) Ltd* [1937] Ch 483 at 488.

merely because the right, recognised by English law as springing from the personal relationship between the parties, is one that is not recognised by the law of the situs.

In that case, an equitable mortgage according to English law had been created over Scottish land by the deposit of title-deeds, together with a memorandum by which the mortgagors agreed to do anything necessary to make the security more effective. The mortgagors, who were partners carrying on business in Scotland and England, became bankrupt, and the mortgagee claimed in the English court to have his debt paid out of the Scottish land in preference to the general body of creditors. The objection raised to this claim was that by the law of Scotland no lien or equitable mortgage on the land was created by the deposit of the title-deeds or by the written memorandum. The court decided in favour of the mortgagee. There was nothing in Scottish law that made it illegal or impossible for the mortgagors to create an effective mortgage according to the terms of their contract, and the fact that what they had done did not create a right in rem according to the law of the situs was no reason why the English court should not enforce the personal obligation by decreeing the execution of an instrument in the proper Scottish form.

The doctrine of *Penn v Baltimore*, however, is subject to two limitations. First, it must be possible for the decree issued by the English court to be carried into effect in the country where the land is situated.[20] This restriction requires no elaboration, for the futility of ordering the defendant to perform some act which would be forbidden by the law of the situs is obvious.[1]

Secondly, the personal obligation which is the basis of the English court's jurisdiction must, to use an expression of Beale, "have run from the defendant to the plaintiff",[2] ie there must be privity of obligation between the parties to the action.

It is firmly established that the court acts only against the actual person who, as a result of his *own* conduct, is under a personal obligation to the plaintiff, and it stops short of exercising the jurisdiction against a third party, even though he may have acquired the land from one who is contractually, or otherwise personally, liable to the plaintiff.[3] There must be privity of obligation between plaintiff and defendant, and that privity must arise from some transaction effected by the plaintiff with the defendant. If A agrees to sell foreign land to B, there is no doubt that A incurs a personal liability that is justiciable in England. But if, in breach of his contract, A sells the land to X, there is no personal equity which B can enforce against X. There is no contract by X with B, no unconscionable conduct by X towards B personally. What is involved in such a case is a claim of title to foreign land advanced by two contesting parties who are strangers to each other so far as mutual dealings are concerned. Such a question of title is, of course, determinable exclusively by the law of the situs and is subject exclusively to the jurisdiction of the courts at the situs.

---

20 *Waterhouse v Stansfield* (1851) 9 Hare 234; cf *Richard West & Partners (Inverness) Ltd v Dick* [1969] 2 Ch 424 at 429–430, 436; *Razelos v Razelos (No 2)* [1970] 1 WLR 392 at 403–405.
1 *Re Courtney* (1840) Mont & Ch 239 at 250–251.
2 (1906) 20 HLR 382, 390.
3 *Martin v Martin* (1831) 2 Russ & M 507; *Waterhouse v Stansfield* (1851) 9 Hare 234; *Norris v Chambres* (1861) 29 Beav 246; affd (1861) 3 De G F & J 583; *Hicks v Powell* (1869) 4 Ch App 741; *Norton v Florence Land Co* (1877) 7 ChD 332.

An apt illustration is *Norris v Chambres*.[4] In that case Sadleir agreed to buy certain Prussian lands from Simons and paid a deposit. Simons refused to complete and sold the land to Chambres, who had notice of Sadleir's contract. Sadleir's representative brought an action in England claiming that he was entitled to a lien on the land. Sir John ROMILLY MR, in dismissing this claim, referred to the cases which had followed *Penn v Baltimore*, and said:[5]

> On examining them, I find that in all of them a privity existed between the Plaintiff and Defendant; they had entered into some contract or some personal obligation had been incurred moving directly from the one to the other. In this case I cannot find that anything of that sort exists ... Simons having received this money repudiates the contract, and sells the estate to a stranger. That constitutes no personal demand which Sadleir could enforce in this country against that stranger. There is no contract between them, there are no mutual rights, and there is no obligation moving directly from one to the other.

There may, of course, be exceptional circumstances in which an equity that has arisen between A and B can be enforced against C under the doctrine of *Penn v Baltimore*. It is always a question of personal obligation. Is the defendant, though not a party to the original transaction which gave rise to the dispute, contractually or otherwise personally bound? Thus in *Mercantile Investment and General Trust Co v River Plate Trust, Loan and Agency Co:*[6]

> An American company created an equitable charge over land in Mexico in favour of certain English debenture-holders. The charge was void by Mexican law for want of registration. The land was later transferred to the defendants, an English company, but *subject to the mortgage, lien or charge now existing* in favour of the debenture-holders.

To an action brought in England to enforce this equitable charge it was objected that there was no privity of obligation between the debenture-holders of the American company and the defendants. The defendants had not issued the debentures, and, by Mexican law, they were the absolute and unfettered owners of the land. NORTH J had no difficulty in disposing of this argument. The defendants had agreed to take the land subject to an express obligation in favour of the debenture-holders, and it was clearly unconscionable that they should rely exclusively on the law of the situs.

Such, then, is the doctrine that the English court invokes to justify an order which, though personal in form, may affect the title to foreign land. It is a doctrine that in some cases has undoubtedly been carried to an extent scarcely warranted by the principles of international law,[7] as, for instance, where an Englishman resident in Chile was ordered to carry out a contract concerning land, binding according to English law, which the Chilean courts had held not to be binding.[8] In fact, Lord ESHER MR once went so far as to say that the decision in *Penn v Baltimore*, "seems to me to be open to the strong objection, that the Court is doing indirectly what it dare not do directly".[9]

---

4 (1861) 29 Beav 246; affd (1861) 3 De G F & J 583. Followed in *Deschamps v Miller* [1908] 1 Ch 856; and see *Re Hawthorne, Graham v Massey* (1883) 23 ChD 743; *Cook Industries Inc v Galliher* [1979] Ch 439, [1978] 3 All ER 945.
5 (1861) 29 Beav 246, at 254–255.
6 [1892] 2 Ch 303.
7 Story, p 758.
8 *Cood v Cood* (1863) 33 LJ Ch 273.
9 *Companhia de Moçambique v British South Africa Co* [1892] 2 QB 358 at 404–405.

An interesting question that has never arisen in England is whether a foreign judgment based on the same principle as that adopted in *Penn v Baltimore*, but affecting *English* land, will be granted extra-territorial effect.[10] If, for instance, a Californian court decrees that X, resident in California, shall reconvey English land to Y, from whom he had obtained it by fraud, will the English court, in proceedings brought by Y, compel X to carry the decree into effect? Comity, if it means anything, would dictate an affirmative answer. However, any attempt by a foreign court to regulate the disposition of land outside its jurisdiction not unnaturally provokes a certain animosity in the state where the property is situated and it is doubtful whether in this particular context the English judges would be imbued with any spirit of reciprocity. The Supreme Court of Canada, indeed, has satisfied itself that English courts do not regard their own decrees in personam affecting land abroad as having any extra-territorial effect, and that therefore no recognition will be granted to similar decrees of foreign courts.[11]

(ii) Questions affecting foreign land arising incidentally in an English action
The second exception, which lacks direct authority but which undoubtedly exists in practice, is apparent from such well-known cases as *Re Duke of Wellington*[12] and *Nelson v Bridport*,[13] to take only two examples.[14] In each of these cases jurisdiction was assumed although quite clearly the title to foreign land was the matter in dispute. Since parties cannot consent to the exercise of a jurisdiction which the court admittedly does not possess,[15] how is this divergence from the general principle to be explained? The usual explanation is that if an estate or a trust, which includes English property and foreign immovables, is being administered in English proceedings,[16] the court is prepared to determine a disputed title to the foreign immovables.[17] Perhaps Lord HERSCHELL had this practice in mind when he accepted that the courts could take jurisdiction to determine incidental matters involving title to foreign land.[18] Although a stern critic might question whether the title to the Spanish land in *Re Duke of Wellington* was a mere incident in the proceedings, there is no doubt that in the course of dealing with such a matter as a trust or a will subject to English law the courts have in fact not hesitated to determine the title to foreign land. The jurisdictional difficulty that arises

10 Dicey & Morris, pp 455–459.
11 *Duke v Andler* [1932] SCR 734; see Gordon (1933) 49 LQR 547; cf *Chapman Estate v O'Hara* [1988] 2 WWR 275. In the USA, although the Supreme Court in *Fall v Eastin* 215 US 1 (1909) held that recognition need not be given to judgments in personam concerning land, most states are prepared to recognise such judgments: Scoles & Hay, pp 931–932; Restatement 2d section 102, comment d.
12 [1948] Ch 118, [1947] 2 All ER 854, supra, p 70.
13 (1846) 8 Beav 547, infra, pp 784–785.
14 See also *Re Piercy* [1895] 1 Ch 83; *Re Hoyles* [1911] 1 Ch 179; *Re Ross* [1930] 1 Ch 377, supra, pp 68–69. Cf *Buttes Gas and Oil Co v Hammer (No 3)* [1982] AC 888, [1981] 3 All ER 616.
15 Duncan and Dykes, *Principles of Civil Jurisdiction*, 258; see also the doubt expressed by SOMERVELL LJ in *The Tolten* [1946] P 135 at 166, [1946] 2 All ER 372 at 388.
16 The jurisdiction of the English court to administer an inter vivos trust of land in a European Community State or an EFTA State which has ratified the Lugano Convention is subject to Arts 1 (1) and 16(1)(a) of the Brussels and Lugano Conventions, infra, pp 286–289, 310–312, 342.
17 *Jubert v Church Commissioners for England* 1952 SC 160; *Re Bailey* [1985] 2 NZLR 656; Morris (1946) 64 LQR 264, 268. Dr Morris suggests that the English and foreign property must be subject to similar limitations, but is this right?
18 *British South Africa Co v Companhia de Moçambique* [1893] AC 602, at 626. See also Westlake, op cit, section 173.

appears to have been canvassed only once,[1] and all that can be said is that the practice comes perilously near to destroying the supposedly universal principle that jurisdiction concerning the title to, or possession of, immovables, resides only in the state in which the property is situated.

(c) Damages for trespass to foreign land

Until fairly recently the limitations at common law extended to prevent jurisdiction in cases where the action raised the issue of the recovery of damages for trespass to foreign land, even though no question of title to the land arose.[2] This rule came in for much criticism and was abolished by section 30(1) of the Civil Jurisdiction and Judgments Act 1982,[3] which provides that

the jurisdiction ... to entertain proceedings for trespass to, or any other tort affecting, immovable property shall extend to cases in which the property in question is situated outside [England] unless the proceedings are principally concerned with a question of the title to, or right to possession of, that property.

(ii) The limitation under the Brussels and Lugano Conventions

The limitation on jurisdiction in respect of foreign immovables under the Brussels and Lugano Conventions stems from Article 16(1)(a), which will only operate in cases where the immovable property is situated in a European Community State (in the case of the Brussels Convention) or in an EFTA Contracting State (in the case of the Lugano Convention).[4] However, unlike many of the jurisdictional provisions under the Conventions, Article 16(1)(a) does not require that the defendant be domiciled in a European Community State or in an EFTA Contracting State. The effect of Article 16(1)(a) is to prevent a court in the United Kingdom from taking jurisdiction in proceedings which have as their object rights in rem in, or tenancies of, immovable property situated in another European Community State or in an EFTA Contracting State,[5] since the courts of the Contracting State in which the property is situated are given exclusive jurisdiction over such proceedings. The proceedings to which Article 16(1)(a) applies are considered in detail in chapter 14, where the Brussels and Lugano Conventions are examined fully.

If Article 16(1)(a) is applicable, the common law rules on jurisdiction in relation to foreign immovables are overriden by this Article.[6] It is important to note that the limitation under Article 16(1)(a) is wider in two respects than that contained under the common law rules. First, Article 16(1)(a) is not confined to proceedings raising the issue of the title to, or the right to

---

1 *Re Duke of Wellington* [1948] Ch 118 at 120, gives the misleading impression that if the parties consent the court can arrogate a jurisdiction that it does not possess. It must be admitted, however, that this was done in *The Mary Moxham* (1876) 1 PD 107. See also *Couzens v Negri* [1981] VR 824.
2 *St Pierre v South American Stores (Gath and Chaves) Ltd* [1936] 1 KB 382 at 396; *Hesperides Hotels Ltd v Aegean Turkish Holidays Ltd* [1979] AC 508, [1978] 2 All ER 1168.
3 Applied in *Trawnik v Lennox* [1985] 2 All ER 368, [1985] 1 WLR 532.
4 See supra, pp 180–181. The proceedings must be in respect of a civil and commercial matter, infra pp 286–290.
5 For the position where the immovable property is situated in Scotland or Northern Ireland see the Modified Convention, discussed infra, pp 336–339 particularly Art 16 (1) of the Modified Convention.
6 Civil Jurisdiction and Judgments Act 1982, s 30 is also subject to the Brussels and Lugano Conventions and the Modified Convention, see s 30(2) as amended by the Civil Jurisdiction and Judgments Act 1991, Sch 2, para 13.

possession of, foreign immovables. The provision has been widely interpreted to encompass, for example, a simple action for unpaid rent in respect of a villa in Italy.[7] Second, apart from the case of short term lets,[8] there are no exceptions to the limitation contained in Article 16(1)(a). It follows that English courts will not be able to take jurisdiction, for example, in a case involving fraud or unconscionable conduct,[9] if Article 16(1)(a) is applicable. However, if the matter affecting the foreign land only arises incidentally, the proceedings will not come within Article 16(1)(a) since they will not have rights in rem "as their object";[10] English courts will, accordingly, be able to take jurisdiction in such a case, as they can do at common law.[11]

What if Article 16(1)(a) is not applicable as, for example, in a case where there is a dispute over the title to land in a non-Contracting State, such as New York? Can the exclusion in the *Moçambique Case* be used to deny jurisdiction to English courts? In cases where the traditional bases of jurisdiction apply, clearly it can. But if jurisdiction has been allocated to the United Kingdom under the Brussels Convention[12] (where, for example, the defendant is domiciled in the United Kingdom) it must be doubtful whether jurisdiction can be declined on the basis of the exclusion contained in the *Mocambique Case*.[13] However, there is some rather questionable English authority to the effect that, in this situation, an English court can use its discretionary powers to stay the proceedings on the basis that New York is the appropriate forum for trial.[14]

(b) FOREIGN INTELLECTUAL PROPERTY RIGHTS

In England it had been assumed until recently that the exception in the *Moçambique Case* was confined to cases involving foreign *immovable* property. However, in *Tyburn Productions Ltd v Conan Doyle*[15] Vinelott J applied the *Moçambique Case* to exclude actions relating to foreign intellectual property rights. The historical distinction between *local* and *transitory* actions was resurrected. Any question of validity of title to and infringement of a foreign copyright, patent or trade mark was a local one for the courts of the country by whose law the copyright, patent or trade mark was created, such rights being territorially limited to that country. It followed that the question raised in the case, namely whether the defendant was entitled to copyright under the law of the United States, was not justiciable in the English courts. This misunderstands the *Moçambique Case*, which was decided on a point of substance and not on the basis of a procedural distinction between *local* and

7 See Case 241/83 *Rösler v Rottwinkel* [1985] QB 33, [1985] ECR 99, discussed infra, pp 311–313.
8 Art 16(1)(b). This provision is differently worded in the Brussels Convention from the Lugano Convention, infra pp 312–313, 343–344.
9 See supra, p 257 for the common law position.
10 Case C-115/88 *Reichert v Dresdner Bank* [1990] ECR 27, particularly at 35 (per the Advocate General).
11 See supra, pp 261–262.
12 Infra, pp 292–324.
13 See, however, for suggestions to the contrary: Droz, paras 165–169; Dicey and Morris, pp 925–926; note by A.M. 1987 SLT 53.
14 *Arkwright Mutual Insurance Co v Bryanston Insurance Co Ltd* [1990] 2 QB 649 at 663; see more generally *Re Harrods (Buenos Aires) Ltd* [1992] Ch 72, discussed infra pp 331–334.
15 [1991] Ch 75; Carter (1990) 61 BYBIL 400; following the High Court of Australia's decisions in *Potter v Broken Hill Pty Co Ltd* (1906) 3 CLR 479; *Steinhardt & Son Ltd v Meth* (1961) 105 CLR 440.

transitory actions.[16] The point of substance related to whether an English court could give an effective judgment. This too concerned VINELOTT J. He concluded that, even if the action was justiciable in England, it would be an exercise in futility to allow the claims sought, since there was no evidence that any decision by an English court would be treated as binding in the United States. This provides a much better basis for the decision.

3. JURISDICTION OVER THE PARTIES

(a) PERSONS WHO CANNOT INVOKE THE JURISDICTION

The one person precluded from suing in an English court is the alien enemy. Before a person can bear this character, there must, of course, be a state of war between the United Kingdom and an enemy country at the time of the attempted proceedings, and whether the countries are still at war despite the cessation of hostilities is conclusively settled by a certificate from the Secretary of State for Foreign and Commonwealth Affairs.[17] Given a state of war, however, the question whether a person is an alien enemy does not depend on his nationality but on where he resides or carries on business. A British subject or a neutral who is voluntarily resident, or who is carrying on business, in enemy territory or in territory under the effective control of the enemy is treated as an alien enemy and is in the same position as a subject of hostile nationality resident in hostile territory.[18] A person of hostile nationality who is within the Queen's peace, as, for example, when he is resident in England under a cartel[19] or by permission of the Crown,[20] is temporarily free from his enemy character and may invoke the jurisdiction.[21]

An alien enemy can neither initiate an action nor continue one that was commenced before hostilities.[22] The disability of suing is based on public policy, but there are no considerations of public policy that make it desirable to suspend actions *against* alien enemies, and it is now well established that they may be sued.[23] Moreover, when sued they can plead a set-off in diminution of the claim of the plaintiff; they can take all the usual procedural steps, and they are at liberty to challenge an adverse judgment by appealing to a higher tribunal.[24]

16 Supra, pp 253–254.
17 *R v Bottrill* [1947] KB 41, [1946] 2 All ER 434, CA.
18 *Porter v Freudenberg* [1915] 1 KB 857 at 869; *Sovracht (vo) v Van Udens Scheepvart en Agentuur Maatschappij (NV Gebr)* [1943] AC 203, [1943] 1 All ER 76. See McNair (1942) 58 LQR 191. For the purposes of the Trading with the enemy Act 1939, which penalises persons trading with the enemy, de facto residence, though not voluntary, is sufficient: *Vamvakas v Custodian of Enemy Property* [1952] 2 QB 183, [1952] 1 All ER 629.
19 *The Hoop* (1799) 1 Ch Rob 196 at 201.
20 Eg when he was registered under the Aliens Restriction Act 1914: *Princess Thurn and Taxis v Moffit* [1915] 1 Ch 58; *Schaffenius v Goldberg* [1916] 1 KB 284.
21 *Johnstone v Pedlar* [1921] 2 AC 262.
22 *Porter v Freudenberg*, supra. An alien enemy, respondent to a petition for the revocation of a patent, has been allowed, however, to amend his specification by way of disclaimer, since this constitutes a defence to the petition: *Re Stahlwerk Becker Aktiengesellschaft's Patent* [1917] 2 Ch 272. His right of action is generally abrogated, but sometimes merely suspended; see *Ertel Bieber & Co v Rio Tinto Co* [1918] AC 260; *Schering Ltd v Stockholms Enskilda Bank Aktiebolag* [1946] AC 219, [1946] 1 All ER 36; Cheshire, Fifoot and Furmston, *The Law of Contract* (12th edn), pp 366–367.
23 *Robinson & Co v Continental Insurance Co of Mannheim* [1915] 1 KB 155; *Porter v Freudenberg*, supra.
24 *Porter v Freudenberg* [1915] 1 KB 857.

(b) PERSONS WHO MAY CLAIM EXEMPTION FROM THE JURISDICTION[25]

(i) Sovereigns and sovereign States[26]

The basic rule at common law was that a foreign sovereign or sovereign foreign State was immune from the jurisdiction of the English courts, though the court would take jurisdiction if the sovereign submitted thereto. This immunity extended both to direct actions against the sovereign and to indirect actions involving his property.[1] However, this whole question was the subject of the European Convention on State Immunity (1972)[2] which led to the law being placed on a statutory basis by the State Immunity Act 1978.[3] Legislative authority for immunity is essential. An argument that the European Community should have an independent claim to sovereign immunity by analogy to a foreign state has been rejected because of the lack of legislative authority for this.[4] When a question of immunity arises under the 1978 Act this must be tried as a preliminary issue before the substantive action can proceed.[5]

Scope of the State Immunity Act 1978 The immunity conferred by the 1978 Act is not limited to those States who are parties to the 1972 Convention but is worldwide in effect.[6] It applies to any foreign or Commonwealth State, other than the United Kingdom, to the sovereign or other head of that State in his public capacity, to the government of that State and to any department thereof.[7] Provision is made for the application of the Act by Order in Council to the constituent territories of a federal State.[8] This is because such constituent territories do not automatically enjoy immunity under the 1972 Convention but only if the federal State so declares.[9] A difficult question before the passing of the 1978 Act was to determine whether a State corporation such as a State Bank, or the United States Shipping Board, could properly claim to be an emanation of the foreign State and thus entitled to

---

25 See Lewis, *State and Diplomatic Immunity* 3rd edn (1989); Sinclair (1980) II Hague Recueil 114; Marasinghe (1991) 54 MLR 664.
26 For proposals for reform see the International Law Commission's Draft Articles, discussed by Greig (1989) 38 ICLQ 243 and 560. We are concerned here with recognised states. On the question of whether an unrecognised state can sue or be sued in an English court, see *Gur Corpn v Trust Bank of Africa Ltd* [1987] QB 599; Warbrick (1987) 50 MLR 84; Beck (1987) 36 ICLQ 348.
 1 There is also a related rule that an English court will not rule directly on the validity of the legislative acts of a foreign sovereign state, see *Buck v A-G* [1965] Ch 745, [1964] 2 All ER 663; *Manuel v A-G* [1983] Ch 77, [1982] 3 All ER 786.
 2 Cmnd 5081; Sinclair (1973) 22 ICLQ 254; Mann (1973) 36 MLR 18.
 3 See Bowett [1978] CLJ 193; White (1979) 42 MLR 72; Mann (1979) 50 BYBIL 43; Delaume (1979) 73 AJIL 185; Lewis [1980] Lloyd's MCLQ 1. For similar legislation abroad see Foreign States Immunities Act 1981 (South Africa); Foreign Sovereign Immunities Act 1976 (USA); and State Immunity Act 1982 (Canada). The 1978 Act also implements the provisions of the 1926 Brussels Convention on Immunity of State-owned Ships, together with the Protocol thereto of 1934.
 4 *J H Rayner (Mincing Lane) Ltd v Department of Trade and Industry* [1989] Ch 72 at 198–203, 223, 252–253, CA; affd [1990] 2 AC 418, 516, HL without deciding this point.
 5 *J H Rayner (Mincing Lane) Ltd v Department of Trade and Industry*, supra at 194, 252; affd by HL, supra, without deciding this point.
 6 For the provisions as to recognition of foreign judgments see, infra, pp 405–406.
 7 1978 Act, s 14(1).
 8 Ibid, s 14(5).
 9 Art 28, see Sinclair (1973) 22 ICLQ 254, 279–280.

immunity.[10] This problem is dealt with in the 1978 Act through the use of the concept of "a separate entity". Such an entity, being distinct from the executive organs of the government of the foreign State and being capable of suing or being sued, is not entitled to immunity unless the proceedings relate to something done by the "separate entity" in the exercise of sovereign authority and the circumstances were such that the State would have been immune.[11] The courts may well have to develop criteria for determining whether a "separate entity" was exercising sovereign authority.[12]

The basic principle of the 1978 Act is that a foreign State is immune from the jurisdiction of the English courts and effect is to be given to that immunity whether or not the State appears in the proceedings.[13] That said, the Act provides a substantial list of exceptions from such immunity.

Exceptions from immunity Section 3[14] provides an exception of major significance. A foreign State is not immune as respects any proceedings relating to a commercial transaction entered into by that State,[15] bearing in mind the wide definition of State already discussed. Until recently, the position at common law was that a foreign State was immune even with regard to its purely commercial activities.[16] However, this wide immunity was rejected in a series of cases, culminating in two decisions of the House of Lords.[17] Instead, the "restrictive"[18] doctrine of immunity was applied, both to actions in rem and in personam, under which a foreign state was entitled to immunity in respect of its governmental acts but not in respect of its commercial transactions.

These common law developments are now, in substance, embodied in the 1978 Act.[19] "Commercial transaction" is defined[20] to include not only contracts for the supply of goods or services but also the provision of finance through loans and the like, and any guarantee or indemnity in respect of such transactions. Even more widely it extends to "any other transaction or activity (whether of a commercial, industrial, financial, professional or other similar character) into which a State enters or in which it engages otherwise

10 *Trendtex Trading Corporation v Central Bank of Nigeria* [1977] QB 529, [1977] 1 All ER 881; *C. Czarnikow Ltd v Rolimpex* [1979] AC 351, [1978] 2 All ER 1043; *I Congreso Del Partido* [1983] 1 AC 244, at 258.
11 1978 Act, ss 14(1), (2).
12 See Sinclair (1973) 22 ICLQ 254, 277–278; *Ferranti-Packard Ltd v Cushman Rentals Ltd* (1981) 115 DLR (3d) 691; *Lorac Transport Ltd v The Ship Atra* (1984) 9 DLR (4th) 129, affd (1986) 28 DLR (4th) 309.
13 1978 Act, s 1.
14 There are transitional provisions in s 23(3)(b).
15 S 3(1)(a).
16 Eg *Kahan v Pakistan Federation* [1951] 2 KB 1003; *Baccus SRL v Servicio Nacional del Trigo* [1957] 1 QB 438, [1956] 3 All ER 715.
17 *The Philippine Admiral* [1977] AC 373, [1976] 1 All ER 78; *Trendtex Trading Corpn v Central Bank of Nigeria* [1977] QB 529, [1977] 1 All ER 881; Lewis [1979] Lloyd's MCLQ 460; *Hispano Americana Mercantil SA v Central Bank of Nigeria* [1979] 2 Lloyd's Rep 277; *Planmount Ltd v Republic of Zaire* [1981] 1 All ER 1110; *I Congreso Del Partido* [1983] 1 AC 244; Fox (1982) 98 LQR 94; Mann (1982) 31 ICLQ 573; *Alcom Ltd v Republic of Colombia* [1984] AC 580, [1984] 1 All ER 1; Ghandi (1984) 47 MLR 597; Lloyd Jones [1984] CLJ 222; Crawford (1984) 55 BYBIL 340; Fox (1985) 34 ICLQ 115. See also *Empresa Exportadora De Azucar v Industria Azucarera Nacional SA, The Playa Larga* [1983] 2 Lloyd's Rep 171.
18 See generally, Sornarajah (1982) 31 ICLQ 661; Crawford (1983) 54 BYBIL 75.
19 See *Planmount Ltd v Republic of Zaire* [1981] 1 All ER 1110; *I Congreso Del Partido* [1983] 1 AC 244 at 260; *Alcom Ltd v Republic of Colombia* [1984] AC 580.
20 S 3(3). See *Alcom Ltd v Republic of Colombia* [1984] AC 580 at 601–603. On the relevance of the common law cases see Fox (1982) 98 LQR 94.

than in the exercise of sovereign authority".[21] Indeed, this commercial exception from immunity extends further to include any obligation of the foreign State which by virtue of a contract, whether or not a commercial transaction, falls to be performed in whole or in part in the United Kingdom.[22] This would include contracts made in the exercise of sovereign authority to be performed here, such as contracts for the building of warships.

There is a variety of other exceptions to immunity. In the case of contracts of employment, there is no immunity in respect of proceedings between the State and an individual where the contract was made in the United Kingdom or the work is to be wholly or partly performed here.[1] There is no immunity as regards proceedings for death or personal injury or damage to or loss of tangible property caused by an act or omission in the United Kingdom;[2] nor is there immunity in the case of proceedings relating to United Kingdom patents, trade marks, and similar rights belonging to the State, or to the alleged infringement in the United Kingdom by the foreign State of such rights, including copyright.[3]

Immunity is excluded in the case of proceedings relating to the State's interest in immovables in England or to an obligation arising from such an interest.[4] Thus the French government, who were tenants of a house in London which was not being used for the purpose of a diplomatic mission,[5] did not have immunity in respect of an action by the landlords for damages sustained as a result of an alleged refusal by the tenants to permit entry to carry out repairs.[6] Furthermore, the State has no immunity in the case of proceedings relating to its interest in other immovable or movable property by way of succession, gift or bona vacantia.[7] There is no requirement that the property be situated in England but the circumstances in which a judgment based on this exception must be recognised elsewhere are limited.[8] In the case of the administration of estates or trusts, or insolvency, the court's jurisdiction is unaffected by the fact that a foreign State may claim an interest in the property.[9] There is also an exception to immunity in the case of a State which is a member of a corporate or unincorporated body, or a partnership,

---

21 S 3(3)(c). Special provision is made in s 10 for ships that are used for commercial purposes.
22 S 3(1)(b). See *JH Rayner (Mincing Lane) Ltd v Department of Trade and Industry* [1989] Ch 72 at 194–195, 222, 252; affd by HL [1990] 2 AC 418 without discussion of this point. The exception from immunity provided by s 3 is inapplicable if the parties to the dispute are States or have otherwise agreed in writing or if the contract (not being a commercial transaction) was made in the territory of the foreign State and the obligation is governed by its administrative law: s 3(2).
1 S 4(1). This is subject to exception in the case of contrary agreement in writing or where the employee is a national of the foreign State or is neither a United Kingdom national nor resident here: ss 4(2) and (5), as amended by Zimbabwe Act 1979, s 6(3) and Sch 3 and by British Nationality Act 1981, s 52(6) and Sch 7 and see the transitional provision in s 23(3)(b). See *Sengupta v Republic of India* [1983] ICR 221.
2 S 5.
3 S 7.
4 S 6(1); and see *The Charkieh* (1873) LR 4 A & E 59 at 97; *Alcom Ltd v Republic of Colombia* [1984] AC 580 at 603.
5 See s 16(1)(b); discussed infra, p 272.
6 *Intpro Properties (UK) Ltd v Sauvel* [1983] QB 1019.
7 S 6(2).
8 See 1978 Act, s 19(3) for the limitations on the recognition here of foreign judgments involving this exemption; and see Art 20(3) of the European Convention on State Immunity (1972) and s 31 of the Civil Jurisdiction and Judgments Act 1982, discussed infra, p 277.
9 S 6(3); *In re Rafidain Bank* (1991) Times, 22 July; cf *United States of America and Republic of France v Dollfus Mieg et Cie SA and Bank of England* [1952] AC 582 at 617–618.

which has members other than States and which is incorporated or constituted under United Kingdom law or is controlled from or has its principal place of business in the United Kingdom.[10] There is no immunity as regards proceedings for VAT, customs or excise duties, or rates on commercial premises.[11]

An important practical exception from immunity is that relating to ships in use, or intended for use, for commercial purposes. In the case of such ships, there is no immunity in Admiralty proceedings (or proceedings on a claim which could be made the subject of Admiralty proceedings) relating to an action in rem against a ship belonging to the foreign State or to an action in personam for enforcing a claim in connection with such a ship.[12]

Finally, there is no immunity if the State has submitted to the jurisdiction of the courts;[13] and there is a related exception in the case where a State has agreed in writing to submit a dispute to arbitration for there is then no immunity with regard to court proceedings which relate to the arbitration.[14] There are detailed rules as to what constitutes submission by the foreign State. Submission may be by prior written agreement[15] or after the dispute has arisen;[16] but a provision in an agreement that the law of a part of the United Kingdom is to govern does not constitute submission.[17] In fact, the only way it could have been regarded as submission would have been if the choice of English law was regarded as an implied choice of English jurisdiction and if that was then regarded as implied submission. Any intervention by a foreign State for the purpose only of claiming immunity or asserting an interest in property in circumstances such that the State would have been entitled to immunity had the proceedings been brought against that State does not amount to submission.[18] A State is, however, deemed to submit if it has instituted the proceedings or, subject to what has just been said, if it intervenes in the proceedings[19] unless it does so in reasonable ignorance of facts entitling it to immunity and immunity is claimed as soon as is reasonably practical.[20]

Indirect impleading It has been assumed so far that the question of the immunity to which a sovereign State is entitled arises in the course of

10 S 8. See *Maclaine Watson & Co Ltd v International Tin Council* [1989] Ch 253 at 282–283.
11 S 11.
12 S 10(1), (2). Special provision is made for actions in rem against one ship in connection with another ship, actions concerning cargo, or proceedings where the foreign State is a party to the Brussels Convention covering the Immunity of State-owned Ships (1926): ss 10(3)-(6), 17(1).
13 S 2(1). Such submission does not imply submission to the enforcement jurisdiction of the courts, see s 13(3), and *Alcom Ltd v Republic of Colombia* [1984] AC 580 at 600.
14 S 9(1). This is subject to contrary provision in the arbitration agreement; nor does it apply to an arbitration agreement between States, s 9(2); and see the transitional provision in s 23(3)(b).
15 See, eg, *A Company Ltd v Republic of X* [1990] 2 Lloyd's Rep 520. See also s 17(2).
16 S 2(2); and see the transitional provision in s 23(3)(a); cf *Duff Development Co Ltd v Kelantan Government* [1924] AC 797; *Kahan v Pakistan Federation* [1951] 2 KB 1003. The head of the State's diplomatic mission in the United Kingdom is deemed to have authority to submit, as is any person who entered into a contract on behalf of the State in matters relating to that contract: s 2(7); cf *Baccus SLR v Servicio Nacional del Trigo* [1957] 1 QB 438 at 473.
17 Ibid.
18 S 2(4).
19 Ibid.
20 S 2(5). Any submission extends to an appeal, but not to a counterclaim unless it arises out of the same legal relationship or facts as the original claim: s 2(6). See also *Kubacz v Shah* [1984] WAR 156.

proceedings in which the State is named as defendant, ie direct impleading. In practice, however, what is far more common is "indirect impleading". In this type of case the issue of State immunity arises either because of inter-pleader proceedings by the State or because one party to the proceedings claims, for example, that the goods in issue[1] are subject to the power of a foreign State and that to proceed with the claim would indirectly implead that State. Before the State Immunity Act 1978 a variety of issues had been held to implead a foreign sovereign, such as an action which puts his title to goods in issue or which relates to property in the possession of the foreign State[2] or which the State has the right to possess,[3] or even property "in the control" of the foreign sovereign.[4] Most cases of indirect impleading involved chattels but the doctrine of immunity was extended to cases where the subject matter of the action was a chose in action to which title was claimed by a foreign State.[5] Finally, the foreign State did not have to prove its title to the property in issue. It was sufficient for evidence to be adduced that the claim of the foreign State was not illusory or founded on a manifestly defective title.[6] It had to be an arguable issue.[7]

The question of "indirect impleading" is not dealt with, as such, in the State Immunity Act 1978 even though it is the most likely circumstance in which the issue of sovereign immunity will arise. Nevertheless, this aspect of sovereign immunity is very substantially regulated. First, it is clear that the immunity, and the exceptions thereto, provided by the 1978 Act are intended to apply whether the foreign State is a party to the action or intervenes by means of interpleader proceedings. This is apparent from section 2(4) which provides that a State does not submit to the jurisdiction merely by intervening in proceedings to assert an interest in property in circumstances such that the State would have been immune if directly impleaded. Secondly, the problems of indirect impleading surface in section 6(4) which provides that a court may entertain proceedings against a person other than a State notwithstanding that the proceedings relate to property in the possession or control of a State or in which a State claims an interest. This is the indirect impleading situation where the State does not necessarily intervene; but the court's power to entertain such proceedings depends on the State not being immune if the proceedings were brought directly against it and, in the case where the proceedings relate to property in which the State claims an interest, the State's claim must be neither admitted nor supported by prima facie evidence.

The result is that in a case of indirect impleading, the law is much as before. There will be immunity unless the case falls within an exception under the 1978 Act, and it is unlikely that the exceptions in the 1978 Act would have altered the decisions in favour of immunity in many of the cases, other than

1 Eg *The Parlement Belge* (1880) 5 PD 197.
2 Eg *Compania Naviera Vascongada v SS Cristina* [1938] AC 485.
3 Eg *United States of America and Republic of France v Dollfus Mieg et Cie SA and Bank of England* [1952] AC 582, [1952] 1 All ER 572.
4 Eg *The Broadmayne* [1916] P 64.
5 *Rahimtoola v Nizam of Hyderabad* [1958] AC 379, [1957] 3 All ER 441.
6 *Juan Ysmael & Co Inc v Indonesian Government* [1955] AC 72 at 88–90. Cf *Shearson Lehman Bros Inc v Maclaine Watson & Co Ltd (International Tin Council intervening) (No 2)* [1988] 1 WLR 16, 29–31, HL—a sovereign asserting a right of property in a document in the possession of a third party.
7 *Rahimtoola v Nizam of Hyderabad* [1958] AC 379 at 410.

those relating to ships,[8] decided at common law,[9] for there is no statutory exception to immunity in most cases involving movables. The requirement of property being in the possession or control of the foreign State indicates little change; though the need to adduce prima facie evidence in support of a claim to an interest in the goods perhaps imposes a heavier burden than at common law. Finally, the reference in section 6(4) of the 1978 Act to "property", without qualification, suggests that the provision covers both corporeal and incorporeal property, ie, choses in action.

Procedural and other miscellaneous matters in the 1978 Act There are a number of other miscellaneous, but significant, matters dealt with by the 1978 Act. Provision is made for the service of process on a foreign State and for a number of other procedural matters.[10] These include immunity from the processes of execution except with the State's written consent or in respect of property in use or intended for use for commercial purposes.[11] It has been held that a credit balance in a bank account kept for the purpose of meeting the day to day expenditure of a foreign embassy was not used for commercial purposes and was therefore immune from the processes of execution.[12] Some of the expenditure would no doubt come within the concept of commercial purposes under the Act, but other expenditure clearly did not, and the bank balance was one and indivisible; it was not susceptible of dissection to reflect the different expenditure. Power is given to provide by Order in Council for the restriction or extension of the Act's immunities and privileges. They may be restricted where they exceed those accorded by the foreign State in relation to the United Kingdom; and they may be extended where they are less than those required by any international agreement between the United Kingdom and the foreign State.[13] Nothing in the list of exceptions to the general principle of immunity is to affect the immunities and privileges conferred by the Diplomatic Privileges Act 1964 or the Consular Relations Act 1968;[14] but the 1964 Act is extended to apply to a head of State, his family and his private servants.[15]

One final issue which may arise is whether the party in question is a foreign State for the purposes of the 1978 Act. This is an issue which arose in relation to sovereign immunity before this Act and the position is, in effect, unchanged. The status of a foreign sovereign is a matter of which the court takes judicial notice, that is to say it is a matter that the court is either assumed to know or to have the means of discovering without embarking upon a contentious inquiry.[16] Where it was doubtful whether a person enjoyed sufficient independence to entitle him to immunity, as, for instance, in the case of a ruler in Malaya[17] or in a case after the Indian Independence Act

---

8 See the exceptions to immunity in the 1978 Act, s 10.
9 Mann (1973) 36 MLR 18, 23–24.
10 1978 Act, ss 12, 13, 14(3)-(5); subject to transitional provisions in s 23(3), (4); see *Westminster City Council v Government of the Islamic Republic of Iran* [1986] 3 All ER 234, [1986] 1 WLR 979.
11 Ibid, s 13.
12 *Alcom Ltd v Republic of Colombia* [1984] AC 580, HL; Ghandi (1984) 47 MLR 597; Lloyd Jones [1984] CLJ 222. The onus is on the judgment creditor to show the commercial purpose.
13 1978 Act, s 15.
14 Infra, pp 271 et seq.
15 1978 Act s 20, discussed infra, pp 276 et seq.
16 *Mighell v Sultan of Johore* [1894] 1 QB 149 at 161.
17 Ibid.

1947 of a former ruler of an independent State in India,[18] the court applied to the Secretary of State for Foreign and Commonwealth Affairs whose answer was final and conclusive, and this rule is embodied in the 1978 Act.[19]

(ii) Ambassadors and other diplomatic officers[20]

It has long been recognised that the representatives in the United Kingdom of a foreign State are sent on the understanding that they shall have an immunity from the civil and criminal jurisdiction of the local courts which reflects that enjoyed by the sovereign whom they represent.[1] The Diplomatic Privileges Act 1708,[2] which was declaratory though not exhaustive of the common law,[3] provided in accordance with this principle that "all writs and processes" against a foreign ambassador or other public minister should be "utterly null and void".[4] At common law the immunity is shared by the members of the foreign envoy's family, if living with him; by his diplomatic family, as it is sometimes called, such as his counsellors, secretaries and clerks; and by his domestic staff, such as chauffeurs.

This principle of immunity is a feature of all systems of law, but since its application has been far from uniform, especially as regards the position of domestic servants, the law on the subject was ultimately codified in 1961 by the Vienna Convention on Diplomatic Intercourse and Immunities. Effect has been given to this convention by the Diplomatic Privileges Act 1964,[5] which, in respect of the matters dealt with therein, replaces any previous enactment or rule of law. It applies not only to diplomatic representatives of foreign countries but also to the diplomatic representatives of Commonwealth countries and the Republic of Ireland and their staffs.[6] Furthermore the Act is retrospective in operation and applies to actions begun before the date it came into force.[7]

The persons entitled to privileges The persons entitled to immunity are allocated to three categories, and the particular privileges allowed them vary according to the category to which they belong. Any doubt as to whether a person is entitled to a privilege is conclusively settled by a certificate given by the Secretary of State.[8] No immunity is conferred until the representative

---

18 *Sayce v Ameer Ruler Sadig Mohammad Abbasi Bahawalpur State* [1952] 2 QB 390, [1952] 2 All ER 64.
19 S 21(a). See *Trawnik v Lennox* [1985] 2 All ER 368, [1985] 1 WLR 532.
20 For a discussion of the historical development, see Young (1964) 40 BYBIL`141.
1 *The Parlement Belge* (1880) 5 PD 197 at 207.
2 See Blackstone's Commentaries, i, 255.
3 *The Amazone* [1940] P 40, [1940] 1 All ER 269.
4 S 3.
5 S 1. See Samuels (1964) 27 MLR 689; Buckley (1965–66) 41 BYBIL 321; and see Hardy, *Modern Diplomatic Law*, pp 52–68; Denza, *Diplomatic Law*, pp 135 et seq; Brown (1988) 37 ICLQ 53. The Act has been amended in minor respects by the Diplomatic and other Privileges Act 1971, and the Diplomatic and Consular Premises Act 1987; and see the State Immunity Act 1978, ss 16(1), 20.
6 Diplomatic Privileges Act 1964, s 8(4), Sch 2, repealing the Diplomatic Immunities (Commonwealth Countries and Republic of Ireland) Act 1952, s 1(1), and thereby limiting the immunity in the case of the staff of Commonwealth High Commissions, eg *Empson v Smith* [1966] 1 QB 426, [1965] 2 All ER 881.
7 *Empson v Smith*, supra.
8 Diplomatic Privileges Act 1964, s 4. See, eg *R v Governor of Pentonville Prison, ex p Teja* [1971] 2 QB 274; *R v Governor of Pentonville Prison, ex p Osman (No 2)* (1988) The Times Dec 24.

of the foreign State has been accepted or received in this country.[9] The three categories are as follows:

(i) *Diplomatic agents* These comprise the head of the mission and the members of his diplomatic staff,[10] as for instance, the secretaries, counsellors and attachés. Arms control inspectors and observers are now included in the definition.[11]

Such a person is exempt from the civil[12] and criminal jurisdiction of the English courts[13] in respect both of his official and private acts, and, though he himself may institute proceedings,[14] no remedy is enforceable against him in the United Kingdom at the instance of either a private citizen or the State. Thus no action will lie against a High Commissioner for unfair dismissal.[15] But this immunity does not import immunity from legal liability.[16] Thus, if he commits a tort against which he has insured himself he can claim to be indemnified by the insurer. If a diplomatic agent is a citizen of the United Kingdom and Colonies[17] or if he is permanently resident in the United Kingdom, his immunity from the civil jurisdiction is limited to official acts performed in the exercise of his functions.[18]

By way of exception to the exemption from civil jurisdiction there are three types of action that lie against a diplomatic agent, namely:

(a) a real action relating to private immovable property in England, unless it is held on behalf of the sending State for the purposes of the mission[19]—it has been decided that a diplomatic agent's private residence was not held for the purposes of the mission;[20]
(b) an action relating to succession in which the diplomatic agent is involved as executor, administrator, heir or legatee in his capacity as a private person;
(c) an action relating to any professional or commercial activity pursued by him in the United Kingdom outside his official functions.[21]

This last exception reverses the previous law, under which a person of diplomatic rank was not liable to be sued in respect of his commercial or private transactions.[22]

9 *R v Governor of Pentonville Prison, ex p Teja,* supra; *R v Lambeth Justices, ex p Yusufu* [1985] Crim L R 510; *R v Governor of Pentonville Prison, ex p Osman (No 2),* supra. However, the position appears to be different in immigration cases: *R v Secretary of State for the Home Department, ex p Bagga* [1990] 3 WLR 1013, at 1021–1023, 1031–1032.
10 Diplomatic Privileges Act 1964, Sch 1, Art 1(a)-(e).
11 Arms Control and Disarmament (Privileges and Immunities) Act 1988. For the position of foreign personnel assisting after a nuclear accident see the Atomic Energy Act 1989, Sch.
12 Including a divorce petition: *Shaw v Shaw* [1979] Fam 62.
13 1964 Act, Sch 1, Art 31(1). Furthermore, the private residence of a diplomatic agent is inviolable, as are the premises of the mission. On diplomatic and consular premises see generally the Diplomatic and Consular Premises Act 1987.
14 *Baron Penedo v Johnson* (1873) 29 LT 452.
15 *Omerri v Uganda High Commission* (1973) 8 ITR 14.
16 *Dickinson v Del Solar* [1930]1 KB 376 at 380.
17 See British Nationality Act 1981, s 61 (3) (a).
18 Diplomatic Privileges Act 1964, s 2(6); Sch 1, Art 38(1). This limited immunity may, however, be extended by Order in Council.
19 See State Immunity Act 1978, s 16(1)(b).
20 *Intpro Properties (UK) Ltd v Sauvel* [1983] QB 1019, [1983] 1 All ER 658. Even if the premises are held for professional purposes, for the immunity to apply there must be proceedings concerning a State's title to or its possession of property.
21 Diplomatic Privileges Act 1964, Sch 1, Art 31(1).
22 *Taylor v Best* (1854) 14 CB 487.

No writ of execution may be issued against a diplomatic agent, except where judgment has been given against him in an action relating to immovable property, to succession or to any private commercial transaction, and even then no measure may be taken that will infringe the inviolability of his person or residence.[1]

The general rule is that a diplomatic agent is exempt from all dues and taxes, personal or real, national, regional or municipal.[2]

The above privileges granted to a diplomatic agent are also possessed by the members of his family forming part of his household, provided that they are of alien nationality.[3]

(ii) *Members of the administrative and technical staff*[4] This category includes such persons as clerks, typists, archivists and radio or telephone operators. Such members of the staff, together with the members of their families, provided that they are neither citizens of the United Kingdom and Colonies nor permanently resident in the United Kingdom, are immune from the civil jurisdiction, but only in respect of acts done within the scope of their duties. They are also on the same footing as diplomatic agents with regard to the exemption from taxes and other dues.[5]

(iii) *Members of the service staff* Members of the service staff, who are defined by the convention as "members of the staff of the mission in the domestic staff of the mission",[6] include such persons as butlers, cooks, maids and chauffeurs. These enjoy no privileges if they are either citizens of the United Kingdom and Colonies or if they are permanently resident in the United Kingdom. Otherwise, they enjoy immunity from the civil jurisdiction of the courts, but only in respect of acts performed in the course of their duties; and they are exempt from income tax on the emoluments paid to them by the sending State and from liability to pay contributions under social security legislation.[7]

Cessation of immunities and privileges The immunities and privileges enjoyed by any person normally cease at the moment when he leaves the United Kingdom[8] or on the expiry of a reasonable time within which to do so, provided that his functions have come to an end. Nevertheless, his immunity continues to endure in respect of acts already done by him in the exercise of his official duties.[9] On the other hand his immunity in respect of acts already done in his private capacity no longer avails him.[10] However, diplomatic immunity which comes into existence after an action has been started will necessitate a stay of those proceedings until such time as the immunity may cease to be enjoyed.[11]

Waiver of privileges It was recognised at common law that a diplomatic

1 Diplomatic Privileges Act 1964, Sch 1, Art 31(3).
2 Ibid, Sch 1, Arts 33, 34, 36.
3 Ibid, Sch 1, Art 37(1); see also *Re C (An Infant)* [1959] Ch 363; Wilson (1965) 14 ICLQ 1265; O'Keefe (1976) 25 ICLQ 329.
4 Diplomatic Privileges Act 1964, Sch 1, Art 1; eg *Empson v Smith* [1966] 1 QB 426, [1965] 2 All ER 881. See also Arms Control and Disarmament (Privileges and Immunities) Act 1988.
5 Diplomatic Privileges Act 1964, Sch 1, Art 37(2).
6 Ibid, Sch 1, Art 1(g).
7 Ibid, s 2(4); Sch 1, Arts 33, 37.
8 *Shaw v Shaw* [1979] Fam 62; see also *Re Regina and Palacios* (1984) 45 OR (2d) 269.
9 Diplomatic Privileges Act 1964, Sch 1, Art 39(2).
10 *Zoernsch v Waldock* [1964] 2 All ER 256 at 265, 266, [1964] 1 WLR 675 at 692.
11 *Ghosh v D'Rozario* [1963] 1 QB 106, [1962] 2 All ER 640.

agent or other member of the diplomatic staff might waive his immunity from the civil and criminal jurisdiction of the local courts, either by expressly consenting through his solicitor to the proceedings, or by entering an appearance to the writ or by commencing proceedings as plaintiff. Since, however, the privilege is the privilege of the sending State, not of the individual diplomat, it was essential that consent to its waiver should have been given by the sending State in the case of proceedings against the head of the mission, and by the head of the mission where the proceedings were against a subordinate member of the staff. It followed that, even if a subordinate member had waived the privilege, he might later obtain a stay of proceedings by showing that he had not acted with the consent of his superior.[12]

These rules have been little affected by the Act of 1964. In the first place, the authority of the sending State to waive the privilege is retained;[13] and it is enacted that a waiver by the head of the mission shall be deemed to be a waiver by that State.[14] The words of this last provision are wide enough to embrace the case where the head of the mission waives his own privilege, not merely that of a subordinate member of the staff.[15] It is enacted that a waiver must always be express.[16] It is possible to waive personal immunity, but at the same time to maintain immunity in respect of a diplomatic document.[17]

Where, under the former law, a person entitled to immunity waived his privilege and commenced an action as plaintiff, it was doubtful whether it was permissible for the defendant to plead a counterclaim. The Act now settles this doubt by providing that:

> the initiation of proceedings by ... a person enjoying immunity from jurisdiction ... shall preclude him from invoking immunity from jurisdiction in respect of any counterclaim directly connected with the principal claim.[18]

The rule at common law that a judgment given against a foreign diplomat cannot be executed, notwithstanding that he has waived his immunity from the jurisdiction,[19] has been confirmed. There can be no enforcement of a judgment unless there has been a separate waiver of the immunity from execution.[20] Failing a separate waiver, the judgment remains unenforceable until the defendant has ceased to be a member of the foreign mission.

Restriction of privileges and immunities　It sometimes happens that the privileges granted to a British mission in a particular foreign State are less than those enjoyed by the mission of that State in the United Kingdom. In that event, an Order in Council may be made withdrawing the statutory immunities and privileges to such extent or in respect of such persons as appears to Her Majesty to be proper.[21] Furthermore, reciprocal arrangements for wider immunities than those contained in the 1964 Act may be continued.[22]

12　*R v Madan* [1961] 2 QB 1, [1961] 1 All ER 588, and authorities there cited.
13　Diplomatic Privileges Act 1964, Sch 1, Art 32(1).
14　Ibid, s 2(3).
15　For the difficulties involved in such a waiver see *Fayed v Al-Tajir* [1988] QB 712 at 733, 737. KERR LJ appears to doubt whether the head of the mission can waive his own privilege (at 737), whereas MUSTILL LJ appears to accept this (at 733).
16　Diplomatic Privileges Act 1964, Sch 1, Art 32(2). See *A Company Ltd v Republic of X* [1990] 2 Lloyd's Rep 520, which held that the waiver must be given to the court itself; Mann (1991) 107 LQR 362.
17　*Fayed v Al-Tajir*, supra.
18　Diplomatic Privileges Act 1964, Sch 1, Art 32(3).
19　*Re Suarez, Suarez v Suarez* [1918] 1 Ch 176.
20　Diplomatic Privileges Act 1964, Sch 1, Art 32(4).
21　Diplomatic Privileges Act 1964, s 3(1); re-enacting the Diplomatic Immunities Restriction Act 1955.
22　Ibid, s 7(1).

International organisations[23] It is clear then, that immunity from jurisdiction is enjoyed by the diplomatic representatives of foreign States who reside in the United Kingdom during the performance of their duties. The International Organisations Act 1968[1] provides that certain privileges may be conferred on persons who are present for a limited time in the United Kingdom as the representatives of some organisation of which the United Kingdom and one or more Sovereign Powers are members.[2] What organisations are eligible and what particular immunities they are to enjoy must be specified by Order in Council.[3] Examples of organisations that have been specified are the United Nations, the Commission of the European Communities, the Council of Europe,[4] the International Labour Organisation, the World Health Organisation and the International Court of Justice.

The maximum immunities that may be granted to an organisation or to a representative thereof vary with each case. Thus, high officers and members of committees and missions may be put on the same footing as heads of diplomatic missions with regard to immunity from suit and legal process, inviolability of residence, exemption from taxes and privileges as to the importation of certain articles, and there is the like inviolability of official premises as is accorded in respect of the premises of a diplomatic agent;[5] but the maximum privileges of other officers and representatives are limited to immunity from suit and legal process in respect of things done in the course of their employment, to exemption from income tax on their official salaries, to exemption from certain other customs duties and taxes and to privileges as to the importation of certain articles.[6]

Special provision is made in the International Organisations Act 1968 for conferring diplomatic exemptions and privileges on officers of specialised agencies of the United Nations,[7] and also on other organisations, including international commodity organisations, of which the United Kingdom is not a member,[8] on persons involved in international judicial proceedings[9] and on representatives at international conferences in the United Kingdom.[10] There is a power under the Diplomatic Immunities Act 1961 similar to that under the International Organisations Act 1968 to confer immunities on the representatives of certain Commonwealth countries and of the Republic of

---

23 In certain circumstances, an international organisation may sue in England, see *Arab Monetary Fund v Hashim (No 3)* [1991] 2 AC 114, [1990] 2 All ER 769, HL; Mann (1991) 107 LQR 357.

1 As amended by the Diplomatic and other Privileges Act 1971; the European Communities Act 1972, s 4(1), Sch 3, Part IV; and the International Organisations Act 1981.

2 Replacing the International Organisations (Immunities and Privileges) Act 1950, as amended by the Diplomatic Privileges Act 1964. The 1968 Act has been extended to Commonwealth organisations, see International Organisations Act 1981, s 1.

3 International Organisations Act 1968, s 1. Orders in Council made under the 1950 Act are to continue to have effect: s 12(5), (6).

4 Of which the European Commission of Human Rights is an organ: *Zoernsch v Waldock* [1964] 2 All ER 256. For immunities for UK representatives to the Consultative Assembly of the Council of Europe, see s 4 of the International Organisations Act 1981.

5 International Organisations Act 1968, Sch I, Pt II; as amended by s 5 of the International Organisations Act 1981.

6 The 1968 Act, Sch I, Pt III; as amended by International Organisations Act 1981, s 5.

7 The 1968 Act, s 2.

8 International Organisations Act 1968, s 4; and s 4A, added by s 2 of the International Organisations Act 1981.

9 The 1968 Act, s 5.

10 International Organisations Act 1968, s 6; see also s 5A added by s 3 of the International Organisations Act 1981.

Ireland who attend conferences in the United Kingdom.[11] A list of such representatives is published in the *Gazette*. If included therein, a representative is entitled to the immunities possessed by an envoy of a foreign sovereign State, while the members of his official staff are in the same position as the retinue of a foreign envoy. A member of the retinue, however, who is a citizen of the United Kingdom and Colonies, and not a citizen of the Commonwealth country concerned, has a limited privilege. He is entitled to immunity only "in respect of things done or omitted to be done in the course of the performance of his duties".[12]

Immunity of foreign sovereigns In placing the whole question of sovereign immunity on a statutory basis, the State Immunity Act 1978[13] has limited the immunity formerly enjoyed by a foreign sovereign or head of State. In so far as the immunities conferred by the Diplomatic Privileges Act 1964 are wider than those under the 1978 Act, it has been thought desirable to apply the appropriate immunities of the 1964 Act to a sovereign or other head of State, the members of his family forming part of his household and his private servants;[14] though without the qualifications in the 1964 Act relating to residence or nationality.[15]

Consular immunities The regulation of consular immunity, so far as foreign consuls and their staffs are concerned,[16] is governed by the Consular Relations Act 1968,[17] giving effect to the Vienna Convention on Consular Relations 1963. Consular officers[18] are not liable to arrest, save in the case of a grave crime,[19] and are only subject to restrictions on personal freedom in execution of judicial decisions of final effect.[20] In the case of civil proceedings, consular officers and employees are not amenable to the jurisdiction of the courts of this country in respect of acts performed in the exercise of consular functions except, in the case of a contractual action, where such officer or employee does not contract expressly or impliedly as an agent of his sending State, and in the case of an action by a third party for damage arising from an accident in the United Kingdom caused by a vessel, vehicle or aircraft.[1] There is power for these various exemptions to be waived by the sending State.[2]

There are provisions dealing also with exemption from social security provisions, taxation, customs and estate duties.[3] Special provision is made for the fact that the varied privileges and immunities shall not be accorded to consular employees and the families of members of a consular post who

11 Diplomatic Immunities (Conferences with Commonwealth Countries and the Republic of Ireland) Act 1961, s 1(1). See Thornberry (1962) 25 MLR 73.
12 Ibid, s 1(4).
13 Supra, pp 265 et seq.
14 State Immunity Act 1978, s 20.
15 Ibid, s 20(2).
16 The position of consular officers from the Commonwealth and the Republic of Ireland is governed by the Diplomatic Immunities (Commonwealth Countries and Republic of Ireland) Act 1952, s 1(2), until such time as an Order in Council applies to them the provisions of the Consular Relations Act 1968 by reason of s 12 of that Act, as amended by the Diplomatic and other Privileges Act 1971.
17 See Woodliffe (1969) 32 MLR 59; and see the State Immunity Act 1978, s 16(1).
18 Defined in Sch I, Art 1.
19 Defined in s 1(2).
20 Sch I, Art 41.
1 Sch I, Art 43. See Lee, *Vienna Convention on Consular Relations*, pp 143–146.
2 Sch I, Art 45.
3 Sch I, Art 48–51.

carry on private gainful occupations in the United Kingdom.[4] Again, as with the Diplomatic Privileges Act 1964, there is provision for those cases where there is already agreement for additional or reduced privileges[5] and for the withdrawal of privileges.[6]

(iii) The Brussels and Lugano Conventions

It is unclear to what extent these rules on sovereign and diplomatic immunity are affected by the Brussels and Lugano Conventions. One initial point that can be made is that these Conventions only apply in relation to civil and commercial matters. If the action concerns the commercial transactions of a foreign State or diplomat this would appear to relate to a civil and commercial matter. However, it is questionable whether an action involving the governmental acts of a foreign State or the official acts of a diplomat (ie the situation where immunity is granted) will come within this concept. As will be seen later, actions involving a public authority acting in the exercise of its powers have been held to fall outside the scope of the Brussels Convention.[7] If the Conventions were to apply in cases involving the governmental acts of a foreign State or official acts of a diplomat, the question would arise of whether the limitations on jurisdiction outlined above would also apply. The problem is an acute one. Much of the law on sovereign and diplomatic immunity stems from international conventions. There could be a clash between obligations arising under these conventions and the obligations that arise under the Brussels and Lugano Conventions. It has been argued[8] that the Civil Jurisdiction and Judgments Act 1982 is drafted on the basis that the limitations in respect of sovereign and diplomatic immunity will still apply.[9] However, it would perhaps be best if the problem were to be side-stepped altogether by interpreting the concept of civil and commercial matters in such a way as to exclude actions involving the governmental acts of foreign states and the official acts of diplomats from the scope of the Brussels and Lugano Conventions.

4. STATUTORY LIMITATIONS ON JURISDICTION

There are a number of statutes, all of which implement international conventions, which preclude the jurisdiction of the English courts over actions in rem and in personam in particular situations.[10] The situations may be defined either by reference to ministerial decision or by the statutes and conventions themselves. The first case may be illustrated by the Supreme Court Act 1981, section 23 of which provides that no court in England shall have jurisdiction to entertain any claim certified by the Secretary of State to be such as falls to be determined under the Rhine Navigation Convention.[11]

---

4 Sch I, Art 57.
5 S 3.
6 S 2.
7 Infra, pp 286–288.
8 Anton, *Civil Jurisdiction in Scotland*, para 3.04.
9 See s 31 of the 1982 Act which deals with judgments against States other than the UK. This section applies to judgments given in, inter alia, Contracting States to the Brussels and Lugano Conventions yet its wording presupposes the continued existence of rules on state immunity.
10 These conventions are not affected by the Brussels and Lugano Conventions; see Art 57 of the Brussels and Lugano Conventions, infra, p 286.
11 See Jackson, *Enforcement of Maritime Claims* (1985), pp 126–127.

Similarly, the jurisdiction of any court in the United Kingdom is excluded under the Nuclear Installations Act 1965 in the case of any claim certified by the Minister to be one which, under any relevant international agreement, falls to be determined by some other United Kingdom or foreign court.[12]

Other statutes, mainly those implementing international transport conventions, stipulate that actions may be brought only under the jurisdictional rules stated in the conventions. For example, the Carriage by Air Act 1961 requires that in the case of international carriage[13] any action for damages must be brought in the territory of one of the High Contracting Parties to the convention,[14] either before the court at the place of destination or before the court having jurisdiction where the carrier ordinarily resides or has his principal place of business or has an establishment by which the contract has been made.[15] Similar jurisdictional rules are prescribed under the Carriage by Air (Supplementary Provisions) Act 1962,[16] the Carriage of Goods by Road Act 1965,[17] the Carriage of Passengers by Road Act 1974,[18] and the International Transport Conventions Act 1983.[19]

---

12 S 17(1).
13 Sch 1, Art 1(2).
14 The Warsaw Convention 1929, as amended at the Hague in 1955.
15 Carriage by Air Act 1961, Sch 1, Art 28(1).
16 Sch, Art VIII.
17 Sch, Art 31(1).
18 Sch, Art 21(1). Other statutes containing specific jurisdictional rules based upon or by reference to international conventions are the Merchant Shipping (Oil Pollution) Act 1971, s 13(2), as substituted the Merchant Shipping Act 1988, s 34, Sch 4, pt I, para 10, the Merchant Shipping Act 1979, s 14 and the Supreme Court Act 1981, ss 20–22.
19 S 1 and Appendix A of the Convention concerning International Carriage by Rail, Cmnd 8535 (1982) which is given the force of law by the 1983 Act.

Chapter 14

Jurisdiction under the Brussels and Lugano Conventions

SUMMARY

1. THE BRUSSELS CONVENTION[1]

The six original members of the European Economic Community entered into a Convention on Jurisdiction and the Enforcement of Judgments in Civil and Commercial Matters in 1968 (the Brussels Convention), which came into force in 1973, and into a Protocol on Interpretation in 1971, which came into force in 1975.[2] The purpose of the Convention is to provide for the free circulation of judgments throughout the Community, thereby inspiring busi-

---

1 This chapter has been written on the assumption that the 1989 Spanish and Portuguese Accession Convention, amending the Brussels Convention, has come into force in all European Community States.
2 Both the original Convention and the Protocol are to be found in OJ 1978, L 304, pp 77 and 97. For commentaries see Hartley, *Civil Jurisdiction and Judgments* (1984); Collins, *The Civil Jurisdiction and Judgments Act 1982* (1983); Anton, *Civil Jurisdiction in Scotland* (1984); Dashwood, Hacon and White, *A Guide to the Civil Jurisdiction and Judgments Convention* (1987); Kaye, *Civil Jurisdiction and Enforcement of Foreign Judgments* (1987); Lasok and Stone, *Conflict of Laws in the European Community* (1987), chs 5–7; O' Malley and Layton, *European Civil Practice* (1989); Droz, *Competence judiciaire et effets des judgements dans le Marché Commun* (1972).

ness confidence and generally encouraging the right conditions for trade. To achieve this aim there had to be harmonisation of the law on jurisdiction throughout the Community.[3] The three members of the Community which joined in 1973, including the United Kingdom, after lengthy negotiations, signed in 1978 a Convention of Accession[4] to the 1968 Convention and the 1971 Protocol. It also contained amendments to both of these.[5] The 1978 Convention of Accession came into force in the original six Member States and in Denmark on 1 November 1986. The legislation required to bring these Conventions (ie the 1968 Convention, the 1971 Protocol and the 1978 Convention of Accession) into effect in the United Kingdom[6] is contained in the Civil Jurisdiction and Judgments Act 1982, the relevant provisions of which came into force on 1 January 1987. Section 2(1) of the 1982 Act gives these Conventions the force of law in the United Kingdom, and Schedules at the end of the Act set out English texts of these Conventions. Since then Ireland has ratified the Conventions. More significantly, there has been the Greek Accession Convention of 1982[7] and the Spanish and Portuguese Accession Convention of 1989 (the San Sebastian Convention).[8] The former only made formal changes; the latter made a significant number of changes of substance. The result of all this is that the law is now contained in the 1968 Brussels Convention and 1971 Protocol as amended[9] by the 1978, 1982 and 1989 Accession Conventions. Before coming onto the substantive law relating to the jurisdiction of the courts under the Brussels Convention three preliminary matters must be mentioned, each of which is affected by provisions in the 1982 Act: the interpretation of the Brussels Convention; the allocation of jurisdiction within the United Kingdom; the special definition of domicil.

(a) INTERPRETATION

(i) **Referrals to the Court of Justice**

The Brussels Convention is not drafted with the precision of a statute. A number of key concepts were deliberately left undefined in the Convention, and the Court of Justice of the European Communities has been left to fill

---

3 See the Preamble to the Convention; the Jenard Report, OJ 1979 C 59, pp 3–8; infra, pp 411–413.
4 OJ 1978, L 304/1.
5 See, generally, the Schlosser Report, OJ 1979, C 59.
6 For the position in Scotland and the special rules on jurisdiction there, see Sch 8 of the 1982 Act (in 1991 the Scottish Courts Administration proposed amendments to this in the light of the 1989 Accession Convention), the Maxwell Report, the Report of the Scottish Committee on Jurisdiction and Enforcement (Lord Maxwell, Chairman, Edinburgh 1980), and Anton, *Civil Jurisdiction in Scotland* ch 10.
7 OJ 1982 L 388/1; see the Evrigenis and Kerameus Report OJ, 1986 C 298/1.
8 OJ 1989 L 285/1; see the accompanying Almeida Cruz, Desantes Real, Jenard Report OJ, 1990 C 189/06. This only applies as between those States which have ratified it (ie Spain, the Netherlands, France, the United Kingdom, Italy, Luxembourg); it is hoped that this process of ratification will have been completed by the end of 1992. The 1989 Accession Convention came into effect in the United Kingdom as from the first of December 1991.
9 All references to the "Convention" (or "Brussels Convention") and "1971 Protocol" are to the amended version. This is set out in SI 1990/2591, Sch 1. This Order also amends the 1982 Act. The 1982 Act has been further amended by the Civil Jurisdiction and Judgments Act 1991, which implements the Lugano Convention, infra pp 340–344. All references to the 1982 Act are to this amended version. For transitional provisions see Art 54 of Sch 1 and Schs 3 and 4 of SI 1990/2591.

in the gaps. The 1971 Protocol authorises this Court to give a ruling on the interpretation of the Brussels Convention (ie the 1968 Brussels Convention, the 1971 Protocol and the three Accession Conventions), on the matter being referred to them by a national court. The Protocol contains two limitations on when a national court can request such a ruling.[10] First, a court can only request a preliminary ruling "if it considers that a decision on the question is necessary to enable it to give judgment".[11] There is nothing to stop English courts from deciding that the meaning of the Convention is clear and that a reference to the Court of Justice is not necessary. However, within a short time of the original Convention (as amended by the 1978 Accession Convention) coming into force the Court of Appeal accepted in two cases[12] that the meaning of the Convention was not clear and made a reference to the Court of Justice.[13] The second limitation is in respect of the courts which can request a ruling from the Court of Justice. In jurisdiction cases, as opposed to those on recognition and enforcement of foreign judgments, the House of Lords must request preliminary rulings, any court when sitting in an appellate capacity[14] may so request, and judges at first instance can never so request.

(ii) The principles and decisions laid down by the Court of Justice

Section 3(1) of the 1982 Act provides that, where the meaning of the Brussels Convention is not referred to the Court of Justice, it must be determined "in accordance with the principles laid down by and any relevant decisions ... [of that court]". There is a substantial body of case law on the Brussels Convention, from references by the original six Contracting States to the Court of Justice, and more recently from references from other Contracting States. The English courts are bound by these decisions and are required to take judicial notice of them.[15] There may be no decision by the Court of Justice on the precise point at issue, but this does not mean that other decisions on the Convention by that Court can be ignored. English courts have to act in accordance with the principles laid down by the Court of Justice in any relevant decision. This means:
(i) English courts must follow the techniques of interpretation which the Court of Justice employs, according to which the meaning of a provision should be ascertained in the light of its purpose rather than by taking its literal meaning.[16]

10 Arts 2 and 3. See Kohler (1982) 7 ELR 3, 4–7. For referrals in cases of recognition and enforcement, see Arts 37 and 41 of the Convention, s 6 of the 1982 Act and infra, p 418.
11 The procedure for references from English courts is contained in RSC Ord 114.
12 *Overseas Union Insurance Ltd v New Hampshire Insurance Ltd* [1992] 1 Lloyd's Rep 218; *Marc Rich & Co AG v Societa Italiana Impianti PA (The Atlantic Emperor)* [1989] 1 Lloyd's Rep 548, CA.
13 These appear as Case C- 351/89 [1992] 2 WLR 586, infra p 327; Case C- 190/89 (1991) Times, 20 September, infra, p 289.
14 See Case 80/83 *Habourdin v Italocremona* [1983] ECR 3639.
15 S 3(1) and (2) of the 1982 Act. Modifications to the 1982 Act and to other laws may become necessary in the light of decisions on interpretation of the Convention by the Court of Justice. There is a power to make these modifications by Order in Council under s 47(1)(a) of the 1982 Act.
16 See generally on interpretation by the Court of Justice: Marsh, *Interpretation in a National and International Context* (1973), pp 82–90; Brown and Jacobs, *The Court of Justice of the European Community* (1977) Ch 12; Bredimas, *Methods of Interpretation and Community Law* (1977); Court of Justice, Judicial and Academic Conference of 27–28 September 1976, papers by Kutscher and Dumon; Rasmussen, *On Law and Policy in the European Court of Justice* (1986).

(ii) English courts must follow the general principles of interpretation in relation to the Convention laid down by the Court of Justice.

The first of these general principles relates to the determination of whose system of law is to be applied in order to define the words and concepts in the Convention. Should it be the community system or that of a particular national system? In the former case a community meaning is found; in the latter, there is a reference to national law. Where a community meaning is given the Court of Justice will define the concept, giving it an independent meaning; it then has a common meaning throughout the Contracting States. A reference to national law means that the Court of Justice is not, in any real sense, defining the concept. It is saying that the concept means what the court first seised of the matter regards it as meaning under its national law. With some concepts, for example, a "civil and commercial matter", under Article 1, if reference was made to national law this would be referring to domestic law; with others, for example, in a contractual matter the place of performance of the obligation in question, under Article 5(1), could be said to be referring to private international law.[17] Many of the concepts in the Convention have different meanings under the separate national laws of the Contracting States and reference to national law inevitably leads to a lack of uniformity in interpretation. The objectives of the Convention require that it should be given a uniform application throughout the Community; accordingly the Court of Justice has generally given its provisions a community meaning.[18] Each provision is looked at separately. The scope of the Convention and of particular provisions has consistently been given a community meaning. As regards other issues, reference to national law has only been made in exceptional cases where, because of the nature of the concept involved, it is thought to be impossible to arrive at a definition without so doing.[19]

The second general principle relates to the method of deciding upon what the community meaning should be. The Court of Justice when defining concepts has considered two factors. First, it looks at the objectives and scheme of the Convention.[20] According to its preamble, the ultimate objective of the Convention is to simplify the formalities on recognition and enforcement of judgments within the community. There is a subsidiary objective of determining the international jurisdiction of courts in the Community, that is, with allocating jurisdiction to the courts of particular Contracting States. The Court of Justice will also look at the objectives of the provision in question (reference to the Reports[21] accompanying the Convention may be helpful in this), and will decide how it relates to other provisions in the Convention.[1] Second, with some concepts the Court of Justice has referred

---

17 See Case 12/76 *Tessili v Dunlop* [1976] ECR 1473, [1977] 1 CMLR 26; discussed infra, p 296.
18 See generally Giardina (1978) 27 ICLQ 263; Kohler (1982) 7 ELR 3 and 103; Layton (1992) Civil Justice Quarterly 28. National courts, however, do not always give a community meaning to undefined or even defined concepts, see Kohler (1985) 34 ICLQ 563.
19 See the opinion of the Advocate General in Case 150/77 *Bertrand v Ott* [1978] ECR 1431, [1978] 3 CMLR 499, and the cases on Art 5(1) infra, pp 294–297. See also Case 129/83 *Zelger v Salinitri (No 2)* [1984] ECR 2397, [1985] 3 CMLR 366, on Art 21.
20 Case 29/76 *Lufttransportunternehmen GmbH v Organisation Européenne pour la Securité de la Navigation Aérienne (Eurocontrol)* [1976] ECR 1541, [1977] 1 CMLR 88.
21 Infra.
1 Case 33/78 *Somafer v Saar-Ferngas* [1978] ECR 2183, [1979] 1 CMLR 490.

to "the general principles which stem from the corpus of the national legal systems".[2] A community meaning does not ignore national laws and reference to bilateral treaties between Contracting States which pre-date the Convention may help in ascertaining shared principles. Now that common law countries are parties to the Convention, the common core will prove much harder to identify. Indeed, with some concepts it may be impossible to identify one at all.

(iii) English courts must follow the more specific principles where the Court of Justice has identified the purpose underlying a particular provision and has laid down policy considerations to be taken into account, in particular, whether a particular provision is to be narrowly or widely interpreted.[3]

(iii) Aids to interpretation

English courts are required to act as if they were the Court of Justice; although it is questionable whether they are equipped to do so. One specific aspect of this question is dealt with in the 1982 Act. The Court of Justice has not infrequently referred to the Jenard Report in order to ascertain the meaning of provisions in the Convention. This Report is a commentary which accompanied the draft Convention and was the work of the rapporteur of the committee of experts which drew up the draft Convention. English law traditionally only allows reference to explanatory reports when interpreting international Conventions after certain conditions have been satisfied, and even then with some reluctance.[4] Section 3(3) of the 1982 Act allows the Jenard Report[5] and the separate Reports accompanying each of the three Accession Conventions,[6] to be considered by English courts, without any conditions being attached to this. Another aspect, not dealt with in the 1982 Act, is the authority to be attached to the decisions of the courts of other Contracting States in relation to the Convention. Whatever the normal attitude is towards the decisions of Continental judges, in this context their decisions ought to be of persuasive authority.[7] Finally, English courts should always be prepared to consider the texts of the Conventions in other languages.[8]

(b) ALLOCATING JURISDICTION WITHIN THE UNITED KINGDOM

The Convention assigns jurisdiction to the courts of Contracting States.[9] The United Kingdom is the Contracting State to the Convention; this raises the particular problem of whether the courts of England, Scotland or Northern Ireland are to have jurisdiction. With some of the provisions in the Con-

---

2 *LTU v Eurocontrol*, op cit.
3 See Collins, pp 14–16; Anton, *Civil Jurisdiction in Scotland* 2.28–2.32; Kohler (1982) 7 ELR 3, and 103; also, generally, infra, pp 286 et seq.
4 See *Fothergill v Monarch Airlines Ltd* [1981] AC 251, [1980] 2 All ER 696; also Bennion, *Statutory Interpretation* (1984), p 538.
5 OJ 1979, C 59.
6 The Schlosser Report OJ 1979, C 59; the Evrigenis and Kerameus Report OJ 1986, C 298/1; the Almeida Cruz, Desantes Real, Jenard Report, OJ 1990, C 189/06.
7 These can be found in Digest of Case Law Relating to the European Communities, D Series. See also Kohler (1985) 35 ICLQ 563.
8 See Art 68; Case 150/80 *Elefanten Schuh GmbH v Jacqmain* [1981] ECR 1671, [1982] 3 CMLR 1; *Newtherapeutics Ltd v Katz* [1991] Ch 226 at 243–245.
9 These are all the Member States of the European Community.

vention it is possible to identify a part or place in the United Kingdom which is to have jurisdiction.[10] It is not possible to do so where, for example, jurisdiction is allocated to the United Kingdom on the basis that the defendant is domiciled within the United Kingdom under Article 2 of the Convention. Section 16 of the 1982 Act solves this problem by introducing a modified version of the Convention,[11] which allocates jurisdiction within the United Kingdom. The Modified Convention is examined in detail towards the end of this chapter. Suffice it to say at this point that it goes further than was strictly necessary by dealing with internal United Kingdom cases (for example, a Scotsman sues in England an English domiciled man in respect of land in England), and not merely with situations where the United Kingdom has been assigned jurisdiction under the Convention (for example, a Frenchman, having been injured in France, sues an English domiciled man in England).

(c)　A SPECIAL DEFINITION OF DOMICIL

Extensive use is made of the concept of domicil for the purpose of deciding when the Convention applies, and, where it does, of allocating jurisdiction[12] to particular Contracting States. However, despite the importance of this concept, it is not defined in the Convention. This raises a serious problem since the meaning of the concept differs from one Contracting State to another.

Article 52 of the Convention deals with the question of which country's definition of domicil is to be used. The first paragraph states that the courts of the Contracting State seised of the matter shall apply their own definition of domicil to determine whether a person is domiciled in that Contracting State. According to the second paragraph,[13] in order to determine whether a person is domiciled in another Contracting State, a court must apply the law of that State; for example, if the United Kingdom courts, having decided (after using their own definition) that a person is not domiciled in the United Kingdom, want to know whether the defendant is domiciled in France they must apply the French definition of domicil.[14]

The effect of these provisions is that the English courts are, initially at least, going to apply their own definition of domicil. What English law usually means by domicil is far removed from what civil law means.[15] The harmonisation of the law on jurisdiction would have been seriously undermined if the traditional English concept of domicil had been used in this context. The 1982 Act therefore contains special provisions on the meaning of domicil for the purposes of the Convention and the 1982 Act. The simplest

---

10 Eg under Art 5. See the Schlosser Report, p 98, and infra, pp 294–306.
11 Set out in the 4th Schedule of the 1982 Act (see infra, pp 334–340). S 39 of the 1982 Act allows for Modified Conventions to be entered into in relation to certain specified territories, closely linked to the United Kingdom, eg the Channel Islands. The United Kingdom can extend the Brussels Convention to non-European territories for whose international relations it is responsible, eg Hong Kong.
12 Infra, pp 290–294. The Modified Convention does likewise, infra, pp 334–339.
13 There was originally a third paragraph dealing with dependent domicils; this was deleted by Art 15 of the 1989 Accession Convention.
14 See O' Malley and Layton, p 1251 and chs 48–55 at para 25 (for the definition of domicil in other European Community States).
15 See the Schlosser Report, pp 95–97.

solution, which would have been to equate an individual's habitual residence with his domicil,[16] was not possible because of the separate reference in the Convention to habitual residence.[17] Section 41 of the 1982 Act adopts a complicated solution, with different rules for each of the contexts under the Convention and Modified Convention in which a person's domicil has to be ascertained. Thus, the rules[18] state when a person is domiciled: (i) in the United Kingdom, (ii) in a particular part of the United Kingdom, (iii) in a particular place in the United Kingdom and (iv) in a state other than a Contracting State. For most of these purposes[19] domicil is equated with the state where (a) a person is resident and (b) the nature and circumstances of his residence indicate that he has a substantial connection with it. Showing a substantial connection is made easier by the use of a presumption (based on residence), which is available under some of these rules, but not others.[20]

As regards companies, the seat of a company or association is treated as its domicil.[21] To determine the seat, each court will apply its own definition,[22] which could mean the courts of several Contracting States deciding that the same company has its seat in their State. The concept of the seat of a company is well known in civil law systems,[1] but has no equivalent under English law, which tends to refer to the place of incorporation of a company. Section 42 of the 1982 Act determines what the seat of a corporation or association is for the purpose of most of the provisions in the Convention.[2] Following the pattern of section 41 there are sub-sections in section 42 defining when a corporation has its seat: (i) in the United Kingdom, (ii) in a particular part of the United Kingdom, (iii) in a particular place in the United Kingdom, and (iv) in a state other than the United Kingdom.[3] There is a basic rule that the seat is where (a) a corporation has its registered office or some other official address; or (b) its central management and control is exercised. In ascertaining where a company has its central management and control it is relevant to look at where the directors are resident, hold meetings and decide major policy issues.[4] Further alternatives are available when the seat is being ascertained in some of the above contexts, but not in others.[5]

There are special rules on domicil for insurance and consumer cases, trusts and for ascertaining the domicil and seat of the Crown.[6]

---

16 See Morris, p 80. In Ireland domicil is, however, equated with ordinary residence: Sch 5, Part I of the Jurisdiction of Courts and Enforcement of Judgments (European Communities) Act 1988.
17 See Art 5(2).
18 See s 41(2) to (7), infra, pp 290–293, 334–339. See generally Kaye (1988) 35 NILR 181.
19 But not when domicil in a particular place in the UK is being ascertained, see s 41(4).
20 The presumption is contained in s 41(6). It can be used for the purposes of s 41(2) and (3), but not s 41(4) and (7). All of the rules of domicil will be examined more fully later on in the context in which they operate, see infra, pp 290–293, 334–339.
21 Art 53 and s 42(1) of the 1982 Act.
22 Art 53, see the Schlosser Report, p 97.
1 See Weser (1961) 10 AJCL 323, 329–330.
2 S 43 defines the seat for the purposes of exclusive jurisdiction under Art 16(2).
3 S 42(3)-(6).
4 See *The Rewia* [1991] 1 Lloyd's Rep 69 at 74; this point was not disputed in the appeal which overruled the decision on other grounds [1991] 2 Lloyd's Rep 325, CA.
5 See infra, pp 290–293, 334–339. When ascertaining whether a corporation has its seat in a Contracting State other than the UK under s 42(6), there is an additional requirement under s 42(7).
6 See ss 44–46.

(d) WHEN DOES THE BRUSSELS CONVENTION APPLY?

(i) The matter must be within the scope of the Convention

None of its provisions, whether on jurisdiction or on recognition and enforcement of judgments, will apply unless the matter is within the scope of the Convention.

Article 1 is designed to deal with the scope of the Convention. But before looking at this two other provisions in the Convention must be mentioned. First, the preamble indicates that the Convention is only concerned with the international jurisdiction of Contracting States. It follows that it will not apply where a dispute involves no foreign element or where the foreign element only involves another part of the United Kingdom.[7] Second, this European Community Convention does not affect certain other conventions on jurisdiction or recognition and enforcement which Contracting States have in the past, or will in the future, enter into, or statutes implementing them.[8] Admiralty jurisdiction in England is an example of one area which is left largely untouched.[9]

(a) Civil and commercial matters Article 1 declares that "This Convention shall apply in civil and commercial matters whatever the nature of the court or tribunal."

No definition is given of "civil and commercial matters",[10] although Article 1 goes on to say that it does not include "revenue, customs or administrative matters".[11] These words were added to make it clear that public law matters are excluded. The difficulty for English lawyers is that in domestic law the distinction between private and public law is not sharply drawn.[12] In civil law jurisdictions there is a clear distinction between the two, although the same criteria are not always applied when drawing the distinction. Some guidance on this definitional problem is given by the Court of Justice in the leading case of *LTU v Eurocontrol*[13] where it was held that a community meaning had to be given to "civil and commercial matters", with the result that the Convention did not apply to the situation where a public authority

---

7 See the Jenard Report, p 8; Anton, *Civil Jurisdiction in Scotland*, paras 1.16–1.18; the Schlosser Report, p 123; Collins, p 17; Hartley, p 41.

8 Art 57 of the Convention, as substituted by the 1989 Accession Convention, and s 9(1) of the 1982 Act; *The Po* [1991] 2 Lloyd's Rep 206; *The Deichland* [1990] 1 QB 361. Art 55 lists bilateral conventions which are in fact superseded by this Convention. For the effect of these provisions on recognition and enforcement of foreign judgments in England see infra, pp 415–416.

9 See supra, pp 217–219, for the effect of the Brussels Convention on admiralty jurisdiction. The provisions in the Convention affecting this are Arts 5(7) and 6A; see the Schlosser Report, pp 108–111, 139–142. In cases where the Convention does apply, Art 2 will operate in relation to an action in rem: *The Deichland* [1990] 1 QB 361.

10 See the Jenard Report, p 9; the opinion of the Advocate General in Case 29/76 *LTU v Eurocontrol* [1976] ECR 1541, [1977] 1 CMLR 88.

11 See the Schlosser Report, p 82. See also *Re State of Norway's Application* [1987] QB 433 at 473–474, affd in *In re Norway's Application (Nos 1 & 2)* [1990] 1 AC 723, HL (a case on the Evidence (Proceedings in Other Jurisdictions) Act 1975, in which the Brussels Convention is discussed, although ultimately the House of Lords regarded it as being of no assistance in interpretation of the 1975 Act, op cit, at 803).

12 See the Advocate General's opinion in *LTU v Eurocontrol*, op cit; the Schlosser Report, p 82; *Re State of Norway's Application*, op cit. See also Philip (1978) II Hague Recueil 1 at pp 63–72.

13 Op cit; see Hartley (1977) 2 ELR 61. The decision is criticised by Giardina (1978) 27 ICLQ 263, 272–274; and by Fletcher, *Conflict of Laws and European Community Law* (1982), p 112.

was acting in the exercise of its powers. The public authority was an international organisation concerned with air safety; it was acting in the exercise of its powers when it sought to collect charges from an airline for the use of its services, the use of the services being obligatory and the rate of charge being fixed unilaterally.

The difficulty with requiring the public authority to be acting in the exercise of its powers, before the matter can be excluded from the Convention, is that it is often hard to tell whether a public authority is acting in a private capacity or in the exercise of its powers.[14] In *Netherlands State v Rüffer*[15] the Court of Justice held that a public authority, in this case the Dutch State, was acting in the exercise of its powers in respect of a public waterway when it sought to recover from a German shipowner the costs of removing a wreck, even though under Dutch law (the Dutch courts being seised of the matter) the action was classified as one in tort. The case was concerned with a community concept and it would therefore be inappropriate to allow Dutch law to classify it according to domestic criteria. The action arose from international treaty obligations and would be regarded by many Contracting States as an administrative one, the common core of the national legal systems being an important consideration when giving a community meaning to this concept.

Article 1 states that the Convention shall apply whatever the nature of the court or tribunal. It follows that the decision of a criminal court is within the Convention provided that it relates to a civil or commercial matter.[16] An example would be where a criminal court awards compensation to an individual injured in a road accident by a careless driver. Similarly, the Convention would also apply to cases brought before tribunals provided that they do not relate to administrative matters.

Width is given to the scope of the Convention by the inclusion of "civil" matters. This covers a number of areas which might otherwise be excluded, for example, certain torts, labour law matters including disputes over contracts of employment,[17] and fines imposed by courts or tribunals provided they are for the benefit of a private plaintiff.[18]

It also includes maintenance, which causes particular problems under the Convention. There is a special basis of jurisdiction under Article 5(2) dealing with maintenance, from which it can be inferred that it comes within the scope of the Convention. Maintenance is another one of the important concepts which is not defined in the Convention.[19] It is clear that it can include lump sum as well as periodical payments.[20] It does not matter that the payments are ancillary to divorce proceedings, and are to be made after the divorce (even though divorce, as a matter of status, is outside the scope of the Convention).[21] The object of maintenance was discussed by the Court

---

14 See the Schlosser Report, pp 83–84.
15 Case 814/79 [1980] ECR 3807, [1981] 3 CMLR 293. For criticism see Hartley, pp 11–15 and (1981) 6 ELR 215. See also *LTU v Eurocontrol*, op cit.
16 See eg Case 157/80 *Rinkau* [1981] ECR 1391, [1983] 1 CMLR 205; Hartley (1981) 6 ELR 483; also Art II of the Protocol attached to the 1968 Convention.
17 See the Jenard Report, pp 9, 24; the Schlosser Report, p 82; the opinion of the Advocate General in *Netherlands v Rüffer* supra; Case 25/79 *Sanicentral GmbH v Collin* [1979] ECR 3423, [1980] 2 CMLR 164 (on which see Collins, p 8).
18 See the Schlosser Report, p 84.
19 See generally the Schlosser Report, pp 101–105.
20 See the Schlosser Report, p 102.
21 However, a foreign maintenance order may be irreconcilable with an English divorce, see *Macaulay v Macaulay* [1991] 1 All ER 865, [1991] 1 WLR 179, infra, pp 717–718.

of Justice in the second *De Cavel* case,[22] where it was held that interim compensatory payments payable on a monthly basis by one spouse to another as part of a French judgment dissolving a marriage were in the nature of maintenance, a crucial point being that they were designed to support that spouse and were based on need. This meant that the case fell within the terms of the Convention. The application of these criteria to the financial orders that can be made by English courts is dealt with later on in the book, where maintenance is considered in detail.[1]

(b) Exclusions Article 1 sets out a number of matters which are excluded from the scope of the Convention, even though they are civil and commercial matters. It is intended that these matters should only be excluded where they are the principal object of the proceedings.[2]

(i) "the status or legal capacity of natural persons, rights in property arising out of a matrimonial relationship, wills and succession"
For English lawyers there are no real problems in understanding what is meant by status[3] or wills and succession. The same cannot be said in respect of the concept of rights in property arising out of a matrimonial relationship. No guidance is given in the Convention as to the meaning of this term. According to the Schlosser Report it is designed to exclude the matrimonial regime used in civil law countries whereby special rules on separation or community of property are established in respect of family assets.[4] The Court of Justice in the first *De Cavel*[5] case held that rights in property arising out of a matrimonial relationship covered not only matrimonial regimes but also any proprietary relationship resulting directly from the marital relationship or its dissolution. It meant the exclusion of protective measures (freezing of assets) relating to the property of the spouses pending divorce proceedings before a French court. The Court of Justice has also held that an action in respect of the husband's management of his wife's property must be considered to be closely connected with the proprietary relationship of the parties flowing from the marriage and was therefore excluded.[6]

There are great difficulties in applying these principles in a common law context. There is no English equivalent of the Continental matrimonial regime. In English law, a dispute concerning matrimonial property may simply be concerned with general property law principles, and the Convention will apply, for example, where there is a dispute between a wife and a mortgagee bank in respect of a matrimonial home mortgaged by the

---

22 Case 120/79 *De Cavel v De Cavel* [1980] ECR 731, [1980] 3 CMLR 1. It does not matter whether it is an interim or final order, see the first *De Cavel* case, Case 143/78 [1979] ECR 1055, [1979] CMLR 547; Hartley (1979) 4 ELR 222. The wording of Art 5(2) was altered by the 1978 Accession Convention expressly to include payments ancillary to divorce proceedings, see the Schlosser Report, pp 84–87.
1 Infra, pp 704–708.
2 See the Jenard Report, p 10. When it comes to recognition and enforcement where an excluded matter has arisen incidentally, see Art 27(4), and infra, p 432.
3 See the Schlosser Report, p 89.
4 At p 87. See also Collins, pp 25–26; Hartley, pp 17–19.
5 Op cit.
6 Case 25/81 *CHW v GJH* [1982] ECR 1189, [1983] 2 CMLR 125. The case involved an application for the delivery up of a document to prevent its use in the main action, and is an example of what is referred to under the Convention as a provisional measure, see Art 24, discussed infra, pp 330–331.

husband.[7] Where a spouse is ordered to make a lump sum payment as part of divorce proceedings the position is less clear. A narrow view would be that marriage gives no property rights, the whole question of financial provision on divorce, being, under English law, one of discretion. A wide view would be that de facto the rights of a spouse in relation to matrimonial property are greater than those of a cohabitant[8] and are therefore rights arising out of a matrimonial relationship. From the point of view of achieving, as far as possible, a uniform application of the Convention throughout the Community, this wide view is the better one. This would exclude from the Convention lump sum payments as part of divorce proceedings, unless they are in the nature of maintenance.[9]

(ii) "bankruptcy, proceedings relating to the winding up of insolvent companies or other legal persons, judicial arrangements, compositions and analagous proceedings"

It is intended that only proceedings arising directly from, and closely connected with, the bankruptcy should be excluded from the Convention.[10] In *Gourdain v Nadler*[11] the Court of Justice held that a French provision, under which a manager of a company in liquidation could be ordered to pay money to form part of the assets of the company, came within the bankruptcy exclusion, the legal foundation of this action being the French law of bankruptcy and it being very closely connected with the winding up proceedings.

(iii) "Social Security"[12]

(iv) "Arbitration"[13]

Arbitration awards cannot be enforced under the Convention.[14] However, the exclusion goes wider than this. In *Marc Rich & Co v Societa Italiana Impianti PA*[15] the Court of Justice held that arbitration is excluded in its entirety, including proceedings brought before the English courts concerning the appointment of an arbitrator. Whether a dispute is excluded from the scope of the Convention is determined by reference solely to the subject matter of the dispute.[16] The fact that, during the course of the dispute, there has to be determined a preliminary issue, whatever that issue may be, cannot affect the exclusion. It followed that the litigation concerning the appointment of an arbitrator was excluded, even though the existence or validity of the arbitration agreement was raised as a preliminary issue in that litigation.[17]

---

7 See *Williams and Glyn's Bank Ltd v Boland* [1981] AC 487, [1980] 2 All ER 408.
8 See *Burns v Burns* [1984] Ch 317, [1984] 1 All ER 244.
9 For maintenance under the Convention, see supra, pp 287–288, infra, pp 299–300.
10 See the Jenard Report, pp 11–12; the Schlosser Report, pp 89–92. See generally Fletcher, *Conflict of Laws and European Community Law* (1982), ch 6.
11 Case 133/78 [1979] ECR 733, [1979] 3 CMLR 180; Hartley (1979) 4 ELR 482.
12 See the Schlosser Report, p 92.
13 Ibid. See Young, *International Commercial and Maritime Arbitration* (ed Rose) pp 77 et seq.
14 See *Allied Vision Ltd v VPS Film Entertainment GmbH* [1991] 1 Lloyd's Rep 392 at 399. They are covered by other conventions, infra, pp 445–453.
15 Case C-190/89 (1991) Times, 20 September; Hartley (1991) 16 ELR 529. The Court of Appeal's decision referring the matter to the Court of Justice is reported at [1989] 1 Lloyd's Rep 548. See also *Union Transport PLC v Continental Lines SA* [1992] 1 WLR 15 at 17–18.
16 For the problem of recognition and enforcement of foreign judgments where a court has taken jurisdiction despite an arbitration clause, see infra, pp 435–436.
17 The latter issue is itself outside the scope of the Convention. But even if it were not, it is clear that the result would have been the same.

(ii) Whether the defendant is domiciled in a Contracting State

It is necessary to distinguish between: (a) bases of jurisdiction (Title II, Sections 1–6); (b) other provisions on jurisdiction in Title II; (c) provisions on recognition and enforcement in Title III. It is only in the first of these, the bases of jurisdiction under the Convention, that an initial basic distinction is drawn between the situation where the defendant is and is not domiciled in a Contracting State.[18] Section 1 of Title II gives one exception where this basic distinction does not operate and, if the wording of individual bases of jurisdiction is studied, at least one more exception emerges. The position can be summarised as follows:

(a) Where the defendant is domiciled in a Contracting State the bases of jurisdiction under the Convention will apply and not the traditional rules of jurisdiction of the forum.

(b) Where the defendant is not domiciled in a Contracting State, in general, the traditional rules of jurisdiction of the forum will apply.

(c) There are exceptions to (b), ie some of the bases of jurisdiction under the Convention (Articles 16 and 17) will apply to defendants, even though they are not domiciled in a Contracting State.

Each of these will be looked at in more detail.

(a) Where the defendant is domiciled in a Contracting State Article 2 in Section 1 contains the most important basis of jurisdiction under the Convention, that a defendant domiciled in a Contracting State is subject to the jurisdiction of the courts of that State. If the defendant is to be sued in the courts of a Contracting State other than that of his domicil, Article 3 provides that this can only be done by virtue of the bases of jurisdiction set out in Sections 2 to 6. This prevents national courts from using their traditional rules on jurisdiction, including their exorbitant rules, against a defendant who is domiciled in a Contracting State. In the United Kingdom's case it is specifically provided in Article 3 that, against such a defendant, jurisdiction can no longer be founded on presence of the defendant in the forum. It is also implicit from Article 3 that service out of the jurisdiction under RSC Order 11 cannot be used.[19] Article 3 does not refer to the domicil of the *plaintiff*. It follows that, for example, a Japanese domiciliary, although not domiciled in a Contracting State, would have to use the bases of jurisdiction under the Convention if he wished to sue in a Contracting State a defendant who was so domiciled.

Articles 2 and 3 require courts to decide whether a defendant is domiciled in a Contracting State. Section 41 of the 1982 Act contains a provision for determining when an individual is domiciled in the United Kingdom.[20] He is so domiciled, if and only if: (a) he is resident in the United Kingdom; and (b) the nature and circumstances of his residence indicate that he has a substantial connection with the United Kingdom. The latter requirement shall be presumed to be fulfilled, unless the contrary is proved, if the individual has been resident in the United Kingdom, or part thereof, for the last three months or more.[21] If the individual is not domiciled in the United Kingdom

---

18 For the position under the Convention as regards other provisions on jurisdiction, see infra pp 325–331; for recognition and enforcement, see infra, p 413.
19 See the Schlosser Report, p 100. RSC Ord 11 is discussed supra, pp 190–210.
20 S 41(2). The Modified Convention will also apply if he is.
21 S 41(6).

it then has to be seen whether he is domiciled in another Contracting State. Section 41 has no provisions for determining this. This is consistent with Article 52 of the Convention, which, it will be recalled,[22] provides that, in order to determine whether a party is domiciled in another Contracting State, the courts shall apply the law of that state.

As regards companies, section 42(3) determines when a corporation has a seat in the United Kingdom. It has, if and only if: (a) it was incorporated in the United Kingdom and has its registered office, or some other official address there; or (b) its central management and control is exercised in the United Kingdom. Section 42(6) determines whether a corporation has its seat in a state other than the United Kingdom; this could be in a Contracting or a non-Contracting State. It uses the same criteria as in section 42(3). The fact that section 42(6) applies for determining whether a corporation has its seat in a Contracting State is consistent with Article 53, which requires Contracting States to apply their own concept of a seat, even when deciding whether a company has its seat in another Contracting State. The danger with this approach is that, to take an example, England may regard the company as having its seat in Italy, whereas Italy, applying its different concept of a seat, may regard it as having its seat in England. Section 42(7) accordingly provides that a corporation shall not be regarded as having its seat in a Contracting State other than the United Kingdom if it is shown that the courts of that state would not regard it as having its seat there. Where this provision applies it is not clear whether the corporation automatically has its seat in the United Kingdom, or, as seems more likely, it does not have a seat anywhere as far as English law is concerned.[1] Under section 42 a company may be domiciled in more than one State. For example, it may be incorporated and have its registered office in Panama but its central management and control in Germany. In such a case the company undoubtedly has a domicil in a Contracting State. The bases of jurisdiction contained in the Brussels Convention will apply and the company cannot be sued in a Contracting State under that State's traditional rules on jurisdiction.[2]

(b) The defendant is not domiciled in a Contracting State Where the defendant is not domiciled in a Contracting State, Article 4 states that the jurisdiction of the courts of each Contracting State shall, subject to the provisions of Article 16, be determined by the law of that State. If, to take an example, an Englishman wishes to sue a Californian domiciliary in England, he would have to do so under the traditional English rules on jurisdiction, which are, by and large, more generous to the plaintiff than their equivalent under the Convention. Article 4 therefore recognises the use of exorbitant jurisdiction by Contracting States in certain circumstances. This has far reaching consequences when it comes to enforcing judgments and declining jurisdiction in cases of *lis pendens*.[3]

Article 4 requires the courts of Contracting States to ascertain when a defendant is not domiciled in a Contracting State. Having decided that an individual defendant is not domiciled in the United Kingdom (under the

---

22 See supra, p 284.

1 This is assuming that s 42(3) does not give the corporation a seat in the United Kingdom, which must be the case, otherwise there would be no need to look at s 42(6) and (7).

2 *The Deichland* [1990] 1QB 361, [1989] 2 All ER 1066, CA; *The Rewia* [1991] 2 Lloyd's Rep 325, CA.

3 See the Jenard Report, pp 20–21, and infra, pp 326–330, 413.

United Kingdom definition), and is not domiciled in another Contracting State (under that State's definition), the defendant must be domiciled in a non-Contracting State. A person must have a domicil in one state or another for the purposes of the Convention and the 1982 Act. In the rare situations where the particular non-Contracting State in which the defendant is domiciled has to be ascertained,[4] this is done by applying section 41(7) of the 1982 Act, which provides that an individual is domiciled in a state other than a Contracting State if and only if (a) he is resident in that state; and (b) the nature and circumstances of the residence indicate that he has a substantial connection with that state.[5] In this particular context there is no presumption to aid in showing the required substantial connection, and it is possible, in rare cases, that an individual may not have a substantial connection with any one state at all. Where this happens one would have to be resigned to saying that the individual is domiciled in a non-Contracting State but it is not clear in which particular one.[6] As regards corporate defendants, section 42(6) will be applied to determine whether a company has its seat in a non-Contracting State.[7]

(c) The exceptions Article 4 mentions just one exception to the rule that national bases of jurisdiction apply where the defendant is not domiciled in a Contracting State; it is contained in Article 16.[8] This gives exclusive jurisdiction in certain circumstances, regardless of the defendant's domicil. Although Article 4 does not mention it, there is another exception to the rule; this is Article 17 (agreements on jurisdiction).[9] This article is drafted in such a way that the defendant is not required to be domiciled in a Contracting State. Other possible exceptions under Article 18 (submission), Article 12 (an agreement in a matter relating to insurance) and Article 15 (an agreement in a consumer contract) are discussed later.[10]

(e) BASES OF JURISDICTION

The first six Sections of Title II set out the bases of jurisdiction under the Convention, with each Section containing one or more bases of jurisdiction. The division into Sections emphasises that different types of jurisdiction are being dealt with. The Convention provides for: (i) general jurisdiction (Section 1), (ii) special jurisdiction (Section 2), (iii) jurisdiction in matters relating to insurance (Section 3), (iv) jurisdiction over consumer contracts (Section 4), (v) exclusive jurisdiction (Section 5), and (vi) prorogation of jurisdiction (Section 6).

In some situations the plaintiff will have to sue the defendant in the courts of the Contracting State which has been allocated exclusive jurisdiction under the Convention. In other situations the courts of more than one Contracting State will have jurisdiction and the plaintiff will be able to choose the

---

4 It may be necessary to ascertain the particular non-Contracting State because of Art 59, discussed infra, pp 441–442.
5 Is state here referring to the political unit, eg the United States, or to a law district, eg New York? When s 41(7) refers to a Contracting State this means a political unit; it is arguable that "a state other than a Contracting State" likewise means a political unit. On the other hand, under s 41 England is applying its own jurisdictional rules and the normal meaning of a state in English private international law is that of a law district.
6 See footnote 4, supra.
7 S 42(7), discussed supra, will not apply.
8 Infra, pp 309–313.
9 See infra, pp 314–322.
10 See Collins, p 51; O'Malley and Layton p 385; infra, pp 306–309, 322.

Contracting State in which to sue the defendant. With the harmonisation of rules on jurisdiction in the different Contracting States, lawyers in the United Kingdom can now advise clients on whether they can sue or be sued not only in the United Kingdom but also in other Contracting States. This task is made easier by the absence from the Convention of provisions giving a discretion to refuse to take jurisdiction.[11]

(i) General jurisdiction

Article 2 provides that "persons domiciled in a Contracting State shall, whatever their nationality, be sued in the courts of that State".

The Convention adopts the principle that, in general, persons should be sued in the courts of the Contracting State where they are domiciled.[12] The words "shall ... be sued" must not be taken literally. Other bases of jurisdiction make it clear that the defendant may, and, in some circumstances, must, be sued in the courts of a Contracting State other than that of his domicil.[13] Mere physical presence in a Contracting State is not enough; the defendant must be domiciled there.

In order to ascertain whether the defendant is domiciled in a Contracting State under Article 2, reference must be made to sections 41 and 42 of the 1982 Act and Article 52 of the Convention, which have already been discussed.[14] Where the Contracting State in which the defendant is domiciled is the United Kingdom the Modified Convention will apply to allocate jurisdiction between the courts of England, Scotland, and Northern Ireland.[15]

(ii) Special jurisdiction

In some cases trial is permitted in the courts of a Contracting State other than the one in which the defendant is domiciled; this is known as special jurisdiction and the relevant provisions are found in Section 2 of the Convention. This form of jurisdiction is justified on the basis that a court of a Contracting State is only given jurisdiction under Section 2 where it is an appropriate forum for trial.[16] It is left to the plaintiff to decide whether he wishes to sue the defendant in the latter's domicil under Article 2, or whether he wishes to sue him in another Contracting State under Section 2. Where the Contracting State given special jurisdiction is the United Kingdom the plaintiff will want to know whether he is to sue in England, Scotland, Northern Ireland or has the choice of suing in any of these. The Modified Convention will not apply[17] to allocate jurisdiction within the United Kingdom. It has no need to. The provisions on special jurisdiction are

---

11 Art 21 deals with the specific problem of *lis pendens* but there is no discretion involved under this provision, see infra, pp 326–330. However, in certain circumstances the English courts can use their traditional doctrine of *forum non conveniens*, infra, pp 331–334.
12 See the Jenard Report, pp 13 and 18–19. See also *SA Consortium General Textiles v Sun and Sand Agencies Ltd* [1978] QB 279 at 295, [1978] 2 All ER 339 at 351; *Citadel Insurance Co v Atlantic Union Insurance Co SA* [1982] 2 Lloyd's Rep 543 at 549.
13 Where Art 21 (*lis pendens*) applies it requires the courts of Contracting States, including the defendant's domicil, to decline jurisdiction.
14 Supra, pp 284–285.
15 Infra, pp 334–340.
16 See the Jenard Report, p 22; Case 12/76 *Tessili v Dunlop* [1976] ECR 1473, [1977] 1 CMLR 26; Case 33/78 *Etablissements Somafer v Saar-Ferngas AG* [1978] ECR 2183, [1979] 1 CMLR 490; Case 34/82 *Peters v Zuid Nederlandse Aannemers Vereniging* [1983] ECR 987.
17 Infra, pp 335–336.

designed to give local as well as international jurisdiction[18] and can be regarded as giving jurisdiction to the courts of a part of the United Kingdom and not merely to the courts of the United Kingdom as a whole. Many of the provisions give jurisdiction to the courts of a place in a Contracting State, and the place in the United Kingdom would be in England, Scotland or Northern Ireland, as indicated by the particular provision. Other provisions give jurisdiction to the courts or a court of a Contracting State, but the context readily identifies which part of the United Kingdom is the appropriate one to have jurisdiction.

(a) Article 5 This is the most important of the three articles in Section 2. Article 5 provides that a person domiciled in a Contracting State may be sued in another Contracting State in seven specified situations. Before looking at these, it is important to realise that the use of the words "may be sued" is not intended to confer on courts a discretion to refuse to take jurisdiction.[19] Rather it emphasises that the plaintiff is allowed (but not required) to sue the defendant in a Contracting State other than where the defendant is domiciled. Nonetheless, the defendant's domicil is the normal place for trial. Article 5 is an exception to this general rule,[20] and the Court of Justice has accordingly interpreted some of its provisions narrowly.[21]

When the issue comes to trial in England the plaintiff has to show a seriously arguable case that the terms of Article 5 are satisfied.[22] The seven situations where the defendant can be sued in a Contracting State other than that of his domicil are as follows:

> **Article 5(1)** in matters relating to a contract, in the courts for the place of performance of the obligation in question; in matters relating to individual contracts of employment, this place is that where the employee habitually carries out his work, or if the employee does not habitually carry out his work in any one country, the employer may also be sued in the courts for the place where the business which engaged the employee was or is now situated.[23]

(i) Which is the obligation in question?
A multiplicity of obligations (which may have different places of performance) can arise in complex contractual cases, yet the Convention gives no indication as to which obligation is being referred to.

In *De Bloos v Bouyer*[1] the Court of Justice went some way towards a community definition for the obligation in question. It held that Article 5(1)

---

18 See the Schlosser Report, p 98; Hartley, p 40.
19 *Tesam Distribution Ltd v Shuh Mode Team GmbH* (1989) Times, 24 October, CA.
20 Case 56/79 *Zelger v Salinitri* [1980] ECR 89, [1980] 2 CMLR 635.
21 See the cases on Art 5(5) infra, pp 302–305.
22 *Tesam Distribution Ltd v Shuh Mode Team GmbH*, op cit, discussing Art 5(1) and (3). This is by way of analogy with Ord 11, r 1(1), supra p 191. See also *Medway Packaging Ltd v Meurer Maschinen GmbH & Co KG* [1990] 2 Lloyd's Rep 112, CA; *Shevill v Presse Alliance SA* [1992] 2 WLR 1, CA; *Mercury Publicity Ltd v Wolfgang Loerke GmbH* (1991) Times, 21 October, CA; *New England Reinsurance Corpn v Messoghios Insurance SA* [1992] 1 Lloyd's Rep 201.
23 Art 4 of the 1989 Accession Convention substituted a new Art 5(1). The major difference is in relation to individual contracts of employment, discussed infra, p 297–299. See generally, Stone [1983] Anglo-Am LR 52; the Jenard Report, pp 23–24, and the *Peters* case, op cit. For the use of this provision where the defendant is domiciled in Luxembourg, see Art I of the Protocol attached to the 1968 Convention. For a transitional provision applicable in contract cases see Art 54, para 3 of the Convention; *New Hampshire Insurance Co v Strabag Bau AG* [1990] 2 Lloyd's Rep 61; appeal dismissed (1991) Times, 26 November.
1 Case 14/76 [1976] ECR 1497, [1977] 1 CMLR 60. See Giardina (1978) 35 ICLQ 263, 269–271; Hartley (1977) 2 ELR 60.

is referring not to any obligation under the contract but to the contractual obligation forming the basis of the legal proceedings; the one which the contract imposes on the defendant, the non-performance of which is relied upon by the plaintiff. Thus an English court had jurisdiction in a case where German defendants broke their obligation to give reasonable notice of termination of an exclusive distribution agreement to an English company in England.[2] If the plaintiff is seeking compensation a decision then has to be made as to whether this claim involves an independent contractual obligation (and therefore within Article 5(1)), or whether it involves a new obligation replacing the unperformed contractual obligation (which would be outside Article 5(1)). There is no consensus amongst the legal systems of the different Contracting States as to which of these two is the source of the right to claim compensation. The national court where trial is sought is therefore left to decide this in the light of the law applicable to the contract under its private international law rules. If English law applies, an obligation to pay unliquidated damages cannot form the basis of jurisdiction under Article 5(1) since this obligation is remedial in character, not an independent contractual obligation.[3]

The difficulty with the *De Bloos* approach is that the plaintiff may make several claims involving different obligations to be performed in different states. This particular problem was solved by the Court of Justice in *Shenavai v Kreischer*.[4] The judge dealing with the case is to identify the principal obligation on which the plaintiff's action is based and jurisdiction is to be determined in accordance with this. Thus, if the defendant shipowners are in breach of obligations under a charterparty to, firstly, nominate a vessel (this obligation to be performed in London) and, secondly, provide a vessel for the carriage of cargo (this obligation to be performed in Florida) the first obligation is the principal one, since it is the performance of this obligation that triggers other obligations.[5] However, it may not always be possible to identify a principal obligation, in which case under Article 5(1) different obligations can end up being subject to the jurisdiction of different Contracting States.[6]

(ii) Where is the place of performance of the obligation in question?
The parties will usually have specified where this is to be under their agreement. This can be done in an informal way, without the formalities required for an agreement as to jurisdiction under Article 17,[7] even though the effect of such a contractual provision is to lead indirectly, by reason of Article 5(1), to a particular court having jurisdiction.[8] The only proviso is that the clause specifying the place of performance must be valid under the law applicable

2 *Medway Packaging Ltd v Meurer Maschinen GmbH & Co KG* [1990] 2 Lloyd's Rep 112, CA. See also *Waverley Asset Management Ltd v Saha* 1989 SLT (Sh Ct) 87.
3 *Medway Packaging Ltd v Meurer Maschinen GmbH & Co KG* [1990] 1 Lloyd's Rep 383 at 389, HOBHOUSE J at first instance. The Court of Appeal did not discuss this point.
4 Case 266/85 [1987] ECR 239; Allwood (1988) 13 ELR 60. See also *Gascoigne v Pyrah* (1991) Times, 26 November.
5 *Union Transport plc v Continental Lines SA* [1992] 1 All ER 161, [1992] 1 WLR 15, HL.
6 See the obiter dicta in the Court of Appeal in *Union Transport PLC v Continental Lines SA* [1991] 2 Lloyd's Rep 48 at 52; this decision was affirmed by the House of Lords, op cit.
7 Art 17 is discussed infra, pp 314–322.
8 Case 56/79 *Zelger v Salinitri* [1980] ECR 89, [1980] 2 CMLR 635; noted by Hartley (1981) 3 ELR 61. See also the decision of the German Federal Supreme Court in *Re The Recovery of Unpaid Customs Duty* [1985] ECC 331.

to the contract.[9] Where the parties have not specified the place of performance, this will be determined by the forum applying its rules of private international law. In *Tessili v Dunlop*[10] the Court of Justice held that the national court before which the matter is brought "must determine in accordance with its own rules of conflict of laws what is the law applicable to the legal relationship in question and define in accordance with that law the place of performance of the contractual obligation in question".[11] Thus in a Scots case[12] involving a Scots bank suing a German domiciled guarantor in Scotland in respect of letters of guarantee, which were silent on the matter, it was held that the place of performance was Scotland. Scots law governed the contract, and according to that law there was an implication that a debtor had to pay a creditor at the latter's place of business. *Tessili* was the first case on interpretation of the Convention decided by the Court of Justice. The refusal to adopt a community definition, and instead to refer the definition to a national court, is understandable in relation to this specific issue.[13] It is not an approach towards interpretation that has been followed by the Court of Justice when interpreting other bases of jurisdiction, nor has it been followed in relation to other issues under Article 5(1).

(iii) What are matters relating to a contract?

Normally there will be a consensus among Contracting States over whether a particular matter does or does not relate to a contract. The *Peters* case[14] arose out of one situation where there is no such consensus. It raised the question of whether an obligation to pay money arising from the relationship between an association and its members came within Article 5(1). Not all Contracting States regard this as a contractual relationship. Nonetheless, the Court of Justice held that this came within Article 5(1). The Court gave a community meaning to the concept of matters relating to a contract and said that it includes relationships which involve close links of the same kind as are created between parties to a contract. This was a somewhat unusual case on its facts. More illuminating is *SPRL Arcado v SA Haviland*,[15] which concerned two claims: one for the payment of commission under a commercial agency agreement; the other for damages for the wrongful premature repudiation of this agreement. The Court of Justice held that both claims came within the community concept of matters relating to a contract. The claim for commission was based on the agreement itself and thus undoubtedly a matter relating to a contract. The claim for damages for wrongful repudiation raised more of a problem, the defendants arguing that this was based on quasi-delict. However, the Court of Justice held that this claim was also a matter relating to a contract, being based on the failure to fulfil a contractual

9 See generally on the law applicable to the contract, infra, pp 457–521.
10 Case 12/76 [1976] ECR 1473, [1977] 1 CMLR 26. See Giardina, op cit, pp 271–272; Hartley (1977) 2 ELR 59.
11 [1976] ECR 1473 at 1485.
12 *Bank of Scotland v Seitz* 1990 SLT 584; cf *Royal Bank of Scotland PLC v Cassa Di Risparmio Delle Provincie Lombard* (1990) Financial Times, 11 December.
13 See Anton, *Civil Jurisdiction in Scotland*, para 5.23.
14 Case 34/82 [1983] ECR 987. See Hartley (1983) 8 ELR 262. See also *Bank of Scotland v Investment Management Regulatory Organisation Ltd* 1989 SLT 432; *Engdiv Ltd v G Percy Trentham Ltd* 1990 SLT 617.
15 Case 9/87 [1988] ECR 1539; Allwood (1988) 13 ELR 366; Briggs [1988] Yearbook of European Law 269; Stone [1988] Lloyd's MCLQ 383.

obligation to give reasonable notice of termination. The Court found confirmation of this from the fact that the Rome Convention on contract choice of law undoubtedly regards such a claim as being contractual in nature.[16]

(iv) Disputes relating to the existence of the agreement

In *Effer v Kantner*[17] the Court of Justice held that jurisdiction under Article 5(1) may be invoked by the plaintiff even where there is a dispute between the parties over the existence of the contract on which the claim is based. The purpose of Article 5(1) is to give jurisdiction to the Contracting State which is best qualified to determine the dispute. The courts of this Contracting State would be too easily deprived of jurisdiction if an allegation that no contract existed was sufficient to prevent the dispute falling within Article 5(1).[18] However, the court whose jurisdiction is invoked under Article 5(1) may, of its own motion, examine its jurisdiction,[19] including the question of the existence of the contract, and decide that it does not have jurisdiction. The power to decide on the existence of the contract is therefore left to the courts of the place of performance of the alleged obligation in question. When it comes to trial in England the plaintiff has to show a good arguable case that the contract exists, which may well involve going into the merits of the case.[20] In *Effer* the issue was as to the formation of a contract between the parties; the idea of "existence" of the contract appears to have a wide meaning and would presumably encompass disputes as to matters as fundamental as non est factum or duress.

(v) Matters relating to individual contracts of employment

The 1989 Accession Convention added a separate provision to Article 5(1) to deal with matters relating to individual contracts of employment.[1] In such cases the place of performance of the obligation in question is "that where the employee habitually carries out his work". The object of this provision is to ensure that the earlier decisions of the Court of Justice in *Ivenel v Schwab*[2] and *Schenavai v Kreischer*[3], which established this principle, are followed by incorporating them into the Convention.[4]

Two policy justifications can be given for this particular rule.[5] First, jurisdiction is allocated to the Contracting State whose law may well be applicable. The Rome Convention on contract choice of law has a special provision

---

16 Infra, p 516. A claim for restitution in respect of a void transaction is outside Art 5(1): *Kleinwort Benson Ltd v Glasgow City Council* (1992) Times, 17 March.
17 Case 38/81 [1982] ECR 825, [1984] 2 CMLR 667; see Hartley (1983) 8 ELR 235. See Art 16, Case 73/77 *Sanders v Van der Putte* [1977] ECR 2383, [1978] 1 CMLR 331.
18 *Quaere* whether the defendant can challenge the plaintiff's allegations as to the obligations under the contract; Hartley, *Civil Jurisdiction and Judgments* (1984) p 48 thinks not.
19 Where Art 20 applies the court will be under a duty to do so, see infra, pp 325–326.
20 *Tesam Distribution Ltd v Shuh Mode Team GmbH* (1989) Times, 24 October, CA; *Medway Packaging Ltd v Meurer Maschinen GmbH & Co KG* [1990] 2 Lloyd's Rep 112, CA. See also *Rank Film Distributors Ltd v Lanterna Editrice SRL* (1991) Financial Times, 14 June (a good arguable case as to the existence of the obligation).
1 See the Almeida Cruz, Desantes Real and Jenard Report, para 23. This adopted, with some modifications, a provision contained in the Lugano Convention 1988, on which see the Jenard and Möller Report OJ 1989 C189/57, pp 72–73. A preliminary draft of the original Brussels Convention had a special provision on contracts of employment, see the Jenard Report, p 24.
2 Case 133/81 [1982] ECR 1891, [1983] 1 CMLR 538; Hartley (1983) 8 ELR 328. The decision is criticised by McClellan and Kremlis (1983) 20 CMLR 529, 542, and by Stone, op cit.
3 Case 266/85 [1987] ECR 239, [1987] 3 CMLR 782.
4 The Almeida Cruz, Desantes Real and Jenard Report, para 23.
5 See the *Ivenel Case*, op cit.

dealing with individual employment contracts.[6] This provides that, in the absence of an express choice by the parties, the applicable law is the law of the country in which the employee habitually carries out his work in performance of the contract. Second, one of the themes shared by the Brussels Convention and the choice of law provisions in relation to contracts of employment is that the weaker party should be protected. Allowing the employee to sue where he works achieves this.

The separate provision in Article 5(1) dealing with contracts of employment, whilst intended to give effect to these two cases, probably extends the law. It is arguable that the *Ivenel Case* was confined to the situation where there were claims relating to different obligations to be performed in different states.[7] There is no such limitation under the separate provision; the courts for the place where the employee habitually carries out his work have jurisdiction, even if the claim involves a single obligation to be performed in one state.

Two major problems arise in relation to this new separate provision. First, what is an individual contract of employment?[8] This phrase is not defined under the Convention. However, it is clear that individual contracts of employment are to be contrasted with collective agreements between employers and workers' representatives.[9] Moreover, guidance can be found in *Shenavai v Kreischer*,[10] where the Court of Justice had to decide whether the case involved a contract of employment. If it did, the principle in the *Ivenel Case* would apply; if it did not, the principle in the *De Bloos Case* would apply. *Shenavai* involved a claim by an architect for fees in connection with the drawing up of plans for the building of houses. The Court of Justice held that this was not a contract of employment and therefore the principle in the *De Bloos Case* would apply. It was said[11] that contracts of employment had certain peculiarities, distinguishing them from other types of contract: they created a lasting bond bringing the worker to some extent within the organisational framework of the business of the employer; "they are linked to the place where the activities are pursued, which determines the application of mandatory rules and collective agreements". The relationship of the parties in a contract of employment has also been described as one of subordination of the employee to the employer.[12] The Court of Appeal has emphasised the personal nature of the relationship between employer and employee and the inequality of bargaining power inherent in this. It has held that a contract appointing an advertising agency as a sole commercial agent was not one of employment.[13]

The second problem is that an employee may habitually carry out his work in several countries. Article 5(1), as amended by the 1989 Accession Convention, goes on to provide that "if the employee does not habitually carry out his work in any one country, the employer may also be sued in the courts for the place where the business which engaged the employee was or

6 The Rome Convention on the Law Applicable to Contractual Obligations (1980), Art 6, discussed, infra pp 495–496.
7 See the opinion of the Advocate General in *Shenavai v Kreischer*, op cit, at 248.
8 See generally Allwood (1987) Yearbook of European Law 131 at 137 et seq.
9 See the Jenard and Möller Report, p 73.
10 Case 266/85 [1987] ECR 239, [1987] 3 CMLR 782.
11 At 255–256. See also Case 32/88 *Six Constructions Ltd v Humbert* [1989] ECR 341; Hartley (1989) 14 ELR 236.
12 The Jenard and Möller Report, p 73.
13 *Mercury Publicity Ltd v Wolfgang Loerke GmbH* (1991) Times, 21 October.

is now situated".[14] This has the virtue of ensuring that jurisdiction under Article 5(1) is not given to a multiplicity of different Contracting States.[15] Furthermore, the law of the country in which is situated the place of business through which the employee was engaged will normally be applied, at least in the absence of a choice of the applicable law by the parties.[16] There is no requirement that the countries in which the employee habitually carries out work are Contracting States. Obviously, though, the place where the business which engaged the employee was or is now situated, must be in a Contracting State. A place of business, in this context, is intended to be understood in a broad sense; "in particular, it covers any entity such as a branch or agency with no legal personality".[17] If the place of business which engaged the employee changes between the time of engagement of the employee and the time when proceedings are brought the employee can bring proceedings in either place.[18] The protective nature of this provision is shown by the fact that only the employee can invoke it; thus, whilst the employee can sue the employer in the courts for the place of business which engaged him, the employer cannot sue the employee there.[19]

Article 5(2) in matters relating to maintenance, in the courts for the place where the maintenance creditor is domiciled or habitually resident or, if the matter is ancillary to proceedings concerning the status of a person, in the court which, according to its own law, has jurisdiction to entertain those proceedings, unless that jurisdiction is based solely on the nationality of one of the parties.[20]

A maintenance creditor has the option to sue in his domicil or habitual residence under Article 5(2) or in the defendant's domicil (under Article 2). This is a rare case where the Convention uses the concept of habitual residence.[1] Domicil is defined under the 1982 Act[2] in a way that is so close to the English concept of habitual residence[3] that the use of habitual residence as an alternative to domicil under Article 5(2) is unlikely to widen the scope of that provision. Nonetheless, Article 5(2) is more obviously pro-plaintiff in its terms than any of the other forms of special jurisdiction in Article 5, and looks more akin to the measures designed to protect the weaker party (in this context the maintenance creditor, usually the wife) found under Sections 3 and 4 of the Convention.[4] At the same time the plaintiff's domicil is an appropriate forum for trial, since a court there is best able to gauge the claimant's needs.[5] The major definitional problem that has arisen so far has been over the meaning of "matters relating to maintenance". This concept

---

14 Cf the earlier decision of the Court of Justice in Case 32/88 *Six Constructions Ltd v Humbert* [1989] ECR 341.
15 The Jenard and Möller Report, p 73.
16 Art 6(2)(b) of the Rome Convention, infra pp 495–496.
17 The Jenard and Möller Report, p 73.
18 Cf the Lugano Convention, infra p 343.
19 Cf the Lugano Convention, infra p 343. This safeguard meets the concern expressed in *Six Constructions Ltd v Humbert* where objection was made to the use of an employer's place of business rule because of a fear that the employer might sue in that state.
20 Maintenance jurisdiction generally is discussed infra, pp 700 et seq.
 1 See generally, Hartley, p 49.
 2 See supra, pp 284–285.
 3 Discussed supra, pp 169–171.
 4 Infra, pp 306–309. For a criticism of the policy in relation to maintenance see Hartley, pp 49–50.
 5 See the Jenard Report, p 25.

has already been discussed in relation to the scope of the Convention.[6] One particular aspect of this which should be mentioned here is the problem posed by the practice of combining maintenance claims (which on their own are within the Convention) with main proceedings for divorce (which on their own are outside the scope of the Convention). The Court of Justice has held that these ancillary claims for maintenance are within the scope of the Convention,[7] and Article 5(2) was amended by the 1978 Accession Convention to give jurisdiction in respect of the maintenance claim to the court which has jurisdiction, according to its own law, to entertain the proceedings as to status.[8] To take an example of how this will affect the jurisdiction of the English courts to grant maintenance: there is jurisdiction to grant a divorce if either party to the marriage is domiciled in England or has been habitually resident here for a period of one year;[9] if one of these bases of jurisdiction is satisfied the English courts will not only be able to grant a divorce but will also be able to grant maintenance where there are maintenance proceedings which are ancillary to the divorce proceedings. Where a maintenance obligation arises from an agreement rather than from a court order, this comes within Article 5(1) rather than Article 5(2).[10]

Article 5(3) in matters relating to tort, delict or quasi-delict, in the courts for the place where the harmful event occurred

The wording of Article 5(3) presupposes that a tort or delict has been committed. As far as trial in England is concerned, the plaintiff has to show a good arguable case that this is so, which involves going into the merits of the case.[11] Article 5(3) would not appear to cover an action to prevent a threatened wrong.[12] This is a serious omission. It means that a plaintiff will have to go to the country where the defendant is domiciled in order to obtain an injunction rather than to the obvious and appropriate country, the one where he is under threat. What is meant by a tort or delict? In some situations, for example where a professional adviser is negligent towards his client, there is liability in tort under English law but there is no liability in delict in civil law systems.[13] There is an obvious danger of Article 5(3) being given a different scope in different Contracting States. The risk of this happening has been reduced by the Court of Justice in *Kalfelis v Schroder*,[14] which gave the concept of "matters relating to tort, delict or quasi-delict" a community definition.[15] The concept was extraordinarily widely defined to include any action which seeks to establish the liability of a defendant and which does

---

6 Supra, pp 287–288.
7 The second *De Cavel* case, Case 120/79 [1980] ECR 731, [1980] 3 CMLR 1.
8 See the Schlosser Report, p 80. This does not apply if the jurisdiction as to status is one based solely on the nationality of one of the parties. English courts do not take jurisdiction on this basis, see infra, pp 630–633.
9 The rules on jurisdiction to grant a decree of divorce, nullity or judicial separation are discussed infra, pp 630–634.
10 See the Schlosser Report, pp 101–102.
11 *Tesam Distribution Ltd v Shuh Mode Team GmbH* (1989) Times, 24 October. See also *Re A Consignment of Italian Wine* [1988] ECC 159, German Federal Supreme Court.
12 Kaye, pp 570–571; cf O'Malley and Layton, p 429; Collins, p 60. See also Art 5(3) of the Modified Convention.
13 There is, however, liability in contract under both English law and civil law.
14 Case 189/87 [1988] ECR 5565; Hartley (1989) 14 ELR 172; Briggs [1988] Yearbook of European Law 272.
15 As the Court had done earlier in relation to the scope of Art 5(1): Case 9/87 *SPRL Arcado v SA Haviland* [1988] ECR 1539.

not involve "matters relating to a contract" under Article 5(1).[16] The case involved a claim for unjust enrichment. If, as is likely, this does not come within the community concept of a contractual matter, it must necessarily come within Article 5(3).[17] The Court of Justice went on to say that if an action is based on both tort/delict and contract the court will only have jurisdiction under Article 5(3) in respect of that part of it based on tort/delict. A plaintiff can always, of course, bring the action in its entirety in the State of the defendant's domicil.

The Jenard Report deliberately left open the question of whether "the place where the harmful event occurred" referred to the place where the act which initiated the damage occurred or the place where the damage took effect. The Court of Justice provided the answer in *Bier BV v Mines de Potasse D'Alsace SA*.[18] This provides a classic example of the situation in which the elements in a tort are split up amongst different states.

> It was alleged that the French defendants had polluted the waters of the Rhine in France. These waters flowed into the Netherlands, where damage was caused to a Dutch horticultural business. The Dutch plaintiffs wished to sue in the Netherlands; so it was necessary to decide on the place where the harmful event occurred.

The Court of Justice, on a reference from the Dutch courts, held that Article 5(3) was intended to cover both the place where the damage occurred and the place of the event giving rise to it, where the two are not identical. The plaintiff therefore has the option of suing either in the place of acting or in the place of damage. The Court of Justice justified this wide interpretation in three ways. First, Article 5(3) is concerned to give jurisdiction to an appropriate forum. Both the place of acting and of damage are appropriate places for trial. Second, it is designed to give the plaintiff the option of suing elsewhere than in the Contracting State where the defendant is domiciled. Applying a place of acting rule on its own would not normally allow this. Applying a place of damage rule on its own would ignore cases where the act took place somewhere other than in the State where the defendant is domiciled. Third, there is artificiality in concentrating on one element in a tort or delict to the exclusion of the other elements.[19]

This decision solves the basic definitional problem in this area. Nonetheless, some difficulties remain. First, it is not always easy to ascertain what the act is which gives rise to the damage. This can be seen from *Minster Investments Ltd v Hyundai Precision and Industry Co Ltd*,[20] a case involving negligent misstatement. The test in the *Bier Case* was thought to be not particularly helpful here since the event giving rise to the liability could be said to be either negligent work of certification of goods which was performed in France

---

16 Supra, pp 296–297.
17 See the earlier case of *Re Jurisdiction in Tort and Contract* [1988] ECC 415, German Federal Supreme Court, in which a claim based on competition law was held to come within Article 5(3). But see *Davenport v Corinthian Motor Policies at Lloyd's* 1991 SLT 774—statutory liability under the Road Traffic Act 1988 held to be not within Art 5(3) of the Modified Convention.
18 Case 21/76 [1978] QB 708, [1976] ECR 1735.
19 This used to be done under the traditional rules on jurisdiction, see *George Monro Ltd v American Cyanamid and Chemical Corpn* [1944] KB 432, [1944] 1 All ER 386. The relevant head of RSC Ord 11 has been altered to provide a rule as wide as that in the *Bier* case, see Ord 11, r 1(1)(f), discussed supra, pp 199–201.
20 [1988] 2 Lloyd's Rep 621; Hartley (1988) 13 ELR 217.

and Korea or, with equal conviction, the receipt of the relevant certificates in England, reliance thereon, and the instructions given from England to pay the Korean sellers of the goods. Steyn J preferred in such a case to use a traditional English formula,[21] and to ask "where in substance the cause of action in tort arises, or what place the tort is most closely connected with". Applying this test to the facts of the case: the essence of the action was the negligent advice and reliance on it and not the historical carelessness leading to this. The place where the harmful event occurred was accordingly in England where the negligently produced certificates were received and relied upon.

Second, there may also be problems in ascertaining where damage occurs.[22] This can arise in personal injury cases[23] but is more likely in cases where the damage is not physical. Financial harm may occur in more than one Contracting State. Thus in *Dumez France and Tracoba v Hessische Landesbank*[24] the immediate victims of the alleged harmful act (of cancelling certain bank loans) committed in Germany were German subsidiary companies, which suffered financial harm in Germany, but as a consequence of this the parent companies also suffered financial loss in France where their head offices were situated. The Court of Justice held that Article 5(3) could not be construed as allowing the parent companies to bring proceedings in France against German defendants. The *Bier Case*, although allowing jurisdiction to be assumed in the State where the harm occurs, was concerned with cases where a direct consequence was felt in a Contracting State (this would be in Germany), not an indirect consequence, as occurred in France. Libel cases can also involve damage in more than one Contracting State. Under English law it is assumed in libel cases that damage occurs where publication takes place. This has meant that a plaintiff was able to sue in England under Article 5(3) a French publisher of a French newspaper, having limited her complaint to publication of the newspaper in England.[25] It mattered not that the newspaper had only a very small circulation in England, compared with that in France.

Third, some torts, at least under English law, do not require proof of damage or injury to be actionable. In such cases the equivalent of the place where damage occurs would have to be utilised, that is the place where the result of the act takes place.[26]

Article 5(4) as regards a civil claim for damages or restitution which is based on an act giving rise to criminal proceedings, in the court seised of those proceedings, to the extent that the court has jurisdiction under its own law to entertain civil proceedings
Article 5(5)[27] as regards a dispute arising out of the operations of a branch, agency or other establishment, in the courts for the place in which the branch, agency or other establishment is situated

21 Taken from cases on the old tort head of Ord 11, RSC; supra, p 199.
22 See the Advocate General's opinion in *Netherlands v Rüffer*, op cit; Anton, *Civil Jurisdiction in Scotland*, para 5.39.
23 *Vile v Von Wendt Zurich Insurance Co* (1980) 103 DLR (3d) 356: the act and injury took place in Quebec, the plaintiff was hospitalised in Ontario, the damage was held to have been sustained there; cf *Thomas v Penna* [1985] 2 NSWLR 171, but now see *Flaherty v Girgis* (1988) 71 ALR 1, HC of Australia.
24 Case C-220/88 [1990] ECR 49; Hartley (1991) 16 ELR 71.
25 *Shevill v Presse Alliance SA* [1992] 2 WLR 1, CA.
26 See the Restatement, Conflict of Laws (1934), s 277.
27 See Fawcett (1984) 9 ELR 326.

This is the Convention equivalent of the traditional English concept of corporate presence within the jurisdiction by virtue of establishing a place of business.[28] There are two requirements under Article 5(5): first, the defendant domiciled in a Contracting State must have a branch, agency or other establishment in another Contracting State. Second, the dispute must arise out of the operations of the branch, agency or other establishment.

(i) A branch, agency or other establishment
A literal interpretation would suggest that these three terms encompass different situations and are there to give width to Article 5(5). The Court of Justice has, instead, applied a teleological interpretation to this provision and has reached a different conclusion.[29] After looking at the purpose of the Convention and the place within it of Article 5(5) as an exception to Article 2, the Court of Justice has decided that this provision should be interpreted narrowly. The "branch", "agency" and "other establishment" are identified by characteristics which are said to be common to all three. These are as follows: the branch, agency or other establishment must (i) have a fixed permanent place of business, (ii) be subject to the direction and control of the parent, (iii) have a certain autonomy[1] and (iv) act on behalf of and bind the parent. These are the characteristics of a typical branch office. Any other method of carrying on business is likely to fall outside the ambit of Article 5(5). The one characteristic that does separate the three terms is that of legal personality. A branch will not have a separate legal personality, whereas an establishment or agent can be a legally independent entity.

The Court of Justice has examined this question in four cases. The *Somafer*[2] case concerned a sales representative.

A French company (Somafer) carried on business in Germany by means of a sales representative who was one of their employees. There was no office or furniture in Germany and Somafer was not entered in a commercial register as a branch. A German company wished to sue Somafer in Germany and the question was whether Somafer had a branch, agency or other establishment in that country.

The Court of Justice stressed the need for a fixed permanent place of business in Germany and the sales representative having the power to act on behalf of and to bind his parent, neither of which would appear to be satisfied on the above facts.

Blanckaert v Trost[3] involved a company carrying on business abroad by means of a commercial agent.

A Belgian manufacturer of furniture appointed a German independent commercial agent to set up a sales network in Germany. The agent was

---

28 Supra, pp 185–188. See *New Hampshire Insurance Co v Strabag Bau AG* [1990] 2 Lloyd's Rep 61 at 69; affd (1991) Times, 26 November. However, the defendant can be an individual with a business establishment who engages in business abroad through a branch etc see *Courtaulds Clothing Brands Ltd v Knowles* 1989 SLT (Sh Ct) 84.
29 Case 14/76 *De Bloos v Bouyer* [1976] ECR 1497, [1977] 1 CMLR 60; Case 33/78 *Somafer v Saar-Ferngas* [1978] ECR 2183, [1979] 1 CMLR 490; Case 139/80, *Blanckaert and Willems v Trost* [1981] ECR 819, [1982] 2 CMLR 1; cf Case 218/86 *Sar Schotte GmbH v Parfums Rothschild SARL* [1987] ECR 4905.
1 The Advocate General in *De Bloos*, op cit, gave his opinion that the autonomy of an agency is less marked than that of a branch.
2 Op cit; see Hartley (1979) 4 ELR 127.
3 Op cit; see Hartley (1981) 6 ELR 481.

free to arrange its own work, was not prevented from representing several other firms competing in the same sector, and transmitted orders to the parent without being involved in their terms or execution.

The Court of Justice, emphasising the need for the intermediary to be under the direction and control of the parent, held that such an agent did not have the character of a branch, agency or other establishment.[4]

The requirement of direction and control had first been introduced in *De Bloos v Bouyer*[5] which concerned an exclusive distributor rather than a commercial agent.

> The defendant French company granted exclusive distribution rights in Belgium for its products to the plaintiff Belgian company. The question arose of whether the plaintiff could sue the defendant in Belgium on the basis that the plaintiff was a Belgian branch, agency or other establishment of the defendant.

The Court of Justice held that it could not do so where the grantee of the concession was not subject to the direction and control of the parent. This would be the situation with a typical grantee. The Court of Justice also made it clear that "an establishment" is based on the same essential characteristics as a branch or agency. Finally, it emerges from the case that Article 5(5) is designed for third parties who wish to sue the parent. It is doubtful whether an intermediary can ever rely on its own presence within a Contracting State to found jurisdiction in an action brought by it against the parent.[6] To allow this would, in effect, give the plaintiff the right to sue in his own residence whenever Article 5(5) is applicable. A third party plaintiff who wishes to found jurisdiction on Article 5(5) will not necessarily be suing in the State where he resides.

The Court of Justice was faced with a case involving a subsidiary company carrying on business through its parent in *Sar Schotte GmbH v Parfums Rothschild SARL*:[7]

> The plaintiff German company provided atomisers to the defendant French company (French Rothschild). The defendant company was a wholly owned subsidiary of a German company (German Rothschild). The plaintiff wished to sue the French defendant in Germany for the price of the atomisers supplied, and argued that German Rothschild was an "establishment" of French Rothschild.

The Court of Justice held that Article 5(5) would apply, even though under company law German Rothschild was an independent company with a separate legal personality.[8] German Rothschild and French Rothschild had the same name and identical management, and German Rothschild negotiated and conducted business in the name of French Rothschild, which used German Rothschild as an extension of itself and would appear as such to third parties. The place of business of the branch etc does not have to be owned by the defendant. The same principles will doubtless also apply in the

---

4 See also *New Hampshire Insurance Co v Strabag Bau AG* [1990] 2 Lloyd's Rep 61 at 68–69; appeal dismissed (1991) Times, 26 November.
5 Op cit; see Hartley (1977) 2 ELR 61.
6 See the Advocate General's opinion at p 1519.
7 Case 218/86 [1987] ECR 4905; Allwood (1988) 13 ELR 213.
8 There was previously considerable uncertainty over this situation: see the opinion of the Advocate General in *De Bloos, Somafer* and *Blanckaert*.

more common situation where a parent carries on business through its subsidiary. This case shows that an "establishment" under Article 5(5) has a different meaning from a "branch" in so far as it covers a body with a separate legal personality. However, this is not much of an advance. German Rothschild only came within Article 5(5) because it acted, in effect, as if it were a branch of French Rothschild. The case is unusual in that a typical parent or subsidiary will act for itself and not on behalf of its subsidiary or parent, and will thus be outside the ambit of Article 5(5).

(ii) The dispute must arise out of the operations of the branch, agency or other establishment

This requirement provides the main difference between Article 5(5) and the traditional English concept of corporate presence, which does not require the dispute to be connected with the presence in England.[9] The provision ensures that the Contracting State given jurisdiction under Article 5(5) is an appropriate one for trial. It presupposes that the branch, agency or other establishment has power to carry out activities itself (albeit on behalf of the parent); this ties in with the requirement, already mentioned, that the intermediary must have a certain autonomy.

In the *Somafer* case the Court of Justice identified three sorts of actions comprised within the concept of a dispute arising out of the operations of a branch, agency or other establishment: (a) actions concerning the management of the intermediary "such as those concerning the situation of the building ... or the local engagement of staff to work there";[10] (b) actions relating to undertakings entered into in the name of the parent in the place where the intermediary is situated and which must be performed there;[11] (c) non-contractual actions arising from the activities of the intermediary. This gives a very narrow interpretation to the concept. It would not cover, for example, the situation where the intermediary simply sells the parent's defective product in France and a purchaser wishes to sue the parent in France, at least not unless the intermediary also gave a contractual undertaking in respect of the product.[12] It is hard to see why, as a matter of policy, the parent should escape from being subject to jurisdiction in France in such a case.

Article 5(6) as settlor, trustee or beneficiary of a trust created by the operation of a statute, or by a written instrument, or created orally and evidenced in writing, in the courts of the Contracting State in which the trust is domiciled[13]

Article 5(7) as regards a dispute concerning the payment of remuneration claimed in respect of the salvage of a cargo or freight, in the court under the authority of which the cargo or freight in question:
(a) has been arrested to secure such payment, or
(b) could have been so arrested, but bail or other security has been given; provided

---

9 Supra, pp 185 et seq.
10 [1978] ECR 2183 at 2192–2193.
11 Criticised by the Advocate General in *Sar Schotte*, op cit, at 4914–4915, as being unduly narrow.
12 It is not clear whether an action based on implied conditions as to merchantability, imposed by law on the seller, would be covered.
13 Trusts are of particular concern to the United Kingdom and this provision was added by the 1978 Accession Convention, see the Schlosser Report, pp 105–108. It does not apply to constructive or implied trusts. In order to determine where the trust is domiciled, see s 45 of the 1982 Act.

that this provision shall apply only if it is claimed that the defendant has an interest in the cargo or freight or had such an interest at the time of salvage[14]

(b) Special jurisdiction under Articles 6 and 6A

Article 6 A person domiciled in a Contracting State may also be sued:
(1) where he is one of a number of defendants, in the courts for the place where any one of them is domiciled;[15]
(2) as a third party in an action on a warranty or guarantee or in any other third party proceedings, in the court seised of the original proceedings, unless these were instituted solely with the object of removing him from the jurisdiction of the court which would be competent in his case;[16]
(3) on a counterclaim arising from the same contract or facts on which the original claim was based, in the court in which the original claim is pending;
(4) in matters relating to a contract, if the action may be combined with an action against the same defendant in matters relating to rights *in rem* in immovable property, in the court of the Contracting State in which the property is situated.[17]

Article 6A Where by virtue of this Convention a court of a Contracting State has jurisdiction in actions relating to liability arising from the use or operation of a ship, that court, or any other court substituted for this purpose by the internal law of that State, shall also have jurisdiction over claims for limitation of such liability[18]

(iii) Jurisdiction in matters relating to insurance

Section 3 of Title II of the Convention (namely Articles 7–12A)[19] deals with matters relating to insurance, although it does not define the term. Section 3 does not apply to cases of reinsurance.[20] Generally, it only applies in the situation where the defendant is domiciled in a Contracting State,[21] although there is the possible exception of the situation where there is an agreement as to jurisdiction under Article 12. An extended meaning is given to domicil in this context.[22] Where an insurer not domiciled in a Contracting State has a branch, agency or other establishment in a Contracting State, and the dispute arises out of the latter's operations, the insurer is deemed to be domiciled in that State.[23] The provisions contained in Section 3 are exclusive.[24]

14 This provision was also added by the 1978 Convention of Accession, see the Schlosser Report, pp 108–109. Salvage of a ship is dealt with under the Brussels Convention of 1952 on the Arrest of Seagoing Ships and the 1968 Convention does not apply.
15 There must exist between the various actions brought by the same plaintiff against the different defendants a connection of such a kind that it is expedient to hear them together to avoid irreconcilable judgments: Case 189/87 *Kalfelis v Schroder* [1988] ECR 5565, discussed supra, pp 300–301. There must also be a valid claim against the defendant domiciled in the forum: *The Rewia* [1991] 2 Lloyd's Rep 325 at 335–336, CA.
16 See Case C-365/88 *Kongress Agentur Hagen GmbH v Zeehaghe BV* [1990] ECR 1845; Hartley (1991) 16 ELR 73.
17 Added by Art 5 of the 1989 Accession Convention; see the Almeida Cruz, Desantes Real and Jenard Report, para 24.
18 The provision was added by the 1978 Accession Convention at the request of the UK, see the Schlosser Report, pp 109–110. See *Saipem SpA v Dredging VO2 BV and Geosite Surveys Ltd, The Volvox Hollandia* [1988] 2 Lloyd's Rep 361; *The Falstria* [1988] 1 Lloyd's Rep 495.
19 See generally, the Schlosser Report, pp 112–117; Anton, *Civil Jurisdiction in Scotland* ch 6; Collins, pp 68–74; Hartley, pp 59–62; O'Malley and Layton, pp 456–492; Kaye, pp 806–823.
20 See the Schlosser Report, p 117. See also *Citadel Insurance Co v Atlantic Union Insurance Co SA* [1982] 2 Lloyd's Rep 543 at 549; Hunter [1987] JBL 344.
21 See Art 7, which says that Section 3 is without prejudice to Art 4; see also Arts 8 and 11.
22 Art 8. For application of this provision within the United Kingdom (the Modified Convention does not have such a provision) see s 44 of the 1982 Act.
23 See, eg, *S & W Berisford plc v New Hampshire Insurance Co* [1990] 2 QB 631.
24 Art 7, which is without prejudice to Arts 4 and 5(5).

Where they apply it is not possible to rely on other bases of jurisdiction under the Convention.[25] It differs from exclusive jurisdiction under Section 5 in two important respects. First, jurisdiction is not assigned to a single Contracting State under Section 3; instead the plaintiff, where he is the weaker party, is allowed a limited choice of forum. Second, the parties may in certain limited circumstances depart from the provisions of Section 3. These two aspects of Section 3 will be examined in more detail.

Section 3 contains protective provisions, designed to protect the party in a weaker position.[26] In a dispute between the policy-holder (ie the other party to the contract of insurance)[1] and the insurer, this will be the policy-holder in those cases where he is faced with a standard form non-negotiable contract. The plaintiff is given a choice of forum when suing the defendant insurer. According to Article 8, where the insurer is the defendant he can be sued: (i) in the Contracting State where he is domiciled; or (ii) in another Contracting State, in the courts for the place where the policy-holder is domiciled;[2] or (iii) if he is a co-insurer, in the courts of a Contracting State in which proceedings are brought against the leading insurer.[3] Article 8 does not say by whom the proceedings have to be brought; presumably this could include not just the policy-holder as plaintiff but also the insured or a beneficiary. In most cases the insured (ie the person who enters into the original contract of insurance) will also be the policy-holder. An example of where he would not be is as follows: A, the owner of a painting, enters into a contract of insurance with the insurer B. A thereby becomes the insured and the policy-holder; but, if he sells the painting to C and assigns with it all his rights under the insurance policy, C may become the policy-holder whereas A remains as the insured.[4] Where the insurer is the plaintiff he is given no choice of forum. According to Article 11 he may bring proceedings only in the courts of the Contracting State in which the defendant is domiciled, whether he is the policy-holder, the insured or a beneficiary.

The policy of favouring the insured party has been strongly criticised by English lawyers; it gives an unwarranted opportunity for the insured to forum-shop, and is based on the erroneous assumption that the insured is always the weaker party, whereas, in reality, the insured may be a wealthy enterprise which is every bit as strong as the insurer.[5] Nonetheless, Section 3 will still operate.[6]

The validity of this criticism is lessened to some extent by the fact that Section 3 can be departed from by an agreement on jurisdiction. Article 12 requires the agreement to satisfy one of five alternatives set out in that Article.[7] These are as follows: (1) the agreement is entered into after the

25 Art 18 may be an exception to this, see the Jenard Report, p 29.
26 See Case 133/81 *Ivenel v Schwab* [1982] ECR 1891, [1983] 1 CMLR 538; Case 201/82 *Gerling v Italian Treasury* [1983] ECR 2503; Anton, *Civil Jurisdiction in Scotland*, para 6.16.
1 See the Jenard Report, p 31; the Schlosser Report, p 117.
2 It is not clear whether the policy-holder must be the plaintiff under this particular alternative.
3 The options are extended in cases of liability insurance, or insurance of immovable property, see Art 9 (which provides that the insurer may also be sued in the courts for the place where the harmful event occurred, in respect of liability insurance or insurance of immovable property) and Art 10.
4 See the Schlosser Report, p 117.
5 Collins, at p 68, and in *Harmonisation of Private International Law by the EEC* (ed Lipstein, 1978), pp 99–100; Kerr (1978) 75 LS Gaz 1190, 1191.
6 See *New Hampshire Insurance Co v Strabag Bau AG* [1990] 2 Lloyd's Rep 61 at 66–68; appeal dismissed (1991) Times, 26 November.
7 See also Art 12A.

dispute has arisen; (2) the agreement allows the policy-holder, the insured or a beneficiary to bring proceedings in courts other than those indicated in Section 3; (3) the agreement is concluded between a policy-holder and an insured with a common domicil or habitual residence in a Contracting State, and confers jurisdiction on that State even if the harmful event were to occur abroad, provided that such an agreement is not contrary to the law of that State; (4) the agreement is concluded with a policy-holder who is not domiciled in a Contracting State except in so far as the insurance is compulsory or relates to immovable property in a Contracting State; (5) the agreement relates to a contract of insurance in so far as it covers one or more of the risks set out in Article 12A. The agreement would presumably also have to satisfy the requirements relating to agreements as to jurisdiction under Article 17 of the Convention.[8] Under Article 17, the defendant does not have to be domiciled in a Contracting State. Article 12 allows all the other provisions in Section 3 (including any requirement as to the defendant being domiciled in a Contracting State) to be departed from. It therefore appears that an agreement conferring jurisdiction in a matter relating to insurance does not require that the defendant be domiciled in a Contracting State.[9] There is a suggestion in the Jenard Report that Section 3 can also be departed from by the defendant submitting to the courts of a Contracting State by entering an appearance under Article 18.[10]

(iv) Jurisdiction over consumer contracts[11]

Section 4 (Articles 13–15) applies where there is a contract concluded by a consumer (defined under Article 13 as a person who concludes a contract for a purpose outside his trade or profession) and the contract is of a type listed in Article 13. This includes a contract for the sale of goods[12] on instalment credit, a term which has been given a community meaning by the Court of Justice.[13] It is expressly provided that Section 4 shall not apply to contracts of transport. It also only applies (apart from agreements as to jurisdiction under Article 15) where the defendant is domiciled in a Contracting State,[14] and this is extended to cover a defendant with a branch, agency or other establishment in one of the Contracting States, provided that the dispute arises out of the latter's operations.[15] Section 4 adopts the same approach towards allocating jurisdiction as does Section 3: the normal rules on jurisdiction do not apply (Section 4 should therefore be interpreted so as to be strictly limited to its objectives);[16] the plaintiff where he is the weaker party is given a choice of forum; and the provisions of Section 4 can be departed from by agreement in certain limited circumstances.

8 *Gerling v Italian Treasury*, op cit.
9 See Collins, p 51.
10 At p 30.
11 See the Schlosser Report, pp 117–120; Anton, *Civil Jurisdiction in Scotland*, ch 6; Hartley, pp 58–62; Collins, pp 74–77; O'Malley and Layton, pp 493–516; Kaye, pp 823–857.
12 This does not include unit trusts: *Waverley Asset Management Ltd v Saha* 1989 SLT (Sh Ct) 87, a case on the Modified Convention.
13 Case 150/77 *Bertrand v Ott* [1978] ECR 1431, [1978] 3 CMLR 499; see Hartley (1979) 4 ELR 47. The 1978 Accession Convention amended the wording of Section 4 to deal expressly with consumers.
14 Art 13, which is without prejudice to Arts 4 and 5(5).
15 Art 13. For the application of this provision within the UK (the Modified Convention does not contain such a provision) see s 44 of the 1982 Act.
16 *Bertrand v Ott*, op cit.

Section 4 is, like Section 3, a protective provision; in this case it is the consumer who is in the weaker position. Under Article 14 he is given the choice of suing the other party to a contract either in the defendant's domicil or in his own domicil. Where the roles are reversed, the other party can only sue the defendant consumer in the latter's domicil. Section 4 can be departed from by an agreement which complies with one of the three alternatives under Article 15 (an agreement which is entered into after the dispute has arisen, or an agreement which allows the consumer to bring proceedings in courts other than those indicated in the Section, or an agreement which confers jurisdiction on the courts of the common domicil or habitual residence of the parties) and, presumably, also complies with Article 17. As with Article 17 the defendant in Section 4 cases probably does not have to be domiciled in a Contracting State.[17] It is likely that Section 4 can also be departed from under Article 18, ie where the defendant submits to the courts of a Contracting State by entering an appearance.

(v) Exclusive jurisdiction

Article 16 allocates jurisdiction to the courts of the Contracting State which is thought to be uniquely well placed to deal with the subject-matter listed in that Article. So strong is this desire to allocate jurisdiction that Article 16 expressly provides that it applies regardless of domicil. It is therefore an exception to the normal rule that the bases of jurisdiction under the Convention only apply where the defendant is domiciled in a Contracting State.[18] Where jurisdiction is assigned to the United Kingdom under Article 16, the Modified Convention will apply to allocate jurisdiction to a part of the United Kingdom. For example, where the proceedings concern the ownership of land in England, the English courts will have exclusive jurisdiction. The jurisdiction under Article 16 is exclusive in the sense that a Contracting State other than the one which has been allocated jurisdiction under it is deprived of jurisdiction, even though it would otherwise have had it under one of the other bases of jurisdiction such as the domicil of the defendant. The courts of Contracting States are required by Article 19 to declare of their own motion that they do not have jurisdiction where they are seised of a claim which is principally concerned with a matter over which the courts of another Contracting State have exclusive jurisdiction by virtue of Article 16. This requirement applies to Contracting States regardless of their own rules on procedure, which may require the jurisdictional point to be raised by one of the parties, and regardless of what steps have been taken by the defendant.[19] It meant a fundamental change of procedure for United Kingdom courts, which had, in the past, only acted after submissions from the parties.[20]

Article 16 applies to proceedings involving: (i) immovable property; (ii) certain company law matters; (iii) validity of entries in public registers; (iv) certain matters involving intellectual property; (v) enforcement of judgments. Article 19 suggests that Article 16 only applies where the claim is principally concerned with one of these matters.[21] Where more than one Contracting

17 See Collins, p 60; O'Malley and Layton, p 385; see the argument on this point in relation to insurance, supra, p 308.
18 Supra, pp 290–291.
19 Case 288/82 *Duijnstee v Goderbauer* [1983] ECR 3663; Hartley (1984) 10 ELR 64.
20 See the Schlosser Report, p 81. New procedural rules are contained in RSC Ord 6, r 7 and Ord 13, r 7B.
21 See Anton, *Civil Jurisdiction in Scotland*, para 7.05.

State is allocated jurisdiction under Article 16 (for example the claim concerns land in two Contracting States) Article 23 provides that any court other than the one first seised shall decline jurisdiction.

There are five heads under Article 16, one for each of the above matters. The reported cases on Article 16 have given a community meaning to its terms and have interpreted the heads in the light of their purpose and their place within the scheme of the Convention. Sometimes this has led to Article 16 being given a narrow interpretation, though on one notable occasion it was given a wide interpretation.[22] The head which has the most startling repercussions is the first one and this will be examined in detail; the remaining four heads will merely be stated.

Article 16 provides that the following courts shall have exclusive jurisdiction, regardless of domicil:

Article 16(1)(a) in proceedings which have as their object rights *in rem* in immovable property or tenancies of immovable property, the courts of the Contracting State in which the property is situated.[23]

The immovable property must be situated in a Contracting State or States. If the dispute relates to property situated in two Contracting States (for example, it concerns the existence of a lease over such property) the Court of Justice in *Scherrens v Maenhout*[24] has held that normally each Contracting State has exclusive jurisdiction over the property situated in the territory of that State. Nonetheless, in certain exceptional circumstances one State may be given exclusive jurisdiction over the entire property. An example given of where this might happen would be where property is subject to a single lease, the land in one Contracting State is adjacent to the land in the other Contracting State and the property is situated almost entirely in one of those two Contracting States. In cases where the property is situated in the United Kingdom, the Modified Convention will apply to allocate jurisdiction to part of the United Kingdom. If the immovable property is situated outside a Contracting State, Article 16(1)(a) will not apply, but, depending on the circumstances, other bases of jurisdiction under the Convention may still be applicable, eg the domicil of the defendant in a Contracting State. Article 16(1)(a) covers two sorts of proceedings: ones which have as their object rights in rem in immovable property and ones which have as their object tenancies of immovable property.

(i) Rights in rem The proceedings must have as their object a right which is enforceable against the whole world (a right in rem), not a right which is merely enforceable against a particular person (a right in personam). Thus proceedings for an order directing the rectification of some register of title have as their object a right in rem; whereas proceedings for an order for specific performance of a contract or for a declaration that the defendant holds property on trust for the plaintiff have as their object a right in personam, and are accordingly outside the scope of Article 16(1)(a).[1] Accord-

---

22 Compare *Duijnstee v Goderbauer*, op cit (on Art 16(4)), and Case 73/77 *Sanders v Van der Putte* [1977] ECR 2383, [1978] 1 CMLR 331, with Case 241/83 *Rösler v Rottwinkel* [1986] QB 33, [1985] 1 CMLR 806.
23 Art 6 of the 1989 Accession Convention substituted a new Art 16(1).
24 Case 158/87 [1988] ECR 3791; Hartley (1989) 11 ELR 57.
 1 *Webb v Webb* [1992] 1 All ER 17, [1991] 1 WLR 1410.

ing to the Court of Justice in *Reichert v Dresdner Bank*[2] what is now Article 16 (1)(a)[3] is only concerned with actions which determine "the extent, content, ownership or possession of immovable property or the existence of other rights *in rem* therein and to provide the holders of those rights with the protection of the powers which attach to their interest". Applying this narrow community definition the Court held that an action whereby a creditor sought to have set aside a gift of the legal ownership of immovable property which he alleged was made by the debtor to defraud his creditors did not come within the scope of what is now Article 16(1)(a). This action did not concern the rules and customs of the situs and accordingly there was no reason why it should come within the exclusive jurisdiction of the courts of the situs.

(ii) Tenancies Article 16(1)(a) also applies to proceedings which have as their object tenancies of immovable property. Leases involve complex social legislation and the courts of the Contracting State where this is in force are best able to apply their own law and are accordingly given exclusive jurisdiction.[4] The difficulty with including tenancies under Article 16(1)(a) is that in some cases a dispute between a landlord and a tenant may relate essentially to the land itself (this is within Article 16(1)(a)); whereas, in other cases the issue may relate more obviously to the contractual rights and obligations between the parties (which are less obviously within the ambit of Article 16(1)(a)).

In *Sanders v Van der Putte*[5] the Court of Justice held that, where the dispute relates to the existence or interpretation of the lease, compensation for damage caused by the tenant,[6] or giving up possession of the premises, it is within what is now Article 16(1)(a). The effect of including disputes relating to the existence of the lease is that a court's jurisdiction under Article 16(1)(a) cannot be defeated by an allegation that the lease is void.[7] The Court of Justice went on to hold that what is now Article 16(1)(a) did not apply to a dispute between an original tenant and a sub-lessee as to the existence of an agreement under which the sub-lessee agreed to rent and run the original tenant's retail business, the emphasis in the agreement being on this latter aspect. What is now Article 16(1)(a) departs from the normal rules of jurisdiction and the Court of Justice was not prepared to give it a wider ambit than is required by its objectives.

Sanders only deals with a limited range of the issues that can arise in disputes between a landlord and a tenant. For example, the Court of Justice gave no answer as to whether claims for the payment of rent and other outgoings are within what is now Article 16(1)(a). Subsequently, the Court of Justice in *Rösler v Rottwinkel*[8] departed from the spirit of narrow interpretation in *Sanders* by holding that what is now Article 16(1)(a) applies to disputes concerning the respective obligations of the landlord and tenant under the agreement.[9] This would cover, for instance, a simple action for

---

2 Case C-115/88 [1990] ECR 27; Hartley (1991) 16 ELR 69. See also the earlier Scots case of *Ferguson's Trustee v Ferguson* 1990 SLT (Sh Ct) 73.
3 Formerly Art 16(1).
4 See the Jenard Report, pp 34–35.
5 [1977] ECR 2383, [1978] 1 CMLR 331; see Hartley (1978) 3 ELR 164.
6 Cf the Schlosser Report, p 120.
7 See also Case 38/81 *Effer v Kantner* [1982] ECR 825, [1984] 2 CMLR 667.
8 [1986] QB 33, [1985] 1 CMLR 806. Criticised by F A Mann (1985) 101 LQR 329 and Hartley (1985) 10 ELR 361.
9 See also the opinion of the Advocate General in *Sanders v Van der Putte*, supra; Anton, *Civil Jurisdiction in Scotland*, para 7.15. Cf the Jenard Report, p 35.

unpaid rent or other outgoings, an action in respect of repairs and decoration of property, and an action in respect of damage to movable property caused by the tenant.[10]

Such disputes are accordingly subject to the exclusive jurisdiction of the Contracting State in which the immovable property is situated. In favour of this, it can be said that one Contracting State will be allocated jurisdiction in respect of most of the disputes that can arise between a landlord and a tenant. This is preferable to having an action which involves, for example, a claim for possession and for unpaid rent split up between different Contracting States. Also the rationale of Article 16(1)(a) leads to a wide interpretation since many Contracting States have social legislation in respect of rents and therefore ought to be able to hear a case which involves a claim for rent in respect of property situated in their territory.

The *Rösler Case* also establishes, by way of contrast, that proceedings which only indirectly concern the use of the property, such as a claim by a landlord for damages for lost enjoyment of a holiday in the property let (and for travel expenses) following the alleged breach by a tenant of a user clause in the lease, do not have as their object the tenancy of immovable property and accordingly fall outside the scope of Article 16(1)(a).

Article 16(1)(b) The *Rösler Case* involved a short term holiday let. Such lets (ie ones for a maximum period of 6 months) are now subject to Article 16(1)(b), which provides as follows:

> however, in proceedings which have as their object tenancies of immovable property concluded for temporary private use for a maximum period of six consecutive months, the courts of the Contracting State in which the defendant is domiciled shall also have jurisdiction, provided that the landlord and the tenant are natural persons and are domiciled in the same Contracting State

This provision was added by the 1989 Accession Convention,[11] and is designed to deal with criticisms levelled at *Rösler v Rottwinkel*. In this case the Court of Justice held, inter alia, that a claim by a plaintiff landlord against a defendant tenant in respect of outgoings, such as water and gas, in relation to the short term holiday let of a villa in Italy, had to be tried in Italy where the property was situated. This was despite the fact that both parties were resident in Germany and that therefore trial in Italy would be very inconvenient to them. Moreover, the drafters of the Convention did not intend to give exclusive jurisdiction to the Contracting State in which the property was situated in cases involving short term holiday lets.[12]

Article 16(1)(b) meets these criticisms by providing that in a case like this the Contracting State in which the defendant is domiciled shall also have jurisdiction. The plaintiff in the *Rösler Case* could now therefore, if he wanted to, sue in Germany. On the other hand, if he preferred, he could still sue in Italy under Article 16(1)(a). Both the Contracting State in which the defendant is domiciled and the Contracting State in which the property is situated have exclusive jurisdiction under Article 16(1).[13] This could result in con-

---

10 It is not clear whether the damage to property mentioned in *Sanders* was only referring to the immovable property.
11 Art 6. See the Almeida Cruz, Desantes Real and Jenard Report, para 25. The 1989 Accession Convention follows the 1988 Lugano Convention (on which see the Jenard and Möller Report OJ 1990 C189/57) with some modifications.
12 See the Jenard and Möller Report, p 75; the Schlosser Report, para 164.
13 See the Jenard and Möller Report, p 75.

current proceedings in two different Contracting States; for example, one party may sue in Italy and the other party in Germany. In such a situation Article 23 will operate so that the court other than the one first seised must decline jurisdiction.[14]

The first requirement that has to be satisfied before jurisdiction is given to the Contracting State in which the defendant is domiciled is that the proceedings have as their object tenancies of immovable property. The meaning of this has already been examined in relation to Article 16(1)(a),[15] where the same phrase is used, and the *Rösler Case* is still no doubt good authority on this point. The other requirements are geared very much to the facts of the *Rösler Case*, the second being that it must be a short term let (for a maximum period of six consecutive months) and the third being that the landlord and the tenant must be natural persons.[16] Legal persons, such as companies, are excluded on the basis that they are generally engaged in commercial transactions. Fourth, both parties must be domiciled in the same Contracting State.[17]

At the same time, Article 16(1)(b) is wide enough to cover a dispute between the landlord and tenant that relates (unlike in the *Rösler Case*) to the land itself, so that inspection of the land may be necessary. The most appropriate place for trial in such a case is the Contracting State in which the land is situated; nonetheless, the Contracting State in which the defendant is domiciled also has jurisdiction, provided that the above requirements are met.

Article 16(2) in proceedings which have as their object the validity of the constitution, the nullity or the dissolution of companies or other legal persons or associations of natural or legal persons, or the decisions of their organs, the courts of the Contracting State in which the company, legal person or association has its seat[18]

Article 16(3) in proceedings which have as their object the validity of entries in public registers, the courts of the Contracting State in which the register is kept

Article 16(4) in proceedings concerned with the registration or validity of patents, trade marks, designs, or other similar rights required to be deposited or registered, the courts of the Contracting State in which the deposit or registration has been applied for, has taken place or is under the terms of an international convention deemed to have taken place[19]

Article 16(5) in proceedings concerned with the enforcement of judgments, the courts of the Contracting State in which the judgment has been or is to be enforced[20]

14 Supra, pp 309–310.
15 Supra, pp 311–312.
16 The Almeida Cruz, Desantes Real and Jenard Report, para 25; cf Art 16(1)(b) of the Lugano Convention, infra pp 343–344.
17 Cf Art 16(1)(b) of the Lugano Convention, infra pp 343–344.
18 It covers proceedings principally concerned with the validity of directors' exercise of their powers: *Newtherapeutics Ltd v Katz* [1991] Ch 226; Kaye (1991) 10 Civil Justice Quarterly 220; Carter (1990) 61 BYBIL 397. See also *Bank of Scotland v Investment Management Regulatory Organisation Ltd* 1989 SLT 432. Partnerships are also included, see the Schlosser Report, p 120. See also s 43 of the 1982 Act for a special definition of the seat of a corporation for the purpose of Art 16(2).
19 See the Schlosser Report, p 124; *Duijnstee v Goderbauer*, op cit; Wadlow (1985) 10 ELR 305.
20 See *Owens Bank Ltd v Bracco* [1991] 4 All ER 833, [1992] 2 WLR 127, CA. The provision does not cover a set-off between the right whose enforcement is being sought and a claim over which the courts of the State would have no jurisdiction if it were raised independently— see Case 220/84 *AS Autoteile Service GmbH v Malhé* [1985] ECR 2267, [1986] 3 CMLR 321;

(vi) Prorogation of jurisdiction

This is referring to jurisdiction selected by the parties. It takes the form of either an agreement on jurisdiction (Article 17), or the defendant's submission to the forum by appearing before its courts (Article 18).

(a) An agreement on jurisdiction[21]

The effect of the agreement
Article 17 is concerned with one type of agreement, ie one which satisfies the requirements in relation to the agreement set out in that article, but it gives the agreement one of two possible effects, depending on where the parties to the agreement are domiciled. The agreement will either give the courts of a Contracting State exclusive jurisdiction or merely preclude the courts of other Contracting States from having jurisdiction.

(i) An agreement giving exclusive jurisdiction Where there is an agreement giving exclusive jurisdiction under Article 17 two consequences follow. First, the courts of the Contracting State selected by the parties have jurisdiction (without any discretionary power in the Convention itself[22] to refuse to take jurisdiction). Second, the courts of this Contracting State have exclusive jurisdiction (ie other Contracting States are deprived of jurisdiction).[23]

An agreement can only give exclusive jurisdiction if one or more of the parties is domiciled in a Contracting State. It is not specified whether the party domiciled in a Contracting State should be the defendant or the plaintiff, and it must be assumed that it can be either.[24] Where the plaintiff is domiciled in a Contracting State and the defendant is not, there is a clash between Article 17 and Article 4 of the Convention. Article 17 will apply if you look only at that Article; but Article 4 declares that where the defendant is not domiciled in a Contracting State each Contracting State shall apply its own law on jurisdiction (subject to Article 16) and not the bases of jurisdiction under the Convention. The intention must be that Article 17 is to operate as an exception to Article 4, along with Article 16, which is specifically mentioned.

(ii) An agreement precluding the courts of other Contracting States from having jurisdiction Article 17 provides that where neither party[25] is domiciled in a Contracting State "the courts of other Contracting States shall have no jurisdiction over their disputes unless the court or courts chosen have declined jurisdiction".

Under this provision the Convention does not give jurisdiction to the court or courts of the Contracting State selected by the parties. Instead, this court

Hartley (1986) 11 ELR 98. It does not prevent a court from granting a world-wide Mareva injunction pending enforcement of the English judgment in a Contracting State: *Babanaft International Co SA v Bassatne* [1990] Ch 13 at 35, 46, CA. See also *Interpool Ltd v Galani* [1988] QB 738, [1987] 2 All ER 981, CA.

21 McClellan [1985] JBL 445; Morse (1989) 1 African J Int Comp L 551.
22 For the circumstances when English courts can stay the proceedings see infra, pp 331–334.
23 According to the Schlosser Report (p 81), the courts of other Contracting States must of their own motion consider if Art 17 applies.
24 Where both are domiciled in the same Contracting State, and particularly where the parties also agree on jurisdiction in that State, there is a basic problem of whether the dispute is international in character: see the Schlosser Report, p 123 and the Jenard Report, pp 37–38; but compare Collins, p 84, O'Malley and Layton, p 553. If the dispute is not international in character it is outside the scope of the Convention; see supra, p 286.
25 This is referring to the original contracting parties.

will apply its national rules on jurisdiction, the defendant being domiciled in a non-Contracting State,[1] and will have to decide whether it has jurisdiction under those rules. However, an agreement on jurisdiction does preclude courts in other Contracting States from having jurisdiction; it is only when the court agreed upon has decided that it has no jurisdiction (or, presumably, has decided, even though it has jurisdiction, that it is going to use a discretion to decline to take jurisdiction) that the courts of other Contracting States can decide whether they have jurisdiction under their national rules.[2]

This is an important development in the law. It means that parties to an international contract who are domiciled in non-Contracting States can oust the jurisdiction of the courts of other Contracting States by putting an English jurisdiction clause in the contract. Moreover, the subsequent English judgment will have to be recognised and enforced in other Contracting States under the Brussels Convention.[3]

The requirements in relation to the agreement

For an agreement to come within Article 17 two requirements must be satisfied: (i) the parties must have agreed that a court or the courts of a Contracting State are to have jurisdiction to settle any disputes which have arisen or which may arise in connection with a particular legal relationship; (ii) the agreement must satisfy certain requirements as to form. Before looking in more detail at these requirements it must be stressed that they apply equally to agreements which give exclusive jurisdiction and to agreements which merely preclude the courts of other Contracting States from having jurisdiction.

(i) The parties must have agreed[4] *that a court or the courts of a Contracting State are to have jurisdiction to settle any disputes which have arisen or which may arise in connection with a particular legal relationship.* Normally, the parties will agree on the court which is to have jurisdiction; however, it can also be conferred by a trust instrument.[5] Article 17 stipulates the form which the agreement must take, and the Court of Justice has held that requirements as to form under national law are no longer applicable.[6] To require parties to comply with two sets of formal requirements would impose such a burden on the parties that this would interfere with normal commercial practices. Where national laws go beyond matters of form and, as a matter of public policy, have a rule prohibiting agreements conferring jurisdiction in certain cases, for example, in contracts of employment, this national law is overridden by the Convention and the agreement will have full effect provided, of course, that it complies with all the other requirements under Article 17.[7] More difficult is the situation where under national law the agreement is void because of general contractual principles. Under English law it is not uncommon for the legality or validity of choice of jurisdiction clauses to be attacked

---

1 Art 4.
2 See the Schlosser Report, p 124.
3 See infra, p 413.
4 See *Dresser UK Ltd v Falcongate Freight Management Ltd* [1992] 2 WLR 319 (relationship between bailor and sub-bailee not based on agreement).
5 Art 17, second paragraph.
6 Case 150/80 *Elefanten Schuh GmbH v Jacqmain* [1981] ECR 1671, [1982] 3 CMLR 1; see Hartley (1983) 8 ELR 237. The Court of Justice classified the Belgian requirement as to the language of the contract as one of form.
7 Case 25/79 *Sanicentral GmbH v Collin* [1979] ECR 3423, [1980] 2 CMLR 164. For a trenchant criticism of the decision see Hartley, pp 72–73, and in (1980) 5 ELR 73.

by one of the parties.[8] It is arguable that, since Article 17 only deals with the form of the agreement, the validity of the agreement, in so far as it relates to issues other than form, should be a matter to be decided by the courts of the Contracting State where trial is sought, applying its rules of private international law.[9] The counter argument, which is much less convincing, is that the Convention lays down the only requirements with which an agreement conferring jurisdiction has to comply.[10] It is possible that the Court of Justice, rather than adopting either of these arguments of principle, may prefer to apply an analogy drawn from decisions on other bases of jurisdiction. It will be recalled that the Court of Justice has held that the contract provision under Article 5(1) cannot be negated by an allegation that the contract does not exist.[11] Exclusive jurisdiction under Article 16(1), likewise, cannot be negated by an allegation that a lease does not exist.[12] Following the principle in these cases, Article 17 should apply where there is prima facie evidence of a valid agreement under the law of the forum. This approach has much to commend it on the ground of pragmatism.

The agreement must confer jurisdiction on the court or courts of a Contracting State. There must be a direct choice of a forum by the parties, for example, "all disputes are to be tried before the French courts". Article 17 does not apply where the parties merely specify the Contracting State which is the place of performance of a contractual obligation, even though the effect of this is to give a Contracting State jurisdiction under Article 5(1).[13] Article 17 only refers to an agreement that the courts of a "Contracting State", in the singular, are to have jurisdiction. However, the Court of Justice in *Meeth v Glacetal Sarl*[14] held that an agreement giving jurisdiction to the courts of two Contracting States was within Article 17. The agreement provided that the parties, who were domiciled in different Contracting States, could only be sued in the courts of their respective States. This could result in two Contracting States having exclusive jurisdiction under Article 17 if each party decided to sue the other. Article 23 would then apply and the court seised of the matter second would defer to the court first seised. The contractual clause in *Meeth* did not give the parties a choice of forum in which to sue. Nonetheless, an English court[15] has held that, as a result of the *Meeth Case*, a clause providing, for example, that "the courts of England and Germany were to have jurisdiction in any proceedings brought by either party" comes within Article 17.

It is not uncommon for the parties to agree to confer non-exclusive jurisdiction on the courts of a Contracting State, for example by providing that

---

8   See supra, pp 237–239.
9   See the opinion of the Advocate General in Case 25/76 *Segoura v Bonakdarian* [1976] ECR 1851, [1977] 1 CMLR 361; in *Sanicentral v Collin*, op cit; and *Elefanten Schuh v Jacqmain*, op cit. See also Collins, p 88; Anton, *Civil Jurisdiction in Scotland*, para 7.26; O'Malley and Layton, pp 564–570; Kaye, pp 1073–1081.
10   See Hartley, p 73.
11   Case 38/81 *Effer v Kantner* [1982] ECR 825, discussed supra, p 297.
12   Case 73/77 *Sanders v Van der Putte* [1977] ECR 2383, [1978] 1 CMLR 331, discussed supra, p 311.
13   Case 56/79 *Zelger v Salinitri* [1980] ECR 89, [1980] 2 CMLR 635, discussed supra, p 295. See Anton, *Civil Jurisdiction in Scotland*, para 7.26. Cf the Schlosser Report, pp 123–124 (there can be an implied agreement).
14   Case 23/78 [1978] ECR 2133, [1979] 1 CMLR 520. See Hartley (1979) 4 ELR 125.
15   *Kurz v Stella Musical Veranstaltungs GmbH* [1992] Ch 196. Quaere the position if the agreement only gave one party a choice of Contracting States in which to sue.

"all disputes shall be subject to the non-exclusive jurisdiction of the English courts". Can such an agreement come within Article 17? HOFFMANN J has held that such an agreement gives jurisdiction to the English courts under Article 17.[16] But does it give exclusive jurisdiction (ie oust the jurisdiction of other Contracting States)? It would be very odd to give exclusive jurisdiction to the courts of a Contracting State under Article 17 when the parties have expressed a wish that it should only have non-exclusive jurisdiction, and HOFFMANN J seems to suggest that such an agreement can confer a non-exclusive jurisdiction under the Convention. This does not accord with the wording of Article 17 which expressly states that the courts of the Contracting State agreed upon are to have exclusive jurisdiction. It is submitted that Article 17 is only concerned with exclusive jurisdiction clauses; such clauses then confer an exclusive jurisdiction under the Convention.

Where the Contracting State whose courts are given exclusive jurisdiction under Article 17 is the United Kingdom, there is the usual problem of allocating jurisdiction within the United Kingdom. Where the Modified Convention applies[17](ie (a) the subject-matter of the proceedings is within the scope of the 1968 Convention and (b) the defendant is domiciled in the United Kingdom or the proceedings are of a kind mentioned in Article 16 (exclusive jurisdiction regardless of domicil)) this will provide the answer.[18] Where the Modified Convention does not apply, the position is less straightforward. It will be necessary to interpret Article 17 as giving jurisdiction not merely to the courts of the United Kingdom, but to the courts of a part of the United Kingdom. This is easy enough where the parties have specifically agreed on trial in England, Scotland, or Northern Ireland. It is not so easy in the unlikely event of the parties merely agreeing on trial in "the United Kingdom", without any further specification.

Where the parties confer jurisdiction on a non-Contracting State, Article 17 will not apply. Other bases of jurisdiction under the Convention may, however, still be applicable, for example Article 2. It has been suggested that national courts can use the choice of jurisdiction clause, if they regard it as valid under their law, as a ground for declining jurisdiction[19] under the Convention. This raises the whole question of whether there is a discretion to stay actions under the Convention, which is considered later in this chapter.

The agreement must be to settle any disputes "which have arisen or which may arise".[20] It follows that an agreement as to jurisdiction may be made after the dispute has arisen, as well as beforehand. The disputes which the agreement is dealing with must be "in connection with a particular legal relationship". This has been interpreted to mean that if the courts of a Contracting State have exclusive jurisdiction under Article 17 the same courts are not precluded from considering a set-off by the defendant against the plaintiff, thereby cutting out superfluous procedure.[21]

(ii) The form of the agreement A choice of jurisdiction clause may be included within the varied terms of a standard form contract and there is a danger

---

16 *Kurz v Stella Musical Veranstaltungs GmbH*, supra. See also O'Malley and Layton, pp 577–581; *S & W Berisford plc v New Hampshire Insurance Co* [1990] 2 QB 631 at 643.
17 See infra, pp 334–336.
18 See infra, pp 336–339.
19 Hartley, p 24; Collins, p 85; O'Malley and Layton, p 557.
20 See *British Steel Corpn v Allivane International Ltd* 1989 SLT (Sh Ct) 57.
21 *Meeth v Glacetal*, op cit. For counterclaims see the Advocate General's opinion in that case and Art 6(3).

of it going unnoticed by one of the parties. Article 17 contains specific requirements[22] as to the form of the agreement in order to prove the genuine consensus of the parties. The agreement must be (a) in writing[23] or evidenced in writing, or (b) in a form which accords with practices which the parties have established between themselves, or (c) in international trade or commerce, in a form which accords with a usage of which the parties are or ought to have been aware and which in such trade or commerce is widely known to, and regularly observed by, parties to contracts of the type involved in the particular trade or commerce concerned. Before looking at these requirements a few words are necessary on the attitude of the Court of Justice towards their interpretation. The Court of Justice has considered, on the one hand, the purpose of the requirements as to form and the place of Article 17 within the Convention, both of which lead to a strict interpretation, and, on the other hand, the need to uphold normal commercial practices, which necessitates that the formal requirements be not unduly onerous.

(a) In writing or evidenced in writing

In writing

This requirement is clearly satisfied where there is a written contract which contains a choice of jurisdiction clause in the text and the contract is signed by both parties. Any variant of this causes problems. Where the choice of jurisdiction clause is contained in general conditions on the back of a written and signed contract there is a danger that, although it is in writing, it will still go unnoticed. Accordingly, the Court of Justice has held that the text of the contract must contain an express reference to these general conditions.[24] Similarly, where the contract refers to earlier offers which had general conditions on the back, the text of the contract must refer expressly to the earlier offers.[1] Where the written contract contains the choice of jurisdiction clause in the text but has only been signed by one party, there is, again, a danger of it going unnoticed by the other party. The Court of Justice has held that the consent of the other party has also to be in writing, either in the document itself or in a separate document.[2] The effect of these cases is that not only must the choice of jurisdiction clause be in writing but also the consensus on its application must be in writing. On the other hand, the mere fact that a written agreement containing a choice of jurisdiction clause has expired is not fatal if it can be shown that under the relevant applicable law the parties can validly extend the initial contract without observing the requirements of writing.[3]

Evidenced in writing

This alternative is designed to deal with the situation where there is an oral

22 There is an extra requirement of form where a person is domiciled in Luxembourg, see the Protocol attached to the 1968 Convention, Art I, second paragraph and Case 784/79 *Porta-Leasing GmbH v Prestige International SA* [1980] ECR 1517, [1981] 1 CMLR 135; noted by Hartley (1981) 6 ELR 62.

23 For the procedural classification of a requirement as to writing under English private international law, see *Leroux v Brown* (1852) 12 CB 801, supra, pp 75–76.

24 Case 24/76 *Colzani v Rüwa* [1976] ECR 1831, [1977] 1 CMLR 345. See also *Marine Contractors Inc v Shell Petroleum Development Co of Nigeria* [1984] 2 Lloyd's Rep 77.

 1 The conditions must have been expressly referred to in the offer and must have been communicated to the other party.

 2 Case 71/83, *Partenreederei MS Tilly Russ v Haven and Vervaebedrijf Nova NV* [1984] ECR 2417, [1985] QB 931, [1984] 3 CMLR 499; see the notes by Wilderspin (1984) 9 ELR 456, and North [1985] Lloyd's MCLQ 177.

 3 Case 313/85 *Iveco Fiat SpA v Van Hool NV* [1986] ECR 3337; Allwood (1987) 12 ELR 461.

contract which is confirmed in writing. In *Galeries Segoura Sprl v Firma Rahim Bonakdarian*[4] the Court of Justice held that, where an oral agreement is made subject to general conditions of sale, the confirmation in writing (accompanied in that case by notification of the general conditions of sale which contain a clause conferring jurisdiction) must be accepted in writing by the other party. It was reasoned that in such a case there is no initial oral agreement as to a clause conferring jurisdiction which is capable of being evidenced by the confirmation in writing. Subsequently, the Court of Justice has shown a concern that the requirements as to form should not be so onerous as to impede normal commercial practices, and has adopted a rather more liberal line. In *Partenreederi MS "Tilly Russ" v Nova NV*[5] it held that where the choice of jurisdiction clause is in writing (in the instant case, in printed conditions in a bill of lading)[6] this can be regarded as written confirmation of an earlier communicated oral agreement between the parties expressly referring to that clause.

The same willingness to recognise that there has been confirmation in writing is evident in the decision of the Court of Justice in *F Berghoefer GmbH and Co KG v ASA SA*.[7] Here it was held that, in the situation where there is an oral agreement expressly dealing with jurisdiction, the formal requirements of Article 17 are satisfied if written confirmation of the agreement by one of the parties was received by the other and the latter raised no objection. It is not required that the confirmation comes from the party who stands to lose from the clause. Thus in the instant case it was a German plaintiff who confirmed the oral agreement that the German courts should have exclusive jurisdiction.

(b) In a form which accords with practices which the parties have established between themselves
This was added by the 1989 Accession Convention.[8] It merely incorporates the effect of certain decisions of the Court of Justice,[9] which has held that the consensus of the parties may be shown by a continuous business relationship between them which was subject to the general conditions containing the jurisdiction clause.

(c) In international trade or commerce, in a form which accords with a usage of which the parties are or ought to have been aware and which in such trade or commerce is widely known to, and regularly observed by, parties to contracts of the type involved in the particular trade or commerce concerned
The 1978 Accession Convention added a provision on trade usage because of fears that the Court of Justice had interpreted the original requirements

---

4 Case 25/76 [1976] ECR 1851, [1977] 1 CMLR 361.
5 Op cit. The case concerned the unamended Convention, ie the version before the 1978 Convention of Accession came into effect.
6 The bill of lading may come into existence after the creation of the contract of carriage to which the jurisdiction clause relates; however, Art 17 does not require the agreement on jurisdiction to be contemporaneous with the original contract. See on this aspect of the case, North [1985] Lloyd's MCLQ 177.
7 Case 221/84 [1985] ECR 2699, [1986] 1 CMLR 13; Hartley (1986) 11 ELR 470. See also Case 313/85 *Iveco Fiat SpA v Van Hool NV* [1986] ECR 3337.
8 Art 7; see the Almeida Cruz, Desantes Real and Jenard Report, para 26; the Jenard and Möller Report, p 77.
9 *Partenreederei M S Tilley Russ v Haven and Vervaebedriff Nova NV*, op cit; *Segoura v Bonakdarian*, op cit.

so restrictively that businessmen would find it hard to meet them.[10] The 1989 Accession Convention introduced the additional requirement that this usage must, on the one hand, be widely known to, and, on the other hand, regularly observed by, parties to contracts of the type involved in the particular trade or commerce concerned.[11]

Which party can allege that the requirements relating to form have not been met? Clearly the party who did not have notice of the choice of jurisdiction clause can do so. This was the position in the *Colzani* and *Segoura* cases. But if this party wishes to rely on the clause, can the other party, who knew about it from the outset, challenge the clause on the basis of lack of compliance with the requirements as to form? Since the purpose of these requirements is to prevent choice of jurisdiction clauses going unnoticed by one of the parties, it is arguable that only the party who did not have notice of the clause should be able to challenge it.[12] On the other hand, if, as the Schlosser Report suggests,[13] the courts of Contracting States must of their own motion determine whether Article 17 operates to prevent them from having jurisdiction, these are requirements which apply regardless of the arguments of the parties, and it should be irrelevant which party raises the issue.

Do the requirements as to form apply in relation to third parties? In *Gerling v Italian Treasury*[14] the Court of Justice held that a third party beneficiary would be entitled to rely on a choice of jurisdiction clause inserted for his benefit in a contract (which satisfied Article 17 requirements) between an insurer and a policy-holder, even though the third party had not satisfied the requirements as to form. The Court pointed out that the provisions on insurance in the Convention were designed to protect the policy holder. It would be pointless to require a third party to go through these formalities; and in those cases where the beneficiary was not told of the jurisdiction clause, impossible for him to do so. Consistent with this, in the more recent *Tilly Russ*[15] case it was held that a third party who, under the applicable national law, stood in the shoes of an original shipper, succeeding to his rights and obligations under a bill of lading (which did comply with Article 17), could not avoid the obligations in respect of jurisdiction under this by arguing that he did not consent to the jurisdiction clause. The same principle as in *Gerling* applied. Seemingly, it did not matter that the case related to marine transport, which is not an area involving protective provisions. Nor did it matter that it related to a third party trying to avoid the burden of a choice of jurisdiction clause rather than to take its benefit. What was important was that under the relevant national law, the third party, upon acquiring the bill of lading, succeeded to the shipper's rights and obligations.

10 See the Schlosser Report, p 125. It may be that both the *Colzani* and *Segoura* cases would now come within this
11 Art 7; see the Almeida Cruz, Desantes Real and Jenard Report, para 26; the Jenard and Möller Report, p 77. This provision accords with Art 9(2) of the 1980 Vienna Convention on International Contracts for the Sale of Goods.
12 For the position in respect of a third party in relation to a contract of insurance, see Case 201/82 *Gerling v Italian Treasury* [1983] ECR 2503.
13 At p 21; see also the *Colzani* case.
14 Case 201/82 [1983] ECR 2503; Hartley (1983) 8 ELR 264.
15 Op cit.

Limitations on the effectiveness of the agreement

First, the third paragraph[16] of Article 17 provides that the courts which have exclusive jurisdiction under Article 16 cannot be deprived of it by an agreement under Article 17, and any agreement which purports to do so shall have no legal force. It also provides that agreements conferring jurisdiction are also of no legal force if they are contrary to Articles 12 or 15. This means that in matters relating to insurance and in consumer contracts any agreement conferring jurisdiction must comply with both the requirements of Article 17 and Articles 12 or 15.

Second, the fourth paragraph of Article 17 provides that, if the agreement conferring jurisdiction was concluded for the benefit of only one of the parties, that party shall retain the right to bring proceedings in any other court which has jurisdiction by virtue of the Convention. Because the agreement is only for one party's benefit, that party is given the right to waive the benefit of it. This is a more limited provision than that contained in the third paragraph; the court of the Contracting State on which jurisdiction has been conferred has jurisdiction but it does not have exclusive jurisdiction. This raises the problem of when an agreement conferring jurisdiction is concluded for the benefit of only one of the parties. The most obvious examples are where one party only is allowed to sue in a named Contracting State,[17] one party is given a wider choice of jurisdiction than the other,[18] and the clause indicates expressly the party for whose benefit it was concluded.[19] On the other hand, it is clear that an agreement conferring jurisdiction is not to be regarded as having been concluded for the benefit of only one of the parties when all that has been established is that jurisdiction is conferred on the courts of the Contracting State in which that party is domiciled.[20] However, it is not clear whether the fourth paragraph would also encompass the situation where the stronger party imposes on the weaker party a standard form of contract which contains a choice of jurisdiction clause.[21] Arguably it should not; it would undoubtedly be an odd result for a Convention which has many provisions designed to protect the weaker party to be interpreted in such a way as to give the stronger party the best of both worlds.

Third, the fifth and final paragraph of Article 17 provides a limitation that is confined to matters relating to individual contracts of employment. This is a new limitation introduced by the 1989 Accession Convention,[22] and is concerned with protecting employees. The agreement on jurisdiction will only take effect if it is entered into after the dispute has arisen or[23] if it is invoked by the employee as plaintiff. The latter alternative means that a plaintiff employee can rely on an agreement conferring jurisdiction entered into before the dispute has arisen. In this situation the agreement does not confer

16 The paragraphing is as set out in OJ, 1989 C 285/1 rather than as set out in Sch 1 of SI 1990/2591 which appears to have incorrectly divided up Art 17 into paragraphs.
17 See Hartley, p 69. See generally Kaye, pp 1089–1093.
18 See the decision of the Court of Justice in Case 22/85 *Anterist v Credit Lyonnais* [1986] ECR 1951, [1987] 1 CMLR 333; Hartley (1986) 11 ELR 471. The case is concerned with what was formerly the third para of Art 17 but which, since the 1978 Accession Convention, is now the fourth para.
19 Ibid.
20 Ibid.
21 See Anton, *Civil Jurisdiction in Scotland*, para 7.26.
22 Art 7; see the Almeida Cruz, Desantes Real and Jenard Report, para 27. The *Elefanten Schuh* and *Sanicentral Cases* would appear to come within this.
23 There is no such alternative under the Lugano Convention, infra p 344.

exclusive jurisdiction since the plaintiff employee, instead of suing in the Contracting State agreed upon, could opt to sue in the State of the defendant's domicil (under Article 2) or in the place of performance of the contract of employment (under Article 5(1)). On the other hand, an employee in the position of defendant cannot rely on an agreement entered into before the dispute has arisen. An employer, whether acting as plaintiff or defendant, can only rely on an agreement conferring jurisdiction entered into after the dispute has arisen.

Fourth, there is one final limitation on the effectiveness of the agreement, which is not mentioned in Article 17. The Court of Justice has held that the defendant's submission to the courts of a Contracting State under Article 18 overrides an agreement conferring jurisdiction under Article 17.[24]

(b) Submission to the forum

Article 18 provides that "... a court of a Contracting State before whom a defendant enters an appearance shall have jurisdiction". This means that where the defendant submits to the courts of a Contracting State he will give that State jurisdiction even though it would not otherwise have had it under the Convention. Where the appearance is before the United Kingdom courts the familiar problem of allocating jurisdiction within the United Kingdom arises.[25] Where the Modified Convention applies this will allocate jurisdiction to a part of the United Kingdom. Where it does not, the Convention itself can be regarded as allocating jurisdiction to the courts of England, Scotland or Northern Ireland, depending on which court the defendant actually appears before.

For Article 18 to apply there are two conditions. First, there is considerable authority for the view that the defendant must be domiciled in a Contracting State.[1] The argument for this is as follows. Article 18 must be read in the light of Articles 3 and 4. Unless there is something in the wording of Article 18 to indicate that it applies regardless of domicil, those articles would confine it to the situation where the defendant is domiciled in a Contracting State. The wording of Article 17 makes it clear that it is intended to apply regardless of domicil; the same cannot be said of Article 18. There is an argument against this, albeit of less weight. Article 17 applies regardless of domicil, and so should Article 18 since both articles are dealing with prorogation of jurisdiction;[2] indeed Article 18 can override Article 17.[3]

Second, the defendant must enter an appearance before a court of a Contracting State. The Convention does not define the meaning of entering an appearance. According to the Jenard Report it will be for the court seised of the proceedings to determine this in accordance with its own rules of procedure.[4] Article 18 does, though, make it clear that not all the situations where the defendant enters an appearance come within its scope.[5] Article 18

---

24 Case 150/80 *Elefanten Schuh GmbH v Jacqmain* [1981] ECR 1671, [1982] 3 CMLR 1.
25 Supra, pp 283–284.
 1 See supra, pp 290–292. See also the Jenard Report, p 38; O'Malley and Layton, p 607; cf Hartley, p 51; Kaye, p 1125.
 2 See *Transocean Towage Co Ltd v Hyundai Construction Co Ltd* [1987] ECC 282, Netherlands Supreme Court.
 3 *Elefanten Schuh v Jacqmain*, op cit; Case 48/84 *Spitzley v Sommer Exploitation SA* [1985] ECR 787, [1985] 2 CMLR 507.
 4 At p 38. See also the opinion of the Advocate General in *Elefanten Schuh v Jacqmain*, op cit.
 5 See the limitations on the application of Art 18, infra.

also only refers to the *defendant* entering an appearance; it would not appear to cover the case where a plaintiff enters an appearance to contest a set-off sought by the defendant in response to the plaintiff's original claim. However, the Court of Justice in *Spitzley v Sommer Exploitation SA*[6] held that a court of a Contracting State, which would not otherwise have had jurisdiction in respect of the set-off, had it under Article 18 because of the plaintiff's appearance before that court. Whilst this interpretation flies in the face of the wording of Article 18, it is not unfair to the parties who have both (one by seeking the original claim, the other by seeking a set-off) elected for trial in that Contracting State. There is also economy of procedure if both the claim and set-off are dealt with in the same Contracting State.

Limitations on the application of Article 18
(i) Article 18 does not apply where the appearance was entered solely to contest jurisdiction. The defendant must be extremely careful as to how he conducts his defence where proceedings are commenced against him in a Contracting State. Where the defendant enters an appearance and fights the action on its merits (for example, denies he is in breach of contract) the court of the Contracting State before which he appears will have jurisdiction. Where the defendant merely denies that the court of a Contracting State has jurisdiction over him (for example, he points out that it is using a traditional exorbitant basis of jurisdiction against him and that this is prohibited by the Convention) the court of the Contracting State before which he appears will not have jurisdiction. A defendant does not submit to the jurisdiction of the English courts merely by acknowledging service and applying to stay the action.[7] The distinction between fighting on the merits and contesting jurisdiction is well known to English lawyers,[8] and is easy to apply where the defendant acts in only one of these ways. What if the defendant appears before the courts of a Contracting State and argues in the alternative, that there is no jurisdiction over him and that, even if there is, he did not, for instance, break the contract? A literal interpretation of Article 18 would suggest that the court before which the defendant has appeared is given jurisdiction in this situation, because the defendant has not appeared *solely* to contest jurisdiction. However, the Convention ought not to be given such a literal interpretation, particularly as the French text of Article 18 does not even contain an equivalent of the word "solely". The Court of Justice in *Elefanten Schuh v Jacqmain*[9] held that one of the objectives of the Convention is to give the defendant the right to defend himself, and he should not be handicapped from going into matters of substance by this having the effect of destroying his arguments as to jurisdiction. It may actually be necessary for him to go into matters of substance in order to protect his property from seizure. The defendant, therefore, does not submit if he argues in the alternative. The danger with this wide interpretation is that spurious arguments as to a lack of jurisdiction may be added on to what is, in essence,

---

6 Case 48/84 [1985] ECR 787, [1985] 2 CMLR 507; Hartley (1986) 11 ELR 98.
7 *The Sydney Express* [1988] 2 Lloyd's Rep 257. See also *Kurz v Stella Musical Veranstaltungs GmbH* [1992] Ch 196 at 201–202; *British Steel Corpn v Allivane International Ltd* 1989 SLT (Sh Ct) 57.
8 Infra, pp 353–354, Collins, pp 92–93.
9 Op cit. Followed in Case 25/81 *CHW v GJH* [1982] ECR 1189, [1983] 2 CMLR 125; Case 27/81 *Röhr v Ossberger* [1981] ECR 2431, [1982] 3 CMLR 29; Case 201/82 *Gerling v Italian Treasury* [1983] ECR 2503. See also *Luis Marburg & Söhne GmbH v Società Ori Martin SpA* [1987] ECC 424, Italian Supreme Court.

a defence based on substance, in order to avoid the application of Article 18. The Court of Justice has stopped the defendant from tacking on arguments as to jurisdiction at a late stage, holding that it must be clear to the plaintiff and the court from the time of the defendant's first defence that it is intended to contest the court's jurisdiction; if not, Article 18 will give jurisdiction to the courts of the Contracting State before which the defendant has appeared.[10] This does nothing to stop the well advised defendant who, at the beginning of proceedings, includes a specious defence which contests jurisdiction.

(ii) Article 18 does not apply where another court has exclusive jurisdiction by virtue of Article 16. Article 18 does not say whether it is subject to Article 17. By only mentioning Article 16 it can be inferred that it is not. The Court of Justice has confirmed this by holding that an appearance under Article 18 overrides an agreement conferring jurisdiction under Article 17.[11] This is only right and proper; both Articles 17 and 18 are dealing with selection of jurisdiction by the parties and a later selection by appearance should take precedence over an earlier selection by agreement.

(f) PROCEDURE—SERVICE OF THE WRIT

Under the traditional English rules on jurisdiction, service of a writ performs the dual functions of providing the basis of jurisdiction and giving the defendant notice of the proceedings. The Convention has bases of jurisdiction which do not depend on service of a writ. Procedure is largely left as a matter for national law, rather than being dealt with by the Convention. The procedure under English law where the Convention applies is as follows.[12] A writ can be issued[13] and served out of the jurisdiction[14] without the leave of the court provided that: (i) the claim is one which by virtue of the 1982 Act the court has power to determine; and (ii) the writ is endorsed with a statement to this effect and with a statement that no proceedings involving the same cause of action are pending elsewhere in the United Kingdom or in another Convention territory. The writ need not be served personally on the defendant and need not be served by the plaintiff or his agent.[15] The precise method for service of the writ abroad depends on whether the defendant is in a country with which there is a convention dealing with the matter.[16] The only thing that the Convention has to say about this is that these conventions on service shall continue to determine the procedure for service between Contracting States, with an additional method of service being added. This is based on co-operation between public officials in Contracting States, with officials in

10 *Elefanten Schuh v Jacqmain*, op cit. Where the challenge to jurisdiction is not a preliminary matter see the Advocate General's opinion in *CHW v GJH*, op cit.
11 *Elefanten Schuh v Jacqmain*, op cit. See also *The Sydney Express* [1988] 2 Lloyd's Rep 257.
12 See Collins, pp 95–96; *Practice Direction* [1987] 1 All ER 160.
13 Ord 6, r 7(1).
14 Ord 11, r 1(2)(a). It deals with service in Scotland and Northern Ireland as well as in other Brussels or Lugano Contracting States.
15 Ord 11, r 5(3); provided it complies with the law of the country where service is effected and complies with a method prescribed by r 6 or r 7.
16 The United Kingdom has entered into bilateral Civil Procedure Conventions, with all the other Contracting States except Luxembourg and Ireland. The United Kingdom is a party to the multilateral Hague Convention of 1965 on the Service Abroad of Judicial and Extrajudicial Documents in Civil or Commercial Matters as are a majority of the other Contracting States, see RSC Ord 11, r 6 and annotations thereto in the *Supreme Court Practice*. In the case of Ireland service must be made by the plaintiff or agent direct, and not through official channels, see RSC Ord 11 r 5(3)(b) and r 6(1)(e).

the Contracting State where the addressee is found forwarding the copy of the judicial documents.[17] The Convention is, however, concerned with the notice of the proceedings that is given to the defendant and, as will be seen later in this chapter,[18] has provisions designed to safeguard his interests.

(g) OTHER PROVISIONS RELATING TO JURISDICTION

There are provisions on jurisdiction in Title II of the Convention dealing with matters other than bases of jurisdiction, for example, dealing with minimum standards in relation to notice of the proceedings and declining jurisdiction in cases of *lis pendens*. These provisions can, as a matter of principle, apply regardless of where the defendant is domiciled.[19] This is subject to the wording of the provision in question which, in some instances, makes it clear that it only relates to the situation where a defendant is domiciled in a Contracting State.

(i) **Safeguarding the rights of the defendant**

The Convention safeguards the rights of the defendant in two ways.

(a) **The duty to examine jurisdiction where the defendant does not enter an appearance**

A court of a Contracting State before which a defendant (domiciled in another Contracting State) is sued, but, does not enter an appearance, is required to examine its own jurisdiction and declare of its own motion that it has no jurisdiction unless this is derived from the provisions of the Convention.[20] Hitherto, an English court has acted on the basis of the submissions of the parties, so that this duty to act on its own motion is a new one.[21]

(b) **Minimum standards in relation to notice**

A court of a Contracting State "shall stay the proceedings so long as it is not shown that the defendant has been able to receive the document instituting the proceedings or an equivalent document in sufficient time to enable him to arrange for his defence, or that all necessary steps have been taken to this end".[22] It is intended that this will only apply where the defendant is domiciled in one Contracting State, is sued in another, and does not enter an appearance.[1] This provision was introduced with civil law systems in mind, under some of which there is a danger of a defendant having a judgment entered against him in default of appearance without having any knowledge of the action.[2] Where the defendant does not enter an appearance, the court of a Contracting State before which an action is brought is required to consider

---

17 Art IV of the Protocol annexed to the 1968 Convention.
18 Infra.
19 See Arts 3 and 4, and supra, pp 290–292.
20 Art 20, para 1.
21 See the Schlosser Report, pp 81–82; for procedural rules that take account of this, see Ord 6, r 7 and Ord 13, r 7B. See also Art 19 and Case 288/82 *Duijnstee v Goderbauer* [1983] ECR 3663. See, generally, Kohler (1985) 34 ICLQ 563, 573–574.
22 Art 20, para 2.
1 See the Jenard Report, pp 39–40. Also Case 228/81 *Pendy Plastic Products BV v Pluspunkt Handelsgesellschaft mbH* [1982] ECR 2723, [1983] 1 CMLR 665; Anton, *Civil Jurisdiction in Scotland*, para 7.33.
2 See Hunnings [1985] JBL 303.

its own procedure, to see that it conforms with these minimum standards, before entering a default judgment. This is not likely to lead to stays of proceedings in England for two reasons. First, the provision is only designed to be a transitional one, and in an increasing number of cases it will not apply. Where the forum and the Contracting State in which the document has to be served have both ratified the Hague Convention of 1965 on the Service Abroad of Judicial and Extrajudicial Documents in Civil and Commercial Matters (the United Kingdom and a majority of the other Contracting States have done so[3]), the detailed provisions on service abroad under Article 15 of that Convention will apply instead, provided that the document instituting the proceedings had to be transmitted abroad in accordance with that Convention.[4] Second, even where the 1965 Hague Convention does not apply, English courts are likely to assume that their procedure for service abroad[5] will comply with the minimum standards for notice set out in the Judgments Convention[6] since the procedure for service abroad,[7] including rules on judgments in default,[8] was introduced after the Civil Jurisdiction and Judgments Act 1982 was passed.

The English procedure will come in for scrutiny from the courts of other Contracting States which are asked to recognise or enforce a judgment of an English court. Conversely, English courts will have to consider foreign procedure when asked to recognise the judgments of other Contracting States.[9]

(ii) Lis pendens—related actions

(a) **Lis pendens** Article 21 provides that "Where proceedings involving the same cause of action and between the same parties are brought in the courts of different Contracting States, any court other than the court first seised shall of its own motion stay its proceedings until such time as the jurisdiction of the court first seised is established.

Where the jurisdiction of the court first seised is established, any court other than the court first seised shall decline jurisdiction in favour of that court."

The Convention will often give jurisdiction to the courts of more than one Contracting State in respect of a single dispute, eg an Italian plaintiff, who is injured in Italy by the negligent driving of a defendant domiciled in France, can sue either in Italy under Article 5(3) or in France under Article 2; there is an obvious need for a provision to deal with the problems of forum shopping, concurrent proceedings and conflicting judgments in the courts of

---

3 Art 15 will not apply in all cases involving Contracting States which are parties to it, eg it will not apply where the address of the defendant is not known: Art 1(2) of the 1965 Hague Convention; see generally O'Malley and Layton, pp 97–102. Art 15 requires actual delivery to the defendant, or to his residence, or compliance with the law of the State addressed for service. See *Noirhomme v Walklate* (1991) Times, 2 August.
4 Art 20, para 3; see also *Pendy Plastic Products v Pluspunkt*, op cit.
5 See supra, p 324. On the length of time a defendant is given to acknowledge service see RSC Ord 11, r 1(3) (generally 21 days).
6 See Collins, p 96.
7 See RSC (Amendment No 2) 1983 (SI 1983/1181 (L 21)).
8 RSC Ord 13, r 7B.
9 See Art 27(2); Case 166/80 *Klomps v Michel* [1981] ECR 1593, [1982] 2 CMLR 773; Hunnings [1985] JBL 303; infra, pp 427–430.

different Contracting States.[10] Whilst Article 21 is limited to concurrent proceedings[11] in Contracting States, it should be noted that it is not limited to proceedings under the bases of jurisdiction set out in the Convention.[12] Article 21 will apply where proceedings involving the same cause of action and parties have been commenced in two Contracting States under their traditional rules on jurisdiction (the bases of jurisdiction under the Convention being inapplicable).[13] The Court of Justice, following a reference from the Court of Appeal, held in *Overseas Union Insurance Ltd v New Hampshire Insurance Co* that there is no requirement that either party be domiciled in a Contracting State.[14] This is clear from the wording and purpose of Article 21. It should also be noted that Article 21 is a purely mechanical rule. The court of the Contracting State first seised of the matter takes priority, and any court of another Contracting State must of its own motion decline jurisdiction, once the jurisdiction of the court first seised is established in that State.[15] The court seised second cannot examine the jurisdiction of the court first seised, except perhaps when the court seised second has exclusive jurisdiction.[16] There is no discretion given to the courts of either Contracting State as to whether they should take jurisdiction. A mechanical rule tends to produce certainty; this does not mean that there are no problems with Article 21.

(i) The two sets of proceedings must involve the same cause of action. According to the Court of Justice in *Gubisch Maschinenfabrik KG v Giulio Palumbo*[17] this, like the other terms in Article 21 concerned with whether a situation of *lis pendens* exists, must be given an independent community meaning. The same cause of action refers to the proceedings being based on the same contractual relationship. There is, though, a separate, albeit closely related, requirement, which does not appear in the English language version of Article 21: the *subject-matter* of the proceedings must be the same. The Court of Justice held that this requirement was satisfied in circumstances where one party brought an action in Italy for the recission or discharge of an international sales contract whilst an action by the other party to enforce the same contract was pending before a court in Germany. The same question of whether the contract was binding lay at the heart of both actions and it was not required that the two claims be entirely identical. Whilst this broad interpretation is understandable it does tend to break down the distinction between this provision and Article 22, which deals with related actions.

10 See Case 42/76 *De Wolf v Cox BV* [1976] ECR 1759, [1977] 2 CMLR 43; noted by Hartley (1977) 2 ELR 146; the case is discussed infra, pp 416–417, 439–440.
11 This means original proceedings, not proceedings for the enforcement of a foreign judgment obtained in original proceedings: *Owens Bank Ltd v Bracco* [1991] 4 All ER 833, [1992] 2 WLR 127, CA.
12 See *The Nordglimt* [1988] QB 183, [1988] 2 All ER 531.
13 See Arts 3 and 4 supra, pp 290–292; the Jenard Report, pp 20–21.
14 Case C-351/89 [1992] 2 WLR 586; Hartley (1992) 17 ELR 75.
15 See the Schlosser Report, p 125; *Re Proceedings in Two Fora* [1987] ECC 273, German Federal Supreme Court. For the procedural provisions under English law which take into account *lis pendens* problems, see supra, pp 324–325.
16 Case C-351/89 *Overseas Union Insurance Ltd v New Hampshire Insurance Co*, op cit. See also *Kloeckner & Co AG v Gatoil Overseas Inc* [1990] 1 Lloyd's Rep 177; infra, p 329.
17 Case 144/86 [1987] ECR 4861; Hartley (1988) 13 ELR 216. Cf *Kloeckner & Co AG v Gatoil Overseas Inc* supra, each purchase and sale agreement stemming from a basic contract was treated as a separate cause of action; *The Maciej Rataj* [1991] 2 Lloyd's Rep 458, proceedings for a declaration not a cause of action.

(ii) The two sets of proceedings must be between the same parties. This requirement has caused the English courts particular problems in relation to actions in rem. As has already been seen,[18] if one action is in personam (against a person) and the other is in rem (against a ship) it has been held that the parties are not the same and Article 21 will not apply.[19]

(iii) Article 21 could lead to a race between the parties, the winner being the one who can show that the court where he brought the action is first seised of jurisdiction. This raises the problem of deciding when a court becomes seised of jurisdiction. The answer is: when proceedings are commenced,[20] and the Jenard Report says that is left to the internal law of each Contracting State to determine.[21] This approach has been confirmed by the Court of Justice.[22] This means that a court in the United Kingdom will apply its own procedural rules to determine the point when proceedings are commenced in that part of the United Kingdom. It will also, of its own motion, have to consider if proceedings have been commenced in another Contracting State and, if so, when.[23] It must apply the procedural law of that other Contracting State to determine the precise moment when proceedings were commenced there. Under English law a court is normally seised of jurisdiction, not when the proceedings are issued, but when they are served on the defendant. However, there is an exception to the effect that the court is seised, if there has been an earlier exercise of jurisdiction, such as the grant of a Mareva injunction, from the moment that jurisdiction is exercised.[24] In other Contracting States a court is likewise seised of jurisdiction when service of the document takes place.[25] It follows that where the parties have raced to start proceedings in England and in, for example, France, the race is run on equal terms.

(iv) Article 21 is limited to concurrent proceedings in different Contracting States. To take an example, it would not apply to concurrent actions in Japan and the United Kingdom. In many such cases (eg a Japanese domiciliary sues a United Kingdom domiciliary in Japan, and there are concurrent proceedings in the United Kingdom where the United Kingdom domiciliary sues the Japanese domiciliary) the Convention would not apply to the action brought in the United Kingdom and the courts would use traditional bases of jurisdiction with the accompanying rules on stays of action, including those specifically dealing with *lis pendens*.[26] In other cases (eg a Japanese domiciliary sues a United Kingdom domiciliary in the United Kingdom,

---

18 Supra, p 219.
19 *The Nordglimt* [1988] QB 183. There must be doubts now over the correctness of this decision, in the light of the Court of Appeal's decision in *The Deichland* [1990] 1 QB 361, supra, p 291, a case on Art 2 of the Convention; see *The Sylt* [1991] 1 Lloyd's Rep 240. Even if Art 21 does not apply, Art 22, infra, pp 329–330, may do so.
20 See the Schlosser Report, p 125. The rule is criticised by Anton, *Civil Jurisdiction in Scotland*, para 7.38.
21 At p 71.
22 Case 129/83 *Zelger v Salinitri (No 2)* [1984] ECR 2397, [1985] 3 CMLR 366; Hartley (1985) 10 ELR 56.
23 At least where the circumstances are such as to lead the court to believe that proceedings may be pending in another Contracting State: Jenard Report, p 41.
24 *Dresser UK Ltd v Falcongate Freight Management Ltd* [1992] 2 WLR 319—an Art 22 case. The position is the same for in rem jurisdiction: *The Freccia Del Nord* [1989] 1 Lloyd's Rep 388.
25 The Schlosser Report, p 125, referring to the six original Contracting States.
26 See supra, pp 231–234, for the relevant English rules.

and there are concurrent proceedings in Japan where the United Kingdom domiciliary sues the Japanese domiciliary), the Convention would apply to the action brought in the United Kingdom. Nonetheless, Article 21 does not apply and there would appear to be no power to decline jurisdiction under any other provision in the Convention,[27] even though it may be inappropriate to take jurisdiction in the light of the other proceedings in the non-Contracting State. The Court of Appeal has got round this difficulty by deciding that, in cases involving an alternative forum which is a non-Contracting State, the English courts can use the traditional English doctrine of *forum non conveniens* (and presumably that of *lis alibi pendens* if proceedings have actually been commenced abroad) to stay the English proceedings.[28]

(v) It may be perfectly clear which court of a Contracting State is first seised of the proceedings, but jurisdiction may be challenged in that court. At one time there was a danger that the court seised of the action second would decline jurisdiction in favour of the court first seised.[1] But, that court might decide subsequently that it had no jurisdiction. Both actions would have been dismissed and starting an action afresh might run into time-bar problems. Article 21 was amended by the 1989 Accession Convention[2] to deal with this problem. The court seised second must of its own motion stay its proceedings until such time as the jurisdiction of the court first seised is established. Once it has been, the court seised second must then decline jurisdiction.

(vi) Article 21 is wide enough to cover cases where two Contracting States have exclusive jurisdiction. Nonetheless, the point is expressly covered by Article 23[3] which, like Article 21, requires a court, other than the one first seised, to decline jurisdiction in favour of that court. Article 23 does not stipulate whether it is referring to exclusive jurisdiction under Article 16 or Article 17,[4] and must be assumed to cover both. More problematical is the situation where a court in one Contracting State regards itself as having exclusive jurisdiction under Article 16 or 17, but a court in another Contracting State, nonetheless, has previously allowed the commencement of proceedings in that State. An English court has held, obiter, that Article 21 does not operate in such a case and the claim brought in the Contracting State with exclusive jurisdiction must be allowed to proceed.[5]

(b) Related actions Article 22 deals with proceedings in two Contracting States where the cause of action is not the same but is related. Related actions are defined as ones which are so closely connected that it is expedient to hear them together to avoid irreconcilable judgments from separate proceedings[6] in courts of different Contracting States. If there is no risk of irreconcilable judgments the actions are not related.[7] The actions are related where the cause of action is the same but the parties are not because one action is in

27 See infra, p 331.
28 *Re Harrods (Buenos Aires) Ltd* [1992] Ch 72, CA discussed infra, pp 332–334.
 1 There was, however, a discretionary power for the court seised second to stay its proceedings.
 2 Art 8; see the Almeida Cruz, Desantes Real and Jenard Report, para 28.
 3 See the Jenard Report, p 42.
 4 On Art 17, see Case 23/78 *Meeth v Glacetal Sarl* [1978] ECR 2133, [1979] 1 CMLR 520.
 5 *Kloeckner & Co AG v Gatoil Overseas Inc* [1990] 1 Lloyd's Rep 177 at 196. This point was left open by the Court of Justice in the *Overseas Union Insurance Case,* op cit.
 6 Art 22, para 3.
 7 *Rank Film Distributors Ltd v Lanterna Editrice Srl* (1991) Financial Times, 14 June. See also *Gascoigne v Pyrah* (1991) Times, 26 November.

personam and the other is in rem.[8] Any court other than the court first seised may (rather than must), while the actions are pending at first instance, stay its proceedings.[9] This appears to give a discretion but it is seemingly not one based on *forum non conveniens*.[10] Normally a stay should be granted in order to avoid irreconcilable judgments.[11] The court seised second can take into account the nature of the proceedings in the court seised first. Thus a stay was refused by an English court in circumstances where the prior proceedings in the Netherlands involved a pre-emptive strike by seeking a delcaration that cargo-owners were not entitled to damages.[12]

(iii) Provisional measures

The Convention allocates jurisdiction to the courts of a Contracting State in respect of the substance of a matter. Nonetheless, under Article 24 application may be made to the courts of another Contracting State, which does not have jurisdiction under the Convention in respect of the main action, for such provisional, including protective, measures as may be available under the laws of that State.[13] This would encompass the English *Mareva* injunction[14] and the Continental saisie conservatoire. Article 24 has been interpreted by the Court of Justice as only applying to provisional measures which relate to matters within the scope of the Convention.[15] It has to be asked what rights a provisional measure seeks to protect, and, if these are outside the Convention, a provisional measure cannot be granted under Article 24. There is no requirement that the main proceedings in the other Contracting State must have actually started when the interim relief is sought.[16]

Article 24 does not allow provisional measures to be granted where none were available beforehand. It requires the courts of the Contracting State before which an application is made to grant the provisional measures which are available under the law of that state.[17] If none are available in the particular circumstances,[18] Article 24 would not help. There was a danger of this happening under English law. A *Mareva* injunction was regarded as being an ancillary order which was only available where the English courts

---

8 *The Nordglimt* [1988] QB 183 at 201.
9 Art 22, para 1. See *Kloeckner & Co AG v Gatoil Overseas Inc* [1990] 1 Lloyd's Rep 177 at 206; Case 150/80 *Elefanten Schuh GmbH v Jacqmain* [1981] ECR 1671, [1982] 3 CMLR 1. For powers to decline jurisdiction where there is consolidation of related actions see para 2, *Owens Bank Ltd v Bracco* [1991] 4 All ER 833, [1992] 2 WLR 127, CA, and Anton *Civil Jurisdiction in Scotland*, para 7.41.
10 See generally Kohler (1985) 34 ICLQ 563, 571–572. See also *The Linda* [1988] 1 Lloyd's Rep 175 at 179; *Virgin Aviation v CAD Aviation* (1990) Times, 2 February.
11 *The Linda*, op cit.
12 *The Maciej Rataj* [1991] 2 Lloyd's Rep 458.
13 See generally, Collins (1981) 1 Yearbook of European Law 249; *The Siskina* [1979] AC 210 at 259–260. For recognition and enforcement of *Mareva* injunctions see Case 125/79, *Denilauler v SNC Couchet Frères* [1980] ECR 1553, [1981] 1 CMLR 62; and infra, pp 416–417.
14 See *Mareva Compania Naviera SA v International Bulkcarriers SA* [1975] 2 Lloyd's Rep 509, CA.
15 Case 143/78 *De Cavel v De Cavel* [1979] ECR 1055, [1979] 2 CMLR 547; Case 25/81 *CHW v GJH* [1982] ECR 1189, [1983] 2 CMLR 125. For the special problem with matrimonial property of not knowing at the time of the interim order what substantive rights are going to be enforced later, see Hartley, pp 17–18.
16 See Anton, *Civil Jurisdiction in Scotland*, para 7.46.
17 *Republic of Haiti v Duvalier* [1990] 1 QB 202 at 212, CA.
18 Eg it may not be available under the law of X, if the parties confer jurisdiction on Contracting State Y and intended provisional measures to be sought there, see Collins, p 90.

had jurisdiction over the main action.[19] If this rule had remained, Article 24 would have been of no practical effect in England. Section 25 of the 1982 Act has altered the rule to prevent this happening.[20] It provides that English courts can grant interim relief where proceedings: (a) have been or are to be commenced[21] in a Brussels Convention Contracting State other than the United Kingdom, or in another part of the United Kingdom; and (b) are proceedings whose subject matter is within the scope of the Convention under Article 1 (whether or not that or any other Convention has effect in relation to the proceedings).[22] There is no requirement that the defendant be domiciled in a Contracting State to the Brussels Convention.[23] The absence of jurisdiction in respect of the substance of the matter is a relevant factor to be taken into account when deciding whether to grant interim relief.[24] The result is that, to take an example, an English court could grant a *Mareva* injunction over assets in England and abroad, pending trial of a civil and commercial matter in France, the object being to preserve the English assets for when the French judgment is enforced in England under the Brussels Convention.[25]

(h) IS THERE A DISCRETION TO STAY PROCEEDINGS?

(i) In the Convention itself

A distinctive feature of the law relating to jurisdiction in common law systems is the presence of a discretionary power to refuse to take jurisdiction on the basis of *forum non conveniens*.[1] There is no such power in civil law systems. Given the civil law origins of the Convention, it is not suprising to find that it contains no general discretion to stay actions on the basis of *forum non conveniens*.[2] Moreover, whilst there is a provision on *lis pendens* in Article 21 this clearly does not involve a discretion.[3]

(ii) Can the traditional English doctrine of forum non conveniens be used?

Section 49 of the 1982 Act provides that:

> Nothing in this Act shall prevent any court in the United Kingdom from staying, sisting, striking out or dismissing any proceedings before it, on the ground of *forum non conveniens* or otherwise, where to do so is not inconsistent with the 1968 Convention . . .[4]

---

19 *The Siskina* [1979] AC 210, [1977] 3 All ER 803. See McLachlan (1987) 36 ICLQ 669.
20 *Babanaft International Co SA v Bassatne* [1990] Ch 13 at 30; *Republic of Haiti v Duvalier*, op cit, at 210; *X v Y* [1990] 1 QB 220 at 227–228. See generally Hogan (1989) 14 ELR 191. S 25 is discussed supra, pp 192–193. See also s 24 (interim relief in cases of doubtful jurisdiction) and s 26 (security in Admiralty proceedings). S 25 also applies to the Lugano Convention.
21 See *Alltrans Inc v Interdom* [1991] 2 Lloyd's Rep 571.
22 Eg the defendant is not domiciled in a Contracting State.
23 *X v Y*, op cit, at 229. This is relevant, though, when it comes to service of the writ abroad, supra, p 193.
24 S 25(2). See *Republic of Haiti v Duvalier*, op cit, at 215–217.
25 See *Republic of Haiti v Duvalier* [1990] 1 QB 202, [1989] 1 All ER 456, CA. The object may be, as in this case, to discover where the assets are. A foreign equivalent of a *Mareva* injunction could not be enforced in England under the Convention see infra, pp 416–417.
1 Supra, pp 221–234.
2 See the opinion of the Advocate General in Case 12/76 *Tessili v Dunlop* [1976] ECR 1473, [1977] 1 CMLR 26; Case 42/76 *De Wolf v Cox* [1976] ECR 1759, [1979] 2 CMLR 43.
3 There is a discretion to stay under Art 22 (related actions) but this is seemingly not one exercised on the basis of *forum non conveniens*, supra, p 330.
4 The Civil Jurisdiction and Judgments Act 1991, Sch 2 para 24, has added to s 49 a reference to the Lugano Convention, discussed infra, pp 340–344.

It follows from this that where the Convention is inapplicable (ie the matter is not within the scope of the Convention)[5] the courts in the United Kingdom will be able to apply their rules on stays of action (whether these are based on *forum non conveniens*, or on a foreign choice of jurisdiction clause) as well as their traditional bases of jurisdiction.

Where the Convention is applicable (ie the matter is within the scope of the Convention), but none of the bases of jurisdiction contained therein apply (the defendant is not domiciled in a Contracting State and Articles 16 and 17 do not apply)[6] the position is more difficult. The traditional English bases of jurisdiction will, in principle, apply, as will the discretion to stay on the basis of *forum non conveniens*. However, because of section 49 the stay of proceedings must not be inconsistent with the Convention.[7] Article 21 on *lis pendens* may operate[8] even where none of the bases of jurisdiction under the Convention apply[9] and the English courts will not be able to exercise their discretion to stay the proceedings on the basis of *lis pendens* if this would be inconsistent with that provision.[10]

Where the bases of jurisdiction under the Convention apply, it has to be decided whether the court of the Contracting State which has been assigned jurisdiction has to take it. If so, to grant a stay would be inconsistent with the Convention and for an English court would also involve being in breach of section 49. Continental lawyers[11] have taken the view that any court of a Contracting State allocated jurisdiction under the Brussels Convention must try the case and that courts in the United Kingdom cannot use their *forum non conveniens* discretion in such circumstances. However, English lawyers have not been prepared to give up their doctrine of *forum non conveniens* so easily, and have distinguished between cases where the alternative forum is a Contracting State and those where it is a non-Contracting State.

The English authorities In *S & W Berisford Plc v New Hampshire Insurance Co*[12] and *Arkwright Mutual Insurance Co v Bryanston Insurance Co Ltd*[13] it was held that there was no general discretionary power to stay the proceedings when jurisdiction had been allocated to England under Article 2 of the Brussels Convention, even if the alternative forum was a non-Contracting State. There are, though, suggestions[14] inconsistent in principle with that approach that a discretion to stay does exist in two specific situations. The first is where jurisdiction has been taken under the Convention, but the parties have agreed on trial in a non-Contracting State.[15] The second situation is where there is a dispute over land in a non-Contracting State.[16]

5 See supra, pp 286–289.
6 For where the bases of jurisdiction do not apply, see supra, pp 290–292.
7 See the judgment of KERR LJ in *The Sennar (No 2)* [1984] 2 Lloyd's Rep 142 at 154, CA.
8 Often it will not, because it is limited to proceedings in two Contracting States.
9 See *The Nordglimt* [1988] QB 183, [1988] 2 All ER 531.
10 See *The Linda* [1988] 1 Lloyd's Rep 175 at 179.
11 See the Schlosser Report, pp 97–99; Kohler (1985) 31 ICLQ 563, 571–574; Droz, p 128.
12 [1990] 2 QB 631, [1990] 2 All ER 321.
13 [1990] 2 QB 649, [1990] 2 All ER 335; Collins (1990) 106 LQR 535; Briggs [1991] Lloyd's MCLQ 10.
14 Based on academic literature. See eg Collins, pp 85; Hartley pp 66, 74, 77–80 who suggests a more general discretion; O'Malley and Layton, pp 30–31.
15 *S & W Berisford Plc v New Hampshire Insurance Co*, op cit, at 643; *Arkwright Mutual Insurance Co v Bryanston Insurance Co Ltd*, op cit, at 663. See also the Schlosser Report, p 124.
16 The *Arkwright Case*, op cit, at 663.

However, the Court of Appeal when faced with essentially the same facts in *Re Harrods (Buenos Aires) Ltd*[17], took a much more radical line. Proceedings were brought in England for, inter alia, the winding up of an English incorporated company. It was argued that the most appropriate forum for trial was Argentina, where the company exclusively carried on its business, and a stay was sought of the English proceedings. The Brussels Convention applied by virtue of the company's English domicil. Nonetheless, it was held that there was power to stay the English proceedings on the ground of *forum non conviens* and a stay was granted. A fundamental distinction was drawn between cases where the alternative forum was, as here, in a non-Contracting State and cases where it was in a Contracting State. The *forum non conveniens* discretion could still be exercised in the former case, but not in the latter. The Court of Appeal accepted the argument[18] that the Convention was intended to regulate jurisdiction as between Contracting States and not as between a Contracting and a non-Contracting State.[19] Exercise of the discretion to stay in a case involving a non-Contracting State would therefore not be inconsistent with the Convention, and was accordingly preserved by section 49 of the 1982 Act.[20]

Two serious criticisms can be levelled at this decision. First, it misunderstands the Convention. The argument used to justify the basic distinction adopted in the case cannot stand up to close scrutiny. The text of the Convention shows that it is not simply concerned with jurisdiction as between Contracting States. Moreover, the use of a discretion to stay, even if confined to cases where the alternative forum is a non-Contracting State, will do the opposite of promoting uniformity of jurisdictional rules throughout the Community. English courts will decline to try cases in cirumstances where most other Contracting States, having no discretionary power to stay proceedings under their national rules, will not do so. Article 2 (and indeed the other bases of jurisdiction under the Convention) should be regarded as being mandatory.

Second, the decision creates new uncertainty in the law. If the alternative forum to England is Germany (a Contracting State) the discretion cannot operate. If the alternative forum is New York (a non-Contracting State) it can. So much is clear. But what if there are connections with three States: England, Germany and New York? DILLON LJ limited the principle in *Re Harrods (Buenos Aires) Ltd* to cases where no other Contracting State was involved. But if only New York is put forward as an alternative forum for trial the rationale of the principle would suggest that the discretion should still operate. Indeed, the Court of Appeal has subsequently applied the doctrine of *forum non conveniens* in this situation.[21] Can the new principle established by the case operate in the situation where exclusive jurisdiction has been allocated to England under Articles 16 or 17? These provisions are more obviously mandatory than Article 2. Nonetheless, the distinction drawn

17 [1992] Ch 72; Briggs (1991) 107 LQR 180; Kaye [1992] JBL 47. For a Continental reaction see Gaudemet-Tallon (1991) 80 Rev crit dr int privé 491.
18 Put forward by Collins, op cit. See also Kaye, pp 1244–1245; Jackson, *Civil Jurisdiction and Judgments—Maritime Claims*, pp 161–161. Cf Mennie [1989] Jur Rev 150 at 167 et seq.
19 See also *Owens Bank Ltd v Bracco* [1991] 4 All ER 833 at 840, CA.
20 This will presumably apply equally to a case of *lis pendens* involving a non-Contracting State. Cf the *Arkwright Case*, op cit.
21 *The Po* [1991] 2 Lloyd's Rep 206. However, in this case England had jurisdiction by virtue of the Collision Convention, preserved by Art 57, and not by virtue of the defendant's domicil in England.

by the Court of Appeal looks to be applicable regardless of the basis of jurisdiction. Finally, should the same principles be taken into account when operating the *forum non conveniens* discretion in cases where the basis of jurisdiction is derived from the Convention as in other cases? The Court of Appeal in *Re Harrods (Buenos Aires) Ltd*, having decided that it had the power to grant a stay of proceedings, simply went on to apply the *Spiliada*[22] principles in the normal way.[22a] However, it has been suggested that, when exercising the discretion, the courts should be reluctant to stay proceedings when jurisdiction has been allocated to England under the Convention;[23] this must be particularly so if England has been allocated exclusive jurisdiction under Articles 16 or 17.

It is hard to resist the conclusion that the decision in *Re Harrods (Buenos Aires) Ltd* is misguided, if not downright wrong.[24] However, the decision has since been followed by a differently constituted Court of Appeal.[25] It is unfortunate that the Court of Appeal in *Re Harrods (Buenos Aires) Ltd* thought it unnecessary to refer the issue of interpretation raised in the case to the Court of Justice.

2. THE MODIFIED CONVENTION[1]

(a) WHEN DOES THE MODIFIED CONVENTION APPLY?

Section 16 of the 1982 Act is headed "allocation within UK of jurisdiction in certain civil proceedings". Section 16(1) states that the Modified Convention in Schedule 4 of the 1982 Act:[2]

> shall have effect for determining for each part of the United Kingdom,[3] whether the courts of law of that part ... have ... jurisdiction in proceedings where:
> (a) the subject-matter of the proceedings is within the scope of the 1968 Convention as determined by Article 1 (whether or not that or any other Convention has effect in relation to the proceedings); and
> (b) the defendant ... is domiciled in the United Kingdom or the proceedings are of a kind mentioned in Article 16 of the 1968 Convention (exclusive jurisdiction regardless of domicile).

It follows from section 16 that for the Modified Convention to apply three conditions must be satisfied.

22 *Spiliada Maritime Corpn v Cansulex Ltd* [1987] AC 460; discussed supra pp 221–231.
22a A stay was granted: *Re Harrods (Buenos Aires) Ltd* [1992] Ch 72 at 107 et seq. However, the dispute was regarded as being primarily one between Swiss shareholders in the company.
23 See *S & W Berisford Plc v New Hampshire Insurance Co*, op cit, at 645–656.
24 Case C-365/88 *Kongress Agentur Hagen GmbH v Zeehaghe BV* [1990] ECR 1845 draws a difficult distinction between jurdisdiction (dealt with by the Convention) and procedure (which is for national law). The example of procedure provided by that case is far removed from the issue of the discretion to stay, which it is submitted is one of jurisdiction.
25 *The Po* [1991] 2 Lloyd's Rep 206.
 1 Sch 4, Civil Jurisdiction and Judgments Act 1982. Amendments to Sch 4 are necessary in the light of the 1989 Spanish and Portuguese Accession Convention. In 1991 the Lord Chancellor's Department put forward proposals for these amendments. This section is written on the assumption that these proposals have been implemented. Implementation is expected sometime in 1992.
 2 For the limited exclusions from Sch 4, see s 17 and Sch 5 (as amended by the Children Act 1989, Sch 13, para 47). For special provisions with respect to trusts and consumer contracts, see s 10.
 3 S 50 defines this as England and Wales, Scotland or Northern Ireland.

(i) The situation must concern allocation of jurisdiction within the United Kingdom[4]

This presupposes that courts in the United Kingdom have jurisdiction. There are two situations where this will be so: first, in Convention cases, that is, where the Convention has allocated jurisdiction to courts in the United Kingdom;[5] second, in internal United Kingdom cases, where for example a Scotsman sues an Englishman in respect of land in England. Rules are needed to determine which part of the United Kingdom should have jurisdiction, although it would have been quite possible to leave the traditional English rules on jurisdiction to do this. The Brussels Convention itself is inapplicable in internal United Kingdom cases.[6]

(ii) The subject-matter of the proceedings must be within the scope of the Convention as determined by Article 1

The scope of the Convention has already been dealt with.[7] Section 16(1)(a) provides that the Modified Convention will apply "whether or not that or any other Convention has effect in relation to the proceedings". In an internal United Kingdom case the proceedings may be within the provisions on the scope of the Convention set out in Article 1 (ie a civil and commercial matter), yet the Convention would not be applied. It will be recalled that the Convention is only concerned with the international jurisdiction of Contracting States.[8] This additional wording in section 16(1)(a) gets over this particular problem.

(iii) The defendant must be domiciled in the United Kingdom or the proceedings must be of a kind mentioned in Article 16 of the 1968 Convention

The Modified Convention is only concerned in Brussels Convention cases with proceedings where jurisdiction is allocated to the United Kingdom under Article 2 (the defendant is domiciled in a Contracting State) or under Article 16 of the 1968 Convention (exclusive jurisdiction regardless of domicil). With both of these articles the Convention confers international jurisdiction (ie on the United Kingdom) and not local jurisdiction (ie on a part of the United Kingdom).[9] Where the Convention assigns jurisdiction to the courts in the United Kingdom under other articles, it is necessary to regard it as allocating jurisdiction to the courts in a part of the United Kingdom. In general, there is no problem where Article 5 applies, as this is designed to give local jurisdiction.[10] Most of the heads of Article 5 are phrased in terms of the courts for a "place" in a Contracting State having jurisdiction.[11] For example, Article 5(3) refers to the courts for the place where the harmful event occurred; ascertaining the "place" where the harmful event occurred inevitably pinpoints a part of the United Kingdom whose courts are to have jurisdiction. Where Articles 17 and 18 apply, as has already been seen,[12] there may be

4 Anton and Collins use the phrase "intra UK".
5 See the Schlosser Report, p 98; supra, pp 283–284 and infra.
6 Supra, p 286.
7 Supra, pp 286–289.
8 See the preamble to the Convention, supra, p 286.
9 See the Schlosser Report, p 98.
10 Ibid.
11 There is, however, a problem with Art 5(6) which gives jurisdiction to the courts of the Contracting State in which a trust is domiciled and does not refer to "the place".
12 Supra, pp 317, 322.

more difficulty in allocating jurisdiction to a part of the United Kingdom.

The requirement under section 16(1)(b) that the defendant be domiciled in the United Kingdom causes the usual definitional problems. In principle, a person is domiciled in England, Scotland, or Northern Ireland, not in the United Kingdom. Section 41(2) of the 1982 Act solves this difficulty by defining for the purposes of the Act whether an individual is domiciled in the United Kingdom. This is only so if: (a) he is resident in the United Kingdom; and (b) the nature and circumstances of his residence indicate that he has a substantial connection with the United Kingdom. Showing this substantial connection is made easier by the introduction of a presumption under section 41(6), according to which, where an individual (a) is resident in the United Kingdom, or in a particular part; and (b) has been so resident for the last three months or more, the requirement as to a substantial connection is presumed to have been fulfilled, unless the contrary is shown. With corporations, section 42(3) basically provides that a corporation has its seat in the United Kingdom if (a) it was incorporated and has its registered office in the United Kingdom; or (b) its central management and control is exercised in the United Kingdom.

(b) INTERPRETATION OF THE MODIFIED CONVENTION

The wording of the Modified Convention closely follows that of the Convention. Section 16(3)(a) of the 1982 Act requires the English courts, although they cannot make referrals to the Court of Justice, to pay regard to the decisions of that Court and to the relevant principles followed by it in relation to the jurisdictional provisions in Title II of the Convention. Also, each Report[13] accompanying the Brussels Convention and the three Accession Conventions may be considered.[14] If the Court of Justice interprets the Brussels Convention in a way of which the United Kingdom disapproves, it can alter the Modified Convention to nullify such decisions in relation to allocating jurisdiction within the United Kingdom.[15]

(c) THE TERMS OF THE MODIFIED CONVENTION

Although there was no necessity for the allocation of jurisdiction within the United Kingdom to be based on the Convention, this is the form it was decided it should take.[16] The effect of this can be seen in two examples. In the first example, the defendant is domiciled in the United Kingdom; the plaintiff will be able to sue him in England (if he is domiciled there),[17] or in Scotland (if special jurisdiction under Article 5 of the Modified Convention gives jurisdiction to Scotland), or in Northern Ireland (if Article 17 of the Modified Convention gives jurisdiction to Northern Ireland—under this provision the jurisdiction given is not exclusive). In the second example, the dispute concerns the ownership of land in England; the plaintiff will have to sue in England being the situs of the land (under Article 16 of the Modified Convention).

13 Supra, p 280.
14 S 16(3)(b) of the 1982 Act.
15 S 47(1)(b) of the 1982 Act.
16 See Anton *Civil Jurisdiction in Scotland*, paras 1–35, 9.01–9.04. This was, in part, because Scotland wished to replace its traditional rules on jurisdiction with new rules based on the Convention.
17 Under s 41 of the 1982 Act a person may have a dual domicil in different parts of the UK, so the plaintiff can sue in either part: *Daniel v Foster* (1989) SLT 90.

The fact that the Modified Convention by and large follows the wording of the 1968 Brussels Convention, (as amended by the three subsequent Accession Conventions of 1978, 1982 and 1989) has meant that the original Modified Convention (based on the 1968 Brussels Convention, as amended by the 1978 Accession Convention), as set out in Schedule 4 of the 1982 Act, has had to be amended[18] to incorporate, where relevant, most of the changes to the Brussels Convention brought about by the 1989 Spanish and Portuguese Accession Convention.[19]

However, right from the outset, when the original Modified Convention came into force in 1987, it was never precisely the same as the Brussels Convention, as at that time. It deliberately adopted a modified version of the Brussels Convention. The subsequent amendments to the Modified Convention have not altered this. The present position is therefore that the Modified Convention, as amended, is different from the Brussels Convention, as amended. The modifications that make it different will now be examined.

The modifications Some of these are necessary to allocate jurisdiction within the United Kingdom. Where the Convention refers to a *Contracting State* the Modified Convention instead refers to a *part of the United Kingdom*. Thus, under Article 2 "persons domiciled in a part of the United Kingdom shall ... be sued in the courts of that part". According to Article 3 they "may be sued in the courts of another part of the United Kingdom only by virtue of the rules set out in Sections 2, 4, 5 and 6 ... [which correspond to the same sections in the Convention]".

In order to determine whether an individual is domiciled in a particular part of the United Kingdom one must refer to section 41(3) of the 1982 Act. This uses the same criteria as are used under section 41(2) when ascertaining whether an individual is domiciled in the United Kingdom, that is, it looks for residence and a substantial connection with that part. The presumption under section 41(6) based on three months' residence is also applicable. Even if the presumption can be rebutted, this is not the end of the matter. Section 41(5) declares that, where the substantial connection cannot be shown in relation to any particular part of the United Kingdom, an individual shall be treated as domiciled in the part of the United Kingdom in which he is resident. Applying these rules, a person could be domiciled in two parts of the United Kingdom at the same time (eg a person has a home in England where he lives all winter but he has spent the previous 3 months of the summer at his home in Scotland), and both parts would have jurisdiction.[20] As far as companies are concerned, section 42(4) provides in broad terms that a company has a seat in a particular part of the United Kingdom only if it has its registered office in that part, or its central management and control is exercised in that part, or it has a place of business in that part. It may also be necessary in the case of some bases of jurisdiction to ascertain the place in the United Kingdom where an individual is domiciled. Section 41(4) provides a definition for determining this.[1]

18 See supra, p 334 footnote 1.
19 The amendments incorporate Arts 5(1), 6(4), 16(1)(a) and 17(5) of the Brussels Convention (as amended by the 1989 Accession Convention) into the Modified Convention. However, Art 16 (1)(b) of the Modified Convention follows the Lugano Convention rather than the Brussels Convention, see infra, p 338.
20 For stays of action, see infra, pp 339–340.
1 S 41(4) has to be used where Art 5(2) or Art 6 are applicable. For companies see s 42(5).

There are also modifications of substance, the most important of which are as follows.[2]

There is an addition to Article 5(3) to deal with threatened wrongs, which gives jurisdiction to the courts for the place in the part of the United Kingdom where the threatened wrong is likely to occur.[3]

There are two additional bases of special jurisdiction under Article 5. Article 5(8) deals, inter alia, with proceedings concerning debts secured on immovable property and gives jurisdiction to the courts of the part of the United Kingdom in which the property is situated. Article 5A deals with certain company law matters and gives jurisdiction to the courts of the part of the United Kingdom in which the company has its seat.

The Lord Chancellor's Department has proposed that there should be an Article 16(1)(b) to deal with short term tenancies of immovable property. This is based on the Lugano Convention rather than the Brussels Convention. This means that, if the proposal is implemented, the courts of the part of the United Kingdom in which the defendant is domiciled are given jurisdiction (as well as those of the part of the United Kingdom in which the property is situated) provided the tenant is a natural person and neither party is domiciled in the part of the United Kingdom in which the property is situated.[4]

Article 17 is altered in three ways. First, the effect of an agreement on jurisdiction is different. Article 17 of the Modified Convention provides that, if the parties have chosen the courts of a part of the United Kingdom, (eg the English courts) as the forum for trial, those courts will have jurisdiction. However, in contrast to Article 17 of the Convention such an agreement on jurisdiction does not give exclusive jurisdiction, and a plaintiff will be able to use the other bases of jurisdiction set out in the Modified Convention to sue in another part of the United Kingdom.[5] There is no requirement in Article 17 of the Modified Convention as to where the parties have to be domiciled, which is consistent with Article 17 of the Convention in so far as that provision deals with agreements which do not give exclusive jurisdiction.[6] If the parties have not specified which part of the United Kingdom has jurisdiction conferred on it (ie the agreement just says that trial is to take place in the United Kingdom), Article 17 of the Modified Convention will not apply, and the other bases of jurisdiction under the Modified Convention will have to be used to allocate jurisdiction within the United Kingdom. Second, there is no requirement in respect of the form of agreement, though there must still be a real agreement between the parties.[7] Third, the agreement, however, must be effective to confer jurisdiction under the law of that part of the United Kingdom whose courts the parties have agreed are to have jurisdiction.[8]

Finally the provisions on jurisdiction in matters relating to insurance and

---

2 See also Arts 13 and 20.
3 See the Schlosser Report, p 111. On Art 5(3) of the Modified Convention generally see *Davenport v Corinthian Motor Policies at Lloyds* 1991 SLT 774.
4 Cf Art 16(1)(b) of the Brussels Convention, supra, pp 312–313. For the differences between Art 16(1)(b) of the Lugano and Brussels Conventions see infra, pp 343–344.
5 See *British Steel Corpn v Allivane International Ltd* 1989 SLT (Sh Ct) 57. Cf *Jenic Properties Ltd v Andy Thornton Architectural Antiques* 1992 SLT (Sh Ct) 5.
6 See supra, pp 314–315.
7 *British Steel Corporation v Allivane International Ltd*, op cit.
8 It is proposed that there should be a limitation in relation to contracts of employment as under Art 17(5) of the Brussels Convention.

exclusive jurisdiction in relation to patents,[9] which are contained in the Convention, are omitted from the Modified Convention. This means that other bases of jurisdiction under the Modified Convention would have to be used in these cases. There is also no provision on *lis pendens* in the Modified Convention.

(d) STAYS OF ACTION

(i) Lis pendens

The absence of a provision on *lis pendens* from the Modified Convention does not cause any problems. Where the Brussels Convention is applicable, Article 21 is worded in such a way as to require all courts in the United Kingdom, whether in England, Scotland, or Northern Ireland, to decline jurisdiction where the courts of another Contracting State are first seised of the action. In internal United Kingdom cases, the Brussels Convention is inapplicable and the traditional English rules on the discretion to stay,[10] including those on *lis pendens*, can be used.

(ii) A general discretion to stay

The wording of the Modified Convention, being based on the Brussels Convention, contains no suggestion that there is a discretion to stay proceedings on the basis of *forum non conveniens*. Section 49 of the 1982 Act merely provides that a stay of action must not be inconsistent with the 1968 Convention.[11] It would, therefore, appear that a discretion to stay actions on the basis of *forum non conveniens* exists under the Modified Convention, where its use is not inconsistent with the 1968 Convention. In deciding whether its use is inconsistent with the 1968 Convention it is important to distinguish between, on the one hand, situations where that Convention applies (as well as the Modified Convention), and, on the other hand, situations where the Modified Convention applies on its own (internal United Kingdom cases).

Where the 1968 Convention applies there is no discretion to stay proceedings on the basis of *forum non conveniens*, at least in cases where the alternative forum is a European Community State.[12] Thus, an English court cannot stay proceedings on the basis that the alternative forum is, for example, France. However, where the Modified Convention then applies to allocate jurisdiction within the United Kingdom it is likely that there is a discretion to stay on this basis. It can be argued that the allocation of jurisdiction within the United Kingdom is a purely internal matter, and other Contracting States can have no objection to a discretion to stay being used to transfer actions from one part of the United Kingdom to another.[13] This is analogous to the reasoning applied by the Court of Appeal in *Re Harrods (Buenos Aires) Ltd*.[14] According to this decision, you can get a stay of English proceedings provided that the alternative forum is a non-Contracting State,

9 For the more general exclusion of patent proceedings from the Modified Convention see Sch 5, para (2) of the 1982 Act, on which see generally Anton, *Civil Jurisdiction in Scotland*, para 9.12.
10 Supra, pp 221–234.
11 Or, as the case may be, the Lugano Convention; discussed infra pp 340–344.
12 See supra, pp 331–334.
13 See the Schlosser Report, p 98; Hartley, p 80; Collins, pp 45–46; Stone (1983) 29 ICLQ 477, 496–499; cf Kaye, p 1245.
14 [1992] Ch 72; supra, pp 331–334.

in that case Argentina. In the light of this decision you should also be able to get a stay in the situation where the alternative forum is Scotland or Northern Ireland. There is, though, the danger with this approach that all the parts of the United Kingdom may stay the proceedings, thereby denying the plaintiff his right, under the Convention, to sue the defendant domiciled in the United Kingdom in that Contracting State.

In internal United Kingdom cases the 1968 Convention is inapplicable and it would appear to be the case that courts in the United Kingdom can use a discretion to stay on the basis of *forum non conveniens* without having to concern themselves with whether this is inconsistent with the Convention.[15]

3. THE LUGANO CONVENTION

The EFTA bloc (Austria, Finland, Iceland, Norway, Sweden and Switzerland) is the single most important trading partner of the European Community, and the need for legal and economic co-operation between the two blocs has been recognised for some time. A convention on jurisdiction and the recognition and enforcement of judgments has been seen as part of this process of co-operation. There are difficulties in the EFTA countries acceding to the Brussels Convention, in particular over the role of the Court of Justice in interpreting that Convention. Instead, a parallel Convention was agreed at Lugano in 1988.[1] This mirrors the Brussels Convention by adopting the same fundamental principles. Nevertheless, as will be seen, the Lugano Convention is an amended version of the Brussels Convention. Although the Lugano Convention is in force,[2] it only applies as between those states which have signed and ratified it (ie France, the United Kingdom, Switzerland, Luxembourg, the Netherlands). Accession is not confined to the present members of the European Communities and the EFTA bloc. The Convention allows for the accession of future European Communities/EFTA Member States[3] and even for third states to be invited to accede to the Convention.[4] In the case of the United Kingdom, as with the Brussels Convention, legislation is required to implement the Convention. This is provided by the Civil Jurisdiction and Judgments Act 1991, which came into force on 1st May 1992. This adds new sections to, and amends, the Civil Jurisdiction and Judgments Act 1982 so as to refer to the Lugano Convention along with the Brussels Convention. When the Lugano Convention comes fully into operation there will be the free circulation of judgments throughout virtually all of Western Europe, and persons domiciled in the region will be free from the risk of exorbitant rules of jurisdiction being exercised against them in another Western European State.

---

15 Hartley, op cit; Collins, op cit; Kaye, p 1245.
1 OJ 1988 L 391/9. This is set out in Sch 3C of the Civil Jurisdiction and Judgments Act 1982, added by s1(1) of the Civil Jurisdiction and Judgments Act 1991. See generally Carpenter, Haymann, Hunter-Tilney, Volken, *The Lugano and San Sebastian Conventions* (1990); Fawcett (1989) 14 ELR 1055; Stone (1988) Yearbook of European Law 105; Beaumont 1991 SLT 111; McCaffrey (1992) Civil Justice Quarterly 12.
2 As from 1 January 1992, following ratification by France and Switzerland, see Art 61, para 3.
3 Art 60(b).
4 Arts 60(c) and 62(1)(b).

(a) WHEN DOES THE LUGANO CONVENTION APPLY?[5]

The Lugano Convention applies in relation to jurisdiction in the situation where the matter is within the scope of the Convention and the defendant is domiciled in a Contracting State (or Article 16 or 17 gives jurisdiction to a Contracting State). This is the same as under the Brussels Convention[6] and presents no problem for EFTA Contracting States. However, Member States of the European Community will be Contracting States to both the Lugano Convention and the Brussels Convention. Given that there are differences between the two Conventions, Member States of the European Community need to know which Convention to apply. Article 54B of the Lugano Convention deals with this.[7] The effect of this provision, as far as EC Contracting States are concerned, is that if a defendant is domiciled in an EC Contracting State the Brussels Convention will still apply in matters of jurisdiction. However, if the defendant is domiciled in an EFTA Contracting State[8] the Lugano Convention will apply. The latter convention will also apply if Articles 16 or 17 confer jurisdiction on the courts of an EFTA Contracting State. The provisions in the Lugano Convention on *lis pendens* and related actions[9] will apply if there are concurrent proceedings in an EC Contracting State and an EFTA Contracting State.

(b) INTERPRETATION[10]

Questions of interpretation of the Lugano Convention cannot be referred to the Court of Justice. This leaves the obvious risk of different interpretations of the Convention in different Contracting States. Protocol 2, annexed to the Convention, seeks to minimise this risk by requiring courts in Contracting States to take account of any principles laid down in any relevant decision delivered by a court of any other Lugano Contracting State concerning provisions of the Convention. United Kingdom courts are compelled by statute to so act when determining the meaning of any provision of the Lugano Convention.[11] Awareness of such decisions is achieved by the establishment of a procedure for the exchange of information concerning relevant judgments.[12]

There is also a risk of a lack of uniformity between the interpretation of the Lugano and Brussels Conventions. There are two declarations annexed to the Lugano Convention which seek to deal with this. The first is concerned with interpretation of the Brussels Convention. Member States of the European Communities declare that "they consider as appropriate that the Court of Justice ... when interpreting the Brussels Convention, pay due account to the rulings contained in the case-law of the Lugano Convention". The second declaration is the corollary of the first, and is concerned with interpretation of the Lugano Convention. In it, the representatives of

5 The Jenard and Moller Report, OJ 1990 C 189/57, pp 67–69.
6 Supra, pp 286–292.
7 See s 9(1A) of the Civil Jurisdiction and Judgments Act 1982, added by s 1(2) of the Civil Jurisdiction and Judgments Act 1991.
8 Or any other Contracting State to the Lugano Convention which is not a member of the European Community.
9 Arts 21 and 22.
10 Minor (1990) 27 CML Rev 507.
11 S 3 B(1) Civil Jurisdiction and Judgments Act 1982, added by s 1(1) of the Civil Jurisdiction and Judgments Act 1991.
12 Protocol 2, Art 2.

the EFTA States declare that when interpreting the Lugano Convention it is appropriate that their courts pay due account to the rulings of the Court of Justice and of courts of the Member States of the European Communities in respect of the provisions of the Brussels Convention which are substantially reproduced in the Lugano Convention. The procedure for exchange of information on judgments extends to decisions of these courts.[13]

There are three obvious aids to interpretation of the Lugano Convention. First, there is the Jenard and Möller Report,[14] which is a commentary on the Convention prepared by the rapporteurs for the working party responsible for the drafting of the Convention. United Kingdom courts may consider this Report when ascertaining the meaning or effect of any provision of the Convention.[15] Second, there are the decisions of the Court of Justice and of courts in EC Contracting States on the interpretation of the Brussels Convention, insofar as the Lugano Convention is based on this Convention.[16] Third, there are the decisions of other Contracting States on the interpretation of the Lugano Convention.[17]

(c) DOMICIL

The special definition of domicil adopted for the purposes of the Brussels Convention is equally applicable for the purposes of the Lugano Convention.[18]

(d) AN AMENDED VERSION OF THE BRUSSELS CONVENTION

(i) The amendments

The Lugano Convention of 1988 was modelled on the Brussels Convention as it stood at that time (ie *prior* to the 1989 Accession Convention of Spain and Portugal). However, it contains a number of significant amendments which are of two types. The first is concerned to deal with special problems faced by the EFTA States. The result has been the introduction into the Lugano Convention of certain new additional defences to recognition and enforcement of judgments.[19] The second and more significant type of amendment is concerned with improving upon the rules at that time contained in the Brussels Convention. The drafters of the Lugano Convention wanted to get rid of uncertainties, give extra protection to employees, and deal more satisfactorily with disputes over short term lets of property. As a result, the Lugano Convention adopted an amended version for certain jurisdictional bases (Articles 5(1), 6, 16 and 17), for the *lis alibi pendens* provision (Article 21), and for the rules on the ascertainment of domicil (Article 52). These improvements were, for the main part, subsequently incorporated into the

13 Ibid.
14 OJ 1990 C 189/57.
15 S 3 B(2) of the Civil Jurisdiction and Judgments Act 1982, added by s 1(1) of the Civil Jurisdiction and Judgments Act 1991.
16 Protocol 2, the preamble and Art 2.
17 Protocol 2, Art 1.
18 Ss 41–46 of the Civil Jurisdiction and Judgments Act 1982 (supra, pp 284–285), as amended by the Civil Jurisdiction and Judgments Act 1991, Sch 2, paras 16–21.
19 See Protocol 1, Art 1a and b; Art 54B, para 3; Art 57, para 4; discussed infra, pp 443–444.

Brussels Convention by the 1989 Accession Convention,[20] and have already been examined earlier in this chapter.[1] Bringing the latest version of the Brussels Convention very largely into line with the Lugano Convention has avoided the awful prospect of having parallel Conventions which otherwise would have contained a disturbingly large number of differences. The Lugano Convention can therefore be seen to have already been very influential in terms of the development of the law in this area

(ii) Differences between the Lugano Convention and Brussels Convention (as amended by the 1989 Accession Convention)

The Lugano Convention and Brussels Convention (as amended by the 1989 Accession Convention) whilst now largely the same are, unfortunately, not completely so. There are differences in substance in relation to Articles 5(1), 16(1)(b) and 17, paragraph 5, which will now be examined.

Article 5(1) In cases involving individual contracts of employment where the employee does not habitually carry out his work in any one country, the Lugano Convention provides that jurisdiction shall be conferred on the courts of the place of performance of the obligation in question which place shall be "the place of business through which he was engaged". The 1989 Accession Convention adopted different wording so that the Brussels Convention now states that "the employer may also be sued in the courts for the place where the business which engaged the employee was or is now situated".[2] This means that under the Lugano Convention, but not the Brussels Convention, an employee, as well as an employer, may be sued in this place. Moreover, under the Lugano Convention the position is unclear in cases in which the place where the business which engaged the employee is situated has changed between the date of engagement and the time when proceedings are brought. Under the Brussels Convention the employee is able to sue in either place.[3]

Article 16(1)(b) This is concerned with short term tenancies of immovable property. In certain circumstances courts in the Contracting State in which the defendant is domiciled are given jurisdiction (as well as those of the State in which the property is situated). The proviso to this under the Lugano Convention is that "the tenant is a natural person and neither party is domiciled in the Contracting State in which the property is situated". The 1989 Accession Convention adopted, and led to the insertion in the Brussels Convention of, a much more restrictive proviso.[4] First, it requires both the landlord and tenant to be natural persons, and not merely the tenant as in the Lugano Convention. Second, it requires both the landlord and tenant to be domiciled in the same Contracting State. To take an example, a French landlord wishes to sue a Swiss tenant following the holiday let of a villa in England. Switzerland has jurisdiction under the Lugano Convention, but, in a parallel case now involving a German tenant, Germany would not have jurisdiction under the Brussels Convention (as amended by the 1989

---

20 See the Almeida Cruz, Desantes Real, Jenard Report on the Spanish and Portuguese Accession Convention: OJ 1990 C 189/06, pp 44–49.
1 Art 5(1) discussed supra, pp 294–299; Art 6(4), supra, p 306; Art 16, supra, pp 309–313; Art 17, supra, pp 314–322; Art 21, supra, pp 326–329; Art 52, supra, pp 284–285.
2 Supra, pp 297–299.
3 The Almeida Cruz, Desantes Real, Jenard Report, para 23.
4 Ibid, para 25. This proviso is discussed supra, p 313.

Accession Convention). One further difference between the two Conventions is that under the Lugano Convention, but not the Brussels Convention, it is possible for Contracting States to enter a reservation not to recognise and enforce judgments of other Contracting States if jurisdiction is based on Article 16(1)(b), and the property is situated in the State which has entered the reservation.[5]

Article 17 paragraph 5 The Lugano Convention introduced a very strict requirement that "In matters relating to individual contracts of employment an agreement conferring jurisdiction shall have legal force only if it is entered into after the dispute has arisen". What this does not allow for is an agreement on jurisdiction which is entered into *before* the dispute has arisen but which is favourable to the employee who now wants to invoke it as plaintiff.[6] The 1989 Accession Convention deals with this situation, as far as the Brussels Convention is concerned, by providing as an alternative that an agreement conferring jurisdiction shall also have legal effect "if the employee invokes it to seise courts other than those for the defendant's domicile or those specified in Article 5(1)".[7]

(e) STAYS OF ACTION

Section 49 of the Civil Jurisdiction and Judgments Act 1982 has been amended[8] to provide that a court in the United Kingdom is prevented from staying proceedings before it not only where this is inconsistent with the Brussels Convention but, alternatively, where this is inconsistent with the Lugano Convention. Much has already been said[9] on the question of when a stay of English proceedings is inconsistent with the Brussels Convention and need not be repeated here. It is likely that the English courts will apply the same principles in relation to the Lugano Convention as they have applied in relation to the Brussels Convention. Thus, for example, if, in a case involving a Swiss defendant, an English court has been allocated jurisdiction under Article 5 of the Lugano Convention, the court will regard itself as having power to stay its proceedings on the basis of *forum non conveniens* if the alternative forum for trial is New York,[10] but not if the alternative forum is Switzerland. However, it is worth noting that for the Lugano Convention to apply in the first place there has to be a specified connection with an EFTA Contracting State, which will normally mean that that State is allocated jurisdiction under the Convention. What the English courts are likely to be doing in Lugano Convention cases is staying their own proceedings on the basis that they lack jurisdiction under the Lugano Convention because, for example, Switzerland has exclusive jurisdiction under Articles 16 or 17, or the defendant is domiciled in Switzerland and England has not been allocated jurisdiction under Article 5.

5 Protocol 1, Art 1b of the Lugano Convention 1988. Discussed infra, p 444.
6 See the Almeida Cruz, Desantes Real, Jenard Report, para 27.
7 Supra, pp 321–322.
8 Sch 2, para 24 of the Civil Jurisdiction and Judgments Act 1991.
9 Supra, pp 331–334.
10 See, in relation to the Brussels Convention, *The Po* [1991] 2 Lloyd's Rep 206.

Chapter 15

Recognition and enforcement of foreign judgments: the traditional rules

SUMMARY

1. INTRODUCTION

(a) THE EFFECT GIVEN TO FOREIGN JUDGMENTS

Unsatisfied foreign judgments give rise to complicated questions of private international law. If a plaintiff fails to obtain satisfaction of a judgment in the country where it has been granted, the question arises whether it is enforceable in another country where the defendant is found. It is clear at the outset that owing to the principle of territorial sovereignty a judgment delivered in one country cannot, in the absence of international agreement, have a direct operation of its own force in another. Levy of execution, for instance, cannot issue in England in respect of a judgment delivered in New York. Nevertheless, the common law systems have long permitted the enforcement of a foreign judgment within certain defined limits, since otherwise one of the essential objects of private international law, the pro-

345

tection of rights acquired under a foreign system of law, would not be fully attained.[1]

(b) THE THEORY UNDERLYING RECOGNITION AND ENFORCEMENT

The attitude adopted by English law from the earliest days has been to permit the successful suitor to bring an action in England on the foreign judgment. But in the last hundred years the courts have changed their view as to the ground upon which this privilege is based. The older cases put it solely on the ground of comity.[2] It is unnecessary, however, to consider this theory further, for it has been supplanted by a far more defensible principle that has been called "the doctrine of obligation".[3] This doctrine, which was laid down in 1842, is that, where a foreign court of competent jurisdiction has adjudicated a certain sum to be due from one person to another, the liability to pay that sum becomes a legal obligation that may be enforced in this country by an action of debt.[4] Once the judgment is proved the burden lies on the defendant to show why he should not perform the obligation.

> The judgment of a court of competent jurisdiction over the defendant imposes a duty or obligation on him to pay the sum for which judgment is given, which the courts in this country are bound to enforce.[5]

In other words, a new right has been vested in the creditor and a new obligation imposed on the debtor at the instance of the foreign court. Lord ESHER once said that "the liability of the defendant arises upon an implied contract to pay the amount of the foreign judgment".[6] This does not mean that the justification for the enforcement of the obligation is an implied contract, but that for procedural purposes the debtor is regarded as having implicitly promised to pay.[7] This may be illustrated by the fact that the creditor's action is barred under the Limitation Act 1980 after six years, not after twelve years as in the case of an English judgment.[8]

The merits of this doctrine, as compared with the principle of comity, are twofold. In the first place the question of reciprocity is eliminated. If A is under a legal obligation to B, there is no more need to consider what treatment is meted out by the foreign court in question to English judgments than there would be to examine the private international law, say, of France, where the obligation resulted from a contract made in France. An obligation, once recognised by English law, must be enforced irrespective of the substantive rules of law obtaining in the country of its creation. In the second place, there is little difficulty in prescribing the defences available to the defendant, for if the ground of his liability is an obligation, then any fact which disproves the existence of an obligation may be pleaded in bar.

1 Bar, p 895.
2 See *Geyer v Aguilar* (1798) 7 Term Rep 681 at 97; Piggott, *Foreign Judgments*, Part i, pp 10 et seq.
3 Piggot, *Foreign Judgments*, pp 10 et seq.
4 *Russell v Smyth* (1842) 9 M & W 810. See also *Adams v Cape Industries Plc* [1990] Ch 433 at 552–553; *Owens Bank Ltd v Bracco* [1991] 4 All ER 833 at 844.
5 *Schibsby v Westenholz* (1870) LR 6 QB 155 at 159.
6 *Grant v Easton* (1883) 13 QBD 302 at 303.
7 Read, *Recognition and Enforcement of Foreign Judgments*, pp 112–113.
8 *Re Flynn (No 2)* (1968) 112 Sol Jo 804; and see *Re Flynn (No 3)* [1969] 2 Ch 403, [1969] 2 All ER 557; *Berliner Industriebank AG v Jost* [1971] 2 QB 463, [1971] 2 All ER 1513.

(c) THE BRUSSELS AND LUGANO CONVENTIONS

One very important recent development is the United Kingdom's accession to the Convention on Jurisdiction and Enforcement of Judgments in Civil and Commercial Matters of 1968 (the Brussels Convention), and to the parallel Lugano Convention. In cases where the rules on recognition and enforcement of foreign judgments under either of these Conventions apply, these rules supersede all other rules on recognition and enforcement. The place of the Brussels and Lugano Conventions within the existing framework of rules on recognition and enforcement of foreign judgments is considered briefly in this chapter and the relevant rules under the Conventions are considered in detail in the next chapter.

(d) FAMILY LAW

It should be stressed that there are special rules dealing with the recognition of foreign divorces, annulments and legal separations, foreign maintenance orders, and foreign orders relating to children. These rules are examined later in the part of the book on family law.

(e) THE EFFECT OF A FOREIGN JUDGMENT ON THE ORIGINAL CAUSE OF ACTION

It is a rule of domestic English law that a plaintiff who has obtained judgment in England against a defendant is barred from suing again on the original cause of action. The same rule now applies in the case of foreign judgments. Section 34 of the Civil Jurisdiction and Judgments Act 1982[9] provides that:

> No proceedings may be brought by a person in England and Wales ... on a cause of action in respect of which a judgment has been given in his favour in proceedings between the same parties or their privies, in a court in another part of the United Kingdom or in a court of an overseas country, unless that judgment is not enforceable or entitled to recognition in England and Wales

The effect of this provision is that, if the judgment is enforceable or entitled to recognition in England and Wales, the plaintiff has to sue on the judgment obtained[10] and cannot bring fresh proceedings based on the original cause of action.[11] The plaintiff is debarred from bringing fresh proceedings in England, despite the parties' agreement on trial here.[12] It is not required that the plaintiff should have been the original party in the overseas proceedings or that such proceedings be exclusively civil in character, provided that the judgment is enforceable or entitled to recognition in England.[13] However, the stronger domestic policy of protecting the interests of minors has meant that this provision may not operate to prevent them from bringing fresh proceedings, when the foreign proceedings were not in their interests and there are questions over their consent to the foreign proceedings.[14]

---

9 The section applies in Northern Ireland, but not in Scotland.
10 In this situation the plaintiff will be able to ask for service of a writ out of the jurisdiction under the Rules of the Supreme Court: see Ord 11, r 1(1)(m), discussed supra, p 202.
11 The section applies regardless of whether the judgment is enforceable or entitled to recognition at common law, by statute, or under the Brussels Convention or Lugano Convention; in the case of either of these two Conventions, s 34 merely confirms the existing rule under the Conventions, see Case 42/76 *De Wolf v Harry Cox BV* [1976] ECR 1759, [1977] 2 CMLR 43, discussed infra, pp 439–440.
12 *The Indian Grace* [1992] 1 Lloyd's Rep 124.
13 *Black v Yates* [1991] 3 WLR 90; [1991] 4 All ER 722.
14 Ibid.

2. RECOGNITION AND ENFORCEMENT AT COMMON LAW

We must now consider the principles on which the successful litigant may take advantage of a foreign judgment at common law.[1] A foreign judgment creditor has an alternative. He may either sue on the obligation created by the judgment, or he may plead the judgment as res judicata in any proceedings which raise the same issue. The common law doctrine is that a foreign judgment, though creating an obligation that is actionable in England, cannot be enforced here without the institution of fresh legal proceedings. Nevertheless, if a fresh action is brought in England on the foreign judgment that action is subject to the Rules of the Supreme Court and, for example, the plaintiff may apply for summary judgment under Order 14 on the basis that the defendant has no defence to the claim.[2] A foreign judgment cannot be enforced by, for example, the appointment of a receiver without such a fresh action in England. Furthermore, any action in England will require the English rules as to jurisdiction and service of writs to be satisfied.[3]

(a) JURISDICTION OF THE FOREIGN COURT[4]: JUDGMENTS IN PERSONAM

The first and overriding essential for the effectiveness of a foreign judgment in England is that the adjudicating court should have had jurisdiction in the international sense over the defendant. A foreign court may give a judgment which, according to the system of law under which it sits, is conclusively binding on the defendant, but unless the circumstances are such as in the eyes of English law justify the court in having assumed jurisdiction, the judgment does not create a cause of action that is actionable in England.[5] In other words, in the view of English law, the foreign court must have been entitled to summon the defendant and subject him to judgment.[6]

Since a foreign judgment is actionable only because it imposes an obligation on the defendant, it follows that any fact which negatives the existence of that obligation is a bar to the action. One of the negativing facts must necessarily be that the defendant owes no duty to obey the command of the tribunal which has purported to create the obligation. There must be a correlation between the legal obligation of the defendant and the right of the tribunal to issue its command. The tests that determine whether obedience is due to an English court should, on grounds of reciprocity, also be adopted when the inquiry relates to the competence of a foreign court. Personal jurisdiction in this country under the traditional rules depends on the right of a court to summon the defendant. Apart from special powers conferred by statute,[7] it is obvious that, since the right to summon depends on the

---

1 The foreign decision must, of course, always be one that is regarded as a judgment: *Berliner Industriebank AG v Jost* [1971] 2 QB 463, [1971] 2 All ER 1513 (entry of a debt in the record as a judgment in bankruptcy proceedings); *Midland International Trade Services Ltd v Sudairy* (1990) Financial Times, 2 May (a decision of an administrative tribunal).
2 *Grant v Easton* (1883) 13 QBD 302.
3 *Perry v Zissis* [1977] 1 Lloyd's Rep 607. Amendments to the Rules of the Supreme Court make this easier: see RSC, Ord 11, r 1(l)(m), supra, p 202.
4 Clarence Smith (1953) 2 ICLQ 510 et seq; Spencer Bower and Turner, *The Doctrine of Res Judicata* (2nd edn), pp 111–130; Pryles (1972) 21 ICLQ 61; Von Mehren (1980) II Hague Recueil 9 at 55 et seq; Briggs (1987) 36 ICLQ 240.
5 See eg *Sirdar Gurdyal Singh v The Rajah of Faridkote* [1884] AC 670.
6 *Pemberton v Hughes* [1899] 1 Ch 781 at 790 et seq; *Salvesen v Administrator of Austrian Property* [1927] AC 641 at 659.
7 Supra, pp 190–211.

power to summon, jurisdiction is in general exercisable only against those persons who are present in England.[8] If the defendant is absent from a country and has no place of business there, then, whether he be a citizen or an alien, he would appear to be immune from the jurisdiction, unless he has voluntarily submitted to the decision of the court.[9]

Let us now consider, in more detail, what are the criteria of jurisdiction in the international sense.

(i) Residence and, possibly, presence of defendant in the foreign country at the time of the suit

(a) An individual defendant There is no doubt that the residence of the defendant within the foreign country is sufficient for jurisdiction.[10] The onus of proving this, and the other bases of international jurisdiction, lies on the plaintiff seeking to enforce the judgment of a foreign court.[11] What is more debateable is whether the mere presence of the defendant in the foreign country for a short time will suffice. The argument in favour of jurisdiction on such a basis is that persons who happen to be within a territorial dominion owe obedience to its sovereign power—obedience, that is to say, to the jurisdiction of its courts and in certain respects to its laws. "By making himself present he contracts—in to a network of obligations, created by the local law and by the local courts."[12] This duty of obedience results from mere presence in the territory, and therefore the length of time for which the presence continues is immaterial.[13] Furthermore, the jurisdiction of the English court may be based on the mere presence of the defendant within the jurisdiction.[14]

This view is supported by *Carrick v Hancock*:[15]

A domiciled Englishman appeared to a writ which was served on him in Sweden while he was on a short visit to that country. It was held that despite his fleeting stay in Sweden an action on the judgment lay against him in this country.

It has been endorsed, obiter, by the Court of Appeal in *Adams v Cape Industries Plc*.[16] The temporary presence must be voluntary, ie not induced by compulsion, fraud or duress.[17] The date of service of process in the foreign country is probably the relevant one for examining whether the defendant is present abroad, rather than the date of issue of proceedings.[18] It is not the date of the cause of action arising.[19]

There is, however, much to be said for the view that casual presence, as

---

8 *Employers' Liability Assurance Corpn v Sedgwick Collins & Co* [1927] AC 95 at 114.
9 *Harris v Taylor* [1915] 2 KB 580 at 589.
10 *Emanuel v Symon* [1908] 1 KB 302 at 309; *Schibsby v Westenholz* (1870) LR 6 QB 155 at 161. Residence implies physical presence; see, however, *Adams v Cape Industries Plc* [1990] Ch 433 at 518.
11 *Adams v Cape Industries Plc*, op cit, at 549–550.
12 Ibid, at 553.
13 *Carrick v Hancock* (1895) 12 TLR 59; *Adams v Cape Industries Plc*, op cit, at 517–518.
14 Supra, pp 183–184.
15 (1895) 12 TLR 59.
16 Op cit, at 517–518. Cf *Re Carrick Estates Ltd and Young* (1988) 43 DLR (4th) 161.
17 *Adams v Cape Industries Plc*, op cit, at 517–518.
18 Ibid.
19 *Emanuel v Symon*, op cit; see also *Re McTavish & Hampton Securities and Investments Ltd* (1983) 150 DLR (3d) 27; *Rafferty's Restaurant Ltd v Sawchuk* [1983] 3 WWR 261; *Re Kelowna and District Credit Union and Perl* (1984) 13 DLR (4th) 756.

distinct from residence, is not a desirable basis of jurisdiction. Where, for instance, both parties are foreigners and the cause of action is based entirely on facts occurring abroad and subject to foreign law, it is strange that the defendant should be bound by the decision of a court in whose jurisdiction he may by chance have been temporarily present. "The court is not a convenient one for either of the parties, nor is it in a favourable position to deal intelligently either with the facts or with the law."[20] Furthermore, any analogy based on the jurisdiction of the English courts is not particularly convincing, since the rules on jurisdiction are operated in conjunction with a discretion to stay the proceedings, and the exercise of the discretion is likely to be an issue when jurisdiction is founded on mere presence.

(b) A corporate defendant A company cannot literally be resident or present in a foreign country. It may though carry on business abroad. The circumstances in which this can amount to an artificial residence or presence in a foreign country were set out recently by the Court of Appeal in *Adams v Cape Industries Plc.*[1] It has to be shown that: (i) the corporation has its own fixed place of business (a branch office) there from which it has carried on its own business for more than a minimal time, or a representative has carried on the corporation's business for more than a minimal time from a fixed place of business;[2] and (ii) the corporation's business is transacted from that fixed place of business. This second requirement is unlikely to cause any difficulties if a branch office is established.[3] However, if business is carried on abroad by a representative the question will arise of whether this person is carrying on the corporation's business or no more than his own. It will then be necessary to look into the functions which this representative has been performing and his relationship with the overseas corporation. This will involve looking at such things as acquisition of business premises, payment of the representative, reimbursement of expenses, the degree of control by the corporation, and display of the corporation's name. The representative's power to bind the corporation contractually is of particular importance. If the representative lacks this power this is a powerful factor pointing against the presence or residence of the overseas corporation.

In the *Adams Case* these principles were applied to the situation where the corporation carried on business abroad by means of a subsidiary company.

The defendants, an English company concerned with mining asbestos, and its world wide marketing subsidiary, another English company, carried on business in the United States through its United States marketing subsidiary, NAAC and its successor CPC, companies incorporated in Illinois. Asbestos mined by the defendants was sold for use in an asbestos factory in Texas. The 206 plaintiffs, who were mainly employees injured whilst working at this factory, commenced proceedings for damages in the United States Federal District Court at Tyler, Texas. The defendants took no part in these proceedings (the Tyler 2 actions), although they had taken part in earlier asbestos-related proceedings involving different plaintiffs (the Tyler

20 Dodd (1929) 23 Ill LR 427, 437–438.
 1 [1990] Ch 433 at 530–531; Collier [1990] CLJ 416; Carter (1990) 61 BYBIL 402. Cases on the jurisdiction of English courts over claims against foreign companies are relevant in this context: see pp 185–188.
 2 Following *Littauer Glove Corpn v F W Millington (1920) Ltd* (1928) 44 TLR 746.
 3 There is no requirement, as under Art 5(5) of the Brussels and Lugano Conventions, that the branch has a certain autonomy, supra p 303.

1 actions),[4] and a default judgment was awarded against them by the U S Court.

SCOTT J dismissed the action to enforce the default judgment in England, and this was affirmed by the Court of Appeal. It was held that the defendants were not present in Illinois, since NAAC and CPC, the representatives of the defendants, were carrying on exclusively their own business and not that of the defendants.[5] Relevant to this was the fact that, inter alia, NAAC leased premises itself, bought and stored asbestos, paid taxes on its profits, had its own creditors/debtors. The position of CPC was even weaker since it was an independently owned company and not even a subsidiary of either of the defendants. Moreover, whilst NAAC and CPC performed valuable services for the defendants as an intermediary, neither had power to, and never did, bind the defendants contractually.

A subsidiary will normally act just for itself and not for the overseas parent.[6] Counsel for the plaintiffs tried to get round this difficulty by arguing that the defendants and NAAC were all part of a single economic unit.[7] This radical idea, which is based on the economic reality of the situation and has found favour in the United States,[8] was rejected by the Court of Appeal, who emphasised the traditional company law notion that parent and subsidiary are separate legal entities. This means that an English company can set up its business abroad in such a way that it is not present/resident there. Provided that the company does not submit to the jurisdiction of the foreign court, judgments against it in that country will not be enforced in England.

What if the defendant had been present/resident in Illinois? Without expressing a final decision on this issue, there are some surprising suggestions, albeit rather hesitant ones, from the Court of Appeal that this would have been sufficient, even though the trial took place in Texas.[9] This was on the basis that the trial took place in a federal district court (ie a United States court) rather than a state of Texas court. This was despite the fact that a federal court judge sitting in Texas has to apply that state's rules on both jurisdiction in personam and choice of law, and a federal judgment is itself a foreign judgment when it comes to its enforcement within the United States.

(ii) Submission of defendant to the foreign court

(a) Submission by virtue of being the plaintiff in the foreign action

It is perfectly clear that, if a person voluntarily and unsuccessfully submits his case as plaintiff to the decision of a foreign tribunal, he cannot afterwards, if sued upon the judgment in England, aver that he was not subject to the jurisdiction of that tribunal.[10]

(b) Agreements to submit
What may be regarded as a particular example of submission arises where the defendant has previously contracted to submit

---

4 This raised arguments in relation to submission, discussed infra, p 358.
5 [1990] Ch 433 at 545 et seq.
6 But see Case 218/86 *Sar Schotte Gmbh v Parfums Rothschild* [1987] ECR 4905, which is concerned with jurisdiction under Art 5(5) of the Brussels Convention, discussed supra, pp 304–305.
7 [1990] Ch 4 33 at 532 et seq; Fawcett (1988) 37 ICLQ 645.
8 See *Bulova Watch Co Inc v K Hattori and Co Ltd* 508 F Supp 1322 at 1342 (1981).
9 [1990] Ch 433 at 550 et seq.
10 *Schibsby v Westenholz* (1870) LR 6 QB 155 at 161; *Novelli v Rossi* (1831) 2 B & Ad 757.

himself to the foreign jurisdiction,[11] as, for instance, in *Feyerick v Hubbard,*[12] where a domiciled British subject resident in London agreed to sell his patent rights to a Belgian, the contract of sale containing a provision that all disputes should be submitted to the jurisdiction of the Belgian courts. A less explicit agreement was held to be sufficient in *Copin v Adamson,*[1] where the facts were as follows:

A domiciled Englishman, resident in England, took shares in a French company whose articles of association provided that all disputes that might arise during liquidation should be submitted to the jurisdiction of a French court, and that process should be served at a domicil to be elected for a shareholder should he fail to elect one himself. On the company going into liquidation the French court gave judgment by default against the Englishman for the amount not paid up on his shares. To an action brought on this judgment in England the defendant pleaded that he was not resident or domiciled in France before judgment, nor was he served with process, nor did he appear, nor had he any knowledge of the proceedings or opportunity to defend himself.

The plea failed. It was held that the articles constituted a contract on the part of every shareholder that he should be bound by a judgment so obtained. "It appears to me", said Lord CAIRNS, "that, to all intents and purposes, it is as if there had been an actual and absolute agreement by the defendant."[2]

If the agreement was entered into under undue influence it will not constitute submission, but the defendant cannot raise in England the issue of undue influence if this defence was available to him in the foreign proceedings and he failed to raise it there.[3]

In *Copin v Adamson* and other cases[4] the agreement to accept the foreign jurisdiction was express and the weight of authority is in favour of the view that an agreement to submit cannot be implied.[5] Despite this body of opinion, DIPLOCK J held in *Blohn v Desser*[6] that a partner in an Austrian firm who was resident in England and took no part in the conduct of the business would be held impliedly to have agreed to submit to the jurisdiction of the Austrian courts.[7] This conclusion has been strongly criticised, extrajudicially,[8]

---

11 *Emanuel v Symon* [1980] 1 KB 302; *Copin v Adamson* (1874) LR 9 Ex 345 at 354.
12 (1902) 71 LJKB 509. Distinguish an agreement which merely selects the law of a foreign country as the governing law of a contract; *Dunbee Ltd v Gilman & Co (Australia) Pty Ltd* [1968] 2 Lloyds Rep 394, NSW CA; infra, p 483.
1 (1874) LR 9 Ex Ch 345; affirmed (1875) LR 1 Ex D 17; *Vallée v Dumergue* (1849) 4 Exch 290.
2 (1875) LR 1 Ex D 17 at 19.
3 *Israel Discount Bank of New York v Hadjipateras* [1983] 3 All ER 129, [1984] 1 WLR 137, CA; discussed infra, pp 371–372.
4 *Bank of Australasia v Harding* (1850) 9 CB 661; *Bank of Australasia v Nias* (1851) 16 QB 717.
5 *Sirdar Gurdyal Singh v The Rajah of Faridkote* [1894] AC 670 at 685–686; *Emanuel v Symon* [1908] 1 KB 302 at 305, 313–314; and see *Gyonyor v Sanjenko* [1971] 5 WWR 381; *Veco Drilling Inc v Armstrong* [1982] 1 WWR 177; *First City Capital Ltd v Winchester Computer Corpn* (1988) 44 DLR (4th) 301.
6 [1962] 2 QB 116, [1961] 2 All ER 1; and see *Sfeir & Co v National Insurance Co of New Zealand Ltd* [1964] 1 Lloyd's Rep 330 at 339–340.
7 In the event, however, the defendant was held not to be liable, since the judgment was not final and conclusive; infra, pp 365–367.
8 Lewis (1961) 10 ICLQ 910; Cohn (1962) 11 ICLQ 583; ibid, Abel, 587; Carter (1962) 38 BYBIL 493; and see the 8th edn of this book, pp 627–628.

and was rejected by ASHWORTH J in *Vogel v R and A Kohnstamm Ltd*[9], who refused to countenance an implied agreement to submit.

In *Adams v Cape Industries Plc*[10] it was argued that the defendants, by their conduct in participating in the earlier asbestos-related actions (the Tyler 1 actions) in the same court, had represented that they would similarly participate in future claims (ie the Tyler 2 actions) brought in that court, and in that sense had impliedly agreed to submit to the jurisdiction. SCOTT J, speaking obiter, seemed to accept that an implied agreement to submit might suffice. However, a clear indication of consent to the exercise of the foreign court's jurisdiction was needed. Furthermore, in the case of a representation, as opposed to a contractual agreement, this would have to be acted upon by the plaintiffs in some way.

(c) Submission by voluntary[11] appearance

(i) An appearance to fight on the merits The defendant submits to the jurisdiction of the foreign court by voluntary appearance if he has fought the action on its merits, and so taken his chance of obtaining a judgment in his own favour.[12]

(ii) An appearance to protest against jurisdiction
The case that for many years caused difficulty was where a defendant entered an appearance with the sole object of protesting against the jurisdiction of the foreign court.

At common law an illogical distinction was drawn between a protest as to the existence of jurisdiction and as to the exercise of a discretion in relation to jurisdiction. In *Henry v Geoprosco International Ltd*[13] the defendant, a company registered in Jersey, appeared before a court in Alberta and argued, unsuccessfully, that service out of the jurisdiction should be set aside, on the ground, inter alia, that the court was not the *forum conveniens*. When it came to enforcement of the Alberta judgment in England, the Court of Appeal held that an appearance, such as this, to ask the court to use its discretion not to exercise its jurisdiction constituted submission. However, the court left open the question of whether an appearance solely to protest against the existence of the jurisdiction of a foreign court constituted submission. Not only was the above distinction unjustifiable, but also its application led to the absurd result that, in certain circumstances, a defendant who appeared before a foreign court to protest that it had no jurisdiction over him would be deemed to have submitted to that court's jurisdiction.

The old law has been replaced by section 33 of the Civil Jurisdiction and

9 [1973] QB 133, [1971] 2 All ER 1428; Cohn (1972) 21 ICLQ 157.
10 [1990] Ch 433 at 463–467. The first instance decision in relation to submission was not challenged on appeal.
11 For the position where there has been undue influence, see *Israel Discount Bank of New York v Hadjipateras* [1983] 3 All ER 129, [1984] 1 WLR 137, CA; discussed supra, at p 352, and infra, at p 381.
12 *Molony v Gibbons* (1810) 2 Camp 502; *Guiard v De Clermont and Donner* [1914] 3 KB 145. On what amounts to an appearance, see *Re Overseas Food Importers & Distributors Ltd and Brandt* (1981) 126 DLR (3d) 422.
13 [1976] QB 726, [1975] 2 All ER 702, CA; Carter (1974–75) 47 BYBIL 379; Collier [1975] CLJ 219; Collins (1976) 92 LQR 268–287; Solomons (1976) 25 ICLQ 665. *Henry v Geoprosco* has not been followed in Canada, see *Clinton v Ford* (1982) 137 DLR (3d) 281; Lange (1983) 61 Can BR 637.

Judgments Act 1982,[1] which is designed to get rid of this absurdity; but, as will be seen, there are still some problems which are caused by the wording of this section.

Section 33 (1) provides that:

> For the purposes of determining whether a judgment given by a court of an overseas country should be recognised or enforced in England and Wales or Northern Ireland, the person against whom the judgment was given shall not be regarded as having submitted to the jurisdiction of the court by reason only of the fact that he appeared (conditionally or otherwise) in the proceedings for all or any one or more of the following purposes, namely:
>
> (a) to contest the jurisdiction of the court;
> (b) to ask the court to dismiss or stay the proceedings on the ground that the dispute in question should be submitted to arbitration or to the determination of the courts of another country;
> (c) to protect, or obtain the release of, property seized or threatened with seizure in the proceedings.

Section 33 only applies to a judgment given by a court of an "overseas country", ie "any country or territory outside the United Kingdom".[2] It does not distinguish between recognition and enforcement at common law and by statute[3] and can, therefore, apply to both, except in so far as section 33(2) applies.

Section 33(2)[4] provides that:

> Nothing in this section shall affect the recognition or enforcement in England and Wales or Northern Ireland of a judgment which is required to be recognised or enforced there under the 1968 Convention or the Lugano Convention.

This means that, although, in principle, section 33 applies to judgments covered by the Brussels Convention or Lugano Convention, it remains subject to these Conventions.[5]

Section 33(1) is a negative provision; it does not define what amounts to submission to the jurisdiction of a foreign court, but merely states that an appearance for one or more specified purposes does not amount to submission. *Henry v Geoprosco*[6] shows that a defendant may, in fact, put in an appearance to argue:

(1) that the foreign court has no jurisdiction because no basis of jurisdiction is applicable;

(2) that the foreign court should use its discretionary powers to set aside service out of the jurisdiction on the basis that it is not the *forum conveniens*;

---

1 For transitional provisions see Sch 13, Pt II, para 9 and *Tracomin SA v Sudan Oil Seeds Co Ltd* [1983] 3 All ER 137, [1983] 1 WLR 1026, CA, which applied this section in the case of a judgment granted before the 1982 Act came into force because the judgment in question was not in one of the specified categories in respect of which s 33 does not have retrospective effect.

2 S 50 of the 1982 Act. For judgments given within the UK, see infra, pp 393–395.

3 As far as enforcement under the Foreign Judgments (Reciprocal Enforcement) Act 1933 is concerned, s 33 of the 1982 Act merely replaces a similarly worded provision under the 1933 Act (s 4(2)(a)(i), discussed infra, at pp 399–400).

4 As amended by the Civil Jurisdiction and Judgments Act 1991, Sch 2, para 15.

5 In cases coming within the Brussels Convention or Lugano Convention, recognition and enforcement is not dependent on whether the defendant has submitted to the foreign court (see infra, p 412) and therefore s 33 is irrelevant, see Collins, *The Civil Jurisdiction and Judgments Act 1982*, p 144.

6 [1976] QB 726, [1975] 2 All ER 702, CA; discussed supra, p 353.

(3) that the foreign court should use its discretionary powers to stay the proceedings on the basis of *forum non conveniens*;

(4) that the foreign court should use its discretionary powers to stay the proceedings because of an agreement on jurisdiction;

(5) that the foreign court should/must[7] stay the proceedings because of an arbitration agreement;

(6) that the foreign court should dismiss or stay the proceedings because of a *Scott v Avery*[8] arbitration clause, ie one which provides not merely for arbitration but that an action cannot be maintained until the matter in dispute has first been referred to and decided by arbitrators.

If a defendant puts in an appearance for any one of these purposes, how is this treated under section 33? The answer is to be found by looking at the six categories above and considering them in relation to the three subsections under section 33(1).

The three purposes for appearance, specified under section 33(1), which do not amount to submission are as follows:

Section 33(1)(a) *an appearance "to contest the jurisdiction of the court"*
Section 33(1)(a) is of the same effect as, and virtually identical in wording to, the end part of section 4(2)(a)(i) of the Foreign Judgments (Reciprocal Enforcement) Act 1933, which it replaces.[9] It follows that, although section 33(1)(a) will be significant in relation to both recognition at common law and under the 1933 Act, it only introduces a major change in the law in respect of recognition at common law.

Section 33(1)(a) follows the 1933 Act in not defining what is meant by contesting the jurisdiction. Given the history of this area of law it is to be regretted that this concept was not clearly spelled out in the 1982 Act. Category (1), of the six categories set out above, clearly comes within section 33(1)(a). There is more difficulty with category (2). A narrow interpretation of section 33(1)(a) would be that only arguments as to the bases of jurisdiction (category (1)) come within it. The distinction drawn in *Henry v Geoprosco* between the existence of jurisdiction and the exercise of a discretion, with category (2) coming within the latter, could still be followed under section 33(1)(a), due to the imprecise wording of this provision. However, it would be better to give a wide interpretation to section 33(1)(a) so that it encompasses any argument in relation to jurisdiction, whether as to the existence of jurisdiction or as to the exercise of a discretion. The wording of the provision allows this interpretation. Moreover, the distinction drawn in *Henry v Geoprosco* was strongly criticised at the time[10] and section 33(1) was intended to overrule that decision.[11] If this wide interpretation of section 33(1)(a) is accepted, it would also encompass category (3).

Section 33(1)(b) *"an appearance to ask the court to dismiss or stay the proceedings on the ground that the dispute in question should be submitted to arbitration or to the determination of the courts of another country"*

7 Under English law, there is a discretion to stay English proceedings where there is a "domestic" arbitration agreement but the stay is mandatory if the arbitration agreement is not "domestic", supra, pp 239–241.
8 *Scott v Avery* (1885) 5 HL Cas 811.
9 See s 54 and Schedule 14 of the 1982 Act, and infra, pp 399–400.
10 See the 10th edn of this book, p 640; Collins (1976) 92 LQR 268, 287; cf Carter (1974–75) 47 BYBIL 379, 381.
11 This becomes even more apparent when one looks at s 33(1)(b), discussed infra.

It was necessary to have a separate provision in section 33(1) to deal with the situation set out in section 33(1)(b) because of a line of reasoning adopted by the Court of Appeal in *Henry v Geoprosco*.[12] There, the defendant appeared and sought a stay of proceedings abroad on the basis, inter alia, that there was a *Scott v Avery* type of arbitration clause in the contract between the parties. According to the Court of Appeal,[13] this defence involved an assertion that the plaintiff had no accrued cause of action, and this meant that the defendants were voluntarily asking the court to adjudicate on the merits of that part of the defence. The defendants had, therefore, submitted to the jurisdiction of the court. Section 33(1)(b) makes it clear that there is no submission in this situation (ie Category 6).[14]

Section 33(1)(b) can also, with some confidence, be said to cover category (5).[15] In the first reported decision on section 33, *Tracomin SA v Sudan Oil Seeds Co Ltd (No 1)*,[16] STAUGHTON J held that Sudanese sellers who appeared before the Swiss courts to ask for a stay of proceedings because of an arbitration clause, which provided that disputes should be submitted to arbitration in London, had not submitted to the jurisdiction of the Swiss courts. The judge did not say whether this situation came within (1)(a) or (1)(b). It is submitted that the more natural place for it is under (1)(b).[17] Section 33(1)(b) does not just deal with agreements on arbitration; it also appears from the context to be designed to deal with agreements on the choice of court (category 4).

Section 33(1)(c) *An appearance "to protect, or obtain the release of, property seized or threatened with seizure in the proceedings"*
Under the common law rules, a defendant who possessed property abroad was placed in a particularly awkward situation. If he ignored the foreign proceedings, he stood to lose his property in the event of a default judgment being granted. On the other hand, if he put in an appearance in order to safeguard his foreign property he stood to lose not only this foreign property but also his English property as well, because his appearance would, in some circumstances, amount to a submission to the foreign court and that court's judgment would accordingly be enforceable in England. Section 33(1)(c) enables the defendant to appear abroad to safeguard his property without running this risk.

Like section 33(1)(a), this provision is closely modelled on the end part of section 4(2)(a)(i) of the Foreign Judgments (Reciprocal Enforcement) Act 1933 which it replaces.[18] Although section 33(1)(c) applies to both recognition

12 [1976] QB 726, [1975] 2 All ER 702; discussed supra, p 353.
13 [1976] QB 726 at 732–735, 750.
14 The Court of Appeal, ibid at 750, said that this defence could be raised as a plea in bar and not merely where a stay is sought; hence s 33(1)(b) refers to an appearance to ask the court to "dismiss" the proceedings, as well as referring to an appearance to ask the court to stay the proceedings.
15 In *Henry v Geoprosco*, op cit, a stay was sought in Alberta on the basis of both categories (5) and (6).
16 [1983] 1 WLR 662, 670–672, affirmed by the Court of Appeal [1983] 1 WLR 1026; the only point raised on appeal was whether s 33, which came into force during the course of the first instance hearing, could apply to an action commenced and a judgement given before the 1982 Act came into force or had been passed; see supra, p 354 (footnote 1).
17 *Quaere*, if there is an agreement to go to arbitration and the appearance is to ask the foreign court to exercise a discretion to stay, can it really be said that the *ground* of the stay is that the dispute should be submitted to arbitration? See the discussion supra, at pp 240–241.
18 See s 54 and Sch 14 of the 1982 Act and infra, pp 399–400.

at common law and under the 1933 Act, it will only effect a major change in the law in respect of recognition at common law, and is a development to be welcomed as bringing uniformity to these two different types of enforcement.

Section 33(1)(c) follows section 4(2)(a)(i) of the 1933 Act in applying regardless of whether the defendant is seeking to protect property that has already been seized in the proceedings, or whether he is acting with foresight to protect property that is merely threatened with seizure. It thus gets rid of the distinction under the common law between the situation where property had already been seized (an appearance to protect this property would not amount to submission)[19] and where the property was merely threatened with seizure (an appearance to protect this property would amount to submission).[1] Now, in neither case is there submission to the foreign court.

Using wording from the 1933 Act as the model for section 33(1)(c), despite all its welcome advantages, does, however, have a serious drawback in that the concept of "to protect, or obtain the release of, property seized or threatened with seizure" is one that is not free from ambiguity.

First, can a defendant who happens to have property in a foreign country appear before a court in that country and then use section 33(1)(c) to deny submission? A defendant can argue that if a judgment is given against him his property will be threatened with seizure in order to satisfy the judgment. However, it should be noted that the seizure or threatened seizure must be "in the proceedings". The clear case where this requirement is satisfied is where property has been seized by the foreign court in order to found jurisdiction against the defendant. This is what the common law decisions had in mind when they allowed an exception to the submission rules in property cases.[2] The 1982 Act would now extend this to the situation where there is a threat of seizure in order to found jurisdiction. It is more questionable whether a threat of seizure after judgment is given, in order to satisfy the judgment, can be said to be "in the proceedings".[3]

Second, if the defendant appears in order to protect his property, is he entitled under section 33(1)(c) to fight on the merits abroad and still claim that he has not submitted? Although the common law made an exception to the voluntary submission rules in certain property cases, there was no express support in those decisions for the proposition that a defendant could fight on the merits and then claim that he had not voluntarily submitted because the appearance was in order to save property which had been seized.[4] It would be unfortunate if section 33(1)(c) was now interpreted so as to allow this. It would be better to confine the operation of the provision to the situation where the defendant appears and, in order to protect his property abroad, challenges the court's jurisdiction.

(iii) Arguing in the alternative

Where the defendant's plea that the foreign court lacked jurisdiction fails and he then goes on to fight the action on its merits, he has clearly submitted

19 *Henry v Geoprosco International Ltd* [1976] QB 726 at 746–747. See also *Clinton v Ford* (1982) 137 DLR (3d) 281.
1 *De Cosse Brissac v Rathbone* (1861) 6 H & N 301; *Voinet v Barrett* (1885) 55 LJQB 39; *Guiard v De Clermont* [1914] 3 KB 145.
2 See *Voinet v Barrett*, op cit, at 42; *Guiard v De Clermont*, op cit.
3 Compare *Guiard v De Clermont* [1914] 3 KB 145 with Dicey and Morris, (9th edn 1973) pp 997–998, and Stone [1983] Lloyd's MCLQ 1, 12–13; Stone (1983) 32 ICLQ 477, 491.
4 Cf Stone [1983] Lloyd's MCLQ 1, 12–13.

to the foreign court's jurisdiction.[5] However, it should not be enough if the defendant merely raises an initial plea on the merits at the same time as his defence as to lack of jurisdiction, but does not go on actually to fight on the merits.[6] A defendant may do this because he is required under some legal systems to plead a defence on the merits at the outset if he is to raise this defence later on, and he may wish to keep alive this possibility.[7] After the defence as to lack of jurisdiction fails, the defendant may decide to take no further part in the proceedings. The defendant should not be regarded as having submitted in this situation.

(iv) Appeals against judgments in default
A foreign judgment that is given against an absent defendant in default of his appearance is clearly not actionable in England, but is this so if he later moves to have the default judgment set aside and is unsuccessful? The answer would seem to depend on the grounds for the appeal. If the appeal is as to the merits of the claim, then this will constitute submission,[8] and will normally amount to submission to the judgment of the court of first instance.[9] However, an appeal, or application for leave to appeal, merely as to a jurisdictional issue would not constitute submission.[10]

(v) Taking procedural steps in the foreign country
In *Adams v Cape Industries Plc*[11] Scott J held that the defendants' participation in a consent order given by the Federal District judge extinguishing the cause of action against them as part of a settlement of the litigation in the Tyler 1 actions amounted to submission to the jurisdiction of the Federal District Court in Texas, in relation to those proceedings. The defendants had thereby waived the jurisdictional objections that they had raised earlier. However, the argument that submission to the Tyler 1 actions was also submission to the Tyler 2 actions (in respect of which the enforcement proceedings were brought), on the ground that there was just one unit of litigation, was rejected. The basis of submission is consent and participation in the order in relation to the Tyler 1 actions was no evidence of consent to the trial of future actions not yet started (the Tyler 2 actions). More generally, it was said[12] that

> If the [procedural] steps would not have been regarded by the domestic law of the foreign court as a submission to the jurisdiction, they ought not, in my view, to be so regarded here.

5 *Boissiere and Co v Brockner & Co* (1889) 6 TLR 85.
6 See Collins, *The Civil Jurisdiction and Judgments Act 1982*, p 144.
7 See eg Case 150/80 *Elefanten Schuh GMbH v Jacqmain* [1981] ECR 1671, [1982] 3 CMLR 1; discussed supra, pp 323–324.
8 *SA Consortium General Textiles v Sun and Sand Agencies Ltd* [1978] QB 279 at 299, 304, 308–309; and see *Guiard v De Clermont* [1914] 3 KB 145.
9 Ibid at 299, 304; cf *Guiard v De Clermont*, supra, at 155. In so far as these cases discuss appeals on jurisdictional issues they must now be read in the light of s 33 of the 1982 Act, discussed supra, pp 354–357.
10 Ibid, at 305, 308–309; s 33 of the 1982 Act. It seems that, in two of the Canadian cases where recognition was denied to a default judgment even though the defendant had moved to set it aside, namely *McLean v Shields* (1885) 9 OR 699; *Esdale v Bank of Ottawa* (1920) 51 DLR 485, the ground on which the defendant moved to set aside the original judgment was want of jurisdiction; see Read, op cit, pp 168–170. In the third it was not clear what the basis for seeking to set aside the original judgment was: *Re Carrick Estates Ltd and Young* (1988) 43 DLR (4th) 161.
11 [1990] Ch 433, supra, pp 350–351.
12 At 461

(iii) Nothing else founds jurisdiction

The results so far of our inquiry into the international competence of foreign courts is that jurisdiction sufficient to render a judgment actionable in England exists in two cases, namely, where the defendant was resident or, possibly, present in the country of the forum at the time of the action, or where he submitted to the jurisdiction. The question now is whether there are any other grounds of competency.[13]

(a) Political nationality Is the fact that the defendant is a national of the foreign country where the judgment has been obtained sufficient to render him amenable to the jurisdiction of the local courts? There is no English authority that contains an actual decision to this effect, but the truth of the proposition has been affirmed obiter in several cases.[14] It is also adopted by certain textbook writers.[15] It has been rejected by the Irish High Court.[16]

It is submitted with some confidence that nationality per se is not, and has been rejected as, a reason which, on any principle of private international law, can justify the exercise of jurisdiction.[17] The argument advanced in its favour, namely that "a subject is bound to obey the commands of his Sovereign, and, therefore, the judgments of his sovereign courts",[18] is no doubt true, but, as Wolff pointed out, it is not the duty of another sovereign to aid the enforcement of the obligation.[19] Indeed the undesirability of such a rule becomes abundantly clear when it is remembered that it is essentially within the competence of a State to decide who are and who are not its nationals. The granting or withholding of nationality is sometimes an instrument of political policy. Even if this is not the case, the legal tie of nationality may have an extremely slender factual basis. If a Romanian court were to give judgment in personam against a person who, though born in Romania, had left that country in his infancy and acquired a domicil in England without taking out letters of naturalisation, it is difficult to appreciate the justification for holding the judgment actionable in England. Again, to make nationality the basis of jurisdiction is scarcely practicable in the case of States, such as the United Kingdom,[20] the USA,[21] Canada or Australia, which contain several separate law districts. Finally, there is no question of reciprocal

---

13 See generally *Adams v Cape Industries Plc* [1990] Ch 433 at 515; and also *Emanuel v Symon* [1908] 1 KB 302 at 309; *Schibsby v Westenholz* (1870) LR 6 QB 155 at 161; *Rousillon v Rousillon* (1880) 14 Ch D 351 at 371. See also *State of New York v Fitzgerald* (1983) 148 DLR (3d) 176.

14 *Douglas v Forrest* (1828) 4 Bing 686; *Schibsby v Westenholz* (1870) LR 6 QB 155 at 161; *Rousillon v Rousillon* (1880) 14 ChD 351 at 371; *Emanuel v Symon* [1908] 1 KB 302 at 309; *Harris v Taylor* [1915] 2 KB 580 at 591; *Forsyth v Forsyth* [1948] P 125 at 132. See also *Gavin Gibson & Co v Gibson* [1913] 3 KB 379 at 388.

15 Westlake, p 399; Foote, p 398; Schmitthoff, *Conflict of Laws* (3rd edn), p 465. It is rejected by Wolff, p 126; Graveson, pp 621–622 (though he suggests exceptions). But see Read, op cit, pp 151–155; Dicey and Morris, pp 447–448.

16 *Rainford v Newell Roberts* [1962] IR 95; Jackson (1963) 26 MLR 563.

17 *Blohn v Desser* [1962] 2 QB 116 at 123; and see *Rossano v Manufacturers' Life Insurance Co Ltd* [1963] 2 QB 352 at 382–383; *Vogel v R and A Kohnstamm Ltd* [1973] QB 133 at 141; *Adams v Cape Industries Plc*, op cit, at 515.

18 Dicey (6th edn), p 357.

19 Wolff, p 126. He further points out that allegiance is not sufficient even in those civil law countries where nationality is the criterion of the personal law.

20 See *Patterson v D'Agostino* (1975) 58 DLR (3d) 63.

21 See *Dakota Lumber Co v Rinderknecht* (1905) 6 Terr LR 210 at 221–224.

recognition, for the British nationality of a defendant does not suffice to found the jurisdiction of the English court.

(b) Domicil If mere allegiance suffices to give jurisdiction, so also, it might be presumed, does domicil. The connection between a man and the country in which he is domiciled is generally a very real one, but the tie of allegiance may be of the loosest description. An ineffective exercise of jurisdiction ought not to be tolerated, and it is undeniable that a judgment based on domicil is superior on the score of effectiveness to one based merely on allegiance. Yet the curious thing is that those writers who are content to make political allegiance a ground of jurisdiction deny without hesitation the sufficiency of domicil. It is suggested that on this point at least they must be right and that domicil alone will not suffice as a ground of jurisdiction.[22]

(c) Locality of cause of action According to the decisions that have dealt with the matter up to the present, it is undoubted that the various circumstances considered above exhaust the possible cases in which a foreign court possesses international competence. Thus it is not sufficient that the cause of action, as, for instance, a breach of contract or the commission of a tort,[1] occurred in the foreign country.[2]

(d) Choice of governing law It has been held by the Supreme Court of New South Wales that an agreement to submit to the jurisdiction of the English courts is not to be inferred from an agreement to make English law the governing law of a contract.[3]

(e) Possession of property It was once thought, on the authority of *Becquet v MacCarthy*,[4] that the possession of immovable property within the foreign country was sufficient to found jurisdiction. It is safe to conclude that this decision would not be followed now for it has since been decided by the Court of Appeal in *Emanuel v Symon*[5] that neither the fact of possessing property in a foreign country nor the fact of making a partnership contract there relating to the property is sufficient to render the possessor amenable to the local jurisdiction.

(f) Foreign judgment based on service out of the jurisdiction The practice, illustrated by Order 11 of the English RSC[6] under which the courts of a country assume jurisdiction over absentees, raises the question whether a foreign judgment given in these circumstances will be recognised in England.[7] The authorities, so far as they go, are against recognition. The question arose in *Buchanan v Rucker*,[8] where it was disclosed that, by the law of Tobago, service of process might be effected on an absent defendant by nailing a copy of the summons on the door of the court house. It was held that a judgment given against an absentee after service in this manner was an international nullity having no extra-territorial effect. Indeed, the suggestion that it should

---

22 Read, op cit, p 160.
1 Eg *Gyonyor v Sanjenko* [1971] 5 WWR 381.
2 *Sirdar Gurdyal Singh v Faridkote* [1894] AC 670 at 684; *Phillips v Batho* [1913] 3 KB 25 at 30; cf *Schibsby v Westenholz* (1870) LR 6 QB 155 at 161.
3 *Dunbee Ltd v Gilman & Co (Australia) Pty Ltd* [1968] 2 Lloyd's Rep 394; and see *Mattar and Saba v Public Trustee* [1952] 3 DLR 399.
4 (1831) 2 B & Ad 951.
5 [1908] 1 KB 302; and see *Sirdar Gurdyal Singh v Faridkote* [1894] AC 670 at 685.
6 Supra, pp 190–211.
7 See Clarence Smith (1953) 2 ICLQ 524–526.
8 (1808) 9 East 192.

be actionable in England prompted Lord ELLENBOROUGH to ask with some disdain:

> Can the island of Tobago pass a law to bind the rights of the whole world? Would the world submit to such an assumed jurisdiction?[9]

A less fanciful process again raised the question in *Schibsby v Westenholz*,[10] where a judgment had been given by a French court against Danish subjects resident in England:

> The mode of citation adopted in accordance with French law was to serve the summons on the Procureur Impérial, the rule being that if a defendant did not appear within one month after such service judgment might be given against him. Although not required by the law, it was customary in the interests of fair dealing to forward the summons to the consulate of the country where the defendant resided, with instructions to deliver it to him if practicable. In the instant case, the defendants were notified of the proceedings in this manner, but they failed to appear and judgment was given against them.

It was held that no action lay on the judgment. Had the principle on which judgments are enforceable been comity the Court of Queen's Bench intimated that having regard to the English practice of service out of the jurisdiction it would have reached a different conclusion. Since, however, the basis of enforcement is that a judgment imposes an obligation on the defendant, it followed that there must be a connection between him and the forum sufficiently close to make it his duty to perform that obligation. No such duty could be spelt out of the inactivity of the defendants, who were aliens resident in a foreign country. WRIGHT J reached the same conclusion in a later case where a New Zealand judgment had been given against an absentee under an assumed jurisdiction substantially similar to that countenanced by the English Order 11.[11]

It is not without significance, however, that in this general context the Court of Appeal in *Travers v Holley*[12] acted on the basis of reciprocity and held that what entitles an English court to assume divorce jurisdiction is equally effective in the case of a foreign court. In a later case, however, HODSON LJ observed that *Travers v Holley* was

> a decision limited to a judgment *in rem* in a matter affecting matrimonial status, and it has not been followed, so far as I am aware, in any case except a matrimonial case.[13]

Thus, any suggestion that the advance towards "internationalism"[14] made by that decision should be extended to jurisdiction assumed under provisions substantially similar to those contained in Order 11 has so far not been

9 Ibid, at 194.
10 (1870) LR 6 QB 155.
11 *Turnbull v Walker* (1892) 67 LT 767.
12 [1953] P 246, [1953] 2 All ER 794; see also *Re Dulles' Settlement* [1951] Ch 842 at 851. For the current law on recognition of foreign divorces, etc see infra, p 655 et seq.
13 *Re Trepca Mines Ltd* [1960] 1 WLR 1273 at 1281–1282; and see *Schemmer v Property Resources Ltd* [1975] Ch 273 at 287; *Henry v Geoprosco International Ltd* [1976] QB 726 at 745; *Felixstowe Dock and Rly Co v United States Lines Inc* [1989] 2 WLR 109 at 121–123. See also *Morguard Investments Ltd v De Savoye* (1991) 76 DLR (4th) 256, S C of Canada.
14 Kahn-Freund, *The Growth of Internationalism in English Private International Law*, pp 30 et seq.

accepted, and the present position is that the rules set out above remain intact.[15]

(b) JUDGMENTS IN REM

(i) The definition of a judgment in rem

The jurisdictional elements that must exist before a foreign judgment in rem can claim recognition in England are not difficult to specify, but it is first necessary to appreciate the correct meaning of this species of judgment. It has been defined as:

> a judgment of a court of competent jurisdiction determining the status of a person or thing (as distinct from the particular interest in it of a party to the litigation); and such a judgment is conclusive evidence for and against all persons whether parties, privies or strangers of the matter actually decided.[16]

The two parts of this definition will now be considered.

(a) The subject matter of a judgment in rem

The *res* which may form the subject-matter of a judgment in rem is not confined to physical things. If the essence of such a judgment is that it constitutes an adjudication on status, it follows that certain decrees declaring the status of persons must also be classed as operating in rem.[17] Thus, the word *res* as used in this context includes those human relationships, such as marriage, which do not originate merely in contract, but which constitute what may be called institutions recognised by the State.[18] A foreign court which issues, for instance, a decree of divorce or nullity of marriage will, if competent in respect of jurisdiction, be deemed to have pronounced a judgment in rem that is conclusive in England and binding on all persons.[1]

There is some authority for the view that judgments in personam that are ancillary to such judgments in rem are equally binding in England. An illustration of this is afforded by *Phillips v Batho*[2] where the facts were these:

> The plaintiff, domiciled in India, obtained a divorce from his wife in an Indian court, and was awarded damages against the defendant, as co-respondent. The defendant was not present in India at the time of the suit, nor did he submit to the jurisdiction. The plaintiff then sued him in England to recover the damages awarded by the Indian judgment.

This judgment, if treated as one in personam, was not actionable in England, since the Indian court had no jurisdiction in personam over the defendant. Neither, in the opinion of the judge, could the plaintiff sue in England on the original cause of action, for the English court had divorce jurisdiction, at that time, only where the parties were domiciled in England. SCRUTTON J

---

15 *Société Cooperative Sidmetal v Titan International Ltd* [1966] 1 QB 828 at 841; and see *Crick v Hennessy* [1973] WAR 74.
16 *Lazarus-Barlow v Regent Estates Co Ltd* [1949] 2 KB 465 at 475, [1949] 2 All ER 118 at 122. And see *Fracis Times & Co v Carr* (1900) 82 LT 698 at 701; Spencer Bower and Turner, *The Doctrine of Res Judicata* (2nd edn), pp 213 et seq.
17 *Salvesen v Administrator of Austrian Property* [1927] AC 641 at 662 (per Lord DUNEDIN), and see per Lord HALDANE, ibid, at 652–653.
18 Cf Lord HALDANE in *Salvesen's Case* [1927] AC 641 at 652–653.
 1 For the estoppel effect of foreign nullity decrees, see *Vervaeke v Smith* [1983] 1 AC 145; discussed infra, pp 387–388 .
 2 [1913] 3 KB 25.

avoided the difficulties by holding that the judgment awarding damages was ancillary to the judgment in rem dissolving the marriage[3] and, as such, was probably conclusive everywhere, and at any rate was conclusive in another part of the Commonwealth.[4] This decision has been subjected to devastating criticism;[5] it has been disapproved in New Zealand,[6] ignored in Canada[7] and is probably wrong. The judgment should be treated as one in personam whose recognition should be denied on the ground of lack of jurisdiction.

(b) The effect of a judgment in rem

The effect, for instance, of a condemnation in the Admiralty court is to vest the ship in the captors and thus to alter its status. Such a judgment differs fundamentally from one in personam. A judgment in rem settles the destiny of the res itself "and binds all persons claiming an interest in the property inconsistent with the judgment even though pronounced in their absence";[8] a judgment in personam, although it may concern a res, merely determines the rights of the litigants inter se to the res. The former looks beyond the individual rights of the parties, the latter is directed solely to those rights.[9]

(ii) Recognition of judgments in rem: the jurisdictional requirements

A foreign judgment which purports to operate in rem will not attract extra-territorial recognition unless it has been given by a court internationally competent in this respect. In the eyes of English law, the adjudicating court must have jurisdiction to give a judgment binding all persons generally.

(a) Judgments relating to immovables

If the judgment relates to immovables, it is clear that only the court of the situs is competent.[10] So English courts will not recognise foreign judgments concerning title under a will to land in England,[11] even though our courts might take jurisdiction to determine the validity of wills as to foreign land.[12] Similarly, though jurisdiction is taken here over actions in personam concerning foreign land,[13] foreign judgments in personam concerning English land are unlikely to be recognised here.[14]

---

3 It has now been decided that an action for damages against an adulterer is not necessarily ancillary to the divorce judgment: *Jacobs v Jacobs and Ceen* [1950] P 146, [1950] 1 All ER 96. Section 4 of the Law Reform (Miscellaneous Provisions) Act 1970 abolished a husband's right to claim damages for his wife's adultery.
4 "A holding which created a new type of judgment—a hybrid obtained by crossing an action *in rem* with an action *in personam*, with the dominant jurisdictional characteristics being possessed by the former." Read, op cit, p 264.
5 Read, op cit, pp 264–267.
6 *Redhead v Redhead and Crothers* [1926] NZLR 131; see Webb & Davis, pp 182–183.
7 *Patterson v D'Agostino* (1976) 58 DLR (3d) 63.
8 *Dollfus Mieg et Compagnie SA v Bank of England* [1949] Ch 369 at 383, [1949] 1 All ER 946 at 957.
9 *Castrique v Imrie* (1870) LR 4 HL 414 at 427.
10 *Re Trepca Mines Ltd* [1960] 1 WLR 1273 at 1277.
11 *Boyse v Colclough* (1854) 1 K & J 124; and see *Re Hoyles* [1911] 1 Ch 179 at 185–186.
12 Supra, pp 260–261.
13 Supra, pp 255–260.
14 See *Duke v Andler* [1932] SCR 734, supra, p 261; see also White (1982) 9 Syd LR 630. Cf *Chapman Estate v O'Hara* [1988] 2 WWR 275.

(b) Judgments relating to movables

In the case of movables, however, the question of competence is not so simple, since there would appear to be at least three classes of judgments in rem.[15]

(i) Judgments that immediately vest the property in a certain person as against the whole world. These occur, for instance, where a foreign court of Admiralty condemns a vessel in prize proceedings.

(ii) Judgments that decree the sale of a thing in satisfaction of a claim against the thing itself. A judgment which orders a chattel to be sold is a judgment in rem if the object of the sale is to afford a remedy, not by execution against the general estate of the defendant, but by appropriating the chattel in satisfaction of the plaintiff's claim. Such a judgment is not the same as the sentence of an Admiralty court in a prize case which immediately vests the property in the claimant, but it is analogous thereto if the money demand of the plaintiff in respect of which it is given is a demand against the chattel and not against the owner personally.[16] In all cases, therefore, the nature of a foreign judgment that has ordered the sale of some chattel must be determined by ascertaining whether according to the foreign law the original action was a suit against the chattel. The subject was elaborately considered by fourteen judges in the leading case of *Castrique v Imrie*:[17]

> The owner of a British ship mortgaged her to X while she was on a voyage. During the voyage the master drew a bill of exchange on the owner for the cost of certain repairs and indorsed it to a Frenchman at Le Havre. The indorsee brought an action on the bill against the master at Le Havre, and obtained a judgment which declared as follows: "The Tribunal condemns Benson in his quality (capacity) of captain of the vessel *Ann Martin*, and *by privilege on that vessel* to pay to the plaintiff" the amount of the bill. The court declared the master to be free from arrest to which otherwise he would have been liable. A higher court, though having an opinion from the Attorney-General that by English law the mortgagee had a better right than the indorsee, affirmed the decision and ordered the ship to be sold. The ship, having been sold, ultimately arrived in England, and the mortgagee brought an action in the Court of Common Pleas to recover her, on the ground that the sale in France was illegal and void.

The decision necessarily depended on the nature of the French judgment. If it was in rem, then the plaintiff must fail, since the ship was in France at the time of the proceedings. If the judgment was in personam it was not binding on the mortgagee, since he had been absent from the French proceedings. The Court of Common Pleas held the judgment to be in personam, but the Exchequer Chamber and the House of Lords reversed this decision.

The "privilege" which the judgment created on the ship was, according to French law, a species of lien, and although the proceedings were started against the master as well as against the ship, the sale was ordered not in execution of the judgment debt, but in enforcement of the lien. A more striking example of the manner in which English courts pay recognition to foreign judgments in rem is afforded by *Minna Craig Steamship Co v Char-*

---

15 Westlake, s 149.
16 *Imrie v Castrique* (1860) 8 CBNS 405 at 411, 412.
17 (1860) 8 CBNS 1; revd, ibid, p 405; reversal affd (1870) LR 4 HL 414.

tered Bank of India,[18] for there the lien that had been declared by a German court was one which conflicted with the principles of English internal law. In this type of case, the only court competent to give a judgment affecting the status of a res that will command general recognition is the court of the country where the res was situated at the time of the action.

(iii) Judgments that order movables to be sold by way of administration.[19] If, in the course of administering an estate in bankruptcy or on death, a foreign court orders the sale of chattels, the sale will be regarded as conferring a title on the purchaser valid in England. In the case of succession on death, jurisdiction to make such an order resides in the court of the country where the deceased died domiciled.[1] The court competent to make an adjudication in bankruptcy will be considered later.[2]

(iii) Enforcement of judgments in rem

Whilst recognition of a foreign judgment in rem may be fairly common and relatively straightforward, enforcement of such judgments in England raises different issues. No foreign judgment relating to immovables abroad can be enforced in England. If the judgment relates to movables, the real issue is whether it was sufficient to pass title to the property, ie a question of recognition rather than enforcement.[3] A rare example of enforcement of a foreign judgment by an action in rem in England is provided by *The City of Mecca*.[4]

A collision had occurred on the high seas between a Spanish ship and a British ship. The owners of the Spanish ship obtained judgment in Portugal for damages for the loss caused by the collision. The British ship returned to England before the damages were paid and the Spanish shipowners sought to enforce the Portuguese judgment in England by an action in rem against the ship.

Sir Robert PHILLIMORE held that the Portuguese judgment was a judgment in rem which could be enforced in England by an action in rem against the ship. Although on appeal this decision was set aside on the ground that the Portuguese judgment was, in fact, a judgment in personam,[5] the first instance decision is still of good authority and has been applied by SHEEN J in *The Despina GK*.[6]

(c) FINALITY OF THE JUDGMENT

A foreign judgment does not create a valid cause of action in England unless it is *res judicata* by the law of the country where it was given. It must be final and conclusive in the sense that it must have determined all controversies between the parties. If it may be altered in later proceedings between the

18 [1897] 1 QB 55; affd, ibid, p 460.
19 Westlake, s 149.
1 See *Re Trufort, Trafford v Blanc* (1887) 36 ChD 600.
2 Infra, pp 912–915.
3 *Castrique v Imrie* (1870) LR 4 HL 414 at 429.
4 (1879) 5 PD 28.
5 (1881) 6 PD 106.
6 [1983] 1 QB 214; see also *SS Pacific Star v Bank of America National Trust and Savings Association* [1965] WAR 159.

same parties *in the same court*, it is not enforceable by action in England.[7] These principles will now be examined.

A provisional judgment is not *res judicata* if it contemplates that a fuller investigation leading to a final decision may later be held. This aspect of the meaning of finality and conclusiveness is illustrated by the leading case of *Nouvion v Freeman*,[8] where the facts were as follows:

X, who had sold certain land in Seville to Y, brought an "executive" action in Spain against Y and obtained a "remate" judgment for a large sum of money. There were two kinds of proceedings under Spanish law: executive or summary proceedings, and "plenary" or ordinary proceedings. In an executive action, on proof of a prima facie case, the judge without notice to the defendant made an order for the attachment of his property. Notice of the attachment was given to the defendant and he was at liberty to appear and defend the action. But the defences open to him were limited in number, and in particular he could not set up any defence that denied the validity of the transaction upon which he was sued. Either party who failed in executive proceedings could institute plenary proceedings before the same judge, and in these could set up every defence that was known to the law.

It was held by the House of Lords, affirming the Court of Appeal, that no action lay on the remate judgment. Since it was liable to be abrogated by the adjudicating court, it was not *res judicata* with regard to either party, neither did it extinguish the original cause of action.

A more modern illustration is afforded by *Blohn v Desser*.[9] In that case, an action was brought against the defendant personally on an Austrian judgment that had been given not against her individually, but against a firm of which she was a member. To have rendered her personally liable under Austrian law would have necessitated a separate action against her individually, but in this event certain defences would have been available to her that could not have been raised in the proceedings against the firm. Therefore, even if the judgment could be regarded as given against her personally, it was not final and conclusive. Again, to take another important example, a judgment in default of appearance does not satisfy the condition of finality if it is given in a country where the defendant is allowed to apply within a limited time for its rescission by the adjudicating court.[10]

The necessity for finality and conclusiveness appears in a slightly different aspect in the cases dealing with foreign maintenance orders. As is the case in England, foreign courts usually have power to vary the amount of maintenance orders. Thus in *Harrop v Harrop*[11] the issue was the recognition of an order for maintenance made in Perak:

The law of Perak on this matter was as follows. A magistrate could order a person to pay a monthly allowance for the maintenance of his wife, and,

---

7 *Nouvion v Freeman* (1889) 15 App Cas 1; *Re Riddell* (1888) 20 QBD 512 at 516; *Blohn v Desser* [1962] 2 QB 116, [1961] 3 All ER 1. Interim payments are now enforceable under the Foreign Judgments (Reciprocal Enforcement) Act 1933, see infra, p 399.

8 (1889) 15 App Cas 1; applied in *Colt Industries Inc v Sarlie (No 2)* [1966] 3 All ER 85, [1966] 1 WLR 1287; *Berliner Industriebank AG v Jost* [1971] 2 QB 463, [1971] 2 All ER 1513; dist in *Audrain v Aero Photo Inc* (1983) 138 DLR (3d) 178.

9 [1962] 2 QB 116, [1961] 3 All ER 1.

10 Wolff, op cit, pp 264, 265. Cf *Barclays Bank Ltd v Piacun* [1984] 2 Qd R 476.

11 [1920] 3 KB 386; and see *Re Macartney* [1921] 1 Ch 522.

if such order was disregarded, could direct the amount due to be levied in the manner in which fines were levied. On application by the husband or wife and on proof of a change in the circumstances of the parties, the magistrate could vary the amount to be paid.

In the present case a magistrate had ordered the payment of a monthly sum, and later, when this fell into arrears, had ordered that payment of the arrears should be enforced by the appropriate method. The wife failed in the action which she brought in England on these orders. SANKEY J in the course of his judgment put the gist of the matter in these words:

> In my view a judgment or order cannot be said to be final and conclusive if (1) an order has to be obtained for its enforcement, and (2) on application for such an order the original judgment is liable to be abrogated or varied.[12]

If a court is empowered to vary the amount of future payments of maintenance but cannot alter its order as to accrued instalments, then instalments that are already due under the foreign judgment may be recovered by action in England.[13] *Harrop v Harrop* is not inconsistent with this rule, for in that case no evidence was given to show that the amount of accrued instalments was unalterable.

The requirement of finality means that the judgment must be final in the particular court in which it was pronounced.[14] It does not mean that there must be no right of appeal. Neither the fact that the judgment may be reversed on appeal, nor even the stronger fact that an actual appeal is pending in the foreign country, is a bar to an action brought in England;[15] though where an appeal is pending the English court has an equitable jurisdiction to stay execution, which it will generally exercise.[16] If, however, the effect under the foreign law of a pending appeal is to stay execution of the judgment, it would seem that, in the interim, the judgment is not actionable in England.[17]

(d) THE JUDGMENT, IF IN PERSONAM, MUST BE FOR A FIXED SUM

As we have seen, the ground on which a foreign judgment is enforceable in England is that the defendant has implicitly promised to pay the amount in which he has been condemned.[18] It follows that there can be no question of enforcing a foreign decree for specific performance or for the specific delivery or restitution of chattels. Moreover, the law implies a promise to pay a definite, not an indefinite, sum.[19] Unless in an action *in personam* the foreign court has definitely and finally determined the amount to be paid, no action

---

12 [1920] 3 KB 386 at 399. Provision for reciprocal enforcement of foreign maintenance orders is now made by statute, infra, pp 714–718.
13 *Beatty v Beatty*, [1924] 1 KB 807; and see *Patton v Reed* (1972) 30 DLR (3d) 494; *Lear v Lear* (1974) 51 DLR (3d) 56; *Stark v Stark* (1979) 94 DLR (3d) 556; *Mclean v McLean* [1979] 1 NSWLR 620.
14 *Beatty v Beatty*, supra, at 815, 816.
15 *Scott v Pilkington* (1862) 2 B & S 11; *Colt Industries Inc v Sarlie (No 2)* [1966] 1 WLR 1287; see also *Four Embarcadero Center Venture v Mr Greenjeans Corpn* (1988) 64 OR (2d) 746; affd (1988) 65 OR (2d) 160.
16 *Scott v Pilkington*, supra; *Nouvion v Freeman* (1889) 15 App Cas 1 at 13; *Four Embarcadero Center Venture v Mr Greenjeans*, supra; cf *Colt Industries Inc v Sarlie (No 2)*, supra.
17 *Patrick v Shedden* (1853) 2 E & B 14; cf *Berliner Industriebank AG v Jost* [1971] 2 QB 463 at 470–471.
18 *Grant v Easton* (1883) 13 QBD 302.
19 *Sadler v Robins* (1808) 1 Camp 253 at 256. But see White (1982) 9 Syd LR 630.

is maintainable in England.[20] In *Sadler v Robins*[1] a court in Jamaica had decreed that the defendant should pay to the plaintiff £3,670 1s 9 1/4d, first deducting therefrom the full costs expended by the defendant, such costs to be taxed by a master of the court. It was held that until taxation the plaintiff had no cause of action in England, since the sum due on the Jamaican decree was indefinite. A sum, however, satisfies the requirement of certainty if it can be ascertained by a simple arithmetical process.[2]

(e) CONCLUSIVENESS OF FOREIGN JUDGMENTS

(i) A foreign judgment is not impeachable on its merits

It is well established that in an action on a foreign judgment the English court is not entitled to investigate the propriety of the proceedings in the foreign court.[3] Erroneous judgments delivered by a foreign court are not void in England.[4] The merits of the case have been argued and determined, and if one of the parties is discontented with the decision his proper course is to take appellate proceedings in the forum of the judgment. The English tribunal, in other words, cannot sit as a Court of Appeal against a judgment pronounced by a court which was competent to exercise jurisdiction over the parties.[5]

(a) Mistakes by the foreign court

(i) Mistakes as to facts or as to law The defendant in England may show that the foreign court had no jurisdiction to try the case, or he may plead a limited number of defences, such as fraud, which will be considered later,[6] but he is not at liberty to show that the court mistook either the facts or the law on which its judgment was founded.[7]

A more difficult question is whether a foreign judgment can be impeached on the ground that the court made an obvious mistake with regard to English law when purporting to give a decision according to that law. It is now decided that such a mistake does not excuse the defendant from performing the obligation that has been laid upon him by the judgment.[8] The doctrine that a foreign judgment cannot be impeached as to merits has been carried to its logical conclusion. Thus in *Godard v Gray*:[9]

> The plaintiffs, who were Frenchmen, sued the defendants (Englishmen) in France on a charter-party, the proper law of which was English law. The charter-party contained the clause: "Penalty for non-performance of this

20 *Sadler v Robins*, supra; *Henderson v Henderson* (1844) 6 QB 288.
1 Supra.
2 *Beatty v Beatty* [1924] 1 KB 807.
3 *Henderson v Henderson* (1844) 6 QB 288; *Bank of Australasia v Nias* (1851) 16 QB 717; *Vanquelin v Bouard* (1863) 15 CBNS 341; *Godard v Gray* (1870) LR 6 QB 139; *Messina v Petrococchino* (1872) LR 4 PC 144; *Vadala v Lawes* (1890) 25 QBD 310 at 316; *Pemberton v Hughes* [1899] 1 Ch 781 at 790; *Merker v Merker* [1963] P 283, [1962] 3 All ER 928. For earlier doubts see *Smith v Nicolls* (1839) 5 Bing NC 208 at 221.
4 *Imrie v Castrique* (1860) 8 CBNS 405 at 428.
5 *Dent v Smith* (1869) LR 4 QB 414 at 446; *Imrie v Castrique*, supra; *Ferdinand Wagner v Laubscher Brothers & Co* [1970] 2 QB 313 at 318.
6 Infra, pp 377–392.
7 *Bank of Australasia v Nias*, supra, at 735; *Godard v Gray*, supra, at 150.
8 *Castrique v Imrie* (1870) LR 4 HL 414; *Godard v Gray* (1870) LR 6 QB 139.
9 (1870) LR 6 QB 139. Approved by Lord SIMON in *Vervaeke v Smith* [1983] 1 AC 145 at 162 (HL). See also *Tracomin SA v Sudan Oil Seeds Co Ltd* [1983] 1 WLR 662 at 674 (STAUGHTON J); *Tracomin SA v Sudan Oil Seeds Co Ltd* [1983] 1 Lloyd's Rep 560 at 577 (LEGGATT J).

agreement estimated amount of freight." The effect of such a clause under English law was not to quantify the damages exactly, but to leave them to be assessed according to the actual loss suffered; but the French court, believing that the language of the charter-party was to be understood in its natural sense, fixed the damages payable by the defendant at the exact amount of freight. When sued on the judgment in England, the defendants pleaded this mistaken view of English law in defence. The plea failed. The court held that there could be no difference between a mistake as to English law and any other mistake.

(ii) A mistake as to its own jurisdiction What, for many years, has been less certain is whether the foreign court must have had internal competence, ie jurisdiction under its own law. LINDLEY LJ once said that the jurisdiction which alone is important in connection with a foreign judgment is the competence of the foreign court in the international sense. "Its competence or jurisdiction in any other sense is not regarded as material by the courts of this country".[10] According to this view, action will lie in England on a foreign judgment although delivered by a court that, according to its own internal law, had no jurisdiction whatsoever over the cause of action. If, for instance, the foreign court has adjudicated on a claim in excess of the legally permitted amount, is it to be no answer to an action on the judgment in England that the court lacked internal jurisdiction? To admit this would be inconsistent with principle. According at any rate to the English rule, a judgment delivered by a court with no jurisdiction is a complete nullity, and it seems curious that what was null and void in the foreign country can be regarded as valid for the purposes of an English action. Such a foreign judgment creates no rights whatsoever in favour of the plaintiff, yet it is because a right has been vested in him that, according to the doctrine of obligation, he may sue on the judgment in England. The dictum of LINDLEY LJ, for it was nothing more, was not applied in *Papadopoulos v Papadopoulos*,[11] where one of the grounds on which the Cypriot decree of nullity was held to be ineffective was that the court had no power by the law of Cyprus to declare the marriage null and void. Similarly, in *Adams v Adams*[12] recognition was refused to a Rhodesian divorce decree because, under Rhodesian law as interpreted in England, the decree was invalid as it had been pronounced by a judge who was not a judge *de iure* of the High Court of Rhodesia.[13]

(iii) A procedural mistake It is essential to observe that if the foreign court is internally competent the fact that it has erred in its own rules of procedure is no answer to an action in England. This is the explanation of *Pemberton v Hughes*,[14] the case in which LINDLEY LJ delivered his dictum. In that case:

A decree for divorce had been pronounced by the competent court in Florida in an undefended suit brought by a husband against his wife, both parties being domiciled and resident in Florida. It appeared that she had received only nine days' notice of the proceedings instead of ten days as

---

10 *Pemberton v Hughes* [1899] 1 Ch 781 at 791. See also *Adams v Cape Industries Plc* [1990] Ch 433 at 549–550, CA; cf the judgment at first instance, at 492.
11 [1930] P 55.
12 [1971] P 188, [1970] 3 All ER 572.
13 Cf *Re James (An insolvent)* [1977] Ch 41 at 65–66, 77–78; see now the requirement of effectiveness for the recognition of foreign divorces, etc, infra, pp 660–661.
14 [1899] 1 Ch 781.

required by the law of Florida. It was held by the Court of Appeal that the decree was final and was binding in England.

LINDLEY LJ in the course of his judgment said:

> All that the English courts look to are the finality of the judgment and the jurisdiction of the court, in this sense and to this extent—namely its competence to deal with the sort of case that it did deal with, and its competence to require the defendant to appear before it.[15]

In other words, the Florida court was not only internally competent to deal with a case of divorce, but also internationally competent, since the defendant was domiciled in Florida. The judge then concluded as follows:

> If the court had jurisdiction in this sense, and to this extent, the courts of this country never inquire whether the jurisdiction has been properly or improperly exercised, provided that no substantial injustice, according to English notions has been committed.[16]

At first sight the decision of the Court of Common Pleas in *Vanquelin v Bouard*[17] may seem difficult to reconcile with this statement of the law.

> This was an action in England on a judgment obtained in France on a bill of exchange. The defendant pleaded that by French law the French court had no jurisdiction, since the defendant was not a trader and was not resident at Orleans where the bills were drawn. The plea was disallowed.

If the plea meant that the French action had been brought in the wrong court[18] and if this were so, it is arguable that the judgment was a nullity. ERLE CJ denied, however, that the court lacked internal jurisdiction. Thus, to repeat the words of LINDLEY LJ, the French tribunal was competent "to deal with the sort of case that it did deal with", though perhaps the defendant might have pleaded in defence that he personally was not within that competence. In explanation of both *Pemberton v Hughes* and *Vanquelin v Bouard* it has been said that:

> The court had competence in the sort of case involved, but there was a mistake or irregularity of procedure in the exercise of that competence which rendered the right created by the judgment merely voidable, capable of being made void by subsequent proceedings.[19]

A significant feature of *Vanquelin v Bouard* is that the defendant let the French proceedings go by default. Further, he did not plead in the English action that the French judgment was a complete nullity.

A more recent example of these rules in operation is provided by *Merker v Merker*.[1] A German court had annulled a marriage, declaring it to be "null and void" in circumstances where, under German law, it should have been declared to be "a non-existent marriage". Although the German court had jurisdiction, its decree would be regarded as a complete nullity by other German courts. Nevertheless, the decree was recognised in England. As the German court had jurisdiction, the English court "must accept the actual

---

15 [1899] 1 Ch 781 at 790.
16 *Pemberton v Hughes* [1899] 1 Ch 781 at 790–791.
17 (1863) 15 CBNS 341.
18 See *Pemberton v Hughes* [1899] 1 Ch 781 at 791.
19 Read, *Recognition and Enforcement of Foreign Judgments*, p 100.
 1 [1963] P 283, infra, p 660.

decision and exclude any evidence impugning it which falls short of showing that it was obtained by fraud or is contrary to natural justice".[2]

(b) Raising defences available abroad

A closely related rule is that defences that were available before the foreign court cannot be raised in England. In such a case the defendant should have raised the defence in the foreign proceedings. Thus in *Ellis v M'Henry*:[3]

> Judgment had been recovered in Canada in an action that would have failed had the defendant pleaded a certain composition deed.

The plaintiff sued on this judgment in England, and the question was whether the defendant was entitled at that stage to set up the deed as a defence. BOVILL CJ dismissed the contention on the basis that this "would go to impeach the propriety and correctness of the judgment, and is a matter which cannot be gone into after the judgment has been obtained".[4]

This doctrine was applied more recently by the Court of Appeal in *Israel Discount Bank of New York v Hadjipateras*:[5]

> A judgment was granted in New York against two defendants in respect of guarantees given by them to the plaintiff bank. The guarantees provided that the defendants submitted to the jurisdiction of the New York courts. The second defendant, who was aged 21 when he entered into his guarantee, alleged that he only did so under the undue influence of his father, the first defendant. He raised this issue for the first time when enforcement of the New York judgment was sought in England, although he could have raised it during the New York proceedings.

The Court of Appeal accepted that, in principle, undue influence could come within the ambit of the defence that enforcement of the judgment would be against public policy, as could duress and coercion.[6] However, since the defence of undue influence was "available" to him in New York (New York law on this defence being the same as English law), he could not now raise it in England. STEPHENSON LJ, relying on *Ellis v M'Henry*, said that "a defendant must take all available defences in a foreign country" [7] and is at fault if he does not do so. Underlying this principle were considerations of "comity and the duty of the courts to put an end to litigation".

Whilst the principle is undeniably a sound one, the question that arises in the instant case is whether an exception should be made to it in cases involving the defence of public policy. Public policy is treated as an exception to normal private international law rules in other areas[8] and could be treated in the same way in this context. It has to be seriously questioned whether it is right to enforce a judgment when an allegation of a matter as serious as undue

---

2 Ibid, at 298–299.
3 (1871) LR 6 CP 228. See also *Henderson v Henderson* (1844) 6 QB 288; *Martelli v Martelli* (1983) 148 DLR (3d) 746; *Dallal v Bank Mellat* [1986] QB 441.
4 Ibid, at 238–239.
5 [1984] 1 WLR 137; Collier [1984] CLJ 47. See also *Tracomin SA v Sudan Oil Seeds Co Ltd* [1983] 1 Lloyd's Rep 560 (LEGGATT J), reversed on another point, [1983] 1 WLR 1026; *ED & F Man (Sugar) Ltd v Yani Haryanto (No 2)* [1991] 1 Lloyd's Rep 429, CA.
6 Per STEPHENSON LJ at 143; GOFF LJ at 147 concurring.
7 At 144, see also O'CONNOR LJ at 146.
8 Supra, pp 128–137.

influence has not been considered in either the foreign or the English proceedings.[9] Moreover, as will shortly be seen, where the defendant is relying
on the analogous defence of fraud, he is allowed to raise this defence in
England even though it was available to him abroad, and was not raised
there.[10] There are therefore weighty arguments against the decision; nonetheless, it is submitted that the Court of Appeal's decision was the right one.
The proper place for defences to be raised is before the foreign court, and it
is not unfair to the defendant to prevent him from raising a defence in
England, provided that the defence was available to him abroad and he
therefore had the opportunity of raising it there.

This inevitably raises the question of what is meant by a defence being
"available" to a defendant abroad. In the instant case it was shown that New
York *law* had a defence of undue influence and it was accepted that this was
the same as the English defence.[11] Presumably, if New York *law* had been
different from English *law* and did not have a defence of undue influence, or
had a narrower concept of undue influence which did not allow the defence
to operate in a situation where the English defence would operate, the defence
would not be "available" abroad and the second defendant would have been
able to raise the issue in England. What is not clear is whether the concept
of availability of a defence abroad is referring solely to the existence of a rule
which allows a particular defence, or whether it is also referring to the
existence of evidence which goes to establish the defence. If new factual
evidence of undue influence had only come to light after the New York
proceedings have ended, it cannot be said, except in the most limited sense,
that the defence was "available" to the defendant abroad. Neither can it be
said that the defendant was at fault in failing to raise the defence. In this
situation the defendant should be allowed to raise the defence in England.[12]

What if the defendant has raised the issue of undue influence during the
foreign proceedings and this plea has failed; can he re-raise the issue in
England? The conclusiveness principle in *Ellis v M'Henry*,[13] which was quoted
with approval in the instant case,[14] prevents the defendant from doing so.

(ii) Estoppel per *rem judicatam*

A cause of action, once it has been adjudicated by a court of competent
jurisdiction, becomes *res judicata*, and as such it raises an estoppel against
the unsuccessful party.

> The rule of estoppel by *res judicata*, which is a rule of evidence, is that where a final
> decision has been pronounced by a judicial tribunal of competent jurisdiction over
> the parties to and the subject-matter of the litigation, any party or privy to such

---

9 See *Syal v Heyward* [1948] 2 KB 443, concerning the analogous defence of fraud, infra,
   pp 377–380. Cf the fraud/public policy defence under the Brussels and Lugano Conventions,
   infra, pp 424–426.
10 Infra, p 380.
11 Because of the presumption that foreign law is the same as English law unless the contrary
   is proved, see [1984] 1 WLR 137 at 140, 146 and generally on the presumption, supra pp
   107–108.
12 The position on this point prior to *Israel Discount Bank of New York v Hadjipateras* [1984]
   1 WLR 137 (CA) was not clear. *De Cosse Brissac v Rathbone* (1861) 6 H & N 301 at 304,
   suggested there was no such defence; but see the criticism of that case in Morris, p 124.
13 (1871) LR 6 CP 228, 238; supra p 371.
14 [1984] 1 WLR 137 at 144 (STEPHENSON LJ).

litigation as against any other party or privy is estopped in any subsequent litigation from disputing or questioning such decision on the merits.[15]

(a) Estoppel as a defence According to this doctrine, at common law, a foreign judgment was conclusive in two respects in favour of the defendant in England.

First, in the situation where the plaintiff lost abroad, the judgment provided the successful defendant in the foreign proceedings with an effective defence if he was sued by the other party in England on the original cause of action. The plaintiff was estopped from denying the conclusiveness of the judgment.[16]

Secondly, in the situation where the plaintiff lost abroad, but had not been awarded full compensation, the common law rule was that the satisfied judgment of the foreign court provided a good defence to an action brought by the plaintiff in England for the residue of his claim.[17]

This common law rule has now been superseded by the much wider statutory rule in section 34 of the Civil Jurisdiction and Judgments Act 1982.[18] Under this section, once a judgment has been obtained by the plaintiff in his favour abroad, it provides a good defence to an action brought by the plaintiff on the original cause of action, even though the judgment has not been satisfied, unless it is not enforceable or entitled to recognition in England and Wales.[19] However, it must still be the case that, if the plaintiff has two causes of action founded on the same damage against separate defendants, as where the drivers of two vehicles have collided and caused him injury, a judgment of a foreign court against one of them does not bar him from suing the other in England.[20] He cannot, however, sustain such an action if the amount awarded him by the foreign judgment is sufficient to compensate him fully for the damage suffered, for English law does not tolerate double satisfaction.[1]

(b) Cause of action and issue estoppel So far as English judgments are concerned, estoppel *per rem judicatam* is a generic term which comprises two species.

The first, called *cause of action estoppel*, "is that which prevents a party to an action from asserting or denying, as against the other party, the existence of a particular cause of action, the non-existence or the existence of which has been determined by a court of competent jurisdiction in previous litigation between the same parties".[2] In such a case, a further action for the same cause can never succeed.

The second species, called *issue estoppel*, becomes relevant where the determination of a cause of action has necessitated the determination of a

---

15 *Carl Zeiss Stiftung v Rayner and Keeler Ltd (No 2)*, [1967] 1 AC 853 at 933, citing Spencer Bower, *The Doctrine of Res Judicata*, p 3. Originally, *res judicata* was called "estoppel by record". The written records of a court which kept records imported such verity that they admitted of no averment to the contrary. But for this form of estoppel it is no longer material whether a court keeps a written record of its proceedings, [1967] 1 AC 853 at 933–4; see also *Carl Zeiss Stiftung v Rayner and Keeler Ltd (No 3)* [1970] Ch 506, [1969] 3 All ER 897.
16 *Ricardo v Garcias* (1845) 12 Cl & Fin 368 at 406.
17 *Taylor v Hollard* [1902] 1 KB 676; *Barber v Lamb* (1860) 8 CBNS 95 at 100.
18 Discussed supra at p 347.
19 In which case, the common law rule would still be of use.
20 See *Kohnke v Karger* [1951] 2 KB 670.
1 Ibid.
2 *Thoday v Thoday* [1964] P 181 at 197.

number of different issues.[3] In the case of an English judgment, the rule then is that the parties to an action are estopped from contesting a particular issue which has already been determined in previous proceedings to which they were also parties.[4] It is immaterial that the cause of action is not the same in both proceedings.[5]

There is abundant authority that cause of action estoppel applies to foreign judgments,[6] and it is now clear that issue estoppel also applies to foreign judgments. In *Carl Zeiss Stiftung v Rayner and Keeler Ltd*[7] a majority of the Law Lords[8] were of the opinion that there can be an issue estoppel in respect of a foreign judgment. However, the doctrine was not applied in that particular case since the essentials for the application of the doctrine[9] were not satisfied. Since then a number of cases have accepted that issue estoppel applies in respect of foreign judgments,[10] and the matter has now been put beyond any doubt by the House of Lords decision in *The Sennar (No 2)*,[11] in which issue estoppel was applied to a Dutch judgment. Lord DIPLOCK said that "it is far too late, at this stage of the development of the doctrine, to question that issue estoppel can be created by the judgment of a foreign court".[12]

(c) Prerequisites of estoppel The same prerequisites apply for a cause of action and an issue estoppel. In both cases an estoppel will not apply unless three conditions are satisfied.[13]

First, the previous decision must have been final and conclusive on the merits,[14] and must have been given by a court of competent jurisdiction.[15]

Second, there must be identity of parties,[16] that is to say, the parties to the

3 The expression "issue estoppel" was coined by HIGGINS J in the Australian case of *Hoystead v Taxation Comr* (1921) 29 CLR 537, 561; on appeal, [1926] AC 155. See generally Spencer Bower and Turner, *The Doctrine of Res Judicata* (2nd edn), pp 149 et seq.
4 *Fidelitas Shipping Co Ltd v V/O Exporteklab* [1966] 1 QB 630 at 640, 642; *Carl Zeiss Stiftung v Rayner and Keeler Ltd (No 2)* [1967] 1 AC 853 at 913–917, 933–935, 964–965.
5 *Marginson v Blackburn Borough Council* [1939] 2 KB 426, [1939] 1 All ER 273.
6 Supra, pp 368–371.
7 [1967] 1 AC 853, [1966] 2 All ER 536.
8 Contra Lord GUEST.
9 Discussed infra, pp 374–376.
10 *Westfal-Larsen and Co A/S v Ikerigi Compania Naviera SA* [1983] 1 All ER 382; *Tracomin SA v Sudan Oil Seeds Co Ltd* [1983] 1 WLR 662 (STAUGHTON J), affd by the Court of Appeal [1983] 1 WLR 1026, CA; *The Jocelyne* [1984] 2 Lloyd's Rep 569 (LLOYD J); *Vervaeke v Smith* [1983] 1 AC 145 at 156, 160, 162 discussed infra, pp 387–388, a case of an English judgment creating an issue estoppel; *The European Gateway* [1987] QB 206.
11 [1985] 1 WLR 490.
12 At 493; the other Law Lords agreed; the case is discussed infra, pp 375–376.
13 *Carl Zeiss Stiftung v Rayner and Keeler Ltd (No 2)* [1967] 1 AC 853 at 909–910, 935, 942, 967–971; *The Sennar (No 2)* [1985] 1 WLR 490 at 493–494, 499.
14 *Carl Zeiss Stiftung v Rayner and Keeler Ltd (No 2)*, op cit, at 918–919, 926, 936, 949, 969–970; *Charm Maritime Inc v Kyriakou and Mathias* [1987] 1 Lloyd's Rep 433; *Tracomin SA v Sudan Oil Seeds Co Ltd* [1983] 1 WLR 662 (STAUGHTON J); *The Sennar (No 2)*, op cit, at 494, 499, discussed infra. An issue estoppel may arise out of a judgment which is subject to appeal, see *Hawke Bay Shipping Co Ltd v The First National Bank of Chicago (The Efthimis)* [1986] 1 Lloyd's Rep 244 at 247.
15 *Carl Zeiss Stiftung v Rayner and Keeler Ltd (No 2)*, op cit at 942; *Tracomin SA v Sudan Oil Seeds Co Ltd* (STAUGHTON J), op cit; *The Sennar (No 2)*, op cit at 499.
16 *Carl Zeiss Stiftung v Rayner and Keeler Ltd (No 2)*, op cit, at 910–913, 928–936, 937, 943–946, 968 et seq; *The Sennar (No 2)*, op cit, at 499; *House of Spring Gardens Ltd v Waite* [1991] 1 QB 241 at 252–254. Even where this is not the case it may, in exceptional cases, still be possible to prevent an issue being relitigated by showing that this would involve an abuse of the process of the court, see eg *J.H. Rayner (Mincing Lane) Ltd v Bank Für Gemeinwirtschaft AG* [1983] 1 Lloyd's Rep 462, CA; see also *Dallal v Bank Mellat* [1986] QB 44; *House of Spring Gardens Ltd v Waite*, op cit at 254–255.

previous decision or their privies must be the same persons as the parties to the later action or their privies.

Third, the cause of action or issue before the court must be identical with that previously determined.[17]

Nonetheless, when it comes to applying these common rules there is an important difference between cases involving a cause of action estoppel and those involving issue estoppel. When applying the doctrine of issue estoppel the need for caution has been stressed.[18] There are good reasons for adopting this attitude. Confronted with an unfamiliar procedure, it may be difficult for an English judge to ascertain, for instance, the exact issues that have been determined by the foreign court and whether each of them has been determined beyond the possibility of further litigation. Issues may not be fully argued abroad because in cases of a trivial nature, the defendant may have regarded it as impracticable, in terms of time and expense, to defend fully. It may then be unjust to estop the defendant from raising these issues in England. Issue estoppel is a rule of evidence and, as such, is no doubt governed by the law of the forum, but this is a case where the law of the forum ought to be applied "in a manner consistent with good sense".[19]

The requirements for an estoppel were discussed by the House of Lords in *The Sennar (No2)*:[20]

> A bill of lading presented by the original sellers of groundnuts to the original buyers contained an exclusive jurisdiction clause, providing that all actions under the contract of carriage should be brought only before the court at Khartoum or Port Sudan and that the law of the Sudan should apply. Nonetheless, GfG, a German company who were subsequent buyers, brought an action in the Netherlands against the defendant shipowners for damages for the equivalent of a tort, claiming that a false date had been put on the bill of lading by the master of the defendant's ship, *The Sennar*, as a result of which they had incurred liabilities. The Dutch court declined jurisdiction, reasoning that GfG could only found a claim on the contract contained in the bill of lading and the contract had in it the Sudanese exclusive jurisdiction clause. The plaintiffs, another German company, who were successors in title to GfG, brought an action in England against the defendants for damages in tort for deceit/negligence in respect of the same cause of action. One of the issues that had to be decided was whether the plaintiffs were estopped by the Dutch decision from asserting that their claim did not fall within the exclusive jurisdiction clause, which only dealt with claims under the contract.

The House of Lords unanimously held that the plaintiffs were estopped from asserting this; the Sudanese exclusive jurisdiction clause applied with the

---

17 *Carl Zeiss Stiftung v Rayner and Keeler Ltd (No 2)*, op cit at 913, 935, 942–944, 967–968; *The Sennar (No 2)*, op cit, at 494–495, 498–500; *Hawke Bay Shipping Co Ltd v The First National Bank of Chicago (The Efthimis)* [1986] 1 Lloyd's Rep 244 at 247; *Siporex Trade SA v Comdel Commodities Ltd* [1986] 2 Lloyd's Rep 428.

18 *Carl Zeiss Stiftung v Rayner and Keeler Ltd (No 2)* [1967] 1 AC 853 at 917, 918 (Lord REID), 925–926 (Lord HODSON), 947 (Lord UPJOHN), 967 (Lord WILBERFORCE); *Westfal-Larsen & Co A/S v Ikerigi Compania Naviera SA* [1983] 1 All ER 382, 385, 388–389. See also *The Sennar (No 2)* [1985] 1 WLR 490 at 500; *Owens Bank Ltd v Bracco* [1991] 4 All ER 833 at 856, CA.

19 [1967] 1 AC 853 at 919.

20 [1985] 1 WLR 490. Only Lords DIPLOCK and BRANDON gave detailed judgments. Lords FRASER, ROSKILL and BRIDGE concurred with these two Law Lords.

result that the English proceedings were stayed.[1] Since the substance of the claim had not been decided by the Dutch court this was not a case of cause of action estoppel but one of issue estoppel. There were, however, problems in the instant case in satisfying two of the prerequisites for an estoppel.

First, was the Dutch decision, which only concerned a preliminary matter of jurisdiction and did not raise the substance of the dispute, decided "on the merits"? Lord BRANDON gave a wide definition to this concept thus:

> Looking at the matter negatively a decision on procedure alone is not a decision on the merits. Looking at the matter positively a decision on the merits is a decision which establishes certain facts as proved or not in dispute; states what are the relevant principles of law applicable to such facts; and expresses a conclusion with regard to the effect of applying those principles to the factual situation concerned.[2]

Lord BRANDON concluded that the Dutch decision was not a procedural one[3] and therefore came within the above definition.[4] Lord DIPLOCK agreed that the Dutch decision was as to the merits. He held that the Dutch court did not simply decide that it did not have jurisdiction; it decided, first, that the only claim against the shipowners was for breach of contract, and, second, that as a result of the Sudanese exclusive jurisdiction clause, that claim was enforceable only in the courts of the Sudan. There was, therefore, a judgment on the merits in respect of these two issues.[5]

Second, was the issue the same in the Dutch and English courts? In the Dutch court, although the action was framed in tort, it could only be founded on the contract. However, in the English court, the action was framed in tort and could also be founded in tort. Nevertheless, the basic issue was held to be the same, ie whether, even though the claim was framed in tort rather than in contract, the exclusive jurisdiction clause applied to such a claim.[6]

There was no need for the exercise of caution in the use of issue estoppel in the instant case[7] since all the issues decided in the Netherlands had been fully litigated. Also the reason why caution is needed is so that issue estoppel does not unjustly prevent *defendants* from raising issues in England. In the instant case, it was being used to prevent *plaintiffs* from relitigating the same claim on another basis in a different jurisdiction.[8] Indeed, there are strong policy reasons why a court should be very willing to use issue estoppel in a case like *The Sennar (No2)*:[9] shipowners are vulnerable to having their ships arrested and to forum shopping by plaintiffs; exclusive jurisdiction clauses are designed to fix the place of trial and therefore plaintiffs should not be able to avoid such clauses by going from one country to another seeking a classification of the cause of action which achieves this objective; having tried this once abroad, a plaintiff should not be able to have another bite of the cherry in England.

---

1   The discretionary power to stay proceedings in this type of case is discussed supra, pp 234–236.
2   At 499; see also p 494 (per Lord DIPLOCK).
3   At 499. Cf *Harris v Quine* (1869) LR 4 QB 653. That case is now affected by s 3 of the Foreign Limitation Periods Act 1984, discussed infra, at p 404.
4   See also *Tracomin SA v Sudan Oil Seeds Co Ltd* [1983] 1 WLR 662 (STAUGHTON J).
5   At 494–495.
6   At 499–500 (per Lord BRANDON).
7   At 500 (per Lord BRANDON).
8   See KERR LJ in the Court of Appeal [1984] 2 Lloyd's Rep 142, 152–153.
9   See generally, Lord DIPLOCK at 493, Lord BRANDON at 501; KERR LJ in the Court of Appeal, op cit, at 149–154.

(iii) Judgments in personam and in rem

The principle of res judicata applies both to actions in personam and actions in rem, for as regards their degree of conclusiveness these actions differ from each other only in the number of persons who are bound by the judgment. A judgment in personam binds the parties and their privies if they litigate the same issue in England. A judgment in rem has a wider operation, since it is conclusive against all the world.[10] Both judgments in rem and judgments in personam are conclusive upon the point decided, but in the former "the point", since it is the determination of status, is conclusive against the whole world, while in the latter, since it is unconcerned with status, is conclusive only between parties and privies.[11]

(f) DEFENCES AVAILABLE TO THE DEFENDANT[12]

Despite the fact that the foreign judgment on which the defendant is sued is final and conclusive, it is still open to him to escape liability not only by pleading that the foreign court had no jurisdiction, but also by pleading any one of seven further defences set out below.

(i) Foreign judgment obtained by fraud

If we omit all reference to private international law for the moment, we find a well-established rule that a domestic judgment may be impeached on the ground that it was obtained by fraud.[13] The unsuccessful party, instead of appealing or applying for a new trial, may bring an independent action to set aside the judgment.[14] It is not a method that is encouraged,[15] or one which, owing to the strict burden of proof imposed on the plaintiff, easily succeeds. It will not succeed unless he alleges and proves that new facts, evidential of fraud, have been discovered since the judgment and that they were not reasonably discoverable at the time of the trial. He must further prove that this new evidence, had it been adduced in the original action, would in all probability have had a material effect on the decision.[16]

Turning now to private international law, it is firmly established that a foreign judgment is impeachable for fraud in the sense that upon proof of fraud it cannot be enforced by action in England.[17]

(a) Types of fraud It is clear that, as in domestic law,[18] a judgment will be denied recognition if the court had been imposed upon by a trick not apparent

10 Supra, pp 362–365. Estoppel in divorce, etc cases is discussed, infra, pp 676–678.
11 *Ballantyne v Mackinnon* [1896] 2 QB 455 at 462.
12 These defences may be pleaded not only by a defendant resisting an action in England on a foreign judgment in favour of the plaintiff, but also by a plaintiff suing in England on the original cause of action who is met by the defence of a foreign judgment in favour of the defendant: *Jacobson v Frachon* (1927) 138 LT 386 (natural justice); *Manolopoulos v Pnaiffe* [1930] 2 DLR 169 (fraud).
13 *Duchess of Kingston's Case* (1776) Smith's *Leading Cases* (13th edn), ii, 641 at p 717; *R v Humphrys* [1977] AC 1 at 21, 30; Gordon (1961) 77 LQR 358–381; 533–559.
14 *Flower v Lloyd* (1877) 6 Ch D 297; *Jonesco v Beard* [1930] AC 298.
15 *Flower v Lloyd (No 2)* (1879) 10 ChD 327 at 333–334, per JAMES LJ, though BAGGALLAY LJ dissented.
16 *Boswell v Coaks (No 2)* (1894) 86 LT 365 n; *Falcke v Scottish Imperial Insurance Co* (1887) 57 LT 39; *Birch v Birch* [1902] P 130.
17 *Vadala v Lawes* (1890) 25 QBD 310 at 316; *Ellerman Lines Ltd v Read* [1928] 2 KB 144.
18 *Duchess of Kingston's Case* (1776) Smith's *Leading Cases* (13th edn), ii, 641 at 651.

at the time of the trial, but discovered later. Thus in *Ochsenbein v Papelier*:[19]

> A French seller, in the course of a dispute in Paris with an English buyer, produced a writ showing that he had begun an action to recover the price of the goods. When remonstrated with, however, he burnt the writ then and there and agreed to refer the dispute to arbitration in London. He nevertheless proceeded with the action behind the buyer's back and obtained judgment by default. The seller brought an action in the Court of Queen's Bench on this judgment, and the Court of Chancery, when asked by the buyer to restrain the action, refused an injunction as being unnecessary. It was unnecessary, because the above facts, if proved, would afford a good defence to the common law action.

The rule that a judgment is impeachable for fraud applies in those rare cases where the foreign court itself has acted in a fraudulent manner. This occurred in *Price v Dewhurst*[1] where, acting under Danish law, certain persons formed themselves into a court for the purpose of administering the property of a deceased testator. On proof that they, or some of them, were interested parties, their decision was treated by SHADWELL V-C as fraudulent and void in so far as it favoured the judges themselves.[2]

(b) Fraud and going into the merits of the foreign judgment When fraud is alleged English courts have gone into the merits of the foreign judgment. This has happened both in the situation where the allegation of fraud has been raised and dismissed abroad, and in the situation where the defendant failed to raise this defence abroad, although it was available to him.

In the case of foreign as distinct from domestic judgments, the Court of Appeal has on no less than four occasions proceeded on the same evidence that was given at the original trial and has sustained a charge of fraud that had been investigated and dismissed by the foreign court. The first of these cases is *Abouloff v Oppenheimer*:[3]

> This was an action brought on a Russian judgment which ordered the return of certain goods unlawfully detained by the defendant, or alternatively, the payment of their value. One defence was that the judgment had been obtained by fraud in that the plaintiff had falsely represented to the Russian court that the defendant was in possession of the goods, the truth being that the plaintiff himself continued in possession of them throughout. It was demurred that this was an insufficient answer in point of law, since the plea was one which the Russian court could, and as a matter of fact did, consider, and that to examine it again would mean a new trial on the merits. The demurrer was overruled.[4]

Lord ESHER, at any rate, had no inhibitions. He said:

> I will assume that in the suit in the Russian courts the plaintiff's fraud was alleged by the defendants and that they gave evidence in support of the charge: I will assume even that the defendants gave the very same evidence which they propose to adduce in this action; nevertheless the defendants will not be debarred at the

19 (1873) 8 Ch App 695.
1 (1837) 8 Sim 279.
2 See also the effect of fraud on the recognition of foreign divorces and annulments, discussed infra, pp 680–685.
3 (1882) 10 QBD 295.
4 It should be noticed, of course, that by demurring to the plea the plaintiff admitted the truth of the facts it alleged.

trial of this action from making the same charge of fraud and from adducing the same evidence in support of it.[5]

The next case is *Vadala v Lawes*,[6] which raised the simple point whether an allegation of fraud which has already been fully investigated by a foreign court can once more be investigated in England. The Court of Appeal unanimously answered the question in the affirmative, and ordered a new trial with a view to discovering whether there had been fraud in relation to certain bills of exchange.

These two cases were followed in the third case, *Jet Holdings Inc v Patel*:[7]

The plaintiffs brought an action in California to recover money allegedly misappropriated by the defendant. The defendant appeared and claimed that he had suffered and been threatened with violence by or on behalf of the president of the plaintiff companies. A default judgment was awarded against the defendant after he failed to attend for a medical examination in California. An action was brought in England to enforce the judgment.

This action failed. The Court of Appeal held that the plaintiffs had implicitly, and even to some extent expressly, asserted to the Californian court that the defendant's account of violence and threats was untrue. If it was true, this, together with the actual incidents of violence relied upon, was capable of amounting to fraud. On the other hand, fraud cannot be a defence if the foreign court has not been deceived,[8] or if what the defendant alleges is plainly untrue.[9] The fraud alleged did not relate, as in the previous two cases, to the cause of action (here, the issue of whether the defendant had misappropriated the money); it was instead an example of what was described as being "collateral" fraud. However, this made no difference to the principles to be applied. In either case, "the foreign courts' views on fraud are neither conclusive nor relevant".[10] The issue of fraud had to go on trial in England, where the facts would be considered afresh to see whether the defendant was entitled to resist enforcement on this basis.

Finally, in *Owens Bank Ltd v Bracco*[11] the Court of Appeal treated the above decisions as binding authorities and held that, as far as fraud is concerned, the enforcement of a foreign judgment is not the same as the enforcement of an English judgment in that there is no requirement of any fresh evidence before an English court can try the issue of fraud.

These four decisions should be contrasted with that of the Court of Appeal in *House of Spring Gardens Ltd v Waite*,[12] where the fact that the issue of fraud had already been litigated in Ireland estopped defendants from alleging, at the enforcement stage, that the prior Irish judgment had been obtained by fraud. What differentiated this case from the first three decisions[13] mentioned

---

5 Ibid, at 306.
6 (1890) 25 QBD 310. See also *Norman v Norman (No 2)* (1968) 12 FLR 39.
7 [1990] 1 QB 335, [1989] 2 All ER 648; Carter (1988) 59 BYBIL 360.
8 If a foreign court still gives judgment for a plaintiff, despite being aware of attempts to mislead that court and of violence against the defendant, enforcement in England would no doubt be against public policy, discussed infra, pp 380–381.
9 [1990] 1 QB 335 at 346.
10 At 345.
11 [1991] 4 All ER 833, CA affd [1992] 2 WLR 621, HL. The case involved enforcement under the Administration of Justice Act 1920, infra p 395. Cf *Keele v Findley* (1990) 21 NSWLR 444.
12 [1991] 1 QB 241, [1990] 2 All ER 990; (1990) 61 BYBIL 405.
13 *Owens Bank Ltd v Bracco*, supra, had not yet been decided.

above was said to be that the issue of fraud had been examined in Ireland in a separate and second action (in 1987) from the original one (in 1983) in respect of which enforcement was sought.[14] It was the judgment in this second action which created the estoppel. The result would have been different and the question of whether there had been fraud re-examined if it had been possible either to impeach the 1987 judgment on the basis that that judgment had itself been obtained by fraud or to produce new evidence of fraud in relation to the 1983 judgment.[15]

The crucial distinction that has to be drawn is between those foreign judgments which create an estoppel in relation to the issue of fraud and those that do not. This was accepted by the Court of Appeal in the most recent case, *Owens Bank Ltd v Bracco*.[16] It is doubtless easier to satisfy the requirements for an estoppel[17] if there has been a separate action abroad dealing solely with the issue of fraud, but it may be possible to satisy these requirements without this. Furthermore the foreign judgment creating the estoppel does not have to have been obtained in the country which granted the original judgment for which enforcement is now sought.[18] The English courts have a discretion to stay the English trial determining whether a foreign judgment was obtained by fraud pending trial of the same issue in another country.[19]

The decision of the Court of Appeal in *Syal v Heyward*[20] takes matters even further, for it allows retrial in England notwithstanding that the plaintiff deliberately refrained from raising in the original trial the facts upon which the allegation of fraud is based. The strange result appears to follow that an English defendant to a foreign action may reserve a defence of fraud available to him with the intention of raising it if he is sued on the judgment in England.[21] This is an indulgence that has nothing to commend it. There can also be a retrial in England even though there has been an attempt to raise the defence of fraud abroad at a late stage and this has not been allowed.[22]

The effect of the above decisions is that the doctrine as to the conclusiveness of foreign judgments is materially and most illogically prejudiced. Moreover, the abandonment of the conclusiveness principle in these cases involving allegations of fraud is in marked contrast to the application of the conclusiveness principle in the analagous area of undue influence in *Israel Discount Bank of New York v Hadjipateras*.[23] However, until the House of Lords decides to the contrary, the law in fraud cases remains as stated by the Court of Appeal in the above cases.

(ii) Foreign judgment contrary to public policy of English law

No action is sustainable on a foreign judgment which is contrary to the

---

14 [1991] 1 QB 241 at 251.
15 Ibid.
16 [1991] 4 All ER 833 at 855–857, CA.
17 Supra, pp 374–376.
18 *Owens Bank Ltd v Bracco*, supra, at 857.
19 Ibid.
20 [1948] 2 KB 443, [1948] 2 All ER 576; approved obiter in *Owens Bank Ltd v Bracco* [1991] 4 All ER 833 at 844, CA. See also *Adams v Cape Industries Plc* [1990] Ch 433 at 568–569.
21 Cowen (1949) 65 LQR 82, 84; though see *Svirskis v Gibson* [1977] 2 NZLR 4 at 10.
22 *Owens Bank Ltd v Bracco*, supra.
23 [1984] 1 WLR 137, CA; discussed supra, pp 371–372. For the position in relation to natural justice: see infra, pp 384–387.

English principles of public policy.[24] There is no need to add anything here to what has already been said about the subject of general public policy,[25] except to give some examples of the application of the doctrine to the particular case of a foreign judgment.[26]

Israel Discount Bank of New York v Hadjipateras[27] shows that undue influence, duress and coercion can come within the ambit of the public policy defence. However, as has already been seen,[28] even though the defence was one of public policy it could not be raised in the instant case because, although it had been available in New York proceedings, it had not been put forward there.

In *Vervaeke v Smith*[29] the House of Lords held that recognition of a Belgian judgment invalidating a sham marriage (ie where the parties had no intention of living together as husband and wife) would be against public policy.[30]

(iii) Foreign revenue, penal or other public laws

English courts will not enforce foreign revenue, penal or other public laws either directly[31] or through the recognition of a foreign judgment.[1] Thus in *US v Inkley*[2] the Court of Appeal refused to enforce a judgment granted in Florida relating to a bail appearance bond, where the purpose of the enforcement action was the execution of a foreign public law/penal process. However, the foreign judgment will be denied recognition only if it falls directly within the area of revenue, penal or other public laws, strictly construed. So, a foreign judgment for costs may be recognised even though the costs would be payable into a foreign legal aid fund.[3] More significantly, it has been said in the Court of Appeal that there is

> nothing contrary to English public policy in enforcing a claim for exemplary damages, which is still considered to be in accord with the public policy in the

---

24 *Re Macartney* [1921] 1 Ch 522 at 527; and see *Dalmia Dairy Industries v National Bank of Pakistan* [1978] 2 Lloyd's Rep 223 at 299–301. The same principal applies in Canada, see eg *Bank of Montreal v Snoxell* (1983) 143 DLR (3d) 349.
25 Supra, pp 128–137.
26 An early example is *Re Macartney* [1921] 1 Ch 522; distd *Stark v Stark* (1979) 94 DLR (3d) 556. There were two other grounds on which *Re Macartney* was based. The first was that the judgment was not final and conclusive, supra, pp 365–367. The second was that the cause of action was unknown in England, a ground which is supported by *De Brimont v Penniman* (1873) 10 Blatch 437; *Mayo-Perrott v Mayo-Perrott* [1958] IR 336; but Read, op cit, pp 293–295, suggests that such a ground is of dubious merit, on the authority of *Burchell v Burchell* (1928) 58 QLR 527. See also *Phrantzes v Argenti* [1960] 2 QB 19, [1960] 1 All ER 778, supra, pp 91–92; Morris, p 120.
27 [1984] 1 WLR 137, CA.
28 Supra, at pp 371–372.
29 [1983] 1 AC 145, HL. The case involved recognition of a foreign nullity decree and is, therefore, discussed more fully infra, pp 676–678.
30 Both at common law and under the Foreign Judgments (Reciprocal Enforcement) Act 1933, on which see infra, p 402. See also *ED & F Man (Sugar) Ltd v Yani Haryanto (No 2)* [1991] 1 Lloyd's Rep 161 at 167; affd by the Court of Appeal but on the basis that there had been a prior English judgment [1991] 1 Lloyd's Rep 429, infra, p 387. The *Vervaeke Case* was also decided on an estoppel point, discussed infra, pp 387–388.
31 Supra, pp 113–122.
1 *USA v Harden* (1963) 41 DLR (2d) 721. See, however, as an exception the Drug Trafficking Offences Act 1986.
2 [1989] QB 255, [1988] 3 All ER 144.
3 *Connor v Connor* [1974] 1 NZLR 632.

United States and many of the great countries of the Commonwealth.[4]

A civil judgment, though combined with a penal judgment, may be actionable in England as creating a separate and independent cause of action, despite the general principle[5] that penalties imposed abroad are disregarded. Thus in *Raulin v Fischer*:[6]

> The defendant, a young American lady, while recklessly galloping her horse in the Bois de Boulogne, ran into the plaintiff, a French officer, and seriously injured him. She was prosecuted by the State for her act of criminal negligence. By French law a person who is injured by a crime may intervene in the prosecution and make a claim for damages, whereupon his civil action is tried together with the prosecution and one judgment is pronounced on both matters. The plaintiff did so intervene. The defendant was convicted of the crime and ordered to pay a fine of 100 francs to the State and 15,917 francs by way of damages and costs to the plaintiff.

It was held on these facts, in an action brought by the plaintiff in England to recover the sterling equivalent of 15,917 francs, that the French judgment was severable. That part of it which awarded the plaintiff damages was not tainted with the penal character of the rest of the proceedings, and therefore might be put in suit in England without involving a recognition of a penal judgment.

(iv) The Protection of Trading Interests Act 1980[7]

The background to this Act is United Kingdom resentment[8] at the extraterritorial application of anti-trust laws by the United States. Diplomatic attempts at solving what is a political as well as an economic and legal problem failed and we now have legal warfare. Under the Act, the Secretary of State is given wide powers to counter foreign measures for regulating international trade which affect the trading interests of persons in the United Kingdom.[9]

Alongside this, there are restrictions on the enforcement of certain overseas

---

4 *SA Consortium General Textiles v Sun and Sand Agencies Ltd* [1978] QB 279 at 300, infra, pp 400–401.
5 Supra, pp 117–121.
6 [1911] 2 KB 93; and see *SA Consortium General Textiles v Sun and Sand Agencies Ltd* [1978] QB 279, infra, pp 400–401; *A-G of New Zealand v Ortiz* [1984] AC 1, at 31–35, CA, discussed supra, pp 118–119.
7 See Huntley (1981) 30 ICLQ 213 at 229–233; Jones [1981] CLJ 41; AV Lowe (1981) 75 AJIL 257; Blythe (1983) 31 AJCL 99; Bridge (1984) 4 Legal Studies 2. For analogous statutes in Australia and Canada see the Foreign Anti-Trust Judgments (Restriction of Enforcement) Act 1979 (Cth) and the Foreign Extraterritorial Measures Act 1984; see generally Patchett, *Recognition of Commercial Judgments and Awards in the Commonwealth* (1984) para 3.24; Castel, *Canadian Conflict of Laws* (2nd edn) (1986) para 178; Castel (1983) I Hague Recueil 9 at pp 79–92; Collins [1986] JBL 372 and 452.
8 See *British Nylon Spinners Ltd v ICI Ltd* [1953] Ch 19, [1952] 2 All ER 780; *Re Westinghouse Electric Corpn Uranium Contract Litigation NDL Docket No 235* [1978] AC 547, [1978] 1 All ER 434. The resentment is also shared by Australia and Canada, see supra, footnote 7.
9 See ss 1–4. See also Protection of Trading Interests (US Antitrust Measures) Order 1983, SI 1983/900; Protection of Trading Interests (Australian Trade Practices) Order 1988, SI 1988/569, on which see *Trade Practices Commission v Australian Meat Holdings Pty Ltd* (1989) 83 ALR 299; Protection of Trading Interests (Hong Kong) Order, SI 1990/2291; and US Reexport Control Order 1982, SI 1982/885.

judgments. Section 5(2) provides that a court in the United Kingdom cannot enforce:[10]

(a) judgment for multiple damages, ie one "for an amount arrived at by doubling, trebling or otherwise multiplying a sum assessed as compensation for the loss or damage sustained by the person in whose favour the judgment is given";[11]

(b) a judgment based on a competition law which is specified in an order made by the Secretary of State;[12]

(c) where a judgment coming within (a) or (b) has been given against a third party, a judgment on a claim for contribution.

Three points should be noted about section 5. First, although the Act does not mention any specific foreign country, the reference to multiple damages shows beyond any doubt that the target at which the Act is aimed is United States anti-trust laws.[13] The litigation in *British Airways Board v Laker Airways Ltd*[14] serves as an illustration. If Sir Freddie Laker had established his anti-trust claim in the United States against British Airways he would have been entitled to multiple damages. However, any award of multiple damages would not have been enforceable in the United Kingdom because of section 5. Second, the prohibition on the enforcement of a judgment for multiple damages applies to all of the judgment and not merely to the non-compensatory part. Third, the prohibition on enforcement does not depend on whether the overseas court applied its anti-trust laws extra-territorially. It has been pointed out[15] that section 5 can apply to the enforcement of a judgment in an anti-trust suit brought by one US corporation against another US corporation, which has assets in the United Kingdom, following anti-trust infringements which took place wholly within the United States. The rationale of this section is not, therefore, that there has been an invasion of United Kingdom sovereignty; instead, it is more akin to that underlying the prohibition of enforcement in cases of foreign penal laws or in cases where enforcement would be against public policy.[16]

Section 5 is a negative provision. More controversial is the accompanying positive provision contained in section 6. This gives a "qualifying"[17] defendant, who has actually paid some or all of the multiple damages, the right to recover in the United Kingdom the non-compensatory part of the payment. This claw-back provision is no doubt designed to discourage private litigants from instigating civil proceedings for multiple damages and to persuade the United States to alter its anti-trust stance in respect of United Kingdom defendants.[18] Section 6 provides a unique cause of action; for this to be of any assistance to a plaintiff in England jurisdictional and enforcement prob-

---

10 Either at common law, or by statute under the Administration of Justice Act 1920, discussed infra, pp 395 et seq, or Part I of the Foreign Judgments (Reciprocal Enforcement) Act 1933, discussed infra, p 397 et seq, see s 5(1). S 5 will not, however, apply to cases coming within the Brussels Convention or Lugano Convention, discussed infra, pp 411–453, but see especially p 424.
11 S 5 (3).
12 S 5(2)(b) and (4).
13 See *British Airways Board v Laker Airways Ltd* [1985] AC 58 at 89 (per Lord DIPLOCK).
14 Ibid; discussed supra at pp 248–249.
15 See *British Airways Board v Laker Airways Ltd* [1984] QB 142 at 161–162 (PARKER J).
16 Ibid, at 162–163; Blythe (1983) 31 AJCL 99, 123.
17 Ie a citizen of the UK, or a body incorporated in the UK, or a person carrying on business in the UK, s 6(1). See also s 6(3) and (4).
18 Blythe, op cit, at pp 126–127.

lems have also to be overcome. The 1980 Act helps with both problems. Section 6(5) provides that "a court in the United Kingdom may entertain proceedings on a claim under this section notwithstanding that the person against whom the proceedings are brought is not within the jurisdiction of the court." A writ will still have to be served on the defendant, but the leave of the court is not required for service out of the jurisdiction.[19] Section 7[20] allows for Orders in Council to be made providing for the enforcement in the United Kingdom of foreign judgments clawing-back sums paid pursuant to an award of multiple damages. This is done on a reciprocal basis[21] so that an overseas country must provide for the enforcement in that country of judgments given in the United Kingdom under section 6. Section 7 applies regardless of whether or not the foreign claw-back provision corresponds to section 6.[22] It follows that an Order in Council could specify that the whole of a foreign judgment, including the claw-back of the compensatory part of an award of multiple damages, is to be enforced in the United Kingdom, even though section 6 does not allow the claw-back of this compensatory part in proceedings in the United Kingdom.[1]

(v) Foreign judgment contrary to natural justice

(a) The meaning of contrary to natural justice Although the judges have frequently asserted that a foreign judgment obtained in proceedings which contravene the principles of natural justice cannot be enforced in England, it is extremely difficult to fix with precision the exact cases in which the contravention is sufficiently serious to justify a refusal of enforcement. SHADWELL V-C once said that "whenever it is manifest that justice has been disregarded, the court is bound to treat the decision as a matter of no value and no substance".[2] But this goes too far. As we have already seen a foreign judgment is enforceable notwithstanding that it patently proceeded upon a wrong view of the evidence or of the foreign law, or even of English law, but it would not be extravagant to suggest that this is a questionable application of natural justice. Such a judgment is in a wide sense unjust, but it is difficult to trace delicate gradations of injustice so as to reach a definite point at which it deserves to be called the negation of natural justice. It is therefore not enough to allege that the decision is very wrong or works injustice in the particular case.[3]

The expression "contrary to natural justice" has, however, figured so prominently in judicial statements that it is essential to fix, if possible, its exact scope. When applied to foreign judgments it relates merely to alleged irregularities in the procedure adopted by the adjudicating court, and has nothing to do with the merits of the case. For many years the courts have been vigilant to ensure that the defendant has been given due notice and a

---

19 RSC Ord 11, r 1(2)(b), see supra, pp 210–211. S 6(5) will not apply in the unlikely event of the jurisdiction rules in the Brussels Convention or Lugano Convention, discussed supra, pp 180–181 et seq, applying (European Community and EFTA States are not likely to give judgments for multiple damages).
20 As amended by s 38 of the Civil Jurisdiction and Judgments Act 1982.
21 See, for example, the United Kingdom-Australia Agreement (1991) Cmnd 1394, Art 2(2) (not yet in force).
22 This is the effect of the amendment introduced by s 38 of the 1982 Act.
1 See Anton, *Civil Jurisdiction in Scotland* (1984), paras 11–15.
2 *Price v Dewhurst* (1837) 8 Sim 279 at 302.
3 *Robison v Fenner* (1913) 3 KB 835 at 842.

proper opportunity to be heard,[4] and natural justice was regarded as being confined to these two requirements. However, there is recent authority to the effect that these are merely instances of a wider principle of natural justice, according to which the court has to consider whether there has been a procedural defect such as to constitute a breach of an English court's views of substantial justice.[5]

(b) Due notice and proper opportunity to be heard Concern over due notice has arisen in the situation where jurisdiction has been exercised over absent defendants. The English courts are reluctant to criticise the procedural rules of foreign countries on this matter and will not measure their fairness by reference to the English equivalents but, if the mode of citation has been manifestly insufficient as judged by any civilised standard, they will not hesitate to stigmatise the judgment as repugnant to natural justice and for that reason to treat it as a nullity. The relevant cases in modern times have been confined to foreign divorces and annulments, and want of notice or of an opportunity to be heard are now dealt with specifically in the Family Law Act 1986.[6] If the foreign court, in proceedings *in personam*, is prepared to dispense with notice of the proceedings, or to allow notice to be served in a manner inadequate to satisfy an English court, it is not for the English court to dispute the foreign judgment,[7] even where the foreign court's jurisdiction is based solely on an agreement by the defendant to submit thereto.[8]

As regards the requirement of a proper opportunity to be heard, it is a violation of natural justice if a litigant, though present at the proceedings, was unfairly prejudiced in the presentation of his case to the court. A clear example of this would be if he were totally denied a right to plead, but the defence of unfair prejudice is not one that is lightly admitted. It is not sufficient, for instance, that his personal evidence was excluded, if the procedural rule of the forum is that parties may not give evidence on their own behalf.[9] The question whether the defendant had a proper opportunity to present his side of the case arose in *Jacobson v Frachon*,[10] where the facts were as follows:

A & Co of London agreed to buy crêpe de Chine from B of Lyons. A & Co brought an action in France for cancellation of the contract and for damages, on the ground that the deliveries of the material were short in quantity and inferior in quality. The French court, before giving judgment, appointed an expert to examine the material in London. The expert, who was a relative of B, made no proper examination, and, though deputed by the court to take evidence, refused to hear the evidence of A & Co and their witnesses. He ultimately made a report adverse to A & Co which was found by ROCHE J to be the uncandid production of a biased and prejudiced mind. Judgment for B was given by the French court. A & Co then sued B in England for breach of the original contract. B pleaded the French

4 *Jacobson v Frachon* (1927) 138 LT 386 at 390 (Lord HANWORTH), 392, (ATKIN LJ); *Buchanan v Rucker* (1808) 9 East 192; *Rudd v Rudd* [1924] P 72.
5 *Adams v Cape Industries Plc* [1990] Ch 433.
6 Infra, pp 678–680.
7 *Jeannot v Fuerst* (1909) 100 LT 816; and see *Vallée v Dumergue* (1849) 4 Exch 290 at 303.
8 *Feyerick v Hubbard* (1902) 71 LJKB 509; *Jeannot v Fuerst*, supra.
9 *Scarpetta v Lowenfeld* (1911) 27 TLR 509; *Robinson v Fenner* [1913] 3 KB 835.
10 (1928) 138 LT 386.

judgment in bar of action, but A & Co replied that this judgment was contrary to natural justice.

The Court of Appeal held that the judgment was not void as contravening the requirements of natural justice, since A & Co had not been prevented from presenting their case to the court. It appeared that by French law the court was not bound by the expert's report, but could reject it if satisfied of its inaccuracy. A & Co therefore were at liberty to produce witnesses to the court and to attack the report. It further appeared that A & Co had taken this course, although without success. It could not, therefore, be said that the court had refused to hear the evidence of the litigant.

(c) Substantial justice Normally, an allegation that there has been a lack of natural justice will involve either or both of the requirements of due notice and a proper opportunity to be heard. However, the Court of Appeal in *Adams v Cape Industries Plc*[11] did not regard the defence as being restricted to these two instances. The ultimate question was whether there was a procedural defect which constituted "a breach of an English court's views of substantial justice".[12] The defendants in the present case had proper notice of the proceedings but chose not to contest them. Nevertheless, it was said, obiter, that there was a breach of natural justice in the way that the Federal District Court judge in Texas had assessed damages in favour of the 206 plaintiffs; this was fixed between the plaintiffs and judge on an average basis per plaintiff rather than on the basis of their individual entitlement according to the evidence. The conclusion of the Court of Appeal that, in such circumstances, a judgment should not be enforced in England is no doubt correct. But it is questionable whether the use of a wide definition of the concept of natural justice was the best way of achieving this result. It opens up a gap between, on the one hand, commercial cases and, on the other hand, cases of recognition of foreign divorces and annulments, where the natural justice defence is expressly confined to instances of want of due notice and opportunity to be heard.[13] Want of substantial justice was a much criticised concept, and is no longer a basis for the refusal of recognition of foreign divorces etc.[14] The use of the concept of substantial injustice in relation to the recognition and enforcement of foreign judgments creates new uncertainty over the ambit of the defence of natural justice. Cases of procedural unfairness which do not involve a lack of due notice or opportunity to be heard would be better dealt with under the defence of public policy.[15]

(d) The availability of a remedy in the judgment-granting country The question was raised in the *Adams Case* of whether the defendants should have sought a remedy in Texas in respect of the lack of natural justice. The Court of Appeal said,[16] using the analogy of fraud,[17] that in cases involving lack of due process and opportunity to be heard it may well be that the defendant does not have to show that he has sought to take advantage of any available remedy in the foreign courts before he can raise the defence of lack of natural justice in England at the enforcement stage. However, in cases involving a

---

11 [1990] Ch 433 at 557 et seq. For the facts of the case see, supra, pp 350–351.
12 At 564.
13 Infra, pp 678–680.
14 Supra, pp 135–137.
15 Supra, pp 380–381.
16 At 568 et seq.
17 Supra, pp 377–380.

lack of substantial justice other than the two primary kinds the position is different; here it is relevant to consider the fact that there is the possibility of the correction of error in the country where the judgment was obtained. Nonetheless, this was not fatal to the use of the natural justice defence on the facts of the case since there was no evidence that the defendants had any knowledge of the method used for the assessment of the damages in the United States until the stage when enforcement of the judgment was sought in England.

What happens if the defendant actually raised the issue of natural justice in the foreign judgment-granting court, and the issue was determined by that court? The *Jacobson Case* suggests that in such a case the defence of lack of natural justice (at least when referring to a lack of due notice and opportunity to be heard) is no longer available. However, this proposition was doubted in *Jet Holdings Inc v Patel*,[18] a case decided on the basis of fraud which also raised the issue of a lack of natural justice. In fraud cases the normal rule is that an English court at the enforcement stage can go into this issue, even though it has previously been litigated in the judgment-granting country.[19] The Court of Appeal expected that the same rule would apply in cases involving a lack of natural justice, although it did not finally decide this point.

(vi) A foreign judgment on a matter previously determined by an English court[20]

A foreign judgment will not be recognised if there has been a prior English judgment in respect of the same matter. The House of Lords so held in *Vervaeke v Smith*:[21]

> In 1954, the appellant, a Belgian domiciled woman, entered into a sham marriage (ie the parties did not intend to live as husband and wife thereafter) with an Englishman (Smith) in order to avoid deportation. In 1970 the appellant married in Italy, Messina, who died on the day of the ceremony. The appellant wished to inherit Messina's property as his "wife". An obvious obstacle to this was her earlier marriage to Smith. She, therefore, sought a decree of nullity in England in respect of her first marriage on the ground of lack of consent. This petition was dismissed;[22] the marriage was not invalidated, even though it was a sham marriage. Later, the appellant went to Belgium and obtained a nullity decree on the ground that the marriage was a sham. Armed with this decree, the appellant returned to England and sought a declaration that the Belgian decree was entitled to recognition here (the first petition), and a declaration that, this being so, the marriage between the appellant and Messina was valid (the second petition). WATERHOUSE J dismissed both petitions and an appeal to the Court of Appeal was dismissed. The appellant then appealed to the House of Lords.

The House of Lords unanimously dismissed both petitions, thereby refusing

18 [1990] 1 QB 335 at 345.
19 Supra, pp 378–380.
20 There is substantially the same defence in cases of recognition under the Brussels Convention or Lugano Convention see infra pp 430–431, 442–443.
21 [1983] 1 AC 145, HL; Lipstein [1981] CLJ 20 (on the Court of Appeal's decision); Carter (1982) 53 BYBIL 302; Jaffey (1983) 32 ICLQ 500; Smart (1983) 99 LQR 24; Jaffey (1986) 5 Civil Justice Quarterly 35.
22 *Messina v Smith* [1971] P 322.

recognition of the Belgian judgment.[23] The earlier English judgment, which determined the validity of the marriage, meant that the matter was *res judicata*.[24] As far as the appellant's first petition was concerned, the English judgment operated as a cause of action estoppel preventing the same matter from being raised before the English courts. It would prevent the appellant from directly seeking a nullity decree in England, and it was said that she should be in no better position by virtue of proceeding indirectly by obtaining a judgment abroad and then seeking recognition of this judgment.[25] The Belgian judgment was in respect of the very matter, ie the validity of the marriage, which had previously been determined in the English judgment. As regards the second petition, the English judgment operated as an issue estoppel preventing the granting of the declaration which the appellant sought.[26] Although the English judgment did not actually determine the validity of the appellant's second marriage, it did decide the issue upon which this was dependent, the validity of the appellant's first marriage.

Vervaeke leaves open two questions.[27] First, what would happen if the English judgment in respect of the same matter is given *after* the foreign judgment for which recognition is sought.[1] The reasoning of the House of Lords could apply equally well to prevent recognition of the foreign judgment in this situation. Second, what would happen where there are two inconsistent foreign judgments given in different States in respect of the same matter, both of which are required to be recognised at common law? This presents more of a problem since the principles in *Vervaeke* do not provide an answer. However, a pragmatic view would be that one of the two judgments should be given priority over the other one, and, on balance, this should be the first judgment.[2]

One final observation should be made in connection with *Vervaeke*. The specific question raised in that case of recognition of a foreign nullity decree following an earlier English decision in the same matter is now dealt with by the Family Law Act 1986.[3] However, *Vervaeke* still remains a good authority on the general principles to be applied in cases involving recognition of foreign judgments (other than divorces, annulments or judicial separations)[4] on matters previously determined by an English court, and has been applied subsequently in a commercial context.[5]

---

23 The case was also decided on the basis of public policy, discussed supra, pp 380–381. It also raised problems of recognition under the Foreign Judgments (Reciprocal Enforcement) Act 1933, discussed infra, pp 402–403.

24 At 156–157 (per Lord HAILSHAM), 158–160 (per Lord DIPLOCK).

25 Per Lord DIPLOCK, at 160. There is, however, a question as to whether the issue was the same in the earlier English judgment and in the present proceedings for recognition of the Belgian judgment, see Jaffey (1983) 32 ICLQ 500.

26 At 156 (per Lord HAILSHAM), at 160 (per Lord DIPLOCK).

27 See generally Stone [1983] Lloyd's MCLQ 1, 22–23. For the solution to these questions where recognition and enforcement comes within the Brussels Convention or Lugano Convention, see infra, pp 430–432.

1 This situation is unlikely to happen because the foreign judgment would normally operate to prevent the English action, see supra, pp 372–376.

2 This is the solution adopted in cases of recognition and enforcement under the Brussels Convention or Lugano Convention, see Art 27(5) of the Conventions discussed infra, pp 431–432. See also s 51(1) of the Family Law Act 1986, discussed infra, pp 676–678.

3 S 51(1); Law Com No 137, para 6.65; see the criticisms of Jaffey (1986) 5 Civil Justice Quarterly 35; infra, pp 676–678.

4 These are dealt with by s 51(1) of the Family Law Act 1986.

5 *E D & F Mann (Sugar) Ltd v Yani Haryanto (No 2)* [1991] 1 Lloyd's Rep 429, CA.

(vii) An overseas judgment given in proceedings brought in breach of agreement for settlement of disputes

Section 32 of the Civil Jurisdiction and Judgments Act 1982 provides an important new defence which is that:

a judgment given by a court of an overseas country in any proceedings shall not be recognised or enforced in the United Kingdom if—

(a) the bringing of those proceedings in that court was contrary to an agreement under which the dispute in question was to be settled otherwise than by proceedings in the courts of that country; and

(b) those proceedings were not brought in that court by, or with the agreement of, the person against whom the judgment was given; and

(c) that person did not counterclaim in the proceedings or otherwise submit to the jurisdiction of that court.

The background to section 32[6] is that some legal systems are much stricter than others in their requirements as to when an arbitration or choice of court agreement is incorporated into a contract. A party who wants to avoid such an agreement may be able to do so by seeking trial in a country which does not accept the agreement as being effective. He may then obtain a judgment as to substance in his favour. If the English courts recognise the agreement, section 32 provides that they shall not recognise and enforce this foreign judgment.

Within a short time of section 32 coming into force the English courts had to consider the operation of this section in *Tracomin SA v Sudan Oil Seeds Co Ltd (Nos 1 and 2):*[7]

A dispute arose between the Sudanese sellers of peanuts and the Swiss buyers. The contracts between the parties contained a clause providing for the settlement of disputes by arbitration in London. Despite this, the buyers brought an action for damages before the Swiss courts. The sellers unsuccessfully sought a stay of those proceedings, relying on the arbitration clause. The Swiss courts decided that the arbitration clause was invalid, because it had not been properly incorporated into the contracts under Swiss law—no evidence of English law, which governed the contracts, having been given. Under English law the arbitration clause had been incorporated into the contracts.

In *Tracomin No 1* the buyers sought an injunction in England restraining the arbitration in London, on the basis that the Swiss judgment created an estoppel in relation to the issue of the validity of the arbitration clause. The Court of Appeal applied section 32 and refused to recognise the Swiss judgment.[8] Sir John DONALDSON (ACKNER and FOX LJJ concurring) confined his comments to the precise point of the appeal, whether sections 32 and 33 applied to a foreign judgment granted before those provisions had come into force.[9] Having decided that in the circumstances of the case[10] they did, it was accepted without argument that the requirements for non-recognition under

---

6 See Collins, *The Civil Jurisdiction and Judgments Act 1982*, pp 141–143.
7 [1983] 1 WLR 1026, CA.
8 Affirming the decision of STAUGHTON J [1983] 1 WLR 662. Swiss judgments are now recognised and enforced under the Lugano Convention, infra, pp 442–444.
9 See Sch 13, Part I, para 2, and Pt II, paras 8(1) and 9(1).
10 The reasoning of the Court of Appeal (at pp 1029–1030) was that Sch 13, Part II, para 8 lists the judgments on which s 32 is not to have retrospective effect; since this judgment did not come within the categories specified therein, s 32 could apply retrospectively to it.

section 32 were satisfied. This is clearly right. The reasons were explained by STAUGHTON J at first instance. There was an agreement under which the dispute was to be settled otherwise than by proceedings in Switzerland, since the arbitration clause had been validly incorporated into the contracts according to the governing law. The decision of the Swiss court that there was no valid arbitration agreement was immaterial because of section 32(3),[11] which provides[12] that a court in the United Kingdom is not bound by any decision of the overseas court relating to any of the matters in, inter alia, section 32(1). The first requirement under section 32(1)(a) was, therefore, satisfied. These Swiss proceedings were not brought with the agreement of the sellers; the second requirement under section 32(1)(b) was, therefore, also satisfied. The sellers, although they appeared, did not, according to section 33(1)(b) of the 1982 Act, submit to the jurisdiction of the Swiss courts since they only appeared in order to ask the court to stay the proceedings on the ground that the dispute should be submitted to arbitration. The third requirement under section 32(1)(c) was, therefore, also satisfied.

In *Tracomin No 2*, which was decided on the next day, the Court of Appeal used their discretionary powers to grant the sellers an injunction restraining the buyers from litigating in Switzerland.[13] The jurisdictional basis for granting this was the existence of the agreement to submit disputes to English arbitration.[14]

(a) The scope of the section Section 32 only applies to a judgment given by a court of an "overseas country", ie any country or territory outside the United Kingdom.[15] This means that it does not apply to the judgments of Scots or Northern Ireland courts.[16]

Section 32(1) does not distinguish between recognition and enforcement at common law and by statute and, as will be seen, the defence can operate in respect of at least some of the forms of statutory recognition and enforcement.[17] However, its impact will be felt most at common law because there was already a similarly worded provision to section 32 under the Foreign Judgments (Reciprocal Enforcement) Act 1933,[18] which it replaces.[19]

---

11 See the decision of STAUGHTON J, op cit at 670.
12 Infra, p 392.
13 Reversing the decision of LEGGATT J [1983] 1 Lloyd's Rep 571 on the exercise of this discretion. See generally on injunctions restraining a party from litigating abroad, supra, pp 241–250.
14 See LEGGATT J [1983] 1 Lloyd's Rep 571, at 576 and the Court of Appeal [1983] 1 WLR 1026 at 1035.
15 See s 50 of the 1982 Act.
16 For recognition of these, see infra, pp 393–395.
17 It applies to judgments recognised and enforced under the Administration of Justice Act 1920, and to most judgments coming under the Foreign Judgments (Reciprocal Enforcement) Act 1933. However, it does not affect judgments given in proceedings which arise under a number of international conventions and which are recognised and enforced under Part I of the 1933 Act (see s 32(4)(b) of the 1982 Act), see infra, p 401. It does not affect judgments required to be recognised or enforced under the Brussels Convention or Lugano Convention (s 32(4), as amended by the Civil Jurisdiction and Judgments Act 1991, Sch 2, para 14), see infra, p 435.
18 S 4(3)(b) of the 1933 Act, see infra, p 401.
19 S 54 of the 1982 Act and Sch 14.

(b) The three requirements for the operation of section 32

(i) There must be an agreement under which the dispute was to be settled otherwise than by proceedings in the courts of the country where the proceedings were brought, and the bringing of the proceedings in that country must be contrary to that agreement (section 32(1)(a)). This requirement would be satisfied in the following examples: proceedings were brought in Norway when an agreement provided that all disputes were to be settled by trial in England; proceedings were brought in New York when an agreement provided that all disputes were to be settled by arbitration in Switzerland;[20] proceedings were brought in Brazil when an agreement provided that all disputes were to be settled by arbitration in Brazil. The agreement for settlement of disputes will normally take the form of a choice of jurisdiction clause or an arbitration clause contained in a written contract between the parties. It could, however, take the form of an agreement made after the dispute had arisen and could, whenever it was made, be an oral agreement.

The party seeking recognition or enforcement of the overseas judgment can, however, challenge the agreement. Section 32(2) provides that the defence under section 32(1) does not apply where the agreement was "illegal, void or unenforceable or was incapable of being performed for reasons not attributable to the fault of the party bringing the proceedings in which the judgment was given". In the absence of a foreign decision creating an issue estoppel,[21] an English court will have to determine these matters itself. A decision on whether an agreement is illegal, void or unenforceable raises a problem of the applicable law. This will be solved by applying the law governing the agreement in accordance with choice of law principles.[1] Thus, in *Tracomin SA v Sudan Oil Seeds Co Ltd*,[2] it will be recalled that the question arose of whether an arbitration clause had been validly incorporated into the contracts. By English law the arbitration clause had been incorporated into the contracts but by Swiss law it had not. STAUGHTON J accepted that English law, as the governing law, should be applied on this question, and that the arbitration clause was validly incorporated into the contracts.[3]

(ii) It must be shown that the person against whom the judgment was given neither brought the proceedings in the first place nor agreed to the proceedings being brought in that court by the other party (section 32(1)(b)). This is a negative requirement and is concerned to ensure that the agreement for settlement of disputes has not been overridden by either of the above two types of conduct.

(iii) It must be shown that the person against whom the judgment was given did not counterclaim or otherwise submit to the jurisdiction of that court (section 32(1)(c)). This shows a similar concern to that shown under section 32(1)(b), but is dealing with the conduct of the party against whom the judgment was given *after* the proceedings have been brought. The losing party abroad must not have submitted to the jurisdiction by putting in a

---

20 See *Deutsche Schachtbau-und Tiefbohrgesellschaft mbH v Shell International Petroleum Co Ltd* [1990] 1 AC 295 at 311; the case went to the House of Lords on a garnishment point, op cit at 323.
21 Supra, pp 372–376 and infra.
1 See Art 1(2)(d) of the Rome Convention, infra, pp 471–472.
2 [1983] 1 WLR 662. Affirmed by the Court of Appeal [1983] 1 WLR 1026; discussed supra, p 389.
3 [1983] 1 WLR 662, 668; the point was not argued before him. The Court of Appeal also implicitly accepted this point [1983] 1 WLR 1026.

counterclaim or in any other way (for example by fighting the action on its merits). It is important to note that, in deciding whether there has been submission, section 33 of the 1982 Act will apply.[4]

(c) Decisions of foreign courts in respect of the above matters

Section 32(3) provides that

> a court in the United Kingdom shall not be bound by any decision of the overseas court relating to any of the matters mentioned in subsection (1) and (2).

Thus, as has already been mentioned, in *Tracomin SA v Sudan Oil Seeds Co Ltd*[5] a Swiss court, applying Swiss law, had held that the English arbitration clause was not validly incorporated into the contracts. When the question of recognition of the judgment arose in England, section 32 was raised as a defence. In deciding that there was a valid agreement on arbitration, STAUGHTON J held that the decision of the Swiss court was immaterial, according to section 32(3).

Section 32(3) does not apply to the decision of a court other than the overseas court which gave the judgment. Instead, the normal principles of issue estoppel[6] will apply, and, according to these principles, issues relating to an agreement on jurisdiction may have to be regarded as being settled by the decision of a foreign court.[7] To take an example, section 32 is raised as a defence to a judgment given in State A and an English court has to decide whether an agreement providing for jurisdiction in State B is valid. The overseas court in State A decided that it was not. The English court is not bound by this decision because section 32(3) applies. However, a court in State C had decided that the agreement was valid. If this judgment is recognised it may create an estoppel in England which prevents any denial that the agreement is valid.

3. DIRECT ENFORCEMENT OF FOREIGN JUDGMENTS BY STATUTE

The common law doctrine that a foreign judgment, though creating an obligation that is actionable in England, cannot be enforced here except by the institution of fresh legal proceedings is subject to important exceptions introduced by a number of statutes, the most important of which are the Civil Jurisdiction and Judgments Act 1982, as amended by the Civil Jurisdiction and Judgments Act 1991 (which deals with both recognition and enforcement within the United Kingdom and under the Brussels and Lugano Conventions); the Administration of Justice Act 1920, Part II; the Foreign Judgments (Reciprocal Enforcement) Act 1933; the European Communities Act 1972 and the State Immunity Act 1978. We will deal with these statutes separately. As far as the Civil Jurisdiction and Judgments Act 1982, as amended, is concerned, the provisions therein on recognition and enforcement within the United Kingdom and under the Brussels and Lugano Conventions will also be dealt with separately.

---

4 See *Tracomin SA v Sudan Oil Seeds Co Ltd* [1983] 1 WLR 1026, CA.
5 [1983] 1 WLR 662 at 670. Affirmed by the Court of Appeal, op cit, without argument on the point.
6 Supra, pp 372–376.
7 See *The Sennar (No 2)* [1985] 1 WLR 490, HL, discussed supra pp 375–376

(a) THE CIVIL JURISDICTION AND JUDGMENTS ACT 1982: RECOGNITION AND ENFORCEMENT WITHIN THE UNITED KINGDOM.[8]

(i) Enforcement of UK judgments in other parts of the UK

Where judgment is given in one part of the United Kingdom (ie England and Wales, Scotland and Northern Ireland) section 18 of the 1982 Act provides for its enforcement in another part of the United Kingdom by way of registration under Schedules 6 (money provisions) or 7 (non-money provisions). A judgment to which section 18 applies can be enforced in another part of the United Kingdom only in this way,[9] ie the common law rules on enforcement cannot be used. Schedules 6 and 7 will only apply where there is a "judgment" as defined under section 18.

Section 18 initially gives a wide definition to the concept of a judgment.[10] It means, inter alia, "any judgment or order . . . given or made by a court of law in the United Kingdom". A judgment of an inferior court is therefore covered, as is a judgment in rem. It also includes "any award or order made by a tribunal" and "an arbitration award".[11] The section then gives a detailed list of judgments which it does not cover.[12] To take some examples, it does not apply to: (i) a judgment given in a magistrates' court; (ii) a judgment given in proceedings relating to bankruptcy or the winding up of a company;[13] (iii) so much of a judgment as concerns the status of an individual;[14] (iv) so much of a judgment as is a provisional measure other than an interim payment; (v) a maintenance order which is enforceable under the separate statutory provisions dealing with enforcement of maintenance orders in another part of the United Kingdom.[15] Finally, to further complicate matters, section 18 contains a few limited specific inclusions within its scope,[16] for example fines for contempt of court.

(a) Enforcement of money provisions In cases where there is a judgment as defined under section 18, the procedure under Schedule 6 for enforcement of money judgments is as follows.[17]

A certificate in respect of the judgment is obtained in the original court, whether it is a judgment of a superior or inferior court. This is then registered in the prescribed manner in the superior court of the other part of the United Kingdom in which enforcement is sought—in England and Wales or Northern Ireland the High Court, in Scotland the Court of Session. A registered certificate is of the same force and effect as a judgment of the registering court, which has the same powers in relation to enforcement as if it had given the original judgment.[18]

8 See generally Hartley, *Civil Jurisdiction and Judgments*, pp 101–101; Collins, *The Civil Jurisdiction and Judgments Act 1982*, pp 131–135; Anton, *Civil Jurisdiction in Scotland*, paras 9.33–9.43; Dicey and Morris, pp 500–503.
9 S 18(8). There is an exception in respect of arbitration awards within s 18(2)(e).
10 S 18(2).
11 Cf the position under the Brussels and Lugano Conventions, infra pp 414, 442.
12 See s 18(3), (5), (6), (7).
13 S 18(3)(c); see also s 18(3)(a) inserted by the Insolvency Act 1985, Sch 8, para 36 and amended by the Insolvency Act 1986, Sch 14. Another statute deals with these matters, see Insolvency Act 1986, s 426, discussed by Woloniecki (1986) 35 ICLQ 644, infra, pp 911–912.
14 S 18(5)(b) and (6), as amended by the Courts and Legal Services Act 1990, Sch 16, para 41.
15 S 18(5)(a); see also s 18(7). The statute in question is the Maintenance Orders Act 1950 (see s 16 of that Act, as amended by the Courts and Legal Services Act 1990, Sch 20).
16 S 18(4).
17 Sch 6, paras 2–6; see also RSC Ord 71, r 37.
18 Sch 6, para 6.

There are few defences to enforcement under Schedule 6. A defendant cannot impeach the judgment on its merits and, unlike at common law, cannot plead that the court in the other part of the United Kingdom lacked jurisdiction. Moreover, the defences available at common law cannot be used, and section 32 of the 1982 Act cannot apply because the judgment is not given by a court of an "overseas" country.

The only defences to enforcement under Schedule 6 that a defendant is allowed under the 1982 Act are to be raised after registration and are as follows: first, the registering court *must* set aside the registration if the procedure in the Schedule has not been complied with; second, it *may* set aside the registration if satisfied that there was an earlier judgment dealing with the matter in dispute given by another court having jurisdiction in the matter.[19] The limited nature of the defences means that the party who objects to the judgment given in the original court has to go there and appeal against it, rather than raise his objections when enforcement of the judgment is sought in another part of the United Kingdom.

This, however, raises the problem of an appeal against the original judgment overturning or amending that judgment. This is met in Schedule 6 by providing that a certificate shall not be issued unless under the law of the part of the United Kingdom in which the judgment was given

(a) either the time for an appeal has expired or the appeal has finally been disposed of; and (b) enforcement is not stayed and the time available for its enforcement has not expired.[20]

Even after registration there is a power given to the registering court to stay proceedings for enforcement pending the outcome of an application, under the law of the part of the United Kingdom in which the judgment was given, to set aside or quash the judgment.[21]

There are special provisions on costs and interest.[1]

(b) Enforcement of non-money provisions The 1982 Act extends the previous statutory law by providing in Schedule 7 for the enforcement of non-money provisions. A non-money provision is defined as "any relief or remedy not requiring payment of a sum of money";[2] this would include an injunction, a decree of specific performance and a declaration as to title. The provisions in this Schedule are very similar to those in Schedule 6. There are, however, some minor procedural differences,[3] and, more importantly, there is a major difference of substance. It is stated that "a judgment shall not be registered ... if compliance with the non-money provisions contained in the judgment would involve a breach of the law of that part of the United Kingdom".[4]

(ii) Recognition of UK judgments in other parts of the UK

Section 19(1) simply states that:

a judgment to which this section applies given in one part of the United Kingdom shall not be refused recognition in another part of the United Kingdom solely on

19 Sch 6, para 10.
20 Sch 6, para 3; criticised by Stone (1983) 32 ICLQ 477, 487–488.
21 Sch 6, para 9.
 1 Sch 6, paras 7 and 8.
 2 Sch 7, para 1.
 3 See Sch 7, paras 2–5; RSC Ord 71, r 38.
 4 Sch 7, para 5(5). Obviously there is no provision on interest as such, but costs carry interest, Sch 7, para 7(2).

the ground that, in relation to that judgment, the court which gave it was not a court of competent jurisdiction according to the rules of private international law in force in that other part.

With a few exceptions, section 19 applies to the same judgments as section 18.[5] It is a curiously worded provision in that it is phrased in negative terms and does not impose a positive duty to recognise judgments.[6] It could be read so as to infer that there are defences available to prevent recognition[7] and that included in these is a defence of lack of jurisdictional competence, provided that this allegation is combined with another defence.

(iii) The effect of a judgment given in another part of the UK

This is dealt with by section 34 of the 1982 Act, which, it will be recalled,[8] abolishes the non-merger rule in respect of foreign judgments. Once a judgment has been given in another part of the United Kingdom, the plaintiff may not bring proceedings in England and Wales on the same cause of action unless that judgment is not enforceable or entitled to recognition in England and Wales.

(b) ADMINISTRATION OF JUSTICE ACT 1920[9]

This Act makes provision for the enforcement within the United Kingdom of judgments obtained in a superior court of any part of the Commonwealth.[10]

(i) When registration of Commonwealth judgments is allowed

A person who has obtained a judgment in a territory forming part of the Commonwealth may within twelve months apply to the High Court in England or Northern Ireland or to the Court of Session in Scotland for its registration, whereupon the court may, if in all the circumstances of the case they think it is just and convenient that the judgment should be enforced in the United Kingdom, order the judgment to be registered.[11] Thus, registration is not a right, as it is in cases of recognition and enforcement within the United Kingdom, but lies wholly within the discretion of the court. A judgment cannot be registered, however, unless it is one under which a sum of money is made payable.[12] Neither can a judgment for multiple damages be registered.[13]

(ii) When registration is not allowed

Under section 9(2) of the 1920 Act registration is not allowed if the original court acted without jurisdiction or if the judgment debtor did not voluntarily submit to the jurisdiction of the adjudicating court, unless he was carrying

---

5 S 19(2); for exclusions from s 19 that are included within s 18, see s 19(3).
6 See generally, Anton, *Civil Jurisdiction in Scotland*, para 9.34.
7 Ie the defences at common law, see Stone [1983] Lloyd's MCLQ 1; Lane (1986) 35 ICLQ 629; cf Anton, *Civil Jurisdiction in Scotland*, para 9.34.
8 Supra, p 347.
9 Some minor amendments have been made to this Act by the Civil Jurisdiction and Judgments Act 1982, s 35; ss 10 and 14 of the 1920 Act are amended.
10 S 13. See generally, Patchett, *Recognition of Commercial Judgments and Awards in the Commonwealth*, chs 1–4.
11 S 9 (1).
12 S 12.
13 Protection of Trading Interests Act 1980, s 5; discussed supra, at pp 382–384.

on business[14] or was ordinarily resident within that jurisdiction. It is assumed that questions of jurisdiction are to be determined by reference to the common law rules as to the jurisdiction of the foreign court.[15] The other defences available under section 9(2) are also similar to those available at common law,[16] namely that the judgment debtor was not served and did not appear in the original proceedings, that the judgment was obtained by fraud,[17] and that the original cause of action was one which, for reasons of public policy or for some other similar reason, could not have been entertained in England. A judgment may not be registered if the judgment debtor satisfies the English court either that an appeal is pending or that he is entitled to appeal against the judgment.[18] The defences mentioned so far are ones laid down by the 1920 Act itself. In addition, the defence laid down by section 32 of the Civil Jurisdiction and Judgments Act 1982, in respect of an overseas judgment given in proceedings brought in breach of an agreement for settlement of disputes,[19] will apply to cases coming within the 1920 Act.

(iii) The effect of registration

A judgment registered under the Act is of the same force and effect, and it may be followed by the same proceedings, as if it had originally been obtained in the registering court.[20] A plaintiff is in no way deprived of his right to sue at common law upon the obligation created by a foreign judgment,[21] but if he sues on a judgment that is registrable under the Act he is not entitled to the costs of the action unless registration has been refused or unless the court otherwise orders.[1]

(iv) Reciprocity

The Act, however, does not render a judgment registrable within the United Kingdom unless its provisions have been extended by Order in Council to the country in which the judgment has been obtained. Reciprocity is essential. When reciprocal provisions have been made by a Commonwealth country for the enforcement of English, Scottish and Northern Ireland judgments, an Order in Council may be made extending the Act to the country in question.[2] The Act has been extended to a substantial number of Commonweath countries.[3]

---

14 See *Sfeir & Co v National Insurance Co of New Zealand* [1964] 1 Lloyd's Rep 330.
15 Supra, pp 348–358.
16 Supra, pp 377 et seq. The common law cases must be referred to for the meaning of these defences: *Owens Bank Ltd v Bracco* [1991] 4 All ER 833, CA
17 *Owens Bank Ltd v Bracco*, supra.
18 S 9(2)(e). There is no such common law defence, see supra, p 367.
19 Supra, pp 389–392.
20 S 9(3)(a), (b); as amended by the Administration of Justice Act 1956, s 40 (b).
21 *Yukon Consolidated Gold Corpn v Clark* [1938] 2 KB 241 at 252, [1938] 1 All ER 366 at 368.
 1 S 9(5).
 2 S 14; as amended by the Civil Jurisdiction and Judgments Act 1982, s 35 (3). The reciprocity is no longer exact in the case of some Commonwealth jurisdictions which now make United Kingdom judgments registrable under their counterparts, not of the 1920 Act, but of the Foreign Judgments (Reciprocal Enforcement) Act 1933; see Dicey & Morris, p 481.
 3 See S I 1985/1994.

(c) FOREIGN JUDGMENTS (RECIPROCAL ENFORCEMENT) ACT 1933[4]

(i) The object of the Act

The policy of facilitating the direct enforcement of foreign judgments in England, and of ensuring that English judgments are enforced abroad,[5] received a further impulse from the Foreign Judgments (Reciprocal Enforcement) Act 1933, which applies the principle of registration, not only to the Commonwealth, but also to foreign countries.

(ii) The countries to which the provisions of the Act are extended

The provisions made by the Act for the registration of foreign judgments in England may be extended by Order in Council to any country which is prepared to afford substantial reciprocity of treatment to judgments obtained in the United Kingdom.[6] It is undesirable that there should be two systems of registration, one for the Commonwealth, the other for countries outside the Commonwealth, and therefore a policy of the gradual supersession of the 1920 Act has been adopted. With this object in view power is given to render the 1933 Act applicable by Order in Council to countries forming part of the Commonwealth, and it is provided that the Administration of Justice Act 1920 shall cease to apply to any such country except those to which it extended at the date of the Order in Council,[7] which was introduced in 1933.[8] However, in order for the 1933 Act to be applied to any particular Commonwealth country, a further specific Order in Council is required, both in the case of a jurisdiction to which the 1920 Act had never been applicable[9] and of one to which it had.[10] Orders to this effect have, however, been made only for Pakistan,[11] Bangladesh,[12] India, the Australian Capital Territory, Jersey, Guernsey, the Isle of Man, and Tonga. The Act has also been extended to Canada.[13]

As regards countries outside the Commonwealth, orders have been made extending the provisions of the Act to Austria, Belgium,[14] France, Israel, Italy, the Netherlands, Norway, the Federal Republic of Germany and

---

4 The 1933 Act is amended by the Civil Jurisdiction and Judgments Act 1982, s 35(1) and Sch 10. Parts of the 1933 Act are repealed by s 54 and Sch 14. The 1933 Act must also now be read in the light of ss 32 and 33 of the 1982 Act, discussed, generally, supra pp 354–357, 389–392 and, more particularly in this context, infra pp 400–401. See generally on the 1933 Act, Vallat, *International Law and the Practitioner*, ch v; Patchett, *Recognition of Commercial Judgments and Awards in the Commonwealth*, chs 1–4.

5 *Yukon Consolidated Gold Corporation v Clark* [1938] 2 KB 241 at 253, [1938] 1 All ER 366 at 368; and see *Ferdinand Wagner v Laubscher Brothers & Co* [1970] 2 QB 313 at 319–320.

6 S 1; as amended by s 35 (1) and Sch 10 of the 1982 Act. Enforcement of a judgment abroad may affect whether security for costs is given in England: *Compagnie Française v Thorn Electrics* [1981] FSR 306; *Porzelack KG v Porzelack (UK) Ltd* [1987] 1 WLR 420.

7 S 7.

8 SR & O 1933 No 1073.

9 *Yukon Consolidated Gold Corpn v Clark*, supra, (Ontario).

10 *Jamieson v Northern Electricity Supply Corpn (Private) Ltd* 1970 SLT 113 (Zambia). If an order is made under the 1933 Act applicable to a country to which there is already an Order in force made under the 1920 Act, then the latter ceases to apply: 1933 Act, s 7(2).

11 See Pakistan Act 1990, Sch, para 8.

12 Bangladesh Act 1973, s 1(1).

13 See the UK/Canada Convention (1984) Cmnd 9337 which was brought into force on 1 January 1987, infra, p 408.

14 Judgments given in Belgium, France, Italy, the Netherlands, and Germany will usually come within the Brussels Convention and will be recognised and enforced under that rather than under the 1933 Act, see infra, pp 411 et seq.

Suriname.[15] These orders provide that judgments in civil and commercial matters shall be mutually recognised and enforced, notwithstanding that the adjudicating court followed rules for the choice of law different from those that would have been followed in the country where enforcement is sought. The provisions of the Act apply also to foreign judgments given in proceedings which arise under a number of international conventions.[16]

(iii) Prerequisites of registration

The successful party to proceedings in a foreign country to which the Act has been extended may apply to the High Court at any time within six years[17] for registration of the judgment in England.[18] A "judgment" now includes certain arbitration awards.[19] It does not, however, include a judgment on a judgment,[20] eg a judgment given in State A providing for the enforcement of a judgment given in State B. The judgment no longer has to be delivered by a superior court.[1] It is, however, required that the judgment was delivered by a recognised court[2] or tribunal;[3] the judgment is final and conclusive or requires an interim payment to be made;[4] a sum of money is adjudged to be payable to the applicant, other than a sum in respect of taxes or in respect of a fine or other penalty.[5] This latter phrase does not include an award of exemplary damages or damages for "resistance abusive" under French law.[6] A judgment is not to be registered if it is one for multiple damages.[7] A judgment is also not to be registered if it has been wholly satisfied or if it cannot be enforced by execution in the foreign country.[8] A judgment, however, is to be deemed final and conclusive, notwithstanding that an appeal may be pending against it or that it may still be subject to appeal in the foreign courts.[9] The Act differs from the earlier Act of 1920 in that no

15 The 1933 Act does not extend to the USA and this has been the source of judicial comment, eg *Perry v Zissis* [1977] 1 Lloyd's Rep 607 at 614, 617. A draft bilateral UK/US recognition convention, quite independent of the 1933 Act, was prepared: (1976) Cmnd 6771; but it was never agreed, see infra, pp 407–408.

16 Eg Carriage of Goods by Road Act 1965, s 4, Sch, Art 31(1). See generally, Dicey and Morris, pp 509–533. The provisions of the 1933 Act may also apply to foreign judgments clawing-back sums paid pursuant to an award of multiple damages: Protection of Trading Interests Act 1980, s 7, discussed supra, pp 382–384.

17 S 2.

18 The judgment can be registered in foreign currency: Administration of Justice Act 1977, s 4(2)(b), supra, p 101; and see *Batavia Times Publishing Co v Davis* (1978) 88 DLR (3d) 144; *Principality of Monaco v Project Planning* (1980) 32 OR (2d) 438; *Clinton v Ford* (1982) 137 DLR (3d) 281.

19 S 10A; added by s 35(1) and Sch 10, para 4 of the 1982 Act.

20 S 1(2A); added by s 35(1) and Sch 10, para 1 of the 1982 Act. For the position under the Brussels Convention, see infra, p 414.

1 Compare the original s 1(1) with the amended version introduced by s 35(1) and Sch 10, paras 1 and 2 of the 1982 Act. See also s 54 and Sch 14 of the 1982 Act.

2 S 1; as amended by s 35(1) and Sch 10, para 1 of the 1982 Act.

3 S11(1); as amended by s 35(1) and Sch 10, para 5 of the 1982 Act.

4 S 1(2); as amended by s 35(1) and Sch 10, para 1 of the 1982 Act.

5 S 1(2); as amended by s 35(1) and Sch 10, para 1 of the 1982 Act.

6 *SA Consortium General Textiles v Sun and Sand Agencies Ltd* [1978] QB 279 at 299–300, 305–306.

7 S 5 of the Protection of Trading Interests Act 1980; discussed supra, at pp 382–384.

8 S 2(1); and see *SA Consortium General Textiles v Sun and Sand Agencies Ltd*, supra, at 297, 300–302.

9 S 1(3). But it is provided by s 5(1) that on an application to set aside registration the court may do so or may adjourn the application if satisfied that an appeal is pending or that the defendant is entitled and intends to appeal; see, for examples where such an application was

discretion is left to the High Court. It is expressly provided that:

> On any such application the court shall, subject to proof of the prescribed matters and to the other provisions of this Act, order the judgment to be registered.[10]

(iv) Setting aside of registration

There are, however, certain circumstances in which, on the application of the party against whom the registered judgment is enforceable, the registration *must* be set aside and other circumstances in which it *may* be set aside.

(a) When registration *must* be set aside

(i) Lack of jurisdiction The first case in which the registration *must* be set aside is if the foreign court acted without jurisdiction.[11] The rules by which the 1933 Act specifies the circumstances in which a foreign court shall be deemed to have had jurisdiction are very similar to the common law rules[12] and vary according to whether the original action was in personam or in rem.

Bases of jurisdiction in personam In the case of a judgment given in an action in personam the original court is deemed to have had jurisdiction on three main bases: residence, submission and having an office or place of business within the foreign jurisdiction.

1. *Residence.* In the case of residence, the 1933 Act provides that there is jurisdiction "if the judgment debtor, being a defendant in the original court, was at the time when the proceedings were instituted resident in, or being a body corporate had its principal place of business in, the country of that court".[13] As residence is required, temporary presence would appear to be excluded.[14] In the case of corporations, the requirement is not just the one at common law or under the 1920 Act of carrying on business,[15] but rather that the *principal* place of business be in the foreign country.

2. *Submission.* The second basis of jurisdiction is submission and three instances of this are provided in section 4(2)(a) of the 1933 Act:[16]

> (i) if the judgment debtor, being a defendant in the original court, submitted to the jurisdiction of that court by voluntarily appearing in the proceedings;[17] or
> (ii) if the judgment debtor was plaintiff in, or counter-claimed in, the proceedings in the original court; or
> (iii) if the judgment debtor, being a defendant in the original court, had before the commencement of the proceedings agreed, in respect of the subject matter of the proceedings, to submit to the jurisdiction of that court or of the courts of the country of that court.

---

refused: *Re A Debtor (No 11 of 1939)* [1939] 2 All ER 400; *SA Consortium General Textiles v Sun and Sand Agencies Ltd* [1978] QB 279 at 297–298, 306–307. See also *Hunt v BP Exploration Co (Libya) Ltd* [1980] 1 NZLR 104. Under the Act of 1920 the fact that an appeal is pending is a bar to registration, supra, p 396.

10 S 2.

11 Compare the Australian position, on which see *Hunt v BP Exploration Co (Libya) Ltd* (1979) 144 CLR 565, and in New Zealand, *Hunt v BP Exploration Co (Libya) Ltd* [1980] 1 NZLR 104.

12 Supra, pp 348 et seq.

13 S 4(2)(a)(iv).

14 Cf the common law position, supra, pp 349–350.

15 Supra, pp 350–351, 395–396.

16 As amended by s 54 and Sch 14 of the Civil Jurisdiction and Judgments Act 1982.

17 Including an appeal, see *SA Consortium General Textiles v Sun and Sand Agencies Ltd* [1978] QB 279 at 309.

What in general constitutes submission through a voluntary appearance to contest the jurisdiction of the court is likely to be determined in the same way as at common law.[18] The likelihood of this being the case is strengthened by the fact that section 33 of the Civil Jurisdiction and Judgments Act 1982, which provides that in three situations there is no submission by voluntary appearance, applies to recognition or enforcement under the 1933 Act as well as to recognition or enforcement at common law.[19] It will be recalled that under section 33 there is no submission where the appearance is to contest the jurisdiction of the court, to seek a stay of proceedings on the ground that there should be arbitration or trial in another country, or to protect property.

Whilst there is no doubt that an express agreement to submit would fall within section 4(2)(a)(iii), there remains the problem of an implied agreement to submit. Despite some faint Scottish indication to the contrary,[20] it is suggested that, as at common law,[1] an implied agreement will never suffice.[2]

The operation of some of these provisions on submission was considered in *SA Consortium General Textiles v Sun and Sand Agencies Ltd*:[3]

The plaintiffs, a French textile company, sold clothing to the defendants, an English company. The goods came from the plaintiffs' branches in Lille and Paris and the invoice from Lille provided that all disputes were to be referred to the commercial court there, whilst the other invoice gave exclusive jurisdiction to the Seine commercial court. The plaintiffs claimed the sums due under both invoices and damages for "resistance abusive" in proceedings before the Lille commercial court. Judgment was given for the plaintiffs in default of appearance, though the defendants had been served with notice of the proceedings. The defendants failed to appeal within the three months period allowed under French law. The plaintiffs then sought enforcement of the Lille judgment in England, whereupon the defendants applied to the President of the Court of Appeal in Douai for leave to appeal, and then in fact appealed to the full Court of Appeal.

The defendants sought, unsuccessfully, to resist the enforcement of the default judgment of the Lille court on a variety of grounds, such as that it could not be enforced by execution in France,[4] or that damages for "resistance abusive" were penal.[5] The main issue, however, was whether the defendants could be taken to have submitted to the jurisdiction of the French courts in respect of both claims. Section 4(2)(a)(iii) of the 1933 Act was interpreted by a majority in the Court of Appeal as not covering an agreement to submit to all the courts of the foreign country by agreeing to submit to one, so that agreement to submit the issues arising under one invoice to the Seine court did not amount to agreement to submit that issue to any other of the courts of

---

18 *Henry v Geoprosco International Ltd* [1976] QB 726 at 751, supra, pp 353 et seq.
19 Supra, pp 353–358. S 33 of the 1982 Act replaces a similarly worded provision contained in the end part of s 4(2)(a)(i), see s 54 and Sch 14 of the 1982 Act.
20 *Jamieson v Northern Electricity Supply Corpn (Private) Ltd* 1970 SLT 113 at 116.
1 Supra, pp 352–353.
2 Thus the decision in *Vogel v R and A Kohnstamm Ltd* [1973] QB 133, [1971] 2 All ER 1428, supra, p 353 would be the same today even though the 1933 Act has now been extended to Israel.
3 [1978] QB 279; Carter (1979) 50 BYBIL 252. The points raised in the case in respect of the 1933 Act are not affected by the alterations made to that Act by s 35(1) of the 1982 Act.
4 1933 Act, s 2(1)(b), supra, p 398.
5 Ibid, s 1(2)(b), supra, p 398.

France, including the Lille court.[6] However, the appeal to the Court of Appeal in Douai on the merits of the claim did amount to submission as to both claims,[7] as did a statement by the defendants' English solicitors, when proceedings against the defendants were contemplated in England, that *all* disputes must be brought before the Lille court.[8]

3. *Jurisdiction based on having a place of business* The third basis of jurisdiction and one not to be found at common law is provided by section 4(2)(a)(v) of the 1933 Act, namely "if the judgment debtor, being a defendant in the original court, had an office or place of business in the country of that court and the proceedings in that court were in respect of the transaction effected through or at that office or place."

Limitations on jurisdiction The three bases of jurisdiction are subject to qualification in that, notwithstanding them, the foreign court shall not be deemed to have had jurisdiction if the case concerned immovables outside the country of the foreign court or if the defendant was under the rules of public international law entitled to immunity from the jurisdiction of the foreign court and did not submit thereto.[9]

Special statutory grounds of jurisdiction Where a foreign judgment is registered under the 1933 Act pursuant to one of the various statutory provisions[10] embodying international conventions, the different statutes provide that the jurisdictional grounds in the 1933 Act shall all be replaced by special jurisdictional grounds relevant to the particular convention in question.[11]

Meaning of action in personam It is expressly enacted that the expression "action in personam" shall not include any matrimonial cause,[12] or any proceedings connected with matrimonial matters, the administration of the estates of deceased persons, bankruptcy, winding up of companies, lunacy or the guardianship of minors.[13]

Statutory grounds of jurisdiction are exclusive In the case of an action in personam, no other ground of jurisdiction will render a foreign judgment registrable under the Act. The fact, for instance, that the plaintiff has obtained leave from the foreign court to serve the writ on the defendant in England does not *per se* generate jurisdiction for the purpose of registration.[14]

Jurisdiction over action in rem The original court is deemed to have had jurisdiction over an action in rem if the subject-matter of the action, whether movable or immovable, was situated in the foreign country at the time of the proceedings.[15]

---

6 [1978] QB 279 at 302–304, 309; cf Lord DENNING MR at 298–299.
7 Ibid at pp 299, 308–309; see supra, p 358.
8 Ibid at pp 299, 307–308; cf GOFF LJ at pp 303–304.
9 S 4(3); as amended by s 54 and Sch 14 of the 1982 Act. S 4(3)(b) of the 1933 Act has been repealed and has been replaced, in effect, by s 32 of the 1982 Act, see supra, p 389.
10 Supra, p 398.
11 Eg Carriage of Goods by Road Act 1965, s 4, Sch, Art 31(1). The defence under s 32 of the 1982 Act will not apply: s 32(4)(b).
12 But see *Vervaeke v Smith* [1983] 1 AC 145, HL, discussed infra, p 403.
13 S 11(2).
14 *Société Cooperative Sidmetal v Titan International Ltd* [1966] 1 QB 828, [1965] 3 All ER 494, infra, pp 409–410; *Coast Lines Ltd v Hudig and Veder Chartering NV* [1972] 2 QB 34 at 45.
15 Section 4(2)(b), subject to the qualifications provided by s 4(3) as amended by s 54 and Sch 14 of the 1982 Act, discussed, supra.

(ii)   Other circumstances where registration must be set aside
There are a number of circumstances in addition to want of jurisdiction[16]
where, according to the 1933 Act,[17] registration *must* be set aside, most of
which are very similar to the common law defences:[18]
  i if the judgment is not one to which the Act applies;
  ii if the judgment debtor, being the defendant in the original proceedings,
     did not (despite service of process in accordance with the foreign law)
     receive notice of the proceedings in sufficient time to enable him to
     defend them and did not appear;[19]
  iii if the judgment was obtained by fraud;[20]
  iv if the enforcement of the judgment would be contrary to public policy
     in England;[21]
  v if the rights under the judgment are not vested in the applicant.
One further instance of where registration *must* be set aside is provided by
section 32 of the Civil Jurisdiction and Judgments Act 1982:[1]
  vi if the judgment was given in proceedings brought in breach of an
     agreement for settlement of disputes.

(b) When registration *may* be set aside Registration *may* be set aside if the
registering court is satisfied that the matter adjudicated upon had already
been the subject of a final and conclusive judgment by a court having
jurisdiction in that matter.[2]

(v)   The effect of a foreign judgment

(a) A judgment which has been registered A judgment registered under the
Act is, for the purposes of execution, of the same force and effect and subject
to the same control as if it had originally been given in the registering court.[3]
One significance of this provision would appear to be that the grounds on
which registration may or must be set aside may be different from those on
which enforcement will be refused. Once the foreign judgment is registered,
then it would appear that not only may the registration be set aside for failure
to satisfy section 4 of the 1933 Act, but also the registered judgment may be
set aside and enforcement refused for any one of the various reasons for

16 S 4(1)(a)(ii).
17 S 4(1)(a).
18 Supra, pp 377–382, 384–387. It is arguable that, as a foreign judgment once registered under
   the 1933 Act shall be of the same force and effect as if it had been a judgment of the English
   court (s 2(2)), it is open to all defences available under English domestic law.
19 This is similar to, but not identical with, the common law defence that the foreign proceedings
   were contrary to natural justice, supra, pp 384–387; and see *Brockley Cabinet Co Ltd v Pears*
   (1972) 20 FLR 333; *Barclays Bank Ltd v Piacun* [1984] 2 Qd R 476.
20 When an application is made on this ground, the same rules apply as apply where the defence
   of fraud is raised to an action at common law on a foreign judgment, supra, pp 377–380;
   Syal v Heyward [1948] 2 KB 443, [1948] 2 All ER 576.
21 For a recognition case where this applied see *Vervaeke v Smith* [1983] 1 AC 145, HL, at 156
   (per Lord HAILSHAM) and 159 (per Lord DIPLOCK); discussed infra, at p 681. This provision
   does not preclude the recognition of a judgment for exemplary damages or damages for
   "resistance abusive" under French law: *SA Consortium General Textiles v Sun and Sand
   Agencies Ltd* [1978] QB 279 at 299–300, 305–306.
 1 Discussed, supra, pp 389–392.
 2 S 4(1)(b); *Vervaeke v Smith* [1983] 1 AC 145, HL at 156 (per Lord HAILSHAM) and 159 (per
   Lord DIPLOCK); discussed infra, p 676.
 3 S 2(2). So a foreign judgment, registered in England, will, for the purposes of the exercise of
   the discretion whether to grant a stay of execution, be treated as if it were an English
   judgment: *Ferdinand Wagner v Laubscher Brothers & Co* [1970] 2 QB 313.

setting aside English judgments[4] which may be appropriate to a foreign judgment.

(b) A judgment which is capable of registration Section 6 of the 1933 Act provides that:

> No proceedings for the payment of a sum payable under a foreign judgment to which this Part of this Act applies, other than proceedings by way of registration of the judgment, shall be entertained by any court in the United Kingdom.

This clearly means that no action for enforcement at common law can be brought on a judgment that is registrable, but, seemingly, *this provision* did not prevent the plaintiff from suing on the original cause of action. However, the plaintiff is now prevented from doing so by section 34 of the Civil Jurisdiction and Judgments Act 1982, which as has been seen[5] abolishes the non-merger rule.

(vi) Conclusiveness of foreign judgments

Section 8[6] of the 1933 Act preserves the common law[7] rules as to the conclusiveness of foreign judgments, but it also provides[8] that a judgment to which the registration provisions of the Act apply, or would apply had a sum of money been payable thereunder, whether or not it can be or is registered, is to be recognised in England as conclusive between the parties in all proceedings founded on the same cause of action.

(a) An exception to the conclusiveness rule However, a foreign judgment is not recognised as conclusive under the Act if the registration has been set aside or, where the judgment has not been registered, it would have been set aside if it had been registered.[9] The grounds on which registered judgments are set aside are contained in section 4 of the Act.[10] The operation of this proviso was considered in *Vervaeke v Smith*,[11] where it was held that a Belgian judgment in respect of the validity of a marriage[12] would not be entitled to recognition under section 8 of the 1933 Act because the matter in dispute had previously been the subject of a final and conclusive judgment in England[13] and also because recognition would be against public policy.[14]

(b) A prerequisite for recognition: the judgment must have been given on the merits The rule in section 8, unlike the general registration provisions, applies to a judgment in favour of a defendant; ie a foreign judgment to which the Act applies in which the plaintiff's claim is dismissed will be recognised in England as conclusive between the parties. However, as with the common law rule on conclusiveness,[15] the judgment must have been given on the

4 See, eg Gordon (1961) 77 LQR 358, 533.
5 Supra, p 347.
6 S 8(3).
7 Supra, pp 368–377.
8 S 8(1).
9 S 8(2). See *Barclays Bank Ltd v Piacun* [1984] 2 QdR 476.
10 Discussed supra, pp 398–402.
11 [1983] 1 AC 145, HL.
12 On the question of whether the judgment (a nullity decree) came within the 1933 Act, see infra, pp 404–405. See also *Maples v Maples* [1988] Fam 14, [1987] 3 All ER 188.
13 Per Lord DIPLOCK at 159–160, Lord HAILSHAM at 156, Lords BRANDON and KEITH concurring at 167. Registration *may* be set aside in such a case according to s 4(1)(b).
14 Per Lord HAILSHAM at 156; Lord BRANDON concurring at 167; Lord DIPLOCK at 159 and 161. Registration *must* be set aside in such a case according to s 4(1)(a)(v).
15 *The Sennar (No 2)* [1985] 1 WLR 490, supra, p 375.

merits. Thus in *Black-Clawson International Ltd v Papierwerke Waldhof-Aschaffenburg AG*:[16]

> The plaintiffs, an English company, became holders of bills of exchange accepted by the predecessors of the defendants, a German company. Just within the six year limitation period under English law, the plaintiffs began proceedings, on the bills which had been dishonoured, in England and in Germany. The limitation period under German law was three years and had expired, and the German trial court dismissed the action on that ground.[17] In the English proceedings, the German defendants argued that the German judgment should be recognised in England under the 1933 Act and, relying on section 8 (1), that it was conclusive between the parties as the English and German proceedings were both founded on the same cause of action.

A majority of the House of Lords held that section 8(1), unlike the main provisions of the 1933 Act, applied to judgments in favour of a defendant as well as of a plaintiff. However, the German judgment, dismissing the action because it was time-barred under the German law as to limitation which merely barred the remedy and did not extinguish the right, was not a decision on the merits even though regarded, in Germany, as a decision on substance. The German judgment was not, therefore conclusive; though the English proceedings were stayed until the outcome of a final German appeal was known.

Black-Clawson remains good authority on the general point that a foreign judgment must be given on the merits in order to come within section 8 of the Act. It is, however, no longer good authority on the specific point of the effect of a foreign judgment involving a limitation period. This is because of section 3 of the Foreign Limitation Periods Act 1984,[18] which treats a foreign judgment on a limitation matter as being conclusive "on its merits". Section 3 applies regardless of whether the foreign court has applied its own law on limitation periods or that of any other country, including England and Wales. It also applies regardless of whether recognition is sought under statutory rules or at common law, and therefore, overturns the common law decision in *Harris v Quine*.[19]

(c) The scope of Section 8: matrimonial causes The provisions on recognition (section 8), unlike those on enforcement, are not confined to cases where there is a money judgment. This raises the major question of whether section 8 can apply to matrimonial causes, for example foreign decrees of divorce or nullity. For many years this question remained unanswered. However, it is now clear that an overseas divorce, etc cannot be recognised under the 1933

---

16 [1975] AC 591, [1975] 1 All ER 810; Jaffey (1975) 38 MLR 585; Carter (1974–1975) 47 BYBIL 381.
17 The analysis of the trial court was that the issue of limitation was one of substance, to be referred to English law as the law governing the contract. English law would class the issue as procedural to be referred to German law as the law of the forum and German law would accept the renvoi and apply its own law. The effect of German law (though regarded as substantive) was to bar the remedy but not extinguish the right. A German appellate court then decided that the English six year period applied. A final appeal to the Federal Supreme Court was pending at the time of the English proceedings.
18 See Law Com No 114 (1982), paras 4.58–4.71; Stone [1985] Lloyd's MCLQ 497; Carter (1985) 101 LQR 68; supra, pp 80–81.
19 (1869) LR4 QB 653, supra, p 376.

Act.[20] The 1933 Act is concerned with "actions",[1] whether in personam or in rem.[2] In matrimonial causes, "proceedings" are brought before the English courts rather than "actions". Moreover, section 8(1) is concerned with judgments which affect "the parties thereto". A judgment of marital status has a wider significance and can affect others, such as the State and children of the marriage.

(d) EUROPEAN COMMUNITY JUDGMENTS

As a result of the European Communities (Enforcement of Community Judgments) Order 1972[3] any Community judgment[4] to which the Secretary of State has appended an order for enforcement shall be registered by the High Court if application is made by the person entitled to enforce it. The judgments to which the Order applies are not those of the national courts of the Member States of the European Community[5] but rather judgments of the courts and institutions of the Community itself, ie judgments of the European Court of Justice, and decisions of the Arbitration Committee of the European Atomic Energy Community, of the High Authority of the European Coal & Steel Community which impose a pecuniary obligation, and of the Council and of the Commission of the European Community which impose a pecuniary obligation on persons other than States.

The effect of registration is that such Community judgments and decisions shall, for all purposes of execution, have the same force and effect as if they were judgments of the High Court. The High Court would appear to have no discretion whether to register such judgments;[6] but the European Court of Justice may order that enforcement of such a registered judgment shall be suspended. Such order then must be registered by the High Court and when registered shall have effect as if it were an order of the High Court staying the execution of the judgment and no steps to enforce the judgment may be taken while the order remains in force.

The judgments which may be registered are not restricted to those under which a sum of money is payable.[7] If, in the case of a community money judgment,[8] it has been partly satisfied at the date of registration, then it is to be registered only in respect of the sum outstanding; and if the judgment is satisfied in whole or in part after registration, then the registration shall be appropriately cancelled or varied.

(e) JUDGMENTS AGAINST STATES

(i) Judgments against the United Kingdom: the State Immunity Act 1978

It will be recalled that the State Immunity Act 1978 implements the European

---

20 *Maples v Maples* [1988] Fam 14, [1987] 3 All ER 188. For recognition of overseas divorces, etc, see infra, pp 655 et seq.
1 See s 4(2); s 4(1)(a)(ii); s 8(2)(b).
2 These terms are defined supra, pp 182, 213–214.
3 SI 1972 No 1590, made under s 2(2) of the European Communities Act 1972.
4 There are similar rules for the registration and enforcement of Euratom inspection orders.
5 As to recognition of which, see infra, pp 411 et seq.
6 Also the defence under s 32 of the Civil Jurisdiction and Judgments Act 1982 will not apply because there is no judgment of a court "of an overseas country" (as defined under s 50).
7 SI 1972/1590, para 2(1); and see *Re Westinghouse Electric Corpn Uranium Contract* [1978] AC 547 at 636.
8 A judgment can be registered in a foreign currency: Administration of Justice Act 1977, s 4(2)(b).

Convention on State Immunity (1972). The major significance of the Convention and of the 1978 Act is to provide for the circumstances when a sovereign State is to be immune from the jurisdiction of our courts.[9] However, provision is also made for the recognition here of judgments given against the United Kingdom by a court in another State which is a party to the 1972 Convention.[10] Recognition must be given to such a judgment if it was a final judgment and if the United Kingdom was not entitled to immunity under the Convention.[11] Such a judgment, and any settlement before a court in a Convention State which is treated under the law of that State as equivalent to a judgment,[12] shall be regarded here as conclusive between the parties.[13] Recognition may, however, be denied on a number of grounds:[1] that recognition would be manifestly contrary to public policy; that a party to the proceedings had no adequate opportunity to present his case; that the procedural requirements of the Convention had not been complied with; if prior similar proceedings between the same parties are pending before a court in the United Kingdom, or before a court in a Convention State whose judgment would be required to be recognised; if there are prior inconsistent judgments of a United Kingdom court or a court in a Convention State; in the case of a judgment concerning the interest of the United Kingdom in movable or immovable property by way of succession, gift or *bona vacantia*, if the foreign court would not have had jurisdiction under rules equivalent to the English rules appropriate to such a claim, or if the foreign court applied a law other than that which would have been applied by an English court and would have reached a different conclusion had it applied that latter law.

(ii) Judgments against other States: the Civil Jurisdiction and Judgments Act 1982

The 1978 Act did not deal with the recognition of foreign judgments against States other than the United Kingdom. These are now dealt with by the Civil Jurisdiction and Judgments Act 1982,[2] section 31 (1) of which provides that:

> A judgment given by a court of an overseas country against a State other than the United Kingdom or the State to which that court belongs shall be recognised and enforced in the United Kingdom, if and only if—
> (a) it would be so recognised and enforced if it had not been given against a State; and
> (b) that court would have had jurisdiction in the matter if it had applied rules corresponding to those applicable to such matters in the United Kingdom in accordance with sections 2 to 11 of the State Immunity Act 1978.

The concept of "a judgment given against a State" is defined under the 1982 Act,[3] as is the concept of a "State" (ie to include the constituent territories

---

9 Supra, pp 265 et seq.
10 1978 Act, ss 18, 19; and see Sinclair (1973) 22 ICLQ 254, 266–267, 273–276.
11 Ibid, s 18(1).
12 Ibid, s 18(3).
13 Ibid, s 18(2).
  1 Ibid, s 19. S 32 of the Civil Jurisdiction and Judgments Act 1982 will not apply, since it only concerns judgments against persons.
  2 S 31. For transitional provisions, see Sch 13, Part II, para 7. S 31 does not, however, deal with judgments against the State to which the court belongs.
  3 S 31(2).

in a federal State).[4] Section 31(1) will not affect judgments given in proceedings which arise under a number of international conventions, and which are recognised and enforced under the 1933 Act.[5]

(f) THE CIVIL JURISDICTION AND JUDGMENTS ACTS 1982 AND 1991: THE BRUSSELS AND LUGANO CONVENTIONS

The jurisdictional provisions of the Brussels Convention and its implementation by the Civil Jurisdiction and Judgments Act 1982 have already been considered,[6] but the Convention provides also for the recognition and enforcement in this country of judgments given in civil and commercial matters in the Contracting States to the Convention. This means that judgments given in another European Community State[7] that are within the scope of the Convention must now be recognised and enforced under this scheme rather than under the 1933 Act[8] or the common law rules.[9] The provisions on recognition and enforcement under the Convention are complex, despite the Convention's aim of simplifying this area of law. Moreover, these provisions are markedly different from the rules on recognition and enforcement at common law or under the 1933 Act.[10] For these reasons, it has been thought best to deal with recognition and enforcement under the Brussels Convention in a separate chapter.[11]

The free circulation of judgments within the European Community, which is provided by the Brussels Convention, is extended to the EFTA bloc[12] by the Lugano Convention.[13] This Convention, which is implemented by the Civil Jurisdiction and Judgments Act 1991 (amending the 1982 Act), is a parallel one to the Brussels Convention, closely based on the latter, but not identical to it. Recognition and enforcement under the Lugano Convention is considered in detail in the same chapter as the Brussels Convention.

(g) CURRENT DEVELOPMENTS

The Brussels Convention and the more recent Lugano Convention have also provided a new impetus for other countries to enter into bilateral recognition and enforcement conventions with the United Kingdom.[14] As will be seen

---

4 S 31(5). If the case is outside the scope of s 31, the 1933 Act may be applicable. However, for a rule preventing enforcement under the 1933 Act of judgments against persons, such as diplomats, entitled to immunity from jurisdiction, see s 4(3)(c) of the 1933 Act.

5 S 31(3).

6 Supra, pp 279 et seq.

7 Ie in Belgium, France, Italy, the Netherlands, Germany, Luxembourg, Denmark, Ireland, Greece, Spain or Portugal.

8 Orders were made extending the 1933 Act to Belgium, France, Italy, the Netherlands and Germany. See supra, pp 397–398. For the relationship between the 1933 Act and the Convention see infra, pp 415–416.

9 The common law rules were used for Luxembourg, Denmark, Ireland, Greece, Spain and Portugal; supra, pp 348 et seq. For the relationship between the common law rules and the Convention see infra, pp 415–416.

10 This is a relevant consideration when deciding whether to award security for costs: *Porzelack KG v Porzelack (UK) Ltd* [1987] 1 All ER 1074, [1987] 1 WLR 420.

11 Infra, pp 411 et seq.

12 Ie Austria, Finland, Iceland, Norway, Sweden and Switzerland. The Convention only applies to the judgments of EFTA States which have ratified it, ie Switzerland.

13 Infra, pp 442–444.

14 It has also led in part to the reconsideration of common law rules and the adoption of a principle of full faith and credit for cases of enforcement within Canada: *Morguard Investments Ltd v De Savoye* (1991) 76 DLR (4th) 256 at 272.

in the next chapter,[15] the Brussels and Lugano Conventions provide for recognition and enforcement in the European Community and EFTA States of judgments given in a Contracting State, even where jurisdiction was taken against a defendant domiciled in a non-Contracting State under an exorbitant basis of jurisdiction. So a judgment of a French court, where the plaintiff is a French national but has no other connection with France,[16] against an American company will be recognised here under the Brussels Convention, though it would not be recognised under the Foreign Judgments (Reciprocal Enforcement) Act 1933. This requirement that English courts must recognise all judgments of the courts of other Contracting States caused considerable anxiety in, for example, the USA[17] and Australia.[18] There is a provision in the Brussels and Lugano Conventions[19] which allows a Contracting State to conclude conventions with other countries under which judgments of the courts of other Contracting States against persons described as habitually resident in such other countries shall not be recognised in the first Contracting State. This was the genesis of a draft UK/USA Judgments Convention.[20] However, this Convention was never implemented because of United Kingdom alarm at the prospect of having to enforce American judgments for large awards of damages. Negotiations with Canada have been more successful and a UK/Canada Convention was brought into force on January 1987.[21] Agreement has also been reached on a UK/Australia Convention, although this is not yet in force.[22]

4. INTERRELATION OF THE COMMON LAW AND STATUTES

One problem which has been touched on already[23] and might usefully be examined a little more fully is that of the interrelation of the common law rules of recognition and those provided by statute (other than the Civil Jurisdiction and Judgments Acts 1982 and 1991[24]), especially in the fields of jurisdiction and defences. It will be recalled[25] that at common law the grounds of jurisdiction of the foreign court which will be recognised in England are

---

15 Infra, pp 411 et seq.
16 Articles 14 and 15 of the Code Civil.
17 Nadelmann (1977) 41 Law and Contemporary Problems 54, 58–62, and see infra, pp 440–441.
18 Pryles and Trindade (1974) 42 Aus LJ 185, 192–195.
19 Art 59, discussed infra, p 441–442.
20 (1976) Cmnd 6771; see Hay and Walker (1976) 11 Texas ILJ 421; Smit (1977) 17 Virginia J of Int L 443; Mathers (1977) 127 NLJ 777; North (1978) 128 NLJ 315; Alford (1979) 18 Colum J Trans L 119; North (1979) 1 Northwestern Journal of Int Law and Business 219; Kerr (1980) Europarecht 353 at pp 356–357.
21 (1984) Cmnd 9337. The Convention is also set out in the Proceedings of the Uniform Law Conference 1982, pp 64–85. See also Patchett, *Recognition of Commercial Judgments and Awards in the Commonwealth* (1984), pp 32–35; Castel, *Canadian Conflict of Laws* (2nd edn) (1986), para 177. The Convention extends the Foreign Judgments (Reciprocal Enforcement) Act 1933 to designated Provinces of Canada (British Columbia, Manitoba, New Brunswick, Newfoundland, Nova Scotia, Ontario, Prince Edward Island, the Yukon Territory, Saskatchewan, Northwest Territories); supra, pp 397–398.
22 (1991) Cmnd 1394. The 1920 Act, supra, pp 395–396, has been extended for a number of years to Australian States.
23 Supra, pp 398–402.
24 For the very different rules for recognition and enforcement under the Brussels and Lugano Conventions, see infra, pp 411–444.
25 Supra, pp 348 et seq.

based on residence and submission. Under section 4(2)(a) of the Foreign Judgments (Reciprocal Enforcement) Act 1933,[26] there are listed five grounds of jurisdiction in actions *in personam*,[1] the underlying bases of which are residence, submission and having an office or place of business within the country. The problems to be examined are whether the statutory regime is to be regarded merely as a codification of the common law principles and, if not, whether in a case which falls outside the statute, the basis of statutory recognition should affect common law recognition. Just such issues arose in *Société Cooperative Sidmetal v Titan International Ltd*:[2]

The defendants, an English company, had agreed to sell steel to the plaintiffs, a Belgian company, and to ship the steel direct to an Italian company who had bought the steel from the plaintiffs. Dissatisfied with the steel, the Italian company sued the plaintiffs in Belgium and the plaintiffs sought to join the defendants as third parties and a Belgian writ was served on them in England. The defendants took no part in the Belgian proceedings, but judgment was given against the defendants and in favour of the plaintiffs. The plaintiffs had the Belgian judgment registered in England under the Foreign Judgments (Reciprocal Enforcement) Act 1933 and the defendants sought to have the registration set aside.

The real issue was whether the Belgian court had jurisdiction such as to permit an English court to recognise and enforce the Belgian judgment. None of the jurisdictional requirements listed in section 4 (2) of the 1933 Act were satisfied, nor were any of the heads of jurisdiction laid down at common law in *Emanuel v Symon*.[3] Nevertheless, it was argued for the plaintiffs that the effect of the 1933 Act was fundamentally to change the basis on which foreign judgments are recognised in England, namely that the 1933 Act approaches the question of recognition "on the principle that, if there is reciprocity between the courts of this country and the courts of the country in which the judgment was obtained, then comity of nations requires that the jurisdiction of the court of that country should be recognised for the purposes of the Act".[4] On such a basis, a Belgian judgment should be recognised either if an English court would have had jurisdiction in similar circumstances, ie service of the writ out of the jurisdiction,[5] or if a Belgian court would have recognised the jurisdiction of the English court in a similar case, mutatis mutandis.

Whilst WIDGERY J accepted that the 1933 Act did not constitute a codification of the common law principles,[6] he was not prepared to accept that that Act had re-introduced comity or reciprocity as the underlying basis for the recognition of foreign judgments either at common law, or under the

---

26 As amended by s 54 and Sch 14 of the Civil Jurisdiction and Judgments Act 1982.
1 Supra, pp 399–401.
2 [1966] 1 QB 828, [1965] 3 All ER 494; Webb (1966) 15 ICLQ 269. Recognition and enforcement of Belgian judgments will usually come now within the Brussels Convention, discussed infra, pp 411–442.
3 [1908] 1 KB 302 at 309.
4 [1966] 1 QB 828 at 845.
5 Cf supra, pp 190–211.
6 [1966] 1 QB 828 at 841, 846. See for the Australian position *Hunt v BP Exploration Co (Libya) Ltd* (1979) 144 CLR 565 and for New Zealand *Hunt v BP Exploration (Libya) Ltd* [1980] 1 NZLR 104. Cf *Re Trepca Mines Ltd* [1960] 1 WLR 1273 at 1281–1282; *Rossano v Manufacturers' Life Insurance Co* [1963] 2 QB 352 at 383.

1933 Act.[7] The bases of jurisdiction laid down in section 4(2)(a) of the 1933 Act are exclusive.[8]

A different question is whether, in so far as the provisions of the 1933 Act are broader than those of the common law, the 1933 Act could influence the development of the common law recognition rules. It is suggested that it could, and should, as in the case of jurisdiction based on having an office or place of business in the foreign country.[9] Certainly it is true in the case of the defence of fraud, illustrated by *Syal v Heyward*,[10] that decisions on recognition at common law may be relied upon for the purposes of the application of the 1933 Act. What one cannot do is to determine the present common law rules by reference to the 1933 Act, for one "cannot ascertain what the common law is by arguing backwards from the provisions of the statute".[11]

---

7 [1966] 1 QB 828 at 841, 847; and see *Blohn v Desser* [1962] 2 QB 116 at 123; *Vogel v R and A Kohnstamm Ltd* [1973] QB 133 at 134; *Henry v Geoprosco International Ltd* [1976] QB 726 at 751.
8 And see *Sharps Commercials Ltd v Gas Turbines Ltd* [1956] NZLR 819.
9 1933 Act, s 4(2)(a)(v), supra, p 401.
10 [1948] 2 KB 443, [1948] 2 All ER 576, supra, p 380. See also *Owens Bank Ltd v Bracco* [1991] 4 All ER 833, [1992] 2 WLR 127, CA supra, pp 379, 396, in relation to the 1920 Act.
11 *Henry v Geoprosco International Ltd* [1976] QB 726 at 751.

Chapter 16

Recognition and enforcement of judgments under the Brussels and Lugano Conventions

SUMMARY

1. THE BRUSSELS CONVENTION[1]

(a) INTRODUCTION

According to its preamble, the Convention on Jurisdiction and Enforcement of Judgments in Civil and Commercial Matters is concerned to facilitate recognition, and to introduce an expeditious procedure for securing the enforcement of judgments obtained in one European Community State throughout the rest of the community.[2] The aim is that judgments should be

---

1 This chapter has been written on the assumption that the 1989 Spanish and Portuguese Accession Convention, amending the Brussels Convention, has came into force in all European Community States.
2 See also Article 220 of the Treaty of Rome. The original Convention, as amended by the 1978, 1982 and 1989 Accession Conventions, is set out in SI 1990/2591, Sch 1. For the history of the Convention and the legislation bringing this into force, see supra, pp 279–280. For commentaries on recognition and enforcement under the Convention see Hartley, *Civil Jurisdiction and Judgments* (1984), ch 5; Collins, *The Civil Jurisdiction and Judgments Act 1982* (1983), ch 5; Anton, *Civil Jurisdiction in Scotland* (1984), ch 8; O'Malley and Layton, *European Civil Practice* (1989) chs 25–29; Kaye, *Civil Jurisdiction and Enforcement of Foreign Judgments* (1987) part 8. For a comparison of the Convention's rules with those at common law and other statutory forms of recognition and enforcement, see Stone [1983] Lloyd's MCLQ 1; Lane (1986) 35 ICLQ 629. See also *Porzelack KG v Porzelack (UK) Ltd* [1987] 1 WLR 420; *De Bry v Fitzgerald* [1990] 1 All ER 560, [1990] 1 WLR 552.

able to circulate freely within the Contracting States to the Convention,[3] which ensures that the economic life of the Community is not disturbed and trade is thereby encouraged. In order to achieve this the Convention provides that: first, the recognition of judgments is automatic, in the sense that none of the usual conditions found in cases of recognition and enforcement at common law or under the Foreign Judgments (Reciprocal Enforcement) Act 1933[4] have to be satisfied before recognition can take place; second, enforcement follows on from recognition and is largely a procedural matter; and third, the defences available under the Convention against recognition and enforcement are limited—in particular, a court in another Contracting State is under a duty to recognise and enforce a judgment even though the court which granted it misapplied the rules on jurisdiction under the Convention.

Such liberal provisions on recognition and enforcement can only work where there is mutual trust amongst the Contracting States. This requires safeguards to be built into the system.[5] The first, and most obvious, one is that the Convention is a double one; that is, it contains direct rules both on jurisdiction and on recognition and enforcement.[6] In order to understand the provisions on recognition and enforcement contained in the Convention, it is essential that its jurisdiction provisions are also borne in mind; for the two sets of rules are each part of a single scheme. The fact that the Contracting States share the same rules on jurisdiction means that when it comes to recognition and enforcement the Convention does not need to impose a requirement that the court in the second State, in which enforcement is sought, should have to check the basis on which the court in the first State, which gave judgment, took jurisdiction. Moreover, the bases of jurisdiction under the Convention are narrow ones; exorbitant bases are prohibited and there are special provisions on natural justice designed to protect the defendant where he has not entered an appearance at the trial.[7] The second safeguard is that there are still defences which can be considered by the court in the Contracting State in which recognition and enforcement of the judgment is sought.[8]

The emphasis under the Convention is away from litigation at the stage of recognition and enforcement (and in the country where this is sought); instead, any disputes as to jurisdiction should be dealt with in the Contracting State in which trial of the substantive issue takes place. A defendant can no longer ignore the original action and decide instead to defend by challenging the recognition and enforcement of the judgment when this is sought in another State. He is virtually forced to defend the original action; once the judgment is given, there will often be nothing he can do to stop its recognition

---

3 All European Community States are now Contracting States to the Convention: ie Belgium, Denmark, Germany, France, Italy, Luxembourg, the Netherlands, the United Kingdom, Ireland, Greece, Spain and Portugal.
4 Supra, pp 348 et seq.
5 See the Jenard Report, OJ 1979, C59/1, p 42; Case 125/79 *Denilauler SNC v Couchet Frères* [1980] ECR 1553, [1981] 1 CMLR 62. See also Fletcher, *Conflict of Laws and European Community Law* (1982), pp 104–109.
6 See generally Bartlett (1975) 25 ICLQ 44; Nadelmann (1967) 67 Col LR 995; Hay (1968) 10 AJCL 149; Newman, in *Legal Problems of an Enlarged European Community* (ed Bathurst 1972), ch 5. For the rules on jurisdiction see supra, pp 292–331.
7 See Articles 3, 19 and 20, discussed supra, pp 290–291, 325–326; the Jenard Report, OJ 1979, C595/1, p 47; Kohler (1985) 34 ICLQ 563.
8 Discussed infra, pp 424–433.

and enforcement in other Contracting States. This is not unfair to a defendant who is domiciled in a Contracting State: the Convention's rules on jurisdiction will frequently mean that the trial takes place in the State of his domicil anyway. Even when he has to go to another State to defend the action, this will still be within the Community. It is more questionable, however, whether the Convention is fair in its treatment of defendants domiciled in non-Contracting States. As will shortly be shown, any judgment given against them in a Contracting State is to be recognised and enforced under the Convention.[9] This is despite the fact that defendants domiciled in non-Contracting States are denied the jurisdictional safeguards available to defendants domiciled in Contracting States; in particular, they are subject to the exorbitant bases of jurisdiction used in Contracting States. These defendants will have to defend away from home and may have to travel long distances in order to do so.

(b) WHEN DO THE RULES ON RECOGNITION AND ENFORCEMENT UNDER THE BRUSSELS CONVENTION APPLY?

Title III (Articles 25–49) of the Convention deals with the recognition and enforcement of judgments. In cases coming within this title traditional national rules cannot be used.[10] Title III applies, regardless of which rules on jurisdiction have been applied in the court which gave the judgment, to the situation where recognition and enforcement is sought in one Contracting State of a judgment given in another Contracting State in respect of a matter coming within the scope of the Convention. As will be seen, it does not cover ex parte orders.

(i) Regardless of which rules on jurisdiction have been applied

Title III of the Convention applies equally to judgments given by the courts of Contracting States granted after jurisdiction was taken under the Convention's rules (contained in Title II) and to judgments granted after jurisdiction was taken under traditional national rules (the defendant being domiciled in a non-Contracting State).[11] It would even apply to the situation where a court has relied upon an exorbitant basis of jurisdiction, eg a German court takes jurisdiction over an American who left his umbrella behind in a hotel room in Germany.[12] It also applies to judgments granted after jurisdiction was taken under other conventions, for example in cases of admiralty jurisdiction.[13] The basic distinction drawn for jurisdictional purposes between situations where the defendant is and is not domiciled in a Contracting State does not apply when it comes to recognition and enforcement of judgments. At this stage, any judgment is entitled to recognition irrespective of the domicil of the defendant.

9 See infra. See also the Jenard Report, p 42. For foreign reaction to the Convention see infra, pp 440–442.
10 The English rules are set out supra, pp 182 et seq.
11 For an example, see Case 178/83 *Firma P v Firma K* [1984] ECR 3033, [1985] 2 CMLR 271. For the rules as to when traditional bases of jurisdiction apply see supra, pp 286–292.
12 Article 23 of the German Code of Civil Procedure. The effect of the Convention on exorbitant bases of jurisdiction is discussed supra, p 290.
13 See Collins, pp 34–35. Of course, if the particular convention also has rules on recognition and enforcement, these will apply rather than the recognition and enforcement rules under the Brussels Convention, see infra, p 415.

(ii) There must be a judgment given in a Contracting State[14]

"Judgment" is widely defined under Article 25 of the Convention as "any judgment given by a court or tribunal of a Contracting State". There is no limitation on the type of court and, therefore, the judgments of inferior as well as of superior courts are covered. The awards of tribunals are also included, provided that the tribunal is of a Contracting State. In other words, the tribunal must be a state rather than a private body. The fact that this requirement would exclude most arbitration awards from Article 25 is of no practical importance since Article 1 excludes arbitration from the scope of the Convention anyway.[15] Neither does it matter what the judgment is called; it includes "a decree, order, decision or writ of execution, as well as the determination of costs or expenses".[16] This is a very wide definition, and it follows, eg, that maintenance orders come within Article 25.[17]

There is no requirement that the judgment must be a final one and it is intended that, in principle, provisional orders will be covered.[18] In contrast to the position in respect of recognition and enforcement in England, at common law or under existing bilateral treaties, the Convention is not limited to money judgments, and can, therefore, include an order for specific performance of an injunction. The Schlosser Report envisages that, on enforcement of a foreign judgment for specific performance, the same penalties for contempt of court should be awarded as if it were an English judgment.[19] It also envisages that a foreign judgment imposing a penalty for disregarding a court order can come within the Convention,[20] although it is not clear whether it will do so when it is a fine which accrues to the State rather than to a judgment creditor.[21] A court order in one State for the enforcement of a judgment given in another State is probably not within Article 25. To decide otherwise would mean, in effect, that a court in Contracting State A would have to recognise a judgment given in a non-Contracting State (X) simply because a court in Contracting State B had recognised the judgment given in State X and had granted an enforcement order in respect of it.[1] This would be contrary to one of the basic principles of the Convention; the

---

14 See Arts 26 and 31. See also *Owens Bank Ltd v Bracco* [1991] 4 All ER 833 at 839–842, CA.
15 See supra, p 289.
16 Article 25. Orders of a procedural nature are not, however, included, see the Schlosser Report, OJ 1979, C59/1, paras 184–187; Anton, *Civil Jurisdiction in Scotland*, para 8.05. For the special rules on recognition and enforcement of authentic instruments and court settlements see Title IV of the Convention (Art 50, as substituted by the 1989 Accession Convention, and Art 51) and s 13 of the 1982 Act. For the recovery of interest on registered judgments, see s 7 of the 1982 Act.
17 See the Schlosser Report, pp 132 and 134; s 5 of the 1982 Act; SI 1986/1962; Collins, pp 123–125; and infra, pp 717–718. Not all maintenance orders come within the Convention, see Art 57, as substituted by the 1989 Accession Convention, discussed infra, p 415.
18 See the Schlosser Report, p 126; Case 143/78 *De Cavel v De Cavel* [1979] ECR 1055, [1979] 2 CMLR 547. This contrasts with the requirement that the judgment be "final and conclusive" under the traditional English rules, see supra, pp 365–367. However, ex parte provisional orders are not included under Title III, see infra, pp 416–417. Moreover, under Article 31 the judgment must be enforceable in the State in which it was given before it can be enforced, see infra, pp 421–422. There may, therefore, be problems even with provisional orders, which are not ex parte.
19 The Schlosser Report, p 132. See Collins, p 116.
20 Ibid. It is implicit from Art 43 that penalties are included in some circumstances; see also Anton, *Civil Jurisdiction in Scotland*, para 8.36.
21 See the Schlosser Report, p 132.
 1 See Hartley, pp 84–85; Collins, p 106; Anton, *Civil Jurisdiction in Scotland*, para 8.05; O'Malley and Layton, p 678; Kaye, p 1357.

Convention is only concerned with recognition of judgments *given in Contracting States* and is not intended to affect the recognition of judgments given in non-Contracting States.

(iii) In respect of a matter coming within the scope of the Convention

Two preliminary points must be made before looking at the scope of the Convention as defined by Article 1. First, Title III is only concerned with the *international* recognition and enforcement of judgments;[2] it will not apply to an internal United Kingdom case as, for example, where an English court is asked to recognise a Scots judgment.[3] Second, Article 57 provides that the Convention "shall not affect any conventions to which the Contracting States are or will be parties and which, in relation to particular matters, govern jurisdiction or the recognition or enforcement of judgments". The effect of this is to preserve a number of conventions dealing with jurisdiction or recognition and enforcement in respect of certain specific matters, such as maintenance obligations towards children, under the Maintenance Orders (Reciprocal Enforcement) Act 1972.[4] It follows that, if another convention is applicable and has rules on recognition and enforcement, these rules will apply and not those contained in Title III of the Brussels Convention. This can be justified on the ground that these other conventions usually involve obligations towards non-Contracting States and should not therefore be altered by a European Community Convention which is confined to Member States of the Community.[5]

What has already been said in the context of jurisdiction[6] about the meaning of civil and commercial matters under Article 1 need not be repeated. It is, however, important to realise that the interpretation of Article 1 can arise at two stages in the litigation process and in the courts of two Contracting States.[7] Where a court of a Contracting State has taken jurisdiction under the rules set out in the Convention, the question of the scope of the Convention will arise both at that stage and at the recognition and enforcement stage in the Contracting State in which recognition or enforcement is sought. Even where the court which gave the judgment decided after full argument that the matter came within the scope of the Convention, the recognising and enforcing court will have to decide the matter afresh, if necessary by referring any question of interpretation to the Court of Justice of the European Communities. If the recognising court considers that the matter does not come within the scope of the Convention, the Convention is being interpreted differently in the Contracting States and a reference to the Court of Justice is desirable. Indeed, many of the cases on the interpretation of Article 1 discussed earlier in chapter 14 are ones where the reference to the Court of Justice came from the court in which recognition and enforcement was sought.[8]

---

2 See Arts 26 and 31, and more generally on the international scope of the Convention, supra, p 286.
3 For rules on this see ss 18 and 19 of the 1982 Act, discussed supra, pp 393–394.
4 Infra, pp 716–717.
5 See the Jenard Report, pp 59–61.
6 Supra, pp 286–289.
7 See Giardina (1978) 27 ICLQ 263, 275.
8 See eg Case 143/78 *De Cavel v De Cavel* [1979] ECR 1055, [1979] 2 CMLR 547; Case 29/76 *LTU v Eurocontrol* [1976] ECR 1541, [1977] 1 CMLR 88; Case 120/79 *De Cavel v De Cavel* (*No 2*) [1980] ECR 731, [1980] 3 CMLR 1.

In contrast to this, where jurisdiction has been taken under national rules, the first time that the scope of the Convention is considered may well be at the recognition and enforcement stage.

Where the matter is not within the scope of the Convention, judgments given in other Contracting States will be recognised and enforced in the United Kingdom at common law or under existing bilateral treaties.[9] The Convention supersedes the bilateral treaties previously entered into by the United Kingdom with many European Community States.[10] These earlier arrangements will, however, still operate where the United Kingdom is asked to recognise and enforce a judgment given in one of these States which is in respect of a matter to which the Convention does not apply.[11] It is for national courts to interpret the scope of these bilateral agreements and where these courts use the concept of civil and commercial matters they may interpret it differently from the community concept under the Convention.

Where a judgment is in respect of several matters, some of which are enforceable under the Convention and others are not, the judgment is split and recognition and enforcement is only authorised for those matters within the scope of the Convention.[12]

(iv) Ex parte orders are not included

In *Denilauler v SNC Couchet Frères*[13] the question arose of whether an order from a French court, during the course of proceedings for payment under a contract (the main action), for a saisie conservatoire freezing certain of the German defendant's assets in Germany, thereby preventing the defendant from thwarting enforcement of the judgment in the main action, was enforceable in Germany under the Convention.

With an ex parte provisional and protective measure,[14] such as the English Mareva injunction or the Continental saisie conservatoire, the defendant is not summoned to appear and it is intended that there should be enforcement without prior service. The Court of Justice held that Title III does not cover decisions resulting from proceedings which by their very nature neither allow the defendant to state his case nor give him an opportunity to do so. However, there is English authority[15] to the effect that, if an English Mareva injunction is made inter partes or after the defendant had an opportunity to resist the plaintiff's application for the order, it is entitled to recognition and

---

9 See Article 56. See Cases 9 and 10/77 *Bavaria Fluggesellschaft Schwabe v Eurocontrol* [1977] ECR 1517, [1980] 1 CMLR 566; Anton, *Civil Jurisdiction in Scotland*, para 3.02; Hartley, pp 11 and 13. For the English rules on enforcement at common law and by statute, see supra, pp 348–410.

10 The UK has bilateral treaties with France, Belgium, the Federal Republic of Germany, Italy and the Netherlands. See also Fletcher, *Conflict of Laws and European Community Law*, pp 138–139.

11 Article 56. See also Cases 9 and 10/77 *Bavaria Fluggesellschaft Schwabe v Eurocontrol* [1977] ECR 1517, [1980] 1 CMLR 566; Hartley (1977) 2 ELR 461. The bilateral treaties also apply to judgments given before the entry into force of the Convention: Art 56, para 2. For transitional provisions generally, see Article 54 as substituted by the 1989 Accession Convention.

12 Article 42. If the excluded matter is only incidentally raised, the recognition rules under the Convention will still apply subject to a defence under Article 27(4), discussed infra, at p 432.

13 Case 125/79 [1981] ECR 1553, [1981] 1 CMLR 62; Hartley (1981) 6 ELR 59.

14 See generally on protective measures and the Convention: Collins (1981) 1 European Yearbook of International Law 249; Lipstein (1987) 36 ICLQ 873; Hogan (1989) 14 ELR 191.

15 *Babanaft International Co SA v Bassatne* [1990] Ch 13 at 31–32, (per KERR LJ who was referring obiter to a pre-judgment Mareva injunction).

enforcement under the Convention, provided at least that the injunction is in aid of substantive proceedings in England.[16] This will be so even if the order relates to assets in another Contracting State.

In deciding to exclude decisions which were not based on adversary proceedings the Court of Justice was influenced by two considerations. First, there are a number of important provisions in Title III which are concerned with whether there has been service of process and compliance with basic requirements of natural justice in the court which granted the judgment.[17] These presuppose that, in principle, both parties can participate in the proceedings, although it may be the case that the defendant, having been summoned, does not actually appear. They are not designed, and by inference neither is Title III, to deal with the situation where the defendant has not even been summoned to appear. Second, the defendant is denied a fundamental right by not being able to put his side of the case in the original proceedings;[18] yet, this is one of the safeguards which is used to justify the liberal provisions on recognition and enforcement under Title III.

The principle in the *Denilauler Case* equally excludes an ex parte permanent injunction if the defendant has not been served with process in the judgment granting State and has not been given an opportunity to be heard before the order was made.[19]

Given that an ex parte protective measure cannot be recognised and enforced in other Contracting States, what the plaintiff has to do is either to wait until the *inter partes* stage is reached and then seek enforcement of the measure under the Convention or to apply under Article 24[20] for a protective measure in the courts of each of the Contracting States in which the defendant has assets. Where the defendant has assets in several Contracting States this involves considerable inconvenience to the plaintiff. On the other hand, it leaves the decision on the granting of the protective measure to the court in the State where the assets are situated, which is the court best able to decide the issue. It also means that there will be a full examination of all the relevant considerations before an order is granted. In certain circumstances an English court may grant a world-wide Mareva injunction (ie over assets abroad).[21] In theory this avoids problems of enforcement of the measure abroad or the need for an application for a protective measure in another Contracting State. In practice it will normally be followed up with one of these steps.

16 Collins doubts whether an English Mareva injunction in aid of foreign substantive proceedings by virtue of s 25 of the Civil Jurisdiction and Judgments Act 1982 is enforceable under the Brussels Convention: (1989) 105 LQR 262 at 293–294.
17 See Art 27(2); Art 46(2); Art 47(1). These provisions are discussed infra, pp 426–430, 420–422.
18 The party against whom the order is directed would know nothing about this in the original State, or in the State where enforcement was sought, until after the enforcement order had been granted. The Advocate General in *Denilauler* gave his opinion that courts in some Contracting States might use the public policy defence to avoid enforcing ex parte protective measures if these were within Title III.
19 *EMI Records Ltd v Modern Music Karl-Ulrich Walterbach Gmbh* [1992] 1 QB 115.
20 Discussed supra, pp 330–331. Under Art 24 a court in a Contracting State can grant a provisional measure even if it does not have jurisdiction under the Convention in respect of the substance of the matter. For doubts on whether the English procedure for providing security for costs comes within Art 24, see *Bank Mellat v Helleniki Techniki SA* [1983] 3 All ER 428 at 434.
21 See *Babanaft International Co SA v Bassatne* [1990] Ch 13, CA; Collins (1989) 105 LQR 262.

(c) PROBLEMS OF INTERPRETATION

The points made in the context of jurisdiction in relation to interpretation of the Convention[22] are equally applicable here, with one additional comment. When it comes to referrals to the Court of Justice the position is considerably more complicated in recognition and enforcement cases.[23] The following courts *must* request a ruling on interpretation if they consider that a decision on the question is necessary to enable them to give judgment:

  (i) the House of Lords;
  (ii) courts to which application has been made under Article 37, para 2, which allows a single further appeal on a point of law from an appeal against the decision *authorising* enforcement. In effect, this will mean the Court of Appeal, the House of Lords hearing an appeal direct from the High Court[24] or, in the case of a maintenance judgment, the High Court;
  (iii) courts to which application has been made under Article 41, which allows a single further appeal on a point of law from an appeal against the decision *refusing* enforcement. This will be to one of the courts in (ii) above.

The following courts *may* request a ruling on interpretation if they consider that a decision on the question is necessary to enable them to give judgment:

  (i) courts of Contracting States when sitting in an appellate capacity;[25]
  (ii) the High Court when hearing an appeal which has been lodged, in accordance with Article 37, against a decision authorising enforcement, or a magistrates' court when hearing an application to set aside registration of a maintenance order.

(d) RECOGNITION[1]

The issue of recognition can arise in three different ways: first, in order for a judgment to be enforced under the Convention, it must first be recognised;[2] second, recognition will apply on its own, without any question of enforcement, where a judgment is used as a defence to a new action;[3] and third, recognition can operate on its own in a more positive way, for example, in order to establish a title to property or by way of a set-off.[4]

Article 26, para 1 provides that "a judgment given in a Contracting State shall be recognised in the other Contracting States without any special procedure being required".[5] The Convention makes recognition of judgments mandatory between Contracting States and does so without any conditions

---

22 Supra, pp 280–283.
23 See Arts 2 and 3 of the 1971 Protocol on Interpretation (as amended); Arts 37 and 41 of the Convention; and s 6 of the 1982 Act. See generally the Schlosser Report, pp 133–134.
24 Administration of Justice Act 1969, s 12.
25 See Case 56/84 *Von Gallera v Maitre* [1984] ECR 1769.
 1 See Section 1 of Title III (Articles 26–30).
 2 See generally Droz, *Competence Judiciaire et Effets des Jugements dans le Marché Commun*, p 273; the opinion of the Advocate General in Case 42/76 *De Wolf v Cox* [1976] ECR 1759, [1977] 2 CMLR 43; see the note on this case by Hartley (1977) 2 ELR 146; also Hartley, p 82.
 3 See, eg *De Wolf v Cox*, supra, discussed infra, pp 439–440.
 4 See Anton, *Civil Jurisdiction in Scotland*, para 8.09. For the position in respect of counter-claims, see Hartley, p 83.
 5 English law has never required any special procedure for recognition. This aspect of para 2, therefore, represents no change in the law of England.

having to be satisfied. In contrast to the rules on recognition at common law and under the Foreign Judgments (Reciprocal Enforcement) Act 1933, it does not have to be shown that the judgment is final and conclusive,[6] or that the foreign court had jurisdiction in an international sense;[7] nor is it required that the foreign judgment was on the merits.[8] The Jenard Report emphasises the point by describing recognition as being automatic under the Convention.[9] This must be qualified by pointing out that there are defences;[10] and a better way of putting it is to say that there is a rebuttable presumption that judgments are to be recognised.[11] A foreign judgment recognised by virtue of Article 26 in principle has the same effects in the State in which enforcement is sought as it does in the State in which it was given.[12]

Section 1 of Title III (Articles 26–30) contains no procedural provisions in respect of recognition. In the situation where recognition is merely a first step towards enforcement, the enforcement procedure under Section 2 (Articles 31–45)[13] will obviously be used. If recognition is used merely as a defence to an action, no procedure is necessary; but this still leaves a minority of cases where there is a need for some procedural rules. Article 26, para 2 provides that, if recognition of a judgment is the principal issue in the dispute, an interested party may apply for the judgment to be recognised in accordance with the enforcement procedure under Section 2.[14] The example given in the Jenard Report[15] is of a negotiable instrument declared to be invalid in Italy and presented to a bank in Belgium. The bank can apply for the judgment in Italy to be recognised using the simplified enforcement procedure in Section 2. If a party opposes recognition, however, he will have to use the normal rules of procedure of the recognising State, and if the outcome of proceedings in a court of a Contracting State depends on the determination of an incidental question of recognition, that court shall have jurisdiction over that question.[16]

(e) ENFORCEMENT[17]

The Court of Justice decided in *De Wolf v Cox*[18] that, in situations where

6 For the traditional English rules requiring this see supra, pp 365–367. However, the Convention does have rules dealing with the case where there is an appeal in the State in which the judgment was granted, see infra, pp 436–439.
7 Cf the traditional English rules, supra, pp 348–358. For the problem of whether the court has internal jurisdiction see Art 28, para 3, discussed infra, p 434.
8 Cf the traditional English rules supra, pp 374–375, 403–404. For the position under the Convention, see Collins, pp 86–87; Anton, *Civil Jurisdiction in Scotland*, para 8.11.
9 At p 74.
10 See infra, pp 424–433.
11 See the opinion of the Advocate General in Case 42/76 *De Wolf v Cox* [1976] ECR 1759, [1977] 2 CMLR 43; also the Jenard Report, at p 43. Certain documents must, nonetheless, be produced by the party seeking recognition, see Article 46.
12 Case 145/86 *Hoffmann v Krieg* [1988] ECR 645.
13 Infra, pp 422–423.
14 The provisions under Section 3 (Arts 46–49) must also be complied with. See, generally, the opinion of the Advocate General in *De Wolf v Cox*, op cit; the Schlosser Report, p 27. If recognition is refused and the applicant wishes to appeal, the enforcement procedure under the Convention (infra, pp 422–423) will be used. In England, Article 26, para 2 must be read in conjunction with RSC Ord 71, r 35.
15 At pp 74–75.
16 Art 26, para 3.
17 See Section 2 of Title III (Arts 31–45). See also ss 4–8 of the 1982 Act; RSC Ord 71.
18 Case 42/76 [1976] ECR 1759, [1977] 2 CMLR 43; Hartley (1977) 2 ELR 146. For further discussion of the case see infra, pp 439–440.

Title III applies, the enforcement procedure in those sections *must* be used. National rules cannot be used as an alternative.

The case concerned a Belgian judgment for a small amount of money, which was recognised by a Dutch court under the Convention. The Dutch court wrongly used Dutch procedure for enforcement, which was cheaper, rather than the procedure under the Convention. This meant that there had to be a new action before the Dutch court, albeit one based on the Belgian judgment, and a judgment as to substance.

The procedure for enforcement involves making an ex parte application in the Contracting State in which enforcement is sought. The other party is informed of this and has rights of appeal and, if he does appeal, the proceedings then become contentious. Before considering the details of this procedure the policy considerations underlying these rules should be examined.

(i) Policy matters

The Convention seeks to simplify enforcement, but, at the same time, provide safeguards for both parties.[19]

(a) Simplifying the procedure The application for an order for enforcement is ex parte, ie the other party will have no warning and is not entitled to make any submissions on the application.[20] This simplifies the procedure, which is in the interests of both parties.

(b) Safeguarding the applicant's interests The applicant's interests are protected in three ways:
(i) By the adoption of a unilateral procedure in respect of the order for enforcement, the party against whom enforcement is sought is prevented from removing his assets out of the jurisdiction in order to thwart the applicant.[21]
(ii) Once there has been a decision authorising enforcement the applicant is entitled as of right to protective measures, such as a Mareva injunction, preventing the other party from removing his assets.[1] The applicant cannot be denied his right to a protective measure by being required, for example, to obtain a court order authorising this, even though this is required by national law.[2] Even before this stage is reached an English court which has given the original judgment may safeguard the applicant's interests by granting a world-wide Mareva injunction over assets in another Contracting

---

19 See the Jenard Report, p 47 et seq; Case 258/83 *Calzaturificio Brennero v Wendel GmbH* [1984] ECR 3971, [1986] 2 CMLR 59; Case 148/84 *Deutsche Genossenschaftsbank v Brasserie du Pêcheur SA* [1985] ECR 1981, [1986] 2 CMLR 496.
20 Art 34. See RSC Ord 71, r 27. For the documents which have to be produced with the application see Arts 46 and 48 and RSC Ord 71, r 28. See also s 11 of the 1982 Act.
21 The Schlosser Report, at p 134; *Denilauler v SNC Couchet Frerès* [1980] ECR 1553, [1981] 1 CMLR 62; Hartley (1981) 6 ELR 59; Case 178/83 *Firma P v Firma K* [1984] ECR 3033, [1985] 2 CMLR 271; Hartley (1985) 10 ELR 233.
1 Art 39, para 2.
2 Case 119/84 *Capelloni v Pelkmans* [1985] ECR 3147, [1986] 1 CMLR 388, Hartley (1986) 11 ELR 96; *Elwyn (Cottons) Ltd v Pearle Designs Ltd* [1989] IR 9; cf RSC Ord 71, r 34(4), which seems to have been drafted on the assumption that English courts would still make orders for protective measures in enforcement cases coming within the Convention.

State, pending proceedings for the enforcement of the judgment under the Convention.[3]

(iii) If an application for enforcement is refused the applicant can appeal against this.[4]

(c) Safeguarding the interests of the party against whom enforcement is sought This party is protected in five ways:

(i) An order for enforcement can be issued only if the judgment is "enforceable" in the Contracting State in which it was granted.[5] The use of the term "enforceable" avoids the definitional problem that is encountered under the traditional English rules which require that a judgment be "final and conclusive".[6] Moveover, it is easy to ascertain whether a judgment is enforceable in the Contracting State in which it was granted. The policy is clear: a foreign judgment should not give the applicant rights which it does not provide in its State of origin. The requirement that the judgment be "enforceable" in the Contracting State in which it was granted is particularly useful in two situations. The first is where an appeal is pending in the Contracting State in which the judgment was given. When the effect of this is to suspend enforcement in that State,[7] the judgment is unenforceable in the State in which it was given and will then be unenforceable in other Contracting States. Secondly, it is useful in preventing the plaintiff from recovering twice;[8] if the judgment has already been enforced in the State in which it was given, it can no longer be said to be enforceable in that State.

(ii) Article 47 (1) provides that before enforcement can take place the party seeking this must produce documents showing that the judgment was served on the other party, who will thereby have had notice of it.

(iii) The application for an order for enforcement may be refused under one of the defences specified in Articles 27 and 28.[9] The enforcing court is under a duty to examine whether one of these defences applies, in so far as this appears from the judgment or is known to the court.[10]

(iv) If the application is successful, the defendant is notified and can appeal against the decision authorising enforcement[11] on the following bases: first, that the rules in Title III of the Convention do not apply; second, that the judgment is not enforceable in the Contracting State in which it was given; third, that one of the defences under Articles 27 and 28 applies.[12]

(v) If an application for enforcement is refused the applicant may appeal

---

3 *Babanaft International Co SA v Bassatne* [1990] Ch 13, CA; criticised by Hogan (1989) 14 ELR 191 at 197 et seq.
4 See infra, p 423.
5 Art 47(1).
6 Cf Hauschild in *Commercial Operations in Europe* (1978) eds Goode and Simmonds, p 65. For the difficulties in defining "final and conclusive" see supra, pp 365–367. The concept of enforceability is not a new one for English lawyers; the 1933 Act requires present enforceability, see supra pp 398–399.
7 See the Schlosser Report, at p 130. Where the appeal does not have this effect Article 38 will come into play, see infra, pp 437–439.
8 See the Schlosser Report, at p 134.
9 Art 34, para 2. These are the only reasons for refusing enforcement. The foreign judgment must, not be reviewed as to its merits, Article 34, para 3. The defences are discussed infra, pp. 424–433.
10 This is by analogy with the position in respect of recognition under Art 26, para 2; see the Schlosser Report, p 127.
11 Art 36. Normally the defendant must appeal at this stage and cannot raise arguments at the stage of execution of the judgment: Case 145/86 *Hoffmann v Krieg*, supra.
12 See the Schlosser Report, p 134. Articles 27 and 28 are discussed infra, pp 424–433.

against this;[13] but the other party must be summoned to appear before the appellate court. If he fails to do so, the natural justice provisions in Article 20 of the Convention will apply,[14] even though this party is not domiciled in a Contracting State and Article 20 would therefore not normally apply. The requirement to summon the other party is a very strict one; it applies even where the application for enforcement has been dismissed in the lower court on the purely formal ground that the correct documents as required under Articles 46 and 47 have not been produced, and even where the enforcement order is applied for in a State which is not the State of residence of the party against whom enforcement is sought.[15] By summoning a party to appear there is an obvious danger (at least where the enforcement order is sought against him in a State other than that of his residence) that he will remove assets from that State before the enforcement order is granted; nonetheless he must still be summoned.[16] A *Mareva* injunction or its Continental equivalent should be sought to prevent him removing assets.

(ii) Procedural rules

These are derived from the Convention, the 1982 Act and new Rules of the Supreme Court.[17] There are separate rules for maintenance orders.[18] The enforcement procedure under the Convention has two stages: the ex parte application and order for enforcement, and subsequent appeals.

(a) The application and order for enforcement The basic provision is Article 31[19] which provides that

> a judgment given in a Contracting State and enforceable in that State shall be enforced in another Contracting State when, on the application of any interested party, it has been declared enforceable there

Where the Contracting State in which enforcement is sought is the United Kingdom, the judgment is enforced in that part (ie England and Wales, Scotland, or Northern Ireland) in which it has been registered for enforcement.[20] If enforcement is required in more than one part of the United Kingdom, the judgment must be registered in each part where enforcement is sought. The application is submitted in England to a Master of the Queen's Bench Division;[21] the procedure for the registration is left to English law,[22] and is similar to that used where there is registration under the traditional rules. The Convention merely lays down requirements as to the documents

13 The procedure is discussed infra, p 423.
14 Art 40, para 2. Article 20 is discussed supra, pp 325–326. For the documents which have to be produced by a party applying for enforcement where there is a default judgment, see Art 46.
15 See Case 178/83 *Firma P v Firma K* [1984] ECR 3033, [1985] 2 CMLR 271, where documents were not produced at the correct time.
16 Ibid.
17 See Sections 2 and 3 of Title III of the Convention, ss 4–3 of the 1982 Act and RSC Ord 71.
18 See s 5 of the 1982 Act, as amended by s 5(5) of the Family Law Reform Act 1987, and generally Hartley, p 99.
19 As substituted by the 1989 Accession Convention.
20 Art 31, para 2. See the Schlosser Report, p 132.
21 Art 32; see also RSC Ord 71, r 26. In the case of a maintenance judgment the application is submitted to a magistrates' court on transmission by the Secretary of State.
22 Art 33. For the procedure see s 4 of the 1982 Act, and generally Collins, pp 116–120. For maintenance orders, see s 5 of the 1982 Act and Collins, pp 123–125. Proving the authenticity of judgments is dealt with by s 11 of the 1982 Act.

to be attached to the application[23] and as to furnishing an address for service.[1] A judgment, the enforcement of which is authorised and registered, is of the same force and effect, and the registering court has the same powers in relation to enforcement, as if the judgment had been given by the registering court in England.[2] Interest for the period after the judgment is given can be recovered on registered judgments provided that, in accordance with the law of the Contracting State in which judgment was given, this is recoverable under the judgment.[3]

(b) The appeal If enforcement is authorised, notice of the registration of the judgment must be served on the party against whom the judgment was given.[4] Article 36 provides that this party has a month from the decision authorising enforcement, or two months where notice was served on a party not domiciled within the jurisdiction, in which to appeal.[5] During this period, and until the appeal has been determined, no measures of enforcement may be taken other than protective ones[6] (eg a *Mareva* injunction). The Court of Justice has held that the right of appeal under Article 36 is only given to the party against whom enforcement is sought and any redress for interested third parties is excluded, even where the national law of the Contracting State in which the enforcement order is granted gives such parties a right of action.[7] In England, the appeal must be made to the High Court in accordance with its rules of procedure.[8] The judgment[9] given on appeal[10] is subject to a single further appeal on a point of law to the Court of Appeal or to the House of Lords (if there is an appeal direct from the High Court to the House of Lords under the leap-frog procedure in the Administration of Justice Act 1969).[11]

A similar procedure for bringing appeals in England is followed where the application is against a *refusal* to grant an order for enforcement.[12]

---

23 Art 33, para 3. For the documents in question see Arts 46 and 47. See also Case 178/83 *Firma P v Firma K* [1984] ECR 3033, [1985] 2 CMLR 271.
1 Art 33, para 2; Case 198/85 *Carron v Germany* [1986] ECR 2437, [1987] 1 CMLR 838; Hartley (1987) 12 ELR 64. See *Rhatigan v Textiles of Confecciones Europeas SA* [1990] 1 IR 126.
2 S 4(3) of the 1982 Act. For maintenance orders see s 5(4) of the same Act.
3 S 7 of the 1982 Act; RSC Ord 71, r 28(1)(b)(ii). For the position in respect of legal aid, see Art 44 of the Convention and s 40 of the 1982 Act.
4 RSC Ord 71, r 32.
5 See also RSC Ord 71, r 33.
6 Art 39; RSC Ord 71, r 34. See Case 119/84 *Capelloni v Pelkmans* [1985] ECR 3147, [1986] 1 CMLR 388; Hartley (1986) 11 ELR 96; Stone (1983) 32 ICLQ 477, 480.
7 Case 148/84 *Deutsche Genossenschaftsbank v Brasserie du Pêcheur SA* [1985] ECR 1981, [1986] 2 CMLR 496—the third party may be able to contest execution though.
8 Art 37. See also RSC Ord 71, r 33. In the case of a maintenance order the appeal is lodged with a magistrates' court.
9 This does not include a preliminary or interlocutory order, see Case 258/83 *Brennero v Wendel GmbH* [1984] ECR 3971, [1986] 2 CMLR 59.
10 This does not include a decision under Art 38, para 1, infra pp 437–439, refusing a stay of proceedings: Case C-183/90 *BJ Van Dalfsen v B Van Loon* [1992] ILPr 5.
11 S 12. See also Art 37, para 2 of the Convention, and s 6 of the 1982 Act. If the action relates to the recognition or enforcement of a maintenance order the single further appeal is to the High Court.
12 See Art 40 of the Convention, and RSC Ord 71, r 33, under which the appellant has only 1 month to appeal even if the notice was served on a party not domiciled within the jurisdiction. The other party must be summoned to appear before the appellate court; this requirement is discussed supra, at pp 421–422. On the single further appeal on a point of law see Art 41 of the Convention and s 6 of the 1982 Act.

(f) DEFENCES

A defendant who wishes to challenge the recognition or enforcement of a judgment can do so by showing that the Convention does not apply[13] or that, in the case of enforcement, the judgment is not enforceable in the Contracting State in which it was given. Using the term in a wide sense these are defences, although strictly speaking it must be part of the plaintiff's case when seeking recognition or enforcement to show that the Convention applies, and, in a case of enforcement, that the judgment is enforceable in the Contracting State in which it was given. The defences proper are contained in Articles 27 and 28. These set out defences to recognition, but since there can be no enforcement without recognition, they are also implicitly defences to enforcement.[14] Article 34 spells this out by providing expressly that the defences specified in Articles 27 and 28 operate as reasons for refusal of an application for an order for enforcement. Subject to the two wider "defences" above, recognition and enforcement will go ahead unless one of the grounds in Articles 27 and 28 applies.[15]

Where a defence under Articles 27 or 28 is established, the judgment will not be recognised or enforced in other Contracting States. Where one of the wider "defences" mentioned above is established, the position is more complicated. If a judgment is not enforceable in the Contracting State in which it was given, it cannot be enforced in other Contracting States. In contrast to this, where the Convention does not apply, it may still be possible for a judgment to be recognised and enforced in another Contracting State under an existing bilateral treaty or at common law.[16]

(i) Defences under Article 27

Article 27 sets out five defences: (a) public policy; (b) natural justice; (c) a conflict with a judgment given in the Contracting State in which recognition is sought; (d) a conflict with a judgment given in a non-Contracting State; (e) preliminary questions as to status and other matters.

(a) Public policy Article 27(1) provides that a judgment shall not be recognised

if such recognition is contrary to public policy in the State in which recognition is sought

(i) *Whose definition of the concept of public policy is to be applied?*
The wording of Article 27(1) strongly suggests that the recognising court is to apply its own concept of public policy when considering this defence. However, because of the differences in the meaning of public policy in the separate Contracting States,[17] it would be most undesirable for national courts to apply their own concept of public policy automatically. National courts are undoubtedly left with some latitude in deciding on the meaning of the concept, but they ought to give it a meaning which is appropriate in

13 See the Schlosser Report, p 134.
14 See also Art 34, para 2.
15 See the Jenard Report, p 43. A defence under Articles 27 and 28 may be raised by the defendant at the appeal stage. It may also be raised by the enforcing court acting on its own motion at the earlier stage of the application for enforcement, see supra, p 421.
16 Supra, pp 415–416.
17 See generally Lloyd, *Public Policy: A Comparative Study in English and French Law* (1953).

the context of the Convention, and the Court of Justice may intervene if they fail to do so.[18]

(ii) What public policy includes

The only guidance given in the Jenard Report on the meaning of public policy is to state that it should only be used in exceptional cases[19] and that it should not be used to criticise the *decision* of the court which gave the judgment. It is the *recognition* of the judgment rather than the judgment itself which must be contrary to public policy.[20] This negative approach is not particularly helpful in understanding what is included within the concept.[21]

The Schlosser Report is more helpful. It envisages that fraud in the proceedings in the Contracting State in which the judgment was given can, in some circumstances, come within the public policy exception.[22] However, it also accepts that there are some situations involving allegations of fraud where it would not be appropriate to use public policy as a defence. Two situations come to mind. First, where the allegation of fraud has been raised and dismissed in the court which gave the judgment, to reopen the matter at the recognition and enforcement stage, in the absence of new evidence, involves both an implicit criticism of the original judgment and going into the substance of the matter. This is prohibited by Article 29.[1] Second, where the issue of fraud *could* have been raised in the State in which the judgment was given, or can still be raised there, it is questionable whether fraud should be available as a defence under Article 27(1). Indeed, PHILLIPS J in *Interdesco SA v Nullifire Ltd*[2] refused to allow the defence of fraud in this situation. To deny a party a defence in these circumstances encourages persons who want to raise the question of fraud to do so in the Contracting State in which the judgment was given,[3] which is the best place for deciding the issue. It is best to confine the public policy defence in cases of fraud to the situation in which (i) there is evidence of fraud which was unavailable and unexamined earlier on in the proceedings, and (ii) the evidence arises at such a late stage that it cannot be raised on appeal in the State which granted the judgment, and the only court in which the fraud can be considered is the recognising court.

---

18 See Anton, *Civil Jurisdiction in Scotland*, para 8.14; Collins, p 108; O'Malley and Layton, p 693; Rasmussen (1978) 15 CMLR 249, 264–266.
19 Followed in Case 145/86 *Hoffmann v Krieg* [1988] ECR 645.
20 See the Jenard Report, at p 44. The recognising court is said to be under a *duty* to verify whether recognition would be contrary to public policy, see the Jenard Report, at p 44. See generally on public policy, Pointon [1975] Legal Issues of European Integration 1, pp 47–48. In Case 27/81 *Rohr v Ossberger* [1981] ECR 2431, [1982] 3 CMLR 29, public policy was raised as a defence but the Court of Justice interpreted Article 18 in such a way that the defence collapsed.
21 It is, however, useful in ascertaining what is not included within the defence, see infra, p 426.
22 See the Schlosser Report, at p 128. There is no provision in the Convention dealing expressly with fraud; it would, therefore, have to come within Article 27(1) if it is to provide a defence; cf the English common law rules, see supra, pp 377–380. For fraud and public policy in the area of recognition of foreign divorces, see *Kendall v Kendall* [1977] Fam 208, [1977] 3 All ER 471; discussed infra, pp 680–685. An example coming within the public policy exception suggested by English lawyers is multiple damages under the Protection of Trading Interests Act 1980, discussed supra, at pp 382–384; see Anton, *Civil Jurisdiction in Scotland*, para 8.16; Hartley, p 89; Stone (1983) 32 ICLQ 477, 480–481.
1 *Interdesco SA v Nullifire Ltd* [1992] 1 Lloyd's Rep 180 at 187. Cf the English common law decisions on fraud discussed supra, pp 377–380. On Article 29 see infra, pp 434–435.
2 [1992] 1 Lloyd's Rep 180.
3 See the Schlosser Report, at p 128; Hartley, pp 85–86; Collins, pp 101–108; O'Malley and Layton, pp 697–698.

(iii) What public policy does not include
It is easier to say what public policy does not encompass than what it does.
As has already been mentioned, the Jenard Report[4] states that the defence
should not be used to criticise the decision of the court which gave the
judgment. Neither can it be applied to review the jurisdiction of the court of
the Contracting State in which the judgment was given.[5] This prevents
it being used to criticise exorbitant jurisdiction taken against defendants
domiciled in non-Contracting States.[6] The defence cannot be used to deny
recognition merely because the recognising court would have applied, under
its private international law rules, a different law from that applied by the
court which gave the judgment.[7] The doctrine cannot be applied where the
foreign court has made a mistake of fact or of law.[8] Public policy will not
protect a defendant whose rights have been infringed by a lack of natural
justice,[9] even *where* there has been a serious irregularity in the procedure in
the original court.[10] Nor can the defence be used when the issue is whether a
foreign judgment is compatible with a judgment given in the state in which
recognition is sought.[11]

In some of the above situations the concept of public policy used in civil
law systems would apply,[12] as would the concept of public policy used in
common law systems.[13] The fact that Article 27 (1) is not intended to apply
in these same situations shows the limited nature of the public policy defence
under the Convention.

(b) Natural justice Article 27(2) provides that a judgment shall not be recognised

> Where it [the judgment] was given in default of appearance, if the defendant was
> not duly served with the document which instituted the proceedings or with an
> equivalent document in sufficient time to enable him to arrange for his defence[14]

There is concern that the rights of the defendant should be fully protected
by the Convention. When a judgment has been given in default of appearance
there is a particular concern as to whether the defendant was given the
opportunity to defend himself properly.[15]

(i) The interaction with jurisdictional provisions on natural justice
Where the natural justice safeguards at the jurisdictional stage of proceedings
apply under Article 20,[16] Article 27(2) operates as a double check on natural

---

4 At p 76. This prevents an examination of the law and procedure of the court which granted
   the judgment; it surely does not prevent the recognising court from considering new evidence
   as to, for example, an allegation that the trial judge was bribed.
5 Art 28, para 3; see also the opinion of the Advocate General in *Rohr v Ossberger*, supra.
6 The Jenard Report, at p 44.
7 See the Jenard Report, p 44; Hartley, p 89; Droz, p 311. This proposition is implicit from
   Art 27(4), see infra, p 432. Cf Forde (1980) 29 ICLQ 259.
8 Art 29 and Art 34, para 3, discussed infra, pp 434–435.
9 This is dealt with under Art 27(2). See also the opinion of the Advocate General in *Rohr v
   Ossberger*, supra.
10 See the Commission's view in *Rohr v Ossberger*, supra.
11 Case 145/86 *Hoffmann v Kreig* [1988] ECR 645. Art 27(3) deals with this, infra pp 430–431.
12 See Forde (1980) 29 ICLQ 259, 272–273.
13 See supra, pp 128–137, 380–382.
14 See generally, the Jenard Report, pp 44–45; Hunnings [1985] JBL 303.
15 See Art 20, discussed supra, pp 325–326; see also Art II of the Protocol annexed to the 1968
   Convention. For the documents which have to be supplied where there is a default judgment,
   see Art 46.
16 Supra, pp 325–326.

justice, with the recognising court examining the same issue that has been examined and decided upon by the court which gave the judgment.[17] In this situation, the defence under Article 27(2) is only likely to be used in exceptional cases.[18]

Where Article 20 does not apply, for example, because the defendant is domiciled in a non-Contracting State, or is not sued in the Contracting State in which he is domiciled, Article 27(2) provides a check on whether basic requirements of natural justice have been satisfied in the Contracting State in which the judgment was given. It is more important to have a check in this situation than in the situation where Article 20 applies, and the defence is correspondingly more likely to be used. The court which gave the judgment may not have even examined the issue of natural justice, and, if it has done so, may only have inadequate procedural safeguards.

(ii) Establishing the defence

Article 27(2) has not infrequently been used as a defence.[19] It comprises the following elements:

1. *the judgment was given in default of appearance.* Article 27(2) does not look at the reasons why a defendant did appear. Whether he appeared merely to contest the jurisdiction of the court, or actually to fight the action on its merits, does not matter; in both cases the judgment would not be considered as being given in default of appearance. Appearances after the judgment has been given raise particularly difficult problems.

In *Klomps v Michel*[20] a judgment which was treated as being in default of appearance was given in Germany.[21] Subsequently, the defendant raised an objection (based on the service of documents) to this judgment before the same German court which had given the judgment in default. This was held to be inadmissible because the time for lodging objections had expired. A Dutch court which was asked to enforce the German judgment referred a number of issues of interpretation of Article 27(2) to the Court of Justice, including whether, in these circumstances, a judgment is to be regarded as given in default.

The Court of Justice held, inter alia, that the judgment was given in default of appearance, despite the fact that the defendant had appeared to have it set aside. The reasoning of the Court was that the defendant had not submitted a defence as to substance, and since the objection he did raise was held to be inadmissible, this left the original decision in default intact.

2. *the defendant was not duly served.* This is a vital question and one that cannot pass unnoticed at the time when recognition and enforcement is sought. Article 46(2)[22] requires the party seeking recognition or enforcement to produce certain evidence which establishes that the party in default was served with the document instituting the proceedings. The concept of due

---

17 Case 228/81 *Pendy Plastic Products v Pluspunkt* [1982] ECR 2723, [1983] 1 CMLR 665; Case 166/80 *Klomps v Michel* [1981] ECR 1593, [1982] 2 CMLR 773, see Hartley's note in (1982) 7 ELR 419. See also Hartley, pp 90–92. The Advocate General in the *Plendy Plastic* case referred to the duty of the court to ascertain whether the requirements of Art 27(2) have been complied with. However, the French Cour de Cassation has held that a court is not required to consider this provision of its own motion: *Wagner v Tettweiler* [1985] ECC 258.
18 See infra.
19 Kohler (1985) 34 ICLQ 563, 576.
20 Case 166/80 [1981] ECR 1593, [1982] 2 CMLR 773.
21 The case involved a German order said to be equivalent to one in default.
22 See also Art 47(1).

service requires reference to the legislation of the State in which the judgment was given and to its conventions on service.[1] In *Klomps v Michel*[2] the Court of Justice held that Article 27(2) does not require proof that the document instituting the proceedings was actually brought to the knowledge of the defendant. No objection was made to the method of notice employed in that case, although it did not involve personal service on the defendant. However, it did comply with the law of the State in which the judgment was given. This is not to say that the recognising court is bound by the findings of the court which gave the judgment; it can properly ask whether, *on the particular facts*, there was due service under the law of the State in which the judgment was given.[3] A document is not duly served if it is not in due form, as where it is not accompanied by a required translation, even though it is served in sufficient time to enable a defendant to enter his defence.[4] Questions concerning issues as to the curing of defects are governed by the law of the State in which the judgment was given.[5]

3. *with the document which instituted the proceedings or with an equivalent document.* In *Klomps v Michel* it was held that this was referring to

> any document ... service of which enables the plaintiff, under the law of the State of the court in which the judgment was given to obtain, in default of appropriate action taken by the defendant, a decision capable of being recognised and enforced under the Convention.[6]

This included an order for payment under German law, but not a subsequent German enforcement order; the latter was the judgment that was enforceable under the Convention and therefore could not be the document which instituted the proceedings. The reference to "an equivalent document" took into account the fact that at the time of the accession of the United Kingdom to the 1968 Convention notice of a writ rather than the writ itself was served out of the jurisdiction under English law. However, subsequent Rules of the Supreme Court provide that the writ itself is served out of the jurisdiction.[7]

4. *in sufficient time to enable him to arrange for his defence.* The concept of sufficiency of time is used to deal with two very different situations.

A genuine question of time The first situation is where there has been due service and the defendant has notice which enables him from that point onwards to defend. Where there has been due service, it can usually be assumed that the defendant is able to defend from that moment onwards; this can be assumed even though there was no personal service on the defendant (Article 27(2) does not require actual knowledge of the document instituting the proceedings). In this first situation there is a straightforward question of whether the defendant has *sufficient time* in which to defend himself.

The *time* in question is that available to the defendant for the purposes of preventing the issue of a judgment in default enforceable under the Convention. In *Klomps v Michel* the judgment in question was the German

1 See the Jenard Report, at p 44; *Klomps v Michel*, op cit.
2 Case 166/80 [1981] ECR 1593, [1982] 2 CMLR 773.
3 See the Advocate General's opinion in *Klomps v Michel*, op cit, and in *Pendy Plastic Products v Pluspunkt*, op cit.
4 Case C-305/88 *Lancray v Peters* (1990) Times, 19 September.
5 Ibid.
6 Op cit, at p 1606.
7 See Rules of the Supreme Court (Amendment No 2), 1983 (SI 1983/1181) discussed supra, pp 190 et seq.

enforcement order; this meant that the period after it was granted, during which objections could be made, was disregarded. Time will begin to run from the date on which service was duly effected.

A more difficult question is whether the time available is *sufficient* to prevent the judgment in default being issued. The recognising court will have to look at all the circumstances of the case. In *Klomps v Michel* the Court of Justice seemed to regard sufficiency of time as being solely a question of fact. But it is hard to see how a court could answer the question without having some yardstick to which the facts can be related. The criterion for sufficiency of time could be left to the law of the State in which the judgment was given, or to the law of the State in which recognition is sought, or it could be left to be determined by an independent community meaning to be given to the concept. It would be wrong to leave the matter to the law of the State in which the judgment was given, since this would not provide the check on abuse of natural justice which Article 27(2) was designed to achieve. The most effective way of achieving this objective would be to give a community definition to the concept of sufficiency of time, although, in the absence of this, national courts may well fall back on their own idea of what is sufficient time.

Inadequacy of service The second situation is where, although there was due service in accordance with the law of the State in which the judgment was given, there may have been inadequate notice to enable the defendant to defend himself from that point onwards. This will only occur in exceptional cases. However, where it does arise the Court of Justice in *Klomps v Michel* and in *Debaecker v Bowman*[8] decided that the recognising court can hold that time has not begun to run, with the result that the defence under Article 27(2) applies. In this situation, the adequacy of the service is being raised, but within the context of sufficiency of time, rather than within the context of whether there has been due service.

In determining whether service has been adequate to enable the defendant to prepare his defence, all the circumstances have to be considered, "including the means employed for effecting service, the relations between the plaintiff and the defendant or the nature of the steps which had to be taken in order to prevent judgment being given in default".[9] It means that, sometimes, personal service will be required and merely serving the writ at the defendant's address, although in accordance with the law of the State in which the judgment was given, would not be enough. The Advocate General in the *Klomps Case* gave as an example the situation where the defendant was in hospital.

The court of the Contracting State in which enforcement is sought may take into account exceptional circumstances which have arisen after service has been duly effected in accordance with the law of the State in which the judgment was given. The Court of Justice so decided in *Debaecker v Bowman*,[10] where it was said that, in deciding whether service had been effected in sufficient time, it was relevant to consider the fact that after fictitious service had been made on the defendant—at a police station in Antwerp—the plaintiff had become appraised of the defendant's post office box address in Essen, but had made no effort to contact him there. However,

8 Case 49/84 [1985] ECR 1779, [1986] 2 CMLR 400; Hartley (1987) 2 ELR 220.
9 *Klomps v Michel*, op cit, at p 1609.
10 [1985] ECR 1779, [1986] 2 CMLR 400.

it was also relevant to consider the fact that the defendant was responsible for the earlier failure of the duly served document to reach him by leaving premises without giving notice and without leaving a forwarding address.

The question of adequacy of service was regarded by the Court of Justice in *Klomps v Michel* and *Debaecker v Bowman* as being solely one of fact. As with the question of sufficiency of time, it would be better to fix some yardstick to which the facts can be related. If this is to be done, it would be desirable to have a community standard rather than leaving the standard to be that of the law of the State in which recognition is sought.

Giving the recognising court the power to consider the adequacy of service is an important measure. Without it there would be no substantial check by the recognising court on whether the defendant was able to prepare his defence in the Contracting State in which the judgment was given. It is a necessary measure in view of the fact that the concept of due service is one that is left to be determined by reference to the law of the State in which the judgment was given, and therefore does not itself provide a proper check on natural justice by the recognising court.

(c) A conflict with a judgment given in the State in which recognition is sought Article 27(3) provides that a judgment shall not be recognised

> if the judgment is irreconcilable with a judgment given in a dispute between the same parties in the State in which recognition is sought

Where there are contemporaneous proceedings between the same parties in two Contracting States, in respect of the same or a related cause of action, the Convention requires one court to decline jurisdiction in favour of the other.[11] The position is more difficult where the cause of action in the two Contracting States is neither the same nor related. There is no provision requiring one of the courts to decline jurisdiction in favour of the other, and there can be conflicting judgments in two Contracting States. Article 27(3) solves this problem, in so far as the conflict is between a judgment given in the Contracting State in which recognition is sought and a judgment given in another Contracting State, by providing that the judgment given in the recognising State takes priority.[12]

All that is required for a defence to operate is that: (i) a judgment has been given in the recognising State—presumably, this can be before or after the judgment is given in the other Contracting State; (ii) it is given in a dispute between the same parties; (iii) this judgment is irreconcilable with the judgment given in the other Contracting State. In order to ascertain this, the Court of Justice in *Hoffman v Krieg*[13] has said that the two judgments should be examined to see whether they entail legal consequences that are mutually exclusive. Applying this test, it was held that a German judgment ordering a husband to pay maintenance to his wife as part of his conjugal obligations was irreconcilable with a subsequent Dutch judgment pronouncing a divorce. It is left to the recognising court to decide whether a judgment has been *given*

---

11 See Section 8 Title II (Arts 21–23) of the Convention, discussed supra, pp 326–330. Nonetheless, even in cases where the cause of action is the same there can still be conflicting judgments, see Hartley, pp 92–93.

12 See the Jenard Report, at p 45.

13 Case 145/86 [1988] ECR 645; Hartley (1991) 16 ELR 64; Briggs [1988] Yearbook of European Law 265; Stone [1988] Lloyd's MCLQ 393. Followed in *Macaulay v Macaulay* [1991] All ER 865, [1991] 1 WLR 179, infra, pp 717–718.

in their State.[14] Where only an interim judgment has been given or where the judgment is subject to an appeal, this may be a difficult decision. Moreover, because the defence does not apply in the situation where proceedings are merely pending in the recognising State, the effect of Article 27(3) will be to induce applicants to race to seek recognition before a conflicting judgment is actually given.

When recognition is sought in England, as far as Article 27(3) is concerned the State in which recognition is sought must be the United Kingdom (ie the Contracting State to the Convention) rather than the individual countries within the United Kingdom. This means that a French judgment will not be recognised in England if it is irreconcilable with a Scots or Northern Ireland judgment.

It has been suggested[15] that a judgment *given* in the State in which recognition is sought (State A) can include the situation where the judgment has in fact been delivered in another State (State B) but is entitled to recognition in State A. The wording of Article 27(3) does not support this wide interpretation. However, in its favour it has to be pointed out that in certain cases it would be the only way of resolving the problem of giving priority to one of the conflicting judgments. The first such case would be where the conflicting judgments are both granted in Contracting States other than the one in which recognition is sought.[16] Article 27(3) will not apply unless this wide interpretation of the word *given* is adopted. The second case is where one of the conflicting judgments is granted in a non-Contracting State. Article 27(5), which is designed to deal with this situation, may not apply (for example, because of the sequence in which the judgments were given).[17] Again, Article 27(3) will only apply if the wide interpretation of the word *given* is adopted.

(d) A conflicting judgment given in a non-Contracting State Article 27(5) provides that a judgment shall not be recognised

> if the judgment is irreconcilable with an earlier judgment given in a non-Contracting State involving the same cause of action and between the same parties, provided that this latter judgment fulfils the conditions necessary for its recognition in the State addressed

This provision, like Article 27(3), is concerned with the situation where there are two irreconcilable judgments and with ensuring that priority is given to one of them.[18] The *lis pendens* provisions in the Convention, requiring one court to decline jurisdiction in favour of another, can only operate where the proceedings are in two different Contracting States.[19] Where the proceedings are in a non-Contracting State and a Contracting State, there is a real possibility of two judgments being given, both of which have to be recognised. This is a serious situation which could give rise to diplomatic problems with non-Contracting States. To avoid this,[20] Article 27(5) gives priority to the

---

14 See the Jenard Report, at p 45.
15 The Jenard Report, p 45; Collins, p 110. Cf Anton, *Civil Jurisdiction in Scotland*, para 8.19.
16 See generally, Hartley, p 93; Anton, *Civil Jurisdiction in Scotland*, para 8.20; Kaye pp 1491–1492; O'Malley and Layton, pp 720–721. Art 21 of the Convention (*lis pendens*) will often prevent this situation from arising, see supra, pp 326–329.
17 See infra.
18 See the Schlosser Report, pp 131–131; cf the Jenard Report, at p 45.
19 See Art 21, discussed supra, pp 326–329.
20 The problem could also be avoided by having a wide general discretion to stay actions. There is some rather questionable authority for this under English law, see supra pp 331–334.

judgment given in the non-Contracting State, and the judgment given in the Contracting State is not recognised.

For Article 27(5) to operate it must be shown that: (i) the judgment given in the non-Contracting State is the earlier one; (ii) it is entitled to recognition;[21] (iii) it is irreconcilable with the later judgment given in the Contracting State; (iv) it involves the same cause of action and the same parties.

There is still a problem where one of these requirements is not satisfied, with the result that Article 27(5) does not apply. If faced with conflicting judgments given in a Contracting and a non-Contracting State, both of which are entitled to recognition, it is possible to solve the conflict by applying the wide interpretation of Article 27(3) set out above[22] to give priority to the judgment of the non-Contracting State. The alternative is that, in the absence of a defence, the judgment given in the Contracting State will have to be recognised under the Convention. Whether the judgment given in the non-Contracting State will also be recognised depends on the traditional national rules in each Contracting State.[23]

(e) Preliminary questions as to status and other matters   Article 27(4) provides that a judgment shall not be recognised

> if the court of the State of origin ... has decided a preliminary question concerning the status ... of natural persons, rights in property arising out of a matrimonial relationship, wills or succession in a way that conflicts with a rule of the private international law of the State in which recognition is sought ... unless the same result would have been reached by the application of the rules of private international law of that State

A judgment will not be outside the scope of the Convention simply because one of the matters excluded from the scope of the Convention arises as an incidental issue in the case. However, Article 27(4) provides a defence in the situation where the excluded matter that has arisen incidentally is as to status[1] or is as to one of a number of other specified matters. On the other hand, where the excluded matter which has arisen incidentally is as to bankruptcy or social security or arbitration, there is no defence under Article 27(4) and, in the absence of any other defence, the judgment will be recognised.

Article 27(4) ensures that the recognising court reserves the right to determine the status of persons under its own rules of private international law.[2] This may be relevant in cases of enforcement of foreign maintenance orders. To take an example, a French court awards maintenance to a woman on the basis that she is the wife of the defendant but if English rules of private international law were applied to the "marriage" it would be held that she was not the defendant's wife. In such a case, an English court can refuse to recognise or enforce the French maintenance award.

The implication can also be drawn from Article 27(4) that the recognising court cannot refuse recognition on the ground that the court in which the judgment was given applied a different law under its choice of law rules

---

21 See the Schlosser Report, at p 131. In England this would be at common law or by statute; see *Owens Bank Ltd v Bracco* [1991] 4 All ER 833 at 841, CA, and generally supra, pp 348–408.
22 Supra, pp 430–431
23 For the English rules see supra, pp 348–408.
 1 See Hartley, in *Harmonisation of Private International Law by the EEC* (ed Lipstein, 1978), p 109.
 2 The Jenard Report, p 46. See Collins, pp 110–111; Anton, *Civil Jurisdiction in Scotland*, para 8.21; Hartley, p 88; Kaye, pp 1492–1497.

from that applicable under the recognising court's own rules of private international law.[3]

(ii) Defences under Article 28

This provides a defence to recognition in two situations; both involve an examination of the jurisdiction taken by the court which delivered the judgment.

(a) The judgment conflicts with Sections 3, 4 or 5 of Title II of the Convention
A judgment will not be recognised if it conflicts with the jurisdictional provisions in Section 3 (insurance matters, Articles 7–12A), Section 4 (consumer contracts, Articles 13–15), or Section 5 (exclusive jurisdiction, Article 16) of Title II of the Convention. Normally, the recognising court cannot review the jurisdiction taken by the court in the Contracting State in which the judgment was granted.[4] Article 28 provides an exception to this which can be justified because Sections 3, 4 and 5 depart from the normal rules of jurisdiction. In examining jurisdiction, the recognising court is bound by the findings of fact on which the court which gave the judgment based its jurisdiction;[5] this avoids unnecessary duplication of effort. The recognising court will, however, examine whether these special rules on jurisdiction were correctly applied by the court which gave the judgment. It appears to be irrelevant whether jurisdiction has been challenged in the court which gave the judgment. Sections 3, 4 and 5 are complex provisions; there is every likelihood of the recognising court interpreting these provisions differently from the way in which they have been interpreted by the court which gave the judgment and holding that the latter court did not have jurisdiction. In order to avoid conflicting interpretations, wherever possible, there should be a referral to the Court of Justice for a definitive interpretation.

(b) The case is provided for under Article 59
A judgment will not be recognised in a case provided for under Article 59.[6] This is concerned with the situation in which a Contracting State has agreed with a non-Contracting State that, in certain circumstances, it will not recognise judgments given in other Contracting States against defendants from that non-Contracting State. This would mean, for example, that if the United Kingdom had entered into a convention with Japan incorporating the obligation under Article 59, a French judgment would not be recognised in England if jurisdiction could only have been taken in France against a Japanese domiciliary on one of the exorbitant bases of jurisdiction referred to in Article 3, para 2[7] of Title II of the Convention. This means that the English court would have to examine the jurisdiction of the French court to see whether it could *only* have been founded on one of the specified exorbitant bases. When examining jurisdiction, it is not clear from the wording of Article 28 whether the recognising court is bound by the findings of fact of the court in which the judgment was given.[8] Because of the United Kingdom's relatively slow progress in entering into Article 59 arrangements with third States (ie non-Contracting States) this defence is of only limited practical importance.

3 The Jenard Report, ibid.
4 Art 28, para 3.
5 Art 28, para 2; the Jenard Report, p 46.
6 Art 28, para 1. Art 59 is discussed infra, pp 441–442.
7 See supra, p 290.
8 Hartley thinks that it is bound, p 87.

(g) NON-DEFENCES

(i) Other defences are not available

The duty to recognise and enforce a judgment under the Convention applies unless one of the defences under Articles 27 and 28 is available; it follows that all other defences are implicitly rejected. The Convention reinforces this point by expressly providing that two very important matters may not be raised as defences.

(a) A review of jurisdiction Article 28, para 3 provides that

the jurisdiction of the court of the State of origin may not be reviewed

This provision is wide enough to exclude two arguments in respect of jurisdiction.[9] First, it prevents any suggestion that the court which gave the judgment must have had jurisdiction in the international sense.[10] Strictly speaking it was not necessary to exclude this expressly since the Convention implicitly does so by providing for recognition and enforcement without any reference to the international jurisdiction of the court which delivered the judgment.[11] Second, it stops any enquiry into the internal jurisdiction of the court which gave the judgment. It cannot be argued that this court misapplied the jurisdictional rules under the Convention.[12] Neither can it be argued that the court which granted the judgment misapplied its traditional national rules on jurisdiction. The prohibition against examining jurisdiction cannot be evaded by using the public policy defence.[13]

It is questionable whether it was right to exclude a defence of lack of internal jurisdiction. It would have been possible under the Convention to lay down a double check on jurisdiction, the court granting the judgment making sure that it has jurisdiction under the Convention, and the recognising and enforcing court checking this. The Convention sets up a system of double checks in respect of natural justice but not in respect of jurisdiction, presumably because it is satisfied that a court will only take jurisdiction under the Convention's rules when it ought to. Despite the safeguards built into the rules on jurisdiction in the Convention, this may be unduly optimistic. It also makes no allowance for the fact that jurisdiction may be taken in a Contracting State under traditional national rules, and those rules may be misapplied.

(b) A review of substance Article 29[14] provides that

under no circumstances may a foreign judgment be reviewed as to its substance

It cannot be alleged that the foreign court made a mistake of fact or a mistake of law. Even though a defence based on an allegation that there has been a mistake of law is not expressly excluded by Article 29, it is implicitly excluded

---

9 For the position where a national court acts in breach of Art 28, para 3, see Kohler (1985) 34 ICLQ 563 at 578–580.
10 The concept of international jurisdiction and how it differs from internal jurisdiction is discussed supra, pp 348, 369.
11 See supra, pp 411–412, 418–419.
12 Subject to the defences under Art 28, discussed supra, p 433.
13 Art 28, para 3.
14 See also Art 34, para 3; and generally, the Jenard Report, p 46.

by the terms of Articles 27 and 28, which provide the *only* defences to recognition.[15]

(ii) The special problem where there is a breach of an agreement for the settlement of disputes

From an English lawyer's viewpoint the most noticeable omission from the defences under Articles 27 and 28 is that of a provision equivalent to section 32 of the Civil Jurisdiction and Judgments Act 1982, which, it will be recalled,[16] provides that an overseas judgment shall not be recognised or enforced in the United Kingdom if it was given in proceedings brought in breach of an agreement for settlement of disputes otherwise than by proceedings in the courts of that country.

(a) A breach of an agreement providing for trial in a particular State Under the Convention there is a duty to recognise and enforce a judgment obtained in another Contracting State, despite the fact that there was an agreement between the parties providing for the trial of disputes in a State (whether a Contracting or non-Contracting State) other than the one in which trial took place. Following from this, because the judgment is required to be recognised or enforced under the Convention, section 32 of the 1982 Act will not apply.[17]

The reason for the absence of a defence under the Convention to deal with this situation is not clear. Admittedly, Article 17[18] will operate in many cases and thereby prevent a court in another Contracting State from taking jurisdiction in defiance of the agreement. But this is not a complete answer. Article 17 will not always apply; for example, it will not do so where the agreement on jurisdiction provides for trial in a non-Contracting State. Even where Article 17 ought to have been applied, there is always the possibility that a court in a Contracting State might misconstrue its provisions and fail to apply them.

(b) A breach of an agreement to go to arbitration There is no defence where recognition or enforcement is sought of a judgment granted by a court in a Contracting State which has taken jurisdiction despite an agreement by the parties to go to arbitration in that or some other State. However, the more basic question arises as to whether there is a duty to recognise or enforce a judgment in the first place in these circumstances. This question has to be asked because Article 1 excludes arbitration from the scope of the Convention. There is no authority directly on the issue of whether this provision excludes not only arbitration proceedings themselves (including arbitration awards[19]) but also, and this is crucial in the present context, judgments of courts where there has been a breach of an agreement to go to arbitration.[20] If such judgments are excluded from the scope of the Convention, the result is that the non-Convention rules on recognition and enforcement will apply, including, in England, section 32 of the 1982 Act and, subject to the terms of that provision, the judgment will not be recognised or enforced. On the other hand, if such judgments are within the scope of the Convention the

15 It does not appear to be a matter of public policy, see supra, pp 424–426.
16 See supra, pp 389–392.
17 Supra, p 390.
18 See supra, pp 314–322.
19 See *Allied Vision Ltd v VPS Film Entertainment GmbH* [1991] 1 Lloyd's Rep 392 at 399.
20 See supra, p 289; Collins, pp 29 and 112; Anton, *Civil Jurisdiction in Scotland*, paras 3.23–3.26, 8.26.

normal duty to recognise and enforce the foreign judgment under the Convention will apply, and section 32 of the 1982 Act will not affect this.

The need to find some means by which a court can refuse to recognise and enforce a judgment based on proceedings brought in breach of an arbitration agreement is even greater than if it is based on proceedings brought in breach of a choice of jurisdiction clause; there is no jurisdictional provision equivalent to Article 17 to stop a court from taking jurisdiction in the former case. This has led to the suggestion that the Convention should be narrowly interpreted so as to exclude from its scope judgments based on proceedings brought in breach of an arbitration agreement.[21]

Against this, it has to be seriously questioned whether the scope of the Convention should be influenced by English preoccupations with discouraging parties from breaching arbitration agreements. The Convention deliberately restricts the number of defences available to recognition and enforcement. It would be wrong to undermine this by introducing by the back door what is not allowed under Articles 27 and 28. More importantly, we now have a decision from the Court of Justice in the *Marc Rich Case*[1] on the scope of the arbitration exclusion, albeit in the context of a different issue in relation to arbitration. This strongly suggests that judgments in cases where there has been a breach of an agreement to go to arbitration are, nonetheless, within the scope of the Convention. The Court of Justice has held that, in determining whether a dispute falls within the scope of the Convention, reference must be made solely to the subject matter of the dispute, rather than to any preliminary issue that has to be resolved in order to determine the dispute. The subject matter of the dispute in the present context is presumably the enforcement of a foreign judgment. This is clearly not part of the process of arbitration, and is accordingly not excluded by the arbitration exclusion.

(h) APPEALS IN THE STATE IN WHICH THE JUDGMENT WAS GIVEN

It is unfair to the judgment debtor for a judgment to be recognised or enforced where there is a possibility of it being altered subsequently on appeal in the Contracting State in which it was granted.[2] Articles 31, 30 and 38 of the Convention may prevent recognition or enforcement in this situation.

(i) Article 31

Article 31 contains a requirement that before enforcement can take place it must be shown that the judgment is enforceable in the State in which it was given.[3] This requirement is not specifically designed to deal with appeals. However, the effect of an appeal in the granting State may be to prevent the judgment from being enforceable there, with the result that the judgment is not enforceable in other Contracting States. This still leaves a problem in

---

21 See Hartley, pp 96–97; Morris, p 112. Cf O'Malley and Layton, pp 364–365; Kaye, pp 147–148.
1 Case C-190/89 *Marc Rich and Co AG v Societa Italiana Impianti PA* (1991) Times, 20 September; supra, p 289.
2 See the Jenard Report, p 52; the opinion of the Advocate General in Case 43/77 *Industrial Diamond Supplies v Riva* [1977] ECR 2175, [1978] 1 CMLR 349. It is equally unfair to the judgment creditor who has lost his action for the judgment to be recognised in other Contracting States when this judgment is subject to an appeal.
3 Supra, pp 421–422.

other cases where the appeal does not have this effect or where recognition alone, and not enforcement, is sought.

(ii) Articles 30 and 38

Articles 30 and 38 of the Convention are specifically designed to deal with the difficulties raised by appeals in the Contracting State in which the judgment was given.

Article 30, para 1 gives the recognising court a power to stay its proceedings if an "ordinary appeal" against the judgment has been lodged in the Contracting State in which the judgment was granted. The idea is that there should be a stay of proceedings until the appeal is finally disposed of. If a stay is granted the judgment cannot be enforced until this is lifted.[4]

Article 38, para 1 gives the court with which an appeal against the decision authorising enforcement is lodged power, in certain circumstances, to stay the proceedings. It is a similar provision to that contained in Article 30, but with the following important differences.[5] First, the party appealing against the decision authorising enforcement must apply for a stay of the proceedings; the court cannot act on its own motion. Second, the power to stay applies not only to cases where an ordinary appeal has been lodged, but also to cases where an ordinary appeal has not been lodged, if the time for such an appeal has not yet expired. In this case, the court may specify the time within which such an appeal is to be lodged. Third, the court with which an appeal has been lodged against a decision authorising enforcement has power to make enforcement conditional on the provision of security,[6] but only when it gives judgment on the appeal, since it is it only at this time that the original judgment can be enforced and the judgment debtor needs this form of protection in case a further appeal succeeds.[7]

Two aspects of Articles 30 and 38 cause particular problems: (i) these provisions are only concerned with "ordinary" appeals; and (ii) the power to stay proceedings is a discretionary one.

(a) An ordinary appeal An "ordinary" appeal must have been lodged against the judgment in the State in which it was given, or, under Article 38 (but not Article 30), the time for an "ordinary" appeal must not yet have expired. In civil law systems, an "ordinary" appeal is often contrasted with an "extraordinary" appeal. The English legal system has no such distinction and this may cause difficulty for both foreign and English courts.

It would be particularly hard for a foreign court, which has been asked to recognise or enforce under the Convention an English judgment subject to an appeal, to determine whether this was an "ordinary" appeal when there is no such concept under English law.[8] The 1978 Accession Convention acknowledged this by introducing an additional paragraph to both Articles 30 and 38.[9] Article 30, para 2 provides that, where enforcement is suspended in the United Kingdom by reason of an appeal, a court in another Contracting State in which recognition is sought may stay the proceedings for rec-

---

4 See Art 39.
5 See the Jenard Report, p 52.
6 Art 38, para 3; formerly para 2 of the original 1968 Brussels Convention.
7 Case 258/83 *Brennero v Wendel GmbH* [1984] ECR 3971, [1986] 2 CMLR 59; Hartley (1986) 11 ELR 95.
8 Since a community meaning is given to the concept, see infra, this would not be an impossible task.
9 See the Schlosser Report, pp 128–130.

ognition.[10] Article 38, para 2 provides that, where the judgment was given in the United Kingdom, "any form of appeal available in the State of origin shall be treated as an ordinary appeal".

This still leaves a problem for English courts; they will have to grapple with an unfamiliar concept when determining whether an "ordinary" appeal has been lodged in the foreign Contracting State in which the judgment was given. An "ordinary" appeal is, however, a concept that has now been defined by the Court of Justice.

> In *Industrial Diamond Supplies v Riva*[11] an Italian court ordered Industrial Diamond Supplies, a Belgian partnership, to pay a sum of money to Riva, a commercial representative residing in Italy. A Belgian court issued an order for enforcement of this judgment in Belgium under the Convention. Industrial Diamond Supplies appealed, asking for a stay of enforcement under Articles 30 and 38. Shortly afterwards, it appealed in Italy against the original order of the Italian court. The enforcing court in Belgium referred to the Court of Justice, inter alia, the question of the meaning of an "ordinary" appeal within Articles 30 and 38.

The Court of Justice gave a community meaning to the concept of an ordinary appeal. This was necessary because some Contracting States do not have the concept, and those that do have it do not always define it in the same way. In deciding what this community definition should be, the Court of Justice was concerned to ensure that the recognising and enforcing court was able to stay the proceedings "whenever reasonable doubt arises with regard to the fate of the decision in the State in which it was given".[12] The court held that an ordinary appeal under Articles 30 and 38 is any appeal which: (a) may result in the annulment or amendment of the original judgment, and (b) for which there is a specific time for appealing which starts to run by virtue of the judgment. It is not an ordinary appeal if it is one which is either dependent on events unforeseeable at the time of the original trial or on action taken by persons extraneous to the case who are not bound by the period for making an appeal.

The first of these two criteria is suitable for an appeal which has actually been lodged, and is relevant to Articles 30 and 38; the second is suitable for the situation where an appeal has not been lodged, but the time for this has not expired, and is therefore only relevant to Article 38. Since the Court of Justice wanted the same criteria to apply to both Articles 30 and 38, it put the two elements together for a common definition of an ordinary appeal. However, adopting this two part definition produces curious results. Where an appeal has been lodged the first part of the definition would be satisfied, since the danger of the original judgment being altered exists. But, if this lodged appeal is of a type for which there is no time limit on when it can be brought, the second part of the definition would not be satisfied. It does not

10 It is not clear whether Art 30, para 1 is replaced by Art 30, para 2 in cases coming within that paragraph. The wording of Art 30 suggests that as an alternative a stay can be granted in the situation where an "ordinary" appeal has been lodged in England, see Hartley, p 95. However, according to the Schlosser Report (p 130), the intention was to replace the concept of an "ordinary" appeal by Art 30, para 2 in the situation where recognition is sought of a judgment from a court in the United Kingdom.
11 Case 43/77 [1977] ECR 2175, [1978] 1 CMLR 349; Hartley (1978) 3 ELR 160, and generally Hartley, p 94. See also the Schlosser Report, p 130. Cf *Interdesco SA v Nullifire Ltd* [1982] 1 Lloyd's Rep 180.
12 At p 2189.

seem right to exclude an appeal which has actually been lodged because it was of a type for which there was no time limit as to when it could have been lodged.[13]

(b) A discretionary power The recognising or enforcing court has a discretion to stay the proceedings; it is under no duty to grant a stay and one can be refused even though an ordinary appeal has been lodged, or, under Article 38, the time for such an appeal has not yet expired. The criteria on which this discretion is to be exercised have not as yet been fully developed by the Court of Justice. The Court of Justice has, however, held that a court, when deciding whether to grant a stay of proceedings may take into account only such submissions as the party lodging the appeal against the decision authorising the enforcement of a judgment was unable to make before the court of the state in which the judgment was given.[14] There is also English authority in *Petereit v Babcock International Holdings Ltd.*[15] The court laid down a general principle that prima facie a foreign judgment should be enforced. In deciding whether to grant a stay pending the result of the appeal abroad the court considered the economic consequences to the parties of, on the one hand, granting a stay and, on the other hand, enforcing the judgment; for what is being decided is which party is to have the use of the judgment money during the period up to the result of the appeal being known. In deciding to grant a stay[16] the judge was influenced by the prospect of the defendant suffering potential losses, in terms of cash flow problems and currency exchange losses, which could not be adequately dealt with by the provision of security by the plaintiff. It also seems that if the appeal abroad is entirely lacking in merit, and will accordingly fail, a stay will be refused.[17] The most likely situation for the exercise of the discretion against a stay is going to arise before courts in other Contracting States which are asked to recognise or enforce judgments given in the United Kingdom and which are subject to an appeal. The extreme width of Articles 30, para 2, and 38, para 2, which are not limited to "ordinary" appeals,[18] needs to be countered by the use of the discretion to refuse a stay.[19]

(i) THE ESTOPPEL EFFECT OF A JUDGMENT OBTAINED IN A CONTRACTING STATE

In *De Wolf v Cox*[20] a Belgian court ordered the defendant Cox, an undertaking with a head office in Holland, to pay a sum of money to the plaintiff De Wolf, a Belgian resident. Instead of seeking to enforce this judgment in the Netherlands under the procedure in the Convention, the plaintiff, because it was cheaper, brought a new action against the defendant in the Netherlands and a judgment was given as to substance. However, the Dutch judgment was in the same terms as the Belgian one, since the Dutch court accepted that it was bound to recognise it under the Convention. There was a reference from the Dutch court to the Court of Justice as to whether, in the above circumstances, the Convention prevents a plaintiff from making an appli-

---

13 Hartley interprets the decision in *Industrial Diamond Suppliers v Riva*, supra, in such a way as to avoid this, p 94.
14 Case C-183/90 *BJ Van Dalfsen v B Van Loon* [1992] ILPr 5.
15 [1990] 2 All ER 135, [1990] 1 WLR 350; Kaye [1991] JBL 261.
16 Conditional on the defendant providing adequate security to protect the plaintiff's position.
17 [1990] 1 WLR 350 at 355.
18 Discussed supra, pp 437–438.
19 See the Schlosser Report, p 130.
20 Case 42/76 [1976] ECR 1759, [1977] 2 CMLR 43; Hartley (1977) 2 ELR 146.

cation in another Contracting State for a fresh judgment as to substance against the other party.

The Court of Justice held that, once a judgment which is enforceable under the Convention has been obtained in one Contracting State, the party who has obtained the judgment in his favour is prevented from bringing a new action before a court in another Contracting State for a judgment in the same terms. The Court came to this conclusion because it foresaw a number of problems that could arise if bringing a new action was allowed. First, it could involve the courts of another Contracting State going into the substance of the dispute when this is a matter for the courts of the Contracting State in which the original judgment was given.[21] Second, if a judgment is given in the second Contracting State which conflicts with that given in the first, it means that the court in the second has failed in its duty to recognise the judgment.[22] Third, the *lis pendens* provisions under the Convention show the general desire to avoid having two sets of proceedings and two judgments in respect of the same cause of action.[23] Fourth, allowing a new action could result in a creditor possessing two orders for enforcement in respect of the same debt.

On the facts of the case, whilst there were two sets of proceedings there were not two inconsistent judgments since the Dutch court recognised the Belgian judgment. The Court of Justice was therefore reacting more against potential problems than actual ones and, by forcing the parties to use the enforcement procedure under the Convention, imposed greater expense upon the parties than would have been the case if the plaintiff had been allowed to bring fresh proceedings in the Netherlands.

The effect of the decision in *De Wolf* is that a judgment given in a Contracting State which is enforceable under the Convention creates what in English law is regarded as an estoppel from the moment that it has been given.[24] The facts of *De Wolf* only concerned the situation where the estoppel principle prevents the plaintiff, having obtained a judgment in his favour, from obtaining another judgment against the same defendant in new proceedings in a different Contracting State. However, this principle must apply equally to prevent a plaintiff who has lost his action from obtaining a judgment against the same defendant in new proceedings in a different Contracting State.

(j) FOREIGN REACTION

(i) The automatic recognition of judgments without jurisdictional safeguards

American lawyers have been outspoken in their criticism of the Convention.[1] The basis of their objection is that the Convention provides for the automatic recognition and enforcement of judgments against defendants domiciled in non-Contracting States,[2] despite the absence of the jurisdictional safeguards provided for defendants domiciled in Contracting States. Minimum stan-

---

21 See Art 29 and Art 34, para 3.
22 See Art 26, discussed supra, pp 418–419.
23 See Art 21, discussed supra, pp 326–329.
24 See supra, p 347 and s 34 of the 1982 Act.
1 Von Mehren (1981) 81 Col LR 1044; Von Mehren (1980) II Hague Recueil 9 at pp 95 et seq; Nadelmann (1967) 67 Col LR 995, reprinted in *Conflict of Laws: International and Interstate*, at p 238; Nadelmann (1967) 5 CMLR 409. See also Bartlett (1975) 25 ICLQ 44; Fletcher, pp 117–120. For Australian reaction see Pryles and Trindade (1974) 42 Aus LJ 185.
2 Supra, p 413.

dards in relation to natural justice[3] do not have to be complied with. The Convention also recognises the use of exorbitant bases of jurisdiction against defendants domiciled in non-Contracting States (but not those domiciled in Contracting States[4]), and under Article 4 para 2 even extends their use. This provision, to take an example, allows a French domiciliary to use Article 14 of the French Civil Code, under which jurisdiction is based on the plaintiff's French nationality, to found jurisdiction against a defendant from a non-Contracting State and to have that judgment recognised and enforced throughout the European Community.

From a Community point of view there is as great a need for the free circulation of judgments where defendants are domiciled in non-Contracting States as there is where they are domiciled in Contracting States,[5] since there is the same risk of a defendant thwarting the plaintiff by moving his assets from one Contracting State to another. It is also understandable that the jurisdictional rules in the Convention, since they are only concerned with allocating jurisdiction to Contracting States, should involve a basic distinction between the situation where the defendant is and is not domiciled in a Contracting State. But when you add these two elements together the result is that defendants domiciled in non-Contracting States are treated unfairly.[6] This whole problem was, seemingly, only recognised at a late stage by the drafters of the Convention who, almost as an afterthought, introduced Article 59 to deal with it.[7]

(ii) Article 59

Article 59 allows a Contracting State to enter into a convention with a third State (ie a non-Contracting State), under which the former agrees not to recognise judgments given against defendants domiciled or habitually resident in the latter where the judgment could only be founded on an exorbitant basis of jurisdiction specified in Article 3, para 2 of the Brussels Convention.

Article 59 is not a satisfactory solution to the problem of unfairness to defendants domiciled in non-Contracting States because:
(i) It requires a convention to be entered into. From the point of view of the third State, it has to go through the difficult process of negotiating treaties with every Contracting State to the Brussels Convention.[8] From the point of view of a Contracting State to the Brussels Convention, it could mean a series of different one-off treaties, which would complicate that State's law on recognition and enforcement. It may not even be possible to agree upon the terms of a treaty. United Kingdom attempts at negotiating a bilateral treaty with the United States incorporating the let-out allowed by Article 59 have

---

3 See Art 20, discussed supra, pp 325–326. The safeguards at the recognition and enforcement stage will, however, apply, see supra, pp 420–422.
4 Supra, p 290.
5 See the Jenard Report, p 20.
6 For an attempt to justify the Convention's treatment of defendants domiciled in non-Contracting States see Hauschild, in *Commercial Operations in Europe*, eds Goode and Simmonds (1978), pp 57–58; see also Kohler (1985) 34 ICLQ 563, 580–581. Cf Nadelmann, *Conflict of Laws: International and Interstate*, at pp 246–248; Nadelmann (1967) 5 CMLR 409, 414–419.
7 For the origins of Art 59, see Nadelmann (1967) 5 CMLR 409.
8 Nadelmann, *Conflict of Laws: International and Interstate*, pp 268–269; Von Mehren, op cit, p 1060.

ended in failure.[9] On the other hand, it has been possible to enter into a treaty with Canada,[10] and with Australia.[11]

(ii) The let-out allowed under Article 59 is unduly narrow. It only protects defendants domiciled or habitually resident in the third State, not those who are nationals or merely resident there. It also only applies to the exorbitant bases of jurisdiction listed in the Convention. Whilst containing many of the well known forms of exorbitant jurisdiction found in the European Community, this is not a complete list; for example, it does not include the English Order 11 of the Rules of the Supreme Court. Neither does it apply to cases where jurisdiction could have been founded on a non-exorbitant basis of jurisdiction. There is a final limitation contained in the second paragraph of Article 59.[12] In broad terms, this provides that the let-out cannot apply where jurisdiction is based on the presence of the defendant's property in the forum and the action relates to this property.

However, the great merit of Article 59 for European Community States is that it puts them in a very strong bargaining position when it comes to negotiating bilateral treaties with third States. The free circulation of judgments founded on exorbitant bases of jurisdiction acts as the stick and the let-out allowed by Article 59 as the carrot to bring third States to the negotiating table.[13]

2. THE LUGANO CONVENTION

The Lugano Convention is concerned with extending the free circulation of judgments beyond the European Communities to the EFTA bloc (Austria, Finland, Iceland, Norway, Sweden and Switzerland). It does this by means of a parallel Convention, based closely on the Brussels Convention, albeit not identical to it. The Lugano Convention, which so far has been ratified by France, Luxembourg, the Netherlands, Switzerland and the United Kingdom, has been examined earlier in the context of jurisdiction.[14] Some of the same issues that were discussed there need to be addressed now in relation to the recognition and enforcement of foreign judgments: when do the rules on recognition and enforcement under the Lugano Convention apply? What are the differences between the Lugano and Brussels Conventions?

(a)   WHEN DO THE RULES ON RECOGNITION AND ENFORCEMENT UNDER THE LUGANO CONVENTION APPLY?

The Lugano Convention applies in the situation where recognition and enforcement is sought in one Contracting State of a judgment given in another Contracting State in respect of a matter coming within the scope of the Convention. This is the same position as under the Brussels Convention[15] and presents no problems for EFTA Contracting States. However, EC States

---

9 See the Draft UK/US Judgments Convention, Cmnd 6771; North (1979) 1 Nw J Int'l Law and Bus 219; Kerr (1980) Europarecht 353, at pp 356–357; supra, pp 408–409.
10 (1984) Cmnd 9337. This was brought into force on 1st January 1987, see supra, p 409.
11 (1991) Cmnd 1394 (not yet in force).
12 This was added by the 1978 Accession Convention.
13 Nadelmann advocates US retaliation against this, *Conflict of Laws: International and Interstate*, pp 267–268.
14 Supra, pp 340–344.
15 Supra, pp 413–417. Title III applies regardless of which rules of jurisdiction have been applied. Ex parte orders are not included.

will be Contracting States to both the Lugano and Brussels Conventions. Given that there are important differences between the two Conventions, it is important for EC States to know which Convention to use. Article 54B of the Lugano Convention deals with the relationship between the two Conventions. The Lugano Convention applies in matters of recognition and enforcement, "where either the State of origin or the State addressed is not a member of the European Communities",[16] but is, of course, a Contracting State to the Lugano Convention (ie has ratified the Convention). Thus if a United Kingdom court is asked to recognise a Swiss judgment, or vice versa, the Lugano Convention will apply. On the other hand, the Brussels Convention will continue to apply where both States are members of the European Communities, for example a United Kingdom court is asked to recognise a French judgment. Of course if both States are members of the EFTA, the Lugano Convention will apply, without reference to Article 54B.

(b) DIFFERENCES BETWEEN THE LUGANO AND BRUSSELS CONVENTIONS

The Lugano Convention contains a number of formal amendments to the terms used in the Brussels Convention. These minor amendments were subsequently incorporated into the Brussels Convention[17] by the 1989 Accession Convention. More importantly, the Lugano Convention introduced four new defences to recognition and enforcement[18] which are not to be found in the Brussels Convention as amended by the 1989 Accession Convention. These came about as the result of special concerns raised by EFTA States, although some of these defences can equally be raised before the courts of EC Contracting States.

First, Article 54B, paragraph 3, introduces a discretionary power to refuse to recognise or enforce a judgment "if the ground of jurisdiction on which the judgment has been made differs from that resulting from this Convention". This is designed to deal with the situation where an EC Contracting State has taken jurisdiction under a differently worded provision of the Brussels Convention, when it should have taken jurisdiction under the Lugano Convention, for example in a case involving a contract of employment.[19] It only applies where recognition or enforcement is sought against a party domiciled in a Contracting State which is a non-EC State; for example a Swiss domiciliary. The defence will not apply if the judgment "may otherwise be recognised or enforced under any rule of law in the State addressed", ie under its common law rules.

Second, there is a new defence under Article 57, paragraph 4,[20] which is concerned with the situation where jurisdiction has been taken under some other convention, for example the Warsaw Convention on international carriage by air of 1929. The EFTA States would not agree to the open system that operates under Article 57 of the Convention.[1] A safeguard was accordingly introduced whereby there is a discretionary power to refuse to recognise or enforce a judgment if the State addressed is not a contracting

---

16 Art 54 B(2)(c) of the Lugano Convention. See also s 9(1A) of the Civil Jurisdiction and Judgments Act 1982, added by s 1(2) Civil Jurisdiction and Judgments Act 1991.
17 See eg Arts 31 and 50; the Almeida Cruz, Desantes Real and Jenard Report, para 29.
18 Art 28, para 2 mentions the defences raised by Arts 54B(3) and 57(4). See also Protocol 1, Art 1a and b.
19 The Jenard and Möller Report, p 68.
20 Ibid, at p 82.
1 Supra, p 415.

party to the Convention under which jurisdiction is asserted and the person against whom recognition or enforcement is sought is domiciled in that State. This defence does not operate solely for the benefit of domiciliaries of the EFTA States; a judgment granted in an EFTA Contracting State could be denied recognition in an EC Contracting State on this ground. Again, the defence will not apply if the judgment may otherwise be recognised or enforced under any rule of law in the State addressed.

Third, Protocol 1[2] provides a safeguard for Contracting States which are unhappy about Article 16(1)(b). This gives exclusive jurisdiction to the State of the defendant's domicil in cases involving short-term holiday lets. Contracting States can reserve the right not to recognise and enforce judgments of other Contracting States if jurisdiction was based exclusively on the domicil of the defendant pursuant to Article 16(1)(b), and the property is situated in the Contracting State which entered the reservation. Thus, if a French landlord brings proceedings in England against an English tenant by virtue of Article 16(1)(b) following a dispute over the rent of a holiday villa in Switzerland, the Swiss courts, if Switzerland had earlier entered a reservation under Protocol 1, would refuse to recognise and enforce the English judgment.

Fourth, Switzerland has the right to declare, at the time of depositing its instrument of ratification, that it will not recognise or enforce a judgment of another Contracting State if the jurisdiction was based only on Article 5(1).[3]

---

2 Protocol 1, Art 1b; see the Jenard and Möller Report, pp 75–76.
3 Protocol 1, Art 1a. The reservation will end on 31 December, 1999.

Chapter 17

Foreign arbitral awards[1]

SUMMARY

A foreign arbitral award is on a similar footing to a foreign judgment in that it may be enforced in England in a variety of ways. An action may be brought at common law to recover the sum awarded. Statutory provision is also made for the enforcement of foreign arbitral awards. Before looking at the various methods of enforcement in detail one general point should be made. The Limitation Act 1980 provides that an action to enforce an award "shall not be brought after the expiration of six years from the date on which the cause of action accrued".[2] This provision applies regardless of the method of enforcement.[3] It has been held that an action to enforce an arbitration award is an independent cause of action.[4] Accordingly, time runs, not from the date of the original breach of contract which had been the subject of the arbitration, but from the date of the failure to honour the arbitration award.[5]

Also, if a foreign award has been entered as a judgment abroad, it seems that this not only can[6] but must be enforced under the rules on enforcement of judgments (provided it is capable of being so enforced) and not as an award.[7]

---

1 Mustill and Boyd, *Commercial Arbitration* (2nd edn, 1989) pp 421–427; Redfern and Hunter, *International Commercial Arbitration*, pp 334–359.
2 S 7. This section does not apply where the submission is by an instrument under seal.
3 *Minister of Public Works of the Government of the State of Kuwait v Sir Frederick Snow & Partners* [1983] 1 WLR 818 at 823–824, CA, see the *obiter dicta* by KERR LJ; the House of Lords affirmed this decision, without discussing this point [1984] 1 AC 426.
4 *Agromet Motoimport v Maulden Engineering Co (Beds) Ltd* [1985] 2 All ER 436, [1985] 1 WLR 762.
5 Ibid.
6 See eg *East India Trading Co Inc v Carmel Exporters and Importers Ltd* [1952] 2 QB 439, [1952] 1 All ER 1053; *International Alltex Corp v Lawler Creations Ltd* [1965] IR 264.
7 S 34 of the Civil Jurisdiction and Judgments Act 1982; supra p 347. Cf Dicey and Morris, pp 564–565. In Australia the common law non-merger rule still applies: *Brali v Hyundai Corpn* (1988) 15 NSWLR 734.

1. ENFORCEMENT AT COMMON LAW

The basic elements for the successful enforcement of a foreign arbitration award in England are that the parties submitted to arbitration, that the arbitration was conducted in accordance with the submission and that the award is both final and valid by the law of the country in which it was made.[8]

There must be a valid submission to arbitration. Where the parties agree in a contract to submit any disputes to arbitration, the validity of such agreement is determined by the proper law of the arbitration agreement.[9] This law will also determine whether the arbitration agreement has been rendered void by subsequent illegality.[10] The proper law of the arbitration agreement is usually the same as the law governing the contract as a whole.[11] The parties can choose the law governing the contract (or indeed the arbitration agreement itself); in the absence of an express choice there is a strong inference that the contract (and thus the arbitration agreement) is governed by the law of the place where the arbitration is to take place.[12] The actual arbitration proceedings, in the absence of an express choice of the law to govern the arbitration proceedings,[13] will be governed by the law of the place of arbitration.[14] That law will determine whether the award is valid,[15] though whether the arbitrator has jurisdiction is a matter for the arbitration agreement and its proper law.[16] The award, to be enforceable in England, must, like a foreign judgment, be final and conclusive.[17] However, the fact that the foreign award is not enforceable in the place where it was made until it has been confirmed by a court probably does not prevent its enforcement in England, provided the law of the place of arbitration regarded the award as final.[18] One justification for this conclusion is that the action in England to enforce the award is an action on the award and not on either the contract to which the award gives effect,[19] or on a foreign judgment. If the foreign arbitral award includes an award of interest, the English court in an action on the award will not make a further award of interest at a higher rate.[20]

It is suggested,[21] though there are few reported decisions, that the rec-

8 *Norske Atlas Insurance Co Ltd v London General Insurance Co Ltd* (1927) 43 TLR 541.
9 *Dalmia Dairy Industries Ltd v National Bank of Pakistan* [1978] 2 Lloyd's Rep 223. This is not affected by the Rome Convention see Art 1 (2) (d), infra, pp 471–472.
10 *Dalmia Dairy Industries Ltd v National Bank of Pakistan* [1978] 2 Lloyd's Rep 223.
11 *Black-Clawson International Ltd v Papierwerke Waldhof-Aschaffenburg AG* [1981] 1 Lloyd's Rep 446 at 455 For the law governing the contract as a whole reference now has to be made to the Rome Convention, infra pp 459–521.
12 Infra, pp 471–472.
13 *International Tank and Pipe SAK v Kuwait Aviation Fuelling Co KSC* [1975] QB 224 at 232–233. See also *Naviera Amazonica Peruvia Sa v Cia International De Seguros Del Peru* [1988] 1 Lloyd's Rep 116 at 119.
14 *James Miller & Partners Ltd v Whitworth Street Estates (Manchester) Ltd* [1970] AC 583, [1970] 1 All ER 796; *Dalmia Dairy Industries Ltd v National Bank of Pakistan* [1978] 2 Lloyd's Rep 223.
15 *Norske Atlas Insurance Co Ltd v London General Insurance Co Ltd* (1927) 43 TLR 541.
16 *Dalmia Dairy Industries Ltd v National Bank of Pakistan* [1978] 2 Lloyd's Rep 223.
17 Ibid, at 246–250.
18 Cf *Union Nationale des Cooperatives Agricoles de Céréales v R Catterall & Co Ltd* [1959] 2 QB 44, [1959] 1 All ER 721; *Dalmia Dairy Industries Ltd v National Bank of Pakistan*, supra, at pp 249–250.
19 *Norske Atlas Insurance Co Ltd v London General Insurance Co Ltd*, supra.
20 *Dalmia Dairy Industries Ltd v National Bank of Pakistan*, [1978] 2 Lloyd's Rep 223 at 272–275, 301–303.
21 See Dicey & Morris, pp 571–574.

ognition or enforcement of a foreign arbitral award may be subject to the obvious defences that the arbitrator lacked jurisdiction,[1] that the award was obtained by fraud,[2] that its recognition or enforcement would be contrary to English public policy[3] or that it was obtained in proceedings which contravene the rules of natural justice.[4]

A foreign arbitral award which does not fall within the various statutory provisions for recognition and enforcement based on international conventions[5] may be enforced either by an action on the award at common law,[6] or by recourse to section 26 of the Arbitration Act 1950 which provides that, with leave of the court,[7] an award may be enforced in the same way as if it were a judgment. This discretionary procedure is not restricted to domestic English awards but is available for the enforcement of foreign awards,[8] though the award will have to satisfy the other requirements for enforcement in the 1950 Act.[9] It will also have to be enforceable here as if it were a judgment and, whilst it is now possible for an award in foreign currency to be enforced in England,[10] it is not possible for an award for a sum to be paid in a foreign country to be enforced here under section 26 of the 1950 Act, though such an award will still be enforceable by action at common law.[11] In the case of a purely domestic award it has been suggested that the discretion under section 26 should be exercised to allow enforcement in nearly all cases, ie unless there is real ground for doubting the validity of the award.[12] Where enforcement of a foreign arbitral award is in issue, the discretion is likely to be exercised with considerably more caution.[13]

2. ENFORCEMENT UNDER THE CIVIL JURISDICTION AND JUDGMENTS ACTS 1982 AND 1991

Foreign arbitral awards and judgments of courts incorporating such awards are not enforceable under the Brussels Convention or under the Lugano

1 *Dalmia Dairy Industries Ltd v National Bank of Pakistan*, supra; and see *Kianta Osakeyhtio v Britain and Overseas Trading Co Ltd* [1954] 1 Lloyd's Rep 247.
2 *Oppenheim & Co v Mahomed Haneef* [1922] 1 AC 482 at 487.
3 *Hamlyn & Co v Talisker Distillery* [1894] AC 202 at 209, 214; *Dalmia Dairy Industries Ltd v National Bank of Pakistan*, supra, at pp 267–269, 299–301.
4 Cf *Dalmia Dairy Industries Ltd v National Bank of Pakistan*, supra, at pp 269–270.
5 Infra, pp 448–453.
6 Ord 11, r 1(1)(m) was introduced under the Rules of the Supreme Court, inter alia, to provide jurisdiction in such cases, see supra, p 202.
7 See RSC Ord 73, r 10.
8 *Dalmia Cement Ltd v National Bank of Pakistan* [1975] QB 9, [1974] 3 All ER 189.
9 Such as the arbitration agreement being in writing: 1950 Act, s 32; it is sufficient if the arbitration agreement itself is in writing, or there is a document which recognises the existence of an arbitration agreement—*Excomm Ltd v Ahmed Abdul-Qawi Bamaodah (The St Raphael)* [1985] 1 Lloyd's Rep 403; and see Dicey and Morris, p 566.
10 *Jugoslovenska Oceanska Plovidba v Castle Investment Co Inc* [1974] QB 292, [1973] 3 All ER 498; *Dalmia Cement Ltd v National Bank of Pakistan*, supra, at pp 23–26; and see *Miliangos v George Frank (Textiles) Ltd* [1976] AC 443, [1975] 3 All ER 801; supra pp 97–106; Law Com No 124 (1983), paras 2.44–2.47 which makes no recommendations for change in the law on this point.
11 See *Dalmia Cement Ltd v National Bank of Pakistan* [1975] QB 9 at 23–27.
12 *Middlemiss and Gould v Hartlepool Corpn* [1972] 1 WLR 1643 at 1647; cf *Re Boks & Co and Peters, Rushton & Co Ltd* [1919] 1 KB 491 at 497.
13 *Dalmia Cement Ltd v National Bank of Pakistan* [1975] QB 9 at 14–15, 23; and see *Union Nationale des Co-operatives Agricoles de Céréales v Catterall* [1959] 2 QB 44 at 52 (an award enforceable under Part II of the 1950 Act, infra, pp 448–450).

Convention.[14] Thus, to take an example, an arbitral award granted in France cannot be enforced in the United Kingdom under the Brussels Convention. However, an arbitration award granted in one part of the United Kingdom can be enforced in another part under the Civil Jurisdiction and Judgments Act 1982. As has already been seen,[15] enforcement in one part of the United Kingdom of a judgment[16] obtained in another part of the United Kingdom is dealt with by section 18 of the Civil Jurisdiction and Judgments Act 1982, which provides for a system of registration of United Kingdom judgments and allows very few defences to enforcement. Section 18 defines a "judgment" very widely and includes "an arbitration award which has become enforceable in the part of the United Kingdom in which it was given in the same manner as a judgment given by a court of law in that part".[17] It should, however, be noted that, unlike other forms of judgment, an arbitration award obtained in the United Kingdom does not have to be enforced under section 18.[18] It is still possible for a plaintiff, if he so chooses, to seek enforcement of the arbitration award at common law or by recourse to section 26 of the Arbitration Act 1950.[19] It should also be noted that section 19 of the 1982 Act, which deals with recognition of United Kingdom judgments, does not apply to arbitration awards.[1]

3. ENFORCEMENT UNDER THE ARBITRATION ACT 1950

Provision is made for the enforcement of certain foreign arbitral awards by Part II of the Arbitration Act 1950, which Act consolidates the Arbitration Acts 1889 to 1934. The background to this provision is afforded by a Protocol of 1923 and a Convention of 1927, both of which were signed by the United Kingdom at Geneva. The former deals with the international validity of arbitration agreements, the latter with the enforcement in one country of arbitral awards made in another.

Part II of the Arbitration Act 1950 applies to foreign arbitral awards[2] made in pursuance of an arbitration agreement to which the 1923 Protocol applies[3] and made between persons who are subject to the jurisdiction of different countries, both of which, by reason of their reciprocal provisions, have been declared by Order in Council to be parties to the 1927 Convention.[4] The award must also have been made in such a country.[5]

Two issues of interpretation arise. It is not immediately apparent when

14 Supra, p 289. As regards judgments incorporating awards (as under s 26 of the 1950 Act) see the Schlosser Report, para 65; O'Malley and Layton, *European Civil Practice*, p 361, n 96; cf Schmitthoff (1987) 24 CML Rev 143 at 154–155.
15 Supra, pp 393–396.
16 The judgment may concern money provisions (Sch 6 of the 1982 Act) or non-money provisions (Sch 7 of the 1982 Act).
17 S 18(2)(e).
18 See s 18(8).
19 Supra, p 447.
 1 S 19(3)(b).
 2 But not to awards made under an arbitration agreement governed by English law: s 40(b), or awards which may be recognised under the Arbitration Act 1975, infra, pp 450–452; see 1975 Act, s 3.
 3 Arbitration Act 1950, Sch 1, para 1.
 4 For a list of the countries which have been declared to be parties to the Convention, see SI 1984/1168.
 5 Arbitration Act 1950, s 35(1).

persons are "subject to the jurisdiction" of different Convention States. Nationality as the basis of the construction of the phrase has been rejected, in favour of a requirement that the parties to the contract submitting to arbitration must both have places of residence and carry on business therefrom in two different Contracting States and also that the contract containing the submission to arbitration results from business so conducted.[6] The second issue is that, although the parties must be subject to the jurisdiction of different Convention States and the award must have been made in such a state, the award need not have been made in either of the parties' State.[7]

In order to implement the Convention of 1927, the 1950 Act provides that a foreign award shall be enforceable in England either by action or, with the leave of the High Court, in the same manner as a judgment is enforced,[8] or indeed, by an action at common law.[9] Further, the award is to be treated as binding for all purposes on the persons between whom it was made, and they are to be entitled to rely on it by way of defence, set-off or otherwise in any legal proceedings in England.[10]

An award, however, is not to be enforceable unless it satisfies certain conditions. It must have

(a) been made in pursuance of an agreement for arbitration valid by the law by which it was governed;[11]
(b) been made by the tribunal provided for in the agreement;
(c) been made in conformity with the procedural rules obtaining in the country where the arbitration was held;
(d) become final in the country in which it was made;[12]
(e) been in respect of a matter which may lawfully be referred to arbitration under English law;

and its enforcement must not be contrary to the public policy or the law of England.[13]

An award is not deemed final if proceedings for testing its validity are pending in the country in which it was made.[14] Moreover, an award is not to be enforceable if it does not deal with all the questions referred to the arbitrator or exceeds the scope of the arbitration agreement,[15] or if the party against whom enforcement is sought was not given sufficient notice of the

---

6 *Brazendale & Co Ltd v Saint Freres SA* [1970] 2 Lloyd's Rep 34.
7 *Union Nationale des Cooperatives Agricoles de Céréales v Catterall* [1959] 2 QB 44, [1959] 1 All ER 721.
8 Arbitration Act 1950, s 36(1), applying s 26 of the 1950 Act. It has been suggested, supra, p 447 that the judicial discretion under s 26 may be exercised less readily in the case of foreign arbitral awards than in the case of domestic awards; see *Dalmia Cement Ltd v National Bank of Pakistan* [1975] QB 9 at 23; and see *Union Nationale des Cooperatives Agricoles de Céréales v Catterall* [1959] 2 QB 44 at 52.
9 Ibid, s 40(a).
10 Ibid, s 36(2).
11 *Kianta Osakeyhtio v Britain and Overseas Trading Co Ltd* [1954] 1 Lloyd's Rep 247.
12 *Union Nationale des Cooperatives Agricoles de Céréales v Catterall* [1959] 2 QB 44, [1959] 1 All ER 721.
13 Arbitration Act 1950, s 37(1); see *Masinimport v Scottish Mechanical Light Industries Ltd* 1976 SLT 245. The reference in s 37(1) of the 1950 Act to enforcement being contrary to "the law of England" probably only refers to rules of a mandatory character relating to the enforcement, rather than the content, of the award; see Dicey and Morris, p 580; and see 1976 SLT 245 at 249.
14 Ibid, s 39.
15 *Kianta Osakeyhtio v Britain and Overseas Trading Co Ltd*, supra.

arbitration proceedings or was under some legal incapacity and was not properly represented.[16]

4. ENFORCEMENT UNDER THE ARBITRATION ACT 1975

The Arbitration Act 1975[17] enabled the United Kingdom to accede to the New York Convention on the Recognition and Enforcement of Foreign Arbitral Awards 1958. The 1975 Act provides for the enforcement in the United Kingdom of "Convention awards", ie awards[18] made, in pursuance of a written arbitration agreement,[19] in a foreign country which is a party to the New York Convention.[20] If it is declared by Order in Council[1] that a State is a party to the New York Convention this is to be conclusive evidence of that fact.[2] The relevant date for ascertaining whether a foreign country is a party to the Convention is the date when proceedings to enforce an award are begun.[3] If a State is a party to the Convention at that date, an arbitration award made there will be a Convention award (provided, of course, that the award was made in pursuance of a written arbitration agreement), even though the State was not a party at the date when the arbitration award was made.[4] An award is "made" when and where it is signed by the arbitrator, even though the arbitration was held in a different state;[5] a fortuitous signature abroad can mean that an English arbitration results in a Convention award.[6] A Convention award can be enforced in two ways,[7] either by action or in the same way as an award can be enforced under section 26 of the Arbitration Act 1950,[8] ie in the same way as if it were a judgment, subject to the discretion of the court which may be exercised with caution in the case of foreign awards.[9]

The effect of an enforceable Convention award is that it is to be treated as binding between the parties for all purposes and can be relied on by any of

16 Arbitration Act 1950, s 37(2).
17 See Lew (1975) 24 ICLQ 870. It is now clear that the 1975 Act applies to awards made before the Act came into force: *Minister of Public Works of the Government of the State of Kuwait v Sir Frederick Snow & Partners* [1984] AC 426.
18 If the award includes an order for costs, this is also enforceable under the Convention, see *Bank Mellat v Helliniki Techniki SA* [1984] QB 291 at 308.
19 1975 Act, s 7(1).
20 Ibid.
 1 See SI 1984/168, SI 1989/1348.
 2 1975 Act, s 7(2); other evidence may be given to show that a State is a party to the Convention, see *Government of the State of Kuwait v Sir Frederick Snow & Partners* [1981] 1 Lloyd's Rep 656 at 666; overruled by the Court of Appeal and House of Lords on another point [1984] 1 AC 426. Cf the 1950 Act which only applies if persons are "subject to the jurisdiction" of different States, supra, p 448.
 3 *Minister of Public Works of the Government of the State of Kuwait v Sir Frederick Snow & Partners* [1984] AC 426. Cf the position under the Arbitration Act 1950, s 35; the Foreign Judgments (Reciprocal Enforcement) Act 1933, s 1(2)(c) (as amended by the Civil Jurisdiction and Judgments Act 1982, Sch 10, para 1(2)).
 4 *Minister of Public Works of the Government of the State of Kuwait v Sir Frederick Snow & Partners*, supra.
 5 *Hiscox v Outhwaite* [1991] 3 All ER 124, [1991] 2 WLR 297, HL unless the arbitration award, or the rules under which the arbitration was conducted, provide to the contrary.
 6 The English courts can still exercise their supervisory jurisdiction under the 1950 and 1979 Arbitration Acts: *Hiscox v Outhwaite*, op cit.
 7 1975 Act, s 3 (1)(a).
 8 Supra, p 447.
 9 See *Dalmia Cement Ltd v National Bank of Pakistan* [1975] QB 9 at 23, supra, p 447.

them by way of defence, set off or otherwise in legal proceedings in the United Kingdom.[10] In order to enforce the award the plaintiff merely has to produce the award and the original arbitration agreement, or certified copies, and a certified translation if either is in a foreign language.[11]

There are, however, a number of grounds on which the defendant may resist enforcement.[12] The court has a discretion[13] to refuse enforcement if the defendant proves any of the following.[14]

(a) that a party to the arbitration agreement was under some incapacity. The question of capacity is to be governed by the law applicable to that party under English contract choice of law rules. Furthermore, enforcement of the award can be refused whichever party to the arbitration agreement lacked capacity;

(b) that the arbitration agreement was invalid[15] under the law to which the parties subjected it, ie the law chosen by the parties.[16] Failing any indication of such law, validity is to be determined by the law of the country where the award was made;[17]

(c) that the defendant was not given proper notice of the appointment of the arbitrator or of the arbitration proceedings or was otherwise unable to present his case;

(d) that the award deals with a difference not contemplated by or not falling within the terms of the submission to arbitration or contains matters beyond the scope of the submission to arbitration;[18]

(e) that the composition of the arbitral authority or the arbitral procedure was not in accordance with the agreement of the parties or, failing such agreement, with the law of the country where the arbitration took place. It can be assumed from this defence that the parties are free to choose the procedural law to govern the arbitration and that, in the absence of choice, the curial law will be that of the country where the arbitration took place;

(f) that the award has not yet become binding on the parties, or has been set aside or suspended by a competent authority of the country in which, or under the law of which, it was made.[19] Under the 1950 Act an award

---

10 1975 Act, s 3(2).

11 Ibid, s 4.

12 The grounds listed in the 1975 Act are the only ones available: s 5(1).

13 Contrast the mandatory provisions of the Arbitration Act 1950, s 37(1), supra, p 449.

14 1975 Act, s 5(2); the reasons for an award can be referred to in order to ascertain whether any of the circumstances under this section apply, see *Mutual Shipping Corpn of New York v Bayshore Shipping Co of Monrovia, The Montan* [1985] 1 WLR 625 at 631. As to the burden of proof, see *Dalmia Dairy Industries Ltd v National Bank of Pakistan* [1978] 2 Lloyd's Rep 223 at 238.

15 See *Dallal v Bank Mellat* [1986] QB 441 at 455–456; Kunzlik [1986] CLJ 377. This may include continuing, as well as initial, validity: *Dalmia Dairy Industries Ltd v National Bank of Pakistan*, supra, at p 238.

16 This would appear to include an inferred choice of the proper law, infra, p 484 and 11th edn (1987), pp 457–461.

17 See *Dallal v Bank Mellat* [1986] QB 441 at 455–456.

18 Subject to the proviso in s 5(4) of the 1975 Act that an award containing decisions on matters not submitted to arbitration may be enforced to the extent that it contains decisions on separate matters which were so submitted. See, on s 5(2)(d), *Agromet Motoimport v Maulden Engineering Co (Beds) Ltd* [1985] 1 WLR 762 at 775–776.

19 See *Rosseel NV v Oriental Commercial and Shipping (UK) Ltd* [1990] 3 All ER 545, [1990] 1 WLR 1387. If an application has been made to a competent authority to set aside or suspend a Convention award, the English court has a discretion to adjourn the enforcement proceedings and to order security to be given: 1975 Act, s 5(5).

is unenforceable, as at common law, if it is not "final",[20] rather than if it is "not yet binding".

There is a further discretion to refuse enforcement of a Convention award which may be exercised by the court either on the application of a party to the arbitration agreement or by the court of its own motion. Enforcement may be refused if the award is in respect of a matter which is not capable of settlement by arbitration, or if it would be contrary to public policy to enforce the award.[21] Whether a matter is capable of settlement by arbitration would appear to be determined by English law as the law of the country where enforcement is sought.[22] Denial of recognition of an award as being contrary to English public policy is less extensive than the equivalent provision under the 1950 Act[1] in that enforcement cannot be denied under the 1975 Act on the ground that it would be contrary to the law of England. What has to be shown is that "there is some element of illegality or that the enforcement of the award would be clearly injurious to the public good or, possibly, that enforcement would be wholly offensive to the ordinary reasonable and fully informed member of the public".[2] Applying this definition, the enforcement of an award arrived at after arbitrators had applied "internationally accepted principles of law governing contractual relations" (the *lex mercatoria*) has been held not to be against public policy.[3] It must finally be noted that enforcement cannot be refused on the basis that the arbitrator made an error of fact or law.[4]

The 1975 Act contains two provisions which interrelate with other bases for enforcement. If a Convention award would also be a foreign award within the meaning of the 1950 Act, that Act is not to apply to it but its enforcement shall be governed by the 1975 Act.[5] Secondly, nothing in the 1975 Act prejudices the right to enforce or rely on an award at common law,[6] eg by an action on the award.

5. ENFORCEMENT UNDER THE ADMINISTRATION OF JUSTICE ACT 1920 AND THE FOREIGN JUDGMENTS (RECIPROCAL ENFORCEMENT) ACT 1933

The provisions of the Administration of Justice Act 1920 whereby judgments given in Commonwealth countries may be registered and enforced in

---

20 Supra, p 449.
21 1975 Act, s 5(3).
22 See Lew (1975) 24 ICLQ 870 at 876.
 1 S 37(1), supra, p 449.
 2 *Deutsche Schachtbau-Und Tiefbohrgesellschaft MBH v Shell International Petroleum Co Ltd (Trading as Shell International Trading Co)* [1990] 1 AC 295 at 316, 322, CA. The case went to the House of Lords (op cit, at 323) on a separate garnishment point, discussed infra, p 819.
 3 Ibid. However, it appears that the parties cannot choose the *lex mercatoria* as the governing law under the Rome Convention on the law applicable to contractual obligations, see infra, p 482.
 4 *Mutual Shipping Corpn of New York v Bayshore Shipping Co of Monrovia, The Montan* [1985] 1 WLR 625 at 631.
 5 1975 Act, s 2.
 6 Ibid, s 6; in *Minister of Public Works of the Government of the State of Kuwait v Sir Frederick Snow & Partners* [1984] AC 426, the defences under the Act were said to cover the whole field of the defences which would be available in a common law action, see pp 446–447.

England[7] apply equally to arbitral awards.[8] The Foreign Judgments (Reciprocal Enforcement) Act 1933[9] now also extends to foreign arbitral awards.[10] However, a foreign arbitral award, which is registrable under the Act, unlike other judgments, does not have to be enforced under the Act.[11] The plaintiff, if he so chooses, can, instead, seek enforcement of the arbitration award at common law or by recourse to section 26 of the Arbitration Act 1950.[12]

6. ENFORCEMENT UNDER THE ARBITRATION (INTERNATIONAL INVESTMENT DISPUTES) ACT 1966

The Arbitration (International Investment Disputes) Act 1966 implements a convention made at Washington in 1965 which established an International Centre for the settlement of investment disputes between Contracting States and the nationals of other Contracting States.[13] Subject to the written consent of the parties, the Centre's arbitration tribunal has jurisdiction to settle any legal dispute arising out of such an investment.[14] An arbitral award made by the Centre's tribunal, if registered in the High Court, has, as respects the pecuniary obligations which it imposes, the same force and effect as if it had been a judgment of the High Court.[15] There is a discretion to stay English proceedings in breach of an agreement to submit to the Centre's arbitration.[16]

---

7 Supra, pp 395–396.
8 Administration of Justice Act 1920, s 12(1).
9 Supra, pp 397–405.
10 S 10A of the 1933 Act, added by Schedule 10, para 4 of the Civil Jurisdiction and Judgments Act 1982. Even before this, the 1933 Act applied to awards made pursuant to the Geneva Convention on the International Carriage of Goods by Road (1956) as embodied in the Carriage of Goods by Road Act 1965; see Dicey & Morris, p 591.
11 See S 10A and s 6 of the 1933 Act.
12 Supra, p 447.
13 1966 Act, Sch, Art 1.
14 Ibid, Art 25. Choice of law rules are provided in Art 42.
15 Ibid, ss 1, 2. The award may be registered in foreign currency: Administration of Justice Act 1977, s 4(2)(a), (b); see also Law Com No 124 (1983), paras 2.44–2.47.
16 Ibid, s 3(2), applying the Arbitration Act 1950, s 4(1), supra, pp 240–241.

Part IV

The law of obligations

SUMMARY

Chapter 18

Contracts

SUMMARY

1. INTRODUCTION

(a) THE NATURE OF THE PROBLEM

The problem of ascertaining the applicable law is more perplexing in the case of contracts than in almost any other area. There are three reasons for this. First, there is the diversity of connecting factors that can be raised by the facts of the case: the place where the contract is made; the place of performance; the domicil, nationality or place of business of the parties; the situation of the subject matter and so on. In most areas of private international law the decisive connecting factor on which ascertainment of the applicable law depends is reasonably clear. There is general agreement, for instance, that it is the place of celebration which indicates the law to govern the formal validity of a marriage. But with contracts the sheer multiplicity of connecting factors makes it hard to identify one single connecting factor as the determinant of the applicable law. Second, contracts are planned transactions and

457

the parties may well have considered the question of what law should govern the contract in the event of a dispute arising between them. They may have made provision in the contract, choosing the applicable law. Third, a wide variety of different contractual issues can arise. For example, there can be a problem over whether a contract has been validly created, concerning how it should be interpreted, about whether it has been discharged. This raises the question of whether the same law should govern all of these issues. Moreover, there are many different types of contract. A sale of goods contract has different features from an insurance contract or a contract for carriage of goods by sea. Should the same law govern regardless of the type of contract involved, or do the special features of particular contracts necessitate special choice of law rules?

(b) VARIOUS SOLUTIONS TO THE PROBLEM[1]

As one would expect from the complex nature of the problem, a wide variety of different solutions have been tried in different countries over the years. In the United States of America a preference was formerly shown for a rigid and inflexible test, represented by the place of contracting in some of the States but by the place of performance in others. However, the choice of law revolution in that country[2] has affected not only tort cases but also contract cases, and a wide range of modern approaches is now used in this area.[3] Most of the countries of the European Continent rejected a rigid test and, instead, adopted the doctrine of autonomy under which the parties were free to choose the governing law, though divergent views obtained on the question whether their freedom was absolute or was restricted to the choice of a law with which the contract was factually connected.[4] In the absence of choice by the parties, most of these countries adopted a flexible approach leaving the judge to select the decisive connecting factors from the various elements of the contract and the circumstances of the case.[5]

English law, until very recently, applied the "proper law of the contract",[6] which was a succinct expression to describe the law governing many of the matters affecting a contract. The doctrine of the proper law was of common law origin and a vast case law developed to take account of the difficulties outlined above. It was both sophisticated and flexible in its approach. The key features of the doctrine were as follows. The parties could choose the proper law, with very little restriction on this right. If the parties did not express a choice, and one could not be inferred by the courts, an objective test was applied. This sought to localise the contract by looking for the system of law with which the transaction was most closely connected. The twin theories which underlay the proper law were therefore the subjective theory, which looked to the intentions of the parties, and the objective theory,

---

1 See generally Lando, 3 International Encyclopaedia of Comparative Law, ch 24; North, (1990) I Hague Recueil, ch 5.
2 Supra, pp 31–37.
3 *Auten v Auten* 308 NY 155, 124 NE 2d 99 (1954)—grouping of contacts; Restatement, 2d, §§ 187, 188; *Lilienthal v Kaufman* 395 P 2d 543 (1964)—governmental interest analysis; *Haines v Mid-Century Insurance Co* 177 NW 2d 328 (1970)—choice influencing considerations. See generally Weintraub (1984) IV Hague Recueil 239; Penn and Cashel [1986] JBL 333 and 497.
4 For a detailed account, see Rabel, ii 370 et seq.
5 See Lando (1987) 24 CMLR 159, 188–199.
6 For a detailed analysis see the 11th edn (1987) of this book, ch 18; Dicey and Morris, chs 32 and 33; Anton, ch 10.

which sought to localise the contract. Special rules were adopted for particular issues. The proper law was usually relevant, but the court was required to go beyond the proper law when considering certain issues. Thus, for example, with the issue of illegality the courts were concerned not only with illegality by the proper law but also with illegality by the law of the place of performance. There were also special rules for particular contracts, such as insurance contracts. These rules either made special provision for ascertaining the proper law or departed from the proper law altogether.

Choice of law in contract is now put on a statutory footing. The Contracts (Applicable Law) Act 1990 has largely replaced the common law rules and the doctrine of the proper law of the contract. The Act implements the EEC Convention on the law applicable to contractual obligations of 1980 (the Rome Convention), and it is with this Convention that this chapter is mainly concerned.

2. THE ROME CONVENTION[7]

(a) PRELIMINARY REMARKS

(i) The history and purpose of the Convention

(a) History of the Convention As early as 1967 there was a proposal from the Governments of the Benelux countries to the Commission of the European Communities for the unification of private international law rules, particularly in the field of contract law. Experts from the then six Member States of the Community prepared a preliminary draft Convention before the United Kingdom, Ireland and Denmark joined the European Community. At that time, this also covered non-contractual obligations. In negotiations between experts from the then nine Member States of the European Community there was extensive revision of the draft Convention, culminating in a final Convention (the Rome Convention) in 1980. This was only concerned with contractual obligations. By the end of 1981 the Convention had been signed by all of the then Member States. However, ratification of the Convention was delayed whilst problems in relation to what powers, if any, the European Court of Justice should have as regards interpretation of the Convention were resolved. In 1988 two protocols on interpretation of the Convention were signed. The Convention was eventually ratified by seven of the Member States which had earlier signed it (Belgium, Denmark, France, Germany, Italy, Luxembourg and the United Kingdom,[8] which provided the requisite seventh ratification[9]) and came into force on 1 April 1991. Since then, the Convention has come into force in Greece, the Netherlands and Ireland. The Convention has not yet come into force in Spain and Portugal and there will need to be an Accession Convention for these remaining two

---

7 (1980) OJ L266 of 9 October; Plender, *The European Contracts Convention* (1991); North (ed), *Contract Conflicts—The EEC Convention on the Law Applicable to Contractual Obligations: A Comparative Study* (1982); Fletcher, *Conflict of Laws and European Community Law* (1982) ch 5; Lasok and Stone, *Conflict of Laws in the European Community* (1987), pp 340–387; Anton, ch 11; North [1980] JBL 382; Bennett (1980) 17 CMLR 269; Williams [1981] Lloyd's MCLQ 250; note (1981) 2 Vir JIL 91; Morse (1982) 2 Yearbook of European Law 107; Weintraub (1984) IV Hague Recueil 239 at 278–290; Williams (1986) 35 ICLQ 1; Lando (1987) 24 CMLR 159; RMM [1991] JBL 205; Young [1991] Lloyd's MCLQ 314.

8 The Convention can be extended to the Channel Isles, the Isle of Man and Gibraltar; see Art 27(2)(b) and s 8 of the Contracts (Applicable Law) Act 1990.

9 See Art 29.

Member States. It is contemplated that any country which in the future joins the European Community should accede to the Convention.[10] The Convention is not open to signature by non-Members of the European Community.[11] However, there is nothing to stop other countries incorporating the rules contained in the Rome Convention into their private international law. Indeed, Belgium, Luxembourg, Denmark, the Netherlands and Germany all did this prior to the Convention itself coming into force in 1991.[12]

(b) The purpose of the Convention According to its preamble, the purpose of the Convention is to establish uniform choice of law rules for contractual obligations throughout the Community.[13] In general terms, the Convention has been seen as a continuation of the work on unification begun by the Brussels Convention on jurisdiction and the enforcement of judgments in civil and commercial matters,[14] and like that Convention is concerned with creating the right conditions for an internal market with the free movement of persons, goods, services and capital amongst the Member States. More particularly, since the law will be the same wherever trial takes place in the Community, it inhibits the forum shopping that the Brussels Convention allows.[15] It was also said that such a Convention would increase legal certainty and make it easier to anticipate more easily the law to be applied.[16]

(ii) The Contracts (Applicable Law) Act 1990

The introduction of the Convention into English law was a matter of considerable controversy with enthusiasts[17] and critics[18] taking polarised positions. The controversy ranged over both the need for harmonisation of contract choice of law rules and the nature and form of the new law. Nonetheless, when the 1990 Act was presented to Parliament it was said[19] that the Convention would produce benefits in terms both of harmonisation and, more questionably, improved certainty in the law. The Convention uses ill defined Continental concepts (for example, mandatory rules and characteristic performance), and when it does use a familiar concept (for example, the parties' freedom to choose the applicable law) this is put in unfamiliar language and in the unfamiliar form of a Code. Moreover, unlike when the Brussels Convention came into force in the United Kingdom, the Rome Convention is not accompanied by decisions of the Court of Justice interpreting it. On the other hand, it is uncontroversial that the substance of the law will be largely unaltered.

The Contracts (Applicable Law) Act 1990 is closely modelled on the Civil Jurisdiction and Judgments Act 1982, which implemented the Brussels

10 See the Joint Declaration attached to the Convention, at III.
11 Art 28 (1).
12 See generally Lando (1987) 24 CMLR 159; Triebel (1988) 37 ICLQ 935; De Boer (1990) 54 Rabels Z 24, 40 et seq.
13 Para 3 of the Preamble.
14 Para 2 of the Preamble. However, there is nothing in Art 220 of the Treaty of Rome about contract choice of law; cf the origins of the Brussels Convention, supra, pp 279–280.
15 See the Giuliano and Lagarde Report (1980) OJ C282 of 31 October, at pp 4–5 which quotes from the address by Vogelaar at the meeting of government experts in 1969.
16 Ibid.
17 North, *Contract Conflicts* at p 23; Jaffey (1984) 33 ICLQ 531.
18 See Mann (1983) 32 ICLQ 265; (1989) 38 ICLQ 715; Briggs [1990] Lloyd's MCLQ 192.
19 See the Lord-Advocate, Hansard, (HL) 12 Dec 1989 vol 513, cols 1258–1260; Lord Chancellor, (HL) 24 April 1990 vol 518, col 439; Solicitor-General, (HC) Second Reading Committee 20 June 1990, cols 3–6.

Convention.[20] The 1990 Act is very short. It provides that the Rome Convention, Luxembourg Convention (the Greek Accession Convention to the Rome Convention) and Brussels Protocol (the first Protocol on interpretation of the Rome Convention) shall have the force of law in the United Kingdom,[1] and sets out the two Conventions and the first Protocol in Schedules to the Act. There is a provision dealing with interpretation of the Conventions and Protocol,[2] which will be examined shortly.[3] Two other important matters are dealt with in the Act. The first is concerned with reservations under the Rome Convention. On ratifying the Convention the United Kingdom, as it was entitled to,[4] reserved the right not to apply Articles 7(1) (mandatory rules of foreign countries) and 10(1)(e) (the consequences of nullity of a contract). Section 2(2) therefore states that these two provisions shall not have the force of law in the United Kingdom. The second is concerned with intra-United Kingdom disputes,[5] as where, for example, there is a trial in England of a dispute involving a Scotsman who contracted in Scotland with an Englishman to deliver goods to England. According to the Convention,[6] the United Kingdom was not bound to apply the rules in the Convention to such a case. However, section 2(3) provides that "the Convention shall apply in the case of conflicts between the laws of different parts of the United Kingdom". This is to be welcomed. To have to apply separate rules for intra-United Kingdom cases would have been an unnecessary complication.

The effect of implementation of the Rome Convention is that, for contracts made after the Convention came into force, the traditional common law rules on contract choice of law are largely replaced by the rules contained in the Convention.[7] Nevertheless, as will shortly be seen, the traditional common law rules will continue to be applied even to contracts made after the Convention came into force in a number of situations. English courts will therefore have to operate two different regimes for contract choice of law: for Convention cases (ie cases coming within the scope of the Convention) there are the Convention rules; for non-Convention cases (ie cases outside the scope of the Convention) there are the traditional common law rules.[8] This undoubted complication in the law could have been avoided if the 1990 Act had provided that the rules in the Rome Convention were to be applied to all contracts made after the Convention came into force, even in non-Convention cases, thereby assimilating the two sets of rules.[9]

(iii) Interpretation[10]

(a) Referrals to the Court Justice Two Protocols on interpretation of the Rome Convention by the Court of Justice were signed in Brussels in

20 Supra, p 280.
 1 S 2(1).
 2 S 3.
 3 Infra, pp 462–463.
 4 Art 22.
 5 Discussed infra, p 469.
 6 Art 19 (2).
 7 As regards statutes, eg the Unfair Contract Terms Act 1977, see infra, pp 500–502.
 8 See the 11th edn (1987) of this book, ch 18. The common law rules were subject to a small number of statutory provisions, ibid.
 9 See North in *Contract Conflicts* at p 12; Fletcher, *Conflict of Laws and European Community Law* (1982), p 155.
10 See Plender, paras 2.01–2.30.

1988.[11] The first Protocol, which is set out in a schedule to the 1990 Act, defines the scope of the jurisdiction of the Court of Justice and the conditions under which that jurisdiction is to be exercised. States accept the jurisdiction of the Court of Justice under this Protocol. The second Protocol confers powers on the Court of Justice to interpret the Rome Convention. The two Protocol system allows some Member States to proceed with allowing referrals to the Court of Justice ahead of other Member States, such as Ireland, which have internal problems relating to allowing such a reference. Neither Protocol has received the requisite number of ratifications, and so is not yet in force.[12]

There was considerable controversy over the whole question of referrals of interpretation to the Court of Justice, but there is no doubt that without this there would be a danger that the courts in each Contracting State would interpret the Convention differently, with the consequent risk that harmonisation of contract choice of law rules within the Community would not be achieved.[13] Two limitations on when a national court can request a preliminary ruling on interpretation are contained in the first Protocol. First, a court can only make such a request "if that court considers that a decision on the question is necessary to enable it to give judgment".[14] There is nothing to stop English courts from deciding that the meaning of the Convention is clear and a reference to the Court of Justice is not necessary. This is the same wording as that adopted in respect of referrals to the Court of Justice in cases of interpretation of the Brussels Convention on jurisdiction and the enforcement of judgments. The second limitation is in respect of the courts which can request a ruling from the Court of Justice. The House of Lords and other courts from which no further appeal is possible, and any court when acting as an appeal court, *may* request a preliminary ruling.[15] Judges at first instance can never so request.

It is noticeable that, in contrast to the Protocol on interpretation of the Brussels Convention,[16] this Protocol states that the specified courts *may* (rather than must) request a ruling if they consider that a decision is necessary to enable them to give judgment. The lack of compulsion on courts to make referrals to the Court of Justice is deliberate. Some Member States, including the United Kingdom, argued that provision for the Court of Justice to have jurisdiction in relation to interpretation of the Convention was undesirable.[17] Many international contracts which have nothing to do with England, nevertheless provide for trial in England and for English law to govern the contract. It was feared that foreign businessmen would, in future, opt for trial outside England and, indeed, outside the Community rather than face the prospect of a compulsory referral to the Court of Justice, which would delay the settlement of their dispute. The power to refer a question of interpretation was therefore made a discretionary one. In exercising this discretion national

11 OJ L48 of 20 February 1989. There is a Report by Professor Tizzano on the Protocols: OJ C219 of 3 September 1990.
12 Furthermore, the Contracts (Applicable Law) Act 1990 in so far as it deals with the first Protocol is not yet in force: SI 1991/707.
13 See Kohler (1982) 7 ELR 103 at 113; the opinion of the Commission of the European Community (1980) OJ L94.39.
14 Art 2.
15 Ibid.
16 Supra, p 281.
17 The Tizzano Report, op cit, sections 23 et seq.

courts can take into account any appropriate factor including the wishes of the parties, who may want a speedy outcome to the litigation.[18] The result is that there are likely to be fewer referrals to the Court of Justice under the Rome Convention than there have been under the Brussels Convention.[19]

There is also no doubt a third limitation on referrals to the Court of Justice, which is not spelt out in the first Protocol. The Court of Justice is concerned with interpretation of the Convention as harmonised European law,[20] and not with interpretation of purely national rules of private international law. Many of the cases on interpretation of the Rome Convention coming before the English courts will arise in the context of whether the court has jurisdiction under Order 11 of the Rules of the Supreme Court.[1] The Court of Justice may well refuse to accept a reference on interpretation of the Convention from the English courts in such a case.[2] The same is doubtless the case in relation to a reference on interpretation arising out of an intra-United Kingdom dispute.

(b) The principles and decisions laid down by the Court of Justice Section 3(1) of the 1990 Act provides that, where the meaning of the Convention[3] is not referred to the Court of Justice, it must be determined "in accordance with the principles laid down by, and any relevant decision of [that Court]".[4] This section adopts the same wording employed in the Civil Jurisdiction and Judgments Act 1982 in relation to interpretation of the Brussels Convention. The effect of section 3(1) is that the English courts have to act in accordance with two different types of authority: first, any relevant decisions of the Court of Justice; second, the principles laid down by the Court of Justice.

If the Court of Justice has previously given a decision on the provision in issue, this must be followed. A relevant decision for these purposes could include one of the decisions of the Court of Justice discussing the Rome Convention[5] in a jurisdiction case on a reference under the Protocol on interpretation of the Brussels Convention. Judicial notice must be taken of any relevant decisions of, or expression of opinion by, the Court of Justice.[6] However, the provision which is in issue may not have been previously discussed by the Court of Justice. In this situation, the English courts must act in accordance with the principles of interpretation previously laid down by the Court of Justice. As yet there have been no referrals under the 1988 Protocol on interpretation of the Rome Convention. This raises two questions. What principles is the Court of Justice likely to apply in relation to interpretation of the Rome Convention? What are the English courts to do in the meantime?

The Court of Justice is likely to apply the same general principles of interpretation to the Rome Convention as it applies to other areas of law.

---

18 Ibid, section 34.
19 See generally Hansard (HL) 24 April 1990 vol 518, col 440.
20 See Art 18, discussed infra, p 464.
1 See Ord 11, r 1 (1)(d)(iii), discussed supra, pp 197–198.
2 But see Plender paras 2.28–2.30. It presumably would accept a reference on the issue of whether Ord 11 RSC is a procedural rule and thus excluded from the scope of the Convention.
3 And the Luxembourg (Greek Accession) Convention and Brussels Protocol.
4 This section is not yet in force.
5 See, eg, Case 133/81 *Ivenel v Schwab* [1982] ECR 1891, [1983] 1 CMLR 538, discussed supra, pp 297–298; Case 9/87 *SPRL Arcado v SA Haviland* [1988] ECR 1539, discussed supra, pp 296–297.
6 S 3(2) Contracts (Applicable Law) Act 1990. This provision is not yet in force.

For example, the meaning of a provision is ascertained in the light of its purpose rather than by looking at its literal meaning. More importantly, the Court of Justice has laid down certain general principles of interpretation in relation to the Brussels Convention.[7] The same principles are likely to be applied by the Court of Justice in relation to another Community Convention which is also concerned with the unification of rules of private international law. The English courts should apply the principles that the Court of Justice is likely to apply. Indeed, the wording of section 3(1) is wide enough to compel the English courts to act in accordance with general principles of interpretation laid down by the Court of Justice in other contexts.

(c) The principle of uniform interpretation One principle that the Court of Justice and national courts are bound to follow is the principle of uniform interpretation, which is set out in the Convention itself. Article 18[8] provides that "In the interpretation and application of the preceding uniform rules, regard shall be had to their international character and to the desirability of achieving uniformity in their interpretation and application". This means that courts should not define concepts by reference to national systems, but instead give independent community meanings to the terms used in the Convention. This provision also has important consequences when it comes to aids to interpretation, which will now be considered.

(d) Aids to interpretation

(i) The Giuliano and Lagarde Report[9]
The Rome Convention is accompanied by the Giuliano and Lagarde Report, which is a commentary by members of the Working Group responsible for drafting the Convention. Section 3(3) of the 1990 Act allows this Report, and the Tizzano Report on the 1988 Protocols on interpretation,[10] to be considered by English courts in ascertaining the meaning or effect of any provisions in the Rome Convention or first Protocol on interpretation. This follows the pattern of the Civil Jurisdiction and Judgments Act 1982, which allowed the Jenard and Schlosser Reports to be considered by English courts when interpreting the new European Community law on jurisdiction and enforcement of judgments.[11] The latter Reports have been constantly referred to by the Court of Justice and national courts when interpreting the Brussels Convention. No doubt the Giuliano and Lagarde Report will be of the same high authority when it comes to interpretation of the Rome Convention.

(ii) Other matters which under English law can be used in interpretation of a Convention
Section 3(3) states that allowing the courts to refer to the Giuliano and Lagarde Report is without prejudice to any practice as to other matters which may be considered. This is the result of an amendment to the Act during its passage through the Lords, when concern was expressed that it should be

---

7 Supra, pp 282–283.
8 The same provision is to be found in Art 7 of the United Nations Convention on Contracts for the International Sale of Goods of 1980.
9 OJ C282 of 31 October 1980.
10 OJ C219 of 3 September 1990.
11 Supra p 283.

made clear that textbook commentaries on the Act could be considered by the courts.[12]

(iii) The decisions of Continental courts

Whatever the normal attitude of English judges towards the decisions of Continental courts, in this context foreign decisions on interpretation of the Rome Convention are of persuasive authority. Article 18 (uniformity of interpretation) enables parties to rely on foreign decisions.[13] This will include the decisions of Continental courts in Member States which have had the Convention as part of their own private international law rules prior to its coming into effect,[14] as well as decisions subsequent to this.

(iv) Texts in other languages

The 1990 Act appears to give the force of law[15] to the Convention in its different language texts, all of which are equally authentic,[16] rather than to the English text, which is merely set out in the Act for ease of reference. Moreover, there is Court of Justice authority to the effect that courts of Member States should always be prepared to consider the texts of the Brussels Convention in other languages.[17] The same principle must apply in relation to the Rome Convention.

(v) The Brussels Convention

It has already been mentioned[18] that the effect of section 3(1) is to oblige English courts to follow decisions on interpretation of the Brussels Convention which are relevant to interpretation of the Rome Convention. The most obvious example is the decision in *Ivenel v Schwab*,[19] which discusses the Rome Convention. Going beyond this, some of the provisions in the Rome Convention use the same concepts as,[20] or are even lifted word for word from,[1] the Brussels Convention. In such a situation, it is only right and proper that the earlier interpretation of this concept or term under the Brussels Convention should be looked at, and, unless there is a good reason to the contrary, followed.

(vi) The traditional common law rules

Much of the Convention appears familiar to English lawyers and there may be a temptation to resort to the old common law rules when interpreting the Convention.[2] However, this is not usually justified and would be a dangerous habit to get into. The provisions in the Convention are not normally based

---

12 Hansard (HL) 5 April 1990 vol 517, cols 1541–1542.
13 The Giuliano and Lagarde Report at p 38.
14 See eg the decisions of courts in the Netherlands: *Compagnie Europeenne Des Petroles SA v Sensor Nederland BV* [1983] 22 ILM 66; *Machinale Glasfabriek De Maas BV v Emaillerie* [1985] 2 CMLR 281; *Buenaventura v Ocean Trade Company* [1984] ECC 183.
15 S 2.
16 See Art 33.
17 Case 150/80 *Elefanten Schuh GmbH v Jacqmain* [1981] ECR 1671, [1982] 3 CMLR 1. See also *Newtherapeutics Ltd v Katz* [1991] ch 226 at 243–245.
18 Supra, p 463.
19 Case 133/81 [1982] ECR 1891, [1983] 1 CMLR 538; discussed supra pp 297–298.
20 See, eg, the concept of a contractual obligation used in Art 1(1) of the Rome Convention and Art 5(1) of the Brussels Convention; discussed supra pp 296–297.
 1 See, eg, Art 5 (certain consumer contracts) of the Rome Convention which borrows from Art 13 of the Brussels Convention, discussed supra, p 308.
 2 This is advocated by the Lord Chancellor, Hansard (HL) 15 Feb 1990 vol 515, col 1489.

on English law or on that of any other country's national law but on a common core of ideas used in Community countries. A rule which may appear at first sight to be the same as the common law rule it has replaced may turn out, on closer examination, to be different in some respect.[3] The aim of uniformity of interpretation throughout the Community will not be achieved if English courts interpret the Convention as a codification of the proper law of the contract. Article 18 (uniform interpretation) serves as a reminder that national courts should not act in this way.[4]

(b) WHEN DOES THE CONVENTION APPLY?

The Convention applies to matters coming within its scope, and it has universal application, ie it applies equally to contracts having no connection with a European Community Contracting State and to contracts with such a connection. Before turning to examine in detail these two aspects of the application of the Convention, four general points need to be made. First, the Convention does not have retrospective effect.[5] It only applies in a Contracting State to contracts made after the Convention has entered into force in that State (1 April 1991 in the case of the United Kingdom); the traditional common law rules will continue to apply to contracts made before the Convention has entered into force. Second, the Convention does not prejudice the application of other international conventions to which a Contracting State is a party, or becomes a party.[6] This means, for example, that, as far as the United Kingdom is concerned, carriage of goods by sea will still be dealt with by the Hague–Visby Rules, implemented by the Carriage of Goods by Sea Act 1971, and not by the Rome Convention. Third, acts of the institutions of the European Communities, for example Community Regulations, laying down choice of law rules relating to contractual obligations, take precedence over the Convention.[7] If, for example, at some future date a Regulation is passed dealing with choice of law for employment contracts, United Kingdom courts will have to apply the choice of law rules in the Regulation rather than the provisions on employment contracts contained in the Rome Convention. Fourth, Contracting States are allowed to introduce unilaterally choice of law rules inconsistent with those contained in the Convention.[8] However, they can only do so in regard to a particular category of contract, for example contracts made by travel agents. Furthermore a process of informing and consulting with other Contracting States must be gone through first.

(i) The scope of the Convention

(a) **Contractual obligations in any situation involving a choice between the laws of different countries** Article 1(1) states that "The rules of this Convention shall apply to contractual obligations in any situation involving a choice between the laws of different countries". There are two separate requirements

---

3 See, eg, inferred choice of the applicable law, discussed infra, pp 484–486.
4 See the Giuliano and Lagarde Report, at p 38.
5 Art 17.
6 Art 21, discussed infra, p 521.
7 Art 20.
8 Art 23. See also Art 24.

under this provision. First, the obligation must be contractual. Second, there must be a choice of law problem.

(i) A contractual obligation

The Convention does not cover, for example, tortious obligations, property rights and intellectual property rights.[9] The position in relation to quasi-contract is more complicated. At first sight the Convention appears to encompass this matter. The Convention contains a provision dealing with "the consequences of nullity of the contract",[10] which under English law is regarded as being a quasi-contractual issue. However, its presence in the Convention is due to the fact that this issue is regarded by other Member States as being contractual. More importantly, a preliminary draft of the Convention[11] which dealt with both contractual and non-contractual obligations included in its provisions on non-contractual obligations a provision dealing with quasi-contract. Issues in quasi-contract should therefore be regarded as being outside the scope of the Convention.[12]

This still leaves the problem of classification. One Contracting State may classify an obligation as being contractual in circumstances where another State would classify it as being tortious. This problem can be avoided if a community meaning is given to the concept of a contractual obligation. Case law on the interpretation of the Brussels Convention supports this. The Court of Justice has consistently given a community meaning to provisions on the scope of the Brussels Convention. In *SPRL Arcado v SA Haviland*[13] the Court of Justice examined the concept of a matter relating to a contract under Article 5(1) of the Brussels Convention (the contract head of special jurisdiction), and held that it was to be given an independent community meaning. A claim for compensation for the wrongful repudiation of a commercial agency agreement was held to be within the meaning of this concept as the basis for such compensation was the failure to comply with a contractual obligation. It was pointed out[14] that the Rome Convention has a specific provision dealing with the applicable law in relation to the consequences of breach.[15]

(ii) A choice between the laws of different countries[16]

A preliminary draft of the Convention stated that it only applied "in situations of an international character".[17] This requirement was criticised[18] for the definitional problems it created, and it was replaced by the more straightforward requirement that there be a situation involving a choice between the laws of different countries. As far as the United Kingdom is concerned this merely makes explicit what was implicit under the traditional

9 See the Giuliano and Lagarde Report, p 10. However, a *contractual obligation* in respect of an intellectual property right, eg a licensing agreement, would presumably come within the scope of the Convention. There was an unsuccessful attempt in the House of Lords to amend the 1990 Act to exclude this: Hansard (HL) 5 April 1990 vol 517, cols 1544–1547.
10 Art 10 (1)(e); discussed infra, pp 517–518, and supra, p 461.
11 Art 13; see generally, Collier in *Harmonisation of Private International Law by the EEC* (ed Lipstein) at 81 et seq.
12 See *Kleinwort Benson Ltd v Glasgow City Council* (1992) Times, 17 March.
13 Case 9/87 [1988] ECR 1539; for the jurisdictional aspects of the case, see supra, p 296.
14 At p 1555.
15 Art 10 (1)(c); discussed infra, pp 516–517.
16 See generally Lando in *Harmonisation of Private International Law by the EEC* (ed Lipstein) p 15; (1987) 24 CMLR 159 at 163–164; Diamond (1986) IV Hague Recueil 236 at 248–251; Plender, paras 3.01–3.03, 3.11–3.18.
17 Art 1 of the preliminary draft Convention.
18 See, eg, Collins (1976) 25 ICLQ 35 at 41.

common law rules on contract choice of law. However, the fact that this is now spelt out in statutory form means that some attention needs to be given to this point. Under English private international law a choice of law problem exists whenever the court is faced with a dispute that contains a foreign element.[19] With a contractual dispute, typical examples of a foreign element are as follows: one of the parties to the contract is a foreign national or is habitually resident abroad; the contract is concluded abroad; the contract is to be performed by one of the parties abroad. In such cases the foreign country has a claim to have its law applied, and the uniform rules in the Convention are intended to apply.

The position is more difficult if the court is faced with a dispute involving a foreign element, but in respect of what is an essentially domestic contract. This can arise in two different types of case. The first is where, for example, there is a purely German contract, which is the subject of trial in England, subsequent to the defendant having moved his business to England after concluding the contract. The situation involves a foreign element in that one of the parties now carries on his business here. However, what is lacking is any relevant connection with a country other than Germany of the sort which would give that other country's law a claim to be applied.[20] Nonetheless, it is desirable that such cases come within the Convention.[1] The object of the Convention of achieving harmonisation of choice of law rules in contract is most likely to be attained if the scope of the Convention is given as wide an interpretation as possible. The above example should therefore be regarded as one involving a choice between the laws of different countries. The second type of case is where there is, for example, a purely English contract, but the parties have agreed that French law shall govern the contract. It is implicit from the terms of Article 3(3)[2] that the Convention will apply in this situation. However, the Convention will not apply if there is a purely English contract which merely incorporates French law by, for example, setting out verbatim a provision of French law as a term of the contract.[3]

There is another problem in relation to the requirement that there is "a choice between the laws of different countries" which is less easily solved. Under English law, if foreign law is not pleaded or proved the court gives a decision according to English law.[4] The courts are free to apply this rule in relation to the Rome Convention because matters of evidence and procedure are excluded from the scope of the Convention.[5] If the English court is going automatically to apply English law it is arguable that this is not a situation involving a choice between the laws of different countries. However, the purpose of the Convention is not going to be met if the English courts allow the parties to side-step the uniform rules contained therein by a simple omission to plead and prove foreign law. It would therefore be better if this sort of case was regarded as coming within the Convention.[6]

---

19 Supra, pp 3 et seq.
20 See the Giuliano and Lagarde Report, at p 10, which presupposes the existence of such a claim.
 1 See Lando, op cit, at pp 15–17. Diamond has no doubts that such cases come within it: op cit, pp 250–251.
 2 Discussed infra, pp 480–482.
 3 Incorporation of foreign law is discussed infra, pp 483–484.
 4 Supra, pp 107 et seq.
 5 Art 1 (2)(h), see infra pp 473–474.
 6 There are problems then of whether the parties have made a choice of the applicable law, infra pp 479–480.

The choice must be between the laws of different *countries*. A country is defined under the Convention in the normal private international law sense as a territorial unit with its own rules of law, in this case relating to contractual obligations.[7] A French court, for example, will have to apply English law, or Scots, or Northern Ireland law under the Convention, even though the United Kingdom is the Contracting State to the Convention. Similarly, an English court may have to apply, for example, Ontario or New South Wales law under the Convention. Indeed, the Convention can apply to an interstate dispute involving connections with the "countries" of California and New York, provided that trial takes place in a Contracting State to the Convention. However, the Convention makes it clear that it is for the United Kingdom to decide whether it wants to apply the rules in the Convention to intra-United Kingdom disputes. It is certainly not bound to do so,[8] but the obvious inconvenience of having a different regime for intra-United Kingdom contractual disputes from all other cases has led to a provision in the Contracts (Applicable Law) Act 1990 applying the Convention to such disputes.[9] The upshot is that England, Scotland and Northern Ireland are separate countries for the purposes of the Convention, even in intra-United Kingdom disputes.

(b) Exclusions[10] Article 1 (paragraphs 2–4) excludes a wide variety of matters from the scope of the Convention. These matters can be put into three main categories. First and foremost, it excludes certain commercial contracts such as arbitration agreements and certain contracts of insurance. Second, it excludes non-commercial contracts, such as agreements to make wills and agreements to pay maintenance. Third, it excludes certain matters which do not involve contract choice of law, such as evidence and procedure, or under the law of some Member States do not involve contract choice of law, such as negotiable instruments and the issue of capacity to contract. The matters excluded from the scope of the convention, and the reasons for their exclusion, will now be examined, in the order in which they are set out in the Convention. These are as follows:

(i) Questions involving the status or legal capacity of natural persons, without prejudice to Article 11[11]
This phrase is a familiar one, and is to be found in the list of exclusions from the Brussels Convention.[12] Questions of status are clearly outside the scope of a Convention concerned with contract choice of law, and do not need expressly to be excluded. The exclusion of legal capacity is more controversial. To common lawyers capacity to contract is a matter falling squarely within the ambit of rules on contract choice of law. But to civil lawyers this is regarded as a matter relating to status, hence its exclusion from the Convention.[13] This particular exclusion only relates to natural persons. The exclusion of the legal capacity of corporations is dealt with under a separate

---

7 Art 19(1).
8 Art 19(2).
9 S 2(3).
10 See Plender, paras 4.01–4.53.
11 Art 1(2)(a).
12 Supra, pp 288–289.
13 See North in *Contract Conflicts*, p 10.

provision.[14] The result of the exclusion is that national courts are left to apply their traditional rules of private international law to the issue of capacity to contract; in England's case this will be the traditional common law rules. However, there is one exception to this. The exclusion of capacity to contract is subject to Article 11 of the Convention, which is a fairly narrow rule designed to protect a party who contracts with a natural person under an incapacity from being caught unawares by this. The English common law rules on capacity to contract, and Article 11, will be examined later on in this chapter in the section on particular issues.[15]

(ii) Contractual obligations relating to:
- *wills and succession,*
- *rights in property arising out of a matrimonial relationship,*
- *rights and duties arising out of a family relationship, parentage, marriage or affinity, including maintenance obligations in respect of children who are not legitimate*[16]

This provision is concerned with non-commercial contracts. Indeed, most disputes relating to the matters in (ii) will not even involve contractual obligations. For example, disputes in relation to wills are not normally contractual, but are concerned with issues such as the validity of the will. This provision makes it clear that, in the rare cases which raise contractual obligations, for example an agreement to make a will, the Convention will not apply.

The phrases "wills and succession" and "rights in property arising out of a matrimonial relationship" are to be found amongst the list of exclusions from the scope of the Brussels Convention,[17] and their meaning has been fully discussed in that context. There is no need under the Rome Convention to distinguish between rights in property arising out of a matrimonial relationship and maintenance since, as we will see next, the latter is also normally excluded from the scope of the Convention.

The third exclusion under (ii), "rights and duties arising out of a family relationship etc.", does not feature in the Brussels Convention and was intended to ensure that contractual obligations relating to any family law matter were excluded from the Convention.[18] In particular, it normally excludes maintenance obligations, which are included within the Brussels Convention.[19] However, the exclusion of maintenance is not all-embracing. The Giuliano and Lagarde Report[20] appears to distinguish between, on the one hand, obligations to pay maintenance which are imposed by law in respect of which there is also an agreement to pay (these are excluded from the scope of the Convention), and, on the other hand, purely contractual obligations to do so (these are within the scope of the Convention). Thus the case of a father who is under a legal obligation to maintain his children after a divorce, but who also agrees to maintain them, although involving a contractual obligation, is excluded from the scope of the Convention. In contrast to this, if a person who is not under a legal obligation to provide

14 Art 1(2)(e), discussed infra, p 472.
15 Infra, pp 510–513.
16 Art 1(2)(b).
17 Art 1(1) of the Brussels Convention; discussed supra pp 288–289.
18 The Giuliano and Lagarde Report, at p 10.
19 See Art 5(2) of the Brussels Convention, discussed supra, pp 299–300.
20 At p 10.

maintenance for a member of the family, nonetheless agrees to do so, as where a child agrees to maintain a parent, this would fall within the scope of the Convention.

(iii) Obligations arising under bills of exchange, cheques and promissory notes and other negotiable instruments to the extent that the obligations under such other negotiable instruments arise out of their negotiable character[1]

Under English law negotiable instruments involve contractual obligations, but have long been subject to special rules, including those contained in the Bills of Exchange Act 1882, rather than being governed by the proper law of the contract.[2] The effect of the exclusion of negotiable instruments from the Convention is to preserve these special rules. The exclusion applies to bills of exchange, cheques and promissory notes, each of which category is well known to English lawyers. It also applies to "other negotiable instruments to the extent that the obligations under such other negotiable instruments arise out of their negotiable character". "Other negotiable instruments" is not defined under the Convention, and Contracting States may have different ideas on whether an instrument is negotiable. However, the Giuliano and Lagarde Report[3] states that it is for the private international law of the forum to determine whether a document is to be characterised as being negotiable. If the transfer takes place in England, the instrument is negotiable if English mercantile custom or a statute so provides. Examples of instruments which are negotiable in England include bonds issued by foreign governments and debentures issued to bearer by English companies. On the other hand, a bill of lading which is transferred in England is not negotiable, and is therefore within the scope of the Convention.

Even if it can be shown that what is involved is a negotiable instrument other than a bill of exchange, cheque or promissory note, the exclusion is limited to cases in which the obligation arises out of the negotiable character of the instrument. This would cover a dispute where, for example, an acceptor of the instrument wants payment but the other party refuses, alleging that the acceptor is not a holder in due course of the instrument. Such a dispute would be outside the scope of the Convention. On the other hand, contracts for the issue of, eg, Government bonds or for purchase/sale of such bonds are not concerned with the negotiable character of the instrument, and are thus within the scope of the Convention.[4]

(iv) Arbitration agreements and agreements on the choice of court[5]

The exclusion of arbitration agreements and agreements on the choice of court was probably the most controversial of the exclusions from the Convention, with the United Kingdom delegation arguing unsuccessfully that such agreements should be subject to the rules contained in the Convention.[6] The exclusion applies not only to arbitration or choice of jurisdiction agreements, ie agreements whose sole or main purpose is to provide for arbitration or a place of trial for a particular dispute, but also to arbitration or choice of jurisdiction clauses contained within a contract, which under English law are themselves regarded as separate agreements. However, when an

---

1 Art 1(2)(c). See the Giuliano and Lagarde Report, at p 11.
2 Infra, pp 522–527.
3 At p 11.
4 Ibid.
5 Art 1(2)(d).
6 For the reasons for this see infra, p 472.

arbitration or choice of jurisdiction clause is excluded,[7] this only affects the clause itself; the remaining clauses in the contract will be within the scope of the Convention and judges and arbitrators will have to apply the rules under the Convention to them. This exclusion obviously relates to any choice of law issues that arise with regard to arbitration agreements and agreements on the choice of court: such as the formation, validity and effects of such agreements. It is also said to relate to any procedural questions that arise in relation to the arbitration.[8]

The result of the exclusion is that national courts will continue to apply their own rules of private international law to arbitration agreements and agreements on the choice of court. In England's case this means the traditional common law rules. Contracts will have to be split up so that a question, for example, of interpretation of a choice of jurisdiction clause will have to be determined under the traditional common law rules, whereas the rest of the contract will be governed by the rules applicable under the Convention. This can lead to different laws governing the agreement on arbitration/choice of court and the rest of the contract.[9] One could end up with a contract which is void according to the rules on the applicable law contained in the Convention, but which contains an arbitration agreement which is valid according to its proper law. It was in order to avoid such splitting of the contract that the United Kingdom argued that arbitration and choice of jurisdiction agreements should not be excluded from the scope of the Convention.

(v) Questions governed by the law of companies and other bodies corporate or unincorporate such as the creation, by registration or otherwise, legal capacity, internal organisation or winding up of companies and other bodies corporate or unincorporate and the personal liability of officers and members as such for the obligations of the company or body[10]

This provision clarifies the point that, if contractual matters are raised in a company law context, they fall outside the scope of the Convention. Examples of matters excluded by this provision are the contract which under English law is contained in the memorandum and articles of association of a company, and a shareholders' agreement to wind up a company. The legal capacity of a company to contract is also excluded from the scope of the Convention.[11] On the other hand, an agreement by promoters to form a company is apparently not excluded from the scope of the Convention.[12] This is presumably on the basis that this is a purely contractual matter and is not governed by company law.

(vi) The question whether an agent is able to bind a principal, or an organ to bind a company or body corporate or unincorporate, to a third party[13]

The exclusion is only concerned with the relationship between a principal

---

. 7 Nonetheless, according to the Giuliano and Lagarde Report, at p 12, the clause remains relevant to the ascertainment of the applicable law under Art 3(1), see infra, pp 484–486.
8 The Giuliano and Lagarde Report, at p 12.
9 See Lipstein in *Harmonisation of Private International Law by the EEC* (ed Lipstein) p 3.
10 Art 1(2)(e); the Giuliano and Lagarde Report, at p 12.
11 This is a total exclusion. For an example of a case raising this issue see *Janred Properties Ltd v Ente Nazionale Italiano per il Turismo* [1989] 2 All ER 444. Cf the position of natural persons under an incapacity—Art 11 may apply, on which see infra, pp 512–513.
12 The Giuliano and Lagarde Report, p 12.
13 Art 1(2)(f). For criticism see Lasok and Stone, *Conflict of Laws in the European Community* (1987), p 354.

and a third party, and is confined to the specific question of whether the principal is bound vis à vis third parties by the acts of the agent.[14] It follows that, for example, a contractual dispute between the principal and agent arising out of the contract of agency is not excluded. The exclusion is therefore a narrow one. However, it does encompass the question of whether an organ of a company can bind the company. This raises the question of ultra vires, which under English law is a question of company law. The exclusion has been explained[15] on the basis that the principle of freedom of contract, which is deeply enshrined in the Convention's rules on the applicable law,[16] is difficult to accept in relation to the matter excluded. As far as English law is concerned the effect of the exclusion is the retention of the common law rule under which the proper law of the contract concluded between the agent and third party governs the question of whether the principal is bound vis à vis third parties by the acts of the agent.

(vii) The constitution of trusts and the relationship between settlors, trustees and beneficiaries[17]
The English concept of a trust is said to define the subject matter of this exception.[18] This raises the question of why this exclusion of the common law trust was introduced. It is presumably because under English law the constitution of trusts and the relationship between trustee/beneficiary and settlor/trustee are not based on contract. The exclusion is for the sake of clarity. There are Continental equivalents of a trust which are contractual in origin and thus appear to come within the Convention. However, these will also be excluded if they exhibit the same characteristics as a common law trust.[19] It is noticeable that the exclusion does not extend to trust property, although this can in fact raise contractual problems. For example, a trustee could invest in property abroad and could then be sued in contract by the vendor of the property. This situation appears to come within the scope of the Convention.

(viii) Evidence and procedure, without prejudice to Article 14[20]
This provision excludes two matters, procedure and evidence. The exclusion of evidence is not total, but is subject to Article 14,[1] which subjects two specific evidential matters, the burden of proof (in so far as this raises rules of substance) and proving a contract, to the rules under the Convention. The exclusion of evidence and procedure was said by the Giuliano and Lagarde Report to require no comment.[2] However, two obvious questions need to be asked. First, why were these matters expressly excluded from the scope of the Convention? Presumably, this is just for the sake of clarity. Procedural and evidential matters would not appear to come within the scope of a Convention which is concerned with contract choice of law (a matter of substance) and therefore do not need expressly to be excluded. Second, there

14 The Giuliano and Lagarde Report, p 13.
15 Ibid.
16 Infra, pp 476–479.
17 Art 1(2)(g). For trusts generally in private international law see infra, ch 35.
18 The Giuliano and Lagarde Report, p 13.
19 Ibid.
20 Art 1(2)(h).
1 Discussed supra, pp 82, 85.
2 At p 38.

is the vital question of when a matter is to be classified as being one of procedure. Procedure is a very different matter from the other matters excluded in that it involves a potential escape device, ie if you classify a matter as being purely procedural you escape from the choice of law rules under the Convention. National courts are likely to resort to their own traditional ideas of what is a procedural matter. However, English courts cannot automatically assume that the classifications which they have adopted in the past will continue to be appropriate under the Convention. For example, the question of whether a contract has to be in writing was classified at common law as being one of procedure. Under the Convention, seemingly, it is to be regarded as a matter of substance raising an issue of formal validity of the contract.[3] The danger of different States classifying the same matter differently can be avoided by adherence to the principle of uniform interpretation. Once it has been decided that the issue is one of evidence or procedure, the effect of the exclusion is that this issue is left to be governed by the forum's rules on private international law. Under English private international law all procedural matters (including evidence) are automatically a matter for the law of the forum.[4]

(ix) Insurance[5]

Finally, certain contracts of insurance are excluded from the scope of the Convention. This is an important exclusion, involving a common type of commercial contract. However, the exclusion is only in respect of contracts of insurance which cover risks situated in the territories of the Member States of the European Community. In order to determine whether a risk is situated in the European Community the court applies its internal law, which means its internal domestic law and not its private international law.[6] The exclusion does not apply to contracts of reinsurance.[7] In so far as insurance comes within the Convention, there are special rules in relation to consumer contracts,[8] which include contracts for the provision of services such as insurance. The exclusion is explained by the fact that it was intended that there should be community Directives containing special choice of law rules for the insurance of risks situated within the European Community. These Directives have now been issued.[9] Contracts of insurance, in so far as they are excluded from the scope of the Convention and not covered by other European Community rules, will be subject to the traditional common law rules,[10] according to which the proper law of the contract is applied, but subject to special rules for ascertaining the objective proper law.

3   The Giuliano and Lagarde Report, at p 31; infra, p 507.
4   Supra, pp 74–75.
5   Art 1(3).
6   Art 1(3); the Giuliano and Lagarde Report, at p 13. For the determination of where a risk is situated see Art 2(d) of Directive 88/357, (1988) OJ L172 of 4 July.
7   Art 1(4). See generally Lasok and Stone, *Conflict of Laws in the European Community* (1987) who argue that there should be special rules for reinsurance, pp 385–386.
8   See Art 5; discussed infra, pp 495–496.
9   See Directives 88/357, (1988) OJ L172 of 4 July; 90/619 (1990) OJ L330 of 8 Nov; discussed in Plender, paras 4.49–4.53. See also the Law Com and Scottish Law Com Report on the Choice of Law Rules in the Draft Non-Life Insurance Services Directive, 11 April 1979. For criticism of the insurance exclusion see North in *Contract Conflicts*, p 11.
10 See Dicey and Morris, pp 1289–1296.

(ii) The universal application of the Convention

The Rome Convention is intended to be of universal or world wide application, ie it applies regardless of whether the contract has any connection with a European Community Contracting State.[11] In particular, there is no need for either party to the contract to be domiciled or resident in a European Community Contracting State. The only thing that matters is that the dispute is tried in a Contracting State to the Convention. Thus a contractual dispute between a New York resident and an Ontario resident which is tried before the Commercial Court in England will be subject to the Convention. This avoids the need to distinguish for choice of law purposes between Contracting States and non-Contracting States, a distinction which would be particularly difficult to apply to contracts which involve connections with both a Contracting and a non-Contracting State.[12]

Article 2[13] provides that

> Any law specified by this Convention shall be applied whether or not it is the law of a Contracting State.

This provision makes it clear that if the uniform rules under the Convention point, for example, to Japanese law as the law governing the contract the courts of Contracting States will apply that country's law, even though Japan is not a Contracting State to the Convention. However, Article 2 only deals with one aspect of the universal application of the rules in the Convention. It says nothing about whether the situation or the parties must have a connection with a Contracting State. It is the Giuliano and Lagarde Report[14] which makes it clear that the Convention is intended to have universal application and, in particular, will apply to nationals of third States and to persons domiciled or resident therein.[15]

(c) THE APPLICABLE LAW

The provisions on the applicable law are at the heart of the Convention. A basic distinction is drawn between the situation where the law is chosen by the parties and the situation where the applicable law is ascertained in the absence of choice. Choice is concerned with the actual intentions of the parties (either expressed by the parties or inferred by the court) and absence of choice requires reference to objective connections localising the contract. The applicable law under the Convention, whether chosen or not, refers to the domestic law of the country in question, and there is no place for the doctrine of renvoi.[16] It is presupposed that there has to be an applicable law at the time when the contract is concluded.[17] The position was the same under the common law rules. This led to the rejection of the concept of a "floating" proper law, ie a proper law which was non-existent at the time when the contract was made but which was crystallised later on by the unilateral act

---

11 See the Solicitor-General in Hansard (HC) Second Reading Committee 20 June 1990, col 4.
12 Lagarde (1981) 22 Virginia J of Int Law 91 at 93.
13 See the Giuliano and Lagarde Report, p 13.
14 At pp 8, 13.
15 See the unsuccessful attempt to amend the 1990 Act so as to limit it to parties habitually resident in a Contracting State: Hansard (HL) 15 February 1990 vol 515 cols 1474–1480.
16 Art 15.
17 See Arts 3(2) and 4(2).

of one of the parties.[18] The position will be the same under the Convention. However, the Convention does allow the parties to vary their choice during the subsequent life of the contract.[19]

(i) The law is chosen by the parties

Any reference to choice of the applicable law raises a number of points which will be examined under the following headings: freedom of choice; limitations on choice; express choice; inferred choice; consent to choice.

(a) Freedom of choice

(i) The basic principle

Article 3 is entitled "Freedom of choice", and paragraph (1) sets out the basic principle that "a contract shall be governed by the law chosen by the parties". The parties' freedom to choose the governing law has been accepted in all the Member States of the Community for many years.[20] In the United Kingdom the philosophical origin of this freedom is to be found in the fidelity of the Victorian judges to the Benthamite dogma of laissez-faire,[1] although authority for allowing the parties expressly to select the governing law predates this.[2] In more modern policy terms, party automony provides the certainty and predictability which are essential in commercial matters. The philosophy of freedom of choice underlies not only the basic principle of allowing the parties to choose the law governing the contract but also some of the more detailed provisions relating to choice. Parties are given the freedom to pick and choose the applicable law so that it governs the whole or merely part of the contract. The parties are free to exercise their choice at any time and to vary their choice. These freedoms will now be examined.

(ii) Dépecage[3]

The last sentence of Article 3(1) provides that

> By their choice the parties can select the law applicable to the whole or a part only of the contract.

The parties are given the freedom to pick and choose (dépecage) the applicable law and thereby sever the contract.[4] The parties can choose different laws for different parts of the contract. Thus there could be an express choice of French law to govern one part, but an express choice of German law to govern the rest of the contract. The choice can be expressed by the parties or inferred by the court. If the parties choose different laws for different parts of the contract the choices must be logically consistent, ie they "must relate to elements in the contract which can be governed by different laws without

---

18 *Armar Shipping Co Ltd v Caisse Algerienne* [1981] 1 WLR 207 at 215–216; *Astro Venturoso Compania Naviera v Hellenic Shipyards SA, The Mariannina* [1983] 1 Lloyd's Rep 12 at 15; *E I Du Pont de Nemours & Co v Agnew and Kerr* [1987] 2 Lloyd's Rep 585 at 592.
19 Art 3(2); discussed infra, pp 478–479.
20 See the Giuliano and Lagarde Report, pp 15–16; Lando (1987) 24 CMLR 159 at 171–179.
1 Graveson, *Lectures on the Conflict of Laws and International Contracts* (1951), pp 6–8.
2 See *Gienar v Meyer* (1796) 2 Hy Bl 603.
3 See generally supra, pp 56–57. See in relation to the Rome Convention: Morse, (1982) 2 Yearbook of European Law 107, pp 117–119.
4 The same freedom is to be found in relation to trusts under Art 9 of the Hague Convention on the law applicable to trusts and on their recognition, implemented by the Recognition of Trusts Act 1987; see infra, p 885.

giving rise to contradiction".[5] The Giuliano and Lagarde Report gives two contrasting examples.[6] An index linking clause may be made subject to a law different from the rest of the contract. On the other hand, it was thought unlikely that repudiation of the contract for non-performance could be subjected to two different laws, one for the vendor and the other for the purchaser. If the chosen laws cannot be reconciled, both choices fail and the rules on the applicable law in the absence of choice[7] have to be used. The parties can choose a law to govern part of the contract but may exercise no choice in respect of the remainder of the contract. In this situation the applicable law for the remainder of the contract must be ascertained, again, by the rules on the applicable law in the absence of choice. The Working Group rejected the notion of a presumption that the law chosen for one part of the contract should govern the entirety.[8]

What is meant by *part* of the contract? Obviously this covers the separate clauses in a contract. Thus the parties can choose one law to govern a particular clause,[9] and a different law to govern other clauses. From the example given above relating to repudiation of the contract, it also appears that *part* can include a particular issue[10] relating to the contract. Accordingly, the parties can choose one law to govern the interpretation of the contract and a different law to govern its discharge. On the other hand, it seems from the same example that the parties are not free to take a single issue, such as repudiation of the contract, and to split this so that one law governs one party's rights and a different law governs the other party's rights. This is regarded as involving two choices which are logically inconsistent. Some contracts are, by their very nature, severable, for example a contract which turns out to consist of several independent contracts. Different laws can clearly be applied to these different contracts, without having to resort to the dépecage provision.[11]

The provision on dépecage probably does not represent a major change in the law as far as England is concerned. In *Forsikringsaktieselskapet Vesta v Butcher*[12] HOBHOUSE J held that, although a reinsurance contract was governed by English law, the inferred intention of the parties was that certain clauses in the contract were to be governed by Norwegian law.[13] Nonetheless, the clear statement in the Convention in relation to dépecage is to be welcomed, and it is likely that new awareness of the possibility of dépecage will lead to an increase in the number of cases in which the parties choose to sever the contract in this way.

---

5 The Giuliano and Lagarde Report, p 17.
6 Ibid.
7 See Art 4, discussed infra, pp 487–495.
8 The Giuliano and Lagarde Report, p 17.
9 Ibid.
10 This is the type of severing of the contract that "dépecage" usually refers to: see supra, pp 56–57. However, see Plender, para 5.13.
11 See, however, Art 4(1) which has a provision on dépecage in relation to contracts which are by their nature severable; infra, pp 488–489.
12 [1986] 2 All ER 488, affd in the Court of Appeal [1988] 3 WLR 565, and House of Lords [1989] AC 852, where the case was decided on the basis of a point of construction of an English contract, rather than on a choice of law point. See generally McLachlan (1990) 51 BYBIL 311. See also *Hamlyn & Co v Talisker Distillery* [1894] AC 202 at 207; *Re Helbert Wagg & Co Ltd's Claim* [1956] Ch 323 at 340.
13 At 505.

(iii) Timing of choice

The first sentence of Article 3(2) provides that:

> The parties may at any time agree to subject the contract to a law other than that
> which previously governed it, whether as a result of an earlier choice under this
> Article or of other provisions of this Convention.

The policy underlying this provision[14] is that of providing maximum freedom
as to when the parties can make their choice.[15] It can be made before the
contract is concluded, at the time of or even after the conclusion of the
contract. If the parties' choice is made for the first time after the conclusion
of the contract, then the applicable law at the time of the conclusion of the
contract will have to be determined by reference to the rules for determining
the applicable law in the absence of choice (Article 4). This law will apply
until the parties subsequently exercise their choice, which may involve a
variation in the applicable law.

(iv) Variation of choice[16]

The parties' freedom to vary the applicable law follows on logically from
their right to choose the applicable law at any time. For example, the parties
may have agreed at the time of contracting that Californian law shall govern
the contract. They have the freedom under Article 3(2) to agree subsequently[17]
that, instead, Japanese law shall govern the contract.[18] It is irrelevant that
Californian or Japanese law might not allow variation. Equally, at the time
the contract is made Luxembourg law may be applicable by virtue of the
rules on the applicable law in the absence of choice (Article 4). The parties
may subsequently agree that New York law shall govern. This subsequent
agreement involves an exercise of the parties' freedom of choice under Article
3(1) and so can be expressed or inferred.[19] If the variation is made during the
course of legal proceedings, it is for the forum's law of procedure to decide
the extent to which this is effective.[20] The rule on variation represents a
welcome change in English law, both in terms of clarifying the position and
in terms of the substance of the rule. Under the common law rules there was
a suggestion that, once the proper law had been determined at the time the
contract was made, it was then unchangeable during the life of the contract,[1]
although it was argued in this book that, in principle, variation should be
allowed.[2]

The Working Group recognised that there were certain dangers in allowing
a variation of the applicable law by the parties. The second sentence of Article
3(2) provides a safeguard in the following terms:

---

14 See the Giuliano and Lagarde Report, p 17.
15 This is referring to the parties' choice under Art 3(1), discussed infra, pp 483–486.
16 See North in *Multum Non Multa: Festshrift fur Kurt Lipstein* (1980) pp 205 et seq; Plender,
    paras 5.15–5.20; Diamond [1979] Current Legal Problems 155, 162–165, who argues variation
    should be a matter for the original governing law; Fletcher in *Conflict of Laws and European
    Community Law* (1982), at 160 argues it should be for both the original and the substitute
    governing laws.
17 For the situation where there is an agreement at the time the contract is made to vary the
    applicable law in the future see infra, p 483.
18 See generally Diamond (1986) IV Hague Recueil 236, 262–264.
19 See the Giuliano and Lagarde Report at p 18; cf Morse, op cit, p 120.
20 The Giuliano and Lagarde Report, p 18.
 1 *Armar Shipping Co Ltd v Caisse Algerienne* [1981] 1 All ER 498, [1981] 1 WLR 207; cf *Black
    Clawson International Ltd v Papierwerke Waldhof-Aschaffenberg AG* [1981] 2 Lloyd's Rep
    446 at 456; *E I Du Pont de Nemours & Co v Agnew and Kerr* [1987] 2 Lloyd's Rep 585 at
    592; see generally Pierce (1987) 50 MLR 176.
 2 11th edn (1987), p 451.

Any variation by the parties of the law to be applied made after the conclusion of the contract shall not prejudice its formal validity under Article 9 or adversely affect the rights of third parties.

As regards formal validity the concern was that the new law chosen by the parties might contain formal requirements which were not known under the law originally applicable. This could create doubts as to the validity of the contract during the period preceding the new agreement between the parties;[3] hence the rule that any variation by the parties is not to prejudice the formal validity of the contract under Article 9. The other danger recognised by the Working Group is in relation to third parties, who may have already acquired rights at the time of the conclusion of the contract between the original contracting parties. These rights cannot be affected by a subsequent change in the choice of the applicable law.

There are two other potential dangers that can arise from the parties' variation of the applicable law. First, the parties might thereby evade the mandatory rules (eg controls on exemption clauses) of the country whose law was originally applicable.[4] However, the normal limitations on the right to choose the applicable law will doubtless apply to a subsequent choice of the governing law in the same way that they apply to an initial choice. As will shortly be seen,[5] there are limitations on choice which deal to some extent with this problem of evasion. Second, the parties might choose a new law which invalidates the contract. Logically, the contract appears to be rendered invalid. This presupposes, however, that the new choice of the applicable law is itself valid. This is a matter for the new law that has been chosen.[6] Thus the validity of a New York choice of law clause (which operates as a subsequent choice) is a matter for New York law.

(v) Choice and the English rules on pleading and proof of foreign law

What happens if the parties choose Utopian law to apply but subsequently neither party pleads Utopian law? The Convention does not provide an answer to this. On the one hand, the English procedural rule preserved by the Convention[7] says that English law must be applied automatically. This would suggest that you can have a procedural variation of the applicable law.[8] On the other hand, Article 3(1) is phrased in strong terms: the "contract *shall* be governed by the law chosen by the parties".[9] But if foreign law has to be applied, this leads on to a practical problem of what an English judge is to do if the parties fail to plead and prove foreign law. In view of this difficulty, English courts are likely to take a pragmatic line and simply apply English law under the English procedural rule. There would be no problem if it could be said that the failure to plead foreign law operates as a new agreement as to the applicable law by the parties replacing the original choice. However, the parties' choice of the applicable law (whether an original or a later choice) must be expressed by the parties or demonstrated with reasonable certainty by the terms of the contract or the circumstances of the case.[10]

3 The Giuliano and Lagarde Report, p 18.
4 See Collins (1976) 25 ICLQ 35 at 44; cf North, op cit, pp 213–214.
5 Infra, pp 480–483.
6 See Art 8(1), infra, pp 505–506.
7 Art 1(2)(h), supra, pp 473–474.
8 See North, op cit, at 214; Diamond, op cit, at 262.
9 The emphasis is the authors'. See also Fentiman (1992) 108 LQR 142 at 144.
10 Art 3(1).

A mere omission to plead and prove foreign law would not appear to satisfy this requirement.[11]

(b) Limitations on choice Any discussion of freedom of choice inevitably leads on to the question of whether there is any restriction on the parties' freedom to choose the governing law. There were a number of such restrictions under the rules prior to the Rome Convention. In particular, in *Vita Food Products Inc v Unus Shipping Co Ltd*[12] Lord WRIGHT said that the parties' choice must be "bona fide and legal" and that there should be "no reason for avoiding the choice on the ground of public policy".[13] The Convention also lays down restrictions on the parties' right to choose the governing law, which will now be examined.

(i) Article 3(3)
The only limitation mentioned in Article 3 itself is contained in Article 3(3) which provides that:

> The fact that the parties have chosen a foreign law, whether or not accompanied by the choice of a foreign tribunal, shall not, where all the other elements relevant to the situation at the time of the choice are connected with one country only, prejudice the application of rules of the law of that country which cannot be derogated from by contract, hereinafter called "mandatory rules".

This provision is concerned with the situation where there is an essentially domestic contract which is turned into a conflict of laws case by virtue simply of the parties' choice of a foreign applicable law. Article 3(3) provides a limitation on the right to choose in this situation, but only to the extent of preserving the *mandatory rules* of the country where all the other relevant connections are situated. According to Article 3(3) mandatory rules are ones that "cannot be derogated from by contract". As an example of English mandatory rules, there are the rules providing controls on exemption clauses contained in the Unfair Contract Terms Act 1977. This Act makes it clear that these controls will, in certain circumstances, apply despite the parties' choice of a foreign law to govern the contract.[14] The effect of Article 3(3) is that if the parties to an entirely German contract, which contains an exemption clause, choose, for example, French law to govern, the court of any Contracting State which tries the case will have to apply any controls on exemption clauses contained in a German equivalent of the 1977 Act. The parties' choice of French law would appear to have been made with a view to evading the German controls on exemption clauses (assuming there are such controls). Article 3(3) will stop many cases of evasion of the law,[15] although it goes wider than this and it will ensure that any German controls on exemption clauses apply even if the parties' have chosen French law for some perfectly legitimate reason, such as the fact that this is the applicable law under some related contract between the parties.

11 See Lando (1987) 24 CMLR 159, 186–188 who suggests that the parties, in cases where the expense of proving foreign law is justified, are to be asked whether they intend to submit their contract to the law of the forum.
12 [1939] AC 277, [1939] 1 All ER 513.
13 At 290.
14 s 27(2); discussed infra, pp 500–501.
15 But not necessarily all cases, see the discussion, infra, p 481, in relation to *Golden Acres Ltd v Queensland Estates Pty Ltd* [1969] Qd R 378; affd sub nom *Freehold Land Investments v Queensland Estates Ltd* (1970) 123 CLR 418. See Lando (1987) 24 CMLR 159 at 182–183; Fawcett [1990] CLJ 44.

There is a number of points that can be made in relation to Article 3(3). First, it requires the parties to have chosen a "foreign" law. This raises a problem in the following type of case: two Californian residents enter into an essentially Californian contract but choose English law to govern the contract. Trial of a subsequent dispute takes place in England. English law is "foreign" to the parties and the contract, but not "foreign" to the forum. Article 3(3) is concerned with the choice of a foreign law and with the situation at the time of the choice. At that time, English law was a foreign one, ie was foreign to the parties and the contract. The result is that Article 3(3) operates and Californian mandatory rules are applicable.[16]

Second, Article 3(3) requires "all the other elements relevant to the situation"[17] to be connected with a country in order that its mandatory rules are to be applied. But when is an element *relevant* to the situation? Take the facts of the well known case of *Golden Acres Ltd v Queensland Estates Pty Ltd*.[18] The case concerned the rate of commission to be paid to an estate agent. Many of the connections were with Queensland, but the plaintiff company was incorporated in Hong Kong. Was the place of incorporation a relevant element, or was the only relevant thing about the company the fact that it acted as an estate agent in Queensland? Under the common law this case was decided on the basis that the choice of Hong Kong law to govern the contract was not made in good faith. Under the Convention the parties' motives are immaterial, but whilst one problem (ascertaining motives) has now disappeared, another problem (ascertaining whether all the relevant elements are with one country) has sprung up in its place.[19]

Third, the structure of the Convention suggests that the country whose mandatory rules have to be applied will be a foreign country and not the forum. However, there is nothing to say that mandatory rules of the forum are excluded under Article 3(3). Indeed, it is important that Article 3(3) should encompass the mandatory rules of the forum, since Article 7(2), although specifically designed to cover the mandatory rules of the forum, is concerned with a different and narrower type of mandatory rule.[20]

Fourth, you have to look to the law of the country with which there are all the other relevant connections to see whether under *that country's law* the domestic rule is one which cannot be derogated from by contract.

Fifth, the effect of applying a mandatory rule is to override the parties' choice of law, rather than to destroy it. Reverting to the earlier example, the German controls on exemption clauses will apply despite a French choice of law clause. Nonetheless, the choice of French law will still operate to govern other issues, such as interpretation of the contract, provided that this is an area where German law does not have mandatory rules.

The sixth and final point about Article 3(3) is that it tells us something, by implication, about freedom of choice. Article 3(3) is only concerned with mandatory rules. It follows that, even if all the other relevant connections are with country X, the choice of the law of country Y will still apply as far

---

16 Where neither party pleads and proves Californian law, presumably English law will apply: Art 1(2)(h).
17 As opposed to relevant to the *contract*.
18 Supra.
19 However, there is no such problem in relation to connections if Art 7(2) is used. This is concerned with the mandatory rules of the forum: infra, p 499. See also Fawcett [1990] CLJ 44 at 58–60.
20 Infra, pp 499–503.

as non-mandatory rules are concerned. This means that the parties can choose, as the applicable law, the law of a country with which there is no relevant connection.

(ii) Other provisions on mandatory rules[1], public policy[2]

These limitations are more appropriately dealt with later on, where they will be looked at in some detail.

This deals with the limitations on choice specifically set out in the Convention itself. Nonetheless, there are a number of other possible limitations which have to be considered.

(iii) Logically consistent choices

As has already been seen,[3] if the parties are choosing two different laws for different parts of the contract, these choices must be logically consistent.

(iv) A meaningless choice of law

In keeping with the above limitation, a meaningless choice of law should be ignored. The difficulty in working out whether a choice of law clause is meaningless can be seen from a case decided under the traditional common law rules. In *Compagnie D'Armement Maritime SA v Cie Tunisienne de Navigation SA*,[4] a contract for the carriage of oil stated that "This contract shall be governed by the laws of the flag of the vessel carrying the goods." This clause (13) was held by the Court of Appeal[5] to be meaningless in the case of a contract which, as here, contemplated that it would be performed in a number of different vessels flying different flags. However, in the House of Lords a bare majority felt able to interpret clause 13 as referring to the law of the flag of the ships "primarily" used to carry the cargo. This was held to be French law. On the other hand, at common law mere difficulty in ascertaining the governing law did not render the choice ineffective.[6] The position would doubtless be the same under the Convention.

(v) Choice of the lex mercatoria

Under Article 3(1) the parties have the right to choose the applicable *law*, and this refers presumably to the law of a country.[7] A problem is raised, however, in cases where the parties specify that the "lex mercatoria"[8] shall govern all disputes between them. Such a choice refers not to the national law of any country but rather to a kind of transnational law consisting of internationally accepted principles of trade law, to be ascertained by arbitrators. Such a reference would therefore appear to be outside the parties' freedom to choose the applicable law.[9]

---

1 Arts 5(2) and 6(1), infra p 495; Art 7, infra pp 493–503; Art 9(6), infra pp 509–510.
2 Art 16, infra pp 503–504.
3 Supra, pp 476–477.
4 [1971] AC 572, [1970] 3 All ER 71.
5 [1969] 3 All ER 589, [1969] 1 WLR 1338.
6 See *The Blue Wave* [1982] 1 Lloyd's Rep 151.
7 See Art 3(3) which specifically refers to the law of a 'country'. For the meaning of country see Art 19(1) and supra p 469.
8 See generally Lando (1985) 34 ICLQ 747; Lord Justice Mustill in *Liber Amicorum for Lord Wilberforce* (eds Bos and Brownlie 1987) at 149; the symposium in (1989) 63 Tulane L Rev, articles by Delaume at 575, Highet at 613, Smit at 631, Park at 647.
9 The position at common law is not clear. Compare *Amin Rasheed Shipping Corpn v Kuwait Insurance Co* [1984] AC 50 at 60, 65, HL, with *Deutsche Schachtbau-Und Tiefbohrgesellschaft MBH v Ras Al Khaimah National Oil Co* [1990] 1 AC 295, at 309–310, CA revsd by HL without discussion of this point in *Deutsche Schachtbau-Und Tiefbohrgesellschaft MBH v Shell International Petroleum Co Ltd* [1990] 1 AC 295; *Home and Overseas Insurance Co Ltd v Mentor Insurance Co (UK) Ltd (in liq)* [1989] 3 All ER 74 at 84–85, CA.

(vi) A "floating" applicable law

The parties presumably cannot choose a "floating" applicable law to govern the contract. The applicable law must exist and be identifiable at the time when the contract is made. It follows that a clause which, for example, gives one party the option to determine the applicable law in the future by selecting the law to govern from a list of possible alternatives, will be ineffective under the Convention, as it was at common law.[10] At least it will be ineffective at the time when the contract is made, and at this stage the applicable law will be determined objectively under Article 4 of the Convention. But what happens if one party makes the selection at some future date? This subsequent choice may have been ineffective under the common law rules,[11] but there can be little doubt that the choice at this future date will be given effect under the Convention, since variation of the applicable law is permissible.[12] The form of the variation is just rather unusual in this situation, in that the agreement is from the outset for a change of the applicable law in the future.

(c) An express choice The parties can express a choice simply by including a choice of law clause in the contract stating that, for example, all disputes shall be governed by English law. Any question as to the validity or existence of this choice is governed by the rules on consent to choice, which will be examined later.[13] Parties may choose a particular law for a variety of reasons.[14] It is usually convenient for a party to have the familiar law of their home state apply. One country's law may be more developed than another's in technical commercial areas such as banking and insurance, when English law is commonly chosen by the parties. It may have become standard practice for a particular country's law to apply to certain transactions. The content of one country's law may be more favourable to one of the parties than that of another. Whatever the law chosen, it is important that the parties should make an express choice, for without this there is considerable uncertainty as to the applicable law.

Under the common law rules it was important to distinguish carefully the express selection of the proper law from the quite different process of the incorporation in the contract of certain domestic provisions of a foreign law, which thereupon became terms of the contract.[15] The same distinction must be drawn under the Convention, for Article 3 is only concerned with selection of the applicable law. Incorporation may be effected either by a verbatim transcription of the relevant provisions or by a general statement that the rights and liabilities shall in certain respects be subject to these provisions. The latter is only a short-hand method of expressing the agreed terms. Thus the parties to an English contract may expressly provide that their duties with regard to performance shall be regulated by certain specific rules contained in

---

10 See *Dubai Electricity Co v Islamic Republic of Iran Shipping Lines, The Iran Vojdan* [1984] 2 Lloyd's Rep 380 at 385; *Cantieri Navali Riuniti SpA v NV Omne Justitia, The Stolt Marmaro* [1985] 2 Lloyd's Rep 428 at 435; cf *Astro Venturoso Compania Naviera v Hellenic Shipyards SA, The Mariannina* [1983] 1 Lloyd's Rep 12 at 15.

11 See *Armar Shipping Co Ltd v Caisse Algerienne* [1981] 1 WLR 207 at 216; cf *Black Clawson International Ltd v Papierwerke Waldhof–Aschaffenburg AG* [1981] 2 Lloyd's Rep 446 at 456; *E I Du Pont de Nemours & Co v Agnew and Kerr* [1987] 2 Lloyd's Rep 585 at 592. See generally Beck [1987] Lloyd's MCLQ 523.

12 Art 3(2), discussed supra, pp 478–479.

13 Art 3(4) discussed infra, p 486.

14 See Collins in *Contract Conflicts*, p 215.

15 See the 11th edn (1987) of this book, pp 456–457.

the Swiss Code. Whether a particular term incorporated in this manner is valid and effective is a matter for determination by the applicable law under the Convention.[16] At common law once a foreign law was incorporated into the contract as a term it remained constant in the sense that it was unaffected by any change in the relevant foreign law occuring after the date of the contract. The position appears to be the same under the Convention.

(d) An inferred choice Article 3(1) provides, as an alternative to an express choice, that there can be a choice "demonstrated with reasonable certainty by the terms of the contract or the circumstances of the case". This provision is concerned with a real choice by the parties, the court inferring what the parties' actual intentions[17] were from the terms of the contract or the circumstances of the case. This concept of an inferred or implied choice is well known in English law, and is to be found in civil law countries as well.[18] Inferred choice under the Convention appears at first sight to be very close to the English law in this area. Nonetheless, there are differences, and cases decided at common law have to be treated with caution.

(i) Drawing the inference
An inference as to the parties' intentions can be drawn from either the terms of the contract or the circumstances of the case.

The terms of the contract The Giuliano and Lagarde Report[19] provides a number of examples of situations where a court may draw an inference as to the parties' intentions. In most of these examples the inference is being drawn from the terms of the contract. Thus an inference can be drawn in cases where: the contract is in a standard form known to be governed by a particular system of law, such as a Lloyd's policy of Marine Insurance; the contract contains a choice of forum clause or an arbitration clause naming the place of arbitration (at least in circumstances indicating that the arbitrator should apply the law of that place); there is a reference to specific articles of the French Civil Code.[20] The reasoning in such cases is that if, for example, the parties intended that trial should take place in England they must also have intended that English law should apply, it being inconvenient and expensive for a foreign law to be applied.

The interesting thing about these examples, from an English point of view, is that the first three are the standard examples of an inferred choice under the common law rules. Thus in *Amin Rasheed Shipping Corpn v Kuwait Insurance Co*[21] Lord DIPLOCK[1] said that the terms of a standard Lloyd's SG form of policy showed by necessary implication that the parties (a Liberian company and a Kuwaiti insurance company) intended that the English law of marine insurance should apply.[2] Kuwait had no law of marine insurance

16 Art 8(1); discussed infra, p 506.
17 See *Hellenic Steel Co v Svolamar Shipping Co Ltd, The Komninos S* [1991] 1 Lloyd's Rep 370 at 374, CA.
18 The Giuliano and Lagarde Report, pp 15–17; Lando (1987) 24 CMLR 171–179. For inferred choice under German law see Von Hoffmann in *Contract Conflicts*, p 221 at 224–225.
19 At p 17.
20 Instead of a choice of French law this may involve an incorporation by reference, supra.
21 [1984] AC 50. The case involved service of a writ out of the jurisdiction under what is now Ord 11, r 1(1)(d)(iii).
1 At 64–67, Lords ROSKILL, BRIGHTMAN and BRANDON concurred. Lord WILBERFORCE reached the same result by applying the objective proper law.
2 See the 11th edn (1987) of this book, at pp 459–460.

at that time, and the parties could not have intended Kuwaiti law to apply. The House of Lords unanimously held that the proper law of the contract was English law. This sort of case presumably will be decided in exactly the same way under the Convention.

These are only examples of situations where it is possible to infer a choice from the terms of the contract, albeit particularly good ones. Could such an inference be drawn, for example, from the fact that the currency in which payment is to be made is that of a particular country? At common law the English courts drew inferences as to parties' intentions from a wide variety of factors relating to the terms of the contract, including this very factor. However, a note of caution should be struck when it comes to inferring a choice under the Convention. First, the inferred choice must be demonstrated "with reasonable certainty". If it is not, you move on to the provisions on the applicable law in the absence of choice (Article 4) to decide the case. Second, you are looking for the actual or real intentions of the parties. It is just about credible to say in a case like *Amin Rasheed* (or in cases involving arbitration or choice of jurisdiction clauses) that the parties had real intentions, but the same cannot be said in a case where all that can be shown is that, for example, there is a clause in the contract relating to the currency in which payment is to be made. In the common law cases, although the language of inferred intent was often used it was by no means clear that the courts were looking for a real or actual intention on the parties' part.[3] The upshot is that it may be harder to draw an inference of intention under the Convention than it was under the common law rules.[4]

The circumstances of the case[5] The inference can be drawn not only from the terms of the contract, but also from the circumstances of the case. The Giuliano and Lagarde Report[6] gives two examples of inferred choice which would seem to fit within this category. The first is the situation where there is an express choice in a related transaction. The second is the situation where there is a previous course of dealing under contracts containing an express choice of the applicable law and this choice of law clause has been omitted in circumstances which do not indicate a deliberate change of policy by the parties. The English courts under the common law rules used the language of inferred intent in similar circumstances. However, they also inferred an intent from the sort of purely objective factors, such as the residence of the parties[7] or the nature and location of the subject of the contract,[8] from which it would be inappropriate to infer an actual intention under the Convention.

---

3 In *Coast Lines Ltd v Hudig and Veder Chartering NV* [1972] 2 QB 34 at 50 it was clear that Stephenson LJ in the Court of Appeal was not. There was much confusion at common law over the meaning of intention, and between the intentions of the parties and objective factors, *infra*, p 488.

4 See Morse, (1982) 2 Yearbook of European Law 107, pp 116–117. The same will be true in Germany, see Triebel (1988) 37 ICLQ 935 at 942. Cf Plender, para 5.07.

5 Cf Art 2 of the (1955) Hague Convention on the law applicable to international sales of goods. It is unclear whether the "circumstances of the case" can include subsequent conduct which shows the parties' earlier intentions at the time of conclusion of the contract, see Plender, paras 5.09–5.11.

6 At p 17.

7 *Jacobs v Credit Lyonnais* (1884) 12 QBD 589.

8 *Lloyd v Guibert* (1865) LR 1 QB 115 at 122–123.

(ii)   Conflicting inferences

The Giuliano and Lagarde Report states[9] that any inference which arises from a choice of jurisdiction clause "must always be subject to the other terms of the contract and all the circumstances of the case" (ie the very matters from which an inference can be drawn). For example, a choice of jurisdiction clause may point to an intention that the law of country A shall apply, whereas a previous course of dealing may point to an intention that the law of country B shall apply. This notion of conflicting inferences is doubtless not confined to the situation where an inferred choice is being drawn from the presence of a choice of jurisdiction clause in the contract. If there are conflicting inferences it cannot be said that the choice has been demonstrated with reasonable certainty, and Article 3(1) does not permit the court to infer a choice of law that the parties might have made if they had no clear intention of making a choice.[10] The result is that you have to turn to the rules on the applicable law in the absence of choice[11] to determine the governing law.

What is less clear is how the inference to be drawn from the terms of the contract and the circumstances of the case stands in relation to the objective connections that the contract has with different countries. For example, a previous course of dealing may raise the inference that English law governs, but many of the objective connections, such as the residence of the parties and the place of performance, could be with France. Under the Convention there is, quite properly, a rigid separation of intention (dealt with under Article 3) from objective connecting factors (dealt with under Article 4). The inference that the parties intended English law to govern can seemingly only be challenged by a conflicting inference, ie by evidence showing a real intention that French law should govern. Some English judges may take a robust view that such an inference can be drawn from the factual connections with France. Nonetheless, it is hard to accept that factual connections of the sort mentioned above are evidence of an actual intention by the parties. The consequence is that, in the above example, English law should apply by virtue of Article 3(1).

(e)   Consent to choice   There can be a dispute as to whether one of the parties has consented to the choice. Article 3(4) provides that issues in relation to the validity and existence of consent are determined in accordance with the special rules in the Convention relating to material validity (Article 8), formal validity (Article 9) and incapacity (Article 11). These provisions will be discussed later in this chapter. Article 3(4) has been criticised.[12] The effect of it appears to be that one party can choose the law to govern the issue of consent to choice. If there is no valid consent to the choice, presumably the applicable law must be determined under the rules on the applicable law in the absence of choice.[13]

---

9   At p 17.
10   The Giuliano and Lagarde Report, p 17.
11   Art 4.
12   See Cavers (1975) 48 So Cal L Rev 603 at 609; Nadelmann (1976) 24 Am J Comp Law 1, 8–9; cf Morse, op cit, at 119.
13   Art 4. Cf the 1985 Hague Convention on the law applicable to contracts for the international sale of goods, Art 10(1) which spells this out.

(ii) The applicable law in the absence of choice

In a surprising number of cases the parties fail to choose the applicable law. This may be because they have contracted without first consulting lawyers, or they cannot agree on the applicable law. The determination of the applicable law in the absence of choice is dealt with under Article 4, which consists of three main parts. First, there is the basic rule that the contract shall be governed by the law of the country with which it is most closely connected.[14] Second, there is a general presumption, based on the concept of characteristic performance, designed to identify the country with which the contract is most closely connected,[15] together with special presumptions[16] for two particular types of contract. Third, there is a provision which, inter alia, states that the presumptions shall be disregarded if it appears that the contract is most closely connected with another country.[17] These provisions seek to combine certainty, provided by the presumptions, with flexibility, provided by the closest connection test and the power to rebut the presumptions. Nonetheless, the scheme of Article 4 raises an initial dilemma, which is as yet unresolved. It is not clear whether what is intended is a three, two or even one stage process. The sequence in which the provisions are set out in Article 4 points to a three stage process.[18] However, the Giuliano and Lagarde Report[19] envisages, at least in many cases, a one stage process which starts and finishes with the presumptions. Against this, it is hard to see how a court can decide whether it is appropriate to rebut a presumption unless it has first applied the closest connection test. This would suggest a two stage process,[20] which starts with a presumption, but then moves on necessarily to consider the closest connection test in order to see whether this presumption can be rebutted. The three parts of Article 4 will now be examined.

(a) The closest connection test

(i) The objective test
Article 4(1) provides that

> To the extent that the law applicable to the contract has not been chosen in accordance with Article 3, the contract shall be governed by the law of the country with which it is most closely connected

Article 4(1) applies in the situation where the law has not been chosen by the parties or their choice has been ineffective.[1] The applicable law is determined by looking objectively at the connections linking the contract to a particular country. This rule is based on the common core of the law in Member States, where the same sort of flexible approach has been commonly used.[2] Under the proper law of the contract approach, in the absence of an express or

---

14 Art 4(1).
15 Art 4(2).
16 Art 4(3) and (4).
17 Art 4(5).
18 See generally Collins (1976) 25 ICLQ 35 at 48.
19 At p 21.
20 Art 6(2) (individual employment contracts), infra, p 495, contains a two stage process.
1 Eg there are two inconsistent choices, see supra p 482; see the Giuliano and Lagarde Report, at p 20.
2 See the Giuliano and Lagarde Report, pp 19–20. This approach is found in the United States under the American Restatement, Second, see Lando (1982) 30 Am J Comp Law 19, 31.

inferred choice, the court looked for the system of law with which the transaction was most closely connected. This took into account such factors as the place of residence[3] or business[4] of the parties, the place where the relationship between the parties was centred,[5] the place where the contract was made[6] or was to be performed,[7] or the nature and subject matter[8] of the contract. These factors are still relevant under the Convention. However, in contrast to the proper law of the contract approach, it is now possible to take account of factors which have supervened after the conclusion of the contract.[9] Article 4 applies a purely objective test,[1C] so it is therefore inappropriate to talk about the intentions of the parties.[11] It follows that the fact that the contract would be valid under one country's law but not under another's could not be considered under Article 4, since this factor is only relevant to the determination of the parties' intentions (ie the parties would expect the contract to be valid[12]). Furthermore, although terms of the contract, such as a choice of jurisdiction or arbitration clause, should presumably be considered in the context of Article 4 in the situation where no clear inference can be drawn from them as to the intentions of the parties under Article 3(1),[13] their relevance when operating the objective test is limited to showing an objective connection with a country, and not as evidence of the parties' intentions. There can be little doubt that when the English courts set out to ascertain the objective proper law of the contract they sought to achieve certain underlying policy objectives, such as giving business efficacy to the contract.[14] English courts are going to find it harder to achieve such objectives under the Convention. The presence of the presumptions and the fact that the law is now codified reduces the flexibility, and thus the room for manoeuvre, for a court that wants to achieve a particular result.[15]

(ii) Severing the contract[16]
The last sentence of Article 4(1) states that

3 *Jacobs v Credit Lyonnais* (1884) 12 QBD 589 at 600, 602.
4 *Re Anglo-Austrian Bank* [1920] 1 Ch 69.
5 *XAG v A Bank* [1983] 2 Lloyd's Rep 535 at 543—banker and customer.
6 *Lloyd v Guibert* (1865) LR 1 QB 115 at 122; *Cantieri Navali Riuniti SpA v N V Omne Justitia, The Stolt Marmaro* [1985] 2 Lloyd's Rep 428 at 433–435.
7 *The Assunzione* [1954] P 150, [1954] 1 All ER 278.
8 *British South Africa Co v De Beers Consolidated Mines Ltd* [1910] 1 Ch 354 at 383, reversed on another point, [1912] AC 52.
9 The Giuliano and Lagarde Report, p 20. For criticism see Lasok and Stone *Conflict of Laws in the European Community*, p 363; Plender, para 6.04. For the position under the common law rules see *Compagnie d'Armement Maritime SA v Cie Tunisienne de Navigation SA* [1971] AC 572, [1970] 3 All ER 71; *Amin Rasheed Shipping Corpn v Kuwait Insurance Co* [1984] AC 50, [1983] 2 All ER 884.
10 This is clear from the title of Art 4 and the opening words of para (1).
11 Under the objective proper law approach the courts often referred to the parties' intentions, in the sense of the intentions that they would have had if they had considered the matter, or ought to have had as reasonable persons, see the 11th edn (1987) of this book, pp 461–462.
12 The position under the proper law was the same: *Monterosso Shipping Co Ltd v International Transport Workers' Federation, The Rosso* [1982] 2 Lloyd's Rep 120 at 131. However, a policy of validation underlies Art 9(1) of the Convention, infra, pp 508–509.
13 Supra, pp 484–486.
14 Wyatt (1974) 37 MLR 399; Jaffey (1984) 33 ICLQ 531, 548–549.
15 However, Jaffey argues that the presumption of characteristic performance will often achieve the desired business efficacy, op cit, 548 et seq.
16 See generally, Diamond (1986) IV Hague Recueil 236 at pp 285–287; Pryles in *Contract Conflicts*, p 323 at 334 et seq; Plender, paras 6.05–6.08.

a severable part of the contract which has a closer connection with another country may by way of exception be governed by the law of that other country.

As has been seen,[17] the parties have the freedom to sever the contract when exercising their choice as to the applicable law. The courts have the same power when determining the applicable law in the absence of choice, and may decide, for example, that one part of the contract has its closest connection with France but another part with Italy.[18] However, severance is an exception to normal principles and the power of severance should be exercised by the courts "as seldom as possible".[19] This provision requires there to be a *severable* part of the contract. In other words, the nature of the contract must be such that part of the contract is independent from the rest and can be severed from it. The Giuliano and Lagarde Report gives, as examples, joint ventures and complex contracts.[20] An English example of severance is provided by *Libyan Arab Foreign Bank v Bankers Trust Co*,[1] a case decided before the Convention came into force. STAUGHTON J held that a single banking contract relating to bank accounts in New York and London was governed in part by New York law (as regards the plaintiffs' New York account) and in part by English law (as regards the plaintiffs' London account). The judge referred to the power to sever a contract under Article 4 of the Convention, and the result would no doubt be the same now that the Convention is in force. Severability under Article 4(1) does not relate to the dispute; a court presumably cannot apply different laws to particular contractual issues, such as interpretation and discharge of the contract.[2] Finally, Article 4(1) is phrased in terms that a severable part of the contract *may* be governed by a different law from the rest of the contract. It is not clear whether this is intended to confer a discretion on the court, which would enable it to refuse to sever the contract, even though part of that contract was independent and severable.

(iii)   The law of the country rather than the system of law
Under Article 4(1) the court has to ascertain the law of the country,[3] rather than the system of law, with which the contract is most closely connected. In many cases the difference between these two formulations may not be significant. However, an example of where it might be important can be seen from the facts of the common law decision in *James Miller & Partners Ltd v Whitworth Street Estates (Manchester) Ltd*.[4] In this case a Scottish company agreed to carry out alterations to an English company's premises in Scotland. The contract was in the standard form provided by the Royal Institute of British Architects. The form, style and legal language of the contract pointed towards English law. If the formulation of the test referred to the system of law you would expect English law to be the applicable law. However, the

---

17 Supra, pp 476–477.
18 Pryles, op cit at 339, suggests that the presumption under Art 4(2) should not be used for ascertaining the law applicable to a severable part of the contract; cf Plender, para 6.08.
19 The Giuliano and Lagarde Report, at p 23.
20 Ibid.
 1 [1989] QB 728, [1989] 3 All ER 252; Carter (1989) 60 BYBIL 502.
 2 Compare the position under Art 3(1), supra, pp 476–477; cf Fletcher *Conflict of Laws and European Community Law* p 161.
 3 For the definition of country see Art 19, discussed supra, p 469.
 4 [1970] AC 583. Under the proper law of the contract approach, connection with the system of law was more commonly required, although two Law Lords in the *James Miller Case* combined the two tests.

other factors in the case (such as the place of performance for both parties) pointed strongly towards Scotland. This would appear to be the *country* with which the contract had the closest connections. Under Article 4(1), Scots law would, accordingly, seem to be applicable.

(iv) The contract

The connection is between the *contract* and the country whose law is to be applied, not between the dispute or transaction and that country.[5] The fact that the connection must be with the *contract* rather than the issue acts to discourage dépecage[6] which, as has been mentioned, is only intended to operate in exceptional circumstances.

(b) The presumptions The difficulty with any objective test that seeks to localise the contract is that of uncertainty. The Convention tries to resolve this uncertainty by the use of presumptions.[7] The Giuliano and Lagarde Report contemplates that the applicable law can be determined solely by applying the presumptions, without searching for the country with the closest connection.[8] The introduction of presumptions turns the clock back as far as English law is concerned. Although popular at one time, presumptions went out of fashion and were rejected,[9] one criticism being the very point that they diverted attention from the necessity to consider every single factor under the objective test. Nonetheless, the common law rule was not as open ended and flexible as might at first appear. In order to promote certainty in the law the courts identified specific factors as having great weight in identifying the closest connection in relation to certain contracts. For example, for insurance contracts the objective proper law would normally be the law of the state where the insurer carried on business.[10]

(i) The general presumption relating to characteristic performance
Article 4(2) provides that

> Subject to the provisions of paragraph 5 [non-application of presumptions] of this Article, it shall be presumed that the contract is most closely connected with the country where the party who is to effect the performance which is characteristic of the contract has, at the time of conclusion of the contract, his habitual residence, or, in the case of a body corporate or unincorporate, its central administration ...

Article 4(2) falls into two parts. First, the characteristic performance under the contract has to be identified. Second, this is given a geographical location by referring to the habitual residence of the party who is to effect the characteristic performance.

---

5   Cf the position at common law, see the 11th edn (1987) of this book, p 464.
6   Vischer in *Harmonisation of Private International Law by the EEC* (ed Lipstein) p 25. See also generally Lando (1987) 24 CMLR 167–169.
7   Cf Art 8, the 1985 Hague Convention on the law applicable to contracts for the international sale of goods.
8   At p 21. The use of presumptions, it is said, "greatly simplifies the problem of determining the law applicable in the absence of choice ... There is no longer any need to determine where the contract was concluded ... Seeking the place of performance becomes superfluous." Cf the Advocate General in Case 266/85 *Shenavai v Kreischer* [1987] ECR 239 at 249.
9   *Coast Lines Ltd v Hudig and Veder Chartering NV* [1972] 2 QB 34 at 47, 50.
10 See Dicey and Morris, pp 1289–1295.

Characteristic performance[11]

Apart from the concept of mandatory rules, this is the most difficult concept used in the Convention. It does not help that the concept is not defined under the Convention nor that its origin is to be found in Swiss private international law.[12] As far as English law is concerned, the place of performance is well known as a connecting factor, but it suffers from the obvious defect that in a typical contract both parties have to perform and may have to do so in different states. The concept of characteristic performance seeks to avoid this difficulty by concentrating on just one performance, the one which is characteristic of the contract as a whole—ie the one which constitutes the essence of the contract. It is this feature of characteristic performance which was used by the Working Group to justify its elevation, above all other connections, to the position of becoming a presumption.[13] More grandiosely, and harder to understand, it was said that "the concept of characteristic performance essentially links the contract to the social and economic environment of which it will form a part".[14]

This still leaves the problem of identifying the characteristic performance. Under Swiss law this depends on the type of contract involved. Again there is no difficulty if only one party has to perform as, for example, in the case of a contract of gift. But more typically, one party will perform services or provide goods, and the other will pay money for these. It is not immediately obvious which of these performances constitutes the essence of the contract. As far as each party is concerned what is important to them is the counter-performance by the other party. However, the Giuliano and Lagarde Report states[15] that the characteristic performance is usually the performance for which the payment is due; for example the delivery of goods, the granting of a right to make use of property, the provision of a service. With a contract of guarantee, it is said that the characteristic performance is always that of the guarantor. The Dutch decision in *Machinale Glasfabriek De Maas BV v Emaillerie Alsacienne SA*[16] provides a good illustration of the operation of these principles. The Dutch courts applied the Convention as part of their own private international law prior to the Convention coming into force. The case involved a Dutch plaintiff suing a French defendant for the price of goods sold and delivered. It was held that under Article 4(2) Dutch law was to be applied. This was on the basis that, in the absence of choice, the party who must perform the characteristic act of performance was the plaintiff company as manufacturer and seller, and the plaintiff had its place of establishment, at the time when the contract was made, in the Netherlands.

A number of criticisms can be levelled at the concept of characteristic performance and at the way it has been defined in the Giuliano and Lagarde Report. First, there are some contracts which cannot be fitted within the concept. With a contract of barter it is impossible to say that one party's

---

11 For criticism of the concept see generally: Collins (1976) 25 ICLQ 35 at 44 et seq; D'Oliveira (1977) 25 Am J Comp Law 303; Juenger in *Contract Conflicts* 300–302; Schultz ibid, pp 186–187; Morse, op cit, pp 126–132; Fletcher, op cit, pp 161–165; Lasok and Stone, op cit, pp 362–363. Cf Lipstein (1981) 3 Northwestern J of Int L and Bus 402; Blaikie (1983) SLT 241; Jaffey (1984) 33 ICLQ 531 at 545 et seq; Plender, paras 6.09–6.18.
12 For the position in Switzerland see the Swiss Federal Statute on Private International Law of December 18, 1987, Art 117. The statute is set out in (1989) 37 Am J Comp Law 193.
13 The Giuliano and Lagarde Report, p 20.
14 Ibid.
15 Ibid.
16 [1985] 2 CMLR 281, [1984] ECR 123.

performance is more characteristic of the contract than the other's.[17] However, the Convention allows for this by providing in Article 4(5) that, if the characteristic performance cannot be determined, the presumption does not apply.

Second, the definition of characteristic performance in terms of the performance for which payment is due does not stand up well to close scrutiny. The payment of money was presumably rejected as the characteristic performance because this is a common feature of many contracts and therefore fails to distinguish between different types of contract. Nonetheless, there are some contracts where the payment of money is arguably the essence of the obligation, for example contracts of pledge or hire-purchase, or repayment of a loan.[18] The Working Group qualified their statement about the payment of money by saying that this is not *usually*[19] the essence of the obligation. Presumably, the payment of money can, in unusual cases, constitute the characteristic performance.

Third, the effect of generally denying that the payment of money constitutes the essence of the contract is to favour the seller of goods over the buyer. This has been justified on the basis that the seller's performance is generally more complicated and to a greater extent regulated by rules of law than that of the buyer.[20] However, it is questionable whether this is sufficient to justify completely ignoring the buyer's performance in most cases.

Fourth, in terms of economic strength, the large enterprise, the manufacturer of goods, the provider of services (such as banks and insurance companies) and the professional is favoured against the other party who may well be in a weaker economic position.[1] It is curious to find a pro-manufacturer stance being taken in a Convention which is sufficiently concerned about protecting weaker parties to have special rules for consumers and employees.

Habitual residence etc.

Despite the emphasis placed on characteristic performance, Article 4(2) does not apply the law of the place of such performance. Instead, reference is made to the country where the party who is to effect the characteristic performance has his habitual residence, or, in the case of a company, its central administration. If the contract is entered into in the course of the trade or profession[2] of the party who is to effect the characteristic performance, reference is made to the principal place of business of that party or to another place of business (if performance is to be effected through that place).[3] Thus in a banking contract the law of the country of the banking establishment with which the transaction is made will normally apply.[4] What-

17 See the representations of the German Government in Case 266/85 *Shenavai v Kreischer* [1987] ECR 239 at 255.
18 Collins (1976) 25 ICLQ 35 at 48; see also Diamond, op cit, p 274. But see the Giuliano and Lagarde Report at p 21.
19 At p 20.
20 See Fletcher, op cit, p 163.
1 For attempts to justify this see Lagarde (1981) 22 Virginia J of Int Law 91 at 97, footnote 32. See also Vischer in *Harmonisation of Private International Law by the EEC* (ed Lipstein) at 28; Lando (1987) 24 CMLR 159 at 202 et seq.
2 There is no guidance in the Convention or Report as to when a contract is entered into in the course of trade or business. The same difficulty arises under the Unfair Contract Terms Act 1977.
3 Art 4(2).
4 The Giuliano and Lagarde Report, at p 21.

ever the merits of the concept of characteristic performance, these become less important when the concept is diluted by the addition of another connecting factor in this way.[5] Moreover, it is questionable whether reference to a personal connecting factor such as habitual residence is appropriate in the context of commercial contracts.[6] Article 4(2) also makes it clear that reference is to be made to the habitual residence or central administration as at the time of the conclusion of the contract, because of the possibility of changes in this connecting factor. It is noticeable that, whilst provision is made for the situation where characteristic performance cannot be ascertained, there is no corresponding provision dealing with the situation where the habitual residence, etc cannot be ascertained.[7] Presumably the forum will have to use its own national definitions of these concepts.[8]

Unless a presumption is easy to apply it will not produce the certainty in determining the objective applicable law that is its raison d'etre.[9] Unfortunately, the presumption in Article 4(2) is a complex one, involving considerable definitional problems. Moreover, with a presumption, one connection is elevated to a position of importance above all others. It is doubtful whether the combination of habitual residence and characteristic performance merits this.

(ii) Special presumptions

Although, in principle, the concept of characteristic performance is applicable regardless of the type of contract involved, it has been thought necessary to have special presumptions relating to immovable property (Article 4(3)) and carriage of goods (Article 4(4)).

With immovable property the presumption is that the contract is most closely connected with the country where the immovable property is situated. However, this provision only applies to the extent that the subject matter of the contract is a right in immovable property or a right to use immovable property.[10] A contract for the sale of property or for the rental of a holiday home would come within this, but a contract for construction or repair would not because the main subject matter of the contract is not the immovable property itself.[11] This presumption, like the general one of characteristic performance, can be rebutted if the contract is more closely connected with another country. The Giuliano and Lagarde Report gives as an example a contract between two Belgians for the rental of an Italian holiday home.[12] It is said that Belgian law would govern this contract.

Contracts for the carriage of goods[13] were regarded by the Working Group as having peculiarities which merited a separate special rebuttable presumption, which refers to the principal place of business of the carrier at the time the contract was concluded. One of a number of alternative connections

5 Cf the Giuliano and Lagarde Report, at pp 20–21. Supported by Jaffey (1984) 33 ICLQ 531.
6 Collins (1976) 25 ICLQ 35 at 45–46; cf Jaffey, op cit, p 557.
7 The preliminary draft Convention contained such a provision in Art 4.
8 "Habitual residence" is discussed supra, pp 169–171. "Central administration" can doubtless be equated with "central management and control", discussed supra, p 285. "Place of business" is discussed supra, pp 186–188.
9 Cf Jaffey (1984) 33 ICLQ 531. See also generally Lando, op cit, 203.
10 See generally Fletcher, p 164; Plender, 6.20–6.24.
11 The Giuliano and Lagarde Report, p 21.
12 Ibid.
13 According to Art 4(4) "carriage of goods" encompasses "single voyage charter-parties and other contracts the main purpose of which is the carriage of goods". See generally Schultz in *Contract Conflicts*, 185 et seq; Fletcher, op cit, pp 164–165; Plender, paras 6.25–6.29.

with that country must also be satisfied, for example, that it is also the place of loading or discharge. If not, presumably no presumption operates. Contracts for the carriage of passengers are subject to the general characteristic performance presumption under Article 4(2).[14] A mixed contract for the carriage of goods and passengers will be subject to two different presumptions with possibly two different applicable laws. With contracts of carriage other international conventions may apply, and these take precedence over the Rome Convention.[15]

(c) Non-application of the presumptions

Article 4(5) provides that

> Paragraph 2 [the basic presumption] shall not apply if the characteristic performance cannot be determined, and the presumptions in paragraphs 2, 3 and 4 [the basic and special presumptions] shall be disregarded if it appears from the circumstances as a whole that the contract is more closely connected with another country.

This deals with two very different situations. The first is where the characteristic performance cannot be determined. In this case it is impossible to apply the basic presumption. The second is where the contract is more closely connected with another country. In this case the presumptions are rebutted.

Impossibility in applying the basic presumption
If the characteristic performance cannot be determined, Article 4(2) [the basic presumption] does not apply and the applicable law has to be determined by using the closest connection approach under Article 4(1). In such cases there will be the usual problems that arise under an objective approach which seeks to localise the contract. The court will have to ascertain all the connections with the different countries, give weight to these, and, if they are evenly balanced between two countries, find one especially important connection which tips the balance in favour of one country. This is what happened with the search at common law for the objective proper law of the contract.[16]

Rebutting the presumptions
All the presumptions under Article 4 are to be disregarded if it appears from the circumstances as a whole that the contract is more closely connected with another country. The power to rebut the presumptions provides flexibility[17] and was thought to be necessary because of the wide variety of different types of contract that have to be dealt with under the Convention, which has few special rules for particular contracts.[18] However, the price for this flexibility is the risk of uncertainty and lack of predictability, thus defeating the object of the presumptions.[19]

When is a contract more closely connected with another country? Lagarde has given an example of a situation where rebuttal might be appropriate. "A subcontract, for example, might be governed by the same law governing the principal contract between the contractor and the employer, rather than by the law of the country in which the subcontractor has his place of business."[20]

14 The Giuliano and Lagarde Report, p 22.
15 Art 21, discussed infra, p 521.
16 See the 11th edn (1989) of this book, pp 464–466.
17 This has been welcomed by an American writer, see Juenger in *Contract Conflicts*, p 307. See also Kay (1989) III Hague Recueil 194. Flexibility can be used to achieve a particular result in a case: Diamond, op cit, pp 284–285.
18 The Giuliano and Lagarde Report, p 22.
19 Reese (1987) 35 Am J Comp Law 395 at 400; Schultz in *Contract Conflicts*, p 187.
20 (1981) 22 Virginia J of Int Law 91 at 97–98.

Of course, rebuttal will not happen in every case. However, it is hard to see how the judge is supposed to know whether it is an appropriate case for rebuttal unless, as a matter of course, he has first applied the closest connection test, and weighed the connections so identified against the presumption. The notion contained in the Giuliano and Lagarde Report that the presumption obviates the necessity for applying the closest connection approach[1] looks somewhat unrealistic. With the closest connection test normally having to be considered by the courts there is a prospect of this test becoming dominant and the presumptions being downgraded.[2] The English courts, in particular, may be inclined to use the flexibility built into Article 4 so as to act as if they were still ascertaining the objective proper law,[3] and thus to reach the same conclusion, though by a rather longer route.

(d) SPECIAL CONTRACTS

In general, the Convention applies the same rules regardless of the type of contract involved. Nonetheless, the Convention acknowledges that particular contracts can produce special problems. The introduction of flexibility into Article 4 by allowing the presumption of characteristic performance to be rebutted was explained on this basis.[4] More particularly, there are special rules in the Convention in relation to contracts for immovable property,[5] carriage of goods,[6] consumer contracts[7] and individual employment contracts.[8] These exceptions have been justified on the basis that application of the normal rules under the Convention may produce inequitable or unrealistic results.[9] As has been seen,[10] the special rules for immovable property and carriage of goods are only concerned with the presumptions used for ascertaining the applicable law in the absence of choice. However, when it comes to consumer contracts[11] and individual employment contracts,[12] the Convention goes further and in Articles 5 and 6 introduces special choice of law rules which are concerned with both choice and the applicable law in the absence of choice. In both situations the aim of these rules is to provide protection for the consumer and the employee. The way this is done is by, firstly, ensuring that the protection given to the consumer or employee by mandatory rules is not thwarted by the parties' choice of the applicable law.[13] Secondly, in the absence of choice pre-eminence is given to the law of the consumer's habitual residence and the employee's habitual place for carrying on work.[14] Finally, the rules in the Convention dealing with the issue of formal validity

---

1 At p 21.
2 For an example of this danger see Diamond [1979] Current Legal Problems 155, 166–167.
3 See generally Fletcher, pp 161–162.
4 The Giuliano and Lagarde Report, p 22.
5 Art 4(3); see also Art 9(6).
6 Art 4(4).
7 Art 5, see also Art 9(5).
8 Art 6.
9 Lagarde (1981) 22 Virginia J of Int Law 91 at 98.
10 Supra, pp 493–494.
11 See Hartley in *Contract Conflicts* at p 111 et seq; Morse (1992) 41 ICLQ 1, 2–11; Plender, paras 7.01–7.24.
12 See Morse in *Contract Conflicts* at p 143 et seq; (1992) 41 ICLQ 1, 11–21; Plender, paras 8.01–8.29.
13 Arts 5(2), 6(1).
14 Arts 5(3), 6(2).

make special provision for consumer contracts[15] and contracts for immovable property.[16]

(e) LIMITATIONS ON THE DOMINANCE OF THE APPLICABLE LAW

(i) Mandatory rules[17]

(a) General comments The concept of mandatory rules is one of the key concepts under the Convention, with no fewer than six different provisions using it. It is a particularly difficult concept for English lawyers to apply because it is not known under English law, at least not under that name. Before turning to look at the definition of the concept under the Convention and at the provisions in which the concept is used, it is important to look at the background to its introduction into the Convention.

(i) The background to the concept
In domestic contract law there are now two very different sorts of rules.[18] There are the traditional rules which are concerned with settling disputes between parties, such as the rules on consideration. There are then the more modern rules which are concerned with protecting some group of persons or the national economic system—rules that arise as the result of state interference with contracts. The concept of mandatory rules only deals with this second class of rules. Consumers and employees provide good examples of groups of persons who are given special protection under the law. There are rules controlling exemption clauses and laying down requirements in relation to hire purchase and consumer credit transactions which are designed to protect consumers. There are also rules on industrial safety and hygiene and in relation to periods of notice for dismissal which are designed to protect employees. When it comes to protecting the national economic system, rules on monopolies, anti-trust, import and export prohibitions, price controls and exchange control legislation[19] are all designed to serve this purpose.

A state's interest in upholding protectionist laws may be so strong that it prohibits the parties from contracting out of such rules in a domestic situation. Going beyond this and into the realms of private international law, the state's interest in upholding certain laws may dictate that those laws must apply even though the issue is, in principle, governed by a different law selected by contract choice of law rules. An exception to the normal choice of law rules is thereby created. This sort of exception is well known in a number of Member States. The Giuliano and Lagarde Report[20] refers to the Dutch decision in the *Alnati Case*[1] which is a predecessor of Article 7(1) of the Convention (the general provision dealing with mandatory rules of a foreign country). The Dutch Supreme Court said that there could be cases

---

15 Art 9(5).
16 Art 9(6).
17 See generally Hartley (1979) 4 ELR 236; Diamond (1986) IV Hague Recueil ch IV; Plender, paras 9.01–9.12.
18 Vischer (1974) II Hague Recueil ch 2; Jaffey (1984) 33 ICLQ 531 at 538 et seq.
19 See the Giuliano and Lagarde Report, p 28; Art 7(2) infra, pp 499–503.
20 At 26.
 1 Nederlandse Jurisprudentie 1967, p 3; Rev Crit 1967, p 522. Though later Dutch decisions seem to have resiled from this approach. See generally Schultsz (1983) 47 Rabels Z 267.

when the interest of a foreign state in having its law applied outside its territory was so great that the Dutch courts should take this into account and give priority to the application of such provisions in preference to the law of another state chosen by the parties. In England there is the Unfair Contract Terms Act 1977 with its provisions restricting the parties' freedom to choose the applicable law.[2] This is an example of what in English law is called an overriding statue,[3] ie the statute overrides normal choice of law rules so as to apply the rules in the statute. Thus the parties may have chosen French law to govern the contract, but in certain circumstances the controls on exemption clauses contained in the 1977 Act will still apply. The Working Group was concerned to retain this sort of exception.

(ii) The definition of mandatory rules

Mandatory rules are defined in Article 3(3) as rules "which cannot be derogated from by contract". This definition applies universally to all of the provisions on mandatory rules. In order to determine whether rules of a particular country are mandatory, reference must be made to the law of that country. For example, if an English court is concerned to ascertain whether a French domestic rule is a mandatory one it has to ask whether under French law that particular rule cannot be derogated from by contract. The essence of mandatory rules is that a rule is applied because *that country's* law requires it to be so applied.[4] This definition of mandatory rules is an unfortunate one in that it can be construed as asking simply whether the parties can agree to depart from the rule in *domestic* cases, rather than the private international question of whether the rule is intended, according to the law of its country of origin, to apply regardless of the governing law.[5] Yet the effect given to mandatory rules under the Convention is to override the normal rules on the applicable law contained in the Convention. If one accepts the above construction of the definition, it follows that mandatory rules may be given a wider effect under the Convention than they have under the law of the country from which they originate. It would have been much better to have had a definition of mandatory rules that clearly reflects the principle that a domestic rule will only be given the effect under the Convention that it has under the law of its country of origin.[6] At the same time, this problem may not be as great as might at first sight appear. As will shortly be seen, it does not arise in relation to what are likely to be the most commonly used provisions in the Convention on mandatory rules. Furthermore, if English law is anything to go by, mandatory rules are likely to be ones which not only cannot be departed from by agreement in a purely domestic context, but which also, according to their country of origin, override normal choice of law principles.[7]

(iii) The provisions on mandatory rules

The concept of mandatory rules is used in no fewer than six different provisions in the Convention. Reference has already been made to three of these

---

2 S 27(2); infra, pp 500–501.
3 See the 11th edn (1987) of this book, pp 466–471.
4 This is particularly clear under Articles 7(1), 7(2) and 9(6).
5 See Jackson in *Contract Conflicts* 59 at 65–66; Plender, para 5.22.
6 See generally Morse, op cit, 123–124.
7 See, eg, the Unfair Contract Terms Act 1977, infra, pp 500–501; the Employment Protection (Consolidation) Act 1978, infra, p 500.

provisions: Articles 3(3) (the limitation on freedom of choice);[8] 5(2) (consumer contracts);[9] 6(1) (individual employment contracts).[10] In each of these provisions mandatory rules operate as a limitation on the freedom to choose the applicable law. These three provisions only apply in very limited circumstances. There is a fourth provision on mandatory rules contained in Article 9(6)[11] which is also very limited, in this case to matters of formal validity in respect of contracts for the use of immovable property. However, there are two general provisons on mandatory rules contained in Article 7(1) and (2) of the Convention, which are of much wider scope. Article 7(1)[12] is concerned with the mandatory rules of a foreign country and Article 7(2)[13] with the mandatory rules of the forum. As far as the United Kingdom is concerned only the latter provision is of direct significance. Section 2(2) of the Contracts (Applicable Law) Act 1990 provides that Article 7(1) shall not have the force of law in the United Kingdom.[14]

(iv) Differences between the separate provisions on mandatory rules
The six provisions on mandatory rules, whilst sharing the same definition of a mandatory rule, are different from each other in three major respect. First, they differ on the question of which country's[15] mandatory rules are being referred to. For example, it may be the forum or that of a foreign country, and if the latter the extent of the connection required with that country may differ. This is a spatial difference which one would expect to find.

Second, and this is much more surprising, the provisions differ as to the type of mandatory rules with which they are dealing. There appear to be two different types of mandatory rules relevant under the Convention.[16] First, there is the basic wide type of mandatory rule, where all that has to be shown is that the definition of a mandatory rule is satisfied, ie under the law of the country with whose rule one is concerned, the rule cannot be derogated from by contract. Articles 3(3), 5(2), and 6(1) are all concerned with this basic wide type of mandatory rule. Second, there are the narrower overriding mandatory rules. With these, it must not only be shown that the rule is a mandatory one, within the above definition, but also that under the law of the country with whose rules you are concerned the mandatory rule overrides the applicable law. Articles 7(1), 7(2) and 9(6) all require this additional element. Thus under Article 7(2) mandatory rules are applied in "a situation where they are mandatory irrespective of the law otherwise applicable to the contract." Under Article 7(1) it must be shown that "those [mandatory] rules must be applied whatever the law applicable to the contract". Under Article 9(6) the mandatory requirements must be "imposed irrespective of the country where the contract is concluded and irrespective of the law governing

8 Supra, p 480–482.
9 Supra, p 495.
10 Supra, p 495.
11 Infra, pp 509–510.
12 Infra, p 503.
13 Infra, pp 499–503.
14 For the power of reservation, see Art 22(1)(a).
15 It has been argued that the European Community should be treated as one country so as to encompass any mandatory rules contained in European Community Regulations and Directives: Lando (1987) 24 CML Rev 160 at 181.
16 The French version of the Convention refers to "dispositions impératives" (see Art 3(3)) and also to "Lois de police" (see the heading to Art 7). See generally Plender, paras 5.21–5.23, 9.06.

the contract." Naturally, a rule falling within this narrower type of mandatory rule will automatically come within the wider type as well. If the parties' right expressly to choose the governing law is taken away, it follows that the domestic rule is one that cannot be contracted out of.

Third, the effect given to a mandatory rule under the Convention differs depending on the provision in question. With Articles 3(3), 5(2) and 6(1) the effect given to the mandatory rule under the Convention is merely to override the parties' freedom to choose the applicable law. With mandatory rules under Articles 7(1), 7(2) and 9(6) the effect given to the rule under the Convention is much greater. The mandatory rule is able to override all of the rules on the applicable law under the Convention (including the rules on the applicable law in the absence of choice).[17]

(b) The mandatory rules of the forum Article 7(2) states that: "Nothing in this Convention shall restrict the application of the rules of the law of the forum in a situation where they are mandatory irrespective of the law otherwise applicable to the contract." The opening words of Article 7(2) make it clear that this provision was put in so that the forum could continue to apply its own mandatory rules to override contract choice of law rules even after the new regime under the Rome Convention entered into force.[18] The existing law is therefore preserved. The Giuliano and Lagarde Report[19] gives some examples of the sort of protectionist domestic rules which Contracting States were anxious to preserve as overriding rules: rules on cartels, competition and restrictive practices, consumer protection and certain rules concerning carriage. Article 7(2), unlike the other provisions on mandatory rules, leads to no difficulty in identifying the country whose mandatory rules are in issue: they are solely the mandatory rules of the forum. However, it is not enough merely to show that the forum has a mandatory rule[20] (ie a rule which cannot be derogated from by contract). It has to be shown that what is involved is "a situation where [the rules] are mandatory irrespective of the law otherwise applicable to the contract". According to the law of the forum the rule must, in the situation in question, be given an overriding effect. This still leaves the problem for the forum of identifying such rules and of identifying a situation when such rules are given overriding effect.

Assuming that England is the forum, English rules expressing a strong socio-economic policy are likely to be contained in statutes, and a statute may state whether it is intended to have overriding effect.[1] The statute could expressly provide that in certain situations: it is to have complete overriding effect; it is to have limited overriding effect; it is to have no overriding effect. Alternatively, the statute may say nothing about its overriding effect, in

---

17 There are problems, however, with statutes of limited overriding effect, discussed infra pp 500–501.
18 See the Giuliano and Lagarde Report, p 28. See also the Lord Advocate, Hansard (HL) 12 December 1989 vol 513 col 1260. An analogous provision is to be found in the Hague Convention on the Law applicable to Trusts and on their Recognition: Art 16, infra, pp 890–891. For the position in relation to torts, see Law Com No 193 (1990), para 3.55.
19 At p 28.
20 Art 7(2) does not actually use the phrase "mandatory rules" but it does refer to rules "in a situation where they are mandatory".
1 See generally on the problems of the interaction between English statutes and the Convention, Morse in *Contract Conflicts* 143 at 163 et seq; Collins (1976) 25 ICLQ 35, at 37–38.

which case it is a matter of statutory construction as to whether, in particular situations, it is intended to have overriding effect. These different possibilities will now be examined.

The statute expressly provides that it is to have complete overriding effect A statute of complete overriding effect is one that, under the law of its country of origin, overrides not only the parties' choice of the applicable law but also the applicable law in the absence of choice, so that forum law is intended to apply even though the objective applicable law is foreign. An example of an English statute which according to its own terms is intended completely to override normal contract choice of law rules is provided in the Employment Protection (Consolidation) Act 1978. Section 153(5) states that for the purposes of the Act it is immaterial whether the law governing the contract is the law of part of the United Kingdom or not. Article 7(2) will only apply in a *situation* where rules are mandatory irrespective of the law applicable to the contract. The 1978 Act is territorially limited to persons ordinarily working in Great Britain. This is the situation where the rules are mandatory irrespective of the law otherwise applicable to the contract.[2]

The statute expressly provides that it is to have limited overriding effect A statute of limited overriding effect is one that, under the law of its country of origin, overrides the parties' freedom to choose the applicable law, but does not override the applicable law in the absence of choice. The Unfair Contract Terms Act 1977 provides an example of an English statute which by its own terms makes it clear that it is of only limited overriding effect. With such a statute the question of whether there is a *situation* where the rules are mandatory irrespective of the law otherwise applicable to the contract becomes particularly important.

The 1977 Act provides a wide ranging set of controls over exemption clauses in many kinds of contract. Some are rendered void; others are subjected to a reasonableness test. What is significant for our purposes is that the 1977 Act also provides for the operation of these controls in the international context. The important provision, which lays down the overriding nature of the rules on exemption clauses under the Act, is section 27(2), which states:

> This Act has effect notwithstanding any contract term which applies or purports to apply the law of any country outside the United Kingdom, where (either or both)—
> (a) the term appears to the court, or arbitrator or arbiter to have been imposed wholly or mainly for the purpose of enabling the party imposing it to evade the operation of this Act; or
> (b) in the making of the contract one of the parties dealt as consumer, and he was then habitually resident in the United Kingdom, and the essential steps necessary for the making of the contract were taken there, whether by him or by others on his behalf.

The essential purpose of this sub-section is easy to state. It is intended to prevent parties to a contract, which is most closely connected with this

---

2 An employee who wants the protection of the 1978 Act is best advised to rely on Art 7(2) rather than Art 6 (individual employment contracts) under which it is necessary to show that English law is applicable in the absence of choice under that Article.

country, from contracting out of the controls of the 1977 Act by a choice[3] of the law of a country outside the United Kingdom. The 1977 Act does not, as such, strike down the choice of a foreign law. It leaves it to take effect, and the foreign law to be applied to the contract, subject to effect being given to the controls of the 1977 Act.[4] However, there is an important limitation on the effectiveness of section 27(2) in that the controls in the 1977 Act do not apply to "international supply contracts".[5] In such contracts the parties will remain free to rely on exemption clauses.

Section 27(2) overrides the parties' freedom to choose a foreign law to govern the contract. Article 7(2) will apply therefore to cases coming within this section.[6] However, section 27(2) is only concerned with the situation where there has been a choice by the parties. In cases where there has been no such choice and the objective applicable law is foreign it seems that the Act's controls on exemption clauses will not apply; it cannot be said that the controls on exemption clauses in the Act apply irrespective of the law that otherwise applies to the contract. Article 7(2) will accordingly not operate in this situation. However, the controls on exemption clauses contained in the Act would, of course, be applicable if the governing law under the Convention is English law.[7]

The statute expressly provides that it is to have no overriding effect Article 7(2) will not be applicable in this case. There does not appear to be an example of such a statute under English law.

The statute has no express provision on its overriding effect but has a provision on its territorial scope In cases where a statute says nothing about its overriding effect it is a matter of construction of the statute to ascertain whether it is intended to have overriding effect in a particular situation.[8] Drawing this inference is much easier if the statute has a provision dealing with its territorial scope, albeit whilst not spelling out explicitly whether it is intended to have overriding effect. This can be illustrated by *Boissevain v Weil*.[9] The case concerned a Defence Regulation, made under the powers conferred by the Emergency Powers (Defence) Act 1939. This regulation made it an offence, subject to severe penalties, for *a British subject*[10] to carry out certain currency transactions. In the House of Lords Lord RADCLIFFE declared that whether such an offence was committed could not depend on whether the law governing a loan contract was English or foreign. In other words, it was a regulation which, in the situation in the case, was construed as being of

3 S 27(2) refers to "any contract term" which applies or purports to apply the law of some other country. This will include an express choice of law clause but it is unlikely to include an inferred choice through an arbitration or choice of court clause in the contract.
4 For the difficulties thereby created see Mann (1974) 90 LQR 42, 51–54; (1977) 26 ICLQ 903, 910.
5 S 26.
6 See the Giuliano and Lagarde Report at 26; Hansard (HL) 12 December 1989 vol 513 col 1260.
7 See, however, s 27(1) of the 1977 Act which imposes a limitation on a right to choose English law as the governing law. This appears to be inconsistent with the Rome Convention, which contains no such limitation.
8 See Pryles in *Contract Conflicts* at 331 et seq.
9 [1949] 1 KB 482, [1949] 1 All ER 146, CA; affd [1950] AC 327, [1950] 1 All ER 728. See also *The Hollandia* [1983] 1 AC 565, [1982] 3 All ER 114, a case on the Carriage of Goods by Sea Act 1971.
10 Defence (Finance) Regulations 1939, reg 2, as amended; Emergency Powers (Defence) Act 1939, s 3, sub-s (1).

complete overriding effect. Article 7(2) would now apply, and the result would be the same under the Convention.

The statute has no express provision as to its overriding effect and no provision on its territorial scope Many statutes say nothing about their extra-territorial scope or their overriding effect. The construction of such a statute to ascertain whether it is intended to have an overriding effect in a particular situation is especially difficult. In *English v Donnelly*[11] a Scots court gave at least limited overriding effect to Scots mandatory hire purchase requirements with the result that the parties were not allowed to contract out of the statute in question by an express choice of law clause. In *Irish Shipping Ltd v Commercial Union Assurance Co plc*[12] STAUGHTON LJ showed some concern that "The intention of Parliament could be frustrated if it were open to the parties to a contract of insurance to exclude the operation of section 1 [of the Third Parties (Rights against Insurers) Act 1930] by choosing a foreign proper law". On the other hand, in *Sayers v International Drilling Co NV*[13] the Court of Appeal did not give overriding effect to the Law Reform (Personal Injuries) Act 1948, which was concerned to protect injured employees from clauses exempting the employer from liability.[14] A majority of the Court of Appeal held that the objectively determined proper law of the contract, Dutch law, applied according to which the exemption clause was valid.

The effect given to the mandatory rule under Article 7(2)[15]
Article 7(2) operates as an exception to the normal choice of law rules under the Convention by giving overriding effect to mandatory rules. Obviously it overrides the rules on the applicable law under Article 3 (choice) and Article 4 (the applicable law in the absence of choice). But Article 7(2) probably has an even wider effect than this. The opening wording of Article 7(2) is that "Nothing in this Convention shall restrict the application of the rules of the law of the forum". This suggests that Article 7(2) should be regarded as a general exception to *all* the choice of law rules contained in the Convention, in the same way that public policy, which is more clearly worded in this respect, provides such an exception.[16] This means that the special rules for particular issues, such as formal validity, and for special contracts will also be overriden.[17] However, there is a particular problem in relation to consumer contracts and individual employment contracts, in that there are provisions on mandatory rules contained in the special regimes set out in Articles 5 and 6. Nevertheless, Article 7(2) should be regarded as overriding the other provisions in the Convention on mandatory rules. The result is that English mandatory rules would take priority over foreign mandatory rules. This has wide implications. For example, in a case where the applicable law under Article 4 of the Convention may be French and English law has mandatory rules, then, in principle, Article 7(2) should operate so that the English mandatory rules override the French ones. However, it must be for English

11　1958 SC 494; see also the High Court of Australia's decision in *Kay's Leasing Corpn Pty Ltd v Fletcher* (1964) 116 CLR 124.
12　[1991] 2 QB 206, [1989] 3 All ER 853.
13　[1971] 3 All ER 163, [1971] 1 WLR 1176, infra, p 562. Cf *Brodin v A R Seljan* 1973 SC 213.
14　However, the case was argued by counsel on the narrow point as to what the proper law of the contract was.
15　The same problem arises in relation to Art 7(1), see infra, p 503.
16　See the Giuliano and Lagarde Report, p 31; infra, pp 503–504.
17　Cf Lasok and Stone at pp 378, 383–384. See also Williams (1986) 35 ICLQ 1 at 24.

law to decide whether its own mandatory rules are of such importance that they should apply in such a case.

(c) The mandatory rules of other countries Article 7(1) provides that:

When applying under this Convention the law of a country, effect may by given to the mandatory rules of the law of another country with which the situation has a close connection, if and in so far as, under the law of the latter country, those rules must be applied whatever the law applicable to the contract. In considering whether to give effect to these mandatory rules, regard shall be had to their nature and purpose and to the consequences of their application or non-application.

Article 7(1) is the widest of the provisions on mandatory rules and is also the least clear. First, which country's mandatory rules are being referred to? The answer is the vague one: any country with which the situation has a close connection. Second, the forum does not have to give effect to the mandatory rules of a country with which there is a close connection. Instead, it is given a discretion as to whether to do so. These two features inevitably lead to uncertainty in the law, and several Contracting States, at the negotiating stage, objected to Article 7(1) on this ground. Because of this the Convention provides that any Contracting State can reserve the right not to apply Article 7(1).[18] The United Kingdom has entered such a reservation, and, in accordance with this, section 2(2) of the Contracts (Applicable Law) Act 1990 provides that Article 7(1) shall not have the force of law in the United Kingdom.[19]

(ii) Public policy[20]

Article 16 of the Convention is entitled "Ordre public" and provides that the "application of a rule of the law of any country specified by this Convention may be refused only if such application is manifestly incompatible with the public policy ('ordre public') of the forum". In civil law countries ordre public operates as a well established exception to normal choice of law rules, as does public policy in common law jurisdictions. Any clash between the civil and common law concepts of public policy is resolved by the reference to the application of a rule of law being "manifestly" incompatible with the public policy of the forum. This word has been regularly used in Hague Conventions on Private International Law in an attempt to restrain the use of the doctrine. This adds nothing as far as English law is concerned since there has long been a reluctance to invoke the public policy doctrine in this country.[1] However, for civil lawyers it makes clear that what is in issue is the narrow concept of international ordre public as opposed to the wide concept

18 Art 22(1)(a).
19 See the Solicitor-General, HC Second Reading Committee 20 June 1990, col 4; Lord-Advocate, HL 12 Dec 1989 vol 513 cols 1258, 1271. See earlier Collins (1976) 25 ICLQ 35 at 49–51; for a more extreme criticism in terms of dissapproval of statutory regulation of contracts see Mann in *Harmonisation of Private International Law by the EEC* (ed Lipstein) 31. Germany also has not included Art 7(1) in its legislation incorporating the Convention into its private international law. Reservations have also been entered by Luxembourg and Ireland.
20 See Philip (1978) II Hague Recueil 1 at 55 et seq; Diamond, op cit, at 292 et seq; Moscani (1989) V Hague Recueil 9; Plender, paras 9.13–9.15. Public policy includes Community public policy: the Giuliano and Lagarde Report, p 38.
1 See the discussion of the public policy defence in relation to the recognition of foreign divorces etc, infra, pp 680–685.

of domestic ordre public. It has to be shown that the *application* of a foreign rule of law is against the forum's public policy. The circumstances of the case have to be considered. If, for example, a contract governed by French law restrains a party from competing in *England* then the application of a French rule allowing restraint of trade would appear to be contrary to the well known English public policy against restraint of trade because of the involvement of England. This limitation is entirely consistent with common law decisions on public policy, which have required some relevant connection with England which justifies English courts in invoking the public policy exception.[2] The intention then is that Article 16 will only be used in exceptional circumstances.[3]

When Article 16 does apply, it provides an exception to all of the preceding choice of law rules contained in the Convention, and is clearer in its wording in this respect than is the mandatory rules exception. Presumably, it can even operate to override the provisions on mandatory rules which are themselves an exception to normal choice of law principles.[4] Thus, an English court could refuse to apply the mandatory rules of a foreign country on the basis that the application of that mandatory rule would be against English public policy. It is possible to envisage this happening in cases where a foreign mandatory rule is in conflict with an English mandatory rule.

Common law cases[5] which involved the consideration of an objectionable foreign law which was held to be contrary to our distinctive English public policy will doubtless be decided in the same way under the Convention, using Article 16. Thus the English court will continue not to enforce such contracts as those in restraint of trade, assigning a cause of action, or contracts for prostitution, provided that the circumstances involve a sufficient connection with England to justify this. However, there was a very different category of public policy cases at common law based on the notion of the comity of nations. Thus in one case[6] the Court of Appeal held that it would be against the comity of nations to enforce a contract, the whole object of which was to import whisky into the United States contrary to the prohibition laws of that country. Such cases do not fit entirely happily within Article 16.[7] This is essentially a negative provision, being concerned with a refusal to apply some objectionable foreign rule.[8] If the English forum's concern, as appears to be the case in the above example, is to uphold a foreign law on a matter of great importance to that foreign country, the appropriate provision to refer to under the Convention is Article 7(1).[9] However, because Article 7(1) is not available in the United Kingdom, resort may have to be made to Article 16, even though this is not what that Article was designed for.

---

2 Supra, pp 128–133. The fact that an agreement also offended the public policy of the foreign place of performance could provide justification: *Lemenda Trading Co Ltd v African Middle East Petroleum Co Ltd* [1988] QB 448, [1988] 1 All ER 513; Carter (1988) 59 BYBIL 356; Collier [1988] CLJ 169.
3 The Giuliano and Lagarde Report, p 38; see also the UK submission in case 150/80 *Elefanten Schuh Gmbh v Jacqmain* [1981] ECR 1671, [1982] 3 CMLR 1.
4 See Fletcher, *Conflict of Laws and European Community Law*, p 172.
5 Supra, pp 128–131.
6 *Foster v Driscoll* [1929] 1 KB 470. English law governed the contract. However, the result would probably have been the same if the contract had been governed by a foreign law, according to which the contract had been enforceable. See also *Regazzoni v KC Sethia (1944) Ltd* [1956] 2 QB 490, affd [1958] AC 301; *Euro-Diam Ltd v Bathurst* [1990] 1 QB 1 at 40.
7 Cf Lasok and Stone, op cit, pp 372–374.
8 The Giuliano and Lagarde Report, at p 38; Philip, op cit, at 57.
9 Supra, p 503.

(f) PARTICULAR ISSUES

The scheme of the Convention is that, having set out the rules on the applicable law, there are then special rules dealing with the particular issues of material validity,[10] formal validity,[11] incapacity[12] and a number of other matters.[13] By implication, all other issues must be governed by the rules on the applicable law set out earlier in the Convention. The point is spelt out by a provision on the scope of the applicable law[14] which gives particular instances of issues governed by the rules on the applicable law. With special rules for particular issues, a problem of classification inevitably arises. Under the common law rules the English courts adopted the system of classification employed in the domestic law of contract. However, under the Convention it is important that the classification of issues is made in the light of the intentions of the drafters of the Convention and of the principle of uniform interpretation.[15] For example, the issue of whether a contract has to be in writing is intended to come within the category of formal validity[16] under the Convention, whereas this was classified as a procedural issue under the common law rules. The provisions in the Convention relating to particular issues will now be examined,[17] after which one issue that causes a special problem for the United Kingdom, that of illegality, will be considered.

(i) Material validity

Article 8 is entitled "Material Validity" and contains two provisions.[18] Before examining these provisions it is necessary to see what is encompassed within the concept of material validity.

What is meant by material validity?

Material validity under the Convention covers a wide variety of different issues. This is apparent from both Article 8(1), which is concerned with "the existence and validity of a contract", and Article 8(2), which deals with the existence of consent. The intention is that not only are issues of material validity in the English sense covered (for example, the issue of illegality), but also issues relating to formation of the contract[19] (for example, offer and acceptance, and consideration). The validity of consent to the contract, (for example, issues of mistake, misrepresentation and duress) is doubtless also covered under Article 8(1). Issues relating to the existence and validity of the contract itself are obviously covered, but so also are such issues in relation to the terms of the contract. As has already been mentioned,[20] the existence and validity of consent to a choice of the applicable law are to be referred to

10 Art 8.
11 Art 9.
12 Art 11.
13 Arts 12, 13, 14.
14 Art 10.
15 The Giuliano and Lagarde Report, p 38.
16 Art 9, infra, pp 507–510; see the Giuliano and Lagarde Report, p 31.
17 That is, apart from Art 12 (voluntary assignment), Art 13 (subrogation) and Art 14 (burden of proof, proving the contract). These matters are more appropriately dealt with elsewhere in the book, see supra, pp 82, 85, infra pp 813–818.
18 Art 8(1) and (2).
19 The Giuliano and Lagarde Report, p 28.
20 See the discussion on Art 3(4), supra p 486.

Article 8.[1] Nonetheless, not all issues of validity are dealt with under Article 8; formal validity has a special rule to itself under Article 9.[2]

(a) The putative applicable law Article 8(1) states that:

> The existence and validity of a contract, or of any term of a contract, shall be determined by the law which would govern it under this Convention if the contract or term were valid.

This means that the normal rules on the applicable law under the Convention are applied to the issue of material validity. The only gloss on this is that with material validity one has to assume that the contract or term is valid in the first place before ascertaining the applicable law. In the terminology of the common law rules the "putative" governing law is applied. As the Giuliano and Lagarde Report explains, "This is to avoid the circular argument that where there is a choice of the applicable law no law can be said to be applicable until the contract is found to be valid."[3] The important point of substance is that the parties are free to choose the governing law under Article 3 of the Convention, for example by putting a choice of law clause in the contract, even though the issue in the case is whether a valid contract exists between them. When it comes to validity of terms of the contract it means that the validity of a New York choice of law clause is governed by New York Law. In other words, the parties are able to pull themselves up by their own bootstraps. The principle has much to commend it. Businessmen use choice of law clauses in order to avoid the problems of ascertaining the objective governing law and their wishes should be respected whatever the issue.[4] However, this can lead to unfairness to one of the parties. The Working Group acknowledged this particular problem and included a safeguard in relation to consent to the contract.

(b) The safeguard in relation to consent[5] This is contained in Article 8(2) which provides that:

> Nevertheless a party may rely upon the law of the country in which he has his habitual residence to establish that he did not consent if it appears from the circumstances that it would not be reasonable to determine the effect of his conduct in accordance with the law specified in the preceding paragraph.

This is designed[6] to cater for the following sort of example: A makes an offer to B, and inserts a choice of law clause in the contract stating that the law of Utopia will govern all disputes between the parties. B remains silent, neither expressly accepting nor rejecting the offer. Under the law of Utopia silence can constitute an acceptance. It would be manifestly unfair for B to be contractually bound. The effect of Article 8(2) is that B can assert that he

---

1 The Giuliano and Lagarde Report, p 28.
2 Capacity is dealt with under Art 11.
3 At p 30.
4 See Dicey and Morris, pp 1197–1199 and the common law case of *Compania Naviera Micro SA v Shipley International Inc, The Parouth* [1982] 2 Lloyd's Rep 351. Cf Briggs [1990] Lloyd's MCLQ 192. For Australian authority applying the law of the forum to the issue of formation of the contract, see *Oceanic Sun Line Special Shipping Co Inc v Fay* (1988) 165 CLR 197, HC of Australia.
5 This has been criticised by Carter as being clumsy and not very adequate (1986) 57 BYBIL 1 at 26, n 108.
6 See the Giuliano and Lagarde Report, p 28.

did not consent to the contract according to the law of his habitual residence. The only proviso is that it would have to appear from the circumstances that it would not be reasonable to determine the effect of his conduct under Utopian law. On the above facts, doubtless it would not be. The circumstances to be taken into account include the parties' previous practices inter se and their business relationship.[7]

Article 8(2) allows a party to rely on the law of his habitual residence to deny the existence of a contract. It cannot be used in a positive way to create a contract which did not exist under the applicable law. It was specifically devised with the question of silence constituting acceptance of an offer in mind. Nonetheless, it is wide enough to cover any issue of offer and acceptance. It is, though, only concerned with the *existence* of consent, not with the *validity* of consent (for example with duress, mistake, misrepresentation). In cases raising these issues Article 8(1) will no doubt apply; but, on its own, without the safeguard contained in Article 8(2). As far as the issue of consent is concerned, the combined effect of Article 8(1) and (2) is that the contract can be invalidated either by reference to the applicable law or by reference to the habitual residence of the party denying that he consented. This suggests that the basic policy in relation to consent is that of invalidating the contract.

(ii) Formal validity

Article 9 of the Convention deals with this issue. It contains general rules relating to the formal validity of contracts, a rule for unilateral acts intended to have legal effect (such as notice of termination of a contract), and special rules for consumer contracts and contracts in respect of immovable property.

(a) What is meant by formal validity? It is not always easy to decide whether a matter is one of form or substance. English lawyers have particular difficulty with the classification of issues as ones of form because of the relative dearth of formal requirements under English law. This has meant that issues have sometimes been given a surprising classification. For example, the issue of whether a contract has to be in writing looks to be one of form, yet traditionally this has been classified under English law as one of procedure, and thus to be determined by the law of the forum.[8] However, it now appears that under the Convention this issue should be classified as one of form. The Giuliano and Lagarde Report gives welcome guidance as to what formal validity encompasses. It includes "every external manifestation required on the part of a person expressing the will to be legally bound, and in the absence of which, such expression of will would not be regarded as fully effective".[9] The following were given as examples of formal requirements:[10] the requirement that there must be two signatures to the contract; that the contract must be made in duplicate; and, of most interest to English lawyers, that a non-competition clause in a contract of employment must be in writing. On the other hand, it was said[11] that it did not include the special requirements

---

7 Ibid.
8 *Leroux v Brown* (1852) 12 CB 801; supra, pp 75–76. See also *G H Montage GmbH v Irvani* [1990] 1 WLR 667 at 684, 690.
9 At p 29.
10 At p 31.
11 At p 29.

which have to be fulfilled where an act is to be valid against third parties, for example the need in English law for a notice of a statutory assignment of a chose in action. It would be best if the concept of formal validity were to be given an independent community meaning. If it is left to national laws to determine whether the issue is one of formal validity, the English courts will need to take a broader view of the concept than they have in the past.

(b) The general rules

(i) The contract is concluded between persons who are in the same country

The first of the general rules on formal validity is contained in Article 9(1) which provides that:

> A contract concluded between persons who are in the same country is formally valid if it satisfies the fomal requirements of the law which governs it under this Convention or of the law of the country where it is concluded.

The policy underlying this provision is clear: to avoid the invalidation of contracts on the basis of formal defects. It does this by a validating rule of alternative reference. The normal rules on the applicable law under the Convention are applied, but if the contract is formally invalid under those rules, as an alternative recourse can be had to the law of the country where the contract was concluded in order to validate it.

The Working Group[12] justified the reference to the law of the place where the contract was concluded on the basis of the historical importance of this law. A modern policy justification would be that disputes as to form arise at the time when and in the country where the contract is concluded. It is therefore convenient that that country's law should be applied to resolve the dispute. There is no problem in determining where a contract was concluded because of the limitation of Article 9(1) to contracts concluded between parties who are in the same country.[13]

When it comes to applying, as an alternative, the law that governs the contract there are a number of difficulties. The first is that this law can be varied by the parties after the contract has been concluded. However, Article 3(2)[14] provides that a subsequent variation will not prejudice the formal validity of the contract. A subsequent variation of the governing law will not be allowed to invalidate the contract. On the other hand, a subsequent variation of the governing law which has the effect of formally validating a contract, invalid at its inception, will presumably be allowed,[15] validating the contract from that date. The second difficulty stems from the fact that different laws may govern different parts of the contract. Which of these governing laws is to determine its formal validity? According to the Giuliano and Lagarde Report "it would seem reasonable to apply the law applicable to the part of the contract most closely connected with the disputed condition on which its formal validity depends".[16] Third, when Article 9 refers to the

---

12 At p 30.
13 Where the contract is concluded by an agent, reference has to be made to the country in which the agent acts: Art 9(3).
14 Supra, pp 478–479.
15 The Giuliano and Lagarde Report, p 30.
16 Ibid.

law that governs the contract, apparently this means the *putative* governing law, ie the law which would govern the contract if it were formally valid.[17]

(ii) The contract is concluded between persons who are not in the same country
If the parties are not in the same country at the time of the conclusion of the contract, the second general rule, which is contained in Article 9(2), applies. According to this:

> A contract concluded between person who are in different countries is formally valid if it satisfies the formal requirements of the law which governs it under this Convention or of the law of one of those countries.

This means that recourse may be had to the law of up to three different countries in order to validate the contract. The rules in Article 9(1) and (2) set out alternatives for validating the contract, rightly without giving a priority to any one alternative.[18]

(iii) Acts intended to have legal effect
The third and last part of the general rules[19] is concerned with formal requirements in respect of acts[20] intended to have legal effect, such as an offer or notice of termination, and is analogous to Article 9(1) in that it refers, as alternatives, to the law applicable under the Convention or the law of the country where the act was done.

(c) The special rules for particular contracts

(i) Consumer contracts
The first of the special rules is concerned with consumer contracts. The formal validity of a consumer contract is governed by the law of the country in which the consumer has his habitual residence.[1] This means that, for consumer contracts,[2] formal validity is governed by the law that governs the substance of the contract, and the consumer is protected by having the law of his habitual residence applied.[3]

(ii) Immovable property
The second special rule is concerned with contracts relating to immovable property. Article 9(6) states that:

> Notwithstanding paragraphs 1 to 4 of this Article, a contract the subject matter of which is a right in immovable property or a right to use immovable property shall be subject to the mandatory requirements of form of the law of the country where the property is situated if by that law those requirements are imposed irrespective of the country where the contract is concluded and irrespective of the law governing the contract.

This provision shows a concern to give effect to the mandatory rules of form of the law of the situs in cases involving immovable property.[4] It is not

---

17 Ibid.
18 Cf the position under the traditional common law rules, see the 11th edn (1987) of this book, pp 479–480.
19 Art 9(4).
20 The act must relate to an existing or contemplated contract: the Giuliano and Lagarde Report, p 29.
1 Art 9(5); see the Giuliano and Lagarde Report, pp 31–32.
2 Ie ones to which Art 5 applies. The contract must be concluded in the circumstances mentioned in Art 5, para 2.
3 Morse criticises this for erring in favour of the consumer, op cit, at 151.
4 See the Giuliano and Lagarde Report, at p 31.

enough to show simply that these rules are mandatory (cannot be derogated from by contract). It must also be shown that the mandatory requirement of form is imposed "irrespective of the country where the contract is concluded and irrespective of the law governing the contract". In other words, according to the law of the situs the mandatory rule has to have overriding effect.[5]

(iii) Capacity

As has already been seen, questions involving the capacity of corporations are excluded altogether from the scope of the Convention.[6] When it comes to natural persons the position is more complex. The status or legal capacity of natural persons is, in general, excluded from the scope of the Convention.[7] Contracting States are therefore left to apply their traditional private international law rules to the issue of capacity to contract. However, this is subject to Article 11 of the Convention. This is a narrow rule concerned with protecting parties who have contracted with a natural person under an incapacity from being caught unawares by this. The traditional English common law rules on capacity will now be examined, and then Article 11 of the Convention.

(a) **The traditional common law rules** What law governs capacity to make a commercial contract is a matter of speculation so far as the English common law authorities are concerned. There is no clear decision and the dicta are not very helpful. It is clear though that the choice lies between the law of the domicil,[8] the law of the place where the contract was made[9] and the proper law in the objective sense.

It may be conceded that in modern conditions of trade domicil is not a satisfactory test. It is incompatible with justice and with the trust that lies at the basis of commercial dealings, for instance, that a person over eighteen years of age should be able to escape liability for the price of goods sold and delivered to him in a London shop on the ground that he is still a minor by the law of his domicil abroad.[10] Indeed, under civil law systems the rule that capacity is governed by the personal law cannot be relied on by a person who, though lacking capacity by his personal law, has capacity according to the law of the place where the contract was made.[11] Under English law, in many cases, contracts by persons under eighteen are not enforceable against them,[12] but the court might well restrict this rule, and it would be reasonable for it to do so, to contracts in respect of which the objective proper law is English law.[13] It is also argued that, in the converse case, capacity conferred by the law of the domicil should not be invalidated by the proper law, ie a

---

5 See the Giuliano and Lagarde Report, p 32, which makes this clear.
6 Art 1(2)(e), supra, p 472.
7 Art 1(2)(a), supra, pp 469–470.
8 *Sottomayor v De Barros* (1877) 3 PD 1 at 5. Although this was a marriage case, COTTON LJ applied his statement in support of the law of the domicil to any contract. He was severely criticised in *Sottomayer v De Barros* (1879) 5 PD 94 at 100: but see *Re Cooke's Trusts* (1887) 56 LJ Ch 637 at 639; *Cooper v Cooper* (1888) 13 App Cas 88 at 99, 100, 108.
9 *Baindail v Baindail* [1946] P 122 at 128, [1946] 1 All ER 342 at 346; and see *Simonin v Mallac* (1860) 2 Sw & Tr 67; *Republica de Guatemala v Nunez* [1927] 1 KB 669 at 689.
10 See Morris, pp 285–288.
11 Wolff, pp 281–282.
12 See Law Com No 134; the Minors' Contracts Act 1987.
13 See Morris, pp 285–287.

person should be regarded as capable if capable by the law of his domicil.[14] So far, however, English courts have not been pressed to adopt such attitudes.

Not only has it been advocated frequently that the law of the place where the contract was made governs the question of capacity[15] but there is also one old English decision to this effect.[16] This view, if it implies that the law of that place exclusively governs the matter, is clearly untenable, for it would enable a party to evade an incapacity imposed upon him by the law that governs the contract in other respects by the simple device of concluding the contract in a country where the law is more favourable. Moreover, the law of the place of contracting is ill adapted to govern the matter if, as may well happen, the parties conclude the contract in a place where they are only transiently present.

Such modern authority as there is would indicate that capacity to conclude a commercial contract is regulated by the proper law of the contract objectively ascertained. This is supported by the Canadian decision in *Charron v Montreal Trust Co*.[17] It was held there that capacity to enter a separation agreement is to be determined by the law of the country with which the contract is most substantially connected,[18] ie the proper law; though in the actual case this was also the law of the place where the contract was made.

More recently, the issue of capacity arose in *Bodley Head Ltd v Flegon*:[19]

The Russian author, Alexander Solzhenitsyn, granted a power of attorney to H, a Swiss lawyer, to deal with his literary works outside Russia. This power stated that Swiss law was applicable to any disputes between the two parties. H assigned certain publication rights to a German publishing house which, in turn, authorised the plaintiff to publish Solzhenitsyn's works in the United Kingdom. The defendant disputed the plaintiff's rights and proposed to publish his own edition of Solzhenitsyn's works. The plaintiff claimed copyright in the works but the defendant argued, inter alia, that the original agreement between Solzhenitsyn and H was invalid as Solzhenitsyn had no capacity under Russian law, which was both the law of the domicil and the law of the place where the contract was made, to enter a contract to appoint an agent to contract abroad on his behalf.

Whilst doubting the correctness of the allegation that Solzhenitsyn was incapable under Russian law, BRIGHTMAN J had no doubt that the question of his capacity was to be decided by Swiss law as the proper law of the contract. Although the point was not discussed, the facts of this case did raise the issue that, in stating that capacity is governed by the proper law of the contract, this expression must be taken to mean the law of the country with which the contract is most substantially connected. Intention cannot here be allowed free play.[20] A person cannot confer capacity upon himself by deliberately submitting himself to a law to which factually the contract is unrelated.

Let us assume, for example, that in *Bodley Head Ltd v Flegon* both H and

14 Dicey & Morris, pp 1202–1207; Restatement, 2d § 198.
15 *Baindail v Baindail* [1946] P 122 at 128, [1946] 1 All ER 342 at 346; Anton, pp 276–278.
16 *Male v Roberts* (1790) 3 Esp 163; and see *Bondholders Securities Corp v Manville* [1933] 4 DLR 699.
17 (1958) 15 DLR (2d) 240.
18 Ibid, at 244–245.
19 [1972] 1 WLR 680.
20 *Cooper v Cooper* (1888) 13 App Cas 88 at 108.

Solzhenitsyn had been domiciled in Russia and that the power of attorney had been granted there, but had been expressed to be governed by Swiss law. The parties would have capacity by Swiss, but not by Russian, law. Objectively regarded, this is a Russian contract void by Russian law and it would be idle to suggest that it is validated by the reference to Swiss law. But if, as was the case, it was made by Solzhenitsyn with a Swiss domiciliary and if it related to acts performable in Switzerland, it is not unprincipled to recognise its validity according to Swiss law. Under the Rome Convention, Swiss law would govern the valid formation of the contract in other respects and it seems only sensible that under the common law rules Swiss law should govern the issue of capacity. It is true, of course, that the defendant would escape from an incapacity imposed upon him by the Russian law of his domicil, but quite apart from the fact that the contract has no material connection with Russia, it does not follow that the Russian rule is intended to affect transactions of a substantially foreign character.

(b) Article 11 Article 11 is entitled "Incapacity"[1] and states that:

> In a contract concluded between persons who are in the same country, a natural person who would have capacity under the law of that country may invoke his incapacity resulting from another law only if the other party to the contract was aware of this incapacity at the time of the conclusion of the contract or was not aware thereof as a result of negligence.

This is an unusual article in that it grafts a specific rule dealing with one aspect of capacity onto national rules of private international law on this topic. The aspect it is concerned with is the position of a party who contracts with a natural person who is under an incapacity but is unaware of this incapacity. In certain circumstances it protects such a party by imposing a limitation on the right of the natural person under the incapacity to invoke his own incapacity. This idea has its origins in the law of certain civil law countries. In order for this limitation to apply, certain stringent conditions have to be satisfied.[2]

First, there must be a contract concluded between persons who are in the same country. The Working Group did not want to prejudice the protection of, for example, minors when a contract was made at a distance. The person under an incapacity must be a natural person. However, there is no such requirement as regards the other party, and this could presumably be a corporation. In cases where the incapacity of a corporation is at issue the traditional common law rules will apply, and in such cases this is not subject to Article 11. Second, it must be a situation where, according to the traditional private international law rules applicable in the forum, a natural person has capacity under the law of the country where the contract was concluded, but lacks capacity under another law. For example, a Contracting State under its traditional private international law rules may apply the proper law (as in the case of England) or the law of the domicil or nationality (as in the case of some civil law countries) to the issue of capacity, and under that law a person lacks capacity. Under Article 11 it is then necessary to turn to the law of the place where the contract was concluded in order to see if there is capacity by that law. There is no difficulty in identifying the

---

1 This includes incapacity in relation to consent to choice: Art 3(4), supra, p 486.
2 The Giuliano and Lagarde Report, p 34.

country where the contract was concluded in cases where (as will always be the case under Article 11) both parties are in the same country at the time of the conclusion of the contract. On the other hand, if a Contracting State to the Convention applies the law of the place of contracting to the issue of capacity under its traditional private international law rules, Article 11 will not operate.

If these requirements are met, the limitation on the right of an incapacitated person to invoke his own incapacity applies. The person under the incapacity can only invoke his own incapacity if the other party was aware of this incapacity or was not aware thereof as a result of negligence. The burden of proof as to this lies on the incapacitated party.[3] If satisfied, the incapacitated party lacks capacity to contract. On the other hand, if the incapacitated party does not satisfy the burden of proof he will have capacity to contract. The limitation is a narrow one. It only affects the rights of the person acting under the incapacity. The other party can raise an incapacity that exists according to the law applied by the traditional private international law rules of the forum even though he or she knew of the incapacity at the time of contracting. Furthermore, it only affects the rights of the person acting under the incapacity when that person is seeking to invoke his own incapacity. It does not prevent, for example, a minor from seeking to uphold a contract, and the other party cannot escape from a contract (valid by the applicable law) by saying that he was unaware that he was contracting with a minor.

(iv) Scope of the applicable law[4]

Article 10 is entitled "Scope of the Applicable Law" and in paragraph (1) gives a number of examples of issues coming within the scope of the law applicable to the contract by virtue of Articles 3–6 and 12.[5] This is not intended to be an exhaustive list,[5a] and it is implicit that all other issues are governed by the rules on the applicable law. The only exceptions are issues classified as ones of formal validity or incapacity. Material validity is, of course, governed by the rules on the applicable law because of Article 8(1). The examples provided by Article 10 are as follows:

(a) Interpretation Under the common law rules the province of interpretation was to discover the true intent and meaning of the parties as expressed by the language of the contract. This was a question of fact. Nevertheless, a question of choice of law could arise, for if an expression was ambiguous and if it bore different meanings in different legal systems, its interpretation had to be determined by reference to one only of these systems. This distinction between fact and law is still valid under the Convention, since the Convention is only concerned with choice of law. When a choice of law problem arises, the Convention adopts the simple solution that the law applicable to the contract will govern the issue of interpretation.[6] A problem which arises from this approach can be illustrated by the situation where the

---

3 Ibid.
4 See Plender, paras 11.01–11.17; Lagarde in *Contract Conflicts* pp 49 et seq.
5 In cases of dépecage the law applicable will be that governing the relevant part of the contract; cf Anton, pp 339–340.
5a "The law applicable to a contract ... shall govern in particular": Art 10(1). See Plender, para 11.02, where it is suggested that "effects of a contract" are omitted from the list.
6 Art 10(1)(a).

contract is governed by Utopian law, but the parties have expressly provided that the contract is to be interpreted according to the law of Ruritania. At common law it seems that Ruritanian law would govern the interpretation of the contract. Under the Convention it appears, at first glance, that Utopian law has to be applied, since this is the law applicable to *the contract*. However, Article 10(1) refers to the law applicable to the contract "by virtue of Articles 3–6". Under Article 3 the parties are able to choose a law for *part* of the contract which may include a specific issue such as interpretation. The law applicable to the issue of interpretation in the above example would accordingly be Ruritanian law, which has been expressly chosen to govern that part of the contract.

(b) Performance

(i) What is encompassed within the concept of performance?
Whilst interpretation of a contract is a fairly self-explanatory category, some explanation is needed of what is encompassed within the concept of performance under Article 10(1)(b). The Giuliano and Lagarde Report gives helpful examples of issues coming within Article 10:

> the diligence with which the obligation must be performed; conditions relating to the place and time of performance; the extent to which the obligation can be performed by a person other than the party liable; the conditions as to performance of the obligation both in general and in relation to certain categories of obligation (joint and several obligations, alternative obligations, divisible and indivisible obligations, pecuniary obligations); where performance consists of the payment of a sum of money, the conditions relating to the discharge of the debtor who has made the payment, the appropriation of the payment, the receipt, etc.[7]

It is not clear whether all of these examples come within Article 10(1)(b) or whether some of them are intended to come within Article 10(1)(c)(failure to perform) or (d) (the various ways of extinguishing obligations). However, it is not necessary to decide this since the position is the same under each of the sub-paragraphs of Article 10(1): the applicable law by virtue of Articles 3 to 6 and 12 governs. Nonetheless, it is important to distinguish all of these cases relating to the substance of performance from "the manner of performance and the steps to be taken in the event of defective performance" because of the special provision in Article 10(2), which deals with the latter.

(ii) The manner of performance: a special rule
Article 10(2) provides that:

> In relation to the manner of performance and the steps to be taken in the event of defective performance regard shall be had to the law of the country in which performance takes place.

This provision deals with the situation where the law of the country of the place of performance is different from the law of the country whose law is applicable under Articles 3–6 and 12 of the Convention.[8] Two questions arise in relation to Article 10(2). The first is a question of definition: what matters fall within the concept of manner of performance? The second is a question

---

7 At pp 32–33.
8 If the two are the same the court would have to apply that country's law as the applicable law.

of substance: what is a court supposed to do if it is faced with a matter of the manner of performance?

The definitional question
The Working Group[9] said that they did not want to give a strict definition to the concept of manner of performance. However, they have provided examples of matters normally falling within this category: rules governing public holidays, the manner in which goods are to be examined, and the steps to be taken if they are refused. Ultimately, it is for the law of the forum to decide if the issue is one relating to the manner of performance. The following have been held to be matters relating to the manner of performance under the old common law rules: questions over the money of payment, ie the currency in which a debt is dischargeable,[10] the date at which lay days begin to run,[11] the hours during which delivery may be tendered,[12] and the meaning to be attributed to the word "alongside" in a stipulation providing that the cargo is "to be taken from alongside the steamer".[13] In all of these examples what is really being talked about are the minor details of performance. These examples would doubtless be classified in the same way under the Convention, for they are entirely compatible with the examples of manner of performance given in the Giuliano and Lagarde Report.[14] The big difference between the Convention and the common law rules is in respect of the rule to be applied to the issue of manner of performance.

The question of substance
This brings us on to the second question in relation to Article 10(2). What is a court supposed to do if it is faced with a matter of the manner of performance? The court does not have to apply the law of the country in which performance takes place. It is merely required to have regard to that law. The court is thus given a discretion as to whether to apply that law or not, as it so chooses.[15] If it does apply that law it can do so in whole or in part. At common law there was no such discretion; if the issue was one relating to the mode and manner of performance the law of the place of performance was applied.[16] The adoption of a discretion under the Convention introduces new and unwelcome uncertainty into this area. Obvious questions are raised. How much regard is to be given to this law? What are to be the criteria for the exercise of the discretion? The only guidance given on this by the Working Group is a reference to the court doing justice between the parties. It is surprising to find a discretion, particularly one to be exercised on such a vague criterion, in a Convention which places such emphasis on achieving uniformity and certainty in the law. And unlike Article 7(1), which is the other provision in the Convention involving the exercise of a discretion,

9 The Giuliano and Lagarde Report, at p 33.
10 *Mount Albert Borough Council v Australasian Temperance and General Mutual Life Assurance Society* [1938] AC 224 at 241.
11 *Norden SS Co v Dempsey* (1876) 1 CPD 654.
12 Dicey & Morris pp 1237–1238; and see *Robertson v Jackson* (1845) 2 CB 412.
13 F A Mann (1937) 18 BYBIL 97, 108, citing *Palgrave, Brown & Son Ltd v SS Turid* [1922] 1 AC 397.
14 For a not very convincing suggestion that manner of performance can include exchange control regulations which make payment illegal see Diamond, op cit, at 296; discussed infra, p 520.
15 The Giuliano and Lagarde Report, at p 33.
16 The 11th edn (1987) of this book, at pp 492–495.

Contracting States are not given a power of reservation in relation to Article 10(2).

(c) Within the limits of the powers conferred on the court by its procedural law, the consequences of breach, including the assessment of damages in so far as it is governed by rules of law[17]

(i) What is encompassed within the concept of consequences of breach?
According to the Giuliano and Lagarde Report[18] "the consequences of breach" encompasses such matters as the liability of the party to whom the breach is attributable, claims to terminate the contract for breach, and any "requirement of service of notice on the party to assume his liability". There is also guidance to be found in the European Court of Justice's decision in *SPRL Arcado v SA Haviland*.[19] This case involved, inter alia, an action for damages for wrongful repudiation of an independent commercial agency agreement. A jurisdictional question arose, namely whether the proceedings related to a contract under Article 5(1) of the Brussels Convention. In deciding that they did, the Court of Justice was influenced by the fact that any choice of law problem in relation to this claim was regarded as being contractual according to Article 10 of the Rome Convention. It was said that this Article "governs the consequences of a total or partial failure to comply with obligations arising under it and consequently the contractual liability of the party responsible for such breach".[20] Finally, a Dutch court,[1] discussing the Convention before it came into effect, has said that "the consequences of breach" must be construed widely and can therefore include strikes. The court ordered striking crew members of a Saudi Arabian ship lying at Rotterdam to return to work on the basis that the strike was unlawful under Philippines law, which was the expressly chosen applicable law. The issues raised by the case were held to fall within Article 10(1)(c). The "consequences of breach" also arguably could encompass the issue of whether specific performance is available as a remedy.[2]

(ii) Assessment of damages
Article 10(1)(c) provides that the consequences of breach include the issue of assessment of damages, but this is only in so far as the assessment is "governed by rules of law". This draws a distinction between circumstances when assessment of damages raises questions of fact and those when it raises questions of law. If the question in relation to assessment is only one of fact (for example, a jury is to calculate the amount of damages) this is a matter purely for the court hearing the action and the applicable law under the Convention will not govern the issue. On the other hand, if the question raised is one of law (the Giuliano and Lagarde Report[3] gives as examples cases where the contract prescribes the amount of damages in cases of non-performance or there is an international convention fixing a limit to the right to compensation) then Article 10(1(c) will apply. Under the English common

---

17 Art 10(1)(c).
18 At p 33.
19 Case 9/87 [1988] ECR 1539.
20 At p 1555.
 1 *Buenaventura v Ocean Trade Company* [1984] ECC 183 at 186.
 2 But see the procedural limitation in relation to Art 10(1)(c), infra p 517; Lasok and Stone, p 370.
 3 At p 33.

law the assessment or quantification of damages is a procedural matter for the law of the forum[4] whereas the questions of heads of damage available and of remoteness of damage are ones of substance for the applicable law. The effect of Article 10(1)(c) is therefore that English courts will now have to apply the law applicable to the contract to the issue of assessment of damages in so far as this raises questions of law.

(iii) The procedural limitation
The scope of Article 10(1)(c) is limited by its opening words:

> within the limits of the powers conferred on the court by its procedural law.

It has been suggested[5] that this would, for example, allow an English court to refuse to award damages in the form of periodical payments (as required by the foreign applicable law) on the basis that, there is no procedural mechanism under English law for the award of damages in this form. It may also allow a let out to an English court which is reluctant to grant specific performance, as required by a foreign applicable law.[6]

(d) The various ways of extinguishing obligations, and prescription and limitation of actions This provision[7] brings together what are, to English eyes, two very different sorts of issue. The first of these is the various ways of extinguishing obligations, of which there is a wide variety: for example, by performance; by bankruptcy; by legislation; by a moratorium; by subsequent impossibility; by novation, ie by a new contract which substitutes an existing obligation for another obligation, as, for example, by changing debtors. Any choice of law problems that arise in relation to these situations are a matter for the applicable law under the Convention, including the provisions on severing the contract.

The second issue covered is prescription and limitation of actions, which is likewise subject to the applicable law as determined by the Convention. This provision was, in part, responsible for the recent changes in the English law on limitation of actions. At one time the matter of limitation was regarded under English law as being a procedural one for the law of the forum. However, as has been seen,[8] the Foreign Limitation Periods Act 1984 changed this rule by adopting the principle that the English court is to apply to the issue of limitation the law which governs the substantive issue according to the English choice of law rules. Thus, even before the Rome Convention came into force the English law on limitation produced the same effect in contract cases as that now produced by Article 10 (1)(d). However, it was an awareness of the latter provision which helped lead to the 1984 Act.[9]

(e) The consequences of nullity of the contract This provision[10], which was added at a very late stage of the negotiation of the Rome Convention, was designed to make it clear that the issue of whether money paid under a void contract is recoverable is to be subject to the rules on the applicable law

---

4 Supra, pp 95–96.
5 See Morse's comments on Art 10(1)(c) in his annotations to the 1990 Act in Current Law Statutes; Plender, para 11.11.
6 Lasok and Stone, p 370.
7 Art 10(1)(d).
8 Supra, pp 79–81.
9 See Law Com No 114 (1982), para 3.9.
10 Art 10(1)(e).

under the Convention.[11] In some Member States the consequences of nullity are regarded as being non-contractual in nature. Indeed, under English and Scots law the right to recover money paid under a void contract forms part of the law of quasi-contract or restitution, not of contract. Because of this, Contracting States were allowed to enter a reservation, reserving the right not to apply Article 10 (1)(e). Accordingly, the United Kingdom has entered a reservation and section 2(2) of the 1990 Act provides that Article 10(1)(e) is not part of United Kingdom law.[12]

(v) The special problem in relation to illegality

Article 8[13] subjects illegality to the normal rules under the Convention. Thus, a court will not enforce a contract which is illegal by the law applicable to the contract. This was equally true under the traditional common law rules.[14] One of the few ways open to United Kingdom courts for dealing with illegality by the law of a particular country is to hold, in cases where there has been no choice by the parties, that the law of that country is the objectively applicable law under Article 4, and there is sufficient flexibility within this Article for the courts to reach this conclusion if they are so minded.

This still leaves the problem of the effect of illegality under a law which is not the law applicable to the contract. There are no special rules under the Convention to deal with this problem. This contrasts with the position under the traditional common law rules, under which there were special rules to deal with issues of illegality.[15] However, Article 7(1) (the discretion to apply the mandatory rules of a foreign country) is a general rule which is effective to deal with the issue of illegality by a foreign law and will no doubt be used for this purpose by those other Contracting States which have not excluded its application. In the absence of this provision in United Kingdom law the only way to deal with the problem of the effect of illegality under a law which is not the applicable law is for English courts to use other rules in the Convention, in particular those contained in Article 10(2) (manner of performance), Article 7(2) (mandatory rules of the forum) and Article 16 (public policy). Four situations involving illegality, which have been much discussed under the common law rules, will now be examined to ascertain what the position will be under the Convention.

An agreement to break a foreign law
At common law such an agreement, even though subject to a foreign law, was probably against the English doctrine of public policy and the comity of nations, and was not enforceable. As has already been seen,[16] cases decided on this basis appear to fall more appropriately within Article 7(1) than within the public policy provision in Article 16. Nonetheless, because of the absence of the former provision in the United Kingdom this type of case will have to be considered under Article 16.

Illegality by the law of the foreign place of performance in cases where the applicable law is English law
This situation arose in the well known case under the common law of *Ralli*

---

11 The Giuliano and Lagarde Report, p 33; North in *Contract Conflicts*, pp 16–17.
12 See the Lord-Advocate, Hansard (HL) 12 Dec 1989 col 1271.
13 Supra, pp 505–506.
14 See *Kahler v Midland Bank Ltd* [1950] AC 24, [1949] 2 All ER 621.
15 See the 11th edn (1987) of this book at pp 482–489.
16 Supra, p 504.

Bros v Cia Naviera Sota y Aznar.[17] This case was concerned not with illegality from the outset of the contract but with the rather different situation of supervening illegality, ie the illegality in the place of performance only arose after the contract had been made. A simple example would be a contract, made in January, the performance of which is rendered illegal by a statute passed in June. The facts of the *Ralli Case* were as follows:

> An English firm chartered a Spanish ship from a Spanish firm to carry jute from Calcutta to Barcelona at a freight of £50 per ton. At the time when payment had fallen due the Spanish Government had issued a decree ordaining that freight on jute must not exceed a figure considerably lower than the contractual freight. Freight was tendered at the rate allowed by Spanish law but the receivers of cargo refused to pay the excess amount.

An action was brought in England to recover freight at the contractual rate. The action failed. The vital point in the case was that the proper law of the contract was English law. The court, therefore, was bound to apply and did in fact apply the internal law, not the private international law, of England. The familiar English cases dealing with impossibility of performance were cited and SCRUTTON LJ summed up their effect on the instant facts in the following words:

> Where a contract requires an act to be done in a foreign country, it is, in the absence of very special circumstances an implied term of the continuing validity of such a provision that the act to be done in the foreign country shall not be illegal by the law of that State.[18]

The position under the Convention with regard to such a case would appear to be as follows. The normal rules for the determination of the applicable law would apply to the issue of illegality by virtue of Article 8. The applicable law was English. Under the English domestic law of contract's doctrine of frustration an agreement to perform that which it later becomes illegal to perform is unenforceable.[19] The result in the case would therefore be the same under the Convention as under the common law rules it replaces, and the action to recover the freight would fail.

Illegality by the law of the foreign place of performance in cases where the applicable law is foreign
No case arose at common law which required the court to consider the effect of illegality at the foreign place of performance on a contract the proper law of which was the law of yet another foreign country. In other words, a case like the *Ralli Case*, but now involving a foreign proper law under which there was no illegality. There were frequent dicta attributing decisive effect to illegality by the law of the place of performance,[20] although it was consistently argued in this book[1] that such an approach was contrary to principle, and not dictated by the authorities.

Turning to the Convention, there is no special rule dealing with illegality

17 [1920] 2 KB 287.
18 At p 304.
19 See Cheshire, Fifoot and Furmston's *Law of Contract* (12th edn) p 570.
20 *Toprak v Finagrain* [1979] 2 Lloyd's Rep 98 at 114; *United City Merchants (Investments) Ltd v Royal Bank of Canada* [1982] QB 208 at 228; revsd by the House of Lords on other points [1983] 1 AC 168, [1982] 2 All ER 720; *XAG v A Bank* [1983] 2 Lloyd's Rep 535 at 543; *Euro-Diam Ltd v Bathurst* [1990] 1 QB 1 at 15; affd by CA at 30; *Libyan Arab Foreign Bank v Bankers Trust Co* [1989] QB 728, [1989] 3 All ER 252.
1 See the 11th edn (1987) pp 486–488.

by the law of the place of performance and on the above facts, there is no illegality under the foreign applicable law. When a foreign country makes conduct illegal this may well involve a foreign mandatory rule, within Article 7(1), which deals with the mandatory rules of a foreign country with which there is a close connection.[2] However, the exclusion of Article 7(1) from United Kingdom law means that the English courts will have no discretion to apply such foreign rules.

If the issue is classified as one relating to the manner of performance under Article 10(2), then it may be appropriate to apply the law, including any rules on illegality, of the country in which performance takes place. The "manner of performance" is, however, a fairly narrow category[3] and it would not be possible to regard the *Ralli Case* as one relating to this issue. It has, nevertheless, been suggested[4] that the concept of manner of performance could include the question of whether payment is illegal because of exchange control regulations; and if these regulations are contained in the law of the place of performance it would then be appropriate to apply that country's law under Article 10(2).

Consideration needs also to be given, in the context of illegality by the foreign law of the place of performance, to the public policy provision of Article 16. The problem with its application in this context is whether a case involving illegality by the law of a foreign place of performance can be regarded as raising public policy considerations for the forum. There was a tendency in the more recent common law decisions discussing the principle of illegality by the law of the place of performance to describe this principle as being rooted in the notion of not acting against the comity of nations.[5] It is, however, submitted that the comity of nations aspect is very much more important in cases where the parties, from the outset, set out to break a foreign law, than it is in cases where the parties act in good faith, but find subsequently that performance becomes impossible because of a change in the law of the place of performance. The upshot is that it is questionable whether cases of illegality by the foreign law of the place of performance can be regarded as falling within Article 16.

Illegality by the law of the English place of performance in cases where the applicable law is foreign
At common law such a contract would not be enforced, and this situation provided an exception to the normal rules on the application of the proper law of the contract.[6] Under the Convention this situation will doubtless involve a mandatory rule of the forum; if so, Article 7(2) will lead to the application of English law and the contract will be unenforceable. Even if not, Article 16 would lead to the same conclusion.

---

2 The place of performance constitutes such a connection: the Giuliano and Lagarde Report, p 27.
3 Supra, pp 514–515.
4 Diamond, op cit, at 296.
5 *Toprak v Finagrain* [1979] 2 Lloyd's Rep 98 at 107; affd by the Court of Appeal at 112, without mentioning this specific point; *United City Merchants (Investments) Ltd v Royal Bank of Canada* [1982] QB 208 at 228, 242, revsd by the House of Lords on other points [1983] AC 168, [1982] 2 All ER 720; *Euro-Diam Ltd v Bathurst* [1987] 1 Lloyd's Rep 178 at 187, [1987] 2 All ER 113 at 120. See also *Lemenda Trading Co Ltd v African Middle East Petroleum Co Ltd* [1988] QB 448, [1988] 1 All ER 513 discussed supra, p 504, note 2. For the application of Art 16 in cases involving the comity of nations, see supra, p 504.
6 Dicey and Morris, pp 1218–1219.

(g) RELATIONSHIP WITH OTHER CONVENTIONS

Article 21 states that "This Convention shall not prejudice the application of international conventions to which a Contracting State is, or becomes, a party". This provision has two effects. First, it makes it clear that existing conventions covering some of the same ground as the Rome Convention are preserved. The United Kingdom has entered into a number of such Conventions in relation to carriage.[7] Cases which fell within one of these Conventions were governed by the rules in the particular carriage Convention (once implemented by legislation) and not by the proper law of the contract.[8] The rules in these carriage Conventions will continue to apply, unaffected by the Rome Convention. Second, it allows Contracting States to enter into new conventions covering some of the same ground as the Rome Convention.[9] This means that Contracting States can become parties to Hague Conventions on Private International Law, such as the Hague Convention on the law applicable to contracts for the international sale of goods of 1985.[10]

---

7 See the Law Commission Consultative Document (August 1974) on the preliminary draft Convention, pp 93–95; Dicey and Morris, pp 1271–1277.
8 *The Hollandia* [1983] 1 AC 565. See also *Kenya Railways v Antares Co Pte Ltd (The Antares) (Nos 1 and 2)* [1987] 1 Lloyd's Rep 424.
9 If a Contracting State wishes to do so, it must follow the consultation procedure set out in Arts 23 and 24.
10 The 1985 Convention is accompanied by an Explanatory Report by Von Mehren. See generally Diamond (1986) IV Hague Recueil 236; McLachlan (1986) 102 LQR 591; Gabor (1986) 7 Northwestern J of Int L and Bus 696. Choice of law problems will still arise despite the 1980 Vienna Convention on contracts for the international sale of goods, which seeks to unify the substantive law in this area. The United Kingdom is considering whether to ratify the 1980 Convention, which is set out in (1980) 19 ILM 668.

Chapter 19

Negotiable instruments[1]

SUMMARY

1. INTRODUCTION

Negotiable instruments, since they represent the medium by which the trade of the modern world is to a certain extent conducted and financed, are a fertile source of problems that can be solved only by a reference to private international law.[2] A bill of exchange drawn in England may be accepted in one foreign country, indorsed in another, and dishonoured in yet another; a foreign bill, exhibiting variations from its English counterpart, may circulate in the United Kingdom; and a bill that has been the subject of a series of purely foreign transactions may raise an issue in English litigation.

A preliminary fact that should be appreciated, since it explains the rules for choice of law adopted in England and indeed in most other countries, is that a negotiable instrument is a document that contains several distinct contracts.[3] Each party who puts his name to the document incurs a separate liability. In the case, for instance, of

a bill of exchange drawn by A on B to the order of C and indorsed by C in favour of D,

the original contract between A the drawer and C the payee is followed by what the Bills of Exchange Act 1882 calls "supervening contracts" made by the acceptor and indorser. The principal debtor on whom the primary liability rests is the acceptor, while the drawer and indorsers are his sureties for the performance of his contract.

Since the liability of the sureties is subsidiary to that of the primary debtor, it is arguable that when a conflict of laws occurs the position of each contracting party should be determined by a single law, namely, the law that governs the acceptance. This, however, is not the view taken by English law.

---

1 On this topic reference should be made to Falconbridge, ch 14; Morris, ch 21; Nygh, ch 20; Byles on *Bills* (26th edn, 1988) ch 25. Negotiable instruments are excluded from the Rome Convention: Art 1 (2)(c), supra, p 471.
2 If the UN Convention on International Bills of Exchange and International Promissory Notes (1989) 28 ILM 170 is adopted by States the problems will be reduced, as will the significance of private international law in the area.
3 See especially Dicey & Morris, pp 1308–1310.

The 1882 Act adopts the general principle that the liability of each separate contracting party is governed by the law of the place where each separate contract is made.[4] There is no right in the parties to select their own governing law. The principle, subject to a few exceptions, is *locus regit actum*.

2. NEGOTIABILITY IN ENGLAND

Whether an instrument is negotiable is to be determined by the law of the country where the "negotiation" takes place. Thus, a question may arise whether a foreign document which is regarded as negotiable in the country of its origin is also negotiable for the purposes of its transfer in England. This question was neatly raised in *Picker v London and County Banking Co*:[5]

> Certain Prussian bonds, which the Court of Appeal assumed to be negotiable by the law of Prussia, came into the possession of X after they had been stolen from the plaintiff. X deposited them with the defendants to secure his overdraft. In an action for their recovery, the defendants claimed a good title to the bonds, on the ground that they had taken delivery of them bona fide and for value.

This claim failed. A negotiable instrument no doubt constitutes cash in the eyes of English law and even if stolen its delivery passes a good title to a bona fide deliveree, but obviously nothing can pass as cash in this country unless it is part of the national currency. The rule, therefore, is that foreign documents may be negotiable in England, but only if they are recognised as negotiable either by statute or by a custom of businessmen in this country.[6]

We will now deal with the rules for the choice of law that apply when a bill drawn in one country is accepted, indorsed or payable in another. The question of what law governs the *transfer* of a negotiable instrument is discussed in a later chapter.[7]

3. FORMAL VALIDITY

It is enacted by section 72 of the Bills of Exchange Act 1882 that the formal validity of a bill, drawn in one country and accepted, negotiated or payable in another, shall be determined by the law of the place of issue, and that the formal validity of each supervening contract, such as acceptance, indorsement or acceptance *supra protest*, shall be determined by the law of the place where such contract is made.[8]

The determination of whether a foreign concept comes within the terms of section 72, for example whether it is a bill or there has been an indorsement of a bill, is a matter of characterisation initially for English law as the law of the forum.[9]

The "place of issue" does not necessarily coincide with the place where the

4 S 72.
5 (1887) 18 QBD 515.
6 *Goodwin v Robarts* (1876) 1 App Cas 476.
7 *Infra*, pp 820–823 et seq.
8 Bills of Exchange Act 1882, s 72(1).
9 *G & H Montage GmbH v Irvani* [1990] 1 WLR 667 at 678 (per MUSTILL LJ), CA. However, in ascertaining the nature of the foreign concept, the obligations it creates under foreign law are relevant (per PURCHAS LJ at 689).

bill is written out or signed by the drawer, for since "issue" means the first delivery of a bill, complete in form, to a person who takes it as a holder,[10] the place of issue is where the first delivery is made. If X signs a promissory note in Florence and posts it to the payee in London, the place of issue is London. Again, the place where each supervening contract is made is the place where that contract is completed by delivery.[11] The law of the place where the contract is made in the rigid sense indicated above, therefore, exclusively regulates formalities and determines, for instance, whether a bill is unconditional[12] or whether an indorsement is made in due form.[13] The formalities of the law of the place where the contract is made are not merely sufficient but essential. Unlike commercial contracts coming within the Rome Convention,[14] it is not enough to show that the formalities of the law governing the contract have been satisfied.

The Bills of Exchange Act 1882, however, raises two exceptions to the predominance of the law of the place where the contract is made.

(i) Foreign stamp laws A bill issued out of the United Kingdom is not invalid by reason only that it is not stamped in accordance with the law of the place of issue.[15] On the principle that claims based on foreign revenue laws will not be enforced,[16] it has long been the rule that a contract made abroad is not void in England merely because it lacks the stamp required by the law of the place where it was made, unless, indeed, that law provides that an unstamped instrument shall be absolutely void.[17] Having regard to the terms of section 72(1), however, it would seem that even in this last case a bill of exchange will not be invalid in England.

(ii) English dealings with foreign bills A bill issued out of the United Kingdom which is formally valid according to the law of the United Kingdom, though not according to the law of the place of issue, is, for the purpose of *enforcing payment* thereof, valid *as between all persons who negotiate, hold or become parties to it in the United Kingdom.*[18] The object of this exception, presumably, is to remove impediments from negotiability; for if the validity of a foreign bill depended on its flawlessness by the law of the place of issue its negotiation in this country might be seriously affected. It must be noticed, however, that the operation of the exception is restricted in two respects.

In the first place, a holder who relies on the exception must prove that both he and the person against whom he seeks to enforce payment became parties to the bill in the United Kingdom. In the second place, the exception is limited to a suit in which the plaintiff seeks to enforce payment of the bill. It has been held, for instance, that an action brought by a holder for a declaration that he is not liable to repay the amount received by him from

---

10 Bills of Exchange Act 1882, s 2.
11 *Chapman v Cottrell* (1865) 3 H & C 865.
12 *Guaranty Trust Co of New York v Hannay* [1918] 1 KB 43 (bill drawn in America on English bank); the Court of Appeal [1918] 2 KB 623 held, however, that the bill was unconditional both by English and by American law, and that the question which law applied did not arise.
13 *Koechlin et Cie v Kestenbaum* [1927] 1 KB 889; infra, pp 820–823.
14 Supra, p 508.
15 S 72(1), proviso (*a*).
16 Supra, pp 114 et seq.
17 *Bristow v Sequeville* (1850) 5 Exch 275 at 279; *James v Catherwood* (1823) 3 Dow & Ry KB 190.
18 Bills of Exchange Act 1882, s 72(1), proviso (*b*).

the acceptor is not an action for "enforcing payment" within the meaning of the 1882 Act.[19] The point, however, is not free from doubt.[20]

4. CAPACITY

No express provision is made in the 1882 Act as to matters of capacity outside domestic law. The issue must be decided by the common law.[21] It has been seen[22] that capacity to enter a commercial contract is to be determined by the proper law of the contract objectively ascertained, and the 1882 Act provides that capacity to incur liability as a party to a bill of exchange is co-extensive with capacity to contract.[23] That being so, and notwithstanding some Commonwealth authority in favour of the law of the place where the contract is made,[1] it is suggested that the proper law governs.

5. INTERPRETATION AND VALIDITY

The Bills of Exchange Act 1882 provides that:

The interpretation of the drawing, indorsement,[2] acceptance or acceptance *supra protest* of a bill is determined by the law of the place where such contract is made.[3]

If, for example, a bill drawn in Poland and accepted in London is expressed to be payable in the Netherlands, the question whether the acceptance is general or qualified is determinable by English law.[4] The difficulty is to ascertain the sense in which the word "interpretation" is employed by the Act. Normally interpretation indicates the process by which certain expressions are construed and their legal meaning determined, as occurs, for instance, where it is decided that the words written by an acceptor indicate a qualified acceptance. But unfortunately it is firmly established that *interpretation* in the present section covers not merely questions of construction but also questions relating to the legal effect, ie to the essential validity, of the various contracts contained in a bill.[5] This means that whether, say, an indorsement constitutes an effective transfer of a bill must in all cases be determined according to the law of the place where the indorsement was

---

19 *Guaranty Trust Co of New York v Hannay* [1918] 1 KB 43. But see SCRUTTON LJ in the Court of Appeal [1918] 2 KB 623 at 670, where the case was decided on a different ground.
20 Falconbridge, op cit, pp 325–327.
21 1882 Act, s 97(2).
22 Supra, pp 511–512.
23 1882 Act, s 22(1).
1 *Bondholders Securities Corporation v Manville* [1933] 4 DLR 699; see also *Re Soltykoff, ex p Margrett* [1891] 1 QB 413.
2 For problems in determining whether there is an indorsement see supra, p 523.
3 S 72(2). On when and where the contract is made see *Banco Atlantico SA v The British Bank of the Middle East* [1990] 2 Lloyd's Rep 504 at 507, CA.
4 *Bank Polski v Mulder & Co* [1942] 1 KB 497, [1942] 1 All ER 396. Cf *Sanders v St Helens Smelting Co* (1906) 39 Nova Scotia LR 370.
5 *Alcock v Smith* [1892] 1 Ch 238 at 256; *Embiricos v Anglo-Austrian Bank* [1905] 1 KB 677 at 683–686; *Koechlin et Cie v Kestenbaum* [1927] 1 KB 889 at 899; and see *Nova (Jersey) Knit Ltd v Kammgarn Spinnerei GmbH* [1977] 1 WLR 713 at 718; *G & H Montage GmbH v Irvani* [1990] 1 WLR 667 at 675, CA; *Banco Atlantico SA v The British Bank of the Middle East* [1990] 2 Lloyd's Rep 504 at 507, CA. Cf *Canada Life Assurance Co v Canadian Imperial Bank of Commerce* (1979) 98 DLR (3d) 670, where the Supreme Court of Canada left the point open.

completed. The subject of transfer, however, is a matter that will be discussed below.[6] The Act makes one exception to the exclusive sovereignty of the law of the place where the contract is made. It provides that:

> Where an *inland bill* is indorsed in a foreign country, the indorsement shall as regards the payer be interpreted according to the law of the United Kingdom.[7]

An *inland bill* is one that is both drawn and payable within the British Islands, or drawn within the British Islands on some person resident there. Any other bill is a foreign bill.[8] This exception confirms the early decision of *Lebel v Tucker*,[9] where

> a bill drawn, accepted and payable in England was transferred to the plaintiff in France by an indorsement which, though valid by English law, was insufficient by French law.

It was held that payment could be recovered from the acceptor. Payment must, therefore, be made to an indorsee of an inland bill if the indorsement is valid by English law, though void by the law of the place of indorsement; but in the case of a foreign bill payment is due on an indorsement valid at the place of indorsement, though void by English law. It must be observed that, since the provision is effective only "as regards the payer", it does not apply to a dispute where two parties claim as holders of a bill indorsed abroad.[10]

6. PRESENTMENT, PROTEST AND NOTICE OF DISHONOUR

When a bill is dishonoured, whether by non-acceptance or non-payment, a holder immediately gets a right of recourse against the drawer and the indorsers, but in order to enforce this right he is, as a general rule, required by English law to give due notice of dishonour to the drawer and to each indorser, and, in the case of a foreign bill, to cause it to be protested.[11] Most foreign countries require the protest of a dishonoured bill. Protest is made by a notary public.

The difficulty of finding the appropriate system of law to govern the problems that may arise on the dishonour of a bill which has circulated in several countries is attacked by section 72(3) of the Bills of Exchange Act 1882. This runs as follows:

> The duties of the holder with respect to presentment for acceptance or payment and the necessity for or sufficiency of protest or notice of dishonour are determined by the law of the place where the act is done or the bill is dishonoured.

This obscure section verges perilously on the unintelligible. As Westlake observes, a reference to the place where an act, such as presentment or protest, is done scarcely meets the difficulty that arises from the act not having been done.[12] He suggests that the words "or not done" must be

---

6　Infra, pp 820 et seq. For a most instructive account of the difficulty see Falconbridge, op cit, pp 327 et seq: see also Chitty on *Contracts*, 26th edn, vol II, paras 2868–2870.
7　S 72(2), proviso.
8　S 4. "British Islands" means the United Kingdom, the Channel Islands and the Isle of Man.
9　(1867) LR 3 QB 77.
10　*Alcock v Smith* [1892] 1 Ch 238.
11　Byles on *Bills*, 26th edn, pp 147 et seq.
12　Westlake, p 322.

interpolated. Dicey & Morris, on the other hand, would prefer to make the words read "where the act is *to be* done".[13] Again, the section refers to three events—presentment, protest and notice of dishonour—and then, on the question of choice of law, indicates two legal systems, the law of the place where the act is done and the law of the place where the bill is dishonoured. But how are these two systems to be distributed between the three events? Is, for instance, a question of presentment to be decided by the law of the place where the act is done, as Dicey & Morris argues,[14] or by the law of the place where the bill is dishonoured, as Westlake says?[15]

However, there is no doubt on the authorities, despite the obscurity of the Act, that the matters mentioned in the section, since they all concern the payment of a bill, come within the principle that the incidents and mode of performance are determinable by the law of the place of performance.[16] In the leading modern case the Court of Appeal applied English law, as the law of the place where payment was due, to the question of whether notice of dishonour or adequate protest had to be given to the defendant.[17]

This rule that the law of the place where a bill is payable exclusively governs the incidents of payment and non-payment holds good only where the person liable is bound to pay in that place. Thus in one case:[18]

> Bills drawn in Poland and accepted generally by the defendants in London were expressed to be payable in Amsterdam. They were not presented for payment in Amsterdam, but after their maturity payment was demanded of the defendants in London. Presentment was necessary by Dutch law, but, owing to the general acceptance, was unnecessary by English law.

The defendants argued that since payment was to take place in the Netherlands the duty of the holder with regard to presentment was governed by Dutch law. TUCKER J held, however, that under section 72(2)[19] the contract of acceptance was subject to English law, and that it was not one which according to English law compelled the acceptor to make payment in the Netherlands.

The Bills of Exchange Act 1882[20] expressly refers the question of date of payment to the law of the place of performance.

> Where a bill is drawn in one country and is payable in another, the due date thereof is determined according to the law of the place where it is payable.

Thus if the law of that country postpones the maturity of a bill owing to war or to a state of emergency, payment cannot be enforced in England until the foreign moratorium is lifted.[1]

13 Dicey & Morris, pp 1326–1328.
14 Ibid.
15 Westlake, pp 322, 323.
16 Foote, pp 460–461.
17 *G & H Montage GmbH v Irvani* [1990] 1 WLR 667 at 680, 687; Lomnicka (1990) 39 ICLQ 914.
18 *Bank Polski v Mulder* [1941] 2 KB 266, [1941] 2 All ER 647. When this case was taken to the Court of Appeal [1942] 1 KB 497, [1942] 1 All ER 396, supra, p 525, the point that the Dutch law of presentment applied was abandoned. See also *Cornelius v Banque Franco-Serbe* [1942] 1 KB 29 at 32, [1941] 2 All ER 728 at 732.
19 Supra, p 525.
20 S 72(5).
1 *Rouquette v Overmann* (1875) LR 10 QB 525; *Re Francke and Rasch* [1918] 1 Ch 470.

Chapter 20

Torts[1]

SUMMARY

1. FOREIGN TORTS

(a) THE THEORIES

When an action is brought in England on a tort that has been committed
abroad, the role of private international law is to specify the legal system
according to which the rights and liabilities of the parties must be determined.
A variety of legal systems have, from time to time, been considered applicable.
The more common views are that either the *lex loci delicti commissi* (the law
of the place where the tort was committed) or the *lex fori* (the law of the
forum) must be chosen, or that these two laws must be combined. A newer
view is that a foreign tort should be adjudged according to the law of the
country with which it has the most significant connection.

---

1 Dicey and Morris, ch 35; Stromholm, *Torts in the Conflict of Laws;* Morse, *Torts in Private
International Law*; Cavers, ch VI; (1970) III Hague Recueil 143–195; Scoles and Hay, ch 17;
Kahn-Freund (1968) II Hague Recueil 166; Shapira, *The Interest Approach to Choice of Law*;
Carter (1981) 52 BYBIL 10; Hanotiau (1982) 30 AJCL 73; Jaffey (1982) 2 LS 98; Fawcett
(1984) 47 MLR 650; for a comparative study Morse (1984) 32 AJCL 51; De Boer, *Beyond
Lex Loci Delicti*; Kaye, *Private International Law of Tort and Products Liability*; Morse
[1989] Current Legal Problems 167.

(i) The law of the forum

To measure the rights and liabilities of the parties by the law of the forum, despite the favour with which this solution was regarded by Savigny,[2] would lead to what COCKBURN CJ, once stigmatised as "the most inconvenient and startling consequences".[3] The most startling and the most unjust would ensue if, in accordance with the law of the forum, the defendant were held responsible for what would be an innocent act in the place where it was committed. If it were the general rule that the law of the forum was the sole arbiter, the plaintiff would be free to choose a forum where the law was more favourable to him than in the place of wrong, provided that he could find one where the defendant happened to be subject to the jurisdiction of the courts of that country.[4]

(ii) The law of the place where the tort was committed[5]

If a plaintiff in English proceedings claims damages for a tort committed against him abroad, it seems eminently reasonable that the court should adopt the law of the place where the alleged infringement of his right occurred.[6] Obviously, any country has a real and legitimate concern with the commission of torts within its borders. Moreover, resort to the law of the place where the tort was committed will give effect in many instances to the natural expectations of the parties. The English driver of a car in France, for instance, reasonably expects that his conduct must conform to the standards of French law in civil as well as criminal respects. He reasonably expects, too, that the same standards will apply to other users of the French roads. The Law Commissions have also pointed out that adherence to the law of the place where the tort was committed would promote uniformity, discourage forum shopping and would accord with the law applied in much of the rest of Europe.[7]

(iii) Proper law of the tort[8]

Dissatisfaction with both of the above laws as the governing law has provoked doubt as to whether, indeed, either can be regarded as the most appropriate law to govern the conduct of the defendant and the rights of the plaintiff.[9] So far as the law of the forum is concerned, it is open to the abuse of "forum-shopping".[10] Nor is the law of the place where the tort was committed necessarily more apt.

If, for instance, an English motor-coach is making a foreign tour and while

---

2 *Private International Law*, Guthrie's translation, pp 205, 206. For a recent justification of the law of the forum see Jaffey (1982) 2 Legal Studies 98 at pp 101–102.
3 *Phillips v Eyre* (1869) LR 4 QB 225 at 239.
4 Hancock, *Torts in the Conflict of Laws*, pp 54 et seq; Morse, op cit, pp 5 et seq.
5 Rabel, vol 2, p 235; and see Morse, op cit, pp 23 et seq, 80 et seq; Jaffey (1982) 2 Legal Studies 98 at pp 102–107.
6 See *Metall und Rohstoff AG v Donaldson Lufkin & Jenrette Inc* [1990] 1 QB 391 at 445–446, CA; overruled on a different point in *Lonrho plc v Fayed* [1991] 3 All ER 303, [1991] 3 WLR 188, HL.
7 Law Com No 193 (1990), Scot Law Com No 129 (1990), para 3.2.
8 Morris (1951) 64 HLR 881; Nygh (1977) 26 ICLQ 932; Mann (1987) 36 ICLQ 437, 438–442.
9 Hancock (1968) 46 Can BR 226.
10 *Boys v Chaplin* [1971] AC 356 at 378, 383, 406; see generally on forum shopping Fawcett (1984) 35 NILQ 141; for the doctrine of *forum non conveniens* as the antidote to the problem see Schuz (1986) 35 ICLQ 374; and supra, pp 221–234.

it is passing through France one of the passengers, all of whom are domiciled and ordinarily resident in England, assaults or defames another, it has been asked whether it is convenient or socially desirable that in an English action the matter should be governed by French law. It has therefore been suggested that a principle better calculated to solve every variety of case would emerge if the judges, adopting the more flexible approach to the subject that succeeded so well in the case of contract, were to develop a doctrine of the proper law of a tort.

> If we adopt the proper law of a tort, we can at least choose the law which, on policy grounds, seems to have the most significant connection with the chain of acts and circumstances in the particular situation before us.[11]

In other words, it is arguable that a foreign tort should be adjudged according to the social environment in which it has been committed.[12]

Support for a solution similar to that of the proper law of the tort is to be found in the United States of America.[13] In *Babcock v Jackson*,[14] a decision of the New York Court of Appeals, the facts were as follows:

> The plaintiff, a gratuitous passenger in the defendant's car, was injured in an accident that occurred in Ontario. At the time the parties, who were New York residents, were on a week-end trip to Canada. The trip had commenced in New York State where the car was licensed, insured and usually garaged. An Ontario statute absolved drivers from liability towards their gratuitous passengers. New York law contained no similar provision. The plaintiff successfully sued the defendant in New York for negligence.

FULD J,[15] expressing the view of the majority of the New York Court of Appeals, embraced the view expressed in the then latest revision of the Conflict of Laws Restatement to the effect that:

11 Morris (1951) 64 HLR 881, 888.
12 Clarence Smith (1957) 20 MLR 447, 460 et seq; Dicey & Morris, pp 1363–1365; see also Baxter (1985) 34 ICLQ 538; cf Jaffey (1982) 2 Legal Studies 98 at pp 107–113. Not only is this type of approach supported by the American Restatement 2d, § 145, but also by the draft Foreign Torts Act produced by the Conference of Commissioners on Uniformity of Legislation in Canada; see Report of Proceedings of their 48th Annual Meeting, p 62; and also Hancock (1968) 46 Can BR 226, especially at pp 244–251; Clarence Smith (1970) 20 UTLJ 81. Dissatisfaction with traditional approaches is seen also in the Hague Convention on the Law Applicable to Traffic Accidents (1968): see Newman (1969) 18 ICLQ 643–646, 664–669; Cavers (1971) 44 So Calif LR 340, 354–359; and in the draft Conflict of Laws (Traffic Accidents) Act produced by the Conference of Commissioners on Uniformity of Legislation in Canada, see Report of Proceedings of their 52nd Annual Meeting, pp 215–266; Castel & Cripeau (1971) 19 AJCL 17; and in the Hague Convention on the Law Applicable to Products Liability (1972), see Reese (1973) 21 AJCL 149; Fischer (1974) 20 McGill LJ 44; Cavers (1977) 26 ICLQ 703. For the Law Commissions' proposals for the reform of English Law see infra pp 564–565.
13 For the development of this approach, see Cavers (1970) III Hague Recueil 75, 143–195; Reese (1976) II Hague Recueil 1, 107–123; Leflar (1977) 41 Law and Contemporary Problems 10; Weintraub (1977) 41 Law and Contemporary Problems 146; Morse, op cit, pp 219 et seq; Korn (1983) 83 Col LR 772; supra, pp 31–38.
14 12 NY 2d 473, 191 NE 2d 279, 240 NYS 2d 743 (1963); reported in England [1963] 2 Lloyd's Rep 286; see (1963) 63 Col LR 1212; and see *Macey v Rozbicki* 18 NY 2d 289, 221 NE 2d 380 (1966); *Tooker v Lopez* 249 NE 2d 394 (1969); *Neumeier v Kuehner* 31 NY 2d 121, 286 NE 2d 454 (1972); *Towley v King Arthur Rings Inc* 40 NY 2d 129, 351 NE 2d 728 (1976); *Cousins v Instrument Flyers Inc* 44 NY 2d 699, 376 NE 2d 914 (1978); *Schultz v Boy Scouts of America Inc* 65 NY 2d 189, 480 NE 2d 679 (1985). For an analysis of the New York decisions see Korn (1983) 83 Col LR 772; De Boer, pp 348–372.
15 For an analysis of the contribution of FULD CJ to the conflict of laws, see Reese (1971) 71 Col LR 548.

The local law of the State which has the most significant relationship with the occurrence and with the parties determines their rights and liabilities in tort[16]

and applied New York law rather than Ontario law, being that of the place where the tort was committed. It is important to note however that the issue before the court was not as to whether the defendant had acted wrongfully but as to the effect of the host driver-guest passenger relationship that existed between the parties. FULD J said explicitly that, if the issue had been the defendant's exercise of due care in the operation of his car, it would have been appropriate to look to the law of the place of the tort so as to give effect to that jurisdiction's interest in regulating conduct within its borders.[17]

In the converse case where the parties were Ontario residents injured in New York, the New York courts first decided still to apply New York law.[18] Such a view would indicate that the forum is extremely prejudiced in favour of the application of its own law. However, the Appellate Division has later vacillated between applying the Ontario guest statute[19] and New York law[1] in such circumstances. When faced, for the first time, with essentially the same problem, the New York Court of Appeals, in a case involving a tort committed in New York, applied the New Jersey charitable immunity rule on the basis of the parties' common domicil in that State.[2]

The interest of the place of the tort has been held to be no greater where the guest-passenger relationship between two parties predominantly connected with the forum arises in the place of the tort.[3] The problem of choice of law has proved to be harder to solve where the guest and the passenger are resident in different states,[4] or where in a fatal accident claim there is a limitation on damages in the jurisdiction where the accident occurs, the defendant is resident and the car involved is registered and insured, but there is no such limitation in the forum which was also the residence of the deceased.[5]

The difficulty in determining the applicable law on this approach is seen most clearly where both the law of the forum and the law of the place of the tort have a sound claim to be applied, where the policies of both appear relevant to the instant case, ie a "true conflict".[6] This may be illustrated by

16 Restatement 2d, Conflict of Laws (1963), Tentative Draft § 379(1). See now Restatement 2d, § 145(1): "The rights and liabilities of the parties with respect to an issue in tort are determined by the local law of the state which, as to that issue, has the most significant relationship to the occurrence and the parties."
17 12 NY 2d 473 at 483.
18 *Kell v Henderson* 270 NYS 2d 552 (1966).
19 *Arbuthnot v Allbright* 316 NYS 2d 391 (1970). This view accords with the Ontario courts' interpretation of the scope of its guest statute: *Gagnon v Lecavalier* (1967) 63 DLR (2d) 12; and see *Martin v Marmen* (1969) 6 DLR (3d) 77. See also *Boxer v Gottlieb* 652 F Supp 1056 (SD NY 1987). See generally on guest statute cases De Boer, op cit, pp 403–456.
1 *Rye v Kolter* 333 NYS 2d 96 (1972); *Bray v Cox* 333 NYS 2d 783 (1972); see also *Himes v Stalker* 414 NYS 2d 986 (1979)—a case concerning the issue of vicarious liability.
2 *Schultz v Boy Scouts of America Inc* 65 NY 2d 189, 480 NE 2d 679 (1985).
3 *Macey v Rozbicki* 18 NY 2d 289, 221 NE 2d 380 (1966); *Tooker v Lopez* 24 NY 2d 569, 249 NE 2d 394 (1969), overruling *Dym v Gordon* 16 NY 2d 120, 209 NE 2d 792 (1965).
4 Eg *Cipolla v Shaposka* 439 Pa 563, 267 A 2d 854 (1970); see (1971) 9 Duquesne LR 347; *Neumeier v Kuehner* 31 NY 2d 121, 286 NE 2d 454 (1972)—forum law not applied; *Rakoric v Croatian Cultural Club* 430 NYS 2d 829 (1980). See also *Schultz v Boys Scouts of America Inc* 65 NY 2d 189, 480 NE 2d 679 (1985).
5 *Miller v Miller* 22 NY 2d 12, 237 NE 2d 877 (1968)—forum law applied.
6 Supra, p 32.

the following decision of the Supreme Court of California, *Bernhard v Harrah's Club*:[7]

> The plaintiff was injured, in California, when his car collided with a car driven by another Californian who had been drinking at the defendant's club in Nevada. Under Californian law a "tavern keeper" is liable if he serves drinks to an intoxicated person who subsequently injures a plaintiff. There is no such liability under the law of Nevada.

The court analysed the policies underlying the two different rules and concluded that Nevada had an interest in protecting its tavern keepers from a civil liability not imposed under the law of the State where they sold drinks. California had an interest in giving the protection of its law to all Californian residents injured in California. Each State "has a legitimate but conflicting interest in applying its own law in respect to the civil liability of tavern keepers".[8] The court declined to apply the law of California simply as the law of the forum but decided to resolve the conflict "by applying the law of the state whose interest would be most impaired if its law were not applied".[9] On this basis, the court favoured the application of its own law.

The hardest problem of all is that where the forum is held not to be one of the interested legal systems, ie a disinterested third state.[10] Such a problem confronted again the California Supreme Court in *Reich v Purcell*.[11] The facts of this case were these:

> There was a collision between two cars in Missouri. One car was owned and driven by the defendant who was resident and domiciled in California. The other car was owned and driven by the wife of the plaintiff. The wife and one of their children were killed in the accident. The plaintiff and his family then resided in Ohio and the deceaseds' estates were administered there. After the accident the plaintiff became domiciled in California. Under the law of Missouri, but not of Ohio or California, there was a limitation on damages in wrongful death actions. The court refused to apply the Missouri limitation and awarded damages under the law of Ohio.

TRAYNOR CJ, expressing the opinion of the court, refused to apply the law of the place of the tort as such and concluded that "as the forum we must consider all of the foreign and domestic elements and interests involved in this case to determine the rule applicable".[12] Any Californian interest based either on the residence of the defendant, the present domicil of the plaintiff or the intended domicil of the deceased was rejected. The forum had, therefore, to decide between the laws of the two other States, Ohio and Missouri. The court examined the interest that Missouri had in its limitation provisions in wrongful death actions, and concluded that the law of the place of the tort has little interest in such compensation rules when none of the parties resides there, for the object of such rules is to protect local resident defendants and

---

7 16 Cal 3d 313, 546 P 2d 719 (1976); Bodenheimer, *Festschrift für F A Mann*, p 123; Weintraub (1977) 41 Law and Contemporary Problems 146, 157–159; note (1982) 95 Harv LR 1079.
8 16 Cal 3d 313 at 319.
9 Ibid, at 320; supra, p 34. See De Boer, pp 282–302.
10 Currie (1963) 28 Law and Contemporary Problems 754; Kay (1989) III Hague Recueil 9 at 73–74.
11 67 Cal 2d 551, 432 P 2d 727 (1967); see (1968) 15 UCLA Law Rev 551–654; and see *Pryor v Swarner* 445 F 2d 1272 (1971). In *Erwin v Thomas* 506 P 2d 494 (1973) forum law was applied where neither the forum nor the place of injury had any interest.
12 (1967) 432 P 2d 727 at 730.

control the distribution of damages to local beneficiaries. Thus, in this case, neither the law of the forum nor the law of the place of the tort was applied, but a third law, that of Ohio, was considered to be the most appropriate.

Ascertaining whether a State is interested in having its law applied in a given case is hard enough in these American inter-State decisions; the difficulties are greatly increased if governmental interest analysis is applied in the international context. The practical problems involved in an English court trying to ascertain, for example, the purpose behind a Maltese law, are such that it is accepted that governmental interest analysis is inappropriate for use in English law.[13] Nonetheless, American developments have not gone unnoticed by English judges.[14] Although there is little judicial support for applying governmental interest analysis here,[15] the movement towards flexibility in the English tort choice of law rules[16] can be seen to have been influenced by American law, in particular by *Babcock v Jackson* and the Conflict of Laws Second Restatement.

(b) PRESENT ENGLISH LAW

The rule for the choice of law that has in fact emerged in England is a compromise. English law, according to the prevalent view, has so intimately blended the law of the place where the tort was committed and the law of the forum that the court is not the mere guardian of its own public policy, but is required to test the defendant's conduct by reference to the English as well as to the foreign law of tort. The rule on the matter is very far from satisfactory. It is the result of the interpretation put by judges and jurists on a certain passage in the judgment of WILLES J, delivered over a hundred years ago in *Phillips v Eyre*.[17] The passage reads as follows:

> As a general rule, in order to found a suit in England for a wrong alleged to have been committed abroad, two conditions must be fulfilled. First, the wrong must be of such a character that it would have been actionable if committed in England. ... Secondly, the act must not have been justifiable by the law of the place where it was done.[18]

These words were repeated by Lord MACNAGHTEN in 1902.[19] They have been taken by later generations to mean that in every action brought in England on a foreign tort the plaintiff must prove that the defendant offended the law both of the place of the tort and of England.[20]

13 Law Com Working Paper No 87 (1984), Scot Law Com Consultative Memorandum (1984), paras 4.36–4.45; Law Com No 193 (1990), Scot Law Com No 129 (1990), Part III; see Fawcett (1982) 31 ICLQ 150; and more generally Brilmayer (1981) 79 Mich LR 1315; Juenger (1984) 32 AJCL 1 at pp 33–37; supra, pp 37–38.
14 See *Boys v Chaplin* [1971] AC 356; discussed infra, pp 534 et seq.
15 Parts of Lord WILBERFORCE's judgment in *Boys v Chaplin*, op cit, use the terminology of interest analysis.
16 See infra, pp 546–547.
17 (1870) LR 6 QB 1.
18 *Phillips v Eyre* (1870) LR 6 QB 1 at pp 28–29. This case has been criticised, and not followed, by the Irish Supreme Court in *Patrick Grehan v Medical Inc and Valley Pine Associates* [1986] IR 528, and by the High Court of Australia, at least in interstate cases, in *Breavington v Godleman* (1988) 169 CLR 41.
19 *Carr v Fracis Times & Co* [1902] AC 176 at 182.
20 One qualification of this rule is that no action will lie in England for trespass to foreign land or for other torts involving foreign land, if the proceedings are principally concerned with a question of title to, or the right to possession of, that land: Civil Jurisdiction and Judgments Act 1982, s 30; discussed supra, p 262.

The rule in *Phillips v Eyre* has, however, been modified by the House of Lords in *Boys v Chaplin*:[1]

Both parties were British servicemen stationed temporarily in Malta. The plaintiff was injured in a road accident by the admitted negligence of the defendant. Both parties were off duty at the time. Under Maltese law the plaintiff was given a right of action to recover pecuniary loss, but no right to compensation for pain and suffering and the plaintiff would be able to recover only £53 special damages. Under English law the damages would be over £2,000.

The crucial issue was, therefore, whether damages should be assessed according to English or Maltese law. The House of Lords was unanimous in deciding that the plaintiff should recover the greater sum under English law. However, this unanimity is clouded by the bewildering variety of reasons for their Lordships' conclusions.

Summarised briefly, the main reasons for their various conclusions would seem to be as follows:

Lord HODSON:[2] The right to claim damages for pain and suffering is a substantive and not a procedural issue. English law is applied as the governing law on the basis of a flexible interpretation of *Phillips v Eyre*, justified on grounds of public policy and in line with the American Restatement.[3]

Lord GUEST: The right to claim damages for pain and suffering should be classified as procedural[4] and be governed by the law of the forum, ie English law. The proper law concept should be rejected.[5]

Lord DONOVAN: The rule in *Phillips v Eyre* should be left unaltered, and, again, English law should be applied as the law of the forum to the procedural issue of the right to claim damages for pain and suffering.[6]

Lord WILBERFORCE:[7] The issue was substantive to be governed by the applicable law. The traditional rule would refer to Maltese law, at least in part, so as to limit the recovery of damages. He was not prepared to accept this conclusion. English law was applied on the ground that the general rule should be departed from here as: "Nothing suggests that the Maltese state has any interest in applying (its) rule to persons resident outside it, or in

1 [1971] AC 356; see McGregor (1970) 33 MLR 1; North & Webb (1970) 19 ICLQ 24; Karsten (1970) 19 ICLQ 34; Carter (1970) 44 BYBIL 222; Clarke (1970) 21 NILQ 47; Baer (1970) 48 Can BR 161; Reese (1970) 18 AJCL 189; Morse, op cit, pp 278 et seq; Briggs (1984) 12 Anglo-Am LR 237; Fawcett (1984) 47 MLR 650.
2 [1971] AC 356 at 377–380.
3 Restatement 2d, § 145(1).
4 There was agreement by the Law Lords that quantification of damages, ie how much could be recovered for a particular head of damages, was a procedural issue. See also *Coupland v Arabian Gulf Oil Co* [1983] 1 WLR 1136 at 1149; affd by the Court of Appeal [1983] 1 WLR 1136 at 1151; infra pp 563–564.
5 [1971] AC 356 at 381–383.
6 [1971] AC 356 at 383, and see Lord UPJOHN in the Court of Appeal: [1968] 2 QB 1 at 32.
7 Lord WILBERFORCE's judgment has been approved in *Church of Scientology of California v Metropolitan Police Commissioner* (1976) 120 Sol Jo 690; *Coupland v Arabian Gulf Oil Co* [1983] 2 All ER 434, [1983] 1 WLR 1136; affd by the Court of Appeal [1983] 3 All ER 226, [1983] 1 WLR 1136; *Armagas Ltd v Mundogas SA* [1986] AC 717 at 740–741, CA; affd by the House of Lords without discussion of this point [1986] AC 717 at 773, [1986] 2 All ER 385.

denying the application of the English rule to these parties."[8] *Phillips v Eyre* must be "made flexible enough to take account of the varying interests and considerations of policy which may arise when one or more foreign elements are present".[9]

Lord PEARSON: The issue before the court was substantive. He accepted the continued application of *Phillips v Eyre*, though considered that it could be applied with flexibility, but not in this case. Nevertheless he applied English law as the substantive law on the basis that forum law plays the dominant role, and determines the cause of action. The law of the forum plays a lesser part and merely requires the act not to be excusable or innocent by that law.[10]

Underlying their Lordships' judgments are a number of sometimes barely articulated policy considerations.[11] There was a concern to take greater account of the involvement of the place of the tort, which can be contrasted with the old fashioned forum preference also evident in the case. There was a desire that the plaintiff should be adequately compensated, which he would not have been if Maltese law had been applied. At the same time, forum shopping should be discouraged.[12] Finally, there was an underlying tension between the need for certainty in the law, and the need for sufficient flexibility to ensure justice in the individual case. Whilst an awareness of these considerations helps in understanding the reasoning used in *Boys v Chaplin*, it does not make it any easier to extract a ratio from the case.

The bewildering variety of opinion[13] expressed by their Lordships has led some to argue that no ratio can be extracted from the case,[14] and others to argue that lower courts can choose whichever ratio they like from the five judgments.[15] However, it is submitted that the case is authority for two propositions.[16] First, the rule in *Phillips v Eyre* is modified so that it now has to be asked whether the conduct of the defendant is actionable, rather than not justifiable, by the law of the place of the tort.[17] Second, the rule is one which is to be applied "with flexibility".[18] Emphasis was placed by the House of Lords on the qualification by WILLES J in *Phillips v Eyre* that his conditions apply "as a general rule". This was seized upon as a justification for diverging from the rule in *Phillip v Eyre* when the special circumstances so demand. As will be seen, these propositions have been accepted by subsequent cases in this area.

---

8 Ibid, at 392.
9 Ibid, at 391.
10 Ibid, at 405–406.
11 See Fawcett (1984) 47 MLR 650; more generally Jaffey (1982) 2 OJLS 368.
12 See also *Breavington v Godleman* (1988) 169 CLR 41.
13 See the analysis in *John Walker and Sons Ltd v Henry Ost and Co Ltd* [1970] 1 WLR 917 at 933–934.
14 McGregor (1970) 33 MLR 1 at 14–15; Gerber (1970) 7 UQdLJ 40, 54.
15 See Lord DENNING in *Paal Wilson & Co A/S v Partenreederei Hannah Blumenthal* [1983] 1 AC 854 at 873–874. This seems to be the view taken in the three English decisions following Lord WILBERFORCE's judgment: *Church of Scientology of California v Metropolitan Police Commr* (1976) 120 Sol Jo 690; *Coupland v Arabian Gulf Oil Co* [1983] 2 All ER 434, [1983] 1 WLR 1136, affd by the Court of Appeal [1983] 3 All ER 226, [1983] 1 WLR 1136; *Armagas Ltd v Mundogas SA* [1986] AC 717 at 740–741, 752–753, CA; affd by the House of Lords without discussion of this point [1986] AC 717 at 773, [1986] 2 All ER 385.
16 Cf Briggs (1984) 12 Anglo-Am LR 237.
17 [1971] AC 356 at 376–377, 381, 387–389, infra, pp 537–540.
18 Ibid, pp 331, 341–343, 352–357, infra, pp 546–549.

The law after *Boys v Chaplin* can be summed up as follows: there is a general rule of double actionability (ie there must be actionability by the law of the forum and the law of the place of the tort), with a flexible exception to this rule.[19] The different parts of this formula and the way in which it has been shaped by *Boys v Chaplin* will now be examined in more detail.

(i) The general rule[20]

(a) **Actionable in England** The first limb of the rule in *Phillips v Eyre* is left intact. This first limb seems to mean that a plaintiff who seeks to recover damages in England for what is an admitted tort according to the law of the place where the tort was committed will fail, unless he proves that had the defendant's act been done in England it would have constituted an actionable wrong by English domestic law. The leading English case in which a plaintiff has been defeated by his failure to satisfy this condition is *The Halley*,[21] where the question was one of vicarious, not direct, liability. It was decided two years before *Phillips v Eyre*.

> Foreign shipowners sued the owners of a British steamer to recover compensation in respect of a collision caused by the negligent navigation of the steamer in Belgian waters. The defendants pleaded that at the time of the collision their steamer was under the charge of a pilot whom they were compelled by Belgian law to employ, and that they were not liable according to English internal law for the negligence of this compulsory pilot.[1] The plaintiffs replied that by Belgian law an owner is liable for faulty navigation, even though due to the negligence of a compulsory pilot.

Judgment was given for the defendants by the Privy Council. SELWYN LJ, after pointing out that if any liability existed in the circumstances it must be the creature of Belgian law, denied that an English court was bound to apply that law in a case where, according to its own principles, no liability whatsoever existed. He affirmed that it was contrary both to principle and authority to give a remedy for an act that constituted no wrong by English law. But it is pertinent to ask why a tenderness, which is withheld in other branches of the law, such as contract, should be shown so generously to the defendant in a case of tort. Why should the plaintiff to an action on a foreign tort be compelled to climb two hurdles instead of one?

The most probable explanation of this strange decision was the necessity, in the opinion of the Privy Council, to enforce the policy of the English legislature as reflected in the Merchant Shipping Act 1854.[2] The policy of England with regard to compulsory pilotage had been expressly declared by the statute, and it must have been tempting to conclude that it should not be sacrificed merely because a contrary policy prevailed in the place of the tort.[3] It is perhaps scarcely surprising that the decision should have been reached in 1868, for at that time the rules for the choice of law were to a considerable extent still immature and in many respects far different from what they have

---

19 This formula is now generally applied in Ontario: *Grimes v Cloutier* (1989) 61 DLR (4th) 505; *Prefontaine v Frizzle* (1990) 65 DLR (4th) 275.
20 Morse, op cit, pp 50 et seq.
21 (1868) LR 2 PC 193.
1   This rule was altered by what is now the Pilotage Act 1983.
2   Hancock, *Torts in the Conflict of Laws*, 91; Kahn-Freund, *Selected Writings*, ch 9, pp 241–244.
3   See Kahn-Freund, op cit, ch 9; and see Hancock (1968) 18 UTLJ 331.

now become. What is surprising is that it should still be regarded with judicial equanimity, despite the greater awareness that now exists with regard to the underlying purpose of private international law. The rule in *The Halley* is open to the basic objections that it places undue emphasis on the accident of the forum, is parochial in appearance and unfair to the plaintiff. It is no longer accepted in the United States of America, where the influence of the forum is generally limited to the exclusion of actions the bringing of which would be contrary to local policy. It has also, seemingly, been rejected in Ireland[4] and in Australia, at least as regards torts committed in Australia.[5] However, despite such dissatisfaction with the first part of the rule in *Phillips v Eyre*, it has survived *Boys v Chaplin*, not only unaltered but unanimously approved and, indeed, almost without criticism.[6] Thus in the recent case of *Metall und Rohstoff AG v Donaldson Lufkin & Jenrette Inc*[7] the Court of Appeal held that claims based on conspiracy, abuse of process, and induce-ment of breach of trust, following events that took place in New York and London, would all fail in England on the ground that they were not available under English law.[8]

The Law Commissions have accepted the above criticisms of the rule in *The Halley*, and have recommended its abolition.[9] If this recommendation is implemented, one effect will be that, for the first time, United Kingdom courts will end up applying foreign laws in relation to torts which are very different from our own law. For example, some foreign laws allow recovery for invasion of privacy, whereas under English law this is not possible. Furthermore, United Kingdom courts will have to quantify the damages in relation to causes of action and heads of damages which are unknown to us. It is not anticipated that this will cause any great practical problem. However, the Law Commissions have spelt out in their draft Bill that a foreign law will not apply: to the extent that it conflicts with public policy; if it is a penal, revenue or other public law; to the extent that it conflicts with a mandatory statutory rule of the forum; to matters of procedure.[10] If the Law Com-missions' proposals are accepted resort to these devices may become much more common in tort cases.

(b) Actionable by the law of the place where the tort was committed

It was recognised in *The Halley*[11] that the law of the place of the tort played as decisive a part as the law of the forum in the determination of the defendant's liability. SELWYN LJ said that there is no objection to an action in England for injuries committed abroad, provided that "such injuries are actionable both by the law of England and also by that of the country where

---

4 *Patrick Grehan v Medical Inc and Valley Pine Associates* [1986] IR 528.
5 *Breavington v Godleman* (1988) 169 CLR 41; Pryles (1989) 63 ALJ 158; Briggs (1989) 105 LQ R 359. See also *Waterhouse v Australian Broadcasting Corporation* (1989) 86 ACTR 1; *Byrnes v Groote Eylandt Mining Co Pty Ltd* (1990) 93 ALR 131. For torts committed outside Australia see *Voth v Manildra Flour Mills Pty Ltd* (1990) 171 CLR 538 at 566–570.
6 [1971] AC 356 at 374, 381, 383, 385–387, 396–398. The only real criticism comes from Lord WILBERFORCE, at 385–387.
7 [1990] 1 QB 391, [1988] 3 All ER 116; overruled on a different point in *Lonrho plc v Fayed* [1991] 3 All ER 303, [1991] 3 WLR 188, HL. The question of the applicable law arose in the context of jurisdiction, supra p 191.
8 Ibid, at 447. See also *Tyburn Productions Ltd v Conan Doyle* [1991] Ch 75 at 87.
9 Law Com No 193 (1990), Scot Law Com No 129 (1990), para 3.6. See also paras 1.6, 3.38.
10 Cl 4, para 3.55.
11 (1868) LR 2 PC 193.

they are committed".[12] Yet, two years later, in *Phillips v Eyre*,[13] WILLES J, when stating the function of the law of the place where the tort was committed, used language which at first sight seems a little obscure. He referred to the matter in two passages. According to the first, the law of the place where the tort was committed must say whether the act of the defendant was "valid and unquestionable", according to the second, whether it was "justifiable". It is the latter of these epithets that has been preferred by later judges.[14] "Justifiable" is a strange word to use in connection with conduct that has caused injury to another, for to justify an act means to show the justice of the act. No doubt it was sufficiently apt to describe the position of the defendant in the circumstances which confronted WILLES J in *Phillips v Eyre*:[15]

> An action was brought in England against the defendant, an ex-Governor of Jamaica, for having assaulted and imprisoned the plaintiff during a rebellion in the island. Judgment was given for the defendant on the ground that his conduct, though originally illegal by Jamaican law, had later been excused by an Act of Indemnity passed by the local legislature.

This was a case in which the legislature took the view that the defendant was justified by the circumstances in acting as he had done. But it does not follow that because a word is appropriate to a particular kind of case it should be used when laying down the broad doctrine applicable to torts in general. The danger is that it may be interpreted in such a way as to warrant the grant of a remedy in England when none is obtainable in the place of wrong. To go thus far is indefensible.

Such a heretical suggestion was, however, translated into practice by the Court of Appeal in *Machado v Fontes*:[16]

> In that case the plaintiff sued the defendant in England for a libel that had been published in Brazil. The defendant pleaded that by Brazilian law no civil action lay for the recovery of damages in respect of such a libel, though he might be criminally prosecuted at the suit of the State. This plea was supported by the argument that, since the libel was not actionable in Brazil, it was not actionable in England.

The Court of Appeal held that the plea was bad and that it must be struck out. LOPES LJ was content to rest on the reasoning that if an act was criminal it was not innocent and therefore not justifiable in the country where it was done. RIGBY LJ agreed. He considered that the change of language from "actionable" to "justifiable" in *Phillips v Eyre* was deliberate. In his view the nature and extent of the remedy in the foreign country was a matter of no importance, for everything must depend on the innocency of the act.

In *Boys v Chaplin*, however, *Machado v Fontes* would appear to have received its quietus at the hands of a majority of their Lordships.[17] The second part of the rule in *Phillips v Eyre* would seem to have been altered in that "actionability by the *lex loci*" is to be substituted for "non-justifiability by

12 Ibid, at 203.
13 (1870) LR 6 QB 1.
14 *Carr v Fracis Times & Co* [1902] AC 176 at 182 (per Lord MACNAGHTEN).
15 (1870) LR 6 QB 1.
16 [1897] 2 QB 231; and see *Scott v Seymour* (1862) 1 H & C 219.
17 See to this effect: *Mitchell v McCulloch* 1976 SLT 2 at 4; *The Adhiguna Meranti* [1988] 1 Lloyd's Rep 384, Hong Kong CA; *Breavington v Godleman* (1988) 169 CLR 41; *Grimes v Cloutier* (1989) 61 DLR (4th) 505; Morse, op cit, pp 303–305.

the *lex loci*". None of their Lordships wished to see a repetition of the decision in *Machado v Fontes*, but their reasons were somewhat varied.[18] Lord PEARSON[19] and Lord DONOVAN[20] would leave the second part of the *Phillips v Eyre* rule unaltered. Their criticism of *Machado v Fontes* was not on the ground of the use of the concept of "not justifiable" but rather that the case involved a blatant instance of "forum shopping". Lord HODSON and Lord WILBERFORCE[1] were clear that one should ask whether the conduct of the defendant was actionable, rather than not justifiable, by the law of the place where the tort was committed. It is submitted that Lord GUEST provides support and thus a majority for the introduction of a rule of double actionability when he said that *the conduct must be actionable by English law and by the laws of the country in which the conduct occurred, the lex loci delicti.*[2] Moreover, since *Boys v Chaplin* numerous English cases,[3] including one decided by the House of Lords,[4] have accepted that the House of Lords in *Boys v Chaplin* modified the law in this way. One must now therefore equate "not justifiable" with "actionable".[5] Although this limb of the rule is not now satisfied if the defendant's conduct is merely criminal under the law of the place of the tort,[6] it does not have to be tortious.[7] Any civil liability will, apparently, suffice. Indeed, it has been argued that actionability in principle, rather than on the facts of the particular case, will suffice.[8] This poses questions of substantive tort law, such as whether the common law defence

---

18 See *John Walker & Son Ltd v Henry Ost & Co Ltd* [1970] 1 WLR 917 at 933–934.
19 [1971] AC 356 at 400–406.
20 Ibid, at 383.
 1 Ibid, at 376–377, 387–389.
 2 Ibid, at 381, italics added.
 3 *Bank Russo-Iran v Gordon Woodroffe & Co Ltd* (1972) Times, 4 October; *Church of Scientology of California v Metropolitan Police Commissioner* (1976) 120 Sol Jo 690; *Coupland v Arabian Gulf Petroleum Co* [1983] 2 All ER 434, [1983] 1 WLR 1136, affd by the Court of Appeal [1983] 3 All ER 226, [1983] 1 WLR 1136; *The Forum Craftsman* [1985] 1 Lloyd's Rep 291 at 296; *Armagas v Mundogas SA* [1986] AC 717 at 740–741, 752–753, CA; affd by the House of Lords without discussion of this point [1986] AC 717 at 773; *Def Lepp Music v Stuart-Brown* [1986] RPC 273; *Intercontex v Schmidt* [1988] FSR 575; *Metall und Rohstoff AG v Donaldson Lufkin & Jenrette Inc* [1990] 1 QB 391, [1988] 3 All ER 116; overruled on a different point in *Lonrho plc v Fayed* [1991] 3 All ER 303, [1991] 3 WLR 188, HL; *Tyburn Productions Ltd v Conan Doyle* [1991] Ch 75; *Adams v Cape Industries plc* [1990] Ch 433 at 509.
 4 *Dimskal Shipping Co SA v International Transport Workers Federation* [1991] 3 WLR 875 at 886 (per Lord GOFF obiter, Lords KEITH, ACKNER and LOWRY concurring).
 5 This is the position in Australia: *Breavington v Godleman* (1988) 169 CLR 41; *Voth v Manildra Flour Mills Pty Ltd* (1990) 171 CLR 538 at 566–570.
 6 Cf *McLean v Pettigrew* [1945] SCR 62; criticised by Swan (1985) 63 Can BR 271. However, in Ontario this case has seemingly been confined to its facts: *Grimes v Cloutier* (1989) 61 DLR (4th) 505; *Prefontaine v Frizzle* (1990) 65 DLR (4th) 275.
 7 *Boys v Chaplin* [1971] AC 356 at 377, 389; *Hesperides Hotels Ltd v Aegean Turkish Holidays* [1978] QB 205 at 221–222, 227, revsd in part [1979] AC 508; *LaVan v Danyluk* (1970) 75 WWR 500 at 502; *Warren v Warren* [1972] Qd R 386 at 388; *Borg-Warner (Australia) Ltd v Zupan* [1982] VR 437 at 454; though cf *Mitchell v McCullouch* 1976 SLT 2 at 3; *Corcoran v Corcoran* [1974] VR 164 at 169.
 8 *Schmidt v Government Insurance of New South Wales* [1973] 1 NSWLR 59 at 63–64; and see *Anderson v Eric Anderson Radio and TV Pty Ltd* (1965) 114 CLR 20 at 42–44. However, later cases held that a good defence under the law of the place where the tort was committed would defeat the plaintiff's claim, see *Cawley v Australian Consolidated Press Ltd* [1981] 1 NSWLR 225; *Carleton v Freedom Publishing Co Pty Ltd* (1982) 63 FLR 326; see generally Handford (1983) 32 ICLQ 452, especially at 461–462, 469–471. These cases now appear to be obsolete in Australia, at least as regards interstate torts, because of *Breavington v Godleman* (1988) 169 CLR 41.

of contributory negligence merely barred the plaintiff's remedy or destroyed his right of action.[9] Such an analysis of actionability does not accord with the requirement of English law that there be civil *liability* under the law of the place of the tort. This was the view taken in *Armagas Ltd v Mundogas SA* by DUNN LJ,[10] who held that it is the relevant claim between the actual parties which must be looked at, and not whether such a claim could in theory be actionable. In other words, the question is whether a party would be likely to succeed in the foreign court.

It only remains to notice that the English court, when it refers to the law of the place where the tort was committed, applies the rules of that law that would be applicable to a purely domestic case, similar to the one under consideration. The purpose of resort to the law of the place of the tort is very largely to give effect to the presumed intentions of the parties. The average person thinks in terms of internal law. It is, therefore, to the internal law of the place of the tort, not to its private international law, that reference is made.[11] If the foreign law of the place of the tort is not pleaded and proved, then the English courts will, under the normal rule,[12] assume that it is the same as English law. Indeed, if the plaintiff does not allege that the defendant's act is wrongful under the law of the place of the tort,[13] a tort claim involving foreign elements may be treated just as though it is a domestic English case.[14]

(c) Interrelation of the two parts of the rule

Problems of the interrelation of the two parts of the rule will disappear if the Law Commissions' recommendations are adopted and the first part of the rule is abolished. In the meantime, such problems continue to bother us.

(i) Jurisdiction or choice of law?[15]

The discussion so far has proceeded on the assumption that the rule in *Phillips v Eyre* as amended by *Boys v Chaplin* provides a rule for choice of law. This has not been universally accepted and three different interpretations of the rule can be suggested. The first is that it provides a double-barrelled choice of law rule, and has nothing to say as to jurisdiction.[16] Secondly, it is a double-barrelled jurisdictional rule, leaving open the choice of law issue;[17] and, thirdly, the first part of the rule is jurisdictional, whilst the second

---

9 See North (1967) 16 ICLQ 379, 390–391.

10 [1986] AC 717 at 752–753; affd by the House of Lords without discussion of this point [1986] AC 717 at 773; Collier [1986] CLJ 20. Cf Briggs (1984) 12 Anglo-Am LR 237.

11 *Haumschild v Continental Casualty Co* 7 Wis 2d 130 at 141–141; 95 NW 2d 814 at 820 (1959); *Pfau v Trent Aluminum Co* 263 A 2d 129 at 136–137 (1970); Restatement 2d § 145, comment h. See also Law Com No 193 (1990), Scot Law Com No 129 (1990), para 3.56.

12 Eg *Bonnor v Balfour Kilpatrick Ltd* 1974 SLT 187, and see supra, pp 107 et seq. See also *University of Glasgow v The Economist* (1990) Times, 13 July.

13 *Yorke v British & Continental SS Co Ltd* (1945) 78 Ll L Rep 181 at 184.

14 Eg *Schneider v Eisovitch* [1960] 2 QB 430, [1960] 1 All ER 169; *Winkworth v Hubbard* [1960] 1 Lloyd's Rep 150; *Astro Vencedor Compania Naviera SA of Panama v Mabanaft GmbH* [1971] 2 QB 588, [1971] 2 All ER 1301.

15 See Morse, op cit, pp 45–50.

16 See McClean (1969) 43 ALJ 183; McLeod, at p 548; Castel, *Canadian Conflict of Laws* (2nd edn 1986), para 469; and see *Kolsky v Mayne Nickless Ltd* [1970] 3 NSWR 511 at 516–517; *Interprovincial Co-operatives Ltd v The Queen* (1975) 53 DLR (3d) 321 at 339–340.

17 See *Anderson v Eric Anderson Radio and TV Pty Ltd* (1965) 114 CLR 20 at 41; Spence (1949) 27 Can BR 661.

constitutes a choice of law rule, ie indicating the application of the law of the place of the tort.[18]

The approach of English law to this issue depends on the interpretation to be given to the speeches in *Boys v Chaplin*, and the position is not wholly clear. Lord DONOVAN and Lord GUEST, without discussing the matter explicitly, both imply that the *Phillips v Eyre* rule goes to the matter of jurisdiction. Lord DONOVAN indicated that in the present case the English court "was competent to entertain the action under the rule in *Phillips v Eyre*";[19] Lord GUEST's statement of the rule was "that to justify an action in England for a tort committed abroad"[20] the conduct must be actionable both by the law of the forum and law of the place of the tort, and he would apply the law of the place as the substantive law. Both comments infer that the jurisdiction of the English court to entertain the action is the issue involved in WILLES J's judgment.

In contrast to this, Lord WILBERFORCE rejects quite clearly the suggestion that the first part of the *Phillips v Eyre* rule relates to jurisdiction and concludes that, under that rule, the substantive law is the law of the forum subject to civil liability under the law of the place.[1] This view has been accepted in the Court of Appeal in *Coupland v Arabian Gulf Oil Co*.[2] Lord PEARSON would appear also to reject any idea that *Phillips v Eyre* relates to jurisdiction when he said of the two conditions in WILLES J's judgment that it shows that "the applicable law, the substantive law determining liability or non-liability, is a combination of the *lex fori* and the *lex loci delicti*".[3]

The views of Lord HODSON are a little difficult to evaluate. He indicates first that the *Phillips v Eyre* rule is the generally accepted choice of law rule;[4] then he says that "WILLES J was not, however, concerned with choice of law but only whether the courts of this country should entertain the action",[5] ie the rule is jurisdictional; but he finally treats the law of England, the law of the forum, as applicable on the basis of a flexible interpretation of *Phillips v Eyre*, ie back to choice of law again.

Whilst it is suggested that, on balance, the traditional interpretation, that *Phillips v Eyre* relates to choice of law and not to jurisdiction, stands, it might be pointed out that to decide otherwise does not provide any easy solution to the choice of law problem. Indeed Lord GUEST regarded the law of the place as the substantive law whilst Lord DONOVAN would apply the law of the forum.[6]

Finally, it is helpful to look at the Australian experience. There has been much discussion by judges and academics of the nature of the double limbed rule, with considerable support for it being regarded as a double limbed jurisdictional rule.[7] The substantive law to be applied should then be,

---

18 Yntema (1949) 27 Can BR 116, 119. Cf *Chaplin v Boys* [1971] AC 356 at 385–387.
19 [1971] AC 356 at 383.
20 Ibid, at 381.
1 Ibid, at 385–387.
2 [1983] 1 WLR 1136 at 1154. For other cases supporting Lord WILBERFORCE's judgment, see supra, p 534. See also *Def Lepp Music v Stuart-Brown* [1986] RPC 273.
3 [1971] AC 356 at 398.
4 Ibid, at 374.
5 Ibid, at 375.
6 [1971] AC 356 at 383; and see Lord UPJOHN in the Court of Appeal [1968] 2 QB 1 at 30–31.
7 See *Anderson v Eric Anderson Radio & TV Pty Ltd* (1965) 114 CLR 20 at 41; *Hartley v Venn* (1967) 10 FLR 151; *Pozniak v Smith* (1982) 151 CLR 38 at 49; cf Sykes and Pryles, pp 552–554. For Canadian authority, see *Gagnon v Lecavalier* (1967) 63 DLR (2d) 12; *Northern Alberta Rly Co v K and W Trucking Co Inc* (1974) 62 DLR (3d) 378.

in the view of many, the law of the forum. However, the recent abolition of the first limb of the rule, at least in interstate cases,[8] means the end of this controversy. The law of the place of the tort rule, when applied on its own, can only be regarded as a choice of law rule. It is to be hoped that United Kingdom law will follow the same path.

(ii)   The double actionability requirement
It is clear that the combined effect of *Phillips v Eyre* and *Boys v Chaplin* is that an action in England based on a tort committed abroad necessitates reference to actionability both by English law and the law of the place of the tort. On the assumption that the rule relates to choice of law, the plaintiff will succeed if the wrong is of such a character that it would have been actionable if committed in England and if it is one which, according to the law of the place of the tort, would impose civil liability on the defendant. According to Lord WILBERFORCE[9] the cause of action must vest in the same person and lie against the same person in both legal systems. In the case, for example, of an action based on wrongful death[10] or, perhaps, in a case of survival of actions[11] this would indicate that there must be a correlation between the two legal systems as to who are the proper parties. Similarly in the case of vicarious liability, it must be asked whether the defendant is vicariously liable under both systems of law.[12]

Under this view the act must, according to the law of the place of the tort, give rise to civil liability actionable at the suit of the plaintiff and the act must give rise there to a civil liability similar to that in respect of which the plaintiff sues in England. A clear illustration of this principle is seen in the Scottish decision in *M'Elroy v M'Allister*[13] where the facts were as follows:

> M'Elroy, while travelling on a lorry, was killed in England as a result of the negligence of the driver. His widow, in her capacity as executrix, sued the driver in Scotland. First, she took advantage of the rule of English internal law that the cause of action of the deceased had survived to her. All the parties came from Glasgow. The rule of Scots internal law, however, was that the right of action of an injured person died with him. Secondly, she claimed damages by way of *solatium*. This claim would be recognised by Scots law but not by English law. Thirdly, she claimed funeral expenses.

As to her first claim, it was necessary for the pursuer, acting on the assumption that *Phillips v Eyre* is accepted by Scots law, to show that the defender's negligence would have satisfied the first condition laid down by WILLES J, had the facts occurred in Scotland. The Court of Session, by a majority, dismissed the claim on the ground that according to Scots law the negligence of the driver was not actionable at the suit of the widow, notwithstanding that it was actionable in the abstract. This supports the view that damages will not be recoverable in the forum for conduct which in the abstract is

8 *Breavington v Godleman* (1988) 169 CLR 41.
9 [1971] AC 356 at 389. Lord WILBERFORCE's judgment has been expressly adopted in a number of cases, supra p 534. Cf Briggs (1984) 12 Anglo Am LR 237.
10 Webb (1961) 24 MLR 467; Morse, op cit, pp 143–144.
11 Webb & Brownlie (1965) 12 ICLQ 1; cf Dicey & Morris, pp 1394–1395, 1399–1400; Morse, op cit, pp 144–147, 161–163; and see *Kerr v Palfrey* [1970] VR 825.
12 See *The Mary Moxham* (1876) 1 PD 107, infra p 543; *Church of Scientology of California v Metropolitan Police Comr* (1976) 120 Sol Jo 690; *Armagas Ltd v Mundogas SA* [1986] AC 717 at 740, CA; affd by the House of Lords [1986] AC 717 at 773, [1986] 2 All ER 385; Morse op cit, pp 151–153; Collins (1977) 26 ICLQ 480.
13 1949 SC 110.

actionable both by the law of the place of the tort and the law of the forum, unless the person to whom the compensation is payable is identical in both laws. As for the second claim, the Court of Session also rejected the pursuer's claim for damages by way of *solatium* since this head of damages was not recoverable under English law.[14] The only claim which did succeed was that for funeral expenses, for which the defender had admitted liability. Here there was correlation between Scots and English law.

The English and Scots case law on the interrelation of the law of the forum and the law of the place of the tort now presents a somewhat complex pattern. However, it would appear that there is support for the following propositions:

No action will lie for an act which, according to either, first, the law of the place where it was committed or, second, English law, imposes no liability whatsoever on the defendant. The first part of this proposition will apply, for instance, if conduct such as conspiracy, which is tortious by English law, is not regarded as wrongful in the foreign country. It is not sufficient for the plaintiff to show merely that the act complained of gave rise to liability in someone other than the defendant.[15] The only rider to this is that the double actionability rule may operate differently so that a defendant is not able to invoke a foreign law to escape liability in cases where the events constituting the tort have occurred in different countries and there is accordingly a definitional problem over the place of the tort.[16]

The second part of the proposition has already been illustrated by *The Halley*[1] and *M'Elroy v M'Allister*.[2]

The defendant can rely on any defence available to him according to either the law of the forum or, provided the defence is not procedural only, the law of the place of the tort. This means that the plaintiff gets the worst of both laws.[3] *McMillan v Canadian Northern Rly Co*[4] illustrates reliance on a defence under the law of the place:

A fireman, in the course of his employment by the respondents, was injured in Ontario owing to the negligence of a fellow servant. He sued in Saskatchewan for the recovery of damages. The defence of common employment was recognised in Ontario but not in Saskatchewan.

Apart from other considerations affecting this case, which are discussed below,[5] it is clear that the appellant could be successfully met in the Saskatchewan action by the defence of common employment.

Another instance in which the defendant may rely on the protection of the law of the place is where he is later excused from liability for his wrong by a

14 And see *Li Lian Tan v Durham* [1966] SASR 143; cf *Kemp v Piper* [1971] SASR 25.
15 *The Mary Moxham* (1876) 1 PD 107. See also *Dimskal Shipping Co SA v International Transport Workers Federation (The Evia Luck) (No 2)* [1989] 1 Lloyd's Rep 166 at 177; appeal allowed on a different point [1990] 1 Lloyd's Rep 319, appeal against the latter decision, dismissed by the House of Lords [1991] 4 All ER 871, [1991] 3 WLR 875.
16 *Metall und Rohstoff AG v Donaldson Lufkin & Jenrette Inc* [1990] 1 QB 391, [1988] 3 All ER 116, CA; overruled on a different point in *Lonrho plc v Fayed* [1991] 3 All ER 303, [1991] 3 WLR 188, HL; infra, pp 553–554.
1 (1868) LR 2 PC 193, supra, pp 536–537.
2 1949 SC 110, supra, pp 542–543.
3 *Boys v Chaplin* [1971] AC 356 at 405. Cf *The Adhiguna Meranti* [1988] 1 Lloyd's Rep 384 at 390, Hong Kong CA.
4 [1923] AC 120.
5 Infra, p 544.

competent authority in the country where he acted, as for instance by an Act of Indemnity.[6]

Again, an action will not be sustainable for an act which, according to the law of the place of the tort, gives rise to a liability that is merely *ex lege*. As we have already seen there is the authority of *Boys v Chaplin* for the view that the defendant's civil liability under the law of the place will enable the plaintiff to succeed in English proceedings. However, liability that is simply *ex lege* does not suffice. This appears to be the effect of the Privy Council decisions in *Walpole v Canadian Northern Railway*,[7] and *McMillan v Canadian Northern Railway*.[8] The facts of the latter case have already been partly given.[9] There was, however, this further obstacle in the way of the appellant's success.

> The Workmen's Compensation Act of Ontario, after providing that an employer should be liable individually to pay compensation at a fixed scale to any workman injured in the course of his employment, directed that no action should lie for the recovery of the compensation, but that all claims should be determined by a Board specially established for the purpose.

The Privy Council in *McMillan's Case* addressed its mind to this problem and decided that the claim of the plaintiff arose, not from the tort, but *ex lege*. The claim, therefore, quite apart from the defence of common employment, was not sustainable in Saskatchewan, since the accident gave rise neither to a cause of action nor to criminal proceedings in the country of its occurrence.

Similarly, in the field of contributory negligence[10] one would expect a claim to fail if under the law of the place of the tort contributory negligence constitutes a complete bar, even though the law of the forum permits apportionment.[11]

There seems little doubt that the defendant can avail himself of similar defences or exculpating factors under the law of the forum.[12]

No action will be sustainable for an act which according to either the law of the forum or the law of the place of the tort gives rise to no civil liability actionable at the suit of the plaintiff.

No action will be sustainable for an act which according to either the law of the place or the law of the forum does not give rise to civil liability similar in nature to that in respect of which the plaintiff sues.

6   *Carr v Francis Times & Co* [1902] AC 176; *Phillips v Eyre* supra, p 538.
7   [1923] AC 113. The same point is made implicitly in *Coupland v Arabian Gulf Petroleum Co* [1983] 1 WLR 1136 at 1143; affd by the Court of Appeal [1983] 1 WLR 1136.
8   [1923] AC 120.
9   Supra, p 543.
10 See Morse, op cit, pp 180 et seq; Brownlie and Webb (1962) 40 Can BR 79; Webb (1966) 44 Can BR 666; North (1967) 16 ICLQ 379.
11 There is Australian authority to the contrary: *Hartley v Venn* (1967) 10 FLR 151; see also *Kolsky v Mayne, Nickless Ltd* [1970] 3 NSWR 511 where the law of the place accepted contributory negligence as a defence subject to apportionment, but under the law of the forum it was no defence at all; but these cases are decided on the principle (no longer applied in Australia) that the governing law is the law of the forum. More recent Australian cases have held that a good defence under the law of the place of the tort will defeat the plaintiff's claim: *Cawley v Australian Consolidated Press Ltd* [1981] 1 NSWLR 225; *Carleton v Freedom Publishing Co Pty Ltd* (1982) 63 FLR 326.
12 This used to be the position in Australia: *Anderson v Eric Anderson Radio and TV Pty Ltd* (1965) 114 CLR 20. But now see *Breavington v Godleman* (1988) 169 CLR 41.

These two propositions are supported in whole or in part by a number of Scottish decisions.[13] The facts of *M'Elroy v M'Allister* have already been given[14] and we have seen first that the pursuer's claim in her capacity as executrix was barred by the rule in *The Halley*, and secondly that the Court of Session rejected her claim for damages by way of *solatium* on the basis that this was not recoverable under the law of the place of the tort.

This first aspect of the *M'Elroy Case* was followed in *James Burrough Distillers plc v Speymalt Whisky Distributors Ltd* in which an action was brought in Scotland for infringement of an Italian trade mark in Italy. This failed. Scots and Italian law conferred a right of action on different parties. Furthermore, the infringement of an *Italian* trade mark would not be actionable if committed in Scotland. The second aspect of the *M'Elroy Case* was followed in *MacKinnon v Iberia Shipping Co Ltd*. The Court of Session held that the plaintiff's claim for *solatium* failed since it was a claim unknown to Dominican law, the law of the place where the tort was committed. In *M'Elroy v M'Allister* the claim for *solatium* was brought by someone other than the party who had been physically injured. *MacKinnon's Case*, however, affirmed a wider rule, for there the plaintiff sued in respect of his own injuries. The plaintiff must show that the law of the place confers upon himself the very right that he seeks to enforce.

In *Mitchell v McCulloch*[15] a claim relating to heads of damage (which included loss of profits of a company of which the injured pursuer was a director) valid under the law of the place was rejected because there was no equivalent liability under the law of the forum.

(iii) What then is the substantive law?
Even though there must be this correlation of actionability between the law of the forum and law of the place of the tort, it must be asked whether this resolves the question which is the substantive law. It is essential to know which it is whenever it is necessary, as in *Boys v Chaplin*, to distinguish a rule of substance from one of procedure,[16] or indeed when the claim under the law of the forum is based on tortious liability but under the law of the place is founded on some other head of civil liability, such as breach of contract.[17] The speeches in the House of Lords in that case provide no clear answer.[18] Lord HODSON and Lord WILBERFORCE would, if they could, have applied a "most significant relationship" concept. However, Lord WILBERFORCE agreed with Lord PEARSON that, if the orthodox *Phillips v Eyre* rule is still applicable, then the two branches thereof must be combined so that the substantive law to be applied is the law of the forum and that as a condition of its application civil liability in respect of the particular claim should exist as between the actual parties under the law of the place of the tort.[19] As Lord PEARSON said, "the substantive law of England plays the dominant role, determining the cause of action, whereas the law of the place in which the act was committed

---

13 *Naftalin v London, Midland and Scottish Rly Co* 1933 SC 259; *M'Elroy v M'Allister* 1949 SC 110; *Mackinnon v Iberia Shipping Ltd* 1955 SC 20; *Mitchell v McCulloch* 1976 SLT 2; *James Burrough Distillers plc v Speymalt Whisky Distributors Ltd* 1989 SLT 561.
14 Supra, p 542.
15 1976 SLT 2.
16 This may be significant in deciding what law is to determine the currency in which damages are to be assessed, see *The Despina R* [1979] AC 685, supra, pp 104–105.
17 Supra, pp 537–540.
18 Lord DONOVAN does not discuss the question of which is the substantive law.
19 [1971] AC 356 at 387–389; and see *Mitchell v McCulloch* 1976 SLT 2 at 5; *The Adhiguna Meranti* [1988] 1 Lloyd's Rep 384 at 390, Hong Kong CA.

plays a subordinate role, in that it may provide a justification for the act and so defeat the cause of action but it does not in itself determine the cause of action".[20]

Lord HODSON's speech does not really clarify this issue. Having determined that WILLES J's judgment does not declare that the tortious act must be determined by the law of the place of the tort,[21] he then decided that as a general principle the law of the place, here Maltese law, was the applicable substantive law. It should, however, be displaced here in favour of English law on grounds of justified flexibility.[22] Lord GUEST considered the substantive law to be the law of Malta, though he applied English law on the ground that the issue before the court was procedural.

Whilst there has been support on one basis or another for the application of the law of the forum as the dominant substantive law,[23] there can be little doubt of the insularity of such an approach.[24] Application of both the law of the forum and the law of the place as the combined governing laws[25] will result in further decisions such as *M'Elroy v M'Allister*[26] where in a multistate tort case there can be recovery based only on exact correlation between the two systems. This is likely to be unduly favourable to the defendant. Few would deny that such a result pays too much regard to the law of the forum and too little to the law of the place. It evidences a failure to realise that the commission of a tort abroad "is of more acute concern to the foreign community than to the community of the forum".[27]

(ii) The exception

(a) Is the proper law of the tort part of English law? There has been a wide spectrum of views expressed as to whether *Boys v Chaplin* is authority for, or against, the proper law of the tort. As has already been mentioned,[1] it has been argued in general terms, by some, that no ratio can be extracted from the case, and, by others, that lower courts can choose whichever ratio they like from the five judgments. More particularly in relation to the proper law of the tort, it has been argued that, in the circumstances of uncertainty following *Boys v Chaplin*, the proper law view should prevail.[2]

There would appear to be a majority of their Lordships opposed to the introduction into English law of the general concept of the proper law of the tort, on the ground, particularly, that it produces uncertainty.[3] Nevertheless, there was acceptance by a majority of their Lordships in *Boys v Chaplin* that some degree of flexibility should be introduced into the choice of law rules.[4] The basis for such an approach stems from the fact that WILLES J prefaced

20 Ibid, at 398.
21 Ibid, at 375.
22 Ibid, at 379–380.
23 See *Kolsky v Mayne Nickless Ltd* [1970] 3 NSWR 511. But now see *Breavington v Godleman* (1988) 169 CLR 41.
24 Cf Ehrenzweig (1968) 17 ICLQ 1.
25 See Lord WILBERFORCE [1971] AC 356 at 389.
26 Supra, pp 542–543.
27 Hancock, *Torts in the Conflict of Laws*, 62; Yntema (1949) 27 Can BR 116, 118 et seq; and also (1951) 4 ILQ 1, 7–10.
1 Supra, p 535.
2 Dicey and Morris, pp 1371–1374.
3 [1971] AC 356 at 381, per Lord GUEST, and see Lord DONOVAN at 383, Lord PEARSON, at 405–406. See also Carter (1981) 52 BYBIL 10 at 25. Even Lord HODSON who, with Lord WILBERFORCE, approved the test as laid down in the American Restatement 2d adverted to the dangers of uncertainty, at pp 377–378.
4 No support for such a view is forthcoming from Lord DONOVAN or Lord GUEST.

his statement of the *Phillips v Eyre* rule with the caveat "as a general rule". The flexibility advocated by Lord HODSON[5] and Lord WILBERFORCE[6], being based on the "significant relationship" test of the recent American Restatement, is more radical than that of Lord PEARSON. He would introduce sufficient flexibility to be able to discourage "forum shopping"[7] if the law of the forum be the substantive law. If the governing law was the law of the place of the tort or a combination of that law and the law of the forum, then he would consider the present case as an exceptional one justifying the ignoring of the provisions of the law of the place of the tort.[8] Thus, the case seemingly decides that there should be a flexible exception[9] but does not decide what this exception should be based upon.

Boys v Chaplin can be seen to have left the law in a state of great uncertainty as to the nature and extent of any exception to the general rule.[10] Judicial law-making of this kind is of little service to private international law. However, in subsequent cases English judges have been untroubled by problems of precedent. Lord WILBERFORCE's judgment has been regarded as the definitive statement on the law relating to tort choice of law[11] and it has been accepted in numerous cases that the proper law of the tort is part of English law.[12] If one assumes that this view is correct, it is at least possible to define the terms of the exception, which you cannot do if you merely regard *Boys v Chaplin* as establishing a "flexible" exception to the general rule. It has been said that "As an exception to the general rule, a particular issue may be governed by the law of the State which, with respect to that issue, has the most significant relationship with the occurrence and the parties."[13] Nonetheless, this still leaves many unanswered questions in relation to the exception.

(b) The unresolved questions[14]

(i) Can the exception be applied in cases where the parties are not from the same State? Lords HODSON and WILBERFORCE only applied the proper law

5 [1971] AC 356 at 378. He would leave latitude to admit or exclude claims in the interest of public policy.
6 Ibid, at 389–393.
7 This is best dealt with at the jurisdictional stage, see Fawcett (1984) 35 NILQ 141; see also Schuz (1986) 35 ICLQ 374. Cf *Breavington v Godleman* (1988) 169 CLR 41.
8 [1971] AC 356 at 406.
9 Cf Briggs (1984) 12 Anglo-Am LR 237.
10 Lords HODSON and WILBERFORCE, whilst in favour of flexibility, also pointed to the dangers of uncertainty: [1971] AC 356 at 378, 406. A flexible exception now seems to have been rejected in Australia, at least in interstate cases: *Breavington v Godleman* (1988) 169 CLR 41.
11 *Church of Scientology of California v Metropolitan Police Commissioner* (1976) 120 Sol Jo 690; *Coupland v Arabian Gulf Petroleum Co* [1983] 1 WLR 1136, [1983] 3 All ER 226; *Armagas Ltd v Mundogas SA* [1986] AC 717 at 740–741, 752–753, CA; affd by the House of Lords without discussion of this point [1986] AC 717 at 773.
12 *Sayers v International Drilling NV* [1971] 1 WLR 1176 at 1180; *Church of Scientology of California v Metropolitan Police Comr*, op cit; *Coupland v Arabian Gulf Petroleum Co*, op cit; *Armagas Ltd v Mundogas SA*, op cit; *Dimskal Shipping Co SA v International Transport Workers Federation (The Evia Luck) (No 2)* [1989] 1 Lloyd's Rep 166; appeal allowed on a different point [1990] 1 Lloyd's Rep 319; appeal against the latter decision dismissed by the House of Lords [1991] 4 All ER 871, [1991] 3 WLR 875. But see *Hesperides Hotels Ltd v Aegean Turkish Holidays Ltd* [1978] QB 205 at 221–222; revsd in part [1979] AC 508, [1978] 1 All ER 227.
13 Karsten (1970) 19 ICLQ 35, 38; and see Dicey and Morris, pp 1373–1378.
14 See Fawcett (1984) 47 MLR 650 and Lowenfeld (1989) 37 Am J Comp Law 353 at 377–380.

as an exception to the general rule. The clear case when this is justified is where the parties are from the same State, and, if the proper law is only to perform a subsidiary role, it must be doubted whether the exception can be applied in the situation where the parties are from different States.[15] Indeed, both Law Lords said that if the defendants were Maltese and the plaintiff English it would be a just result to apply the general rule.[16]

(ii) In *Boys v Chaplin* the proper law also happened to be the law of the forum.[17] Will the exception be applied in cases where the proper law happens to be the law of the place of the tort or the law of a third country?[18] In principle, there is no reason why the proper law exception should not be applied in such cases;[1] and there is some more recent authority, albeit in *obiter dicta*, directly supporting this.[2]

(iii) If the use of the exception does lead to the application of the law of a third country, will the law of the forum be retained to limit the application of the foreign proper law? In other words, does the proper law exception displace both parts of the general rule (ie the law of the forum and the law of the place of the tort) or merely the second limb of the general rule (ie the law of the place of the tort)? Lords HODSON and WILBERFORCE would appear to favour the former view,[3] but, of course, they were talking in the context of a case which did not involve a third country. The policy considerations[4] that led all five Law Lords to support the requirement of actionability in England under the first limb of the rule in *Phillips v Eyre* under the general rule are equally applicable under the exception. If the English courts are unwilling to trust the unfettered use of the law of the place of the tort, there must be at least a possibility that they will be equally unwilling to trust the unfettered use of the proper law and will limit the use of the exception by requiring actionability under the law of the forum to be shown in cases where the proper law is the law of a third country.

(iv) Will the exception apply where it has the effect that the plaintiff will recover less than under the general rule? Lords HODSON and WILBERFORCE were influenced in adopting the exception by an awareness that the plaintiff would thereby recover full compensation, and there must be some doubt as to whether they would be prepared to apply the exception if the plaintiff would be more adequately compensated by application of the general rule.[5]

---

15 See Karsten, op cit, at p 42; Morse, op cit, at pp 287–288. Cf *Sayers v International Drilling Co NV* [1971] 1 WLR 1176 at 1181.
16 [1971] AC 356 at 379, 392.
17 This was also the case in *Church of Scientology of California v Metropolitan Police Comr* (1976) 120 Sol Jo 690; and in the following Australian cases: *Kemp v Piper* [1971] SASR 25 at 38; *Warren v Warren* [1972] QdR 386 at 392; *Corcoran v Corcoran* [1974] VR 164 at 171–171.
18 See generally on the exception Kahn-Freund (1968) II Hague Recueil 1, 63–129; McGregor (1970) 33 MLR 1, 15–21; Dicey and Morris, pp 1373–1378.
1 Lord WILBERFORCE's judgment supports this, see [1971] AC 356 at 391.
2 *Sayers v International Drilling Co NV* [1971] 1 WLR 1176 at 1181; *Coupland v Arabian Gulf Oil Co* [1983] 1 WLR 1136 at 1149; affd by the Court of Appeal [1983] 1 WLR 1136.
3 [1971] AC 356 at 392; see also *Coupland v Arabian Gulf Oil Co*, op cit, at 1149; Morse (1984) 33 ICLQ 449 at 456.
4 Supra, p 535.
5 See also *Church of Scientology v Metropolitan Police Comr* (1976) 120 Sol Jo 690, where the Court of Appeal said that if there was no double actionability the plaintiff might come within the exception; see also *Coupland v Arabian Gulf Petroleum Co*, op cit, at 1149.

(v) Will the exception apply, if, unlike in *Boys v Chaplin*, it gives no recovery at all? Lord HODSON's judgment[6] can be read to the effect that he would not support the use of the exception in such a case, whereas Lord WILBERFORCE's judgment[7] suggests that he would. The need adequately to compensate the plaintiff in this situation is even more urgent than it is in cases where some recovery is given under the general rule, and for this reason the use of the exception should not be ruled out simply because there is no overlap whatsoever between the law of the forum and the law of the place of the tort under the general rule.

(vi) Is the exception applicable if the issue is changed? Lord WILBERFORCE[8] was careful to segregate the issue in the case. The law of the place of the tort is much more relevant to some issues, eg standard of care, than to others,[9] and there must be some doubt whether the exception can ever be applied to one of these issues in respect of which the law of the place of the tort is particularly important.

(c) The Law Commissions' proposals[10]

It has been proposed that there should be an exception to the rules on the prima facie applicable law.[11] Under this exception the applicable law is that of the country or territory with which the tort or delict has the most real and substantial connection. Unlike under the present law, the exception would apply in two very different situations. The first is a very narrow situation and is concerned with certain of the cases where there are problems in ascertaining the place where the tort was committed. More will be said about this when discussing more generally the place of the tort.[12] The second and more general situation is where it would be "substantially more appropriate" that a law other than that indicated under the general rules on the prima facie applicable law should apply, having regard amongst other things to factors relating to the parties and to all of the surrounding circumstances.

Does this proposed general exception provide any more certainty than the present law? Some at least of the unresolved questions under the present law appear to remain unresolved. It is still not clear whether the exception can be applied in cases where the parties are not from the same state. Perhaps significantly, all of the Law Commissions' examples of cases where the exception might be appropriate actually involve two parties from the same state. It is also not clear if the exception will apply when it gives the plaintiff less recovery than under the general rules. The use of the dangerous word "appropriate" would allow in a consideration of this factor when deciding whether to apply the exception. On the other hand, the list of relevant factors and examples given by the Law Commissions does not include this particular factor. Finally, it is very unclear what significance if any, is to be attached to the particular issue that arises in a case. The Law Commissions made no express reference to this matter. However, they were concerned that the rule of displacement under the exception should operate when the tort as a whole

6 Op cit, at 379.
7 Op cit, at 391. See also *Church of Scientology v Metropolitan Police Comr* (1976) 120 Sol Jo 690; *Warren v Warren* [1972] QdR 386.
8 At 392.
9 Morse, op cit, at pp 291–294.
10 Law Com No 193 (1990), Scot Law Com No 129 (1990); discussed infra, pp 564–565.
11 Paras 3.8–3.12.
12 Infra, p 557.

has a closer connection with a country other than that selected by the general rules. This surely means that you have to consider what the issue was.

2. TORTS IN ENGLAND

Where a tort is alleged to have been committed in England, then the English courts have always applied English law to such a claim, for there is a coincidence of forum law and the law of the place of the tort. This has been the case however foreign the parties and however limited the connection with England, as may be illustrated by *Szalatnay-Stacho v Fink*:[13]

> The defendant, an official of the Czech Government, then in exile in England during the Second World War, sent to the President of the Czech Republic, also in England, documents alleging misconduct by the plaintiff, the Czech Acting Minister in Egypt. These documents which were published in England were clearly defamatory of the plaintiff. Under Czech law the documents were absolutely privileged, but under English law only the defence of qualified privilege was available.

The Court of Appeal decided that English law was applicable to this tort committed in England, but that the conduct of the defendant fell within the defence of qualified privilege. Indeed, it was suggested that foreign law could only be applied in a case such as this if it was expressly provided for by legislation.[14]

The application of English law in cases like this is an inevitable result of the application of the general two-part rule in *Phillips v Eyre*. If, however, the defendant pleaded a contractual defence or exemption from liability then, provided such a defence was permitted under English law,[15] its effect would be referred to the law applicable to the contract.[16]

What remains to consider is whether the "flexibility" introduced by *Boys v Chaplin* would permit English law to be displaced as both law of the place and law of the forum in the case of a tort committed in England, in favour of the application of some more appropriate law. Could Czech law now be applied in *Szalatnay-Stacho v Fink*? Could Maltese law be applied to a motor accident in England involving only two Maltese?[17] Whilst the judgments of both Lord HODSON[18] and Lord WILBERFORCE[19] in *Boys v Chaplin* are expressed in terms broad enough to allow both heads of the *Phillips v Eyre* rule to be supplanted by a more appropriate foreign law, Lord PEARSON's[20] concept of flexibility was far more limited and would seem to allow the court to disregard one or other, but not both, of the heads of *Phillips v Eyre*. That being so, it is arguable that an English court could not avoid the application of English law to a tort committed in England.[21] This seemingly was the view of the

13 [1947] KB 1. See also *Borg-Warner (Australia) Ltd v Zupan* [1982] VR 437 at 450. Cf *Bagg v Budget Rent-A-Car* [1989] 4 WWR 586.
14 Ibid, at 13.
15 See *Brodin v A/R Seljan* 1973 SC 213, infra, p 563.
16 *Galaxios Steamship Co Ltd v Panagos Christofis* (1948) 81 Ll L Rep 499; *Kahler v Midland Bank Ltd* [1950] AC 24, [1949] 2 All ER 621; *Zivnostenska Banka National Corporation v Frankman* [1950] AC 57, [1949] 2 All ER 671; North (1977) 26 ICLQ 914, 915–920.
17 Dicey and Morris, p 1409.
18 [1971] AC 356 at 377–380.
19 Ibid, at 389–392.
20 Ibid, at 406.
21 And see *Interprovincial Co-operatives Ltd v The Queen* (1975) 53 DLR (3d) 321 at 339–340.

Court of Appeal in *Metall und Rohstoff AG v Donaldson Lufkin & Jenrette Inc*[22] where it was said that, if the tort was committed in England, the court could wholly disregard the rule in *Boys v Chaplin*. In particular, no recourse could be had to a foreign law to claim an exemption from liability.[23]

The Law Commissions have proposed[24] that for torts that "relate to, or the consequences of, any conduct the most significant elements of which took place in a part of the United Kingdom" the law of that part of the United Kingdom shall apply. Surprisingly, there is no proper law exception to this rule. The Law Commissions were concerned that a person who acts in the United Kingdom in accordance with our law should not be held liable by the application of a foreign law. Equally, of course, a person will not be able to escape liability by invoking a foreign law. Be that as it may, it is hard to justify the application of English law in the situation where the tort has the most real and substantial connection with a foreign country. It is a matter for regret that the Law Commissions have adopted such an inflexible approach for torts committed in the United Kingdom.[25] There is though a special provision for defamation cases involving publication both in the United Kingdom and abroad, according to which, where a statement is published abroad and is simultaneously or previously published in the United Kingdom, the applicable law is that of the relevant part of the United Kingdom.[26]

3. THE PLACE OF A TORT[27]

It is now necessary to consider how one determines where a tort is committed in order to identify the law of the place of the tort.[28] In the normal case, where the facts and events that are said to constitute the tort have all occurred in one country, there is, of course, no difficulty in deciding where the alleged wrong was committed. But a more complicated situation arises if the facts have occurred some in one country, some in another. For example, if a fire, that has been negligently started by A on the English side of the Scottish border, spreads into Scotland and burns down B's house, in which country has the tort been committed? The importance of ascertaining this is evident, since the two laws may differ fundamentally on the question of A's liability, and there are different tort choice of law rules for torts committed in England and torts committed abroad.[29] The possible solutions for defining the place of the tort will now be examined.

22 [1990] 1 QB 391, [1988] 3 All ER 116, CA; overruled on a different point in *Lonrho plc v Fayed* [1991] 3 All ER 303, [1991] 3 WLR 188, HL.
23 At 446–447. This was in the context of the foreign law of the place where acts of inducement of breach of contract occurred, rather than a foreign proper law, granting exemption from liability, see infra pp 553–554.
24 Law Com No 193 (1990), Scot Law Com No 129 (1990), paras 3.14–3.18.
25 See North (1991) 42 NILQ 183, 196–198. In some circumstances, if the tort is committed in the forum this may also be the state with the closest connection: *Kim v Yun* (1991) 4 OR (3d) 455.
26 Paras 3.28–3.33.
27 Wolff, pp 493 et seq; Morse, op cit, pp 111 et seq; Lorenzen (1931) 47 LQR 483, 491 et seq; Webb & North (1965) 14 ICLQ 1314; Fridman (1974) 24 U Tor LJ 247; Kahn-Freund (1974) III Hague Recueil 139, 405–406.
28 Cf Robb (1977) 8 Sydney LR 146, 149–151.
29 See *Metall und Rohstoff AG v Donaldson Lufkin & Jenrette Inc* [1990] 1 Q B 391 at 446; overruled on a different point in *Lonrho plc v Fayed* [1991] 3 All ER 303, [1991] 3 WLR 188, HL; supra, pp 536 and 550.

(a) THE THEORIES

Three different tests have been proposed for the determination of the matter.

First, the place where the defendant did the acts from which the harm ensues constitutes the place of the tort. Many arguments have been advanced in favour of this solution.[30] It is, however, not free from ambiguity. The defendant may have acted in more than one place. He may, for instance, have written a defamatory letter in one country and have posted it in another.

The second theory prefers the country in which the harm ensues. There is American support for this view: thus, Beale says that "the place of wrong is the place where the person or thing harmed is situated at the time of the wrong."[1] On the other hand, Cook is of opinion that the theory has been adopted without an adequate discussion of the issues involved.[2] Indeed, the problem of determining the place of the tort disappears if one adopts the approach to choice of law in tort now current in the USA.[3] Again, it may be noted that this second theory is not free from obscurity. A plaintiff may be injured in State A but hospitalised in State B.[4] Damage may also occur in more than one country. Moreover, harm that is of a non-physical nature, such as financial harm[5] or damage to reputation, cannot be localised physically except by resort to a fiction.

According to the third theory, favoured by Cook,[6] the place of a tort is the place where the law is most favourable to the person wronged. The plaintiff can, at will, fix the place of the tort in any country in which any of the operative facts occurred. This solution, thus baldly stated, favours the plaintiff unduly.

(b) PRESENT ENGLISH LAW

(i) The status of the authorities

There are very few cases where the problem of locating the commission of a tort has arisen in the choice of law context.[7] However, until recently the problem did arise in another context in English private international law. It was sometimes necessary for the court to decide where an alleged tort had

---

30 They are summarised by Lorenzen in (1931) 47 LQR 483, 493.
1 *Conflict of Laws*, vol 2, p 1287; and see Leflar, pp 365–373.
2 *Logical and Legal Bases of the Conflict of Laws*, p 319.
3 *Babcock v Jackson*, supra, pp 260–261; Restatement 2d § 145. The problem has, however, resurfaced in New York where increasing significance has been given to the law of the place of the tort; see *Schultz v Boys Scouts of America Inc* 65 NY 2d 189, 480 NE 2d 679 (1985).
4 *Vile v Von Wendt* (1980) 103 DLR 3d 356; *Brix-Neilsen v Oceaneering Australian Pty Ltd* (1982) 2 NSWLR 173; *Flaherty v Girgis* (1986) 63 ALR 466; cf *Thomas v Penna* [1985] 2 NSWLR 171.
5 See *Metall und Rohstoff AG v Donaldson Lufkin & Jenrette Inc*, op cit; overruled on a different point in *Lonrho plc v Fayed* [1991] 3 All ER 303, [1991] 3 WLR 188, HL; infra, pp 553–554.
6 Op cit, p 345. See also Morse, op cit, pp 124 et seq.
7 The cases are: *Church of Scientology v Metropolitan Police Comr* (1976) 120 Sol Jo 690; *Armagas Ltd v Mundogas SA* [1986] AC 717 at 740–741, CA—this case actually discussed the problem; affd by the House of Lords [1986] AC 717 at 773; *Metall und Rohstoff AG v Donaldson Lufkin & Jenrette Inc* [1990] 1 QB 391, [1988] 3 All ER, 116; overruled on a different point in *Lonrho plc v Fayed* [1991] 3 All ER 303, [1991] 3 WLR 188, HL, infra. The problem has arisen in the choice of law context in one or two Scottish cases: eg *Soutar v Peters* [1912] 1 SLT 111; *John Walker & Sons Ltd v Douglas McGibbon & Co Ltd* 1972 SLT 128; and in Canada: *Interprovincial Co-operatives Ltd v The Queen in right of Manitoba* (1975) 53 DLR (3d) 321.

been committed when hearing an application for leave to serve process out of the jurisdiction. Order 11, Rule 1(1)(h) of the old Rules of the Supreme Court provided that at the discretion of the court such leave could be given "if the action begun by the writ is founded on a tort committed within the jurisdiction."[8] There was, of course, no compelling reason to suppose that the problem should be solved in precisely the same way in connection with choice of law as it was in connection with jurisdiction. Nonetheless, in the few cases where the problem arose in the choice of law context the same definition of the place of the tort was applied as in the jurisdictional context.[9]

It has always been questionable whether jurisdictional cases should be used as authority in the choice of law context. It should not be forgotten that a decision whether to grant leave for service out of the jurisdiction is discretionary. Furthermore, whilst a court may be prepared to hold that a tort is committed in several places for the purposes of a jurisdictional rule,[10] it should insist on one single place of the tort in the choice of law context. Thus the jurisdictional test adopted by the Supreme Court of Canada,[11] under which "it would not be inappropriate to regard a tort as having occurred in any country substantially affected by the defendant's activities and whose law is likely to have been in the reasonable contemplation of the parties"[12] is unworkable in the choice of law context,[13] since it could lead to the result that a tort may be committed in more than one State at once.

The use of cases decided under RSC Order 11 becomes even more questionable now that the new tort head of Order 11[14] does not even require the place of the tort to be ascertained. What one is talking about therefore is the use of cases decided under a now obsolete head of Order 11. This means that, if a question of jurisdiction arises, the new tort head of Order 11 is used. Whereas, if the question is one of choice of law (and this may arise in the same case), the place of the tort is ascertained by reference to cases decided under the old tort head of Order 11.

This is what happened in the leading case of *Metall und Rohstoff AG v Donaldson Lufkin & Jenrette Inc*:[15]

8 The new rule, which is differently worded, is contained in Ord 11, r 1(1)(f); see supra, pp 199–201.
9 See in respect of defamation, *M Isaacs & Sons Ltd v Cook* [1925] 2 KB 391 at 400, and *Church of Scientology v Metropolitan Police Commissioner* (1976) 120 Sol Jo 690, which can be compared with the Ord 11 case of *Bata v Bata* [1948] WN 366; see infra, p 555. See in respect of fraudulent misrepresentation, *Armagas Ltd v Mundogas SA* [1986] AC 717 at 740, CA; affd by the House of Lords [1986] AC 717 at 773; the Court of Appeal applied the Ord 11 case of *Diamond v Bank of London and Montreal Ltd* [1979] QB 333, [1979] 1 All ER 561; discussed infra, p 556.
10 Eg *Abbott-Smith v Governors of University of Toronto* (1964) 45 DLR (2d) 672 at 680, 694; *Moran v Pyle National (Canada) Ltd* (1973) 43 DLR (3d) 239 at 242; *Handelskwekerij GJ Bier BV v Mines de Potasse d'Alsace SA* Case 21/76 [1976] ECR 1735, [1978] QB 708; discussed supra, p 301.
11 *Moran v Pyle National (Canada) Ltd* (1973) 43 DLR (3d) 239; Hurlburt (1974) 52 Can BR 470; Blom (1974) 9 UBCL Rev 389; Collins (1975) 24 ICLQ 325. Applied in: *Skyrotors Ltd v Caviere Technical Industries Ltd* (1980) 102 DLR (3d) 323; *Petersen v AB Bahco Ventilation* (1980) 107 DLR (3d) 49; *Ichi Canada Ltd v Yamauchi Rubber Industry Co* (1983) 144 DLR (3d) 533. Cf *Macgregor v Application des Gaz* [1976] QdR 175. The same is true of the jurisdictional test adopted in Ireland in *Patrick Grehan v Medical Inc and Valley Pine Associates* [1986] IR 528.
12 *Moran*, op cit, at p 250; *Petersen v AB Bahco Ventilation* (1980) 107 DLR (3d) 49 at 57.
13 Collins (1975) 24 ICLQ 325, 328. This was acknowledged in *Moran* at 242.
14 Ord 11, r 1 (1)(f); see supra, pp 199–201.
15 [1990] 1 QB 391; [1991] 3 All ER 303, overruled on a different point in *Lonrho plc v Fayed* [1991] 3 WLR 188; Briggs (1989) 105 LQR 359; Fentiman [1989] CLJ 191.

The plaintiffs, a Swiss company, started proceedings in England against the defendants (two United States companies) for, inter alia, inducing a breach of contract. The alleged acts of inducement took place largely in New York at a series of meetings attended by the defendants and AML, a subsidiary company. The consequence of these meetings was that AML, who acted as the plaintiffs' brokers, committed breaches of contract in England which caused serious injury in England to the plaintiffs. As has been seen,[16] the Court of Appeal applied the new tort head of Order 11 in relation to the issue of jurisdiction. The question though arose of where the tort was committed for choice of law purposes.[17]

The Court of Appeal adopted the familiar test to be found in the old Order 11 cases, and held that "as a matter of substance" the torts were committed in London. In determining this, the issue had to be looked at broadly; the breaches and resulting damage in London had to be considered alongside the acts of inducement in New York. Since the torts were committed in England, English law applied, with the result that the plaintiffs would recover damages. Under New York law they would not do so.

Whilst following cases on jurisdiction the Court of Appeal was only too well aware of the choice of law repercussions of the finding as to the place of the tort, and of the implications of this for the recovery of damages by the plaintiffs. The court was concerned that a defendant who had done acts abroad directed against persons in England, or which were foreseeably likely to injure persons here, should not necessarily be able to claim exemption from liability by invoking the law of the country where the acts were done. There are two ways of avoiding this possibility. The first is to find that the tort was committed in England, as happened here. The second is to say in the above situation that, even though the tort is committed abroad, the plaintiff may still recover despite the absence of actionability by the law of the place of the tort. There is support in the Court of Appeal[18] for this by way of a public policy exception to the double actionability rule. This would operate in the situation, outlined above, that concerned the court.

(ii) The different torts

According to the *Metall und Rohstoff Case* it seems that the same test applies regardless of the tort involved, ie "where in substance did this cause of action arise?"[19] Nonetheless, it is necessary to look at the different torts to see how this test operates in relation to particular torts.

(a) Negligence The "substance" test was first used in negligence cases under the old tort head of Order 11.[20] In fact, what these cases have looked for is

---

16 Supra, p 200.
17 This was in the context of whether the plaintiffs had established a good arguable case for the purposes of jurisdiction under Ord 11 RSC, supra, p 191.
18 Op cit, at 446–447.
19 See also *Voth v Manildra Flour Mills Pty Ltd* (1990) 171 CLR 538 at 567, HC of Australia.
20 *Distillers Co (Bio-Chemicals) Ltd v Thompson* [1971] AC 458 at 468; *Castree v Squibb Ltd* [1980] 1 WLR 1248 at 1252; *Multinational Gas and Petrochemical Co v Multinational Gas and Petrochemical Services Ltd* [1983] Ch 258 at 267, 272–273, 284; see also *Cordoba Shipping Co Ltd v National State Bank, Elizabeth, New Jersey, The Albaforth* [1984] 2 Lloyd's Rep 91 at 96.

a wrongful act within the forum.[1] Considerable ingenuity has been shown in order to find this. Thus in *Castree v Squibb Ltd*,[2] where a user of a machine manufactured in Germany was injured in England, the substantial wrongdoing (ie the wrongful act) was held to be putting on the English market a defective machine with no warning as to its defects. The Court of Appeal in the *Metall und Rohstoff Case* placed reliance on this decision when adopting the "substance" test. It is likely that the same reasoning as in the *Castree Case* would be applied in the choice of law context. When applying the "substance" test the search would therefore be for a wrongful act committed in England. Both the Supreme Court of Canada[3] and the High Court of Australia[4] have applied the wrongful act test in cases where the need to determine the place of the tort arose for the purposes of ascertaining the applicable law. The alternative and perhaps preferable approach towards applying the "substance" test would be to emphasise the fact, if such be the case, that the injury took place in England. This is what happened in the *Metall Und Rohstoff Case* itself, although this was not a case on negligence. If you take the facts of *Castree v Squibb Ltd*, which is by no means an untypical case, the result would be the same whichever of these two approaches was adopted. There would be a tort committed in England, thereby avoiding the possibility of a defendant, who had injured someone in England, from invoking a foreign law to escape liability.

(b) Defamation[5] In *Bata v Bata*,[6] where defamatory letters had been written by the defendant in Zurich and posted to certain addresses in London, it was argued on the basis of the rule for negligence that the tort had been committed in Switzerland where the letters had been written and that therefore leave to serve the defendant out of the jurisdiction should not be granted. The Court of Appeal, however, held that, since publication is the material element that completes the tort of libel, the cause of action had arisen in England.[7] This reasoning was seemingly applied by the Court of Appeal in the choice of law case of *Church of Scientology v Metropolitan Police Commissioner*.[8] English police officers published an allegedly libellous report to a German Police Authority. The court acted on the basis that the tort was committed in

---

1 This was the traditional test used in *Monro (George) Ltd v American Cyanamid and Chemical Corpn* [1944] KB 432, [1944] 1 All ER 386. See more recently *Camera Care Ltd v Victor Hasselblad AB* [1986] ECC 373.
2 [1980] 2 All ER 589, [1980] 1 WLR 1248; Carter (1981) 52 BYBIL 319; Carter (1984) 55 BYBIL 347; see also *Distillers Co (Bio-Chemicals) Ltd v Thompson* [1971] AC 458, [1971] 1 All ER 694; cf the unsuccessful attempt to find a wrongful act in England in *Multinational Gas and Petrochemical Co v Multinational Gas and Petrochemical Services Ltd* [1983] Ch 258 at 267, 272–273, 284. For a Scots case which reached the same result as *Castree* applying different reasoning, see *Russell v F W Woolworth & Co Ltd* 1982 SLT 428.
3 *Interprovincial Co-operatives Ltd v The Queen in Right of Manitoba* (1975) 53 DLR (3d) 321.
4 *Voth v Manildra Flour Mills Pty Ltd* (1990) 171 CLR 538—the question of the applicable law arose in the context of the exercise of the *forum non conveniens* discretion.
5 See Handford (1983) 32 ICLQ 452 at 463–468.
6 [1948] WN 366, 92 Sol Jo 574.
7 See too, *Kroch v Rossell et Cie* [1937] 1 All ER 725 where it was enough for publication that a few copies of a foreign newspaper had been sold in England. A similar rule has been applied in public nuisance: *Town of Peace River v British Columbia Hydro and Power Authority* [1972] 5 WWR 351; Webb & North (1965) 14 ICLQ 1314, 1341–1344. See also *Diamond v Bank of London and Montreal Ltd* [1979] QB 333 at 346; Law Com No 193 (1990), Scot Law Com No 129 (1990), paras 3.32–3.33 for discussion of the problem of simultaneous publication in both the UK and abroad.
8 (1976) 120 Sol Jo 690.

Germany. In *Jenner v Sun Oil Co*[9] an action was brought against the owners of a radio station who were alleged to have defamed the plaintiff by remarks broadcast in the United States and heard in Ontario. The Ontario High Court granted leave, holding that an alleged tort had been committed in Ontario.[10]

(c) Fraudulent misrepresentation In *Cordova Land Co v Victor Bros Inc*,[11] WINN J concluded that it was not appropriate to concentrate on either the moment when the tort was complete, ie when the misrepresentation was relied on, or when it became actionable, ie when damage was suffered. Rather one must look at "the substance of the wrong conduct alleged to be a tort".[12] This could be read as getting very close to a requirement that *all* the elements of the tort must have occurred in England for service out of the jurisdiction.[13] However, WINN J was seemingly not as restrictive as this in his approach. He was concerned to ascertain the place where the misrepresentation was made, and the substance of the wrong was held to have taken place in the United States since clean bills of lading were issued by ships' masters and handed over to the shippers there. The later case of *Diamond v Bank of London and Montreal Ltd*[14] concerned a different situation, that is where fraudulent misrepresentations are made by telex or telephone. The Court of Appeal held that the substance of the tort was committed within the jurisdiction, on the basis that a misrepresentation made by telephone or telex is committed where the message is received and acted on (in this case England), and not in the country from which it is sent (in this case the Bahamas). This rule applies equally to negligent misrepresentations.[15] However, if the negligent misrepresentation is part of an allegation of professional negligence, by, for example, an accountant (with the essence of the cause of action being the provision of a bad service) it makes more sense to refer to the cases on negligence and to look for the wrongful act.[16]

There is little doubt that these Order 11 cases would be followed if the question of the place of the tort arose in the choice of law context. The Court of Appeal in the *Metall und Rohstoff Case* relied upon them when adopting the "substance" test. Moreover, the *Diamond Case* was followed in the Court of Appeal in *Armagas Ltd v Mundogas SA*,[17] the other English case apart from *Metall und Rohstoff* to discuss, albeit very briefly, the problem of the place of the tort in the context of choice of law. The Court of Appeal held that the tort of fraudulent misrepresentation was committed in Denmark

9 [1952] 2 DLR 526; see also *Pindling v National Broadcasting Corpn* (1985) 14 DLR (4th) 391.
10 See also *Gorton v Australian Broadcasting Commission* (1973) 22 FLR 181. The problem was mitigated in New Zealand and New South Wales by drafting the rules for service out of the jurisdiction more widely: *Adastra Aviation Ltd v Airports (NZ) Ltd* [1964] NZLR 393; *Distillers Co (Bio-Chemicals) Ltd v Thompson* [1971] AC 458.
11 [1966] 1 WLR 793; and see *R v Robert Millar (Contractors) Ltd* [1970] 2 QB 54 at 62–64.
12 [1966] 1 WLR 793 at 798; and see *Buttigeig v Universal Terminal and Stevedoring Corpn* [1972] VR 626 at 629.
13 And see *Abbott-Smith v Governors of University of Toronto* (1964) 45 DLR (2d) 672 at 687, 694–697; but see *Distillers Co (Bio-Chemicals) v Thompson* [1971] AC 458 at 466–467.
14 [1979] QB 333, [1979] 1 All ER 561; Carter (1979) 50 BYBIL 241; and see *Original Blouse Co v Bruck Mills* (1963) 42 DLR (2d) 174; cf *Petersen v A/B Bahco* (1980) 107 DLR (3d) 49.
15 *Diamond v Bank of London and Montreal*, op cit; see also *Cordoba Shipping Co Ltd v National State Bank, Elizabeth, New Jersey, The Albaforth* [1984] 2 Lloyd's Rep 91; *Canadian Commercial Bank v Carpenter* (1989) 62 DLR (4th) 734.
16 *Voth v Manildra Flour Mills Pty Ltd* (1990) 171 CLR 538 at 566–570.
17 [1986] AC 717, CA.

where the misrepresentation was orally communicated and acted upon.[18] In affirming this decision, Lord KEITH, who gave the judgment of the House of Lords,[19] accepted without going into the point in any detail, that the tort was committed in Denmark.[20]

(d) Economic torts In the *Metall und Rohstoff Case*[1] the Court of Appeal held that the substance of the tort of inducing a breach of contract was committed in London where the breaches of contract and resulting damage occurred, rather than in New York where the acts of inducement took place. On the other hand, PHILLIPS J seems to have assumed, without argument, that the economic torts of intimidation and interference with contractual rights are committed where the industrial action complained of took place.[2]

(e) Passing off This tort is seemingly committed in the country in which the act of misrepresentation takes place.[3]

(iii) A different approach

The Law Commissions in their Report[4] have sought to avoid the problem of defining the place of the tort and accept that in complex cases, such as the *Metall und Rohstoff Case*, this is merely a fiction. Instead, their proposals directly identify the applicable law, without recourse to the law of the place of the tort.[5] This is not quite as radical as may at first appear. For the first two of the rules on the prima facie applicable law are based on the notion of the place of injury or damage, which is, of course, just one way of defining the place where a tort is committed. Nonetheless, the formal absence of the concept of the place of the tort has meant that rules on the applicable law have been recommended which are geared to choice of law considerations and are not there by virtue of dubious analogies with Order 11 cases. Thus a place of injury rule has been justified as the prima facie applicable law in cases of personal injury on the ground that this fits in with the modern view of the law of tort that this is concerned to protect the interests of an injured person.[6] The particular problem of identifying any single connection as the basis for the applicable law in a case like *Metall und Rohstoff* is acknowledged by having a special rule for the prima facie applicable law in cases other than those of personal injury, damage to property, or death. This states that the prima facie applicable law is that of the country in which the most significant elements in the sequence of events occurred. If there is no such single country the proper law is applicable as an exception to the rules on the prima facie applicable law.

18 Ibid, at pp 740–741.
19 [1986] AC 717 at 773, [1986] 2 All ER 385.
20 Ibid, at 783.
1 Supra. See also *Ichi Canada Ltd v Yamauchi Rubber Industry Co* (1983) 144 DLR (3d) 533; *Elguindy v Core Laboratories Canada Ltd* (1987) 60 OR (2d) 151. Cf *Atlantic Underwriting Agencies Ltd v Cia Di Assicurazione Di Milano SPA* [1979] 2 Lloyd's Rep 240, an earlier Ord 11 case.
2 *Dimskal Shipping Co SA v International Transport Workers Federation, The Evia Luck (No 2)* [1989] 1 Lloyd's Rep 166 at 177; appeal allowed on a different point [1990] 1 Lloyd's Rep 319; appeal against the latter decision dismissed [1991] 4 All ER 871, [1991] 3 WLR 875, HL.
3 *Intercontex v Schmidt* [1988] FSR 575 at 578.
4 Law Com No 193 (1990), Scot Law Com No 129 (1990), paras 3.6–3.8.
5 Infra, pp 564–565.
6 Law Commission Working Paper No 87 (1984); Scottish Law Commission Consultative Memorandum No 62, para 4.70.

4. MARITIME TORTS[7]

The law that governs maritime torts depends on whether they have been committed within the territorial waters of some State[8] or on the high seas.

In the former case, the ordinary doctrine as laid down in *Phillips v Eyre*, as amended by *Boys v Chaplin*[9] applies. The place of the tort is deemed to be the littoral State rather than the country of the ship's flag.[10] The Scottish Court of Session in *Mackinnon v Iberia Shipping Co Ltd*[11] rejected the argument, attractive on the score of common sense, that the distinction between torts having consequences external to the ship and those having purely internal consequences—a distinction that affects torts on the high seas—should be extended to the case of torts in territorial waters.[12]

The High Court has jurisdiction to entertain an action in respect of injurious acts done on the high seas,[13] even though both the litigants are foreigners.[14] It is a little difficult, however, to specify with absolute certainty the law which the court will follow in determining the rights and liabilities of the parties. It seems clear, in the first place, that the law of the flag is the decisive factor wherever the acts complained of have all occurred on board a single vessel, for a ship is regarded for certain purposes as a floating island over which the national law prevails.[15] If, therefore, the tort is committed on board an English vessel, English law will alone apply; but if it is committed wholly on a foreign ship and an action is brought in England, the plaintiff, if the analogy of wrongs done in a foreign country is followed, will have to prove that the act is actionable both by the law of the flag and by English law. Where a flag is common to a political unit containing several different systems of law, as in the case of Canada or the USA, the law of the flag means the law of the port at which the ship is registered.[16]

It is scarcely possible, however, that the law of the flag should govern all wrongs committed on the high seas. Suppose that the act giving rise to the dispute is external to the foreign ship in the sense that it has affected persons or property not on board, as, for example, where it is negligent navigation leading to a collision or to the destruction of a submarine cable. Is such an act on all fours from the point of view of choice of law with an act, such as an assault, that took place entirely on the ship? Before we can answer this

---

7 See Sundström, *Foreign Ships and Foreign Waters* (1971); Winter (1954) 3 ICLQ 115.
8 See Hancock, pp 261–271.
9 Supra, pp 533 et seq; cf *Sayers v International Drilling Co NV* [1971] 3 All ER 163, [1971] 1 WLR 1176, infra, pp 561–563.
10 *The Arum* [1921] P 12; and see *The Mary Moxham* (1876) 1 PD 107; *The Waziristan* [1953] 2 All ER 1213, [1953] 1 WLR 1446.
11 [1954] 2 Lloyd's Rep 372, 1955 SLT 49; Carter (1957) 33 BYBIL 342–343.
12 In *Sayers v International Drilling Co NV* [1971] 3 All ER 163, [1971] 1 WLR 1176, infra, pp 561–563, Nigerian law, in whose territorial waters the oil-rig was situated at the time of the accident, was ignored. This fact lends some support to the application of this distinction to torts within territorial waters.
13 *The Tubantia* [1924] P 78.
14 *Chartered Mercantile Bank of India v Netherlands India Steam Navigation Co* (1883) 10 QBD 521 at 536–537.
15 *R v Anderson* (1868) LR 1 CCR 161 at 168; *R v Keyn* (1876) 2 Ex D 63 at 94. But not for the purpose of jurisdiction, *Chung Chi Cheung v R* [1939] AC 160, [1938] 4 All ER 786; *O'Daly v Gulf Oil Terminals (Ireland) Ltd* [1983] ILRM 163.
16 *Canadian National Steamship Co v Watson* [1939] 1 DLR 273; and see *Gronlund v Hansen* (1969) 4 DLR (3d) 435.

question we must ascertain the law by which the liability for what may be called acts external to a foreign ship are determined.

There is no doubt that the commonest kind of external act, namely, one that causes a collision, is governed solely by the general maritime law as administered in England, and not by that combination of English and foreign law which is required by the general principle laid down in *Phillips v Eyre*, as amended by *Boys v Chaplin*.[17] "All questions of collision are questions *communis iuris*"[18] and must be decided by the law maritime.[19]

The natural inference to draw from the expression "general maritime law" is that there exists a body of law which is universally recognised as binding on all nations in respect of acts occurring at sea. There is, however, no such law.[20] The expression, in truth, means nothing more than that part of English law which, either by statute or by reiterated decisions, has been evolved for the determination of maritime disputes.[21] It is the law which, despite the views of Westlake,[22] must be applied to all questions of collision unless international regulations have been laid down by a convention between States.[23] It may be asked, indeed, whether the bewildering number of laws that might require consideration would not make it impossible to apply the general rule as laid down in *Phillips v Eyre*, as amended by *Boys v Chaplin*.[24]

If, for instance, an action were brought in England in respect of a collision between two foreign ships of different nationality, the almost impossible feat of referring to three laws would impede any attempt to apply the ordinary rule. The impediment would become insuperable if a third ship of yet another nationality had contributed to the collision.

The question that now arises is whether this maritime law must be applied to all external acts, ie to all cases where the alleged wrong consists of some act, other than a collision, done by a foreign ship to the property of another, as, for example, where a submarine cable is fouled[25] or where possession is seized of a wreck that is being salved by a third party.[26] In many such cases, unlike the case of a collision, there would be little difficulty in applying the principle of *Phillips v Eyre* as amended by *Boys v Chaplin*, but in others it would be almost impossible. If, for instance, two or more foreign ships flying different flags were involved in a dispute concerning the capture of whales[27] it might be virtually impossible to refer to each law, since the act might be

17 Supra, pp 533 et seq. However, in *Gronlund v Hansen* (1969) 4 DLR (3d) 435, a Canadian court seemed prepared to apply the original *Phillips v Eyre* rule to a claim arising from a death resulting from a collision on the high seas.
18 *The Johann Friedrich* (1839) 1 Wm Rob 36 at 37.
19 *The Wild Ranger* (1862) Lush 553; *The Zollverein* (1856) Sw 96; *The Leon* (1881) 6 PD 148; *Chartered Mercantile Bank of India, London and China v Netherlands India Steam Navigation Co Ltd* (1883) 10 QBD 521; Dicey & Morris, pp 1411–1413; Foote, pp 524–525.
20 *Lloyd v Guibert* (1865) LR 1 QB 115 at 123–125.
21 *The Gaetano and Maria* (1882) 7 PD 137 at 143.
22 *Private International Law*, pp 290–291.
23 The collision regulations at present in force are those which are laid down by various international conventions and given effect by the Merchant Shipping Acts 1894–1988. Damage to structures erected for the exploitation of the sea-bed of the Continental Shelf over which the United Kingdom exercises rights falls under the Continental Shelf Act 1964, as amended by the Oil and Gas (Enterprise) Act 1982, see Dicey & Morris, pp 1411–1413.
24 Supra, pp 533 et seq.
25 *Submarine Telegraph Co v Dickson* (1864) 15 CBNS 759.
26 *The Tubantia* [1924] P 78.
27 Dicey & Morris, p 1410; and see *Aberdeen Arctic Co v Sutter* (1862) 4 Macq 355.

innocent in one of the countries and wrongful in the others. Again, it seems a little strained to treat the law of the flag in maritime wrongs as being equivalent to the law of the place where the tort was committed in the case of torts on land. The reason why English law requires proof that a wrong committed in a foreign country is actionable by the law of the place of the tort is that the offending act has been committed within the exclusive jurisdiction of a foreign sovereign, but, as BRETT LJ has shown, there is no such thing as exclusive jurisdiction over the high seas.[1] If the place where a wrong is committed is subject to no exclusive jurisdiction, it is surely a misnomer to speak of a law of the place of the tort. It is possible to speak of a law of the place of the tort only where all the acts have occurred on board a single foreign ship. Finally, the sphere of authority possessed by the general maritime law has been described in such comprehensive terms by the judges that it would appear to cover all torts committed on the high seas;[2] including an action under the Fatal Accidents Acts arising from a collision between a Latvian trawler and a Panamanian tanker off the coast of the USA.[3]

In conclusion, therefore, the rules adopted by English courts for the choice of law, so far as regards torts committed at sea, may be stated as follows: first, a plaintiff who sues in England in respect of acts, all of which have occurred on board a single foreign vessel, must prove that the conduct of the defendant was actionable by the law of the flag, and that it would have been actionable had it occurred in this country.[4]

Secondly, all other acts occurring on the high seas and later sued upon in England must be tested solely by English maritime law.[5]

The Law Commissions have recommended that the reformed rules will not apply to torts and delicts occurring on the high seas to which, at present, our choice of law rules do not apply.[6]

5. AVOIDING THE TORT CHOICE OF LAW RULES

One way in which a plaintiff may avoid both the harsh consequences of the general double actionability choice of law rule for torts laid down in *Boys v Chaplin* and the uncertainties of the proper law of the tort exception is to persuade the court that the issue before it is not one of tort at all, but is to be classified in some other way, with a different choice of law rule. The most obvious example of this is seen in *Boys v Chaplin* itself where a minority in the House of Lords was prepared to apply English law as the law of the

---

1 *Chartered Mercantile Bank of India v Netherlands India Steam Navigation Co* (1883) 10 QBD 521 at 536–537.
2 Ibid; and see *Lloyd v Guibert* (1865) LR 1 QB 115 at 125; *The Gaetano and Maria* (1882) 7 PD 37; ibid, p 137 at 143; *Davidsson v Hill* [1901] 2 KB 606; *The Esso Malaysia* [1975] QB 198, [1974] 2 All ER 705.
3 *The Esso Malaysia*, supra.
4 *Quaere* whether the exception to the general rule can ever be applied.
5 For torts committed on board aircraft or resulting from aerial collisions, see Shawcross & Beaumont, *Air Law* (4th edn) Re-issue 1986, vol I, paras 93–98; VII, 71–73; McNair, *Law of the Air* (1964) 3rd edn, pp 259–271, 281–295; Dicey & Morris, pp 1415–1417. There appear to be no English authorities on this issue. The rules contained in the Warsaw Convention may be applicable; see generally McGilchrist [1983] Lloyd's MCLQ 685; *Goldman v Thai Airways International Ltd* [1983] 3 All ER 693, [1983] 1 WLR 1186.
6 Law Com No 193 (1990), Scot Law Com No 129 (1990), para 3.27.

forum to an issue classified by them as procedural. Although the argument that the issue whether damages can be recovered for pain and suffering is procedural rather than substantive is unsupportable,[7] there are other situations where a plaintiff may well benefit from such a reclassification of the issue.

For example, whether one spouse is liable to the other in tort may be classified as a matter of status to be referred to the law of the domicil;[8] whether a child can sue his parents may be similarly so classified.[9] Another situation where the choice of law rule in tort has been avoided is where the issue has been classified as contractual or quasi-contractual. This device has been utilised in the case of a claim by a victim of a road accident under legislation permitting a direct action against the wrongdoer's insurance company. In such circumstances the claim has been classed as contractual, as a statutory extension of contractual liability or as quasi-contractual, to be governed by the law govering the insurance contract.[10] Similarly, a claim between joint tortfeasors has been classified as quasi-contractual and thus governed by the law govering the obligation.[11] On the other hand, the right to an indemnity has been regarded as being *sui generis* and not to be classified as either tortious or contractual.[12]

6. MIXED QUESTIONS OF TORT AND CONTRACT[13]

In the situation where there is a claim in tort to which a contractual defence is raised, there are difficult problems as to the interrelationship of the separate tort and contract choice of law rules. Unfortunately, the few reported cases

7 Supra, pp 93–95.

8 This is the general view in the USA: *Haumschild v Continental Casualty Co* 7 Wis 2d 130, 95 NW 2d 814 (1959); cf *Schwartz v Schwartz* 103 Ariz 562, 447 P 2d 254 (1968) where the same conclusion was reached applying the choice of law rule of the Restatement 2d § 145. Australian courts have taken different views on this matter. *Warren v Warren* [1972] QdR 386 at 390–391 supports application of the law of the domicil, but in *Schmidt v Government Insurance Office of New South Wales* [1973] 1 NSWLR 59 it is assumed that interspousal immunity is governed by the *Phillips v Eyre* rule; see especially at p 71. This is also true of *Corcoran v Corcoran* [1974] VR 164; but there the law of the forum, which was also the law of the domicil, was applied relying on the "flexibility" exception to the double actionability rule, supra, pp 546–547. See Morse, op cit, pp 155 et seq. The Law Commissions reached no conclusion on the characterisation of intra-family immunities: Law Com No 193 (1990), Scot Law Com No 129 (1990), paras 3.45–3.46.

9 *Balts v Balts* 273 Minn 419, 142 NW 2d 66 (1966); and *see Emery v Emery* 45 Cal 2d 421, 289 P 2d 218 (1955); cf *Pierce v Helz* 314 NYS 2d 453 (1970).

10 *Plozza v South Australian Insurance Co Ltd* [1963] SASR 122, especially at 128; *Stewart v Honey* [1972] 2 SASR 585; *Schmidt v Government Insurance Office of New South Wales* [1973] 1 NSWLR 59 at 70; *Hodge v Club Motor Insurance Agency Pty Ltd* (1974) 22 FLR 473; cf *Hall v National and General Insurance Co Ltd* [1967] VR 355; *Ryder v Hartford Insurance Co* [1977] VR 257; and see *Harker v Caledonian Insurance Co* [1977] 2 Lloyd's Rep 556. This opportunity to avoid the application of the restrictive choice of law rules in tort was not taken in *Li Lian Tan v Durham* [1966] SASR 143. See Morse, op cit, pp 163 et seq; Blaikie [1984] Jur Rev 112.

11 *Plozza v South Australian Insurance Co Ltd*, supra, at p 127; *Stewart v Honey*, supra, at p 592; and see *Nominal Defendant v Bagot's Executor and Trustee Co Ltd* [1971] SASR 347 at 365–367; revd on other grounds (1971) 124 CLR 179; but see *Baldry v Jackson* [1977] 1 NSWLR 494. See Morse, op cit, pp 208–210.

12 *Borg-Warner (Australia) Ltd v Zupan* [1982] VR 437.

13 See Kahn-Freund (1968) II Hague Recueil 129–157; Collins (1967) 16 ICLQ 103; North (1977) 26 ICLQ 914; Morse, op cit, pp 187 et seq.

in this area have failed to raise squarely the issues involved. The leading English case is *Sayers v International Drilling Co NV*:[14]

> The plaintiff was an Englishman who entered a contract of employment with a Dutch company, the defendants, to work on their oil rigs. The plaintiff was sent to work on a rig in Nigerian territorial waters and was injured by the alleged negligence of his fellow employees. The contract contained a clause excluding all remedies for such injuries, other than those expressly provided by the contract. Such a clause was valid under Dutch law in the case of international contracts, but void under English domestic law by reason of the Law Reform (Personal Injuries) Act 1948.[15]

The Court of Appeal held unanimously that the plaintiff's claim for damages for his personal injuries should fail, though two bases for this conclusion are to be found in the judgments. A majority decided that the proper law of the contract was Dutch law. Though the factors were fairly evenly balanced as between English law and Dutch law, the facts that the contract was to be performed outside the United Kingdom and that the form of the contract was such that it could be applied to employees of different nationalities tipped the scales in favour of Dutch law. Applying that law as the proper law of the contract, the majority held that the exemption clause was valid and any claim in tort was defeated thereby.[16]

Lord DENNING MR adopted a less orthodox approach. He was prepared to hold that the claim was one in tort and that tortious liability is governed by the proper law of the tort which, apart from any contractual issues, he concluded was Dutch law. The proper law of the contract was, apart from any tort issues, English law. However, he felt that "it is obvious that we cannot apply two systems of law, one for the claim in tort, and the other for the defence in contract. We must apply one system of law by which to decide both claim and defence".[17] This he held to be Dutch law.

The end-result is that all members of the Court of Appeal agreed on the application of Dutch law, two because the issue was characterised as one in contract and the other because it was regarded as a hybrid. It is suggested that both approaches fail properly to classify the issues raised by a case such as this where an exemption clause is pleaded as a defence to an action in tort. The claim is essentially one in tort, being whether the plaintiff can recover damages for his personal injuries, and should be referred to the law of the place of the tort and the law of the forum in order to determine whether it is actionable under both laws. This then raises the issue whether a contractual exemption clause can provide a good defence under either system of law. If

---

14 [1971] 3 All ER 163, [1971] 1 WLR 1176; see Collins (1972) 21 ICLQ 320; Carter (1971) 45 BYBIL 404.
15 S 1(3).
16 If the case arose now, the Unfair Contract Terms Act 1977 would have to be considered, as would the Rome Convention, supra pp 459–521. However, the result would probably be the same. It is likely that Dutch law would be applicable under the Convention: Art 6(2); supra p 495. The Court of Appeal, unfortunately, did not address the issue whether the English domestic rules in the 1948 Act should be regarded as mandatory ones. There is thus no authority to suggest that such rules are within Art 7(2) of the Convention. The rules in the 1977 Act are not mandatory ones in a case like *Sayers*, supra pp 500–501. See generally, Morse in *Contract Conflicts* p 158 et seq; Morse (1982) 2 Yearbook of European Law 107, 141–142; Lasok and Stone, *Conflict of Laws in the European Community* pp 375–376.
17 [1971] 1 WLR 1176 at 1181.

the answer to that is in the affirmative,[18] then the question is whether this contractual exemption clause is effective and that is for the law governing the contract to decide.[19]

On the facts of the present case, it is not clear what was the law of the place of the tort. The accident took place on a Dutch rig in Nigerian territorial waters and it is arguable that in the case of matters purely internal to the rig Dutch, rather than Nigerian, law should be regarded as the law of the place.[20] However that issue may be resolved, it was for Dutch or Nigerian law as the law of the place and English law as the law of the forum to decide whether an exemption clause could provide a defence in such a case as this; and only after satisfaction on that point was reached should reference have been made to the effect of the clause under Dutch law as the law governing the contract. There is much to be said for the view that English law, as the law of the forum, would and should have denied effect to the exemption clause as a defence to an action in tort. Certainly, the Court of Session in a very similar case, *Brodin v A/R Seljan*,[21] has insisted on the application of the statutory prohibition against exemption clauses:

> The deceased, a Norwegian, domiciled in Scotland, was injured on board an oil tanker as it was docking in Scotland. He later died. The law of the forum and the law of the place of the tort were, therefore, Scottish. The proper law of the deceased's contract of employment was Norwegian and it contained an express choice of law clause which also excluded liability for personal injuries. Such an exemption is void under Scottish domestic law by reason of the Law Reform (Personal Injuries) Act 1948.[22]

The Court of Session held that Scottish law alone was applicable to a claim for damages by the deceased's widow and that no defence based on such an exemption clause was available, irrespective of its effects under Norwegian law. The court was applying what we would now describe as a mandatory rule[1] of the forum. Such an analysis is far more satisfactory than that of the Court of Appeal.[2]

Obviously, there is no problem if the contract between the parties does not contain any clause which provides a defence. This is the explanation of the most recent decision in this area, *Coupland v Arabian Gulf Oil Co*:[3]

> A claim was brought, inter alia, in tort in England against a Libyan national oil company by a Scots resident who had been injured in Libya whilst working as an employee of the company.

---

18 Eg *Canadian Pacific Rail Co v Parent* [1917] AC 195 where an exemption clause was effective under the law of the place though not under the law of the forum.
19 Whether the law governing the contract is determined by the conflict rules of the forum or of the law of the place of the tort is a matter of debate; see Collins (1967) 16 ICLQ 103, 115; North (1977) 26 ICLQ 914, 925–927; Morse, op cit, pp 213.
20 See [1971] 1 WLR 1176 at 1181; though cf *Mackinnon v Iberia Shipping Co Ltd* 1955 SLT 49, supra, p 545.
21 1973 SC 213.
22 S 1(3).
1 Supra, pp 496–503.
2 Similar problems on the interrelation of contractual and tortious liability are posed by a contractual release from tortious liability; see *Scott v American Airlines Inc* [1944] 3 DLR 27; North (1977) 26 ICLQ 214, 227–231; Morse, op cit, p 210.
3 [1983] 2 All ER 434, [1983] 1 WLR 1136; Carter (1983) 54 BYBIL 301; Morse (1984) 33 ICLQ 449.

The Court of Appeal held[4] that this was a straightforward case where there was actionability under both the law of the forum and the law of the place of the tort, and therefore the case could proceed on the basis of the ordinary principles of the English law of negligence. It was held that, as far as the tort claim was concerned, the contract between the parties, the proper law of which was Libyan, was irrelevant since it contained no term which restricted or limited the claim in tort, such as an exemption clause. Because the contract provided no defence to the tort claim it was not necessary for the court to determine the question of the law to be applied in respect of a contractual defence to a tort claim, and the court did not do so. The only reference to this matter in the Court of Appeal came from GOFF LJ who said that "on ordinary principles the contract is only relevant to the claim in tort in so far as it does, on its true construction in accordance with the proper law of the contract, have the effect of excluding or restricting the tortious claim."[5] However, this statement fails to analyse the issues involved and is not sufficiently clear for any definite conclusions to be drawn from it.[6]

Disappointingly, there is no recommendation from the Law Commissions in relation to this difficult area of mixed tort and contract.[7] It seems that agreement could not be reached on the vexed question of characterisation raised in this area.

7. REFORM

At one time there were proposals for an EEC Convention on non-contractual and contractual obligations. This was subsequently confined to the area of contractual obligations.[8] Nonetheless, it provided the impetus for the English and Scottish Law Commissions to re-examine choice of law in tort and delict, and produce a joint Report.[9] The recommendations contained in this Report have been examined at various points in this chapter; they will now be summed up here. It has been recommended that the much criticised first limb of the rule in *Phillips v Eyre*, requiring actionability by English law before the plaintiff can recover damages in England, should be abolished.[10] There would be general rules based on the law of the place of the tort, but phrased in terms of the prima facie applicable law, with a proper law exception.

The Report proposes three rules[11] for the prima facie applicable law: in cases of personal injury and damage to property this should be the law of the country or territory where the person was when he was injured or the property was when it was damaged; in cases of death it should be the law of the country or territory where the deceased was when he was fatally injured; in all other cases it should be the law of the country or territory in which the most significant elements in the sequence of events occurred. These rules are

---

4 [1983] 1 WLR 1136 at 1151 et seq.
5 Op cit, at 1153.
6 Cf Carter, op cit at 305.
7 Para 3.49–3.50. Cf Law Commission Working Paper No 87 (1984), paras 6.51–6.53, which recommended the same approach as is proposed in this book.
8 Supra, pp 459–521.
9 Law Com No 193 (1990); Scot Law Com No 129 (1990); Carter (1991) 107 LQR 405. For reform in Australia see ALRC Discussion Paper 44 (1990).
10 Para 2.11.
11 Paras 3.6–3.7.

designed to provide certainty and to avoid having formally to identify the place where the tort was committed.

Flexibility is provided by a proper law exception,[12] which applies in two situations. The first is where, under the third of the above rules, the country in which the most significant elements occurred cannot be identified. The second is where it is substantially more appropriate that another law should apply. The applicable law under the exception is that of the country or territory with which the tort or delict has the most real and substantial connection.

There are no special rules for particular issues and torts, apart from those cases of defamation where a statement is published in the United Kingdom and abroad.[13] In particular, there is no recommendation in relation to contractual defences to claims in tort and delict. There is, though, a recommendation in relation to public policy and certain other related exceptions.[14] If a tort is committed in the United Kingdom, the law of the relevant part of the United Kingdom applies, without the possibility of using the proper law exception.[15]

12 Paras 3.8–3.12.
13 Paras 3.32–3.33.
14 Para 3.55.
15 Para 3.16.

Part V

Family law

SUMMARY

Chapter 21

Marriage[1]

SUMMARY

1 Maddaugh (1973) 23 UTorLJ 117; Swan (1974) 24 UTorLJ 17, 18–41; Jaffey (1978) 41 MLR 38; North (1980) I Hague Recueil 9; Jaffey (1982) 2 OJLS 368, 369–373; North (1990) I Hague Recueil 9, 49–96 and see Audit, *La Fraude à la Loi*, pp 308–323.

1. THE MEANING OF "MARRIAGE"

It is important to observe at the outset that the contract in which a marriage originates differs fundamentally from a commercial contract,[2] since it creates a status that affects both the parties themselves and the society to which they belong. It is *sui generis*. It is fulfilled on the solemnisation of the marriage ceremony, and thereafter there is a change in the law that governs the relationship between the parties.

The occasions are frequent and various on which the existence of a marriage must be established as a preliminary to legal proceedings. The matter may concern many different parts of the law. Thus the institution of a matrimonial cause, such as a petition for divorce or judicial separation, implies that the parties are related to each other as husband and wife. If a person claims an inheritance or money due under an insurance policy as the widow or widower of the deceased; if a beneficiary under a will claims to be free from liability to inheritance tax as being the surviving spouse of the testator; in each case a preliminary to success is proof that a regularly constituted marriage exists. The existence of the marriage tie is equally essential in several departments of criminal law, as, for instance, where a person is prosecuted for bigamy. Again, social security benefits and the operation of the immigration laws may depend on the existence of a valid marriage. All these matters, and indeed many others, may raise a problem of private international law, since the parties in question may, for instance, have gone through a marriage ceremony abroad which, though valid by the law of the place of celebration or by the law of the domicil, does not create the status of marriage according to English law.

Since the consensual union of man and woman, the one common factor of every marriage,[3] may possess diverse features according to the law to which it is subject, each legal system must determine what its attributes shall be in order to create the relationship of husband and wife. In 1866 Lord

2 Under the Law Reform (Miscellaneous Provisions) Act 1970, s 1, an agreement to marry does not have effect as a contract.
3 *Corbett v Corbett (orse Ashley)* [1971] P 83; Matrimonial Causes Act 1973, s 11 (c); and see *Re North and Matheson* (1974) 52 DLR (3d) 280.

Penzance defined marriage "as the voluntary union for life of one man and one woman to the exclusion of all others".[4] Although, as we shall see,[5] in the intervening century English law has come to accept as valid for many purposes marriages which are polygamous in nature or in fact, the requirement of a life long union (despite the prevalence of divorce) is still a necessary characteristic of marriage in the eyes of English law.

This requirement does not mean that a marriage must be indissoluble, but that in the eyes of the law of the place of celebration it must be potentially indefinite in duration. The facility with which, according to that law, it may be dissolved is irrelevant to its nature at the time of its creation. The one essential in this respect is that the parties have married in a form which envisages that, in the ordinary course of things, they will cohabit as man and wife for the rest of their lives. This was affirmed in *Nachimson v Nachimson*,[6] where a marriage had been solemnised in Moscow in 1924 between parties domiciled in Russia. At that date unilateral divorce was permissible by Russian law. In a suit for judicial separation brought in England, it was argued that the marriage was "of such a flimsy nature" that it could not be regarded as a union for life.[7] This argument was dismissed by the Court of Appeal as untenable. It was demonstrated that the dissolubility of a marriage can have no effect on its original character, for the valid creation of any contract, whether matrimonial, commercial or otherwise, stands apart from the conditions of its avoidance.[8] The remedy of divorce is an incident not of the marriage contract, but of the resulting status and, as such, is not necessarily the concern of the law of the country of domicil at the time of marriage.

The ease of international travel has, in the field of family law and elsewhere, given added impetus in recent decades to the development of private international law rules. Of particular importance in relation to marriage and matrimonial causes has been the incidence of immigration into this country of many people from differing social, cultural and religious backgrounds. Until the middle of the nineteenth century, our choice of law rules relating to marriage were undeveloped and simple. All matters were to be referred to the law of the country where the marriage was celebrated. However, in 1861, the House of Lords in *Brook v Brook*[9] drew a distinction between the rules governing formalities and those governing capacity to marry. The facts were these:

> A marriage was celebrated in Denmark between a domiciled Englishman and his deceased wife's sister, also domiciled in England. The marriage was legal by Danish law, but illegal at that date (1850) by English law.

Although the marriage was valid by Danish law, the place where it was celebrated, the House of Lords was unwilling to allow the man to evade the prohibitions of English law, the law of his domicil. In applying English law and holding that the marriage was void, Lord CAMPBELL LC drew the following distinction:

> But while the forms of entering into the contract of marriage are to be regulated by the *lex loci contractus*, the law of the country in which it is celebrated, the

4 *Hyde v Hyde* (1866) LR 1 P & D 130 at 133.
5 Infra, pp 621 et seq.
6 [1930] P 217.
7 Ibid, at 220, per counsel.
8 *Warrender v Warrender* (1835) 2 Cl & Fin 488 at 533.
9 (1861) 9 HL Cas 193.

essentials of the marriage depend upon the *lex domicilii*, the law of the country in which the parties are domiciled at the time of the marriage, and in which the matrimonial residence is contemplated.[10]

In the light of this decision, two major choice of law issues have to be examined: the choice of law rules governing the formal validity of a marriage and those rules governing its essential validity or capacity, and it is necessary in addition to consider the special problems posed by polygamous marriages.

2. FORMALITIES OF MARRIAGE[11]

(a) THE GENERAL RULE

(i) The rule

There is no rule more firmly established in private international law than that which applies the maxim *locus regit actum* to the formalities of a marriage, ie that an act is governed by the place where it is done. Whether any particular ceremony constitutes a formally valid marriage depends solely on the law of the country where the ceremony takes place.[12] The absolute nature of both the positive and negative aspects of this principle has frequently been stressed by the courts. "Every marriage must be tried according to the law of the country in which it took place",[13] and if it is good by that law, then, so far as its formal validity alone is concerned "it is good all the world over, no matter whether the proceedings or ceremony which constituted marriage according to the law of the place would or would not constitute marriage in the country of the domicil of one or other of the spouses".[14] The reverse is equally true. "If the so-called marriage is no marriage in the place where it is celebrated, there is no marriage anywhere, although the ceremony or proceedings if conducted in the place of the parties' domicil would be considered a good marriage."[15]

Furthermore, the predominance of the law of the place of celebration is not disturbed even though the sole object of the parties in celebrating their marriage abroad is to evade some irksome requirement of the law of their domicil.[16] Thus in *Simonin v Mallac*:[17]

Two persons, French by domicil, contracted a marriage in London which, though formally valid according to English law, would have been void if tested by French law since the parental consent required by the Code

10 Ibid, at 207.
11 See Sykes (1952) 2 ICLQ 78; Mendes da Costa (1958) 7 ICLQ 217; Parry, 8 British Digest of International Law, pp 513 et seq; Palsson, *Marriage and Divorce in Comparative Conflict of Laws*, ch 6; North (1980) I Hague Recueil 9, 69–77.
12 *Scrimshire v Scrimshire* (1752) 2 Hag Con 395; *Dalrymple v Dalrymple* (1811) 2 Hag Con 54; *Warrender v Warrender* (1835) 2 Cl & Fin 488 at 530; *Harvey v Farnie* (1882) 8 App Cas 43 at 50; *Berthiaume v Dastous* [1930] AC 79, PC; *Kenward v Kenward* [1951] P 124, [1950] 2 All ER 297; and see *R v Bham* [1966] 1 QB 159; *Re X's Marriage* (1983) 65 FLR 132; *Burke v Burke* 1983 SLT 331. As to the method of proving a foreign marriage in English proceedings, see Dicey & Morris, pp 613–620. If there is no ceremony and the courts of the country where the parties are domiciled and resident recognise a marriage by repute, then so will the English courts: *Re Green* (1909) 25 TLR 222.
13 *Herbert (Lady) v Herbert (Lord)* (1819) 3 Phillim 58 at 63.
14 *Berthiaume v Dastous* [1930] AC 79 at 83.
15 Ibid. This general rule is subject to certain exceptions, discussed, infra, pp 577 et seq.
16 Eg *Scrimshire v Scrimshire* (1752) 2 Hag Con 395; *Ogden v Ogden* [1908] P 46.
17 (1860) 2 Sw & Tr 67.

Napoléon had not been obtained. The wife later petitioned for a decree of nullity.

The court dismissed the petition, for, since the necessary consent, as we have seen,[18] was nothing more than a formality, its absence could not affect a marriage celebrated in England.[1] If, however, a marriage, valid as to form under the law of the place of celebration, but formally void according to the personal law of the parties is later annulled in the courts of their domicil, the decree of nullity will be recognised as effective by an English court even if the marriage was celebrated in England.[2]

One conclusion to be drawn from the rule that the law of the place of celebration governs the formal validity of a marriage is that no marriage in England is formally valid unless it complies with the requirements of English law as laid down in the Marriage Act 1949.[3] Therefore a marriage according to Romany custom,[4] a marriage in polygamous form[5] or a marriage in an unregistered building[6] are, in the absence of any further civil ceremony, void. Indeed such a marriage is regarded not so much as a void marriage, but as no marriage at all.[7] If there is a civil ceremony as well, it is this alone which the law recognises.[8]

(ii) Retrospectivity

It seems almost axiomatic that the question whether the status of husband and wife has been acquired must be determined once and for all by reference to the law of the place of celebration as it stood at the time when the parties went through the ceremony of marriage. According to this view, the verdict of that law at that time, whether in favour of, or adverse to, the acquisition of a married status, will be unaffected by a later change in its provisions. Otherwise the relationship between the parties will remain insecure. In *Starkowski v A-G*,[9] however, this conclusion was not fully accepted by the House of Lords, which held that a marriage void at the time of its celebration may be validated by a subsequent and retroactive change in the law of the place of celebration:[10]

H and W, Polish both by nationality and domicil, were married in Austria on May 19, 1945. The marriage was void by Austrian law since the

---

18 Supra, p 50.
1 And see *Ramos v Ramos* (1911) 27 TLR 515 where failure to register a marriage as was required by the law of the domicil did not affect the validity of the marriage.
2 Infra, pp 657 et seq; see *Salvesen v Administrator of Austrian Property* [1927] AC 641; *De Massa v De Massa* [1939] 2 All ER 150n; *Galene v Galene* [1939] P 237, [1939] 2 All ER 148; *Merker v Merker* [1963] P 283, [1962] 3 All ER 928.
3 Proposals for reform are put forward in Law Com No 53 (1973): Report on Solemnisation of Marriage in England and Wales.
4 National Insurance Decision No R (S) 4/59.
5 Cf *R v Ali Mohamed* [1964] 2 QB 350n; *R v Bham* [1966] 1 QB 159, [1965] 3 All ER 124, infra, p 622.
6 Marriage Act 1949, s 41. There is special provision for the marriage of Quakers and Jews and for marriage by Registrar General's licence and by Archbishop's licence.
7 Law Com No 53 (1973), para 120.
8 *Qureshi v Qureshi* [1972] Fam 173 at 186.
9 [1954] AC 155, [1953] 2 All ER 1272; and see *Re Howe Louis* (1970) 14 DLR (3d) 49.
10 If an act such as registration is required for the retrospective validation of a marriage, then the marriage remains invalid until that act is done: *Pilinski v Pilinska* [1955] 1 All ER 631; see Thomas (1954) 3 ICLQ 353; Mendes da Costa (1958) 7 ICLQ 217, 251–260; Sinclair (1952) 29 BYBIL 479, (1953) 30 BYBIL 523.

ceremony was religious. On June 12, a daughter, Barbara, was born to them. As from June 30, Austrian legislation retrospectively validated such religious marriages, subject to their registration in a public register. In 1949, by which time H and W had both acquired a domicil in England, their marriage was registered in Austria, so that, by Austrian law, the parties were then regarded as having been lawfully married since May 19, 1945. In 1950 W and X went through a ceremony of marriage at Croydon. They had a son, Christopher, born before this marriage.

The issue before the House of Lords was whether Christopher was legitimate. If the marriage between H and W was still valid in 1950, W and X were bigamously married, and Barbara was legitimate, Christopher illegitimate; if it was void, Barbara was illegitimate, but Christopher had been legitimated by the ceremony of 1950. Thus the crucial question was whether the validity of the marriage between H and W was determinable according to the state of Austrian law on May 19 or on June 30, when the retrospective legislation came into force. It was held that the latter was the appropriate date.

The answers to the two main arguments against this solution were not altogether convincing. The objection that the status of parties domiciled in England can scarcely be altered by the law of a country with which they are no longer connected was ruled out on the ground that the Austrian legislation dealt with formalities rather than with status. The objection, that the parties to a void marriage will be unable to rely on their unmarried status if the ceremony remains liable to validation, was met by the reflection that validation will normally not be long delayed.

If the marriage between W and X had preceded the retrospective validation of the marriage between W and H, then it is suggested that the validation would not be recognised so as to nullify the second marriage which was wholly valid when entered into.[11] Similarly, if an English court had granted a decree of nullity in relation to the first marriage, the validity of that decree ought not to be affected by any later act of registration.[12] If the marriage between W and X came after the retrospective validation of the earlier marriage, but W was domiciled at the time of her second marriage in a country which did not recognise the effect of the validation, then the second marriage ought to be regarded in England as valid.[13]

(iii) What are matters of form?

The statement that a marriage good by the law of the place of celebration is good all the world over is accurate only if confined to the question of formal validity. Essential validity is, as we shall see,[14] a matter for the personal law of the parties. This distinction may raise the question whether a particular rule obtaining in the place of the ceremony affects form or essence. Some matters seem clearly to be formal in character, such as whether a religious or civil ceremony is required, the time and place of the ceremony, the need for witnesses, registration of the marriage, prior notification of the ceremony

---

11 This point is left open by the House of Lords in *Starkowski v A-G* [1954] AC 155 at 168, 171–172, 176, 182; but support for this conclusion is provided by *Ambrose v Ambrose* (1961) 25 DLR (2d) 1.

12 *Salvesen v Administrator of Austrian Property* [1927] AC 641 at 651.

13 See Law Commission Working Paper No 89 (1985), para 2.11. The Commission recommended, at paras 4.1–4.13, that there should be no legislative reform of the rules on retrospectivity, a view adopted in Law Com No 165 (1987), para. 2.13.

14 *Infra*, pp 586 et seq.

or a requirement of premarital blood tests. It has been established, for instance, that a rule which permits a marriage by proxy must be classified as formal since it is concerned with the manner in which the marriage ceremony may be performed.[15] Thus, if a woman, domiciled and resident in England, executes a power of attorney appointing X to act as her representative in the celebration of a marriage between her and Y in a country where marriage by proxy is recognised,[16] and the ceremony is in fact performed, the formal validity of the marriage cannot be impugned. A marriage ceremony solemnised in such a manner, though not possible in England, is not regarded as contrary to English public policy.[17] The other important area where the issue of the classification of a particular rule as one of capacity or form has arisen is that of parental consent to marry. It has been seen[18] that English law classifies this as a question of form in relation to consent both under English and under foreign law.[19]

(iv) Marriages in foreign consulates and embassies

It is not wholly clear what the present law is as to celebration of marriages in consulates and embassies. The question of the formal validity of a marriage celebrated in a foreign consulate abroad was considered in *Radwan v Radwan (No 2)*:[20]

In 1951, the husband, domiciled in Egypt married Ikbal in Egypt in polygamous form. In 1952, he married the petitioner, Mary, a domiciled Englishwoman, in the Egyptian Consulate General in Paris, in polygamous form and their matrimonial home was established in Egypt. In 1953, the husband divorced Ikbal by *talak*. In 1956 the husband and Mary came to live in England and acquired a domicil here. In 1970, the husband obtained a *talak* divorce from Mary in the Egyptian Consulate General in London and then Mary petitioned the English courts for divorce.

This matrimonial saga raises a number of separate issues, not all of which were considered in a logical sequence in the proceedings and some of which must be dealt with at greater length elsewhere. First, it was held that the *talak* divorce in the Egyptian Consulate General could not be recognised in England because the diplomatic premises were to be regarded as English and not Egyptian territory.[1] There was, however, the logically anterior question of the validity of the marriage in the Egyptian Consulate General in Paris and this was considered in the later proceedings in the case.[2] Two questions had to be examined—whether the parties had capacity and whether the marriage was formally valid. CUMMING-BRUCE J decided that, although Mary was incapable by English law of entering a polygamous marriage, she was

---

15 *Apt v Apt* [1948] P 83, [1947] 2 All ER 677; *Ponticelli v Ponticelli* [1958] P 204, [1958] 1 All ER 357; *Birang v Birang* (1977) 7 Fam Law 172.
16 Cf National Insurance Decision No R (G) 3/74.
17 *Apt v Apt*, supra; *Ponticelli v Ponticelli*, supra.
18 Supra, pp 49–50.
19 *Simonin v Mallac* (1860) 2 Sw & Tr 67; *Ogden v Ogden* [1908] P 46; *Lodge v Lodge* (1963) 107 Sol Jo 437; see also *Bliersbach v McEwen* 1959 SC 43; Anton & Francescakis [1958] Jur Rev 253.
20 [1973] Fam 35.
 1 *Radwan v Radwan* [1973] Fam 24; Polonsky (1973) 22 ICLQ 343. The divorce recognition aspect of the case is considered infra, p 669.
 2 [1973] Fam 35.

capable by Egyptian law, the law of the intended matrimonial home.[3] As to formal validity, the court held that the Egyptian Consulate General in Paris was to be regarded as French, and not Egyptian, territory.[4] French law must, as the law of the place of celebration, be applied to questions of formal validity. The court presumed the marriage to be formally valid in the absence of decisive evidence of French law to rebut this presumption.

Whilst this case provides clear authority for the view that a marriage abroad in a foreign embassy or consulate[5] must comply with the formalities of the receiving state, there remains the problem of marriages in England in foreign diplomatic premises.[6] There is some authority for the view that such marriages are formally valid if both parties are nationals and, perhaps, domiciliaries of the foreign state.[7] The opinion has been expressed at the diplomatic, rather than judicial, level that marriages in a foreign embassy between nationals of the sending State will be regarded as valid, but that, apart from diplomatic convention, consular marriages must comply with the formalities of English law.[8] The rejection of the idea of extra-territoriality is certainly consistent with the reasoning in *Radwan v Radwan (No 2)*[9] where the decision that the marriage in Paris must comply with French law was supported by reference to the earlier conclusion[10] that the divorce in London must be regarded as an English and not an Egyptian divorce.

(v) Renvoi

It has been assumed up to this point that formalities are to be governed by the internal law of the law of the place of celebration; but there is some authority that the doctrine of renvoi[11] applies in this area with the result that a marriage will be formally valid if it complies with the formal requirements of whatever law is selected by the choice of law rules of the place of celebration. In *Taczanowska v Taczanowski*,[12] two Polish nationals, domiciled in Poland were married in Italy in 1946 in a military camp, the husband being a member of the Allied occupation forces in Italy. The ceremony did not comply with the formal requirements of Italian law, but the court considered[13] the rule of Italian law that the marriage would be regarded as valid by the Italian courts if it complied with the formal requirements of Polish law, the law of the parties' common nationality. In fact the marriage was not formally valid under Polish law, though it was held valid in England as an exception to the general rule of reference to the law of the place of celebration.[14] Nevertheless, it seems to have been assumed that the English courts would have regarded the marriage as formally valid had Polish law so regarded it, applying the renvoi doctrine of transmission from Italian law.

3 This aspect of the case is discussed, infra, pp 592, 617–618.
4 See also *R v Turnbull, ex p Petroff* (1971) 17 FLR 438.
5 Marriages abroad in British consulates are discussed, infra, pp 577–578.
6 And see *Khan v Khan* (1960) 21 DLR (2d) 171 at 176.
7 *Bailet v Bailet* (1901) 17 TLR 317; and see *Pertreis v Tondear* (1790) 1 Hag Con 136; *Ruding v Smith* (1821) 2 Hag Con 371 at 386.
8 Parry, 8 *British Digest of International Law*, pp 631–645.
9 [1973] Fam 35, [1972] 3 All ER 1026.
10 *Radwan v Radwan* [1973] Fam 24, [1972] 3 All ER 967.
11 Supra, pp 58 et seq.
12 [1957] P 301, [1957] 2 All ER 563; and see *Hooper v Hooper* [1959] 2 All ER 575, [1959] 1 WLR 1021.
13 Ibid, at 305, 318.
14 Infra, pp 582–585.

What is the position if a marriage satisfies the formal requirements of the domestic law of the place of celebration, but not those of the country referred to by its choice of law rules? Although there is no direct authority on this issue,[15] it has been suggested that, in the interests of upholding the validity of marriage, the English courts should regard the marriage as valid if it complies either with the domestic law of the place of celebration or with the system of law which would be applied by that country's choice of law rules. The Law Commission,[16] whilst supporting generally the application of the doctrine of renvoi in the case of formal validity of marriage in the interests of upholding the validity of marriages and promoting uniformity of status,[17] rejected such an alternative reference rule, despite its convenience, on the ground that it could lead to the marriage being regarded here as formally valid, though not so regarded in the place of celebration.

(b) EXCEPTIONS TO THE GENERAL RULE

There are two statutory exceptions and one common law exception to the rule that the law of the place of celebration governs formalities.

(i) The two statutory exceptions

(a) **Consular marriages** What is generally called a "consular marriage" is the first exception. The Foreign Marriage Act 1892, as amended by the Foreign Marriage Act 1947 and the Foreign Marriage (Amendment) Act 1988, provides that all marriages between parties, one of whom at least is a United Kingdom national,[18] solemnised before a "marriage officer" in a foreign country[19] in the manner prescribed by the Act, shall be as valid as if it had been solemnised in the United Kingdom with a due observance of all forms required by law.[20] The persons who may be appointed marriage officers include British ambassadors, High Commissioners and consular officers, but they must hold a marriage warrant from the Secretary of State.[21]

The 1892 Act lays down various requirements as to such matters as parental consent,[1] the giving of notice of the marriage[2] and the registration of the marriage.[3] Section 8 is the most important section and it provides that every marriage must be solemnised at the official house[4] of the marriage officer, with open doors, in the presence of two or more witnesses and according to such form as the parties see fit to adopt. Where a statement that the parties know of no impediment to their marriage would not otherwise be included in the ceremony adopted, they must each declare:

15 In *Hooper v Hooper* [1959] 2 All ER 575, [1959] 1 WLR 1021 a marriage in Baghdad was held formally invalid for failure to comply with the requirements of English law, which law was to be applied under Iraq choice of law rules; but it does not appear from the brief report whether the domestic law of Iraq had been satisfied.
16 Law Commission Working Paper No 89 (1985), paras 2.39–2.42; and see the views of the Irish Law Reform Commission: LRC 19–1985, p 152.
17 A view not broadly supported on consultation: Law Com No 165 (1987), para 2.5.
18 Defined in s 1(2) of the 1892 Act, added by s 1(2) of the 1988 Act.
19 This means any country outside the Commonwealth.
20 S 1; eg *Ramsay-Fairfax v Ramsay-Fairfax* [1956] P 115.
21 S 11; and see Law Commission Working Paper No 89 (1985), para 2.15.
1 S 4, as substituted by s 2 (1) of the 1988 Act.
2 Ss 2, 3.
3 S 9.
4 Defined in SI 1970/1539, para 5.

I solemnly declare that I know not of any lawful impediment why I *AB* [*or CD*] may not be joined in matrimony to *CD* [*or AB*]

Similarly, if not otherwise stated in the ceremony adopted, each party must make the following declaration:

I call upon these persons here present to witness that I *AB* [*or CD*] take thee *CD* [*or AB*] to be my lawful wedded wife [*or husband*].[5]

It has been held[6] that section 8 is the crucial section of this Act and is mandatory in nature whilst other sections, namely 2, 3, 4, 7 and 9, are administrative or procedural and are only directory in nature. Failure to comply with these latter sections does not render the marriage invalid.

A marriage contracted under these statutory provisions is necessarily valid in England from the point of view of form, even though it might be void under the law of the country where it took place.[7] However, any real danger that a marriage solemnised under the Act may be regarded as void in the law of the place of celebration has been virtually eliminated by the Foreign Marriage Order 1970.[8] This provides that a marriage officer must not solemnise a marriage in a foreign country unless he is satisfied:[9]

(a) that at least one of the parties is a United Kingdom national; and
(b) that the authorities of that country will not object to the solemnisation of the marriage; and
(c) that insufficient facilities exist for the marriage of the parties under the law of that country; and
(d) that the parties will be regarded as validly married by the law of the country in which each party is domiciled.

Furthermore, the 1892 Act provides that a marriage officer is not required to solemnise a marriage if to do so "would be inconsistent with international law or the comity of nations".[10] It is far from clear what this means and, indeed, whether it is of any force in the light of the conditions just listed above. However, nothing in the 1892 Act is to confirm, impair or affect the validity of a marriage celebrated abroad other than as the Act provides.[11] This means that a marriage valid under some other exception to the general rule is still to be regarded as valid.

(b) Marriages of members of British forces serving abroad Section 22 of the Foreign Marriage Act 1892,[12] as substituted by the Acts of 1947 and 1988, provides as follows:

(1) A marriage solemnised in any foreign territory[13] by a chaplain serving with any part of the naval, military, or air forces of His Majesty[14] serving in that territory

---

5 Ibid, s 8 (2)-(4), as substituted by s 4 of the 1988 Act.
6 *Collett v Collett* [1968] P 482.
7 *Hay v Northcote* [1900] 2 Ch 262. In this case the marriage was held to be valid despite its annulment in the common domicil of the parties, but such an annulment would now be recognised here, infra, pp 657 et seq.
8 SI 1970/1539.
9 Ibid, para 3(1), as amended by SI 1990/598.
10 Foreign Marriage Act 1892, s 19.
11 Ibid, s 23.
12 For Orders in Council made under the Act, see SI 1964/1000; SI 1965/137; SI 1990/2592.
13 This is defined, in s 22(2), as any territory other than the Commonwealth, colonies, British protectorates and other territories under the protection or jurisdiction of the Crown. The original section 22 was limited to "British lines."
14 The original section 22 was limited to the army.

or by a person authorised ... by the commanding officer of any part of those forces serving in that territory shall, subject as hereinafter provided, be as valid in law as if the marriage had been solemnised in the United Kingdom with a due observance of all forms required by law.

(1A) Subsection (1) above shall not apply to a marriage unless—

(a) at least one of the parties to the marriage is a person who—

   (i) is a member of the said forces serving in the foreign territory concerned or is employed in that territory in such other capacity as may be prescribed by Order in Council; or

   (ii) is a child of a person falling within sub-paragraph (i) above and has his home with that person in that territory; and

(b) such other conditions as may be so prescribed are complied with.

(1B) In determining for the purposes of subsection (1A) above whether one person is the child of another—

(a) it shall be immaterial whether the person's father and mother were at any time married to each other; and

(b) a person who is or was treated by another as a child of the family in relation to any marriage to which that other is or was a party shall be regarded as his child.

"Foreign territory" includes, inter alia, ships which are for the time being in the waters of any foreign territory.[15] A marriage celebrated under the Act is valid whether the armed forces are on active service, or in the occupation of foreign territory after the successful conclusion of hostilities, or merely stationed there. There is no necessity for one of the parties to be a British subject,[16] but Commonwealth forces are excluded.[1]

(ii) The common law exception

(a) Meaning of "common law marriage"[2] It has long been admitted that there may be peculiar circumstances which allow a marriage not solemnised according to the law of the place of celebration to be recognised as valid if it satisfies the forms required by the common law of England. Before discussing the nature of these circumstances, it must be made clear what is meant by a "common law marriage", or, as it is better called, a "canon law marriage", since it emerged at a time when the canon law governed the matrimonial affairs of Christians throughout Western Europe.[3]

The only essential to the formal validity of a marriage required by the canon law and by the original common law was that the parties should take each other as man and wife. In 1843, however, the further common law condition was added that an episcopally ordained priest or deacon, whether of the English or Roman Catholic Church, should perform the ceremony. This was decided by the House of Lords in *R v Millis*,[4] where it was held, though in a rather unsatisfactory manner,[5] that a marriage celebrated in

15 S 22(3).
16 *Taczanowska v Takzanowski* [1957] P 301, [1957] 2 All ER 563.
1 Foreign Marriage Act 1947, s 3.
2 Hall [1987] CLJ 106.
3 *Lazarewicz v Lazarewicz* [1962] P 171 at 177, [1962] 2 All ER 5 at 7. There is Irish authority that a potentially polygamous marriage is excluded: *Conlon v Mohamed* [1989] ILRM 523.
4 (1843–4) 10 Cl & Fin 534.
5 The four judges of the Irish Court of Queen's Bench were equally divided, and PERRIN J, who had held the marriage valid, formally withdrew his judgment in order that an appeal might be taken to the House of Lords. The case was there argued before six Law Lords and ten judges. A unanimous opinion of all the judges in favour of the invalidity of the marriage was read by TINDAL CJ, who explained, however, that lack of time had prevented a proper investigation of the case. The Law Lords were, however, equally divided.

Ireland by a Presbyterian minister according to the rites of the Presbyterian Church[6] was invalid. Lord HARDWICKE's Marriage Act[7] did not extend to Ireland, and therefore marriages in that country were governed by the common law. This rule, that no common law marriage is valid without the intervention of an episcopally ordained priest, is one that almost certainly lacks historical justification;[8] but its applicability to English common law marriages seems clear, though may well be thought undesirable.[9]

There are several situations in which a marriage may be celebrated out of England and we shall have to consider them in turn to determine whether the marriage is formally valid if it satisfies the requirements of the common law.

(b) Where the common law is in force in the foreign country The first situation is where the common law of England continues to govern the parties even in the foreign country where they take each other as husband and wife. This can be illustrated by the early days of colonialism. It was consistently recognised as a matter of constitutional law that the British settlers in such countries as Australia took English common law with them, but only so much of it as was suitable to the local conditions.[10] Tested by this principle, it seems clear that the rule of the common law requiring the intervention of an episcopally ordained priest could scarcely be extended to a marriage contracted in a colony during the early days of the colonisation when there was no Church establishment and no division of the country into parishes.[11] The weight of judicial opinion was for many years in favour of treating the rule in *R v Millis* as being confined to marriages in England and Ireland,[12] and in *Catterall v Catterall*[13] Dr LUSHINGTON held that a marriage which had been celebrated at Sydney in 1835 by a Presbyterian minister was valid at common law.

The position may be illustrated by two cases from a more modern setting. In *Wolfenden v Wolfenden*:[14]

A Canadian, whose domicil of choice appears to have been English, went through a ceremony of marriage with a Canadian woman in China. The ceremony was performed, not by an episcopally ordained priest, but by the local minister of the Church of Scotland Mission. A Chinese Order in Council was in force which, after reciting that a treaty had given His Majesty the King jurisdiction in the Republic of China, proceeded to establish a system of judicature there and provided that the civil jurisdiction of every court acting under the Order should "as far as circumstances permit be exercised on the principle of and in conformity with English law for the time being in force."

6 Whose ministers are not episcopally ordained.
7 Of 1753.
8 The majority of canonists and historians consider the decision in *R v Millis* to be wrong; see Pollock & Maitland, *History of English Law*, vol II, pp 370–372; *Merker v Merker* [1963] P 283 at 293–294; and see Lucas [1990] CLJ 117.
9 Hall [1987] CLJ 106, 120.
10 Blackstone, *Commentaries on the Laws of England*, i, 108.
11 *Maclean v Cristall* (1849) Perry's Ori Cas 75.
12 *Beamish v Beamish* (1861) 9 HL Cas 274 at 348, 352; *Lightbody v West* (1903) 18 TLR 526.
13 (1847) 1 Rob Eccl 580. There was in fact a local marriage statute which had not been observed, but Dr LUSHINGTON had already held in *Catterall v Sweetman* (1845) 1 Rob Eccl 304 that the statute did not avoid all marriages failing to satisfy its requirements.
14 [1946] P 61, [1945] 2 All ER 539. A similar case was *Phillips v Phillips* (1921) 38 TLR 150.

LORD MERRIMAN P held that the marriage was valid at common law. The parties had freely consented to it and the circumstances precluded the presence of an episcopally ordained priest.

A similar decision was reached in *Penhas v Tan Soo Eng*.[15] Certain charters of justice issued in the first half of the nineteenth century introduced English law into Singapore, but provided that it should be administered in such a manner as the religions, manners and customs of the inhabitants would admit. Therefore, a marriage ceremony in 1937 between a Jew and a Chinese woman, both British subjects domiciled in Singapore, at which the man observed the Jewish custom but the woman followed the Chinese rites, was held to be valid at common law. The parties intended the composite ceremony to record that they took each other as man and wife. The rule in *R v Millis* was inapplicable.

It has never been doubted, of course, that a marriage in a foreign country, where local formalities are non-existent or where those that exist are inapplicable to an English marriage, is valid if it is contracted in the presence of an episcopally ordained priest.[16] What is not clear is whether the requirement of celebration by an episcopally ordained priest can be ignored even if there is no difficulty in obtaining his services. The weight of authority favours compliance with the requirement in such a case.[17]

Strictly speaking, a marriage held to be valid in the types of case just considered is not a true exception to the doctrine *locus regit actum* for, so far as the parties are concerned, the law of the place of celebration is none other than the common law.[18]

(c) Insuperable difficulty The second exceptional situation is where the parties, though not subject to the common law in the foreign place of celebration have, nevertheless, without regard to the local formalities, taken each other as man and wife at a ceremony performed, usually, by an episcopally ordained priest. In such a case the marriage will be regarded as valid if compliance with the local formalities had been prevented by some insuperable difficulty.[19] What is meant by insuperable difficulty has been expressed in various ways. LORD STOWELL considered that "legal or religious difficulties" might justify a relaxation of the principle *locus regit actum*.[20] LORD ELDON was clear that the parties might invoke the common law if they could not avail themselves of the law of the place of celebration or if there was no local law. He accordingly held that a marriage between Protestants at Rome solemnised by a Protestant priest was valid, since no Catholic priest would be allowed to perform the ceremony.[1] The parties must have found it impossible, or virtually impossible,[2] to comply with the local law. It is not enough that they found it inconvenient, embarrassing or distasteful so to

---

15 [1953] AC 304.
16 *Limerick v Limerick* (1863) 32 LJPM & A 92; *Phillips v Phillips* (1921) 38 TLR 150.
17 *Taczanowska v Taczanowski* [1957] P 301 at 326; *Collett v Collett* [1968] P 482 at 487; *Kuklycz v Kuklycz* [1972] VR 50; cf *Preston v Preston* [1963] P 411 at 436.
18 *Taczanowska v Tacanowski* [1957] P 301 at 327, 328.
19 *Kent v Burgess* (1840) 11 Sim 361.
20 *Ruding v Smith* (1821) 2 Hag Con 371.
 1 *Lord Cloncurry's Case* (1811), cited by Cruise, *Dignities and Titles of Honour*, 276; and see the *Sussex Peerage Case* (1844) 11 Cl & Fin 85 at 92, 102.
 2 *Preston v Preston* [1963] P 411 at 432; or perhaps where conformity with the local law would be contrary to conscience: *Kochanski v Kochanska* [1958] P 147 at 151–152.

comply, as in *Kent v Burgess*[3] where a marriage in Belgium was held void for non-compliance with Belgian residence requirements, there being no insuperable difficulty in the parties waiting the prescribed six months period.

Australian courts have considered that "insuperable difficulty" existed in Germany in 1945 at a time when no register offices were open and the registrars had left their posts,[4] and in the Ukraine in 1942 as the German army advanced,[5] but not in Saigon in 1978.[6] The marriages in the first two cases were upheld as valid according to the common law.[7]

Although it has usually been the case that, when a marriage has been upheld under this exceptional head of insuperable difficulty, it has been celebrated by an episcopally ordained priest,[8] it is suggested that this is not a necessary requirement and that celebration by some other clergyman or even by none at all will suffice.[9]

(d) Marriages of military forces in belligerent occupation [10] Circumstances can be envisaged where, although compliance with the local law is not impossible, it might be thought unreasonable. Such a problem arose in Europe at the end and in the aftermath of the Second World War when many people married without recourse to the civilian, often Nazi, authorities. The problem is illustrated by the leading decision in *Taczanowska v Taczanowski*:[11]

> Two Polish nationals, domiciled in Poland, were married in Italy in 1946 by a Polish Army Chaplain, an episcopally ordained priest of the Catholic Church, and therefore according to the English common law. The husband was serving in the Polish 2nd Corps, an independent command in belligerent occupation of Italy. The ceremony did not comply with the local forms and was therefore void by Italian domestic law, but it would be recognised as valid by that country's private international law if it was valid by the national law of the parties. It was, however, not valid by Polish law. The parties came to England in 1947 and, in 1955, the wife petitioned for a decree of nullity on the ground that the marriage was void for non-compliance with the local forms.

The Court of Appeal felt that they were not bound to apply the law of the place of celebration, Italian law, when the parties were presumed not to have submitted themselves to that law. It was considered that there is often no submission by a member of the military forces in occupation of a country, and such was held to be the case here. As Italian law was not applicable and the law of the parties' domicil was considered irrelevant,[12] English common

---

3 (1840) 11 Sim 361.
4 *Savenis v Savenis* [1950] SASR 309.
5 *Kuklycz v Kuklycz* [1972] VR 50; cf *Persian v Persian* [1970] 2 NSWR 538.
6 *Re X's Marriage* (1983) 65 FLR 132.
7 It is an interesting question whether laws prohibiting inter-racial marriages could be regarded as creating insuperable difficulty; cf *Conlon v Mohamed* [1989] ILRM 523.
8 Eg *Savenis v Savenis* [1950] SASR 309 (Roman Catholic priest); *Kuklycz v Kuklycz* [1972] VR 50 (Greek Orthodox priest).
9 As in the first common law marriage exception, discussed supra, pp 580–581.
10 See Mendes da Costa (1958) 7 ICLQ 217; Andrews (1959) 22 MLR 396; Brownlie & Webb (1963) 39 BYBIL 457.
11 [1957] P 301, [1957] 2 All ER 563.
12 As the court was not concerned with a question of capacity; see also *Kochanski v Kochanska* [1958] P 147 at 154–155; *Kuklycz v Kuklycz* [1972] VR 50 at 52; cf *Maksymec v Maksymec* (1955) 72 WN (NSW) 522.

law was applied and the validity of the marriage upheld.[13] The result was that the Court of Appeal, animated perhaps by a desire to save other similar marriages, said to number between three and four thousand, recognised as valid at common law a marriage void both by the law of the place of celebration and by the personal law of the parties.

A further step was taken in *Kochanski v Kochanska*.[14] Here, two Polish nationals, occupants of a displaced persons' camp in Germany, to whom everything German was anathema, were married by a Catholic priest without compliance with the local forms. Although this case was distinguishable from previous decisions in that neither party to the marriage could be described as a member of the armed forces of occupation, SACHS J upheld the validity of the marriage. He concluded there was no submission to the local law; and having thus eliminated German law, the judge held the marriage to be valid on the ground that the ceremony satisfied the common law; though he would have preferred to fall back on the Polish law of the domicil had authority justified that course.

In moving beyond the narrow category of members of the armed forces of occupation, SACHS J gave support to the general idea that the requirement of compliance with the law of the place of celebration is based on submission thereto by the parties. In the case before him there was no submission and so the common law was applied. Such a general principle of submission underlies the decision in *Lazarewicz v Lazarewicz*,[15] where a Polish corporal, serving with the Polish army in Italy, was married in 1946 at Barletta in Italy to an Italian national. The ceremony, performed at a Polish refugee camp by a Catholic priest, did not comply with Italian law. PHILLIMORE J distinguished the case before him from the two earlier cases on the ground that there was evidence of the parties' intention to submit to Italian law.

> The husband had married not as a member or within the lines of the army of occupation, but as an ordinary sojourner in and subject to the laws of the foreign State.[16]

Reliance on the common law was, therefore, precluded and the marriage was void.

This decision adds further support to a general theory that the basis of the rule *locus regit actum* is the presumed intention of the parties to submit themselves to the law of the place of celebration. It is suggested, however, that this theory of submission, if it purports to represent a general principle applicable to marriages other than those in an occupied country or in a country where it is insuperably difficult to comply with the local law, is neither supported by previous authority nor free from other objections. Clear authority against such a general rule is provided by the statement of the Privy Council in 1930 that:

> If the so-called marriage is no marriage in the place where it is celebrated it is no marriage anywhere, although the ceremony or proceeding if conducted in the place of the parties' domicil would be considered a good marriage.[17]

13 The argument of the husband that the marriage was valid by virtue of the Foreign Marriage Act 1892, s 22 failed, since the Polish army chaplain was not officiating under the orders of a commanding officer of the British army serving abroad, supra, pp 578–579.
14 [1958] P 147; followed in *Jaroszonek v Jaroszonek* [1962] SASR 157; cf *Fokas v Fokas* [1952] SASR 152; *Grzybowicz v Grzybowicz* [1963] SASR 62.
15 [1962] P 171, [1962] 2 All ER 5; and see *Dukov v Dukov* (1968) 13 FLR 149.
16 *Merker v Merker* [1963] P 283 at 295, [1962] 3 All ER 928 at 934.
17 *Berthiaume v Dastous* [1930] AC 79 at 83.

Again, if this rule stated in such categorical terms by the Privy Council is to give way to the presumed intention of the parties, certainty will be displaced by uncertainty, unless it is made clear what evidence suffices to establish an intention not to submit to the law of the place of celebration.[1] It will be seen[2] that evidence that the parties did not wish to observe the local law obviously cannot suffice. In the result, the suggestion that the control of the law of the place of celebration depends on the intention of the parties, whatever its future fate may be, confused what was formerly reasonably clear.

Later decisions do not rely on the dangerous concept of submission. In *Merker v Merker*,[3] Sir JOCELYN SIMON P was faced with another marriage in occupied enemy territory:

> The parties were Polish domiciliaries who were serving in the Polish Armoured Division, part of the allied forces occupying Germany. They were married in a local German church by a Catholic priest, a Polish army chaplain. German local law was not complied with. Later a German court granted a decree declaring the marriage to be null and void. After the wife had become resident in England, she petitioned for a declaration as to her status.

The first issue before the court was that of the validity of her marriage.[4] One of the arguments put to the court was that a person marrying in a foreign country could elect whether to submit to the local law or not, and, if he did not submit, then English common law, as the law of the forum, should determine the validity of his marriage. Such a general principle was emphatically rejected, for its effect "would be to leave the rule in *Berthiaume v Dastous*[5] in tatters and to introduce anarchy in a field where order and comity are particularly required".[6] Sir JOCELYN SIMON P confined the principle of *Taczanowska's Case* to cases of:

> Marriages within the lines of a foreign army of occupation (which constitute, so to speak, an enclave within which it is reasonable to hold that the local law has no application), or of persons in a strictly analogous situation to the members of such an army, such as members of an organised body of escaped prisoners of war.[7]

Applying such a narrow principle, the marriage before him was, nevertheless, valid according to English common law.

This more restrictive decision was followed by that of the Court of Appeal in *Preston v Preston*[8] where the court had to consider the validity at common law of a marriage, in the same camp as that in *Kochanski v Kochanska*,[9] which had failed to comply with the law of the place of celebration. On the evidence before it, the court considered that the camp in question was part of the organisation of the allied forces of occupation. ORMEROD LJ interpreted *Taczanowska's Case* as deciding that persons who marry in a foreign country are assumed to have submitted to the local law except in the case of the

---

1 Carter (1957) 33 BYBIL 335.
2 *Merker v Merker* [1963] P 283 at 295, [1962] 2 All ER 928 at 933; *Preston v Preston* [1963] P 411 at 427, [1963] 2 All ER 405 at 414.
3 [1963] P 283.
4 The problems stemming from recognition of the German decree are considered infra, p 660.
5 Supra, p 572.
6 [1963] P 283 at 295; see also *Milder v Milder* [1959] VR 95.
7 [1963] P 283 at 295.
8 [1963] P 411.
9 Supra, p 583.

members of forces in belligerent occupation.[10] The general rule that persons are deemed to submit to the marriage laws of the place of celebration cannot be evaded merely because the parties claim that they did not intend to submit to that law. The circumstances where this general rule is inapplicable were narrowly, though not explicitly, defined.[11]

The conclusion to be drawn is that the principle of submission canvassed in the *Taczanowska Case* and other decisions is very limited. It is relevant only to marriages contracted by a member of a conquering force in the conquered country.[12] This is the one type of case in which it is not unreasonable to offer the parties an alternative to the law of the place of celebration, for the incongruity of compelling a conqueror to submit to the conquered is obvious.[13]

(e) Marriages on the high seas There is little authority as to what constitutes a valid marriage solemnised in a merchant ship while on the high seas.[14] The general principle is that the law of the flag governs transactions on board a vessel, for, as BYLES J once said, a British ship is regarded as a floating island on which British law prevails.[15] This raises two difficulties in the case of British ships.

First, since there is no one system of law common to all the countries that employ the British flag, which particular legal system constitutes the law of the flag? The alternative seems to lie between English law and the municipal law of the country in which the ship is registered. The latter is the more reasonable rule and the one that is generally advocated.[16]

Presuming this view to be correct, the second difficulty is to discover from the authorities what part of English law governs a marriage on a ship that is registered in England. Is it the common law or the common law as regulated by statute? The latter alternative appears clearly to be excluded. There is no statute that deals particularly with marriages at sea[17] and the "floating island" theory can scarcely be pressed so far as to suggest that the Marriage Acts are applicable.[18] Except where modified by statute, the common law is in force on a ship, as in the analogous case of a colony. To make the analogy complete it must also be conceded that only so much of the law is imported into the ship as is suitable to the local conditions. That raises the further question whether it suffices that the parties have freely taken each other for man and wife, or whether, in accordance with *R v Millis*,[19] it is necessary that the ceremony should have been performed by an episcopally ordained

10 This casts doubt on the decision in *Kochanski v Kochanska*, supra, and also on *Oleszko v Pietrucha* (1963) Times, 22 March, where the parties were members of what was considered to be a displaced persons' camp.
11 [1963] P 411 at 427–428.
12 Eg *Rosenthal v Rosenthal* (1967) 111 Sol Jo 475; cf *Dukov v Dukov* (1968) 13 FLR 149.
13 As, perhaps, also with members of an organised body of escaped prisoners of war: *Merker v Merker* [1963] P 283 at 295.
14 White (1901) 17 LQR 283; Charteris (1907) 19 Jur R 178.
15 *R v Anderson* (1868) LR 1 CCR 161 at 168; but see *R v Carr* (1882) 10 QBD 76 at 85.
16 Dicey & Morris, p 608; and see *Bolmer v Edsell* 90 NJ Eq 299 (1919); cf *Fisher v Fisher* 250 NY 313 (1929). Compare the rule relating to torts committed on board a ship, supra, pp 558–560.
17 The provisions of the Merchant Shipping Act 1894, ss 240(6) and 253 (1)(viii), requiring particulars of marriages celebrated at sea to be entered in the ship's log have been repealed without replacement by the Merchant Shipping Act 1970, ss 100(3), 101(4), Sch 5.
18 Indeed the theory itself is now hard to sustain: *R v Gordon-Finlayson, ex p Officer* [1941] 1 KB 171 at 178–179; *Oteri v R* [1976] 1 WLR 1272 at 1276.
19 (1844) 10 Cl & Fin 534.

clergyman. That the presence of an episcopally ordained clergyman is sufficient for validity seems generally to be admitted,[20] but that it is essential appears unwarranted.[21] The impossibility of procuring a clergyman on the high seas is even more apparent than in the case of a remote part of China, and it is difficult to resist the conclusion that the rule laid down in *Wolfenden v Wolfenden*[22] applies equally to a ship. The argument sometimes advanced, that a ship must sooner or later put into a port where advantage may be taken of the facilities offered by the local law or by the Foreign Marriage Acts, is of little weight. It can be countered by the reflection that the same facilities were open to parties in a remote part of China if they were prepared to make the necessary journey.

It is sometimes suggested that the absence of a clergyman is fatal to the validity of a marriage at sea, unless it is a *marriage of necessity*. What this ambiguous expression means is not clear but there is little doubt that it is taken from the Irish case of *Dumoulin v Druitt*[23] in 1860, which is no longer a safe guide. In that case:

A woman stowaway was discovered on a troopship during a voyage to Australia. The commanding officer ordered that she and one of the soldiers on board should immediately be married, and the marriage was celebrated in his presence. In fact, as soon as the ship arrived in Sydney, the woman left her "husband" and went to live with the officer who had acted as clerk in the marriage ceremony. Later they married, in the lifetime of the soldier, and the issue arose as to the validity of her ship-board marriage.

The court held that the rule in *R v Millis*[1] applied and that the ship-board marriage was void on the ground that the marriage was not one "of necessity", since the vessel would touch at places where a clergyman would be obtainable.[2] Having regard to *Wolfenden v Wolfenden*,[3] it would seem that this peculiar reasoning need no longer be considered seriously.

It is submitted, then, that if parties, whatever their domicil or nationality, voluntarily take each other as man and wife while at sea in a vessel registered at an English port, the marriage is formally valid in the eyes of English law provided, probably, there is some element of urgency about their marriage.[4]

3. CAPACITY TO MARRY[5]

(a) INTRODUCTION

We turn now to consider the second major issue relating to choice of law in the context of marriage, namely, the law to govern capacity or, as it is sometimes described, essential validity. There is general agreement that this terminology includes matters of legal capacity such as consanguinity and

20 Elphinstone (1889) 5 LQR 44, 53.
21 *Merker v Merker* [1963] P 283 at 294.
22 [1946] P 61.
23 (1860) 13 ICLR 212.
 1 (1844) 10 Cl & Fin 534; supra, pp 579–580.
 2 Cf *Maclean v Cristell* (1849) Perry's Ori Cas 75; and also *Culling v Culling* [1896] P 116, where the validity of a marriage on board a warship before the ship's captain was upheld; see now the Foreign Marriage Act 1892, s 22, supra. pp 578–579.
 3 [1946] P 61, [1945] 2 All ER 539, supra, pp 580–581.
 4 Dicey & Morris p 608.
 5 See Jaffey (1978) 41 MLR 38; (1982) 2 OJLS 368; North (1980) 1 Hague Recueil 9, 53–69; Fentiman [1985] CLJ 256.

affinity, bigamy and lack of age. Consideration is given later to the law to govern matters of consent[6] and physical incapacity.[7] The fact that capacity as a term encompasses a wide range of matters does not necessitate the conclusion that all matters of capacity should be subject to the same choice of law rule—a matter to which we shall return.[8] A further preliminary point which ought to be borne in mind is that, provided that a person has capacity under the relevant law, the fact that he is, for example, under age according to English law will not invalidate the marriage in the eyes of English law as the law of the forum—at least if the marriage is not in England.[9]

There are two main views as to the law which should govern capacity to marry—the dual domicil doctrine, and the intended matrimonial home doctrine.[10] These must now be examined more closely.

(b) THE TWO MAIN THEORIES

(i) The theories stated

The traditional and still prevalent view is that capacity to marry is governed by what may conveniently be called the *dual domicil doctrine*. This prescribes that a marriage is invalid unless, according to the law of the domicil of both contracting parties at the time of the marriage, they each have capacity to contract that particular marriage.[11] This is said to be true whether the incapacity is "absolute", ie one which forbids a person, such as a child below a particular age, to marry anyone; or "relative", ie one which forbids two individual persons, such as an uncle and niece, to marry each other.[12] Under this doctrine, a marriage, for instance, between a man of the Jewish faith domiciled in Egypt and a woman of the same faith domiciled in England, the latter being his niece, is invalid, since a marriage between persons so related, though permissible in Egypt,[13] is prohibited by English law.

The alternative doctrine, and the one which has been supported strongly in earlier editions of this book,[14] is that which submits the question of capacity to what may briefly be termed the law of the *intended matrimonial home*. More fully stated, the doctrine is this.

> The basic presumption is that capacity to marry is governed by the law of the husband's domicil at the time of the marriage, for normally it is in the country of that domicil that the parties intend to establish their permanent home. This presumption, however, is rebutted if it can be inferred that the parties at the time of the marriage intended to establish their home in a certain country and that they did in fact establish it there within a reasonable time.

---

6 Infra, pp 644–648.
7 Infra, pp 648–652.
8 See *Radwan v Radwan (No 2)* [1973] Fam 35 at 51, infra, pp 592, 617.
9 Eg *Mohamed v Knott* [1969] 1 QB 1, [1968] 2 All ER 563, infra, p 625.
10 Some more recently developed alternative approaches are examined, infra, pp 601–603.
11 Dicey & Morris, pp 622 et seq; Wolff, pp 332–337.
12 Westlake, s 21, p 57.
13 Cf *Cheni v Cheni* [1965] P 85, [1962] 3 All ER 873.
14 Eg 7th edn (1965), pp 276 et seq.

(ii) Evaluation of the two theories

Postponing for the moment a consideration of the actual decisions, the question may now be asked—What are the respective merits and demerits of the two rival doctrines?

(a) The intended matrimonial home doctrine On social grounds it can be argued that the doctrine of the dual domicil is inferior to that of the intended matrimonial home. Marriage is an institution that closely concerns the public policy and the social morality of the State.

The general laws which dictate its incidents, however, vary considerably between different countries, and where a woman domiciled in one country marries a man domiciled in another the question naturally arises—which State is to control the incident of capacity? Which State is in the nature of things entitled to demand pre-eminent consideration for its code of social morality? One clear answer might be—the State in which the parties set up their home.

A choice of law rule commands little respect if it is framed without regard to its impact on the social life of the community that will be most intimately affected by its operation. It seems reasonably clear that whether the inter-marriage of two persons should be prohibited for social, religious, eugenic or other like reason is a question that affects the community in which the parties live together as man and wife.[15]

In support of the argument that it is the law there in force which should be allowed to assess the propriety or impropriety of the marriage one might take the example of the extreme case of an absolute incapacity. If an English girl, aged fifteen and a half, contrary to the law of England, marries a foreigner domiciled in a country whose law permits marriage at this early age, it might be doubted whether it is justifiable to regard the marriage as void, for the social life of England is unaffected if the girl goes to live with him in his country, as the girl proposes to sever her connection with this country. As against that, however, it is arguable that rules as to the age of marriage are designed to protect minors whether they intend to live abroad or not. It is also arguable that a matter so important as capacity to marry should not be determined by the intentions of the parties.[16]

Apart from social considerations, principle might seem to support the view that, where the parties are domiciled in different countries before their marriage, questions of the essential validity of the marriage, including their personal capacity, should be governed by the law of the place where they establish their joint home.[17] This is at least compatible with the rule that capacity to enter into a commercial contract is governed by the law of the country with which the contract has the closest connection.[18] Broadly speaking, domicil signifies the country with which the *propositus* is most closely connected since it is there that he has established his home.[1]

But owing to the peculiar reverence that English law still pays to the domicil of origin, it may well happen that the country in which a party is

15 Report of the Royal Commission on Marriage and Divorce (1956) Cmnd 9678, para 889; and see *Bliersbach v McEwen* 1959 SLT 81 at 89.
16 Anton, p 429; and see *Cooper v Cooper* (1888) 13 App Cas 88 at 108; *Muhammad v Suna* 1956 SC 366 at 370.
17 *Lawrence v Lawrence* [1985] Fam 106 at 127.
18 Supra, pp 487 et seq.
 1 *Warrender v Warrender* (1835) 2 Cl & Fin 488 at 536.

technically domiciled immediately prior to marriage in no sense represents his or her home, whether actual or contemplated. Could it be said, for instance, that George Bowie, the work-shy Scotsman in *Ramsay v Liverpool Royal Infirmary*,[2] had his home in, or any substantial connection with, Scotland? Finally, not only is just one law to be applied under the intended matrimonial home theory, but it may be more effective than the dual domicil test in supporting a policy of upholding the validity of marriages and of giving effect to the legitimate expectations of the parties.[3]

When one turns to the disadvantages of the intended matrimonial home theory, then several objections of a practical matter may be advanced against it.[4] It may be objected that any rule is undesirable which renders it impossible to decide whether a marriage is valid or void at the time of its celebration.[5] Such may be the case if it is doubtful whether the parties genuinely intend to establish their home in the alleged country. Again, it may be asked what is the position if they delay unreasonably in going to the chosen country or never go there at all, or intend never to set up a matrimonial home?[6] Answers to these criticisms have been propounded. First, the question whether a marriage is void for incapacity, unless it arises incidentally in the course of some other proceedings, will require the institution of a nullity suit for its answer, by which time it will be known whether the alleged intention of the parties was in fact fulfilled. The difficulty with such an answer is that it ignores the fact that a marriage which is void ab initio does not require a decision of a court to determine the parties' status. If it is void, it is void. If the parties have to wait and see what law is to govern their capacity, then their marital status remains in doubt. The second suggested answer is that it is not true that the status of the parties will remain indeterminate, for if the place of their future home is doubtful it is presumed to be in the domicil of the husband at the date of their marriage. However, in that case it is not easy to find merit in a discriminatory solution which refers the issue of a wife's capacity to marry to the law of the husband's ante-nuptial domicil.

It is also the case that arguments of principle have been advanced against the intended matrimonial home theory, it being suggested that post-nuptial intentions should be irrelevant when determining ante-nuptial capacity, and that it enables rules which are the legitimate concern of the domiciliary law to be evaded by an intention to set up home elsewhere.

(b) The dual domicil theory The greatest merit of the dual domicil theory is that it refers capacity to marry to that law which, up to that time, has governed the status of each party.[7] The law of the domicil is the law of the country to which a person "belongs".[8] Furthermore, it preserves equality of the sexes by looking to the law of each party's domicil.[9] This is of added weight since a wife no longer takes automatically her husband's domicil on marriage.[10]

2 [1930] AC 588, supra, pp 146–147.
3 Law Commission Working Paper No 89 (1985), para 3.34; and see Jaffey (1978) 41 MLR 38; (1982) 2 OJLS 368.
4 Law Commission Working Paper No 89 (1985), para 3.35; and see Glenn (1977) 4 Dalh LR 157.
5 Dicey & Morris, p 625; and see *Lawrence v Lawrence* [1985] Fam 106 at 127–128.
6 Eg *Vervaeke v Smith* [1983] 1 AC 145.
7 *Lawrence v Lawrence* [1985] Fam 106 at 127.
8 Hartley (1972) 35 MLR 571, 576.
9 Morris, p 159.
10 Domicile and Matrimonial Proceedings Act 1973, s 1.

Varied criticisms have been made of the dual domicil theory. It tends towards the invalidity of marriages.[11] If the domiciliary laws differ as to the validity of the marriage, the marriage will be regarded as invalid. It is also said to be inefficacious as a practical working rule, in that it is a rule which admits of its own evasion. Suppose, for instance, that a woman domiciled in England wishes to marry her uncle who lives and is domiciled in Egypt. English internal law would prohibit the marriage. Being properly advised, however, she travels to Cairo for the marriage ceremony with the intention of remaining there for the rest of her married life, and thus acquires a domicil of choice, the law of which permits a marriage between an uncle and a niece. She is now of full capacity in the eyes of English private international law. It is said that the protection supposedly afforded to an English woman by the dual domicil rule is somewhat illusory. The evasion involved here amounts to as substantial a step as deciding to establish a matrimonial home in Egypt. However, this should not detract from the view, expressed earlier,[12] that if the woman is under sixteen she should remain subject to incapacity by English law, so long as it remains the law of her domicil.

Another criticism which might be voiced is that, because of the inflexibility of many of the rules relating to acquisition and loss of a domicil, a person's capacity to marry may be determined by the law of a country he has never visited. Such criticism may, however, provide a reason for changing the rules relating to domicil,[13] rather than those concerning capacity to marry.

(iii) The rule as deducible from the English decisions[14]

We must now turn from theory and attempt to ascertain whether judicial authority in England supports the view that capacity to marry is governed by the law of the pre-marriage domicil of each party, or by the law of the intended matrimonial home. Many of the relevant decisions,[15] it is submitted, are rather inconclusive. It will be seen that in such cases the decision would have been the same whether it had been based on the application of the law of the matrimonial home or on the dual domicil theory.

Inconclusive decisions For example, in *Brook v Brook*,[16] where, it will be recalled,[17] a Danish marriage was held void because both spouses lacked capacity under English law, the law of their domicil and of the intended matrimonial home, Lord CAMPBELL LC had this to say:

> But I am by no means prepared to say, that the marriage now in question ought to be or would be held valid in the Danish courts, proof being given that the parties were British subjects domiciled in England, that England was to be their matrimonial residence, and that by the law of England such a marriage is prohibited.

11 Hartley (1972) 35 MLR 571, 578.
12 Supra, p 588.
13 Supra, p 175. It has been proposed by the Irish Law Reform Commission that reference should be made to the law of the country of habitual residence rather than of domicil in determining capacity to marry; see LRC 19–1985, pp 112–114
14 And see North, *Private International Law of Matrimonial Causes*, pp 119 et seq.
15 *Mette v Mette* (1859) 1 Sw & Tr 416; *Brook v Brook* (1861) 9 HL Cas 193; *Re De Wilton* [1900] 2 Ch 481; *Re Paine* [1940] Ch 46; *Pugh v Pugh* [1951] P 482, [1951] 2 All ER 680; and see *In the Will of Swan* (1871) 2 VR (IE & M) 47. In *Ali v Ali* [1968] P 564, [1966] 1 All ER 664, infra, pp 614–615, CUMMING-BRUCE J at 576–577, suggested that both views were tenable and neither concluded by authority. On the facts of the case, the law of the domicil and the law of the intended matrimonial home were both English law.
16 (1861) 9 HL Cas 193.
17 Supra, pp 571–572.

The doctrine being established that the incidents of the contract of marriage celebrated in a foreign country are to be determined according to the law of the country in which the parties are domiciled and mean to reside, the consequence seems to follow that by this law must its validity or invalidity be determined.[18]

It is not possible to conclude in favour of one theory or the other on the basis of this case.[19]

Mette v Mette[20] is the earliest decision on this matter in which the parties were domiciled in different countries prior to their marriage:

A domiciled Englishman contracted a marriage in Frankfurt with his deceased wife's half-sister, a domiciled German woman. This marriage, then prohibited by English law but valid by German law, was held to be void.

This decision does not conclude the controversy, since it is again compatible both with the dual domicil doctrine and the doctrine of the intended matrimonial home. The man was domiciled in England until his death, both parties contemplated a matrimonial residence in England, and therefore English law, as being the law of the matrimonial home, was the appropriate legal system to determine the matter. In the words of the judge, the husband "remained domiciled in this country, and the marriage was with a view to subsequent residence in this country".[1] The *ratio decidendi* is in fact rather doubtful. After remarking that "there could be no valid contract unless each was competent to contract with the other", words which suggest a preference for the dual domicil doctrine, Sir CRESSWELL CRESSWELL finally concluded that since the husband had remained domiciled in England, and the marriage was with a view to subsequent residence there, the English prohibition was necessarily operative.[2]

Support for the intended matrimonial home theory Having considered and discarded such rather inconclusive decisions, one must turn to those which provide more specific support for one theory or the other, starting with those in favour of the intended matrimonial home view. The most persuasive early decision is that in the Australian case of *In the Will of Swan*,[3] where the issue was whether a marriage, which was celebrated on a temporary visit to Scotland between parties domiciled in the State of Victoria, could be held to revoke a will made by the husband before marriage. The wife was the niece of the husband's deceased wife and it was assumed that the marriage, though voidable by Victorian law, was void by Scots law. In upholding the validity of the marriage and thus of the revocation of the will, MOLESWORTH J said "The validity of marriages as to ceremonial and so forth depends upon the law of the place of the marriage, but ... the policy of the occurrence of such marriages and their results, should depend, I think, upon the laws of the country of the parties in which they are afterwards probably to live."[4] No doubt, however, a similar result would have been achieved through the dual domicil test.

18 (1861) 9 HL Cas 193 at 213; see also at 224, 230–231, 239.
19 Though see, at 212, Lord CAMPBELL's explanation of *Warrender v Warrender* (1835) 2 Cl & Fin 488. See also *Sottomayer v De Barros* (1877) 3 PD 1, infra, pp 595–597.
20 (1859) 1 Sw & Tr 416.
 1 Ibid at 424.
 2 Ibid at 423–424.
 3 (1871) 2 VR (IE & M) 47; Fleming (1951) 4 ILQ 389, 392–393.
 4 Ibid, at 50. This latter law was presumed to be Victorian.

There are, moreover, judicial pronouncements which refer the question of the legality of a marriage to the law of the matrimonial domicil; though in all these cases the remarks are made obiter as no issue of capacity to marry was directly involved. In the first of these, *De Reneville v De Reneville*,[5] Lord GREENE MR had this to say:

> The validity of a marriage so far as regards the observance of formalities is a matter for the *lex loci celebrationis*. But this[6] is not a case of forms. It is a case of essential validity. By what law is that to be decided? In my opinion by the law of France, either because that is the law of the husband's domicil at the date of the marriage or (preferably, in my view) because at that date it was the law of the matrimonial domicil in reference to which the parties may have been supposed to enter into the bonds of marriage.[7]

A further judgment which shows a similar trend is that of DENNING LJ in *Kenward v Kenward*,[8] where he affirmed, with no ambiguity, that the "substantial validity" of a marriage contracted between persons domiciled in different countries is governed by the law of the country where they intend to live and on the basis of which they have agreed to marry.

More recently, in *Radwan v Radwan (No 2)*[9] CUMMING–BRUCE J, after a careful review of the authorities, held that capacity to contract a polygamous marriage is governed by the law of the intended matrimonial home,[10] a conclusion of some significance, for the wife was domiciled in England whilst the husband's domicil and the law of the intended matrimonial home was Egyptian. However, he did not maintain that the matrimonial home view provides the universal test, for he said that "Nothing in this judgment bears upon the capacity of minors, the law of affinity, or the effect of bigamy upon capacity to enter into a monogamous marriage."[11]

Support for an approach at least similar to the intended matrimonial home test has been voiced most recently in two decisions more directly concerned with the recognition of foreign decrees. In *Vervaeke v Smith*[12] where the main issue was the recognition of a foreign nullity decree relating to a sham marriage, Lord SIMON of Glaisdale gave support to a choice of law rule which amounted to applying the law of the country with which the marriage has the most real and substantial connection.[13] Similar support is found for such an approach in the judgment of Lincoln J, at first instance, in *Lawrence v Lawrence*,[14] a decision on the effect of the recognition of a foreign divorce

5 [1948] P 100, [1948] 1 All ER 56. See also a similar statement by BUCKNILL LJ in *Casey v Casey* [1949] P 420 at 429, 430, [1949] 2 All ER 110 at 115, 116.
6 Ie the effect on the marriage of the impotence and wilful refusal of one of the parties, see infra, pp 648–652.
7 [1948] P 100 at 114, and see BUCKNILL LJ, at pp 121–122. In *Ponticelli v Ponticelli* [1958] P 204 at 214, [1958] 1 All ER 357 at 362, SACHS J assumed that the personal capacity of a spouse is governed by "the lex domicilii which normally coincides with the law pertaining to the country of the husband's domicil at the time of the marriage".
8 [1951] P 124 at 144–146, [1950] 2 All ER 297 at 309–311; see also *Bliersbach v McEwen* 1959 SC 43 at 55.
9 [1973] Fam 35, [1972] 3 All ER 1026, infra, p 617.
10 The whole question of capacity to enter a polygamous marriage is considered in more detail, infra, pp 617 et seq.
11 [1973] Fam 35 at 54. For discussion of whether different rules should apply to different forms of incapacity, see infra, pp 600–601.
12 [1983] 1 AC 145, infra, p 677.
13 Ibid, at 166.
14 [1985] Fam 106 at 112–115. The Court of Appeal did not think that the case raised general issues relating to the law governing capacity to marry.

on capacity to remarry,[15] but which also provides a rare example of a case where the dual domicil test would mean that the marriage was void, whilst the application of the intended matrimonial home/real and substantial connection test had the result that the marriage was valid.[16] Although both judges formulated their real and substantial connection test as an application of the "intended matrimonial domicil" doctrine, it is more convenient to consider a real and substantial connection test separately and more fully below.[17]

Support for the dual domicil theory We must now turn to those decisions which can be said to support the dual domicil theory, and which, it is submitted, are of greater weight than those cited in favour of the opposite theory.[18] There was clear reliance on the dual domicil theory in *Re Paine*:[19]

An English testratrix left a sum of money on trust for her daughter, W, for life, and, if she died leaving any child or children surviving, then on trust for her absolutely.

W was a British subject domiciled in England. In 1875 she travelled to Germany and married H, her deceased sister's husband, a German subject. H had lived in England for some time shortly before the marriage,[1] and he and his wife continued to live there until their respective deaths. H died in 1919, W died some twenty years later. One daughter of the marriage survived W.

In these circumstances the legacy to W would not become absolute unless the surviving daughter was her legitimate child, for the rule then was that a reference in a will to a "child" meant a legitimate child only, unless a different intention could be determined from the context.[2] Whether the daughter was legitimate depended on whether the marriage in 1875 was valid. At that time a marriage between a woman and her deceased sister's husband was prohibited by English law, but allowed by German law. BENNETT J adopted the dual domicil doctrine and held the marriage to be void because of the incapacity attaching to W under the law of her pre-marriage domicil. However, the result was exactly what it would have been had he applied the doctrine of the intended matrimonial home.[3] Since England was the country where the wife was domiciled, where the man was resident before the marriage, where they intended to reside together and where in fact they resided throughout their married lives, the decision that English law must prevail could scarcely have been different.

A later case, which raised a question of capacity in the narrow sense of the term, is *Pugh v Pugh*,[4] where the facts were these:

A British officer, domiciled in England but stationed in Austria, married

15 Infra, pp 603–605.
16 [1985] Fam 106 at 112.
17 Infra, pp 601–602.
18 See *Lawrence v Lawrence* [1985] Fam 106 at 122.
19 [1940] Ch 46. This decision is at first sight difficult to reconcile with that of ROMER J in *Re Bischoffsheim* [1948] Ch 79, [1947] 2 All ER 830, infra, pp 750–751, where, however, the question of the legitimacy of the children was held not to depend on the validity of their parent's marriage.
1 See the facts as reported in (1940) 161 LT 266 at 267.
2 See now the Family Law Reform Act 1987, s 19.
3 *Radwan v Radwan (No 2)* [1973] Fam 35 at 50.
4 [1951] P 482, [1951] 2 All ER 680; cf *Vida v Vida* (1961) 105 Sol Jo 913; and see North, *Private International Law of Matrimonial Causes*, p 120; (1980) I Hague Recueil 9, 57–69.

a Hungarian girl in Austria in 1946. The girl, whose domicil of origin was Hungarian, had gone to Austria with her parents to escape from the Russian advance. She was only fifteen years of age and therefore, if her capacity had been governed by English domestic law, the marriage would undoubtedly have been rendered void by the Age of Marriage Act 1929 which prohibited a marriage "between persons either of whom is under the age of sixteen".[5] By Austrian law the marriage was valid, and by Hungarian law it had become valid in that it had not been avoided before she had attained the age of seventeen.

The wife submitted that the marriage was void for want of capacity, first because the husband was a British subject with an English domicil and therefore bound by the 1929 Act; secondly, and alternatively, because the essential validity of the marriage was determinable by English law as being either the law of the husband's domicil or the law of the country of the proposed matrimonial home. PEARCE J granted a decree of nullity, holding that the wife was entitled to succeed on both submissions. The 1929 Act, he said, was intended to affect "all persons domiciled in the United Kingdom wherever the marriage might be celebrated".[6] He also agreed with the second submission, "since by the law of the husband's domicil it was a marriage into which he could not lawfully enter".[7] This passage, coupled with the citation of *Re Paine*,[8] undoubtedly suggests that the judge applied English law as being the law of the husband's domicil before marriage, though the fact remains that the decision is compatible with the doctrine of the intended matrimonial domicil.

More recently, the dual domicil theory has been approved expressly, though again in circumstances where a similar result would have been achieved by the intended matrimonial home test.[9] However, a more significant decision is that of Sir JOCELYN SIMON P in *Padolecchia v Padolecchia*.[10] The facts were as follows:

The husband, at all times domiciled in Italy, married there in 1953. He was later granted a divorce decree, by proxy, by a Mexican court, which decree would not be recognised in Italy. He went to live in Denmark and, on a one day visit to England in 1964, he "married" the respondent who was resident and domiciled in Denmark. They both returned to Denmark to live and then the husband petitioned the English court for a decree of nullity on the ground that he was already married when he "married" the respondent.

Having decided that the court had jurisdiction,[11] Sir JOCELYN SIMON P had to determine by what law to test the petitioner's capacity to marry the respondent.[12] There was no doubt that, by Italian law, the law of his domicil,

---

5 See now the Marriage Act 1949, s 2.
6 [1951] P 482 at 493, [1951] 2 All ER 680 at 687.
7 [1951] P 482 at 494, [1951] 2 All ER 680 at 688.
8 Supra, p 593.
9 Eg *R v Brentwood Superintendent Registrar of Marriages, ex p Arias* [1968] 2 QB 956, [1968] 3 All ER 279; *Crickmay v Crickmay* (1967) 60 DLR (2d) 734.
10 [1968] P 314, [1967] 3 All ER 863; and see *Szechter v Szechter* [1971] P 286 at 295.
11 This aspect of the case is considered infra, p 634.
12 Had the issue been classified as one concerned with the recognition of foreign divorces the outcome would have been the same, as the petitioner was domiciled at all material times in Italy, by whose law the Mexican decree was not recognised: [1968] P 314 at 338. It also seems most unlikely that the Mexican decree would be recognised under the Family Law Act 1986, infra, pp 657 et seq.

the divorce would not be recognised and hence that he had no capacity to marry. The position was probably the same under Danish law, though the evidence of Danish law was not wholly satisfactory. Had the case turned on Danish law, which would seem certain to be classed as the law of the intended matrimonial home, then further investigation of that law would have been necessary. However, the judge had no doubts that the capacity of the petitioner had to be referred to Italian law, the law of his domicil. His examination of the position under other possibly relevant laws seems to have been on the hypothesis that one of them might have been considered to be the law of the domicil.[13]

This decision would seem to provide a clear and explicit authority for the dual domicil theory.[14] Further support for this view may be drawn from two statutory provisions.[15] The first is the Marriage (Enabling) Act 1960 which modified the former rules of affinity. It has long been the rule that, after the death of his wife, a man may marry her sister, aunt or niece; and may also marry the wife of his brother, uncle or nephew after her husband is dead. The Act of 1960 eliminated the condition that the wife, brother, uncle or nephew must be dead at the time of the proposed marriage.[16] Thus, for example, it is now permissible for a man to marry the sister of his divorced wife while the latter is still alive. Having made this change in English internal law, the Act lays down a rule for the choice of law by providing that no such marriage shall be valid "if either party to it is at the time of the marriage domiciled in a country outside Great Britain, and under the law of that country there cannot be a valid marriage between the parties".[17] Despite the argument that this choice of law provision was not discussed in Parliament,[18] it does provide a clear statutory reference to the dual domicil theory, though in admittedly limited circumstances.[19]

The second statutory provision is section 11(d) of the Matrimonial Causes Act 1973 which stipulates that a marriage celebrated abroad is void if it is an actually or potentially polygamous marriage and either spouse was domiciled in England at the time of the marriage.[20]

(c) FURTHER ISSUES

It is now necessary to consider a number of further issues related to the operation of either the dual domicil or the intended matrimonial home approaches.

(i) The rule in *Sottomayer v De Barros (No 2)*[1]

The rule in *Sottomayer v De Barros (No 2)*[2] provides what may appear to be

---

13 Further support for the approach in this case may be drawn from *Shaw v Gould* (1868) LR 3 HL 55; *Schwebel v Ungar* (1963) 42 DLR (2d) 622; (1964) 48 DLR (2d) 644, supra, pp 54–55; Lysyk (1965) 43 Can BR 363, 368–370; and see *Ungar v Ungar* [1967] 2 NSWR 618.
14 See also National Insurance Decision No R (G) 3/75.
15 The Marriage (Scotland) Act 1977, ss 1(1), 2(1), specifically refer to persons domiciled in Scotland in relation to the questions of lack of age and consanguinity and affinity; and see also ss 3(5), 5(4).
16 Marriage (Enabling) Act 1960, s 1(1).
17 Ibid, s 1(3); see *Crickmay v Crickmay* (1967) 60 DLR (2d) 734.
18 See 7th edn (1965), p 288.
19 See *Radwan v Radwan (No 2)* [1973] Fam 35 at 51.
20 The provision is discussed more fully, infra, pp 618–621.
 1 See Clarkson (1990) 10 Legal Studies 80, 84 et seq.
 2 (1879) 5 PD 94; see also *Ogden v Ogden* [1908] P 46.

an exception to the two choice of law theories which have just been examined. Two related decisions need to be considered together here:

> The husband and wife were first cousins. They were presumed to be domiciled in Portugal by whose law marriage between first cousins was prohibited in the absence of a Papal dispensation. They married in England and lived together in the same house, though without consummating the marriage, for 6 years.

The Court of Appeal held[3] that the question of capacity must depend on the law of the domicil. If they were both domiciled in Portugal, the marriage would be void. This decision provides some further support for the dual domicil theory, though it is not conclusive for it appears that the parties never intended to live together as man and wife, never really had a matrimonial home and so reference to the law of Portugal as the law of the husband's domicil is compatible with the statement of the intended matrimonial home doctrine.[4]

The actual determination of the parties' domicil fell to be considered in later proceedings,[5] where it was decided that the husband was domiciled in England but the wife in Portugal. What effect, then, did this conclusion have on the validity of the marriage? If it is true to say that a marriage is invalid where either party is incapacitated by his or her personal law, the decision in this case should have been adverse to the legality of the union, but Sir JAMES HANNEN P held that it constituted a valid marriage. It must be admitted that he did not base his decision on the matrimonial residence of the parties in England, but on the fact that the law of the place of celebration was English. Impressed by the "injustice which might be caused to our own subjects if a marriage were declared invalid on the ground that it was forbidden by the law of the domicil of one of the parties",[6] he refused to give effect to the prohibition imposed on the wife by Portuguese law. The decision has never been overruled. How, then, is it to be rendered compatible with the dual domicil doctrine? The difficulty is usually surmounted by framing an exception to that doctrine. It has been formulated as follows:

> The validity of a marriage celebrated in England between persons of whom the one has an English, and the other a foreign, domicile is not affected by any incapacity which, though existing under the law of such foreign domicile, does not exist under the law of England.[7]

In other words, capacity must be tested by the law of the domicil of each party, but when one of them has an English domicil, a foreign incapacity affecting the other and unknown to English law must be utterly disregarded if the marriage takes place in England. This suggested rule has been stig-

3 *Sottomayor v De Barros* (1877) 3 PD 1.
4 Supra, p 587. It should be mentioned, however, that in the lower court the Queen's Proctor had argued, unsuccessfully, for the application of English law as that of the intended matrimonial home: (1877) 2 PD 81 at 82.
5 *Sottomayer v De Barros (No 2)* (1879) 5 PD 94.
6 (1879) 5 PD 94 at 104.
7 Dicey & Morris, pp 638–639. In addition to *Sottomayer v De Barros (No 2)* (1879) 5 PD 94, the exception is supported by dicta: *Ogden v Ogden* [1908] P 46 at 74–77; *Chetti v Chetti* [1909] P 67 at 81–88; *Vervaeke v Smith* [1981] Fam 77 at 122 (the point was not referred to in the House of Lords: [1981] 1 AC 145); and see *R v Brentwood Superintendent Registrar of Marriages, ex p Arias* [1968] 2 QB 956 at 968–969; see also *MacDougal v Chitnavis* 1937 SC 390; cf Anton, pp 431–432. The exception can also be relied on to justify the decision in *Perrini v Perrini* [1979] Fam 84, [1979] 2 All ER 323.

matised as "anomalous"[8] and as "unworthy of a place in a respectable system of the conflict of laws".[9] The rule has been subject to cogent criticism from the Law Commission.[10] It is xenophobic in that it gives preference to the law of the place of celebration of the marriage if that is English, but not if it is foreign. It is likely to lead to "limping" marriages, valid in England but not in the country of the domicil of one spouse. The case for the abandonment of the rule seems clear.

The *Sottomayer* decision could, on the facts, though not on the reasoning, be regarded as supporting the intended matrimonial home theory. A better view would be to regard this decision as an inelegant exception to the dual domicil theory and, if it is to remain, one to be interpreted as restrictively as possible by confining it, for example, "to a condition imposed by the law of the domicil that a specified consent or consents should be given".[11] Even if such restrictive interpretation is not accepted, there has been a narrowing of the scope of the rule by reason of the Marriage (Enabling) Act 1960,[12] for a marriage covered by that Act is not validated if either party is domiciled in a country under whose law there cannot be a valid marriage between the parties. To apply *Sottomayer v De Barros (No 2)* other than to cases of invalidity caused through want of consents would mean that its application would depend on the particular degree of affinity in question.

(ii) The role of the law of the place of celebration[13]

How far is the law of the place of celebration relevant to capacity to marry? This issue has arisen in two contexts. The first is whether there are issues as to essential validity which should be referred exclusively to the law of the place of celebration. Some support for such an approach is to be found in the speech of Lord SIMON of Glaisdale in *Vervaeke v Smith*[14] where he suggested that matters of "quintessential validity", such as whether, as in the case before him, a sham marriage could constitute a marriage at all, might be referred to the law of the place of celebration. It seems hard to justify such an approach in the case of matters going to the fundamental nature of marriage, but not in the case of other issues of essential validity, especially as the parties may have had only a limited connection with the place of celebration.[15] Furthermore, the authorities on which the judge relied either ante-date the distinction which has been maintained since the mid nineteenth century between form and essential validity[16] or were primarily concerned with formal validity.[17]

The second context in which the application of the law of the place of celebration has arisen is in deciding whether the rules of that law relating to essential validity must be satisfied in addition to those of the parties' personal

8 *Radwan v Radwan (No 2)* [1973] Fam 35 at 50.
9 Falconbridge, *Conflict of Laws*, 711.
10 Law Commission Working Paper No 89 (1985), para 3.17; and see paras 3.45–3.48. See also Law Com No 165 (1987), paras 2.7–2.8, 2.15.
11 As can be implied from *Miller v Teale* (1954) 92 CLR 406 at 414; and see Nygh, p 358.
12 Supra, p 595.
13 Clarkson (1990) 10 Legal Studies 80, 81–84.
14 [1983] 1 AC 145 at 165–166.
15 For a detailed rejection of the law of the place of celebration as the law generally to be applied to issues of essential validity, see Law Commission Working Paper No 89 (1985), paras 3.21–3.23.
16 *Warrender v Warrender* (1835) 2 Cl & Fin 488 at 530.
17 *Berthiaume v Dastous* [1930] AC 79 at 83.

law.[18] Clear authority for the rejection of any reference to the law of the place of celebration is found in *In the Will of Swan*.[19] There have, in more recent years, been dicta[20] and the decision in *Breen v Breen*[21] which have indicated that the law of the place of celebration is relevant and should be considered in addition to the personal law, so that a marriage will be regarded as invalid if the parties lack capacity by the law of the place of celebration, even though they are capable under their personal law.

In *Breen v Breen*,[22] the parties were at all relevant times domiciled in England. They married in Ireland during the lifetime of the husband's former wife, that first marriage having been dissolved by an English court. The second wife petitioned for a decree of nullity on the grounds that the divorce decree would not be recognised in Ireland and that, therefore, her "husband" lacked capacity to marry by Irish law. KARMINSKI J concluded, after examination of the Constitution of Ireland, that since the English divorce decree would be recognised in Ireland the second marriage was valid. However the only connection with Ireland that this marriage had was that it was celebrated there, yet reference was made to Irish law on an issue of capacity. One can conclude that as an authority for referring issues of capacity to the law of the place of celebration, this case is "a sorry and inarticulate precedent [which] should be considered insufficient to establish a rule of very doubtful merit".[1]

While it is true that the law of the place of celebration cannot always be disregarded,[2] a distinction should be drawn between cases where the law of the place of celebration is that of the forum and other cases. An English registrar, for instance, cannot be required to sanction a marriage if it would be void for incapacity by English law and an English court is unlikely, for policy reasons, to uphold such a marriage.[3] It is probably true to say that all marriages celebrated in England must comply with English law, not only as to formal validity but also as to matters of essential validity.[4]

On the other hand, incapacity by the law of a foreign place of celebration should be ignored, as is illustrated by the Canadian decision in *Reed v Reed*:[5]

> The husband and wife were first cousins domiciled in British Columbia. The wife was aged 18 and could not marry in British Columbia without parental consent which was refused. As a consequence the parties were married in the State of Washington where all the necessary formal requirements were satisfied, but under whose law first cousins lacked capacity to marry.

18 Bradshaw (1986) 15 Anglo-Am LR 112; and see Law Com No 165 (1987), para 2.6.
19 (1871) 2 VR (IE & M) 47, supra, pp 591–592.
20 Eg *Lendrum v Chakravarti* 1929 SLT 96 at 103. It is not clear why reference was made in *Schwebel v Ungar* (1963) 42 DLR (2d) 622 at 633–634 to the proposition that the law of the place of celebration might be relevant to capacity to marry without applying it. In that case an incapacity did exist by the law of the place of celebration, which was also the law of the forum, but the marriage in question was upheld: see Lysyk (1965) 43 Can BR 363, 369–370.
21 [1964] P 144; Unger (1961) 24 MLR 784.
22 [1964] P 144.
1 Unger (1961) 24 MLR 784, 787.
2 And see the Marriage (Scotland) Act 1977, s 2(3)(a).
3 Support might be inferred from *Padolecchia v Padolecchia* [1968] P 314 at 335; *Vervaeke v Smith* [1983] 1 AC 145 at 152; and also from *Pugh v Pugh* [1951] P 482 at 491–492.
4 The Marriage (Scotland) Act 1977, ss 1(2), 2(1)(a) provide expressly that a marriage celebrated in Scotland is void if the requirements as to age or consanguinity and affinity are not satisfied.
5 (1969) 6 DLR (3d) 617.

The wife petitioned, unsuccessfully, in British Columbia for a nullity decree. Lack of parental consent was characterised as an issue of form to be referred to the law of the place of celebration, Washington, by which law the marriage was formally valid. Consanguinity was a matter of capacity to be referred to the law of the domicil, British Columbia, by which law the parties were capable. The court declined to apply the law of the place of celebration to the issue of capacity.

(iii) Public policy

Where a foreign domiciliary law governs the capacity of the parties to a marriage, it will not be recognised if it is repugnant to public policy.[6] The court has a discretionary power to repudiate a capacity or an incapacity on the ground that to give effect to it would be unconscionable.[7] This discretion, however, is to be exercised sparingly.[8] Thus, so far as repudiation of capacity is concerned, in *Cheni v Cheni*,[9] a case which is considered later in another context,[10] it was argued that a marriage celebrated in Cairo between an uncle and a niece, both domiciled in Egypt, was incestuous by the general consent of Christendom or at least by the general consent of civilised nations. Sir JOCELYN SIMON P disagreed. He insisted that a reasonable tolerance must be shown in applying the doctrine of public policy.[11] Marriages between uncle and niece were accepted by general Jewish law and by many Lutheran churches, and were not totally condemned even by the Catholic Church. It would, therefore, be unjustifiable to stigmatise as unconscionable a capacity acceptable "to many peoples of deep religious convictions, lofty ethical standards and high civilisation".[12]

It does seem clear, however, that the courts would be prepared, albeit with caution, to deny recognition to a wide variety of incapacities imposed by the law of the domicil such as incapacity to marry at all,[13] or inability to marry other than according to the tenets of a particular faith,[14] or incapacity to marry outside one's caste[15] or race.[16]

(iv) Renvoi

There is some authority that a reference to the personal law as governing issues of capacity should include a reference to its rules of private inter-

---

6 There is also a minor statutory restriction, namely that imposed on descendants of George II by the Royal Marriages Act 1772; see Dicey & Morris, pp 634–636; MacNeill (1922) 38 LQR 74; Parry (1956) 5 ICLQ 61.
7 *Cheni v Cheni* [1965] P 85 at 98, [1962] 3 All ER 873 at 882.
8 *Vervaeke v Smith* [1983] 1 AC 145 at 164.
9 Supra.
10 Infra, p 613.
11 And in *Mohamed v Knott* [1969] 1 QB 1, [1968] 2 All ER 563, infra, p 625, the validity of the foreign marriage of a 13-year-old Nigerian girl was upheld.
12 [1965] P 85 at 99.
13 Eg because the person is a monk or a nun: *Sottomayer v De Barros (No 2)* (1879) 5 PD 94 at 104.
14 Cf *Gray (orse Formosa) v Formosa* [1963] P 259, [1962] 3 All ER 419; *Lepre v Lepre* [1965] P 52; and see *Papadopoulos v Papadopoulos* [1930] P 55 at 64; cf *Corbett v Corbett* [1957] 1 All ER 621 where incapacity to marry outside the Jewish faith was recognised.
15 *Chetti v Chetti* [1909] P 67.
16 *Sottomayer v De Barros (No 2)*, supra, at 104; cf *Conlon v Mohamed* [1989] ILRM 523.

national law, ie that the doctrine of renvoi applies in this context. In *R v Brentwood Superintendent Registrar of Marriages, ex p Arias*[17] the facts were these:

> The husband, an Italian national domiciled in Switzerland, was married to a Swiss wife. He obtained a divorce in Switzerland. His wife remarried. He wished to remarry in England, but his Swiss divorce was not recognised in Italy.

The court upheld the Registrar's objections to the marriage. The husband's capacity to marry was referred to the law of Switzerland, his ante-nuptial domicil and the intended matrimonial home. It was agreed on the facts that Swiss law would refer the issue of his capacity to Italian law. This seems clearly to be an application of the doctrine of renvoi, though the matter is not discussed by the court; and it had the consequence that the husband was incapable of remarrying even in the country of his domicil and not-withstanding the remarriage in the same country of his first wife.[18]

(v) Should the same rule apply to all issues of capacity?

The discussion of the law governing capacity to marry has, so far, proceeded on the assumption that all incapacitating factors give rise to the same problems and are susceptible of the same solution in choice of law terms. Whilst it is true that, on the balance of the authorities, the ante-nuptial domiciliary law determines issues of capacity[19] such as consanguinity and affinity,[20] lack of age,[1] and, indeed, bigamy,[2] it has been suggested that:

> It is an over-simplification of the common law to assume that the same test for purposes of choice of law applies to every kind of incapacity—non age, affinity, prohibition of monogamous contract by virtue of an existing spouse, and capacity for polygamy. Different public and social factors are relevant to each of these types of incapacity.[3]

There is no doubt that there are issues relating to capacity which are governed by special rules. For example, the rules governing capacity to marry following

---

17 [1968] 2 QB 956; and see the Marriage (Scotland) Act 1977, s 3(5).
18 The Law Commission has supported the application of renvoi to capacity to marry; see Working Paper No 89 (1985), para 3.39, Law Com No 165 (1987), para 2.6; and so has the Irish Law Reform Commission: LRC 19–1985, p 153. The decision in the *Brentwood Case* would now be different by reason of the Family Law Act 1986, s 50, infra, pp 603–605.
19 The questions whether consent and physical incapacities, such as impotence or wilful refusal to consummate, are to be regarded as matters of essential validity governed by the law of the domicil are considered, infra, pp 644 et seq, as these issues will tend normally to arise in the context of nullity petitions.
20 Eg *Mette v Mette* (1859) 1 Sw & Tr 416; *Brook v Brook* (1861) 9 HL Cas 193; *Sottomayer v De Barros* (1877) 3 PD 1; *Re Paine* [1940] Ch 46. The effect of the Marriage (Enabling) Act 1960, s 1(3) has already been considered supra, p 595.
1 *Pugh v Pugh* [1951] P 482.
2 *Padolecchia v Padolecchia* [1968] P 314, [1967] 3 All ER 863.
3 *Radwan v Radwan (No 2)* [1973] Fam 35 at 51; and see Jaffey (1978) 41 MLR 38; Downes (1986) 35 ICLQ 170.

a divorce are now governed by specific statutory provisions,[4] and, as the passage just quoted illustrates, there is some authority for saying that, even though the dual domicil test applies to many forms of incapacity, the intended matrimonial home test ought to apply to capacity to enter a polygamous marriage.[5] It has also been suggested that different rules should apply to matters of "quintessential validity" as compared with other issues of essential validity.[6]

The virtue of a situation in which different choice of law rules may be applied to different issues of essential validity is that it enables the courts to retain the flexibility necessary to reach just results in difficult cases. It is hard to argue against a desire for justice but, in fact, in that way lies uncertainty, anarchy and ultimately injustice. Whilst a limited number of exceptions from a general choice of law rule may be justifiable, it is not acceptable to permit the judge to decide which rule to apply essentially by reference to the factual circumstances of a particular case.[7] It is suggested, for example, that there is no justification for applying the intended matrimonial home test to determine whether a man may marry polygamously[8] but the dual domicil test to determine whether he may marry his niece[9]—especially if she is to be his second wife! There would appear to be no social or policy factors justifying a different approach to the two types of case.

(d) ALTERNATIVE APPROACHES

It has been assumed so far that, in determining the general choice of law rule to select the law to govern the essential validity of marriage, the choice lies between the dual domicil or the intended matrimonial home approaches. Whilst it is true that the case law overwhelmingly supports one or other of these approaches, consideration has been given in recent years to other ways of determining the applicable law, some of which will be examined here.

(i) Real and substantial connection[10]

In *Vervaeke v Smith*,[11] Lord SIMON of Glaisdale suggested that the "quintessential validity" of a marriage, this being in the case before him the validity of a "sham" marriage, should be governed by the law of the country "with which the marriage has the most real and substantial connection". A similar test was applied by LINCOLN J in *Lawrence v Lawrence*[12] to the issue of capacity to marry after a foreign divorce.[13] This approach has received some

---

4 Family Law Act 1986, s 50, infra, pp 603–605. The courts have also been prepared to accept the need for a special rule as to capacity in this context, see *Lawrence v Lawrence* [1985] Fam 106 at 114–115, 134.
5 Discussed more fully, infra, pp 617–621.
6 *Vervaeke v Smith* [1983] 1 AC 145 at 165–166.
7 Sykes and Pryles, p 428.
8 *Radwan v Radwan (No 2)* [1973] Fam 35, [1972] 3 All ER 1026.
9 Eg *Cheni v Cheni* [1965] P 85, [1962] 3 All ER 873.
10 See supra, pp 592–593.
11 [1983] 1 AC 145 at 165–166.
12 [1985] Fam 106 at 112–115; though no specific support for this approach is to be found in the judgments in the Court of Appeal. See also *Entry Clearance Officer, Dhaka v Ranu Begum* [1986] Imm AR 461 at 464–465, 466–467; *R v Immigration Appeal Tribunal, ex p Rafika Bibi* [1989] Imm AR 1.
13 Infra, pp 603–605.

academic support in the past[14] and these two decisions have prompted further support.[15] It has, however, been vigorously rejected by the Law Commission:

> It is an inherently vague and unpredictable test which would introduce an unacceptable degree of uncertainty into the law. It is a test which is difficult to apply other than through the courtroom process and it is therefore unsuitable in an area where the law's function is essentially prospective, ie a yardstick for future planning.[16]

It does seem to be a retrograde step to introduce into the field of validity of marriage a test which, because of its inherent uncertainty, was abandoned in the field of divorce recognition in 1971.[17] It also seems unworkable where there is a real and substantial connection with more than one country.[18]

(ii) Alternative reference

A criticism that can be advanced against the dual domicil approach is that it favours invalidity, because the marriage will be invalid if either party lacks capacity by their ante-nuptial domiciliary law. To counter this disadvantage, and in order to differentiate between rules designed to protect the public interest and those designed to protect the parties, it has been suggested[19] that, in cases other than those such as non-age, impotence or wilful refusal, where the purpose of the rule is to protect the parties, the marriage should be regarded as valid if either the dual domicil or the intended matrimonial home tests is satisfied. This embodies a clear policy in favour of upholding the validity of marriages, and this is a policy which has, in the present context, attracted some judicial support.[20] There are, however, major disadvantages with such an alternative reference approach which led to its rejection by the Law Commission.[21] Not only does it suffer from many of the disadvantages of the intended matrimonial home test, it may also require the substantive marriage laws of three different legal systems to be investigated. Furthermore, it does seem to depend on a distinction being made between grounds of invalidity on the basis of some form of assessment of the purpose of individual invalidating rules, thus introducing into the field of family law many of the problems of American "interest analysis".[22] Finally, it seems unwarranted to give such prominence to a policy in favour of the upholding of marriages that it becomes the fundamental basis of the choice of law rule.

---

14 Sykes suggested that essential validity should be governed by the proper law of the contract to marry, ie the law of that country with which the contract has the most real connection: (1955) 4 ICLQ 159, 168.
15 Fentiman [1985] CLJ 256; Smart (1985) 14 Anglo-American LR 225; Fentiman (1986) 6 OJLS 353, 354–360.
16 Working Paper No 89 (1985), para 3.20. This approach (and the next two examined here) were not discussed further in Law Com No 165 (1987).
17 By the recognition of Divorces and Legal Separations Act 1971, abrogating the decision in *Indyka v Indyka* [1969] 1 AC 33, [1967] 2 All ER 689; see now the Family Law Act 1986, Part II, infra, pp 657 et seq.
18 *R v Immigration Appeal Tribunal, ex p Rafika Bibi* [1989] Imm AR 1 at 4–5.
19 Primarily by Jaffey (1978) 41 MLR 38; (1982) 2 OJLS 368; and see Royal Commission on Marriage and Divorce (1956), Cmd 9678, para 891.
20 *Lawrence v Lawrence* [1985] Fam 106 at 115, 134; and see *Minister of Employment and Immigration v Narwal* (1990) 26 RFL (3d) 95.
21 Working Paper No 89 (1985), para 3.27.
22 See North (1980) I Hague Recueil 9.

(iii) Elective dual domicil test

Concern for upholding the validity of a marriage has led to the suggestion[1] that, instead of declaring a marriage invalid if either party lacks capacity under his or her ante-nuptial domiciliary law, the marriage should be valid if it is so regarded under either law. Where, however, the issue arises prior to the celebration of the marriage, as where a registrar refuses a licence, it is suggested that the orthodox dual domicil test be applied.[2] This approach also was provisionally rejected by the Law Commission[3] for much the same reasons as the alternative reference test was rejected. It does not appear justified to prefer the rules of one party's domiciliary law to those of the other—to do so could lead to evasion and limping marriages. This approach would, again, give undue prominence to a domestic policy in favour of upholding the validity of marriages.

(e) CAPACITY AND RECOGNITION OF FOREIGN DIVORCES OR ANNULMENTS

(i) Effect of valid divorce or annulment on capacity to remarry[4]

An allegation of incapacity to marry on the grounds of bigamy involves most frequently in private international law a question of the recognition of a foreign divorce or annulment. In such a case the marriage will be bigamous only if the English courts decline to recognise the foreign divorce or annulment. Whilst the whole general question of the rules for the recognition of foreign divorces or annulments is considered later,[5] it is necessary at this point to examine the effect of such recognition on capacity to re-marry.

The first problem to consider, taking the case of a foreign divorce, is that which arises where the divorced spouse is domiciled in one foreign country and is divorced in another, and the divorce is recognised in England but not in the country of the domicil. Here there is a conflict of private international law rules—a problem of the "incidental question".[6] If we ask whether the spouse has capacity to remarry, reference to the law of his domicil will reveal he is already married. If we ask whether he is single because validly divorced, our divorce recognition rules will reveal that he is single, with the corollary that he ought to be free to remarry.

Until recently the resolution of this conflict necessitated separate examination of the effects of recognising foreign divorces and annulments and of whether the remarriage was in the United Kingdom or abroad. If the foreign divorce was recognised and the marriage was in the United Kingdom, any incapacity under the law of the domicil was, by statute, to be ignored.[7] If the remarriage was abroad the statute was silent and it was a matter of doubt as to whether recognition of the divorce carried with it capacity to remarry.[8] However, in 1985 in *Lawrence v Lawrence*[9] the Court of Appeal upheld the

---

1 Hartley (1972) 35 MLR 571, 576–578.
2 Ibid, at p 578.
3 Working Paper No 89 (1985), para 3.38.
4 See Law Com No 137; Scot Law Com No 88 (1984), paras 2.35, 6.49–6.60.
5 Infra, pp 655 et seq.
6 Supra, pp 53–57.
7 Recognition of Divorces and Legal Separations Act 1971, s 7; reversing *R v Brentwood Superintendent Registrar of Marriages, ex p Arias* [1968] 2 QB 956, [1968] 3 All ER 279.
8 See Law Com No 137; Scot Law Com No 88 (1984), para 6.52.
9 [1985] Fam 106. The decision attracted much comment, see: Carter (1985) 101 LQR 496, (1986) 57 BYBIL 441, Collier [1985] CLJ 378; Jaffey (1985) 48 MLR 465; Downes (1986) 35 ICLQ 170; Lipstein (1986) 35 ICLQ 178.

validity of a marriage abroad, following a divorce in Nevada, which was recognised in this country but not in Brazil, the country of the remarrying wife's domicil.[10] Unanimous in their conclusion in favour of the validity of the second marriage, the judge at first instance and the members of the Court of Appeal reached it by different routes. One was to apply the law of the country with which the marriage had the most real and substantial connection, which was held to be England as the intended matrimonial home (LINCOLN J[11] and Sir David CAIRNS[12]). Another was that recognition of the divorce carried with it the right to remarry, even abroad, ie a judicial extension of the statutory rule for United Kingdom marriages to foreign marriages (ACKNER LJ[13] and Sir David CAIRNS[14]); The third was that, if a foreign divorce is recognised on the basis that it was obtained in the country of the domicil, determined in the foreign rather than the English sense,[15] then this domiciliary law (here Nevada) and not that of the domicil determined by our law (Brazil) governed the issue of capacity to remarry (PURCHAS LJ[16]).

In the case of a foreign annulment followed by the remarriage of one of the former spouses, there is authority that, if the foreign annulment is recognised in England, a remarriage in England will be regarded as valid even though the annulment is not recognised in the country of that spouse's domicil.[17] This conclusion mirrored for nullity the then current statutory rule in divorce; and there is no direct authority on the validity of a remarriage abroad. Finally, there are the cases of a divorce or nullity decree granted in England and followed by a marriage in England or elsewhere. Would a party to such a decree be regarded as incapable of marrying if the decree was not recognised in the country of his domicil? Despite some English authority to the contrary,[18] it seems only right that an English court should regard an English divorce, for example, as permitting a divorced spouse to remarry and not to be in a less advantageous position than that of a person whose foreign divorce is recognised here.

This confused state of affairs was examined by the Law Commission in 1984[19] with the conclusion that the same rule should apply to divorces and annulments, whether granted here or obtained elsewhere and recognised here, and whether followed by a marriage in the United Kingdom or abroad. In all cases the fact that the divorce or annulment was not recognised in the country of the domicil or anywhere else should not affect the validity of a later marriage; and this proposal is now embodied in section 50 of the Family Law Act 1986:

Where, in any part of the United Kingdom—
(a) a divorce or annulment has been granted by a court of civil jurisdiction, or

10   It is not easy to reconcile this conclusion with the decision of the House of Lords in *Shaw v Gould* (1868) LR 3 HL 55, infra, pp 747–750.
11   [1985] Fam 106 at 114–115; and see supra, pp 601–602.
12   Ibid, at 134.
13   Ibid, at 124–125.
14   Ibid, at 134–135.
15   See Family Law Act 1986, s 46(1), (5), infra, pp 658–659.
16   [1985] Fam 106 at 131–134. This approach is strongly, and rightly, criticised by Carter (1985) 101 LQR 496, 500–501; Jaffey (1985) 48 MLR 465, 468–469.
17   *Perrini v Perrini* [1979] Fam 84, [1979] 2 All ER 323.
18   *Breen v Breen* [1964] P 144, [1961] 3 All ER 225, supra, p 598, where following a divorce in England reference was nevertheless made to Irish law as that of the place of celebration to determine capacity to remarry.
19   Law Com No 137, Scot Law Com No 88 (1984), paras 6.49–6.60.

(b) the validity of a divorce or annulment is recognised by virtue of this Part,[20] the fact that the divorce or annulment would not be recognised elsewhere shall not preclude either party to the marriage from re-marrying in that part of the United Kingdom or cause the remarriage of either party (wherever the re-marriage takes place) to be treated as invalid in that part.

The effect of this provision is to provide one clear straightforward rule embodying a principle which may well already be the law.[21]

(ii) Effect on capacity to marry of non-recognition of a divorce or annulment

Section 50 of the 1986 Act only applies where a foreign divorce or annulment is recognised in England. There can be a similarly difficult, but converse, case where a foreign divorce or annulment is recognised by the law of the domicil, or the country of the intended matrimonial home at the time of the remarriage, but not in England. There is Canadian authority in *Schwebel v Ungar*[1] for resolving this incidental question in a converse way to that to be found in section 50, ie by regarding the main question as that of capacity to marry, holding the spouse capable notwithstanding the non-recognition of the divorce under the forum's divorce recognition rules. The Law Commission examined this problem but concluded that no legislative provision should be made for it.[2] The Commission's reasons are essentially practical ones—there is no point in introducing legislation to resolve a problem unlikely to arise in real life. In the case of a re-marriage in this country, conflict between the recognition and capacity rules is not likely to arise given that capacity by English law will be required.[3] In the case of re-marriage abroad, there is the further factor that our recognition rules are so broad that conflict with the law governing capacity is unlikely, except where recognition is denied in England on grounds of public policy. In such a case recognition of the later re-marriage might well be justified.

(iii) Prohibitions against remarriage

There is one final problem which relates to foreign divorces and capacity to marry. Some foreign divorce decrees though purporting to dissolve the marriage provide restrictions or prohibitions on remarriage by one or both of the parties. Restrictions of this kind appear to fall roughly into two classes, namely, those that are directed against the guilty party and those that postpone the date at which either party may contract a further marriage.[4]

To take the latter class first, it may be said that a decree which forbids the parties to remarry before a certain period has elapsed has not finally and conclusively restored the parties to the status of celibacy. It is somewhat analogous to the English decree nisi. The dissolution of the marriage occurs only on the lapse of the specified period, not at the issue of the decree nisi.

---

20 Infra, pp 655 et seq.
21 See, eg Lipstein (1986) 35 ICLQ 178; *cf Lawrence v Lawrence* [1985] Fam 106 at 131–132 per PURCHAS LJ; Carter (1986) 57 BYBIL 441, 444.
1 (1963) 42 DLR (2d) 622; affd (1964) 48 DLR (2d) 644, supra, pp 54–55.
2 Law Com No 137; Scot Law Com No 88 (1984), para 6.60; cf Jaffey (1985) 48 MLR 465, 469; Briggs (1989) 9 OJLS 251, 258.
3 Supra, pp 597–599.
4 On this subject see M Mann (1952) 42 *Transactions of the Grotius Society* 133, 138–141; Hartley (1967) 16 ICLQ 680, 694–699.

This view was adopted for English law in *Warter v Warter*,[5] where the parties, who had been divorced in Calcutta, were prohibited by the Indian law of their domicil from marrying again before six months. It was held that a marriage in England contracted by the wife within six months with a domiciled Englishman was invalid.[6]

On the other hand, a decree which finally dissolves the marriage, but which by way, presumably, of punishment, imposes a restriction on the guilty party, is regarded by English law as imposing a penalty. We have already seen that the penal laws of foreign countries may be disregarded in England.[7] Thus in *Scott v A-G*:[8]

> Two persons domiciled in South Africa were divorced in that country, and thereupon became subject to a rule of South African law which provided that the guilty party could not remarry as long as the other party remained unmarried. The wife, who was the guilty party, remarried in England, her former husband being still unmarried.

This second marriage was upheld by the English court on the ground that the restriction on remarriage was a penalty, and therefore inoperative out of the jurisdiction under which it was inflicted.[9] The correctness of this decision would seem, indeed, to rest on an even simpler reason. Since the decree had effected a complete dissolution of the marriage according to South African law, the woman, being no longer a wife, was free to acquire her own separate domicil.[10] She had in fact acquired a new domicil in England at the time of her remarriage, and therefore there was no possible ground on which her capacity to marry could be referred to South African law.[11]

4. REFORM OF GENERAL RULES

There have been various initiatives for reform of the choice of law rules relating to marriage. None has borne significant fruit. On the broader international scene, the Hague Conference on Private International Law in 1978 agreed a Convention on Celebration and Recognition of the Validity of Marriages, but few states have ratified it[12] and the United Kingdom has rejected it,[13] rightly so because the Convention rules are both unacceptable and incomplete.[14]

---

5 (1890) 15 PD 152; but see now *Boettcher v Boettcher* [1949] WN 83; *Buckle v Buckle* [1956] P 181, [1955] 3 All ER 641. See the Australian case, *Miller v Teale* (1954) 92 CLR 406; Webb (1956) 5 ICLQ 137.
6 But why was it not held valid under the exceptional rule in *Sottomayer v De Barros (No 2)* (1879) 5 PD 94, supra, pp 595–597?
7 Supra, pp 117–121.
8 (1886) 11 PD 128.
9 As explained in *Warter v Warter* (1890) 15 PD 152 at 155.
10 She would now, of course, always be free to acquire a separate domicil, supra, pp 163–165.
11 (1886) 11 PD 128 at 131; and see Wolff, p 379.
12 Though it has been accepted in Australia and implemented in the Marriage Amendment Act 1985, see Nygh, pp 345–348; Sykes and Pryles, pp 439, 444–448; Neave (1990) 4 Aus J Fam Law 190.
13 Law Com No 165 (1987), para 1.2.
14 For a range of criticisms of the Convention, see Battiffol (1977) 66 Rev crit dr int pr 451; Glenn (1977) 55 Can BR 586; Rees (1977) 25 AJCL 393; (1979) 20 Vir JIL 25; Lalive (1978) 34 Annuaire suisse de droit international 31; North (1981) 6 Dalh LJ 417, 430–433; (1990) I Hague Recueil 9, 74–81.

Closer to home, the Irish Law Reform Commission[15] had no doubt that, in the absence of effective international agreement, reform of the Irish choice of law rules was needed to eradicate uncertainty and complexity and to ensure that practical difficulties for the non-lawyers who have to apply them are avoided. In the Commission's view, this was a task requiring legislative reform and restatement. In making a wide range of recommendations, heavy reliance was placed on a Working Paper (No 89) produced in 1985 by the English and Scottish Law Commissions on the same topic.[16] This examined both the desirability of reform of particular rules and, where appropriate, what specific changes might be made. Few, if any, of the Commissions' provisional proposals were radical. They were primarily concerned to produce clarity and certainty. Confirmation that the law of the place of celebration should govern formal validity amounted to nothing new, nor did the idea that there should be some exception founded on the lines of the present common law marriage exception.[17] Again, the provisional proposals that essential validity should be governed by the dual domicil test, that renvoi should apply to the law governing both formal and essential validity and that there should be a public policy safeguard to enable a foreign law not to be applied either confirmed existing law or did little more than resolve matters of current debate.[1] More substantial were the suggestions that the rule in *Sottomayer v De Barros (No 2)*[2] be abolished and that, in determining essential validity, reference should be made in all cases to the law of the place of celebration as well as to that of the domicil.[3] There were also detailed proposals for minor reforms of the Foreign Marriage Act 1892 and its related delegated legislation.

The Irish recommendations have not been implemented and the provisional proposals in Great Britain have, with the exception of the reform of the Foreign Marriage Act 1892,[4] been abandoned.[5] The Law Commissions decided against recommending comprehensive legislation primarily because, in their view, there were no major areas "where, in practice, the law seems to go wrong, ie to lead to an undesirable result",[6] because satisfactory resolution of uncertainties in the law would require complex legislation, and because statutory intervention was thought undesirable whilst the law is still in a state of development. These reasons for doing nothing are not convincing. The solution of complex problems does not necessarily lead to complex legislation. There can be little doubt that aspects of the current law are undesirable; nor can there be doubt that other elements of the marriage choice of law rules are uncertain or unclear. It is perverse then to rely, as in effect the Commissions do, on that uncertainty as a reason for doing nothing, in the hope that the courts will in due course provide the appropriate new, clear rules.[7] The experience of the last hundred years is unlikely to convince those varied officials who have to advise on and apply marriage choice of

15 LRC 19–1985.
16 For criticisms, see Fentiman (1986) 6 OJLS 353, 354–360.
17 Supra, pp 579 et seq.
 1 Supra, pp 586 et seq.
 2 (1879) 5 PD 94, supra, pp 595–597.
 3 Cf supra, pp 597–599. This view was, rightly, abandoned in the Law Commissions' Report: Law Com No 165 (1987), para 2.6.
 4 See the Foreign Marriage (Amendment) Act 1988, supra, pp 577 et seq.
 5 Law Com No 165 (1987), paras 2.13–2.14.
 6 Ibid, para 2.13.
 7 Ibid, para 2.14.

law rules that the much needed clarification will in fact be forthcoming through judicial decisions.

5. POLYGAMOUS MARRIAGES[8]

(a) INTRODUCTION

A marriage which is both formally and essentially valid under the laws to be applied under our rules of private international law may still be regarded as invalid—or as a marriage to which no effect will be given—if it is actually or potentially polygamous. There has been a steady erosion, this century, of the circumstances in which a different attitude is taken by the law to polygamous marriages from that taken to monogamous marriages, but differences still remain, though mainly in the case of actually polygamous marriages.

The high water mark of the dislike of polygamy is to be seen in the judgment of Lord PENZANCE in *Hyde v Hyde*:[9]

> An Englishman, who had embraced the Mormon faith, married a Mormon lady in Utah according to the Mormon rites. After cohabiting with her for three years and having children by her, he renounced his faith and soon afterwards became the minister of a dissenting chapel in England. He petitioned for a decree of divorce after his wife had contracted another marriage in Utah according to the Mormon faith.

Lord PENZANCE assumed that a Mormon marriage was potentially polygamous, and he refused to dissolve the marriage. He defined "marriage, as understood in Christendom ... as the voluntary union for life of one man and one woman to the exclusion of all others."[10] The matrimonial laws of England are adapted to the Christian marriage, he thought, and are wholly inapplicable to polygamy. Parties to a polygamous marriage, therefore, "are not entitled to the remedies, the adjudication, or the relief of the matrimonial law of England".[11] Although the determination of the nature of the marriage is no longer of importance in deciding whether the parties are entitled to matrimonial relief from the English courts,[12] it is still, as will be seen,[13] of some importance in other areas of the law, such as its effect on succession, a later re-marriage, or social security entitlement.

(b) NATURE OF A POLYGAMOUS MARRIAGE

Some further consideration must be given to Lord PENZANCE's definition. Although the form of marriage recognised by English law is generally described as a "Christian marriage",[14] this reference to religion is misleading. Whatever may be the religion of the parties or of the country in which they marry, their union is a marriage in the English sense provided that, in the eyes of the relevant law, it possesses the two attributes of indefinite duration and the exclusion of all other persons. Monogamy, for instance, is not and

8 Beckett (1932) 48 LQR 341; Morris (1953) 66 Harv LR 961; Hartley (1969) 32 MLR 155; Poulter (1976) 25 ICLQ 475; Jaffey (1978) 41 MLR 38; James (1979) 42 MLR 533.
9 (1866) LR 1 P & D 130.
10 Ibid, at 133. For a modern assessment, see Poulter (1979) 42 MLR 409.
11 Ibid, at 138.
12 Matrimonial Causes Act 1973, s 47, replacing, with minor amendments, s 1 of the Matrimonial Proceedings (Polygamous Marriages) Act 1972, discussed infra, pp 628–629.
13 Infra, pp 621–626.
14 Eg *Warrender v Warrender* (1835) 2 Cl & Fin 488 at 532.

never has been the monopoly of Christianity. Given these two attributes, the union constitutes an English marriage notwithstanding that it may have been contracted in what mid-Victorian judges called an "infidel country", or contracted between non-Christians.[15]

The exclusion of polygamy from the English concept of marriage has been held to extend to a marriage that is potentially polygamous though in fact monogamous. If a husband is entitled by the law that determines the nature of his marriage to take a plurality of wives, his marriage is considered to be polygamous notwithstanding that at the time when the question is raised he has not exercised that right nor ever intends to.[16] If the marriage is potentially polygamous at its inception then, though it may be possible to change it into a monogamous marriage, it retains its polygamous nature until such change is actually made.

Thus in *Sowa v Sowa*,[17] a polygamous marriage was celebrated in Ghana where the parties were domiciled. Prior to the ceremony the husband promised the wife that he would go through a later ceremony which, according to the law of Ghana, would convert the union into a monogamous marriage. He failed to carry out his promise.

It was held that, despite his promise and despite the fact that the husband had not taken an additional wife, the marriage continued to be regarded as polygamous. In conformity with this reasoning, *Mehta v Mehta*[18] indicates that a marriage that is monogamous in its inception is not to be regarded as potentially polygamous merely because the husband is free later to change his religion and join a polygamous sect. Although the suggestion in this case that the inception of the marriage is the only time for determining its nature has been disapproved,[1] such marriage will remain monogamous until there has been the requisite change.

One problem with determining the nature of a marriage concerns the border-line between polygamy and concubinage. In *Lee v Lau*,[2] a marriage in Hong Kong in which the husband, under Chinese customary law, though not permitted to remarry during the lifetime of his first wife, could take *"tsipsis"*, ie concubines or secondary wives, was held to be potentially polygamous. In the words of the judge: "Under a Chinese customary marriage, even if the title of 'wife' is given only to the woman who was joined to the man at the marriage ceremony, that ceremony cannot be said to bring about a union to the exclusion of all others, since the husband can take fresh partners to whose status some legal recognition is given."[3]

---

15 *Brinkley v A-G* (1890) 15 PD 76 (marriage in Japan between an Englishman domiciled in Ireland and a Japanese woman); *Spivack v Spivack* (1930) 99 LJ P 52 (Jewish marriage); *Penhas v Tan Soo Eng* [1953] AC 304 (marriage between a Jew and a non-Christian solemnised according to mixed Chinese and Jewish rites); and see *Ali v Ali* [1968] P 564 at 576.
16 *Hyde v Hyde* (1866) LR 1 P & D 130; *Sowa v Sowa* [1961] P 70; *Cheni v Cheni* [1965] P 85 at 88–89. What law determines the nature of his marriage is discussed infra, pp 610–612.
17 [1961] P 70, [1961] 1 All ER 687.
18 [1945] 2 All ER 690.
1 Infra, pp 613–616.
2 [1967] P 14, [1964] 2 All ER 248; cf *Ng Ping On v Ng Choy Fund Kam* [1963] SR (NSW) 782; and see *Re Ah Chong* (1913) 33 NZLR 384; *Yuen Tse v Minister of Employment* (1983) 32 RFL (2d) 274; *Tang Lau Sau-kiu v Tang Lei* [1987] HKLR 85 at 90.
3 *Lee v Lau* [1967] P 14 at 20.

(c) WHAT LAW DETERMINES THE NATURE OF A MARRIAGE?

In effect, the inquiry here is to identify the law that determines whether the union conforms to the English concept of marriage. As we have seen, two requirements must be satisfied, the first of which is that the union is potentially for an indefinite period. The relevant law to govern this question is clear beyond all doubt, namely that of the place of celebration.[4]

On the other hand the law that determines whether the marriage is monogamous or polygamous has not yet been settled beyond all doubt.

If, for instance, a woman domiciled in England marries a Muslim in London and then cohabits with him in Pakistan where he is domiciled, what law determines whether her marriage is monogamous or polygamous in nature?[5]

The choice lies between English law as the law of the place of celebration and the law of her ante-nuptial domicil and Pakistani law as the law of his ante-nuptial domicil and, presumably, of both their post-nuptial domicils. There is, unfortunately, no case in which this issue has been squarely raised and fully discussed. Whichever be the law, there is much to be said for the view that its function is to determine the nature and incidents of the marriage according to its own view, but not necessarily to impose that classification on the court of the forum. This approach may be seen from *Lee v Lau*[6] where Chinese customary law, being the law to which it was considered that reference should be made to determine the nature of the marriage, regarded the marriage as monogamous. Nevertheless CAIRNS J considered that, although reference should be made to the law of the place of celebration to determine the nature and incidents of the union by that law, the ultimate decision on the classification of the nature of the marriage, as with issues of classification generally, must be made by the law of the forum.

There is much in favour of the view that the appropriate law by which to test the monogamous or polygamous character of a marriage is the law of the domicil. To apply the law of the place of celebration runs against the fundamental principle that matters of status, especially the status of husband and wife, are regulated by the law of the domicil. The proposition that the nature of a marriage should be determined by the law of the domicil, not by the law of the place of celebration, is certainly not devoid of judicial support.[7]

Some further support for the application of the law of the domicil might be derived from *Hussain v Hussain*[8] where the Court of Appeal held that a marriage in Pakistan in Moslem form between a man domiciled in England and a woman domiciled in Pakistan could not be classified as potentially polygamous for the purpose of determining the effect of the Matrimonial Causes Act 1973 on the man's capacity to marry. It seems clear that the law

---

4 *Nachimson v Nachimson* [1930] P 217.
5 The question whether it is a *valid* marriage, of whatever nature, is discussed, infra, pp 617–621.
6 Supra, p 609; and see *Hassan v Hassan* [1978] 1 NZLR 385 at 390.
7 *Warrender v Warrender* (1835) 2 Cl & Fin 488 at 535; *Kenward v Kenward* [1951] P 124 at 145; *Russ v Russ* [1964] P 315 at 326; *Ali v Ali* [1960] P 564 at 576–577; and see Briggs (1983) 32 ICLQ 737, 738. It seems also to have been assumed in *Radwan v Radwan (No 2)* [1973] Fam 35, [1972] 3 All ER 1026 that the law of the domicil or of the intended matrimonial home determined that the marriage in question was polygamous, because the place of celebration was held (at pp 42–43) to be France.
8 [1983] Fam 26, [1982] 3 All ER 369, discussed more fully, infra, pp 619–621.

of the place of celebration was not applied to determine the nature of the marriage; so English law as the law of the forum, of the man's domicil, or of the intended matrimonial home must have been. Regrettably, the judgment of ORMROD LJ does not indicate with any clarity the basis on which this characterisation was made. He merely stated[9] that the cases in support of the law of the place of celebration were of less authority now that the English courts had jurisdiction to entertain proceedings in relation to polygamous marriages.[10] Unfortunately, the widening of the jurisdiction of the courts in no way affects the need to characterise the nature of a marriage for all other purposes.[11] It is hard to disagree with the conclusion that, on the issue of the law to determine the nature of a marriage, the decision in *Hussain* is "no more than a decision, albeit a strange one, on the construction of a particular statutory provision, albeit an important one".[12]

Determination of the nature of a marriage by reference to the law of the domicil does, however, create a number of real difficulties. It would until 1972[13] have denied the matrimonial relief of the English courts to persons who married in England, if domiciled in a country which regarded the marriage as potentially polygamous. Furthermore, now that a married woman may have a domicil separate from her husband,[14] the problem would arise of deciding whether the domicil of the husband or of the wife, if different, should determine the nature of the marriage. If such a difficulty is to be avoided, and surely it should be, then the nature of a marriage ought to be determined by the law of the place of celebration. Furthermore, to do otherwise would mean acceptance of the fact that a marriage in an English register office could be a polygamous marriage. Such a conclusion should be reached only on the clearest authority. There is a further argument against reference to the law of the domicil. In some jurisdictions both monogamous and polygamous marriages are recognised and therefore the nature of a particular marriage in such a country depends on the form of the ceremony by which it is celebrated. This, as has been seen,[15] indicates a matter to be considered by the law of the place of celebration.[16]

When one turns to consider what authority there is for reference to the law of the place of celebration, it is true that one will find that a number of the cases often cited in favour of this view[17] have, as the result of careful analysis, been properly described as "either irrelevant or ambiguous".[18] *Hyde*

---

9 Ibid at 31.
10 See now Matrimonial Causes Act 1973, s 47, infra, pp 628–629.
11 See Schuz (1983) 46 MLR 653, 656; Briggs (1983) 32 ICLQ 737, 738–739; Carter (1982) 53 BYBIL 298, 300–301.
12 Carter (1982) 53 BYBIL 298, 302.
13 Matrimonial Proceedings (Polygamous Marriages) Act 1972, s 1; now Matrimonial Causes Act 1973, s 47.
14 Domicile and Matrimonial Proceedings Act 1973, s 1.
15 Supra, pp 572 et seq.
16 Eg *Sowa v Sowa* [1961] P 70, [1961] 1 All ER 687; *Kassim v Kassim* [1962] P 224; and see *Mohamed v Knott* [1969] 1 QB 1, [1968] 2 All ER 563; Nygh, p 337; Mendes da Costa (1966) 44 Can BR 293, 302.
17 *Hyde v Hyde* (1866) LR 1 P & D 130; *Chetti v Chetti* [1909] P 67; *R v Hammersmith Marriage Registrar* [1917] 1 KB 634, CA; *R v Naguib* [1917] 1 KB 359; *Maher v Maher* [1951] P 342, [1951] 2 All ER 37 (This last case was overruled as regards another point by *Russ v Russ* [1964] P 315, [1962] 3 All ER 193, CA); *Risk v Risk* [1951] P 50, [1950] 2 All ER 973. The Scottish decision in *Lendrum v Chakravati* 1929 SLT 96 favours the law of the place of celebration.
18 Bartholomew (1964) 13 ICLQ 1022, 1058.

v Hyde[19] itself is not clear on this matter for it is not certain whether the husband was domiciled in Utah where the marriage was celebrated, and so there may have been no conflict between the law of the domicil and of the place of celebration.

It is clear that the crucial case for the determination of this issue is one where the law of the place of celebration is different from that of the domicil.[20] Such a case was *Re Bethell*:[1]

> The deceased had "married" a native girl in Bechuanaland (now Botswana) at a ceremony in accordance with the custom of her tribe, the Barolong tribe, by whose custom marriage was considered to be potentially polygamous. Just after his death, a child was born and a question arose whether the child was legitimate for the purposes of an English will.

Having accepted the uncontroverted evidence that the deceased was domiciled in England at the time of his marriage, STIRLING J nevertheless concluded that the marriage was a Barolong marriage and thus polygamous. It is clear that the deceased's domiciliary law did not determine the nature of the marriage, though whether in considering Barolong custom STIRLING J can be said to be referring to the law of the place of celebration is a little doubtful without evidence of the law prevailing in Bechuanaland at that time.[2]

Reference to the law of the place of celebration was assumed to be beyond doubt in *Qureshi v Qureshi*:[3]

> The parties were both Moslems. The husband was domiciled at all material times in Pakistan. The wife was apparently domiciled before her marriage in India and, after her marriage, she assumed her husband's domicil in Pakistan. By both personal laws the marriage was potentially polygamous. They married in an English register office, followed by a religious ceremony. The question arose of recognition in England of an extra-judicial divorce by *talak*.[4]

Although not essential to his decision, Sir JOCELYN SIMON P had no doubt that this was a monogamous marriage, for the marriage "having taken place in England, where monogamy is the rule, must be regarded as monogamous for the purpose of invoking the jurisdiction of the court".[5]

One may conclude that, other than on the issue of capacity to marry,[6] all marriages in England are to be characterised as monogamous and that all marriages of English domiciliaries in a foreign country, according to polygamous forms or custom, will be regarded as polygamous. If there is a civil ceremony in England, followed by a religious one, it is the former which constitutes the legal monogamous marriage.[7]

---

19 (1866) LR 1 P & D 130.
20 In *Iman Din v National Assistance Board* [1967] 2 QB 213 at 218–219, SALMON LJ went so far as to infer that whether a marriage is polygamous is determined by reference to both the personal law of the parties and the law of the country in which it was celebrated: *sed quaere*.
1 (1888) 38 Ch D 220.
2 Bartholomew (1964) 13 ICLQ 1022, 1052–1053.
3 [1972] Fam 173, [1971] 1 All ER 325; and see *Chetti v Chetti* [1909] P 67; *Ohochuku v Ohochuku* [1960] 1 All ER 253.
4 Discussed, infra, pp 664 et seq.
5 [1972] Fam 173 at 182.
6 Infra, pp 617–621.
7 *Qureshi v Qureshi* [1972] Fam 173 at 186.

(d) CAN THE NATURE OF A MARRIAGE CHANGE?

One issue which has caused difficulty in the past is whether the nature of a marriage as monogamous or polygamous is to be determined as at the date of the marriage or of later legal proceedings. In other words, can the nature of a marriage change? This issue has usually arisen in the context of a claimed change in character from potentially polygamous to monogamous and has diminished in importance as the differences between the two kinds of marriage have narrowed.[8] Earlier cases rejected any possibility of change,[9] but it is now apparent from more recent decisions that English courts will recognise a change in the nature of a marriage after its inception. This is seen quite clearly from *Cheni v Cheni*,[10] where the facts were these:

> Two Sephardic Jews, uncle and niece domiciled in Egypt, were married in Cairo and a child was born to them two years later. By Jewish and Egyptian law the marriage was potentially polygamous in the sense that if no child was born within ten years the husband might take another wife subject to the approval both of his first wife and of the Rabbinical court. Five years after the parties had acquired an English domicil, the wife petitioned for a decree of nullity on the ground that she and her husband were within the prohibited degrees of consanguinity.

The court had no jurisdiction at that time[11] to entertain this suit if the marriage was potentially polygamous. Sir JOCELYN SIMON P was satisfied that at its inception it was undoubtedly of that nature, because of the remote possibility of an additional wife being taken, but he then held that the decisive date for considering its polygamous potential was the inception of the instant proceedings. By that date the birth of the child had rendered the marriage monogamous, and the court assumed jurisdiction.

It is now accepted that there is a variety of ways in which the nature of a marriage may be changed from polygamous to monogamous. Furthermore, given that the nature of the marriage can change, then a corollary is that the relevant time for determining the nature of the marriage is that of the commencement of the proceedings in question.[12] Various examples of change from potentially polygamous to monogamous can be given, but it must always be remembered that the marriage must initially be regarded as valid. So a purported change in the nature of a *void* polygamous marriage will not turn it into a *valid* monogamous marriage. If the personal law of the parties refers the nature of their marriage to their religious law, then a change of religion may be held to alter the nature of the marriage.[13] If the law under which the marriage was celebrated later forbids polygamy, then such legislative action will render the marriage monogamous from henceforth,[14] and

8 Infra, pp 621 et seq.
9 See *Hyde v Hyde* (1866) LR 1 P & D 130; *Mehta v Mehta* [1945] 2 All ER 690; *Sowa v Sowa* [1961] P 70, [1961] 1 All ER 687.
10 [1965] P 85, [1962] 3 All ER 873.
11 See now Matrimonial Causes Act 1973, s 47.
12 *Cheni v Cheni* [1965] P 85 at 92; *Parkasho v Singh* [1968] P 233 at 254–255.
13 *Sinha Peerage Claim* (1939) 171 Lords Journals 350, [1946] 1 All ER 348 n. See also *Cheni v Cheni* [1965] P 85 at 90–91. An interesting, though undecided, issue is whether the change of religion of only one of the spouses has this effect: *A-G of Ceylon v Reid* [1965] AC 720, [1965] 1 All ER 812 suggests that it might. See Webb (1965) 14 ICLQ 992, 996–997.
14 *Parkasho v Singh* [1968] P 233, a decision on the effect of the Hindu Marriage Act 1955 prohibiting polygamy for Hindus in India, as to which the National Insurance Commissioners had much earlier reached the same conclusion: Decision No R (G) 2/56; and see *Poon v Tan* (1973) 4 Fam Law 161; *R v Sagoo* [1975] QB 885, [1975] 2 All ER 926.

it has been seen that the birth of a child to the spouses can change the nature of their marriage under the relevant religious law.[15]

There is some authority that, where there is a marriage in polygamous form followed by a later marriage between the same parties in monogamous form, the parties are to be regarded as monogamously married. In *Ohochuku v Ohochuku*[16] a potentially polygamous marriage in Nigeria was followed four years later by a ceremony of marriage in monogamous form in England, between the same parties. Unable to grant a decree of divorce of the first marriage, the court dissolved the later marriage, thus apparently ignoring the polygamous nature of the union ascribed to the parties at the date of their first marriage. It is suggested that this decision is out of harmony with *Baindail v Baindail*[17] and *Thynne v Thynne*,[18] both decided by the Court of Appeal. As we shall see, it was held in the former case that a polygamous marriage valid according to the law of the parties' domicil is valid in the eyes of English law and therefore that it is an effective bar to a subsequent marriage with a third person in England.[19] *Thynne v Thynne* decided that what a decree of divorce dissolves is not any particular ceremony, but the existing status of the parties as husband and wife.[20] The parties in the *Ohochuku Case* possessed a polygamous status according to the law of Nigeria where they were still domiciled and where the first marriage was celebrated. To nullify the English ceremony, therefore, could not affect their status still subsisting under the Nigerian marriage and transform them from polygamists to monogamists,[1] unless it can be argued that by the later marriage the nature of the first marriage was altered and that therefore the parties acquired a monogamous status.[2]

Finally, *Ali v Ali*[3] provides authority for the proposition that, if a husband changes his domicil from a country which permits polygamy to one which does not, this change of domicil renders the marriage monogamous. The facts were these:

The parties, both domiciled in India, there entered into a valid potentially polygamous marriage. Later they came to England and the wife left the husband. The husband acquired an English domicil in 1963 and he petitioned for divorce on the ground of the wife's desertion, and she cross-petitioned on the grounds of the husband's cruelty until she left him and of his adultery in 1964. The court's jurisdiction depended at that time on

15 *Cheni v Cheni*, supra, p 613.
16 [1960] 1 All ER 253; cf National Insurance Decision No R (G) 11/53; *Sowa v Sowa* [1961] P 70, supra p 609.
17 [1946] P 122, [1946] 1 All ER 342.
18 [1955] P 272, [1955] 3 All ER 129.
19 Infra, p 622.
20 And see *Peters v Peters* (1968) 112 Sol Jo 311.
 1 The decision may perhaps be supported on the ground that the Nigerian law of the subsisting domicil would regard the decree as effective to dissolve the polygamous marriage, a question which the judge was not prepared to consider.
 2 *Cheni v Cheni* [1965] P 85 at 91; *Ali v Ali* [1968] P 564 at 578; *Parkasho v Singh* [1968] P 233 at 242; cf Carter (1965–1966) 41 BYBIL 443. Even so, if the Nigerian marriage was valid, how could they be married again in England? See *Ali v Ali*, supra, at p 578.
 3 [1968] P 564, [1966] 1 All ER 664; and see *R v Sagoo* [1975] QB 885, [1975] 2 All ER 926; National Insurance Decision No R (G) 3/75; *Re Hassan and Hassan* (1976) 69 DLR (3d) 224. A similar conclusion had been reached much earlier by the National Insurance Commissioners, see Decision No R (G) 12/56.

whether the marriage, at the time of the proceedings, was to be regarded as polygamous or monogamous.

CUMMING-BRUCE J concluded that the husband's acquisition of an English domicil and continued residence in England precluded him, divorce apart, from marrying a second wife in the lifetime of the first. This prohibition on remarriage was considered to have impressed a monogamous character on his previously polygamous marriage, even though there was no conscious act on the part of the parties directed to this end. Furthermore the court rejected the argument that the mutability of a marriage depends on whether the facts relied upon to effect the change are capable of taking place in the place of celebration, or probably, according to its law.[4] In other words, although the nature of the marriage is decided by the law of the place of celebration, the issue of mutability is not determined at the time of the marriage.

Though the logic of such a conclusion may be attacked,[5] it did have the practical advantage of allowing those who contracted valid potentially polygamous marriages to come within the jurisdiction of the English courts for the purposes of matrimonial relief as soon as they became domiciled in England. This advantage is far less substantial now that the matrimonial jurisdiction of the English courts has been opened to the parties to potentially and actually polygamous marriages.[6] However, various difficulties with the decision in *Ali v Ali* must still be examined. If change of domicil changed the nature of the marriage in that case, why was not a similar change effected in *Hyde v Hyde*[7] itself? The only explanation offered by CUMMING-BRUCE J was that in 1866 the importance of domicil affecting capacity to marry was not fully appreciated, nor was the issue of the mutability of the nature of the marriage put before the court in that case; but it must be admitted that this reasoning is not wholly convincing.[8]

Another problem arises from the *Ali v Ali* situation, caused by the fact that a married woman can now have an independent domicil. Let us assume that a husband and wife, both domiciled in Pakistan, marry there according to polygamous form. Is the nature of their marriage changed if only one of them becomes domiciled in England, or if both become domiciled here and the husband alone returns to Pakistan, and reacquires a domicil there? Now that the main raison d'être for the decision in *Ali v Ali*, namely the rule denying English matrimonial relief to the parties to a polygamous marriage, has disappeared, both the decision and the difficulties posed by it may, one hopes, be regarded as of little more than academic interest.

A marriage that is in fact polygamous cannot be changed to a monogamous one by, for example, a change of domicil by one[9] of the wives or by both;[10] but the problem might arise in the case of a marriage which, though once in fact polygamous, has ceased to be so, eg by divorce or by the death of a wife before the change. If, after the acquisition of an English domicil, the marriage

---

4 [1968] P 564 at 575; cf Carter (1963) 39 BYBIL 474, 478. See the rejection of a similar argument in *Parkasho v Singh* [1968] P 233 at 244–245; cf Carter (1967) 42 BYBIL 300–301; and see the slight doubts of CUMMING-BRUCE J in *Radwan v Radwan* [1973] Fam 24 at 27.
5 Carter (1965–1966) 41 BYBIL 442–444; Mendes da Costa (1966) 44 Can BR 293, 307–310; Tolstoy (1968) 17 ICLQ 721; cf Morris (1968) 17 ICLQ 1014.
6 Infra, pp 628–629.
7 (1866) LR 1 P & D 130.
8 Law Com No 42 (1971), para 12.
9 Eg *Onobrauche v Onobrauche* (1978) 8 Fam Law 107.
10 Eg *Re Sehota* [1978] 3 All ER 385, [1978] 1 WLR 1506.

ceased to be in fact polygamous, then that fact combined with the English domicil might well render the marriage monogamous.[11]

The discussion of mutability has centred so far on the change from a polygamous to a monogamous nature. Some consideration must be given to the possibility of change from monogamy to polygamy. If a marriage may be changed from polygamy to monogamy then it might seem logical to recognise a change the other way, based on similar circumstances, eg change of religion or change of law.[12] It has, however, been suggested that a marriage has the benefit of any doubt as to monogamy, ie that "it is sufficient that it is either monogamous in its inception or has become so by the time of the proceedings".[13] This would mean that even though it might be possible to change the nature of a marriage from monogamous to polygamous such change would not affect the attitude of English law towards it. Such an approach would afford a convenient way of dissipating the force of the argument that all monogamous marriages are potentially polygamous in that the spouses are free to change their religion or domicil and thus the nature of their marriage.[14]

There are very real difficulties with a view that, if parties marry in monogamous form, for example in England, one party (normally the husband) may change the whole nature of their marriage by changing his religion or domicil and thereby rendering the marriage potentially polygamous. To deny these difficulties would be to deny that polygamy is a different social and legal institution from monogamy.[15] The problem is seen most sharply where there is a possibility of a man being monogamously married to his first wife and polygamously married to his second, as where a husband domiciled in England marries his first wife, an English domiciliary, in England in a monogamous form and then, having acquired a domicil in Pakistan, marries a second wife, a Pakistan domiciliary in Pakistan in polygamous form.[16] It would seem most unfair to the first wife that her marriage should, by the unilateral act of her husband, be changed in nature from monogamous to polygamous. This raises two issues—whether the second marriage is valid and, if so, what effect it has on the first marriage and on the rights of the first wife. Such authority as there is points in favour of the validity of the second marriage, which would satisfy all our general choice of law rules.[17] It seems also to be the case that the fact that the husband has entered a second valid polygamous marriage does not change the nature of the first marriage as monogamous, leaving the first wife free, for example, to petition for divorce on the basis of adultery by the husband in taking a second wife.[18]

11 Law Com No 42 (1971), para 13.
12 See *A-G of Ceylon v Reid* [1965] AC 720 for consideration of this problem under the law of Ceylon; but their Lordships, at 734, declined to express any opinion on "the situation in a purely Christian country"; and see Pearl [1972 A] CLJ 120, 139–142; cf *PP v White* (1940) 9 MLJ 214.
13 *Cheni v Cheni* [1965] P 85 at 90. This is supported, further, by *Mehta v Mehta* [1945] 2 All ER 690 at 693, *Parkasho v Singh* [1968] P 233 at 243–244.
14 See *Cheni v Cheni* [1965] P 85 at 90; *Parkasho v Singh* [1968] P 233 at 244.
15 See Carter (1982) 53 BYBIL 298, 299–300.
16 The problem is the same if the husband was, at all times, domiciled in Pakistan.
17 *Drammeh v Drammeh* (1970) 78 Ceylon Law Weekly 55, PC, infra, pp 629–630; *A-G of Ceylon v Reid* [1965] AC 720, [1965] 1 All ER 812. In *Nabi v Heaton* [1981] 1 WLR 1052 at 1056–1057, VINELOTT J declined to decide the question; and see infra pp 624–625.
18 See infra, pp 629–630; and see Law Com No 146; Scot Law Com No 98 (1985), paras 4.10–4.24.

(e) CAPACITY TO CONTRACT A POLYGAMOUS MARRIAGE

(i) Common law choice of law rules

There has long been controversy in identifying the law that governs capacity in the case of a polygamous union, and the present law on this issue is a confusing mixture of common law and statute. The Law Commission has made proposals for reform,[1] but they have not yet been implemented. There is support at common law for this issue to be referred to the ante-nuptial domicil of both parties,[2] the law of the intended matrimonial home[3] or the law of the place of celebration.[4] One argument in favour of the last view is that it is that law which determines whether a marriage is polygamous or monogamous[5] but this is not sufficient to outweigh the view that issues of marital status are to be referred to the law of the domicil and it is suggested that capacity to marry more than one spouse is an issue affecting status.[6] Indeed, there was a clear rejection of reference to the law of the place of celebration by CUMMING-BRUCE J in *Ali v Ali*.[7] He concluded that a husband domiciled in England and intending to reside there[8] did not have capacity to confer the status of "wife" on anyone else, no matter where he purported to "marry" a second wife.[9]

If the law of the place of celebration is rejected, the choice lies between the law of the intended matrimonial home and the law of the domicil, and, as has been seen, there is authority in support of both. The fullest fairly recent discussion of the choice of law issue is to be found in *Radwan v Radwan (No 2)*[10] which supports the intended matrimonial home approach. Here, CUMMING-BRUCE J applied the law of Egypt to determine the issue of capacity to enter an actually polygamous marriage celebrated in the Egyptian Consulate General in Paris between a domiciled Egyptian and a domiciled English woman, the parties intending to live in Egypt, which in fact they did. It was the judge's considered view that the law to determine capacity to enter a polygamous marriage, if no other question of capacity, should be that of the intended matrimonial home.

This decision was greeted with widespread,[11] though not unanimous,[12] criticism—primarily for its rejection of the dual domicil approach and for indicating that a special capacity rule in the case of polygamous marriages

---

1 Law Com No 146; Scot Law Com No 96 (1985).
2 Eg *Re Ullee* (1885) 53 LT 711 at 712; *Lendrum v Chakravarti* 1929 SLT 96 at 99.
3 *Kenward v Kenward* [1951] P 124 at 145; *Radwan v Radwan (No 2)* [1973] Fam 35, [1972] 3 All ER 1026.
4 *Kaur v Ginder* (1958) 13 DLR (2d) 465. In *Sara v Sara* (1962) 31 DLR (2d) 566, varied on other grounds (1963) 36 DLR (2d) 499, it seems to have been assumed that capacity by the law of the place of celebration is all that is required.
5 Supra, pp 610–612.
6 The reference in *Kaur v Ginder*, supra, to the law of the place of celebration was on the basis that power to enter a polygamous marriage was more an issue of form than capacity.
7 [1968] P 564, [1966] 1 All ER 664, supra, pp 614–615.
8 Thus avoiding a choice on the general question of capacity to marry between the ante-nuptial domiciliary laws of both parties and the law of the intended matrimonial home; see supra, pp 590 et seq.
9 [1968] P 564 at 576–577; but cf *A-G of Ceylon v Reid* [1965] AC 720, [1965] 1 All ER 812.
10 [1973] Fam 35, [1972] 3 All ER 1026.
11 Karsten (1973) 36 MLR 291; Pearl [1973] CLJ 43; Wade (1973) 22 ICLQ 571.
12 See Jaffey (1978) 41 MLR 38; Stone [1983] Fam Law 76; *Hassan v Hassan* [1978] 1 NZLR 385 at 389–390.

can be justified.[13] There is certainly a weight of authority supporting the view that capacity to contract a polygamous marriage is to be determined by the law of the ante-nuptial domicil,[14] whether the marriage is actually[15] or potentially[16] polygamous. Two further factors support this approach. In a number of cases since 1973 in which the validity of a polygamous marriage has arisen, the court or tribunal has simply applied the law of the domicil without any consideration of whether that country was the same as that of the intended matrimonial home.[17] The second factor is that Parliament seems also to have assumed that the dual domicil test was the law. In the case of both potentially and actually polygamous marriages celebrated outside England and Wales after 31 July 1971, the Matrimonial Causes Act 1973[18] provides that the marriage is void if either party was domiciled in England at the time of the marriage. This is a clear statutory reference to the ante-nuptial domicil. It is necessary now to look more closely at this provision and its effects.

(ii) Matrimonial Causes Act 1973

In the context of capacity to enter a polygamous marriage, it is necessary to consider sections 11 and 14 of the Matrimonial Causes Act 1973. They provide as follows:

> 11. A marriage celebrated after 31 July 1971 shall be void on the following grounds only, that is to say ...
>   (b) that at the time of the marriage either party was already lawfully married ...
>   (d) in the case of a polygamous marriage entered into outside England and Wales, that either party was at the time of the marriage domiciled in England and Wales.
> For the purposes of paragraph (d) of this subsection a marriage may be polygamous although at its inception neither party has any spouse additional to the other.
>
> 14. Where, apart from this Act, any matter affecting the validity of a marriage would fall to be determined (in accordance with the rules of private international law) by reference to the law of a country outside England and Wales, nothing in section 11 ... above shall—
>   (a) preclude the determination of that matter as aforesaid; or
>   (b) require the application to the marriage of the grounds ... there mentioned except so far as applicable in accordance with those rules.[19]

Two rather different issues arise. The first is whether, in relation to marriages celebrated after 31 July 1971, these provisions embody a choice of law rule;

---

13 This opposition was not unexpected; see [1973] Fam 35 at 54, and see supra, p 592.
14 It may well be that the decision in *Re Bethell* (1888) 38 Ch D 220 can only be justified on the ground that the "husband" had no capacity by English law, the law of his domicil, to enter into a polygamous marriage. In *Risk v Risk* [1951] P 50, [1950] 2 All ER 973, the court declined jurisdiction to consider this issue on the ground that the marriage, whether valid or not, was polygamous.
15 *Crowe v Kader* [1968] WAR 122; *Ishiodu v Entry Clearance Officer, Lagos* [1975] Imm AR 56.
16 *Ali v Ali* [1968] P 564 at 576–577; *Afza Mussarat v Secretary of State for the Home Department* [1972] Imm AR 45; cf Hartley (1969) 32 MLR 155, 158–160.
17 Eg *Hussain v Hussain* [1983] Fam 26, [1982] 3 All ER 369; *Zahra v Visa Officer, Islamabad* [1979–80] Imm AR 48; *Rokeya Begum v Entry Clearance Officer, Dacca* [1983] Imm AR 163; National Insurance Decision No R (G) 3/75.
18 S 11(d), re-enacting in substance the Matrimonial Proceedings (Polygamous Marriages) Act 1972, s 4.
19 For a provision similar to s 14, see the Marriage (Prohibited Degrees of Relationship) Act 1986, s 1(7).

and the second is to determine the effect of the provisions in cases to which they apply. As to the first issue, although as has been seen[20] some recent decisions have proceeded on the basis that section 11 of the 1973 Act applies whenever one party is domiciled in England, that approach was specifically rejected by CUMMING-BRUCE J in *Radwan v Radwan (No 2)*.[1] In considering the statutory predecessors of sections 11 and 14,[2] the judge concluded that the Law Commission,[3] the government and Parliament had laboured under a misapprehension as to the common law rules on capacity.[4] His conclusion that the choice of law rule is that the law of the intended matrimonial home should apply has the following effect. Section 11 will not apply in those cases where the parties did not intend to set up a matrimonial home in England, as was the position in *Radwan* itself. This is because section 14 expressly preserves the application of the substantive law of another country held to be applicable under our rules of private international law. Put another way, section 11(d) can only apply to invalidate a marriage if one party was domiciled in England *and* the parties intended to live in England. Of course, if *Radwan* is not followed, section 11(d) will apply whenever one party is domiciled in England, irrespective of the intended matrimonial home.

We must now turn to examine the effect of section 11 in those polygamous marriage cases where validity is governed by English law. From 1973 until 1983, anxiety had been expressed over the impact of section 11(d) in the following type of circumstance. An immigrant to this country from Pakistan becomes domiciled here and then returns to Pakistan to marry, for the first time, in Moslem form bringing his new wife back to England with him. This marriage was regarded as potentially polygamous with the result, so it was thought, that the marriage was void under section 11(d)—a conclusion which was much criticised.[5] Had the Pakistani been only resident, and not domiciled, here, his marriage would have been valid[6] and, indeed, would become monogamous in character on his acquisition of an English domicil.[7] Furthermore, if the marriage had taken place in England, being monogamous in fact and in character, it would also have been valid.

Sustained criticism of the effect of section 11(d) in the case of a potentially polygamous marriage prompted the Law Commission to consider the case for reform. The day that its Working Paper was due to be sent for printing,[8] the Court of Appeal in *Hussain v Hussain*[9] cast a wholly new light on the effect of section 11 of the 1973 Act. The facts were as follows:

> The husband and wife married in Pakistan in 1979. They were Moslems and they married in a form appropriate for polygamous marriages. At all times the marriage was in fact monogamous. At the time of the marriage the husband was domiciled in England and the wife in Pakistan. When,

---

20 Supra, p 618.
1 [1973] Fam 35, [1972] 3 All ER 1026.
2 Namely, s 4 of the Matrimonial Proceedings (Polygamous Marriages) Act 1972 and s 4 of the Nullity of Marriage Act 1971.
3 The predecessor of s 11 is based on Law Com No 42 (1971).
4 [1973] Fam 35 at 52.
5 See Hartley (1971) 34 MLR 305, 306–307; Cretney (1972) 116 Sol Jo 654; Poulter (1976) 25 ICLQ 475, 503–508; James (1979) 42 MLR 533, 536.
6 Eg *Ishiodu v Entry Clearance Officer, Lagos* [1975] Imm AR 56.
7 Supra, pp 614–615.
8 Working Paper No 83 (1982), para 1.3.
9 [1983] Fam 26, [1982] 3 All ER 369.

on the subsequent breakdown of the marriage, the wife petitioned in England for judicial separation, the husband argued that the marriage was void by reason of section 11(d) in that it was polygamous in nature and that he was domiciled in England at the relevant time.

The Court of Appeal rejected the husband's argument and held the marriage to be valid. In so doing, they met many of the criticisms of section 11(d) and achieved a good deal, though not all, of the reform sought by the Law Commission; but they also created a range of further problems and turned on its head the law as it had been assumed to be for a decade by lawyers, immigrants and government officials alike.[10]

The reasoning of the Court of Appeal was as follows. Section 11(d) prevents an English domiciliary from entering a polygamous marriage, whether actually or potentially polygamous, but "a marriage can only be potentially polygamous if at least one of the spouses has the capacity to marry a second spouse".[11] However, in the case of a person domiciled in England, there is no capacity to enter an actually polygamous marriage because section 11(b) of the 1973 Act renders a person who is actually married incapable of marrying a second spouse.[12] On this reasoning, the marriage in question was valid. It was not to be regarded as potentially polygamous, and thus falling within section 11(d), because the wife was incapable, under the Moslem law of Pakistan, of marrying a second husband, and the husband was incapable under English law, namely section 11(b) of the 1973 Act, of marrying a second wife.

Whilst the actual decision of the Court of Appeal has been welcomed, the process of reasoning by which it was reached and the implications to be drawn from it have been widely criticised.[13] The reasoning ignores the part played by the law of the place of celebration in determining whether a marriage is to be characterised as polygamous,[14] and could lead to the conclusion that a marriage which is, in fact and form, monogamous, would be void under section 11(d) because the husband's domiciliary law permitted polygamy. ORMROD LJ stated that it was no longer necessary to characterise the nature of the marriage by the law of the place of celebration "for jurisdiction purposes".[15] Whilst that is true,[16] it is also irrelevant, because the issue before the court was not one of jurisdiction but of capacity to marry, and the validity of a polygamous marriage continues to affect a wide range of matters, such as social security, taxation and immigration, to say nothing of matrimonial relief. The implications to be drawn from the decision are also worrying. It only applies to marriages celebrated after 31 July 1971 because that is the limit of the scope of section 11. This means that the validity of earlier polygamous marriages is governed by the common law under which a marriage in circumstances similar to *Hussain* will be void. Furthermore, even in the case of a marriage after 31 July 1971, it will be void

10 Law Commission Working Paper No 83 (1982), paras 4.3–4.39.
11 [1983] Fam 26 at 32.
12 The Court of Appeal assumed that s 11 (a) of the 1973 Act applies to all English domiciliaries, without examining the claims of the intended matrimonial home rule laid down in *Radwan v Radwan (No 2)* [1973] Fam 35, supra, p 617, and see *R v Junaid Khan* (1987) 84 Cr App Rep 44.
13 Carter (1982) 53 BYBIL 298; Briggs (1983) 32 ICLQ 737; Pearl [1983] CLJ 26; Schuz (1983) 46 MLR 653; Poulter (1983) 13 Fam Law 72.
14 Supra, pp 610–612.
15 [1983] Fam 26 at 31.
16 See Matrimonial Causes Act 1973, s 47, infra, pp 628–629.

if the position of the parties in *Hussain* is reversed, ie if the wife is domiciled in England and the husband in Pakistan. This is because the marriage will now be regarded as polygamous in nature, and thus within section 11(d), as the husband is capable under his personal law of marrying a second wife.[17]

This unsatisfactory state of the law on capacity to enter a polygamous marriage has led the Law Commission to recommend[18] further reform in the wake of *Hussain*. The essence of the proposals, which have not yet been implemented, is that section 11(d) of the 1973 Act should be repealed and that men and women domiciled in England should have capacity to enter a marriage outside the United Kingdom which, though polygamous in form, is monogamous in fact, ie a potentially polygamous marriage. The new rules would apply to all marriages, whenever celebrated; though it was thought necessary to exclude from validation any marriage which had already been declared void by a nullity decree,[19] or, in the case of a marriage not covered by *Hussain*, if either spouse had entered a later marriage which would be rendered invalid by the retrospective validation of the earlier one.[20] There would, however, be no change in the present rule that there is no capacity under English law to enter an actually polygamous marriage.[1]

(f) RECOGNITION OF POLYGAMOUS MARRIAGES IN ENGLAND

In considering what recognition will be extended by an English court to a valid marriage that is found to be potentially or actually polygamous, it should be observed in the first place that no recognition is possible unless the marriage has been validly created in the eyes of English private international law. In short it must have been contracted between parties of full capacity and in accordance with the formal requirements of the law of the place of celebration.

Polygamous marriages are now recognised for a wide variety of purposes. There was once a tendency for the courts to disregard such marriages for all purposes on the inadmissible ground that "it is a union falsely called marriage" and one that merits no recognition in a Christian country. This disdainful attitude towards an institution favoured by many people across the world is, however, a thing of the past. In *Baindail v Baindail*,[2] Lord GREENE MR stressed that, since the status of a person depends on his personal law, the status of husband and wife conferred on the parties to a polygamous marriage by the law of their domicil must be accepted and acted on in other countries. Although he was careful to add that it must be accepted for certain purposes only, and not for all, the present state of the law is that a polygamous marriage is recognised for most purposes. The balance of definition has tipped from defining those instances where, exceptionally, such a marriage will be recognised to defining those few instances where it may not. A variety of situations needs to be considered.

The position used to be that neither party to a polygamous marriage could invoke "the remedies, the adjudication or the relief" given either by the

17 Eg Social Security Decision No R(SB) 17/84.
18 Law Com No 146; Scot Law Com No 96 (1985), Pt II.
19 Ibid, para 2.21.
20 Ibid, paras 2.24–2.26. There are some other proposals dealing with retrospective effect in relation to property rights, pensions, tax and titles of honour; see para 2.33.
1 Ibid, paras 4.2–4.8.
2 [1946] P 122 at 127–128, [1946] 1 All ER 342 at 345.

High Court,[3] or by magistrates' courts,[4] in the exercise of their matrimonial jurisdiction. However, such matrimonial or declaratory relief may now be granted, under section 47 of the Matrimonial Causes Act 1973, whether the marriage is actually or potentially polygamous.[5]

The English courts are prepared to recognise that a polygamous marriage can constitute a valid marriage[6] and therefore one which constitutes a bar to a later marriage. This means that the second "spouse" is entitled to a nullity decree on the grounds of bigamy.[7] It might be thought that, in such a case, the spouse who "married" twice would also be guilty of the crime of bigamy. It has now been decided, however, in a lower court,[8] and approved by the Court of Appeal,[9] that a party to an existing polygamous marriage is not "married" for the purpose of founding a criminal charge of bigamy against him. These decisions create an unfortunate distinction between the civil and the criminal law conceptions of bigamy.[10]

Turning to succession,[11] it seems fairly clear that the children of both a potentially and an actually polygamous marriage can succeed to property in England.[12] The only real doubt[13] on the issue of succession by children concerns whether a child of a polygamous marriage can succeed to a title of honour, as an "heir" to real property or to an entailed interest.[1] This problem was discussed by Lord MAUGHAM in *The Sinha Peerage Claim*,[2] which con-

3 *Hyde v Hyde* (1866) LR 1 P & D 130.
4 *Sowa v Sowa* [1961] P 70, [1961] 1 All ER 687.
5 Infra, pp 628–629.
6 But the Irish courts have held that it cannot constitute a "common law" marriage: *Conlon v Mohamed* [1989] ILRM 523.
7 [1946] P 122, [1946] 1 All ER 342; and see *Srini Vasan v Srini Vasan* [1946] P 67; *Hashmi v Hashmi* [1972] Fam 36, [1971] 3 All ER 1253; Hartley (1967) 16 ICLQ 680, 691–694.
8 *R v Sarwan Singh* [1962] 3 All ER 612; Polonsky [1971] Crim LR 401.
9 *R v Sagoo* [1975] QB 885, [1975] 2 All ER 926; Carter (1974–75) 47 BYBIL 374; Morse (1976) 25 ICLQ 229. The Court of Appeal held that *R v Sarwan Singh*, supra, was wrongly decided, but only on the ground that no consideration had been given as to whether the marriage had become monogamous. The general principle was approved that "the marriage which is to be the foundation for a prosecution for bigamy must be a monogamous marriage": [1975] QB 885, at 889; Smith and Hogan, *Criminal Law* 6th edn (1987), pp 708–710.
10 Celebration of a "marriage" in England in polygamous form, in a private house, is not considered to be celebration of a "marriage" within the meaning of s 75(2) of the Marriage Act 1949, under which it is an offence knowingly and wilfully to solemnise a marriage in an unregistered building: *R v Bham* [1966] 1 QB 159, [1965] 3 All ER 124; and see *R v Ali Mohamed* [1964] 2 QB 350 n. On the other hand, it might be noted that the parties to a valid polygamous marriage are married for the purposes of the crime of conspiracy so that the spouses are unable to conspire together: *Mawji v R* [1957] AC 126, [1957] 1 All ER 385. If it is invalid it is of no effect in the law of evidence: *R v Junaid Khan* (1987) 84 Cr App Rep 44.
11 Though the determination of legitimacy is now of very limited relevance (infra, p 746), it might be noted that children of a valid potentially polygamous marriage are to be regarded as legitimate: *Sinha Peerage Claim* (1939) 171 Lords Journal 350, [1946] 1 All ER 348n; *Baindail v Baindail* [1946] P 122 at 127–128. It would also appear that children of an actually polygamous marriage are to be regarded as legitimate: *Hashmi v Hashmi* [1972] Fam 36; and see *Yuen Tse v Minister of Employment and Immigration* (1983) 32 RFL (2d) 274. For criticism of *Hashmi*, see Goldberg & Lowe (1972) 35 MLR 430; Carter (1971) 45 BYBIL 413, 414.
12 Cf *Bamgbose v Daniel* [1955] AC 107, [1954] 3 All ER 263; and see National Insurance Decision No R (G) 11/53. In *Re Bethell* (1888) 38 Ch D 220, such a child was unable to succeed, but this is probably because the polygamous marriage there would not be regarded in England as a valid marriage, given the husband's incapacity by his domiciliary law, supra, pp 617 et seq; cf Hartley (1969) 32 MLR 155, 171–172.
13 See Law Commission Working Paper No 83 (1982), para 4.42.
1 See Megarry and Wade, *The Law of Real Property*, 5th edn (1984), p 556.
2 [1946] 1 All ER 348n.

cerned succession to a title of honour. In fact, the marriage of the claimant's father, celebrated in polygamous form, was held to have become monogamous by change of religion.[3] In holding that the claimant could succeed to the title, Lord MAUGHAM declined to express a view on succession as "heir" or to entails. It seems, however, that he was primarily concerned with problems which could arise in the case of an actually polygamous marriage: "If there were several wives, the son of a second or third wife might be the claimant to a dignity to the exclusion of a later born son of the first wife. Our law as to heirship has provided no means of settling such questions as these."[4] These problems relate only to actually polygamous marriages and it seems safe to assume, with the Law Commission,[5] that although a child of an actually polygamous marriage cannot succeed as "heir" no such disability attaches to the child of a potentially polygamous marriage.

In the case of intestate succession by the widow of a potentially polygamous marriage, there is Privy Council authority in favour of her being able to succeed.[6] Such English authority as there is supports the view that such a widow would also be able to succeed under the Administration of Estates Act 1925.[7] There appears to be no good reason for not applying a similar rule in the case of succession by the wives of an actually polygamous marriage,[8] and this approach is supported by *Re Sehota*.[9] Here the deceased husband was validly polygamously married to two wives. He left the whole of his estate to the second wife and the first wife applied successfully for reasonable provision as a "wife" out of the estate, under the Inheritance (Provision for Family and Dependents) Act 1975.

Polygamous marriages are recognised for the purpose of determining other property rights. In *Shahnaz v Rizwan*,[10] a Moslem woman, whose potentially polygamous marriage celebrated in India had been validly dissolved, was held entitled to recover deferred dower from her former husband. The agreement recorded in the marriage certificate placed the husband under a contractual obligation to pay a certain sum by way of dower in the event of a divorce. WINN J was careful to emphasise[11] that the wife's right arose not out of the relationship of husband and wife, but out of a contract made in contemplation and in consideration of a marriage that was lawful in the eyes of English law. There is statutory recognition of actually and potentially polygamous marriages for the purposes of the protection granted to a spouse by the Matrimonial Homes Act 1983;[12] and it has been held that the summary procedure, under section 17 of the Married Women's Property Act 1882,

3 Supra, p 613.
4 [1946] 1 All ER 348 at 349.
5 Law Com No 146, Scot Law Com No 96 (1985), paras 3.5–3.6.
6 *Coleman v Shang* [1961] AC 481, [1961] 2 All ER 406.
7 In *Re Sehota* [1978] 1 WLR 1506, it was suggested (at 1511) that questions of succession had never fallen within the ambit of the rule in *Hyde v Hyde* (1866) LR 1 P & D 130; and see *Chaudhry v Chaudhry* [1976] Fam 148 at 152.
8 See *Cheang Thye Phin v Tan Ah Loy* [1920] AC 369; cf *The Six Widows Case* (1908) 12 Straits Settlements LR 120; though it must be admitted that there might be difficulty with distribution of the personal chattels.
9 [1978] 3 All ER 385, [1978] 1 WLR 1506.
10 [1965] 1 QB 390, [1964] 2 All ER 993; and see *Qureshi v Qureshi* [1972] Fam 173, [1971] 1 All ER 325.
11 Because of the then existing inability of the court to grant matrimonial relief in the case of polygamous marriages.
12 S 10(2).

for determining property disputes between husband and wife extends to polygamous marriages.[13]

Statutory recognition of polygamy is provided by social security legislation. Various social security benefits were denied to a wife or widow whose marriage was actually or potentially polygamous.[14] The relevant legislation was amended to allow a polygamous marriage celebrated outside the United Kingdom to be treated as a valid marriage, provided it had at all times been monogamous. However, these amendments were too restrictive in that they denied benefit not only in the case of a marriage which was actually polygamous, but also in the case of a marriage which was actually monogamous, though had once been polygamous. In the case of benefits such as widow's benefit, maternity benefit and child benefit which fall within the Social Security Act 1975 and the Child Benefit Act 1976, the present position is governed by regulations made under those Acts.[15] They allow a valid polygamous marriage to be treated as a monogamous marriage if it has either always been actually monogamous or for any day throughout which it was, in fact, monogamous.[16] This means that when a marriage becomes monogamous through death or divorce or until it ceases to be monogamous by reason of a second valid marriage there is a right to qualification for these social security benefits.

A rather different approach has been adopted towards income support and its predecessor benefits. In *Iman Din v National Assistance Board*[17] a husband and wife were married in Pakistan in 1948, this marriage being actually polygamous as the first wife did not die until 1949. Shortly after they had come to England in 1961, the husband abandoned his wife and four of their children, who then received assistance from the National Assistance Board. The question before the court was whether the words "wife" and "children" under section 42(1)(a) of the National Assistance Act 1948 included the wife and children of a polygamous marriage, for, if so, the husband could be ordered to contribute to the maintenance of his family. SALMON LJ asked himself: "is there any good reason why the appellant's wife and children should not be recognised as his wife and children for the purpose of the National Assistance Act 1948? I can find no such reason, and every reason in common sense and justice why they should be so recognised".[18] Here the status of the wife was recognised, though it should be borne in mind that the marriage was, at all material times, actually monogamous. The present position with regard to income support is that a crucial factor is the nature of the relationship between a man and a woman who are members of the same household, rather than whether they are validly married. The result is that the relevant legislation[19] extends to cases of actually polygamous marriages.[20]

The question of the application of tax legislation to polygamous marriages

13 *Chaudhry v Chaudhry* [1976] Fam 148, [1976] 1 All ER 805—a case of a potentially polygamous marriage.
14 Decision Nos R (G) 18/52; R (G) 11/53; R (G) 3/55; R (G) 7/55; and see Ogus and Barendt, *The Law of Social Security*, 3rd edn (1988), pp 352–353, Pearl [1978–79] JSWL 24.
15 Social Security Act 1975, s 162b, SI 1975 561; Child Benefit Act 1976, s 9(2)(a), SI 1976 965.
16 SI 1975 561, rr 1(2), 2(2); SI 1976 965, r 12.; and see National Insurance Decision Nos R (G) 2/75; R (G) 3/75.
17 [1967] 2 QB 213, [1967] 1 All ER 750; Partington (1967) 16 ICLQ 805.
18 [1967] 2 QB 213 at 220.
19 Social Security Act 1986; SI 1987 1697, r 18.
20 SI 1987 1697, r 2(1); Ogus & Barendt, op cit, pp 424, 427.

came before the courts in *Nabi v Heaton*[1] where the facts were these.

The taxpayer claimed relief on the ground that his wife was wholly maintained by him[2] from 1970 to 1976. He had come to England from Pakistan
in 1965 and married his first wife in England in 1968. They soon separated
and in 1969, whilst still domiciled in Pakistan, he there married his second
wife. She lived in Pakistan, maintained by him from England, until she
came to join him here in 1975 when he divorced his first wife. The allowance
was claimed in respect of the second wife.

Although logically the first question to ask was whether the second marriage
was to be regarded in England as valid,[3] VINELOTT J felt it unnecessary to
answer it because he concluded that the taxpayer failed whether or not the
second marriage was a valid actually polygamous marriage.[4] The reason for
his conclusion was that he decided that reference to "his wife" in the Income
and Corporation Taxes Act 1970 had to be construed in the singular.[5]
Although it was the practice of the Revenue to grant the relief claimed in the
case of potentially polygamous marriages,[6] VINELOTT J's decision would deny
the relief in respect of any wife in the case of a valid actually polygamous
marriage. When the taxpayer appealed, the Crown obviously had second
thoughts, accepting that the appeal should be allowed by consent;[7] from
which one may conclude that, in practice, the relief will now be extended to
all wives.

Other examples can be provided of the acceptance of polygamous marriages in English law. It seems generally agreed[8] that a wife, or wives, of a
polygamous marriage should be able to claim under the Fatal Accidents Act
1976 on the basis of dependence on the deceased husband. Finally, one of
the most striking examples of recognition of the marital status conferred by
a polygamous marriage is provided by *Mohamed v Knott:*[9]

A Nigerian domiciled in Nigeria there married a thirteen year old girl,
according to Moslem law. This marriage was potentially polygamous and
was valid under Nigerian law. Three months later they both came to
England and a complaint was made against the husband that the girl was
in need of care and protection within the meaning of section 2 of the
Children and Young Persons Act 1963. The justices refused to recognise
the marriage and concluded that a thirteen year old girl living with a man
twice her age was in need of care and protection.

The Divisional Court differed and decided that this was a valid though
potentially polygamous marriage, which should be recognised as conferring
the status of a "wife" on the girl.[10]

It is possible now to draw a number of general conclusions as to the
recognition afforded today by English law to polygamous marriages. The

1 [1981] 1 WLR 1052, appeal allowed by consent [1983] 1 WLR 626; see Carter (1981) 52
  BYBIL 322.
2 Income and Corporation Taxes Act 1970, s 8(1); see now Income and Corporation Taxes
  Act 1988, s 257(1).
3 Supra, pp 617 et seq.
4 [1981] 1 WLR 1052 at 1056–1057.
5 Ibid at 1057–1059. Contrast the more generous approach in *Iman Din v National Assistance
  Board* [1967] 2 QB 213, [1967] 1 All ER 750, supra, p 624.
6 Ibid at 1059.
7 [1983] 1 WLR 626.
8 Law Com No 42 (1971), para 124; Hartley (1969) 32 MLR 155, 169–170.
9 [1969] 1 QB 1, [1968] 2 All ER 563; Karsten (1969) 32 MLR 212.
10 Whilst the court considered that an order under the 1963 Act could be made in respect of a
   married woman, it declined to make one in this case.

wheel has almost come full circle since 1866.[11] Instead of such marriages, whether actually or potentially polygamous, being denied recognition for all purposes, they are now widely recognised. The general pattern of legislative interpretation over the last two decades has been a liberal one, so that the term "wife" is generally taken to include the wives in an actually polygamous marriage. There is now a presumption in favour of the recognition of a polygamous marriage unless a good contrary reason can be shown. This has led to the suggestion that the rule in *Hyde v Hyde* has been entirely abolished.[12] If that is to be taken to mean that all *actually* polygamous marriages have the same effect and recognition as monogamous ones, it is too extravagant a statement. Obvious continuing areas of difference are capacity to marry[13] and the rules as to social security benefits. It is, however, worth examining whether there are, or should be, any differences between monogamous and *potentially* polygamous marriages.

The Law Commission has identified[14] only two possible differences—the present rules on capacity to marry and succession as an "heir" to real property, an entailed interest or a title of honour. The first difference will disappear if the Commission's proposals for reform are implemented.[15] The second difference is more apparent than real because the restrictions on succession would seem to be limited to the children of actually polygamous marriages.[16] The Law Commission's conclusion is that, provided a marriage remains actually monogamous, there should be no difference between a marriage celebrated in a monogamous form and a potentially polygamous one, and that, if the Commission's recommendations on capacity to marry are implemented, all references to potentially polygamous marriages can safely be removed from the statute book.[17] The concept will be dead.[18] Indeed it seems hard to disagree with the comment that the "use of the concept of a potentially polygamous marriage . . . involves an unnecessary and undesirable complication in an area of law which is sufficiently difficult without it".[19]

---

11 *Hyde v Hyde* (1866) LR 1 P & D 130.
12 *Re Sehota* [1978] 1 WLR 1506 at 1511.
13 Where it has been recommended that English domiciliaries should continue to be incapable of contracting actually polygamous marriages, supra, p 621.
14 Law Com No 146, Scot Law Com No 96 (1985), para 3.5.
15 Supra, p 621.
16 Supra, pp 622–623.
17 Law Com No 146, Scot Law Com No 96 (1985), paras 3.5–3.10.
18 As it seems to be in the USA: *Royal v Cudahy Packing Co* (1922) 190 NW 427 at 428.
19 Palsson, *Marriage and Divorce in Comparative Conflict of Laws* (1974), p 155.

Chapter 22

Matrimonial causes[1]

SUMMARY

1. INTRODUCTION

Matrimonial causes are now generally taken to include petitions for divorce, nullity of marriage, judicial separation and presumption of death and dissolution of marriage.[2]

The rules relating to the jurisdiction of the courts and to the recognition of foreign divorces, annulments and judicial separations are, in essence,

---

1 See North, *Private International Law of Matrimonial Causes*; (1990) I Hague Recueil 9, 97–126.

2 Two other matrimonial causes have been abolished in recent times: the action for restitution of conjugal rights by the Matrimonial Proceedings and Property Act 1970, s 20, and the action for jactitation of marriage by the Family Law Act 1986, s 61. Jactitation of marriage was a rare proceeding which could be brought against a person who persistently boasted that he or she was married to the petitioner. The relief granted was a decree of perpetual silence. See Law Com No 132 (1984), paras 4.1–4.11.

identical for all three matrimonial causes.[3] So they will be examined together, identifying where appropriate any rules which do not apply to all three. It will be seen that the one major area of difference remaining concerns the determination of the law to be applied by the English courts.[4] We shall then go on to examine, separately, proceedings for presumption of death and dissolution of marriage.

Before these various matrimonial causes are considered, it is necessary to discuss a further preliminary issue, namely whether an English court will assume jurisdiction to grant matrimonial relief in the case of an actually or potentially polygamous marriage.

2. POLYGAMOUS MARRIAGES AND MATRIMONIAL RELIEF[5]

(a) AT COMMON LAW

Until 1972, the rule of English law was that the parties to a polygamous marriage were "not entitled to the remedies, the adjudication, or the relief of the matrimonial law of England."[6] It meant that the courts would decline to grant a divorce,[7] a decree of nullity even where the petitioner claimed lack of capacity to enter a polygamous marriage,[8] or a decree of judicial separation.[9] Although the restrictive nature of this rule could be avoided in part by such devices as holding that the law of the place of celebration determined the nature of the marriage,[10] so that all valid marriages in England were regarded as monogamous, or that the nature of a marriage might change by, for example, acquisition of an English domicil,[11] more fundamental reform was called for in view of the number of immigrants from jurisdictions where they had contracted valid marriages in polygamous form. A substantial number of people, permanently resident though not domiciled in England, were denied all matrimonial relief.

(b) MATRIMONIAL CAUSES ACT 1973, SECTION 47

All this has now changed. Section 47(1) of the Matrimonial Causes Act 1973[12] provides that:

> A court in England and Wales shall not be precluded from granting matrimonial relief or making a declaration concerning the validity of a marriage by reason only that the marriage in question was entered into under a law which permits polygamy.

This section makes available to the parties to a polygamous marriage, whether

---

3 All actions for divorce, nullity or judicial separation must be started in a divorce county court, with transfer to the High Court (or indeed vice versa) to be made under a flexible system whereby the criteria are to be laid down by direction: Matrimonial and Family Proceedings Act 1984, ss 33(1), 37–39; Matrimonial Proceedings (Transfers) Act 1988; *Practice Direction (Family Division: Business: Distribution)* [1988] 1 WLR 558.
4 Infra, pp 639 et seq.
5 See North, op cit, ch 7.
6 *Hyde v Hyde* (1866) LR 1 P & D 130 at 138.
7 *Hyde v Hyde*, supra; *Muhammad v Suna* 1956 SC 366.
8 *Risk v Risk* [1951] P 50, [1950] 2 All ER 973.
9 Cf *Nachimson v Nachimson* [1930] P 217.
10 Supra, pp 610–612.
11 Supra, pp 613–616.
12 Re-enacting, with minor amendments, s 1 of the Matrimonial Proceedings (Polygamous Marriages) Act 1972.

potentially or actually so,[13] a wide range of matrimonial relief,[14] namely decrees of divorce, nullity, judicial separation, presumption of death and dissolution of marriage, orders for financial provision in the cases of neglect to maintain, variation of maintenance agreements, orders for financial relief or relating to children which are ancillary to any of the preceding decrees or orders,[15] orders made under Part I of the Domestic Proceedings and Magistrates' Courts Act 1978,[16] orders for financial relief after a foreign divorce, annulment or legal separation,[17] and any declaration under Part III of the Family Law Act 1986 involving a determination as to the validity of a marriage.[18] Indeed it has been said that the effect of section 47 of the 1973 Act is to abolish entirely the old rule, so that all forms of relief which can be classed as matrimonial are now available in the case of polygamous marriages.[19]

(c) REMAINING PROBLEMS

Whilst polygamous marriages will, for the purposes of such relief, normally be treated just as if they were monogamous marriages, they do pose certain peculiar problems, especially in the, albeit rare, cases of actually polygamous marriages. Indeed, in such cases the 1973 Act makes specific provision for the making of rules of court to require notice of the proceedings to be served on any spouse other than one who is party to the proceedings and to confer on such a spouse a right to be heard.[20]

Where a party to an actually polygamous marriage brings proceedings for divorce alleging irretrievable breakdown of the marriage,[21] difficulties may arise over adultery, unreasonable behaviour or desertion as proof of break-down.[22] If a wife alleges that her husband has committed adultery with another wife, such a claim will usually fail because "it is an essential element of adultery that intercourse has taken place outside the marriage relationship ie between persons not married to each other. This being so, intercourse with a wife could not be adultery".[23] In terms of policy, this conclusion seems right if both marriages were entered into in polygamous form. It has been said[24] that in such a case there has been no breach of the obligation of fidelity imposed by the law governing the marriage. Difficulties arise, however, in the case of a valid monogamous marriage, followed by a valid polygamous one,[25] as in the decision of the Privy Council in *Drammeh v Drammeh*:[26]

H, domiciled in The Gambia, married W1 in England in monogamous

---

13 Matrimonial Causes Act 1973, s 47(4); see eg *Onobrauche v Onobrauche* (1978) 8 Fam Law 107; *Quoraishi v Quoraishi* [1985] FLR 780, CA.
14 Matrimonial Causes Act 1973, s 47(2).
15 *Chaudhry v Chaudhry* [1976] Fam 148 at 151.
16 See 1978 Act, Sch 2, para 39.
17 Matrimonial and Family Proceedings Act 1984 Sch 1, para 15, infra, pp 709–714.
18 Matrimonial Causes Act 1973, s 47(3), as substituted by the Family Law Act 1986, Sch 1, para 14.
19 *Re Sehota* [1978] 3 All ER 385 at 389, [1978] 1 WLR 1506 at 1511.
20 Matrimonial Causes Act 1973, s 47(4); see Family Proceedings Rules 1991, r 3.11.
21 Ibid, s 1.
22 Ibid, s 1(2)(a), (b) and (c).
23 Law Com No 42 (1971), para 50; and see *Onobrauche v Onobrauche* (1978) 8 Fam Law 107.
24 Clive, *The Law of Husband and Wife in Scotland*, 2nd edn (1982), p 129.
25 The question of the validity of the second marriage where the first was monogamous is discussed supra, p 616.
26 (1970) 78 Ceylon Law Weekly 55.

form. Both professed the Christian faith. H then returned to The Gambia, reverted to his Moslem faith and married W2 in polygamous form. W1 petitioned for divorce, before the courts of The Gambia, alleging adultery by H with W2.

The Privy Council upheld the decision that W1 was entitled to a divorce, holding that even if the marriage to W2 was a valid polygamous marriage under the law of The Gambia, this should not affect the rights of W1 stemming from her valid English monogamous marriage. The nature of her marriage was not changed by H's unilateral change of faith. So far as W1's marriage was concerned, H had committed adultery with W1.[1] Had W1 chosen, as well she might, to have petitioned for divorce in England, it seems likely that an English court would have reached the same conclusion as the Privy Council.[2] When the Law Commission considered the effect of a later polygamous marriage on an earlier marriage, whether in monogamous or polygamous form, it concluded that legislative intervention was neither necessary nor desirable.[3]

If a wife's divorce petition is based on the husband's unreasonable behaviour,[4] then the court will have to examine all the circumstances of the marriage[5] and it has been held that the taking by the husband of a second wife is unreasonable behaviour towards the first.[6] Similarly, if a husband's petition is based on desertion by the first wife,[7] the fact that he has validly married a second wife has been held to give the first wife reasonable grounds for leaving him.[8]

3. DIVORCE, NULLITY AND JUDICIAL SEPARATION

(a) JURISDICTION[9]

(i) Bases of jurisdiction

The Domicile and Matrimonial Proceedings Act 1973, Part II, provides two broad bases of jurisdiction for divorce, nullity and judicial separation—domicil and habitual residence. These are the only two bases of jurisdiction, and they provide uniform bases throughout the United Kingdom.[10]

Domicil
The English courts have jurisdiction to entertain proceedings for divorce, nullity and judicial separation (whether the marriage is alleged to be void or voidable) if either of the parties to the marriage is domiciled in England at the time when the proceedings are begun.[11] Jurisdiction is based on the domicil of either party whether petitioner or respondent (or, in the case of

1 See also *A-G of Ceylon v Reid* [1965] AC 720 at 729; *Lendrum v Chakravarti* 1929 SLT 96 at 99.
2 Law Com No 146 (1985), para 4.16.
3 Ibid, para 4.23.
4 Matrimonial Causes Act 1973, s 1(2)(b).
5 *Gollins v Gollins* [1964] AC 644.
6 *Poon v Tan* (1973) 4 Fam Law 161.
7 Matrimonial Causes Act 1973, s 1(2)(b).
8 *Quoraishi v Quoraishi* [1985] FLR 780, CA.
9 See North, op cit, chapters 2–4.
10 For Scotland, see Domicile and Matrimonial Proceedings Act 1973, s 7; for Northern Ireland, see now the Matrimonial Causes (Northern Ireland) Order, SI 1978/1045 (NI 15), art 49.
11 S 5(2)(a).

nullity, even if neither[12]), bearing in mind that one spouse can acquire a domicil separate from that of the other. Thus a husband domiciled abroad may petition for divorce on the jurisdictional ground that his wife, the respondent, is domiciled in England, even though he has never visited England.

The time at which domicil is to be determined is (with one exception relating to nullity petitions[13]), as at common law,[14] the time when proceedings are commenced, not at the later time when the case is tried. If the rule were otherwise, a respondent domiciled in England could frustrate a petition brought by the other spouse, domiciled and resident abroad, by changing his domicil between the presentation of the petition and the hearing of the case. The rule is "once competent, always competent"[15] and this will be so even if the party domiciled in England at the time of the proceedings has since changed his domicil, disassociated himself from the determination of his status by an English court and even taken proceedings in the court of his new domicil.[16]

Habitual residence[17]

The English courts have jurisdiction to hear petitions for divorce, nullity or judicial separation if either party, husband or wife, was habitually resident in England throughout the period of one year up to the date when the proceedings were begun.[1] As with domicil, the relevant date is one year's habitual residence up to the date of commencement of proceedings, rather than of trial or judgment. This time factor is even more significant in the case of habitual residence than domicil for it is easier to change one's residence than domicil and thus frustrate the petitioner. There seems little doubt that ante-nuptial residence will qualify for the determination of the one year period.[2] It will also be the case that a spouse, who has never been to England and has no personal connection with England whatsoever, will be able to petition on the basis of the respondent's habitual residence in England.

The residence to found jurisdiction must be "habitual". This is not easy to define[3] and indeed it was thought that "habitual residence" was similar to the concept of "ordinary residence", a view which has been adopted by the House of Lords[4] in a different context. This approach has been applied by BUSH J to the issue of divorce jurisdiction in *Kapur v Kapur*,[5] saying:

In my view, there is no real distinction to be drawn between "ordinary" and

12 For a nullity petition relating to a void marriage may be brought by a person, other than a spouse, who has an interest in so doing: eg *Faremouth v Watson* (1811) 1 Phillim 355; *Sherwood v Ray* (1837) 1 Moo PCC 353; *Bevan v M'Mahon* (1859) 2 Sw & Tr 58; *Faull v Reilly* (1970) 16 FLR 150; *Dunne v Brown* (1982) 60 FLR 212; see Law Com No 132 (1984), paras 3.29–3.33 where the continuation of the present rule is recommended.
13 Infra, p 633.
14 *Leon v Leon* [1967] P 275.
15 Ibid, at 284.
16 Cf ibid, at 284. This is subject to the rules relating to staying of matrimonial proceedings, infra, pp 635–639.
17 Hall (1975) 24 ICLQ 1.
1 S 5(2)(b); again, with an exception in relation to nullity petitions, infra, p 633.
2 Cf *Navas v Navas* [1970] P 159, [1969] 3 All ER 677.
3 See supra, pp 169–171; North, op cit, pp 13–15.
4 *Barnet London Borough Council v Shah* [1983] 2 AC 309.
5 [1984] FLR 920 at 926. Dicta in *Cruse v Chittum* [1974] 2 All ER 940 at 943 differentiating between ordinary and habitual residence were rejected as inconsistent with *Shah's Case*, supra.

"habitual residence". It may be that in some circumstances a man may be habitually resident without being ordinarily resident, but I cannot at the moment conceive of such a situation ... "Habitually" means settled practice or usually, or, in other words, the same as ... ordinary residence—a voluntary residence, with a degree of settled purpose.

The essence of the concept of "habitual residence" is less demanding in terms of intention than the concept of domicil[6] but "a residence must be more than transient or casual; once established, however, it is not necessarily broken by a temporary absence."[7] Indeed, a respondent has been held[8] to be habitually resident here for the purposes of divorce jurisdiction even though she spent one third of the relevant year either on holiday in Spain or visiting her children in the USA and Canada. What is unclear is whether a person may have more than one habitual residence.[9] Tax cases[10] and a divorce decision[11] indicate a possible duality of ordinary residence, but such a possibility seems to have been rejected for habitual residence in the context of adoption.[12] Given the breadth of the present matrimonial jurisdictional rules, no harm would come from the wider view and, indeed, injustice might be avoided if our courts did decide that one party had been sufficiently strongly connected with England for a year, notwithstanding an equal connection elsewhere.

Jurisdiction to entertain other matrimonial proceedings in respect of the same marriage
Although domicil and habitual residence are determined as at the date when proceedings are begun, section 5(5) of the Domicile and Matrimonial Proceedings Act 1973 makes provision for jurisdiction to be assumed in other circumstances. If proceedings are pending for divorce, judicial separation or nullity in which the court has jurisdiction by reason of the grounds laid down in the 1973 Act, then the court has jurisdiction to entertain other proceedings, in respect of the same marriage, for divorce, judicial separation or nullity even though there would be no jurisdiction under the 1973 Act.

The jurisdictional grounds in the case of divorce, judicial separation and nullity are identical[13] and so the purpose of this somewhat cryptic provision seems to be to deal with two jurisdictional problems. For example, let us assume that a husband, habitually resident in England at the date the proceedings are begun, petitions for nullity but, before the petition is heard, abandons his English residence. The wife, domiciled and resident abroad, wishes to cross-petition for divorce. At that time, there is no apparent jurisdictional basis for her petition; but section 5(5) confers jurisdiction because proceedings for nullity are pending in respect of which the court does have jurisdiction. Secondly, the English court appears also to have jurisdiction where the petitioner changes his mind, as in the case where a spouse petitions for judicial separation, jurisdiction being based on his habit-

6 *Adderson v Adderson* (1987) 36 DLR (4th) 631.
7 Law Com No 48 (1972), para 42. See also Council of Europe Resolution (72)1: Standardisation of the Legal Concepts of Domicile and "Residence", Rule 9.
8 *Oundjian v Oundjian* [1979] 1 FLR 198.
9 North, op cit, p 15; and see *Barnet London Borough Council v Shah* [1983] 2 AC 309 at 344–345.
10 Eg *IRC v Lysaght* [1928] AC 234.
11 *Hopkins v Hopkins* [1951] P 116, [1950] 2 All ER 1035.
12 Blom (1973) 22 ICLQ 109, 135–136.
13 Save that provision is made in the case of nullity for the situation where one spouse has died and this is, of course, quite irrelevant to divorce or judicial separation: s 5(3)(c), infra, p 633.

ual residence, and then, before the petition is heard but after he has lost his English habitual residence, amends his petition to one for divorce. Finally, there is one further complication in that section 5(5) applies to cases where jurisdiction is conferred by reason of that sub-section itself. For example, proceedings are pending for divorce, jurisdiction being based on habitual residence; then a cross petition is brought for divorce even though the original jurisdictional grounds no longer exist, jurisdiction being conferred by section 5(5); the original proceedings are abandoned; the cross-petitioner then wishes to amend the petition to one for nullity. The court has jurisdiction, again under section 5(5), to hear the final nullity petition so long as the cross-petition is still pending.

Nullity petitions: domicil or habitual residence before death
There is one basis of jurisdiction which applies only to nullity petitions. If either party to the marriage has died before the date when the proceedings for nullity were begun, the court has jurisdiction if the deceased was domiciled at death in England, or had been habitually resident in England for the year immediately preceding the death.[14] The reason for this special jurisdictional rule is that, whilst divorce and judicial separation petitions can only be brought if both spouses are alive, the validity of a marriage may need to be tested in a nullity petition notwithstanding the death of one spouse or even after the death of both, as where succession issues are involved. We have seen already[15] that it is possible for a person not a party to the marriage to petition for the annulment of a void marriage.

(ii) Impact of the statutory bases

(a) No discretion If the statutory bases of jurisdiction are satisfied, the court does not have a general discretion to refuse to hear the petition. We shall see[16] that there is a discretion to stay the proceedings in cases where to proceed would lead to a clash with foreign proceedings, but there is no other discretion. For instance, leave is not required to serve the petition on a respondent overseas.[1] The position has been summed up by BUSH J in a case where the respondent wife was resident in Ireland and could not afford to contest the English divorce proceedings:

> If a court has jurisdiction ... there is no way in which the court could decline jurisdiction on the ground of hardship, apparent unfairness or any other ground.[2]

(b) Effect on the common law rules In the case of divorce and judicial separation, the jurisdictional bases under the 1973 Act are markedly broader than the common law rules which they replaced. With nullity petitions, the effect of the statutory jurisdictional rules is one of great simplification, but one notable basis of jurisdiction has been lost. It was the case that celebration of the marriage in England conferred jurisdiction over a nullity petition relating to a void marriage.[3] The loss of this head of jurisdiction could create some difficulty in one situation. If two people with only a transient connection

---

14 Domicile and Matrimonial Proceedings Act 1973, s 5(3)(c).
15 Supra, p 631.
16 Infra, pp 635–639.
1 Family Proceedings Rules 1991, r 10.6, infra, pp 634–635; cf RSC Ord 11, r 1(1), supra, pp 190 et seq.
2 *Kapur v Kapur* [1984] FLR 920 at 922.
3 *Simonin v Mallac* (1860) 2 Sw & Tr 67; *Ross-Smith v Ross-Smith* [1963] AC 280, [1962] 1 All ER 344; *Padolecchia v Padolecchia* [1968] P 314, [1967] 3 All ER 863.

with England marry here, when domiciled and resident abroad, the English court will have no jurisdiction to rule upon the formal validity of that English marriage[4] unless and until one of the parties acquires an English domicil or resides here for a year.[5]

(c) Retention of domicil as a jurisdictional basis It might be asked why the much criticised connecting factor of domicil should be retained as a jurisdictional basis. Despite the improvements afforded by the Domicile and Matrimonial Proceedings Act 1973 in the cases of married women and minors, it is still a difficult and complex factor to apply in particular cases. What would be lost if it was abandoned altogether? Such a move would, however, lead to hardship in a number of cases where the spouses, though not resident in England, retain strong links with England, such as those who spend long periods abroad either in the service of the Crown as diplomats or administrators or in a purely business capacity. It is undesirable to deny them access to the matrimonial jurisdiction of the courts of the country to which they consider they "belong".

(d) Dangers inherent in the habitual residence basis It is, undoubtedly, true, however, that most petitioners whether or not domiciled in England will rely on habitual residence as the basis of jurisdiction as it is so much easier to prove and domicil will, in practice, be reserved for those exceptional cases where there is no, or insufficient, residence. Paradoxically, the very utility of habitual residence as a connecting factor leads to difficulties. There is a danger of the English courts being used as a haven by those who are unable to obtain divorces or other matrimonial decrees in the country of their domicil or nationality. This danger is, of course, reduced both by the cost of establishing residence here for a year and the factors of immigration controls and the granting of work permits. Even in those cases where one spouse is habitually resident here, there is a further difficulty in that the English decree may be denied recognition elsewhere, especially in the country of the domicil,[6] on the basis that the foreign jurisdiction does not accept, for recognition purposes, such wide jurisdictional grounds as the English courts now have. The marriage will, therefore, limp, but the parties may regard a limping marriage as better than no decree at all.

These broad jurisdictional grounds may also have the effect that there are several countries which, simultaneously, claim jurisdiction over the parties to entertain the proceedings.[7] The need for power to stay actions in certain such cases, and other procedural issues must now be considered.

(iii) Procedural issues

(a) Service of the petition A copy of every petition for divorce, nullity or judicial separation must be served personally or by post on the respondent and every co-respondent,[8] and there is no need to obtain the leave of the

---

4 Cf *Padolecchia v Padolecchia* [1968] P 314 at 334–335; *Prawdzic-Lazarska v Prawdzic-Lazarski* 1954 SC 98 at 103.
5 Cf Law Com No 48 (1972), para 60.
6 See, eg the Irish Domicile and Recognition of Foreign Divorces Act 1986, s 5; and see *Gaffney v Gaffney* [1975] IR 133 at 150; *KED (KC) v MC* [1987] ILRM 189; cf *M (C) v M (T)* [1988] ILRM 456; and see *CM v TM* [1991] ILRM 268.
7 *Gadd v Gadd* [1984] 1 WLR 1435 at 1439.
8 Family Proceedings Rules 1991, r 2.9(1).

court for service out of the jurisdiction.[9] An order for substituted service may be made in appropriate circumstances,[10] and service may even be dispensed with altogether in any case in which service is impracticable or dispensation otherwise appears necessary or expedient.[11] This discretion is unfettered, but it will be exercised in favour of the petitioner only in exceptional cases, as, for instance, when the possible methods of substituted service are likely to be ineffective.[12]

(b) Staying proceedings[13] The breadth of the English jurisdictional rules introduced by the Domicile and Matrimonial Proceedings Act 1973 has the consequence that there is a greater risk of divorce and other matrimonial proceedings in respect of the same marriage being pursued in England and in some other country simultaneously. Indeed there could be several jurisdictions potentially in conflict, as where a wife habitually resident in England, but domiciled in Ireland, petitions for divorce from a husband habitually resident in Ontario, but domiciled in New York. There are two related problems in that the other proceedings may either be in some other part of the British Isles or in some politically foreign country; and the provisions in Schedule 1 of the Domicile and Matrimonial Proceedings Act 1973 for the staying of the English proceedings vary as between these two cases. In both, however, there is an obligation on the petitioner, or a cross-petitioner, when proceedings are pending before the English court to furnish particulars of any proceedings[14] in respect of that marriage, or affecting its validity, which he knows are continuing in another jurisdiction.[15]

Mandatory stays
Paragraph 8 of Schedule 1 provides for a mandatory stay. Where it appears before the beginning of the trial[16] of proceedings for divorce, and only divorce,[17] that proceedings for divorce or nullity are continuing elsewhere in the British Isles,[18] that the parties to the marriage have resided together after its celebration, that the place where they resided together when those proceedings began or where they last resided together before those proceedings began is that other jurisdiction in the British Isles, and that either of the parties was habitually resident there for a year ending with the date on which they last resided there together, the English court must, on the

---

9 Ibid, r 10.6(1).
10 Ibid, r 2.9(9).
11 Ibid, r 2.9(11).
12 *Luccioni v Luccioni* [1943] P 49, [1943] 1 All ER 384 (no dispensation); *Weighman v Weighman* [1947] 2 All ER 852 (dispensation); *Paolantonio v Paolantonio* [1950] 2 All ER 404 (dispensation); *Spalenkova v Spalenkova* [1954] P 141, [1953] 2 All ER 880 (no dispensation); and see *Whitehead v Whitehead* [1963] P 117 at 138, [1962] 3 All ER 800 at 811, 812. Different considerations are relevant in the case of a petition for presumption of death and dissolution of marriage: *N v N* [1957] P 385, [1957] 1 All ER 536; infra, pp 691–692.
13 Schuz (1987) 17 Fam Law 438; (1989) 38 ICLQ 946.
14 Including non-judicial proceedings of a description prescribed by rules of court: Sch 1, paras 5 and 6; see Family Proceedings Rules 1991, rr 2.3, 2.27.
15 Domicile and Matrimonial Proceedings Act 1977, s 5(6), Sch 1, para 7.
16 Trial of a preliminary issue of jurisdiction does not constitute trial of the proceedings for this purpose: Sch 1, para 4(1). Nor does trial of an issue as to custody or financial relief: *Thyssen-Bornemisza v Thyssen-Bornemisza* [1986] Fam 1, [1985] 1 All ER 328.
17 Where the proceedings are not only proceedings for divorce, then references to divorce apply only to the extent to which the proceedings are for divorce: Sch 1, para 8(2).
18 Defined by Sch 1, para 2, to mean Scotland, Northern Ireland, Jersey, Guernsey and the Isle of Man.

application of one of the spouses,[19] order the English proceedings to be stayed.[20]

The salient features of this mandatory stay are that it only applies to English divorce proceedings and then only when the parties to the marriage are closely and clearly connected with the other jurisdiction in the British Isles. If the English proceedings are other than for divorce, or if the other British proceedings are other than for divorce or nullity, or if the residential connections with the other British jurisdiction are not all satisfied, this does not mean that the other proceedings cannot be stayed. It means, merely, that there will be no mandatory stay and that the question must be considered instead in the context of the court's *discretion* to stay the other proceedings. The object of the fairly elaborate criteria as to mandatory stays is to ensure that the proceedings are heard in the more appropriate forum; though it is possible to point to cases where the criteria produce the less appropriate forum.[21]

Discretionary stays
Paragraph 9 of Schedule 1 makes provision for discretionary stays. Where it appears before the beginning of the trial of any matrimonial proceedings[1] before the English courts that any proceedings[2] are pending in another jurisdiction in respect of, or capable of affecting, the validity or subsistence of the marriage in question, then the English court has a discretion to stay its own proceedings. It has been held that proceedings in India for maintenance and for an injunction to allow the wife to reoccupy the matrimonial home do not affect the validity or subsistence of the marriage.[3] This discretion is wider than in the case of the mandatory staying provisions in that it applies to proceedings before both other British and foreign courts and it also applies to a much wider range of proceedings before both the English and the other courts.[4] In this case, the court may act not only on the application of a spouse but also of its own motion, and so it might exercise its discretion to stay proceedings in circumstances covered by the mandatory staying provisions where a spouse has not sought such a stay.

The basis on which the court's discretion is to be exercised is stated to be that the balance of fairness and convenience between the parties, having regard to all relevant factors, including the convenience of witnesses and

---

19 But not by the court's acting of its own motion, see Law Com No 48 (1972), paras 90–93. See Family Proceedings Rules 1991, r 2.27(1).
20 Sch 1, para 8(1); see *T v T (Custody: Jurisdiction)* [1992] 1 FLR 43. There are similar provisions requiring divorce proceedings in Scotland or Northern Ireland to be stayed when proceedings for divorce or nullity are continuing elsewhere in the British Isles: Sch 3, para 8; Sch 5.
21 North, op cit, pp 37–38.
 1 These are defined as proceedings for divorce, judicial separation, nullity, and declarations as to the validity or subsistence of the petitioner's marriage: Sch 1, para 2. Proceedings for presumption of death and dissolution of marriage and for declarations of legitimacy or parentage are not included. Trial of an ancillary issue as to custody or financial relief is not trial of the matrimonial proceedings: *Thyssen-Bornemisza v Thyssen-Bornemisza* [1986] Fam 1, [1985] 1 All ER 328.
 2 The foreign proceedings may be of any kind, both as to the relief sought and the nature of the proceedings, including presumably administrative proceedings, so long as they are of a description prescribed by rules of court: Sch 1, paras 5 and 6; see Family Proceedings Rules 1991, rr 2.3, 2.27.
 3 *Kapur v Kapur* [1984] FLR 920 at 922.
 4 Insofar as it applies also to cases covered by the mandatory staying provisions, the court shall not exercise its discretionary power whilst an application for a mandatory stay is pending: Sch 1, para 9(3).

delay or expense likely to result from a decision whether or not to stay the proceedings, is such that it is appropriate for the proceedings before the other court to be disposed of first.[5] It will depend on the facts of each case as to how the judge will draw this balance, but guidance has now emerged from the small number of reported cases directly concerned with the exercise of the discretion.[6] What is clear is that, in determining the principles for the exercise of the discretion under the 1973 Act, the courts are to apply the general approach to the operation of the doctrine of *forum non conveniens* under the inherent jurisdiction which was developed in the context of commercial cases.[7] This means that the discretion under paragraph 9 of Schedule 1 of the 1973 Act ought to be exercised to grant a stay if the defendant can point to another forum which is the appropriate one for trial of the proceedings provided that the plaintiff does not show that justice cannot be done there. Indeed, it has been suggested that, with the general common law development of *forum non conveniens*, the statutory provisions relating to matrimonial causes are no longer necessary.[8]

The drawing together of the statutory and common law approaches was achieved by the House of Lords in *De Dampierre v De Dampierre:*[9]

The husband and wife were both French nationals who married in France in 1977. Two years later they moved to London. Then, in 1984, the wife established an antiques business in New York and in 1985 she took their child to live there with her. The wife refused to return and the husband started divorce proceedings in France, whereupon the wife then petitioned for divorce in England. The husband sought to have the English proceedings stayed. This was resisted by the wife who claimed that, if she was found to be solely responsible for the breakdown of the marriage, she would receive less financial support from a French court than from an English one.

The English court had jurisdiction to entertain the wife's petition on the basis of the husband's habitual residence in England; but it was pointed out that this was just the type of case which would raise issues as to staying proceedings, given that domicil was no longer the exclusive ground of jurisdiction.[10] The House of Lords granted a stay, having little doubt that France was the more appropriate forum, given the wife's tenuous links with England and that "she voluntarily severed all connections with England before instituting her English divorce proceedings".[11] If France was the natural forum, then the issue had to be addressed as to whether substantial justice could be done

5 Sch 1, para 9(1)(b), (2).
6 *Mytton v Mytton* (1977) 7 Fam Law 244; *Shemshadfard v Shemshadfard* [1981] 1 All ER 726; *Gadd v Gadd* [1985] 1 All ER 58, [1984] 1 WLR 1435; *Thyssen-Bornemisza v Thyssen-Bornemisza* [1985] FLR 670, affd [1986] Fam 1, [1985] 1 All ER 328; *K v K* [1986] 2 FLR 411, [1986] Fam Law 329; *De Dampierre v De Dampierre* [1988] AC 92, [1987] 2 All ER 1.
7 *Spiliada Maritime Corpn v Cansulex Ltd* [1987] AC 460, [1986] 3 All ER 843, supra, pp 221 et seq.
8 Schuz (1989) 38 ICLQ 946, 949.
9 [1988] AC 92, esp at pp 102, 108–109; and see *Gadd v Gadd* [1985] 1 All ER 58, [1984] 1 WLR 1435; *K v K* [1986] 2 FLR 411; See also *Kornberg v Kornberg* (1991) 76 DLR (4th) 379.
10 In the Court of Appeal: [1987] 1 FLR 51 at 55.
11 [1988] AC 92 at 102. Another factor as to the appropriateness of the forum might be the language in which the proceedings are to be conducted and the availability of witnesses: *Shemshadfard v Shemshadfard* [1981] 1 All ER 726 at 734–735.

there. In particular, what weight was to be given to the fact that the wife was likely to receive a lower level of financial support from a French than from an English court? In earlier decisions, this had proved to be a factor of considerable significance. For example, in *Gadd v Gadd*,[12] the fact that a wife would receive no financial support in divorce proceedings in Monaco tipped the scales in favour of refusing a stay. Courts should be less influenced by the issue of whether or not financial relief is available in the foreign court, given that the factor of advantage to the plaintiff is of less significance since the *Spiliada Case*,[13] and that the English courts now have power to grant such relief after a foreign divorce.[14] Certainly, in *De Dampierre*, the House of Lords did not find the difference between French and English matrimonial relief a convincing reason for refusing a stay of the English proceedings.[15] In earlier cases, as well as the availability of remedies,[16] other factors existing at the time of the application for a stay[17] which have been taken into account are whether any English decree or financial provision order will be recognised in the other country[18] or whether continuation of the English proceedings will lead to a speedier outcome of the issue.[19]

Finally, it should be mentioned that the English proceedings cannot be stayed once the trial of the main issues has begun, save that the court may stay the proceedings at a later time if the petitioner has failed to furnish particulars of concurrent proceedings in another jurisdiction.[20]

General matters

In the case of both mandatory and discretionary stays, the English court has a power, on application by one of the parties to the proceedings, to discharge the order if the other proceedings are stayed or concluded, or if there has been unreasonable delay in prosecuting them.[1] Once a mandatory stay has been discharged the proceedings cannot again be mandatorily stayed,[2] though a discretion to stay remains but cannot normally be exercised once the trial of the English proceedings has begun. Special provision is made for the granting of ancillary relief in the case where English proceedings are stayed because proceedings are pending in another British jurisdiction.[3] It should be mentioned that the staying provisions contained in the Domicile and Matrimonial Proceedings Act 1973 are in addition to, and not in substitution for, any other power to stay proceedings.[4] The inherent power to stay was

---

12 [1985] 1 All ER 58, [1984] 1 WLR 1435.
13 [1987] AC 460 at 482–484, supra, pp 223 et seq.
14 Matrimonial and Family Proceedings Act 1984, Part III, infra pp 709–714; referred to in *Gadd v Gadd* [1984] 1 WLR 1435 at 1442.
15 [1988] AC 92 at 102, 110.
16 And see *Mytton v Mytton* (1977) 7 Fam Law 244; *Thyssen-Bornemisza v Thyssen-Bornemisza* [1985] FLR 670.
17 *Shemshadfard v Shemshadfard* [1981] 1 All ER 726 at 735.
18 *Thyssen-Bornemisza v Thyssen-Bornemisza* [1985] FLR 670 at 687.
19 Ibid.
20 Sch 1, para 9(4). Trial of a preliminary issue of jurisdiction will, also, not terminate the power to order a stay: Sch 1, para 4(1).
1 Sch 1, para 10(1).
2 Sch 1, para 10(2).
3 Sch 1, para 11. These provisions are considered more fully in the context of jurisdiction to grant ancillary relief, infra, pp 700–701.
4 S 5(6)(b). This seems to have been overlooked by DUNN LJ in *Gadd v Gadd* [1984] 1 WLR 1435 at 1438.

rarely used in matrimonial proceedings,[5] but, as we have seen, there is now little difference between the statutory power to stay and the developed common law doctrine of *forum non conveniens*.

(c) Restraining foreign proceedings The English court has long had the inherent power, in matrimonial proceedings, to restrain by injunction a party who wished to pursue foreign matrimonial proceedings;[6] but it is a power which has been sparingly and carefully exercised. Recently, the Privy Council has laid down the principles on which this inherent power is to be exercised in the commercial context[7] and the Court of Appeal has made clear in *Hemain v Hemain*[8] that such principles are to be applied in matrimonial cases.[9]

(b) CHOICE OF LAW

(i) Divorce and judicial separation[10]

At common law, the sole basis of the jurisdiction of the English courts in divorce was domicil[11] and no choice of law problem arose. English law was applied and this could be justified either as the application of the law of the domicil[12] to issues affecting status or as the application of the law of the forum on the basis that dissolution of a marriage is a matter which "touches fundamental English conceptions of morality, religion and public policy",[13] and one which is governed exclusively by rules and conditions imposed by the English legislature.

The need for a choice of law rule arises when the court possesses jurisdiction on some basis other than domicil, as may be illustrated by *Zanelli v Zanelli*:[14]

An Italian national, domiciled in England, married an Englishwoman in England in 1948. Later he was deported from this country and thereupon reverted to his Italian domicil. The Matrimonial Causes Act 1937, which was then in force, had given the English court jurisdiction in divorce (and also judicial separation) in such a case,[15] but it did not impose a rule for the choice of law.

5 *Sealey (orse Callan) v Callan* [1953] P 135, [1953] I All ER 942, a divorce case where the court, in fact, declined to stay the English proceedings; and see *Baroness von Eckhardstein v Baron von Eckhardstein* (1907) 23 TLR 539 and 593 (judicial separation).
6 See *Orr-Lewis v Orr-Lewis* [1949] P 347, [1949] 1 All ER 504, where, in the exercise of its discretion, the divorce court declined to issue an injunction; contrast *Bryant v Bryant* (1980) 11 Fam Law 85 where an injunction was issued restraining a husband from taking steps to have a Canadian divorce decree nisi made absolute in order to protect the wife's position in seeking relief from the English courts, and see infra, pp 709 et seq. In *Christian v Christian* (1897) 78 LT 86 the English court hearing judicial separation proceedings did restrain the husband from pursuing divorce proceedings in Scotland.
7 *Société National Industrielle Aerospatiale v Lee Kui Jak* [1987] AC 871, [1987] 3 All ER 510 supra, pp 241 et seq where the new principles are fully discussed.
8 [1988] 2 FLR 388, supra, p 247.
9 See also *Kornberg v Kornberg* (1991) 76 DLR (4th) 379.
10 North, op cit, pp 146–151; North, (1980) I Hague Receuil 9, 77–88; and see for judicial separation Grodecki (1957) 42 *Grotius Society* 23, 41–43.
11 *Le Mesurier v Le Mesurier* [1895] AC 517.
12 *Lord Advocate v Jaffrey* [1921] 1 AC 146 at 152.
13 Wolff, p 374; and see *Holland v Holland* 1973 (1) SA 897 (T) at 902.
14 (1948) 64 TLR 556; see also *Niboyet v Niboyet* (1878) 4 PD 1 at 9.
15 S13 (re-enacted in the Matrimonial Causes Act 1973, s 46(1)(a), itself repealed by the Domicile and Matrimonial Proceedings Act 1973). Jurisdiction could be assumed in the case of a petition by a wife, on the basis of the husband's domicil in England prior to his desertion or deportation.

The court, applying English domestic law but without any consideration of the choice of law issue, granted the wife a decree of divorce, despite the rule of the Italian law of her domicil at that time that divorce was not permissible. A similar approach, namely the uniform application of English law, is to be seen in the case of judicial separation not only where, at common law, jurisdiction was taken on the basis of domicil,[16] but also on the basis of residence[17] or of a matrimonial home within the jurisdiction,[18] even though the parties were domiciled elsewhere.

The English common law rules were later extended to permit divorce and nullity (but not judicial separation) decrees to be granted on the basis of three years' residence in England by a wife,[19] and at that point a statutory choice of law rule was introduced both for this case and for that exemplified in *Zanelli v Zanelli*, ie the domicil of the wife in England immediately prior to the husband's desertion or deportation. This choice of law rule provided that the court should apply "the law which would be applicable thereto if both parties were domiciled in England at the time of the proceedings".[20]

Strangely, this rule was cast in terms which pointed more to the law of the domicil than to the law of the forum. The latter approach could have been expressed far more simply by just saying that English law was applicable. Whilst the two statutory jurisdictional grounds available to the wife prevented considerable hardship in the case of divorce, they did not provide nearly so far-reaching an inroad into the basic jurisdictional rule dependent on domicil as has the Domicile and Matrimonial Proceedings Act 1973. Habitual residence is now, in practice, the main jurisdictional basis. The two statutory grounds available to a wife have been abolished and so also has the attendant choice of law provision.[21] There is now no statutory choice of law rule. It was undoubtedly the intention of the Law Commission, in proposing the reforms which led to the 1973 Act, that English law should be applied;[22] but this does raise the issue whether such a rule is desirable.

Whilst some civil law jurisdictions are prepared to consider the relevance of the divorce law of countries other than the forum,[23] the general approach of the common law is to apply the law of the forum.[24] It is not self-evidently correct that this should be so. One argument in favour of the law of the forum is that divorce law may be regarded as part of the public law of the forum and so should be applied as part of that country's mandatory laws, governing the continuance of a marital relationship within that particular society.[25] This argument is strongest in a jurisdiction, like many in the USA, with narrow jurisdictional rules and narrow rules for the recognition of

16 *Eustace v Eustace* [1924] P 45.
17 *Armytage v Armytage* [1898] P 178; *Ward v Ward* (1923) 39 TLR 440.
18 *Wells v Wells* [1960] NI 122.
19 Law Reform (Miscellaneous Provisions) Act 1949, s 1(1), re-enacted in the Matrimonial Causes Act 1973, s 46(1)(b), and repealed by the Domicile and Matrimonial Proceedings Act 1973.
20 Ibid, s 1(4), re-enacted in the Matrimonial Causes Act 1973, s 46(2).
21 Domicile and Matrimonial Proceedings Act 1973, s 17(2).
22 Law Com No 48, paras 103–108.
23 Eg France, see Batiffol & Lagarde, *Droit International Privé*, 7th edn (1983) vol II, pp 79–82; and see Palsson, *International Encyclopedia of Comparative Law*, vol III, ch 16, pp 129 et seq; Anton, p 467.
24 Palsson, op cit, pp 126–129; though see *Alton v Alton* 207 F 2d 667 at 684–685 (1953).
25 Wolff, *Private International Law*, 2nd edn, (1950) 373–374; Cavers (1970) III Hague Recueil 75, 245–246.

foreign divorces. In this country—where both sets of rules are broader—it may be much less obvious that parties have a close connection with the forum, especially if they can obtain a divorce abroad and readily have it recognised here even though obtained on grounds unavailable under English law.[26] A further argument in favour of the law of the forum is that it would cause delay and create expense to apply foreign law to English petitions for divorce or judicial separation, most of which are undefended; and it has also been suggested that to "require English courts to dissolve marriages on exotic foreign grounds would be distasteful to the judges and unacceptable to public opinion".[27] These are dangerous arguments if carried too far. It is always easier and cheaper to apply the law of the forum, but nowhere else in our choice of law rules, save in the case of torts, do we apply the law of the forum as such.[28] If we are prepared to take jurisdiction over "exotic foreigners", under our broad jurisdictional rules, it is arguably no more distasteful to apply their personal law to the dissolution than to apply it, as we do,[29] to the creation of their marriage.

There are certainly those who advocate the application of the party's personal law, ie the law of their domicil, to divorce and judicial separation—that being the law which should govern matters of status. Indeed, Weintraub has taken this argument to a logical conclusion, namely that exclusive jurisdiction should be conferred on the courts of the domicil.[1] The main argument in favour of applying the law of the domicil is that dissolution of the marriage affects the status of the parties no less than does the creation of the marriage and is a substantive, not just a procedural, matter. Whilst the public policy of the forum may have a role to play, as elsewhere in choice of law matters,[2] this should not, it is said, be to the exclusion of other laws. There is, however, a practical difficulty with the application of the law of the domicil. Now that a wife may acquire a separate domicil which she is more likely to have done if the marriage has broken down and one spouse is petitioning for a divorce, which spouse's domicil is to be regarded as the relevant one for choice of law purposes? The answer to such a question can be little more than arbitrary and militates against the application of the law of the domicil.

The arguments on choice of law in divorce and judicial separation have been summed up thus:

> The decision on choice of law rules in divorce must depend upon a balance between principle, which undoubtedly points to the application of the personal law, and pragmatism which favours the *lex fori*. It is no surprise that the civil law supports the former and the common law the latter. What is worrying about the common law approach is that a rule which was historically justified by its jurisdictional link has been maintained with little real consideration of the implications of breaking that jurisdictional link.[3]

The Matrimonial Causes Act 1973, unlike its predecessors, is silent on choice of law matters relating to divorce and judicial separation, though the fact that there is no express saving for the rules of private international law in

---

26 See infra, p 664.
27 Morris, p 192.
28 And that rule is far from being free of criticism, supra pp 536–537.
29 Supra, pp 586 et seq.
1 *Commentary on the Conflict of Laws*, 3rd edn (1986) 261; and see Scoles & Hay, p 475.
2 Supra, pp 128–137.
3 North (1980) I Hague Recueil 9, 87–88.

the case of divorce and judicial separation, such as there is in the case of nullity,[4] provides some tacit support for the application of the law of the forum. There is no doubt, however, that in practice English law is applied to all petitions for divorce or judicial separation which come before the English courts.[5] The rules of English law existing at the time of the proceedings are applied and they will decide whether there is a good cause for divorce or judicial separation, and will determine the form of relief and the conditions on which the decree will be granted. Any other legal system, such as the law under which the parties married, the law of their domicils or nationalities, or the law of the place where the facts on which the petition is based took place, is completely irrelevant.[6] It should be mentioned that under English law it does not matter that the facts evidencing breakdown of the marriage did not constitute a basis for divorce in the country where they took place,[7] or in the country of the parties' domicils.[8] Nor does it matter that the ground for divorce was not a ground under English law at the time that the cause arose.[9]

(ii) Nullity[10]

(a) Introduction Whilst divorce gives rise to few choice of law problems, the same cannot be said for nullity. The reasons for this are varied. A nullity decree is concerned with the validity of the creation of a marriage, unlike divorce which dissolves a marriage which is admittedly validly created. This means that the choice of law issues in nullity are essentially the same as those already examined in the context of marriage. The question to be asked is the same—is the marriage valid or invalid? General issues of formal and essential validity have already been examined[11] as matters relating to marriage. But others such as lack of consent and physical defects are considered here because they tend to arise in nullity petitions. Another reason why choice of law in nullity is a more difficult area than divorce is that the effects of annulment vary according to the particular ground in issue and they vary in relation to the same ground even within the United Kingdom. Some defects avoid a marriage *ab initio*, ie render it void, whilst others merely render it voidable. These distinctions can readily be exemplified. If one party is below the minimum age of marriage or is already married, English law regards the marriage as void.[12] If, however, a decree is granted in England on the ground of lack of consent, the marriage will be regarded as voidable.[13] In Scotland, on the other hand, lack of consent renders the marriage void *ab initio*. Again, impotence or wilful refusal to consummate the marriage renders it voidable under English law;[14] whereas in Scotland, although impotence also renders the marriage voidable, wilful refusal has no effect on its validity.

---

4 Matrimonial Causes Act 1973, s 14, infra, pp 652–653.
5 *Quoraishi v Quoraishi* [1985] FLR 780, esp at 783.
6 *Czepek v Czepek* [1962] 3 All ER 990.
7 Eg *Czepek v Czepek*, supra; and see *Holland v Holland* 1973 (1) SA 897 (T). It would be no defence to a divorce petition in England that the adultery took place in Dublin.
8 See *Quoraishi v Quoreishi* [1985] FLR 780, [1985] Fam Law 308, CA; *Grummett v Grummett* (1965) 7 FLR 415.
9 Eg *Pratt v Pratt* [1939] AC 417, [1939] 3 All ER 437.
10 North, op cit, ch 8; Law Commission Working Paper No 89 (1985), Pt V.
11 Supra, pp 572 et seq.
12 Matrimonial Causes Act 1973, s 11.
13 Ibid, s 12.
14 Ibid.

The difference between void and voidable marriages is significant. "A void marriage is no marriage. Considered literally the expression is self-destructive and contradictory. But without misleading anyone it serves to denote the situation where a ceremony of marriage does not bring about a marriage".[15] No proceedings are necessary to establish the fact of its nullity, though it may in practice be wise to take them, eg to obtain maintenance for the "wife" and any child of the "marriage" or to still doubts as to one's status where the position is disputed. Moreover, any member of the public may treat the marriage as void, notwithstanding the absence of a decree, as, for instance, by withholding payment of money that is due to the woman conditionally on her being the wife of the man.

On the other hand "A voidable marriage is one that will be regarded by every court as a valid subsisting marriage until a decree annulling it has been pronounced by a court of competent jurisdiction."[16] So the effect of a defect, like impotence, that renders a marriage voidable in England is such that the status of the parties as husband and wife, having sprung from a contract free from imperfection, cannot be affected until the existence of the defect has been proved, and therefore the rule is that the marriage is valid and must be treated as such by every court and every person until it has been judicially declared void. No one but the parties themselves can be heard to deny that they are married or can challenge, by nullity proceedings or otherwise, the validity of their marriage. Until either of them obtains a decree of nullity, all the normal consequences of the married status ensue, both inter se and as regards third parties.

There are also further differences in relation to the effects of an annulment. The annulment of a void marriage has retrospective effect; it declares the marriage never to have existed. However, the position is different in England in the case of a voidable marriage. Although the annulment of such a marriage had retrospective effect at common law, the position in the case of nullity decrees granted after 31 July 1971 is that the decree operates to annul the marriage prospectively only from the date of the decree absolute. Until that time the marriage must be treated as subsisting.[17]

A further difficulty in nullity cases is the all too common disregard of the elementary and primary distinction between jurisdiction and choice of law. The tendency of the judges, in cases involving lack of consent or physical incapacities, after surmounting the problem of jurisdiction, has been to apply the internal law of England as a matter of course.[18] Not only does this mean that the principles on which the choice of law depends are undeveloped, but it is particularly regrettable that the personal law should be deprived of its control over the married status.

(b) Classification of the nature of the defect The ascertainment of the proper law in a nullity suit depends on analysing the various defects that may constitute cause for annulment, in order to determine their intrinsic nature. Once this is done, the legal system to which a particular defect is subject should become apparent. The consequence of this analysis is that, once the court has jurisdiction, then, in order to determine the law applicable to some

---

15 *Ross Smith v Ross Smith* [1963] AC 280 at 314, [1962] 1 All ER 344 at 361–362.
16 *De Reneville v De Reneville* [1948] P 100 at 111, [1948] 1 All ER 56 at 60.
17 Matrimonial Causes Act 1973, s 16.
18 Eg *Easterbrook v Easterbrook* [1944] 1 All ER 90; *Hunter v Hunter* [1944] P 95, [1944] 2 All ER 368; *Buckland v Buckland* [1968] P 296, [1967] 2 All ER 300.

alleged defect, it applies its own characterisation to decide whether the defect is as to form or essential validity. If, for example, it is the former, then it applies the rules of the law of the place of celebration to the issue in question. This may be illustrated by the British Columbia decision in *Solomon v Walters,*[19] where the facts were these:

A marriage had been celebrated in Nevada between the husband, domiciled in British Columbia, and the wife, apparently domiciled in Alberta. The wife petitioned in British Columbia for a nullity decree on the ground of lack of parental consent as required by Nevada law, though by the domestic law of British Columbia the marriage was unaffected by the defect; by Nevada law it was rendered voidable.

The judge, having classified the defect as one of form, applied Nevadan law and granted a decree of nullity. If the defect is as to capacity, then as has been seen,[1] the court should apply the ante-nuptial domiciliary law of the party alleged incapable.

It remains to consider other, more problematical, choice of law areas namely lack of consent and personal physical defects.

(c) Lack of consent: is it formal or essential? What is not considered finally settled by authority is whether defects affecting consent to marry are to be classified as akin to form and thus to be governed by the law of the place of celebration or as personal defects, thus raising questions of essential validity to be referred to the personal law of the parties.[2] There are a variety of different grounds on which an allegation of lack of consent can be based,[3] not all of which are sufficient in English domestic law. It may be argued that one party was mistaken as to the identity of the other party[4] or as to the nature of the ceremony, eg thinking that it was a betrothal rather than a marriage ceremony,[5] or that the marriage was entered into as the result of fraud[6] or fear caused by duress or coercion,[7] or during mental illness,[8] or there may have been a mistake as to the legal effects of the ceremony,[9] or as to the attributes of the other party,[10] or cases where one party has made mental reservations as to the effect of the ceremony.[11] What is remarkable is that the English courts for many years failed to realise that a choice of law problem existed in such cases and invariably applied English law. It is a masterly understatement to say that "there has been some difference of

19 (1956) 3 DLR (2d) 78; and see *Lepre v Lepre* [1965] P 52 at 60, where the law of the place of celebration considered the marriage to be valid rather than voidable or void.
1 Supra, pp 586 et seq.
2 Woodhouse (1954) 3 ICLQ 454.
3 Neville Brown (1968) 42 Tul LR 837.
4 Cf *C v C* [1942] NZLR 356.
5 *Valier v Valier* (1925) 133 LT 830; *Parojcic v Parojcic* [1958] 1 All ER 1, [1958] 1 WLR 1280; and see *Ford v Stier* [1896] P 1; and similarly *Mehta v Mehta* [1945] 2 All ER 690: belief that the marriage ceremony was merely one of conversion to Hinduism.
6 *Johnson v Smith* (1968) 70 DLR (2d) 374.
7 *Hussein v Hussein* [1938] P 159, [1938] 2 All ER 344; *H v H* [1954] P 258, [1953] 2 All ER 1229; *Parojcic v Parojcic* [1958] 1 All ER 1, [1958] 1 WLR 1280; *Buckland v Buckland* [1968] P 296, [1967] 2 All ER 300; *Szechter v Szechter* [1971] P 286, [1970] 3 All ER 905.
8 Cf *Re Park's Estate* [1954] P 89, [1953] 2 All ER 1411.
9 *Way v Way* [1950] P 71 at 79–80, approved, [1951] P 124, at 133–134; *Kassim v Kassim* [1962] P 224, [1962] 3 All ER 426.
10 Cf *Mitford v Mitford* [1923] P 130.
11 *Bell v Graham* (1859) 13 Moo PCC 242; *Silver v Silver* [1955] 2 All ER 614, [1955] 1 WLR 728; cf *Johnson v Smith* (1968) 70 DLR (2d) 374.

opinion as to what law applies".[12] Indeed virtually the only cases in which there has been any discussion of the issue have been those where it was not necessary for the decision.

Application of the law of the forum
The only solution supported by all the direct authorities is reference to English law as the law of the forum in "consent" cases, but this is, in truth, an abdication from the problem. Since the decisions can be explained as having been reached *per incuriam*, reference to the law of the forum should only be accepted on such merits of principle as it may have. It has been suggested[13] that the law of the forum can be applied to cases of mistake as to the legal nature of the ceremony and to sham marriages, but not to cases of mistake as to the legal effects of the marriage which should be referred to the law of the mistaken party's ante-nuptial domicil.[14] The justification that the former concern issues of fact more appropriate for the forum than the issues raised in the latter case is not convincing, for the determination of a factual question such as whether or not duress existed does not of itself resolve the problem of the effect of such duress on the validity of the marriage.

The common judicial attitude of ignoring choice of law issues so far as the parties' consent is concerned may be illustrated by *Buckland v Buckland*[15] where a marriage celebrated in Malta between two Maltese domiciliaries was declared a nullity by an English court on the ground that the petitioner had gone through the ceremony because of fear of an unjust prosecution if he did not. No reference was made to any law other than English law. The only connection with England was that, by the date of the proceedings, the petitioner had become domiciled here. The question of determination of the applicable law could be referred to other legal systems, whose varied claims we must now examine.

Application of the law of the place of celebration
In *Parojcic v Parojcic*,[16] DAVIES J referred the question of the effect of duress to English law as the law of the place of celebration. Despite this dictum, the view that that law should govern only "the method of giving consent as distinct from the fact of consent"[17] seems preferable, for, even in the sphere of commercial contracts, the issue of the parties' consent is not referred to the law of the place of contracting.[18] Indeed, it would seem that a marriage may comply with all the formal requirements of the law of the place of celebration and yet lack essential validity because of lack of consent.[19] Although reference to the law of the place of celebration is in accordance with many of the cases, there are certainly others which militate against it.[20]

Application of the law of the domicil
The same can also be said of the opinion that "no marriage is (*semble*) valid if by the law of either party's domicile he or she does not consent to marry

12 *Mahadervan v Mahadervan* [1962] 3 All ER 1108 at 111. This is omitted from the report in [1964] P 233.
13 Webb (1959) 22 MLR 198, 202–204.
14 Cf *Kassim v Kassim*, supra.
15 [1968] P 296, [1967] 2 All ER 300; see also *Kassim v Kassim*, supra.
16 [1958] 1 WLR 1280 at 1283.
17 *Apt v Apt* [1948] P 83 at 88.
18 Supra, pp 505–507.
19 *Nane v Sykiotis* (1966) 57 DLR (2d) 118 at 122.
20 *Bell v Graham*, supra; *Mehta v Mehta*, supra; *Apt v Apt* [1948] P 83 at 88; and see *H v H* [1954] P 258; *Silver v Silver*, supra; *Kassim v Kassim*, supra; *Buckland v Buckland*, supra.

the other".[1] There are at least three English decisions[2] in which the validity of a marriage, so far as consent is concerned, has been considered without reference to the domiciliary law of one or both of the parties. The weight of opinion does, however, favour reference of the issue of consent to the law of the domicil. The view that lack of consent is a personal defect was accepted by HODSON J in *Way v Way:*[3]

> The petitioner, a British subject domiciled in England, went through a ceremony of marriage at Archangel with the respondent, domiciled in Russia, as the result of which he believed that he had been legally married. He later claimed annulment on the grounds, (1) that certain formalities required by Russian law had been omitted, (2) that the marriage was void for want of consent, since he believed at the time of the ceremony that his wife would be allowed to accompany him to England (which was not permitted by the Soviet authorities) and also that it was the duty of both parties to live together. According to Russian law he was mistaken in both respects.

HODSON J first held that there had been no neglect of the Russian formalities. He then propounded the doctrine that "questions of consent are to be dealt with by reference to the personal law of the parties rather than by reference to the law of the place where the contract was made", with the result that "the matrimonial law of each of the parties" had to be applied.[4] He then held that, by English law, the personal law of the petitioner, consent is not nullified by a mistake of the kind pleaded, ie mistake as to attributes, a finding with which it is impossible to disagree.

The Court of Appeal[5] held the marriage to be void on the ground that the Russian formalities had not, in fact, been observed, and therefore anything that was said about the law to govern the question of consent was *obiter*. However, Sir RAYMOND EVERSHED MR was "prepared to assume" that HODSON J was correct in referring the question to the personal law of the parties.[6]

This decision to refer issues of consent to the law of the domicil was followed in *Szechter v Szechter:*[7]

> The husband, his first wife and his secretary, Nina, were all domiciled in Poland. The secretary was imprisoned for "anti-state activities" and her health deteriorated rapidly. In order to obtain her release from prison, the husband secretly divorced his first wife and in 1968 married Nina in prison. Shortly thereafter she was released from prison and all three came to England and became domiciled there. Nina petitioned for annulment of her marriage on the grounds of duress, so that the husband and first wife could resume their married life.

These facts undoubtedly raise an issue of choice of law. Polish law was the law of the place of celebration and the law of the domicil of both parties at

1 Dicey & Morris, p 642.
2 *Silver v Silver*, supra; *Kassim v Kassim*, supra; *Buckland v Buckland*, supra; and see *Cooper v Crane*, supra; *H v H*, supra; and see also *Parojcic v Parojcic* [1958] 1 WLR 1280 at 1283.
3 [1950] P 71, [1949] 2 All ER 959.
4 [1950] P 71 at 78, [1949] 2 All ER 959 at 963.
5 *Kenward v Kenward* [1951] P 124, [1950] 2 All ER 297.
6 [1951] P 124 at 133, [1950] 2 All ER 297 at 302.
7 [1971] P 286, [1970] 3 All ER 905; cf *Feiner v Demkowicz* (1973) 42 DLR (3d) 165; *Re Suria's Marriage* (1977) 29 FLR 308.

the time of the marriage. English law was the law of the forum and the law of the domicil at the time of the proceedings. Both legal systems agreed that the marriage was void for duress. However, Sir JOCELYN SIMON P concluded that it was for Polish law, as the law of the domicil of the parties at the time of the marriage, to determine the validity of the marriage.[8] In so doing, he approved the proposition in Dicey & Morris[9] that "no marriage is valid if by the law of either party's domicile one party does not consent to marry the other".[10] The editors of that work have, however, accepted[11] the suggestion made in these pages[12] that the issue of a party's alleged lack of consent to marry should be determined by reference to that person's ante-nuptial domiciliary law, and not to the law of both parties' ante-nuptial domicils. It seems adequate to analyse the issue of consent as a personal issue to be referred to the law governing capacity, without requiring a wife to have consented not only according to her own law but also according to her husband's, or vice versa.

Application of the law of the domicil to issues of consent has been supported more recently by the Court of Appeal in *Vervaeke v Smith*.[13] A major issue in this case was whether the English courts would recognise the validity of a Belgian nullity decree;[14] but the Court of Appeal also gave some consideration to the original validity of the marriage in question. The marriage had taken place in England between a woman domiciled in Belgium and a man domiciled in England. This was essentially a sham marriage whose purpose was to give the woman British nationality. Such a marriage, though valid under English law, was void under Belgian law. Nevertheless, its validity was upheld under the exception to the dual domicil rule provided by *Sottomayer v De Barros (No 2)*[15] in that the marriage was valid by English law, that of the domicil of one party and the place of celebration.[16]

Reform

In their examination of the choice of law rules relating to marriage, the Law Commission considered the issue of the law to be applied to matters of consent.[17] They suggested that, although some arguments can be advanced in favour of the application of the law of the forum, issues of consent are concerned with the essential or substantive validity of a marriage and that "it would be contrary to principle and inconvenient in practice to fragment

---

8 Nevertheless, he satisfied himself that the marriage was also invalid under English domestic law. Indeed so extensive was his examination of English law, that, had the marriage been valid by Polish law, the impression is given that he would, nevertheless, have held it to be void as contrary to English public policy; see Hartley (1972) 35 MLR 571, 580; cf Carter (1971) 45 BYBIL 406, 409.

9 Dicey & Morris (8th edn, 1967), p 271. The proposition in the 11th edn (1987), p 642, is in substantially the same terms.

10 [1971] P 286 at 294–295.

11 See now Dicey & Morris 11th edn (1987), p 644.

12 8th edn, p 396.

13 [1981] Fam 77 at 122.

14 Infra, pp 676–678.

15 (1879) 5 PD 94, supra, pp 595–597.

16 The House of Lords did not discuss the application of the *Sottomayer* rule; though Lord SIMON of Glaisdale was prepared to regard this issue of reality of consent as one of "quintessential validity" to be governed by the law of the country with which the marriage had the most real and substantial connection: [1983] 1 AC 145 at 166, supra, pp 601–602.

17 Law Commission Working Paper No 89 (1985), paras 5.6–5.24. Their Report, Law Com No 165 (1987), adds little to this discussion, see paras 2.4, 2.8.

the question of essential validity."[18] This led to the conclusion that the law of the domicil should govern issues of consent, as it probably does already; and the Law Commission favoured reference to the domiciliary law of the person whose consent is alleged to be defective, rather than the formulation approved in *Szechter v Szechter*.[19]

(d) Physical defects[20] It remains to identify the law which governs other personal physical defects. These can encompass a wide range of grounds of invalidity, as is illustrated by those which render a marriage voidable under section 12 of the Matrimonial Causes Act 1973: impotence, wilful refusal to consummate the marriage, mental disorder such as to render the person unfitted for marriage, venereal disease and that the woman was pregnant by another man. In the context of English law, a nullity petition on the ground of the respondent's pregnancy or suffering from venereal disease may only be brought if the petitioner is unaware of this fact and so such grounds could be regarded more properly as relating to the reality of the petitioner's consent and thus to be governed by the law appropriate to that issue.[1] However, other legal systems do not necessarily take the same approach and, in any event, the consent classification cannot so readily be applied to issues such as wilful refusal or impotence. Two issues are raised: what are the current choice of law rules to govern these personal physical defects and are the rules appropriate and adequate?

What is the present law?
It is not easy to resolve the first issue and state the current law with any confidence. The main defects to consider are impotence and wilful refusal, but the authorities are far from clear as to what law is to govern these defects. There is some authority to support the application of the law of the domicil, of the place of celebration or of the forum. The difficulty with the decisions is that in all but one of the cases[2] English law has been applied, often with little or no consideration of the choice of law issue. Even when that issue is considered, the varied dicta seem to be at odds with the facts of the reported decisions. For instance, in *Robert v Robert*[3] wilful refusal is characterised as an "error in the quality of the respondent"[4] to which the law of the place of celebration should be applied;[5] yet against such classification may be cited *Way v Way*,[6] where English law was applied to a nullity petition based on wilful refusal arising from a marriage celebrated in Russia; and *Ponticelli v Ponticelli*,[7] where English law was applied though the place of celebration was Italy.

The confused state of the cases can be further illustrated by the fact that

18 Ibid, para 5.18.
19 [1971] P 286, [1970] 3 All ER 905; supra, pp 646–647.
20 Bishop (1978) 41 MLR 512; Law Commission Working Paper No 89 (1985), paras 5.25–5.43; Law Com No 165 (1987), para 2.9.
1 Supra, pp 644 et seq.
2 *Robert v Robert* [1947] P 164, [1947] 2 All ER 22.
3 Ibid.
4 Ibid, at 167–168. This is criticised by Morris, p 171, note 53.
5 Though the court did consider that, if the defect was to be classified as a question affecting the capacity of one of the parties to contract a marriage, then the law of the domicil was applicable and this is supported by the citing of *Sottomayor v De Barros* (1877) 3 PD 1, and see *Addison v Addison* [1955] NI 1 at 30.
6 [1950] P 71 at 80.
7 [1958] P 204, [1958] 1 All ER 357.

application of the law of the husband's domicil at the time of the marriage is supported by some decisions[8] on impotence and wilful refusal but is inconsistent with others.[9] Again, application of English law as the law of the forum finds support in some cases,[10] but not in all.[11]

What ought the law to be?
If the cases provide no clear guide to the law to govern nullity petitions based on personal physical defects, are there obvious principles which might guide courts in the future? Application of the law of the place of celebration can be rejected. The defects in question cannot be classified as relating to formalities of marriage. Support in principle can be found for the application of both the law of the domicil and the law of the forum. If one regards defects such as impotence, pregnancy by another man, mental disorder, and the fact that the respondent was suffering from venereal disease, as matters of essential validity akin to capacity, then the relevant law to determine the effect of such alleged invalidity is that of the domicil.[12] It is, however, more difficult to adopt that approach in the case of wilful refusal to consummate the marriage. It is a post-nuptial defect and it might be thought inappropriate to apply the law of the domicil existing at the time of the marriage to a ground of annulment more akin to a ground of divorce. Indeed, the divorce analogy would provide support for applying the law of the forum.[13]

The easy answer would be to have different choice of law rules for ante-nuptial and post-nuptial defects, for impotence and wilful refusal. This is, however, an impracticable solution because the two grounds are frequently pleaded in the alternative and, as the Law Commission has pointed out, "it would be undesirable and inconvenient if different choice of law rules were to apply, depending on whether non-consummation was due to inability to consummate or unwillingness to do so".[14] This means that either the law of the domicil or the law of the forum must apply to both impotence and wilful refusal.

The arguments in favour of the law of the forum are good but not good enough. It is easier, and cheaper, to apply the law of the forum than any other law; but that argument can be used in relation to choice of law in any context but is not accepted, except in torts (where reference to the law of the forum is much criticised)[15] and in divorce. Wilful refusal, though not impotence, may be like divorce in its post-nuptial character, but it is significant that English law has chosen to regard it as a ground of annulment.

8 *Way v Way*, supra; *Ponticelli v Ponticelli*, supra.
9 *Easterbrook v Easterbrook* [1944] P 10; *Hutter v Hutter*, [1944] P 95, unless one can explain them on the ground that, when the foreign law is not pleaded, it is the same as English law. In so far as *Ramsay-Fairfax v Ramsay-Fairfax* [1956] P 115 at 125 can be considered an authority on choice of law, it militates against this view, unless Scots law, the law of the husband's domicil, is not only considered to be the same as English law (which is not the case), but it is accepted that this is a reason for applying English law as such.
10 *Easterbrook v Easterbrook*, supra; *Hutter v Hutter*, supra; *Magnier v Magnier* (1968) 112 Sol Jo 233.
11 *Robert v Robert* [1947] P 164, [1947] 2 All ER 22 and see *Ponticelli v Ponticelli* [1958] P 204 at 214–216; *Sangha v Mander* (1985) 47 RFL (2d) 212 at 216.
12 See *Robert v Robert* [1947] P 164 at 168; and see *Ramsay-Fairfax v Ramsay-Fairfax* [1956] P 115 at 125.
13 Supra, pp 639–642; for rejection of the analogy, see *Sangha v Mander* (1985) 47 RFL (2d) 212 at 216–217.
14 Law Commission Working Paper No 89 (1985), para 5.30.
15 Supra, pp 529, 536–537.

That being so, to apply the law of the domicil will ensure consistency with the treatment of all grounds of invalidity. It will also confirm the view that these personal defects go to the essential validity of a marriage and that all aspects of essential validity are to be governed by the law of the domicil.[16] Finally, it is hard to disagree with Lord Reid when he pointed out that application of the law of the forum is wrong in principle, saying: "Suppose a case where the law of the parties' domicile gives no relief on this ground [ie wilful refusal[17]], it seems to me quite contrary to principle that the wife should be able to come here and seek relief on that ground."[18]

Returning to the authorities, the most persuasive decision in favour of the application of the law of the domicil is *Ponticelli v Ponticelli*,[19] where the facts were these:

The parties married by proxy in Italy. The wife was domiciled in Italy and the husband was domiciled in England. When the husband petitioned for a nullity decree on the ground of wilful refusal, the court had to face the choice of law issue, for wilful refusal was not in the circumstances a ground for annulment in Italian law.

SACHS J rejected a classification of wilful refusal as akin to an issue of form and so he rejected the law of the place of celebration, here Italian law, as the appropriate law.[20] He did not favour the analogy of wilful refusal with divorce, and so his arguments militated against the application of the law of the forum,[1] though he applied English law but rather because it was the law of the husband's domicil[2] at the time of the marriage and of the petition,[3] and it was also the law of the intended matrimonial home. Furthermore, he rejected any attempt to distinguish between the choice of law rules for wilful refusal and for impotence. He considered they should both be regarded as matters of personal capacity,[4] to be governed by the law of the domicil, for "it is surely a matter of some importance that the initial validity of a marriage should, in relation to all matters except form and ceremony . . ., be consistently decided according to the law of one country alone . . . and that consistency cannot be attained if the test is *lex fori*".[5]

Even if it is agreed that physical personal defects are to be governed by the law of the domicil, that is not an end of difficulties. It remains to determine which spouse's domiciliary law is to be applied and whether the domicil, and thus the applicable law, is to be determined at the date of the marriage or at the date of the nullity petition. Although in *Ponticelli* reference was made to the law of the husband's domicil, there seems little doubt that, now that a married woman is capable of acquiring a separate domicil, reference must be

16 *De Reneville v De Reneville* [1948] P 100 at 114; *Szechter v Szechter* [1971] P 286 at 295; *Sangha v Mander* (1985) 47 RFL (2d) 212 at 217–218.
17 As is the case in Scotland.
18 *Ross Smith v Ross Smith* [1963] AC 280 at 306; and see *Ponticelli v Ponticelli* [1958] P 204 at 215.
19 [1958] P 204, [1958] 1 All ER 357 and see more recently *Sangha v Mander* (1985) 47 RFL (2d) 212.
20 Thereby rejecting *Robert v Robert* [1947] P 164, [1947] 2 All ER 22.
1 He regarded *De Reneville v De Reneville*, supra, as supporting his view.
2 The question of which spouse's domiciliary law should be applied is discussed infra.
3 [1958] P 204 at 216, though reference to domicil at the time of the petition seems hard to justify.
4 See *Ramsay-Fairfax v Ramsay-Fairfax* [1956] P 115 at 133.
5 [1958] P 204 at 215–216.

made to the wife's domicil where appropriate. Various differing ways have been suggested to determine the relevant domiciliary law to be applied. One approach is to look at the law of each spouse's domicil and to annul the marriage if there are grounds for so doing under either law.[6] This tips the scales firmly in favour of annulling a marriage, with the result that the petitioner would succeed even though there were no grounds for annulment under the law of his domicil and even though he was the person alleged to lack capacity. The balance can be redressed by always applying the law of the petitioner's domicil;[7] but under this approach a nullity decree will be denied in, say, a case of wilful refusal if that does not constitute a ground of annulment under the law of the petitioner's domicil even though it is a ground under that of the respondent, the respondent being the person who has refused. A third approach, which avoids this difficulty, is to apply the law of the domicil of the spouse who is alleged to be incapable, taking that in the case of non-consummation to be the spouse who is unable, or refuses, to consummate the marriage. In its turn, this approach would deny annulment in the case where wilful refusal was a ground for nullity under the law of the petitioner's, but not the respondent's domicil, assuming the refusal to be by the respondent.

No answer is perfect; but it is suggested that the third approach is the more appropriate in that it accords with the general choice of law rule relating to matters of essential validity, ie the application of the ground of invalidity under the domiciliary law of the person alleged to be incapable.[8] This would still leave it open to a court to conclude that, in the special circumstances of a non-consummation, it would be right to apply the law of the person who is rendered unable to consummate the marriage by reason of the conduct of the other party.

Finally, there is the question of the time at which the law of the domicil is to be determined. The general rule applicable to matters of essential validity is that the applicable law is that of the domicil immediately preceding the marriage—the ante-nuptial domicil.[9] There should be no doubt that this is the relevant time in all cases of alleged invalidity except wilful refusal.[10] The more doubtful case is that of wilful refusal. If it is also to be regarded as a straightforward issue of capacity, then the relevant time is again that of the marriage.[11] If, however, it is regarded more properly as an anomalous ground of nullity more like a ground for divorce, since it is post-nuptial, then the relevant date for determining domicil might be thought to be that of the proceedings.[12] However, the Law Commission would seem to be right in indicating that, if domicil is to be the test for determining the governing law in all issues of essential validity, consistency requires the domicil to be determined at the same time in all cases, ie immediately before the marriage,

---

6 Palsson, *Marriage in Comparative Conflict of Laws* (1981), pp 314–315.
7 Jaffey (1978) 41 MLR 38; Bishop (1978) 41 MLR 512.
8 And see Anton, p 442.
9 Supra, pp 574 et seq.
10 *De Reneville v De Reneville* [1948] P 100 at 114. This may have been lost sight of in *Savelieff v Glouchkoff* (1964) 45 DLR (2d) 520; Lysyk (1965) 43 Can BR 107, 121–121.
11 Cf *Robert v Robert* [1947] P 164 at 167–168.
12 Such a view might be supported by *Way v Way* [1950] P 71 at 80. In *Ponticelli v Ponticelli* [1958] P 204 it is expressly stated, at 216, that the husband was domiciled in England both at the date of the marriage and of the petition; cf *De Reneville v De Reneville* [1948] P 100 at 114 where Lord GREENE's reference to the date of the marriage is made without qualification of the case of wilful refusal.

especially as wilful refusal and impotence are often pleaded in the alternative.[13]

(e) Annulment on grounds unknown to English law There is a further issue, closely connected with the question whether English law as the law of the forum should be applied to cases of impotence and wilful refusal. This is whether the English courts will annul a marriage on grounds unknown to English law. There is clear statutory provision for the application of foreign law to any question affecting the validity of a marriage. Section 14(1) of the Matrimonial Causes Act 1973 qualifies the grounds of annulment of void and voidable marriages laid down by that Act[14] by stating that, where any matter affecting the validity of a marriage would, in accordance with the rules of private international law, fall to be determined by a foreign law, nothing in the nullity provisions of the 1973 Act should preclude the application of the foreign law or require the application of the English law of nullity.[15]

There is no doubt that this provision contemplates that English courts will apply foreign law to nullity petitions in appropriate circumstances and, equally, there is no doubt that English courts will annul marriages on the basis of foreign rules as to invalidity. As has been seen when considering the validity of a marriage,[16] the English courts will annul a marriage celebrated in a foreign country if the formalities of the law of the place of celebration are not complied with, irrespective of the English law on such matters.[17] Similarly, the English courts will annul a marriage, even if celebrated in England, on a ground laid down by the parties' ante-nuptial domiciliary laws, whether or not that ground is co-extensive with a similar English ground. For instance, a marriage has been treated as void because the parties were within the prohibited degrees of relationship under their foreign domiciliary law, though not under English law.[18]

There appears to be no authority on whether an English court will annul a marriage on a ground which, under the law of the domicil, renders the marriage voidable but which falls quite outside the grounds on which a marriage might be declared voidable under English domestic law. Whilst agreeing that any determination of the question whether English courts would annul a marriage in such circumstances is speculative,[19] it is suggested that an English court should be prepared fully to accept the general principle that questions as to the essential validity of the marriage are to be referred to the law of the domicil. In that event, it is suggested that it matters not whether the English court applies foreign grounds verbally similar to English grounds such as consanguinity or non-age, even though the substance of the rule be different, or a foreign ground which is a variant of the English ground, such

13 Law Commission Working Paper No 89 (1985), para 5.41.
14 Ss 11–13.
15 S 14(2) also provides that the grounds on which a marriage is to be declared void, laid down in s 11, are without prejudice to other grounds under which a marriage celebrated under the Foreign Marriage Acts 1892–1947 or a common law marriage celebrated abroad might be declared void. See also the Marriage (Prohibited Degrees of Relationship) Act 1986, s 1(7).
16 Supra, pp 572 et seq.
17 *Berthiaume v Dastous* [1930] AC 79 (marriage with religious, but no civil, ceremony); *Kenward v Kenward* [1951] P 124, [1950] 2 All ER 297 (failure to comply with the Russian Marriage Code).
18 *Sottomayor v De Barros* (1877) 3 PD 1.
19 Morris, pp 209–210.

as declaring a marriage voidable on the ground that at the time of the marriage another woman was pregnant by the husband,[20] or a foreign ground substantially different from any under English law, such as the incapacity of a person of one religion to marry a member of another[21] or annulment on the ground of a mistake as to the attributes of the other spouse.[1] It must not be forgotten that the English courts would always retain the power, as in the case of other issues of validity,[2] to refuse to apply a foreign provision laying down a rule of invalidity where the application of that rule would be contrary to English public policy.[3]

(f) What law determines whether a marriage is void or voidable? It has been suggested[4] that, as the annulment of a voidable marriage and a divorce decree both only have prospective effect, the law of the forum should be applied to the former as to the latter. This would have the disadvantage of requiring the choice of law rule to depend on whether the marriage was void or voidable, and of deciding by what law that issue is to be determined—a difficult problem to which we must now turn.

It has been seen that different legal systems attribute different effects to invalidating factors. A clear example is provided by lack of consent which renders a marriage void under Scots law but voidable under English law.[5] This poses a problem. If an English court annuls the marriage of parties both domiciled in Scotland, applying the Scottish law on consent, is the marriage to be regarded in England as void or merely as voidable? At first sight it might seem that an English court ought to apply its own criteria for determining whether the problem is one of alleged voidness or of alleged voidability.[6] A moment's reflection, however, reveals the illogicality of this suggestion. Whether a marriage is void or voidable is merely a facet of the question whether it is valid or invalid. The law that determines its validity or invalidity must also determine what is meant by invalidity, that is, whether it means voidness or voidability. The role of the proper law, whether it is the law of the place of celebration or the law of the parties' domicils, is to determine whether the alleged defect is sufficient ground for annulment and if so what consequences ensue, assuming its existence to be proved. One of these consequences is the extent of the invalidity of the union, ie whether the marriage is merely voidable or void.

So far as authority is concerned, the weight of opinion supports the approach of characterisation by the law governing the substantive issue rather than by the law of the forum.[7] Nevertheless, it has been argued[8] that

20 This used to be a ground in New Zealand. The English rule is limited to the case of a wife being pregnant by another man: Matrimonial Causes Act 1973, s 12(*f*).
21 Eg *Lendrum v Chakravarti* 1929 SLT 96; though see *MacDougall v Chitnavis* 1937 SC 390; cf *Corbett v Corbett* [1957] 1 All ER 621, [1957] 1 WLR 486, a decision on recognition of a foreign decree.
1 Cf *Mitford v Mitford* [1923] P 130, also a decision on recognition.
2 Supra, p 599.
3 *Vervaeke v Smith* [1983] 1 AC 145, [1982] 2 All ER 144 provides some support for the view that English courts might not apply foreign rules invalidating sham marriages.
4 Law Commission Working Paper No 89 (1985), para 5.47.
5 Supra, p 642.
6 This seems to have been what was done in *Corbett v Corbett* [1957] 1 All ER 621, [1957] 1 WLR 486.
7 See *De Reneville v De Reneville* [1948] P 100 at 114; *Casey v Casey* [1949] P 420 at 429–430; *Merker v Merker* [1963] P 283 at 297; *Szechter v Szechter* [1971] P 286 at 294; and see Law Commission Working Paper No 89 (1985), para 5.53.
8 Morris (1970) 19 ICLQ 424.

it is for English law as the law of the forum and not for some foreign governing law to determine whether a marriage is void or voidable,[9] and that any argument based upon or by analogy with *De Reneville v De Reneville*[10] "seems to have been overtaken by oblivion and no longer represents the law".[11] The main support for such a view would appear to be an unarticulated assumption in the House of Lords decision in *Ross-Smith v Ross-Smith*[12] where it was held that there was jurisdiction to annul a void but not a voidable marriage celebrated in England, even though the husband who was alleged to be impotent or wilfully to have refused to consummate the marriage was domiciled at all material times in Scotland. No reference was made to whether the marriage was void or voidable under Scots law. If their Lordships merely assumed[13] that Scots and English law was the same on the question whether impotence and wilful refusal rendered a marriage voidable,[14] this was a strange assumption.[15] Nevertheless, although a link in the chain of reasoning in the House of Lords is missing,[16] this is a feature all too common in nullity cases and the silence of the House of Lords on this issue provides scant authority against reference to the law of the domicil and in favour of the law of the forum.

In conclusion, it is English law as the law of the forum which has to classify the type of defect as one of formalities (governed by the law of the place of celebration) or as a personal defect (governed by the law of the domicil). Once that classification is made, the effect of the defect on the validity of the marriage will be determined not by the law of the forum but by that law which, according to English choice of law rules, governs alleged defects of that kind. Any other approach would be highly unsatisfactory where the marriage was void under the governing law, but entirely valid under the law of the forum. To give the marriage full effect under the law of the forum notwithstanding its invalidity under the governing law would be to deprive the choice of law rule of any real impact.

(g) The law to govern the effect of a nullity decree[17] Although it is right to determine whether a ground of invalidity renders a marriage void or voidable by the law applicable to that ground, the effect of any decree of nullity is a matter for the law of the forum which granted it.[18] So, if an English court grants a decree annulling a marriage, it is for English law, as the law of the forum governing procedure, to determine the effect of its own decree. That being so, the law of the domicil or of the place of celebration, depending on the type of defect in question, will decide whether the marriage is void or voidable, but English law will decide whether, in the light of that classification, the decree should have retrospective effect.

9 Ibid.
10 [1948] P 100.
11 Morris (1970) 19 ICLQ 424, 427–428.
12 [1963] AC 280.
13 No evidence of Scots law would be necessary on this point as the House of Lords takes judicial knowledge of Scots law.
14 Lysyk (1965) 43 Can BR 107, 119–120.
15 Anton, p 440.
16 Morris (1970) 19 ICLQ 424, 428.
17 North, op cit, p 135; Law Commission Working Paper No 89 (1985), paras 5.54–5.55.
18 For the effect of a foreign decree, see infra, pp 688–689.

(c) RECOGNITION[19]

(i) Introduction

Until 1972, recognition of foreign divorces and legal separations was governed by common law rules. These rules were substantially, but not wholly, replaced by statutory grounds of recognition in the Recognition of Divorces and Legal Separations Act 1971, which was passed to implement the Convention on the Recognition of Divorces and Legal Separations adopted in 1970 by the Hague Conference on Private International Law. There had previously been criticism of the common law rules and the implementation of the Convention in the 1971 Act provided an opportunity to introduce reforms rather broader in scope than the Convention required. However, the 1971 Act did not extend to the recognition of foreign annulments which continued to be governed by common law recognition rules. The uncertainty of those rules and the fact that different regimes applied to divorce and nullity recognition was a source of criticism[20] which led the Law Commission in 1984 to examine the varied rules for the recognition of divorces, annulments and legal separations and to propose that essentially the same statutory rules should apply in the case of all three matrimonial causes, and that those rules should be based on the Recognition of Divorces and Legal Separations Act 1971, subject to a number of amendments.[21] These recommendations have been substantially carried into effect by Part II of the Family Law Act 1986.[1]

The general effect of the new statutory rules is that, subject to a few minor exceptions mentioned later,[2] the same recognition rules apply to all three matrimonial causes. Furthermore, the common law rules of nullity recognition,[3] and those common law rules relating to the recognition of divorces and legal separations which survived the 1971 Act,[4] have now been replaced by the new statutory regime irrespective of where the divorce, annulment or legal separation was obtained and of whether it was obtained before or after the 1986 Act came into force.[5]

Different rules are provided for the recognition of divorces, annulments and judicial separations granted in other jurisdictions within the British Isles[6] and of divorces, annulments and legal separations[7] obtained in politically foreign countries. These two situations must be considered separately.

---

19 McClean, *Recognition of Family Judgments in the Commonwealth* (1983), chs 2 & 3; Gordon, *Foreign Divorces: English Law and Practice* (1988).
20 Eg Carter (1979) 50 BYBIL 250, 252; Collier [1979] CLJ 289, 290.
21 Law Com No 137 (1984).
 1 Which came into force on 4 April 1988. For discussion of Part II of the 1986 Act, see Pearl [1987] CLJ 35. The major difference between the Law Commission proposals and the 1986 Act is that the latter introduces separate, and more restrictive, recognition rules for foreign extra-judicial divorces obtained where there have been no judicial or other proceedings; discussed infra, pp 673–675.
 2 Infra, pp 662–663, 678.
 3 See 10th edn, pp 406–416; and see Law Com No 137 (1984), Pt II.
 4 Ibid, pp 366–369.
 5 This is subject to rules preserving the effect of common law recognition in very limited circumstances, infra, p 686.
 6 This means the United Kingdom, the Channel Islands and the Isle of Man: see Interpretation Act 1978. Sch 1.
 7 The differing use of "judicial separation" and "legal separation" in the 1986 Act is discussed, infra, p 663.

(ii) Divorces, annulments and judicial separations granted elsewhere in the British Isles

Any decree of divorce, nullity, or judicial separation granted by a court of civil jurisdiction[8] in any part of the British Isles must be recognised in any part of the United Kingdom,[9] irrespective of when it was granted.[10] So, the English courts must[11] recognise any divorce, etc granted elsewhere in the British Isles and, similarly, such divorces, etc must be recognised in Scotland and Northern Ireland.[12]

Although such divorces, etc cannot be denied recognition on jurisdictional grounds,[13] two qualifications on recognition are provided. First, an English court can refuse recognition to a divorce or a judicial separation granted elsewhere in the British Isles at a time when there was no subsisting marriage between the parties, according to English law, including English rules of private international law.[14] This would cover such situations as where a marriage in England was invalid under English domestic law or a marriage abroad failed to satisfy English rules of private international law. In such circumstances, the English court has a discretion[15] to refuse recognition to, say, a Scottish divorce decree dissolving that marriage. It may be noted that this provision does not apply to recognition of nullity decrees for which, given the invalidity of the marriage, it might be thought inappropriate. However, the second qualification does extend to other British nullity decrees, as well as to divorces and judicial separations.[16] It gives the English court a discretion to deny recognition on a *res judicata* basis, ie if the other British decree was granted at a time when it was irreconcilable with a decision on the validity of the marriage previously given either by an English court or given elsewhere and entitled to be recognised in England. So a Scottish decree annulling or dissolving an English marriage can be denied recognition if there

---

8 The significance of this is that extra-judicial divorces, etc are excluded: see Family Law Act 1986, s 44 (1); Law Com No 137 (1984), para 4.14, and infra, pp 670–671. There is one minor exception to the denial of recognition to extra-judicial divorces obtained in England, relating to those obtained before 1974, see infra, p 686.
9 Family Law Act 1986, ss 44(2), 54(1).
10 Ibid, s 52(1)(a), (3). This marks a change from the Recognition of Divorces and Legal Separations Act 1971 which only applied to the recognition of British divorces granted after the Act came into force. There is a number of transitional provisions which apply both to the recognition of other British and overseas divorces, etc and which are discussed infra, p 686.
11 Subject to s 51 of the 1986 Act, infra, pp 676–686.
12 The Isle of Man has enacted legislation similar to Part II of the 1986 Act: the Recognition of Divorces etc Act 1987; and there is also legislation, based on similar rules in the Recognition of Divorces and Legal Separations Act 1971, s 1, in the Channel Islands, see North, op cit, pp 309–310, 324–326, 343–346.
13 Since 1974, the bases of divorce jurisdiction have been the same in England, Scotland and Northern Ireland: Domicile and Matrimonial Proceedings Act 1973, Parts II and III, Matrimonial Causes (Northern Ireland) Order, SI 1978/1045, Art 49 (replacing Pt IV of the 1973 Act). However, until 1974, there were differences eg between England and Scotland. The Scottish courts, but not the English, would grant a decree of divorce where a respondent was domiciled within the jurisdiction at the time of his adultery but not at the time of the proceedings: *Clark v Clark* 1967 SC 269; North op cit pp 26–27, 167–168. So a Scottish divorce granted in such circumstances before 1974 will be recognised in England.
14 1986 Act, s 51(2)(a).
15 Under the 1971 Act, s 8(1)(a) refusal of recognition was mandatory. For the reasons for the change to a discretionary rule, see Law Com No 137 (1984) paras 4.6 and 6.66, and infra, p 678.
16 S 51(1)(a).

is already an English decree, or a French decree recognised in England, to similar effect. In the case of a divorce or judicial separation, if there is a previous decision ending the marriage, the court's discretion can be exercised under either of the two heads just mentioned.[17]

Because of the mandatory wording of the Family Law Act 1986, section 44(2) of which states that divorce, etc decrees granted elsewhere in the British Isles *shall be recognised* in England, such other British decisions cannot now[18] be denied recognition in England even though they may contravene the rules of natural justice or be manifestly contrary to English public policy.[19] The justification for this is that it was "thought that in such circumstances the complaining party should seek to have the decree set aside by the court which granted it,[20] or on appeal from that court, and that it would be objectionable to allow a court in another part of the British Isles[21] to refuse to recognise the decree".[1] However, an English court is not required under Part II of the 1986 Act to recognise any findings of fault or any maintenance, custody or other ancillary order made in the other British proceedings.[2]

(iii) Divorces, annulments and legal separations obtained overseas

(a) **Introduction** Part II of the Family Law Act 1986 deals with a range of matters relating to the recognition in England of divorces, annulments and legal separations which have been obtained in a country[3] outside the British Isles, referred to in the 1986 Act as an "overseas divorce", etc.[4] No distinction is drawn in the 1986 Act, as there was in the 1971 Act,[5] between different kinds of foreign divorce, etc dependent on whether their recognition fell within or outside the Hague Convention of 1970. The consequence, as recommended by the Law Commission,[6] is a less complex set of recognition rules, especially in relation to issues of jurisdiction.[7] The issues to be examined here include the jurisdictional bases for recognition, the requirement of effectiveness of the divorce, etc in the country where it was obtained, the grounds on which recognition may be denied and the special problems and rules relating to different kinds of extra-judicial divorce.

(b) **General matters** The recognition rules laid down in Part II are exclusive.[8] It is not possible for the recognition of a foreign divorce, annulment or legal separation to be governed by common law recognition rules, whether or not

---

17 The two grounds for denying recognition are examined more fully in the context of the recognition of overseas divorces, etc, infra, pp 676–678.
18 Cf *Bonaparte v Bonaparte (otherwise Megone)* [1892] P 402.
19 These are reasons for denying recognition to divorces, etc obtained in other, foreign countries: 1986 Act, s 51(3), infra, pp 678–686.
20 See *Gaffney v Gaffney* [1975] IR 133.
21 This must mean "the United Kingdom".
1 Law Com No 34 (1970), p 43; and see Law Com No 137 (1984), para 4.7.
2 1986 Act, s 51(5); for recognition of maintenance and custody orders generally, see infra, pp 714 et seq, 731 et seq.
3 The meaning of "country" is discussed more fully, infra, pp 661–662.
4 S 45. Recognition by virtue of any other statute is, however, preserved: s 45(b), discussed infra, p 664.
5 Contrast ss 2–5 with s 6 of the 1971 Act; and see North, op cit, pp 172–176.
6 Law Com No 137 (1984), paras 6.3–6.6.
7 Though the eradication of complexity has been somewhat offset by the decision, not recommended by the Law Commission, to have special rules for the recognition of some extra-judicial divorces, infra, pp 673–675.
8 S 45.

it was obtained[9] before or after the 1986 Act came into effect.[10] As a result, the extension of the statutory regime for recognition to foreign annulments has the effect that it is now clear that an annulment of a void marriage will not be recognised on the basis that it was obtained in the country where the marriage was celebrated.[11] Furthermore, the general rule is that recognition is mandatory,[12] provided that the requirements of Part II (as to jurisdiction, etc) are satisfied and that one of the statutory grounds for denying recognition[13] is not relevant.

(c) Jurisdictional rules Section 46(1) of the 1986 Act provides a number of jurisdictional grounds for the recognition of overseas divorces, annulments and legal separations which have been obtained by judicial or other proceedings.[14]

(i) Domicil
An overseas divorce, etc will be recognised if either party, whether petitioner or respondent, to the marriage was domiciled in the country where it was obtained[15] at the date of the commencement of the foreign proceedings.[16] In the case of the recognition of foreign divorces and legal separations, this involves a very slight limitation on the recognition rules available under the 1971 Act where it was possible for a divorce, etc to be recognised in England if its validity was recognised in the country of each spouse's domicil, though obtained in neither.[1] The Law Commission[2] concluded that there was no case for the retention of such an extended rule relating to domicil, given that there is no equivalent rule in relation to the other jurisdictional heads of habitual residence and nationality,[3] and that the old rule was inequitable if one of the spouses was domiciled in England and the other abroad. In such a case the divorce, etc would only be recognised if recognised in England which was the very matter in issue; so recognition would have to be refused.[4] There is, therefore, no counterpart of such an extended domiciliary rule in the 1986 Act[5] where there are foreign proceedings.[6]

It has been assumed so far, as is usual in private international law, that domicil means domicil in the English sense. However, section 46(1)(b) requires an overseas divorce, etc to be recognised if either party is domiciled

9 S 52, subject to certain saving provisions, discussed infra, p 686.
10 S 52(1).
11 As in *Merker v Merker* [1963] P 283, [1962] 3 All ER 928; Law Com No 137 (1984), paras 6.33–6.34.
12 S 45.
13 S 51, infra, pp 676 et seq.
14 See the definition of "proceedings" in s 54. The jurisdictional rules relevant to extra-judicial divorces obtained without proceedings are discussed infra, pp 673–675.
15 S 46(1)(b)(ii).
16 S 46(3)(a).
1 Recognition of Divorces and Legal Separations Act 1971, s 6(3)(b); based on the common law decision in *Armitage v A-G* [1906] P 135.
2 Law Com No 137 (1984), paras 6.27–6.30.
3 Infra, p 659. Though the rules in the 1986 Act in relation to domicil are in other respects much wider than those in s 6 of the 1971 Act, where the domicil connection had to be satisfied in relation to both parties: see Law Com No 137 (1984), paras 6.21–6.26.
4 See North, op cit, p 185.
5 Though there are saving provisions which preserve the validity of divorces and legal separations obtained before the 1986 Act came into effect and which would have been recognised under the now-abandoned rule: s 52(5)(b), (e), infra, p 686.
6 The common law rule is retained in cases where there are no proceedings: s 46(2), infra, pp 674–675.

in the foreign country in either the English or the foreign sense of domicil,[7] this latter being a ground of jurisdiction provided in the 1970 Hague Convention and in the 1971 Act. So an overseas divorce may have to be recognised on the basis of such foreign concept of domicil,[8] even though neither spouse was domiciled in the foreign country in the English sense of the term.[9]

It is possible that a country may have different concepts of domicil for different purposes;[10] and so section 46(5) of the 1986 Act makes clear that the concept of domicil relevant for recognition purposes is that used in the foreign country "in family matters".[11]

(ii) Habitual residence

An overseas divorce will be recognised if it was obtained in a country in which, at the time of the commencement of the proceedings,[12] either spouse was habitually resident.[13] No length of period of residence is specified or required;[14] and jurisdiction may be founded on the habitual residence of either spouse, whether petitioner or respondent.

(iii) Nationality

A similar rule applies in the case of nationality, so that divorces, etc obtained in a country of which, at the time of the proceedings,[15] either party was a national will be recognised in England.[16] No definition of nationality is provided,[17] but there seems little doubt that, in the case of a person with dual nationality, recognition will be given to divorces, etc obtained in either country of the nationality.[18]

(d) The time at which the jurisdictional rules must be satisfied As we have seen, the general rule is that the jurisdictional connection must be satisfied at the date of the commencement of the foreign proceedings by which the divorce, etc was obtained.[19] There are, however, two exceptions to this. The first is relevant only to the recognition of foreign annulments. It is possible both in this country and elsewhere for an annulment of a void marriage to be obtained by a person other than a spouse and for that to be done after the death of either or both spouses. Our own jurisdictional rules make special

---

7 S 46(5). The same applies where there are no proceedings, infra, p 675.
8 See *Lawrence v Lawrence* [1985] Fam 106 at 121.
9 Recognition does not depend, under the 1986 Act, on the foreign court having assumed jurisdiction on the basis of domicil, infra, p 664.
10 Indeed England has a special concept of domicil for the purposes of the Civil Jurisdiction and Judgments Acts 1982 and 1991, supra, pp 284–285, 342.
11 This is consistent with Art 3 of the 1970 Hague Convention. It also involves dropping the requirement, to be found in s 3(2) of the 1971 Act, that the foreign country uses its concept of domicil as a ground of jurisdiction in divorce, etc. The Law Commission considered such a limitation to be ineffective, unnecessary and illogical, especially in the case of extra-judicial divorces: Law Com No 137 (1984), para 6.18.
12 This head is inapplicable if there are no proceedings, infra pp 673–675.
13 S 46(1)(b)(i), (3)(a). See, eg *Cruse v Chittum* [1974] 2 All ER 940; *Kendall v Kendall* [1977] Fam 208, [1977] 3 All ER 471; *Joyce v Joyce* [1979] Fam 93 at 105; *Quazi v Quazi* [1980] AC 744 at 788, 821; Social Security Decision No R (P) 2/90.
14 Cf the English jurisdictional test, supra, pp 631–632, where the meaning of "habitual residence" is discussed.
15 Again, this head is inapplicable if there are no proceedings, infra, pp 673–675.
16 S 46(1)(b)(iii), 3(a); see eg *Broit v Broit* 1972 SLT (Notes) 32; *Quazi v Quazi* [1980] AC 744 at 805, 813, 821; *Lawrence v Lawrence* [1985] Fam 106 at 121.
17 Though see s 54(2).
18 *Torok v Torok* [1973] 1 WLR 1066 at 1069.
19 S 46(3)(a).

provision for such a case,[20] as does section 46(4) of the 1986 Act in the case of recognition of an overseas annulment. If the annulment was obtained after the death of a party to the marriage, the jurisdictional requirements of domicil, habitual residence or nationality are satisfied if the appropriate connection existed at the date of the death.[1]

The second exception concerns cross-proceedings, where it is sufficient if the jurisdictional grounds of habitual residence, nationality and domicil in the English or the foreign sense existed either at the date of the original proceedings or of the cross-proceedings.[2] This applies irrespective of which proceedings led to the foreign divorce, etc. For example, if a wife petitioned for divorce in a jurisdiction where she was habitually resident and the husband cross-petitioned, and a decree was granted to him, it would be recognised even though he was not resident or domiciled in, or a national of, that jurisdiction, or even if at the date of the cross-petition the wife had ceased to be resident there. Of course, even if this special jurisdictional provision is satisfied, it is necessary to satisfy all the other requirements of Part II of the 1986 Act for the divorce, etc to be recognised.[3]

(e) Effectiveness Not only must one of the various jurisdictional requirements be satisfied at the relevant time, but it is also necessary that the overseas divorce, etc be "effective under the law of the country in which it was obtained".[4] This requirement of effectiveness was also to be found in the 1971 Act[5] but did not there extend to recognition on the jurisdictional basis of domicil in the English sense. Following the recommendations of the Law Commission,[6] this requirement applies, under the 1986 Act, also to the domicil basis[7] and is extended, as is the whole of Part II of the 1986 Act, to the recognition of overseas annulments. This marks a change from the common law rules as to nullity recognition where, for example, a German decree was recognised in England even though it was regarded in Germany as invalid and of no effect there.[8]

Various examples of legal ineffectiveness might be provided, as, for instance, where a foreign divorce does not, in the foreign country, dissolve a marriage until a specified period has elapsed,[9] or whilst an appeal is pending,[10] or until a decree absolute is pronounced.[11] It is also possible[12] that, under the

20 Domicile and Matrimonial Proceedings Act 1973, s 5(3)(c), supra, p 633.
 1 See Law Com No 137 (1984), para 6.32.
 2 S 47(1)(a).
 3 S 47(1)(b); and see Law Com No 137 (1984), para 6.39.
 4 S 46(1)(a).
 5 S 2(b).
 6 Law Com No 137 (1984), paras 6.12–6.13.
 7 An example of a divorce recognised under common law domicil rules where the effectiveness requirement would not have been satisfied is provided by *Har-Shefi v Har-Shefi (No 2)* [1953] P 220, [1953] 2 All ER 373; though see now the 1986 Act, ss 44(1), 52(5), infra, pp 670–671, 686.
 8 *Merker v Merker* [1963] P 283. It might be argued that a foreign decree, though invalid in the country where granted, is effective there until actually set aside: *Kendall v Kendall* [1977] Fam 208 at 214.
 9 Eg *Martin v Buret* 1938 SLT 479.
10 Eg *Torok v Torok* [1973] 3 All ER 101, [1973] 1 WLR 1066; cf Social Security Decision R(P) 2/90, at p 6.
11 Eg *De Thoren v Wall* (1876) 3 R (HL) 28. A further example in the case of an extra-judicial divorce by *talak* might be a delay whilst conciliation proceedings are continuing: National Insurance Decision Nos R(G) 5/74; R(G) 2/75.
12 North, op cit, pp 175–176.

law of the foreign country, the divorce, etc might be regarded as ineffective there because that country's rules as to service on the parties or as to the jurisdiction of its courts had not been satisfied, even though the jurisdictional requirements of the 1986 Act[13] had been. This might be so even if the procedural defects did not fall within the heads listed in the 1986 Act[1] as grounds for denying recognition.[2]

(f) Meaning of "country" So far, in examining the jurisdictional and other rules of Part II of the 1986 Act, it has been assumed that the requirement of a connection with the "country" in which the divorce, etc was obtained causes no difficulty.[3] There are, however, political countries which comprise different territories[4] and those territories may have different substantive or jurisdictional rules for obtaining divorces, etc. There were problems with the 1971 Act in deciding whether some or all of the references in that Act to "country" meant the political state or the individual territory.[5] In order to try to resolve these difficulties, section 49 of the 1986 Act[6] provides express modifications of the provisions of Part II of that Act in those cases where, in a country comprising different territories, there are different systems of law in force in relation to divorce, annulment or legal separation.[7] The general approach is to say that, in such cases, any requirement of domicil (in the English or foreign senses) or habitual residence in a country, and indeed effectiveness under the law of that country, means domicil or habitual residence in an individual territory.[8] This means that, as each American state has its own divorce, etc laws, New York or California is to be treated as a separate country for the purposes of determining domicil or habitual residence. On the other hand Canada and Australia, both also federal states, have federal divorce laws;[9] so one must ask whether in divorce proceedings a spouse was habitually resident or domiciled in Canada or Australia, rather than in an individual province or state.

Nationality as a connecting factor poses rather different problems. Federal and other non-unitary states do not have different nationality rules, depending on a person's connection with a particular territory within the state. This

---

13 S 46(1)(b), supra, pp 658–659; see eg *Papadopoulos v Papadopoulos* [1930] P 55.
 1 S 51, infra, pp 676 et seq; eg *Pemberton v Hughes* [1899] 1 Ch 781.
 2 Particular problems of effectiveness relating to extra-judicial divorces are discussed, infra, pp 672–673.
 3 Part II of the 1986 Act does not define "country" apart from saying that it includes a colony or other dependent territory of the United Kingdom (eg Hong Kong or Gibraltar), but that a person is to be treated as a national of such a territory only if it has a law of citizenship or nationality separate from that of the United Kingdom and he is a citizen or national of that territory under that law: s 54(2).
 4 Eg the USA, Canada, Australia, the United Kingdom.
 5 North, op cit, pp 173–175, 177, 179, 181–181; Law Com No 137 (1984), para 6.15.
 6 Following recommendations made in Law Com No 137 (1984), para 6.16.
 7 S 49(1).
 8 S 49(2), (4), (5), amending where appropriate the main jurisdictional rules in s 46(1)(b), supra, pp 658–659, and also the special jurisdictional rules where there are no proceedings, in s 46(2)(b), infra, pp 673–675; as well as the rules for the conversion of a legal separation into a divorce (s 47(2), infra, pp 662–663) and relating to proof of finding of facts in the foreign proceedings (s 48, infra, p 663). Also amended are the provisions of s 52(3) and (4); but this appears to be a slip, which it is hoped will be corrected, as the appropriate provisions to be amended appear to be those in s 51(3) and (4). None of the provisions mentioned above are amended in relation to nationality, which is dealt with by s 49(3), infra, p 662.
 9 The position would be different in Canada with regard to legal separation which, unlike divorce, is a provincial rather than a federal matter.

would suggest that a connection with a territory is satisfied for jurisdictional purposes if either party is a national of the political state as a whole. This means that if a divorce, etc is obtained in New York, it will be recognised in England even though the only relevant connection for the purposes of the 1986 Act is that one spouse is a United States citizen.[10] The provisions which state that connection by domicil or habitual residence with a territory will suffice[11] do not extend to connection by nationality.

It is necessary in the case of connection by nationality, as in other cases, not only that the divorce, etc was obtained in the country of the nationality but also that it was effective "under the law of the country in which it was obtained".[12] This raises the issue as to the meaning of "country" in this latter context. If, for instance, a divorce is obtained in California by an American citizen, and the only jurisdictional test which is satisfied is that of nationality, does the divorce have to be effective in California or throughout the USA? The 1971 Act was unclear on this question and academic views differed as to the answer;[13] but section 49(3)(a) of the 1986 Act now makes it clear, that, in such a case, effectiveness "throughout the country in which [the divorce] was obtained" is necessary.[14] So, in the example just given, the Californian divorce will only be recognised here if it is recognised throughout the USA. Indeed, it has been thought to be "absurd" to recognise a divorce obtained in one American state which would not be recognised elsewhere in the USA.[15] Furthermore, the Law Commission, on whose recommendations this provision is based, concluded that the new approach

is unlikely to lead to denial of recognition because most federal countries have uniform divorce laws (eg Australia, Canada, Switzerland) or uniform jurisdictional rules or make provision for giving full faith and credit throughout the federal country to a divorce, etc obtained in one territory thereof.[16]

(g) Two procedural issues

(i) Conversion of legal separation into divorce
Some jurisdictions permit a legal separation automatically to be converted into a divorce at the end of a prescribed period. If the legal separation would be recognised on the jurisdictional grounds[17] of habitual residence, nationality, or domicil in the English or the foreign sense, then the later divorce will be recognised even though the jurisdictional criteria cannot be satisfied at that later date.[18] The conversion must, however, be in the country

---

10 S 46(1)(b)(iii).
11 S 49(2),(4),(5).
12 S 46(1)(a), supra, pp 660–661.
13 Contrast Dicey and Morris, pp 698–700; Clive, *Husband and Wife* (2nd edn, 1982), pp 654–656.
14 There is a similar provision in s 49(3)(b) in relation to the effectiveness of the conversion into a divorce of a legal separation obtained in a country of which one party was a national, infra.
15 Morris (1975) 24 ICLQ 635, 641; and see Law Com No 137 (1984), para 6.16.
16 Law Com No 137 (1984), para 6.16; though some problems may still remain where there is no uniform approach, as with legal separation in Canada: North, op cit p 282.
17 Including the provisions as to cross-proceedings in s 47(1).
18 S 47(2).

where the legal separation was obtained and the new divorce must be effective under the law of that country.

(ii) Findings of fact
If any finding of fact on the basis of which jurisdiction was assumed, such as to the domicil in the foreign sense,[19] habitual residence[20] or nationality[1] of the parties,[2] is made in the foreign divorce, etc proceedings, it shall be conclusive evidence of the fact found if both spouses took part in the proceedings.[3] In any other case, eg an *ex parte* divorce, it shall be sufficient proof of that fact unless it is challenged and the contrary is shown.[4]

(h) Meaning of divorce, annulment or legal separation As foreign matrimonial proceedings may differ markedly from English ones, it is necessary for the English court to decide whether the foreign proceedings come within one of the categories of divorce, annulment[5] or legal separation within the meaning of Part II of the 1986 Act. It has been held, for example, that the termination of a marriage by the husband's unilateral decision to change his religion and become a Moslem, which was evidenced by a declaration before witnesses in Malaysia, could be regarded here as neither a divorce nor an annulment.[6] In the case of legal separations, it should be noted that, although the rules for the recognition of other British decrees refer to decrees of "judicial separation",[7] those for recognition of separations obtained outside the British Isles refer to "legal separations".[8] A legal separation is not defined in the 1986 Act, nor indeed in the 1970 Hague Convention on which the Act is based. It must be assumed that the Act extends to all foreign decrees or orders which are similar in character to an English decree of judicial separation and, indeed, to any order or decree made by a foreign court which has the effect that the parties are no longer obliged to live together, but not the effect of dissolving the marriage. The consequence of the use of different terminology is that, for example, a non-cohabitation order made in Northern Ireland will not be recognised in England because it is not a decree of judicial separation.[9] On the other hand, had it been made outside the British Isles, it is likely to be recognised as a legal separation.[10]

19 It is not appropriate for a finding by a foreign court as to domicil in the English sense to be binding on an English court: see Law Com No 137 (1984), para 6.40.
20 Eg *Cruse v Chittum* [1974] 2 All ER 940; cf Social Security Decision R (P) 2/90.
 1 Eg *Torok v Torok* [1973] 1 WLR 1066 at 1069.
 2 S 48(2).
 3 S 48(1)(a), as in *Lawrence v Lawrence* [1985] Fam 106 at 121; and appearance is to be treated as taking part in proceedings: s 48(3).
 4 S 48(1)(b); eg *Mamdani v Mamdani* [1984] FLR 699 at 700. The court is not required under Part II of the 1986 Act to recognise any findings of fault made in any divorce, nullity or separation proceedings or any maintenance, custody or other ancillary order made in such proceedings: s 51(5); see *Sabbagh v Sabbagh* [1985] FLR 29. For recognition of maintenance and custody orders generally, see infra, pp 714 et seq, 731 et seq.
 5 A non-exclusive definition of annulment is provided in s 54(1) to include "any decree or declaration of nullity of marriage, however expressed".
 6 *Viswalingham v Viswalingham* (1979) 1 FLR 15. As the marriage was held to be ended under the law of Malaysia, the common domicil of the parties, prima facie this would be recognised in England; but recognition was in fact denied on public policy grounds.
 7 1986 Act, s 44(2).
 8 Ibid, ss 46–52.
 9 North, op cit, pp 278–280.
10 Ibid, pp 286–287.

(i) Irrelevance of the foreign jurisdictional rules or of the grounds for granting the divorce, etc It should be pointed out that, as was the case at common law,[11] the grounds on which the foreign divorce, etc were obtained are irrelevant to the question of recognition.[12] It is immaterial that the divorce, etc was obtained on a ground unknown to English law. This is illustrated clearly by the fact that, at common law, a foreign nullity decree has been recognised annulling a marriage, validly celebrated in England, on the ground of what English courts would class as formal invalidity.[13] A corollary of this is that a foreign divorce or annulment will be recognised though granted on grounds unknown to English law,[14] even where one spouse was domiciled in England.[15]

Furthermore, again as at common law, the jurisdictional basis assumed by a foreign court is similarly irrelevant. The English court is concerned only with the factual jurisdictional circumstances in the foreign country when the divorce, etc was obtained.

(j) Other statutory grounds of recognition Section 45(b) of the 1986 Act preserves the rules for the recognition of overseas divorces, annulments and legal separations which exist by virtue of any other enactment. However, at the same time, the 1986 Act repeals[16] as spent legislation most, if not all, of the other statutory provisions[17] under which overseas divorces, etc might be recognised, whilst also preserving the validity of past divorces, etc which would be recognised under that spent legislation, and might not be recognised under the 1986 Act.[18] Furthermore, it has been made clear[19] that an overseas divorce, etc, not recognised under the 1986 Act, cannot be recognised under the Foreign Judgments (Reciprocal Enforcement) Act 1933.[20]

(iv) Extra-judicial divorces, annulments and legal separations[1]

(a) Introduction Divorces may be obtained not only in judicial proceedings but also extra-judicially in a variety of ways. These include divorce by mutual consent,[2] by administrative process[3] or, more commonly, under religious laws.[4] For instance, Jewish Rabbinical law allows a husband to dissolve his marriage by delivering to his wife a letter of divorce, called a *gett* and, though this necessitates his appearance before a Rabbinical court, the proceeding is a formality and is not accompanied by a judicial finding and pronouncement.[5]

11 *Indyka v Indyka* [1969] 1 AC 33 at 66.
12 Subject to any public policy factor, infra, pp 680–685.
13 *De Massa v De Massa* (1931), reported in [1939] 2 All ER 150n: *Galene v Galene (otherwise Galice)* [1939] P 237, [1939] 2 All ER 148.
14 *Corbett v Corbett* [1957] 1 WLR 486 at 490.
15 *Mitford v Mitford and Von Kuhlmann* [1923] P 130.
16 S 68(2) and Sch 2.
17 The main ones are the Colonial and Other Territories (Divorce Jurisdiction) Acts 1926 to 1950 and the Matrimonial Causes (War Marriages) Act 1944, s 4: see Law Com No 137 (1984), paras 6.44–6.48.
18 S 52(5)(c), (d); and see Law Com No 137 (1984), pp 115–116.
19 *Maples v Maples* [1988] Fam 14, [1987] 3 All ER 188.
20 Supra, pp 397–405.
 1 North, op cit, ch 11; (1975) 91 LQR 36; Young (1987) 7 Legal Studies 78; Edwards (1988) 18 Fam Law 419; Pilkington (1988) 37 ICLQ 131.
 2 National Insurance Decision No R(G) 1/72.
 3 *Manning v Manning* [1958] P 112, [1958] 1 All ER 291.
 4 Gordon, *Foreign Divorces: English Law and Practice* (1988), chs 1–3.
 5 Eg *Har-Shefi v Har-Shefi (No 2)* [1953] P 220, [1953] 2 All ER 373; *Broit v Broit* 1972 SLT (Notes) 32; *Maples v Maples* [1988] Fam 14, [1987] 3 All ER 188; and see Berkovits (1988) 104 LQR 60, 81–93.

Under Moslem law, a husband is permitted to divorce his wife without any reference to a court. Such a divorce, by *talak*, merely requires him to state unequivocally three times his intention to repudiate the marriage. In some countries, no further formality is required than this—what is often called a "bare" *talak*.[6] In other jurisdictions where Moslem law is applied, it is necessary also either to register such a divorce with a court or administrative body[7] or, as under the Pakistan Muslim Family Laws Ordinance 1961,[8] to go through procedures giving the opportunity of conciliation proceedings.[9] Moslem law also provides other forms of divorce, such as by *khula*, a form of divorce by agreement on the suggestion of the wife.[10]

Examples of extra-judicial annulments are very much less easy to provide,[11] not least because few countries recognise religious or administrative annulment of marriage. However, examples can be provided of annulment by an ecclesiastical rather than civil tribunal.[12]

At common law, English courts were originally very reluctant to recognise the effectiveness and validity of extra-judicial divorces;[13] but attitudes changed and it came to be accepted that they should normally be recognised if the general jurisdictional criteria for recognition had been established.[14] Indeed, in 1970 recognition was given to a *talak* divorce pronounced in England, dissolving the marriage celebrated in England of spouses domiciled in Pakistan.[15]

The rules for the recognition of foreign extra-judicial divorces and legal separations were placed by the Recognition of Divorces and Legal Separations Act 1971 on the same general statutory basis as the rules for the recognition of foreign divorces and legal separations obtained by court order; though the grounds for recognising extra-judicial divorces and legal separations obtained without there having been any proceedings (such as a bare *talak*) were narrower[16] than for those which involved some form of proceedings as in the case of a *gett*.[17] There were also special rules generally denying recognition to extra-judicial divorces and separations obtained in the British Isles but recognised as valid elsewhere.[18] This pattern has substantially

---

6 Eg *Sharif v Sharif* (1980) 10 Fam Law 216 (Iraq); *Zaal v Zaal* (1982) 4 FLR 284 (Dubai); *Chaudhary v Chaudhary* [1985] Fam 19, [1984] 3 All ER 1017 (Kashmir).
7 Eg *Russ v Russ* [1964] P 315, [1962] 1 All ER 649 (Egypt).
8 See *Qureshi v Qureshi* [1972] Fam 173, [1971] 1 All ER 325; *R v Registrar General of Births, Deaths and Marriages, ex p Minhas* [1977] QB 1, [1976] 2 All ER 246; *Quazi v Quazi* [1980] AC 744, [1979] 3 All ER 897; *R v Secretary of State for the Home Department, ex p Fatima* [1986] AC 527, [1986] 2 All ER 32.
9 See *Radwan v Radwan* [1973] Fam 24, [1972] 3 All ER 967 (Egypt).
10 *Quazi v Quazi* [1980] AC 744, [1979] 3 All ER 897.
11 Cases of extra-judicial separation have not come before the courts for many years: *Connelly v Connelly* (1851) 7 Moo PCC 438; North, op cit, p 280.
12 *Di Rollo v Di Rollo* 1959 SC 75; *Butterley v Butterley* (1974) 48 DLR (3d) 351; see North, op cit, pp 264–266.
13 Eg *R v Hammersmith Superintendent Registrar of Marriages, ex p Mir-Anwarrudin* [1917] 1 KB 634.
14 Though the extra-judicial annulment in *Di Rollo v Di Rollo*, supra, was denied recognition on grounds of public policy.
15 *Qureshi v Qureshi* [1972] Fam 173, [1971] 1 All ER 325. Recognition was denied at common law if the spouses were domiciled in England: [1972] Fam 173 at 199; *Radwan v Radwan* [1973] Fam 24, [1972] 3 All ER 976.
16 Jurisdiction could only be based on domicil in the English sense under s 6 of the 1971 Act.
17 Jurisdiction could also based on habitual residence, nationality or domicil in the foreign sense under ss 2–5 of the 1971 Act.
18 See the 1971 Act, ss 1, 6; Domicile and Matrimonial Proceedings Act 1973, s 16.

been retained in Part II of the 1986 Act, with the addition that the recognition rules now extend to the recognition of extra-judicial annulments.[19] The Law Commission[20] had proposed a more liberal approach[1] so that, for example, "bare" *talaks* would fall within the broader recognition rules applicable where there had been some proceedings. On the other hand, they also proposed that the requirement of some form of proceedings, albeit more liberally interpreted,[2] should apply to all divorces, etc irrespective of the jurisdictional basis of recognition. This would have had the effect that an entirely informal divorce could no longer be generally recognised[3] even though obtained in the country of the spouses' common domicil. This essentially more liberal approach was rejected[4] for three reasons, namely because of problems of proof in the case of informal divorces, because such divorces tend to discriminate against women (being usually obtained by men) and because they often provide little or no financial protection for the wife and family. These arguments are not wholly convincing. The last is met by the provisions in Part III of the Matrimonial and Family Proceedings Act 1984 allowing the courts to grant financial relief even though a foreign divorce is recognised here.[5] If there is force in the first two arguments they militate against any recognition of such informal divorces, but in fact they are to continue to be recognised, provided they are obtained or recognised in the country of the domicil in the English sense.[6] It is not easy to see why a domicil connection provides any greater protection than one based, say, on habitual residence.[7]

The result is that, in relation to extra-judicial divorces, etc, Part II of the 1986 Act still follows very much the approach of the 1971 Act. We shall have, therefore, to consider separately the rules relating to extra-judicial divorces, etc obtained in the British Isles and overseas, and to determine where a divorce, etc is obtained, given that the recognition rules depend on this factor even though, because of the very informality of many of the divorces, etc under consideration, the parties may regard the place where it takes place as totally unimportant. In the context of overseas divorces, etc, it is necessary also to look separately at those obtained by some form of proceedings and, indeed, to consider what constitutes "proceedings".

(b) General issues Before examining the particular rules relating to the recognition of extra-judicial divorces, etc, it is necessary to examine, first, two of these interrelated general issues. As there are different rules for extra-judicial divorces, etc obtained in the British Isles and overseas, and for overseas divorces, etc depending on whether or not they were obtained by "proceedings", we shall consider here the two questions: where is an extra-judicial divorce, etc obtained? and what constitutes proceedings?

19 Ss 44, 45; following the recommendations of the Law Commission: Law Com No 137 (1984), para 6.9.
20 Law Com No 137 (1984), para 6.11.
1 Similar to that in Australia: Family Law Act 1975, s 104.
2 It was suggested that the statutory phrase "judicial or other proceedings" should include acts which constitute the means by which the divorce, etc may be obtained and which are done in compliance with the procedures required in the country where it was obtained.
3 Under s 6 of the 1971 Act.
4 473 HL Official Report cols 1082, 1103 (1986); see Young (1987) 7 Legal Studies 78, 81–83.
5 Infra, pp 709–714.
6 S 46(2), infra, pp 674–675.
7 S 46(1).

(i) Where is an extra-judicial divorce, etc obtained?
This question may be asked in two main contexts. First, it is necessary that
an overseas divorce, etc be effective in the country where it was obtained and
that one of the relevant jurisdictional links with that country is satisfied.[8]
The second context, which has proved in practice to be the more important,
is to determine whether the divorce, etc was obtained in the British Isles or
overseas. The significance of this is that the divorce, etc will normally be
denied recognition if obtained in the British Isles.[9]

It might be thought that the proceedings or act[10] by which an extra-judicial
divorce, etc is obtained could only occur in one country. Whilst this is usually
true, particular difficulty has been caused by Moslem divorces by *talak*
especially where this religious requirement is also combined with a need for
some further type of proceedings, as is illustrated by a decision under the
Recognition of Divorces and Legal Separations Act 1971, *R v Secretary of
State for the Home Department, ex p Fatima*:[11]

> The husband was a Pakistan national who married there in 1968, but had
> lived in England ever since. In 1978, he purported to divorce his wife by
> *talak* and in 1982 wished to marry Ghulam Fatima; but she was refused
> entry to this country by an immigration officer at Heathrow Airport. The
> reason was because he concluded that the husband's *talak* divorce would
> not be recognised in this country and so the husband was not free to marry
> again here.

The crucial issue with which the House of Lords was faced was to determine
where the *talak* divorce in 1978 was obtained. If it was obtained in Pakistan,
where it was effective, it would be recognised here as a divorce obtained in
the country of the nationality.[12] If it was obtained in England, it would be
denied recognition.[13] The circumstances were that it was a "trans-national"
divorce:[14] some proceedings took place in England, others in Pakistan under
the Muslim Family Laws Ordinance 1961 in force there. What happened was
that the husband had pronounced the *talak* in England and made a statutory
declaration to that effect to an English solicitor. Copies of this were sent to
Pakistan both to the wife and, as required by the Ordinance, to the Chairman
of the relevant local union council; and it would appear that all the necessary
conciliation procedures in Pakistan were complied with, the effect of which
was that the divorce became effective there 90 days after receipt of notice of
the *talak* by the chairman. Lord ACKNER concluded that the divorce was not
obtained by proceedings wholly in Pakistan because the pronouncement of
the *talak* in England was an essential part of the proceedings.[15] This led him
to the conclusion that the divorce was obtained by proceedings which took
place in both countries and that recognition must be denied, because section
2 of the 1971 Act required an overseas divorce to be obtained by means of

8 1986 Act, s 46.
9 Ibid, s 44, infra, pp 670–671.
10 The need to decide where a divorce, etc was obtained arises whether or not it was obtained
  by judicial or other proceedings.
11 [1986] AC 527, [1986] 2 All ER 32; affirming the CA, [1985] QB 190; Berkovits (1988) 104
  LQR 60.
12 Supra, p 659.
13 Infra, pp 670–671.
14 [1985] QB 190 at 197, 207.
15 [1986] AC 527 at 533–534; and see *Quazi v Quazi* [1980] AC 744 at 817, 826.

judicial or other proceedings in a country outside the British Isles and to be effective under the law of that country.

Such a result is wholly consistent with the policy of denying recognition to extra-judicial divorces, etc which have been obtained by proceedings in England,[16] but it does highlight the particular weight which the legislation places on where a divorce, etc is obtained, a factor which, if the divorce, etc is informal, is likely to be perceived by the layman to be irrelevant. If the husband in this case had had the advice, or the funds, to go to Pakistan to pronounce the *talak*, it would have been recognised here.[17]

A difficult question is whether the same result is compelled under the 1986 Act which is worded slightly differently. Section 46(1) requires an overseas divorce obtained by proceedings to be effective in the country where it was obtained but does not, in so many words, require the proceedings to be in that country. This has led to the suggestion[18] that where the proceedings take place in more than one country, as in *Ex p Fatima*, the divorce may still be recognised if that element of the proceedings which renders the divorce effective takes place in the overseas country with which the necessary jurisdictional links may be established. So, it is argued,[19] a *talak* pronounced in England by a Pakistan national but perfected by proceedings in Pakistan is obtained (and effective) in Pakistan and should be recognised in England. There is considerable force in this argument, though it appears to be founded on legislative oversight, rather than conscious policy.[20] Furthermore, other provisions of the 1986 Act, like their predecessors in the 1971 Act, are drafted on the basis that the divorce was obtained in the foreign proceedings.[21] This is particularly true of those provisions concerned with the giving of notice of the proceedings to the parties.[22] It is nonetheless undesirable to say, as was said by Lord ACKNER in *Ex p Fatima*, that there "must be a single set of proceedings which have to be instituted in the same country as that in which the relevant divorce was ultimately obtained".[23] This may be too sweeping a statement.[24] It is surely understandable to deny recognition to a divorce obtained by proceedings partly in this country and partly abroad, given the prohibition on recognition of extra-judicial divorces, etc obtained in the British Isles.[1] It is less justifiable to deny recognition to, say, a *talak* pronounced in Dubai followed by conciliation proceedings in Pakistan, given that the divorce is effective in each of the countries where some of the proceedings took place.

If a divorce, etc is obtained in a consulate or embassy, it is to be taken to be obtained in the country where the consulate or embassy is situated, not in the country of the sending state. So it has been held that an extra-judicial

16 1986 Act, s 44(1), infra, pp 670–671.
17 See [1985] QB 190 at 199–200.
18 Pilkington (1988) 37 ICLQ 130, 132–136; and see Young (1987) 7 Legal Studies 78, 87; Berkovits (1988) 104 LQR 60, 79–80; Gordon, op cit, pp 101–104.
19 Pilkington (1988) 37 ICLQ 130, 135.
20 Section 46(1) is essentially to the same effect as Clause 3(1)(a) of the Law Commission's draft Bill on which the 1986 Act is based and the Commission expressed itself content with the decision in *Ex p Fatima*: see Law Com No 137 (1984), para 6.11 and p 94.
21 Eg ss 47(1), 48(1), supra, pp 660, 663.
22 S 51(3), infra, pp 678–679.
23 [1986] AC 527 at 534.
24 Indeed it was made in answer to a question posed by Lord ACKNER which was restricted to proceedings which took place both in the British Isles and overseas: [1986] AC 527 at 533.
1 1986 Act, s 44(1), infra, pp 670–671.

divorce obtained in the Consulate-General of the United Arab Republic in London was obtained in England and was not an overseas divorce.[2]

(ii) What constitutes proceedings?

The significance of this question is that, where the divorce, etc is obtained by judicial or other proceedings, the jurisdictional bases of recognition are much wider than if there are no proceedings[3]—being limited in the latter case to domicil.[4] This is much the same as the position under the 1971 Act[5] in which context the courts have had to consider the same question. Whilst there is no definition of "judicial or other proceedings" in the 1986 Act,[6] it has been suggested[7] that the phrase is limited to cases involving some act external to the parties themselves, such as registration, conciliation proceedings or some other form of approval.[8] The House of Lords has held in *Quazi v Quazi*[9] that a divorce obtained in Pakistan by *talak* and which then involved the procedures of the Pakistan Muslim Family Laws Ordinance 1961—namely the giving of notice to the wife and to the chairman of the local union council, with the prospect of conciliation proceedings—had been obtained by means of judicial or other proceedings. On the other hand, after a period of uncertainty, the Court of Appeal[10] has concluded that a "bare" *talak*, ie where there is no more than an oral pronouncement by the husband three times, whether or not before witnesses, that he divorces his wife, does not constitute proceedings.[11] It has been suggested by OLIVER LJ that proceedings "must impart a degree of formality and at least the involvement of some agency, whether lay or religious, of or recognised by the state having a function that is more than simply probative,"[12] and would exclude "a private act conducted entirely by parties inter se or by one party alone, as a proceeding, even though the party performing it may give it an additional solemnity or even an efficacy by performing it in the presence of other persons whose only involvement is that they witness the performance".[13] On this approach, it can be concluded that a divorce in Thailand by mutual consent based simply on an agreement signed by the spouses,[14] or a divorce by consent under Chinese customary law, even if the agreement is presented to, and authenticated by, a local body,[15] will not be regarded as having been obtained

---

2 *Radwan v Radwan* [1973] Fam 24, [1972] 3 All ER 967, supra, pp 575–576; and see *Chaudhary v Chaudhary* [1976] Fam 148, [1975] 3 All ER 687.

3 1986 Act, s 46(1).

4 S 46(2), infra, pp 673–675.

5 Contrast the broad recognition rules of ss 2–5 with the more limited domicil ground of s 6 which was the only ground of recognition if there were no proceedings.

6 S 54(1) and nor was there in the 1971 Act; and see *Quazi v Quazi* [1980] AC 744 at 788–789. Contrast the proposed definition in Law Com No 137 (1984), pp 122–123.

7 North, op cit, pp 225–230; Polonsky (1973) 22 ICLQ 343, 345.

8 Including the delivery of a *gett* before a Rabbinical court, even though there is no judicial investigation: *Broit v Broit* 1972 SLT (Notes) 32; and see Gordon, *Foreign Divorces: English Law and Practice* (1988) pp 96–97.

9 [1980] AC 744, [1979] 3 All ER 897; Karsten (1980) 43 MLR 202.

10 This point had been left open by the House of Lords in *Quazi v Quazi* [1980] AC 744, 817.

11 *Chaudhary v Chaudhary* [1985] Fam 19, [1984] 3 All ER 1017; Canton (1985) 48 MLR 212. This confirms the view of WOOD J in *Sharif v Sharif* (1980) 10 Fam Law 216 in contrast to those of BUSH J in *Zaal v Zaal* (1982) 4 FLR 284 at 286–288 and TAYLOR J in *R v Secretary of State for the Home Department, ex p Ghulam Fatima* [1985] QB 190 at 195.

12 [1985] Fam 19 at 41.

13 Ibid.

14 Eg *Ratanachai v Ratanachai* [1960] CLY 480; *Varanand v Varanand* (1964) 108 Sol Jo 693.

15 Eg *Lee v Lau* [1967] P 14, [1964] 2 All ER 248.

by proceedings.[16] In taking this approach, the Court of Appeal does seem to have rejected the more liberal line of Lord SCARMAN in *Quazi v Quazi*.[17] He defined "proceedings" as "any act or acts officially recognised as leading to divorce in the country where the divorce was obtained and which itself is recognised by the law of the country as an effective divorce". On this basis, he was prepared to recognise, as obtained by proceedings, a divorce by *khula* in Thailand which involved no more than a written agreement witnessed by two persons.[18] The problem with Lord SCARMAN's approach is that it is so wide that it would include virtually every kind of effective divorce, etc and thus deprive of any content the special rules in Part II of the 1986 Act governing divorces, etc obtained where there are no proceedings.[19] Finally, there seems little doubt that, if the termination of a marriage by one spouse's unilateral declaration of his change of religion could be regarded as a divorce,[20] it is certainly not obtained by proceedings.[1]

(c) Extra-judicial divorces and annulments obtained in the British Isles The type of situation with which we are concerned here is illustrated by the case of the pronouncement of a *talak* in England,[2] whether it is a "bare" *talak* or one followed by further procedures in, say, Pakistan.[3] The common law position was that such divorces, if recognised as valid under the common law recognition rules, ie if recognised by the law of the domicil,[4] would be recognised in England—despite the fact that the *talak* was pronounced here.[5] The Recognition of Divorces and Legal Separations Act 1971 left this position unaffected;[6] but two years later section 16(1) of the Domicile and Matrimonial Proceedings Act 1973 denied recognition to any such divorces obtained after 1973. It provided that "no proceedings" in the British Isles "shall be regarded as validly dissolving a marriage unless instituted in the courts of law" there. This general approach is maintained in section 44(1) of the Family Law Act 1986, but with rather different wording:[7]

> No divorce or annulment obtained in any part of the British Isles shall be regarded as effective in any part of the United Kingdom unless granted by a court of civil jurisdiction.

This means that extra-judicial divorces and annulments wholly obtained in any part of the British Isles will not be valid in England, including of course such divorces and annulments obtained in England.[8] What is made unclear

16 *Chaudhary v Chaudhary* [1985] Fam 19 at 42, 47.
17 [1980] AC 744 at 824.
18 Ibid.
19 S 46(2), infra, pp 673–675.
20 Supra, p 663.
1 *Viswalingham v Viswalingham* (1979) 1 FLR 15 at 19, supra, p 663.
2 Including a consulate or embassy here, supra, pp 668–669.
3 A trans-national divorce, supra, pp 667–668.
4 Under the rule in *Armitage v A-G* [1906] P 135.
5 *Har-Shefi v Har-Shefi (No 2)* [1953] P 220, [1953] 2 All ER 373; *Qureshi v Qureshi* [1972] Fam 173, [1971] 1 All ER 325; provided in fact the law of the domicil did regard it as effective; National Insurance Decisions No R(G) 5/74, No R(G) 2/75.
6 Such divorces fell through the provisions of the Act: North, op cit, p 223.
7 The Law Commission's draft Bill followed the wording of s 16(1) of the 1973 Act: Law Com No 137 (1984), p 90.
8 Eg *Chaudhary v Chaudhary* [1985] Fam 19 at 28; *Maples v Maples* [1988] Fam 14, [1987] 3 All ER 188; and see Young (1987) 7 Legal Studies 78, 84–86. A difficult "incidental question" (supra, pp 53–57) will arise if the spouses are domiciled in a country where the extra-judicial divorce in England is recognised and one of them remarries either there or in England. Does that spouse have capacity to remarry? See North, op cit, pp 224–225.

by the change in wording between the 1973 Act and the 1986 Act is whether a trans-national divorce with proceedings taking place, for example, partly in England and partly in Pakistan[9] is one "obtained in England".[10] If it is now to be regarded (contrary it is suggested to the intentions of Parliament) as obtained in Pakistan, then the denial of recognition in section 44(1) will be ineffective.

The inclusion of annulments marks an extension from the 1971 Act; but in the absence of evidence of extra-judicial separations in the British Isles it was not felt necessary to provide for their denial of recognition.[11] A further change is that the 1986 Act avoids a number of detailed problems caused in the earlier legislation by the use of the term "proceedings", which led to doubts as to the scope of the denial of recognition to extra-judicial divorces obtained in the British Isles and, in particular, as to whether it applied to wholly informal divorces such as "bare" *talaks*.[12] There now seems little doubt that any form of extra-judicial divorce or annulment obtained in the British Isles will be denied effect in England.

Finally, the 1986 Act follows the pattern of the earlier legislation[13] and preserves the effect of an extra-judicial divorce obtained in the British Isles before 1974 and which would be recognised under the common law rules then applicable.[14] This saving provision is limited to divorces and does not apply to extra-judicial annulments.

(d) Recognition of extra-judicial divorces, etc obtained overseas It is necessary to examine separately the recognition rules for extra-judicial divorces, etc obtained overseas depending on whether or not there are "judicial or other proceedings".[15]

(i) Where there are proceedings
The basic approach where there are proceedings is that recognition of the divorce, etc is governed by the general rules as to recognition already discussed in relation to judicial divorces, etc. So, the divorce, etc must have been obtained in a country where one party to the marriage was domiciled (in the English or the foreign sense) or habitually resident or of which one party was a national,[16] and it must have been effective under the law of that country.[17] All the other provisions of Part II of the 1986 Act applicable to judicial divorces, etc apply to divorces, etc obtained by other types of proceedings.[18] It might be noted that, as at common law,[19] an extra-judicial divorce, etc obtained by proceedings can be recognised in England despite the fact that both spouses are domiciled here. So, a *talak* obtained in Pakistan by a

9 Eg *R v Secretary of State for the Home Department, ex p Fatima* [1986] AC 527, supra, pp 667–668.
10 Pilkington (1988) 37 ICLQ 131, 136, discussed supra, p 668.
11 Law Com No 137 (1984), p 91.
12 *Chaudhary v Chaudhary* [1985] Fam 19 at 28, 39, 42, 47; North, op cit, pp 224–230.
13 Domicile and Matrimonial Proceedings Act 1973, s 16(3).
14 Family Law Act 1986, s 52(4), (5)(a); eg *Chaudhary v Chaudhary* [1976] Fam 148, [1975] 3 All ER 687.
15 1986 Act, s 54(1). The meaning of this phrase has been discussed supra, pp 669–670.
16 S 46(1)(b), supra, pp 658–659.
17 S 46(1)(a), infra, pp 672–673.
18 Ss 46(4), 47(1)—supplementary rules on jurisdiction, supra, pp 659–660; s 48 on proof of facts, supra, p 663; s 49—the meaning of "country", supra, pp 661–662; s 51—the grounds for refusing recognition, infra, pp 676 et seq; and s 52—transitional provisions, infra, p 686.
19 Eg *Manning v Manning* [1958] P 112, [1958] 1 All ER 291.

husband who is a Pakistan national can be recognised here, notwithstanding the English domicil of both spouses.[20]

The application of these general rules as to recognition in the context of divorces, etc obtained by extra-judicial proceedings does raise a number of special problems. The jurisdictional rules assume that the divorce, etc is *obtained* by the particular proceedings,[1] that the divorce, etc is effective under the law of *the country* where it was obtained[2] and that the connecting factors of habitual residence, domicil or nationality in the country where it was obtained are satisfied at the date of the commencement of the proceedings.[3] These requirements mean that it is necessary to determine whether a divorce, etc is obtained by going through all, or only part of, the proceedings and to identify the date of the commencement of the proceedings by which it was obtained. These issues have arisen in the context of "trans-national" *talak* divorces,[4] where it has been held that, though conciliation proceedings are required, and have taken place, in Pakistan, the earlier pronouncement of the *talak* in England was the commencement of the proceedings by which the divorce was obtained.[5]

Particular concerns arise, in the context of the recognition of extra-judicial divorces, etc, in relation to the requirement that the divorce be effective "under the law of" the country where it was obtained.[6] The effectiveness of a divorce, nullity or legal separation decree will be tested in terms of its validity in the courts which granted it, but it will often be necessary to determine in the case of an extra-judicial divorce, etc whether it satisfies the domestic law requirements of the country where it was obtained. For example, in *Quazi v Quazi*[7] whilst the House of Lords was satisfied that the *talak* divorce obtained in Pakistan had satisfied the procedural requirements of that country's Muslim Family Laws Ordinance 1961 (and thus was effective there[8]), much greater doubt was expressed as to the effectiveness under Thai law of the divorce by *khula* obtained in that country.[9] It may also be the case that the country where the extra-judicial divorce, etc was obtained requires the parties to go through civil judicial proceedings, and the courts in Ontario have denied recognition on this basis to an extra-judicial annulment.[10] However, it is possible in the case of an extra-judicial divorce, etc for its validity to be tested not simply according to the domestic law of the country where it was obtained but according to that country's rules of private international law. Take the following example:

> Husband and wife are Jews, both Israeli nationals domiciled in Israel, but habitually resident in British Columbia in Canada. They are divorced by "gett" before a Rabbinical court in British Columbia.

The requirements of the 1986 Act that there be judicial or other proceedings if recognition is to be based jurisdictionally on habitual residence are sat-

---

20 See 1986 Act, s 46(1)(b)(iii). It might, however, be denied recognition on the grounds of public policy, infra, pp 680–685.
1 S 46(1).
2 S 46(1)(a).
3 S 46(1)(b), (3)(a).
4 Supra, pp 667–669.
5 *R v Secretary of State for the Home Department, ex p Fatima* [1986] AC 527 at 533, supra, pp 667–668.
6 North, op cit, pp 231–232.
7 [1980] AC 744, supra, pp 669–670.
8 Ibid at 805, 818, 824–826.
9 Ibid at 824; and see Carroll (1985) 48 MLR 434, 437–438.
10 *Butterley v Butterley* (1974) 48 DLR (3d) 351.

isfied.[11] The extra-judicial divorce is not valid under the domestic law of British Columbia but it will be recognised there under that province's divorce recognition rules.[12] On that basis it should be considered to be "effective" under the law of British Columbia and thus be recognised in England.[13]

(ii) Where there are no proceedings

We are concerned here with the special recognition rules for extra-judicial divorces, etc obtained overseas without any proceedings.[14] This type of case can best be illustrated by such Moslem religious divorces as consensual divorce by *khula*[15] or divorce by "bare" *talak*.[16] Under the Recognition of Divorces and Legal Separations Act 1971, such a divorce could only be recognised if the spouses were domiciled (in the English sense) in the country where it was obtained, or if it was recognised in the country or countries of their domicil.[17] It was not enough that one spouse was habitually resident[18] in, or a national of,[19] the country where the divorce was obtained. It was not, however, a specific statutory requirement that the divorce should be effective in the country in which it was obtained.[20]

As has been indicated earlier,[21] the Law Commission's proposals[22] to have one set of recognition rules for all overseas divorces, etc, coupled with a broadening of the concept of proceedings, was not accepted. Part II of the Family Law Act 1986 follows the general approach of the 1971 Act and provides special, and limited, recognition rules for overseas divorces, etc obtained where there are no proceedings. The central provision is section 46(2):

> The validity of an overseas divorce, annulment or legal separation obtained other-wise than by means of proceedings shall be recognised if—
> (a) the divorce, annulment or legal separation is effective under the law of the country[23] in which it was obtained;
> (b) at the relevant date[24]—
>   (i) each party to the marriage was domiciled in that country; or
>   (ii) either party to the marriage was domiciled in that country and the other

---

11 S 46(1).
12 Because it is recognised in Israel: see *Walker v Walker* [1950] 4 DLR 253; *Viccari v Viccari* (1972) 7 RFL 241, applying *Armitage v A-G* [1906] P 135.
13 Indeed a divorce obtained in England in similar circumstances before 1974 was recognised here: *Qureshi v Qureshi* [1972] Fam 173, [1971] 1 All ER 325; and see the 1986 Act, s 52(5)(a), infra, p 686.
14 As to what constitutes "proceedings", see supra, pp 669–670.
15 See *Quazi v Quazi* [1980] AC 744 at 824.
16 *Chaudhary v Chaudhary* [1985] Fam 19, [1984] 3 All ER 1017.
17 1971 Act, s 6, as substituted by the Domicile and Matrimonial Proceedings Act 1973, s 2.
18 Eg *Chaudhary v Chaudhary* [1985] Fam 19, [1984] 3 All ER 1017.
19 Eg *Sharif v Sharif* (1980) 10 Fam Law 216; *Chaudhary v Chaudhary* [1985] Fam 19, [1984] 3 All ER 1017.
20 This was because the requirement of effectiveness in s 2 of the 1971 Act did not apply to recognition on the domicil basis under s 6 of that Act.
21 Supra, pp 665–666.
22 Law Com No 137 (1984), para 6.11.
23 "Country" in s 46(2) means territory within a political state if each territory has different laws on divorce, etc: s 49(1), (4), supra, pp 661–662.
24 This means the date on which the divorce, etc was obtained: s 46(3)(b), with appropriate amendments in the rare case of an extra-judicial annulment without proceedings after the death of one spouse; (s 46(4)), supra, pp 659–660. Although the special rules on cross-proceedings (s 47(1)) and proof of facts made in foreign proceedings (s 48) cannot apply where there are no proceedings, the special jurisdictional rule on conversion of a legal separation into a divorce (ss 47(2), 49(4), supra, pp 662–663) does, in theory at least, apply to an extra-judicial divorce, etc obtained without proceedings.

party was domiciled in a country under whose law the divorce, annulment or legal separation is recognised as valid; and

(c) neither party to the marriage was habitually resident in the United Kingdom throughout the period of one year immediately preceding that date.

It will be seen that the divorce, etc must be obtained in one country and be effective there. This can raise the same type of problem as has been discussed in relation to divorces obtained by proceedings in the case of a trans-national divorce.[1] It will be necessary to decide where, in the case of a divorce by mutual agreement, as in the Moslem *khula*, the divorce is obtained if the spouses are in different countries. It is also necessary that the divorce, etc be "obtained" in the country of the domicil. Where there are no proceedings, a divorce is not obtained in the sense of being granted or approved by a third party; it is only obtained in the sense of being obtained by reason of legal provision made for it.

The rules laid down in section 46(2) of the 1986 Act reveal three particular changes from the rules applicable under the 1971 Act, in addition to their extension to extra-judicial annulments.

(i) The first is that there is now an express statutory requirement that the divorce, etc be effective in the country in which it was obtained[2] and, indeed, recognition may be refused if no official documents can be produced certifying that effectiveness.[3]

(ii) The second change concerns the jurisdictional test. Section 46(2) follows the pattern of the 1971 Act in limiting the jurisdictional basis to domicil. It also provides, as did the 1971 Act,[4] that such a divorce, etc will be recognised not only if it was obtained in the overseas country in which both spouses were domiciled, but also if it was obtained in the overseas country in which one spouse was domiciled and was recognised in the country of the domicil of the other spouse.[5] So, if a husband domiciled in Dubai obtains a "bare" *talak* there which is recognised in Pakistan where the wife is domiciled, the essential requirements of section 46(2) are satisfied.[6] There is no express requirement that the country of one spouse's domicil in which the divorce, etc is recognised is an overseas country, to the exclusion of a part of the British Isles, including even England. Nevertheless, if one spouse was domiciled in England recognition would be refused. There is here a circular problem, which also arose under the 1971 Act.[7] The divorce will be recognised only if recognised in England and than is the very matter at issue. That being so, recognition must be refused.[8] However, the domicil test under section 46(2) is more narrowly drawn than under the 1971 Act. Although recognition was allowed under the 1971 Act if the overseas divorce, etc was obtained in a country in which neither spouse was domiciled, but was recognised either in

1 Supra, pp 667–668.
2 S 46(2)(a).
3 S 51(3)(b)(i), infra, pp 685–686.
4 S 6(3)(a).
5 This is a statutory perpetuation of the common law recognition rule in *Armitage v A-G* [1906] P 135. Recognition may be refused if no official document certifying effectiveness in the country of the domicil of the second spouse can be produced: s 51(3)(b)(ii), infra, pp 685–686.
6 The result would be the same if the situations were reversed, ie if the husband, domiciled in Pakistan, obtained the divorce in Dubai—provided it is valid in both countries. It does not matter with which of the spouses the two jurisdictional links are established.
7 S 6; see North, op cit, p 185.
8 As was probably the case in *R v Secretary of State for the Home Department, ex p Fatima* [1986] AC 527, especially at 535.

their common domicil or in the countries of their separate domicils,[9] there is no such jurisdictional basis of recognition under the 1986 Act.

(iii) The third change from the jurisdictional rules under the 1971 Act is that, under those provisions, the reference to domicil was to domicil in the English sense. However, domicil under section 46(2) of the 1986 Act includes, rather surprisingly, domicil in both the English sense and that of the country where the divorce was obtained or recognised.[10] So a "bare" *talak* obtained in, say, Dubai will be recognised in England if the spouses were domiciled in Dubai according to the law of Dubai on domicil in family matters, even though not so domiciled according to English law.

There is one major limitation on the recognition of overseas divorces, etc obtained where there are no proceedings, and that is the provision in section 46(2)(c) that recognition will be denied, despite the validity of the divorce, etc under the law of the domicil, if either party had been habitually resident in the United Kingdom for a year immediately preceding the date on which the divorce was obtained. The major purpose of this provision, like its counterpart in the earlier legislation,[11] is to prevent circumvention of the rule that, in the case of British divorces, etc, recognition will only be given to those "granted by a court of civil jurisdiction".[12] It is not possible for the ban on extra-judicial divorces in the British Isles to be evaded by one spouse going to the country of his domicil to pronounce a "bare" *talak*, relying on the fact that it will be recognised in England if recognised in the country of the other spouse's domicil, if either spouse has been habitually resident for one year anywhere in the United Kingdom, not just in England. In fact this type of anti-evasion provision is less necessary under the 1986 Act than under the previous legislation, because, under the old law, without such a prohibition, a "bare" *talak* pronounced in, for example, France by a husband on a day trip there would have been recognised in England if recognised in the domicil of both spouses.[13] This cannot happen under the 1986 Act because the divorce, etc has to be obtained in the country of the domicil of one spouse and be effective under that law. It is, therefore, rather surprising to find that the anti-evasion provision in section 46 of the 1986 Act applies if *either* spouse had been habitually resident in the United Kingdom for one year, whereas the old law required them *both* to have been.[14] Finally, it should be emphasised that this limitation on recognition of divorces, etc obtained in, or recognised under the law of, the spouses' domicils applies only to extra-judicial divorces, etc obtained "otherwise than by means of proceedings". There is no general prohibition on the recognition in England of a divorce obtained in, for example, Pakistan, under the Muslim Family Laws Ordinance 1961, even if the spouses have both been habitually resident here for years and even if they are both domiciled here, provided one of them is a Pakistan national.[15]

9 S 6(3)(b). An overseas divorce or legal separation which would have been recognised under this provision and which was obtained before Part II of the 1986 Act came into force will continue to be recognised: Family Law Act 1986, s 52(5)(b)(e).
10 S 46(5), supra, pp 658–659.
11 Domicile and Matrimonial Proceedings Act 1973, s 16(2); *Sharif v Sharif* (1980) 10 Fam Law 216.
12 1986 Act, s 44(1); see Law Com No 137 (1984), para 6.30.
13 1971 Act, s 6(3)(b).
14 Domicile and Matrimonial Proceedings Act 1973, s 16(2).
15 1986 Act, s 46(1); see *R v Secretary of State for the Home Department, ex p Fatima* [1985] QB 190 at 199–200. If recognition is to be denied in such a case, it would have to be on one of the discretionary grounds in s 51, most probably the public policy ground, infra, pp 680–685.

(v) Grounds for non-recognition of divorces, annulments and legal separations

(a) Introduction

Not only does Part II of the 1986 Act provide an exclusive list of the jurisdictional bases on which overseas divorces etc may be recognised here,[16] it also provides in section 51 an exclusive list of the grounds on which recognition may be denied both to other British and to overseas divorces, etc.[1] There are only two discretionary grounds on which another British divorce, etc may be denied recognition: *res judicata* and that there was no subsisting marriage between the parties at the time of the divorce, etc.[2] On the other hand, an overseas divorce, etc may be denied recognition, not only on these grounds but also, if there have been judicial or other proceedings, on the grounds of want of notice of, or opportunity to take part in, the proceedings. Where there were no proceedings, recognition may be denied to an overseas divorce, etc if there is no certificate as to its effectiveness where it was obtained or, when recognition depends on reference to the law of the domicil of one of the parties in another country, if there is no certificate as to its validity under the law of that country. Finally, recognition will be denied to all overseas divorces if recognition would be manifestly contrary to public policy. It was thought to be inappropriate to allow a court in the United Kingdom to deny recognition to another British decree, etc on any of these further grounds. If it is felt necessary to attack a British decree on one of those bases, that should be done in the court which granted it.[3] All the grounds of non-recognition mentioned so far are discretionary. There are, however, two further circumstances in which an overseas divorce, etc *must* be denied recognition, both of which have already been fully considered, namely if the jurisdictional requirements for recognition under the 1986 Act are not satisfied,[4] or if the divorce, etc is not effective in the country where it was obtained.[5] There is nothing in Part II of the 1986 Act to indicate that the right to challenge the recognition of a divorce, etc is confined to a party to the marriage. There certainly seems to have been no such restriction at common law,[6] and Part III of the 1986 Act contemplates the making of declarations as to the validity or invalidity of a divorce, etc obtained outside England and Wales on the application by a person other than a party to the marriage.[7]

The various grounds for non-recognition laid down in section 51 of the 1986 Act must now be considered in more detail.

(b) Res judicata

In the 1971 Act there was no ground of non-recognition based specifically on *res judicata*. Instead, another British or a foreign divorce or legal separation would be denied recognition if it was obtained at a time when there was no subsisting marriage between the parties.[8] One purpose of

---

16 It being borne in mind that recognition of other British divorces, etc is automatic so far as jurisdiction is concerned.
1 The limiting of the grounds of non-recognition to those provided by the 1986 Act is effected by s 45.
2 Supra, pp 656–657.
3 Supra, p 657.
4 S 46(1), (2), supra, pp 658–659, 673–675.
5 Ibid, supra, pp 660–661, 672–673.
6 Eg *Pemberton v Hughes* [1899] 1 Ch 781; *Powell v Cockburn* (1976) 68 DLR (3d) 700.
7 S 55, infra, pp 695–696.
8 1971 Act, s 8(1), and there is a similar ground of non-recognition in s 51(2) of the 1986 Act, infra, p 678.

this provision was, however, to deal with issues of *res judicata*,[9] as where the marriage has already been brought to an end by either an English divorce or nullity decree or a foreign one which was recognised here. Whilst such an approach may be appropriate for the recognition of divorces and legal separations, it is not appropriate in the case of annulments where the whole issue in the foreign nullity proceedings for which recognition is now sought here may be to declare that the marriage was void *ab initio*. On the other hand, there is common law authority that a foreign nullity decree may be denied recognition on the basis of *res judicata*, as in *Vervaeke v Smith*:[10]

> In 1970, the wife sought to have her English marriage in 1954 annulled on the ground that her husband was already married at the time, even though he had gone through divorce proceedings in Nevada in 1946, and that it was a "sham" marriage, being celebrated simply to enable her to acquire British nationality. The English court refused to grant her a nullity decree— because the Nevada divorce was recognised in England and the fact her marriage was a "sham" was no ground for annulling it.[11] The wife then, in 1972, obtained a nullity decree from a Belgian court on the ground, considered but rejected in England, that the marriage was a "sham".

It was held, in the lower courts,[12] that the Belgian decree satisfied the common law jurisdictional rules for the recognition of foreign annulments.[13] Nevertheless, recognition was denied, on the basis of the doctrine of *res judicata*.[14] The House of Lords had no doubt that the issue before the Belgian courts was the very point earlier decided in the English courts.[15]

It was thought that it would be desirable to retain the effect of this decision in any statutory regime for recognition of annulments, but that it would be inappropriate to extend the existing statutory rule from divorces to annulments. So, a new head of non-recognition based more specifically on *res judicata* had to be introduced.[16] To this end, section 51(1) of the 1986 Act[17] provides:

> Subject to section 52 of this Act, recognition of the validity of—
> (a) a divorce, annulment or judicial separation granted by a court of civil jurisdiction in any part of the British Islands, or
> (b) an overseas divorce, annulment or legal separation, may be refused in any part of the United Kingdom if the divorce, annulment or separation was granted or obtained at a time when it was irreconcilable with a decision determining the question of the subsistence or validity of the marriage of the

9 Implementing Art 9 of the 1970 Hague Convention: see Law Com No 34 (1970), para 16 and App B (notes on clause 8); Law Com No 137 (1984), paras 4.66, 6.64.
10 [1983] 1 AC 145, [1982] 2 All ER 144; Carter (1982) 53 BYBIL 302; Jaffey (1983) 32 ICLQ 500; [1986] Civil Justice Quarterly 35.
11 *Messina v Smith* [1971] P 322, [1971] 2 All ER 1046.
12 [1981] Fam 77.
13 The wife had a real and substantial connection with Belgium at the relevant time: *Indyka v Indyka* [1969] 1 AC 33, [1967] 2 All ER 689; *Law v Gustin* [1976] Fam 155, [1976] 1 All ER 113.
14 And also on more general public policy grounds, infra, pp 680–682. Estoppel is discussed generally, supra, pp 372–376.
15 [1983] 1 AC 145 at 156, 160, 161–163.
16 See Law Com No 137 (1984), paras 4.6, 6.65–6.66.
17 See the critical discussion in Jaffey [1986] Civil Justice Quarterly 35, 44–45, 47–49.

parties previously given (whether before or after the commencement of this Part) by a court of civil jurisdiction in that part of the United Kingdom or by a court elsewhere and recognised or entitled to be recognised in that part of the United Kingdom.

A number of points might be emphasised in relation to this statutory head of non-recognition. It is discretionary, as the common law rule was and as the other statutory heads are under section 51. It applies to the recognition in England of all three kinds of matrimonial decision: divorces, annulments and legal separations; and whether they were granted elsewhere in the British Isles or obtained in some other foreign country. Furthermore, the earlier irreconcilable decision which brings the provision into play may be either an earlier English decision, as was the case in *Vervaeke v Smith*, or it could be an earlier decision from a court elsewhere but which is recognised in England under Part II of the 1986 Act. This statutory head does, however, only apply to an earlier decision of a court, and so the fact that there had been an earlier extra-judicial divorce which was recognised here would not bring the provision into play.[18] Because the earlier decision must be one relating to the "subsistence or validity" of the marriage, the provision would seem inapplicable where there has been an earlier decision refusing to grant a divorce or legal separation unless that was because there was held to be no marriage between the parties.[19]

(c) No subsisting marriage The English court has a discretion to refuse recognition to a divorce or legal separation, whether granted elsewhere in the British Isles, or obtained overseas, if it was obtained at a time when, according to English law, there was no subsisting marriage between the parties.[20] Under the 1971 Act, denial of recognition on this ground was mandatory[1] but, because of the possible overlap with the *res judicata* ground, it was thought more appropriate that this head also should become discretionary.[2] This head is limited to the recognition of divorces and legal separations because it is inappropriate in the case of annulments whose purpose is to declare that the marriage is invalid. Whilst there is some overlap with section 51(1), as where there is a prior "decision" dissolving or annulling the marriage, there are other cases for which this further provision is required. It may be, for example, that the marriage in question is regarded by English law (and this includes our rules of private international law) as void ab initio, even though there has been no annulment of it. Furthermore, the *res judicata* provisions of section 51(1) would not apply where the marriage is terminated by an extra-judicial annulment which is recognised here.

(d) Want of notice of the proceedings Recognition may be refused to an overseas[3] divorce, etc which has been obtained by judicial or other proceedings if it was obtained without such steps having been taken for giving notice of the proceedings to a party to the marriage as, having regard to the nature of the proceedings and all the circumstances, should reasonably have

18 Though it would be relevant under s 51(2), infra.
19 See Jaffey [1986] Civil Justice Quarterly 35, 47–48.
20 S 51(2).
1 1971 Act, s 8(1).
2 Law Com No 137 (1984), para 6.66.
3 This does not apply to the recognition of other British divorces, etc, supra, pp 656–657.

been taken.[4] This provision would seem to embody the common law rules for denying recognition to a divorce or annulment on the grounds of want of notice of the proceedings;[5] so lack of notice will not normally affect the recognition of a foreign divorce, etc if the foreign court's rules as to service or dispensation therefrom had been complied with.[6] This is subject to the qualification that such rules are themselves not unreasonable.[7] Indeed, "it cannot be sufficient merely to comply with local procedure, otherwise the provisions of the Act would be nugatory".[8] Recognition should still be denied where the lack of notice is consequent upon the petitioner's fraud.[9]

In determining whether to deny recognition because of want of notice, the court will have to examine a wide range of factors, including whether one party has already decided not to take part in the foreign proceedings.[10]

The application of this ground of non recognition may not prove to be easy in the case of extra-judicial divorces, etc. It is only relevant to those cases of extra-judicial divorce, etc, which have been obtained by means of judicial or other proceedings. So there must have been sufficient formality for these to be considered to be "proceedings";[11] but recognition may only be denied if the steps taken to give notice are inadequate with regard, inter alia, to the nature of the proceedings. It may be, therefore, that it is thought unreasonable to have to give notice of exiguous proceedings. This would certainly be compatible with the approach to the recognition of extra-judicial divorces at common law where recognition was given to informal divorces in the absence of any notice to the other spouse.[12] Indeed, it has been suggested that the requirement, in what is now the 1986 Act, to have regard to the nature of the proceedings in deciding whether to deny recognition must "contemplate the possibility of proceedings which preclude the possibility of notice or participation".[13]

(e) **Want of opportunity to take part in the proceedings** Recognition of an overseas[14] divorce, etc obtained by proceedings may be refused if it was obtained without a party to the marriage having been given (for any reason other than lack of notice) such opportunity to take part in the proceedings as, having regard to the nature of the proceedings and all the circumstances, he should have been given.[15] There may be cases where a party is prevented by external events from taking part in the proceedings, as in time of war; but even then an English court has recognised a German nullity decree obtained in wartime despite the fact that the English respondent was unable to go to

---

4 S 51(3)(a)(i). This marks a slight, but possibly significant, change in approach from its predecessor, s 8(2) of the 1971 Act, which referred to a divorce, etc obtained by one spouse without adequate notice to the other. That wording meant that the subsection could not apply where a petitioner was tricked into petitioning for divorce but had had insufficient notice: *Kendall v Kendall* [1977] Fam 208, infra, p 683.
5 *Kendall v Kendall* [1977] Fam 208 at 212–213.
6 *Igra v Igra* [1951] P 404; *Hornett v Hornett* [1971] P 255, [1971] 1 All ER 98.
7 *Macalpine v Macalpine* [1958] P 35 at 45; *Sabbagh v Sabbagh* [1985] FLR 29 at 33–34.
8 *Sabbagh v Sabbagh* [1985] FLR 29 at 33; and see *Joyce v Joyce* [1979] Fam 93 at 111.
9 *Macalpine v Macalpine* [1958] P 35, [1957] 3 All ER 134.
10 Eg *Sabbagh v Sabbagh* [1985] FLR 29.
11 Supra, pp 669–670.
12 Eg *Maher v Maher* [1951] P 342 at 344–345.
13 *Chaudhary v Chaudhary* [1985] Fam 19 at 44; and see at 48.
14 But not a British divorce, etc, supra, pp 656–657.
15 S 51(3)(a)(ii).

Germany.[16] More recently, the courts have examined a range of matters as relevant to the issue of opportunity to take part in the proceedings. These include the failure of lawyers in the foreign country to comply with the respondent's instructions,[17] whether the respondent has the financial resources and time to attend or be represented in the foreign proceedings,[18] or even the fact that the husband has the wife's passport.[19] The "opportunity" is not to be limited to the mere taking part in the proceedings; it must be an effective opportunity to place views before the court.[20] However, the opportunity to take part in the proceedings does not necessarily require the spouse to attend the proceedings,[1] and it has been held in one case that five days' notice of foreign nullity proceedings was sufficient.[2] In the case of an extra-judicial divorce, etc the exiguous nature of the proceedings will not, as in the case of lack of notice,[3] necessarily constitute grounds for denial of recognition. Finally, the discretionary nature of the power to refuse recognition must be stressed.[4] Even if the necessary opportunity is lacking, the court may still recognise the foreign divorce, etc.[5]

(f) Public policy[6] As has been mentioned earlier,[7] recognition can only be refused on the grounds laid down in the 1986 Act. One of these is that recognition would be manifestly contrary to public policy.[8] There was a similar discretionary ground for denying recognition at common law on public policy grounds, the decisions on which will be considered first as they continue to provide guidance for the exercise of the statutory discretion.

The common law rules
The residual discretion[9] at common law to refuse to recognise a foreign divorce, annulment or legal separation where such recognition would be contrary to English public policy led, for example, to a foreign divorce being denied recognition where there had been fraud as to the jurisdiction of the foreign court[10] or duress had been exercised on the petitioner.[11] Recognition would also be refused if acceptance of the foreign legal rules being applied would be contrary to English public policy. Although it has been said in the context of the recognition of foreign divorces that the residual discretion to

16 *Mitford v Mitford* [1923] P 130.
17 *Newmarch v Newmarch* [1978] Fam 79 at 90–94.
18 *Joyce v Joyce* [1979] Fam 93, [1979] 2 All ER 156; *Quazi v Quazi* [1980] AC 744 at 780; *Sabbagh v Sabbagh* [1985] FLR 29 at 34; *Mamdani v Mamdani* [1984] FLR 699, [1985] Fam Law 122.
19 *Sharif v Sharif* (1980) 10 Fam Law 216 at 217.
20 *Joyce v Joyce* [1979] Fam 93 at 111–112.
 1 *Sabbagh v Sabbagh* [1985] FLR 29 at 34; cf *Joyce v Joyce* [1979] Fam 93 at 113.
 2 *Law v Gustin* [1976] Fam 155, [1976] 1 All ER 113.
 3 Supra, p 679.
 4 *Chaudhary v Chaudhary* [1985] Fam 19 at 43–44, 48.
 5 As in *Newmarch v Newmarch* [1978] Fam 79, infra, p 683, where the factors relevant to the exercise of the discretion are discussed; and see Dickson (1979) 28 ICLQ 132.
 6 Carter (1984) 55 BYBIL 111, 127–130.
 7 Supra, p 676.
 8 S 51(3), infra, pp 682–685.
 9 *Qureshi v Qureshi* [1972] Fam 173 at 201.
10 *Middleton v Middleton* [1967] P 62, [1966] 1 All ER 168. There is some authority for denying recognition to a foreign nullity decree if there had been fraud as to the merits of the foreign petition: *Von Lorang v Administrator of Austrian Property* [1927] AC 641 at 663, 671–672; but disapproval of such an approach in the field of divorce recognition is seen in *Middleton v Middleton* [1967] P 62 at 69; *Kendall v Kendall* [1977] Fam 208 at 213.
11 *Re Meyer* [1971] P 298, [1971] 1 All ER 378.

deny recognition was one sparingly to be exercised,[12] the courts became increasingly willing to deny recognition, especially to foreign nullity decrees, on the ground that either the foreign legal rule, or its application in the particular circumstances,[13] was offensive to the judicial sense of "substantial justice".[14] So recognition was denied to a Maltese nullity decree based on a provision of Maltese law that the marriage of a Maltese domiciled Roman Catholic was void if he had not married in a Roman Catholic church.[15] The Maltese husband had in fact married in a register office in England and recognition of the Maltese decree would have involved acceptance of the invalidity of this English marriage.

Although the breadth of that approach was much criticised,[16] and the courts have remained uncertain whether a foreign divorce should be denied recognition on the sole basis that the decree was granted on racial or religious grounds,[17] the high water mark for the denial of recognition at common law on the ground of want of "substantial justice" was reached in the House of Lords decision in *Vervaeke v Smith*.[18] It will be recalled[19] that the petitioner had entered into a "sham" marriage in England in 1954 in order to obtain British nationality. Having failed to have that marriage annulled in England,[20] she obtained a nullity decree in Belgium annulling it and sought to have that decree recognised here. Recognition was refused, not only on the basis that the matter was already *res judicata*,[1] but also because recognition would offend English public policy. Sham marriages are void in Belgium, but valid in England;[2] yet even though courts elsewhere in the United Kingdom are prepared to regard such marriages as invalid,[3] the House of Lords regarded the English rule as embodying a principle of English public policy so strong that it had to be applied in the international context. Lord HAILSHAM LC stated that the English rule:

> is a doctrine of public policy and so at least in the present case takes the case outside the rules for the recognition of foreign, and, in particular, Belgian, decrees, that is at least as regards a marriage celebrated in England between a British national and an alien for an extraneous purpose of the kind contemplated by the parties in the present case, viz. using the marriage as a vehicle for conferring British nationality on the alien partner so as to save her from deportation for a criminal offence.[4]

These were arguments, it must be stressed, for *upholding* the validity of the marriage and denying effect to the Belgian decree!

Other arguments in favour of non-recognition of the Belgian decree for

---

12 *Varanand v Varanand* (1964) 108 Sol Jo 693; *Qureshi v Qureshi* [1972] Fam 173 at 198–199, 201.
13 Carter (1978) 49 BYBIL 295, 297.
14 *Pemberton v Hughes* [1899] 1 Ch 781 at 790; *Middleton v Middleton* [1967] P 62 at 69–70.
15 *Gray v Formosa* [1963] P 259.
16 Carter (1962) 38 BYBIL 497; Lewis (1963) 12 ICLQ 298. The decision was followed only with misgivings in *Lepre v Lepre* [1965] P 52, [1963] 2 All ER 49 and a different approach was taken by the courts in Australia & South Africa: *Vassallo v Vassallo* [1952] SASR 129; *De Bono v De Bono* 1948 (2) SA 802.
17 Contrast *Igra v Igra* [1952] P 404 with *Re Meyer* [1971] P 298 at 310.
18 [1983] 1 AC 145; Smart (1983) 99 LQR 24; Jaffey (1983) 32 ICLQ 500.
19 Supra, p 677.
20 *Messina v Smith* [1971] P 322, [1971] 2 All ER 1046.
 1 Supra, pp 676–678.
 2 [1983] 1 AC 145 at 152–153.
 3 *Orlandi v Castelli* 1961 SC 113; *Akram v Akram* 1979 SLT (Notes) 87.
 4 [1983] 1 AC 145 at 156–157.

public policy reasons were advanced by Lord SIMON of Glaisdale.[5] The essence of his approach was that no case had been made out why English law "should surrender its own concept of the public policy involved and defer to that of Belgian law as expressed in the Belgian judgment."[6] This approach is both suspect and dangerous. It is suspect because there is a variety of instances where English courts have accepted the validity of foreign decrees without anxiety that the foreign law applied is different from the English rule, and have done so even where the effect has been to render void a marriage celebrated in England and valid by English law.[7] The approach is dangerous because it would undermine the whole structure of our choice of law rules. Frequently our courts apply foreign law different from our own law, but it is only rarely that public policy is felt to justify not applying the foreign law[8] and certainly the courts do not, and could not, weigh the policy of English law against that of the foreign law in every case.

The extraordinary conclusion in this case[9] can, perhaps, only really be explained by the fact that denying effect to the Belgian decree would render invalid the petitioner's second marriage and prevent her from succeeding as a widow to the second husband's estate, she having been a prostitute and he having managed her activities.[10] There is real danger in the adoption of so broad and vague an approach to the issue of public policy. It renders the law unpredictable on a matter vital to social stability and human happiness.

> It is a common, natural and reasonable thing for people to adjust their lives according to the ostensible effect of a judgment disposing of their status pronounced by a competent court.[11]

The more likely it is that a foreign divorce, etc will be denied recognition on unpredictable grounds of public policy, the harder is it for those reasonable expectations to be met.[12]

Under the 1986 Act
Denial of recognition to an overseas[13] divorce, etc on public policy grounds is specifically provided for in section 51(3) of the 1986 Act. The court has a discretion to refuse recognition if such recognition "would be manifestly contrary to public policy". It seems very likely that the courts will, in applying this provision, seek guidance from the common law decisions just discussed in deciding whether recognition would be contrary to public policy.[14] It should be emphasised that, again, the court has a discretion; there is no requirement that recognition be refused on this basis and there is some authority for the unusual view that the discretion would be exercised in favour of recognition even if such recognition would be manifestly contrary

5 Ibid, at 163–167.
6 Ibid, at 164.
7 Eg *Galene v Galene* [1939] P 237, [1939] 2 All ER 148.
8 Supra, pp 128–137.
9 Given that it was stated that the power to deny recognition should be exercised "with extreme reserve": [1983] 1 AC 145 at 164.
10 Ibid, at 153; but Lord SIMON rejected these factors: ibid at 166.
11 *Merker v Merker* [1963] P 283 at 301.
12 See Lewis (1963) 11 ICLQ 298, 301.
13 But not a British divorce, etc, supra, pp 656–657.
14 It is suggested that WOOD J was wrong, in *Chaudhary v Chaudhary* [1985] Fam 19 at 29, to indicate that there also coexisted a common law basis for denial of recognition on public policy grounds. Recognition is exclusively governed by what is now Part II of the 1986 Act and the grounds for denying recognition are limited to those in the Act: s 45.

to public policy.[15] Section 51(3) refers to recognition being "manifestly"[16] contrary to public policy. This does no more than confirm the stated attitude at common law that the discretion is one to be exercised sparingly. Indeed "manifestly" has been held to add nothing to the common law rule;[17] but the courts may prove to be willing to maintain the breadth which the common law rule had reached, and there is some evidence that the courts will deny recognition where the application of the foreign rule is, in the particular circumstances, felt to be contrary to public policy.[18]

The principles on which the statutory discretion should be exercised have been stated thus:

> In exercising its discretion ... this court should have regard to all the surrounding circumstances which would include a full investigation of the facts relied upon to support a refusal of recognition; the likely consequences if the petitioning spouse had been given the opportunity to take part in the proceedings; an assessment of what the legitimate objectives of the petitioning spouse are, and to what extent those objectives can be achieved if the foreign decree remains valid, and what the likely consequences to the spouses and any children of the family would be if recognition were refused.[19]

In applying such principles, it has been held that the fact that a foreign decree has a different effect from an English one is not, as such, grounds of public policy for denying recognition to the former.[20] The operation of such principles might be illustrated by *Kendall v Kendall*:[1]

> H and W lived together in Bolivia. W decided to leave Bolivia, with their children, in 1974. Before leaving she signed documents, in Spanish which she did not read, which H told her were documents to permit her to take the children out of the country. In 1975 the Bolivian courts granted a decree of divorce, purporting to be a decree granted to W as petitioner. It was probably the case that the documents W signed constituted a power of attorney enabling a decree to be granted without W's presence before the court.

As H was habitually resident in Bolivia at the time of the decree it ought, prima facie, to be recognised here.[2] It could not be denied recognition for want of notice under the relevant provisions of the Recognition of Divorces and Legal Separations Act 1971[3] because they only related to lack of notice of, or want of opportunity to take part in, the proceedings in the case of the respondent.[4] Here, the party disadvantaged was W, the apparent petitioner. However, HOLLINS J concluded that recognition of the decree would manifestly be contrary to public policy, the Bolivian court having been deceived,

15 *Newmarch v Newmarch* [1978] Fam 79 at 97.
16 The term is only in the statute in order to conform with Art 10 of the 1970 Hague Convention: Law Com No 34 (1970), p 43.
17 *Sharif v Sharif* (1980) 10 Fam Law 216 at 217–218; *Chaudhary v Chaudhary* [1985] Fam 19 at 28–29.
18 Eg *Newmarch v Newmarch* [1978] Fam 79, [1978] 1 All ER 1; Carter (1978) 49 BYBIL 295, 297; *Joyce v Joyce* [1979] Fam 93 at 114; Dickson (1980) 43 MLR 81, 84–85; *Chaudhary v Chaudhary* [1985] Fam 19 at 39–40, 43–45.
19 *Newmarch v Newmarch* [1978] Fam 79 at 95.
20 Social Security Decision No R(G) 1/85.
1 [1977] Fam 208, [1977] 3 All ER 471.
2 See now the 1986 Act, s 46(a)(i).
3 S 8(2)(a).
4 There is no such restriction in s 51(3)(a) of the 1986 Act, supra, pp 678–680.

not just as to facts alleged in the petition, but as to the fundamental issue of whether W was petitioning at all.

Finally, particular problems in relation to public policy may arise in the context of the recognition of extra-judicial divorces, etc. The recognition of extra-judicial divorces as such is not contrary to public policy.[5] However, when it was thought[6] that recognition of a "bare" *talak*, ie one delivered without any further proceedings, fell within the broad recognition rules of the Recognition of Divorces and Legal Separations Act 1971,[7] it was suggested that, though it would not be right to lay down a general rule for "bare" *talaks*, such a divorce could be denied recognition on the public policy grounds that it was done in secrecy and without the wife being in any way aware that it was about to happen.[8] It is now the case that specific provision is made in the 1986 Act for the recognition of "bare" *talaks* and other divorces, etc where there are no proceedings, but only on the limited jurisdictional basis of domicil.[9] It cannot, therefore, be the case that "bare" *talaks* would be denied recognition, as such, on public policy grounds, because Parliament has provided clearly for their recognition. However, the courts will remain free to take account of the particular circumstances of a case as justifying denial of recognition.

It has also been suggested that recognition should be denied on public policy grounds to an extra-judicial divorce, etc if both parties were domiciled in England when it was obtained.

> It must plainly be contrary to the public policy of the law in a case where both parties to the marriage are domiciled in this country to permit one of them, whilst continuing his English domicile, to avoid the incidents of his domiciliary law and to deprive the other party to the marriage of her rights under that law[10] by the simple process of taking advantage of his financial ability to travel to a country whose laws appear temporarily to be more favourable to him.[11]

This suggestion was made in the context of the recognition of a "bare" *talak* and the problem cannot in fact now arise there because recognition is based on the domicil of the parties.[12] This approach has, however, been welcomed[13] as more widely appropriate to the case of extra-judicial divorces, etc where there are proceedings and which could be recognised, even though both spouses are domiciled in England, because obtained for example in the country of which one spouse was a national.[14] There are difficulties with so broad an approach. Why should such a rule be limited to extra-judicial divorces, etc as there may well be judicial divorces, etc where a spouse domiciled in England takes advantage of his financial resources to obtain a valid divorce abroad, to the disadvantage of the other spouse, also domiciled

5 *Quazi v Quazi* [1980] AC 744 at 781–782.
6 That was shown to be incorrect in *Chaudhary v Chaudhary* [1985] Fam 19.
7 Ie those based on nationality, habitual residence and domicil in the foreign sense, under ss 2–5 of the 1971 Act.
8 *Zaal v Zaal* (1982) 4 FLR 284 at 288–289; and see *Quazi v Quazi* [1980] AC 744 at 783; *Chaudhary v Chaudhary* [1985] Fam 19 at 28–29, 39–41, 43–45.
9 S 46(2)(b), supra, pp 673–675.
10 But see now the Matrimonial and Family Proceedings Act 1984, Part III, infra, pp 709–714; Pilkington (1988) 37 ICLQ 131, 137–141.
11 *Chaudhary v Chaudhary* [1985] Fam 19 at 45.
12 1986 Act, s 46(2), supra, pp 673–675.
13 Carroll (1985) 101 LQR 175, 177; for a markedly different approach, see Gordon (1986) 16 Fam Law 169.
14 1986 Act, s 46(1), supra, pp 671–672.

in England? If all divorces, etc obtained in such circumstances are to be denied recognition on public policy grounds, this seems to run counter to the policy of Parliament, for the legislation does not in terms preclude their recognition nor could it under the 1970 Hague Convention on which the 1986 Act is still based.[15]

(g) Special rules for extra-judicial divorces, etc where there are no proceedings It will be recalled[16] that where a divorce, etc is obtained overseas but there are no judicial or other proceedings, eg a "bare" *talak*, the only jurisdictional basis for recognition is domicil in the English sense. However, even if the overseas divorce, etc satisfies that jurisdictional test and is effective in the relevant country of the domicil,[17] it may be denied recognition on any one of the following three bases for non-recognition already discussed: *res judicata*, no subsisting marriage or that recognition would manifestly be contrary to public policy.[18] However, the two bases concerned with notice of, or opportunity to take part in, the proceedings[19] are not applicable, for obvious reasons, where there are no proceedings. Instead, a foreign divorce, etc obtained without proceedings may be refused recognition if "there is no official document certifying that the divorce, annulment or legal separation is effective under the law of the country where it was obtained".[20] This does not go to issues of justice as between the parties but, rather, its purpose would seem essentially to be evidential. An official document is defined as one "issued by a person or body appointed or recognised for the purpose"[1] in the foreign country. So the operation of the provision will depend on whether court or other officials in the country where a bare *talak* or the like is obtained are prepared to provide such certification for the purposes of English proceedings, and certificates may not be easy to obtain.[2] Whilst proof of effectiveness of such divorces has been shown on occasions to be a problem,[3] one would hope that an English court is unlikely to deny recognition if it is satisfied as to the effectiveness of the divorce, etc even though no certificate is forthcoming. If that is so, it is hard to see what real purpose this provision serves.[4]

This provision on certification assumes that the divorce, etc is obtained in the country where both parties were domiciled at that time,[5] but there is a variant of it to deal with the case where the divorce, etc is obtained in the country where one spouse was domiciled and is recognised in the country of the domicil of the other spouse.[6] In such a case, recognition may be denied not only if there is no official certificate as to the effectiveness of the divorce where it was obtained, but also if there is no "official document" certifying

15 Art 1 of the Hague Convention envisages the recognition of at least some extra-judicial divorces and legal separations.
16 Supra, pp 673–675.
17 Supra, pp 660–661, 674; contrast pp 672–673.
18 S 51(1), (2), (3)(c).
19 S 51(3)(a).
20 S 51(3)(b)(i).
 1 S 51(4).
 2 See Lord MESTON, 473 HL Official Report col 1094 (1986).
 3 *Quazi v Quazi* [1980] AC 744 at 824.
 4 No guidance can be found from Law Com No 137 (1984) because this basis of non-recognition is not one recommended by the Law Commission, who did not propose special rules for divorces, etc obtained where there were no proceedings.
 5 S 46(2)(b)(i), supra, pp 673–674.
 6 S 46(2)(b)(ii), supra, pp 674–675.

that it is recognised as valid in the country of the domicil of the other spouse.[7] So, if a husband domiciled in Dubai there obtains a "bare" *talak*,[8] his wife being domiciled in Pakistan, the divorce may be denied recognition if there is no official certificate as to its effectiveness in Dubai or that it will be recognised in Pakistan.

(vi) Retrospectivity

The general rule in Part II of the 1986 Act is that its provisions govern the recognition of both British and overseas divorces, annulments and legal separations whether they were obtained before or after the 1986 Act came into force.[9] There are two kinds of limitation on this general retrospective effect. The first is that, in so far as the rules of the 1986 Act are narrower than those prevailing under earlier legislation or at common law, recognition will continue to be given to certain divorces, etc which would have been recognised under the old law.[10] So, for example, an extra-judicial divorce obtained in the British Isles before 1974 and recognised at common law because recognised under the law of the domicil[11] will continue to be recognised,[12] as will an overseas divorce or legal separation obtained before the 1986 Act came into force which was recognised here because recognised in, though not obtained in, the country of the spouses' domicil.[13] There is, however, no general saving of the validity of annulments which would have been recognised at common law, but not under the 1986 Act.[14]

The second kind of limitation on the retrospective effect of Part II of the 1986 Act concerns any divorce, etc, whether British or overseas, and whether or not obtained by means of proceedings, which was obtained before Part II came into effect. Although the recognition of such a divorce, etc will be governed by the general recognition rules, these are subject to two qualifications. The first is that these rules shall not affect any property to which any person became entitled before the commencement of the 1986 Act.[15] The most common instance of this will be where the estate of a deceased person has been distributed on the basis that a marriage had, or had not, been effectively ended by a divorce or annulment. The second qualification is that the rules "shall not affect the recognition of the validity of the divorce, annulment or separation if that matter has been decided by any competent court in the British Islands" before the commencement of the 1986 Act.[16] The type of situation envisaged here is where, for example, a foreign divorce has already been refused recognition by a Scottish court. In such a case, the recognition rules of the 1986 Act are inapplicable, with the corollary that the English court should follow the Scottish decision.[17]

---

7 S 51(3)(b)(ii).
8 Cf *Zaal v Zaal* (1982) 4 FLR 284.
9 1986 Act, s 51(1), (2), (3).
10 S 52(4), (5).
11 *Qureshi v Qureshi* [1972] Fam 173, [1971] 1 All ER 325.
12 1986 Act, s 52(5)(a).
13 S 52(5)(b), (e).
14 Eg annulment of a void marriage obtained in the country of its celebration: *Merker v Merker* [1963] P 283, [1962] 3 All ER 928, supra, p 658.
15 S 52(2)(a).
16 S 52(2)(b).
17 Law Com No 34 (1970), p 45.

(vii) Effect of a foreign divorce, annulment or legal separation[18]

One problem which is untouched by the 1986 Act is as to the effect to be given in England to a divorce, annulment or legal separation obtained outside England (described here as a "foreign" divorce, etc[19]) and whose recognition is governed by Part II of that Act. This is left to the common law and it is convenient to consider the three matrimonial causes separately.

(a) **Divorce** The effect of a foreign divorce on the married status of the parties is obvious. If, in the eyes of English law, the divorce is valid, it effectively terminates that status;[20] if it is void for want of jurisdiction, the status remains unchanged. Nevertheless, the divorce may have an effect with regard to certain subsidiary purposes other than the assessment of status. The question of the effect of a foreign divorce seldom arises in practice, but three situations merit some discussion.

First, although a valid divorce terminates the married status of the parties, it does not automatically terminate a maintenance order in favour of the wife made by an English court at a time when they were living permanently in England.[1] It lies within the discretion of the court to retain, vary or discharge it, and in exercising this discretion it is relevant to consider whether the wife participated in the divorce proceedings, whether the question of maintenance was raised in the foreign court and whether the ground for divorce was insufficient by English law.[2]

It is rare that a foreign divorce will be denied recognition here for want of jurisdiction, because of the breadth of our recognition rules. However, should it be held invalid for lack of jurisdiction, then, though it leaves the married status of the parties undisturbed,[3] it is not altogether devoid of effect. It may at least require consideration in the context of desertion and estoppel. There is little authority on the question whether the effect of an invalid divorce is to exclude from consideration the period during which the respondent may have been in desertion prior to the divorce. This may be a critical factor if the petitioner later institutes divorce proceedings in England on the ground that the marriage has broken down in that the respondent has deserted the petitioner for a period of at least two years immediately preceding the presentation of the petition.[4] Although no doubt the answer depends on the conduct of the parties, it would appear from the two relevant decisions, both concerned with a Jewish divorce by delivery of a *gett*, that the desertion is not terminated unless the respondent initiated or instigated the foreign suit or at least freely consented to its institution.[5]

Another question is whether a foreign divorce, invalid for want of jurisdiction, is affected by the doctrine of estoppel.[6] What is at any rate clear is that there is no estoppel so far as the married status of the parties is concerned.

18 North, op cit, pp 135, 191–201, 266–268, 287–292.
19 Including both those granted elsewhere in the British Isles and those obtained overseas.
20 For discussion of its effect on capacity to remarry, see supra, pp 603–605.
1 See infra, pp 708–709.
2 *Wood v Wood* [1957] P 254, [1957] 2 All ER 14; Carter (1957) 33 BYBIL 336; *Qureshi v Qureshi* [1972] Fam 173 at 200–201; *Newmarch v Newmarch* [1978] Fam 79.
3 Subject to problems of the "incidental question", discussed, supra, pp 53–57, and see North, op cit, pp 199–200.
4 Matrimonial Causes Act 1973, s 1(2)(c).
5 *Joseph v Joseph* [1953] 2 All ER 710, [1953] 1 WLR 1182 (desertion terminated); *Corbett v Corbett* [1957] 1 All ER 621, [1957] 1 WLR 486.
6 Estoppel in general is discussed, supra, pp 372–376.

Neither party is precluded from denying that in the eyes of English law the parties are still husband and wife.[7] What is not clear is whether the doctrine of estoppel can be invoked for other purposes. Can, for instance, a woman who has obtained an invalid divorce in a foreign country claim a widow's share of her deceased husband's estate? To succeed, she must show that she was the "wife" of her late husband at the time of his death, which involves relying on the invalidity of the divorce. But can it not be maintained that she is estopped from impugning the decision of the court whose jurisdiction she herself invoked? This question has met with conflicting answers in Canada,[8] though the Supreme Court of Canada[9] has expressed itself in favour of there being no conclusive overriding principle of estoppel and certainly there is no estoppel in the case of a person not a party to the foreign divorce;[10] but so far as English courts are concerned, there is in principle no room for estoppel, since the paramount issue from which all else flows is the marital status of the parties at the time of the husband's death, and of that there can be no doubt.[11]

(b) Annulment[12] In considering the effect in England of a foreign annulment which is recognised here, it is necessary to investigate what effect the annulment has in the country where it was obtained and compare that effect with the effect of an English nullity decree. Where the foreign annulment has the same effect on the status of the parties as an equivalent English decree, there will be little difficulty in giving full effect to it.[13] Difficulty may arise where, for example, a decree annulling a voidable marriage is retrospective in effect, whilst an equivalent English decree is only prospective in effect.[14] This problem has arisen in a decision concerned with the recognition in Scotland of a Northern Ireland nullity decree. It concerned a claim to social security: *Social Security Decision No R(G) 1/85* where the facts were these:

The wife lived in Scotland. Her first husband died in 1966 and she received a widow's pension ever since. In 1980, in Northern Ireland she went through a ceremony of marriage with M with whom she lived for just seven weeks before returning to Scotland. As soon as she married, her widow's pension ceased to be paid. In 1982, she obtained a decree absolute from the Northern Ireland court declaring her second marriage void on the ground of non-consummation because of M's impotence. In the light of that, she sought, in Scotland, to have her widow's pension reinstated retrospectively. The effect in Northern Ireland of the nullity decree was that the marriage was voidable, and the decree had only prospective effect.[15]

---

7 *Travers v Holley* [1953] P 246 at 254; and see *Bonaparte v Bonaparte* [1892] P 402; *Schwebel v Schwebel* (1970) 10 DLR (3d) 742; *Gaffney v Gaffney* [1975] IR 133. Indeed it has been said, in *Hornett v Hornett* [1971] P 255 at 261, that "there are great difficulties about applying a doctrine of estoppel to a legal decree affecting status"; and see Carter (1971) 45 BYBIL 410.
8 Castel, *Canadian Conflict of Laws*, 2nd edn (1986) pp 317–320; Battersby (1977) 16 UW Ont LR 163.
9 *Downton v Royal Trust Co* (1972) 34 DLR (3d) 403.
10 *Fromovitz v Fromovitz* (1977) 79 DLR (3d) 148.
11 And see *Gaffney v Gaffney* [1975] IR 133.
12 See Law Com No 137 (1984), paras 2.32–2.38. The Law Commission recommended (at para 6.60) that the effect in this country of a foreign annulment should not be the subject of legislation; and see Jaffey (1983) 32 ICLQ 500.
13 *Von Lorang v Administrator of Austrian Property* [1927] AC 641 at 654–655. For its effect on capacity to marry, see supra, pp 603–605.
14 Matrimonial Causes Act 1973, s 16, supra, p 643.
15 Matrimonial Causes (Northern Ireland) Order 1978, Art 18.

However an equivalent decree in Scotland would render the marriage void and have retrospective effect. The two issues for the Social Security Commissioner were whether the Northern Ireland nullity decree should be recognised in Scotland and, if so, whether it should be given prospective or retrospective effect. If the former, the wife would lose; if it had the Scottish retrospective effect, she would succeed.

The Commissioner had no hesitation in holding that the Northern Ireland nullity decree should be recognised in Scotland.[16] Having rejected arguments that to recognise the Northern Ireland effect of the decree as prospective only would be contrary to Scottish public policy or that the effect was simply a matter of procedure to be ignored in Scotland,[17] he followed the approach recommended by the Law Commission[18] that the foreign effects of the annulment should normally be recognised and gave the Northern Ireland decree only prospective effect. To do otherwise would have given the decree greater effect in Scotland than it had in Northern Ireland and differing effects as between the two "spouses" who were domiciled in different countries.

Where the foreign annulment is not recognised, it should be treated in the same way as a foreign divorce that is not recognised.[19] There is Canadian authority[1] for the application of the doctrine of estoppel; but it is suggested that an English court should deny operation to the doctrine, whether the matter at issue is the direct one of marital status or a less central question such as succession.

(c) **Legal separation** An English decree of judicial separation entitles the petitioner to live apart from the respondent,[2] but does not dissolve the married status of the parties.[3] It is permanent in the sense that it remains in operation unless and until a discharge of the decree is ordered. Turning to the effect of a foreign legal separation which is recognised in this country, this was considered at common law in *Tursi v Tursi*:[4]

Two Italian subjects, domiciled in Italy, married there in 1942. The husband deserted the wife and never returned to her. In 1947, the wife obtained in Rome a decree of judicial separation, substantially similar in effect to an English decree, on the ground of the husband's desertion. In 1955, the wife, who had been resident in England since 1949, petitioned for divorce on the ground of the husband's desertion for three years,[5] he being still domiciled and resident in Italy.

In deciding to recognise the foreign decree granted by the law of the domicil, SACHS J had to consider its effect under English law. He held that it should have the same effect with respect to desertion as an English decree of judicial

16 Applying common law recognition rules, based on the fact that M, though not the wife, was domiciled in Northern Ireland.
17 Social Security Decision No R(G) 1/85, 8–10.
18 Law Com No 137 (1984), para 2.33; North, op cit, p 267; cf Smith (1980) 96 LQR 380, 390–393.
19 Supra, p 687.
 1 *Re Capon* (1965) 49 DLR (2d) 675; *Schwebel v Schwebel* (1970) 10 DLR (3d) 742.
 2 Matrimonial Causes Act 1973, s 18(1).
 3 Though if a spouse dies intestate whilst such a decree is in force, his property will devolve as if the other spouse was dead: Matrimonial Causes Act 1973, s 18(2).
 4 [1958] P 54, [1957] 2 All ER 828.
 5 The equivalent ground of divorce under the Matrimonial Causes Act 1973, s 1(1) and s 1(2)(c) is breakdown of marriage as evidenced by two years' desertion immediately preceding the petition.

separation, namely that a decree of judicial separation did not put an end to desertion, as at common law,[6] but that the wife could treat any period of desertion occurring before the decree as occurring immediately before the petition for divorce.[7] There seems no reason why the same conclusion should not be reached, under the Matrimonial Causes Act 1973, in respect of a petition for divorce on the ground of breakdown of marriage being evidenced by two years' desertion, so that a period of desertion preceding a foreign legal separation may be deemed to precede the English petition.[8] Similarly, it may be argued that the provision barring one spouse, judicially separated from the other, from succeeding to the latter's estate on intestacy[9] applies equally to foreign legal separations.[10]

More recent discussion of the effect to be given to a foreign legal separation which is recognised here is found in *Sabbagh v Sabbagh*:[11]

> The spouses were married in Brazil in 1965, where they were domiciled. Shortly thereafter they came to England and acquired a domicil here; but in 1980 the marriage broke up. The husband returned to Brazil and became domiciled and habitually resident there, whilst the wife remained in England. In 1983 the husband obtained a decree of judicial separation in Brazil, the effect of which was to freeze the proprietary rights of the parties, without dissolving the marriage. The wife then petitioned for divorce in England and two issues arose: should the Brazilian decree be recognised and, if so, what effect did recognition have on the rights of the English court to grant the wife financial and other relief on her divorce petition?

There was no doubt in the mind of BALCOMBE J that the Brazilian decree, being a decree of the country of the petitioner's domicil and habitual residence,[12] should be recognised.[13] What effect was to be given to it? If its effect was the same as that of an English decree of judicial separation, it would prevent the English court from itself making a decree.[14] However, the effects of the Brazilian decree on the property rights of the parties were not to be recognised here. This was not required by the statute[15] and "there is no basis here for the contention that the Brazilian decree of judicial separation will have the effect of excluding the English court's powers to deal with the wife's financial application once she has been granted a decree of divorce in England".[16]

---

6 *Harriman v Harriman* [1909] P 123.
7 Under s 7(3) of the Matrimonial Causes Act 1950.
8 Matrimonial Causes Act 1973, s 4(3), as amended by the Domestic Proceedings and Magistrates' Courts Act 1978, s 62.
9 Ibid, s 18(2).
10 Dicey & Morris, p 722.
11 [1984] FLR 29.
12 Applying s 3 of the Recognition of Divorces and Legal Separations Act 1971; see now s 46(1) of the 1986 Act.
13 None of the grounds for non-recognition in s 8 of the 1971 Act (s 51 of the 1986 Act) were made out.
14 [1984] FLR 29 at 35.
15 S 8(3) of the 1971 Act; now s 51(5) of the 1986 Act; supra, pp 657, 663.
16 [1984] FLR 29 at 36. The availability of financial relief after foreign divorces, etc is discussed generally, infra, pp 708–714.

4. PRESUMPTION OF DEATH AND DISSOLUTION OF MARRIAGE[17]

An English court may dissolve a marriage where a suit is brought for a decree of presumption of death of one of the parties and also for the dissolution of the marriage. Section 19 of the Matrimonial Causes Act 1973 allows any married person, who alleges reasonable grounds for supposing that the other party is dead, to petition the court not only to have it presumed that such party is dead, but also to have the marriage dissolved. Strictly speaking, once a person is dead in the eyes of the law, it is superfluous to dissolve his marriage, but nevertheless its express dissolution is desirable to meet the contingency of the presumption being proved wrong. Such decrees are, therefore, *sui generis*, because in the case of divorce the court proceeds on the assumption that the respondent is alive, whilst here the opposite is assumed.[18]

Jurisdiction

The jurisdiction of the English court is now based, under section 5(4) of the Domicile and Matrimonial Proceedings Act 1973, on grounds very similar to those for divorce.[19] The sole grounds are that:

(a) the petitioner, whether husband or wife, is domiciled in England at the date when the proceedings are begun;[1] or

(b) the petitioner has been habitually resident in England throughout one year ending with the date of the institution of the proceedings.[2]

Choice of law

So far as choice of law is concerned, the problem is similar to that in divorce.[3] The courts appear consistently to have applied English law, even though the petitioner was domiciled elsewhere,[4] but their statutory obligation to do so[5] has been repealed.[6]

Recognition

The rules as to recognition of foreign decrees of presumption of death and dissolution of marriage are not wholly clear, for no statutory provision has expressly been made for them.[7] Such a foreign decree if granted in circumstances which, *mutatis mutandis*, would have conferred jurisdiction on an English court will be recognised here.[8] So, we will recognise decrees granted in the country where the petitioner was domiciled or had been

---

17 North, op cit, pp 68–71, 151, 297–299; and see Kelly and Varsanyi (1971) 20 ICLQ 535.
18 *Wall v Wall* [1950] P 112, at 122–123, 125; *N v N* [1957] P 385 at 391.
19 Those grounds are discussed, supra, pp 630–632, and their detailed examination is not repeated here. It might be noted that there is here no statutory ground of jurisdiction based on the court having jurisdiction over other proceedings involving the same marriage. Nor is any statutory provision made for the staying of proceedings for presumption of death and dissolution of marriage; see the definition of "matrimonial proceedings" in Sch 1, para 2 of the Domicile and Matrimonial Proceedings Act 1973.
1 S 5(4)(*a*).
2 S 5(4)(*b*).
3 Discussed, supra, pp 639–642; see North, op cit, p 151.
4 *Wall v Wall* [1950] P 112, [1949] 2 All ER 927.
5 Matrimonial Causes Act 1973, s 19(5), re-enacting s 14(5) of the Matrimonial Causes Act 1965.
6 Domicile and Matrimonial Proceedings Act 1973, s 17(2).
7 See North, op cit, pp 297–299.
8 *Szemick v Gryla* (1965) 109 Sol Jo 175.

habitually resident for one year.[9] It is quite possible that the common law rules for divorce recognition might be applied so as to permit recognition in England of a decree granted in a jurisdiction with which the petitioner had a "real and substantial connection".[10] If the foreign decree can, properly, be classed as a decree of divorce[11] then it may be recognised under the rules laid down in Part II of the Family Law Act 1986.[12] Neither that Act nor the Convention on which it is based defines what is meant by a "divorce". However a foreign decree of presumption of death not coupled with one for dissolution of marriage might well not be recognised in England, on the ground that it was merely a matter of procedure and not of substantive law.[13]

9 Cf s 5(4) of the Domicile and Matrimonial Proceedings Act 1973.
10 Cf *Indyka v Indyka* [1969] 1 AC 33, [1967] 2 All ER 689; North (1968) 31 MLR 257, 281.
11 On the question of classification, see North, op cit, p 203.
12 Supra, pp 657 et seq; and see Law Com No 48 (1972) para 74, n 21.
13 *Re Wolf's Goods* [1948] P 66, [1947] 2 All ER 841; though see *In the Goods of Schlesinger* [1950] CLY 1549.

Chapter 23

Declarations

1. INTRODUCTION

The courts have had power, both under their inherent jurisdiction[1] and by statute,[2] to make declarations as to status. The purpose of such a declaratory judgment is not to determine the rights of the parties and to grant the appropriate relief but merely to affirm what their rights are without any reference to their enforcement. The courts for many years had statutory power[3] to grant declarations of legitimacy,[4] legitimation, of the validity of a marriage or that the petitioner is a British subject. They have exercised their inherent powers to declare that a foreign divorce or annulment should, or should not, be recognised in England.[5] There was no power, however, to declare the invalidity of a marriage by declaration: that had to be done in nullity proceedings.[6] Whether a marriage could be declared valid under the inherent jurisdiction was a matter of doubt and uncertainty.[7] Certainly declarations have been made as to the subsisting validity of a marriage;[8] but it has also been said[9] that declarations as to the initial validity of a marriage

1 Under RSC Ord 15, r 16.
2 Matrimonial Causes Act 1973, s 45.
3 Ibid.
4 But not of illegitimacy: *Mansel v A-G* (1877) 2 PD 265; affd (1879) 4 PD 232; *B v A-G* [1966] 2 All ER 145n, [1967] 1 WLR 776.
5 *Har-Shefi v Har-Shefi* [1953] P 161, [1953] 1 All ER 783; *Law v Gustin* [1976] Fam 155, [1976] 1 All ER 113; *Kendall v Kendall* [1977] Fam 208, [1977] 3 All ER 471; *Lepre v Lepre* [1965] P 52 at 57; *Lawrence v Lawrence* [1985] Fam 106, [1985] 1 All ER 506.
6 *Kassim v Kassim* [1962] P 224, [1962] 3 All ER 426.
7 See Law Com No 132 (1984), paras 2.7–2.8; North, op cit, ch 6.
8 Eg *Garthwaite v Garthwaite* [1964] P 356, [1964] 2 All ER 233; *Re Meyer* [1971] P 298, [1971] 1 All ER 378.
9 *Collett v Collett* [1968] P 482, [1967] 2 All ER 426; *Aldrich v A-G* [1968] P 281, [1968] 1 All ER 345; *Vervaeke v Smith* [1981] Fam 77, [1981] 1 All ER 55, affd [1981] Fam 77, CA, [1983] 1 AC 145; *Williams v A-G* [1987] 1 FLR 501; though this was actually done in *Woyno v Woyno* [1960] 2 All ER 879, [1960] 1 WLR 986.

could only be made in the exercise of the statutory powers. The significance of this is that the jurisdictional grounds varied as between the two heads of jurisdiction and, furthermore, various procedural safeguards were available under the statutory jurisdiction but not in the exercise of the inherent powers.

2. REFORM

The Law Commission, in 1984, expressed concern as to the general state of the law on declarations in family matters. They identified five main defects in the then law:[10] it was unclear what types of declaration could be made under the inherent jurisdiction; the procedural safeguards applicable to declarations under the Matrimonial Causes Act 1973 did not extend to the inherent jurisdiction; the jurisdictional criteria enabling the court to make declarations under RSO Ord 15, r 16 were unclear; the jurisdictional criteria for making declarations under the 1973 Act were anomalous; and there seemed little value in the declaration under the 1973 Act as to "the right to be deemed a British subject". They proposed a clean sweep and a fresh start, recommending "a new legislative code, based on consistent principles [to] replace the existing hotchpotch of statutory and discretionary relief".[11] That has been achieved, following the Law Commission's detailed proposals, in Part III of the Family Law Act 1986.[12] In that year, the Law Commission also recommended that there should be a power to grant declarations of parentage and that such declarations should be governed by essentially the same rules as those contained in the 1986 Act for other declarations, particularly those of legitimacy.[13] That recommendation has been implemented by amendments to Part III of the 1986 Act, as introduced by the Family Law Reform Act 1987.[14]

3. FAMILY LAW ACT 1986, PART III

The effect of Part III of the 1986 Act is to state what declarations may be granted under the Act and what are the relevant jurisdictional rules for each class of declaration.[15] It is proposed to consider separately the three classes of declaration, ie declarations as to marital status, as to parentage, legitimacy or legitimation and as to adoptions effected overseas. There will then be examined a number of matters which are common to all three classes. It ought to be noted at the outset that the various types of declaration listed in Part III may only be granted by the court[16] on the basis of the rules there laid down; section 45 of the Matrimonial Causes Act 1973 is repealed[17] and

10　Law Com No 132 (1984), para 2.12.
11　Ibid, para 2.13.
12　There are transitional provisions relating to proceedings already begun under the old law when Part III came into effect: 1986 Act, s 68(3).
13　Law Com No 157 (1986), para 3.14.
14　S 22.
15　For the relevant Rules of Court, see SI 1988/226.
16　The High Court or a county court: s 63.
17　This means that there is no longer a statutory power to grant a declaration that the applicant is a British subject. Any inherent power to make a declaration that a person is a British citizen is unaffected, as in *Bulmer v A-G* [1955] Ch 558, [1955] 2 All ER 718; *A-G v Prince Ernest Augustus of Hanover* [1957] AC 436, [1957] 1 All ER 49; *Motala v A-G* [1990] 2 FLR 261, revsd on another point [1991] 4 All ER 682, [1991] 3 WLR 903, infra, pp 751–752.

the inherent jurisdiction under the Rules of the Supreme Court is inapplicable to matters falling within Part III.[18]

(a) DECLARATIONS AS TO MARITAL STATUS

There are five declarations which the court may make in this category,[19] all of which had been made under the old law, namely:

that the marriage was valid at its inception;

that it did subsist on a date specified in the application;

that it did not so subsist;

that the validity of a divorce, annulment or legal separation obtained outside England and Wales is entitled to recognition here; and

that such a divorce, etc is not entitled to recognition here.

The jurisdictional rules for granting any of those five types of declaration are modelled on those for granting nullity decrees,[20] namely that either party to the marriage should, at the date of the application, be domiciled in England or have been habitually resident here for a year. If a party to the marriage is dead then the jurisdictional requirements of domicil or one year's habitual residence have to be satisfied at the date of death.[21] The jurisdictional connection is not with the applicant but rather with a party to the marriage and this accounts for the need for a rule, as in nullity, dealing with the case where a party to the marriage has died.[22] The reason for the connection being with the party to the marriage is because section 55 of the 1986 Act allows anyone to apply for one of the five listed declarations. If, however, the applicant is not a party to the marriage, the court has a discretion to refuse to hear the application if it considers that the applicant does not have a sufficient interest in the determination of the application,[1] a test similar to that applied in the case of nullity petitions.[2] As under the old law, a declaration may not be made that a marriage was at its inception void.[3] That is to be determined by means of a nullity petition, the powers to grant which are unaffected by Part III of the 1986 Act.[4] In this way, a party will be unable to avoid the ancillary relief powers of the court available on a nullity petition, by seeking instead a declaration where such powers are unavailable.[5]

The Domicile and Matrimonial Proceedings Act 1973 provides[6] that, in the case of any petition for a declaration as to the validity of a marriage of

---

18 S 58(4). It is unlikely that foreign declaratory judgments in personam would be recognised here—and no rules have been devised for the recognition of foreign declarations in rem. This is probably because it would usually require an English declaration to recognise the foreign one: see North, *Private International Law of Matrimonial Causes*, p 300.

19 S 55(1). See also Family Proceedings Rules 1991, rr 3.12, 3.16.

20 Supra, pp 630–633.

21 S 55(2). The effect of these rules is to abolish the common law ground of jurisdiction that a declaration could be granted as to the validity of a foreign divorce if that was a necessary step in adjudicating on a matter within the jurisdiction of the court: *Lepre v Lepre* [1965] P 52, [1963] 2 All ER 49; see Law Com No 132 (1984), para 3.45.

22 This can be very useful, as in *Re Meyer* [1971] P 298, [1971] 1 All ER 378.

1 S 55(3).

2 Supra, p 631. See Law Com No 132 (1984), paras 3.29–3.33 for discussion of the issue of who should be able to apply for these declarations.

3 S 58(5)(a).

4 S 58(6).

5 *Kassim v Kassim* [1962] P 224, [1962] 3 All ER 426. It will, however, be possible for a petitioner to seek in the alternative a nullity decree or a declaration as to the validity of the marriage: Law Com No 132 (1984), paras 3.26–3.27.

6 Sch I, para 9.

the petitioner or as to the subsistence of such a marriage, the court has a discretion to stay the English proceedings before the beginning of the trial thereof. This would seem to cover all five declarations as to marital status falling within section 55 of the 1986 Act. The statutory discretion is the same as that in divorce proceedings and has been fully discussed in that context.[7]

(b) DECLARATIONS AS TO PARENTAGE, LEGITIMACY AND LEGITIMATION

Section 56 of the 1986 Act[8] retains and slightly extends the previous statutory power[9] to make declarations as to legitimacy and legitimation,[10] and introduces a new power to make declarations of parentage. The court may make four kinds of declaration in this category:

that a person is or was the applicant's parent,

that the applicant is the legitimate child of his parents, and

that the applicant has, or has not, become a legitimate person.[11]

Declarations as to legitimation may relate to legitimation by statute, or to foreign legitimations which are recognised here either under statutory provisions or at common law.[12] It should be noted that the court is expressly prohibited from making a declaration that a person is or was illegitimate.[13] There was no power to make such a declaration either under the Matrimonial Causes Act 1973 or under the inherent jurisdiction, and the Law Commission saw no case for introducing such a power.[14] Its absence does not prevent a court from finding that a person is illegitimate in the course of other proceedings; but it cannot make a declaration to that effect binding *in rem*.[15] Only a person alleging that he is the child of someone may apply for a parentage declaration; and an application for a declaration as to legitimacy or legitimation may only be made by the person whose status is in issue. The old law had a similar rule in the case of legitimacy but allowed a person to seek a legitimation declaration in relation to himself or any ancestor.[16] No good reason for the distinction can be identified and the former legitimacy rule is adopted in the 1986 Act.[17]

The jurisdictional rules for granting any of these declarations are the simple and familiar ones that the applicant is, at the time of the application, domiciled in England or has been habitually resident here for one year immediately preceding that date.[18]

7 Supra, pp 635–639.
8 As substituted by s 22 of the Family Law Reform Act 1987; and see Family Proceedings Rules 1991, rr 3.13, 3.16.
9 See Matrimonial Causes Act 1973, s 45; see *Motala v A-G* [1990] 2 FLR 261, revsd on another point [1991] 4 All ER 682, [1991] 3 WLR 903, infra, pp 751–752.
10 Such declarations are still needed notwithstanding the major reforms of the law relating to legitimacy contained in the Family Law Reform Act 1987, infra, p 746; see Law Com No 118 (1982), para 10.2; Law Com No 157 (1986), para 3.14.
11 These may be sought in the alternative: s 56(2).
12 S 56(5). Recognition of foreign legitimations is discussed infra, pp 756–760.
13 S 58(5)(b).
14 Law Com No 132 (1984), para 3.22.
15 On the effect of declarations, see infra, p 698.
16 Matrimonial Causes Act 1973, s 45(2).
17 See Law Com No 132 (1984), paras 3.34–3.36.
18 S 56(3); and see Law Com No 132 (1984), paras 3.34–3.36; *Motala v A-G* [1990] 2 FLR 261, revsd on another point [1991] 4 All ER 682, [1991] 3 WLR 903.

(c) DECLARATIONS AS TO FOREIGN ADOPTIONS

Although recognition in England of adoption orders made elsewhere in the British Isles is automatic,[19] this is not true of foreign adoptions, whether their recognition falls under statutory or common law rules.[20] Whilst there is no reported case of an application for a declaration as to the validity of a foreign adoption,[21] the Law Commission concluded[1] that it would be desirable to take the opportunity to make clear provision for such declarations and to provide appropriate procedural safeguards.[2] Under section 57(2) of the Family Law Act 1986[3] the court may grant a declaration that the applicant either is or is not the adopted child of a particular person.[4] The only person who can apply for a declaration as to the validity of a foreign adoption is the child himself and he can apply whether recognition of the foreign adoption is governed by the statutory or common law recognition rules.[5] Again, the jurisdiction of the court is based on the domicil of the applicant in England at the date of the application or his habitual residence here for one year immediately preceding that date.[6]

(d) LIMITS ON THE COURTS' POWERS

The basic approach of Part III of the 1986 Act is that the court may make the declarations listed there in family matters but may make no others.[7] So there is express provision, as has been mentioned earlier, that no court may make a declaration as to the initial invalidity of a marriage or that a person is illegitimate,[8] and that the declarations available under Part III of the 1986 Act may only be made under that Part.[9] This latter provision excludes any possibility of the exercise of an overlapping jurisdiction under the inherent powers of the court under RSC Ord 15, r 16.[10] It is also not possible for a court to make a "negative declaration", ie to declare the opposite of what is sought,[11] eg that a marriage was not subsisting on a particular date when a declaration is sought that it was.[12] There is nothing, however, to prevent a petitioner in that case from petitioning for the two declarations in the alternative, and indeed the Act expressly refers to this possibility in relation to declarations as to legitimation and adoption.[13]

---

19 Adoption Act 1976, s 38(1)(c).
20 Infra, pp 764–769; and see Law Com No 132 (1984), para 3.15.
21 The issue of the validity of a foreign adoption has always arisen in the course of other proceedings such as entitlement under a settlement (*Re Valentine's Settlement* [1965] Ch 831, [1965] 2 All ER 226), a will (*Re Marshall* [1957] Ch 507, [1957] 3 All ER 172), or an intestacy (*Re Wilson* [1954] Ch 733, [1954] 1 All ER 997).
1 Law Com No 132 (1984), paras 3.15–3.16.
2 Infra, p 698.
3 And see Family Proceedings Rules 1991, rr 3.15, 3.16.
4 These declarations may be sought in the alternative: s 57(1).
5 S 57(1).
6 S 57(3).
7 It might also be noted that the power to grant declarations under the Greek Marriages Act 1884 is abolished as is the right to petition for jactitation of marriage: ss 61, 62: and see Law Com No 132 (1984), paras 4.1–4.13.
8 S 58(5).
9 S 58(4).
10 S 58(3); and see Law Com No 132 (1984), para 3.28.
11 S 58(3); and see Law Com No 132 (1984), paras 3.24–3.27.
12 Under s 55(1).
13 Ss 56(2), 57(1). As has been mentioned, supra, p 695, it is also possible to petition for a nullity decree and a declaration of initial validity in the alternative.

(e) SAFEGUARDS AND OTHER PROCEDURAL MATTERS

All declarations made under Part III of the 1986 Act are binding *in rem*, ie they bind not only the parties but all other persons including the Crown.[14] It is important that in matters of personal status some finality is brought to the proceedings in order to still any doubts on the issue, and declarations as to the validity of a marriage for example are very close in nature to decrees of divorce or nullity which do operate in rem. Although it is always possible for a declaration, like any other judgment, to be rescinded for fraud, the binding nature conferred on declarations under Part III does call for a number of procedural safeguards to protect the interests of third parties and of the public.

The first concern is that a declaration should only be granted on convincing evidence, and it is provided that the truth of the proposition to be declared has to be proved "to the satisfaction of the court".[15] A further safeguard is provided by involvement of the Attorney-General to enable him to protect the public interest.[16] The outcome of a petition for a declaration could be very relevant, for example, on issues of nationality[17] or immigration. To meet these concerns, it is provided that the court may at any stage of the proceedings, either of its own motion or on the application of a party to the proceedings, direct that all papers be sent to the Attorney-General who may, whether or not he has been sent the papers, intervene in the proceedings.[18] It is also desirable that adequate provision be made for giving notice of the proceedings to all interested parties and to the Attorney-General, and power is given to make rules of court for that purpose.[19]

Finally, there is the issue whether declarations under Part III should be available as of right, or only within the discretion of the court. The power of the court to grant a nullity decree is not discretionary[20] and it has been said that "the right to obtain a declaration of status is a human right which should not be subject to the court's discretion".[21] Consequently, section 58(1) of the 1986 Act requires the court to make a declaration if the truth of the proposition to be declared is proved to the satisfaction of the court. There is, however, one exception to this in that the court may refuse to grant a declaration if to do so "would manifestly be contrary to public policy". This follows the approach of the earlier law, when courts were prepared to refuse a declaration as to the subsisting validity of a marriage, under section 45 of the Matrimonial Causes Act 1973, on grounds of public policy:

> It cannot be the intention of the statute that a decree must be pronounced (to the permanent prejudice of the Crown) when, although there has been no fraud at the hearing, the whole history is of fraud and perjury and the facts to found a decree have been brought about by criminal acts and offences and a fraudulent, deceitful course of conduct.[22]

14 S 58(2). This follows, in part, the approach of the Matrimonial Causes Act 1973, s 45; and see Law Com No 132 (1984), paras 3.41–3.42.
15 S 58(1).
16 See Matrimonial Causes Act 1973, s 45(6); cf *Williams v A-G* [1987] 1 FLR 501, [1987] Fam Law 160.
17 Eg *Puttick v A-G* [1980] Fam 1, [1979] 3 All ER 463.
18 S 59.
19 S 60; and see Law Com No 132 (1984), paras 3.60–3.63. In the case of declarations of parentage and of legitimacy, if a declaration is made the Registrar General must be notified: Family Law Act 1986, s 56(4).
20 *Kassim v Kassim* [1962] P 224 at 234.
21 Law Com No 132 (1984), para 3.39.
22 *Puttick v A-G* [1980] Fam 1 at 22.

Chapter 24

Financial relief

SUMMARY

In many petitions for matrimonial relief, the parties are not only, or indeed primarily, concerned with the determination of their matrimonial status, but are also concerned with the powers of the court to make orders as to financial support, rights to the matrimonial home and property, and the like.[1] These forms of relief, often ancillary to that obtained in the main matrimonial

---

1 Their other main concern is with orders concerning the welfare of the children, infra, pp 719 et seq.

proceedings, give rise to three main questions of private international law—the jurisdiction of the English court, the power to order relief after a foreign divorce, annulment or legal separation, and the recognition of foreign decrees or orders in relation to financial relief.

1. JURISDICTION OF THE ENGLISH COURT

As the types of relief available to the parties to a marriage are varied, the jurisdictional issues raised thereby must be considered separately. The position is further complicated by the fact that general jurisdiction over claims for maintenance is conferred by the Civil Jurisdiction and Judgments Acts 1982 and 1991. There are also special rules, under Part III of the Matrimonial and Family Proceedings Act 1984, as to the powers and jurisdiction of the English courts to grant financial relief following the obtaining of a foreign divorce, annulment or legal separation. It is necessary, therefore to examine separately the jurisdictional rules governing the various heads of English financial relief and those which are uniform within the European Community and the EFTA Contracting States[2] under the Civil Jurisdiction and Judgments Acts 1982 and 1991, before considering the position under Part III of the 1984 Act.

(a) GENERAL JURISDICTIONAL RULES

(i) Relief ancillary to an English decree of divorce, nullity or judicial separation

On granting a decree of divorce, nullity or judicial separation,[3] or at any time thereafter, the English court may make an order for the payment of periodical payments, which may be ordered to be secured, or that a lump sum shall be paid by one spouse to the other,[4] or that similar payments may be made by one spouse to or for the benefit of a child of the family,[5] or that a spouse shall transfer to or settle property on the spouse or a child or for the benefit of a child,[6] or the court may order the variation of any settlement made on the parties to the marriage or order the extinction or reduction of the interest of either party thereunder.[7]

The court has jurisdiction to make such orders and grant such ancillary relief whenever it has jurisdiction in the main proceedings for divorce, nullity or judicial separation.[8] This means, essentially, if either party is domiciled, or has been habitually resident for one year, in England.[9] On the basis of jurisdiction in the main suit, an order for periodical payments has been made against a husband domiciled and resident in France and with no assets in England but where there was a real probability of his appearing before

---

2 Currently, only Switzerland.
3 Provision is also made for the payment of maintenance pending the suit: Matrimonial Causes Act 1973, s 22.
4 Matrimonial Causes Act 1973, s 23(1)(a)-(c).
5 Ibid, s 23(1)(d)-(f). This relief may be ordered before a decree is granted, or if the proceedings are dismissed: ibid, s 23(2).
6 Ibid, s 24(1)(a),(b).
7 Ibid, s 24(1)(c) and (d), infra, pp 892–893. For consent orders, see Matrimonial and Family Proceedings Act 1984, s 7.
8 *Cammell v Cammell* [1965] P 467, [1964] 3 All ER 255.
9 Domicile and Matrimonial Proceedings Act 1973, s 5. This jurisdiction is unaffected by the Civil Jurisdiction and Judgments Acts 1982 and 1991, infra, pp 704–707.

the English courts.[10] As the power to make orders for ancillary relief is discretionary,[11] the court will decline jurisdiction where an order would be quite ineffective,[12] as where the respondent had no connection with England and the English order would not be recognised in the foreign country.[13] The fact that there has been a judicial separation abroad which is recognised here does not prevent the English court from granting relief ancillary to a later English divorce petition.[14]

The power to make orders for ancillary relief may be exercised at any time after the granting of the main decree,[15] and there is authority for the opinion that, so long as there was jurisdiction in the main suit, ancillary relief may still be granted notwithstanding that the jurisdictional ground such as domicil or habitual residence no longer exists.[16]

It will be recalled that the jurisdiction of the English courts to grant decrees of divorce, nullity and judicial separation is subject to a discretionary power in the court to stay the proceedings if similar proceedings are continuing in another jurisdiction.[17] If English proceedings are stayed because similar proceedings are continuing in another jurisdiction in the British Isles, the English court does not have power to make, inter alia, orders for periodical payments or the payment of lump sums, save in circumstances of urgency. Furthermore, any order, other than a lump sum order, already made in connection with the stayed proceedings ceases to have effect three months after the proceedings were stayed.[18] If an order for periodical payments or any provision relating to a child which could be made under section 8 of the Children Act 1989 has been made in the other British proceedings, then any English order made in connection with the stayed English proceedings in relation to the same matters shall cease to have effect and no such order may be made.[19]

(ii) Failure to provide reasonable maintenance

The court has power to order periodical payments, which may be ordered to be secured, or lump sum payments to be made to a spouse or to or for the benefit of a child if the other spouse has failed to provide reasonable maintenance.[20] This relief may be sought during the continuance of the

10 *Cammell v Cammell*, supra; and see the power to vary a marriage settlement exercised over foreign settlements in *Nunneley v Nunneley* (1890) 15 PD 186; *Forsyth v Forsyth* [1891] P 363; and see *Hunter v Hunter and Waddington* [1962] P 1, [1961] 2 All ER 121, infra, pp 892–893.
11 Matrimonial Causes Act 1973, ss 23, 24.
12 *Tallack v Tallack* [1927] P 211; *Goff v Goff* [1934] P 107; *Wyler v Lyons* [1963] P 274, [1963] 1 All ER 821.
13 *Tallack v Tallack*, supra. The court also has power, under the Matrimonial Causes Act 1973, s 37, to restrain or set aside transactions intended to prevent or reduce relief and will, in appropriate circumstances, exercise this power in relation to immovables abroad: *Hamlin v Hamlin* [1986] Fam 11, [1985] 2 All ER 1037.
14 *Sabbagh v Sabbagh* [1985] FLR 29. This would not have been possible if the earlier decree had been one of divorce or nullity or if the English decree sought had also been one of judicial separation, see ibid, at pp 35–36. Relief after a foreign divorce, etc is discussed more fully, infra, pp 708 et seq.
15 Matrimonial Causes Act 1973, ss 23(1), 24(1).
16 *Moss v Moss* [1937] QSR 1; Nygh, p 354.
17 Supra, pp 635–639.
18 Domicile and Matrimonial Proceedings Act 1973, Sch 1, para 11(2).
19 Ibid, para 11(3), as amended by the Children Act 1989, Sch 13, para 33, Sch 15.
20 Matrimonial Causes Act 1973, s 27. The differing obligations of maintenance on a husband and a wife are laid down in s 27(1), as substituted by s 63 of the Domestic Proceedings and Magistrates' Courts Act 1978; and see the Matrimonial and Family Proceedings Act 1984, s 4; Family Law Reform Act 1987, Sch 2, para 52.

marriage and is not ancillary to a petition for divorce, nullity or judicial separation. Indeed it assumes that the spouses are still married, though such relief may be granted after there has been a decree of judicial separation.[21] The court has jurisdiction to make such orders on three bases:[1]

(a) Domicil of the applicant or respondent in England at the date of the application.
(b) Habitual residence of the applicant in England for one year immediately preceding the application.
(c) Residence of the respondent in England on the date of the application.[2]

(iii) Alteration of maintenance agreements

The court has power to order alterations, by variation or revocation, in a maintenance agreement on application by either of the parties thereto.[3] The court must be satisfied that the financial circumstances of the parties have changed or that the agreement fails to make proper arrangements for a child of the family. Jurisdiction is based on the domicil or residence in England of each party to the agreement at the time of the application.[4] If an application is made to a magistrates' court, both parties must be resident in England and one must be resident in the commission area for which the court is appointed.[5]

(iv) Financial provision in magistrates' courts[6]

(a) Under the Domestic Proceedings and Magistrates' Courts Act 1978 Magistrates' courts have power under Part I of the Domestic Proceedings and Magistrates' Courts Act 1978 to order either party to a marriage to make financial provision for the other spouse or for a child of the family. Jurisdiction to make such orders, and other orders covered by Part I of the 1978 Act,[7] is based on either the applicant or respondent ordinarily residing within the commission area for which the particular magistrates' court is appointed.[8] This is a matter of internal jurisdiction only.[9] The one truly international jurisdictional provision in the 1978 Act is that the domicil of the parties is irrelevant to matters of jurisdiction.[10] All other issues remain to be deter-

21 *King v King* [1954] P 55, [1953] 2 All ER 1029.
1 Matrimonial Causes Act 1973, s 27(2), as amended by the Domicile and Matrimonial Proceedings Act 1973, s 6(1). This is subject to the effects of the Civil Jurisdiction and Judgments Acts 1982 and 1991, infra, pp 704–707.
2 Jurisdiction to make these orders used to be the same as to grant a decree of judicial separation. This third head preserves what was one of the common law jurisdictional grounds in judicial separation. For the meaning of "residence", see *Sinclair v Sinclair* [1968] P 189, [1967] 3 All ER 882 and cases there cited.
3 Matrimonial Causes Act 1973, s 35.
4 Ibid, s 35(1). If an agreement provides for the continuation of payment after the death of one party, and that party died domiciled in England, the court has jurisdiction over any application by the survivor or the personal representatives of the deceased: s 36.
5 Ibid, s 35(3).
6 For the impact on these rules of the Civil Jurisdiction and Judgments Acts 1982 and 1991, see infra, pp 707–708.
7 The Act also gives magistrates' courts power, for example, to make orders for the protection of a party to the marriage or of a child of the family (ss 16–18, as amended by the Courts and Legal Services Act 1990, Sch 20).
8 S 30(1).
9 The only international jurisdictional rules were contained in s 30(3), dealing with conflicts of jurisdiction within the United Kingdom, but they were repealed, without replacement, by the Courts and Legal Services Act 1990.
10 S 30(5).

mined, as they were with the forerunners of this Act, by the common law. The general principle is that, if the defendant is resident outside the United Kingdom, an English magistrates' court will lack jurisdiction.[11] However, it is arguable that a claim for financial provision is not a matter of status but is to be regarded simply as an action in personam,[12] in which event mere presence within the jurisdiction should suffice.[13] There is some authority[14] that any want of jurisdiction cannot be cured by submission because, in the case of an inferior court such as a magistrates' court, submission cannot extend "a limited and circumscribed jurisdiction"[15] conferred by statute. However, the only jurisdiction conferred by the 1978 Act relates to intra-United Kingdom jurisdiction and it is suggested that, if a claim for financial provision is characterised as an action in personam, submission by a respondent resident outside the United Kingdom should confer jurisdiction.

(b) Under the Maintenance Orders (Facilities for Enforcement) Act 1920 and the Maintenance Orders (Reciprocal Enforcement) Act 1972 If the defendant resides in a country outside the United Kingdom, the English courts may have jurisdiction to make a maintenance order against him if the circumstances are such that either the Maintenance Orders (Facilities for Enforcement) Act 1920[16] or the Maintenance Orders (Reciprocal Enforcement) Act 1972[17] is applicable.[1] Both these statutes deal with the problem of reciprocal enforcement of maintenance orders and the former will be repealed when the latter is brought wholly into force.[2] As the basis of the operation of both statutes is reciprocity, they both deal with the recognition of foreign maintenance orders as well as the jurisdiction of the English court, but only the latter aspect is considered here.[3]

The 1920 Act applies only to those Commonwealth countries to which it has been extended by Order in Council. If a defendant is resident in such a country, then an English magistrates' court may make a provisional order against him in his absence, even though the applicant's basis of complaint did not arise in England.[4] A copy of such an order is then sent by diplomatic channels to the Commonwealth country where the defendant resides with a view to its being confirmed by the courts of that country. In other words, there are proceedings in England for a provisional order, followed by proceedings in the foreign country for confirmation thereof.

Part I of the 1972 Act establishes a similar procedure but it is wider in scope. It applies to all countries with whom reciprocal agreements have been reached and not just Commonwealth countries.[5] It contains a wider definition of the type of orders to which it applies than does the 1920 Act. Furthermore,

11 *Forsyth v Forsyth* [1948] P 125, [1947] 2 All ER 623.
12 See *Berkley v Thompson* (1884) 10 App Cas 45 at 49.
13 *Forsyth v Forsyth* [1948] P 125 at 136; *Collister v Collister* [1972] 1 WLR 54 at 59.
14 *Forsyth v Forsyth*, supra, at p 132.
15 *Re Dulles' Settlement* [1951] Ch 265 at 274.
16 See Dicey & Morris, Fourth Cumulative Supp, pp 143–145; McClean, *Recognition of Family Judgments in the Commonwealth* (1983), ch 5.
17 As amended by the Domestic Proceedings and Magistrates' Courts Act 1978, ss 54–61; McClean, op cit, chs 6 & 7.
1 Dicey & Morris, Fourth Cumulative Supp, pp 146–150.
2 Maintenance Orders (Reciprocal Enforcement) Act 1972, s 22(2)(a).
3 Recognition is discussed, infra, pp 715–717.
4 *Collister v Collister* [1972] 1 All ER 334, [1972] 1 WLR 54.
5 Indeed the 1920 Act is being replaced in the case of Commonwealth countries by new Orders made under the 1972 Act, see eg SI 1983/1124, 1125.

the "shuttlecock" procedure of provisional order in one country followed by confirmation in the other applies also to variation and revocation of maintenance orders.[6] Such variation or revocation may be made either by the court which made the original provisional order or the court which confirmed it.

Part II of the 1972 Act gives effect to the United Nations Convention on the Recovery Abroad of Maintenance (1956). If a person, usually the wife, in the United Kingdom claims maintenance from a person "subject to the jurisdiction" of a convention country, she makes an application through the clerk of the magistrates' court in the area where she resides. This application is forwarded through diplomatic channels to that foreign country and there are no judicial proceedings in England. In the converse case, where a foreign application is received in England by the clerk of the magistrates' court in the area where the defendant resides, the court proceeds just as if the complainant was before the English court.[7]

Under section 40 of the 1972 Act,[8] special recognition arrangements may be made with countries designated by Order in Council, applying modified versions of either Part I or Part II to such countries. Under this provision, there are, for example, reciprocal arrangements applying an amended version of Part I to Ireland[9] and to countries which are parties to the 1973 Hague Convention on the Recognition and Enforcement of Decisions Relating to Maintenance Obligations.[10] A modified version of Part II has been applied to a majority of the states in the USA.[11]

(b) CIVIL JURISDICTION AND JUDGMENTS ACTS 1982[12] AND 1991

The jurisdictional provisions discussed so far vary according to the court in which the proceedings for financial relief are brought and according to the kinds of relief available in that court. More broadly defined rules as to jurisdiction over financial relief are provided by the Civil Jurisdiction and Judgments Act 1982 and the Civil Jurisdiction and Judgments Act 1991 which amends the 1982 Act. Although the general provisions of these Acts have already been considered in detail in relation both to jurisdiction[13] and to recognition,[14] it is necessary to return in the present context to examine the operation of those rules in the field of financial relief, and to consider what forms of financial relief fall within these Acts and what are the relevant jurisdictional rules.[15]

6 1972 Act, ss 5, 9, as amended by the Domestic Proceedings and Magistrates' Courts Act 1978, s 54, the Civil Jurisdiction and Judgments Act 1982, Sch 11, para 12, and the Maintenance Enforcement Act 1991, Sch 1, para 14. For an example see *Killen v Killen* 1981 SLT (Sh Ct) 77.
7 Under s 28A of the 1972 Act (amended by the Matrimonial and Family Proceedings Act 1984, s 26) an English magistrates' court can entertain an application for maintenance even though the spouses' marriage has been dissolved or annulled.
8 As amended by the Civil Jurisdiction and Judgments Act 1982, Sch 11, para 17.
9 SI 1974/2140; see *Macaulay v Macaulay* [1991] 1 All ER 865, [1991] 1 WLR 179; and see *Sachs v Standard Chartered Bank (Ireland) Ltd* [1987] ILRM 297.
10 SI 1979/1317; SI 1981/837, 1545, 1674; SI 1983/885, 1523 SI 1987/1282; and see *Armitage v Nanchen* (1983) 4 FLR 293.
11 SI 1979/1314; SI 1981/606; SI 1984/824.
12 See now SI 1990/2591 for the substituted Sch 1 to the 1982 Act, implementing the San Sebastian Convention on the Accession of Spain and Portugal; supra, p 280.
13 Supra, pp 279–344.
14 Supra, pp 411–444.
15 See SI 1986/1962. The rules relating to recognition and enforcement are examined infra, pp 717–718.

(i) What are maintenance orders?

The Brussels Convention (applicable to European Community States) brought into force by the 1982 Act includes "matters relating to maintenance",[16] but this concept is not defined in the Convention;[17] nor is it defined in the parallel Lugano Convention[18] (applicable to European Community and EFTA Contracting States) brought into force by the 1991 Act.[19] Financial relief in its common form of periodical payments falls within the meaning of maintenance, as may be illustrated by *De Cavel v De Cavel*[20] where an order, made in the course of divorce proceedings, for interim payments to be paid on a monthly basis was held to be within the Brussels Convention. The court did, however, stress that the payments were designed to support the spouse and were based on need. It is also authoritatively stated that maintenance can include lump sum orders.[21] The fact that a financial relief order is ancillary to a divorce decree or other judgment outside the Brussels or Lugano Conventions does not mean that the financial relief order is excluded. Indeed specific mention is made of such a case in the jurisdictional context, in Article 5(2) of both Conventions.

Applying these criteria to the various financial orders that can be made by English courts, it is clear that financial orders (periodical or lump sum) made during the subsistence of a marriage, both for a spouse and for children being designed for support, must rank as maintenance within the Conventions. The position where there is a divorce, or annulment, is more difficult. Financial orders for periodical payments to be made to a child or spouse are designed to support that person and must therefore be within the Conventions. The position in respect of lump sum payments is more problematical. Sometimes these are undoubtedly concerned with the support of a spouse and will constitute "maintenance". Other lump sum payments may be more in the nature of compensation or a division of matrimonial property and will fall outside the meaning of maintenance. The effect of this is that they will fall outside the special jurisdictional rules for "maintenance".[22] Such non maintenance lump sum payments are also likely to fall outside the scope of the Brussels and Lugano Conventions altogether as being caught by the exclusion of rights in property arising out of a matrimonial relationship.[23] It is not clear whether orders made by the English courts under Part III of the Matrimonial and Family Proceedings Act 1984 after the marriage has been ended by a foreign divorce or annulment[1] fall within the meaning of maintenance, and it can be argued that, as the marriage is already at an end before the proceedings in England begin, such orders are not "maintenance" orders.[2]

---

16 See Art 5(2).
17 See Schlosser Report, pp 101–105.
18 Art 5(2).
19 Where a case involves both a European Community state and an EFTA Contracting State, Art 54B of the Lugano Convention indicates whether the rules of that Convention or of the Brussels Convention are to be applied, discussed supra, p 341.
20 Case 120/79 [1980] ECR 731, [1980] 3 CMLR 1. It does not matter whether the order is interim or final: *De Cavel v De Cavel* Case 143/78 [1979] ECR 1055, [1979] 2 CMLR 547.
21 Schlosser Report, p 102.
22 Art 5(2), infra, pp 706–707.
23 Art 1(2)(1), discussed supra, in this context, pp 288–289.
 1 Infra, pp 709–714.
 2 The inter-relation of Part III of the 1984 Act with the Civil Jurisdiction and Judgments Acts 1982 and 1991 is discussed, infra, pp 711–712.

(ii) Jurisdictional rules

(a) General rules A person who is seeking an order for financial relief which falls within the Brussels or Lugano Conventions has a number of jurisdictional options open to him. First, he can sue under any of the generally applicable jurisdictional rules of the Conventions. This means that the English courts will have jurisdiction if the respondent is domiciled here[3] within the special meaning of domicil for the purposes of the Conventions and the 1982 Act, as amended by the 1991 Act;[4] if the parties have chosen the jurisdiction of the English courts;[5] or if the respondent submits to the jurisdiction of the English courts.[6]

(b) Special rules In addition to the rules of general application just discussed, Article 5(2)[7] of the Conventions provides special jurisdictional rules for maintenance cases, stating that claims may be brought against a respondent domiciled in another Contracting State,[8] as follows:

> In matters relating to maintenance, in the courts for the place where the maintenance creditor is domiciled or habitually resident or, if the matter is ancillary to proceedings concerning the status of a person, in the court which, according to its own law, has jurisdiction to entertain those proceedings.

The effect of this provision is to add two more bases of jurisdiction.[9] An English court will be able to entertain maintenance proceedings against a defendant domiciled in other Contracting State if the petitioner is domiciled here in the Convention sense or is habitually resident here. Given the breadth of the special concept of domicil, there may not be much difference between the two. More accurately, the jurisdictional link must be with the maintenance creditor. So, what happens if the maintenance debtor wants to sue, for example, for a reduction in his periodical payments? The English courts will have jurisdiction if one of the general jurisdictional bases is satisfied, the most obvious being if the maintenance creditor is domiciled here.[10] What if he is only habitually resident here? Undoubtedly the maintenance creditor can bring proceedings here, by reason of Article 5(2), but can the maintenance debtor sue here on the basis of the creditor's habitual residence? Opinions are divided on this, but if, in a case under the Brussels Convention, the European Court of Justice follows the authoritative Schlosser Report,[11] jurisdiction will be denied.[12]

Article 5(2) of both Conventions also confers jurisdiction on the English courts if the maintenance proceedings are ancillary to "proceedings con-

---

3 Art 2 of both Conventions, supra, pp 290–291, 293, 340 et seq.
4 S 41 of the 1982 Act, as amended by the 1991 Act, Sch 2, para 16 supra, pp 284–285, 342.
5 Art 17 of both Conventions supra, pp 314–322, 340 et seq.
6 Art 18 of both Conventions supra, pp 322–324, 340 et seq.
7 Discussed more fully, supra, pp 299–300.
8 Ie not in the United Kingdom; but the 1982 Act, Sch 4 provides identical provisions for the case where he is domiciled elsewhere in the United Kingdom.
9 If a maintenance obligation arises from an agreement and not from a court order, Art 5(2) will be inapplicable; but the special contractual head of jurisdiction under Art 5(1) may be applicable, supra, pp 294–299. Art 5(1) is not identical in the Brussels and Lugano Conventions, see, supra, p 343.
10 In such a case the maintenance creditor's domicil also satisfies Art 2 of both Conventions.
11 Para 107. It will be recalled (supra, p 283) that the 1982 Act, s 3(3)(b) gives particular force to this and other reports. See also the 1991 Act, s 1.
12 Collins, *The Civil Jurisdiction and Judgments Act 1982*, p 58; Anton, *Civil Jurisdiction in Scotland*, para 5.33; Kaye, *Civil Jurisdiction and Enforcement of Judgments*, p 545; cf Hartley, *Civil Jurisdiction and Judgments*, pp 49–50.

cerning the status of a person", provided the court already has jurisdiction over those status proceedings under the relevant English jurisdictional rules. This is important because, as we have seen,[13] many applications for financial relief are made in conjunction with divorce proceedings. Whilst no definition is provided in the Conventions of proceedings concerning status, there seems little doubt that it will cover proceedings for divorce, nullity or judicial separation. So, an English court will be able to make a maintenance order in such proceedings over a respondent domiciled in another Contracting State[14] if the court has jurisdiction over the main proceedings on the basis of the domicil or one year's habitual residence of either party.[15]

Maintenance orders are often varied and sometimes revoked. A court which made the original order may only vary or revoke it if it still has jurisdiction under one of the Conventions at the later date.[16] There should be no problem with maintenance orders made in England which are ancillary to divorce, etc proceedings, because the English court, under our rules, retains jurisdiction to vary or revoke the order, even though the original basis of jurisdiction has gone.[17] If, however, jurisdiction is based on the domicil or habitual residence of the maintenance creditor under Article 5(2), an English court will be unable to vary or revoke its own order if the maintenance creditor is neither domiciled nor habitually resident here at the time of the later proceedings, assuming that the maintenance debtor is still domicil in a Contracting State.[18] If he is not, the Conventions will cease to apply and the English courts will have to decide the jurisdictional issue for themselves and, following the approach to variation of orders ancillary to divorce, etc proceedings, ought to take jurisdiction.

(c) INTER-RELATION OF THE 1982 AND 1991 ACTS WITH OTHER BASES OF JURISDICTION

Finally, there is the question of the inter-relation of jurisdiction under the 1982 and 1991 Acts with the other jurisdictional bases already discussed. Difficulty arises from the fact that, for example, the jurisdictional rules of the Brussels Convention and the 1982 Act provide that only the courts given jurisdiction under the Convention may exercise it.[19] This means that, in the case of a respondent who is domiciled (in the Convention sense) in another part of the United Kingdom or in another Contracting State to the Brussels Convention and the proceedings concern "maintenance" in the Convention sense, there may be circumstances in which an English court is deprived of jurisdiction. There is no difficulty with the jurisdiction ancillary to divorce, etc proceedings because the Brussels Convention itself provides for that.[20] Nor is there any difficulty[21] with jurisdiction under Part II of the Maintenance

---

13 Supra, pp 700–701.
14 There is a limitation in Art 5(2) of both Conventions in cases where jurisdiction is taken on the basis of nationality, but this is irrelevant in the United Kingdom where there is no such jurisdiction basis.
15 Domicile and Matrimonial Proceedings Act 1973, s 5, supra, pp 630–633.
16 Jenard Report, p 25; Schlosser Report, paras 107–108.
17 Supra, p 701.
18 And will have to recognise a variation or revocation made by a court in another Contracting State.
19 The same approach is taken in the Lugano Convention and the 1991 Act.
20 As does the Lugano Convention.
21 This is because Art 57 (as substituted by the 1989 Accession Convention) gives overriding effect to other Conventions which govern jurisdiction or recognition and enforcement to which the parties to the 1968 Convention are, or become, parties. Art 57 of the Lugano Convention is to similar effect.

Orders (Reciprocal Enforcement) Act 1972, which applies to all European Community states except Ireland. There is probably no difficulty either in the case of Ireland, because the amended version of Part I of the 1972 Act applicable to Ireland under section 40 of the 1972 Act[22] would seem to constitute a convention containing jurisdictional rules within the meaning of Article 57 of the Brussels Convention.[1] However, in the case of the amended version of Part I of the 1972 Act which, under section 40, gives effect to the 1973 Hague Maintenance Convention,[2] there is more difficulty. The 1973 Convention extends to a number of European Community states[3] but the jurisdictional provisions in the Order in Council[4] which provides an amended version of Part I of the 1972 Act are not derived from that Convention. Similar difficulties arise in relation to the Lugano Convention because the 1973 Hague Convention applies to a number of EFTA states also.[5] This suggests that Article 57 of the Brussels and Lugano Conventions does not apply, with the apparent result that, if the case falls within the 1982 or 1991 Acts, the parties cannot use the procedures provided under section 40 of the 1972 Act. Furthermore, the English courts will be unable to exercise any of their other heads of jurisdiction where the respondent is domiciled in a Contracting State and the claim is within the terms of the Brussels or Lugano Convention. This will, for example, exclude jurisdiction to make orders for failure to provide maintenance on the basis of the respondent's residence in England,[6] or the jurisdiction of the magistrates' courts to make orders based on the residence of the respondent,[7] or orders under the Maintenance Orders (Facilities for Enforcement) Act 1920 or under Part I of the Maintenance Orders (Reciprocal Enforcement) Act 1972 (in the case of a person domiciled in a Contracting State to which Part I does not apply.)

2. FINANCIAL RELIEF AFTER A FOREIGN DIVORCE, ANNULMENT OR LEGAL SEPARATION

There are two issues to be examined in this context: the effect of a foreign divorce, annulment or legal separation on a pre-existing English order for financial relief, and the powers of the English court to grant such relief notwithstanding a prior foreign divorce, etc.

(a) EFFECT OF FOREIGN DIVORCE, ETC ON FINANCIAL RELIEF ALREADY GRANTED IN ENGLAND

Under English domestic law, a maintenance order granted by a magistrates' court may be continued in the discretion of the magistrates even after the marriage has been dissolved in England.[8] The Court of Appeal has decided that the position is the same if the marriage is dissolved by a foreign divorce

---

22 Supra, p 704.
 1 Art 57 of the Lugano Convention is to similar effect. See supra, pp 286, 341, 415, 443–444.
 2 Supra, p 704.
 3 Denmark, France, Germany, Italy, Luxembourg, the Netherlands, Portugal and Spain.
 4 SI 1979/1317, supra, p 704.
 5 Finland, Norway, Sweden and Switzerland.
 6 Matrimonial Causes Act 1973, s 27(2), supra, pp 701–702.
 7 Supra, pp 702–703.
 8 *Bragg v Bragg* [1925] P 20; and see Matrimonial Causes Act 1973, s 28; Domestic Proceedings and Magistrates' Courts Act 1978, s 4.

recognised in England;[9] and the same principle has been applied to an interim order for maintenance made by a divorce county court, notwithstanding a later foreign divorce recognised here.[10] The English court retains its discretion to continue, vary or discharge the English maintenance order, but the changed marital circumstances of the parties may well affect their financial position and the view taken thereof by the court, as where dower became payable on the termination of a marriage by *talak*.[11]

(b) POWERS OF ENGLISH COURT TO GRANT FINANCIAL RELIEF DESPITE AN EARLIER FOREIGN DIVORCE, ANNULMENT OR LEGAL SEPARATION

(i) The common law position

Until Part III of the Matrimonial and Family Proceedings Act 1984 came into force on September 16 1985, the general rule was that, once a marriage had been dissolved or annulled, the English court's power to grant financial relief came to an end.[12] No ancillary relief could be granted on the basis of a foreign divorce. The more liberal the English rules for the recognition of foreign divorces, etc the greater the problem for spouses who wished to seek financial relief in England.[13] Various devices were utilised by the courts to minimise the difficulties of those who sought financial relief in England, such as expediting English proceedings if there were parallel foreign ones,[14] or granting relief in favour of a child though none could be granted to a parent.[15] Useful though these devices were, the law was undoubtedly unsatisfactory in that, if the foreign proceedings had included no, or inadequate, financial provision for an English spouse, usually the wife, she could find herself destitute in this country with social security as her only source of financial support. This could be so even though her husband lived in England and had substantial assets here. Furthermore, the inability of the English courts to grant relief if a foreign divorce was recognised here led regularly to challenges to the validity of such divorces for recognition purposes. This problem[16] led to proposals for reform being made by the Law Commission[17] which were carried into effect by Part III of the Matrimonial and Family Proceedings Act 1984, which applies whether the foreign divorce was obtained before or after Part III came into effect.[18]

(ii) Part III of the Matrimonial and Family Proceedings Act 1984[19]

In considering the powers of the English court[20] to grant matrimonial relief after a foreign divorce, etc, it is necessary to consider the orders which the

9 *Wood v Wood* [1957] P 254, [1957] 2 All ER 14.
10 *Newmarch v Newmarch* [1978] Fam 79, [1978] 1 All ER 1.
11 *Qureshi v Qureshi* [1972] Fam 173 at 200–201.
12 *Moore v Bull* [1891] P 279.
13 Eg *Turczak v Turczak* [1970] P 198, [1969] 3 All ER 317.
14 Eg *Torok v Torok* [1973] 3 All ER 101, [1973] 1 WLR 1066; *Bryant v Bryant* (1980) 11 Fam Law 85.
15 Under what is now s 23(3) of the Matrimonial Causes Act 1973. See *P (LE) v P (JM)* [1971] P 318, [1971] 2 All ER 728; *Hack v Hack* (1976) 6 Fam Law 177.
16 Exemplified by *Quazi v Quazi* [1980] AC 744, [1979] 3 All ER 897.
17 Law Com No 117 (1982).
18 *Chebaro v Chebaro* [1987] Fam 127.
19 See Family Proceedings Rules, 1991, rr 3.17–3.19; and see Gordon, *Foreign Divorces: English Law and Practice*, ch 11.
20 Part IV of the 1984 Act confers similar, but more limited, powers on the Scottish courts, following the report of the Scottish Law Commission in Scot Law Com No 72 (1982).

court may make, the bases of jurisdiction available for the making of such orders and certain limitations or controls on the courts' powers.

(a) Orders which the court can make The powers conferred by Part III of the 1984 Act apply to the High Court, and certain divorce county courts, but not to magistrates' courts. The general approach is that the court can make any of the orders which it could make on granting an English decree of divorce, annulment or judicial separation,[1] including consent orders, orders for the transfer of tenancies[2] and orders relating to children.[3] So, notwithstanding a foreign divorce, the English court will, for example, be able to make periodical payments orders, lump sum orders, and property adjustment orders. In deciding whether to make any of the orders which it could make on granting a decree, the court must have regard to a range of matters[4] which are essentially the same as if it was granting a decree itself.[5] In addition, section 18(6) provides as follows:

> Where an order has been made by a court outside England and Wales for the making of payments or the transfer of property by a party to the marriage, the court in considering in accordance with this section the financial resources of the other party to the marriage or a child of the family shall have regard to the extent to which that order has been complied with or is likely to be complied with.

The purpose of this provision is to enable the court to take account of any foreign order which has been made and of its likely effectiveness. Furthermore, the English court is free, if it thinks it appropriate, to make an order in relation to matrimonial assets which are abroad, just as would seem to be the case in normal English matrimonial proceedings.[6]

(b) Jurisdiction of the English courts There are three main bases of jurisdiction laid down by section 15(1) of the 1984 Act. They are similar to, but not identical with, the bases of jurisdiction on which the English courts may grant a decree of divorce, nullity or judicial separation.[7] The three bases are as follows:

(a) the domicil in England and Wales of either party to the marriage. This can be at one of two dates—either the start of the English proceedings for relief[8] or the date when the foreign divorce, etc took effect in the foreign country;[9]

(b) the habitual residence in England and Wales of either party to the marriage for one year ending on either of the two dates relevant to

---

1 Supra, pp 700–701.
2 Ss 17, 19, 21–22. There are also provisions similar to those in the Matrimonial Causes Act 1973 for avoiding transactions designed to defeat applications for financial relief (s 23) and, for preventing transactions intended to defeat prospective applications (s 24). The court's powers are limited to orders relating to the matrimonial home (s 20) when jurisdiction is taken solely on the basis of the presence of that home in England, infra, p 711.
3 Children Act 1989, s 8(4)(g).
4 S 18.
5 See Matrimonial Causes Act 1973, ss 25, 25A.
6 *Razelos v Razelos (No 2)* [1970] 1 WLR 392 at 400–401; and see *Hunter v Hunter* [1962] P 1, [1961] 2 All ER 121; *Tallack v Tallack* [1927] P 211; *Hamlin v Hamlin* [1986] Fam 11, [1985] 2 All ER 1037.
7 Supra, pp 630–633.
8 Technically, the date of the application for leave, under s 13 of the 1984 Act, infra, pp 712–713.
9 For detailed discussion of the reasons for selecting these alternative dates see Law Commission Working Paper No 77 (1980), paras 33–38.

domicil, ie the date of the English proceedings or that on which the foreign divorce became effective;

(c) either or both of the parties to the marriage had at the date of the English proceedings a beneficial interest in possession in a dwelling-house[10] in England and Wales which was at some time during the marriage a matrimonial home of the parties to the marriage.

In the view of the Law Commission, the use of the same jurisdictional criteria of domicil and habitual residence as apply to divorce petitions strikes the proper balance of formulating "jurisdictional rules strict enough to prevent persons, whose marriage is insufficiently connected with this country to make it appropriate for the English court to adjudicate on financial matters, from invoking the court's powers; but not so strict as to exclude meritorious cases".[11] The third head of jurisdiction, that there had been a matrimonial home in England, might be thought to cause more problems in terms of striking the correct balance and, indeed, was provisionally rejected by the Law Commission at one stage.[12] However, such a head of jurisdiction was felt necessary[13] in order to give the court power to deal with the quite common situation where the parties, though living abroad at the date of the divorce, had lived here previously and where their only substantial asset is the former matrimonial home. The danger perceived by the Law Commission[14] that the matrimonial home head of jurisdiction could be too wide, in giving the court power to make orders in relation to all the property of persons who had left England long ago, is met by limiting the orders which the court may make, when exercising this head of jurisdiction alone, to orders relating to the former matrimonial home.[15]

Provision is also made in Part III of the Matrimonial and Family Proceedings Act 1984 to dovetail these new rules of jurisdiction into the structure of the Civil Jurisdiction and Judgments Act 1982, as now amended by the Civil Jurisdiction and Judgments Act 1991. It will be recalled[16] that the 1982 and 1991 Acts extend the jurisdiction to grant maintenance orders, that no definition of maintenance orders is to be found in those Acts or the Conventions scheduled to them, and that it is possible that the European Court of Justice in a case falling under the Brussels Convention and the 1982 Act might decide that an order made under Part III of the 1984 Act is not within that Convention because it is first granted after the spouses' marriage has come to an end. Nevertheless, this possibility cannot be relied on; though, even if the Conventions are applicable, they will not apply to those orders under the 1984 Act which concern "rights in property arising out of a matrimonial relationship".[17] In order to deal with the possibility of clashes between the jurisdictional rules of the 1982 Act, as now amended by the 1991 Act, and of the 1984 Act, section 15(2) of the 1984 Act provides that in any

10 Defined in s 27 in terms identical to those in the Matrimonial Homes Act 1983, s 10(1).
11 Law Commission Working Paper No 77 (1980), para 31, and see Law Com No 117 (1982), paras 2.7–2.8.
12 Ibid, para 44.
13 Law Com No 117 (1982), paras 2.8–2.9.
14 Ibid, para 2.10.
15 1984 Act, s 20; and there is in such cases no power to make interim maintenance orders under s 14.
16 Supra, pp 704–707.
17 Art 1(1). The meaning of this exclusion from the scope of the Convention is not clear, see supra, pp 288–289.

case, jurisdiction over which falls to be governed by the 1982 and 1991 Acts, the English court cannot take jurisdiction if the provisions of those Acts are not satisfied even if those of the 1984 Act are; and, conversely, must take jurisdiction if the provisions of the 1982 and 1991 Acts are satisfied, even if those of the 1984 Act are not. Assuming that some orders, at least, made under Part III of the 1984 Act fall within the 1982 and 1991 Acts, the latter Acts apply in all cases where a defendant is domiciled in a country which is a Contracting State to the Brussels Convention or to the Lugano Convention,[18] and in such cases the court of the defendant's domicil will have jurisdiction[19], as will that where the "maintenance creditor" is domiciled or habitually resident.[20] Where the maintenance order is ancillary to divorce or similar proceedings, the court which has jurisdiction over those proceedings may also make a maintenance order.[1] An example might help to illustrate the inter-relation of the two sets of jurisdictional provisions. Assume the parties to the former marriage are now both domiciled and habitually resident in France, the former matrimonial home being in England. Despite section 15(1)(c) of the 1984 Act, the English courts cannot take jurisdiction to make orders in relation to the matrimonial home, because the 1982 Act confers jurisdiction on the French courts. Conversely, if the former spouses are domiciled and habitually resident in France (where the former matrimonial home is) at all relevant times, the English court will still retain jurisdiction if, at the time of the proceedings under the 1984 Act, either party is domiciled in England using the special concept of domicil provided for the purposes of the 1982 Act.[2]

(c) "Filter" mechanisms In making proposals for giving the courts power to make financial relief orders after foreign divorces, etc the Law Commission was much concerned that the relief should be "confined to those cases in which it is appropriate for the English court to intervene".[3] In addition to rules as to jurisdiction, Part III of the 1984 Act contains two further means for limiting relief to appropriate cases. The first is a filter mechanism for applications to the court. Under section 13 of the 1984 Act no application for a financial relief order can be made unless the leave of the court has been obtained, and "the court shall not grant leave unless it considers that there is substantial ground for the making of an application";[4] but the existence of a foreign financial provision order is no bar as such to the English application.[5] This is because the foreign order may be inadequate or inappropriate. Furthermore, leave may be granted subject to conditions,[6] such as an undertaking not to enforce a foreign order. If, however, the court con-

---

18 Art 2 of both the Brussels and Lugano Conventions.
19 By reason of the amendments to the 1982 Act made by the 1991 Act.
20 Art 5(2) of both Conventions.
1 Ibid. Arts 16–18 of the two Conventions also provide certain exclusive grounds of jurisdiction, and for jurisdiction to be conferred by submission, see supra, pp 309–324.
2 S 41, supra, pp 284–285. There is no provision in the 1984 Act for the allocation of jurisdiction to different parts of the United Kingdom, as there is in Part II of the 1982 Act. This suggests that if, for example, the respondent is domiciled anywhere in the United Kingdom for the purposes of the 1982 Act, the English court will have jurisdiction to make orders under Part III of the 1984 Act.
3 Law Com No 117 (1982), para 2.1.
4 And it is necessary for the applicant to place all the material facts before the court: *W v W* [1989] 1 FLR 22.
5 S 13(2).
6 S 13(3).

cludes that it would not be appropriate (under the second filter mechanism) for an order to be made, it should refuse leave.[7]

The second control or filter mechanism operates at the time of the actual hearing of the application, ie once leave to apply has been given[8] and even if the jurisdictional rules are satisfied. Under section 16 the court has to be satisfied that in all the circumstances of the case it is appropriate for a court in England and Wales to make the order and the court is directed to consider a wide range of matters in determining the appropriateness of the venue. These include[9] the connection of the parties with England, with the country where the divorce was obtained or with any other country, the relief ordered in a foreign country and the likely effectiveness of that order, whether there is a right to apply for relief abroad, and the likelihood of any order made under Part III of the 1984 Act being enforceable. In determining the appropriateness of the English court granting relief, the court will have regard, where there are proceedings in a foreign country, to the general law relating to the doctrine of *forum non conveniens*.[10]

(d) Other matters Part III of the 1984 Act gives the English court power to make orders for financial relief not only when a foreign divorce is recognised here, but also when a foreign annulment or legal separation is recognised.[11] The case for having the same powers in the case of divorce and annulment is strong. In both cases the marriage is at an end[12] and the rules for the recognition of foreign divorces and annulments are now the same.[13] They are also the same in the case of legal separations but in that case the marriage still subsists and there would be no bar to taking divorce proceedings in England and there seeking the usual ancillary relief.[14] If, however, it was not wished to seek divorce, proceedings could be brought on the ground of failure to provide maintenance.[15] The powers of the English court are less extensive in such a case than those provided in Part III of the 1984 Act, and so it was felt desirable[16] to make the latter powers available also in the case of legal separations.

The powers of the court under Part III of the 1984 Act depend not only on there having been a foreign divorce, annulment or legal separation but also on its being entitled to be recognised in England.[17] However, the powers are limited to divorces, etc obtained in an "overseas country" which is defined as one outside the British Isles.[18] This means that the English court has no power to make an order under Part III following, for example, a Scottish divorce or Northern Ireland annulment. It was thought more appropriate and not too inconvenient in such a case for the party seeking relief to return

7 *Holmes v Holmes* [1989] Fam 47, [1989] 3 All ER 786, CA.
8 The court has power to make interim orders between the granting of leave to apply and the full hearing of the application: ss 14, 21.
9 S 16(2).
10 *Holmes v Holmes*, supra; and see supra, pp 221 et seq.
11 S 12(1).
12 If a party remarries, then he or she loses the right to apply for relief under the 1984 Act: s 12(2), (3).
13 Family Law Act 1986, Part II, supra, pp 655 et seq.
14 *Sabbagh v Sabbagh* [1985] FLR 29.
15 Matrimonial Causes Act 1973, s 27; supra, pp 701–702.
16 See Law Commission Working Paper No 77 (1980), para 64.
17 S 12(1)(b); and see Law Commission Working Paper No 77 (1980), para 59. The rules for recognition are discussed supra, pp 655 et seq.
18 S 27.

to the court which granted the original decree.[19] Furthermore, the powers are limited to divorces obtained "by means of judicial or other proceedings",[20] thus excluding informal divorces despite the fact that, if obtained in the country of the domicil, they will be recognised here.[21]

3. CHOICE OF LAW

This is little doubt that, when an English court is considering an application for maintenance or similar relief, it applies English domestic law, irrespective of the domicil of the parties or any other factors connecting them with some other jurisdiction.[22] However, in cases to which the Maintenance Orders (Facilities for Enforcement) Act 1920 or the Maintenance Orders (Reciprocal Enforcement) Act 1972 apply, there may be a limited number of circumstances where foreign law is relevant by reason of the reciprocal provisions.[1]

4. RECOGNITION AND ENFORCEMENT OF FOREIGN ORDERS

All forms of financial relief, such as orders for periodical payments, the payment of lump sums or maintenance orders granted by a foreign court may be regarded as foreign judgments in personam.[2] Usually, the foreign court has a power to vary the amounts of such payments, in which event the order will not be recognised in England as it is not "final or conclusive".[3] Where the power to vary is prospective only, then any arrears of past payments may be recovered in England.[4] This is an atypical situation and the rules for the recognition and enforcement of foreign orders have not been left to the common law but are essentially statutory in formulation.

(a) RELIEF ANCILLARY TO A FOREIGN DIVORCE, ANNULMENT OR LEGAL SEPARATION

The main statutory provision in this area is negative in effect, for the Family Law Act 1986 provides that nothing in that Act shall be construed as requiring the recognition of any maintenance, custody or other ancillary order made in any foreign proceedings for divorce, annulment or legal separation.[5] In such cases, recognition depends on the common law rules for the recognition of foreign judgments,[6] unless covered by any of the statutory provisions considered below. Recognition of a foreign maintenance order ancillary to a foreign divorce, etc will be denied recognition in England if the English court,

19 Law Commission Working Paper No 77 (1980), paras 65–66.
20 S 12(1)(a).
21 Supra, pp 673–675.
22 Eg *Sealey v Callan* [1953] P 135, [1953] 1 All ER 942; and see Law Commission Working Paper No 77 (1980), para 56.
1 See Dicey & Morris, Fourth Cumulative Supp, pp 155–156.
2 Discussed supra, pp 348 et seq, and see especially the critical discussion of *Phillips v Batho* [1913] 3 KB 25, supra, pp 362–363. See McClean, *Recognition of Family Judgments in the Commonwealth* (1983), ch 4.
3 Supra, pp 365 et seq.
4 *Beatty v Beatty* [1924] 1 KB 807; and see *G v G* [1984] IR 368; *Sachs v Standard Chartered Bank (Ireland) Ltd* [1987] ILRM 297.
5 S 51(5).
6 Supra, pp 348 et seq.

under its rules for the recognition of foreign divorces, etc, considers the foreign court to have lacked jurisdiction.[7] For "if the main order goes, then any order which is merely ancillary to that order should go with it".[8]

(b) MAINTENANCE ORDERS MADE ELSEWHERE IN THE UNITED KINGDOM

A maintenance order made elsewhere in the United Kingdom may, under Part II of the Maintenance Orders Act 1950,[9] be registered in an English court if the person liable to make the payments resides here and it is regarded as convenient that the order should be enforceable here.[10]

This procedure applies to a wide range of orders, including those for periodical payments ancillary to decrees of divorce, nullity or judicial separation, or for failure to provide reasonable maintenance, and orders for maintenance or other financial provision made by magistrates' courts.[11] Registration is in the discretion of the court making the original order and not the court which is asked to register it, as is also normally the case with variation or discharge of a registered order; but once registered, the order may be enforced as if an order of the registering court.[12]

(c) RECOGNITION UNDER THE MAINTENANCE ORDERS (FACILITIES FOR ENFORCEMENT ACT) 1920

Under the Maintenance Orders (Facilities for Enforcement) Act 1920 it will be recalled[13] that provision is made for the reciprocal enforcement of maintenance orders between England and those Commonwealth countries to which the Act has been extended by Order in Council. The "shuttlecock" procedure applicable to English proceedings is equally applicable to foreign proceedings, so that if a provisional order is made in a Commonwealth country in the absence of the defendant, it may be confirmed by the English magistrates' court in the area where the defendant resides.[14] The defendant may raise any defence which he might have raised in the foreign proceedings and the English court has a discretion whether or not to confirm the foreign provisional order.

There are further reciprocal provisions in the 1920 Act whereby an English

7 *Simons v Simons* [1939] 1 KB 490, [1938] 4 All ER 436; and see *Papadopoulos v Papadopoulos* [1930] P 55.
8 *Simons v Simons*, supra, at p 499.
9 Such orders remain within the 1950 Act even though they cover matters considered to be "maintenance" within the Brussels Convention scheduled to the Civil Jurisdiction and Judgments Act 1982. This means that the 1950 Act and not the Convention applies to them: see 1982 Act, s 18(5)(a). The same is true of the Lugano Convention and the Civil Jurisdiction and Judgments Act 1991.
10 Such orders are brought within the provisions of the Maintenance Orders Act 1958 as to registration and enforcement by reason of the amendments to that Act contained in the Administration of Justice Act 1977, s 3, Sch 3; Civil Jurisdiction and Judgments Act 1982, Sch 11, para 2; and the Matrimonial and Family Proceedings Act 1984, s 46(1), Sch 1, paras 4 and 5.
11 Discussed, supra, pp 700–703.
12 Recognition of liability orders, made elsewhere in the United Kingdom under the Child Support Act 1991, is to be governed by regulations made by the Secretary of State: Child Support Act 1991, s 39. The jurisdiction of a child support officer to make an original maintenance assessment is based on the relevant person's habitual residence in the United Kingdom: 1991 Act, s 44.
13 Supra, p 703.
14 S 4 of the 1920 Act, amended by the Maintenance Enforcement Act 1991, Sch 1, para 1.

maintenance order may be registered in the Commonwealth country[15] or a Commonwealth order may be registered in England.[16] These provisions assume that the court making the original order had jurisdiction to make it but that there is difficulty in enforcing it in that jurisdiction, as where the defendant was resident in the Commonwealth country when the order was made, but is resident in England when enforcement is sought. If a certified copy of the maintenance order is sent from the Commonwealth court to the prescribed officers of the English court, registration is mandatory and the order has the same effect as if it was an English order, though there is no power to rescind or vary such an order.[17]

(d) RECOGNITION UNDER THE MAINTENANCE ORDERS (RECIPROCAL ENFORCEMENT) ACT 1972

There is reciprocal machinery, similar to that contained in the 1920 Act, for the recognition of maintenance orders made in any foreign reciprocating country.[18] A foreign provisional order made in the absence of the defendant may be sent to the English court within whose jurisdiction the defendant resides and that court has a discretion whether or not to confirm the order.[19] The defendant may raise any defences open to him in the original proceedings; but, once confirmed, the order is registered and has effect as if made by the English court. Normally, variation or revocation of such orders may be made by either the English or the foreign court.[20]

As with the 1920 Act, there is also provision for the registration of a foreign order in an English court[21] and vice versa.[1] Again, it is assumed that the original court had jurisdiction to make the order, but it is more convenient for it to be enforced in the other country. If a certified copy of a foreign order is sent to the prescribed officer of the magistrates' court where the defendant resides, registration is mandatory and the order has effect as if made by the English court.

We have seen[2] that section 40 of the 1972 Act allows Part I of the Act to be applied, by Order in Council, in amended form to specified countries. These amended versions extend to recognition as well as to jurisdiction.[3] The variations can be illustrated by the fact that, although registration (and thus recognition) of a certified foreign order is mandatory under the 1972 Act itself,[4] there are a number of grounds on which it can be refused under the version implementing the 1973 Hague Convention on the recognition of

---

15 S 1.
16 S 2.
17 *Pilcher v Pilcher* [1955] P 318, [1955] 2 All ER 644.
18 S 1.
19 S 5(5), including a foreign provisional order varying an original English order: *Horn v Horn* [1985] FLR 984.
20 Eg *Hinkley v Hinkley* (1984) 38 RFL (2d) 337.
21 S 6, as amended by the Civil Jurisdiction and Judgments Act 1982, Sch 11, para 10.
 1 S 2, as amended by the 1982 Act, Sch 11, para 9.
 2 Supra, p 704.
 3 The implementation of international Conventions under this power, as well as under Part II itself, is effective even if the other State is a Contracting State to the Brussels or Lugano Conventions, notwithstanding the Civil Jurisdiction and Judgments Acts 1982 and 1991; see the Brussels Convention Art 57 (as substituted by the 1989 Accession Convention) and the Lugano Convention, Art 57, and supra, p 708.
 4 S 6.

maintenance orders,[5] including that "registration is manifestly contrary to public policy."[6]

(e) RECOGNITION UNDER THE CIVIL JURISDICTION AND JUDGMENTS ACTS 1982 AND 1991

The general rules laid down in the Civil Jurisdiction and Judgments Acts 1982 and 1991 and the Brussels and Lugano Conventions for the recognition and enforcement in England of judgments obtained in other European Community or EFTA states which are Contracting States to those Conventions[7] extend to maintenance orders,[8] provided they fall within the meaning of "maintenance" under the Conventions.[9] So a maintenance order made elsewhere in such a European Community or EFTA Contracting State can be enforced in England if registered here under the 1982 or 1991 Acts.[10] The application for registration is sent to the magistrates' court in the place where the respondent is domiciled (in the sense used in the 1982 and 1991 Acts) and the decision on registration is taken by the prescribed officer of the court. Once it is registered, the order is treated for enforcement purposes as if it were an English order made by the court and the methods of enforcement are the same as for an English affiliation order.[11]

There are three particular issues which arise in connection with the recognition and enforcement of maintenance orders under the 1982 and 1991 Acts. The first arises from Article 27(4) of the Brussels and Lugano Conventions[12] which provides, in effect, that, if the court which made the order has decided a preliminary question as to the status or legal capacity of the parties, or as to rights in property arising out of a matrimonial relationship, in a way which conflicts with an English rule of private international law, the order is not to be recognised here; unless we would have reached the same result applying our rules of private international law. So, if a French court awards maintenance to a woman who is regarded as a "wife" under French law, but whose marriage is invalid according to our choice of law rules, the French maintenance order is not to be recognised or enforced in England.

The second issue concerns a particular example of a problem discussed earlier,[13] namely that of conflicting judgments covered by Article 27 (3) of the two Conventions. Maintenance orders fall within the Conventions but divorce decrees do not. If for example, therefore, the parties have been divorced in a European Community state where enforcement is sought of a

---

5 SI 1979/1317, para 6(6).
6 Ibid, para 6(6)(a); *Armitage v Nanchen* (1983) 4 FLR 293.
7 Supra, pp 411 et seq. The 1982 Act does not apply to the enforcement of a maintenance order made elsewhere in the United Kingdom (1982 Act, s 18(5)(a)). These continue to be governed by the Maintenance Orders Act 1950, supra, p 715.
8 Schlosser Report, pp 132, 134; and see 1982 Act, s 5.
9 Supra, pp 299–300, 705.
10 Art 31 of the two Conventions. For the detailed procedures for registration, see the 1982 Act, s 5; SI 1986/1962; Collins, *The Civil Jurisdiction and Judgments Act 1982*, p 124.
11 1982 Act, s 5(4)(b). Interest is payable on the order according to the law of the country making the order (s 7(1)) but, in the case of a maintenance order, only if the order is reregistered in the High Court under s 2A of the Maintenance Orders Act 1958 (1982 Act, s 7(4)). Sums payable in England under the foreign order are to be paid in sterling, converted as at the date of registration: 1982 Act, s 8.
12 Supra, p 432.
13 Supra, pp 430–431.

maintenance order granted in another European Community state, such enforcement may be refused under the Brussels Convention on the ground that the award of maintenance in the first state depends on the parties' still being married.[14] Whether, however, an English court could refuse enforcement in such a case is debatable, given the powers under Part III of the Matrimonial and Family Proceedings Act 1984 to award maintenance after divorce.[15]

The third issue concerns the inter-relation of the recognition and enforcement provisions of the 1982 and 1991 Acts with other legislation and conventions. It seems clear that, where there are conventions with States which are Contracting States to the Brussels or Lugano Conventions,[16] the procedures available thereunder are still available[17] and, indeed, that the maintenance creditor can choose whether to follow those procedures or the procedures of the 1982 or 1991 Acts.[18] However, where two conventions apply and they contain similar provisions, they are likely to be interpreted in the same way.[19]

---

14 Case 145/86 *Hoffmann v Krieg* [1988] ECR 645; *Macaulay v Macaulay* [1991] 1 All ER 865, [1991] 1 WLR 179.
15 Supra, pp 709–714.
16 As under the Maintenance Orders (Reciprocal Enforcement) Act 1972, supra, pp 703–704, 716–717.
17 1982 Act, Sch 1, Art 57; 1991 Act, Sch 1, Art 57.
18 *Macaulay v Macaulay* [1991] 1 All ER 865, [1991] 1 WLR 179; and see Anton, *Civil Jurisdiction in Scotland*, para 8.54.
19 *Macaulay v Macaulay*, supra.

Chapter 25

Children[1]

SUMMARY

1. INTRODUCTION

We are concerned in this chapter to look at the private international law rules regulating orders concerning children below the age of majority. The most important of these, so far as English law is concerned, are orders determining with whom a child shall live or with whom he may have contact;[2] but there are other significant orders to be examined, primarily those appointing a guardian for a child and also orders relating to children made under the inherent jurisdiction of the court in wardship proceedings. Although "custody" is a term which has now been abandoned by English domestic law, it remains of importance in defining the types of foreign orders and rights which may fall to be recognised and enforced in England.[3]

Until recently, many of the private international law rules in this field were provided by an unclear and inconsistent mixture of statutory provision and common law decisions.[4] Indeed the English jurisdictional rules to make orders concerning the welfare of children were a mixture of very broad and very narrow rules, statutes and common law, detail and vagueness, clarity and confusion, and the rules were, above all, bewilderingly complex.[5] By contrast, the rules for the recognition or enforcement of orders made outside England, whether elsewhere in the British Isles or overseas, were simple. Whilst such orders

1 See North (1990) I Hague Recueil 9, 127 et seq.
2 Under the Children Act 1989, s 8.
3 Infra, pp 731 et seq.
4 See Law Com No 138 (1985), Part II.
5 Ibid, paras 2.5–2.32, 2.48–2.52.

would be given "grave consideration"[6] in England, they had no direct effect here and their relevance lay only in assisting an English court in deciding whether to exercise its own discretion to make an order, and if so, to what effect.

It became increasingly to be realised that, in an age of great mobility, a situation in which there are no rules for the recognition of other countries' custody and similar orders, at least on a reciprocal basis, was capable of engendering great anguish for the parents and for children who might be shuttled from country to country. The legal position was in danger of verging on anarchy; and indeed, the Law Commission described the position as "a state of legal disorder".[7] It was the source of potential and, sometimes, actual conflict between the courts in England and Scotland, with each claiming jurisdiction, making conflicting orders and not recognising orders made in the other country.[8] On the broader international scene, child abduction by, or on behalf of, one parent often unsuccessful in custody proceedings became so serious an international issue that action at last was taken.

Action in this country has covered four main areas. First, the Child Abduction Act 1984[9] introduces new criminal offences governing the taking of a child under 16 out of the United Kingdom without consent. The statute covers abduction both by a parent and by others. Secondly, more effective powers have been given to the courts to order the disclosure of the whereabouts of a child, to order its recovery, to order the surrender of the child's passport and to prohibit the removal of the child from the United Kingdom;[10] and the administrative procedures to prevent children being removed by stopping them at airports or ports have been improved.[11]

These two types of development are, of course, of great practical importance but do not involve rules of private international law. The third and fourth areas of development are much more directly our concern. English courts now may have the duty under two international conventions, brought into effect by the Child Abduction and Custody Act 1985, to recognise custody rights arising under the law of, or orders made in, foreign countries which are parties to the relevant conventions. Furthermore, under Part I of the Family Law Act 1986,[12] English courts may be obliged to recognise and enforce such orders as are listed in section 1 of that Act (essentially orders relating to the custody, care or control of a child) and which are made elsewhere in the United Kingdom or the Isle of Man.[13] Orders falling under

6 *McKee v McKee* [1951] AC 352 at 365.
7 Law Com No 138 (1985), para 1.9.
8 Eg *Johnstone v Beattie* (1843) 10 Cl & Fin 42; *Babington v Babington* 1955 SC 115; *Hoy v Hoy* 1968 SC 179; though courts have tried more recently to avoid such conflicts: *Re H* [1965] 3 All ER 906, [1966] 1 WLR 381; *Re L* [1974] 1 All ER 913, [1974] 1 WLR 250; *Campbell v Campbell* 1977 SLT 125; *Thomson, Petitioner* 1980 SLT (Notes) 29; *Girven, Petitioner* 1985 SLT 92.
9 Amended by the Family Law Act 1986, s 65 and the Children Act 1989, Sch 12, paras 37–40, Sch 15. For evidence of its use, see [1991] Fam Law 202; and see *R v C (Kidnapping: Abduction)* [1991] 2 FLR 252.
10 Family Law Act 1986, ss 33–37; Children Act 1989, s 13; *Practice Direction (Disclosure of Addresses: 1989)* [1989] 1 WLR 219.
11 *Practice Direction (Minor: Preventing Removal Abroad)* [1986] 1 WLR 475.
12 References to the 1986 Act are to the Act as later amended, most significantly by the Children Act 1989, Schs 13, 15, and by SI 1991/1723.
13 The 1986 Act has been extended to the Isle of Man by SI 1991/1723 but for ease of exposition the term United Kingdom or reference to a part thereof will be used (inaccurately) in this chapter to include the Isle of Man and any other dependent territory to which the 1986 Act may be extended.

Part I of the 1986 Act are formally described as Part I orders.[14] This development is closely connected with the fourth one, the provision of coherent statutory jurisdictional rules for the making of such orders, which rules are essentially common throughout the United Kingdom. The Law Commission and the Scottish Law Commission, on whose recommendations[15] Part I of the 1986 Act is based, concluded that, if there was to be a scheme for intra-United Kingdom recognition of such orders, the acceptability of such a scheme would be advanced by there being uniform jurisdictional rules throughout the United Kingdom for the making of the orders—a step which would also provide the opportunity of curing the varied defects in the then existing English rules. The new jurisdictional rules are, however, limited to the making of such orders as are defined by section 1 of the Act (ie Part I orders). This leaves the jurisdictional rules for the making, for example, of guardianship orders to the separate systems within the United Kingdom and thus without any uniform approach to the matter of recognition.[16]

We must now turn to consider these new statutory rules governing the jurisdiction of the English courts, such common law jurisdictional rules as there are for the making of orders relating to guardianship and under the inherent, wardship jurisdiction, the relevant choice of law rules and, finally, the varied provisions for the recognition and enforcement of "custody" or "access" orders made elsewhere.

2. JURISDICTION: RESIDENCE, CONTACT, ETC ORDERS

(a) WHAT ARE RESIDENCE, CONTACT, ETC ORDERS?

The Children Act 1989 has introduced major changes in the law relating to children and, in particular, as to the orders which the court may make concerning them. Gone is the terminology of custody, guardianship, custodianship orders; indeed the wardship jurisdiction is now described as the inherent jurisdiction. Instead the court may make orders under section 8 of the Children Act 1989 which are contact, prohibited steps, residence or specific issue orders—generally described as "section 8 orders". The powers of the court to make such orders[1] may be exercised in a range of "family proceedings"[2] which include both proceedings under the statutory jurisdiction[3] and under the inherent jurisdiction of the High Court in relation to children.[4] The court also has power to make orders for the appointment of a guardian of a child[5] which, again, are regarded as orders made in family proceedings;[6] but they are not "section 8 orders" and jurisdiction over them and certain other orders made under the inherent jurisdiction must be considered separately.[7]

14 See Children Act 1989, Sch 13, para 62(2)(a).
15 Law Com No 138 (1985).
16 Infra, pp 728–730.
1 Under Children Act 1989, ss 9–11.
2 1989 Act, s 8(3).
3 Ibid, s 8(3)(b), (4); namely Matrimonial Causes Act 1973; Domestic Violence and Matrimonial Proceedings Act 1976; Adoption Act 1976; Domestic Proceedings and Magistrates' Courts Act 1978; Matrimonial Homes Act 1983, ss 1, 9; Matrimonial and Family Proceedings Act 1984, Part III; Children Act 1989, Parts I, II, IV.
4 Ibid, s 8(3)(a).
5 Ibid, ss 5, 6.
6 Because made under Part I of the 1989 Act.
7 Infra, pp 728–730.

Part I of the Family Law Act 1986[8] lays down the jurisdictional rules of the English courts to make what are now "section 8 orders" in relation to children under the age of eighteen.[9] The same jurisdictional rules also apply to an order made in the exercise of the inherent jurisdiction of the High Court with respect to a child "so far as it gives care of a child to any person or provides for contact with, or the education of, a child".[10] The exercise of the inherent jurisdiction to make such orders or "section 8 orders" is described as that of the High Court and would seem to be limited to that jurisdiction.[11]

(b) BASES OF JURISDICTION

(i) **Introduction**

The principles on which the jurisdictional rules under Part I of the Family Law Act 1986 are founded are these: that they should be uniform throughout the United Kingdom, be designed to reduce the likelihood of courts in more than one part of the United Kingdom having concurrent jurisdiction, normally result in the case being heard in the country with which the child has the closest long-term connection, and be clear and systematic.[12] These objectives are achieved in the following ways. First, there are essentially identical jurisdictional rules in Part I of the Family Law Act 1986 for England and Wales, Scotland, and Northern Ireland.[13] Secondly these rules in places interlock, with the result that a court in one country will usually not have jurisdiction if a court elsewhere does; and, thirdly, the rules are exclusive: Part I orders falling within the 1986 Act may only be made if the jurisdictional provisions of that Act are satisfied.[14]

In examining the jurisdictional rules for making Part I orders, it is necessary to look separately at the special rules for orders made in matrimonial proceedings, ie proceedings for divorce, nullity or judicial separation,[15] at the general rules for orders made in other proceedings, at special rules for proceedings under the inherent jurisdiction and, finally, at jurisdiction to vary Part I orders. Before looking at the details of the rules, it might help to consider the overall structure of the scheme. There is in essence a hierarchy of jurisdictional rules, designed to ensure that the courts of one country in the United Kingdom have priority, with the result that courts elsewhere in the United Kingdom with weaker jurisdictional links are unable to take

8   As amended by the Children Act 1989.
9   Family Law Act 1986, s 7(a); though under the Children Act 1989, s 9(7) such orders will only be made in relation to children of sixteen or over in exceptional cases.
10 1986 Act, s 1(1)(d), but excluding an order varying or revoking such an order; see *F v S (Wardship: Jurisdiction)* [1991] 2 FLR 349, [1991] Fam Law 312. The various orders relating to children falling within Part I of the 1986 Act are hereafter described as "Part I orders". The term will also include orders made by other courts in other parts of the United Kingdom, which orders also fall within Part I of the 1986 Act, given that the jurisdictional rules laid down therein are uniform throughout the United Kingdom, infra.
11 1989 Act, s 8(3) (a). The power to transfer family proceedings from the High Court to a county court, though it includes wardship proceedings, excludes applications for a child to be or cease to be a ward of court and "any proceedings which relate to the exercise of the inherent jurisdiction of the High Court with respect to minors": Matrimonial and Family Proceedings Act 1984, s 38(2)(b), as amended by the Children Act 1989, Sch 13, para 51.
12 Law Com No 138 (1985), para 3.10.
13 Chapters II, III and IV respectively of Part I. There is also power under s 43 of the 1986 Act to extend Part I by Order in Council to the rest of the British Isles and to any colony and, as has been seen, this has been done in the case of the Isle of Man: SI 1991/1723.
14 S 2.
15 1986 Act, s 7(b).

jurisdiction, thus avoiding the problem of conflicting orders in all save the most exceptional cases. The basic hierarchy is as follows: a court in which matrimonial proceedings are continuing has prime jurisdiction, followed in descending order by the courts of the country where the child is habitually resident or, lastly, is merely present.[16] The British nationality[17] or English domicil of the child do not confer jurisdiction on the courts.

(ii) Matrimonial proceedings

The English courts have power in proceedings under the Matrimonial Causes Act 1973 for divorce, nullity and judicial separation to make section 8 orders relating to children.[18] The jurisdictional basis for so doing is that the court has jurisdiction over the matrimonial proceedings, ie if either spouse was domiciled in, or had been habitually resident for one year in, England at the date of the commencement of the proceedings.[19] These rules remain essentially unaffected by the Family Law Act 1986;[20] but there are two respects in which the rules are dovetailed in with those applicable in the other parts of the United Kingdom. First, if the English proceedings are merely for judicial separation, the English court will lose its power to make a section 8 order therein if, after the granting of the decree of judicial separation and at the date of the application,[21] divorce or nullity proceedings are continuing in Scotland or Northern Ireland.[22] It seems only right that the court dealing with the continued existence of the marriage should assume the position of primacy. Secondly, an English court in which the appropriate matrimonial proceedings are continuing may conclude that it is more appropriate for an application for a Part I or similar[23] order to be determined in another country, whether elsewhere in the United Kingdom or abroad. In that event it may direct that no section 8 order be made by an English court in those matrimonial proceedings.[24] The need for this provision is caused by the fact that matrimonial proceedings once begun, and not dismissed, may continue indefinitely[1] even though, for instance, a divorce has been granted. This could have the result that the English divorce court retained its prime jurisdiction to make a section 8 order long after all the parties had ceased to have a close, or any, connection with England. A power to decline jurisdiction where appropriate seemed desirable.[2]

16 There is also a power, which does not conform with this hierarchy, to make an emergency order relating to a child, under the inherent jurisdiction of the court (as defined by the 1986 Act, s 1(1)(d)): 1986 Act, s 2(3)(b), infra, p 725.
17 See Law Com No 138 (1985), paras 4.41–4.47.
18 Children Act 1989, s 8; see *T v T (Custody: Jurisdiction)* [1992] 1 FLR 43.
19 Domicile and Matrimonial Proceedings Act 1973, s 5, supra, pp 630–633. It is irrelevant that the jurisdictional link ceases to exist during the course of the proceedings.
20 Ss 2(1), 2A. It is necessary that the matrimonial proceedings are still continuing or, if the proceedings have been dismissed, that the section 8 order was applied for before they were, or is being made forthwith: s 2A(1).
21 Or when the court is considering making the order if no application is made: 1986 Act, s7(c).
22 S 2A(1)(2). By reason of s 2A(3), the English court would not lose its jurisdiction if a court in another part of the United Kingdom had declined jurisdiction or stayed the proceedings before it, on the ground that it was more appropriate that an application for a Part I order be made in a court elsewhere.
23 See s 42(7)(b).
24 S 2A(4) It can always reinstate the basis of jurisdiction by revoking such direction.
1 English proceedings are treated by s 42(2) of the 1986 Act as continuing until the child is 18.
2 Law Com No 138 (1985), para 4.97.

(iii) Other proceedings

Habitual residence There are two main bases of jurisdiction to make Part I orders in proceedings, other than matrimonial proceedings—the habitual residence and the presence of the child in England.[3] Habitual residence is now a widely accepted connecting factor for matrimonial jurisdiction[4] and it is worth noting that, unlike divorce jurisdiction, no period of habitual residence is specified. This is hardly surprising, given that Part I orders may be made in relation to very young children. Although, as is usual, the habitual residence in England of the child has to be determined as at the date of the application for the Part I order,[5] there is a danger that one parent, by taking the child to another jurisdiction, often wrongfully, could change his habitual residence and thus deprive the English court of its jurisdictional power to make a Part I order. To combat this, the 1986 Act[6] provides that, if a child under 16 who is habitually resident in England is removed from or leaves England[7] and goes to another country either in contravention of an English court order or without the consent of anyone having the right to determine where he resides,[8] then if he becomes habitually resident in that other country, he is still treated as continuing to be habitually resident in England for a year from the date he left, or until he becomes 16 or there is agreement to his living elsewhere.[9]

Presence The second basis of jurisdiction is the presence of the child in England at the date of the application for the Part I order.[10] Presence is a basis of the inherent jurisdiction,[11] and its retention as the residual basis of jurisdiction was thought desirable in order to ensure that a range of appropriate cases could be entertained by courts here. For example, if a child habitually resident abroad is brought here against the wishes of the person entitled to exercise parental responsibilities in relation to the child[12] in the country of habitual residence, that person would be deprived of any effective remedy[13] unless the English court took jurisdiction on the basis of the presence of the child here.[14]

The presence basis of jurisdiction was described above as "residual" and it is only available if no court elsewhere in the United Kingdom can exercise jurisdiction. So, an English court cannot exercise jurisdiction to make a Part I order in the case of a child present here[15] if it is habitually resident in another part of the United Kingdom.[16] It is more appropriate that the proceedings should take place in that other part.

3 1986 Act, ss 2(2), (3), 3.
4 Supra, pp 169–171, 631–632.
5 S 7(c). If no application is made, the date is that when the court is considering making the order. It is irrelevant that the jurisdictional link is later broken.
6 S 41; cf *Scullion v. Scullion* [1990] SCLR 577.
7 S 41 also covers the case where the child was temporarily out of England, for example, on holiday or at school, and is not returned when he should have been.
8 But this excludes an unmarried father with no right to determine the child's residence: *F v S (Wardship: Jurisdiction)* [1991] 2 FLR 349, [1991] Fam Law 312.
9 Provided in this last case, there has been no contravention of a court order.
10 Ss 2(2), (3), 3. As to the relevant date, see s 7(c), supra, n 5.
11 Infra, pp 728–730.
12 Cf Children Act 1989, ss 2, 3.
13 Unless the child could be returned under the provisions of the Child Abduction and Custody Act 1985, infra, pp 733–734.
14 For other examples, see Law Com No 138 (1985), para 4.25.
15 Except in emergency proceedings under the inherent jurisdiction, infra, p 725.
16 1986 Act, s 3(1)(b).

Matrimonial proceedings elsewhere in the United Kingdom If matrimonial proceedings for divorce, nullity or judicial separation are continuing elsewhere in the United Kingdom, then the English court must not exercise jurisdiction to make a Part I order despite the habitual residence or presence of the child in England.[17] English jurisdiction must yield to the primacy of the country of the matrimonial proceedings, unless and so long as the courts in Scotland or Northern Ireland have directed that no Part I order be made in those proceedings, or have stayed the proceedings for a Part I order, because it would be more appropriate for the Part I proceedings to be entertained in England.[18]

(iv) Emergency jurisdiction

Whilst there is much to be said for a carefully constructed, interlocking set of jurisdictional rules within the United Kingdom, there is a danger that a hierarchy of jurisdictions may provide too cumbersome a set of rules to deal with those cases, not infrequent, where courts are called upon to act very quickly in matters concerning the welfare of children. To deal with this difficulty, section 2(3)(b) of the 1986 Act confers an emergency basis of jurisdiction on a court to make an order in exercise of the inherent jurisdiction of the High Court with regard to children,[19] "if the child concerned is present in England and Wales on the relevant date and the court considers that the immediate exercise of its powers is necessary for his protection". As the Law Commission said: "Where a child is in immediate danger, his protection must take precedence over procedural considerations."[20] The effect of section 2(3)(b) is to allow the inherent jurisdiction of the High Court to be exercised to make such "emergency orders" even though the child is habitually resident elsewhere in the United Kingdom, or divorce, etc proceedings between its parents are continuing in Scotland or Northern Ireland. However, the English "emergency order" can be superseded at any time by the order of a court in the country with primacy of jurisdiction.

(c) VARIATION AND DURATION

(i) Variation

One characteristic of orders relating to the welfare of children is that parents may well return to the courts to claim that their circumstances, or those of the child, have changed and to seek the variation of the order. Such applications inevitably pose jurisdictional problems. Should the court which made the original order retain jurisdiction to vary it, even though in the meantime its jurisdictional link with the child has been broken?[21] The general approach of Part I of the 1986 Act is that the power to vary[1] continues despite the loss of jurisdiction. There are, however, two different cases to consider. The first is where the English jurisdictional link is broken but no new link exists with another part of the United Kingdom, and the second is where such a new link does exist.

In the first case, the power to vary continues unaffected by the break in

17 S 3(2).
18 S 3(3).
19 Within the limits set by the 1986 Act, s 1(1)(d).
20 Law Com No 138 (1985), para 4.19.
21 The answer in the past was unclear; see Law Com No 138 (1985), para 2.33.
 1 As to what constitutes a variation, see the 1986 Act, ss 1(2), 42(5), (6).

the jurisdictional link. In the second case, if the English section 8 order was made in matrimonial proceedings, then that basis of jurisdiction in fact continues unaffected in principle by the fact, for example, that the child later acquires an habitual residence in Scotland. There are just two qualifications to this. First, an English court will lose its jurisdiction to vary a section 8 order made in matrimonial proceedings if it was made in such proceedings which are no longer continuing, or in judicial separation proceedings which are still continuing but where a decree has been granted.[2] If the original English order was made in proceedings other than matrimonial proceedings, jurisdiction to vary it will continue despite the loss of the English jurisdictional connection and the establishment of one elsewhere in the United Kingdom unless that new link is based on matrimonial proceedings. So if an order is made in England in relation to a child who is present here, it can be varied even though the child later acquires an habitual residence in Scotland. If, however, the parents start divorce proceedings in Scotland, the English power to vary is lost.[3]

(ii) Duration

In the discussion so far of variation, it has been assumed that a court elsewhere in the United Kingdom, though it may have acquired jurisdiction to do so, has not yet made an order. What if it has made an order? How does this affect the jurisdiction of the English court to vary the earlier order? We shall see later[4] that a subsequent order made elsewhere in the United Kingdom will be entitled to recognition and enforcement in England. A corollary of that is that the English order, in so far as it deals with the same matters, ceases to have effect once the other later order comes into force,[5] and the power to vary the English order is thereupon lost.[6]

(d)   WAIVER, STAY AND REFUSAL OF APPLICATION

The two main principles underlying the jurisdictional rules—a clear hierarchy of jurisdictional rules coupled with a desire that an application for an order relating to the welfare of a child is to be heard by the court with the most appropriate links with the issue—are bound at times to come into conflict. The system in the 1986 Act has three devices built into it to provide flexibility and to minimise such conflicts. The first concerns the matrimonial proceedings jurisdiction—the jurisdictional connection with primacy over the others. As we have seen,[7] the English court hearing matrimonial proceedings may waive its jurisdiction to make a section 8 order, whether or not any application has already been made for such an order in the divorce, etc proceedings. It will do so where it thinks it more appropriate for the pro-

---

2   1986 Act, s 6(3A). The English court will not lose its jurisdiction to vary if Part I proceedings before the other court have been stayed or if that court has directed that the Part I proceedings be taken in England: s 6(4).
3   S 6(3). The English court will not lose its power, in proceedings under the inherent jurisdiction, in an emergency to vary a Part I order relating to a child then present in England: ss 6(5), 7.
4   Infra, pp 731–733.
5   See *Re K (A Minor: Wardship: Jurisdiction: Interim Order)* [1991] 2 FLR 104, [1991] Fam Law 226; *T v T (Custody: Jurisdiction)* [1992] 1 FLR 43.
6   1986 Act, s 6(1), (2), (7), (8).
7   Supra, p 723.

ceedings to be determined outside England and Wales.[8] The effect of this will be to make available elsewhere in the United Kingdom the habitual residence or presence bases of jurisdiction, as the case may be; though the power of the English court to waive its jurisdiction is not limited to cases where there is a more appropriate court elsewhere in the United Kingdom.[9] The criterion for the court hearing matrimonial proceedings is "appropriateness". Although cases prior to the 1986 Act had rejected the doctrine of *forum non conveniens* in child custody cases,[10] it would appear that "appropriateness" is not directly concerned with the welfare of the child, but rather with the suitability of the court to entertain the proceedings.[11] This was certainly the view of the Law Commission who gave,[12] as an example of appropriate circumstances for a waiver of jurisdiction, the case where a divorce had been granted in England five years earlier, with no application for an order relating to a child, but where, at the time of the later application for such an order, the parents and the child were habitually resident in another country.[13]

The second element of flexibility is particularly relevant where there are two sets of proceedings continuing simultaneously, but no Part I order has been made in either. This could happen, for example, where proceedings are started in England for a Part I order, in relation to a child who is habitually resident here, followed by divorce proceedings in Northern Ireland where the father is habitually resident. In such a case, the English court has a power to stay its proceedings if it thinks it appropriate to do so.[14] If the circumstances were reversed so that the Northern Ireland divorce proceedings were first in time, the primacy of those proceedings would deprive the English court of jurisdiction.[15] Nevertheless, just as the Northern Ireland court can waive its jurisdiction in the first place,[16] so it can stay its proceedings,[17] thus allowing the English Part I order proceedings to start.[1] The power to stay also applies in the simpler case where, after the English proceedings were started, the jurisdictional link is broken but then there is no new link with another part of the United Kingdom, as where a child habitually resident in England at the start of the proceedings becomes habitually resident in Norway before a Part I order is made.

The third situation is concerned with the case where the issue in question has already been determined in proceedings elsewhere. This situation is separate from that of recognition of any other order. No matter where the other order has been made and irrespective of whether or not it may be recognised and enforced here, the English court may itself decline jurisdiction, on any basis, to make a Part I order.[2] The court is to be free to take the view

---

8 1986 Act, s 2A(4).
9 The power of the Scottish court is so limited: s 13(6).
10 Eg *Re R* (1981) 2 FLR 416.
11 And see *Spiliada Maritime Corpn v Cansulex Ltd* [1987] AC 460 at 474–475.
12 Law Com No 138 (1985), para 9.97.
13 It might also be noted that, in family law matters, there is an increasing willingness to rely on the general principles of *forum non conveniens, supra*, pp 221 et seq, 636–638.
14 S 5(2)(a); see, eg, *Hill v Hill* (OH) [1990] SCLR 238. It can also lift the stay as appropriate: s 5(3).
15 S 3(2).
16 S 21(5), the equivalent of s 2A(4), *supra*, p 723.
17 S 22(2)(b). The English equivalent is s 5(2)(b).
 1 S 3(3)(b).
 2 S 5(1). This may be very significant where the child has been "kidnapped" from another jurisdiction. The difficulties arising in such cases are discussed more fully, *infra*, p 742.

that it does not wish to interfere with a decision as to the child's welfare which has already been made.[3]

3. JURISDICTION: GUARDIANS, PARENTAL RESPONSIBILITY AND THE INHERENT JURISDICTION

Although residence, contact and other orders under section 8 of the Children Act 1989 are the most important and most common orders to be made in relation to children, there are three other forms of order of significance whose jurisdictional rules must be considered, namely orders appointing a person as a guardian, orders as to the welfare of a child made under the inherent jurisdiction of the High Court and orders that a father is to have parental responsibility for a child. We shall consider together the jurisdictional rules relating to the first two categories of orders.[4] The effect of orders appointing a person as guardian, ie to take parental responsibility[5] for a child,[6] goes further than matters covered by section 8 orders and, by extending to all matters of parental responsibility, includes for example the right to deal with the property of the child.[7] The second category is that of the inherent jurisdiction of the High Court, normally exercised through wardship proceedings,[8] where we have to distinguish between the jurisdictional rules for making orders under the inherent jurisdiction giving the care of a child to any person, or providing for contact with or the education of the child, which are governed by the Family Law Act 1986,[9] and the jurisdictional rules governing the exercise of the inherent jurisdiction making a child a ward of court. The difference is important because the High Court[10] may make orders under the inherent jurisdiction in wardship proceedings relating to matters other than the care of the child, such as orders as to his property;[11] and, indeed, the jurisdictional rules of the Family Law Act 1986 concerning orders as to the care of the child will only apply if the court had had jurisdiction to entertain the original wardship application.[12] Although a child becomes a ward of court on the making of the application,[13] the wardship lapses unless a wardship order is made within the prescribed period and no order as to the care of the child will be made if it is shown that the jurisdictional criteria were not satisfied.

What then are the relevant jurisdictional rules?[14] They are substantially governed by case law rather than by statute. We must examine first the

3 This general system of interlocking rules makes it very important for the court to be aware of other proceedings which relate to the child, whether in the United Kingdom or elsewhere, including administrative proceedings; see 1986 Act, ss 39, 42(7).
4 Orders relating to the maintenance of children have been considered, supra, pp 700 et seq.
5 Defined in the Children Act 1989, s 3.
6 Children Act 1989, s 5.
7 Ibid, s 3(1).
8 See Law Com No 138 (1985), para 1.25.
9 1986 Act, s 1(1)(d).
10 Wardship jurisdiction is limited to the High Court.
11 Lowe & White, *Wards of Court* 2nd edn (1986), p 126.
12 Because s 1(1)(d) refers to orders made in the exercise of the inherent jurisdiction, which latter must be validly established.
13 Law Reform (Miscellaneous Provisions) Act 1949, s 9(1); and he cannot then marry, or be taken out of the jurisdiction, subject to the Family Law Act 1986, s 38; and see Law Com No 138 (1985), para 1.26.
14 See Lowe & White, op cit, pp 17–28.

inherent jurisdiction of the High Court to make a child a ward of court which is founded on the prerogative power of the Crown acting in its capacity as *parens patriae* to do what is necessary for the welfare of children. It has long been held that this royal prerogative delegated to the courts should benefit those who owe allegiance to the Crown. It is, therefore, well established that the High Court may exercise this jurisdiction in respect of any British subject[15] under 18, even though he possesses no property in England and even if he is out of the country at the time of the proceedings.[1] Jurisdiction has also been extended to an alien child who, at the time of the proceedings, is either (i) physically present though not domiciled in England,[2] or (ii) is ordinarily resident, though not in fact present, in England.[3] In the case of a person too young to decide for himself where to live, his ordinary residence is the matrimonial home if his parents live together, but the home where he normally lives if they are separated.[4] Neither the English domicil of the child,[5] nor his possession of property[6] in England, suffice to found jurisdiction. In fact there is no reported case of jurisdiction being assumed over a child who was neither resident nor present in England.[7] In a case of "kidnapping",[8] the court would no doubt bear the same factors in mind, giving predominance to the welfare of the child,[9] as in considering an application for an order as to the care of a child.[10]

In the past, orders made by the High Court under the inherent jurisdiction in wardship proceedings have quite often been for the appointment of a guardian to a child.[11] This power is abolished by the Children Act 1989[12] which introduces both in its place and in place of the previous statutory rules[13] relating to the making of guardianship orders a new statutory regime for the appointment of a guardian under that Act.[14] This statutory power to appoint a guardian may be exercised by the High Court, a county court or a magistrates' court,[15] thus raising the question as to the jurisdictional rules applicable to these different courts. No provision is made in the 1989 Act to

15 Which would probably now mean a "British citizen" within the meaning of the British Nationality Act 1981.
1 *Hope v Hope* (1854) 4 De G M & G 328; *Re Willoughby* (1885) 30 ChD 324; *Harben v Harben* [1957] 1 All ER 379, [1957] 1 WLR 261; *Re P (GE)* [1965] Ch 568 at 582, 587, 592; *McM v C (No 2)* [1980] 1 NSWLR 27; *Romeyko v Whackett (No 2)* (1980) 25 SASR 531; *Brown v Kalal* (1986) 7 NSWLR 423; cf *McM v C* [1980] 1 NSWLR 1.
2 *Re D* [1943] Ch 305, [1943] 2 All ER 411; *Re P (GE)* [1965] Ch 568 at 582, 588, 592; *J v C* [1970] AC 668 at 700–701, 720; *Re A* [1970] Ch 665, [1970] 3 All ER 184.
3 *Re P (GE)* [1965] Ch 568 at 584–586; and see *Scheffer v Scheffer* [1967] NZLR 466; *Holden v Holden* [1968] VR 334; *Nielsen v Nielsen* (1970) 16 DLR (3d) 33; *Glasson v Scott* [1973] 1 NSWLR 689; *Re Allison* (1979) 96 DLR (3d) 342.
4 *Re P (GE)* [1965] Ch 568 at 585–586.
5 Ibid, at 583–584, 589–590, 592–593.
6 *Brown v Collins* (1883) 25 ChD 56.
7 See Law Com No 138 (1985), para 2.11.
8 See Lowe & White, *Wards of Court* 2nd edn (1986), ch 17.
9 Children Act 1989, s 1(1).
10 Infra, p 742; and see Lowe & White, op cit, pp 355–361.
11 Eg *Hope v Hope* (1854) 4 De G M & G 328; *Re Willoughby* (1885) 30 ChD 324.
12 S 5(13). The appointment of a guardian of the estate of a child may be made under the inherent jurisdiction, if so provided by rules of court: Children Act 1989, s 5(11), (12).
13 Eg the Guardianship of Minors Act 1971.
14 S 5.
15 Children Act 1989, s 92(7); subject to the Lord Chancellor making orders under Sch 11 of the 1989 Act as to the allocation of jurisdiction (s 92(6), (8)) and to limits on the jurisdiction of a magistrates' court to make orders concerning the property of a child (s 92(4)).

indicate what English links, if any, must be shown by the child or the applicant[16] for the order appointing a guardian. Furthermore, an order appointing a guardian, not being a Part I order, falls outside the jurisdictional rules contained in Part I of the Family Law Act 1986.[17] We are are cast back on common law rules. It was assumed, under the previous legislation, that the jurisdictional criteria for the High Court to make a guardianship order were the same as for making such orders under the inherent jurisdiction. That line cannot now be followed as the inherent jurisdiction to appoint guardians has, essentially, been abolished. Furthermore, no jurisdictional provision is made for the making by a county court or a magistrates' court of an order appointing a guardian.[18] It is a major defect of the Children Act 1989 that the creation of jurisdictional rules is left, in this context, to judicial development with no guidance offered as to the form such development should take.

A similar problem arises with the third category of order to be considered in this context. Under section 4 of the Children Act 1989,[19] a court may, in relation to a child whose parents are not married, make an order on the application of the father that he is to have parental responsibility[20] for the child. It is quite possible that a foreign father might seek an order in relation to a child in this country or indeed even possible that an English father might wish such an order to be made in relation to a child living abroad. However the 1989 Act provides no jurisdictional rules for the making of such orders and one can only surmise that appropriate rules will be developed judicially by analogy to those applicable to orders of guardianship and those made under the inherent jurisdiction.

4. CHOICE OF LAW

There seems little doubt that, when an English court takes jurisdiction to make orders with respect to children in family proceedings under the Children Act 1989 or under the inherent jurisdiction of the High Court, it will apply English law as the law of the forum. Indeed, the application of the law of the domicil to guardianship orders was rejected long ago.[1] The application of English law is reinforced by the requirement imposed on the court to regard the welfare of the child as the paramount consideration.[2]

---

16 The court also has power to appoint a guardian even though no application has been made; Children Act 1989, s 5(2).
17 This also means that such orders fall outside the rules for the recognition and enforcement of United Kingdom orders, infra, pp 731–733.
18 There was at least a provision in the Guardianship of Minors Act 1971, s 15(2A), (2B) making clear that a magistrates' court could make an order even though a party to the proceedings was resident abroad; reversing a common law rule to the contrary effect: *Collister v Collister* [1972] 1 WLR 54 at 59.
19 See s 4(1)(a).
20 Defined in s 3 of the 1989 Act.
 1 *Johnstone v Beattie* (1843) 10 Cl & Fin 42 at 114.
 2 Children Act 1989, s 1(1).

5. RECOGNITION AND ENFORCEMENT

(a) INTRODUCTION

The historic attitude of English courts to the recognition of orders relating to children, such as custody, guardianship and wardship orders, made in other countries has been simple. Though they might be given careful consideration by an English court in deciding whether and, if so, what order to make, they were never recognised as such. The reasons for this attitude were primarily[3] because the English courts are instructed to take the welfare of the minor as the paramount consideration,[4] and this could conflict with recognition of a foreign order; and because such orders relating to children are never final, being always subject to review by the court which made it.[5] This attitude contrasts strikingly with that, for example, in Canada, Australia and the USA, where there has for some time been legislation regulating the recognition of such foreign orders. The last few years have marked a significant change in the English attitude with new legislation governing the recognition and enforcement of orders falling under Part I of the Family Law Act 1986 and made elsewhere in the United Kingdom and with two international conventions, given the force of law here, which provide for the recognition of custody orders granted in, or custody rights under the law of, a number of foreign countries. The historic denial of recognition now only applies to orders granted in those countries not covered by the new legislation; though, even under the new legislation, the courts will have power to deny recognition.[6] These varied rules must be considered in turn.

(b) ORDERS GRANTED IN SCOTLAND AND NORTHERN IRELAND

In 1985 the Law Commissions recommended not only, as we have seen, that there should be uniform jurisdictional rules throughout the United Kingdom for the making of orders which were then described as "custody orders", but also as a corollary that such orders should be recognised and enforceable elsewhere in the United Kingdom. In this way, protracted, expensive and disruptive proceedings might be avoided. The Commissions said:

> In broad terms, our proposals are that the custody orders of the courts of each country [in the United Kingdom] should be recognised in the other countries but should only be enforceable if centrally registered in the courts of the receiving country and should only be enforced through the process of the receiving country.[7]

These proposals are carried into effect in that form by Part I of the Family Law Act 1986.[8]

The recognition and enforcement provisions of the 1986 Act apply to exactly the same range and type of orders, ie Part I orders, as do the jurisdictional provisions.[9] However, whilst the English jurisdictional provisions govern all Part I orders made in relation to children under the age of

3 See Law Com No 138 (1985), para 2.45.
4 Now embodied in the Children Act 1989, s 1(1).
5 *McKee v McKee* [1951] AC 352 at 364–365.
6 Infra, pp 736–737, 738–740.
7 Law Com No 138 (1985), para 3.19.
8 See Family Proceedings Rules 1991, Part VII, Ch. 3. There is power under s 43 of the 1986 Act to extend Part I of the Act by Order in Council to the rest of the British Isles and to any colony, and this power has been exercised, as has been seen, in relation to the Isle of Man: SI 1991/1723.
9 1986 Act, s 1, supra, pp 721–722.

18, the recognition and enforcement provisions are limited to orders applying to children under the age of 16, and they cease to have effect when the child reaches this age. There are various reasons for this difference:[10] Scottish orders can only be made up to the age of 16; the recent international conventions are limited to children under 16;[11] English orders in relation to 16 and 17 year olds are rare and their enforcement would be difficult against the wishes of the child.

All Part I orders made elsewhere in the United Kingdom[12] and still in force in relation to a child under 16 must be recognised in England;[13] and this will be of practical importance to third parties, such as social workers and school teachers, to know that rights conferred by, say, a Scottish order are to be recognised here. A Scottish or Northern Ireland order cannot, however, be enforced in England until it has been registered here,[14] and proceedings taken in England for its enforcement.[15] Registration is effected by applying to the court which made the order which, provided the order is still in force, passes a certified copy of the order and other relevant documents to the High Court[16] for registration.[17] If the order ceases to have effect, other than by revocation,[18] as where it is superseded by a later order, its registration will be cancelled by the English court.[19]

Once registered in England, the Scottish and Northern Ireland order can be enforced in exactly the same way as if it was an English Part I order.[20] However, enforcement proceedings may be stayed on the application of any interested party on the ground that he has taken or intends to take other proceedings, whether in the United Kingdom or elsewhere, as a result of which the order may cease to have effect or have a different effect.[1] So although the merits of the order cannot be attacked in the country of registration,[2] a parent might convince the English court that he was going to attack them before the Scottish court which made the order, or there argue that that court lacked jurisdiction, or, indeed, that he proposes to apply to another court for a new order. In all such cases, the English court has a discretion to stay the enforcement proceedings and, indeed, to lift any stay.[3] If the English court is satisfied that the original order, now registered in England, has ceased to have effect, it will dismiss the enforcement proceedings.[4]

10 Law Com No 138 (1985), para 1.22.
11 Infra, pp 734, 737.
12 Subject to transitional provisions in ss 1 (3), 32 and 40, this includes orders made before as well as after Part I of the 1986 Act came into effect.
13 1986 Act, s 25(1). No recognition is given to parts of the order which may relate to enforcement, such as a requirement to hand over the child at a particular time or place: s 25(2). This is so as to ensure that all matters of enforcement are in the hands of courts in the receiving country.
14 Ss 25(3), 27.
15 S 29. They will fail if, by then, the order has ceased to have effect where granted: *T v T (Custody: Jurisdiction)* [1992] 1 FLR 43.
16 S 32(1).
17 S 27.
18 If the order is cancelled, this is notified by the court which made the order: s 28(1).
19 S 28(2).
20 S 29; and see *Woodcock v Woodcock* 1990 SLT 848.
 1 S 30.
 2 It is suggested that the Court of Session was incorrect in *Woodcock v Woodcock* 1990 SLT 848 at 853 in indicating the contrary.
 3 S 30(3).
 4 S 31. It is relevant in the context of enforcement, as of jurisdiction, that the English court knows of similar proceedings elsewhere, including administrative proceedings, ss 39, 42(7).

Whilst it is to be hoped that the system for the recognition and enforcement throughout the United Kingdom of orders made in one part thereof will eradicate the conflicts which arose in the past, particularly between English and Scottish courts,[5] attention has to be drawn to the fact that the recognition and enforcement procedures apply only to orders falling under Part I of the 1986 Act. They do not apply, for example, to guardianship orders whose recognition and enforcement remain governed by common law rules.[6] There is, however, power under the Children Act 1989[7] for the Secretary of State to make regulations to give effect in Northern Ireland to prescribed orders made in England and falling under the Act, and vice versa.[8] Such regulations could cover guardianship orders.

(c) CHILD ABDUCTION AND CUSTODY ACT 1985[9]

The recognition, and thus enforceability, of custody orders obtained outside the United Kingdom falls into three categories, two governed by the Child Abduction and Custody Act 1985, and the third by the common law. We shall consider them in that order. The Child Abduction and Custody Act 1985[10] gives effect to two international conventions relating to the recognition of foreign custody rights and orders, both of which are scheduled to the Act and provides very similar mechanisms for their operation.[11] The first is the Hague Convention on the Civil Aspects of International Child Abduction (1980), to which 23 other countries are currently parties,[12] and which is implemented by Part I of the 1985 Act. The second is the European Convention on Recognition and Enforcement of Decisions concerning Custody of Children and on the Restoration of Custody of Children (1980)—the Council of Europe Convention. There are currently twelve other parties[13] to this Convention which is implemented by Part II of the 1985 Act.

(i) Part I of the 1985 Act: the Hague Convention[14]

The prime concern of the Hague Convention is the restoration of children who have been wrongfully removed, whether or not this is in breach of a custody order in one of the Contracting States.[15] So it goes wider than the recognition and enforcement of custody orders and protects rights to custody

---

5 Supra, p 720. Contrast the balanced approach under the 1986 Act as evidenced by *Re K (A Minor: Wardship)* [1991] 2 FLR 104, [1991] Fam Law 226.
6 Infra, pp 740 et seq.
7 S 101.
8 There is also power to make similar regulations in relation to the Isle of Man and the Channel Islands: s 101(3).
9 See Family Proceedings Rules 1991, Part VI.
10 As amended by the Family Law Act 1986, ss 67, 68, Sch 1, para 28, and by the Children Act 1989, Sch 13, para 57, Sch 15.
11 In relation to both there is power to order the disclosure of a child's whereabouts: 1985 Act, s 24A; and see *Re D (A Minor) (Child Abduction)* [1988] FCR 585, [1989] 1 FLR 97 n.
12 See SI 1991/2870.
13 SI 1990/2289.
14 On the Convention, see McClean, *Recognition of Family Judgments in the Commonwealth* (1983), pp 276–285; Nygh, pp 405–410; Sykes and Pryles, pp 542–546; Anton (1981) 30 ICLQ 537; Eekelaar (1982) 32 U Tor LJ 281, 305–325; Farquhar (1983) 4 Can Jo Fam L 5; Shapira (1989) II Hague Recueil 127, 189–200; Davis (1990) 4 Aus J Fam L 31. A report by the Hague Conference on the operation of the Convention is to be found in (1990) 29 International Legal Materials 220.
15 It can also be utilised to secure rights of access: Art 21; and see *B v B (Minors: Enforcement of Access Abroad)* [1988] 1 All ER 652, [1988] 1 WLR 526; *C v C (Minors) (Child Abduction)* [1992] 1 FLR 163.

even where there has been no order. Essential elements of the Convention are that it applies to a child under the age of 16 who was habitually resident in a Contracting State at the time when he was wrongfully removed or retained.[16] The House of Lords[17] has made clear that both removal and retention are single events, so that if a child is wrongfully removed before the Convention came into force but not returned after that date such latter conduct does not constitute "retention" within the meaning of the Convention[18] and section 2 of the Act. This means that, for those purposes, removal and retention are mutually exclusive concepts:

> Removal occurs when a child, which has previously been in the state of its habitual residence, is taken across the frontier of that state; whereas retention occurs where a child, which has previously been for a limited period outside the state of its habitual residence, is not returned to that state on the expiry of such limited period.[19]

The habitual residence of the child is the crucial connecting factor[20] and it is not defined in the Convention. It is essentially a question of fact.[1] The child's habitual residence is usually determined by the parents. So a removal from one country with the consent of both parents will change the child's habitual residence even though one parent later changes his or her mind.[2] However, a child's habitual residence cannot be changed by one parent without the consent of the other;[3] and a wrongful removal of the child will not alter his habitual residence for the purposes of the Convention.[4] Removal or retention is wrongful if it is, at that time,[5] in breach of custody rights under the law of the child's habitual residence which were being exercised.[6] These rights include those which can be attributed to one parent,[7] or to both jointly,[8] and which can arise "by operation of law or by reason of a judicial or administrative decision, or by reason of an agreement having legal affect under the law" of the child's habitual residence.[9]

---

16 Art 4.
17 *Re H (Minors) (Abduction: Custody Rights)* [1991] 2 AC 476, [1991] 3 All ER 230; and see *Kilgour v Kilgour* 1987 SLT 568; *B v B (Minors: Enforcement of Access Abroad)* [1988] 1 All ER 652, [1988] 1 WLR 526; *Re Gollogly and Owen's Marriage* (1989) 13 Fam LR 622.
18 [1991] 2 AC 476 at 499; cf *Re J (A Minor) (Abduction: Custody Rights)* [1990] 2 AC 562 at 578–579.
19 Ibid, at 500.
20 Eg *V v B (A Minor) (Abduction)* [1991] FCR 451, [1991] 1 FLR 266.
 1 *Re J (A Minor) (Abduction: Custody Rights)* [1990] 2 AC 562 at 578–579.
 2 Ibid, at 572 (CA); *Dickson v Dickson* [1990] SCLR 692.
 3 Provided both have the right to determine the child's residence.
 4 *Re S (A Minor) (Abduction)* [1991] FCR 656, [1991] 2 FLR 1; *Re H (Minors) (Abduction: Custody Rights)* [1991] 2 AC 476 at 484–485, CA, affd, ibid, at 491, HL.
 5 *Re Barraclough's Marriage* (1987) 11 Fam LR 773; *Re Gollogly and Owen's Marriage* (1989) 13 Fam LR 622; *Re Brandon's Marriage* (1990) 14 Fam LR 181.
 6 Art 3. In determining "wrongfulness" reference is to be made to the law of the state of the child's habitual residence: Arts 14, 15; and see 1985 Act, s 8; *C v C (Minors) (Child Abduction)* [1992] 1 FLR 163. An English court can, therefore, make a declaration as to wrongfulness for the benefit of a foreign court considering whether to order the return of a child: *In Re J (Abduction: Ward of Court)* [1989] Fam 85, [1989] 3 All ER 590. There is, however, no absolute guarantee that it will be followed abroad, just as there is no obligation on an English court to follow a foreign court's ruling; see *Re J (A Minor) (Abduction: Custody Rights)* [1990] 2 AC 562 at 577–578.
 7 Including, it appears, removal which is wrongful because in breach of the rights of the remover: *Re H (A Minor) (Abduction)* [1990] 2 FLR 439; *C v C (Minors) (Child Abduction)* [1992] 1 FLR 163.
 8 Art 3.
 9 Ibid.

So, the Convention includes, but is not limited to, custody rights arising from a court order. Rights of custody are not defined exclusively but include rights relating to the care of the person of the child and to determine his place of residence.[10] They also include, in England, custody rights attributed to a court when a child is made a ward of court.[11] If, however, one parent had no such rights under the law of the child's habitual residence at the time of removal or retention by the other parent, then such conduct is not wrongful and falls outside the Convention even if such rights are acquired later.[12] Furthermore, the wrongful removal or retention under the Convention must be "international" in nature,[13] ie the child must have been taken from, or retained outside, the country of his habitual residence in which the custody or access rights existed.[14] In other words, what is involved is wrongful removal from, or retention out of, that country, rather than just from or out of the care of the parent having custody rights.

The Convention requires administrative structures and procedures to be established to enable a child to be returned to the country from which it has been wrongfully removed or outside which it has been wrongfully retained. If we assume that a child has been wrongfully removed from France to England, the procedures to ensure its return to France are as follows.[15] The parent or other person claiming the child applies to the Central Authority in France or in any other Contracting State for assistance in securing the return of the child. The application, which has to contain essential particulars of the child, the grounds of the claim and available information as to the child's whereabouts,[16] is sent without delay by the Central Authority which receives it to the Central Authority in the country where the child is thought to be.[17] In the case of a child thought to be in England, the application is sent to the Lord Chancellor,[18] who must then cause to be taken all appropriate measures to discover the whereabouts of the child, to prevent further harm to him and to try to secure the voluntary return of the child.[19] He must also initiate, or facilitate, the institution of judicial or administrative proceedings to secure the return of the child[20] without considering the merits of any custody issue;[1] and any judicial proceedings in England are in the High Court.[2] If less than one year has elapsed between the date of the wrongful removal and the

---

10 Art 5(a). See *C v C (Abduction: Rights of Custody)* [1989] 1 WLR 654; *C v C (Minors) (Child Abduction)* [1992] 1 FLR 163; but see the predicament of an unmarried father as illustrated by *F v S (Wardship: Jurisdiction)* [1991] 2 FLR 349 at 354.
11 *Re J (Abduction: Ward of Court)* [1989] Fam 85, [1989] 3 All ER 590. A Canadian court has held that rights of custody may be attributed to a North American Indian Tribe: *S (SM) v A(J)* (1990) 65 DLR (4th) 222.
12 *Re J (A Minor) (Abduction: Custody Rights)* [1990] 2 AC 562.
13 *Re H (Minors) (Abduction: Custody Rights)* [1991] 3 AC 476, [1991] 3 All ER 230.
14 *B v B (Minors: Enforcement of Access Abroad)* [1988] 1 WLR 526 at 532.
15 Similar procedures apply, mutatis mutandis, where a parent in England seeks the recovery of a child wrongfully taken or retained abroad; see eg *Re J (Abduction: Ward of Court)* [1989] Fam 85, [1989] 3 All ER 590.
16 Art 8.
17 Art 9.
18 1985 Act, s 3.
19 Arts 7, 11.
20 The return of the child is to the country of its habitual residence: *Re A (A Minor) (Abduction)* [1988] 1 FLR 365 at 373.
1 Art 19.
2 1985 Act, s 3. Once an application has been made to the court, it may give interim directions to secure the welfare of the child or to prevent a change in circumstances: s 5; see *Re D (A Minor) (Child Abduction)* [1988] FCR 585, [1989] 1 FLR 97 n.

English proceedings, the child must[3] be ordered to be returned forthwith; if more than a year has elapsed, the return of the child must be ordered "unless it is demonstrated that the child is now[4] settled in its new environment".[5] Settlement in this context means more than mere adjustment to surroundings. It involves both the physical element of being established in a community and an environment, and an emotional constituent of security and stability.[6] Even if settlement is established, the court still has a discretion to order the return of the child.[7] Furthermore, if notice of a wrongful removal has been received in England the merits of the custody issue cannot be determined here until a decision has been taken on the return of the child or unless an application for its return is not made within a reasonable time.[8]

Although the purpose of the Hague Convention and Part I of the 1985 Act is to ensure the speedy return of a child without consideration of the merits of the custody issue,[9] there are three grounds on which return may be refused. Such refusal is discretionary. The first is if the child objects to being returned "and has attained an age and degree of maturity at which it is appropriate to take account of its views".[10] The other two require opponents of the child's return to establish *either* that the person or body in the other country having care of the child was not actually exercising custody rights at the time of removal, or consented to or subsequently acquiesced in[11] the removal or retention; *or* "that there is a grave risk that his or her return would expose the child to physical or psychological harm or otherwise place the child in an intolerable position".[12] Courts in England, and elsewhere, have had the opportunity on a number of occasions to consider the scope of this third ground and the circumstances in which it should be applied. Whilst it may be clear that a child will suffer psychological harm if its return is ordered, the court has to determine whether that is outweighed by the harm that would ensue if no order was made. What is clear is that the harm must be substantial[13] and the risk of it must be "grave", ie greater than would

3 Subject to the discretionary grounds for refusal of return, infra, pp 736–737.
4 This means the date of the commencement of the proceedings: *Re N (Minors) (Abduction)* [1991] 1 FLR 413 at 417.
5 Art 12. There is also power to stay or dismiss the application if it is thought that the child has been taken to another state. The Convention powers are in addition to any other powers to order the return of the child: Art 18.
6 *Re N (Minors) (Abduction)* [1991] 1 FLR 413, [1991] Fam Law 367; and see *Re S (A Minor) (Abduction)* [1991] 2 FLR 1 at 23–24; *Graziano v Daniels* (1991) 14 Fam LR 697.
7 See *Re S (A Minor) (Abduction)* [1991] FCR 656, [1991] 2 FLR 1.
8 Art 16. Issues which in England are held to go to the merits are listed in the 1985 Act, s 9, as amended by the Children Act 1989, Sch 15. Furthermore, if an order is made by the High Court for the return of the child, any similar English order ceases to have effect: ss 25, 27, Sch 3 (as amended by the Children Act 1989, para 57, Sch 15).
9 See *Re E (A Minor) (Abduction)* [1989] 1 FLR 135 at 145; *P v P (Minors) (Child Abduction)* [1992] 1 FLR 155. Speed is most strikingly illustrated by *Re J (A Minor) (Abduction: Custody Rights)* [1990] 2 AC 562 where less than 3 months elapsed between a request being made by the Australian Central Authority for the return of a child in England and the HL decision.
10 Art 13; and see *Re G (A Minor) (Abduction)* [1990] FCR 189, [1989] 2 FLR 475; *Re S (A Minor) (Abduction)* [1991] FCR 656, [1991] 2 FLR 1. In *Re R (A Minor: Abduction)* [1992] 1 FLR 105 the court declined to order the return of a teenage child who had threatened suicide if her return was ordered.
11 See *Re A and Another (Minors: Abduction)* [1991] FCR 460, [1991] 2 FLR 241; *Re A (Minors) (Abduction: Custody Rights)* [1992] 2 WLR 536.
12 Art 13. These three criteria must be read disjunctively: *Director General of Family and Community Services v Davis* (1990) 14 Fam LR 381.
13 *Re Gsponer's Marriage* (1988) 94 FLR 164 at 177; *Director General of Family and Community Services v Davis* (1990) 14 Fam LR 381.

normally be expected if a child was taken from one parent and passed to another. In assessing the degree of risk, the court may look at the practical consequences involved in the return of the child, such as financial provision or accommodation.[14] It is striking, however, that the courts take a good deal of convincing that return should be refused on this ground to which they have given a strict and narrow interpretation.[15] So English courts have ordered the return of a child to Australia even though the mother would have serious accommodation problems there;[16] and a Scottish court has concluded that a child is unlikely to be placed in an intolerable position by being returned to Canada even though a grandparent who was likely to look after the child spoke no English.[17] Indeed an intolerable situation has to be "something extreme and compelling".[18] The courts have regularly emphasised that they are not here concerned with the "paramount consideration" of the child's welfare, but rather with whether the child should be returned speedily to the jurisdiction most apppropriate for the determination of that issue.[19] This cannot be thwarted by a parent refusing to return with the child and then arguing that the child will suffer grave psychological harm from being separated from that parent. To accept such an argument would "drive a coach and four through the Convention, at least in respect of applications by young children".[20] Though the burden of establishing grave risk is high, it is not impossibly so, and a Scottish court has refused to return a child to Canada in the face of evidence of the Canadian father's depression and alcoholism.[1]

(ii) Part II of the 1985 Act: the Council of Europe Convention[2]

This Convention governs the recognition and enforcement of decisions relating to custody, whether made by a judicial or administrative authority, in force in relation to children under 16.[3] A decision relating to custody is one which "relates to the care of the person of the child, including the right to

---

14 *Re A (A Minor) (Abduction)* [1988] 1 FLR 365, [1988] Fam Law 54; *MacMillan v MacMillan* 1989 SLT 350.

15 In exercising its discretion, the court may well be influenced by undertakings given by the parties: *C v C (Abduction: Rights of Custody)* [1989] 2 All ER 465, [1989] 1 WLR 654; *Re G (A Minor) (Abduction)* [1990] FCR 189, [1989] 2 FLR 475; McClean (1990) 106 LQR 375.

16 *Re A (A Minor) (Wrongful Removal of Child)* [1988] Fam Law 383; and see *C v C (Abduction: Rights of Custody)* [1989] 1 WLR 654; *Re E (A Minor) (Abduction)* [1989] 1 FLR 135, [1989] Fam Law 105; *Re G (A Minor) (Abduction)* [1989] 2 FLR 475, [1989] Fam Law 473; *V v B (A Minor) (Abduction)* [1991] FCR 451, [1991] 1 FLR 266; *Parsons v Styger* (1989) 67 OR (2d) 1.

17 *Viola v Viola* 1988 SLT 7.

18 *Re N (Minors) (Abduction)* [1991] 1 FLR 413 at 419; *Re R (A Minor: Abduction)* [1992] 1 FLR 105 at 107.

19 Eg *C v C (Abduction: Rights of Custody)* [1989] 1 WLR 654 at 661; *V v B (A Minor) (A Minor) (Abduction)* [1991] 1 FLR 266 at 273; *Re Gsponer's Marriage* (1988) 94 FLR 164 at 178–180.

20 *C v C (Abduction: Rights of Custody)* [1989] 1 WLR 654 at 661; and see *V v B (A Minor) (Abduction)* [1991] 1 FLR 266 at 274.

1 *MacMillan v MacMillan* 1989 SLT 350; see Anton, pp 531–532.

2 See Jones (1981) 30 ICLQ 467; Shapira (1989) II Hague Recueil 127, 200–206. The Council of Europe has reviewed the operation of the Convention: DIR/JUR (89)1.

3 1985 Act, Sch 2, Art 1. It does not apply to a child under 16 if he has the right to decide the place of his residence under the law of his habitual residence, nationality or of the Contracting State where recognition and enforcement is sought.

decide on the place of his residence or to the right of access to him".[4] Let us assume that such a decision has been made in Belgium and the person who obtained it wishes to have it recognised and enforced in England. The procedure is much the same as under the Hague Convention.[5] An application, accompanied by the relevant documents and information as to the child's whereabouts,[6] is made to the Central Authority in any Contracting State and, if it is not sent in our example to the English Central Authority (who is the Lord Chancellor[7]), it must be sent directly and without delay to the Lord Chancellor by the Central Authority in the Contracting State to which the application was made.[8] Unless it is manifestly clear that the conditions of the Convention are not satisfied,[9] steps must be taken in England without delay to find the child, prevent any prejudice to his or the applicant's interests, and to secure the recognition and effective enforcement of the Belgian decision.[10] The foreign decision will be recognised here, unless the High Court[11] has declared that such recognition shall be denied on any of the stated grounds.[12] It cannot, however, be enforced in England until it is registered in the High Court, and registration can be refused if the custody decision would not be recognised here, if it is not enforceable where it was made or if an application under the Hague Convention is pending.[13] Once registered, the foreign decision can be enforced as if it was an English one,[14] and registration or an application for registration of a foreign custody decision will limit the powers of the English courts in English proceedings relating to the welfare of the child started later than the foreign ones.[15]

Although the basic approach of the Convention is that all custody decisions given in one Contracting State should be recognised and enforced in all others[16] without any review of the substantive custody issue,[17] there are quite broad and elaborate grounds on which recognition and enforcement may be refused:[18]

(i) Where the decision was given in the absence of the defendant or his lawyers and the defendant was not duly served with the necessary documents, unless he concealed his whereabouts,[19] *or*

4 Ibid. The Convention can also be utilised to secure rights of access: Art 11; and "rights of access" is defined for English purposes by s 27(4) of the 1985 Act, added by the Children Act 1989, Sch 13, para 57.
5 It also works in a similar way where it is sought to enforce an English order in a foreign country.
6 Listed in Art 13.
7 1985 Act, s 14.
8 Art 4.
9 Art 4(4).
10 Art 5(1). If the child is thought to be in another Contracting State, the application must be passed on to the Central Authority there.
11 1985 Act, s 27(2).
12 Ibid, ss 15(2), 27(1).
13 Ss 15(2)(b), 16. If the original decision is varied or revoked, the registration can be varied or cancelled: s 17.
14 S 18; and the court has interim powers once an application for registration has been made: s 19.
15 S 20, as amended by the Children Act 1989, Sch 15. If there is an earlier English custody order, it will cease to have effect on registration of the foreign one: ss 25, 27, Sch 3, as amended by the Children Act 1989, Sch 13, para 57, Sch 15.
16 Art 7.
17 Art 9(3).
18 1985 Act, s 15(2)(a).
19 Eg *Re G (A Minor) (Child Abduction: Enforcement)* [1990] FCR 973, [1990] 2 FLR 325.

the jurisdiction of the authority making the decision was not based on the habitual residence of the defendant or of the child, or the last common habitual residence of both parents which is still the habitual residence of one of them.[20]

(ii) The decision is incompatible with a custody decision which became enforceable in the State addressed before the child was improperly[1] removed unless the child had been habitually resident in the requesting State for one year before his removal.[2]

(iii) Where the effects of the custody decision are "manifestly incompatible with the fundamental principles of the law relating to the family and children in the State addressed".[3]

(iv) The effects of the original decision are manifestly no longer in accordance with the welfare of the child, by reason of changes in circumstances, including lapse of time, but excluding the change in the residence of a child improperly removed.[4]

(v) At the time of the original proceedings, the child was a national of, or habitually resident in, the State addressed and there was no such connection with the State of origin, or the child was a national of both States and habitually resident in the State addressed.[5]

(vi) The original decision is incompatible with a decision of, or enforceable in, the State addressed, proceedings in which were begun before the submission of the request for recognition and enforcement, and if refusal of recognition and enforcement of the original decision is in accordance with the welfare of the child.[6]

It will be noted first, that this catalogue of grounds for refusal is lengthy and, second, that, in a number of instances, it may be necessary to consider the substantive merits of the original decision, despite the general requirement of recognition and enforcement.[7] The most significant of these instances is (iv), above, namely that the effects of the original decision are manifestly no longer in accordance with the welfare of the child. This has led an English court to refuse the return of young children who had lived in England for a year since the making of the foreign order, even though their original removal was wrongful;[8] and has led a Scottish court to refuse to order the return of a teenager against his wishes when such return would have disrupted his schooling.[9] More recently, the English courts have adopted what seems to be a more robust view and have ordered the return of children who have been in this country for a year or more.[10]

The Convention distinguishes between cases of improper removal and others, with more limited bases for refusal of recognition in the former

20 Art 9(1)(a), (b).
1 1985 Act, s 15(3). Improper removal is defined in Art 1(d), and see Art 12.
2 Art 9(1)(c).
3 Art 10(1)(a). This may, in this country, include the welfare principle; see *Re G (A Minor) (Child Abduction: Enforcement)* [1990] FCR 973, [1990] 2 FLR 325.
4 Where practicable, the views of the child are to be sought: Art 15.
5 Art 10(1)(c).
6 Art 10(1)(a); see *Campins-Coll, Petitioner* 1989 SLT 33.
7 Art 7, coupled with the prohibition on review of the substance of the foreign decision, in Art 9(3).
8 *F v F (Minors) (Custody: Foreign Order)* [1989] Fam 1; Hall [1989] CLJ 189.
9 *Campins-Coll, Petitioner* 1989 SLT 33.
10 *Re K (A Minor) (Abduction)* [1990] FCR 524, [1990] 1 FLR 387; *Re G (A Minor) (Child Abduction: Enforcement)* [1990] FCR 973, [1990] 2 FLR 325.

case;[11] but the United Kingdom in exercising a power of reservation under the Convention[12] has extended the full range of grounds for refusal of recognition and enforcement to all custody decisions, whether or not there was wrongful removal.

(iii) The Conventions compared[13]

Some ten countries are, like the United Kingdom, parties to both Conventions.[14] There would seem to be nothing to prevent a person, whose claim could fall under both Conventions, choosing which, or both, procedures to follow; though an application under the Hague Convention will prevent registration of a foreign custody decision under the Council of Europe Convention.[15] Whilst there are considerable similarities between the two Conventions—they both apply to children under the age of 16, and their procedures follow the same pattern—there are also major differences. The Hague Convention protects custody rights, whether or not there has been a custody order; but this protection is only provided in cases of wrongful removal of children habitually resident in a Contracting State. The Council of Europe Convention is limited to the registration and enforcement of foreign custody decisions, but applies in all circumstances and not just in improper removal cases. One further significant difference is that the grounds, under the Hague Convention, for refusing to return the child are narrower than those under the Council of Europe Convention for refusing recognition and enforcement of the foreign decision. This suggests that, given a choice, the Hague Convention is to be preferred.[16]

(d) COMMON LAW RULES[17]

(i) Recognition of foreign orders

Despite the recent statutory developments, the common law rules as to the recognition of foreign orders continue to be important. This is because the 1985 Act and its Conventions still apply to only a relatively small number of countries and so the common law rules apply in the case of all orders (whether custody, guardianship or wardship orders) made in other countries outside the United Kingdom, to any orders made in countries covered by the two Conventions which do not fall within their definitions of "rights of custody"[1] or "decision relating to custody",[2] and to any orders made elsewhere in the United Kingdom which are not "Part I orders" within the meaning of the 1986 Act.[3] The common law position is simple. No automatic recognition or enforcement is given to a foreign custody order.[4] However potent may be

11 Arts 8 and 9.
12 Art 17, and see 1985 Act, s 12(2).
13 Eekelaar (1982) 32 U Tor LJ 281, 321–325.
14 Austria, France, Germany, Luxembourg, The Netherlands, Norway, Portugal, Spain, Sweden and Switzerland.
15 1985 Act, s 16(4)(c).
16 North (1990) I Hague Recueil 9, 150–151.
17 See McClean, *Recognition of Family Judgments in the Commonwealth* (1983), pp 252–262.
 1 Child Abduction and Custody Act 1985, Sch 1, Art 5(a).
 2 Ibid, Sch 2, Art 1(c).
 3 Orders made elsewhere in the United Kingdom which affect the property rather than the person of the child fall outside Part I of the Family Law Act 1986 and so their recognition is governed by common law rules: see Law Com No 138 (1985), para 123.
 4 For ease of exposition, we shall take recognition of custody orders as the prime example.

arguments of comity or reciprocity, they are held to be outweighed by the principle that the welfare of the child is the paramount consideration of the English court in all proceedings concerned with the upbringing of the child on the administration of its property.[5] Even though a custody order has been made by a foreign court, the English judge can still make such order as he thinks is in the best interest of the child;[6] for "national status is merely one of the factors which the judge in exercising his discretion will take into consideration".[7]

The leading common law authority is *McKee v McKee*:[8]

Husband and wife, American citizens, separated and agreed in writing that neither of them, without the permission of the other, would remove their son out of the USA. A year later the husband obtained a decree of divorce from a Californian court and an order awarding him the custody of the child and confirming the written agreement. About four years later, the same court, on the applications of both parties, awarded custody to the wife, whereupon the husband took his son to Ontario without the leave or knowledge of his wife. The wife thereupon took *habeas corpus* proceedings in Ontario. The trial judge, after a careful review of the circumstances, awarded custody of the child to the husband, but his decision was reversed by the Supreme Court of Canada.

The Privy Council restored the Ontario decision. The two charges levelled against the husband, that he had broken the agreement with his wife and had flouted the order of the Californian court, had been adequately considered by the trial judge, who, in the opinion of the court, was justified in concluding that in the light of the other circumstances the interests of the child would best be served by leaving him in the custody of his father. The order of the Californian court was a factor of great importance, but it was not decisive.

It is the law ... that the welfare and happiness of the infant is the paramount consideration in questions of custody ... To this paramount consideration all others yield. The order of a foreign court is no exception. Such an order has not the force of a foreign judgment: comity demands not its enforcement, but its grave consideration. This distinction ... rests on the peculiar character of the jurisdiction and on the fact that an order providing for the custody of an infant cannot in its nature be final.[9]

What is the effect of giving a foreign order "grave consideration"? It certainly does not prevent the English court from making a contrary order if the judge thinks it in the best interests of the child to do so;[10] but it must not be forgotten that the judge who made the first order will have had the advantage of seeing the parties and hearing cross-examination of witnesses.[11] The court

5 See Children Act 1989, s 1.
6 *Re G (JDM)* [1969] 1 WLR 1001 at 1004; *J v C* [1970] AC 668 at 700–701, 714, 720.
7 [1970] AC 668 at 701; cf *Re B (Infants)* [1971] NZLR 143.
8 [1951] AC 352, [1951] 1 All ER 942.
9 [1951] AC 352 at 365; and see *Re B's Settlement* [1940] Ch 54, [1951] 1 All ER 949n; *Re G (JDM)* [1969] 1 WLR 1001.
10 *McKee v McKee* [1951] AC 352 at 364–365; *J v C* [1970] AC 668 at 700–701, 714, 720, 728; *Re L* [1974] 1 WLR 250 at 264; *Re C* [1978] Fam 105, [1978] 2 All ER 230; *Re R* (1981) 2 FLR 416 at 425; *Sinclair v Sinclair* 1988 SLT 87.
11 *McKee v McKee*, supra at 360; *Re Kernot* [1965] Ch 217, [1964] 3 All ER 339; *Re S(M)* [1971] Ch 621, [1971] 1 All ER 459.

will be influenced by a variety of factors in deciding whether to make an order in terms similar to, or different from, those of the foreign order. If the foreign order was made some years ago, and the family circumstances have changed, the English order may well be in different terms and a further significant time factor is that the children will be older and their views more important.[12] Furthermore, attitudes towards the basic common law rule are changing,[13] with the acceptance of statutory provisions within the United Kingdom and elsewhere of Conventions providing for the speedy return of children. This has led to suggestions that the provisions of the Hague Convention should be applied where there has been wrongful removal of a child from a country not, at the relevant time, a party to that Convention.[14] Indeed the Court of Appeal has recently made clear, in *Re F (A Minor) (Abduction: Custody Rights)* that, certainly where removal is wrongful, there are two contexts in which the court must consider the welfare of the child:

> The first is the context of which court shall decide what the child's best interests require. The second context, which only arises if it has first been decided that the welfare of the child requires that the English rather than a foreign court shall decide what are the requirements of the child, is what orders as to custody, care and control and so on should be made.[15]

There are decisions under the common law rules, just as there are under the recent Conventions, involving cases where children have been brought within the jurisdiction of the English courts by one parent against the wishes of the other, often in flagrant contempt of the order of a foreign court;[16] though in other cases the "kidnapping" has been done before there has been a foreign order,[17] sometimes to frustrate foreign proceedings.[18] These cases raise the issue whether the English court should, despite any foreign custody order, examine the merits of the case concerning the child or make a summary order and just send the child back to the jurisdiction from which he has come. *Re F (A Minor) (Abduction: Custody Rights)*[19] now establishes[20] that the first task for the court in assessing the welfare of the child is to decide whether the return of the child to the country from which it has been wrongfully taken should be ordered. The general principle to be applied, following the policy of the Hague Convention,[1] is that any long term decision as to the custody of a child should be determined in the courts of its residence, and an English court is likely only to refuse to order the return of a child if circumstances exist similar to those provided for in the Hague Convention.[2]

12 *Re T* [1969] 1 WLR 1608, at 1611; and see *E v F* [1974] 2 NZLR 435.

13 *McKee v McKee*, supra, has been described as "somewhat discredited": *Re Taylor's Marriage* (1988) 92 FLR 172 at 178.

14 *Re F (A Minor) (Abduction: Custody Rights)* [1991] Fam 25, [1990] 3 All ER 97; *G v G (Minors) (Abduction)* [1991] 2 FLR 506; *Re Lavitch* (1985) 24 DLR (4th) 248; *Re H's Marriage* (1985) FLC 80, 164; *Re Barrios and Sanchez's Marriage* (1989) 96 FLR 336.

15 [1991] Fam 25 at 31.

16 Eg *McKee v McKee* [1951] AC 352, [1951] 1 All ER 942; *Re H* [1965] 3 All ER 906, [1966] 1 WLR 381; *Re E(D)* [1967] Ch 761, [1967] 2 WLR 1370; *Re T* [1968] Ch 704, [1968] 3 All ER 411; *Re L* [1974] 1 All ER 913, [1974] 1 WLR 250; *Re C* [1978] Fam 105, [1978] 2 All ER 230; *Re R* (1981) 2 FLR 416; *Re G* (1983) 5 FLR 268.

17 Eg *Re T* [1968] Ch 704, [1968] 3 All ER 411; *Re L* (1983) 4 FLR 368.

18 Eg *Re B* (1982) 4 FLR 492.

19 [1991] Fam 25, [1990] 3 All ER 97.

20 Cf *Re L* [1974] 1 All ER 913, [1974] 1 WLR 250; *Re R* (1981) 2 FLR 416, 11 Fam Law 57.

1 See also *Re Barrios and Sanchez's Marriage* (1989) 96 FLR 336.

2 Art 13, supra, pp 736–737.

It is only then, in the relatively rare case of immediate return not being ordered, that the English court will decide what order, in the best interests of the child, to make under section 8 of the Children Act 1989.[3]

(ii) Effect of a foreign order in England

Although, as we have seen, there are no rules at common law for the recognition and enforcement of foreign custody and guardianship orders, they may well not be devoid of effect here. Whilst there is no clear judicial authority in the case of custody orders, the Law Commission has suggested "that in practice a third person, such as an English headmaster, would be held to have acted properly if he acted on the assumption that a custody order made [elsewhere] was effective in England and Wales."[4]

There is some old authority in relation to foreign guardianship orders which supports the idea that effect will be given to such an order in this country as it affects third parties, even though the English courts will remain free to make their own order.[5] A major question which arises is whether the foreign guardian is entitled to exercise in England those rights over the person and property of his ward that are recognised by English internal law. It is clear in the first place that, with or without an English order, his powers are limited to those recognised by English internal law.[6] This rule is in sharp contrast with the practice adopted in civil law countries, where it is admitted in general that a tutor appointed under the personal law of the child enjoys the same rights over his ward's movable property in other countries as he possesses in the country of his appointment. The problem is, then, whether a foreign guardian is justified if he acts in England within the limits of English internal law. The answer would appear to be that he occupies in effect the same position as a person appointed in England as the child's guardian. What he does within the limits of English internal law will be recognised as validly done provided that his authority has not been challenged;[7] but if his position or his authority is challenged, then, as in the case of an English guardian, it lies within the discretion of the court whether he should be replaced by another person or whether his acts or proposed acts should be approved. Perhaps the major difference in this respect between a foreign and an English guardian is that the court would be more ready to displace the former than the latter.[8]

So, a foreign guardian whose authority was unchallenged here would act properly if he took the child abroad, as he would be doing no more than an English guardian could do in exercising parental responsibility for the child.[9] Conversely, the English courts have recognised a foreign guardian and ordered that his ward, the young Prince Rainier of Monaco, at school in England, be delivered up to him.[10]

---

3 Supra, p 721.
4 Law Com No 138 (1985), para 5.6.
5 See Dicey and Morris, pp 802–804.
6 *Johnstone v Beattie* (1843) 10 Cl & Fin 42 at 114.
7 *Nugent v Vetzera* (1866) LR 2 Eq 704 at 712.
8 Old cases in which foreign guardianship orders were recognised without regard to the paramount importance of the welfare of the child would not, in that respect, now be followed, ie *Nugent v Vetzera* (1866) LR 2 Eq 704; *Re Savini, Savini v Lousada* (1870) 18 WR 425.
9 Children Act 1989, s 5(6); and see *Nugent v Vetzera* (1866) LR 2 Eq 704 at 714; provided the removal was done with the appropriate consent required under the Child Abduction Act 1984, s 1, supra, p 720.
10 *Monaco v Monaco* (1947) 157 LT 231.

With regard to property rights, English practice has, also, shown a tendency to recognise the right of a foreign guardian to claim movable property in England.[11] Again, however, if his right is challenged it is at the discretion of the court whether, having regard to the interests of the child, the property shall be delivered to the guardian or to some other person.[12] The question generally arises where money is due to a foreign child under an English settlement, will or intestacy. Where the money has not been paid into court, it has been said that the trustees are legally discharged if they make payment to the foreign guardian and take his receipt.[13] Where the money is in court, then the court is entitled, but not compelled, to order payment to the guardian, and whether it does so or not depends on whether it is satisfied that the property will be properly administered for the child's benefit.[14]

11 *Mackie v Darling* (1871) LR 12 Eq 319; *Re Crichton's Trust* (1855) 24 LTOS 267; *Re Browne's Trust* (1865) 12 LT 488.
12 *Ex p Watkins* (1752) 2 Ves Sen 470; *Re Hellman's Will* (1866) LR 2 Eq 363; *Re Chatard's Settlement* [1899] 1 Ch 712. Cf *Dharamal v Lord Holm-Patrick* [1935] IR 760: A, domiciled in Indore in India, not entitled as of right to Irish Sweep winnings of his daughter, aged 7, though by the law of Indore he could give a good discharge.
13 *Re Chatard's Settlement* [1899] 1 Ch 712 at 716.
14 Children Act 1989, s 1.

Chapter 26

Legitimacy, legitimation and adoption

SUMMARY

1. INTRODUCTION

The three matters that require consideration in this chapter are legitimacy, legitimation and adoption. Legitimacy ordinarily means the status acquired by a person who is born to parents who are married to one another at the time of the birth. Legitimation means that a person who has not been born to married parents acquires the status of a legitimate person as the result of some act, such as the subsequent marriage of his parents, that occurs after the date of his birth. Adoption, in English law, involves the extinction of the parental links between the child and the natural parents and the creation of similar links between the child and the adoptive parents.

Whether a person is legitimate or has been legitimated or adopted has, in the past, been of considerable importance in the field of succession. If the will of a domiciled Englishman contained a gift to the "children" of a specified person it had to be asked whether this included not only legitimate children but also those who were illegitimate, legitimated or adopted. English domestic law has moved from a position in which it was rare that a will or intestacy applied to other than legitimate children to the situation where, as a consequence of a process culminating in the Family Law Reform Act 1987, there has been a very substantial assimilation of the rights of children, irrespective of the circumstances of their birth.[1] This legislation does not, however, abolish the distinction between legitimacy and illegitimacy, nor the concept of legitimation. Though they have become far less important, it will still be necessary to determine whether or not the parents of a child are married, or whether the child is legitimate, for the purposes, for example, of citizenship[2] or domicil, as well as in determining the rights of the father.[3]

The general effect of these developments has been to diminish, though not to the point of disappearance,[4] the need for rules of private international law to determine a person's legitimacy or the validity of his legitimation. It might, for example, also be necessary for a child domiciled in England to have his legitimacy determined for the purposes of succession under a foreign law. There has, on the other hand, been if anything an increase in the need to determine the validity in this country of foreign adoptions, resulting from the increase in the number of foreign children adopted, sometimes abroad, by English parents.

We have examined already[5] the powers and jurisdiction of the English courts to make declarations relating to legitimacy, legitimation and adoption. We have now to consider in relation to legitimacy and legitimation the choice of law rules relevant to the determination of these issues and in relation to adoption the further questions of the rules for the jurisdiction of the English courts to make adoption orders and for the recognition of foreign adoptions.

2. LEGITIMACY[6]

(a) LEGITIMACY TO BE GOVERNED BY THE LAW OF THE DOMICIL

Before the passing of the Legitimacy Act 1959, the rule of domestic English law was that no child acquired the status of legitimacy unless he was born in lawful wedlock, that is, born of parents whose marriage was valid at the time of his birth. This exclusive test, however, was exceptional, for most countries, including Scotland, had long recognised the doctrine of the putative marriage, according to which a child even of a void marriage is also legitimate.[7] A

1 1987 Act s 1.
2 See British Nationality Act 1981, s 50(9).
3 Children Act 1989, s 2.
4 See Law Com No 132 (1984), paras 3.9–3.14; Law Com No 157 (1986), para 3.14.
5 Supra, pp 696–697.
6 Welsh (1947) 63 LQR 65; Lipstein (1954) *Festschift für Ernst Rabel*, vol I, p 611.
7 For example, the French Code, CC 201, provides that a marriage which has been contracted in good faith produces its civil effects, both as regards the spouses and the children, despite the fact that it has been declared void: Amos and Walton, *Introduction to French Law* (3rd edn), pp 66–67.

common, though not a universal, qualification of this doctrine is that the spouses should have *bona fide* believed in the validity of their marriage. A question of choice of law might therefore arise if a child were born out of lawful wedlock in the country where X and Y, his parents, were domiciled and where the doctrine of the putative marriage was recognised.

The view expressed by several writers, that in such circumstances the English test of birth in lawful wedlock becomes applicable, is open to the insuperable objection that it fails to appreciate the true function of English law in such a case. If an English will bequeaths a legacy to the "legitimate children" of parents who were domiciled abroad at the time of their son's birth and if his legitimacy is disputed, there are two separate questions to be resolved. The first is a question of construction—what did the testator intend by his use of the phrase "legitimate children"? This is a matter for English domestic law as the law governing succession. If the answer is that he referred to legitimate children, then the second question, whether the children are in fact legitimate, is a question not of construction, but of status determinable by the law of their domicil. The subject of inquiry is not whether the marriage of the legatee's parents is valid, but whether he is legitimate in the eyes of the law of his domicil—the only law that is entitled to pass upon his status.[8] English law is, indeed, relevant so far as concerns the construction of the will, but as ROMER J said in one case:

> The only relevant rule of construction is that a bequest in an English will to the children of A means to his legitimate children[9] and that does not carry the matter very far, for the question remains who are his legitimate children, and that is not a question of construction at all, it is a question of law.[10]

(b) SHAW V GOULD

(i) The decision

This principle, that any person legitimate according to the law of his domicil, though not born in lawful wedlock, is legitimate for the purpose of succeeding to movables under an English will or intestacy has been repeatedly affirmed in a stream of cases from at least 1835 onwards;[11] but, with two exceptions,[12] these statements were all made in cases concerned with legitimation. It is sometimes said, therefore, that they are of little value having regard to the decision of the House of Lords in *Shaw v Gould*,[13] which raised a question of legitimacy. The facts of this case were as follows:

> Funds were bequeathed by a testator domiciled in England in trust for Elizabeth Hickson for life and after her death in trust for her children. English land was also devised after her death to "her first and other sons *lawfully begotten*". Elizabeth, at the age of sixteen, was induced by fraud, without the knowledge of her family, to marry a domiciled Englishman,

8 See, for example, *Re Andros* (1883) 24 ChD 637 at p 639 where the position is stated with great clarity.
9 Before the operation of what is now the Family Law Reform Act 1987, s 19.
10 *Re Bischoffsheim* [1948] Ch 79 at 86, [1947] 2 All ER 830 at 833, 834.
11 *Doe d Birtwhistle v Vardill* (1835) 2 Cl & Fin 571 at 573, 574; *Re Don's Estate* (1857) 4 Drew 194 at 197–198; *Re Goodman's Trusts* (1881) 17 ChD 266 at 291, 296–297; *Re Andros* (1883) 24 ChD 637 at 639; *Re Bischoffsheim* [1948] Ch 79 at 92, [1947] 2 All ER 830 at 836.
12 *Re Bischoffsheim*, supra; *Motala v A-G* [1990] 2 FLR 261, revsd on another point [1991] 4 All ER 682, [1991] 3 WLR 903; and see *Hashmi v Hashmi* [1972] Fam 36, [1971] 3 All ER 1253; *Re Karnenas* (1978) 3 RFL (2d) 213.
13 (1868) LR 3 HL 55.

named Buxton, at Manchester. Her friends, however, succeeded in taking her away just after the ceremony, and she never lived with her husband for a single day. Sixteen years later, Elizabeth, having become engaged to a domiciled Englishman named Shaw, devised a scheme for obtaining a divorce in Scotland from Buxton. Shaw acquired a domicil in Scotland, and Buxton was paid £250 to go to that country for forty days. The marriage was dissolved by the Court of Session. Elizabeth then married Shaw in Edinburgh and had by him two daughters and one son, all of whom were born in the lifetime of Buxton. At the time of the present action Buxton, Elizabeth and Shaw were dead. The questions before the English court were whether the daughters and son were entitled under the will of the testator to the funds as being the "children" of Elizabeth, and also whether the son was entitled to the land as being her "son lawfully begotten". Evidence was given that by Scots law the divorce and second marriage were valid; also, that children born of a putative marriage, ie one regular in point of form but void owing to the prior existing marriage of one of the parties, were regarded as legitimate, provided that the parents were justifiably ignorant of the prior existing marriage.

It was the opinion of the Scottish advocates who gave evidence that justifiable ignorance existed if the parents believed in the validity of the divorce. The House of Lords unanimously held that the children were not entitled to take under the will.[14]

The reason that appears to have impressed their Lordships was the supposedly logical one that since Buxton, and therefore Elizabeth, remained domiciled in England, the Scottish divorce was not recognised in England; therefore the union between Elizabeth and Shaw was not a valid marriage according to English law; and that therefore the children were not born to lawfully married parents (being the test of legitimacy according to English domestic law). Lord COLONSAY, though impressed with the logic of the reasoning, was perplexed with doubts as to whether the status of legitimacy ought to be denied to the children. He felt that this denial was difficult to reconcile with general principles of jurisprudence or with the generally recognised rules of international law.[15]

(ii) Criticisms

It is difficult to resist the conclusion that the House of Lords lost its direction through its persistent concentration on one general principle to the exclusion of others. It certainly was a general principle that a divorce not recognised as valid by the law of the husband's domicil is invalid in England. But another principle, affirmed many times by the judiciary, is that legitimacy is determined by the law of the father's domicil at the time of the child's birth. Both these principles demanded attention in *Shaw v Gould*. There is nothing inconsistent in them. They are not mutually antagonistic. It was easy to argue in this manner:

The father cannot be granted the status of a husband, since the woman whom he purported to marry is, owing to the continuance of her earlier marriage, the wife of another man. Therefore the children of the father by this woman cannot be regarded as legitimate.

14 Though see now the Family Law Reform Act 1987, s 19.
15 (1868) LR 3 HL 55 at 96–97.

Nevertheless, the conclusion is a non sequitur. The issue was the status of the children, not of their parents. The fact that Mrs Buxton could not claim to be Mrs Shaw was not necessarily a bar to the legitimate status of the children. The legitimacy of a child happened at the time of the case to depend according to English domestic law on the validity of the marriage of which he was born; but this is not and was not the case in all legal systems. If the two questions are separable by the law of the child's domicil of origin, they should be kept separate by an English court when dealing with a private international law case. The courts of other countries have found no difficulty in this. Thus in South Africa it was held that the children of a polygamous union, born when the father was domiciled in India, were to be regarded as legitimate in Natal, which was his domicil at death. For the purpose of fixing the rate of succession duty payable on the father's death, the status of the mother as a "wife" was tested by the internal law of Natal; but the status of the children was referred to their domicil of origin.[16]

> It is essential [said INNES CJ] to bear in mind the distinction between the points to be decided in each instance. With regard to the wife, the issue is the validity of the marriage to which she was a party; with regard to the children, the issue is their right to the status of legitimacy. The wife's position cannot be considered apart from the marriage, but the position of the children may be.[17]

It is submitted that in any event *Shaw v Gould* ought to be regarded as an abnormal decision and one to be interpreted in the light of the exceptional circumstances involved. "My opinion in this case", said Lord CHELMSFORD, "is founded entirely upon the peculiar circumstances attending it."[18] It was, indeed, distinguished by a number of special features among which may be mentioned the following:

> The Scots divorce was granted in 1846, eleven years before judicial divorce was possible in England and at a time when the prevalent view, in accordance with the unanimous opinion of the judges in *Lolley's Case*,[1] was that no foreign proceeding in the nature of a divorce could affect a marriage that had been contracted in England. In fact, in the court of first instance, KINDERSLEY V-C said: "By the English law of marriage, an English marriage is absolutely indissoluble by the sentence of any court (of course I am speaking of the law as it stood at the time of the transactions in question which was long before the Act establishing the Divorce Court). ... Any decree or judgment or sentence of any foreign court, purporting to dissolve such marriage, is treated as a mere nullity."[2] It must be observed, however, that this view did not appeal to the House of Lords.
>
> The conduct of the Shaws was calculated to arouse the suspicion of any court. In the greatest secrecy and with every precaution against discovery,

---

16 *Seedat's Exors v The Master* 1917 AD 302.
17 Ibid at 311–312. In the New York case of *Re Hall* (1901) 61 App D 266, a woman obtained a divorce in Dakota that was not regarded as valid in New York. She then married a man domiciled in Dakota and a child was born of the marriage. It was held that the child was legitimate for the purposes of taking under the will of a testator who died domiciled in New York.
18 *Shaw v Gould* (1868) LR 3 HL 55 at 79.
1 (1812) Russ & Ry 237. The view was finally repudiated in *Harvey v Farnie* (1882) 8 App Cas 43.
2 *Re Wilson's Trusts* (1865) LR 1 Eq 247 at 257–258.

they contrived a scheme to obtain a divorce in a court which, to their knowledge, had no jurisdiction in the eyes of English law.[3]

The children were legitimate by Scots law if either of the Shaws was justifiably ignorant that there was an impediment to their marriage, ie in their case, a prior invalid divorce. After a careful examination of the facts, KINDERSLEY V-C found himself unable to agree that even Mrs Shaw was justifiably ignorant of the true position.

(c) OTHER AUTHORITIES

It is significant that in the much later case of *Re Stirling*,[4] SWINDEN EADY J was far from repudiating the suggestion that a child might be legitimate although the previous divorce of one of his parents was invalid. It was not necessary, however, to decide the point, for it was held that the doctrine of putative marriage, on which the argument for the child turned, did not obtain in Scotland unless at least one of the parties was ignorant of the impediment that invalidated the second marriage. The party had to be mistaken as to some fact. The ignorance alleged was that the mother of the child was unaware that her divorce from her first husband was invalid, but this was an error of law, not of fact.

Another authority that is sometimes said to support *Shaw v Gould* is *Re Paine*[5] which has already been discussed in another connection.[6] The question there, it will be recalled, was whether the children of W were legitimate for the purpose of the effect of a disposition to W contained in an English will.

> In 1875 W, when domiciled in England, was married in Germany to the widower of her deceased sister. At that date a marriage between such persons was prohibited. The husband was held to have been domiciled in Germany at the time of the ceremony. The parties cohabited in England until the husband's death in 1919.

BENNETT J adopted the dual domicil doctrine of capacity and held the three children of the union to be illegitimate, since they had sprung from a void marriage. But, as in *Shaw v Gould*, the possibility that the children might be legitimate according to the German law of their domicil of origin, despite the absence of lawful wedlock between their parents, was not canvassed.

However, despite all attempts to rationalise *Shaw v Gould*, the fact remains that, until the decision of ROMER J in *Re Bischoffsheim*,[7] it seemed to provide an embarrassing obstacle to the prevalent judicial view that the legitimacy of a child is a matter for the law of his domicil of origin. This view, however, was translated into action in *Bischoffsheim's Case* where the facts were these:

> In 1919 W was married in New York to H, the brother of her deceased husband. It may be taken that at that time both parties were domiciled in England. The marriage was void by English law, but valid by the law of New York. After they had acquired a domicil in New York a son was born to them. The question was whether the son was the legitimate child of his mother so as to entitle him to benefit under the will of a testator who had died domiciled in England.

3 For the details see ibid, at 260–262.
4 [1908] 2 Ch 344.
5 [1940] Ch 46.
6 Supra, p 593.
7 [1948] Ch 79, [1947] 2 All ER 830.

Romer J found in favour of the son on the following principle:

> Where succession to personal property depends upon the legitimacy of the claimant, the status of legitimacy conferred on him by his domicil of origin (ie the domicil of his parents at birth), will be recognised by our courts; and that if that legitimacy be established, the validity of his parents' marriage should not be entertained as a relevant subject for investigation.[8]

He distinguished *Shaw v Gould* by showing that since in that case the Lords chose to concentrate their attention on the validity of the divorce they were bound to find it invalid and consequently to fix the children's domicil of origin in England. This left no room for a claim based on the ground that their legitimacy stood apart from the validity of the divorce and that if so their domicil of origin was in Scotland.[9]

It has been argued that this decision should be dismissed as being inconsistent with higher authority, an opinion that has been expressed on several occasions.[10] To do so would have the startling result that in the same context legitimacy is subject to one rule, legitimation to another. Where a question has arisen of succession under an English testacy or intestacy, it has long been settled that if a claimant has been legitimated by the law of the country where at the time of his birth (and of the subsequent marriage) his father was domiciled, English law "recognises and acts on the status thus declared by the law of the domicil".[11] There is no substantial difference between legitimacy and legitimation[12] and no reason of logic or convenience why the law should relegate them to mutually exclusive categories. If from the date of the act of legitimation the child assumes the status that he would have possessed had he been born legitimate, it is incomprehensible that these two causes of the same result should be subject to divergent rules for the choice of law.

Happily, any such divergence of approach is clearly rejected by Sir Stephen Brown P in *Motala v A-G*:[13]

> H and W, domiciled at all material times in India, went to live in Northern Rhodesia (now Zambia) where in 1950 they went through a ceremony of marriage according to Sunni Moslem law. The marriage was invalid under the law of Northern Rhodesia and, in 1968, the parties went through another ceremony of marriage there, valid by that law. The first marriage was, however, regarded as valid by Indian law. The question arose of the legitimacy of some of the spouses' children in the context of their claims to British citizenship.

An immediate question to be considered was whether the children had been legitimated by their parents' subsequent marriage. This was referred to Indian

---

8 [1948] Ch 79 at 92, [1947] 2 All ER 830 at 836. Approved by the Privy Council in *Bamgbose v Daniel* [1955] AC 107 at 120, [1954] 3 All ER 263; and see *Re Jones* (1961) 25 DLR (2d) 595, infra, p 756; *Re Karnenas* (1978) 3 RFL (2d) 213.
9 [1948] Ch 79 at 92, [1947] 2 All ER 830 at 835.
10 Morris (1948) 12 Conveyancer (NS) 223; F A Mann (1948) 64 LQR 199; Falconbridge, *Conflict of Laws* (2nd edn), pp 747 et seq. On the other hand, it is approved by Wolff, p 388; Nygh, p 414.
11 *Re Goodman's Trusts* (1881) 17 Ch D 266 at 299; and see *Boyes v Bedale* (1863) 1 Hem & M 798; *Re Andros* (1883) 24 Ch D 637; *Re Grey's Trusts* [1892] 3 Ch 88.
12 *Re Bischoffsheim* [1948] Ch 79 at 92, [1947] 2 All ER 830 at 836.
13 [1990] 2 FLR 261, revsd. on another point by the House of Lords: [1991] 4 All ER 682, [1991] 3 WLR 903; and see *R v Secretary of State for the Home Department, ex p Brassey* [1989] 2 FLR 486 at 494; *A-G for Victoria v Commonwealth of Australia* (1961–1962) 107 CLR 529 at 596; *In Re Sit Woo-tung* [1990] 2 HKLR 410.

law, being that of the domicil of the parents and of the children at all material times, and Indian law did not recognise legitimation by subsequent marriage. That left the question of legitimacy which was answered by means of the same process. Legitimacy, being regarded as an issue of status, was referred to the law of the children's domicil of origin, India, which law regarded the children as legitimate because Indian law regarded the parents' first marriage as valid. *Shaw v Gould* was distinguished as being concerned with the validity of the Scottish decree, and the decision in *Re Bischoffsheim* was approved.

What is striking about this decision is that the children were regarded in England as legitimate, notwithstanding the fact that their parents' marriage was, in the eyes of English private international law, invalid. Had the parents petitioned for a declaration as to the validity of their first marriage, it would have been refused on the ground that the marriage was invalid as to form according to the law of the place of celebration.[14] This strengthens the view that a child's legitimacy depends on the law of his domicil of origin.

(d) EFFECT OF DOCTRINE OF PUTATIVE MARRIAGE

It is submitted, then, that even if there had been no statutory alteration of English domestic law in 1959 the courts would have endorsed the approach to the subject made in *Bischoffsheim's Case* and would have restricted the decision in *Shaw v Gould* to the exceptional circumstances of the case. This submission was considerably fortified once the doctrine of putative marriage was accepted in the Legitimacy Act 1959.[15] Birth in lawful wedlock no longer represents the sole test of legitimacy according to English domestic law; for it is now provided that, where the father is domiciled in England, a child born of a void marriage is to be treated as legitimate if both or either of his parents reasonably believed that the marriage was valid.[16] Where, therefore, the father is domiciled in a foreign country where a similar doctrine is recognised, there would be less justification even than formerly for denying the legitimate status of a child born of a void marriage.[1]

(e) MEANING OF "DOMICIL OF ORIGIN"

ROMER J's statement[2] that the domicil of origin means the country in which the parents are domiciled at the birth of the child is not supported by indisputable authority. Some of the judges have preferred to refer to the domicil of the father,[3] though others, probably having in mind the usual case where the father and mother possess a common domicil, have with ROMER J, preferred to speak of "the domicil of the parents", a view which, if adopted, would require the law of each domicil to be satisfied. It is, of course, true that to attribute to the child the domicil of his father where his parents have different domicils is to beg the question of his legitimacy, for, since the domicil of a child is said to be that of his father if legitimate but of his mother if illegitimate,[4] it would appear to be impossible to fix his domicil until the question of his legitimacy has been settled.

14 See *Berthiaume v Dastous* [1930] AC 79, supra, pp 572–573.
15 See now Legitimacy Act 1976, infra, pp 755–756.
16 Ibid, s 1, Sch 1.
 1 Jones (1959) 8 ICLQ 722, 725.
 2 *Re Bischoffscheim* [1948] Ch 79 at 92.
 3 Eg *Yuen Tse v Minister of Employment and Immigration* (1983) 32 RFL (2d) 274.
 4 Supra, p 159.

This vicious circle[5] would disappear if it could be said that the legitimacy of a child was to be referred to the domicil of one of his parents, but that his domicil of origin depended on the validity of his parents' marriage. Some nineteenth-century cases[6] on the domicil of origin of a child are compatible with such a view. The present difficulty stems from Lord WESTBURY's statement that "the law attributes to every individual as soon as he is born the domicil of his father, if the child be legitimate, and the domicil of his mother if illegitimate".[7] As in *Shaw v Gould*, the questions of the legitimacy of a child and of the validity of his parents' marriage seemed to nineteenth century judges inextricably to be the same. The later acceptance that a child might be legitimate notwithstanding the invalidity of his parents' marriage[8] must inevitably cast doubt on the acceptability of Lord WESTBURY's views.[9]

If one must accept that Lord WESTBURY's statement has stood the test of time too well and cannot now be confounded, the vicious circle must be broken; for logic must not be allowed to impede the best solution of the problem. It is not easy to determine whether the domicil of the father or of the mother should predominate. Especially now that a wife does not automatically take her husband's domicil on marriage, the problem cannot be evaded by general reference to the domicil of the mother. There is, however, much to be said in favour of reference to the domicil of the mother for it is with the mother that the young child is likely to make his first home. Nevertheless, the solution most favourable to the child, it is submitted, is that the domicil of the natural father should be decisive.[10] It would seem that it is this relationship on which most emphasis is placed by the Continental legal systems.[11] In the leading case of *Re Grove*,[12] STIRLING J, after citing authority for the view that "the status of a person, his legitimacy or illegitimacy, is to be determined everywhere by the law of his country of origin",[13] ie the law of the place where his parents were domiciled at his birth, went on to say:

If the parents have different domicils (as may happen where they are not married), the authorities shew that the domicil of the father is to be regarded, and not that of the mother.[14]

This is admitted without question in cases of legitimation. Moreover, it is significant that the operation of the Legitimacy Act 1976 recognising the legitimacy of a child born of a void marriage is confined to a case where the father is domiciled in England at the time of the child's birth.[15] The fact that

5 Dicey & Morris, p 831.
6 For example, in *Forbes v Forbes* (1854) Kay 341 at 343 it is said that "every person born in wedlock acquires by birth the domicil of its father."
7 *Udny v Udny* (1869) LR 1 Sc & Div 441 at 457.
8 Eg putative marriage under the Legitimacy Act 1976, s 1, infra, pp 755–756.
9 The vicious circle also disappears under the view in the Restatement 2d, §287 that a child's legitimacy may be determined as to one parent only by reference, normally, to the domicil of that parent, so that a child may be legitimate with respect to one parent, but illegitimate with respect to the other.
10 Schmitthoff, *Conflict of Laws*, 3rd edn, p 283; contra, Dicey & Morris, p 831.
11 Guttman (1959) 8 ICLQ 678, 685.
12 (1888) 40 Ch D 216.
13 These words are from the judgment of JAMES LJ in *Re Goodman's Trusts* (1881) 17 Ch D 266 at 296.
14 *Re Grove*, supra, at 224. See also *Re Don's Estate* (1857) 4 Drew 194 at 198; *Re Andros* (1883) 24 Ch D 637 at 642; *R and McDonell v Leong Ba Chai* [1954] 1 DLR 401 at 403; *Perpetual Executors and Trustees Association of Australia Ltd v Roberts* [1970] VR 732 at 756–757; and see *Hashmi v Hashmi* [1972] Fam 36.
15 S 1(2).

the legitimacy may not be recognised in the separate domicil of the mother is irrelevant.

The decisive date for fixing the domicil of origin is the birth of the child. A child, no doubt, is for various purposes deemed at birth to have been in existence from the time of conception,[16] and if the parents change their domicil between the time of conception and of birth it is arguable that the law of the father's domicil at the former time deserves consideration.[17] Although there is no authority in point it is probable that the English courts would regard the domicil at the time of birth as decisive. A somewhat analogous question arises in the case of a posthumous child whose mother has changed her domicil since the death of the father. Is the law of the father's domicil at the time of his death or the law of the mother's domicil at the time of the child's birth to determine the question of legitimacy? The latter is probably the correct solution because the domicil of origin of a posthumous child is that of his mother.[18]

(f) RELEVANCE OF THE INCIDENTS OF STATUS

The question whether a child is legitimate or not by the law of the domicil is to be determined by examining the incidents of his status under that law rather than the title used to describe it. If the law of the domicil is the law of a country such as New Zealand[1] where there is no distinction drawn between legitimate and illegitimate children, then as the child would have all the incidents of the status of a legitimate child in England, though only described in New Zealand as a "child",[2] he should be regarded in England as legitimate, though not born to parents who are married. Indeed, the Supreme Court of Canada[3] has concluded that a child born in Mexco to parents who are not married, who was described by Mexican law as illegitimate, was to be considered to have the status of a legitimate child in Canada. Under Mexican law she had all the capacities and obligations of such a child, though certain social limitations attached to her position in Mexico causing her to be described there as "illegitimate".

(g) WHERE BIRTH TO PARENTS WHO ARE MARRIED DOES NOT CONFER LEGITIMACY

The rule suggested above[4] allocates a question of legitimacy to the law of the domicil of origin. Principle requires that this personal law should apply exclusively, since it is the only law competent to determine the status of the child. Nevertheless, if a case were to arise in which a child, though born to married parents, was for some reason not regarded as born legitimate, as for example because he was not conceived during the marriage, it is probably a safe assumption that an English court would be satisfied with the practically universal test of birth to parents married to one another. This break with

---

16 *Re Salaman* [1908] 1 Ch 4; *Re Callaghan* [1948] NZLR 846. But see *Elliot v Lord Joicey* [1935] AC 209.

17 Taintor (1940) 18 Can BR 589, 596–597.

18 There seems to be no English authority on the domicil of a posthumous child, but academic opinion favours the view that it is the same as the mother's: Westlake (7th edn), s 250; Dicey & Morris, p 126.

1 Status of Children Act 1969 (New Zealand).

2 Ibid, s 3.

3 *Re MacDonald* (1962) 34 DLR (2d) 14, affd (1964) 44 DLR (2d) 208; and see *Khoo Hooi Leong v Khoo Hean Kwee* [1926] AC 529 at 543; *In Re Sit Woo-tung* [1990] 2 HKLR 410.

4 Supra, p 752.

principle might be justified by the paramount importance of communicating to the child the beneficial status of legitimacy if some rational ground for doing so exists.

(h) PUTATIVE MARRIAGES

It remains to add a few words on the doctrine of the putative marriage under the Legitimacy Act 1976.[5] The main provision is as follows:

> The child of a void marriage, whenever born,[6] shall ... be treated as the legitimate child of his parents if at the time of the insemination resulting in the birth or, where there was no such insemination, the child's conception (or at the time of the celebration of the marriage if later) both or either of the parties reasonably believed that the marriage was valid.[7]

This provision, however, does not apply unless the father of the child was domiciled in England at the time of the birth or, if he died before the birth, was so domiciled immediately before his death.[8] Where this condition is not satisfied, the legitimacy of a child born of a void marriage must be determined, as we have seen, by the law of his domicil of origin.

In a provision that is susceptible of more than one interpretation,[9] a void marriage for the purposes of the Act is defined as

> a marriage, not being voidable only, in respect of which the High Court has or had jurisdiction to grant a decree of nullity, or would have or would have had such jurisdiction if the parties were domiciled in England and Wales.[10]

The purport of this language certainly does not leap to the eye, but its probable object is to exclude any union which in the eyes of English law has no claim to be a marriage at all, as for example one springing from concubinage.

The impact of the introduction of the doctrine of putative marriage into English law on the private international law rules relating to legitimacy is interesting. The provisions of the Legitimacy Act 1976 apply only if the husband was domiciled in England at the time of the birth. Let us assume, therefore, that the parents of a child are domiciled at all material times in a foreign country which recognises the doctrine of putative marriage. If birth in lawful wedlock is the test of legitimacy, the English courts would regard the child as illegitimate, even though the courts of his domicil regard him as legitimate, as would the English courts had his father been domiciled in England at the time of his birth. Such an unreasonable conclusion has been rejected by the courts of British Columbia in *Re Jones, Royal Trust Co v*

---

5 First introduced by the Legitimacy Act 1959, s 2. Special provision is introduced in the Family Law Reform Act 1987, s 27 to deal with the status of a child born to a married couple by artificial insemination, with the semen of a man other than the husband. However, no choice of law rule is laid down, though the provisions are limited to the case of a child born in England.

6 Provided the child was born after the marriage was entered into: *Re Spence* [1989] 2 All ER 679.

7 S 1(1), amended by the Family Law Reform Act 1987, s 28(1). A presumption of reasonable belief is introduced by s 28(2) of the 1987 Act.

8 S 1(2).

9 For various views on its almost identical predecessor, s 2(5) of the Legitimacy Act 1959, see Jones (1959) 8 ICLQ 725, 726; Tucker (1960) 9 ICLQ 321, 322; Kahn-Freund (1960) 23 MLR 58, 59.

10 S 10(1).

Jones[11] thereby adding support to the view that legitimacy should be determined by the law of the domicil. The facts were these:

A testator left property to H and his children. H married W1, by whom he had 2 children. H left W1 and acquired a domicil in California. Later W1 divorced him in Nevada and H married W2 by whom he had a son, X. There was doubt as to the validity of the marriage between H and W2 because the Nevada divorce might not be recognised in California. However, Californian law accepted the doctrine of putative marriage and regarded X as legitimate. California being X's domicil of origin, the Canadian court decided that X was legitimate without deciding whether his parents' marriage was valid. X could, therefore, take under the will.

3. LEGITIMATION[12]

In the various legal systems of the world two main methods are found by which a person, not born with the status of legitimacy, may be later legitimated. These are: subsequent marriage of the parents and recognition of the child by the father. Each of these methods requires separate consideration. Here again, however, it should be emphasised that our concern is to examine the law which should determine the status. It is, for example, for the law governing succession to decide whether a child who has been legitimated may or may not succeed by will or under an intestacy.

(a) LEGITIMATION BY SUBSEQUENT MARRIAGE

(i) Introduction

It has long been accepted that children born before marriage were made legitimate by the subsequent marriage of their parents. This rule became part of canon law about the twelfth century, and was later adopted by practically all the legal systems on the Continent and in South America. It has received statutory recognition in most of the common law world. Until the Legitimacy Act of 1926, however, it formed no part of the law of England and Wales or of Ireland, though it obtained in Scotland, the Isle of Man and the Channel Islands.

(ii) Common law rule

The role of private international law is to choose the system of law which shall determine whether legitimation by this method is effective or not. The rule finally established at common law by *Re Grove*,[13] after some hesitation,[14] is that a foreign legitimation by subsequent marriage is not recognised in England unless the father is domiciled, *both at the time of the child's birth and also at the time of the subsequent marriage*, in a country whose law allows this method of legitimation.[15]

11 (1961) 25 DLR (2d) 595.
12 On the subject generally see Taintor (1940) 18 Can BR 589 and 691; F A Mann (1941) 57 LQR 112; Lipstein (1954) *Festschrift für Ernst Rabel*, vol I, p 611. For problems connected with legitimation under a foreign statute, see Dicey & Morris, pp 852–856.
13 (1887) 40 Ch D 216.
14 See, for example, *Boyes v Bedale* (1863) 1 Hem & M 798, disapproved in *Re Goodman's Trusts*, infra.
15 *Re Goodman's Trusts* (1881) 17 Ch D 266; *Re Andros* (1883) 24 Ch D 637; *Re Grove* (1887) 40 Ch D 216; and see *Motala v A-G* [1990] 2 FLR 261 at 267.

A simple illustration of the working of the rule is afforded by the case of *Re Goodman's Trusts*,[16] where a domiciled Englishwoman had died intestate in respect of a large sum of money, and it was necessary to decide which of her brother's children were entitled to share therein, as being her "next of kin" under the Statutes of Distribution. The relevant events in her brother's life were chronologically as follows.

(a) While domiciled in England he had three children by Charlotte Smith, to whom he was not married.
(b) He acquired a Dutch domicil, and had a fourth child, Hannah, by Charlotte Smith.
(c) He married Charlotte Smith in Amsterdam.
(d) While still domiciled in the Netherlands he had a fifth child, Anne, by Charlotte Smith.

Legitimation by subsequent marriage was part of Dutch law. It was, therefore, held on the above facts that Hannah and Anne were alone legitimate for the purposes of the English intestacy. It was only in their cases that at the two critical moments, birth and marriage, the law of the father's domicil recognised this particular form of legitimation.

(iii) Under the Legitimacy Act 1976

The operation of the common law rules, though not abrogated, was immensely curtailed by the Legitimacy Act 1926[17] which made legitimation by subsequent marriage part of the law of England. The present law is to be found in the Legitimacy Act 1976, section 2 of which provides that, where the parents of an illegitimate person marry, the marriage shall, if the father is *at the date of the marriage* domiciled in England and Wales, render that person, if living, legitimate from the date of the marriage.

With regard to persons who are not domiciled in England and Wales, section 3 of the Legitimacy Act 1976 provides as follows:

Where the parents of an illegitimate person marry one another and the father of the illegitimate person is not at the time of the marriage domiciled in England and Wales but is domiciled in a country by the law of which the illegitimate person became legitimated by virtue of such subsequent marriage, that person, if living, shall in England and Wales be recognised as having been so legitimated from the date of the marriage[18] notwithstanding that, at the time of his birth, his father was domiciled in a country the law of which did not permit legitimation by subsequent marriage.

This section is one that affects private international law, and it discards the old rule that the law of the father's domicil at the time of the child's birth must be taken into account. The law of the father's domicil at the time of the marriage is the sole decisive factor.[19] It is this law that decides, for instance, whether something more than mere marriage, such as a formal acknowledgment, is necessary to effect legitimation.

16 (1881) 17 Ch D 266.
17 S 1; the status of a person legitimated thereunder is preserved by the Legitimacy Act 1976, Sch 1, para 1.
18 This applies even though the father or mother was married to a third person at the time of the child's birth; cf Legitimacy Act 1926, s 1(2) since repealed.
19 See *Heron v National Trustees Executors and Agency Co of Australasia Ltd* [1976] VR 733.

(b) LEGITIMATION BY RECOGNITION

It has been assumed so far that the foreign legitimation is by subsequent marriage. However, in several states in Europe and in North and South America a father is allowed to legitimate his child by formally recognising it to be his own. The first question that this raises in private international law is—By what legal system will the English courts determine the validity of this particular form of legitimation? Is it sufficient that it is valid by the law of the father's domicil at the time of recognition, or, like legitimation by subsequent marriage before the Legitimacy Act 1926, must it also be valid by the law of the father's domicil at the time of the child's birth? The matter has been considered in only one case—*Re Luck's Settlement Trusts*[20]—where the facts were as follows:

Under the will of George Luck, a British subject domiciled in England, funds were held in trust for all his children attaining twenty-one. Each child was to receive the income of his share for life, and after his death the capital was to be divided equally among his children at twenty-one. The marriage settlement of George limited further sums in the same manner, except that only those grandchildren born within twenty-one years of the death of the survivor of George and his wife were to take a share of the capital. The survivor died in 1896. Therefore, no grandchild was entitled under the settlement trusts unless he was alive and legitimate in 1917 at the latest.

Charles was a son of George Luck. He married in 1893, but in 1906, while still married, he became the father of an illegitimate son, David, in California. At this time both he and David's mother were domiciled in England. After the dissolution of his first marriage he married a second wife. In 1925 he signed a formal document with the assent of his second wife by which he acknowledged David to be his legitimate son and adopted him as such.[1] At this time Charles was domiciled in California. It was assumed by the Court of Appeal that David's mother was also domiciled there. By the law of California the acknowledgement in 1925 operated to legitimate David from his birth in 1906.

The question that arose on these facts was whether David was entitled to a share under the will and marriage settlement of his grandfather, George. At that time, to take under the latter he was required to be a legitimate grandchild alive as such in 1917.

The Court of Appeal held that David was entitled neither under the will nor under the settlement. The reasoning was that legitimation by subsequent marriage is disregarded at common law unless allowed by the law of the father's domicil at the time both of the birth and the marriage; that the relevant judgments regard this rule, not as confined to the single case of a subsequent marriage but as applicable to all forms of legitimation; and that in any case both convenience and principle demand the application of a uniform rule to all forms. Therefore David was disqualified, since at the time

---

20 [1940] Ch 864, [1940] 3 All ER 307; and see *R and McDonnell v Leong Ba Chai* [1954] 1 DLR 401.

1 It is important to notice, as F A Mann has shown ((1941) 57 LQR 112, 119), that the Californian method was not adoption, but legitimation by recognition. The unwary might assume from the judgments in the Court of Appeal that it was equivalent to adoption in the English sense.

of his birth his father was subject to English law, by which legitimation by recognition is not allowed.

The common law rule based on the child's capacity at birth was never in fact extended to cases other than legitimation by subsequent marriage. It was curtailed substantially even in this connection by the Legitimacy Act 1926;[2] and gratuitously to prolong its life and to extend its operation is a retrograde step. In fact the decision has been most generally criticised on the ground that, though it is obviously convenient that one principle should govern all types of legitimation, it is a little eccentric to choose one whose operation has been greatly curtailed by statute.[3]

It is therefore to be hoped that, if the occasion arises, the House of Lords will prefer the dissenting judgment of SCOTT LJ, who argued in a convincing manner and at no little length that status, the outstanding characteristic of which is its "quality of universality", once determined by the law of the domicil, must be judicially recognised all the world over. At a time when David and his father and mother were domiciled in California, his father made a certain declaration according to Californian law. The effect of this by that law was to clothe David with the status of a legitimate person. Therefore, "that status, established by the law of that foreign country, was under English law one which it was the duty of the English court to recognise, and *prima facie* to enforce in accordance with its nature and attributes as determined by the law of that country".[4] It is the law of the domicil at the time when the legitimation is effected that should alone be considered.

It might also be added that the Legitimacy Act 1976 in referring to the recognition of legitimation at common law talks of a "legitimation (whether or not by virtue of the subsequent marriage of his parents)".[5]

4. ADOPTION[6]

A variety of issues arise from consideration of the private international law rules relating to adoption. There are wide differences between the laws of different countries on a number of matters, such as who can adopt, or be adopted, and the effects of adoption on, for instance, succession rights. For example, the requirements of English law that the person to be adopted must be unmarried and under the age of 18[7] are not found in all legal systems. In examining the rules as to the jurisdiction of the English court to make adoption orders, the relevant choice of law rules and the rules for the recognition of foreign adoptions, it will be necessary to differentiate between the rules generally applicable to these issues and the particular rules which govern "regulated adoptions", that is, adoptions which fall within the provisions of the 1964 Hague Convention on Adoption.

---

2 S 8(1).
3 Beckett (1944) 21 BYBIL 209; Taintor (1940) 18 Can BR 589, 652; F A Mann (1941) 57 LQR 112, 120.
4 [1940] Ch 864 at 888, [1940] 3 All ER 307 at 325.
5 1976 Act, s 10(1).
6 Morris, *Festschrift für F A Mann*, 241.
7 Adoption Act 1976, s 72(1).

(a) ADOPTION PROCEEDINGS IN ENGLAND

(i) Introduction

Adoption, the process by which a child is brought permanently into the family of the adopter, was introduced into England by the Adoption of Children Act 1926, which was ultimately replaced by the consolidating legislation of the Adoption Act 1976.[8] Unlike the case in some other countries, adoption can be effected only by the order of a court,[9] after a judicial inquiry directed mainly to ensuring that such an order will be for the welfare of the child. The effect of an order is to take away from the child whatever legal benefits nature conferred upon him and to transfer all obligations towards him to the adoptive parents who by nature have no obligation towards him at all.[10] There is a complete and fundamental change in the status of the child. He becomes a child in law of his adoptive parent or parents to the exclusion of his natural parents.

The jurisdiction of the English court to make an adoption order and the law to be applied by the court depend on two different sets of statutory rules, namely general rules and Convention rules, ie those which implement the 1964 Hague Convention on Adoption.

(ii) General rules

Jurisdiction Under the general rules, jurisdiction is stated to depend primarily on domicil. The applicant for the order must be domiciled[11] in some part of the British Isles.[12] Where the application is by a married couple, only one of them needs to satisfy the domicil requirement.[13] The domicil of the child is not relevant.[14] Criticism has been voiced[15] of the fact that there is no specific requirement, as there was under the Adoption Act 1958,[16] that the applicant and the child reside in England. It appears at first sight, from the Adoption Act 1976, that the domicil of the applicant is the only jurisdictional criterion and that residence or habitual residence are irrelevant. However, even if the applicant is domiciled in England, the court may still be unable to make an adoption order. For example, if the child is not in Great Britain when the application is made, the 1976 Act provides that only the High Court has

8   Only brought into force on 1 January 1988, and since amended by the Children Act 1989, Sch 10, Part I.
9   This can be the High Court, county court, or magistrates' court: Adoption Act 1976, s 62; but see *Practice Direction (Family Division: Transfer of Business)* [1986] 2 All ER 703, [1986] 1 WLR 1139; *Re N and L (Minors) (Transfer of Business)* [1987] 2 All ER 732, [1988] 1 FLR 48.
10 Adoption Act 1976, s 12, amended by the Children Act 1989, Sch 10, para 3.
11 Ibid, s 15(2)(a).
12 Ie the United Kingdom, the Channel Islands and the Isle of Man.
13 Adoption Act 1976, s 14(2)(a).
14 If the child is a foreign national, notice of the application should be given to the Home Secretary to enable him to intervene in the proceedings, as where he suspects the purpose of the adoption is to avoid immigration controls: *Re H(A Minor) (Adoption: Non-Patrial)* [1982] Fam 121, [1982] 3 All ER 84; *Re W (A Minor) (Adoption: Non-Patrial)* [1986] Fam 54, [1985] 3 All ER 449; though it should be borne in mind that a de facto, extra-legal, adoption may satisfy immigration rules: *R v Immigration Appeal Tribunal, ex p Tohur Ali* [1988] 2 FLR 523, [1988] Fam Law 289; *R v Immigration Appeal Tribunal, ex p Gurdev Singh* [1989] 1 FLR 115, [1989] Fam Law 110.
15 Morris, *Festschrift für F A Mann* 241, 242–245.
16 S 1(5).

jurisdiction to make an adoption order.[17] However, even then the court may be unable or unwilling to do so. For instance, the court may not make an order unless it is satisfied that the relevant adoption agency or local authority has had sufficient opportunity to see the child and the applicant in "the home environment".[18] This is impossible if either the child or the applicant lives abroad.[19] It is similarly impossible for an applicant resident abroad to give notice of his intention to apply for an adoption order to the local authority "within whose area he has his home".[20] In the light of these difficulties SHELDON J declined jurisdiction to entertain an adoption application by an English domiciliary resident in Hong Kong in relation to his wife's two children who were at boarding school in England and spent their holidays in Hong Kong.[21] All this suggests that the single statutory jurisdictional criterion of domicil is misleading and, given that the adoption provisions of the Adoption Act 1976 are very hard to satisfy in the case of a person resident abroad, it would have been better if the general jurisdictional criterion had been that of habitual residence.

Choice of law The absence of any requirement that the child should be domiciled in England raises a question of choice of law. If an applicant, domiciled in England, applies for an adoption order in respect of a child domiciled abroad, will the court have regard to the substantive requirements of the foreign law of the domicil, which may differ widely from their English equivalents in such matters as the age of the respective parties and the consents of relatives? The terms of the English legislation are, indeed, such that an adoption order made by the court would not be vitiated by a failure to take account of the foreign law, yet it is submitted that to refer exclusively to the law of the forum would be contrary to principle and often prejudicial to the well-being of the child. The admitted and basic feature of status as fixed by the law of the domicil is its universality.[22] The status attributed to a child in his domicil of origin is entitled to universal respect. It is, therefore, undesirable for the English court to make an adoption order which affects to destroy that status and to substitute another that is fundamentally different. Moreover, such an order would scarcely be recognised in the domicil of origin, with the result that the child would be the child of X in England but of Y in all other countries, a situation which seems strangely at odds with the statutory requirement that, in reaching any decision relating to adoption, first consideration shall be given to the need to safeguard and promote the welfare of the child.[23]

The contrary view, that the English statute must be exclusively applicable on practical grounds, has been vigorously advanced by Kahn-Freund:[24]

Adoption in particular is now ... so intimately linked with the activities of the

17 S 62(3).
18 S 13(3).
19 Eg *Re Y (Minors)* [1985] Fam 136, [1985] 3 All ER 33.
20 S 22(1), amplified by Children Act 1989, Sch 10, para 10.
21 *Re Y (Minors)* [1985] Fam 136, [1985] 3 All ER 33; and see 1976 Act, s 71(1A), substituted by the Children Act 1989, Sch 10, para 30(9).
22 *Re Luck's Settlement Trusts* [1940] Ch 864 at 894, [1940] 3 All ER 307 at 329.
23 Adoption Act 1976, s 6.
24 *The Growth of Internationalism in English Private International Law* (The Lionel Cohen Lectures, 6th series, 1960), 62–66; and see Dicey and Morris, pp 867–869.

welfare authorities that it has become almost impossible to view an English adoption otherwise than in a purely English context.[25]

It might, indeed, be extremely difficult to blend two opposing systems of adoption law, but none the less the fact remains that to impose a status on a child in conflict with that which he possesses in his domicil of origin, to create as it were a limping child,[26] would be a doubtful blessing to bestow upon him.[1]

A resolution of the conflict between principle and the wording of what is now section 14 (1) of the Adoption Act 1976[2] was found in *Re B (S) (An Infant)*,[3] where the facts were as follows:

An application was made by proposed adopters for the consent of the natural father to the adoption to be dispensed with. The natural father was domiciled in Spain and the child and the adoptive parents were resident in England where the adoptive parents were domiciled. It was assumed that the child was domiciled in Spain,[4] and this raised the issue whether Spanish law should be considered relevant to the application.

GOFF J decided that the court had jurisdiction to make an adoption order "notwithstanding that by the law of the infant's domicil the court there could not make an order or could only make one having different consequences."[5]

Nevertheless, he admitted that the law of the domicil is not to be ignored for "the true impact of the domiciliary law is purely as a factor—albeit an important one—to be taken into account in considering whether the proposed order will be for the welfare of the infant, a matter upon which the Statute expressly provides[6] that the court must be satisfied before making an order."[7] Moreover, GOFF J took the view that "welfare", as used in the statute, "does not mean simple physical or moral well-being, but benefit in the widest sense which must include consideration of the effect the order, if made, will have on the infant's status."[8] If the adoption will not be recognised by such law, though here there was evidence that Spain would recognise the English order, then the court will have to weigh the serious disadvantages of being a "limping child" against the benefits which may accrue from adoption. This means that there will be cases, albeit rare ones, where an English adoption order will be made in circumstances where it will not be recognised by the law of the domicil. Indeed jurisdiction has been exercised[9] to make an adoption order

25 Kahn-Freund, op cit, pp 65–66.
26 Despite the comment in Morris, 3rd edn, p 255, it is suggested that neither the phrase nor, particularly, its implications for the child, is amusing.
1 In the reverse case, where a person domiciled abroad wishes to adopt abroad a child who is in England, the court under s 55 of the Adoption Act 1976 (amended by the Children Act 1989, Sch 10, para 22) will only enable the applicant to take the child abroad (by vesting in the applicant the parental rights and duties relating to the child) if, essentially, the court is as satisfied as if the application was for an English adoption order.
2 What was then the Adoption Act 1958, s 1(1).
3 [1968] Ch 204; Blom-Cooper (1968) 31 MLR 219; Carter (1967) 42 BYBIL 309–310.
4 The natural parents were divorced and the court would not decide whether in such a case a child took the domicil of the mother to whom custody had been awarded.
5 [1968] Ch 204 at 210.
6 Adoption Act 1958, s 7(1)(b); see now Adoption Act 1976, s 6.
7 [1968] Ch 204 at 211; approved in *Re G (An Infant)* [1968] 3 NSWR 483 at 485–486.
8 Ibid.
9 *Re R (Adoption)* [1966] 3 All ER 613, [1967] 1 WLR 34; cf *Re A (An Infant)* [1963] 1 All ER 531, [1963] 1 WLR 231.

in the case of a twenty-year old[10] political refugee without any reference at all to the law of his foreign domicil.

In all the relevant English decisions, there is no doubt that the courts have not considered the problem of the effect of the adoption order on the status of the natural parents. Whilst jurisdiction can be exercised without reference to their domicil, one might question[11] whether an order which deprives them in England of the status of parent should be made without consideration not only of their interests in relation to matters such as consent, but also the effect of the adoption order under the law governing their status.[12] Not only a child but also a parent can "limp". The Supreme Court of Canada, in 1981, decided[13] (though without detailed consideration of the choice of law issues) that the question whether a child was one who could be adopted should be referred not only to the domiciliary law of the applicants and of the child, but also at least in contested cases to that of the natural parents.

(iii) Convention rules

General In 1964 the Tenth Session of the Hague Conference on Private International Law produced a Convention on Adoption which was signed in 1965.[14] This Convention, which was ratified by the United Kingdom in 1978, relates to jurisdiction, choice of law and recognition of foreign adoptions.[15] The relevant provisions are now to be found in the Adoption Act 1976.

Jurisdiction The Convention, and the implementing legislation in section 17 of the 1976 Act, do not apply to internal adoptions, ie those where the adoptive parents and the child possess the same nationality and are living in the country of which they are nationals.[16] The effect of section 17 is to extend the jurisdiction of the High Court in cases of "convention adoptions", ie where at least one party is connected by nationality or habitual residence with a country which is a party to the Hague Convention,[17] other than the one granting the adoption, in this case England. The extended jurisdiction enables the court to grant adoptions on the following bases when application is made for a "Convention adoption order".[1] Where the applicants are a married couple they must both be United Kingdom nationals[2] or nationals of a Convention country and both be habitually resident in Great Britain, or both be United Kingdom nationals and be habitually resident in British

---

10 At that time the age of majority was still twenty-one.
11 See Blom-Cooper (1968) 31 MLR 219.
12 In *J v C* [1970] AC 668, the House of Lords granted custody of a child to foster parents against the desire of the unimpeachable natural parents in Spain. Their Lordships were at pains to indicate they were not considering an application for an adoption order, see at pp 692, 714, 719, thus suggesting greater weight would be paid to the interests of the natural parents in the case of adoption because of its permanent effect.
13 *Paquette v Galipeau* [1981] 1 SCR 29; and see *Re L (HK)* [1989] 1 WWR 556.
14 Cmnd 2615. See Graveson (1965) 14 ICLQ 528; Lipstein [1965] CLJ 224; Unger (1965) 28 MLR 463.
15 For discussion of the recognition rules, see infra, pp 765–767.
16 Adoption Act 1976, s 17(3). Does "living in" mean "habitually resident in"? Cf Hague Adoption Convention 1964, Art 2(b).
17 The only other countries which are parties to the Convention so far are Austria and Switzerland.
1 Adoption Act 1976, s 17(1).
2 For the meaning of "United Kingdom national", see Adoption Act 1976, s 72(1); SI 1978/1432, para 7, as amended by the British Nationality Act 1981, s 51(3)(a)(ii), itself amended by SI 1986/948, Art 7(9)(a).

territory[3] or a Convention country.[4] A single applicant must satisfy the same criteria of nationality and habitual residence.[5] The child to be adopted must be under eighteen[6] and not have been married and, again, jurisdiction is based on habitual residence in British territory or a Convention country and nationality of the United Kingdom or a Convention country.[7] All these jurisdictional criteria must be satisfied both at the time of the application and when the order is made.[8]

Choice of law The law to be applied to convention adoptions is a mixture of English law and the law of the nationality of the applicants and of the child.[9] If the child is not a United Kingdom national, then the law of the Convention country of which he is a national must be applied to matters of consents and consultations,[10] other than those with respect to the applicant and members of his family.[11] The English court must also refuse to make an adoption order if the adoption would be prohibited by a provision of the applicant's national law[12] which has been notified to the United Kingdom government under the Convention.[13] There are special rules for the ascertainment of nationality and of the internal law of a foreign country.[14]

(b) RECOGNITION OF FOREIGN ADOPTIONS

There may be a variety of circumstances in which a court in England is faced with the decision whether to recognise an adoption which has taken place abroad. The issue may arise incidentally in the course of other proceedings and the main examples in the reported cases concern property rights—eg whether a child adopted abroad can take under a will,[15] in an intestacy[16] or a settlement,[17] or whether a parent can succeed on his adopted child's intestacy.[18] The recognition of a foreign adoption may also affect the powers of the English court to make an adoption order itself,[19] social security issues,[20] or rights of entry to the United Kingdom as an immigrant.[1] Finally, it is possible that a child might wish simply to seek from the English courts a

---

3 Defined in the Adoption Act 1976, s 72(1) as the United Kingdom, Channel Islands, Isle of Man or a colony where so designated; and the United Kingdom has been designated as "British territory": SI 1978/1432, para 5.
4 Adoption Act 1976, s 17(4).
5 Ibid, s 17(5).
6 Ibid, s 72(1).
7 Ibid, s 17(2).
8 Ibid, s 17(1).
9 Blom, (1973) 22 ICLQ 109, 136–142.
10 Adoption Act 1976, s 17(6).
11 Ibid, s 17(7).
12 Ibid, s 17(4), (5).
13 Ibid, s 17(8), see SI 1978/1431.
14 Ibid, ss 70, 71.
15 *Re Marshall* [1957] Ch 507, [1957] 3 All ER 172; and see *Perpetual Trustee Co Ltd v Montuori* [1982] 1 NSWLR 710.
16 *Re Wilson* [1954] Ch 733, [1954] 1 All ER 997.
17 *Re Valentine's Settlement* [1965] Ch 831, [1965] 2 All ER 226; *Spencer's Trustees v Ruggles* 1982 SLT 165.
18 *Re Wilby* [1956] P 174, [1956] 1 All ER 27.
19 *Re H (An Infant)* (1973) 4 Fam Law 77.
20 Eg National Insurance Decisions Nos R(F) 1/65; R(F) 3/73.
1 Eg *Mathieu v Entry Clearance Officer, Bridgetown* [1979–80] Imm AR 157; *Secretary of State for the Home Department v Lofthouse* [1981] Imm AR 166.

declaration as to his status and thus whether his foreign adoption will be recognised here.[2]

In examining the rules for the recognition of foreign adoptions, three different situations must be distinguished. They are recognition of adoption orders made elsewhere in the British Isles and recognition either under common law rules or under the Adoption Act 1976 of adoption orders made in other foreign countries.

(i) Recognition of adoptions made elsewhere in the British Isles

Any adoption order made in Scotland, Northern Ireland, the Channel Islands, or the Isle of Man will be recognised and given effect to in England.[3]

(ii) Recognition of adoptions made in other foreign countries

Under the Adoption Act 1976[4] The 1976 Act provides two sets of rules dealing with the recognition of foreign adoptic 1 orders. These depend on whether the adoption is an "overseas adoption" or a "regulated adoption". An overseas adoption is defined as "an adoption of such a description as the Secretary of State may by order specify, being a description of adoptions of children appearing to him to be effected under the law[5] of any country outside Great Britain".[6] By Order in Council, it has now been stated that adoptions in and under the law of a large number of Commonwealth countries,[7] the USA, South Africa[8] and all Western European countries are to be included in the definition "overseas adoption,"[9] whether or not they were made before the legislation came into effect.[10] A "regulated adoption" is an overseas adoption of a type which has been designated as that of an adoption regulated by the 1964 Hague Convention on Adoption.[11] Regulated adoptions are limited to those of countries which are parties to the 1964 Convention,[12] though all regulated adoptions are also overseas adoptions. The latter include those from many countries which are most unlikely to accede to the Hague Convention.

Basic rules as to recognition

The basic recognition rule, provided by the 1976 Act,[13] is that all overseas adoptions, including, therefore, all regulated adoptions, are to be recognised in England and to have the same incidents and effects as if they were made in England under that Act. The recognition of this wide range of foreign adoptions is not dependent, in any way, on reciprocity between England and the "overseas adoption" country. The overseas adoption, to be recognised

---

2 The bases on which the court will grant a declaration in relation to a foreign adoption are considered, supra, p 697.
3 Adoption Act 1976, s 38(1)(c).
4 Replacing the Adoption Act 1968.
5 Wherever the 1976 Act refers to the internal law of a country and a country has more than one system of internal law, the relevant system is to be determined by reference to any rule in that country indicating the relevant system and, failing that, it is the system most closely connected with the case; Adoption Act 1976, s 71(2).
6 Adoption Act 1976, s 72(2).
7 Cf *Mathieu v Entry Clearance Officer, Bridgetown* [1979–80] Imm AR 157.
8 Eg *Secretary of State for the Home Department v Lofthouse* [1981] Imm AR 166.
9 SI 1973/19.
10 Ibid, para 3(2); and see *Secretary of State for the Home Department v Lofthouse*, supra.
11 1968 Act, s 5(2); SI 1978/1432, para 3.
12 Austria and Switzerland: SI 1978/1431.
13 S 38(1)(d).

under these statutory rules, must be effected under legislative provisions and not under customary or common law and must relate to the adoption of someone who, at the time of the foreign adoption application, is under the age of eighteen and has not married.[14]

Furthermore, section 53 of the 1976 Act lays down the only other grounds[15] on which an overseas adoption[16] (including a regulated adoption) may be denied recognition and regarded as invalid in Great Britain either as the result of a specific application[17] or when the matter arises in any other proceedings,[18] such as a succession claim. There are just two grounds, that the adoption is contrary to public policy and that the authority which purported to authorise the adoption was not competent to entertain the case.[1] The first of these grounds is one which undoubtedly justifies denial of recognition of a foreign adoption at common law.[2] Apart from these grounds of non-recognition, an overseas adoption must be recognised even though there is no link, such as is required by English law,[3] between the country where the adoption is effected and the adoptive parents.

Recognition of other adoption decisions
There are further rules in relation to the recognition of decisions made overseas in adoption proceedings and these necessitate the identification of two further kinds of adoption order, namely a "specified order" and a "Convention adoption order". The former is any provision for the adoption of a child effected under enactments similar to sections 12(1) and 17 of the 1976 Act which are in force in Northern Ireland or any British territory[4] outside the United Kingdom.[5] The latter means an order made, in England or Scotland, as a Convention adoption order under section 17 of the Adoption Act 1976.[6] If an authority,[7] ie a court or administrative agency, of a Convention country or a specified country has power under the law of that country to authorise, or review the authorisation of, a regulated adoption or a specified order, or to give or review a decision revoking or annulling a regulated adoption, a specified order or a Convention adoption order, then any such determination must be given effect to in England.[8] This means that not only must an annulment by a Northern Irish court of a Northern Irish adoption order[9] be recognised in England, so must an Austrian annulment of a Convention adoption order made in England.[10]

14 SI 1973/19, para 3(3).
15 1976 Act, s 53(5).
16 And any "determination" under s 59(1), infra, and see s 53(2)(b).
17 Ibid, s 53(2).
18 Ibid, s 53(3).
 1 Ibid, s 53(2)(a). In determining this latter issue, the court is bound by any finding of fact made by the overseas authority and stated by them to be made for the purpose of deciding whether they were competent: 1976 Act, s 54(3).
 2 Infra, p 769; *Re Valentine's Settlement* [1965] Ch 831 at 842.
 3 Supra, pp 760–761.
 4 Defined in the 1976 Act, s 72(1).
 5 1976 Act, s 72(1).
 6 Ibid.
 7 Ibid, s 54(3).
 8 Ibid, s 59(1), as amended by the Children Act 1989, Sch 10, para 26(1).
 9 Ie a specified order.
10 Ie "a Convention adoption order".

Annulment of "convention adoptions"

The English courts have power, normally within two years of its making,[11] to annul a "convention adoption"[12] on three grounds; namely if the adoption was contrary to a provision in the adopter's national law[13] which had been notified to or by the United Kingdom under the Convention,[14] if the adoption contravened the law as to consents in the national law of the person to be adopted,[15] provided in both cases the adoption could be impugned under those respective laws at the time it purported to take effect under the law of the country in which it was made[16] and, thirdly, if the adoption could be impugned on any other ground under the law of the country where it was effected.[17] The jurisdiction of the English courts to annul convention adoptions on these grounds depends on either the person adopted or the adopter or adopters being habitually resident in England immediately before the application is made.[18]

Finally, it might be emphasised that these statutory recognition rules are in addition to and not in substitution for the common law rules of recognition.[19] If an "overseas adoption" is denied recognition under the statutory rules because, for example, made under customary law, it may still be possible for the adoption to be recognised or given effect under the common law rules for recognition. Furthermore, although the list of countries whose adoptions have been included under the definition of overseas adoptions is extensive, it is not world-wide. In the case of such other countries[20] and those "overseas adoptions" which, as has just been seen, fall outside the legislative rules, it is necessary to have resort to the common law recognition rules, to which we must now turn.

At common law Although the question of the extent to which, at common law, the English courts will recognise and give effect to an adoption order made abroad is of much less significance in the light of the statutory recognition provisions, it is still of some importance and is a question which has not been fully answered by the courts.

The leading case on this subject is *Re Valentine's Settlement*.[1] The facts were these:

A British subject, domiciled in what was then Southern Rhodesia, in 1946 made an English settlement of a fund on trust for her son Alastair for life and then to his children. Alastair had married only once and had one child, Simon, by the marriage. He and his wife had adopted two other children—Carol in 1939 and Timothy in 1944. These adoptions took place in South Africa where at the date of their respective adoptions Carol and Timothy were domiciled. Under the law of Southern Rhodesia an adoption order

11 SI 1984/265, para 37(2).
12 Ie one made in a convention country.
13 Adoption Act 1976, s 70 contains rules to assist the court in determining nationality.
14 1976 Act, ss 53(1)(a), 54(4); see SI 1978/1431; SI 1978/1432, para 8.
15 Ibid, s 53(1)(b).
16 Ibid, s 54(4).
17 Ibid, s 53(1)(c). There is also power to annul a convention adoption where a child has been adopted by one parent and the child is later legitimated by the marriage of his parents: s 52(3).
18 Ibid, s 54(2).
19 Ibid, s 38(1)(e).
20 Cf *Re H (An Infant)* (1973) 4 Fam Law 77.
1 [1965] Ch 831; and see National Insurance Decisions Nos R(F) 1/65; R(F) 3/73.

could not be made in respect of any child who was not resident and domiciled there: so no Southern Rhodesian adoption order was made. Alastair and his wife were themselves domiciled and resident in Southern Rhodesia at all material times, and Alastair died domiciled there in 1962 without having exercised a power of appointment under the settlement. The trustees issued a summons to determine whether the trust fund devolved on Simon or equally between Simon, Carol and Timothy.

The short question was as to whether the two adopted children were "children" of Alastair within the meaning of the settlement. The Court of Appeal by a majority answered this question in the negative. The whole Court was clearly prepared to countenance the recognition of foreign adoptions in some circumstances.[2] Lord DENNING MR stated that "we should recognise an adoption order made by another country when the adopting parents are domiciled there and the child is resident there."[3] It was held, however, that the South African adoptions could not be recognised in the instant case because the adopting parents were not domiciled in South Africa.[4]

A number of further issues arise. The first is whether it is right to concentrate exclusively on the domicil of the adopters and ignore the domicil of the child or of the natural parents. The view was expressed obiter by Lord DENNING MR[5] that it would not have been necessary to show in addition that the children were domiciled in South Africa at the time of the adoptions. Residence would have sufficed.[6] The basis of this reasoning was that, as an English court then[7] required the adoptive parents to be resident and domiciled in England and the child to be resident there, our recognition rules should be based on an analogy with our jurisdictional rules. Is it right that, for instance, the English court should recognise an adoption in India,[8] where the adopters are domiciled, of a child domiciled in Bangladesh? Is it sufficient that one of these laws is satisfied, and if so which should it be? Or, must both be satisfied?[9] There is no agreement on the question among foreign legal systems. In some, the personal law of the child governs; in others, the personal law of the adopters is preferred; but in many, the doctrine of cumulation prevails by which the personal law of all three parties must be satisfied.[10] Whilst one may argue that the only law to pronounce on status is that of the

2 The earlier contrary decision in *Re Wilby* [1956] P 174, [1956] 1 All ER 27 was said to have been wrongly decided.
3 [1965] Ch 831 at 842; and see National Insurance Decision No R(F) 1/65; *Perpetual Trustee Co Ltd v Montuori* [1982] 1 NSWLR 710; *R v Secretary of State for the Home Department, ex p Brassey* [1989] FCR 423, [1989] 2 FLR 486; *Patel v Visa Officer, Bombay* [1990] Imm AR 297; *MF v An Bord Uchtala* [1991] ILRM 399.
4 It was further held that, even if the South African adoptions were to be recognised, Carol and Timothy would be treated in English law (the law governing the settlement) as if they had been adopted in England. They would, therefore, be unable to take as the settlement was made before 1 January 1950, and English adopted children by virtue of s 5(2) of the Adoption of Children Act 1926 would have had no rights under it.
5 [1965] Ch 831 at 842–843.
6 This was approved in *Re B (S) (An Infant)* [1968] Ch 204 at 209–210.
7 See now Adoption Act 1976, s 14(2)(a), supra pp 760–761.
8 India is not one of the Commonwealth countries whose adoptions are recognised as "overseas adoptions", supra, pp 765–766.
9 See the discussion by Kahn-Freund, *The Growth of Internationalism in English Private International Law*, 82–88.
10 F A Mann (1941) 57 LQR 112, 123; Wolff, op cit, 398; Jones (1956) 5 ICLQ 205, 210–219. For a fuller discussion, see de Nova (1961) III Hague Recueil 75–153; Lipstein (1963) 12 ICLQ 835.

domicil, the jurisdiction of the English court is based on the domicil of the adoptive parents—that of the child and the natural parents is ignored. It seems reasonable to recognise a foreign jurisdiction exercised in similar circumstances. There is no justification, by analogy with English jurisdictional rules, for looking especially to the domicil of the natural rather than the adoptive parents.[11] If the domicil of the adopters is accepted as the main jurisdictional criterion for recognition, then it is suggested that, on the analogy of the common law rule for divorce recognition in *Armitage v A-G*,[12] an adoption should be recognised here as conferring the status of a child on the adopted person if recognised in the country (or countries) of the adopters' domicils even though actually effected elsewhere.[13]

Another issue is whether it is still appropriate to demand that the child be resident in the country where the adoption is effected. That criterion was relied on in *Re Valentine's Settlement* because at that time there was a similar requirement for the jurisdiction of the English courts. There is no longer such a requirement[14] and so jurisdictional reciprocity would support its abandonment when considering recognition of foreign adoptions.[15] Finally, it is not clear whether the English courts will be prepared to recognise foreign adoptions in wider circumstances such as those where, *mutatis mutandis*, an English court would not have jurisdiction, but where there was a "real and substantial connection" with the foreign court.[16]

We have seen that the statutory rules relating to the recognition of "overseas adoptions" provide that such an adoption may be denied recognition on grounds of public policy.[17] Public policy is similarly relevant to the recognition of foreign adoptions at common law. Adoption law in other countries may be very different from ours, as with adoption of adults and married persons in the USA.[18] Whilst great caution should be exercised in denying recognition on public policy grounds, the courts have power to do so both in relation to the incidents of the adoption, such as whether the child can succeed to the adoptive parents, and, in an extreme case, to the adoption's effect on the status of the parties, ie as to whether the parent and child relationship has been created at all.[19]

(c) EFFECT OF FOREIGN ADOPTIONS[20]

Before 1976, the law governing the effect in England of a foreign adoption recognised here was both complex and uncertain. Now, under Part IV of the Adoption Act 1976, the law is simple to state. If a foreign adoption is recognised in England, whether by reason of its being an "overseas adop-

---

11 Cf [1965] Ch 831 at 854.
12 [1906] P 135, supra, p 658.
13 Some support for this may be drawn from *Re Valentine's Settlement* [1965] Ch 226 at 234 at first instance; and see ibid at 855.
14 Supra, pp 760–761.
15 On the analogy of the common law divorce recognition rule in *Travers v Holley* [1953] P 246, [1953] 2 All ER 794. Though regret has been suggested earlier, supra, p 761, that the jurisdiction of the English courts is not based on habitual residence.
16 Cf *Indyka v Indyka* [1969] 1 AC 33, [1967] 2 All ER 689; North (1968) 31 MLR 257, 280–281.
17 Supra, p 766.
18 Scoles & Hay, p 547.
19 *Re Valentine's Settlement* [1965] Ch 831 at 842, 854.
20 Morris, *Festschrift für F A Mann* 241, 251–255.

tion",[1] or because it is recognised at common law, it has the same effect as an English adoption.[2] If, for example, a child, adopted in New York, claims to succeed to the movable property of an adoptive parent dying domiciled in England, the adoption will be recognised as an "overseas adoption" and the child will, under English law as the law governing succession, have the same rights as an English adopted child.[3] This rule applies to succession, testate and intestate, and other dispositions of property from 1976 onwards.[4] It includes the disposal of entailed interests[5] but not, in the absence of a contrary intention, property limited to devolve with a title of honour.[6] So far as entitlement to British nationality is concerned, this is governed, in the case of a person adopted abroad, by the relevant United Kingdom legislation. The effect of the adoption is not determined by the law of the country of adoption.[7]

It is important to distinguish between the question of recognition and the determination of, for example, the succession rights of an adopted child once his status has been recognised. This latter issue should be determined by the appropriate law to govern matters of succession.[8] This means that the provisions of the Adoption Act 1976, giving a child whose foreign adoption is recognised here the same succession rights as an English adopted child, are only relevant if English law governs the succession. If the law governing succession is foreign, it will be for that law to decide whether, and if so what, succession rights are given to an adopted child, even though the adoption is recognised here.

1 Supra, pp 765 et seq.
2 Adoption Act 1976, ss 38, 39.
3 See the Family Law Reform Act 1987, ss 1, 18, 19.
4 Adoption Act 1976, s 39(5).
5 Ibid, s 46(5).
6 Ibid, s 44.
7 *R v Secretary of State for the Home Department, ex p Brassey* [1989] FCR 423, [1989] 2 FLR 486.
8 See *Re Valentine's Settlement* [1965] Ch 831 at 843–845, rejecting suggestions to the contrary in *Re Marshall* [1957] Ch 507, [1957] 3 All ER 172.

Chapter 27

Mental disorder

SUMMARY

1. INTRODUCTION

People suffering from mental disorder can give rise to a variety of legal problems, not only generally, but also in regard to rules of private international law. Some of these arise incidentally in other contexts. For example, special rules have had to be devised for determining the domicil of mentally disordered persons because they may be incapable of exercising a free choice as to where they are to live.[1] The inability of such people to grant full consent can affect issues relating to their marriage[2] or to contracts which they purport to have entered into. There is no direct authority on whether the issue of the capacity of a mentally disordered person should be governed by the law of his domicil or by the law governing the contract. Following the analogy of other contractual issues of capacity,[3] it is suggested that the law governing the contract should apply.

Mental disorder may be, more directly, the source of private international law problems. It will be necessary, for example, to decide when an English court has jurisdiction to order the detention of a mentally disordered person or to place the management of his affairs in the hands of the court, what law is to be applied in such circumstances and the extent to which the English courts will recognise the powers conferred by a foreign court or under foreign law on someone (a curator) to manage the affairs of a mentally disordered person.

---

1 Supra, pp 162–163.
2 Supra, pp 644 et seq.
3 Supra, pp 510–513. The capacity of a mentally disordered person could also arise in a tort claim: see Dicey & Morris, p 1396.

2. JURISDICTION OF THE ENGLISH COURTS

(a) CONTROL OF THE PERSON

Under Part II of the Mental Health Act 1983, a person may be compulsorily admitted to hospital and detained there, or may be placed under guardianship. It seems clear that, as the steps taken under the 1983 Act are for the protection of the mentally disordered person and the public, the powers of the court can be exercised over anyone present in England, irrespective of their domicil or nationality.[4] It would seem that, conversely, if the person is not present in this country, there is no jurisdiction over his person; though the court could order that he be returned within the jurisdiction of the court.[5]

(b) CONTROL OF A PATIENT'S PROPERTY

The management of the property and affairs of a person who is, by reason of mental disorder, incapable of managing them himself is, under English law, committed to the Lord Chancellor and certain judges of the Supreme Court nominated by him and to the Master and other officers of the Court of Protection.[6] The usual method of exercising this management is by the appointment of a receiver, who is invested with certain powers of dealing with the property of the patient and whose authority is restricted to the exercise of the particular powers so given.[7]

The jurisdiction of the Court of Protection[8] extends to any person incapable by reason of mental disorder of managing his affairs who is actually present in England, whatever his nationality or domicil and even though his property is, except for a few personal belongings, all situated abroad.[9] The jurisdiction likewise extends to any such person, whatever his nationality or domicil, who is outside the country provided that he has property in England.[10] British nationality or English domicil would not of itself appear to justify an exercise of the jurisdiction.

The exercise of the jurisdiction where a foreign element arises is, however, qualified in two ways. First, the Court of Protection cannot make an order directly affecting property situated in a country where the authority of the court is not recognised, but it achieves its object by directing the receiver to take such steps as may be necessary to effect the purposes of the court, eg by appointing an attorney to act in the name of the patient in selling property and accounting to the receiver for the proceeds. Secondly, the court acts in accordance with the comity of nations and refrains from making orders that would be regarded as an infringement of a foreign jurisdiction.

Under section 110 of the Mental Health Act 1983, the powers of the English court over the property and affairs of a mentally disordered person also extend to his affairs and property (other than land) elsewhere in the United Kingdom, provided a receiver or person holding an equivalent office has not been appointed in the other part of the United Kingdom. There

---

4 Eg *Re Sottomaior* (1874) 9 Ch App 677.
5 See *Re Wykeham* (1823) Turn & R 537.
6 Mental Health Act 1983, Pt VII.
7 Ibid, s 99.
8 In this context, the expression "Court of Protection" includes also the Lord Chancellor and the "nominated judges".
9 *Re Houstoun* (1826) 1 Russ 312; *Re Princess Bariatinski* (1843) 1 Ph 375; *Re Burbidge* [1902] 1 Ch 426.
10 *Ex p Southcote* (1751) 2 Ves Sen 401; *Re Scott* (1874) 22 WR 748.

are reciprocal provisions relating to the powers of a receiver or equivalent appointed in Scotland or Northern Ireland over property or affairs in England.

3. CHOICE OF LAW

There seems little doubt that, when exercising powers over the person, property or affairs of a mentally disordered person, the English court will apply English law. The one specific statutory provision relating to choice of law is section 97(4) of the Mental Heath Act 1983 which limits the effect of a will which a judge has authorised to be made on behalf of a patient.[11] The will is limited in its effect to matters governed by English law—and so has no effect in relation to foreign immovables or to the movable property of a person domiciled outside England unless the law of his domicil, by renvoi, refers the issue of his testamentary capacity to English law.

4. POSITION OF A FOREIGN CURATOR

The question may arise whether someone appointed abroad to exercise powers in relation to the person, property or affairs of a mentally disordered person, whom we shall describe as a "foreign curator", can exercise any rights in England. It is necessary to consider, first, whether such a foreign curator will be recognised in England at all and then, if so, what rights he can exercise here.

(a) RECOGNITION

Before a foreign curator can enforce in England any rights relating to the property or affairs of a mentally disordered person, the English courts must be satisfied, first, that the curator is entitled, according to the law under which he was appointed, to take proceedings in England (ie abroad) to recover the property or manage the affairs of the patient.[12] Secondly, the English court must be prepared to recognise that the curator was appointed under the law of a country with which the patient was sufficiently closely connected. Will, for example, a foreign curator be recognised in England if appointed in a country in which the patient was present, even though domiciled elsewhere, possibly even in England? Whilst in many cases, the patient will be domiciled and present in, and a national of, the country where the curator was appointed,[13] presence alone will suffice.[14] The English courts have recognised a curator appointed in New York to manage the affairs of a widow domiciled in England;[15] though the rights of the curator in relation to proceedings in England concerning the patient's property are less extensive than if the patient had been domiciled in New York.[16]

11 Mental Health Act 1983, s 96(1)(e).
12 *Re Barlow's Will* (1887) 36 Ch D 287, on which see *Didisheim v London and Westminster Bank* [1900] 2 Ch 15 at 49–50, and see *Re Piper* [1927] 4 DLR 924.
13 Eg *Re De Linden* [1897] 1 Ch 453.
14 *Re De Larragoiti* [1907] 2 Ch 14.
15 *New York Security and Trust Co v Keyser* [1901] 1 Ch 666.
16 Infra, pp 774–775.

(b) PERSON OF THE PATIENT

It is clear that a foreign curator can exercise, as of right, no control in this country over the person of the patient.[17] The English court can, however, authorise the handing over of the mentally disordered person into the care of the foreign curator and the person's removal abroad.[18] In the case of a person who is neither a British nor Commonwealth citizen with a right of abode in the United Kingdom, and who is detained in hospital as a patient receiving mental treatment, the Secretary of State can authorise the patient's removal to a country outside the British Isles.[19] The Secretary of State has to be satisfied as to the arrangements made for such removal, and that it is in the interests of the patient, and the exercise of his powers requires the approval of a Mental Health Review Tribunal. Provision is also made relating to the removal of patients to and from Scotland, Northern Ireland, the Isle of Man and the Channel Islands on the authority of the Secretary of State or other appropriate authority.[20]

(c) PROPERTY AND AFFAIRS IN ENGLAND

With regard to the powers of a foreign curator over the property or affairs in England of a mentally disordered person, it must first be observed that the curator has no power to bring an action for the recovery of immovables.[1] In the case of movables, he similarly has no power if a receiver has been appointed in England, because in that case all powers to deal with the person's property and affairs are vested in the Court of Protection.[2] Subject to this, the rule has now been established that a foreign curator can sue in England as of right to claim money or property due to the mentally disordered person and to demand, and to give valid receipts for, property belonging to the patient which is held by persons in England.[3] This principle was finally laid down by the Court of Appeal in the leading case of *Didisheim v London and Westminster Bank*,[4] where the facts were as follows:

> A lady, domiciled and resident in Belgium, had securities of great value deposited with the defendant bank in London. She became insane in fact, though without being so found judicially, and Didisheim was appointed her provisional administrator by the Belgian court. Didisheim, having applied to the bank without success for the securities, brought an action for their recovery.

The Court of Appeal held that Didisheim was entitled to call for the securities and to give the bank a good discharge:

> On general principles of private international law, the courts of this country are

---

17 *Re Houston* (1826) 1 Russ 312.
18 Eg *Re Sottomaior* (1874) 9 Ch App 677.
19 Mental Health Act 1983, s 86.
20 Ibid, ss 80–85; Mental Health (Scotland) Act 1984, ss 77–79.
 1 *Grimwood v Bartels* (1877) 46 LJ Ch 788.
 2 *Re RSA* [1901] 2 KB 32.
 3 *Didisheim v London and Westminster Bank* [1900] 2 Ch 15; and see *Scott v Bentley* (1855) 1 K & J 281; *Re De Linden* [1897] 1 Ch 453; *Thiery v Chalmers Guthrie & Co* [1900] 1 Ch 80; *Kamouh v Associated Electrical Industries International Ltd* [1980] QB 199 at 205–206; *Re FN and the Mental Health Act 1958* [1984] 3 NSWLR 520.
 4 [1900] 2 Ch 15.

bound to recognise the authority conferred on him by the Belgian courts, unless lunacy proceedings in this country prevent them from doing so.[5]

The court, however, ordered Didisheim to pay all the costs of the action, since the bank was justified in not complying with his demands until he had established his title by a successful action in the High Court. At the present day, however, an English debtor in like circumstances is not justified in insisting on the protection of an order of the court. *Didisheim's Case* has definitely established the right of a foreign curator to demand property. If therefore, an English debtor insists on proceedings, he acts with an unreasonable excess of caution and will have to pay his own costs.[6]

Some limitations on the decision in *Didisheim's Case* must be noticed. The foreign curator has no greater rights than his English counterpart. So, if there are funds in court, the payment out of which is in the discretion of the court, payment to a foreign creditor who claims the funds will be subject to such discretion.[7] Furthermore, in *Didisheim's Case*, the owner of the property was an alien domiciled abroad over whom the court had no jurisdiction personally. If the patient is domiciled in England, then the foreign curator does not have a right to claim property in England, though the court has a discretion to order payment of appropriate sums.[8]

Although the principle established by *Didisheim's Case* is of great benefit to foreign curators, its usefulness is limited not only by the fact that it has no application to immovable property but also because it does not enable the foreign curator to reduce into possession stock and shares registered in the name of the patient. The reason for this is that stock and shares can only be transferred by an instrument of transfer executed by the registered holder or by a person having authority to execute the document on his behalf, and a foreign curator is not recognised as having this power.

It is not, however, necessary in every case where stock and shares are concerned to appoint a receiver in England or to have independent medical evidence of mental incapacity, for the Court of Protection is empowered, if satisfied that the foreign curator has been appointed on the ground that the patient is incapable by reason of mental disorder of managing his property, to direct any stock or shares standing in the name of the patient to be transferred to the curator or otherwise dealt with as he may direct.[9] The power is discretionary, and the court will not direct the capital to be transferred unless satisfied that it is required for the patient's maintenance or that there is other sufficient reason justifying a transfer.[10]

5 Ibid, at 51.
6 *Pelegrin v Coutts & Co* [1915] 1 Ch 696.
7 *Re Garnier* (1872) LR 13 Eq 532; *Re De Linden* [1897] 1 Ch 453.
8 *New York Security and Trust Co v Keyser* [1901] 1 Ch 666.
9 Mental Health Act 1983, s 100.
10 *Re Knight* [1898] 1 Ch 257; *Re De Larragoiti* [1907] 2 Ch 14.

Part VI

The law of property

SUMMARY

Chapter 28

The distinction between movables and immovables

SUMMARY

1. INTRODUCTION

English private international law, in order to arrive at a common basis on which to determine questions involving a foreign element, classifies the subject-matter of ownership into movables and immovables, and thus adopts a distinction that is accepted in other legal systems,[1] though even common law jurisdictions cannot agree whether some kinds of property are movable or immovable.[2] The first task of the court in a private international law case when required to decide some question of a proprietary or possessory nature is to decide whether the item of property which is the subject of the dispute is a movable or an immovable. On this preliminary decision depends the legal system that will be applicable to the case. Rights over immovables are determined by the law of the situs; rights over movables are not necessarily governed by that law. In the sphere of private international law, then, the common law distinction between realty and personality is abandoned, even though the case concerns a common law country where it is recognised in the sphere of domestic law. The importance of not confusing the domestic distinction between realty and personality with the private international law distinction between movables and immovables can scarcely be exaggerated. They do not cover the same ground. The one cuts across the other in the sense that personality includes both movables and immovables. Thus "realty" is not synonymous either with "land" or with "immovables", for though a life tenant, for instance, holds an interest in realty, a leaseholder holds an interest in personality. For the purpose of private international law, however,

---

1 *Re Hoyles* [1911] 1 Ch 179 at 185. For a critical examination of the relevant authorities, see Clarence Smith (1963) 26 MLR 16.
2 Eg the right of a mortgagee. England and Ontario consider it to be immovable: *Re Hoyles* [1911] 1 Ch 179; *Re Ritchie* [1942] 3 DLR 330; whereas New Zealand and Australia consider it to be movable: *Re O'Neill* [1922] NZLR 468; *Re Greenfield* [1985] 2 NZLR 662 at 664; Wills Amendment Act 1955, s 14(4); *Haque v Haque (No 2)* (1965) 114 CLR 98; see Nygh, pp 438–440; Sykes & Pryles, pp 648–651, 658–660.

a lease creates an interest in an immovable and is subject to the law of the situs.[3]

2. CLASSIFICATION BY THE LAW OF THE SITUS

The question whether the subject-matter of ownership is a movable or an immovable generally presents no difficulty. English law and most other legal systems accept that interests in land, whether classified according to their nature, such as legal estates and equitable interests; or limited in duration, such as fees simple, entails and terms of years; or independent of the right to possession of the land, such as easements, profits and rentcharges, are interests in an immovable. A more complex problem arises in those cases where a right over what is physically a movable is regarded by a particular legal system as a right over an immovable. For instance, the owner of such obvious chattels as title-deeds, fixtures, fish in a pond and the key of a house is regarded by English internal law as having an interest in land. Again, it seems obvious at first sight that a building erected for the purposes of an exhibition, and which cannot be removed without losing its identity, must be in the same category as normal buildings, yet in the USA[4] and in Germany[5] its owner has been deemed to hold an interest in a movable. If, therefore, the subject-matter of ownership is regarded as an immovable by one system of law but as a movable by another, to which law is the decision left? The answer given by English law and by most foreign legal systems is: the law of the situs. If the law of the situs attributes the quality of movability or of immovability to the object in question, the English court which is seised of the matter must proceed on that basis.[6]

3. SOME EXAMPLES

(a) MORTGAGES

Mortgages provide an important illustration of this classification. It has been held that the right vested in a mortgagee of English land must be regarded by English law, as being that of the situs, as an interest in an immovable, notwithstanding that it is classified by English domestic law as personalty and that the debt, not the charge, is the principal characteristic of the transaction.[7]

(b) TRUSTS FOR SALE

A further and important illustration is provided by *Re Berchtold*.[8] This case turned on the English doctrine of conversion,[9] namely, that:

Money directed to be employed in the purchase of land, and land directed

3 *Freke v Carbery* (1873) LR 16 Eq 461; *Duncan v Lawson* (1889) 41 Ch D 394; *Re Caithness* (1891) 7 TLR 354.
4 Eg *Public Service Co of New Hampshire v Voudonas* 84 NH 387, 157 A 81 (1930).
5 BGB, s 95; Cohn, *Manual of German Law* (2nd edn) vol I, p 72.
6 *Johnstone v Baker* (1817) 4 Madd 474n; Westlake, s 160, approved in *Re Hoyles* [1910] 2 Ch 333 at 341, [1911] 1 Ch 179; *Macdonald v Macdonald* 1932 SC (HL) 79.
7 *Re Hoyles* [1911] 1 Ch 179.
8 [1923] 1 Ch 192; and see *Philipson-Stow v IRC* [1961] AC 727 at 762.
9 On the uses to which this doctrine may be put in a conflict of laws situation, see Hancock (1965) 17 Stan LR 1095.

to be sold and turned into money, are to be considered as that species of property into which they are directed to be converted.[10]

What this equitable doctrine means in effect is that where there is such a direction the realty is treated as personalty for certain purposes, or in the reverse case that the personalty is treated as realty for certain purposes. If, for instance, land is conveyed to trustees on trust for sale and to pay the proceeds to A, and A dies before the actual sale, a bequest by him of all his personalty will include the money eventually arising from the sale. This, of course, does not alter the fact that until sold the land is still an immovable. This becomes material if the beneficiary under the trust dies domiciled in a foreign country before the conversion has actually been effected. *Re Berchtold* is just such a case:

A died intestate, domiciled in Hungary, being entitled to a freehold interest in English land which was subject to a trust for sale but which had not been sold. The English rule for the choice of law is that intestate succession is governed by the law of the situs in the case of immovables, but by the law of the domicil in the case of movables. It was, therefore, vital to decide whether the freehold interest, despite the doctrine of conversion, was still to be regarded as an interest in an immovable.

It was argued with some plausibility that by reason of the trust for sale the land was already money in the eyes of equity, that money is a movable, and that therefore the devolution was governed by Hungarian law.

The fallacy of this argument was demonstrated by RUSSELL J. The primary question before the court was whether the subject-matter in which the deceased was interested was immovable. This had nothing to do with a subsequent question that might arise under the doctrine of conversion, namely, whether realty was to be treated as personalty, or vice versa. It was held that the unsold land was an immovable, notwithstanding the binding direction for its conversion into money, and that therefore the appropriate law to govern its devolution on intestacy was the law of the situs.

As an Irish judge said in a case where land in Ireland, subject to an existing trust for sale, had been disposed of by the will of a domiciled Scotsman:

It is still immovable property in fact and the disposition of it is a disposition of immovable property and not of something else, namely, the money by which, if sold, it would be represented, but which before the sale does not in fact exist.[11]

These two decisions were distinguished by MORTON J in a later case where the distinction between realty and personalty, and therefore the doctrine of conversion, were not strictly relevant:[12]

English land that was subject to an English settlement had been sold under the Settled Land Act 1882 and the proceeds had been invested in English debenture stock. The beneficiary under the settlement died intestate in 1897 domiciled in Ontario.

So far it seems obvious that the stock was in fact a movable and that therefore under the relevant doctrine of private international law its devolution was

10 *Fletcher v Ashburner* (1779) 1 Bro CC 497, 499; Hanbury and Maudsley, *Modern Equity* (13th edn) pp 805–810; Pettit, *Equity and the Law of Trusts* (6th edn), ch 30.
11 *Murray v Champernowne* [1901] 2 IR 232.
12 *Re Cutcliffe's Will Trusts* [1940] Ch 565, [1940] 2 All ER 297.

governed by the law of the deceased's domicil. The Settled Land Act 1882, however, provided that:

> Capital money arising under this Act while remaining uninvested and securities on which an investment of any such capital money shall be made, shall, for all purposes of disposition, transmission and devolution, be considered as land.[13]

In order to choose the governing law the primary question was whether the stock was a movable or an immovable. It was held that it was an immovable and subject as such to the English law of devolution. The decision has been attacked on the ground that the domestic doctrine of conversion was erroneously applied at the stage when the case was being considered internationally.[14] But this is to misinterpret the ratio decidendi. How could the decision have been otherwise? The stock was physically situated in England. English law, therefore, had to determine whether it was to be treated as a movable or an immovable. An English statute peremptorily demanded that for all purposes, ie presumably including the choice of the applicable law, it should be regarded as land.

(c) ANNUITIES

The character of annuities and other periodical payments depends on whether they issue out of, or are charged on, land. An annuity in the strict sense represents a right to a movable, but a rent charged on land is an interest in an immovable.[15]

4. RELEVANCE OF DISTINCTION BETWEEN REALTY AND PERSONALTY

Once the choice of law has been made, there may come a stage at which the distinction between realty and personalty then becomes relevant. This occurs where the choice falls on a law that recognises the distinction. The chosen law now has control of the case and it must be allowed to operate in its own way. In *Re Berchtold*,[16] for instance, the effect of deciding that the intestate died entitled to an immovable was to let in English law as the law of the situs, with the result that the immovable, being regarded as money under the domestic doctrine of conversion, devolved as personalty according to the rules of English internal law.

5. DISTINCTION BETWEEN TANGIBLE AND INTANGIBLE MOVABLES

The subject-matter of ownership, if not immovable, is properly divisible into choses in possession, ie tangible physical objects, and choses in action, such as debts, patents, copyright, goodwill, stocks and shares. The classification of movables usually preferred, however, by private international lawyers is into tangible things and intangible things.[17] This is not only a linguistic

---

13 S 22(5); see now Settled Land Act 1925, s 75(5).
14 By Falconbridge (1940) 18 Can BR 568.
15 *Chatfield v Berchtoldt* (1872) 7 Ch App 192.
16 Supra, pp 780–781.
17 For a criticism of the distinction see Cook, pp 284 et seq.

solecism, since it is scarcely possible to move a thing that cannot be touched, but it provokes an unfortunate tendency to ascribe to a disembodied thing, such as a debt, the physical attributes of a corporeal object as, for instance, a definite situs. Although Lord HALSBURY once remarked that he was "wholly unable to see that goodwill itself is susceptible of having any local situation",[18] it is of course necessary for certain purposes, such as jurisdiction or probate, to assign a situs not only to goodwill, but to choses in action generally.[19] This is not without its dangers. Since the situs principle has furnished a simple and effective rule for questions relating to a physical thing, the natural inclination is to extend it to all questions and to regard it as the general determinant of rules for the choice of law concerning choses in action. This is a false analogy. Moreover, it frequently leads to forcing a rule, eminently adapted to one set of circumstances, to fit circumstances for which it is entirely inappropriate. It is reasonably clear that the appropriate law to govern goodwill or a debt depends on quite different considerations from those that are relevant to a physical thing. An English manufacturer, for instance, having sold goods on credit to a foreigner who has places of business in France, Switzerland and Italy, assigns the debt to a Dutchman. If the right of the assignee to sue the debtor is disputed, is the question to be governed by the law of the situs? If so, what is the situs? The traditional answer, that it is the country where the debtor resides, is calculated to increase rather than to dispel uncertainty in commercial transactions. Obviously some different approach to the problem is required from that which has proved useful in another field. Although it might seem less harmful to adopt the distinction between choses in possession and choses in action, the division into tangible and intangible movables is now widely accepted and will be followed here. Nevertheless, one must be aware of the danger of straining rules to fit categories.

---

18 *IRC v Muller & Co's Margarines Ltd* [1901] AC 217 at 240.
19 See Dicey & Morris, pp 907–916. Goodwill is deemed to be situated in each country in which the business to which it is attached is carried on: *Reuter (RJ) Co Ltd v Mulhens* [1954] Ch 50 at 95, 96, [1953] 2 All ER 1160 at 1183.

Chapter 29

Immovables

SUMMARY

1. JURISDICTION

An English court, as we have seen earlier,[1] will not take jurisdiction to determine the issue of title, or right to possession of, foreign land. This rule stems from two sources. The first is the common law rule in *British South Africa Co v Companhia de Mocambique*.[2] Second, in the case of land within a Contracting State to the Brussels or Lugano Conventions, the rule derives from the Civil Jurisdiction and Judgments Acts 1982 and 1991 which give exclusive jurisdiction in proceedings "which have as their object rights *in rem* in immovable property or tenancies of immovable property" to the courts of the country in which the property is situated.[3]

2. CHOICE OF LAW

(a) THE LAW OF THE SITUS RULE

In the United States[4] and in most European countries the general rule is that the law of the situs is the governing law for all questions that arise with regard to immovable property.[5] The rule was authoritatively stated for English law in *Nelson v Bridport*,[6] where Lord Nelson, in his capacity as Duke of Bronte,

---

1 Supra, pp 253 et seq.
2 [1893] AC 602.
3 Sch 1, Art 16 (1)(a) of both Conventions. Art 16 (1)(b) of both Conventions, though not in identical terms, deals with jurisdiction over disputes concerning short term tenancies, supra, pp 309–313, 343–344.
4 Scoles & Hay, pp 715–716; Leflar, pp 473–475; and see Restatement 2d §§ 222, 223.
5 This proposition is so clear as scarcely to require authorities, but see *Birtwhistle v Vardill* (1840) 7 Cl & Fin 895; *Coppin v Coppin* (1725) 2 P Wms 291; *Re Duke of Wellington* [1947] Ch 506, [1947] 2 All ER 854, affirmed [1948] Ch 118; Dicey & Morris, Rule 118, p 936; Westlake, s 156; Story, Ch X.
6 (1846) 8 Beav 547.

had attempted to devise his Sicilian estate in a manner contrary to the law of Sicily. Lord LANGDALE MR said:[7]

> The incidents to real estate, the right of alienating or limiting it, and the course of succession to it, depend entirely on the law of the country where the estate is situated. Lord Nelson having accepted the Sicilian estate could deal with it only as the Sicilian law allowed; he had a right to appoint a successor, but no right to modify the estate, interest, or powers of disposition to which the successor was entitled by the law of Sicily. The successor became the holder of the estate subject to the incidents annexed to it by the grant and the law of Sicily and no others. Among the incidents was a particular course of succession different from that which Lord Nelson had directed, and the necessary consequence appears to be that no operation or effect could be given to the expressed wish and intention as to the succession to the estate itself, beyond that which the law of Sicily allowed.

Whilst the law of the situs rule may have been authoritatively stated, it has come under increasing criticism in recent years.[8] Indeed the rule has been condemned as a "taboo".[9] There is no doubt, however, that the law of the situs has a powerful interest in its rules being applied to a wide range of matters—essentially "in the manner in which land is used, occupied or developed".[10] This concern is seen at its strongest in the case of the transfer of title to land.[11] At the end of the day, only the law of the situs can control the way in which land, which constitutes part of the situs itself, is transferred. So uniformity with the law of the situs is necessary in terms of effectiveness and justifies an English court applying that foreign law. Indeed this attitude is reinforced by the refusal of English courts to adjudicate on issues relating to title to foreign land[12] or to recognise foreign judgments to such effect.[13] In other cases, however, "where the parties are non residents and the policy of the situs does not concern the use, tenure or marketing of its land",[14] the case for the application of the law of the situs is much weaker. Although the courts have been prepared to apply a law other than that of the situs to govern a contract for the sale of land,[15] a foreign implied marriage settlement[16] or the formal validity of a will of immovables,[17] the generality of the law of the situs rule remains in force as is illustrated by the law on intestate succession[18] to immovables and on the essential validity of a will relating to immovables.[19] It seems unlikely that the entrenched position of the law of the situs as the choice of law rule for immovables is going to be altered other than by legislation.[20]

---

7 Ibid, at 570.
8 Cavers (1970) III Hague Recueil 75, 196 et seq.
9 Hancock (1964) 15 Stan LR 561; (1965) 17 Stan LR 1095; (1966) 18 Stan LR 1299; (1967) 20 Stan LR 1; Weintraub (1966) 52 Cornell LQ 1; Morris (1969) 85 LQR 339.
10 Scoles & Hay, p 714.
11 Eg *Re Ross* [1930] 1 Ch 377; *Re Duke of Wellington* [1947] Ch 506.
12 Supra, pp 253 et seq.
13 Supra, p 363.
14 Hancock (1966) 18 Stan LR 1299, 1321.
15 See now supra, p 493.
16 *Re De Nicols (No 2)* [1900] 2 Ch 410, infra, pp 873–874.
17 Infra, pp 852–853.
18 Infra, pp 851–852.
19 Infra, p 853.
20 As in the case of the formal validity of wills, infra, pp 852–853.

Meaning of the "law of the situs"

Before giving specific illustrations of the situs doctrine in operation it is essential that the true meaning of the expression "the law of the situs" should be understood. Most decisions and most writers have proceeded on the assumption that it means the relevant rule applicable at the situs to a purely domestic situation involving no foreign element at all. The assumption, however, is scarcely warranted. This, as we have seen in considering the renvoi doctrine, is one of those exceptional cases in which the court of the forum refers to the whole law of the foreign situs.[1] It may be that a court at the situs, if required to give a decision, would apply the relevant rule of its own law applicable to a purely domestic situation. This, however, is not necessarily so and the whole law of the foreign situs might either include its rules of private international law or might involve an examination of the rule applicable to a domestic situation to see whether it extended to a case with international elements. So, in order to determine this, the relevant rule should be examined in the light of its reason, the purpose that it is designed to effect and the policy on which it is based. It does not follow that a rule of land law designed to promote the welfare of persons domiciled in a country or to regulate local transactions should necessarily be extended to transactions completed abroad between domiciled foreigners. The truth of this is well brought out by Cook in his discussion of the New Hampshire case of *Proctor v Frost*,[2] where the facts were these:

> By the statute law of New Hampshire a wife was incapable of becoming surety for her husband, but by the law of Massachusetts she was free from this incapacity. A married woman entered into a transaction in Massachusetts, where she was domiciled, by which she became surety for her husband. By way of security she executed in that State a mortgage of her land in New Hampshire.

There was no dispute that her capacity to execute the mortgage as a surety fell to be determined by the law of the situs, but that did not inevitably mean that the New Hampshire statute applied to the instant case. A correct decision on that question could scarcely be reached without first considering the purpose of the statute. Was this purpose to regulate the conveyance of New Hampshire land, or was it to protect wives against the importunities of embarrassed husbands? If it was the latter, it would be unseemly and inexpedient to extend this paternal solicitude to wives domiciled in foreign jurisdictions. In the result the Supreme Court of New Hampshire considered that the object of the statute was to protect married women within the jurisdiction, and they therefore held the mortgage to be valid.[3] This decision stands out as one of the few in which the matter has been approached in this manner.

It will be found, almost without exception, that the term "the law of the situs" is interpreted in its narrow literal sense as meaning that rule which applies to an analogous situation free from all trace of foreign elements. This narrow meaning must, of course, be adopted when the dispute concerns the

---

1 Eg *Re Ross* [1930] 1 Ch 377; *Re Duke of Wellington* [1947] Ch 506, [1947] 2 All ER 854, supra, p 68.
2 89 NH 304, 197 A 813 (1938); Cook, p 274; and see the articles by Hancock in note 9, supra.
3 Though their decision to apply the law of Massachusetts, essentially by way of renvoi, (see 197 A 813 at 815) as the place of execution of the mortgage, rather than as the place of the wife's domicil, is hard to justify: Cook, p 275.

legal effects of a conveyance, as, for example, when the question is whether there has been an infringement of the rule against perpetuities or whether the interest created is legally possible;[4] but there is no reason why it should be regarded as the only possible meaning.

(b) SPECIFIC ISSUES

Problems relating to choice of the law applicable to immovables may arise in a variety of contexts. Some of these are considered separately in later chapters, such as administration of estates of immovables and succession thereto, the effect of marriage on property, both movable and immovable, and bankruptcy. Nevertheless, some of the cases to be discussed in this chapter will be drawn from those fields, especially succession, where they illustrate principles generally applicable to immovables.

(i) Capacity to take and transfer immovables

Unless a person has capacity by the law of the situs to take immovables, he will be excluded from ownership. In *Duncan v Lawson*,[5] for instance, it was admitted that a bequest by a domiciled Scotsman of English leaseholds to trustees on trust for sale and out of the proceeds to pay certain legacies to charities was void as infringing the Mortmain and Charitable Uses Act 1888[6] (since repealed), for whether a charity was competent to take English freeholds and leaseholds, even under a foreign will, must depend on English law. The same is true of capacity to transfer immovables, whether by sale, gift, mortgage or devise. If full age is attained in country A at 18 and in country B at 25, a person 22 years old, domiciled in A, cannot execute a valid conveyance of lands lying in B; whereas a person of the same age, even though domiciled in B, can effectually convey land in A.[7]

It was definitely established by *Bank of Africa Ltd v Cohen*[8] in relation to capacity to transfer land abroad that the law of the situs rule is part of English law. The facts were these:

The defendant, a married woman domiciled in England, entered into a deed in England by which she agreed to make a mortgage of her land at Johannesburg in favour of the plaintiffs. The mortgage was intended to secure money lent to her husband. The Roman-Dutch law prevailing in the Transvaal ordained that a married woman could not be bound as a surety unless she specifically renounced the benefits of the Senatus consultum Velleianum, and also the benefits of another law, de authentica. The evidence went to show that this renunciation had not been made in the formal manner required by the local law. In an action brought in England for specific performance of the English transaction, judgment was given both by the court of first instance and also by the Court of Appeal in favour of the defendant.

The decision was based on the defendant's lack of capacity.

---

4 Cook, p 270.
5 (1889) 41 ChD 394; and see *A-G v Parsons* [1956] AC 421.
6 *Hewit's Trustees v Lawson* (1891) 18 R 793.
7 Cf *Sell v Miller* 11 Ohio State 331 (1860); Scoles and Hay, pp 717–718; Leflar, pp 479–481; Restatement 2d, § 223.
8 [1909] 2 Ch 129.

In the words of BUCKLEY LJ:[9]

> Mr Dicey's language I think is correct, that a person's capacity to make a contract with regard to an immovable is governed by the lex situs.

This decision is far from satisfactory. If the facts raised a true question of capacity, it did not follow that the object of the South African rule was to protect married women domiciled in other countries.[10] If a question of form was involved, it is difficult to distinguish the case from that of *Re Courtney*,[11] where a contrary decision was reached. Again, since the married woman had made a contract valid by English law, the governing law, was she not bound to do everything required by South African law to render it effective?

There is no English authority on the law governing capacity to transfer land in England when the transferor is domiciled abroad. However, there is clear Canadian authority in favour of applying the law of the situs in such a case. In *Landry v Lachapelle*,[12] the facts were these:

> The husband and wife were domiciled in Quebec. The wife owned land in Ontario. She conveyed the land to her husband, to be owned by them as joint tenants. As a married woman, she had capacity to do this under the law of Ontario, but not of Quebec.

The Ontario Court of Appeal identified the issue as one relating to title, not to the validity of any contract. "The crucial question ... may be stated as follows:—Is the law of Ontario inconsistent with the law of Quebec as regards the conveyance to the defendant of the lands in question? If so, the Ontario law must govern."[13]

It does not necessarily follow, however, that the substantive rules of law to be applied in the situs in the case of a foreign domiciliary are necessarily the same as would be applied to someone domiciled in the situs. It has been seen from *Proctor v Frost*[14] that the New Hampshire court declined to apply the New Hampshire statute on the ground that it was not meant to apply to mortgages of New Hampshire land executed by married women domiciled elsewhere. Although, by a process of renvoi, they went on to apply Massachusetts law, they could just as well have determined (and with the same outcome) that the wife had capacity under New Hampshire law, given that the statutory restriction on capacity did not apply to her as a foreign domiciliary.

(ii) Formalities of alienation

The formal validity of a transfer of immovables is determined by the law of the situs.[15] This is generally taken to mean that a transfer must comply with the formalities prescribed by the internal law of the situs for a purely domestic transaction containing no foreign element. For example, in *Adams v Clutterbuck*[16] it was held that a conveyance between two domiciled Englishmen of shooting rights in Scotland was valid, notwithstanding the fact that it was

---

9 Ibid, at 143.
10 See this aspect of the matter discussed supra, pp 786–787.
11 (1840) Mont & Ch 239, supra, pp 258–259.
12 [1937] 2 DLR 504.
13 Ibid, at 508.
14 89 NH 304, 197 A 813 (1938), supra, p 786.
15 Dicey & Morris, p 939. On the other hand, a contract to transfer an interest in land does not have to satisfy the formal requirements of the law of the situs: *Re Smith, Lawrence v Kitson* [1916] 2 Ch 206, infra, p 791.
16 (1883) 10 QBD 403.

not under seal as required by English, but not Scots, law. Again it has been held in a case decided before the Wills Act 1837 that a devise which was valid by the law of the testator's domicil was ineffectual to pass English land, since it was not attested by three witnesses as then required by the Statute of Frauds.[17] Nevertheless, it does not inevitably follow that a local formality must in all circumstances be observed. Everything depends on how it is regarded by the law of the situs itself. This law may, indeed, regard it as essential for every conveyance, no matter where or by whom executed. On the other hand it may regard the formality as necessary only for conveyances completed within the jurisdiction.[1]

(iii) Essential validity of transfers

The general rule laid down in *Nelson v Bridport*,[2] as we have already seen,[3] is that no disposition, though made in a country where it may be regular, can create an interest in immovables that is contrary to the law of the situs. The law of the situs obviously must decide whether an interest in land is permissible in nature or extent. That law governs exclusively the tenure, title and descent of immovables.[4] Although it is a general principle that a legal title duly acquired in one country is a good title all the world over,[5] yet, where the title concerns immovables, it must conform to the law of the situs. Thus a disposition of English land, whether by will or otherwise, which contains limitations that infringe the rules as to perpetuities and accumulations is void.[6]

A common application of the general principle occurs in the case of those restraints on alienation which are found in most systems of law. Prohibitions against alienation between certain persons, or for certain purposes or beyond a certain amount, are frequently met with, and in fact most of the civil law systems of law forbid testators to dispose of more than a certain proportion of their property. When the subject-matter of alienation is an immovable the application of such restraints depends solely on the law of the situs.[7]

The treatment by the courts of the English mortmain statutes, which imposed severe restrictions on devises of land to a charity, provided an apt illustration of this general principle until those statutes were swept away in 1960.[8] Since, broadly speaking, the policy was to prevent the excessive accumulation of land by way of devise in the hands of perpetual bodies, it followed that the decisive factor in considering the validity of a charitable devise was not the domicil of the testator, but the country where the land was situated. A devise or gift of English land contrary to the statutes was void, even though valid by the law of the donor's domicil,[9] but whether a

---

17 *Coppin v Coppin* (1725) 2 P Wms 291.
1 In the USA many statutes have expressly provided that a transfer shall be valid if the formalities of the place of execution are observed; see the Uniform Acknowledgements Act 1957; Leflar, p 481; Restatement 2d §223, comment e.
2 (1846) 8 Beav 547.
3 Supra, pp 784–785.
4 *Fenton v Livingstone* (1859) 33 LTOS 335. Contrast the law governing the essential validity of contracts relating to land, infra, pp 791–792.
5 *Simpson v Fogo* (1863) 1 Hem & M 195, infra, pp 797 et seq.
6 *Re Grassi, Stubberfield v Grassi* [1905] 1 Ch 584 at 592; *Freke v Carbery* (1873) LR 16 Eq 461.
7 *Re Hernando* (1884) 27 Ch D 284 (English land); *Re Ross* [1930] 1 Ch 377 (foreign land).
8 Charities Act 1960, s 38.
9 *Curtis v Hutton* (1808) 14 Ves 537; *Duncan v Lawson* (1889) 41 ChD 394.

gift of foreign land was void for the same reason depended on the law of the situs.[10]

A somewhat troublesome case in this connection is *Re Piercy*,[11] where an unduly ephemeral operation was allowed to the law of the foreign situs. The facts, so far as relevant to the present discussion, were these:

> A testator, domiciled in England, devised his Sardinian land to trustees on trust for sale, and to hold the same until conversion and the proceeds of sale after conversion on certain trusts for his children for their respective lives, with remainder to their issue. Italian law would regard the children as entitled to their shares absolutely, since it did not allow trusts of that kind to be imposed on land in Italy.

The unsophisticated might conclude that the land must be allowed to remain subject to Italian law, and that any move to subject it, directly or indirectly, to the English trusts would be contrary to principle as being a contravention of the law of the situs. NORTH J, however, was of a different opinion. He admitted, indeed, that the land was subject to Italian law as long as it remained unsold, but, apart from that concession, he directed the trustees to sell the land and to hold the proceeds on the trusts declared by the will. His reasoning, ingenious if not sound, was that by Italian law it was not illegal for the testator to direct the sale of his land, that Italian law qua the law of the situs would continue to govern the land in the hands of the purchaser, but that it had nothing whatever to do with the proceeds of sale, for by that time the land would have been placed beyond the reach of Italian law. But, by Italian law, the beneficiaries under such a disposition become absolute legal owners of the land, the executors and trustees having nothing more than a mere right of administration.[12] No dealing with the land could be effective unless it complied with Italian law, and by that law the sale directed by the judge was illegal.[13] Was it not, therefore, a deliberate evasion of Italian law to place the land in the hands of a nominal owner whose true position was only that of a trustee?[14] What probably weighed with the judge was that the land had become money under the equitable doctrine of conversion, but whether such a conversion has been effected depends on the law of the situs, and by Italian law the answer was most definitely in the negative.

(iv) Contracts

The recognition of the paramountcy of the law of the situs does not, however, conclude all difficulties. The generality of the rule and the sweeping manner in which it is usually stated are apt to lead to error unless we notice the distinction between an actual transfer of land and a contract to transfer.[15] So far as formalities are concerned, any transaction or instrument that purports to change, then and there, the ownership of immovables must satisfy the formal requirements of the law of the situs. But a different position arises

10 *Re Hoyles, Row v Jagg* [1911] 1 Ch 179. It seems no longer necessary to consider the unsatisfactory decision in *Canterbury (Mayor) v Wyburn* [1895] AC 89 (PC); though see Hancock (1964) 16 Stan LR 561, 599–604.

11 [1895] 1 Ch 83; apparently approved in *Philipson-Stow v Inland Revenue Comrs* [1961] AC 727 at 744–745.

12 Wolff, p 592.

13 Cf the remarks of Lord REID in *Philipson-Stow v Inland Revenue Comrs* [1961] AC 727 at 748, [1960] 3 All ER 814 at 823.

14 Cf *Brown v Gregson* [1920] AC 860 at 886.

15 Dicey & Morris, p 939.

where the inquiry relates not to the actual transfer of some interest, but to the rights and liabilities of the parties under a contract relating to immovables. A contract by A that he will transfer some interest in land to B brings into play the choice of law rules governing the validity of a contract, now to be found in the Rome Convention on the Law Applicable to Contractual Obligations, scheduled to the Contracts (Applicable Law) Act 1990.[16]

Form Under Article 9(1) of the Convention, a contract is binding, so far as relates to form, if it satisfies the requirements of the law of the place of contracting or of the law applicable to it under the other Convention rules.[17] So if A and B, two domiciled Englishmen, make a contract in London in such terms that its governing law is that of England, there is no doubt that it is exclusively subject to English law. The mere fact that it relates to foreign land does not affect the contractual rights and liabilities of the parties. Furthermore, a contract will be regarded as formally valid if so valid under its governing law or the law of the place of contracting, even if not formally valid under the law of the situs. This can be illustrated, at common law, by *Re Smith, Lawrence v Kitson:*[18]

> The testator had executed a deed in England by which he charged his land in the West Indies as security for the repayment to his sisters of £1,000, and agreed to execute a legal mortgage whenever required to do so. This deed was not sufficient by the law of the situs to constitute a valid incumbrance on the land. In an administration action brought against the trustees of the will it was held that the sisters were entitled to have a legal mortgage executed in their favour according to the requirements of the local law.

There is, however, a special rule in Article 9(6) of the Convention which deals with the formal validity of a contract the subject matter of which is a right in immovable property or the right to use immovable property. Such a contract shall:

> "be subject to the mandatory requirements of form of the law of the country where the property is situated if by that law those requirements are imposed irrespective of the country where the contract is concluded and irrespective of the law governing the contract."

It is thought that such mandatory requirements, which must under the law of the situs have overriding effect, are "probably rather rare",[19] though there may be some such rules under Scots law.[20]

Essential validity Under Article 3(1) of the Convention, the parties are free to choose the law to govern their contract relating to immovables;[1] but, in the absence of choice, the essential validity of the contract will, by reason of Article 4[2] and much as it was at common law,[3] be governed by the law of the country with which the contract is most closely connected. In the nature of

16 Supra, pp 459 et seq.
17 Supra, pp 507–510.
18 [1916] 2 Ch 206.
19 Report on the Convention by Giuliano and Lagarde, OJ C282, 31 October 1980, p 32.
20 Anton, p 606.
1 Supra, pp 476–486. Reference is made to Arts 3 and 4 by Art 8 on material validity.
2 Supra, pp 487–495.
3 See *British South Africa Co v De Beers Consolidated Mines Ltd* [1910] 2 Ch 502, revsd on other grounds [1912] AC 52; *Re Anchor Line (Henderson Bros) Ltd* [1937] Ch 483, [1937] 2 All ER 823; cf *Carse v Coppen* 1951 SC 233 at 247–248.

events, this is likely to be the law of the situs, and this is reinforced by a rebuttable presumption in Article 4(3) "that the contract is most closely connected with the country where the immovable property is situated."[4]

Capacity   It would seem, on principle, that the distinction between an actual transfer and a contract to transfer must also be relevant in a question of capacity. Where a person contracts in one country to transfer land in another country his capacity should be tested by the law[5] governing the essential validity of the contract. The difficulty, however, of maintaining this view is that, if the contracting party were subject to some incapacity in the true sense, eg minority, by the law of the situs though not by the governing law, it would be futile to subject him to a decree of specific performance that the local law would forbid him to implement. The most that could be done would be to hold him liable in damages.

4 Supra, p 493. The Convention rules governing the validity of contracts relating to immovable
   property are, of course, subject to all the other general provisions of the Convention,
   discussed supra, pp 466 et seq.
5 Supra, pp 510–513.

Chapter 30

The transfer of tangible movables

SUMMARY

1. INTRODUCTION

Our task in this chapter is to ascertain the legal system according to which the various problems that may arise from an assignment of movables[1] must be determined. We are not concerned here with what are usually called general assignments, under which, on the occasion of marriage, death and bankruptcy, the entirety of a person's property may pass to another. Our inquiry is confined to particular assignments inter vivos of isolated or individual movables, of which the commonest examples are sales, gifts, mortgages and pledges. Further, the present discussion is limited to tangible movables.

This is one of the most intractable topics in English private international law, for of the few relevant authorities most are antiquated and they do not reveal with any certainty what principles govern the subject as a whole. One common but fallacious assumption is that all problems must be referred to one single law. In the course of time varied views on what this is have been advanced. The law of the situs of the property, the law of the place of the parties' domicil or of the transferor, the law of the place of acting, the proper law of the transfer—each of these has had its advocates. The assumption, however, is untenable. It represents an oversimplification of the position, for

---

1 On this subject see especially, Lalive, *The Transfer of Chattels in the Conflict of Laws*; Zaphiriou, *The Transfer of Chattels in Private International Law*; Falconbridge, *Conflict of Laws* (2nd edn), 442 et seq; Benjamin's *Sale of Goods*, 3rd edn (1987), paras 2464–2492; Morris, pp 350–357; Nygh, pp 453–463; Sykes and Pryles, pp 663–704; Morris (1945) 22 BYBIL 232; Chesterman (1973) 22 ICLQ 213; North (1990) I Hague Recueil 9, 259 et seq; Prott (1989) V Hague Recueil 215, 262–281.

it is based on the fallacy that the possible questions arising out of a transfer of movables all fall into the same category and are all of the same juridical nature. This is not so. Suppose, for instance, the following facts:

> A, resident and domiciled in England, sells goods lying in a Barcelona warehouse to B, a Dutch businessman. He transmits the bill of exchange and the bill of lading to B to secure acceptance. B fails to accept the bill of exchange but takes the bill of lading to Antwerp and transfers it there to C, a Belgian businessman. Meanwhile, the goods have been shipped from Barcelona en route to Holland. The ship is wrecked off the coast of France, but the goods are salvaged and sold by the judicial authorities in Bordeaux to D.

A number of questions, some contractual others proprietary, differing fundamentally in character, may arise from these facts, and it does not require much acumen to appreciate that each one of these cannot satisfactorily be submitted to one system of law. Litigation may occur between A and B as to the formal or essential validity of the original transfer. A may claim as against B that he is entitled to stop the goods in transit. C may claim a derivative title from B which he alleges renders stoppage unlawful. D may claim that the effect of the judicial sale in France has been to divest all previous owners, original as well as derivative, of their former titles. If it is true to say that questions arising out of the transfer and acquisition of property in corporeal movables are determinable by one single law, what is that law in the instant case? Is Spanish law, which happened to be the law of the situs at the time of the original transfer, to determine inter alia the essential validity of the transaction between A and B, the effect of a failure by a Dutch buyer to accept a bill of exchange received by him from an English seller, and the title of a Frenchman who buys goods in France publicly sold by a French judicial authority? Further, the law of the situs has not remained constant. Is it Spanish law for some questions, French law for others? If so, how are the questions to be classified for this purpose? If the law of the situs is disenthroned as the one governing system and replaced by the law of the place of acting, or by the law with which the original transfer is most closely connected, or by the law of the domicil of any of the possible contestants, the mind recoils from the strange conclusions that might be reached by a court. MAUGHAM J once said obiter:

> I do not think that anybody can doubt that with regard to the transfer of goods the law applicable must be the law of the country where the movable is situate.[2]

This rule, though undoubtedly correct in general, is not without its exceptions. The truth is that the search for the proper law to govern questions arising out of the transfer of corporeal movables will produce nothing but confusion and obscurity unless certain elementary distinctions are made. Before suggesting how this should be done, it is proposed to consider the various theories that have been advanced.

---

2 *Re Anziani* [1930] 1 Ch 407 at 420. See also *Bank voor Handel en Scheepvaart NV v Slatford* [1953] 1 QB 248 at 257, [1951] 2 All ER 779 at 786 per DEVLIN J: "There is little doubt that it is the lex situs which as a general rule governs the transfer of movables when effected contractually."

2. THE VARIOUS THEORIES

In choosing the proper law to govern the transfer of movable objects, arguments may be advanced in favour of the law of the domicil, the law of the situs, the law of the place of acting, or the proper law of the transfer. It will be well to consider the relative merits of these legal systems before attempting a final statement of the law.

(a) THE LAW OF THE DOMICIL

Historically, the starting-point is the maxim mobilia sequuntur personam—goods follow the person. "Personal property", some English writers have said, "has no locality". Although sweeping statements to the effect that rights over movables are to be governed by the law of the owner's domicil may be found in the earlier English authorities,[3] it is now generally agreed that to allow either party to invoke the law of his domicil in the case of a dispute arising out of a transfer of chattels would be commercially impracticable and contrary both to natural justice and to the normal expectations of the parties themselves. Indeed, it has been said by the Privy Council that the maxim mobilia sequuntur personam means, not that movables are deemed to be situated where their owner is domiciled, but merely that their devolution on his death is governed by his personal law.[4] It might, moreover, be prejudicial to innocent third parties, as can be seen from a hypothetical case.

A, a domiciled Englishman, by a transaction which is valid by English law but void by the law of Illinois, executes a bill of sale in favour of X, another domiciled Englishman, over goods that are situated in Chicago, Illinois. Later, Y, also domiciled in England, causes a writ of attachment to be levied on the goods in Chicago in respect of a debt due to him from A. The attachment suit proceeds to judgment and the goods are sold in satisfaction of Y's debt.

The result of holding in such a case that the original transaction conferred a valid and prior title to the goods on X, since it conformed to the law of the common domicil of A and X, would be to impose liability for conversion on the sheriff and the officer who conducted the sale in Chicago. Yet it is obvious that, though the sheriff must be presumed to know the law of the place where the goods are situate, he cannot be expected to investigate the law of their owner's domicil.

Again, whose domicil is decisive? Suppose, for instance, that the question is whether goods stored in Rotterdam belong to a domiciled Englishman or to a domiciled Frenchman. In such a case no decision is possible on the basis of the law of the domicil if the laws of France and of England differ, for there is no guide as to which of these laws shall be chosen. If the law of the plaintiff's domicil is chosen on the ground that the question of his title has been raised, this is a circular argument, since the sole issue is whether he possesses a title. The result is the same if the law of the defendant's domicil is chosen. Moreover, if the decisive factor is the domicil of one of the parties, the governing law would vary according to which of them began proceedings.

---

3 *Sill v Worswick* (1791) 1 H Bl 665, at 690; *Re Ewing's Estate* (1830) 1 Cr & J 151 at 156.
4 *Alberta Provincial Treasurer v Kerr* [1933] AC 710 at 721.

(b) THE LAW OF THE SITUS

An alternative to the law of the domicil is the law of the situs. This has obvious virtues. Where claimants have different domicils or where they rely on transactions in different countries, the law of the situs has the great advantage of being a single and exclusive system that can act as an independent arbiter of conflicting claims. Moreover, its right of control satisfies the expectations of the reasonable man, for a party to a transfer naturally concludes that the transaction will be subject to the law of the country in which the subject-matter is at present situated. If a movable which is vested in A as the result of a transaction with B governed by English law is taken by B to France and there sold to C in circumstances which, by French law but not by English law, confer a valid title on C, it would be a travesty of justice to determine the mutual rights of A and C by English law, the relevancy of which would be entirely unknown to C.

Nevertheless there may be cases where reference to the law of the situs appears arbitrary. If, for example, goods deposited temporarily in a Hamburg warehouse are sold by their owner, London importers, to another London dealer by a contract effected in England, there may seem to be no obvious reason why any question concerning the title to the goods should be governed by German law. However, there would seem to be good policy reasons to support reference to the law of the situs. "Two decisive considerations are, firstly, that the country of the situs has the effective power over the chattel, secondly that the exclusive application of the law of the situs alone can fulfil the need for security in international property transactions."[5]

As can be seen from the example suggested earlier,[6] difficulties may arise where the situs of the goods changes during the course of events leading to litigation. If this is so then the problem will be to identify the law of the particular situs that must govern.[7]

(c) THE LAW OF THE PLACE OF ACTING

There is little to be said in favour of the law of the place of acting. Here, as in other areas of law, the mere fact that a transaction is completed in a particular place is no adequate reason for admitting the control of the local law. If, for instance, an Englishman executes a document in Edinburgh granting a lien over his furniture in London to another Englishman it is unthinkable that this slight and perhaps accidental connection with Scotland should require the possessory rights of the parties to be determined by Scots law. Yet, curiously enough, there are decisions, dealing, however, with negotiable instruments, which contain strong dicta in favour of the law of the place of acting. Thus in *Alcock v Smith*, ROMER J said:

> Generally, the rights of transferor and transferee, on a transfer in one country of a document of title to a debt or to an interest in personal property, are governed by the law of the country where the transfer takes place, although the debt may be due from persons living in, or the personal property may be situate in, a foreign country.[8]

5　Lalive, op cit, p 115.
6　Supra, p 795.
7　Morris (1945) 22 BYBIL 232, 233; infra, pp 797 et seq.
8　[1892] 1 Ch 238 at 255. See also *Embiricos v Anglo-Austrian Bank* [1905] 1 KB 677 at 683, 685.

On appeal, KAY LJ in terms said the same thing,[9] but it seems clear from the illustrations he gave that he had in mind a case where the law of the place of acting and the law of the situs coincided. Since the place of acting and the situs are necessarily the same in the transfer of a negotiable instrument, it is probable that in these cases the judges, despite their reference to the law of the place of acting, were in fact speaking in terms of the law of the situs.[10]

(d) THE LAW GOVERNING THE TRANSFER

The last law that may be chosen to govern questions arising out of a transfer of movables is the law of the country with which the transfer has the most real connection, or more shortly, the law governing the transfer, analogous to the law governing a contract. Its ascertainment will in most cases cause no difficulty, as for instance where the law of the place of acting and the law of the situs are identical or where two English businessmen meet in Paris and complete a transfer there of goods situated in England. But a more complex problem may arise, as where A, resident and domiciled in England, sells goods lying in a Naples warehouse to B, who is resident and domiciled in the Netherlands. Without more facts it is scarcely possible to say what the proper law would be in such a case. Before it could reach a decision, the court would require to know, inter alia: Where was the transfer effected? If reduced to writing, was it drafted in terms peculiar to English or Dutch law? Were the goods only temporarily in Italy? The danger, however, to avoid is the assumption that the law of the situs always constitutes the proper law.

It would seem that of the four laws proposed the choice lies between the law of the situs and the proper law of the transfer. Nevertheless, it cannot be said that either governs exclusively all the issues arising from a particular transfer. The choice between them depends, basically, on whether the issue under consideration is contractual or proprietary.

3. THE MODERN LAW

(a) THE GENERAL RULE

The questions which arise in relation to a transfer of tangible movables may include a variety of matters, such as whether the transfer is void for incapacity, whether it is formally or essentially valid, whether it is voidable for misrepresentation or other cause, whether the property in the movables has passed to the transferee, whether the transferor has a lien on the goods or a right to stop them in transit, and what is the nature of the interest created by the transfer. Some of these questions are of a contractual, others of a proprietary, character.

It is clear that the contractual rights and obligations fall to be determined by the proper law of the transfer. This category includes such questions as whether there is an implied condition that the subject-matter of the transfer is of merchantable quality or fit for a particular purpose, or whether the transfer itself is formally valid.

The solution is not so obvious, however, where the question relates not to the purely contractual rights but to claims to some possessory or proprietary right in the chattel itself. If, in such a case, the law of the situs and the proper

9 Ibid, at 267.
10 Lalive, op cit, p 79.

law of the transfer are not coincident, which is to prevail? Although the authorities are few and whilst there is some support for reference to the proper law,[11] it is now established that the proprietary effect of a particular assignment of movables is governed exclusively by the law of the country where they are situated at the time of the assignment.[12] An owner will be divested of his title to movables if they are taken to a foreign country and there assigned in circumstances sufficient by the local law to pass a valid title to the assignee. The title recognised by the law of the foreign situs overrides earlier and inconsistent titles, no matter by what law they may have been created. As DIPLOCK LJ has said:[13]

> The proper law governing the transfer of corporeal movable property is the lex situs. A contract made in England and governed by English law for the sale of specific goods situated in Germany, although it would be effective to pass the property in the goods at the moment the contract was made if the goods were situate in England would not have that effect if under German law ... delivery of the goods was required in order to transfer the property in them.

The application of the law of the situs rule must prevail on practical grounds of business convenience.[14] If by a transaction subject to English law a man obtains possession of goods of which he becomes neither the legal nor the ostensible owner, and then sells and delivers them to a buyer in France, the latter should be entitled to assume that the French rule applies. He should not be required to investigate the foreign title of the seller.

The leading authority for the application of the law of the situs is *Cammell v Sewell*,[15] where the facts were these:

> A Russian seller shipped in Russia a cargo of timber on a Prussian vessel to English importers in Hull who insured the cargo with the plaintiffs as underwriters. The vessel having been wrecked off the coast of Norway, the timber was sold to X at a public auction held at the instance of the master in Norway. An action, brought by the underwriters in the Norwegian court to set aside the sale, failed. X shipped the timber to England and transferred it to the defendants. The underwriters sued the defendants for its value.

By English law, the auction sale had not affected the title vested in the English importers by the original contract and which was now vested in the plaintiffs. The defendants, however, did not deny the effect of that contract. Their case was that, by virtue of what happened in Norway at the time when the timber was there, they had acquired a title which under Norwegian law overrode that of the earlier English purchaser. The Court of Exchequer gave judgment for the defendants on the ground that the decision of the Norwegian court was a judgment in rem which vested the property in X as against the whole world. On appeal, a majority of the Court of Exchequer Chamber, without giving a definite decision on the point, were of opinion that the judgment

11 Eg *Inglis v Usherwood* (1801) 1 East 515 where Russian law was the law of the situs, the law of the place of acting, and also, apparently, the proper law of the transfer.
12 *Cammell v Sewell* (1858) 3 H & N 617; on appeal (1860) 5 H & N 728; *Winkworth v Christie Manson and Woods Ltd* [1980] Ch 496, [1980] 1 All ER 1121.
13 *Hardwick Game Farm v Suffolk Agricultural Poultry Producers Association* [1966] 1 WLR 287 at 330, affd by the House of Lords [1969] 2 AC 31; and see *Bank voor Handel en Scheepvart NV v Slatford* [1953] 1 QB 248 at 257.
14 *Re Anziani* [1930] 1 Ch 407 at 420.
15 (1858) 3 H & N 617; on appeal (1860) 5 H & N 728.

was not a judgment in rem, but they decided that the title conferred on X by Norwegian law must prevail. CROMPTON J said:

> We think the law on this subject was correctly stated by the Lord Chief Baron ... when he says, "If personal property is disposed of in a manner binding according to the law of the country where it is that disposition is binding everywhere."[1]

No doubt exclusive reference to the law of the situs will cause hardship to the previous owner if without his knowledge his movables are dealt with in a foreign country. Thus, CROMPTON J acknowledged that the English law as to the distraint of a foreigner's goods for rent due from a tenant, or as to the title to stolen property acquired by a purchaser under a sale in market overt, might appear harsh.

> But [he said] we cannot think that the goods of foreigners would be protected against such laws, or that if the property once passed by virtue of them it would again be changed by being taken by the new owner into the foreigner's own country.[2]

This approach was applied by SLADE J in *Winkworth v Christie, Manson and Woods Ltd*[3] to the converse case of goods stolen in England, sold abroad and brought back to England.

> Works of art were stolen from the plaintiff's house in England. They were taken to Italy and there sold to the second defendant, an Italian, who then sent them back to England to be auctioned by the first defendants. It was agreed that, under Italian law, though probably not under English law,[4] the second defendant acquired a title to the goods good against the world. It was crucial to decide whether title to the goods was governed by Italian law, as the law of the situs at the time of the transfer to the second defendant.

Although it appeared hard on the plaintiff to see goods stolen from him in England being properly offered for sale in England by the defendants, SLADE J upheld the law of the situs rule and would not accept that there should be any exception to it on the basis that the goods had been returned to England:

> Security of title is as important to an innocent purchaser as it is to an innocent owner whose goods have been stolen from him. Commercial convenience may be said imperatively to demand that proprietary rights to movables shall generally be determined by the lex situs.[5]

Furthermore, the fact that the goods were wrongfully removed from England to Italy was held not to affect the fact that their situs at the time of the transfer to the second defendant was Italian. SLADE J was not prepared to attribute a fictional English situs to them:

> Intolerable uncertainty in the law would result if the court were to permit the introduction of a wholly fictional English situs when applying the principle to any

1 (1860) 5 H & N 728 at 744–745.
2 Ibid, at 744; and see at 741, 743. In *Alcock v Smith* [1892] 1 Ch 238 at 267, KAY LJ said: "The goods of a foreigner sold in market overt by one who had no title to them could not be recovered from the purchaser." It seems likely that such a view would also be taken of transfers under such provisions as the Sale of Goods Act 1979, s 25, the Hire Purchase Act 1964, s 27 and the Factors Act 1889, ss 2, 8 and 9 (the 1889 and 1964 Acts as amended by the Consumer Credit Act 1974, s 192, Sch 4, Pt 1).
3 [1980] Ch 496, [1980] 1 All ER 1121; Carter (1981) 52 BYBIL 329; Knott [1981] Conv 279; and see *Todd v Armour* (1882) 9 R 901.
4 Ibid, at 500.
5 Ibid, at 512.

particular case, merely because the case happened to have a number of other English connecting factors.[6]

It was accepted[7] that there is a number of exceptions to the law of the situs rule; such as, for example, the rules applicable to goods in transit with a casual or unknown situs at the relevant time.[8] Again, bankruptcy and succession are governed by separate choice of law rules.[9] Further, the law of the situs will not be applied if there is a mandatory statutory provision of English law which the courts are required to apply; though it should be pointed out that it is very rare for an English provision to be so interpreted. However, SLADE J was prepared to accept two further exceptions. The first is where the purchaser claiming title did not act bona fide. This is a dubious exception. If good faith is required by the law of the situs, as it was in the present case, this is no exception. It can only be an exception if the English requirement of good faith is to be insisted upon, notwithstanding its absence under the law of the situs. It is suggested that this exception can only be justified, if at all, as an example of the broader public policy exception and that would mean that it would not apply in every case where the English concept of good faith had not been satisfied; but only in the rare case where the application of the law of the situs in the particular circumstances was quite unacceptable to English public policy. SLADE J himself described this second public policy exception as applicable to a case "where the content of the particular foreign law on which [the defendant] relied was so outrageous that this court regarded it as wholly contrary to justice and morality".[10] This is no more than the application of a general rule of private international law.[11]

(b) DERIVATIVE CLAIMS

The principle of the law of the situs rule is that a title to movables acquired in one country by A under a transaction with B is good all over the world,[12] unless and until it is displaced by a new title vested in C as the result of an assignment effective by the law of the country to which the movables have been taken. As has been seen from the issue of market overt, the principle extends to a case where C claims derivatively from one of the parties to the earlier transaction. The conditional sale is the fertile begetter of this type of problem, not indeed in England but in federal States where it is a matter of daily occurrence to move chattels from one law district to another.[13]

Suppose, for instance, that a car is delivered by A to B under a hire-purchase transaction concluded in England. By English law, which is both the law of the situs and the proper law of the transaction, the ownership of the car remains in A until all the instalments of the price have been paid. B takes the car to the Netherlands and sells it to C, a bona fide

---

6 Ibid, at 509.
7 Ibid, at 501, 514.
8 See infra, pp 806–807.
9 See infra, pp 837 et seq, 911.
10 [1980] Ch 496 at 510.
11 See supra, pp 128 et seq.
12 *Simpson v Fogo* (1863) 1 Hem & M 195 at 222 where PAGE-WOOD V-C said: "A good title acquired in one country shall be a good title all over the globe."
13 For a discussion of the relevant authorities in Australia, Canada and the USA see Davis (1964) 13 ICLQ 53; and see Nygh, pp 458–460; Castel, *Canadian Conflict of Laws* 2nd edn (1986) ch 24; McLeod, *The Conflict of Laws*, 339–342; Juenger (1978) 26 AJCL (Supp) 145. For the European position, see Schilling (1985) 34 ICLQ 86.

purchaser. Suppose also that Dutch internal law requires hire-purchase agreements to be recorded in a public register, and holds that whether a sale by the hirer binds the owner depends on whether the agreement has been recorded. Later C brings the car to England in the course of his holiday. A then brings an action against him claiming the return of the car or alternatively the payment of damages.

These facts raise the question whether the rights of the parties are determinable by Dutch or by English law. It would seem that on general principles English law should be preferred, for the alleged derivative title of C should depend on A's title from which its derivation is claimed. However, expediency demands that the bone fide assignee of movables shall be protected if he acts according to the law of their situation, and there can be no doubt that a derivative title to them, recognised as valid by that law, will be recognised as valid by English law. What this means in the present context is that, where there have been two transactions relating to the same subject-matter, the first in one situs, the second in another situs to which the subject-matter has been transferred, it is the law of the second situs that governs the conflicting claims of the parties.[14]

Two North American cases might be discussed as illustrations of the problem where goods are removed from one state to another, there having been a reservation of title in the first state. The first case is the Canadian decision in *Century Credit Corporation v Richard*:[15]

> X sold and delivered a car, in Quebec, to Y under a conditional sale agreement. This agreement reserved title in X, the unpaid seller, until full payment of the purchase price. Under Quebec law this agreement did not have to be, and was not, registered. Y took the car to Ontario and sold it to Z who was unaware of X's reservation of title. Under Ontario law such conditional sale agreements were required to be registered. Furthermore, under Ontario law, Y could pass a good title to Z despite any defects in his own title.

The Ontario court held that Z's title, good under the law of Ontario, prevailed against X. The reasoning was that, so far as the requirement of registration was concerned, X had made a valid reservation of title under Quebec law which was not affected by taking the car to Ontario. Ontario courts should recognise the validity of X's claim as against Y.[16] However, the sale of the car by Y in Ontario amounted, under Ontario law, to an overriding of X's reservation of title.

The second case is *Goetschius v Brightman*:[17]

> Y obtained possession of a car in California from X under a conditional sale contract by which the title remained in X until the whole price had been paid. The contract expressly provided that the car should not be removed from California. Y, however, took it to New York and there sold it to the defendants. The conditional sale was recorded neither in New York nor in California. By the domestic law of California applicable to a purely domestic case, the title of X would prevail over that of the defend-

14 Davis (1964) 13 ICLQ 53, 56.
15 (1962) 34 DLR (2d) 291; and see *Price Mobile Homes Centres Inc v National Trailer Convoy of Canada* (1974) 44 DLR (3d) 443; *Re Delisle* (1988) 52 DLR (4th) 106.
16 See, eg, *Taylor v Lovegrove* (1912) 18 ALR (CN) 22.
17 (1927) 245 NY 186.

ants; by the equivalent law of New York the title of the defendants would be preferred. The plaintiff was the assignee of X.

The New York court, though it applied New York law as being the law of the situs, found for the plaintiff. The judgment can be summarised as follows. The law that governs the interpretation and effect of the conditional sale is Californian law; by that law the title of the plaintiff is superior to that of the defendants; but, since the defendants bought the car while it was present in New York, it does not follow that New York law will recognise the superiority of the plaintiff's title.

No rule of comity requires this State to subordinate its public policy in regard to transfers made within the State of property situated here to the policy of the State where the owner of the property resides or where he acquired title.[18]

The law of New York applies as being the law of the situs. But what is the New York rule applicable to the circumstances of this case? The law of a particular situs may prescribe that a person in the position of the present plaintiff may be divested of his title if the chattel has been removed out of his State with or without his consent. That, however, is not the rule in New York, for the rule is that an owner shall not lose his title if the chattel is brought here without his consent. It is true that a conditional sale is void by New York statutory law against a purchaser unless it is filed, but this is confined to sales effected in New York, not in some other State or country.[19]

(c) RETENTION OF TITLE CLAUSES[1]

There has been a number of recent Scottish and Irish decisions in which the effect of retention of title clauses in international contracts has had to be considered.[2] Foreign suppliers of goods have included terms in contracts of sale to Scottish or Irish buyers which purport to incorporate the provisions of the seller's law,[3] allowing him to reserve title to goods which he has delivered until they have been fully paid for. Almost inevitably in this type of case, the situs of the goods will change with their delivery, raising issues as to what law is to govern the operation of the reservation of title clause. This may be illustrated by *Zahnrad Fabrik Passau GmbH v Terex Ltd*:[4]

---

18 Ibid, at 191.
19 In the converse case where title would not appear to have been effectively reserved in one jurisdiction and the chattel is taken to another jurisdiction where the reservation of title was effective, there is a tendency in the courts to protect the original owner's title, either by generous interpretation of the domestic law of the original jurisdiction (eg *A J Smeman Car Sales v Richardsons Pre-Run Cars* (1969) 63 QJPR 150; *Davis* (1970) 2 ACLR 50) or, apparently, of its territorial scope (eg *Marvin Safe Co v Norton* 48 NJL 410, 7 A 418 (1886); cf *Charles T Dougherty Co Inc v Krimke* 144 A 617 (1929)).
1 North (1990) I Hague Recueil 9, 265–273; Benjamin's *Sale of Goods*, 3rd edn (1987), paras 2485–2492.
2 *Hammer and Sohne v HWT Realisations Ltd* 1985 SLT (Sh Ct) 21; *Zahnrad Fabrik Passau GmbH v Terex Ltd* 1986 SLT 84; *Armour v Thyssen Edelstahlwerke AG* [1991] 2 AC 339, [1990] 3 All ER 481, HL; *Re Interview Ltd* [1975] IR 382; *Kruppstaal AG v Quitmann Products Ltd* [1982] ILRM 551.
3 Often the foreign law is not pleaded, eg *Aluminium Industrie Vaassen BV v Romalpa Aluminium Ltd* [1976] 2 All ER 552, [1976] 1 WLR 676; *Emerald Stainless Steel Ltd v South Side Distribution Ltd* 1983 SLT 162; *Deutz Engines Ltd v Terex Ltd* 1984 SLT 273; *Armour v Thyssen Edelstahlwerke AG* [1991] 2 AC 339 at 350; or the parties may agree (rightly or wrongly) that the foreign law is the same as that of the forum, as in *E Pfeiffer Weinkellerei-Weineinkauf GmbH & Co v Arbuthnot Factors Ltd* [1988] 1 WLR 150.
4 1986 SLT 84.

Plaintiffs in Germany agreed to supply vehicle components to a manu-facturer in Scotland under a contract containing a reservation of title clause, the law governing the contract appearing to be German law. The components were used in the construction of earth-moving equipment and, when the Scottish buyer became insolvent, the plaintiffs claimed title to the goods supplied by them.

Notwithstanding the fact that German law may have been the law governing the contract, the court concluded that, as the dispute was as to title to the goods, this issue fell to be decided by Scots law as that of the situs of the goods. The reason given for applying Scots law was that title was alleged by the defendants to have been acquired there by accession once the components were included in the equipment. A fuller analysis might have been to ask whether title was properly reserved in Germany when that was the situs of the goods and then to ask, when the goods were moved to Scotland, whether the reserved title was overriden by accession under the law of the new situs.[5]

(d) MEANING OF "THE LAW OF THE SITUS"

In determining the meaning and content of the law of the situs, there are two problems to consider. The first is whether, when English law refers to the law of the situs, the doctrine of renvoi[6] applies; ie will the English court apply the law, not of the situs itself, but of whichever country is selected as applicable by the choice of law rules of the law of the situs? Some tentative support for the application of renvoi in this context can be derived from *Winkworth v Christie, Manson and Woods Ltd* where SLADE J said:

It is theoretically possible that the evidence as to Italian law would show that the Italian court would itself apply English law. In this event I suppose it would be open to the plaintiff to argue that English law should, in the final result, be applied by the English court by virtue of the doctrine of renvoi.[7]

The second problem is illustrated by the reasoning in *Goetschius v Bright-man*. It concerns the identification of the substantive rules which are to be applied once the appropriate legal system has been selected. This can be exemplified by reference to the hypothetical case, given earlier.[8] There the English judge must apply Dutch law, as that of the situs. He must ascertain as a fact what rule a court at the situs would apply in the instant circumstances. It is essential to appreciate that this will not necessarily be the rule that a Dutch court would apply to a domestic case containing no foreign element.[9] That court, if required to adjudicate between A and C, would be confronted with a private international law case. It would therefore be obliged to examine its own internal law in order to ascertain whether the necessity of recording a hire-purchase agreement applied to an agreement made abroad between two foreigners. This would necessitate an investigation into the policy of the law. Was the object to protect persons in the Netherlands who paid money on the faith of an ostensibly good title? If so registration would be necessary in the case of all movables within the jurisdiction, no matter where or between

5 If there is no further act in the second situs, the issue then will be whether the law of that situs accepts a reservation of title valid under the law of the first situs, see *Armour v Thyssen Edelstahlwerke AG* [1991] 2 AC 339.
6 Supra, pp 58 et seq.
7 [1980] QB 496 at 514.
8 Supra, pp 800–801.
9 Cook, pp 263 et seq.

whom the hire-purchase agreement had been made. If this were the correct interpretation of the registration law, then an English court, if seised of the case, should decide in favour of C. But the policy of the Dutch law might be different. Its design might be to strike only at agreements concluded in the Netherlands. Or, though its object might not be restricted in this way, the Dutch courts, in the case of agreements concluded abroad, might have made the validity of a foreign agreement not registered in the Netherlands turn on whether the owner had or had not consented to the removal of the movables to another country.

This simple truism, that the law of the situs means the law that a court at the situs would apply to the case in hand and not necessarily the domestic law applicable to a purely domestic case, illustrates the correct role of private international law so far as individual assignments of movables are concerned. Its role is to choose what law shall determine the conflicting claims of the parties. Its function in this regard is completed as soon as it has ruled that the law of the situs, or the law chosen by that country's choice of law rules under the renvoi doctrine, governs. Once this ruling has been given, once the choice of law has been made, we pass from the sphere of private international law, and it merely remains for the English court to ascertain as a fact what particular principle a court at the situs would follow in the actual circumstances. This appears to be an obvious and elementary observation, but it is sometimes overlooked, with the result that the complications of a part of the law not remarkable for its simplicity are needlessly increased. In dealing with the choice of law problem that arises where the subject-matter of a hire-purchase agreement is removed to a foreign country and there sold, authors sometimes say that the governing law depends on whether the removal was with or without the consent of the owner. If the removal was without his consent, they say that the question arising between the owner and the purchaser is governed by the law to which the hire-purchase agreement is subject; otherwise it is governed by the domestic rule of the law of the situs. This distinction, however, forms no part of the English rule for the choice of law. The law of the situs of the goods at the time of their sale is chosen because, in the words of Wolff, "the place where a thing is situate is the natural centre of rights over it",[10] and it therefore follows that whether those rights depend on consent to removal or on any other factor is a matter solely for the law of that place to determine.

The authorities, so far as they go, appear to support the proposition that the English court, when required to apply English law as being the law of the situs in a case containing a foreign element, does not necessarily apply the ordinary domestic law of England. *Dulaney v Merry & Son*,[11] though it concerned a general assignment, may be given by way of analogy.

> Two domiciled Americans executed a deed in Maryland by which they assigned all their property wherever situate to another domiciled American for the benefit of their creditors. The deed was valid by the law of Maryland, but it was not registered under the English Deeds of Arrangement Act 1887.[12]

The question was whether the assignee was entitled to goods situated in

10 *Private International Law* (1950) 2nd edn, p 512.
11 [1901] 1 KB 536.
12 See now the Deeds of Arrangement Act 1914.

England. This was determinable by the law of the situs, English law. Had a similar assignment been effected in England between English traders concerning goods situated in England alone, there is no doubt that the deed would have been void. But this was a private international law case, and therefore a necessary inquiry was whether the English statute was designed to strike at all assignments, wherever made, affecting goods in England, or whether its operation was confined to assignments made in England. After stating that the English legislature may enact rules as to the passing of the property in goods situated in England notwithstanding what the law might be in the country of the owner's domicil, CHANNELL J said that the question before him reduced itself to the construction of the Act of 1887. After subjecting this to a critical examination, he came to the conclusion that the policy of the Act as disclosed by its language was not to bring within its provisions an assignment by foreign debtors affecting goods abroad as well as goods in England. By internal English law, therefore, the Maryland assignment was valid with regard to the English goods.[13]

(e) ATTACHMENT OF MOVABLES BY CREDITORS

The control of the law of the situs extends also to the attachment of movables by a creditor. The creditor enjoys the rights recognised by the law of the country where the movables are situated at the time of the attachment.[14] Those rights prevail against all persons claiming under some other law. Thus in *Liverpool Marine Credit Co v Hunter*:[15]

A British ship was mortgaged in England by X, a British subject, to Y, another British subject. It was later arrested at New Orleans, Louisiana, by certain British subjects who were creditors of X. The mortgage was void according to the law of Louisiana. In order to avoid a sale of the ship by the New Orleans court, Y gave bonds to the creditors for the amount of their debts. Y subsequently sued in England to restrain the creditors from suing on the bonds. Judgment was given for the creditors.

The mortgagee's argument was that the defendants had been guilty of inequitable conduct in taking legal action in the USA, but it was held that, since the creditors owed no duty to the mortgagee, they were clearly entitled to avail themselves of the local procedure in respect of property within the jurisdiction. This, like *Cammell v Sewell* and *Winkworth v Christie, Manson and Woods Ltd*, was a case where the owner's rights in chattels were overridden by the operation of the law of the situs.

A similar situation arose in *Inglis v Robertson*,[16] where the facts were these:

G, a domiciled Englishman, the owner of whisky stored in a warehouse at Glasgow, held delivery warrants issued by the warehouse-keeper stating that the whisky was held to G's order or "assigns by endorsement hereon". G, in return for a loan, delivered in London to Inglis, an English merchant, a letter of hypothecation stating that the whisky was deposited with him as security for the loan, with power of sale. He indorsed the warrants and handed them to Inglis. Inglis gave no notice of his right to the warehouse-

13 But cf the present position as to bankruptcy, infra, pp 904 et seq.
14 But, for the distinction between the assignment of a movable and its attachment, see Lalive, op cit, p 156.
15 (1867) LR 4 Eq 62; on appeal (1868) 3 Ch App 479; cf Lalive, op cit, p 69.
16 [1898] AC 616.

keeper. Robertson, claiming as personal creditor of G, arrested the whisky in the hands of the warehouse-keeper.

Presuming that by English law Inglis, claiming through G, had a better right to the whisky than Robertson, would that conclude the matter in his favour? It would not do so if Scottish law were applicable, for the rule in Scotland is that a pledgee who wishes to make his pledges effective in such circumstances must give notice to the warehouse-keeper, otherwise his right is subordinated to the claims of the pledgor's creditor. The House of Lords gave judgment for Robertson. Lord WATSON refused to discuss the internal law of England. After stating that Robertson had done what was necessary by Scottish law to acquire a real right against the whisky, he proceeded as follows:

> It would ... be contrary to the elementary principles of international law, and, ... without authority, to hold that the right of a Scottish creditor when so perfected can be defeated by a transaction between his debtor and the citizen of a foreign country which would be according to the law of that country, but is not according to the law of Scotland, sufficient to create a real right in the goods.[17]

Again:

> The crucial question in this case is whether the right ... vests in the pledgee of the documents, not a jus ad rem merely, but a real interest in the goods to which these documents relate. That is a question which I have no hesitation in holding must, in the circumstances of this case, be solved by reference to the law of Scotland. The whisky was in Scotland, and was there held in actual possession by a custodian for [G] as the true owner. That state of the title could not, so far as Scotland was concerned, be altered or overcome by a foreign transaction of pledge which had not, according to the rules of Scottish law, the effect of vesting the property in the whisky, or, in other words, a jus in re, in the pledgee.[18]

(f) GOODS IN TRANSIT

The transfer of movables while they are in course of transit raises a difficult question of choice of law.[19]

> Suppose, for instance, that goods have been dispatched overland from London to Vienna, and that before reaching their destination they have been the subject of a sale or some other commercial transaction. The problems that such circumstances raise become more complex if the parties have different domicils, or if the transaction is effected in some country other than Austria or England.

What law should be applied in such a case has not arisen in the English courts, the probable explanation being that goods in transit are generally represented by a bill of lading or other documentary symbol of ownership

---

17 Ibid, at 625.
18 Ibid, at 626.
19 For a fuller discussion see Lalive, op cit, pp 186–193; Wolff, pp 519–521; Sassoon, *C.I.F. and F.O.B. Contracts*, (1984) 3rd edn, para 742.

which is capable of an independent dealing.[20] Jurists have advocated several laws, such as the law of the situs, the law of the owner's domicil, the law of the place of ultimate destination, the law of the place of dispatch and the proper law of the particular transfer. Objections may be raised to each of these. The law of the situs, owing to its inconstancy, is an impracticable choice unless the movables have come to a definite resting-place at the time of the transfer.[1] The domicil of the owner is not a suitable criterion of the law to govern a mercantile transaction. The law of the stipulated place of destination, though an appropriate choice in many circumstances, suffers from the disadvantage that it may be and frequently is altered during the course of the transit. The law of the place of dispatch is not well adapted to govern a transfer effected abroad when the transit is nearing completion. The proper law is, no doubt, suitable to govern questions dependent upon the effect of a particular transaction, but scarcely apposite to every question.

The truth again is that no one law can be made the exclusive arbiter of disputes arising out of a transfer of goods in transit. The problems must be broken down. A dispute between the parties to a particular transaction, as, for example, a mortgage of the goods granted by the assignee, will be governed by the proper law of the transaction.[2] If the movables come to rest sufficiently to admit of a dealing with them, as where they are seized by creditors in accordance with the local law or wrongfully sold by the carrier, the question of title must clearly be determined by the law of the situs.[3] If the transit is by sea in a single ship, there is much to be said for applying the law of the flag.[4]

(g) GIFTS

Some special comment should be made on the transfer of movables by gift. The more common context for this issue to arise is that of donatio mortis causa—a gift in contemplation of death. Where such a gift has been characterised as a transfer of property,[5] then its validity and effect are governed by the law of the situs.[6] Even though FARWELL J in *Re Craven's Estate*[7] characterised such a gift as a testamentary disposition and applied the law of the testatrix's domicil, English law, by which law an effective parting with

---

20 See, eg the delivery warrants in *Inglis v Robertson*, supra. There is, however, no clear authority on what law governs the transfer of a bill of lading or other document of title to goods. The three possibilities seem to be the proper law of the bill of lading, the law of the situs of the bill at the time of its endorsement, and the law of the situs of the goods at that time. The point is important, since in some countries, eg France, the endorsement of a bill of lading does not pass the property in the goods; Hellendall (1939) 17 Can BR 7, 18–25. It is suggested that the correct choice is the law of the situs of the bill of lading at the time of its endorsement; see Zaphiriou, op.cit, pp 199–209.

1 Eg *Cammell v Sewell* (1858) 3 H & N 617, on appeal (1860) 5 H & N 728; and see *Hardwick Game Farm v Suffolk Agricultural Poultry Producers Assocn* [1966] 1 WLR 287 at 300; affd by the House of Lords [1969] 2 AC 31.

2 In *North Western Bank v Poynton* [1895] AC 56, the House of Lords was prepared to apply the English proper law of a transfer between A and B to the right of creditors to seize the subject-matter in Scotland; though there was agreed to be no difference between English and Scots law; see Anton, pp 613–615.

3 *Cammell v Sewell* (1860) 5 H & N 728.

4 Cf *Lloyd v Guibert* (1865) LR 1 QB 115.

5 See Lalive, op cit, pp 26–29.

6 *Re Korvine's Trust* [1921] 1 Ch 343.

7 [1937] Ch 423, [1937] 3 All ER 33 and see the fuller report in (1937) 53 TLR 694.

dominion was necessary to make the gift valid, he did refer to the law of the situs to determine what was sufficient to pass the dominion.[8]

There is very little authority on transfer of movables by gift inter vivos, but it is suggested that the validity of such transfers of property should be governed by the law of the situs.[9] In *Cochrane v Moore*[10] a donor, apparently domiciled and resident in England, purported, by words of gift spoken in England, to give to the defendant a quarter share in a horse at all relevant times stabled in Paris. Later the plaintiff advanced money on the security of the horse and, when the horse was sold, he claimed that he was entitled to the whole proceeds of the sale. The issue whether any title had passed by the gift was decided solely by reference to English law, whereunder delivery was held to be necessary. However, as French law was not pleaded or referred to, the case is hardly strong authority against the application of the law of the situs.

The American decision in *Morson v Second National Bank of Boston*[11] is of interest in this context. The donor, whilst travelling in Italy with the donee, handed her an envelope containing shares in a Massachusetts company, thus purporting to transfer to her the title to the shares; later, the donor, whilst still in Italy, signed and delivered the stock certificate to the donee. This was adequate under Massachusetts law, but not under Italian law, to effect transfer of legal title to the shares. It was concluded by the Massachusetts court that the law of the situs should determine whether there had been a completed gift of a tangible chattel and, had the shares been tangible chattels, Italian law, as the law of the situs, would have governed. This rule for the choice of law was, however, inapplicable since a transfer of shares falls to be governed by the law of the country in which the issuing company has been incorporated. On the other hand, the validity of the transfer of the actual certificate was subject to the law of the situs.[12]

8 Ibid, at 430; and see (1937) 53 TLR 694 at 698.
9 Zaphiriou, op cit, pp 57–58.
10 (1890) 25 QBD 57.
11 306 Mass 589, 29 NE 2d 19 (1940).
12 The rules as to assignment of shares in English private international law are discussed infra, pp 823–825.

Chapter 31

The assignment of intangible movables

SUMMARY

1. INTRODUCTION

Intangible movables may be divided into rights which are mere rights of action, and rights which are represented by some document or writing that is not only capable of delivery but in the modern commercial world is negotiated as a separate physical entity. A debt, arising from a loan or from an ordinary commercial contract, is an example of the first class; while the second class is chiefly exemplified by negotiable instruments and shares. It is proposed here to keep the two classes separate, and to deal first with debts, secondly with negotiable instruments, and thirdly with shares.

2. DEBTS

(a) THE SITUS OF A DEBT[1]

We have seen that the determination of the situs of immovable and tangible movable property may be necessary in order to determine the applicable law. It is possible also that a debt may be deemed by English law to have a definite locality of its own for several different purposes, such as the exercise of jurisdiction,[2] the payment of taxes, and the grant of probate or of letters of administration.[3] The test by which the locality is determined has been explained by ATKIN LJ in the following words:

> The test in respect of simple contracts was: Where was the debtor residing? ... The reason why the residence of the debtor was adopted as that which determined where

---

1 Rogerson [1990] CLJ 441.
2 Kaye [1989] JBL 449.
3 See, for example, *A-G v Bouvens* (1838) 4 M & W 171 at 191; *Stamps Comrs v Hope* [1891] AC 476 at 481–482; *A-G v Lord Sudeley* [1896] 1 QB 354 at 360–361; *Re Maudslay, Sons and Field* [1900] 1 Ch 602; Falconbridge (1935) 13 Can BR 265.

the debt was situate was because it was in that place where the debtor was that the creditor could, in fact, enforce payment of the debt.[4]

This rule, that an intangible movable, such as a right to recover a loan[5] or money due under an insurance policy,[6] is situated in the country where the debtor resides,[7] because that is where it can be enforced,[8] is a general but not a universal rule. It has been held that a debt which arises under an irrevocable letter of credit is situated in the place where it is in fact payable against the documents,[9] rather than the place of residence of the bank. The general rule of reference to the residence of the debtor encounters an apparent difficulty where, as will often occur in the case of a company, the residence extends to two or more countries. Although the place of residence is chosen because it is there that recovery by action is possible, eg where the company can be found for service,[10] it is not clear what the situs of a debt is (if any) where a country in which the debt may be payable is not that of the residence of the debtor. One view is that the residence of the debtor is "an essential element in deciding the situs of the debt".[11] If, however, the debtor resides in two or more countries, then it is suggested that the debt is situated in the one in which

> it is required to be paid by an express or implied provision of the contract or, if there is no such provision, where it would be paid according to the ordinary course of business.[12]

If, however, the debtor resides only in one country, it is there alone that the debt is situated notwithstanding that it may be expressly or implicitly payable elsewhere.[13] This does not, however, deal adequately with the case where the debtor is not resident in any country where the debt is payable. An Australian court[14] has rejected the idea that such a debt has no situs and relied on the second part of the above quotation's reference to the place of payment in the ordinary course of business, notwithstanding the fact that the debtor is not resident there.

---

4 *New York Life Insurance Co v Public Trustee* [1942] 2 Ch 101 at 119; *Kwok Chi Leung Karl v Comr of Estate Duty* [1988] 1 WLR 1035 at 1040.
5 *Re Helbert Wagg & Co Ltd's Claim* [1956] Ch 323, [1956] 1 All ER 129.
6 *New York Life Insurance Co v Public Trustee* [1924] 2 Ch 101; *Jabbour v Custodian of Israeli Absentee Property* [1954] 1 All ER 145, [1954] 1 WLR 139.
7 *Swiss Bank Corpn v Boehmische Industrial Bank* [1923] 1 KB 673 at 678; *Sutherland v German Property Administrator* (1933) 50 TLR 107.
8 *Alloway v Phillips* [1980] 3 All ER 138, [1980] 1 WLR 888. In *Brooks Associates Inc v Basu* [1983] QB 220, [1983] 1 All ER 508, it was held that a debt due from the National Savings Bank could be attached in England even though the head office of the Bank was in Scotland.
9 *Power Curber International Ltd v National Bank of Kuwait SAK* [1981] 1 WLR 1233 at 1240.
10 *Kwok Chi Leung Karl v Comr of Estate Duty* [1988] 1 WLR 1035 at 1041.
11 *Deutsche Bank und Gesellschaft v Banque des Marchands de Moscou* (1930) unreported, CA, cited in *Re Helbert Wagg & Co Ltd's Claim* [1956] Ch 323 at 343, [1956] 1 All ER 129 at 136.
12 *Jabbour v Custodian of Absentee's Property of State of Israel* [1954] 1 All ER 145 at 152, [1954] 1 WLR 139 at 146; *Re Russo-Asiatic Bank* [1934] Ch 720; *Rossano v Manufacturers' Life Insurance Co Ltd* [1963] 2 QB 352 at 378–380. A debt due from a bank to a customer, for instance, is deemed by the general law to be situated at the branch where the account is kept: *Clare & Co v Dresdner Bank* [1915] 2 KB 576; *Joachimson v Swiss Bank Corpn* [1921] 3 KB 110 at 127.
13 *Re Helbert Wagg & Co Ltd's Claim* [1956] Ch 323, [1956] 1 All ER 129.
14 *Cambridge Credit Corpn Ltd v Lissenden* (1987) 8 NSWLR 411.

(b) THE VARIOUS THEORIES

The conflict of opinion that impedes the search for the proper law to govern an assignment of tangible movables has been equally evident in the corresponding case of debts. Various theories have been propounded. The law of the place where the creditor is domiciled; the law of the place where the debt may be said to have an artificial situation; the law of the place where the assignment is made; the proper law of the assignment; the proper law of the transaction that created the debt; all these legal systems have found their advocates.

There appears to be neither authority nor reason for choosing the law of the domicil as such, either of the creditor or the debtor, as the law to govern an assignment of a debt, and in fact cases may be put in which the choice would lead to absurdity. If a domiciled Englishman, having acquired a right to receive a sum of money from a Belgian by reason of some commercial transaction governed by the law of France, were to assign that debt first to one man in Italy and then to another in Switzerland, it is difficult to adduce any principle that would justify the settlement of a dispute between the parties according to the law either of England or of Belgium. On the contrary, the assignee of a debt could not reasonably be expected to realise that he was subjecting his rights to the law of the domicil of either the creditor or the debtor, especially as the place of domicil might well be an unknown quantity.

Although, as we have seen, a debt may possess a definite, though artificial, situation for certain purposes this does not necessarily imply that its assignment should be governed by the law of its situs, and there is authority rejecting reference to the law of the situs.[15]

English judges have more regularly said that an assignment is to be governed by the law of the place where it is executed.[16] Another theory is that the governing system is the *lex actus*, ie the law of the country with which the assignment is most closely connected. This is preferable to the law of the place of acting, since it does not depend on the chance place of execution, but nevertheless it would seem to be less convenient than still another law which will now be discussed.

It is submitted that there is an obvious answer to the question—What is the most appropriate law to govern questions arising from the voluntary assignment of an intangible movable? The appropriate law is not the law governing the validity of the assignment, but the law governing the validity of the original transaction out of which the intangible movable arose. It is reasonable and logical to refer certain questions relating to a debt to the transaction in which it has its source and to the legal system which governs that transaction. If the transaction under which A lends money or sells goods to B is connected with no other country but England, A acquires a right that is admittedly governed by English law. The right thus created under the aegis of English law should, so far as its assignability is concerned, be governed throughout its existence by English law. Again, reference to such law is logical to determine questions of priorities.[17] This is not to deny that certain questions might be determinable by the governing law of the assignment

---

15 *Re Anziani* [1930] 1 Ch 407.
16 *Lee v Abdy* (1886) 17 QBD 309; *Alcock v Smith* [1892] 1 Ch 238; *Embiricos v Anglo-Austrian Bank* [1905] 1 KB 677; *Republica de Guatemala v Nunez* [1927] 1 KB 669; *Re Anziani* [1930] 1 Ch 407.
17 Infra, pp 816–817.

itself, as for example those concerned with the formal validity of a particular assignment and arising between the parties or their representatives. But when the question travels beyond these boundaries—when, for example, it is denied that the right is capable of assignment—a solution must obviously be sought elsewhere. What is more reasonable than to refer to the law that admittedly continues to govern the subject-matter of the assignment? One undeniable merit of this is that, where there have been assignments in different countries, no confusion can arise from a conflict of laws since all questions are referred to a single legal system. The same merit is not shared by the law of the situs, since this follows the residence of the debtor and is not therefore a constant.

An illustration may be given to show that the application of the law governing the validity of the original transaction out of which the debt arose is at least logical.

> If an Englishman contracts a debt as the result of the purchase of goods from another Englishman in London, his obligation, if expanded in words, is to pay not only the seller but also an assignee of the seller, provided however that the assignment is regarded as good by English law. What governs his liability to the seller must also govern his liability to any person deriving title from the seller.

In such a case the attention of the debtor, when he assumes that role, is confined solely to the legal system under which he contracts the obligation, and the reasonable inference is that any transfer of the obligation made by the creditor shall be governed by the law of England as being the legal system to which the subject-matter of the transfer owes its existence.

Let us turn from the debtor and, taking the test of the reasonable man, contemplate the attitude of mind of an assignee. If B, the debtor under the original transaction from which the obligation sprang, takes up his residence in Italy, and A, the creditor, makes in France an assignment of the debt to X, it is reasonable to presume that X, as a prudent businessman, will concentrate his attention on the transaction which gave rise to B's obligation to pay, for it is the benefit of that obligation of which he is a purchaser. It will naturally occur to him that an obligation having its origin in, and drawing its protection from, English law, will in all respects be subject to that law, just as much as if the subject-matter of the assignment were goods situated in England or shares in an English company, and we should naturally expect him to inquire what is necessary under English law for the completion of an effective assignment. What would not occur to him would be to consider the law of Italy merely because of the debtor's presence in that country. It would, perhaps, be convenient to allow the law of France, as the law governing the assignment, to govern the rights of A and X inter se, but, to take only one example, it cannot solve a question of priorities between X and an assignee claiming under an assignment made in some other country, except in the simplest case.

It is suggested, then, that the most appropriate law to govern the question at any rate of priorities is the law governing the transaction by which the subject-matter of the various assignments was created.[18]

---

18 This principle seems to have been adopted by Warrington J in *Kelly v Selwyn* [1905] 2 Ch 117, infra, p 816; and see *Banque Paribas v Cargill International SA* [1992] 1 Lloyd's Rep 96 at 100; contrast Goode, *Commercial Law* (1982), pp 932–933 who would apply the law of the situs of the debt.

(c) THE MODERN LAW

Leaving theory on one side, we must examine the present state of the law governing the assignment of a debt. An initial distinction has to be drawn, because there are two types of assignment, the voluntary and the involuntary. The former occurs where the creditor of his own volition transfers his right to another person; the latter, where his right is transferred against his will by operation of law, as, for example, where in the course of execution the debt is attached as being part of his assets.

Furthermore, the questions in which the issue is the validity or effect of an assignment fall into two classes. The issue may depend solely on the validity and effect of the assignment itself, as, for example, where the dispute relates to capacity, form or essential validity; or it may depend on the validity and effect of the original transaction by which the debt was created, as, for example, where the question is whether the debt is capable of assignment, or to which of two or more competing assignees it is payable.

(i) Voluntary assignments

Although the two issues just mentioned must be considered separately in the case of voluntary assignments, the source of the modern law on both of them is the same, namely the Contracts (Applicable Law) Act 1990 and Article 12 of the (1980) Rome Convention on the Law Applicable to Contractual Obligations which is implemented by the Act.[19] This has made a major improvement to the relevant choice of law rules where the voluntary assignment is effected by a contract between assignor and assignee, having "the welcome effect of replacing a highly unsatisfactory and retrograde jurisprudence with rules which are at once both logical and practically defensible".[20]

(a) **Questions dependent solely on the validity and effect of the assignment** Issues of form and essential validity are governed by Article 12(1) of the Rome Convention which provides:

> The mutual obligations of assignor and assignee under a voluntary assignment of a right against another person ("the debtor") shall be governed by the law which under this Convention applies to the contract between the assignor and assignee.[21]

It will be seen that the effect of this provision is to require the application, to most questions which arise between assignor and assignee, of the law which governs the validity and effect of the contract between them. So, in the case of essential validity, reference must be made to the law chosen by the parties where a choice is made or, in the absence of choice, to that determined by reference to the presumptions in Article 4 of the Convention.[1] This general approach confirms the view most recently adopted by the English

---

19 Supra, pp 459 et seq. Art 13 deals with the related matter of subrogation (which may result from both voluntary and involuntary assignment) but is limited to rights which are contractual in nature; see Fletcher *Conflict of Laws and European Community Law* (1982), p 177.

20 Fletcher, op cit, p 176.

21 It might have been thought clearer to deal with the rights as between assignor and assignee after examining, for example, the question of assignability (Art 12(2)); but the reasons for this order are explained in the Report on the Rome Convention by Giuliano and Lagarde, OJ C282, 31 October 1980, pp 34–35.

1 Supra, pp 476–495.

courts.[2] Turning to formalities, the assignment will be formally valid, under Article 9 of the Convention,[3] if it satisfies the formal requirements of the governing law, or of the law of the place where it was concluded if both parties were in the same country, or, if they were in different countries, of the law of one of those countries.[4]

There remains the issue of capacity which, save in one limited respect,[5] falls outside the ambit of the Rome Convention. So here, as in contract generally, reference must continue to be made to common law rules, and assuming that the contractual assignment of a debt stands in this respect on the same footing as a commercial contract, then the issue of capacity is to be governed by the proper law of the contract.[6] On this footing, the governing law will be the law of the country with which the assignment itself is most closely connected. This seems correct on principle, but unfortunately, in the few cases that have raised the question, the courts have shown a preference for the law of the place of acting. In *Lee v Abdy*:[7]

> A policy of life insurance issued by an English company was assigned in Cape Colony by a husband to his wife. The assignment was valid by English law, but was invalid by the law of Cape Colony, where the parties were domiciled, because the assignee was the wife of the assignor. The insurance company, when sued by the wife for the recovery of the money, pleaded that the assignment was void.

It was held that the law of Cape Colony governed the assignment. There is much to be said for the view that the proper law of the assignment was the law of the Cape, for it was there that the parties were domiciled and the assignment was effected, but the judgments leave little doubt that the mechanical test of the place of the transaction was applied by the court.

In *Republica de Guatemala v Nunez*,[8] SCRUTTON LJ said that:

> in cases of personal property, the capacity of the parties to a transaction has always been determined either by the lex domicilii or the law of the place of the transaction; and where, as here, the two laws are the same it is not necessary to decide between them.[9]

It is a little surprising to meet the suggestion that the capacity of a person to enter into a commercial contract is determined by the law of his domicil; little less surprising is the suggestion that the determining law is the law of the place of acting, if that expression is to be taken literally. Is an assignment by an Englishman to his wife of a debt situated in London and governed by English law to be held void, merely because he executes the instrument of transfer in Cape Town while on a short visit to South Africa?

The only question is whether the judges in these two cases meant the idea of the application of the law of the place of acting to be taken literally and rigidly, or whether they intended to indicate the law governing the assignment.

2 *Trendtex Trading Corpn v Credit Suisse* [1980] QB 629 at 658, affd on other grounds [1982] AC 679 [1981] 3 All ER 520; and see *Lee v Abdy* (1886) 17 QBD 309 at 313; contrast *Re Anziani* [1930] 1 Ch 407.
3 Supra, pp 507–510.
4 This marks a distinct improvement on the confused state of the old law on formal validity stemming from *Republica de Guatemala v Nunez* [1927] 1 KB 669.
5 Article 11, supra, pp 512–513.
6 Supra, pp 510–512.
7 (1886) 17 QBD 309.
8 [1927] 1 KB 669.
9 Ibid, at 689; and see LAWRENCE LJ at 701.

The law of the place of contracting has so often in the past constituted the proper law of the contract that judges have tended to adopt the former expression when their intention seems to have been to refer to the proper law. This was especially true in the late nineteenth century when *Lee v Abdy* was decided. In fact in that case DAY J stated the rule for contracts in language that was scarcely felicitous. He said:

> The general rule, ... is that the validity and incidents of a contract *must be determined* by the law of the place where it is entered into.[10]

Just as there has been a development in the general common law rules of contract in favour of the proper law as the law to govern capacity,[11] so also should there be a similar development in the particular context of assignment.[12]

(b) Questions dependent on the nature of the right assigned The assignment of a debt may raise questions that cannot be answered without considering the legal effect of the transaction to which the debt owes its origin. In such cases it is imperative, if a satisfactory solution is desired, to be guided exclusively by the law governing that transaction. This was the view taken in a number of common law authorities,[13] and it is the view now adopted as English law by reason of Article 12(2) of the Rome Convention which provides:

> The law governing the right to which the assignment relates shall determine its assignability, the relationship between the assignee and the debtor, the conditions under which the assignment can be invoked against the debtor and any question whether the debtor's obligations have been discharged.

It will be seen that a number of different types of problem may fall to be governed by the law governing the validity of the debt, the most important of which are whether the debt may be assigned, and the issue of priorities between successive assignments. These issues may be exemplified by common law decisions.

Assignability
The primary question is whether the right may be assigned at all. This may be illustrated by *Trendtex Trading Corpn v Credit Suisse:*[14]

> A Swiss company sued a Nigerian bank in England for failing to honour a letter of credit. The Swiss company then assigned this cause of action to one of its creditors, a Swiss bank, the assignment taking place in Geneva. The Swiss company then later took proceedings in England against the Swiss bank, alleging that the assignment was void, such a right of action being incapable of assignment as it offended against English rules relating to maintenance and champerty.

So there was an assignment in Switzerland of an English right of action. Which law governed its assignability? The Court of Appeal held that the

---

10 Italics supplied.
11 Supra, pp 511–512.
12 Cf *Lowenstein v Allen* [1958] CLY 491.
13 *Compania Colombiana de Seguros v Pacific Steam Navigation Co* [1965] 1 QB 101 at 128–129; and see *Pender v Commercial Bank of Scotland* 1940 SLT 306; *Bankhaus H Aufhauser v Scotboard Ltd* 1973 SLT (Notes) 87.
14 [1980] QB 629, [1980] 3 All ER 721. Whether a copyright may be assigned has been held to be determined by the law governing the creation of the copyright: *Campbell Connolly & Co Ltd v Noble* [1963] 1 All ER 237, [1963] 1 WLR 252.

Swiss company's right of action against the Nigerian bank was English, having been reduced into possession by the issue of the writ in England. In examining the nature and attributes of this right of action, it was necessary to refer to the legal system under which it arose, English law. Neither its content nor its characteristics could be altered merely because it had been the subject of a later transaction that in certain respects was subject to a foreign system of law. Such questions as whether the assignment was voidable for fraud or unenforceable for lack of a written memorandum might be determinable by Swiss law, but the primary and fundamental question,[15] whether the subject-matter was even capable of assignment, fell to be determined by English law.[16]

Priorities

The law governing the transaction under which a debt arose is also the most satisfactory legal system by which to determine the ranking of competing claimants where the creditor has made more than one assignment. A true question of priorities arises where there have been two or more valid and competing assignments, the ranking of which is doubtful, as may be illustrated by *Kelly v Selwyn*,[17] where the facts were these:

By an assignment executed in 1891 in New York, where he was then domiciled, X assigned to his wife his interest in certain English trust funds. Notice was not given to the trustees until twelve years later, since none was required by the law of New York. In 1894 X assigned the same interest to the plaintiff by a deed executed in England. Immediate notice of this was given to the trustees.

It was held that the plaintiff ranked first, since the rights of the claimant fell to be regulated by English law. WARRINGTON J said:

The ground on which I decide it is that, the fund here being an English trust fund and this being the Court which the testator may have contemplated as the Court which would have administered that trust fund, the order in which the parties are to be held entitled to the trust fund must be regulated by the law of the Court which is administering that fund.[18]

The judge's language is somewhat ambiguous, leaving it a little doubtful whether he chose English law as that of the forum, the situs or the law governing the validity of the debt. It is suggested, however, that the decisive factor in the mind of the judge, if his language is considered as a whole, was that the subject-matter of the assignment consisted of a trust fund, the governing law of which was English law.[19] Such an analysis is supported by *Le Feuvre v Sullivan*[20] where the law of the forum was the law of Jersey, but English law, which would appear to have been the law governing the debt,[1]

---

15 Ibid, at 652.
16 In the House of Lords ([1982] AC 679) the choice of law issues were not addressed with any clarity. The House of Lords took the view that, under English law, the cause of action could not be assigned, but that nevertheless it was for Swiss law to determine the effect of the invalidity of the assignment on the agreement as a whole between the parties, there being issues involved other than just the validity of the assignment, supra, p 130.
17 [1905] 2 Ch 117; and see *Le Feuvre v Sullivan* (1855) 10 Moo PCC 1. In *Republica de Guatemala v Nunez* [1927] 1 KB 669, there were successive assignments but they were, for different reasons, held to be invalid.
18 Ibid, at 122.
19 Morris, p 363.
20 (1855) 10 Moo PCC 1.
 1 Ibid, at 13.

was relied on to determine priorities. This is the approach now confirmed in the Contracts (Applicable Law) Act 1990 implementing the 1980 Rome Convention on the Law Applicable to Contractual Obligations; and Article 12(2) of that Convention also applies the law governing the debt to such questions as whether notice of an assignment must be given to the debtor and whether an assignee takes subject to equities.

Substance or procedure?
The question whether an assignee must join the assignor as a party to his action raises the conflict between substance and procedure. Suppose, for instance, that

> a Frenchman assigns by way of charge to another Frenchman a sum of money due from a French debtor, the assignment being made in France and according to the law of that country.

According to the rules of private international law, the assignment has universal validity. According to English domestic law, the assignment is valid, but the assignee cannot recover the money unless he makes the assignor a party to the action against the debtor. If this rule as to joinder of parties is to be regarded as a procedural rule for the purposes of private international law,[2] it is governed by the law of the forum and it must be obeyed in an action brought in England notwithstanding that it is not recognised by French law. Such old authorities as there are would indicate, however, that the rule as to joinder of parties is substantive[3] and thus governed by the law governing the debt.[4]

Voluntary non-contractual assignments It has been assumed, so far, that the assignments under consideration have been effected, as is usually the case,[5] by a contract between assignor and assignee. This does not necessarily have to be the case as a voluntary assignment may, for example, be effected by gift.[6] This raises the issue whether such non-contractual assignments fall within the scope of Article 12 of the Rome Convention, given effect in this country by the Contracts (Applicable Law) Act 1990. It will be recalled[7] that Article 12(1) makes provision for the law to be applicable to the mutual obligations of assignor and assignee under a voluntary assignment, but without at that point restricting the provision to contractual assignments. However, the law to be applied is that which "applies to the contract between the assignor and assignee". If there is no such contract, then the rule cannot apply, leaving one with the conclusion that the Rome Convention, which is in terms to govern "contractual obligations",[8] does not in fact govern the voluntary non-contractual assignment of rights, even of contractual rights. The consequence of this is that reference must continue to be made to the common law rules[9] which have been described (as seen earlier) as "a highly

2 See supra, pp 85 et seq.
3 *Innes v Dunlop* (1800) 8 Term Rep 595; *O'Callaghan v Thomond* (1810) 3 Taunt 82; cf *Regas Ltd v Plotkins* (1961) 29 DLR (2d) 282.
4 Art 12(2) of the Rome Convention.
5 Eg *Lee v Abdy* (1886) 17 QBD 309; *Trendtex Trading Corpn v Credit Suisse* [1980] QB 629, [1980] 3 All ER 721.
6 See *Re Westerton* [1919] 2 Ch 104; *Republica de Guatemala v Nunez* [1927] 1 KB 669; *Re Anziani* [1930] 1 Ch 407.
7 Supra, pp 813–814.
8 Art 1(1).
9 See 11th edition of this book (1987), pp 807–815.

unsatisfactory and retrograde jurisprudence".[10] Whilst there is some evidence of recent improvement,[11] it is to be hoped that the courts will now abandon the old rules and apply the provisions of Article 12 by analogy to cases of voluntary non-contractual assignments.

(ii) Involuntary assignments

The problem that affects private international law in the case of the involuntary assignment of a debt, as for instance where a customer's credit balance at a bank is vested by legislation in a custodian of enemy property,[12] is best illustrated by the process known as garnishment in England and by arrestment in Scotland[13] and many other countries. This is a process by which a judgment creditor attaches a sum of money that is due to the judgment debtor from a third party, called the garnishee. If the necessary proceedings are taken the court may order that the garnishee shall pay the money direct to the judgment creditor.

In purely domestic proceedings, where the parties and the relevant transactions are connected solely with England,[14] the garnishee is, of course, effectively discharged from further liability once he has paid the judgment creditor. The position, however, is not so straightforward in a case containing a foreign element. The first problem arises where the garnishee may be in one country and the debt situated in another. In garnishment proceedings in England, it is necessary that the garnishee be within the jurisdiction,[15] albeit temporarily, or have submitted to the jurisdiction.[16] It is not, however, necessary that the judgment debtor be within the jurisdiction nor, strictly speaking, that the debt be situated within the jurisdiction. If the debt is enforceable within the jurisdiction, even though payable elsewhere, the court has jurisdiction to garnish it.[17] There is a risk in the case of a debt that is not situated within the jurisdiction that the garnishee, having already complied with an order made in one country, will remain liable to pay his debt a second time if he is sued by the judgment debtor in a foreign court which refuses to recognise the validity of the order.[18] That risk is met by the court having a discretion whether or not to assume jurisdiction, being prepared to decline where the risk of the garnishee being ordered to pay twice is real.[19] It is usually the case that the court will assume jurisdiction to make a garnishment order, confident that no such risk will materialise, as is illustrated by *Swiss Bank Corpn v Boemische Industrial Bank*:[20]

---

10 Fletcher, *Conflict of Laws and European Community Law* (1982), p 176.

11 See *Trendtex Trading Corpn v Credit Suisse* [1980] QB 629, [1980] 3 All ER 721, affd on other grounds [1982] AC 679, [1981] 3 All ER 520.

12 See eg *Arab Bank Ltd v Barclays Bank (Dominion, Colonial and Overseas)* [1954] AC 495, [1954] 2 All ER 226.

13 For reform proposals, see Scottish Law Commission Discussion Paper No 90 (1990), Extra-territorial Effect of Arrestments and Related Matters.

14 Cf *Brooks Associates Inc v Basu* [1983] QB 220, [1983] 1 All ER 508, supra, p 810, n 8.

15 RSC, Order 49, r 1(1).

16 *SCF Finance Co Ltd v Masri (No 3)* [1987] QB 1028, [1987] 1 All ER 194; Kaye [1989] JBL 449, 455–459.

17 *Deutsche Schachtbau Und Tiefbohrgesellschaft GmbH v Shell International Petroleum Co Ltd* [1990] 1 AC 295, CA, revsd in part, ibid, 323, HL.

18 *Martin v Nadel* [1906] 2 KB 26.

19 *SCF Finance Co Ltd v Masri (No 3)* [1987] QB 1028 at 1044; *Interpool Ltd v Galani* [1988] QB 738 at 741.

20 [1923] 1 KB 673.

The plaintiffs had recovered judgment for a large sum of money against the defendants, a company carrying on business exclusively in Czechoslovakia. The defendants kept an account at a London bank where their balance was over £9,000. The plaintiffs issued a garnishee summons against the bank.

It was objected that to make a garnishee order in these circumstances would be inequitable, since the bank, if sued later in Czechoslovakia, would probably be ordered to pay the sum over again to the defendants. The Court of Appeal nevertheless made the order in the confident belief that, having been made in the country where the debt was normally and properly recoverable, its validity and effect would not be repudiated in Czechoslovakia.

It must not be assumed, however, that, where the debt is situated in England, there will never be a risk of double jeopardy and that jurisdiction will always be assumed, as the unusual decision in *Deutsche Schachtbau v Shell International Petroleum Co Ltd*[21] illustrates. The facts were these:

The defendants (Shell) owed $4.8 million to Rakoil, the National Oil company of the Gulf state of R'As al-Khaimah in respect of oil which Shell had bought. This debt was situated in England. The plaintiffs were in dispute with Rakoil over an oil concession agreement, and they took this dispute to arbitration in Switzerland where they were awarded $4.6 million. The plaintiffs then obtained leave to enforce this award against Rakoil in England, and wished to obtain an order to garnish the debt owed by the defendants to Rakoil. Meanwhile a civil action was successfully brought in R'As al-Khaimah by that state (not Rakoil) claiming the English debt owed by the defendants to Rakoil. This left the defendants in the position that, if a garnishment of their debt was allowed in England, they would still be liable effectively for the same debt, though technically to another party, in R'As al-Khaimah.[22]

A majority in the House of Lords concluded that, even though the debt was situated in England, the exercise of jurisdiction in garnishment proceedings was discretionary and that it would be inequitable to exercise it here, bearing in mind that "the garnishee does not have to establish a certainty, or a very high degree of risk, of being compelled to pay the debt twice over; he has only to establish a real risk of being required to do so".[23]

The law of the situs of the debt is not only relevant in determining the question of jurisdiction, it is also relevant to the effect of the garnishment as regards third parties.[24] If, for example, an involuntary assignment occurs after a voluntary assignment has already been made, the law of the situs determines whether the rights of the voluntary assignee have been postponed or defeated; if the involuntary assignment occurs first, the law of the situs determines what rights, if any, the voluntary assignee has acquired.

---

21 [1990] 1 AC 295; see Briggs [1988] Lloyd's MCLQ 429.
22 Even though the judgment there might not be recognised in England.
23 [1990] 1 AC 295 at 359.
24 *Re Queensland Mercantile and Agency Co* [1891] 1 Ch 536, affd [1892] 1 Ch 219.

3. NEGOTIABLE INSTRUMENTS[25]

If a transfer of a negotiable instrument has been made abroad and its validity is disputed in an English action, the court is confronted with a problem of choice of law. What the choice should be depends on the manner in which the problem is analysed. It may be regarded as raising a question of form or interpretation to be governed by the Bills of Exchange Act 1882; or as the transfer of a chattel, in which case the law of the situs will be applicable; or as an assignment of a contractual right and therefore subject to the law governing the contract. *Koechlin et Cie v Kestenbaum*,[26] the leading decision on the matter, definitely treats the question as one of form or interpretation, and the doubt whether the Court of Appeal did not reach this conclusion by reading too much into the earlier authorities is one that can be resolved only by the House of Lords.

The common law authorities[27] which preceded the Bills of Exchange Act 1882, with one exception,[28] showed a marked tendency to determine the validity of an indorsement by the law which governs the original contract of the acceptor or maker.

The relevant sub-sections of the Bills of Exchange Act 1882 are as follows:

72.—Where a bill drawn in one country is negotiated, accepted or payable in another, the rights, duties, and liabilities of the parties thereto are determined as follows:

(1) The validity of a bill as regards requisites in form is determined by the law of the place of issue, and the validity as regards requisites in form of the supervening contracts, such as acceptance, or indorsement, or acceptance suprà protest, is determined by the law of the place where such contract was made. Provided that—

(a) Where a bill is issued out of the United Kingdom it is not invalid by reason only that it is not stamped in accordance with the law of the place of issue;[29]

(b) Where a bill, issued out of the United Kingdom, conforms as regards requisites in form, to the law of the United Kingdom, it may, for the purpose of enforcing payment thereof, be treated as valid as between all persons who negotiate, hold, or become parties to it in the United Kingdom.

(2) Subject to the provisions of this Act, the interpretation of the drawing, indorsement, acceptance, or acceptance suprà protest of a bill, is determined by the law of the place where such contract is made.

The question now is whether these sections are concerned with the subject of transfer at all, and whether it is possible to ascertain from them the legal system that determines the validity and effect of an indorsement, or of a delivery, of a negotiable instrument.

25 See Falconbridge, pp 341–357. For discussion of the contractual aspects of negotiable instruments, see chapter 19, supra.

26 [1927] 1 KB 889.

27 *Trimbey v Vignier* (1834) 1 Bing NC 151; *Lebel v Tucker* (1867) LR 3 QB 77; *Re Marseilles Extension Rail and Land Co* (1885) 30 Ch D 598.

28 *Bradlaugh v De Rin* (1868) LR 3 CP 538.

29 It is also enacted by the Finance Act 1933, s 42, that a bill of exchange which is presented for acceptance, or accepted or payable, outside the United Kingdom shall not be invalid by reason only that it is not stamped in accordance with the law for the time being in force relating to stamp duties. Such bill may be received in evidence on payment of the proper duties and penalties under the Stamp Act 1891, ss 14, 15(1).

There have been only three relevant cases since the Act.[1] The first of these was *Alcock v Smith*:[2]

A bill of exchange, drawn by and on English firms, and payable in England to the order of X, was indorsed and delivered in Norway by X to Y. While in the hands of Y it was seized by a judgment creditor in Norway, and in the due course of Norwegian law was ultimately sold by public auction to Z. In fact, Z had no title to the bill by English law, but according to Norwegian law the property was duly passed to him as a result of the sale. In the action subsequently brought in England, it was held that the effect of the transactions in Norway must be governed by Norwegian law, and therefore that the title acquired thereunder by Z must prevail over one which by English law would have been stronger.

The judgments paid little heed to the statutory provisions, but in general adopted the view that Norwegian law applied because it was the law of the place of acting. ROMER J, indeed, held that the word "interpretation" in section 72 (2) was wide enough to cover the "legal effect" of a contract and that therefore statutory effect had been given to the principle of the application of the law of the place of acting. In the Court of Appeal, however, no reliance was placed on the Act.

The facts of the second case, *Embiricos v Anglo-Austrian Bank*,[3] were these:

A cheque on a London bank was drawn in Romania in favour of the plaintiffs, who specially indorsed it there to a firm in London and placed it in an envelope addressed to that firm. The cheque was stolen from the envelope in Romania by a clerk of the plaintiffs. Three days later the cheque, bearing an indorsement which purported to be that of the London firm but which was in fact a forgery, was presented for payment at a bank in Vienna. The Vienna bank cashed the cheque in good faith, indorsed it to the defendants, who were their London agents, and the latter collected the amount from the bank on which the cheque was drawn. The plaintiffs then sued the defendants in damages for conversion. Austrian law provided that, notwithstanding the theft and forgery, the Viennese bank acquired a good title to the cheque and judgment was given for the defendants.

In this case the title that was acquired under the law of the country where the instrument was situated at the time of the transaction was upheld by the English court.

Again Austrian law was chosen as being the law of the place of acting (though perhaps what was in the mind of the court was the law of the situs, since this necessarily coincided with the law of the place of acting),[4] and again the judgments attributed only trifling importance to the Bills of Exchange Act 1882. ROMER LJ thought that section 72(2) recognised the law of the place of acting as being applicable to the matter, an opinion which WALTON J was prepared to share if "interpretation" includes "legal effect". VAUGHAN WILLIAMS LJ was not clear that the sub-section covered the case, but according to STIRLING LJ its applicability was worthy of serious consideration.

Section 72, which, it will be observed, was only a secondary consideration

1 *Alcock v Smith* [1892] 1 Ch 238; *Embiricos v Anglo-Austrian Bank* [1904] 2 KB 870; affd [1905] 1 KB 677; *Koechlin v Kestenbaum* [1927] 1 KB 616; revsd [1927] 1 KB 889.
2 Supra.
3 [1904] 2 KB 870; affd [1905] 1 KB 677.
4 Supra, p 811.

in these two decisions, played, however, a decisive part in *Koechlin et Cie v Kestenbaum*,[5] which is the most recent case on the subject:

> In that case a bill of exchange was drawn in France by X on the defendants in London to the order of Y, who was X's father. It was accepted, payable in London, by the defendants. The bill was indorsed not by the payee, Y, but by X, and was then transferred for value to the plaintiffs in France. X's indorsement was affixed on behalf of, and with the authority of, Y. On presentment the defendants refused payment, on the ground that the bill did not bear the signature of Y by way of indorsement.
>
> English law requires that a bill payable to order shall be indorsed by the payee, or by an agent who expressly signs per pro the payee. French law, however, permits a valid indorsement to be made by an agent in his own name, provided that he so acts with the authority of the payee.
>
> Therefore, whether the plaintiffs were entitled to payment depended on whether the validity of the indorsement was to be determined by English or by French law.

BANKES LJ held that the proper law to govern the validity of a transfer had been definitely settled by the Bills of Exchange Act, section 72, in favour of the law of the place of acting, here French law. In his opinion this legal system was deliberately applied by the Court of Appeal in the *Embiricos Case* long after the passing of the Act. The bill, he said, was drawn and indorsed in France in a form recognised by French law, and therefore it became valid in England by virtue of section 72(1).

SARGENT LJ agreed, the essence of his judgment being contained in the following words:

> In my judgment the question whether this bill could properly be indorsed in the name of the payee ... only or could rightly be indorsed by the son, ..., in his own name if he had authority in fact to do so is purely a question of form, and is therefore covered in terms by s 72, sub-s (1); but if it is not covered by that subsection it is covered by sub-s (2), in view of the very wide effect of the decision in *Embiricos v Anglo-Austrian Bank* ... If the indorsement in fact made is, according to the law of the place where it is made, sufficient to give a title to the indorsee, it appears to me that by the express terms of the Act the indorsee is entitled to sue. The effect is not to increase the liabilities of the acceptor, but merely to enlarge the methods by which the right to enforce those liabilities can be transferred by the person originally entitled to them to some subsequent indorsee.[6]

This case is a definite authority in favour of the law of the place of acting, though it is remarkable that it attributes to the judges who decided *Embiricos v Anglo-Austrian Bank* a confidence in the applicability of the Bills of Exchange Act 1882 that is not very apparent from their judgments.

It is necessary in stating the law with regard to the transfer of negotiable instruments to deal with both inland and foreign bills of exchange. An "inland bill" is one which is both drawn and payable within the British Isles, or one which is drawn within the British Isles upon some person resident there.[7] It is expressly provided by the Bills of Exchange Act 1882[8] that, when such a bill is indorsed in a foreign country, the indorsement shall, *as regards the payer*, be interpreted according to the law of the United Kingdom. This

5 [1927] 1 KB 889.
6 Ibid, at 898–899.
7 Bills of Exchange Act 1882, s 4.
8 S 72(2) proviso.

confirms the decision in *Lebel v Tucker*,[9] and means that the acceptor of an inland as contrasted with a foreign bill is liable only to holders who claim under an indorsement valid by English law. The enactment, however, is expressly confined to the liability of the payer.

Secondly, we must contrast the transfer of a foreign bill, ie one which does not satisfy the definition given in the preceding paragraph. The rule here is that whether a transfer is valid or not is determined by the law of the place where the transfer is effected, ie in the words of the Act, "where such contract is made".[10] This rule applies equally to a promissory note and to a cheque.[11] The position was thus stated by SARGENT LJ in *Koechlin v Kestenbaum*:[12]

> The result [of the 1882 Act] was that any one dealing with a foreign bill of exchange was in a less certain position than a person dealing with an inland bill, because in the case of an indorsement abroad on a foreign bill he might find substituted for the person to whom he was originally liable as acceptor not merely a person to whom the transfer would have been good if made in England, but a person to whom the transfer by indorsement would be good if made according to the law of the country in which it was made. That is rendered perfectly clear by s. 72, sub-ss 1 and 2, of the Act. The matter was carried probably further than was contemplated by the actual language of the sub-sections by the decision in *Embiricos v Anglo-Austrian Bank*.

The result of this distinction is scarcely satisfactory to the commercial world, but it certainly shows how important it is that as wide a unification as possible of the internal laws relating to negotiable instruments should be effected.

4. SHARES

A share of stock is intimately connected with the place where the issuing company has its residence, since the general rule is that it can be effectively transferred only by a substitution of the name of the transferee for that of the transferor in the register of shareholders. This register is normally kept by the company at its principal place of business, though there may be branch registers in other countries for the purpose of recording transactions that are effected there.[13] Despite the fact that a share is generally represented by a certificate which may be pledged and otherwise dealt with as a document of value, it still remains true that by English law entry on the register constitutes, and alone constitutes, legal ownership. The rule of private international law is that shares are deemed to be situated in the country where they can be effectively dealt with as between the shareholder and the company.[14] In other words, shares that are transferable only by an entry in the register are deemed

---

9 (1867) LR 3 QB 77.
10 Bills of Exchange Act 1882, s 72(1), (2); *Embiricos v Anglo-Austrian Bank* [1904] 2 KB 870; affd [1905] 1 KB 677; *Alcock v Smith* [1892] 1 Ch 238; *Koechlin v Kestenbaum* [1927] 1 KB 889.
11 *Embiricos v Anglo-Austrian Bank*, supra.
12 [1927] 1 KB 889 at 898–899.
13 For instance, the Companies Act 1985, s 362, provides that an English company may keep a branch register (called an overseas branch register) in any of a scheduled list of countries for members there resident. No transaction affecting shares so registered shall be registered in any other register: Sch 14, Pt II, para 5.
14 On the situs of letters of allotment, see *Young v Phillips* [1984] STC 520.

to be situated in the country where the register or branch register is kept.[15] If a company keeps registers in two or more countries, in any of which transfers may be registered, the question where any particular shares are situated depends on the country in which according to the ordinary course of business the transfer would be registered.[16]

A question of choice of law may arise with regard to a transfer of shares. Foreign companies, for instance, frequently issue certificates which, according to the legal system that governs the incorporation of the company, can be transferred in such a manner that, even prior to registration, the transferee acquires, as against the transferor, both the legal and the equitable title to the shares. If, in such a case, the certificate is transferred in a country other than that in which the register of shareholders is kept, it becomes important to ascertain the country whose law will determine the validity and effect of the transfer. The effect of such a transfer may require consideration from two entirely different aspects, namely, first, its effect as against the company, and secondly, its effect as regards the parties to the transfer and persons claiming under them.

Questions of the first type are determined by the law of the situs of the shares.

If, for instance, the certificates of a company incorporated in New York have been transferred in England, New York law must decide whether the mode in which the transfer has been effected entitles the transferee to be registered as a shareholder. The corporate rights of the transferee depend entirely on that law.

The second type of question, on the other hand, is determined by the proper law of the transaction, which in practically all cases will be the law of the place where the certificate has been delivered. Thus, to take the illustration of the New York company given above, the question whether the transferee is entitled by virtue of the transaction to retain the certificates as against the transferor must be determined by English law. If English law decides in favour of the transferee, then, whether he can demand to be registered as a shareholder is a matter for the law of New York.[17]

This second type of question might be illustrated by *Re Fry*:[18]

X was resident in New Jersey and domiciled in Florida. Whilst in New Jersey he executed transfers of shares, which he owned in an English company, by way of gift to a private company and to his son. The share certificates were sent to England to be registered but, under the Defence Regulations 1939, the English company could not register the shares without Treasury consent. The necessary forms were sent to X who signed and returned them but died before consent was actually obtained. As English law, the proper law of the transfers, had not been complied with, the transfers were incomplete and invalid.

15 *Brassard v Smith* [1925] AC 371; *Baelz v Public Trustee* [1926] Ch 863; *London and South American Investment Trust v British Tobacco Co (Australia)* [1927] 1 Ch 107; *Erie Beach Co v A-G for Ontario* [1930] AC 161; *R v Williams* [1942] AC 541, [1942] 2 All ER 95.
16 *R v Williams*, supra; *Treasurer of Ontario v Blonde* [1948] AC 24; *Standard Chartered Bank Ltd v IRC* [1978] 3 All ER 644, [1978] 1 WLR 1160.
17 Falconbridge, op cit, pp 590–591.
18 [1946] Ch 312, [1946] 2 All ER 106.

The leading authority for both these rules is *Colonial Bank v Cady*:[19]

> The executors of a deceased Englishman, owner of certain New York railroad shares, who desired to be registered as owners in the books of the company, sent the certificates to London brokers for transmission to New York. At the request of the brokers the executors signed the certificates in blank. The brokers deposited the certificates with the Colonial Bank as security for a debt, and later became bankrupt.

The question whether the deposit conferred a legal title on the bank depended on whether the transaction was to be governed by English or by New York law. By English law no title passed, but by New York law the delivery of the certificates operated to vest in the bank both the legal and the equitable ownership of the shares. It was held that, as the deposit was made in England, its effect must be determined by English law.

> I agree, [said Lord HERSCHELL] that the question, what is necessary or effectual to transfer the shares in such a company, or to perfect the title to them, must be answered by a reference to the law of the State of New York. But I think that the rights arising out of a transaction entered into by parties in this country, whether, for example, it operated to effect a binding sale or pledge as against the owner of the shares, must be determined by the law prevailing here.[20]

In the court below, BOWEN LJ simplified the problem with terse felicity:

> The key to this case is whether the defendants [the bank] have a right to hold these pieces of paper, these certificates. What the effect upon their ulterior rights in America would be, if we were to declare that they were entitled to these pieces of paper, is another question.[1]

---

19 (1890) 15 App Cas 267; in the Court of Appeal, sub nom *Williams v Colonial Bank* (1888) 38 Ch D 388.
20 (1890) 15 App Cas 267 at 283.
 1 (1888) 38 Ch D 388 at 408.

Chapter 32

Administration of estates

1. INTRODUCTION

The modern legal systems which have had their origin in English law differ fundamentally from the civil law jurisdictions with regard to the procedure by which property is administered after the death of its owner. In England the only person entitled to deal with the property is the person to whom a grant has been made by some public authority. This grant of the right of administration is made, according to the circumstances, to either an executor or an administrator. It is made to:

an executor, when some person has been appointed as such by the will; or to

an administrator cum testamento annexo, when a will has omitted to appoint an executor, or when the appointment fails, as, for instance, by the death or renunciation of the executor; or to

an administrator, when the deceased has died intestate.

The executors and administrators or, to use a comprehensive expression, the personal representatives become subject to two distinct duties. First, they must clear the estate of liabilities by the payment of funeral expenses and debts; secondly, they must distribute the residue of the estate among the beneficiaries according to the limitations of the will or the rules of intestacy. These two functions, debt-administration and beneficial distribution, are governed by different principles of private international law.

In the civil law countries, however, in the rare case where personal representatives are appointed, their duties and functions are generally of a supervisory nature widely different from those of their English counterparts.[1] The general civil law rule is that the entire property of a deceased person passes directly to his heirs, testate or intestate, or to his universal legatee,

---

1 See, for example, *Re Achillopoulos* [1928] Ch 433 at 435.

subject, of course, to their acceptance; and these successors, broadly speaking, continue the existence of their predecessor.[2] For instance, unless they accept the inheritance with the benefit of an inventory, their liability for the debts of the deceased is not limited to the assets but is enforceable against their private property.

Thus the striking difference between English and civil law practice is that in the latter case the property passes on death directly to the successor, but that in England it cannot be dealt with by anyone without a public grant.[3] It is important, however, to observe at once that the automatic transfer recognised by civil law systems can have no operation on property of the deceased situated in England. Succession to movables is governed by the law of the deceased's domicil,[4] but, no matter what that domicil may be, nobody can rightfully and effectually obtain possession of movable property situated in England unless he gets an English grant of probate or of administration.[5] Authority to administer English assets requires without exception an English grant.

2. ENGLISH GRANTS

(a) JURISDICTION OF ENGLISH COURTS

One of the cardinal rules of private international law, as we shall see later,[6] is that the movable property of a deceased person, so far as concerns either testate or intestate succession, is regulated by the law of that country in which he died domiciled. It might be thought, therefore, that the courts of that domicil have jurisdiction to make a grant of administration, merely on the ground of domicil and regardless of whether there are assets actually within the jurisdiction. Theoretically this principle is tenable, but there are two facts that militate against its application.

First, such a grant would be ineffective if there were no assets within the jurisdiction.

Secondly, the jurisdiction of the old ecclesiastical courts, of which the High Court exercising jurisdiction in probate matters[7] is the successor, was universally founded on the presence within the jurisdiction of movables belonging to the deceased.

The rule, in fact, for many years has been that an English court can grant

---

2 Distinguish the English personal representative, who, strictly speaking, does not represent the deceased at all.

3 But the Revenue Act 1889, s 19, provides that where a policy of life insurance has been effected by a person who dies domiciled elsewhere than in the United Kingdom, a grant of representation shall not be necessary to establish the right to receive the money payable; see *Haas v Atlas Assurance Co Ltd* [1913] 2 KB 209, where SCRUTTON J gives the genesis of the provision. For another case where no grant is necessary, see *Vanquelin v Bouard* (1863) 15 CBNS 341, infra, pp 833–834; and see the Administration of Estates (Small Payments) Act 1965.

4 See infra, pp 837 et seq.

5 *New York Breweries Co v A-G* [1899] AC 62. It should be noted, however, that an executor derives his title from the will, not from the grant of probate.

6 Infra, pp 837 et seq.

7 Supreme Court Act 1981, s 25. Under Sch 1, paras 1 and 3, non-contentious or common form probate business is assigned to the Family Division and all other probate business to the Chancery Division. As to what is included in non-contentious business, see *Re Clore* [1982] Fam 113 at 116; affd [1982] Ch 456, [1982] 3 All ER 419.

administration only if there is property in England,[8] though it now has statutory authority to make a grant notwithstanding that the deceased left no estate,[9] provided, probably, that the testator died domiciled in England.[10]

(b) SEPARATE WILLS

Testators quite often have property both in England and abroad and, in such cases, they sometimes make separate wills, one disposing of their English property and the other of the foreign. This may be important if, for example, the law of the situs of foreign immovables has restrictive rules as to who may inherit them. In such cases, the normal practice is only to admit to probate the English will,[11] but it is possible also to admit to probate here the foreign will, provided there is some appropriate reason for so doing.[12]

(c) SITUS OF ASSETS

Except in the case of tangible movables there may be some difficulty in establishing the situation of property, especially in the case of choses in action such as debts and shares.[13] For the purposes of jurisdiction to make a grant of probate or administration, however, it has long been settled with respect to choses in action and titles to property that judgment debts are assets where the judgment is recorded; leases, where the land lies; specialty debts, where the instrument happens to be; and simple contract debts, where the debtor resides at the time of the testator's death.[14] Securities, such as bonds, promissory notes and bills of exchange which are transferable by delivery only, are assets if situated in England.[15] A share of stock, transferable only by registration, is situated, not in the place where the certificates happen to be, but in the country where the shares may effectively be dealt with as between the shareholder and the company, ie in the country where registration must be effected.[16]

(d) PERSONS TO WHOM GRANT WILL BE MADE

Who are the persons in whose favour this jurisdiction ought to be exercised? Where the deceased dies domiciled in England, probate of his will is normally granted to the executors named in it.[17] On intestacy, letters of administration are usually granted to a person taking a beneficial interest in the estate.[18] What happens if the deceased died domiciled abroad? A case that commonly

8 *Evans v Burrell* (1859) 28 LJPM & A 82; *In the Goods of Tucker* (1864) 34 LJPM & A 29; Dicey & Morris, pp 981–983.
9 Supreme Court Act 1981, s 25(1); see *In the Estate of Wayland* [1951] 2 All ER 1041.
10 *Aldrich v A-G* [1968] P 281 at 295.
11 If the English will refers to and incorporates the foreign will, then the latter must be included in the probate; *Re Western's Goods* (1898) 78 LT 49; and see *Re Tinkler* [1990] 1 NZLR 621.
12 *Re Wayland's Estate* [1951] 2 All ER 1041.
13 Dicey & Morris, pp 907 et seq.
14 *A-G v Bouwens* (1838) 4 M & W 171 at 191.
15 *Winans v A-G* [1910] AC 27.
16 *A-G v Higgins* (1857) 2 H & N 339; *Brassard v Smith* [1925] AC 371; *Erie Beach Co v A-G for Ontario* [1930] AC 161; *R v Williams* [1942] AC 541, [1942] 2 All ER 95; *Standard Chartered Bank Ltd v Inland Revenue Commissioners* [1978] 3 All ER 644, [1978] 1 WLR 1160; supra, pp 823–824.
17 Tristram and Coote's *Probate Practice*, 27th edn (1989), ch 4. Under the Supreme Court Act 1981, s 116, the court has a discretion to appoint someone else; see *IRC v Stype Investments (Jersey) Ltd* [1982] Ch 456, [1982] 3 All ER 419.
18 Tristram and Coote's *Probate Practice*, 27th edn (1989), ch 6.

arises is where a person dies domiciled abroad, leaving the bulk of his property in the foreign country and a smaller amount in England. The ideal here, just as in the case of bankruptcy,[19] is to have one administration in the domicil for the whole of the property, but such principle of unity is not found in practice and is attainable only by international agreement.[20] A separate grant of administration must be obtained from the English court with regard to the property in England. In such a case, the administration in England is said to be "ancillary", whilst that in the country of the deceased's domicil is the "principal" administration.

The English court will normally make a grant to a person who has been entrusted with the administration of the deceased's estate by a court in the country of the deceased's last domicil.[1] In some countries, grants of representation, in the English sense, are not made by courts or it may be that no application may in fact have been made in the country of the domicil. In such cases an English grant may be made to the person beneficially entitled to the estate by the law of the place where the deceased died domiciled.[2] In these cases, the making of a grant is discretionary and the court may make a grant to such persons as it thinks fit, whether or not there is someone who fits in to the above categories.[3] For example, in *Re Kaufman's Goods*[4] the deceased died domiciled in the Netherlands and the only person entitled to the estate under Dutch law died before the estate could be administered. The court made a grant, in the interests of convenience, to the deceased's brother who would have been entitled under English law to a grant if the deceased had died domiciled in England.

If the foreign domiciliary's will is in English or Welsh, then the court may grant probate to any executor named in the will.[5] It has also been held that a rule of the law of the foreign domicil restricting the authority of such an executor to a period of one year from the death of the testator must be disregarded in the English administration.[6] Furthermore, if the will, in whatever language, describes "the duties of a named person in terms sufficient to constitute him executor according to the tenor of the will"[7] probate may be granted to that person.

When the person who has been authorised to administer the estate in the country of the deceased's domicil seeks a grant of probate in England, the English court does not examine the grounds of his appointment under the foreign law.[8] But the domiciliary executor or heir has no absolute right to administer the English assets. The court has a discretion, and although there are few cases where it refuses to follow the foreign grant, it will certainly do

19 Infra, pp 904 et seq.
20 See, eg, the Hague Convention on the International Administration of the Estates of Deceased Persons (1972) which provides one international initiative, but one with a low success rate; see Law Com No 107 (1981) para 2.45; and also Nadelmann (1973) 21 AJCL 136, 139–149.
1 Non-Contentious Probate Rules 1987 (SI 1987, No 2024), r 30(1)(a).
2 Non-Contentious Probate Rules 1987, r 30(1)(b).
3 Ibid, r 30(1)(c).
4 [1952] P 325, [1952] 2 All ER 261; and see *Bath v British and Malayan Trustees Ltd* [1969] 2 NSWR 114.
5 Non-Contentious Probate Rules 1987, r 30(3)(a)(i).
6 *Re Goenaga's Estate* [1949] P 367. See Morris (1950) 3 ILQ 243 where it is shown that the decision, though correct in principle, is irreconcilable with *Laneuville v Anderson* (1860) 2 Sw & Tr 24.
7 Non-Contentious Probate Rules, 1987, r 30(3)(a)(ii).
8 *Re Hill's Goods* (1870) 2 P & D 89; *Re Humphries's Estate* [1934] P 78.

so if the foreign grantee is incompetent according to English law to act as administrator. Thus no grant will be made to a minor.[9] A further example is provided by the fact that where a minority or life interest arises in an estate the grant of probate must normally be made to not fewer than two individuals or to a trust corporation.[10] Even if the law of the domicil allows one person to administer the estate, the court will not in such a case make a grant to just one individual.[11]

If a justification for the English court following the grant made in the foreign country is thought to be that of consistency with the rule that succession to a deceased's movable estate is governed by his domicil on death,[12] this would seem to break down if the deceased's estate consists of immovables, succession to which is governed by the law of the situs.[13] Indeed the High Court of Australia has refused to follow the law of the domicil, England, and make a grant to the English personal representative in the case of a will of movables and immovables. The court required the title to administer the will, and its validity, to be determined by the law of the situs.[14] English law does not adopt so purist an approach, which is highly inconvenient where, as is often the case, the estate consists of both movables and immovables. The English court will make a grant following the one made in the domicil, even though the estate includes immovables.[15] Where, however, the whole or substantially the whole of the estate in England consists of immovables, the court may make a grant, in respect of the whole estate, in accordance with the law which would have been applicable if the deceased had died domiciled in England,[16] ie English law.

Under the Consular Conventions Act 1949 a grant of administration may be made to the consular officer of a foreign State where the executor or other such person is a national of that State and is not resident in England and where no other application is made by a person duly authorised by power of attorney.[17] A "foreign State" means one with which a Consular Convention has been concluded and so declared by Order in Council.[1]

(e)   TITLE OF ADMINISTRATOR UNDER AN ENGLISH GRANT

Although the theory may be that an English grant extends to property no matter where situated, it is obviously of no practical importance, for whether the administrator is entitled to the property of the deceased in a foreign country must necessarily depend on the local law. The one certainty is that an administrator acting under an English grant, who does succeed in obtaining property in a foreign country, is accountable for it as administrator in England.[2]

His title extends not only to property situated in England at the death of

---

9 *Re D'Orleans's (Duchess) Goods* (1859) 1 Sw & Tr 253; presumably *Re Da Cunha's Goods* (1828) 1 Hag Ecc 237 would not now be followed.
10 Supreme Court Act 1981, s 114(2).
11 Non-Contentious Probate Rules, 1987, r 30(2).
12 Infra, pp 837 et seq.
13 Infra, pp 851 et seq.
14 *Lewis v Balshaw* (1935) 54 CLR 188.
15 *Re Meatyard's Goods* [1903] P 125.
16 Non-Contentious Probate Rules 1987, r 30(3)(b).
17 S 1(1).
  1 For a list of current Orders in Council see Halsbury's *Statutes of England*, 4th edn, vol 10, p 444.
  2 *Dowdale's Case* (1604) 6 Co Rep 46b; *Stirling-Maxwell v Cartwright* (1879) 11 ChD 522.

the deceased,[3] but also to all property that comes to England thereafter.[4] Property, however, which comes to England after the death of the deceased does not pass to the administrator under an English grant if it has previously been appropriated abroad by an administrator acting under the law of the foreign situs.[5]

3. CHOICE OF LAW

Where an ancillary administrator has been authorised to deal with the English assets of a person dying domiciled abroad, the rule is that, though beneficial distribution is governed by the law of the domicil, the administration of the assets is governed exclusively by English law.[6] Thus the duty of an executor who receives a grant of administration from the English court is to pay all debts, whether domestic or foreign, according to the rules of English law. No distinction must be made between English and foreign creditors; no regard must be had to the corresponding rules of the law of the deceased's domicil. A foreign creditor seeking payment here must take the law of England as he finds it. He can neither claim an advantage which his own or any other foreign law may allow him, nor can he be deprived of an advantage which belongs to him by English law though not by the law of the deceased's domicil. In particular, the priority of debts[7] and their extinction by lapse of time[8] are matters to be governed exclusively by English law. If, for instance, certain foreign debts owed by the deceased are statute-barred by English law but not so barred by the law of the domicil, the principal administrator in the country of the domicil is not entitled as of right to demand that the surplus English assets shall be handed over to him in order to satisfy the claims of the foreign creditors.[9] The only difficulty is to determine at what stage administration ends and beneficial distribution begins.[10] It has been held, for instance, that though all debts have been paid and a net residue ascertained, yet, if the beneficiaries are minors, the right of an administrator under the Administration of Estates Act 1925,[11] to postpone the realisation of the English assets is still exercisable, since postponement is a matter of administration.[12]

After all debts have been paid by an ancillary administrator according to the law of England, the usual procedure is for him to remit any surplus assets to the principal administrator in the country of the deceased's last domicil, in order that they may be distributed among the beneficiaries according to

---

3 Administration of Estates Act 1925, s 1; *IRC v Stype Investments (Jersey) Ltd* [1982] Ch 456 at 473.
4 See, eg, *Whyte v Rose* (1842) 3 QB 493 at 506; Dicey & Morris, pp 990–991.
5 *Currie v Bircham* (1822) 1 Dowl & Ry KB 35; Dicey & Morris, p 991.
6 *Re Kloebe* (1884) 28 Ch D 175; *Re Lorillard* [1922] 2 Ch 638; *Preston v Melville* (1841) 8 Cl & Fin 1 at 12, 13; *Enohin v Wylie* (1862) 10 HL Cas 1 at 13, 14.
7 *Re Kloebe* (1884) 28 Ch D 175.
8 *Re Lorillard* [1922] 2 Ch 638.
9 Ibid.
10 *Re Kehr* [1952] Ch 26, [1951] 2 All ER 812.
11 S 33.
12 *Re Wilks* [1935] Ch 645; cf *Re Northcote's Will Trusts* [1949] 1 All ER 422; *Re Kehr* [1952] Ch 26, [1951] 2 All ER 812.

the law of the domicil.[13] But this remission of assets is not a matter of course. It is within the discretion of the English court whether surplus assets shall be remitted to the domicil for purposes of beneficial distribution or whether that distribution shall be made from England. The sole function of the law of the domicil with regard to English assets is to regulate their beneficial distribution, not to allocate them in payment of debts. An immoderate use was made of this rational principle in the much debated case of *Re Lorillard*:[14]

> The testator, domiciled in New York, died leaving assets and creditors both in England and America. Administration proceedings were taken in both countries. The New York assets were exhausted, leaving unpaid certain creditors whose debts were statute-barred by English law but not so by the law of New York. There was a surplus of English assets after all creditors entitled under English law had been paid.

Eve J made an order that, if the American creditors did not within two months establish that their debts were payable by English law, the executor must not remit the assets in this country to the New York executor, but must distribute them among the beneficiaries. The Court of Appeal refused to interfere with the exercise by Eve J of his discretion.

It certainly seems a strange exercise of judicial discretion to enrich beneficiaries at the expense of creditors entitled to payment in the place of the principal administration.[15] In any event, this attack on the creditors will not always succeed. It succeeded in the instant case because the beneficiaries were resident in England, but had they resided in New York or, indeed, in any other country where statutes of limitation were not then classified as procedural,[16] they would have been liable at the suit of the creditors to disgorge what they had received.

4. FOREIGN ADMINISTRATORS

The rule is absolute that the status of an administrator appointed by a foreign court is not recognised in England. His title relates only to property that lies within the jurisdiction of the country whence he derives his authority, and therefore he has no right to take or to recover by action property in England without a grant from the English court.[17] If, without the support of a grant, he succeeds in obtaining property in England, he is clearly liable as executor

13 *Re Achillopoulos* [1928] Ch 433; *Re Manifold* [1962] Ch 1, [1961] 1 All ER 710; *In the Estate of Weiss* [1962] P 136, [1962] 1 All ER 308; and see *Scottish National Orchestra Society Ltd v Thomson's Executor* 1969 SLT 325; *Re Lord Cable* [1977] 1 WLR 7 at 25–26.

14 [1922] 2 Ch 638. The decision has been severely criticised by Nadelmann (1951) 49 Michigan LR 1129, 1148–1149.

15 But the decision was approved in *Government of India v Taylor* [1955] AC 491 at 509, [1955] 1 All ER 292 at 298, per Lord Simmonds; same case sub nom *Re Delhi Electric Supply and Traction Co Ltd* [1954] Ch 131 at 161, [1953] 2 All ER 1452 at 1466, per Evershed MR, and at pp 165–166 and pp 1468–1469 respectively, per Jenkins LJ. On this aspect of the case see M Mann (1954) 3 ICLQ 502, 504–506. See also *Permanent Trustee Co (Canberra) Ltd v Finlayson* (1968) 122 CLR 338; Nygh, pp 513–514.

16 For the changes in English law introduced by the Foreign Limitation Periods Act 1984, see supra, pp 79–81.

17 For discussion generally of the right to sue in a representative capacity, see supra, p 86–87.

de son tort to account for the assets received.[18] As TEMPLEMAN J said in *IRC v Stype Investments (Jersey) Ltd*:

> If a stranger so deals with proceeds of sale of English property belonging to a deceased in such manner as to submit the proceeds of sale to another jurisdiction and is unable to pay and account for the proceeds of sale to the English representatives when constituted in England, the stranger has intermeddled with the estate and constituted himself an executor de son tort.[19]

Since a foreign administrator has no right to sustain actions or to receive property in this country qua representative of the deceased,[20] it would appear clear on principle that a debtor from whom he receives payment is not discharged from liability to an English administrator.[1] As Story says,[2] however, there is much room for discussion and doubt on this matter. On the one hand, the domestic rule of English law is that "where an executor de son tort is really acting as executor, and the party with whom he deals has fair reason for supposing that he has authority to act as such, his acts shall bind the rightful executor, and shall alter the property".[3] On the other hand, there is the undoubted fact that a foreign administrator, as such, has no authority to receive or otherwise deal with English assets. There is no English case directly in point, but if a debtor had reasonable grounds for believing that the foreign administrator was the bona fide representative of the deceased, it would seem justifiable to depart from strict principle and to regard the payment as a valid discharge. The majority of courts in the USA adopt this view.[4]

But although a foreign administrator is not permitted to sue in England as the representative of the deceased, it has long been established that he may enforce by action a right that is personal to himself and which he is entitled to assert in his own individual capacity, even though it is connected with the estate that he is administering.[5] If, for instance, in his official capacity he recovers judgment abroad against a debtor, he has effectually reduced the debt into his possession, and can sue on the judgment in England without taking out a separate administration.[6] In *Vanquelin v Bouard*:[7]

> A widow in France became donee of the universality of the succession of her deceased husband. By French law she was, as such donee, *personally* liable for her husband's debts and *personally* entitled to his property. She paid to an indorsee the amount of a bill of exchange that her husband had drawn, and later brought an action in England to recover this amount from the acceptor.

It was held that there were two grounds on which the widow must succeed. First, the right that she sought to enforce was not one that formed part of

18 *New York Breweries Co v A-G* [1899] AC 62; and see *Beavan v Lord Hastings* (1856) 2 K & J 724.
19 [1982] Ch 456 at 474.
20 It even appears that a foreign personal representative cannot sue on behalf of the deceased's dependants under a Fatal Accidents Acts claim: *Finnegan v Cementation Co Ltd* [1953] 1 QB 688, though see the criticisms at pp 699–700.
1 Westlake, s 98; cf Dicey & Morris, pp 997–998.
2 Section 514.
3 *Thomson v Harding* (1853) 2 E & B 630 at 640.
4 Scoles & Hay, p 849; Restatement 2d, §322.
5 *Vanquelin v Bouard* (1863) 15 CBNS 341.
6 *Re Macnichol* (1874) LR 19 Eq 81; and see *Peterson v Bezold* (1970) 17 DLR (3d) 471.
7 (1863) 15 CBNS 341.

the husband's estate at the time of his death but, since it arose from a payment made by her since the death, was a right that she had acquired personally. Secondly, her position as donee gave her, according to French law, a personal right to recover the sum from the acceptor.

The liabilities to which an administrator is subject are imposed on him in his capacity as the lawful representative of the deceased, and since the status of a representative appointed abroad is not recognised in England, it follows that a foreign administrator as such is not liable to be sued in this country.[8] This is so even though he brings foreign assets to England. He cannot sue, neither can he be sued, in his capacity as administrator, but an action might lie, at the suit of a creditor or beneficiary, for the judicial administration of any unappropriated assets.[9]

But just as a foreign administrator can enforce in England a right that attaches to him personally, so he can be sued on a claim that is sustainable against him not in his representative, but in his personal, capacity, eg as trustee for legatees,[10] or as an executor de son tort.[11] An action will not lie against an administrator if it is based on a transaction entered into by the deceased, but it will lie on a transaction effected by the administrator after taking office. Thus, for instance, he will be liable on any contract connected with the winding-up of the estate that he makes in England.[12] Indeed, the liability in this country of a foreign executor would seem to go further than this, for if in any way he has changed his character from that of an executor to that of a trustee he would seem to incur liability within the principle of *Penn v Baltimore*.[13]

5. COMMONWEALTH AND OTHER UNITED KINGDOM GRANTS

A grant of administration made in any country to which the Colonial Probates Act 1892[14] has been extended by Order in Council may be sealed with the seal of the English probate registry, ie "resealed", and thus made effective with regard to English assets. An Order in Council, however, is not made until the country in question has made adequate provision for the recognition within its territory of English grants. The Act has been applied to most Commonwealth countries[15] and continues to apply to South Africa.[16] Resealing is discretionary and the court will not normally reseal a grant unless it

8 *Beavan v Lord Hastings* (1856) 2 K & J 724; *Degazon v Barclays Bank International Ltd* [1988] 1 FTLR 17; *Nova v Grove* (1982) 140 DLR (3d) 527; *Canadian Commercial Bank v Belkin* (1990) 73 DLR (4th) 678; Dicey & Morris, pp 999–1001.
9 *Logan v Fairlie* (1825) 2 Sim & St 284; *Tyler v Bell* (1837) 2 My & Cr 89 at 110; Dicey & Morris, pp 999–1001.
10 Dicey & Morris, pp 999–1001.
11 *New York Breweries v A-G* [1899] AC 62; cf *Charron v Montreal Trust* (1958) 15 DLR (2d) 240; *Re Pemberton* (1966) 59 DLR (2d) 44; *Canadian Commercial Bank v Belkin* (1990) 73 DLR (4th) 678 at 684–685.
12 See the American case, *Johnson v Wallis* (1889) 112 NY 230; Restatement 2d, §359.
13 *Bond v Graham* (1842) 1 Hare 482 at 484; *Ewing v Orr-Ewing* (1885) 10 App Cas 453. *Penn v Baltimore* (1750) 1 Ves Sen 444 is fully discussed, supra, pp 256 et seq.
14 As amended by the Administration of Estates Act 1971, s 11, and the Supreme Court Act 1981, Sch 5.
15 Colonial Probates Act 1892; extended to protected States and mandated territories by the Colonial Probates (Protected States and Mandated Territories) Act 1927, s 1. For the countries to which the legislation applies, see Halsbury's *Statutes of England*, 4th edn, vol 17, p 254.
16 South Africa Act 1962, s 2 and Sch 2.

was made to the person entitled to an English grant where the deceased died domiciled abroad,[17] eg the person entrusted with the administration of the estate by the court of the deceased's last domicil or the executor named in a will in English or Welsh.[18] Notice of the resealing is sent to the court which made the original grant.[19]

The position in the United Kingdom is that, since 1972, under section 1 of the Administration of Estates Act 1971,[20] a grant of administration in Scotland or Northern Ireland is directly effective in England without the need for resealing.[1] Similarly, English grants may be directly recognised in Scotland[2] and Northern Ireland;[3] Scottish in Northern Ireland;[4] and vice versa.[5]

---

17 Supra, pp 828–829.
18 Non-Contentious Probate Rules 1987, r 39(3).
19 Ibid, r 39(6).
20 See *Practice Direction* [1971] 1 WLR 1790.
 1 The provision is retrospective: Administration of Estates Act 1971, s 1(6).
 2 Ibid, s 3(1).
 3 Ibid, s 2(1).
 4 Ibid, s 3(1).
 5 Ibid, s 2(2).

Chapter 33

Succession[1]

SUMMARY

1. INTRODUCTION

Presuming that the estate of the deceased has been cleared of debts and all taxes and duties paid, the duty of the administrator is to distribute the property among those to whom it beneficially belongs. These persons are to be identified by the choice of law rules relating to succession and these rules may vary according to whether the estate consists of movables or immovables and whether the deceased left a will or died intestate. It is also necessary to examine the rules relating to the exercise of powers of appointment by will.

Most foreign countries have adopted the principle of unity of succession by which questions relating to intestacy or wills are governed by one single law, the personal law of the deceased, irrespective of the nature of the subject-

---

1 See Miller [1988] Conv 30; (1990) 39 ICLQ 261; Scoles (1988) II Hague Recueil 9, 54–89; North (1990) I Hague Recueil 9, 273–282.

matter. The common law of England has consistently adhered to what is called the principle of scission by which the issues are dealt with separately, with the result that the destination of movables on the death of the owner is governed by the law of his domicil, whilst the destination of immovables is governed by the law of the situs.[2] It is for that reason that we have to examine succession to movables separately from succession to immovables.

2. MOVABLES

(a) INTESTATE SUCCESSION

The rule has been established for well over two hundred years that movable property in the case of intestacy is to be distributed according to the law of the domicil of the intestate at the time of his death.[3] This law determines the class of persons to take, the relative proportions to which the distributees are entitled, the right of representation, the rights of a surviving spouse and all analogous questions.

The fate of movables situated in England and belonging to an intestate who has left no relatives recognised as his successors by the law of his domicil has already been fully discussed.[4] Summarily stated, the rule, which derives from the principle that the authority of the law of the domicil is rigorously confined to questions of succession, is this:

If, by the law of the domicil, the movables pass to the state or some other body in the domicil by way of succession, English law gives effect to this ruling;[5] if, on the other hand, they are claimed by some body in the domicil as being no-one's property, they pass to the English Crown as bona vacantia. In this latter case, there is no question of succession to be referred to the law of the domicil.[6]

(b) WILLS

The general rule established both in this country and in the USA is that testamentary succession to movables is governed exclusively by the law of the domicil of the deceased as it existed at the time of his death.[7] When a

2 For a fuller account of the opposing principles, see Wolff, pp 567 et seq; Cohn (1956) 5 ICLQ 395. For criticism of the idea of scission, see *Re Collens* [1986] Ch 505 at 512–513. The Hague Conference on Private International Law concluded, in 1988, a Convention on the Law Applicable to Succession to the Estates of Deceased Persons. This Convention adopts the principle of unity of succession, applying the same rules to movables and immovables, and to testate and intestate succession. In most cases the law to be applied would be that of the deceased's habitual residence at the time of death. The Convention is not yet in force and has not been signed or ratified by the United Kingdom. For varied assessments of the Convention's merits, see von Overbeck (1989) 46 Annuaire suisse de droit international 138; Lagarde (1989) 78 Rev crit dr int privé 249; North (1990) I Hague Recueil 9, 278–282; Schoenblum (1991) 32 Va J Int L 83.
3 *Pipon v Pipon* (1744) Amb 25.
4 Supra, pp 50–52.
5 *In the Estate of Maldonado* [1954] P 223; Lipstein [1954] CLJ 22.
6 *Re Barnett's Trusts* [1902] 1 Ch 847; *In the Estate of Musurus* [1936] 2 All ER 1666; cf *Re Mitchell, Hatton v Jones* [1954] Ch 525, [1954] 2 All ER 246, on which see Ing, *Bona Vacantia*, pp 57–62.
7 A subsequent change in the law of the domicil is in general of no effect: *Lynch v Provisional Government of Paraguay* (1871) LR 2 P & D 268; and see *Re Aganoor's Trusts* (1895) 64 LJ Ch 521; but see the Wills Act 1963, s 6(3), infra, p 842; cf succession to immovables where the relevant date is that of the proceedings: *Nelson v Lord Bridport* (1846) 8 Beav 547.

testator dies domiciled abroad leaving assets in England, it is true that probate must be taken out in England, and it is also true that the assets must be administered in this country according to English law, but nevertheless all questions concerning beneficial succession under a will must be decided in accordance with the law of the domicil. The duty of the executor is to ascertain who, by the law of the domicil, are entitled under the will, and that being ascertained to distribute the property accordingly.[8] It is necessary, however, to deal separately with the various questions that arise in the case of wills.

(i) Capacity

The capacity of a testator to make a will is determined by the law of his domicil;[9] and there is no distinction between "lack of capacity due to immaturity or status and incapacity arising from ill health."[10] The meaning of this statement is clear enough if he is domiciled in the same country at the time both of his making the will and of his death. If this is a foreign country, his capacity by English law is immaterial. Thus, in a case decided when a married woman possessed no testamentary capacity at common law,[11] the English court granted probate of the will of a married woman, a domiciled Spaniard, on proof that by Spanish law a wife was empowered to bequeath her movables.[12]

But what is the position where the testator has changed his domicil after making his will? Is the determinant of the governing law his domicil at death or at the time when he made the will? There is no decision on the matter. Some writers hold that it means the former.[13] This is curious, for by English internal law, and presumably by other municipal systems, the decisive moment for testing capacity is the time when the will is made. A will made by a minor or by a person of unsound mind cannot be validated by subsequent events. No will can be valid unless it is valid when made. On principle it makes no difference that the subsequent event consists in a change of domicil to a new country where the law has a more favourable rule for capacity. For instance:

> A domiciled Hungarian, twenty-two years of age, and therefore (it is assumed) lacking testamentary capacity by Hungarian law, makes a will, but ultimately dies domiciled in England.

It is submitted that the will is void. What is invalid for incapacity in its origin can scarcely be automatically validated by the change of domicil. If, on the other hand,

> a domiciled German, sixteen years of age, makes a will, as he is permitted to do by German law, but ultimately dies domiciled in England,[14]

it is submitted that the will is valid. In fact it is difficult to disagree with the

---

8 *Enohin v Wylie* (1862) 10 HL Cas 1 at 19.
9 *In the Estate of Fuld (No 3)* [1968] P 675 at 696; and see *Re Lewal's Settlement Trusts* [1918] 2 Ch 391.
10 [1968] P 675 at 696.
11 Until the Married Women's Property Act 1882, a married woman could dispose by will of her separate estate or exercise a power of appointment, and she could bequeath personalty with the assent of her husband, but otherwise she had no testamentary capacity.
12 *In the Goods of Maraver* (1828) 1 Hag Ecc 498.
13 Westlake, s 86; Scoles & Hay, pp 783–786; Stumberg, p 376.
14 Cohn, *Manual of German Law* (2nd edn), vol 1, §614.

view that testamentary capacity, in the sphere of both internal law and private international law, is governed by the law of the testator's domicil at the time when the will is made.[15]

The capacity of a legatee to take a bequest is determined by either the law of his domicil,[16] or the law of the testator's domicil. These determine, for instance, whether he is of full age or whether an unincorporated association is capable of receiving a legacy. Thus, in the case of *Re Hellmann's Will*,[17] the court did not apply the law of the legatee's domicil exclusively, but adopted the principle that where these two laws as to capacity conflict that is selected which is most favourable to the propositus.

A domiciled Englishman bequeathed legacies to each of the two children of a domiciled German. The children were a daughter aged 18 and a son aged 17. By German law girls attained majority on completing their eighteenth year; boys, on completing their twenty-second year.

It was held that the legacy to the daughter might be paid to her on her own receipt, since she was of age by the law of her domicil; and that the legacy might be paid to the son as soon as he attained majority according to English law or according to German law, whichever first happened.

(ii) Formal validity

In the view of the common law, domicil was the only connecting factor that determined the law to govern the formal validity of a will of movables. The formal requirements of the law of the country where the testator was domiciled at the time of his death had to be satisfied. His nationality, his domicil at the time of making the will and the place where he executed his will were inadmissible factors. The disadvantages of so rigid a principle were brought to light by the case of *Bremer v Freeman* in 1857,[18] where it was held that the will made in the English form of a British subject who died domiciled in France was invalid, since it neglected the formalities prescribed by French law. This decision led to the passing of the Wills Acts 1861, often known as Lord Kingsdown's Act, which was designed to offer testators a wider choice of laws so far as formalities were concerned. That Act, however, though a welcome step forward, was disfigured by several serious blemishes.[19] It was badly drafted and was, for example, confined to wills of British subjects, differentiating moreover between realty and personalty rather than between movables and immovables.

The 1861 Act was repealed and replaced by the Wills Act 1963[1] which applies to a will, whether of movables or immovables, made by any testator, irrespective of his domicil or nationality, provided that he died on or after 1 January 1964, even though it was executed before that time. A will made

15 See *Re Lewal's Settlement* [1918] 2 Ch 391; and see Dicey & Morris, pp 1009–1010; Wolff, pp 581–582; cf Nygh, p 518.
16 *Re Hellmann's Will* (1866) LR 2 Eq 363; *Re Schnapper* [1928] 1 Ch 420; and see *Re Pemberton* (1966) 59 DLR (2d) 44.
17 Supra. By German law the boy's father was entitled as guardian to receive the legacy. Lord ROMILLY MR, however, refused to permit payment to him and ordered that during the minority the money should be treated as a minor's legacy.
18 (1857) 10 Moo PCC 306.
19 Morris (1946) 62 LQR 170, 173–176.
 1 This enabled the United Kingdom to ratify the 1961 Hague Convention on the Formal Validity of Wills, Cmnd 1729 (1961).

before 1964 that satisfies the Wills Act 1861, is, however, admissible to probate notwithstanding the repeal of that Act.[2]

The gist of the Act of 1963 is that it increases the relevant connecting factors by adding nationality and habitual residence to those which were already recognised by common law and the Wills Act 1861, namely domicil and the place of acting. It provides that "a will shall be treated as properly executed" if its execution conforms to the internal law in force in any one of the following territories:[3]

(a) The territory where the will was executed, even if the testator was on a temporary visit.[4]

Where a will is made on board a vessel or aircraft whether civil or not, the identity of the law of the place of execution receives special statutory treatment. If at the time of execution the aircraft is grounded in a particular territory or the vessel is within territorial waters, the testator may comply with the internal law of that territory. Alternatively he may comply with the internal law of the territory with which, having regard to its registration and other relevant circumstances, the vessel or aircraft, whether in course of transit or not, has the closest connection.[5] Judged by this test, the law of the place of acting will normally be the law of the flag, which is represented by the law of the territory where the ship or aircraft is registered if the flag is common to a political unit containing a variety of legal systems.[6]

(b) The territory where the testator was domiciled either at the time of making the will or at death.

(c) The territory where the testator was habitually resident either at the time of making the will or at death.

This provides one of the earliest examples of our adoption of the test of habitual residence, bridging the gap between the common law's reliance on domicil and the civil law's on nationality.

(d) The State of which the testator, either at the time of making the will or at death, is a national.

This extension of the civil law principle of nationality, though it is a departure from the common law, does at least unify English and European rules so far as the formal validity of wills is concerned and will often save a will that under the old law would have failed. For instance, a will made at Zurich in Dutch form by a citizen of the Netherlands, domiciled and habitually resident at all material times in France, is properly executed even though it may be formally void in the eyes of French and Swiss law.

Where, however, reliance is placed on the national law of the testator, there are two situations in which it may be difficult to determine the relevant internal law. The first is where he is simultaneously a national of more than one country. The problem then is to decide whether it is necessary to select one particular nationality to denote the internal law or whether the will will be formally valid if it satisfies the internal law of any of the nationalities. If the former approach is to be adopted, it has been suggested that the court should select either the nationality in which the testator

2 Wills Act 1963, s 7(1), (2), (3), (4). For notes on the Act, see Morris (1964) 13 ICLQ 684; Kahn-Freund (1964) 27 MLR 55.
3 S 1.
4 Eg *Re Wynn* [1983] 3 All ER 310, [1984] 1 WLR 237; and see *Re Kanani* (1978) 122 Sol Jo 611.
5 S 2(1)(a).
6 Cf supra, pp 558–560.

is habitually and principally resident, or the nationality of the country with which in the circumstances he appears to be in fact most closely connected.[7]

The other approach, namely of upholding the validity of the will if any of the relevant laws is satisfied, is said to conform more closely with the intentions of those who drafted the 1961 Hague Convention on which the Wills Act 1963 is based.[8]

The second situation that causes difficulty is where the State of which the testator is a national comprises various systems of internal law, as is the case for instance in the United Kingdom or the USA. The 1963 Act solves the problem by providing that the system to be applied shall be ascertained as follows. First, if there is in force throughout the State a rule indicating which of the various systems can properly be applied to the case in question, that rule shall be followed. Failing such a rule, the system shall be that with which the testator was most closely connected at the relevant time.[9]

The first of these rules is likely to be of little practical benefit because there will be few composite states which have a unified conflict of laws rule but different domestic rules as to the formal validity of wills. It is reasonable to assume that under the second rule the court, in its search for the country with which the testator was most closely connected at the relevant time, will attribute most importance to his domicil and habitual residence. Where, however, he is domiciled and resident other than in the composite state of which he is a national, as is likely to be the case where he is relying on the law of his nationality as the basis of formal validity, the one remaining factor of significance seems to be the situation of his assets. The relevant time at which the connection must exist is specified in the 1963 Act as

the time of the testator's death where the matter is to be determined by reference to circumstances prevailing at his death, and the time of execution of the will in any other case.[10]

More generally, it will have been observed that the time at which the connecting factors of domicil, habitual residence or nationality may indicate an applicable law is either when the will is executed or when the testator dies. In effect, therefore, there are seven statutory rules for the choice of law.[11] It would seem that if in fact a will satisfies the requirement of any one of these possible laws it is valid as regards form even though the validating law was not deliberately chosen by the testator. This is the reasonable implication of the statutory provision that "a will shall be treated as properly executed if its execution conformed"[12] to one of the prescribed laws.

A testator, for instance, domiciled in country X makes a will in country Y which is formally valid under the law of X but not under the law of Y. He

---

7 This is the test laid down by the Hague Convention on Conflict of Nationality Laws (1930). If, however, the propositus is a national of the forum, it is generally agreed that that nationality prevails; see Rabel, vol 1, p 120.
8 Mann (1986) 35 ICLQ 423.
9 S 6(2).
10 S 6(2)(b).
11 In the case of immovables it is also sufficient to comply with the law of the situs: s 2(1)(b), infra, pp 852–853. The Law Reform Committee of British Columbia, in its Report on the Making and Revocation of Wills (1981), has recommended (p 107) that a will should also be formally valid if it complies with the law of the situs of movables either at the time the will was made or at the date of death.
12 S 1.

believes that he has satisfied the requirements of the law of the place of execution.

It might be thought that the will is void, since the intention was to conform to the rules of the law of the place of execution, not of the law of the domicil. But the paramount intention of the testator in such a case is to make a valid will and if he achieves this purpose under one possible law his erroneous belief that he is achieving it under another is immaterial.[13]

The merit of the statutory provision that the legal system to govern formalities, whether it be based on nationality, domicil, habitual residence or place of execution, means the internal law of that system, is that the doctrine of renvoi stands excluded. This is fortified by the definition of "internal law" as the "law which would apply in a case where no question of the law in force in any other territory or State arose."[14] Nevertheless, for three reasons, this does not mean that renvoi is wholly inapplicable in the case of the formal validity of wills. First, there is the transitional point that the Wills Act 1861 is still applicable to a will made before 1964 and the doctrine of renvoi has been applied under that Act.[15] Secondly, the Wills Act 1963 does not, despite the references to domicil, abolish the old common law rule whereby the formal validity of a will may be referred to the law of the testator's domicil on death,[16] including any further legal system referred to by that law.[17] Thirdly, the Wills Act 1963 does not take away the right to prove in England a will which has been accepted by a court of the deceased's last domicil,[18] even if that acceptance was based other than on that country's internal law.[19]

In considering, under the Wills Act 1963, whether a will has been properly executed, regard must be had to the internal law as it existed at the time of execution, but any later alteration of the law, operating retrospectively to that time, may be taken into account if it validates, but not if it invalidates, the will.[20]

Although it is clear that the capacity of a testator is governed by his personal law, and therefore not necessarily by the law that governs the formal validity of his will, it may sometimes be troublesome to determine whether or not a given rule affects capacity.

Suppose, for instance, that the testator, Dutch by nationality and by domicil, makes a holograph will in France and leaves assets in England. Both Dutch and French law recognise holograph wills, but Article 992 of the Netherlands Civil Code forbids a Dutch national to make such a will abroad.

If the proper execution of the will is questioned in England, the court must determine the scope of the rule contained in Article 992. If it imposes an

---

13　Wolff, p 586.
14　S 6(1).
15　*In the Goods of Lacroix* (1877) 2 PD 94; *In the Estate of Fuld (No 3)* [1968] P 675, [1965] 3 All ER 776.
16　*In the Goods of Deshais* (1865) 4 Sw & Tr 13 at 17.
17　*Collier v Rivaz* (1841) 2 Curt 855; cf *Bremer v Freeman* (1857) 10 Moo PCC 306; and see Morris, p 396; Nygh, p 520.
18　*Enohin v Wylie* (1862) 10 HL Cas 1; *Doglioni v Crispin* (1866) LR 1 HL 301.
19　Tristram & Coote's *Probate Practice*, 27th edn (1989), pp 94, 97–99, 395.
20　S 6(3). If this extends to alterations in the law made after the death of the testator, it reverses the effect of *Lynch v Provisional Government of Paraguay* (1871) LR 2 P & D 268, supra, p 837.

incapacity upon the testator, it must be enforced; if it relates to formalities, it must be ignored. Such a problem is dealt with by the following section of the Wills Act 1963:[1]

> Where (whether in pursuance of this Act or not) a law in force outside the United Kingdom falls to be applied in relation to a will, any requirement of that law whereby special formalities are to be observed by testators answering a particular description, or witnesses to the execution of a will are to possess certain qualifications, shall be treated, notwithstanding any rule of that law to the contrary, as a formal requirement.

In the hypothetical case suggested above, therefore, the will made in France would be formally valid in the eyes of English law.

International form of will Increased mobility has meant an increase in the number of people who make wills in a country in which they are not domiciled or habitually resident or of which they are not nationals. Undoubtedly the Convention which led to the Wills Act 1963 has done much to assist with this problem; but a further step has been taken with the United Kingdom's ratification of the Washington Convention on International Wills (1973).[2] The Annex to the Convention is brought into force by section 27 of the Administration of Justice Act 1982 and is scheduled to that Act. Its essential provision[3] is that a will will be formally valid in all the Contracting States irrespective of where it was made, the location of the assets or the nationality, domicil or residence of the testator if it complies with the formalities laid down in the Convention. The main formalities[4] are that the will be in writing (in any language) and signed or acknowledged by the testator in the presence of two witnesses and an "authorised person" (which in England will be a solicitor or a notary public'),[5] who have then to attest the will in the presence of the testator. The authorised person has to attach to the will a certificate in the form prescribed by the Convention[6] authenticating the will and its proper execution.

In essence, the Convention provides a new, additional form for a will which a Contracting State must recognise as formally valid. It may also be recognised in a non-Contracting State under general choice of law rules, as where that State looks to the law of the domicil of the testator and the testator was domiciled in a State which is a party to the Convention and his will had complied with the Convention even though not with the formal requirements of his domiciliary law.[7]

1 S 3.
2 Nadelmann (1974) 22 AJCL 365; Brandon (1983) 32 ICLQ 742; Kearney (1984) 18 Int Lawyer 613.
3 Art 1.
4 Arts 2–5.
5 1982 Act, s 28(1).
6 Art 10.
7 The Administration of Justice Act 1982, ss 23–26 also implements another international convention, namely the Council of Europe Convention on the Establishment of a Scheme for the Registration of Wills (1973) which may also be of practical assistance to the person who makes a will away from home. It provides for the establishment of national registration schemes for wills and access to them from other Contracting States.

(iii) Essential validity

The essential, or material, validity of a will, and of any particular gift of movables therein is determined by the law of the country in which the testator was domiciled at death.[8] This rule is not affected by the Wills Act 1963. A will may be admitted to probate under that statute as having complied with the formalities of one of the legal systems that it makes available, but the actual effect of its dispositions must be measured by the law of the testator's domicil at death. The grant of probate is conclusive proof that the instrument proved is the will of the testator but it is not conclusive as to the validity of the dispositions.

If, for instance, a British subject dies domiciled in France, having made a will in England according to English law, probate is necessarily granted. But if he has neglected to leave to his children that portion of the estate required by French law, the English court allows the will to take effect only as it would do in France. If French law regards the testamentary dispositions as ineffective, the court directs the property to be distributed according to the French law of intestacy;[9] if French law requires only part of the estate to go to the children, the will would be valid as to the rest with the bequests proportionately reduced.[10]

The principle that the law of the domicil at death is decisive is well illustrated by the reverse case to that just given. An example is afforded by *Re Groos, Groos v Groos*[11] where the facts were as follows:

A Dutch lady made her will in the Netherlands constituting her husband heir of her movable property except for the "legitimate portion to which her descendants were entitled". She died domiciled in England, leaving her husband and five children surviving. By Dutch law the "legimate portion" of the children was three-fourths of the estate, but by English law it was nothing. It was held that, since the will operated under English law, the whole estate passed to the husband.

Whether a beneficiary is entitled to take under a will is determined by the law of the testator's domicil if the question turns on a rule of substantive law, not on procedure. In the case of *Re Cohn*:[12]

A testatrix and her daughter, both domiciled in Germany, were killed in an air raid in London in circumstances which left it uncertain which of them died first. The daughter's estate was entitled to movables under her mother's will, but only if she were the survivor. In such a case the English rule is that the younger person is presumed to have survived the elder,[13] but the presumption by German law was that they died simultaneously.

These presumptions were classified as falling within the sphere of substantive law, and it was held that the German view must be adopted. On the other hand, the English rule relating to the burden of proof of testamentary capacity

---

8 *Thornton v Curling* (1824) 8 Sim 310; *Campbell v Beaufoy* (1859) John 320; *Macdonald v Macdonald* (1872) LR 14 Eq 60; *Re Groos, Groos v Groos* [1915] 1 Ch 572; *Phillipson-Stow v IRC* [1961] AC 727 at 761; *Re Levick's Will Trusts* [1963] 1 All ER 95, [1963] 1 WLR 311.
9 *Thornton v Curling*, supra; *Campbell v Beaufoy*, supra.
10 Eg *Re Annesley* [1926] Ch 692; *Re Adams* [1967] IR 424, especially at 452–458.
11 [1915] 1 Ch 572.
12 [1945] Ch 5; Morris (1945) 61 LQR 340.
13 Law of Property Act 1925, s 184.

has been classified as procedural and governed by the law of the forum.[14]

Other examples of questions of substance are whether a gift to an attesting witness, or to the relative of an attesting witness, is valid,[15] whether the testator acted under duress or undue influence,[16] and whether a beneficiary is put to his election.[17] Similarly, legislation empowering the court to make an order for such provision out of the estate as is adequate to support the dependants of the deceased would appear to be a matter of substance applicable only if the testator died domiciled within the jurisdiction.[18]

It should not be assumed that because a testator dies domiciled in England his will is therefore inevitably subject to all the rules of English domestic law concerned with essential validity. This fact has not always been admitted. It has been said,[19] for instance, that whether a restraint on marriage or a gift to a charity is valid, or whether a limitation is void as infringing the rule against perpetuities,[20] must be determined by the law of the testator's domicil no matter what the domicil of the beneficiary may be. It is submitted that this view is neither consonant with principle nor warranted by the authorities. It entirely ignores the essential difference between the right to give and the right to receive. The two are not necessarily analogous. The right of a testator to give, as for example whether he is free to bequeath the whole of his property as it pleases him or on the contrary whether he must reserve a legitimate portion for his children, is of necessity governed by the English law of succession from which his testamentary power of disposition is derived. But there is no reason why this law should restrict the right of a foreign legatee to enjoy a gift in accordance with the terms of the will, provided that the legacy is valid according to his personal law and provided that the limitations imposed on its enjoyment do not offend some rule of public policy so sacred in English eyes as to demand extra-territorial application.

Suppose that a testator domiciled in England bequeaths a sum of money to a legatee domiciled in France, and that the legacy, though valid by French law, is void by English internal law as being obnoxious to the perpetuity rule.

Is the legacy void? The answer must be in the affirmative if the English policy is to insist on the early vesting of interests regardless of where the property is to be enjoyed and administered. Such a suggestion is untenable. The object of the perpetuity rule is to restrict the withdrawal of property from the channels of commerce, a purpose which is clearly local, and which, therefore, cannot justifiably be invoked to destroy a bequest of money that is to be

---

14 *In the Estate of Fuld (No 3)* [1968] P 675 at 694–699.
15 *Re Priest* [1944] Ch 58. This case has been much discussed; see RMW (1944) 60 LQR 114; Morris (1945) 61 LQR 124; (1946) 62 LQR 172, 173; Kahn-Freund (1946) 7 MLR 238; Wolff, p 586. See now the Wills Act 1968.
16 *In the Estate of Fuld (No 3)* [1968] P 675 at 698–699.
17 See *Re Ogilvie* [1918] 1 Ch 492, 500; *Re Mengel's Will Trust* [1962] Ch 791, [1962] 2 All ER 490; Dicey & Morris, pp 1028–1033. Election is discussed more fully in the context of succession to immovables, infra, pp 856–858.
18 *Pain v Holt* (1919) 19 SR (NSW) 105; *Re Herron* [1941] 4 DLR 203; *Re Terry* [1951] NZLR 30; *Re Greenfield* [1985] 2 NZLR 662. The English legislation is limited in terms to testators dying domiciled in England: Inheritance (Provision for Family and Dependants) Act 1975, s 1(1); and see *Mastaka v Midland Bank Executor and Trustee Co Ltd* [1941] Ch 192.
19 Westlake, p 154.
20 Ibid.

enjoyed and administered in a foreign country. As Lord COTTENHAM said in an early case:

> The rules acted upon by the courts in this country with respect to testamentary dispositions tending to perpetuities relate to this country only. . . . The fund [given by the English will] being to be administered in a foreign country is payable here though the purpose to which it is to be applied would have been illegal if the administration of the fund had been to take place in this country.[1]

This conclusion has several times been reached by the New York Court of Appeals[2] and on one occasion at least by an Australian court.[3] In the laconic words of one judge: "It is no part of the policy of the State of New York to interdict perpetuities or gifts in mortmain in Pennsylvania or California."[4]

Again:

> Suppose that a testator, domiciled in England, leaves a sum of money in trust that the income thereof shall be used for purposes most conducive to the good of religion in a certain diocese in country X, and that persons domiciled in X are appointed to administer the trust.[5]

The trust is invalid by English law as not being charitable;[6] but, if it is valid by the law of X, must the court forbid payment of the money to the trustees? Such a ruling would be indefensible. English law confines the definition of a charity within comparatively narrow limits, presumably with the object of restricting the amount of money that may be withdrawn from circulation, but it cannot justifiably claim to impose this policy on foreign countries. The decisive factor is the law of the country where the trust is to be administered, ie its proper law, not the law that governs the instrument of gift.[7] Three conditions must be satisfied before transfer of the money to the foreign country will be authorised.

First, the charitable bequest must be valid according to its proper law, the law of the country where it is to be administered.

Secondly, there must be persons in that country willing and competent to undertake the task of administration.[8]

Thirdly, the purposes for which the bequest is to be employed must not conflict with some rule of English public policy intended to operate extra-territorially. It can scarcely be maintained that a rule which confines within

---

1 *Fordyce v Bridges* (1848) 2 Ph 497 at 515. An English testator gave the residue of his personal estate to trustees on trust to convert it into money and lay it out in the purchase of land in England or Scotland according to the limitations of a Scottish entail. Such limitations infringed the English rule against perpetuities. The trustees were allowed to purchase land in Scotland in accordance with the terms of the will.
2 Gray, *The Rule against Perpetuities*, 4th edn (1942), §263.2; Morris and Leach, *The Rule against Perpetuities*, 2nd edn (1962), pp 22–23; and see *Re Chappell's Estate* 124 Wash 128, 213 P 684 (1923).
3 *Re Mitchner* [1922] St R Qd 252.
4 *Chamberlain v Chamberlain* (1870) 43 NY 424 at 434.
5 The American position relating to charitable gifts is discussed by Hancock (1964) 16 Stan LR 561.
6 *Dunne v Byrne* [1912] AC 407.
7 The majority decision of the Supreme Court of Canada to the contrary: *Jewish National Fund Inc v Royal Trust Co* (1965) 53 DLR (2d) 577, has been strongly criticised: Nygh, pp 475–476; Picarda, *The Law and Practice Relating to Charities* (1977), pp 580–582; Waters, *Law of Trusts in Canada*, 2nd edn (1984), pp 1126–1127.
8 *New v Bonaker* (1867) LR 4 Eq 655.

narrow limits the possible beneficiaries of a charitable gift is intended to be anything more than local in its operation.[9]

It would seem, then, that the principle which refers questions of substantial validity to the law of the testator's domicil is not unqualified.

(iv) Construction

The province of construction is to ascertain the expressed intentions of the testator, ie the meaning which the words of the will, when properly interpreted, convey. If the intention is expressed in a manner that leaves no room for doubt, the aid of private international law is unnecessary, for the duty of any court, no matter in what country it may sit, is to give effect to expressed intentions, and, these being clear, there can be no occasion to test the language of the will by reference to any particular legal system. If, however, the language of the will leaves the intention doubtful, or if it uses expressions which are ambiguous or equivocal or if the testator has failed to provide for certain events which have not been covered by his dispositions, a problem of choice of law arises, for it is essential that the doubtful intention of the testator should be ascertained by reference to rules of construction obtaining in one particular system of law. The consequences may be serious according as this law or that law is chosen, for when it is said that the intention of the testator is the sovereign guide in questions of construction, this does not mean that his language is necessarily to be construed in a manner that would commend itself to an intelligent man, but that it must be read in the light of those technical rules of construction recognised by the governing legal system.

It will be seen, therefore, that in choosing a law to govern construction it is desirable to discover that system with which the testator was most intimately acquainted, and which it is just to presume that he had in mind when drafting his will.[10] Certain expressions, such as "next of kin", bear different meanings in different countries, and it is obvious that the intention of a testator may be defeated unless the legal system with reference to which he wrote his will is correctly ascertained.

The law with which the ordinary person is most familiar is the law of his existing domicil, and, despite the fact that certain authorities choose the domicil at death as the controlling factor,[11] it is more consonant with the desire of the court to implement the intention of the testator to say that the law of the domicil at the time when his will is made governs its construction, unless there is evidence indicating that his mind was directed to some other legal system. This approach is supported by section 4 of the Wills Act 1963 which provides that the "construction of a will shall not be altered by reason of any change in the testator's domicile after the execution of the will".[12]

In most cases, of course, the domicil does not change after the will has been made and examples can readily be provided of the application of the law of the domicil, being unchanged between the making of the will and

9 *Oliphant v Hendrie* (1784) 1 Bro CC 571; *Mackintosh v Townsend* (1809) 16 Ves 330; *A-G v Mill* (1827) 3 Russ 328 at 338; affirmed by the House of Lords (1831) 2 Dow and Clark 393; *Fordyce v Bridges* (1848) 2 Ph 497 at 515.

10 See *Re McMorran* [1958] Ch 624 at 634, [1958] 1 All ER 186 at 191; *Durie's Trustees v Osborne* 1960 SC 444 at 450–451; *Re Adams* [1967] IR 424 at 458–461.

11 *Re Cunnington* [1924] 1 Ch 68; *Trotter v Trotter* (1828) 4 Bli NS 502; *Yates v Thompson* (1835) 3 Cl & Fin 544.

12 And see *Philipson-Stow v IRC* [1961] AC 727 at 761, [1960] 3 All ER 814 at 830. Cf *Re Levick's Will Trusts* [1963] 1 All ER 95, [1963] 1 WLR 311.

death. Where, for instance, a domiciled Englishman bequeathed a legacy to the "next of kin" of a foreigner, it was held that the legatees must be ascertained according to English law.[13] Whether a gift in the will of a domiciled Englishman was a satisfaction of a debt due under a Scottish settlement was tested by reference to English law.[14] Words of value or of quantity or of measurement, which vary in meaning in different countries, have been interpreted according to the law of the testator's domicil.[15]

There is, however, no absolute rule that the interpretation of a will depends on the law of the testator's domicil. It is merely a prima facie rule that is displaced if the testator has manifestly contemplated and intended that his will should be construed according to some other system of law.[16] Thus where a domiciled Frenchwoman left an unattested will valid by the law of France, in which she said that the will was to "be considered in England the same as in France", STIRLING J held, on the question whether the document operated as the execution of a power, that the testatrix wrote with reference to English law.[17]

(v) Revocation

Since the rules relating to revocation vary from country to country, the problem is to ascertain the law that determines what suffices to revoke an existing will. According to English internal law, a will may be voluntarily revoked either by a fresh will or by its destruction, or obliteration, with the intention of revoking it, by the testator himself or by some authorised person in his presence. Further, its automatic revocation may result from the later marriage of the testator. These three methods will serve as the basis on which to discuss the problem of the choice of law.

Revocation by later will   A will purporting to revoke an earlier will is formally valid and effective if it satisfies the requirements of any one of the laws by which, under the Wills Act 1963, its formal validity is determinable. Suppose, for instance, that a testator domiciled in England makes a will in the English form revoking an earlier will that he had made when domiciled in France. The revocation is effective even if ineffective according to French law.

The Wills Act 1963, however, goes further. It provides that the revoking will shall be effective if it complies with the requirements of any one of the laws qualified to govern the formal validity of the *earlier* will.[18] The mere fact that, at the time of his death, the testator has become subject to another testamentary law is not to upset what he lawfully and intentionally did according to a law that governed him in the past. Thus, to reverse the illustration suggested above, the revocation would be effective if contained

---

13 *Re Fergusson's Will* [1902] 1 Ch 483. But see *Re Goodman's Trusts* (1881) 17 Ch D 266, supra, p 757; cf the Scottish view: *Mitchell's Trustee v Rule* 1908 SLT 189; *Smith's Trustees v Macpherson* 1926 SC 983; Anton, pp 692–694.
14 *Campbell v Campbell* (1866) LR 1 Eq 383.
15 *Saunders v Drake* (1742) 2 Atk 465.
16 *Pierson v Garnet* (1786) 2 Bro CC 38; Westlake, s 123; cf *Re Cunnington* [1924] 1 Ch 68.
17 *Re Price, Tomlin v Latter* [1900] 1 Ch 442. In *Re Wynn* [1983] 3 All ER 310, [1984] 1 WLR 237, English law was applied to determine whether a will which revoked previous wills but made no fresh dispositions of the testatrix's property (apparently both movable and immovable) could have the effect of excluding her husband from taking on intestacy, even though it was not decided where the testatrix was domiciled at the material time.
18 S 2(1)(c).

in a will that was formally void by English law but valid according to the law of France.

It should be noted, however, that a testator may make a valid English will which does not revoke an earlier will in foreign form where the latter deals solely with property in a foreign country and the English will deals only with English property, even though it contains a revocation clause.[19]

Revocation by destruction of the will The Private International Law Committee recommended in 1958 that the effect of the destruction of a will should be determinable by any one of the laws capable of governing the formal validity of the testator's will, had he chosen to make one.[20] This proposal has not been accepted by the legislature. The Wills Act 1963 deals only with a testamentary revocation. Hence, the problem of choice of law in the case of acts such as destruction of the will, or obliteration of some of its provisions, must be solved on the basis of the common law principle of domicil.[1] But what is the decisive domicil in this context? The question is superfluous if the testator has lived in the same country throughout his life, since there is only one possible domiciliary law. It requires an answer, however, if he possessed one domicil at the time of the act of destruction, and another at the time of death, for what is an effective revocation by the earlier law of the domicil, may be ineffective by the later.

Suppose, for instance, that a testator domiciled in Quebec sent written instructions to his solicitor to destroy his will. The will was accordingly burnt and was thereby revoked in the eyes of Quebec law. The testator died domiciled in England. English internal law would not regard the revocation as effective since the burning was not carried out in the presence of the testator.[2]

Since the testator died subject to English law, could it successfully be contended that his will, presuming its contents to be ascertainable, was still operative? It is submitted that such a contention would be ill-founded. The legal effect of the act of destruction fell to be determined at the time of its performance. The testator intended to revoke his will. He fulfilled his intention by an act that was regarded as final and effective by the law to which he was then subject. There was no other law available to him.[3] The mind recoils from the suggestion that the effect of such an act within the law might be nullified or changed merely because at some later period in his life he happened to be subjected to a different legal system. It requires something more than this to undo what has lawfully and intentionally been done in the past.

The same reasoning applies to the reverse case. If the act of destruction were sufficient by English law but insufficient by Quebec law, the will would remain unrevoked. A chance change of domicil could scarcely infuse life into an act that was legally abortive at birth.[4]

Revocation by marriage The rule of English law is that a will is revoked by marriage unless it is explicitly expressed to be made in contemplation of

---

19 *In the Estate of Wayland* [1951] 2 All ER 1041; *Guardian Trust and Executors Co of New Zealand Ltd v Darroch* [1973] 2 NZLR 143.
20 (1958) Cmd 491, p 8.
 1 Cf *Valasco v Coney* [1934] P 143.
 2 Wills Act 1837, s 20.
 3 See *Re Traversi's Estate* 189 Misc 251, 64 NYS 2d 453 (1946).
 4 Mann (1954) 31 BYBIL 217, 231.

marriage.[5] Few other legal systems have adopted the rule and so choice of law problems may arise. When a person marries after making a will and then dies leaving movables in some other country, the question may arise whether the law of his domicil at the time of marriage or at the time of death determines the effect of marriage on the will.[6] The answer to this question depends on whether the rule as to revocation by marriage is to be classified as a rule of matrimonial law or of testamentary law. If it is a rule concerning husband and wife, then its effect must be tested by the law of the domicil at the time of marriage; if, on the other hand, it has nothing to do with the matrimonial régime at all, its effect is to be measured by the law of the domicil at the date of death. It would seem scarcely open to doubt that it is essentially a doctrine connected with the relationship of marriage, and that this is so was affirmed in the case of *Re Martin, Loustalan v Loustalan*,[7] where:

A woman, after making a will, married a man domiciled in England and subsequently died domiciled in France. By English internal law a will is revoked by marriage, but this is not so under French law.

In order to decide whether the will was revoked it was necessary to decide whether this was a matrimonial question governed by English law or a testamentary question governed by French law. VAUGHAN-WILLIAMS LJ in the Court of Appeal held[8] that the question was one of matrimonial law, English law applied and the will was revoked.

As the relevant domicil is that at the time of the marriage, the effect of a change of domicil may be shown by the following two examples:

A makes a will while domiciled in England; then he acquires a domicil in Scotland (where marriage does not revoke a will); then marries in Scotland, and ultimately dies domiciled in England.[9]

In this case the will stands. English law applies only as being the governing testamentary law under which A dies, and therefore its doctrine as to the effect of marriage cannot affect a marriage that took place when the parties had a foreign domicil. The reverse case to that just put is as follows:

A makes a will while domiciled in Scotland then acquires an English domicil and later marries in England.

Here the question as to revocation is governed by English law as being the law applicable to all matters concerning the matrimonial regime.

It has been assumed so far that the spouses have a common domicil on marriage. However, this may not always be the case, given that a wife may have a domicil independent from that of her husband.[10] As domicil for the purposes of revocation of a will by marriage is to be determined as at the time of marriage, there may be some cases where a wife retains her separate domicil notwithstanding her marriage. If so, the law of that country will determine whether her will is revoked by marriage.

So far as English law is concerned, a marriage which is void under English

---

5 Wills Act 1837, s 18 (as substituted by the Administration of Justice Act 1982, s 18); Law of Property Act 1925, s 177.
6 There is also the fundamental question as to whether the relevant marriage was valid; see *Re Fleming, deceased* [1987] ILRM 638.
7 [1900] P 211; and see *Re Micallef's Estate* [1977] 2 NSWLR 929.
8 Ibid, at 240.
9 *In the Goods of Reid* (1866) LR 1 P & D 74; cf *In the Estate of Groos* [1904] P 269.
10 Domicile and Matrimonial Proceedings Act 1973, s 1.

rules of private international law will have no effect on the will;[11] but a voidable marriage will revoke it.[12]

3. IMMOVABLES

(a) INTESTATE SUCCESSION

We have seen earlier[13] that, under the principle of scission, succession to immovables is governed, not by the law of the testator's domicil, but by the law of the situs.[14]

Accordingly, where the owner of immovables dies intestate, the order of descent or distribution prescribed by the law of the situs is applied by the English court no matter what his domicil may have been.[15] This rule can be attacked on a number of grounds.[16] It is an historical anomaly from the time before 1926 when intestate succession to land was subject to rules different from intestate succession to personalty. Domestic legislation on intestate succession would seem to be based on the assumption, erroneous in fact, that succession to all the intestate's property will be governed by the same law. This is particularly striking with regard to the statutory legacies which go to a surviving spouse under the law of England[17] and of Northern Ireland.[18] Can a widow claim two such statutory legacies, one based on land in England and the other on personalty in Northern Ireland?[19]

The operation of the rule may be illustrated by two decisions. The first is an Irish case, *Re Rea:*[20]

A domiciled Irishman died intestate without issue in Ireland owning land in both Ireland and Victoria. In such circumstances a widow was entitled by a Victorian statute to a charge of £1,000 on land in the colony and by an Irish statute to a charge of £500 payable out of the real and personal estate in Ireland. The land in Victoria having been sold and the proceeds remitted to Ireland, it was held that the widow was entitled to the £1,000 under the Victorian statute, as well as the £500 under the Irish statute, since her rights were those conferred by the law of the situs.

The second, and more recent, decision is *Re Collens:*[1]

The deceased died in 1966. He was intestate and died domiciled in Trinidad

---

11 *Mette v Mette* (1859) 1 Sw & Tr 416.
12 *Re Roberts* [1978] 3 All ER 225, [1978] 1 WLR 653.
13 Supra, pp 836–837.
14 This would seem to mean the law of the situs at the date of the proceedings, rather than at the time of death: *Nelson v Lord Bridport* (1846) 8 Beav 547.
15 *Balfour v Scott* (1793) 6 Bro Parl Cas PC 550; *Duncan v Lawson* (1889) 41 Ch D 394; cf *Re Ralston* [1906] VLR 689. When the immovables are situated in a country that adopts the principle of unity of succession this means that, subject to the acceptance of the renvoi doctrine by the law of the situs, the order of descent may be that of England; cf *Re Duke of Wellington* [1947] Ch 506, [1947] 2 All ER 854; supra, p 70.
16 See Morris (1969) 85 LQR 339, 348–352.
17 Administration of Estates Act 1925, s 46(1)(i), para (3), as amended by Intestates' Estates Act 1952, s 1; Family Provision Act 1966, s 1(1)(b).
18 Administration of Estates Act (Northern Ireland) 1955, s 7, as amended by Family Provision Act (Northern Ireland) 1969, s 1(c).
19 Morris & North, p 575. A clear negative answer has been given in Canada: *Re Thom* (1987) 40 DLR (4th) 184.
20 [1902] 1 IR 451.
1 [1986] Ch 505, [1986] 1 All ER 611.

and Tobago, leaving property there, in Barbados and in England. The property in England included immovable property. There was a dispute over succession to the estate and it was agreed that the deceased's second wife should receive $1 million in settlement of any claim to the property in Trinidad and Tobago, but that succession to the estate in Barbados and England should be governed by their respective laws. It was not contested that English law as the law of the situs governed the intestate succession to the English immovables. The question for the court was whether the second wife could take, not only the $1 million agreed under the law of the deceased's domicil, but also the statutory legacy due to a widow under the English law of intestacy.

Sir NICOLAS BROWNE-WILKINSON V-C was reluctant to see the widow succeed both under the law of the domicil and to the statutory legacy under English law as the law of the situs. Nevertheless he was unable to interpret either the English statutory provisions or the choice of law rules so as to lead to any other result. Though he saw force in the criticisms of this state of the law, he felt obliged to conclude that "my job is to administer the law as it now is".[2]

(b) WILLS

The general rule in the case of testamentary succession to immovables is, as with intestate succession, that it is the law of the situs of the immovables which governs. Though there are fewer authorities relating to wills of immovables, it may be helpful to consider the various issues that may arise in the same order as with wills of movables.

(i) Capacity

There seems little doubt that the law of the situs exclusively determines whether the testator has capacity to make a will of immovables,[3] and also probably capacity to take a bequest.

(ii) Formal validity

At common law, a will of immovables had to comply with the formal requirements of the law of the situs.[4] However, as with wills of movables,[5] the common law principles have been much enlarged by the Wills Act 1963. It is sufficient for the will to comply with any one of the seven laws specified in section 1 of the Act in relation to movables, namely the territory where the testator was domiciled or habitually resident or of which he was a national, either when the will was executed or when the testator died, or the territory where the will was executed. Furthermore, the common law rule, ie compliance with the formalities of the law of situs, is also retained in the case of immovables.[6] However, reference in the Wills Act to the law of the situs is in terms of "the internal law in force in the territory where the property

---

2 Ibid, at 513.
3 See *Re Hernando, Hernando v Sawtell* (1884) 27 Ch D 284, where the proposition, so far as related to English land, was undisputed; and see Mental Health Act 1983, s 97 (4)(a).
4 *Coppin v Coppin* (1725) 2 P Wms 291, supra, p 789; *Pepin v Bruyere* [1900] 2 Ch 504.
5 Supra, pp 839–843.
6 Wills Act 1963, s 2(1)(b).

was situated"[7] and the reference to the "internal law" of the situs seems to exclude the doctrine of renvoi.[8]

(iii) Essential validity

There is no doubt that the law of situs, including its choice of law rules, (ie the doctrine of renvoi[9] is applicable) governs matters of essential validity. This rule has been applied to such issues as whether the bequest contravenes the rule against perpetuities or against accumulations,[10] whether gifts to charities are valid,[11] whether a proportion of the estate has to be left to the children or to a surviving spouse,[12] whether a power to assign part of the estate is valid,[13] and, indeed, whether the land can be devised at all.[14]

A matter of considerable practical importance is whether a court can order payment to be made out of the estate for the support of dependants. In the case of movables, we have seen[15] that, under the Inheritance (Provision for Family and Dependants) Act 1975, an English court can only make such an order if the testator died domiciled in England. It might, therefore, have been expected that, in the case of an estate of immovable property, the 1975 Act would have been applicable if England was the law of the situs.[16] Unfortunately the 1975 Act is seriously defective[17] in that the court can only make an order in the case of immovables, as well as movables, if the testator died domiciled in England.[18] This means that, in the case of a testator who dies domiciled in a country which applies the law of the situs rule such as New South Wales[19] or New Zealand[20] no provision for support can be made out of the English immovable property. The foreign court has no power because of the English situs and the English court has no power because of the foreign domicil.

(iv) Construction

A somewhat difficult question arises with regard to the construction of wills of immovables. It has been seen that a bequest of movables is construed according to the law intended by the testator, which is generally the law of his domicil at the time when he prepared his will.[21] The problem is whether the English authorities extend the same rule to wills of immovables, or whether they require that exclusive respect shall be paid to the law of the situs.

It is submitted that there is little difficulty if we resort to first principles, and determine what are the natural provinces of the law of the domicil and

7 Ibid.
8 Cf wills of movables; supra, p 842.
9 Supra, pp 58 et seq.
10 *Freke v Carbery* (1873) LR 16 Eq 461.
11 *Duncan v Lawson* (1889) 41 Ch D 394; supra p 787.
12 *Re Hernando* (1884) 27 Ch D 284; *Re Ross* [1930] 1 Ch 377; and see *Re Bailey* [1985] 2 NZLR 656.
13 *Public Trustee v Vodjdani* (1988) 49 SASR 236.
14 *Nelson v Bridport* (1846) 8 Beav 547.
15 Supra, p 845.
16 See eg *Re Paulin* [1950] VLR 462 at 465.
17 Morris (1946) 62 LQR 170, 178–179; cf Law Com No 61 (1974) paras 258–262.
18 1975 Act, s 1(1).
19 *Pain v Holt* (1919) 19 SRNSW 105.
20 *Re Bailey* [1985] 2 NZLR 656.
21 Supra, pp 847–848.

of the law of the situs respectively in this matter. It must be conceded that the object of all courts, when dealing with a will, is first to ascertain the intention of the testator and then to give effect to that intention so far as is consonant with the governing law. In the ascertainment of this intention, where the will has reference to more countries than one, it may be a matter of great moment whether the testator's language is read in the light of this or that legal system, for it frequently happens that the same word or phrase, such as "heirs of the body", bears a different signification in different countries. It follows, therefore, in such a case that the result which the testator intended will not ensue unless we discover the system of law which he had in mind when he wrote the will. The presumption should be in favour of the law of the domicil at the time of the making of the will, for that is the system of law under which he lives and with which he is expected to be familiar.

It may, of course, be some other system, such as the law of the situs, for the inquiry turns wholly on intention, and if there is anything clearly indicative of a desire to exclude the law of the domicil, the will must be construed accordingly.[22] Thus, if a domiciled Englishman, possessing land in Scotland, were to adopt in his will the expression "tailzied fee", it would be reasonable to conclude that he wished Scottish law to govern his disposition; similarly, if he made one will for the land and a separate will for his English property.[1]

Where a testator is domiciled in one country and has land in another, the fact to be borne in mind, then, is that the law of the situs, as such, has no paramount claim to exclusive recognition.[2] Otherwise the result may be to defeat a testator's intention, for he may leave property, not to named persons, but to those persons who would be entitled were he to die intestate. It is obvious, in such a case, that his intention is to benefit the successors admitted by the law of his domicil, since it is that system with which he is familiar, and it can scarcely be denied that arbitrarily to make a new will for him by admitting a different line of succession imposed by the law of a foreign situs, merely because the will includes a certain amount of land situated abroad, would constitute a departure from principle.

The adoption of this principle does not infringe any local rule of the law of the situs; nor does it derogate from the sovereign power of the country in which the land is situated. All courts, in administering private international law, desire to give effect to expressed intentions, provided that this does not conflict with the public policy of the forum or of the situs, and it is a matter of indifference that A takes land under a will that has been construed according to the law of the testator's domicil, though B would have taken had the construction been that of the law of the situs. This, however, gives us the clue to the limits of the doctrine. If the rules of the law of the situs make it illegal or impossible to give effect to the will as construed by the system of law intended by the testator, the general principle must perforce give way, and the construction adopted must be that of the law of the situs.[3] Or again, if the interest arising from a will that has been so construed possesses incidents different in the situs from those recognised by the law of the domicil, the law of the situs must prevail, for it is that law which determines the nature and extent of estates and interests in immovables. The

22 *Public Trustee v Vodjdani* (1988) 49 SASR 236.
 1 As in *Re Duke of Wellington* [1947] Ch 506, [1947] 2 All ER 854.
 2 Cf *Re Osoba, Osoba v Osoba* [1979] 1 WLR 247 at 250.
 3 *Philipson-Stow v IRC* [1961] AC 727 at 761, [1960] 3 All ER 814 at 831.

testator may, indeed, make his own dictionary, but the law of the situs has the last word.

The law may, then, be stated as follows:

A will of immovables must be construed according to the system of law intended by the testator. This is presumed to be the law of his domicil at the time when the will is made, but the presumption will be rebutted if evidence is adduced from the language of the will proving that he made his dispositions with reference to some other legal system. If, however, the interest that arises from such construction is not permitted or not recognised by the law of the situs the latter law must prevail.

It now remains to examine the English authorities with the view of discovering whether the principle that has been stated above is accepted in this country.[4]

It was decided in *Studd v Cook*,[5] an appeal to the House of Lords from the Court of Session in Scotland, that the size of estate which a devisee takes depends on the law of the testator's domicil. In that case:

A domiciled Englishman devised land in both England and Scotland to the use of X for his life, without impeachment of waste, remainder to the use of the first and every other son of X, "successively, according to their respective seniorities, in tail male". By English law X took a mere life interest, but by Scottish law he was entitled to the fee simple. It was held that the testator clearly intended the limitations of his will to be understood in their English sense, since he had used technical language familiar to English conveyancing, and that therefore his intention was effective so far as the law of Scotland permitted.

This case is distinguishable from *Re Miller, Bailie v Miller*,[6] where a different principle was at stake.

By a trust disposition, made in Scottish form but sufficient to constitute a valid will by English law, A, a domiciled Scotsman, gave his lands in Scotland and England "for behoof of my eldest son, James ... and the heirs male of his body in fee", with remainders over. James died without issue and without having executed any disentailing assurance of the English land. He made, however, a trust disposition in Scottish form, executed in the manner required by English law for the execution of wills, by which he disposed of the whole of his real and personal property.

By English law, as it then stood, the will of James was ineffectual to pass the estate tail in the English land. By Scottish law the will of A did not create a strict entail but gave James an interest that he could dispose of either inter vivos or by will. It was held that the question whether James had power to dispose of his London house by will must be decided according to English law

It would seem that this decision is not inconsistent with *Studd v Cook*. The latter decided that a will should be construed according to the law of the domicil in order to ascertain the size and nature of the interest that the testator intended to give. *Re Miller* did not raise a question of construction only. What the advocates of Scottish law attempted in effect to maintain was

4 Cf Sykes & Pryles, pp 774–777.
5 (1883) 8 App Cas 577.
6 [1914] 1 Ch 511. See also *Nelson v Bridport* (1846) 8 Beav 547; *Philipson-Stow v IRC* [1961] AC 727 at 761.

that A's disposition did create an estate tail, but at the same time an estate tail with Scottish and not English incidents. According to Scottish law, the interest of A was at least a species of estate tail, for, failing a disentailing assurance or a testamentary disposition, it would pass to his male issue, or if no such issue, to the remainderman. A devisable estate tail, however, was unknown in England before 1926; and to frame a settlement under English law which would correspond to the limitations as recognised by Scottish law would be a task of extreme nicety. The question was not—Which of the various estates recognised by English law did A intend to create? Rather it was—Did English law recognise the estate that A had purported to create?

(v) Election

The idea that a will of immovables does not necessarily depend in all matters on the law of the situs may also be illustrated by decisions dealing with the doctrine of election.

> Suppose, for instance, that a domiciled Englishman makes a will by which he devises his son's foreign land to X but gives £50,000 out of his own property to his son. The rule of domestic English law applicable to these circumstances is that, if the testator clearly intended to dispose of the land in favour of X, the son cannot claim the whole of the £50,000 unless he adopts the testamentary disposition of the land. He must elect, ie he must either keep the land and have the legacy correspondingly reduced, or must recognise the whole of the will by taking his legacy in full and abandoning the land to X. Election is based on the presumption that a testator intends his will to take effect in its entirety.

The rule of English private international law is now well settled that, where a testator disposes of property in more countries than one, the question whether a beneficiary is put to his election is governed by the law of the testator's domicil.[7] This is so even though the subject-matter of the election is land situated abroad, for, though the courts of the domicil cannot withhold the land from the person to whom it belongs according to the law of the situs, they can, in the administration of the movables which is their particular province, insist that if he retains the land contrary to the will he shall compensate the disappointed beneficiaries by relinquishing the whole or part of the legacy.[8] The English court in adopting this attitude does not interfere with the law of the situs. The foreign heir comes to the court, not as heir to the land, over which the court has no jurisdiction, but as legatee of movable property which is being administered in England. It can thus be said to him: "We have no power to dispense with the provisions of the foreign law relating to wills of land, but you come to us as legatee under the will of a testator domiciled in England; and if you claim the legacy you must also recognise

---

7 *Orrell v Orrell* (1871) 6 Ch App 302; *Dewar v Maitland* (1866) LR 2 Eq 834; *Re Ogilvie* [1918] 1 Ch 492. This rule was overlooked by COHEN J in *Re Allen's Estate* [1945] 2 All ER 264, as to which case see *Re Mengel's Will Trusts* [1962] Ch 791; Dicey & Morris, pp 1028–1029; Morris (1945) 10 Conv (NS) 102; (1946) 24 Can BR 528.

8 There is a conflict of authority in the USA in the case of immovables as to whether the law of the domicil or the law of the situs applies: Leflar, p 557. The Restatement 2d, §242 supports the law of the situs. In the case of movables, whilst the predominant view is that expressed in the Restatement 2d, §265 that the law of the domicil applies, this conclusion has been justified by reference to a balancing of the predominant interests of the jurisdictions involved: *Re Clark's Estate* 21 NY 2d 478, 236 NE 2d 152 (1968); *Re Mulhern's Estate* 297 NYS 2d 485 (1969).

the disposition which the will has purported to make of the land." It is always open to the heir to ignore the English administration and to claim the land under the territorial law.[9]

If a case, then, involving the doctrine of election falls to be considered in England the court turns to the law of the testator's domicil. That domicil may be English or foreign. If it is English, the court merely considers whether the domestic doctrine of election is applicable to the circumstances in question; if it is foreign, its sole guide is the law of the foreign domicil.[10] In *Balfour v Scott*:[11]

A person domiciled in England died intestate leaving immovables in Scotland. The heir to the Scottish land was also one of the next of kin, and as such he claimed a share of the English movables. It was objected to this claim that by the law of Scotland an heir could not share in movables unless he consented to the immovables being massed with the movables so as to form one common subject of division. This, however, was not the English rule, and it was therefore held that the heir could take his share as one of the next of kin without complying with the rule of the law of the situs.

So far as concerns private international law the question of election generally arises where the testator devises his own land away from the heir by a will that is void, either formally or essentially, according to the law of the situs, but bequeaths by a valid will a legacy to the rejected heir. The question arises here whether the heir must elect, ie if he claims the land on the ground that the will is invalid, can he retain the legacy in full or must he make compensation out of it to the disappointed devisee?

This situation was possible in England prior to 1837 *in a purely domestic case*, for, until the law was altered by the Wills Act 1837, the formalities necessary for a valid will varied according as the subject-matter of the disposition was realty or personalty. In this state of the law it was established as early as 1749 in *Hearle v Greenbank*[12] that, if a testator devised his English freeholds to a stranger and bequeathed legacies to the heir-at-law in a will that was valid as to personalty but void as to realty, the heir was not bound to elect, unless there was an express direction that anyone who disputed any part of the will should forfeit all benefits.[13] He was entitled both to the land and to the legacies. Although this situation can no longer arise in the case of an English will disposing of English property, it may well do so where the testator is domiciled abroad. Suppose that:

A testator domiciled in Italy makes a will by which he devises his English entailed interests to X and bequeaths a legacy to Y, who is his heir-at-law according to English law. The will is formally valid by Italian law but ineffective by English law.

In such a case as this it has been held, following the principle of *Hearle v*

---

9 The present account of election is confined to a case where movables are bequeathed to the owner of the foreign land and in such a case the law of the domicil governs. If English land is left to the foreign heir and foreign land left away from the heir, then English law as that of the situs governs, irrespective of domicil.
10 *Dundas v Dundas* (1830) 2 Dow & Cl 349.
11 (1793) 6 Bro Parl Cas 550.
12 (1749) 1 Ves Sen 298.
13 *Boughton v Boughton* (1750) 2 Ves Sen 12.

Greenbank, that the English heir is not put to his election.[14] He can claim the land as heir against the invalid will of realty, and retain the legacy under the bequest which, since its validity falls to be determined by the law of the domicil, is invulnerable. This is an example of that "special tenderness" which the courts have always shown to the heir-at-law of English land,[15] though now that the heir has been abolished for fee simple estates in England it is doubtful whether a similar indulgence will be extended to those relatives who are entitled to the residuary estate of an intestate person. It is an inequitable privilege established by the courts at a time when they particularly favoured the heir-at-law and frowned on any attempt to defeat his rights.

This tenderness has never been shown to a foreign heir, ie to the heir entitled to take foreign land under the rules of intestate succession recognised by the law of the situs. The attitude of English law with regard to election in a case of this sort can be illustrated from *Re Ogilvie*,[16] where the facts were as follows:

A domiciled Englishwoman devised her land in Paraguay to a charity and gave legacies to the persons who were the obligatory heirs of the land according to Paraguayan law. The charitable devise was void by the law of the situs to the extent of four-fifths, which was the portion reserved for the obligatory heirs. Moreover, according to the law of the situs, the right of an heir to his legal portion was not affected by any other benefit that he might have received under the will.

In a case of this description, English law, as being the law of the testator's domicil, determines whether the foreign heir is to be put to his election. This raises the question of construction whether the testator has manifested an intention to pass the foreign land for, if he has, then despite the invalidity of the will by the law of the situs the doctrine of election becomes applicable.[17] The rule evolved by English courts on this matter is that the foreign property must be described either specifically or by necessary implication.[18] Thus, if a testator uses only general descriptive words, as for example where he says, "I devise all my estate, whatsoever or wheresoever, whether in possession or reversion", he is taken to intend that his disposition shall be restricted to such land as he is empowered to pass by a will executed in that particular form.[19] There was no difficulty of this sort in *Re Ogilvie*, since the testatrix had shown a plain intention to pass the Paraguayan property, and therefore it was held that the obligatory heirs must elect between what they took under the law of the situs owing to the invalidity of the charitable devise and what they were given in the shape of legacies by the will.[1]

(vi) Revocation

As with the case of a will of movables,[2] a will relating to immovables may be revoked by a later valid will and its validity will depend on the rules

14 *Re De Virte* [1915] 1 Ch 920.
15 *Re Ogilvie* [1918] 1 Ch 492 at 496.
16 [1918] 1 Ch 492.
17 *Trotter v Trotter* (1828) 5 Bli NS 502.
18 *Maxwell v Maxwell* (1852) 16 Beav 106; *Orell v Orell* (1871) 6 Ch App 302.
19 *Maxwell v Maxwell*, supra.
 1 Cf the Scottish decision in *Brown v Gregson* [1920] AC 860, where it was held that a foreign heir will not be put to his election if it would be impossible by the law of the situs to give effect to the disposition of the foreign land intended by the testator.
 2 Supra, pp 848–851.

discussed earlier.[3] It should be mentioned that the provisions of the Wills Act 1963 relating to the testamentary revocation of an earlier will apply to a will of immovables as to a will of movables.[4] In the case of revocation by destruction or obliteration of the will, there is United States authority for referring this issue to the law of the situs, as in *Re Barrie's Estate*[5] where the testatrix, who was domiciled in Illinois, wrote "void" across the will several times, and the effect of such an act was determined not by the law of Illinois but by that of Iowa, the situs of her immovable property.

Finally, in the case of revocation by subsequent marriage, we have seen[6] that, in the case of movables, such revocation is generally to be regarded as an aspect of matrimonial law to be governed by the domiciliary law at the time of marriage rather than of death. Such an approach would indicate that, in the case of the revocation of a will of immovables by a subsequent marriage, reference should also be made to the law of the domicil at marriage and not to the law of the situs. Despite one English decision to the contrary,[7] it is suggested that the view just expressed is correct and support for it is to be found in the Australian decision of *Re Micallef's Estate:*[8]

> The testator, who was at all material times domiciled and resident in Malta, owned land in New South Wales. In 1970 he made a valid will disposing of all his property, including the land. He married in Malta in 1972 and died in 1973. Under Maltese law, the marriage did not revoke the will; under New South Wales law it did.

The court could find no policy justifying the imposition of New South Wales law on Maltese parties to a Maltese marriage. Furthermore, there was no justification for departing from the rule applicable to movable property:

> I can see no logical or other reason for making any distinction between movable and immovable property in applying the foreign law relating to the marriage and its consequences to a will of one of the parties to the marriage. If marriage is the reason for the rule in England and English law recognises the foreign law of the marriage as governing the parties to the marriage, the nature or location of the property dealt with by the will is immaterial.[9]

4. POWERS OF APPOINTMENT EXERCISED BY WILL[10]

Under English law, instead of disposing directly of his property, a person, either in a settlement or in his will, can nominate a person who, in his own will,[11] shall have the power to specify the ultimate recipient of the property which is the subject matter of the original settlement or will. For example A in his will could leave the property to trustees to pay the income to B and then to transfer the capital to whoever B, in his will, appointed. In this case, A is described as the donor of the power of appointment and B is the donee

---

3 Supra, pp 852 et seq.
4 1963 Act, s 2(1)(c), supra, pp 848–849.
5 240 Iowa 431, 35 NW 2d 658 (1949).
6 Supra, pp 849–851.
7 *Re Caithness* (1891) 7 TLR 354.
8 [1977] 2 NSWLR 929; and see *Davies v Davies* (1915) 24 DLR 737 at 740.
9 Ibid, at 933.
10 Fridman (1960) 9 ICLQ 1.
11 It could also be a further settlement, inter vivos, but our concern here is with powers exercised by will.

of the power, or appointor. Whoever B selects as the beneficiary is described as the appointee.

There are two kinds of powers of appointment—general and special—and we shall see that this may be of significance in determining the appropriate choice of law rules. If the donee of the power, B in the above example, can appoint anyone he chooses, including himself, the power is general. If, however, the donor of the power, A, limits, in the instrument creating the power, the people or class of people among whom B can appoint, the power is special. One significance of the difference is that in the case of a special power B, the appointor, is clearly seen to be disposing of A's property, rather than his own, for A, the donee, has determined the class within which B must choose. In the case of a general power, though it may still in strict theory be true that B is disposing of A's property, this is more apparent than real, as B has the same freedom of choice as if the property was his own, including the power to appoint himself.

Choice of law problems may arise from powers of appointment exercised by will in a number of ways. It may be that the donor, the appointor and appointee all have different domicils. Whilst it might seem logical to refer the essential validity of, for instance, the will of the donor which created the power (the instrument of creation) to the law of his domicil on death and the validity of the exercise of the power by will (the instrument of appointment) to the law of the donee's domicil on death, problems arise if the donee dies domiciled in a civil law country, such as France, where the concept of a power of appointment is unknown. The only practical answer would seem to be to refer to the law governing the instrument of creation. There is the further problem that, in the case of immovables, the law of the situs may be different from that of any of the relevant domicils, though most of the cases are in fact concerned with movables.[12]

It can readily be argued that the law governing the instrument of creation should govern in the case of a special power, for the donee is manifestly no more than the agent for disposal of the appointor's property. As we have seen, this is less obviously true in the case of a general power which then poses a preliminary choice of law problem. If the main choice of law rule may depend on whether a power is special or general, by what law is that issue to be determined? After examining that question, we shall consider the other more general choice of law matters relating to powers of appointment exercised by will.

(a) SPECIAL AND GENERAL POWERS

It is not always easy in a domestic system of law to decide whether a power is general or special.[13] Furthermore, and more significantly, different legal systems which are familiar with powers of appointment may classify them differently.[14] As a matter of principle, it seems right that the nature of the power, ie as to whether it is special or general, should be determined by the law governing the instrument which created the power.

---

12 It should be assumed that the discussion relates to movables, unless immovables are referred to.
13 Eg Megarry and Wade, *The Law of Real Property*, 5th edn (1984), pp 491–492.
14 See Dicey & Morris, p 1049.

(b) CAPACITY

Considerations different from those relevant to testamentary capacity[15] apply to the question of capacity to exercise a testamentary power of appointment given by an English instrument to an appointor domiciled abroad. The obvious principle here is that, just as in the case where a testator disposes of his own property, capacity must be tested by the law of the appointor's domicil. There is indeed no doubt that, if the domiciliary law's rule on the matter is satisfied, the appointment is good. It is enough, whether the power is general or special, that the appointor is of full capacity by the law of his own domicil, even though he is incapable by the law that governs the instrument by which the power was created, ie the will. For example, in *Re Lewal's Settlement Trusts*,[16] the wife had a general power of appointment under an English marriage settlement. She had originally been domiciled in England but on her marriage had acquired the French domicil of her husband. In her will, made when she was aged 19, she appointed her husband her "legataire universel", and ten years later she died domiciled in France. Under English law, she had no capacity to exercise the power, being under twenty one; under French law, she was capable of disposing of half the property she could have disposed of had she been twenty one. The court applied French law[17] to the issue of her capacity, with the result that half the property subject to the power went to her husband, and the other half went as in default of appointment.

But this does not conclude the matter. What of the converse case, ie where the appointor has capacity by the law governing the instrument by which the power was created, but not under the law of his domicil? The view taken by English law is that the instrument which creates the power, not the one by which the power is exercised, is the governing instrument, and that the appointor is a mere agent to carry out the wishes of the donor. The appointee takes under the instrument of creation, not under the will of the appointor. It follows, therefore, that an appointment is valid if the appointor has capacity by the law that governs the instrument of creation, though he may be incapable by the law of his own domicil. It may well be objected that even if the appointor is regarded as merely the agent of the donor he should not be free to do what, according to the law to which he is subject, he is incapable of doing. Nevertheless, to treat him as an agent is not unreasonable in the case of a special power, for here, as has been seen, his function is to select the beneficiaries from the class already designated by the donor. He is in no sense disposing of his own property. But there is little to justify a reference to the law governing the instrument of creation in the case of a general power, for the appointor in such a case can scarcely be regarded as a mere agent to implement the wishes of the donor.

The correct rule probably is, therefore, that the testamentary exercise of a general power is invalid for want of capacity unless the appointor is capable by the law of his domicil; but that in the case of a special power the exercise is valid if he is capable either by the law of his domicil or by the law that governs the instrument of creation.[18]

15 Supra, pp 838–839, 852.
16 [1918] 2 Ch 391.
17 The English marriage settlement did also provide that the appointment should be made by will "executed in such manner as to be valid according to the law of" the appointor's domicil.
18 Cf Scoles & Hay, p 816; Fridman (1960) 9 ICLQ 1, 2–11. For a full discussion of the whole subject see Dicey & Morris, pp 1039–1041.

(c) FORMAL VALIDITY

A power of appointment exercisable by will is frequently given by an English settlement or an English will to a person who ultimately dies domiciled in a foreign country or who makes his will in a foreign country. In such a case it is essential to ascertain the legal system that determines whether the formalities attending the testamentary exercise of the power are sufficient. The Wills Act 1963 has extended and amended the previous law. The position now is as follows.

First, a will so far as it exercises a power of appointment is to be treated as properly executed if it complies with the requirements of any one of the legal systems specified in the Act.[19] Thus the connecting factors now qualified to determine the governing law are the place of execution of the will or the nationality, domicil or habitual residence of the testator or the law of the situs in the case of immovables.

Secondly, the will is to be treated as properly executed if its execution conforms to the law that governs the essential validity of the instrument creating the power.[20] If the power is created by an English instrument, it will be validly executed if it conforms with English law;[1] and if creation is by a foreign instrument, then there should be conformity with that foreign law.[2]

There is a further provision in the 1963 Act, resolving some tiresome problems in the law before 1964,[3] that the testamentary exercise of a power of appointment is not formally invalid by reason only of a failure to observe a formality required by the instrument of creation.[4]

(d) ESSENTIAL VALIDITY

The determination of the law to govern the essential validity of a disposition resulting from the exercise of a power of appointment depends on whether the power is general or special. The effect of the appointment in the case of a special power is determined by the legal system to which the instrument that created the power is subject, for, since the appointor is merely the agent through whom the donor of the power designates the beneficiaries, the latter take under the instrument of creation.

> But the power in this case is a special power, and the execution of such a power does not bring the appointed property into the will of the appointor at all, but operates as a nomination of the persons whose names are to be inserted in the settlement as entitled in remainder in lieu of the power of appointment. There is therefore no disposition of property belonging to the testatrix.[5]

In the case in which these words were spoken:

> A domiciled Frenchwoman, who had a special power of appointment given by an English settlement, was held capable under English law of exercising it in a manner that was incompatible with the French doctrine of community.

In the case of general powers, the property given thereunder may be treated

19 Supra, pp 839–843, 852–853.
20 Wills Act 1963, s 2(1) (d). Essential validity of wills is discussed, supra, pp 844–847, 853.
 1 Eg *Murphy v Deichler* [1909] AC 446.
 2 See (1958) Cmnd 491, para 11(c).
 3 See, eg, *Barretto v Young* [1900] 2 Ch 339.
 4 Wills Act 1963, s 2(2).
 5 *Pouey v Hordern* [1900] 1 Ch 492 at 494.

by the donee either as if it were his own, ie as a mass combined with his own, or quite separately therefrom. It is a question of construction as to how it is to be considered.[6] In the first case, where the donee treats the settled property as his own, the Court of Appeal in *Re Pryce*[7] held that the operation and effect of the donee's appointment must be determined by the law that governs the will by which he exercises the power, ie by the law of his last domicil. DANCKWERTS J in *Re Waite's Settlement*[8] preferred to apply the law governing the instrument creating the power, rather than the law of the donee's domicil, despite the fact that the case related to a general power where the funds were massed, but his decision was disapproved in *Re Khan's Settlement*.[9] The facts of that case were:

> The testator, the Nawab of Bhopal, domiciled in India, made a settlement in which he reserved to himself a general power of appointment by will. This settlement was to be governed by English law, apart from a clause referring to his heirs under Indian law. His English will gave legacies to three of his seven heirs, in excess of the free estate under the will, and then executed the power of appointment in favour of all his heirs. Under Indian law, the domiciliary law, the consent of all heirs was necessary before payment of legacies to any heirs could be made, and this consent was refused. Thus, if Indian law governed, the legacies could not be paid out of the free estate or the settlement funds, whilst there was no such restriction under English law, the law governing the instrument of creation.

RUSSELL LJ concluded that he was bound to follow *Re Pryce*[10] rather than *Re Waite's Settlement*.[11] He decided that the free estate and the settled fund formed one mass, the distribution of which was to be governed by Indian law, and the legacies could not be paid. He thought

> it a logical consequence of the grounds of those decisions in cases of blending or massing ... that the settled funds are subjected to the whole succession law of the domicile of the appointor, including any restriction on testation.[12]

If in the case of a general power the settled funds are not treated as having been taken out of the settlement and massed with the donee's own funds, then, as in *Re Mégret*,[13] the validity of the exercise of the power of appointment is governed, not by the law of the domicil of the donee, but by the law governing the instrument of creation, as in the case of special powers. This can be justified on the ground that in neither of these cases is the donee in reality disposing of his own funds.

The cases so far discussed all concern movable property. In the case of the essential validity of the exercise by will of a general power of appointment over immovables, there is clear authority that this should be governed by the law of the situs of the property.[14]

---

6 *Re Pryce* [1911] 2 Ch 286 at 295.
7 Ibid; and see *Re Lewal's Settlement Trusts* [1918] 2 Ch 391.
8 [1958] Ch 100, [1957] 1 All ER 629; and see *Re McMorran* [1958] Ch 624 at 633–634; for criticisms, see Dicey & Morris, pp 1048–1049.
9 [1966] Ch 567, [1966] 1 All ER 160; cf *Re Fenston's Settlement* [1971] 1 WLR 1640 at 1647.
10 [1911] 2 Ch 286.
11 Supra.
12 [1966] Ch 567 at 578.
13 [1901] 1 Ch 547; and see *Re Pryce* [1911] 2 Ch 286 at 296–297; cf Fridman (1960) 9 ICLQ 1, 9–10.
14 *Re Hernando* (1884) 27 ChD 284; and see *Murray v Champernowne* [1901] 2 IR 232.

(e) CONSTRUCTION

In accordance with the principle applicable to wills generally, the construction of a power of appointment is governed by the law intended by the testator [or appointor] which, in the case of movables, is presumed to be that of his domicil when the will was made.[15] This appears to be true whether the power is special[16] or general.[17] If it appears that the testator intended a law other than that of his domicil at the time of making the will to apply, as in *Re Price*,[18] then that other law governs the construction.

But the question has arisen whether the intention of the testator is decisive if it indicates a foreign law that has no knowledge of powers.

Suppose, for instance, that a testator, domiciled in France and having a general power of appointment by virtue of an English settlement, makes a valid will according to French law. The will does not refer in any way to the power but merely disposes of the property in general words. A power to dispose of property not belonging to the donor (which is the true nature of a power of appointment) is unknown to French law.[19] The will, therefore, if construed according to French law, can scarcely be said to constitute an execution of the power. Can English law be applied to the issue of construction?

After considerable judicial conflict this question has been answered in the affirmative.[20] The French court, being ignorant of the peculiar power of disposition thus given by an English instrument, would have to turn to English law (with reference to which the testator obviously wrote) in order to ascertain the nature of the right and the manner in which it might be exercised.

A consequence of this conclusion is that section 27 of the Wills Act 1837 may apply to wills of persons domiciled other than in England. Under section 27 a general devise or bequest is construed as exercising a general power of appointment unless a contrary intention appears in the will. In the above example, the testator's French will falls to be construed in accordance with section 27 as exercising a general power of appointment.[1] Were the power merely special, it would not be held to be exercised under section 27.

(f) REVOCATION

A power of appointment over movables exercisable by will may be revoked under the law of the donee's domicil.[2] A power over movables or immovables will be revoked if it is revoked by a later will properly executed under the

---

15 Supra, pp 847–848.
16 *Re McMorran* [1958] Ch 624; and see *Re Walker* [1908] 1 Ch 560.
17 *Durie's Trustees v Osborne* 1960 SC 444; Gareth Jones (1961) 10 ICLQ 624.
18 [1900] 1 Ch 442; and see *Mitchell and Baxter v Davies* (1875) 3 R (Ct of Sess) 208.
19 Contrast the position in Scotland: *Re McMorran* [1958] Ch 624 at 634–635; *Durie's Trustees v Osborne*, supra.
20 *Re Simpson* [1916] 1 Ch 502; *Re Wilkinson's Settlement* [1917] 1 Ch 620; *Re Lewal's Settlement* [1918] 2 Ch 391; *Re Waite's Settlement* [1958] Ch 100; *Re Fenston's Settlement* [1971] 3 All ER 1092. Decisions to the contrary are *Re D'Estes' Settlement Trusts* [1903] 1 Ch 898; *Re Scholefield* [1905] 2 Ch 408.
 1 Eg *Re Lewal's Settlement*, supra; cf *Re Fenston's Settlement*, supra, where the will, as construed by the law of the domicil, contained no "bequest" to anyone.
 2 *Velasco v Coney* [1934] P 143. Presumably, compliance with the law of the situs is required in the case of immovables.

Wills Act 1963.[3] Under section 2(1)(d) of the 1963 Act,[4] a will so far as it exercises a power of appointment is validly executed if it complies with the law governing the essential validity of the power. This does not apply, however, to a will which merely revokes a power of appointment without providing another power in its place. Finally a power exercisable by will may be revoked by the subsequent marriage of the testator according to the law of his domicil at the time of his marriage, rather than of his death.[5] Where, however, the testator is domiciled in England at the time of his marriage then, under section 18(2) of the Wills Act 1837,[6] an exercise of a power of appointment by will takes effect, "notwithstanding the subsequent marriage unless the property so appointed would in default of appointment pass to his personal representatives".

3 Ss 1, 2(1)(b), (c), supra, pp 839–843, 852–853.
4 Supra, p 862.
5 Supra, pp 849–851, 859.
6 As substituted by the Administration of Justice Act 1982, s 18.

Chapter 34

Matrimonial property[1]

1. INTRODUCTION

The problem that confronts us in this chapter is how to determine what system of law regulates the rights of a husband and wife in the movable and immovable property which either of them may possess at the time of marriage or may acquire afterwards. Important consequences may ensue according as this or that law is chosen. For instance, the result of choosing one particular legal system may be that the property of the wife passes entirely to the husband, as was substantially the case in England prior to 1883. Again, if an Englishwoman marries a Belgian and Belgian law is regarded as the governing system, it may be that the parties become subject to "community of goods" under which everything that belongs to either spouse at the time of marriage or that is acquired by either afterwards is owned by them jointly. They become joint co-owners of everything by the mere fact of marriage.[2]

In determining the choice of law rules for identifying the appropriate matrimonial property regime, it will be necessary to look separately at two types of case—first where the parties have not made an ante-nuptial contract and, secondly, where there is such a contract.

---

1 Marsh, *Marital Property in the Conflict of Laws* (1952); Goldberg (1970) 19 ICLQ 557; McLachlan (1986) 12 NZULRev.66; Scoles (1988) II Hague Recueil 9, 17–53. There is a Hague Convention on the Law Applicable to Matrimonial Property (1976) but it has not been signed by the United Kingdom: see Philip (1976) 24 AJCL 307; Glenn (1977) 54 Can BR 586.

2 For a valuable exposition of the different systems found in the world see Rheinstein and Glendon, *International Encyclopedia of Comparative Law*, vol iv, ch 4 (1980), pp 47–118. There is a tendency in civil law countries now to allow the spouses the separate administration of their property during marriage, but to constitute the community of property on death or divorce; for France, see Amos and Walton, *Introduction to French Law*, 3rd edn (1966), pp 379–392; for Germany, see Leyser (1958) 7 AJCL 276.

2. ASSIGNMENT WHERE THERE IS NO ANTE-NUPTIAL CONTRACT[3]

(a) MOVABLES

The primary rule is that the effect of marriage on the proprietary rights of the parties in movables is determined by the law of the husband's domicil. In the words of LINDLEY MR:

> It is not necessary to cite authorities to shew that it is now settled that, according to international law as understood and administered in England, the effect of marriage on the movable property of spouses depends (in the absence of any contract) on the domicil of the husband in the English sense.[4]

This statement,[5] clear though it appears on the surface, raises two problems that, owing to the scarcity of authority, are by no means easy to solve. First, what is meant by "the law of the husband's domicil"? Secondly, what is the effect if the law of the husband's domicil is subsequently changed?

(i) Application of law of husband's domicil

According to the traditional view, the determining domicil is that which the husband possesses *at the time of the marriage*.[6] On the whole it is an unobjectionable view, for in the vast majority of cases the matrimonial home is established in the country where the husband is domiciled before the marriage and is retained by the parties throughout their joint lives.

An alternative solution is to submit the question to the law of the intended matrimonial domicil.[7] There must no doubt be a presumption that the rights of a husband and wife to each other's movables are governed by the law of the husband's domicil at the time of the marriage. But it can be argued that this presumption should be rebutted if, in pursuance of their previous agreement, the parties in fact acquire a fresh domicil within a reasonable time after the marriage. The merit of this approach to the problem is that it meets the not unusual case where the parties intend to settle immediately after marriage in another country and in fact do so.

That a rigid application of the law of the husband's domicil at the time of the marriage may cause hardship can be illustrated by the facts of the South African case, *Frankel's Estate v The Master*:[8]

> H, whose domicil of origin was German, and W, domiciled in Czechoslovakia, were married in Czechoslovakia in 1933. At the time of the

---

3 Cf Goldberg (1970) 19 ICLQ 557 who maintains that there is always a contract which may be express, implied or presumed.

4 *Re Martin, Loustalan v Loustalan* [1900] P 211 at 233. For an example of the application of this rule see *Re Bettinson's Question* [1956] Ch 67, [1955] 3 All ER 296; and see *Razelos v Razelos (No 2)* [1970] 1 All ER 386 n, [1970] 1 WLR 392. There are statutory choice of law rules in Canada, as in Ontario where the law to be applied is usually that of the parties' last common habitual residence: Family Law Act 1986, s 15; and see *Pershadsingh v Pershadsingh* (1988) 40 DLR (4th) 681; *Mittler v Mittler* (1988) 17 RFL (3d) 113.

5 The statement, like choice of law rules generally, is subject to the application of a foreign law not being contrary to the public policy of the forum: *Vladi v Vladi* (1987) 39 DLR (4th) 563.

6 Dicey & Morris, pp 1066–1067; Westlake, s 36; *Welch v Tennent* [1891] AC 639 at 644. For a case where a retrospective change in the law to a community regime was accepted, see *Topolski v R* (1978) 90 DLR (3d) 66.

7 *Corbet v Waddell* (1879) 7 R (Ct. of Sess) 200 at 208; and see Anton, pp 585–586; Story, paras 191–199; Westlake, s 36.

8 1950 (1) SA 220 (AD), analysed by Ellison Kahn (1950) 3 ILQ 439.

marriage the parties had definitely agreed that they would leave Europe for good and settle permanently in Johannesburg. They established their home in that city four months after the marriage. After working there for four years, they moved to Durban with the intention of remaining there permanently. Eleven years later, H died. According to the law of South Africa, the parties had married in community of property, but according to German law the doctrine of community was inapplicable. If South African law applied, as W claimed, death duties were not payable. The Appellate Division of the Supreme Court of South Africa held unanimously that German law applied.

Thus the proprietary rights of the parties were subjected to the law of Germany, a country which the husband had abandoned and which, it may be surmised, he would be little inclined to revisit. He was to this extent indelibly impressed against his will and against the will of his wife with the civil status of a German. Indeed, South African courts have applied the law of the domicil at marriage including retrospective changes in that law effected after the spouses had become domiciled in South Africa.[9] On the other hand, reliance on the intended matrimonial domicil does suffer from the disadvantage, here as elsewhere,[10] that it may not have been acquired yet, and, that being so, there is no certainty that it will ever be acquired.

Whether the test of the intended matrimonial domicil is accepted by English law was not squarely raised until the case of *Re Egerton's Will Trusts*,[11] where ROXBURGH J stated the law to this effect:

> There is a presumption that the mutual property rights of spouses are determined by the law of the husband's domicil at the time of the marriage. This presumption may be rebutted by an express contract that some other law shall apply.[12] Further, rebuttal may be inferred from the conduct of the parties if the circumstances justify the inference.

Thus, it is now judicially admitted that the law of the husband's domicil at the time of the marriage will be ousted if the intention to adopt the law of another domicil can be spelt out of the facts of the particular case. A tacit agreement is sufficient to rebut the primary presumption.

But what the judge repudiated is the suggestion that an ante-nuptial agreement to establish the matrimonial home in another country, even though carried out with reasonable promptitude, is per se sufficient to rebut the presumption and to let in the law of the new domicil. To have this effect, the circumstances must warrant the inference that the parties intended not merely to acquire a new domicil, but also to subject their proprietary rights to the law of that domicil. The judgment makes it clear that everything must turn on the precise facts of each case, including the reliability of the evidence by which the alleged agreement to change the domicil is supported, the length of time that may have elapsed before the fulfilment of that agreement and even the financial circumstances of the spouses.[13]

In *Egerton's Case* itself the particular circumstances did not warrant any such inference. The facts were these:

In 1932, the testator domiciled in England married a woman domiciled in

9 *Sperling v Sperling* 1975 (3) SA 707 (AD).
10 This is discussed generally, supra, pp 588–589.
11 [1956] Ch 593, [1956] 2 All ER 817; Carter (1957) 33 BYBIL 345.
12 *Re Martin, Loustalan v Loustalan* [1900] P 211 at 240.
13 [1956] Ch 593 at 605, [1956] 2 All ER 817 at 824.

France. The parties agreed, before the marriage, to settle in France, but the testator did not acquire a French domicil until some time after September, 1934, which he retained until his death. The question to be decided was whether his estate should be administered on the footing that he and his wife were subject to the French regime of community of property at the time of the marriage.

ROXBURGH J held that the parties' agreement to settle in France did not render their proprietary rights subject to French law. The equivocal nature of the agreement which contemplated no immediate change of home, but only one that should be effected "as soon as possible"; the long period that in fact elapsed before the new domicil was acquired; the lack of any evidence that the parties even appreciated the difference between the property regimes of the two countries: all these precluded the inference that in the minds of the parties the law of England was to be supplanted by that of France. On the other hand, it is submitted that in *Frankel's Case* the only reasonable intention to attribute to the parties was to sever all links with the German domicil of origin of the husband as quickly as possible.[14]

Although it has been assumed so far that the choice of the governing law lies between that of the husband's domicil and that of the intended matrimonial home, it must not be forgotten that a wife has been capable of acquiring a domicil independent of her husband since 1974.[15] The effect of this may be that the courts will be more inclined to select a law other than that of the husband's domicil to govern the rights of husband and wife to movable property.

(ii) Effect of a change of domicil

Even though it may be clear what is meant by "the law of the husband's domicil", a second question may arise—What is the effect of a subsequent change of the marriage domicil? Are the mutual proprietary rights of the spouses affected by the change? Many legal systems adopt what has been called the doctrine of immutability,[16] according to which the rights of property in movables as fixed by the law of the marriage domicil are unaffected by the acquisition of a fresh domicil. Thus the established rule in France is that the law of the matrimonial domicil governs the rights of the spouses in movables, whether existing at the time of marriage or acquired later, and continues to govern them despite a change of domicil. This is so even with respect to movables acquired in the new domicil.[17] The prevailing rule in the United States is not so comprehensive. The law of the marriage domicil continues to govern movables owned at the time of marriage, but movables acquired later are subject to the law of the parties' domicil at the time of acquisition.[18]

---

14 *Devos v Devos* (1970) 10 DLR (3d) 603 might similarly be criticised, for there the matrimonial domicil was held to be Belgian, where the husband was domiciled at the time of the marriage, even though the parties emigrated to Canada less than three months later. Contrast *Vien Estate v Vien Estate* (1988) 49 DLR (4th) 558.
15 Domicile and Matrimonial Proceedings Act 1973, s 1.
16 Wolff, pp 360–361.
17 Batiffol & Lagarde, *Droit international privé*, 7th edn (1983), vol II, pp 356–365; and see Juenger (1981) 81 Col LR 1061, 1062–1066.
18 Scoles and Hay, pp 456–461; Juenger, op cit; cf Restatement 2d §258 which adopts a "most significant relationship" test, though retaining emphasis on the law of the domicil at the time of acquisition; see *Re Crichton's Estate* 20 NY 2d 124, 228 NE 2d 799 (1967) (the Louisiana courts have been constrained by the US Constitution to uphold this decision despite their clear view that the New York decision was erroneous: *Crichton v Successor of Crichton* 232 So 2d 109 (1970); though see now La Civ Code 2334 (1980)); cf *Wyatt v Fulrath* 16 NY 2d 169, 211 NE 2d 673 (1965).

It has been said that, according to English private international law, if the marriage domicil is abandoned, the proprietary rights of the spouses are governed by the law of the new domicil. It is extremely doubtful, however, whether English law is committed to this doctrine of mutability.[19] The one case invariably cited in its support is the Scots decision in *Lashley v Hog*,[20] but when analysed this appears to be quite irrelevant to the controversy. The facts were these:

> Hog, a native of Scotland, married an Englishwoman at a time when he was domiciled in England. There was no marriage settlement. After living fifteen years in England the parties acquired a domicil in Scotland. Hog survived his wife and died in 1789. After his death, his daughter, Mrs Lashley, brought an action in the Scottish court claiming as the representative of her mother a share in her father's movables which, according to the then law of Scotland, were subject to the doctrine of community of goods. The basis of her claim was that, on the change of domicil from England to Scotland, her father's proprietary rights vis-à-vis his wife became restricted by the Scottish rule of community.

The House of Lords held that Scottish law governed Mrs Lashley's claim, and that she was entitled in right of her mother to a share of the movables owned by her father at the time of her mother's death.[21]

What was the ratio decidendi? Was it that the rights of the wife with regard to the matrimonial property were enlarged as a result of the change of domicil? It would seem not. The view of the House of Lords was that the matter "turned on testamentary and not on matrimonial law".[1] The so-called community of goods did not give the wife on marriage a proprietary interest similar to that recognised, for instance, by Belgian law, but only a hope of succeeding to the property.[2] The question therefore, was not: Were the rights of the wife enlarged by the change of domicil? but, What were the succession rights of the wife or her representative on the death of her husband? Thus Lord HALSBURY, speaking of the decision in a later case, said:

> If the wife by the marriage in Scotland[3] acquired no proprietary rights whatever, but only what is called a hope of a certain distribution upon the husband's death, it is intelligible that that right of distribution, or by whatever name it is called, should be dependent upon the husband's domicil, as following the ordinary rule that the law of a person's domicil regulates the succession of his movable property. But if by the marriage the wife acquires as part of that contract relation a real proprietary right, it would be quite unintelligible that the husband's act[4] should dispose of what was not his; and herein, I think, is to be found the key to Lord ELDON's judgment.[5]

The last sentence of this statement is a repudiation of the doctrine of mutability, for if the wife's acquired rights cannot be defeated by a change of domicil, neither can they be enlarged.

A more decisive authority than *Lashley v Hog* must be found, then, before

---

19 Marsh, op cit, pp 103–108.
20 (1804) 4 Paton 581; analysed by Goldberg (1970) 19 ICLQ 557, 580–584.
21 See now the Married Women's Property (Scotland) Act 1920, s 7.
 1 Westlake, p 74; cf Dicey & Morris, pp 1068–1071.
 2 Falconbridge (1937) 53 LQR 537, 539–540. For the purposes of private international law, it is treated in Scotland as a right of succession; Anton, pp 672–673.
 3 The marriage in fact took place in London.
 4 Ie the act of changing his domicil.
 5 *De Nicols v Curlier* [1900] AC 21 at 27.

it can be categorically asserted that the proprietary relations between husband and wife change with a change of their domicil (the doctrine of mutability). It is a strong assertion to make, for, as Westlake says, "justice is shocked by allowing the husband to affect the wife's position by a change for which he does not require her assent",[6] and which, of course, now does not affect her domicil. What is shocking is suspect, and it is in fact doubtful whether English law has adopted the doctrine of mutability to its full extent.

The law, then, is far from certain, but nevertheless an attempt must be made to state the modern rule. The clue to it seems to be the distinction between inchoate and vested rights. Even if the doctrine of mutability is part of English law it can scarcely operate without restriction, for not only justice but principle demands that a spouse shall not by reason of a change of domicil be divested of a right of property actually acquired under the law of the marriage domicil, even though enjoyment of the right may be postponed until the death of the other spouse.[7] Under the Dutch system of community of goods, for instance, all movables belonging to husband and wife fall on marriage into the common ownership of both. Thus, on marriage, the wife becomes co-owner of movables then belonging to the husband. She also becomes co-owner of future movables when and as they are acquired.[8] If parties domiciled in the Netherlands at the time of marriage acquire a fresh domicil in England where the husband dies, the wife cannot on principle be deprived by her husband's will of what she owned when she reached England. No doubt the will of her husband, since he dies domiciled in England, is governed by English law, and English internal law does not recognise community of goods, but that cannot entitle him to dispose of what is not his. His power of testamentary disposition is limited by the extent of his title. If he dies intestate, his distributable assets are diminished by the rights of property therein owned by his wife.

But vested rights must be distinguished from those that are inchoate. When the Dutch couple change their domicil from the Netherlands to England, it cannot be said that either of them has a vested right of property in movables not yet acquired. At the most they have the hope of acquiring. It is a hope that is not recognised by the law to which they are now subject and which alone can make its voice effective. If, therefore, it should ultimately be decided that the proprietary rights of spouses change with a change in their domicil, this would presumably be subject to the exception that rights vested in either party under the law of some previous domicil remain unaffected. Indeed this view has been accepted in Canadian courts:

> The law appears to be that the mutual rights of husband and wife as to personal property are governed by the law of the matrimonial domicile, and such rights are not affected by a subsequent change, but rights acquired after such change are, of course, governed by the law of the actual domicile.[9]

The solution that the rights of the spouses in movable property change with a change of domicil, though leaving acquired rights unaffected, is complicated by the provision of the law of domicil whereby a wife may now have a domicil

6 *Private International Law* (7th edn), p 73.
7 Dicey & Morris, pp 1068–1071.
8 Rheinstein and Glendon, *International Encyclopedia of Comparative Law*, vol iv, ch 4 (1980), pp 52–57.
9 *Pink v Perlin & Co* (1898) 40 NSR 260 at 262; *Re Heung Won Lee* (1963) 36 DLR (2d) 177.

independent of that of her husband.[10] To continue our example of spouses domiciled at marriage in the Netherlands, if only one spouse later becomes domiciled in England, the other remaining domiciled in the Netherlands, the court will be faced with the difficult question whether after-acquired property is governed by English law or by the community rules of Dutch law. It seems wrong that the rights of the spouse domiciled in the Netherlands should be prejudiced by the other spouse's change of domicil and it is suggested that only when both spouses abandon their Dutch domicil should the community regime be abandoned also.

(b) IMMOVABLES

Discussion so far has been concerned with the effect of marriage on the spouses' movable property in the absence of a marriage contract. The leading decision in relation to immovables is *Welch v Tennent*,[11] a Scottish appeal to the House of Lords whose facts were these:

> Husband and wife were domiciled in Scotland. The wife owned land in England which she sold with her husband's agreement and the proceeds of sale were paid to him. Later the parties separated and the wife claimed that the proceeds of sale be paid to her, arguing that under Scots law she was entitled to recall any donation made by her to her husband.

Lord HERSCHELL disposed very rapidly of the argument that Scots law might be applied, saying:

> The rights of the spouses as regards movable property must, in the circumstances of this case be regulated by the law of Scotland, but it is equally clear that their rights in relation to heritable estate are governed by the law of the place where it is situate.[12]

English law was applied and the husband was entitled to keep the proceeds of sale of the land.

3. ASSIGNMENT WHERE THERE IS AN ANTE-NUPTIAL CONTRACT

(a) THE GENERAL RULE

When we turn to the situation where the parties have entered an ante-nuptial contract,[13] it must be borne in mind that the choice of law issues which may arise are governed by common law rules. This is because the Rome Convention on the Law Applicable to Contractual Obligations[14] does not apply to contractual obligations relating to "rights in property arising out of a matrimonial relationship".[15] If the parties have made an ante-nuptial contract to regulate their future proprietary relationship, then the difficulties, just discussed, concerning the identification of the governing laws or the effect of a change of domicil do not arise. The contract continues to govern

10 Supra, pp 163–165.
11 [1891] AC 639; and see *Callwood v Callwood* [1960] AC 659 at 683–684; *Tezcan v Tezcan* (1990) 68 DLR (4th) 277 at 284–285.
12 Ibid at 645.
13 Where an ante-nuptial agreement is embodied in a trust, as in *Re Fitzgerald* [1904] 1 Ch 573, the rules relating to the essential validity of trusts fall to be considered; see chapter 35.
14 Brought into force by the Contracts (Applicable Law) Act 1990, supra, pp 459 et seq.
15 Art 1(2) (b), supra, p 470.

the proprietary rights of the parties not only in the matrimonial domicil, but also in any other domicil that may later be acquired. It must be recognised no matter where it may be put in suit,[16] (subject to any overriding provisions of the law of the forum)[17] and it applies whether the property in question is movable[18] or immovable.[19] It may either define precisely what the rights shall be or state the system of law by which they are to be regulated.[20]

No distinction in this respect is made between an express and a tacit contract, as is illustrated by *De Nicols v Curlier*:[21]

H and W, French both by nationality and by domicil, were married in Paris without making an express contract as to their proprietary rights. Nine years after their marriage, they came to England, acquired a domicil here and prospered as the owners of the Cafe Royal, in Regent Street. The husband died in 1897 leaving a considerable fortune in movable and immovable property. In his will, he disposed of all of his property without taking account of the wife's entitlement to a half share in the property under the French system of community of property. The issue was whether the spouses' change of domicil from French to English affected their legal position in relation to the property.

The position of the movable property was considered by the House of Lords first, and separately from that of the immovables. The expert evidence accepted by the court was that according to French law parties who marry without an express marriage contract are bound by a tacit contract to abide by the system of community. Therefore, said Lord Macnaghten:

if there is a valid compact between spouses as to their property, whether it be constituted by the law of the land or by convention between the parties, it is difficult to see how that compact can be nullified or blotted out merely by a change of domicil.[22]

The question then arose whether the French contract or English law as that of the situs determined the rights of the surviving wife to the English immovables of her deceased husband. Kekewich J held,[23] after further argument, that the French implied contract must operate according to the intention of the parties so as to bind the immovable property of the deceased, unless there was any overriding rule of English law that would render it unenforceable. The only possible rule was the provision of section 4 of the Statute of Frauds 1677, requiring a written memorandum in the case of a contract concerning land;[24] but the judge held that, since this particular contract constituted a partnership between the spouses in the eyes of French law, it fell within the rule of English law that a parol agreement for a partnership is not caught by the statute and is enforceable despite the lack of written evidence. The accuracy of the view expressed by Kekewich J that the contract implied by French law included foreign immovables is open to

16 *Anstruther v Adair* (1834) 2 My & K 513; *Montgomery v Zarifi* (1919) 88 LJPC 20; *De Nicols v Curlier* [1900] AC 21 at 46; *Re Hannema's Marriage* (1981) 54 FLR 79.
17 Eg *Stark v Stark* (1988) 16 RFL (3d) 257.
18 *De Nicols v Curlier* [1900] AC 21.
19 *Re De Nicols* [1900] 2 Ch 410.
20 *Este v Smyth* (1854) 18 Beav 112.
21 [1900] AC 21.
22 Ibid, at 33.
23 *Re De Nicols* [1900] 2 Ch 410.
24 See now Law of Property (Miscellaneous Provisions) Act 1989, s 2.

doubt.[1] His decision might have been based more surely on counsel's other argument, namely that the land represented the investment of money acquired by the husband during marriage, and that the wife could follow the money, to which she was admittedly entitled, into whatsoever form it had been converted.

Support for the application to immovables of the law governing the ante-nuptial contract is provided by *Chiwell v Carlyon*,[2] a case which appeared before both the English and the South African courts.

In 1887 H married W at Kimberley in South Africa. No express ante-nuptial contract was made. The parties were domiciled at the time in South Africa, and while still so domiciled they made a joint will disposing of their joint estate, ie of the movables and immovables that they held in community. In 1892, after the parties had settled in England, certain land in Cornwall was bought by H and conveyed to him. W died in 1893, H in 1895.

The question that arose before the Chancery Division was whether the Cornish land passed under the will of the joint estate. STIRLING J felt that the law of the previous domicil at the time of their marriage could not be disregarded and he submitted two questions to the Supreme Court in the Cape of Good Hope. The second[3] question was this:

Assuming H and W to have been domiciled in South Africa at the time of their marriage, but subsequently to have acquired an English domicil before the purchase of the land, would this change have any effect by South African law on their respective rights in regard to the land?

The Supreme Court held that this question must be answered in the negative. The marriage created a universal partnership between husband and wife in all property, movable and immovable, belonging to either of them before marriage or coming to either during marriage.

It is competent [said DE VILLIERS CJ] for the intended spouses, before marriage, to regulate their respective rights by express contract, but in the absence of such an express contract, they are understood to enter into a tacit contract that community of property between them shall prevail.[4]

This tacit contract of community extended to foreign land. It was unaffected by a change of domicil.

On receipt of this opinion from the South African court, STIRLING J decided that

in any event the joint estate passing under the said will includes all property which according to the law of the Cape of Good Hope would fall within the community of property which would have been created by the marriage of the testator and testatrix, if they were domiciled at the Cape of Good Hope at the time of their marriage.[5]

1 Or indeed that French law would today consider there was a tacit contract in such a case; see Nygh, pp 382–383.
2 (1897) 14 SC 61 (South Africa); and see *Tezcan v Tezcan* (1990) 68 DLR (4th) 277 at 285.
3 The first question was whether the South African community system applied to immovables acquired outside South Africa. The Supreme Court held that it did. Had it decided the opposite, that would have been the end of the claim, as in *Callwood v Callwood* [1960] AC 659, [1960] 2 All ER 1.
4 (1897) 14 SC 61 at 65.
5 This case is not reported in England, but the Public Record Office reference to the Entry Books of Decrees and Orders [Supreme Court of Judicature] is 1897 A 2919.

He thereupon made an order declaring that the Cornish land passed under the will apparently in accordance with the tacit contract, though the decision is perhaps also explicable on other grounds.[6]

It remains now to consider specifically what law governs the three questions of capacity, formal validity and essential validity in the case of marriage contracts.

(b) CAPACITY[7]

The combination of circumstances which most neatly raises the question of capacity occurs where a woman, being a minor according to the law of her English domicil, makes a marriage contract in England prior to her marriage with a foreigner, by the law of whose domicil the woman is not subject to any incapacity. A variation, which occurred in *Viditz v O'Hagan*,[8] arises if the contract is made in a country which is the domicil neither of the woman nor of the man.

If in these cases we reason by analogy to commercial contracts, the proper law of the contract governs,[9] but if by analogy to the contract to marry, then the law of the parties' domicil[10] is the governing system. It is submitted, however, that on principle the proper law of the agreement should govern, and that the proper law is prima facie deemed to be the law of the matrimonial domicil.[11] It is that law which is universally recognised as controlling the personal and proprietary relations of the parties during their marriage, and it is difficult to appreciate why the one question of capacity to make a marriage contact should be withdrawn from that law and referred to the pre-existing law of the woman's domicil, in the above example.

Yet it is sometimes said that capacity in this connection must be determined by the law of each party's domicil. Under this view, if the woman is subject to an incapacity by the law of her pre-nuptial domicil, though not by the law of her intended husband's domicil, the contract is void.[12] At the same time it is reasonably clear that the judgments which lay down this rule are based on hasty generalisations drawn from obscure dicta and partly from the writings of Continental jurists.

The relevant cases[13] in chronological order are: *Re Cooke's Trusts*,[14] *Cooper v Cooper*,[15] and *Viditz v O'Hagan*.[16]

The facts of *Re Cooke's Trusts* were that a domiciled Englishwoman under

6 One possible ground is that the land represented money already owned by the parties in South Africa. Another, that it was merely a question of testamentary construction.—What did the parties intend? Being subject to and conversant with South African law at the time of making the will, they would naturally contemplate that the common property would include everything regarded as such by that law.

7 On this difficult subject see Dicey & Morris, pp 1061–1063; Morris (1938) 54 LQR 78; cf Goldberg (1970) 19 ICLQ 557, 569–573. Capacity to contract is largely unaffected by the Contracts (Applicable Law) Act 1990, supra, pp 510–513.

8 [1900] 2 Ch 87, infra, p 877.

9 It should be the proper law objectively ascertained, rather than deemed to be chosen by the parties; see supra, p 511.

10 As to the law of the parties' domicil, see supra, pp 586 et seq.

11 On the meaning of this, see supra, pp 867–869.

12 Wolff, pp 366–367.

13 The practical significance of all three cases is now much less, given that the age of majority has been reduced to 18: Family Law Reform Act 1969, s 1.

14 (1887) 56 LJ Ch 637.

15 (1888) 13 App Cas 88.

16 [1899] 2 Ch 569; revsd [1900] 2 Ch 87.

twenty-one married a Frenchman in France. Prior to the marriage, she made a notarial contract in France, which excluded the French doctrine of community of goods, and gave her "the entire administration of her property and the free enjoyment of her income". There were three children of the marriage. After having lived in Jersey for eight years separately from her husband, she went through a ceremony of marriage with X in 1853 under the mistaken belief that her husband was dead. She resided with X and with her three children in New South Wales until her death in 1879. Her French husband did not die until 1877. She made a will leaving all her property to X. It was argued that the notarial contract was valid, and that it precluded the testatrix from depriving her children of the vested interests in her property given to them by French law.

STIRLING J, after deciding that the woman died domiciled in New South Wales, held that her capacity to make the notarial contract was governed by English law, as being the law of her pre-marriage domicil. The consequence was that in his opinion her minority rendered the contract "void".[17] The reasoning which led the judge to this conclusion was not impressive. All that he did was to follow *Sottomayor v De Barros*,[18] relying on statements that personal capacity to contract is governed by the law of the domicil.[19] The decision is of little value on the question of capacity, for the right of the Englishwoman to dispose of her property by will was in no way restricted by the French contract on which the children relied. As Dr Morris has said:

> If a woman makes an ante-nuptial contract which merely excludes communauté des biens [community of goods] and gives her full powers of disposition, it is difficult to see how the children of the marriage can complain if they take nothing under the will.[1]

The decision, in other words, would have been the same had she been of full age when she made the contract.

The facts of *Cooper v Cooper*,[2] a Scottish appeal to the House of Lords, were as follows:

> A domiciled Irishwoman of 18 made an ante-nuptial contract in Dublin with her intended husband, a domiciled Scotsman, by which she purported to relinquish the proprietary rights that she would be entitled to under Scottish law on the death of her husband. Both parties contemplated, in accordance with what proved to be the fact, that the matrimonial home would be established in Scotland. The husband died thirty-five years after his wife attained her majority. On his death she sued to set aside the contract on the ground that at the time of its execution she was a minor by Irish law.

It was held that the woman's capacity must be governed by the law of Ireland, since that country was not only her domicil but also the place where the contract was made. Lord MACNAGHTEN rejected the notion that Scottish law, as being the law of the matrimonial domicil, applied, saying:

> It is difficult to suppose that Mrs Cooper could confer capacity upon herself by contemplating a different country as the place where the contract was to be fulfilled,

17 Though see *Edwards v Carter* [1893] AC 360.
18 (1877) 3 PD 1.
19 Ibid, at p 5. This is no longer regarded as being so, see supra, pp 511–512.
1 (1938) 54 LQR 78, 81.
2 (1888) 13 App Cas 88.

if that be the proper expression, or by contracting in view of an alteration of personal status which would bring with it a change of domicil.[3]

In any event the decision is not readily explicable. By Irish law, as well as by English law, a marriage contract was voidable, in the sense that it was to be treated as valid unless repudiated by the minor within a reasonable time after the attainment of majority.[4] Since there had been no repudiation within thirty-five years after the event, why was the contract not valid even by the law of the minor's pre-marriage domicil? The true explanation seems to be that the House of Lords considered Scots law as well as Irish law to be a governing factor. By Irish law she might repudiate the contract or leave it in operation. By Scots law, the law of her new domicil, she could do nothing but repudiate it, since to ratify it or to leave it unrepudiated would constitute a gift that was revocable as being a gift between husband and wife.[5] The decision is far from convincing as an authority in support of the view that capacity to make a marriage settlement depends on the law of the domicil at the time of the contract.

Viditz v O'Hagan[6] is a curious case, in which the facts were these:

A domiciled Englishwoman, under twenty-one, made a marriage contract at Berne in view of her approaching marriage with a domiciled Austrian. The contract was voidable by English law, ie it could be rescinded by her after she attained majority, though it would become irrevocable if not rescinded within a reasonable time after that event. The rule of Austrian law, the law of the matrimonial domicil, was that the husband and wife might revoke the settlement agreement at any time. Twenty-nine years after the settlement, ie long after it had become irrevocable by English law, the husband and wife executed an instrument in the Austrian form by which they exercised the right of revocation. They then brought the present action against the English trustees claiming a declaration that the agreement had been annulled. It was held by the Court of Appeal that they were entitled to the declaration, since the power of revoking the settlement agreement was a matter for Austrian law.

In other words, by English law the wife could repudiate the contract, provided that she did so within a reasonable time after attaining her majority; by Austrian law, to which she later became subject, she could always repudiate it. Therefore the joint operation of the two laws rendered effective what the parties had done.

Neither *Cooper v Cooper* nor *Viditz v O'Hagan*, then, justifies the view that the law of each party's domicil governs capacity, for if this were the law the contract in each case would have been valid as not having been repudiated within a reasonable time.

(c) FORMAL VALIDITY

What is the appropriate legal system to determine the formalities that must be observed in the case of a marriage contract? If, for instance, an Englishwoman marries a man domiciled in a country where such a contract is void unless

3 (1888) 13 App Cas 88 at 108.
4 *Edwards v Carter* [1893] AC 360.
5 Morris, p 418, citing Lord LINDLEY in *Viditz v O'Hagan* [1900] 2 Ch 87 at 96, 98; cf Anton, pp 576–580.
6 [1900] 2 Ch 87.

made by notarial act, and she wishes to make a settlement agreement with ordinary English limitations, it is important to know whether the English or the foreign form must be followed. The proper course is to execute the settlement as an English deed and then to re-execute it as a notarial act, but if this is not done a difficult question arises. If the deed is executed in the foreign country it neglects the forms required by the law of the place of contracting; if in England, it requires the parties to act under a transaction that is devoid of effect by the law of the matrimonial domicil.

Although the traditional view formerly was that a contract must observe the forms required by the law of the place of contracting, it has been accepted at common law, as well as under the Contracts (Applicable Law) Act 1990,[7] that formalities, like essential validity, may be governed by the proper law. At common law, the form required by the law of the place of contracting is sufficient[8] but not essential. The English cases clearly show that in the case of marriage contracts relating to property it is sufficient to adopt the formalities of the proper law as an alternative to those of the law of the place of contracting.[9]

The exact point arose in *Van Grutten v Digby*:[10]

Prior to a marriage between an Englishwoman and a domiciled Frenchman, a deed of settlement in the English form and containing the usual English limitations was executed at Dunkirk. The settlement was wholly void by French law, since it had not been executed before a notary public. Five years later the husband claimed that, owing to the formal invalidity of the contract by French law, the settled property was subject to the doctrine of community of goods.

Lord ROMILLY held, however, that the contract was binding on both parties.

I hold it to be the law of this country [he said] that if a foreigner and an English-woman make an express contract previous to marriage, and if on the faith of that contract the marriage afterwards takes place, and if the contract relates to the regulation of property within the jurisdiction and subject to the laws of this country, then, and in that case, this court will administer the law on the subject as if the whole matter were to be regulated by English law.[11]

(d) ESSENTIAL VALIDITY

The essential validity of a marriage contract is governed by its proper law. It seems clear that there may be express selection of the governing law, at least if it is connected with the transaction.[12] In the absence of choice, the proper law will be the law of the country with which the contract is most closely connected. In effect, the principles on which the proper law is to be determined are much the same as those relevant at common law to determine the proper law of a commercial contract. However, the nature of the subject matter is such that certain factors may predominate in significance, not

---

7 Supra, pp 507–510.
8 Eg *Guépratte v Young* (1851) 4 De G & Sm 217.
9 As to what is the proper law see infra, under (d) essential validity; see also *Ex p Spinazzi* 1985 (3) SA 650.
10 (1862) 31 Beav 561; see also *Watts v Shrimpton* (1855) 21 Beav 97; *Re Barnard, Barnard v White* (1887) 56 LT 9; *Re Bankes* [1902] 2 Ch 333.
11 (1862) 31 Beav 561 at 567.
12 *Re Fitzgerald, Surman v Fitzgerald* [1904] 1 Ch 573 at 587–588; *Montgomery v Zarifi* 1918 SC (HL)128; Anton, p 580; cf *Re Bowen's Estate* 351 NYS 2d 113 (1973).

least being the matrimonial domicil.[13] Indeed there would appear to be a presumption in favour of the law of the matrimonial domicil, but this may well be rebutted by other circumstances.[14] Furthermore, it will be of significance that the spouses may have separate domicils both before and after their marriage, given that a wife may have a domicil independent of her husband. Other factors to which consideration may be given include: the nature and situation of the property; whether the form and contents of the document are appropriate to one law, but not to another; the place where the accounts, the shares and other indicia of title are kept; the fact that the contract is invalid under the law of the matrimonial domicil.

The proper law, once it has been identified in accordance with these principles, continues to govern the marriage contract even though the interested parties may establish their home in a country where a different law prevails.[15] Where there is a marriage settlement creating trusts of that settlement, then the essential validity of such trusts falls to be governed by the law determined by reference to the Recognition of Trusts Act 1987.[16]

---

13 Supra, pp 867–869.
14 *Re Fitzgerald* [1904] 1 Ch 573; and see *Re Hannema's Marriage* (1981) 54 FLR 79, 7 Fam L R 542.
15 *Re Hewitt's Settlement* [1915] 1 Ch 228.
16 Infra, pp 880 et seq.

Chapter 35

Trusts

SUMMARY

1. INTRODUCTION

The common law rules concerning the validity of trusts in the international context were described in 1951 as "simply specific rules, evolved to meet particular difficulties. They do not reflect, or form part of a fully-developed system, and it is a matter for remark that they deal with so few of the many possible situations which may possibly arise."[1] In the intervening years the case law remained thin, with patchy analysis of the issues and uncertainty as to the relevant rules in a number of areas. It is, therefore, not surprising that the Recognition of Trusts Act was passed in 1987 to enable the United Kingdom to give effect to the Convention, formally concluded in 1986 by the Hague Conference on Private International Law, on the Law Applicable to Trusts and on their Recognition.[2] This Convention is implemented by being scheduled, with some omissions,[3] to the 1987 Act.[4]

---

1 Keeton (1951) 4 Current Legal Problems 111, 119.
2 See Actes et Documents de la Quinzième session, Vol II, especially the official Explanatory Report, at p 370, by von Overbeck; Hayton (1987) 36 ICLQ 260; Gaillard and Trautman (1987) 35 Am Jo Comp L 307; Klein, in *Mélanges Paul Piotet* (1990), p 467.
3 It would have been more helpful to have scheduled a fuller version. Indeed reference is made in this chapter to some provisions which have not been scheduled.
4 1987 Act, s 1(1).

It has to be said that the main reason for the initiation of work on this Convention was not the unsatisfactory nature of the private international law of trusts in those countries familiar with the law of trusts, but rather the fact that issues involving the validity of trusts or the powers of trustees may arise in countries where the trust concept is unfamiliar.[5] This accounts for the fact that the Hague Convention and the 1987 Act not only lay down choice of law rules but also extend to the question of the recognition of trusts, a particular problem if they are unknown in the domestic law.[6] Earlier impetus for work on the private international law rules relating to trusts had been provided by the accession of countries where trusts are familiar (the United Kingdom and Ireland) to the European Community Convention on jurisdiction and enforcement of judgments in civil and commercial matters.[7] This necessitated the amendment of the original 1968 Convention to include a specific head of jurisdiction relating to trusts,[8] with the corollary that, for example, an English judgment relating to trusts will have to be recognised throughout the European Community.

In considering the private international law rules governing trusts which are laid down in the Recognition of Trusts Act 1987 and its scheduled Convention,[9] it is necessary first to examine a range of preliminary issues before turning to the specific rules governing choice of law and the recognition of trusts.

2. PRELIMINARY ISSUES

(a) DEFINITION OF A TRUST

A major objective of the Convention is "to establish common provisions on the law applicable to trusts and to deal with the most important issues concerning the recognition of trusts";[10] but these common provisions are to be applied in countries some of which are familiar with the trust concept and others of which are not. Furthermore, as the Convention is an "open" and not a "reciprocal" Convention, the law to be applied to the validity or recognition of a trust may not be that of a Contracting State.[11] This has led to the decision to include, in Article 2 of the Convention, a description, if not a definition, of a trust for the purposes of the Convention:

5 Actes et Documents de la Quartorzième session, Vol I, p 189.
6 The Convention rules apply to trusts regardless of the date on which they were created: Art 22; though other states have a power (not exercised by the United Kingdom) to limit the rules to trusts created after the Convention came into force in those states. S 1(5) of the 1987 Act makes clear that Art 22 is not to be construed as affecting the law to be applied to anything done or omitted to be done before the Act came into force.
7 Supra, pp 279 et seq, 411 et seq.
8 Art 5(6); though the Convention does not apply to issues relating to the creation of testamentary trusts: Art 1; see Collins, *The Civil Jurisdiction and Judgments Act 1982*, p 64, supra, pp 288–289. Trusts are, however, specifically excluded from the 1980 Rome Convention on the Law Applicable to Contractual Obligations: see Contracts (Applicable Law) Act 1990, Sch 1, Art 1(2) (g), supra p 473.
9 The new rules apply to conflicts between the laws of parts of the United Kingdom as they do more generally internationally; though there is a power in the Convention (Art 24) which would have allowed the exclusion of intra-United Kingdom conflicts.
10 Convention, Preamble.
11 Though there is a power for Contracting States to make a reservation limiting the application of the rules on recognition to a trust the validity of which is governed by the law of a Contracting State: Art 21.

For the purposes of this Convention, the term "trust" refers to the legal relationships created—*inter vivos* or on death—by a person, the settlor, when assets[12] have been placed under the control of a trustee for the benefit of a beneficiary or for a specified purpose.

A trust has the following characteristics—

(a) the assets constitute a separate fund and are not a part of the trustee's own estate;

(b) title to the trust assets stands in the name of the trustee or in the name of another person on behalf of the trustee;

(c) the trustee has the power and the duty, in respect of which he is accountable, to manage, employ or dispose of the assets in accordance with the terms of the trust and the special duties imposed upon him by law.

The reservation by the settlor of certain rights and powers, and the fact that the trustee may himself have rights as a beneficiary, are not necessarily inconsistent with the existence of a trust.

The effect of this is to include within the Convention the classic concept of trust known to the common law world, whilst also making it possible to extend the Convention to trust-like institutions familiar to other jurisdictions.

(b) TYPES OF TRUST FALLING WITHIN THE 1987 ACT

The definition of a trust in Article 2 ensures that the rules of the Convention apply both to trusts created *inter vivos* and on death, and that they apply both to trusts for the benefit of specific beneficiaries and for "a specified purpose", thus including charitable trusts. Under Article 3, it is stated that "The Convention only applies to trusts created voluntarily and evidenced in writing". Whilst this does not require the trust to be in writing, merely evidenced in writing, it would appear to exclude purely oral trusts, trusts which are created by judicial decision, and trusts created by statute. All three such categories of trust are, however, covered by the 1987 Act, though in differing ways.

In the case of a trust created by judicial decision, the Convention[13] gives Contracting States the power to extend the provisions of the Convention to such trusts and this has, in fact, been done in the 1987 Act.[14] It should be noted that the extension is unlimited in that it applies to trusts created by virtue of a judicial decision whether in the United Kingdom or elsewhere. This means that trusts created by judicial decision elsewhere in the European Community or in the EFTA States will fall to be recognised under the Civil Jurisdiction and Judgments Acts 1982 and 1991 respectively.[15] If the trust is created by judicial decision in some other country its recognition will depend on whether that foreign judgment falls to be recognised under the general rules for the recognition of foreign judgments.[16]

Turning to oral trusts and trusts created by statute, not only do they fall outside the Convention, but there is no express power to extend the Convention provisions to them. Nevertheless, in the interests of ensuring that as many kinds of trust as is appropriate are governed by the same rules, the 1987 Act applies the rules in the Convention on both choice of law and recognition to "any other trusts of property arising under the law of any part

12　No distinction is drawn between movable and immovable property.
13　Art 20.
14　S 1(2).
15　Supra, pp 411 et seq.
16　Supra, pp 345 et seq.

of the United Kingdom".[17] There is no doubt that this includes purely oral trusts arising under English law as well as trusts created by the operation of a statute[18] or by specific action under a statute.[19]

Although the rules of the Convention are to be applied to a wide variety of trusts, not every type of trust is included. For example, the validity of an oral trust which arises under the law of some country outside the United Kingdom will have to be determined by an English court according to the common law rules of private international law, which, notwithstanding the 1987 Act, will remain applicable to such a trust.[20] The extension of the provisions of the Convention to trusts of property created by judicial decision will ensure that many instances of constructive trust are included, but not cases where constructive trusts are created as a form of personal remedy.[1]

(c) VALIDITY OF THE INSTRUMENT OF CREATION OF THE TRUST

In the case of a voluntary testamentary or *inter vivos* trust, there is an important preliminary issue to be faced, namely whether the instrument which creates the trust, ie the will or the settlement, is valid according to the relevant governing law. It is made quite clear, by Article 4 of the Convention, that this preliminary issue as to validity falls outside the scope of the Convention. The relevant choice of law rules will be those governing, for example, the formal or essential validity of wills[2] or, in the fairly rare cases where there is a settlement, those governing the validity of contracts[3] or deeds. In the case of a testamentary trust it will also be for the law governing the validity of the will to determine, for example, whether the testator is required to leave a fixed portion of his estate to his wife or children rather than on trust for other beneficiaries.[4]

(d) TRANSFER OF TRUST ASSETS

Not only does a voluntary trust depend on there being a valid instrument of creation, it is also necessary that the transfer of the trust assets is valid and this further preliminary issue is also excluded from the Convention by reason of Article 4 as being an act "by virtue of which assets are transferred to the trustee". The choice of law issue as to whether a trustee has effective legal title to the assets to hold them for the beneficiaries will normally be governed by the general rules applicable to the transfer of property, eg the law of the situs in the case of tangible movables[5] and of immovables.[6] If the instrument of creation of the trust is valid under its governing law, the trust will, nevertheless, fail if the law of the situs does not permit the transferee to hold the property other than absolutely, as where the concept of the trust is

17 S 1(2).
18 Eg under the Law of Property Act 1925, ss 34–36; Administration of Estates Act 1925, s 33; Administration of Justice Act 1925, s 42; *Re Kehr* [1952] Ch 26, [1951] 2 All ER 812.
19 Eg under the Mental Health Act 1983, s 96(1)(d).
20 Though there are unlikely to be major differences between the two sets of rules, see infra, pp 884 et seq. For the common law rules, see the 11th edn of this book, ch 35.
 1 See Hayton (1987) 36 ICLQ 260 at 264. Whether most forms of resulting trust are included is unclear, see Hayton, op cit, 263–264.
 2 Supra, pp 839 et seq, 844 et seq.
 3 Supra, pp 457 et seq.
 4 Eg *Re Hernando* (1884) 27 Ch D 284; *Re Annesley* [1926] Ch 692; *Re Ross* [1930] 1 Ch 377; and see supra, pp 845, 853.
 5 Supra, pp 797 et seq.
 6 Supra, pp 784 et seq.

unknown to that legal system. *Re Pearse's Settlement*[7] provides an illustration of this type of problem:

> In 1897, the settlor conveyed property to trustees to hold on the trusts of a marriage settlement. In all respects this was an English settlement. She agreed to settle after-acquired property on the same trusts. In 1901 she became entitled to land in Jersey and the question was whether that land was caught by the covenant to settle after-acquired property. There was no doubt as to the validity under English law of the instrument creating the trust. However, under the law of Jersey, the settlor could not transfer land in Jersey to trustees, in the absence of adequate pecuniary consideration. That being so, the court held that the Jersey land was not subject to the covenant to settle after-acquired property because the trustees could not, under the law of the situs, have those trust assets conveyed to them.

3. CHOICE OF LAW

(a) CHOICE BY THE SETTLOR

Article 6 of the Convention embodies party autonomy by providing:

> A trust shall be governed by the law chosen by the settlor. The choice must be express or be implied in the terms of the instrument creating or the writing evidencing the trust, interpreted, if necessary, in the light of the circumstances of the case.

This makes clear that either an express or an implied choice by the settlor of the governing law is permitted. Such a rule confirms what had generally been accepted to be the position at common law in relation both to testamentary[8] and inter vivos[9] trusts, and whether the case is one of choice of a foreign law by an English domiciled testator or settlor or of English law by a foreign domiciliary.[10] To be effective the choice must be of the substantive law of the jurisdiction chosen[11] and cannot include its private international law rules; ie the doctrine of renvoi is excluded here as elsewhere in the Convention.[12] No guidance is provided by the Convention on what will be held to constitute an implied choice of the applicable law; though there is certainly a suggestion at common law in the case of testamentary trusts that the testator was presumed to intend that the law of his domicil governed the validity of such trusts.[13] In the case of inter vivos trusts there is a degree of common law authority indicating circumstances from which the settlor's intention can be determined.[14] For example, reference has been made to such factors as the

---

7 [1909] 1 Ch 304.
8 See, eg, *Re Lord Cable* [1977] 1 WLR 7 at 20; *Re Healy's Will* 125 NYS 2d 486 (1953).
9 See, eg, *Este v Smith* (1854) 18 Beav 112 at 122; *Re Hernando* (1884) 27 Ch D 284 at 292–293; *Re Fitzgerald* [1904] 1 Ch 573 at 587; *Augustus v Permanent Trustee Co (Canberra) Ltd* (1971) 124 CLR 245; *Re Pratt* 8 NY 2d 855, 168 NE 2d 709 (1960).
10 Cf *Canterbury Corpn v Wyburn and Melbourne Hospital* [1895] AC 89.
11 This includes, here as elsewhere in the Convention, the law of a part of a multi-territory State which has its own law of trusts, eg of a part of the United Kingdom or of a state within the USA: 1987 Act, s 1(4), and Art 23 of the Convention (not scheduled to the Act).
12 Art 17; though see Art 15, discussed infra, p 891.
13 Eg *Peillon v Brooking* (1858) 25 Beav 218; *Re Aganoor's Trusts* (1895) 64 LJ Ch 521; *Re Lord Cable* [1977] 1 WLR 7 at 20; though this was not an invariable rule, see *A-G v Campbell* (1872) LR 5 HL 524.
14 See *Revenue Comrs v Pelly* [1940] IR 122.

place of making the original contract or deed,[15] the situs of the property subject to the trust[16] and the place of registration of the trustee company[17] or the place of administration of the trust.[18]

The Convention allows "a severable aspect of the trust" to be governed by a different law from that otherwise applicable.[19] So, a testator or settlor could choose English law to govern the administration of a trust but New York law to govern all other matters relating to the trust—or he could choose the law to govern just one aspect, leaving the determination of the law to govern the others to be decided by the rules applicable in the absence of choice. If there are trust assets in different jurisdictions it is an interesting question of construction of the Convention as to whether choosing different laws to govern the different assets is permitted as "a severable aspect" of the trust.

There are some limits on the freedom of the settlor to choose the governing law. If he should choose the law of a country which "does not provide for trusts or the category of trust involved"[20] then such a meaningless choice is ineffective and the trust is governed by the law applicable in the absence of choice.[1] Mandatory rules of the forum, mandatory rules of other countries applicable by reason of the forum's private international law rules, and the forum's rules on public policy may be applied notwithstanding the choice of another applicable law.[2] One factor which may inhibit choice of the applicable law is that recognition of a trust may be refused if the significant elements of the trust are, but for the choice of the applicable law, the place of administration and the habitual residence of the trustee, more closely connected with a State or States which do not have the institution of the trust or the category of trust involved.[3] So life may not be breathed into a trust in such circumstances by the choice of the law of a common law country.

(b) ABSENCE OF CHOICE

If the settlor has not chosen the law to govern the validity of the trust, or has made an ineffective choice by selecting the law of a country where the trust concept is unknown, then Article 7 provides for the determination of the applicable law as follows:

> Where no applicable law has been chosen, a trust shall be governed by the law with which it is most closely connected.
> In ascertaining the law with which a trust is most closely connected reference shall be made in particular to—
> (a) the place of administration of the trust designated by the settlor;
> (b) the situs of the assets of the trust;
> (c) the place of residence or business of the trustee;
> (d) the objects of the trust and the places where they are to be fulfilled.

The basic rule that a trust should be governed by the law of the country with

---

15 *Harris Investments Ltd v Smith* [1934] 1 DLR 748.
16 Ibid; *Lindsay v Miller* [1949] VLR 13.
17 *A-G v Jewish Colonization Association* [1901] 1 KB 123.
18 *Chellaram v Chellaram* [1985] Ch 409 at 424–425.
19 Art 9.
20 Art 6.
 1 Art 7, infra. If that law also does not provide for trusts, then the Convention rules cease to apply: Art 5.
 2 Arts 15, 16, 18, discussed infra, pp 890–891.
 3 Art 13, infra, p 890.

which it is most closely connected[4] is in substance the same rule as applied at common law, in the absence of choice, both in the case of testamentary[5] and *inter vivos*[6] trusts. The application of such a closest connection test may be illustrated by *Iveagh v IRC*.[7]

A settlement, dated 1907, was prepared by English solicitors and executed in England. The share certificates relating to the trust assets were kept in a bank in London. At the date of the settlement all the relevant parties were domiciled in Ireland where the day to day management of the trust was carried on. It became important, for the purposes of estate duty, to determine the law governing the settlement.

Whilst UPJOHN J thought the question was not easy to answer, his quest was to establish "the proper law of the settlement". He placed little reliance on the nature and situation of the trust property, there being investments in many parts of the world. Far more importance was attached to the Irish domicil of the settlor and of the life tenant in reaching the conclusion that the governing law was Irish law. If, however, the trust assets consist of immovable property it is likely that greater significance will be afforded to the law of the situs of the property.[8]

Although Article 7 provides a list of factors for the court to consider, it is not an exclusive list and a court would remain free, as in *Iveagh's Case*, to attach importance, for example, to domicil.[9] What is not clear is the relative weight to be given to all the factors, whether or not listed in Article 7. All that can really be said is that it will vary with the circumstances of each individual case,[10] though there may be a tendency to favour the application of the law of a country under which the trust is valid.[11]

What is not made clear expressly by Article 7 is the time at which the factors determining closeness of connection must be considered. It is suggested, however, that, as express provision is made later in relation to change of the applicable law,[12] the appropriate time to consider the factors should be that of the creation of the trust. This would follow the common law position where changes in the identity, and thus the domicil or residence, of the trustees,[13] or in the place of investment[14] taking place after the trust was created were to be ignored.

Just as with a choice of the applicable law, there are certain limits on the

---

4 In theory, at least, Art 9 would allow different laws to be applied to different aspects of the trust more closely connected with different jurisdictions. If the court decides, unusually, that the most closely connected law is that of a country which does not provide for trusts or for trusts of this kind, then the Convention is inapplicable: Art 5.
5 See *A-G v Campbell* (1872) LR 5 HL 524 in the case of movables. The position in relation to immovables was less clear, see the 11th edn of this book, pp 884–885.
6 Eg *Iveagh v IRC* [1954] Ch 364; *Chellaram v Chellaram* [1985] Ch 409, [1985] 1 All ER 1043; *Perpetual Executors and Trustees Association of Australia Ltd v Roberts* [1970] VR 732.
7 [1954] Ch 364, [1954] 1 All ER 609.
8 Art 7, para (b); and see, eg, *Freke v Lord Carbery* (1873) LR 16 Eq 461; *Peabody v Kent* 153 App Div 286, 13 NYS 32 (1912); affd 213 NY 154, 107 NE 51 (1914).
9 And see *Re Hewitt's Settlement* [1915] 1 Ch 228; *Re Lord Cable* [1977] 1 WLR 7 at 20.
10 See Wallace (1987) 36 ICLQ 455, 468–469.
11 Hayton (1987) 36 ICLQ 260, 272.
12 Art 10, infra, p 889.
13 *Iveagh v IRC* [1954] Ch 364 at 370; and see *Re Hewitt's Settlement* [1915] 1 Ch 228 at 233–234; *Duke of Marlborough v A-G* [1945] Ch 78 at 85.
14 *Iveagh v IRC*, supra: and see *Re Fitzgerald* [1904] 1 Ch 573 at 588; *Duke of Marlborough v A-G*, supra.

application of the most closely connected law. The forum's mandatory rules and rules of public policy remain applicable despite the close connection of the trust with another law;[15] also applicable are the mandatory rules of other countries which are to be applied by reason of the forum's private international law rules.[16]

(c) SCOPE OF THE APPLICABLE LAW

Article 8 makes it clear that the applicable law determined by reference to Articles 6 or 7 is to govern "the validity of the trust, its construction, its effects and the administration of the trust". The basic starting point is, therefore, that the same law governs all these issues; though, as has been seen, it is possible for a severable aspect of a trust to be governed by a different law.[17] This generality of approach has the effect that normally the same law will apply to a testamentary or inter vivos trust even though the trust property consists of both movable and immovable property.

Article 8 goes on to list a non-exclusive range of matters which are to be governed by the applicable law, namely:

(a) the appointment, resignation and removal of trustees, the capacity to act as a trustee, and the devolution of the office of trustee;
(b) the rights and duties of trustees among themselves;
(c) the right of trustees to delegate in whole or in part the discharge of their duties or the exercise of their powers;
(d) the power of trustees to administer or to dispose of trust assets, to create security interests in the trust assets, or to acquire new assets;
(e) the powers of investment of trustees;
(f) restrictions upon the duration of the trust, and upon the power to accumulate the income of the trust;
(g) the relationships between the trustees and the beneficiaries including the personal liability of the trustees to the beneficiaries;
(h) the variation or termination of the trust;[18]
(i) the distribution of the trust assets;
(j) the duty of trustees to account for their administration.

The reference of these matters to the law determined by Articles 6 or 7 very much follows the common law approach in the case of inter vivos trusts as may be illustrated by *Augustus v Permanent Trustee Co (Canberra) Ltd.*[19]

The settlor executed a voluntary deed of settlement in the Australian Capital Territory. He was resident and domiciled in New South Wales. The trusts were in favour of the settlor's children and grandchildren; and those who were alive at the date of the settlement were also domiciled and resident in New South Wales. The trustee was a corporation registered in Canberra which was where the funds were paid over by the settlor. The trust was void for perpetuity under the law of the Australian Capital Territory, but valid under the law of New South Wales.

In the High Court of Australia, WALSH J held that the issue of validity was to be determined by the proper law of the trust and, there being a clause in the trust deed which was interpreted as a reference to the law of New South

15 Arts 16, 18, infra, pp 890–891.
16 Art 15, infra, p 891.
17 Art 9, supra, p 885.
18 Discussed more fully, infra, pp 892–893.
19 (1971) 124 CLR 245; and see *Lindsay v Miller* [1949] VLR 13.

Wales, he upheld the validity of the trust, applying the law of that State.

Article 8 specifically states that the applicable law is to govern the construction of the trust. Where no view, express or implied, has been indicated by the testator or settlor, no problem arises and the most closely connected law will be applied.[20] It may be, however, that it is possible to determine the law which was intended to govern the construction or interpretation of the trust and it would seem to be the case that, under the Convention, as under the common law, the court's first task is to try to find whether there is any such intention on the part of the testator or settlor.[1] If so then the intended law should be applied by reason of Article 6 even though it may only be applied to this severable aspect of the trust.[2]

The law to govern the administration of the trust is also specifically included within the terms of Article 8. This means that, where there is a choice, express or implied, of the law to govern the administration of the trust, effect will be given to that choice,[3] even though a different law is held to govern the validity of the trust.[4] Indeed it may also be the case that the closest connection test, in the absence of choice, leads to a different law being applied to administration from that applied to validity.[5] One or two words of caution are necessary here, however. It may not always be easy to determine the place of administration, as where a testator leaves property in two countries creating separate administrations in each with the trustees' investment powers varying as between the applicable laws of the two separate places of administration.[6] Whilst here it could be argued that there are two separate administrations governed by separate laws, that escape is not available where there are issues which affect the administration of the trust as a whole, such as the appointment of a new trustee. For such an issue the law of just one place of administration needs to be identified; and whilst there is some common law authority supporting reference to the place where the bulk of the assets is held,[7] a better view is to identify the place of administration by reference to the place of residence of all, or a majority, of the trustees.[8] It has been assumed so far that it is easy to decide whether a matter refers to validity or administration but this may not always be the case.[9] Indeed the categorisation may vary as between legal systems, thus requiring the choice of a legal system to resolve the issue. Whilst the Convention is silent on this issue, it has been suggested that it is for the law governing validity to determine the matter.[10]

20 As at common law in *Re Levick's Will Trusts* [1963] 1 WLR 311 at 319; *Philipson-Stow v IRC* [1961] AC 727, [1960] 3 All ER 814; *Perpetual Executors and Trustees Association of Australia Ltd v Roberts* [1970] VR 732.
 1 Eg *Re Pilkington's Will Trusts* [1937] Ch 574, [1937] 3 All ER 213; *Trustees Executors and Agency Co Ltd v Margottini* [1960] VR 417; *Philipson-Stow v IRC*, supra, at 761.
 2 Eg *Spencer's Trustees v Ruggles* 1982 SLT 165.
 3 As at common law, see *Chellaram v Chellaram* [1985] Ch 409 at 431–432.
 4 Art 9 in allowing a different law to be applied to a severable aspect of a trust makes specific reference to matters of administration.
 5 Eg *Re Wilks* [1935] Ch 645; *Re Kehr* [1952] Ch 26, [1951] 2 All ER 812.
 6 Eg *Re Tyndall* [1913] SASR 39.
 7 *Permanent Trustee Co (Canberra) Ltd v Permanent Trustee Co of New South Wales Ltd* (1969) 14 FLR 246 at 252–253.
 8 *Re Smyth* [1898] 1 Ch 89 at 94.
 9 *Chellaram v Chellaram* [1985] Ch 409, [1985] 1 All ER 1043; and see Wallace (1987) 36 ICLQ 454, 474–475.
10 Hayton and Marshall, *Cases and Commentary on Trust Law*, 8th edn (1986), p 778.

(d) VARIATION OF THE APPLICABLE LAW

There is no doubt that a trust must have a law or laws governing its validity, construction and administration from the moment of its creation. If further assets are later transferred to the trustees that will not, as such, affect the law applicable to the trust. Article 10 of the Convention envisages, however, that as with contracts[11] the law to govern some or all aspects of a trust may be varied during the lifetime of the trust, for example, by a later express choice of the governing law, the trust up to that point having been governed by the law determined under Article 7. Article 10 does not lay down a substantive rule that such variation is permitted but rather provides a choice of law rule for resolving this issue by stipulating that "the law applicable to the validity of the trust shall determine whether that law or the law governing a severable aspect of the trust may be replaced by another law". So, if English law is the law already applicable to the trust, it will decide whether or not, for example, a provision in the trust allowing the trustees to replace the law governing all or part of the trust shall have effect.[12] It should be noted that Article 10 assumes that one law can be identified as that applicable to the validity of the trust even though different aspects of the trust are expressly governed by different laws. So if validity is expressly governed by English law and administration by New York law, it is for English law to decide whether the law governing the administration of the trust may later be varied.

4. RECOGNITION

Chapter III of the Hague Convention is concerned with the recognition of trusts and, as such, is of more practical importance for the recognition of trusts in civil law countries where the concept of the trust is unfamiliar—though it is no doubt important that English trusts secure recognition in other Contracting States. The approach of the Convention is, in Article 11, almost to state the obvious by providing that a trust created in accordance with the choice of law rules laid down in the Convention shall be recognised as a trust. It goes on, however, to provide (really for the benefit of countries where the trust is unfamiliar) what are the implications and effects of recognition:

> Such recognition shall imply, as a minimum, that the trust property constitutes a separate fund,[13] that the trustee may sue and be sued in his capacity as trustee, and that he may appear or act in this capacity before a notary or any person acting in an official capacity.
>
> In so far as the law applicable to the trust requires or provides, such recognition shall imply, in particular—
>
> (a) that personal creditors of the trustee shall have no recourse against the trust assets;
>
> (b) that the trust assets shall not form part of the trustee's estate upon his insolvency or bankruptcy;
>
> (c) that the trust assets shall not form part of the matrimonial property of the

---

11 Supra, pp 477–479.

12 Change could also be effected by agreement of the beneficiaries, though this really amounts to the making of a new settlement: *Duke of Marlborough v A-G* [1945] Ch 78 at 85; *Iveagh v IRC* [1954] Ch 364 at 370.

13 The trustee is entitled, under Art 12, to register trust assets in his capacity as trustee provided such registration is not prohibited by or inconsistent with the law of the country where registration is sought.

trustee or his spouse nor part of the trustee's estate upon his death;
(d) that the trust assets may be recovered when the trustee, in breach of trust, has mingled trust assets with his own property or has alienated trust assets. However, the rights and obligations of any third party holder of the assets shall remain subject to the law determined by the choice of law rules of the forum.[14]

It is noticeable that these provisions concentrate, at least on their face, on the position of the trustee though they do by inference provide safeguards for beneficiaries. Attention has been drawn to the fact that the last part of paragraph (d) will restrict the ability of a beneficiary to trace trust assets into hands of a third party where the assets are situated in a country where the trust concept is unknown.[15]

There are, however, limitations on the recognition to be given to a foreign trust. There are, first, the generally applicable limitations which allow for the application of the public policy or mandatory rules of the forum or those designated by its choice of law rules.[16] If these last rules prevent the recognition of a trust, then Article 15 stipulates that "the court shall try to give effect to the objects of the trust by other means". This is a very vague exhortation and is likely to prove particularly difficult to operate in civil law countries.

A further limitation on recognition is provided by Article 13:

No State shall be bound to recognise a trust the significant elements of which, except for the choice of the applicable law, the place of administration and the habitual residence of the trustee, are more closely connected with States which do not have the institution of the trust or the category of trust involved.

This is designed to protect the interests of states where the trust concept is unknown and has, therefore, been excluded from the provisions of the Convention scheduled to the 1987 Act. Nevertheless, lawyers in this country need to be aware that the provision may limit the recognition abroad of a trust expressed to be governed by English law but which is generally more closely connected with a "non-trust" state.[17]

5. MANDATORY RULES AND PUBLIC POLICY

The provisions of the Convention dealing with mandatory rules and public policy apply, normally, both to the question of the determination of the applicable law and to that of the recognition of a foreign trust.

(a) MANDATORY RULES

Article 16 embodies the generally accepted private international law provision that, notwithstanding choice of law or recognition rules, the mandatory

---

14 Art 14 permits, also, the application of rules of law more favourable to recognition.
15 Hayton (1987) 36 ICLQ 260, 275–276.
16 Arts 15, 16 and 18, infra, pp 890–891.
17 It is also the case that a Contracting State may reserve the right to apply the recognition provisions only to trusts whose validity is governed by the law of a Contracting State: Art 21 (not included in the provisions scheduled to the 1987 Act as the United Kingdom has not exercised this power of reservation).

rules[18] of the forum may continue to be applied.[19] It does so by describing such rules as "provisions of the law of the forum which must be applied even to international situations".[20] Article 16 goes on to allow a court to apply the mandatory rules of another sufficiently closely connected state. Such a provision was no more acceptable to the United Kingdom in the context of trusts than of contract[1] and a power of reservation[2] was exercised to exclude it.

Rather more complex, and loosely drafted, provisions as to mandatory rules are to be found in Article 15 which states that the "Convention does not prevent the application of provisions of the law designated by the conflicts rules of the forum, in so far as those provisions cannot be derogated from by voluntary act". There is here a somewhat broader description than under Article 16 of the rules which the forum may apply notwithstanding the provisions of the Convention. Although Article 15 merely gives the forum court power to continue to apply those rules, the 1987 Act requires an English court to do so.[3] What is striking is that the mandatory rules in question are not those of the forum but rather of another country (not that governing the trust) the application of whose law has been determined by "the conflicts rules of the forum". Those conflicts rules must be rules other than those contained in the Convention, ie rules applicable to an issue classified as other than one concerning the validity or recognition of a trust. Article 15 then goes on to give a non-exclusive list of such issues:

(a) the protection of minors and incapable parties;
(b) the personal and proprietary effects of marriage;
(c) succession rights, testate and intestate, especially the indefeasible shares of spouses and relatives;
(d) the transfer of title to property and security interests in property;
(e) the protection of creditors in matters of insolvency;
(f) the protection, in other respects, of third parties acting in good faith.

(b) PUBLIC POLICY

Article 18 contains the provision generally to be found in Hague Conventions allowing the forum to disregard the Convention provisions "when their application would be manifestly incompatible with public policy".[4] This would enable an English court to impose some limit on the freedom to choose the applicable law under Article 6 if, for example, there had been an attempt to evade the English rule against perpetuities by the choice of a foreign law to govern what was essentially an English trust.[5]

---

18 Examples that have been given of such rules include those designed to prevent the export of currency or of cultural heritage objects: Hayton (1987) 36 ICLQ 260, 278.
19 S 1(3) of the 1987 Act makes clear that, if there are such mandatory rules, then an English court must apply them.
20 Contrast the rather different description in Art 7(2) of the 1980 Rome Convention on Contractual Obligations, scheduled to the Contracts (Applicable Law) Act 1990, supra, pp 499–503.
1 See Rome Convention, Art 7(1), supra, p 503.
2 Art 16, third para.
3 S 1(3).
4 Art 19 preserves the powers of states in fiscal matters. It appears not to have been thought necessary to include this in the provisions scheduled to the 1987 Act.
5 Dicey & Morris, p 1074 and Fourth Cumulative Supplement, p 255.

6. VARIATION OF TRUSTS AND SETTLEMENTS

(a) VARIATION OF TRUSTS ACTS 1958

Section 1 of the Variation of Trusts Act 1958 provides that where property, whether movable or immovable, is held on trusts arising under any will, settlement or other disposition, the court may, if it thinks fit, approve any arrangement varying or revoking all or any of the trusts. The courts have held that the power of the English courts to exercise their jurisdiction under this provision is not limited to trusts governed by English law,[6] because to take such a restrictive view would mean

> that the court would be unable to vary a settlement made (say) in 1920 and governed by (say) Australian law, even though the beneficiaries, the trustees and the trust property had been for many years in this country. It would be unfortunate if the court had no jurisdiction in such a case.[7]

The power under the 1958 Act has to be set against the provision in Article 8 of the Trusts Convention which makes clear that "the variation or termination of the trust"[8] is a matter to be governed by the law applicable to the trust and not, for example, by the law of the forum. How do these two statutory provisions interrelate? The 1958 Act, as its long title states, is concerned with the jurisdiction of the courts, whereas Article 8 of the Trusts Convention is concerned with choice of law matters. On that basis the court still retains the power under the 1958 Act to vary a trust governed by foreign law but there would seem to be two limitations on the exercise of that power. The first is that the court should proceed with caution in deciding whether to assume jurisdiction in such a case, following the advice of Cross J in *Re Paget's Settlement*:

> Where there are substantial foreign elements in the case, the court must consider carefully whether it is proper for it to exercise the jurisdiction. If, for example, the court were asked to vary a settlement which was plainly a Scottish settlement, it might well hesitate to exercise its jurisdiction to vary the trusts, simply because some, or even all, the trustees and beneficiaries were in this country. It may well be that the judge would say that the Court of Session was the appropriate tribunal to deal with the case.[9]

The second limitation is that, in exercising the jurisdiction under the 1958 Act, the court should apply to the variation the substantive law of the country governing the trust, identified by reference to Articles 6 or 7 of the Convention. If the law governing the trust does not permit variation, then the jurisdiction under the 1958 Act should not be exercised.

(b) VARIATION OF MARRIAGE SETTLEMENTS

There is power in the English court when granting a divorce, nullity or judicial separation decree, or at any time after the decree, to vary any settlement of movable and immovable property made on the parties to the

---

6 *Re Ker's Settlement Trusts* [1963] Ch 553, [1963] 1 All ER 801; *Re Paget's Settlement* [1965] 1 All ER 58, [1965] 1 WLR 1046.
7 *Re Paget's Settlement*, supra, at 1050.
8 Art 8, para (h).
9 [1985] 1 WLR 1046 at 1050. It has, however, to be noted that the judge was in fact prepared to vary a trust which may have been governed by New York law.

marriage, whether by an ante-nuptial or a post-nuptial settlement.[10] The court can also extinguish or reduce the interest of either of the parties to the marriage under such a settlement.[11] The court has jurisdiction to order such variations whenever it has jurisdiction in the main proceedings for divorce, nullity or judicial separation.[12] However, this application of English law as the law of the forum has not been restricted to settlements governed by English law or of English property. For example, in *Nunneley v Nunneley and Marrian*,[13] the English court varied a settlement made in Scotland and in Scottish form of movables and immovables in Scotland. Is this power now limited by the Recognition of Trusts Act 1987 to settlements governed by English law? It would certainly seem undesirable that the power of the court in such family proceedings should be limited by the choice of law rules in the 1987 Act; and the exclusion of those rules might well be supported by reference to Article 15[14] which allows the English forum still to apply its conflict rules, here in fact leading to the application of the substantive law of the forum, to inter alia "the personal and proprietary effects of marriage".[15]

The fact that the English court would seem to continue to have power to apply English law to the variation of such marriage settlements does not mean that all foreign elements are to be ignored. The jurisdiction of the court is discretionary and it may well choose not to exercise its power if its order would be ineffective in the foreign country, as where the respondent had no connection with this country, no property here and where any English order would not be recognised in the foreign country.[16] Indeed, such ineffectiveness may justify setting aside service of the writ on the foreign trustees.[17]

10 Matrimonial Causes Act 1973, s 24(1)(c). See also the orders which can be made after a foreign decree, under the Matrimonial and Family Proceedings Act 1984, s 17, supra, pp 709 et seq.
11 Ibid, s 24(1)(d).
12 *Cammell v Cammell* [1965] P 467, [1964] 3 All ER 255, supra, pp 700–701.
13 (1890) 15 PD 186; and see *Forsyth v Forsyth* [1891] P 363.
14 Supra, p 891.
15 Reliance might also be placed on the over-riding public policy of the forum under Art 18.
16 *Tallack v Tallack and Broekema* [1927] P 211; cf *Hunter v Hunter and Waddington* [1962] P 1, [1961] 2 All ER 121.
17 *Goff v Goff* [1934] P 107; *Wyler v Lyons* [1963] P 274, [1963] 1 All ER 821.

Part VII

Corporations and bankruptcy

SUMMARY

Chapter 36

Corporations

Corporations raise a variety of conceptual problems, such as: To what extent do they constitute legal persons? What law, or laws, govern their creation and their dissolution? The first of these is a question of status, but the further questions raise issues relating to property.[1]

1. STATUS

Matters of status concerning a corporation fall to be determined by the law of its domicil,[2] and these would seem to include, not only its creation and dissolution, but also all those matters that are regulated by its instrument of incorporation. The well-known words of BOWEN LJ, spoken with reference to an English company, seem equally applicable to a foreign corporation.

> What you have to do is to find out what the statutory creature is and what it is meant to do; and to find out what this statutory creature is you must look at the statute only, because there, and there only, is found the definition of this new creature.[3]

Questions concerning the status of the "statutory creature", such as whether the individual members are personally liable,[4] whether its transactions are ultra vires,[5] or whether it may be represented in legal proceedings by its directors,[6] are determined by the rules of its constitution as interpreted by the law of its domicil. The only gloss to make on the statement of BOWEN LJ is that in many legal systems an association of persons may be endowed with the attribute of legal personality without any express statutory incorporation or anything corresponding to it. Thus in civil law countries many unincorporated associations, including partnerships, are persons in the eyes of the law. In these cases, it is to be presumed that the status ascribed to the association by the law of the country in which it has been formed will be

---

1 Matters such as the creation, capacity or winding up of a company are governed by company law and are accordingly excluded from the scope of the Contracts (Applicable Law) Act 1990, see Sch 1, Art 1(2)(e), supra, p 472.
2 Smart [1990] JBL 126.
3 *Baroness Wenlock v River Dee Co* (1883) 36 Ch D 675, note at p 685.
4 *General Steam Navigation Co v Guillou* (1843) 11 M & W 877.
5 *Risdon Iron and Locomotive Works v Furness* [1906] 1 KB 49 at 56–57.
6 *Banco de Bilbao v Sancha* [1938] 2 KB 176 at 194–195, [1938] 2 All ER 253 at 260.

recognised by English courts.[7] In the case of an organisation created by international treaty, it will not be recognised as having legal personality in England (in the absence of special statutory provision);[8] but an organisation will be recognised if it is accorded juridical personality in, and is created by, the laws of a foreign country recognised by the Crown.[9]

The correct role of the law of the domicil in an English action concerning a foreign corporation is well illustrated by *Metliss v National Bank of Greece and Athens SA*,[10] where the facts were as follows:

> In 1927 the National Mortgage Bank of Greece issued sterling mortgage bonds, repayable as to principal in 1957 with interest thereon meanwhile. The bonds were guaranteed by the National Bank of Greece. It was agreed that questions arising between the bank and bondholders should be settled by arbitration in London in accordance with English law. No interest was paid after April 1941. In 1949 a Greek decree imposed a moratorium suspending all obligations and rights of action on the bonds, and another decree in 1953 dissolved the guarantor bank and amalgamated it and the Bank of Athens (which had hitherto been unconnected with the bonds) into a new banking company under the style of the National Bank of Greece and Athens—the defendants in the instant case. This decree provided that the new bank should be the "universal successor" to the rights and obligations of the former banks.
>
> The Bank of Athens, having traded in England before its amalgamation, had acquired assets which were still in the country, and therefore the plaintiff, one of the bondholders, brought an action against the defendant bank for the recovery of arrears of interest, contending that it had succeeded to the obligations of the now defunct guarantor bank.

The first defence was that no action lay against the defendant bank, since it had not been a party to the issue of the bonds. In order to answer this, it thus became necessary to examine Greek law which alone was competent to pronounce whether the "statutory creature" that it had created was an available debtor to the plaintiff. It was admitted that the English court was bound to recognise the Greek dissolution of the banks and the birth of the newly formed National Bank of Greece and Athens into which those banks had been amalgamated. The only arguable question was whether there was an equal duty to recognise that the obligation undertaken by one of the defunct corporations to guarantee payment of interest on the bonds had passed to the new bank under the doctrine of universal succession. The answer is scarcely in doubt. It is wholly irrelevant that English internal law subscribes to no general doctrine by which the personality of a former entity is assumed by a successor. What is decisive is that according to English private international law the sphere of influence of the law of the domicil in the present context is to determine the status of artificial entities originating in the domicil. In the instant case the new entity, the defendant bank, had succeeded to the obligations of its predecessors as a result of the status imposed on it by Greek law, and it is difficult to find any rational ground on which the English court could admit its status as a justiciable person, but

---

7 *Von Hellfeld v Rechnitzer and Mayer Freres & Co* [1914] 1 Ch 748; *Skyline Associates v Small* (1974) 50 DLR (3d) 217.
8 *J H Rayner (Mincing Lane) Ltd v Department of Trade and Industry* [1990] 2 AC 418.
9 *Arab Monetary Fund v Hashim (No 3)* [1991] 2 AC 114.
10 [1958] AC 509, [1957] 3 All ER 608.

deny its liability for an obligation attached to that status. This would be to accept one facet of the governing law of the status but to repudiate another.

Admitting, however, that the bank was liable to be sued for arrears of interest, there was yet another argument to be met. It was said that if Greek law was followed on the question of universal succession it must also be followed with regard to the moratorium. But to say this was to distort the correct role of the law of the domicil. Its function was to determine whether the defendant bank was a competent debtor, but, having settled this primary question of status, it was not entitled to determine what constituted liability in the case of an obligation subject exclusively to internal English law.

A later Greek attempt to extricate the defendant bank from its obligations was unsuccessful.

A further decree, issued by the Greek Government on 16 July 1956, after the decision of the court of first instance in the *Metliss Case*, amended the amalgamation decree of 1953. It provided that the defendant bank should become the universal successor to the rights and obligations of the amalgamated banks *except for the obligations to which such banks were liable, whether as principals or guarantors, under bonds payable in gold or foreign currency*. The retrospective effect of this decree according to Greek law was that the defendant bank was no longer liable to discharge the former obligations of the original guarantor bank in respect of the sterling bonds. Certain bondholders, having been refused payment of interest that fell due after 16 July 1956, sued the bank in London for recovery of these debts.

Was the release of 1956 effective? It had, indeed, already been decided in the *Metliss Case* that the Greek decree of 1953, by endowing the bank with the status of universal successor, had rendered it liable. The argument accepted by the Court of Appeal was that since Greek law, as the admitted arbiter of the status of the bank, possessed the power of endowment it equally possessed the power of disendowment. It could abrogate the liabilities that it had formerly transferred.[11] The House of Lords, however, demonstrated the fallacy of this reasoning. The liability under the contract of guarantee, having been transferred to the bank in 1953, was an existing, albeit inchoate, obligation at the time of the 1956 decree. Moreover, it was a liability contained in a contract governed exclusively by English internal law. In technical language, English law was the law governing the contract[12] and therefore the well-established rule applied that that law alone determined whether the contract could be discharged, extinguished or otherwise affected.[13]

2. WINDING UP OF FOREIGN CORPORATIONS[14]

When considering the jurisdiction of the English courts to wind up foreign companies,[15] it is normally true to say that there can be no question of a foreign company being wound up in England, for its extinction, no less than

11 See *Adams v National Bank of Greece and Athens* [1960] 1 QB 64 at pp 81–2.
12 Supra, pp 457 et seq.
13 *Adams v National Bank of Greece and Athens* [1961] AC 255, [1960] 2 All ER 421. For a full account of the litigation, see Grodecki (1961) 24 MLR 701. For further proceedings, see *National Bank of Greece SA v Westminster Bank Executor and Trustee Co (Channel Islands) Ltd* [1971] AC 945.
14 Smart, *Cross-Border Insolvency* (1991).
15 Lipstein [1952] CLJ 198; Smart (1990) 39 ICLQ 827.

its birth, is a matter solely for the law of the country in which it has been incorporated. Once dissolved according to this law it necessarily becomes a non-existent person in the eyes of the common law. As such, it can no longer sue, or be sued or be wound up; it cannot acquire rights or incur liabilities, and such assets as it possesses in England pass to the Crown as bona vacantia.[16]

At common law, debts due to or from a branch which continued to trade in this country after the dissolution of the parent company were irrecoverable, since it had no locus standi in the courts. Such a branch has been described as "a submerged wreck, floating on the ocean of commerce";[17] the branch's assets were neither distributable by a liquidator among creditors nor liable in respect even of transactions effected in England after and perhaps in ignorance of the dissolution, though the agent who had acted for this non-existent principal would no doubt be personally liable.

The cure for these ills, however, is to be found in the provisions of what is now the Insolvency Act 1986[18] which govern the winding-up of unregistered companies.[19] Section 221(5) provides that any unregistered company may be wound up at the discretion of the court, if the company is dissolved, or has ceased to carry on business, or is carrying on business only for the purpose of winding up its affairs, or if the company is unable to pay its debts, or if the court is of the opinion that it is just and equitable that the company should be wound up.[20] The expression "unregistered company" includes inter alia "any association and any company" but not, of course, a company registered in the United Kingdom.[1] It should, however, be noted that an "unregistered company" now no longer includes a partnership.[2] Moreover, these provisions have been held not "to confer on the court jurisdiction to wind up an international organisation established by treaty between sovereign States, including an organisation of which the United Kingdom is itself a member."[3] The expression "unregistered company" does not refer in terms to foreign corporations, but nevertheless it is well settled that they may be wound up under the statutory provisions.[4] The Act expressly provides that an unregistered company may be wound up if it *is dissolved*,[5] and since these words have been construed as equivalent to *has been dissolved*,[6] it follows that the English branch of a Russian bank dissolved many years ago is subject

16 *Re Wells* [1933] Ch 29.
17 *Re Russian Bank for Foreign Trade* [1933] Ch 745 at 764.
18 Previously, these provisions were contained in various Companies Acts.
19 An English court has jurisdiction to wind up any company registered in England: Insolvency Act 1986, s 117(1). There is no jurisdiction to wind up a company registered in Scotland (Insolvency Act 1986, s 120(1)) or Northern Ireland (Insolvency Act 1986, s 441). It may be that there is jurisdiction in the case of a company registered in Northern Ireland which has carried on business in Great Britain, but has now ceased to do so: Dicey & Morris, p 1145. For the effect of winding up orders, both English and foreign, see Dicey & Morris, pp 1147–1152.
20 An unregistered company whose principal place of business is Scotland or Northern Ireland and which has no principal place of business in England is not to be wound up in England: Insolvency Act 1986, s 221(2), (3).
 1 Insolvency Act 1986, s 220.
 2 This is the effect of the Insolvency Act 1985, s 235(3), Sch 10, Pt IV; cf *Russian and English Bank v Baring Brothers & Co* [1936] AC 405 at 432, [1936] 1 All ER 505 at 522.
 3 *Re International Tin Council* [1987] Ch 419 at 451; affd [1988] Ch 309, [1988] 3 All ER 257; a case on ss 665–671 of the Companies Act 1985, now ss 220–226 of the Insolvency Act 1986.
 4 *Re Mercantile Bank of Australia* [1892] 2 Ch 204.
 5 Insolvency Act 1986, s 221(5)(a).
 6 *Re Family Endowment Society* (1870) 5 Ch App 118 at 136.

to this particular jurisdiction of the High Court on the petition either of the branch itself or of a creditor.

In order to invoke the jurisdiction conferred by section 221(5)(a) of the Act, it is not necessary to show that the dissolved company had established a definite branch or place of business in England,[7] nor indeed that it had carried on any business within the jurisdiction,[8] unless, of course, jurisdiction is founded on a past or present carrying on of business within the jurisdiction. Since the object of the section is to provide machinery whereby any assets found in the country may be collected and distributed among the creditors, it follows that proof by the petitioning creditor[9] of the existence of such assets, which frequently will imply the carrying on of business in some sense of the term, is sufficient to justify the making of a winding-up order. This is so even though the sole asset is a claim to the benefit of an insurance policy, the benefit of which will pass directly to the petitioning creditor[10] and will not be available to the liquidator.[11] Where the sole asset is such a claim, it will only found jurisdiction if the petitioning creditor shows that it has a reasonable chance of success.[12] Is it, however, essential to show that there are assets within the jurisdiction? It would appear not, provided that a sufficient connection with the jurisdiction is shown, that there is no more appropriate jurisdiction and that there is a reasonable possibility of benefit to the creditors from the winding up.[13] The jurisdiction conferred by the Act has been invoked on the basis that such reasonable possibility of a benefit could be established from the fact that there were assets coming into the hands of the petitioners in England from an outside source—a state-run redundancy fund—rather than from the company. These assets would only be available once a winding up order had been made.[14]

The difficulties caused by confiscatory legislation in Russia after the revolution of 1917[15] prompted the insertion of an additional section in the Companies Act 1929 which now appears as section 225 in the Insolvency Act 1986. It is to this effect:

> Where a company incorporated outside Great Britain which has been carrying on business in Great Britain ceases to carry on business in Great Britain, it may be wound up as an unregistered company under this Act, notwithstanding that it has been dissolved or otherwise ceased to exist as a company under or by virtue of the laws of the country under which it was incorporated.

The prevalent view is that the section merely confirms a jurisdiction that has long existed and removes any possible doubts as to its exercise in the case of

---

7 *Banque des Marchands de Moscou v Kindersley* [1951] Ch 112, [1950] 2 All ER 549; *Re Azoff-Don Commercial Bank* [1954] Ch 315, [1954] 1 All ER 947; *Re Compania Merabello San Nicholas SA* [1973] Ch 75, [1972] 3 All ER 448.
8 *Re Compania Merabello San Nicholas SA*, supra, at 86–88.
9 *Re Allobrogia SS Corpn* [1978] 3 All ER 423 at 430.
10 Under the Third Parties (Rights against Insurers) Act 1930, s 1(1); as amended by the Insolvency Act 1986, s 439(2) and Sch 14.
11 *Re Compania Merabello San Nicholas SA*, supra; *Re Allobrogia SS Corpn* [1978] 3 All ER 423.
12 *Re Allobrogia SS Corpn*, supra, at 430.
13 *Re A Company (No 00359 of 1987)* [1988] Ch 210.
14 In *Re Eloc Electro-Optieck and Communicatie BV* [1982] Ch 43, [1981] 2 All ER 1111, the company had no assets in England, although it did carry on business here.
15 See, eg, *Re Russian Bank for Foreign Trade* [1933] Ch 745.

such associations as the Russian banks.[16] In particular, its reference to "carrying on business" in Great Britain imposes no limitation on the general jurisdiction conferred by section 221(5)(a).[17] In effect, the words only indicate that some assets on which a winding-up order can operate must be found in Great Britain.

This spectacle of winding up an extinct entity is bound to disturb the logician.[18] He may justifiably ask several questions. How can you liquidate a body that has already been annihilated, unless it has been expressly reanimated by the Act, which is not in fact the case? Since all the assets of a dissolved corporation pass to the Crown as bona vacantia, what remains to be distributed among the creditors? Who are the creditors, what are the debts for it is well settled that debts due to or from a corporation are extinguished on its dissolution?[19] In the leading case of *Russian and English Bank v Baring Brothers & Co* [20] the House of Lords by a bare majority[1] surmounted these difficulties by holding that a dissolved company is implicitly revivified by the Act for winding-up purposes. In the words of Lord ATKIN:[2]

> The legislature has provided that a dissolved foreign corporation may be wound up in accordance with the provisions of the Companies Act. The provisions of the Companies Act as to winding-up are only applicable to corporations which are in existence. Are we to say that the legislative enactment is completely futile: or is there another solution? My Lords, I think that we are entitled to imply, indeed I think it is a necessary implication, that the dissolved foreign company is to be wound up *as though it had not been dissolved*,[3] and therefore continued in existence.

Thus, the consequences normally flowing from the dissolution of a company are disregarded in the English liquidation. The company is an existing person; the liquidator may bring actions on its behalf;[4] and its assets do not pass to the Crown as bona vacantia until the claims of creditors have been satisfied.[5] The doctrine or pretence of revivification, in fact, means that the dissolution, but the dissolution alone, is to be ignored.[6] The results caused solely by the dissolution are reversed. Thus, for example, a creditor may prove for a debt which is recoverable and therefore situated in England, but not for one which is situated in Russia and which has for some reason such as illegality or confiscation been extinguished by Russian law.[7] In such a case, the annihilation of the debt is not due solely to the dissolution of the corporate debtor.

The provision in the Insolvency Act 1986, that a company may be wound up notwithstanding its dissolution in the country of its incorporation, necessarily implies the recognition of the other statutory provisions relating to

16 *Russian and English Bank v Baring Brothers & Co* [1936] AC 405 at 424, [1936] 1 All ER 505 at 516.
17 *Banque des Marchands de Moscou v Kindersley* [1951] Ch 112 at 131, [1950] 2 All ER 549 at 560; *Re Compania Merabello San Nicholas SA,* supra, at 86; and see *IRC v Highland Engineering Ltd* 1975 SLT 203.
18 M Mann (1952) 15 MLR 479; (1955) 18 MLR 8.
19 Blackstone's *Commentaries*, p 484, cited in *Re Higginson and Dean* [1899] 1 QB 325 at 330.
20 [1936] AC 405, [1936] 1 All ER 505.
1 Lords BLANESBURGH, ATKIN, and MACMILLAN.
2 [1936] AC 405 at 427, [1936] 1 All ER 505 at 518.
3 Italics supplied.
4 *Russian and English Bank v Baring Brothers & Co* [1936] AC 405, [1936] 1 All ER 505; *TM Burke Estates Pty Ltd v PJ Constructions (Vic) Pty Ltd* [1991] 1 VR 610.
5 *Re Azoff-Don Commercial Bank* [1954] Ch 315, [1954] 1 All ER 947.
6 M Mann (1954) 3 ICLQ 689, 691.
7 *Re Banque des Marchands de Moscou* [1954] 2 All ER 746, [1954] 1 WLR 1108; M Mann (1954) 3 ICLQ 689.

winding up, including that which directs that the surplus assets of a dissolved company shall be distributed among "the persons entitled to it".[8] In the case of a foreign company, therefore, it must be ascertained whether the law under which it was incorporated recognises the existence of any such persons and if this is found to be the case their rights must be satisfied before the Crown can establish its claim to the surplus as bona vacantia.[9]

A question on which two judges have differed[10] is whether debts alleged to have been contracted in the interregnum between the dissolution of the company and the order for winding-up can rank for payment, since the logical difficulty again arises that the non-existent company was at that time incapable of entering into binding transactions. It is suggested that WYNN-PARRY J reached the correct solution by carrying the doctrine of revivification to its logical conclusion and holding that the dissolution of the company before the creation of the debt must be ignored.[11] In an earlier case, however, which was not brought to the notice of the judge, VAISEY J had reached the opposite conclusion.[12]

8 Insolvency Act 1986, s 154.
9 *Re Banque des Marchands de Moscou (Koupetschesky)* [1958] Ch 182, [1957] 3 All ER 182; M Mann (1958) 21 MLR 95.
10 VAISEY J in *Re Banque des Marchands de Moscou, Wilenkin v The Liquidator* [1952] 1 All ER 1269; WYNN-PARRY J in *Re Russian Commercial and Industrial Bank* [1955] Ch 148, [1955] 1 All ER 75; M Mann (1955) 4 ICLQ 226.
11 *Re Russian Commercial and International Bank*, supra.
12 *Re Banque des Marchands de Moscou, Wilenkin v The Liquidator* [1952] 1 All ER 1269.

Chapter 37

Bankruptcy[1]

1. JURISDICTION OF THE ENGLISH COURTS

(a) INTRODUCTION

Under the Bankruptcy Act 1914, the jurisdiction of the English courts depended, in essence, on the commission of an act of bankruptcy by a debtor, as defined in that Act.[2] Following proposals for the reform of this area of the law,[3] a completely new regime for dealing with insolvency was introduced

---

1 See Smart, *Cross-Border Insolvency* (1991).
2 Bankruptcy Act 1914, s 1(1), (2).
3 Report of the Review Committee on Insolvency Law and Practice (1982), Cmnd 8558. Paragraphs 529–533 and 1902–1913 are particularly relevant in the present context.

by the Insolvency Act 1985, since consolidated in the Insolvency Act 1986.[4] It is with the rules for the jurisdiction of the English courts[5] provided by the 1986 Act[6] that we will here be concerned.

(b) PETITIONS BY CREDITORS OR THE DEBTOR

There are four main bases of jurisdiction laid down by section 265 of the Insolvency Act 1986 for the presentation of a bankruptcy petition by the debtor himself or by a creditor.[7] Such a bankruptcy petition cannot be presented to the English courts unless the debtor is connected with England by either domicil, presence, residence or carrying on business here. All require a link between the debtor and England; no longer can jurisdiction depend on the commission of an act of bankruptcy. Each of the four connecting factors will be examined in turn.

(i) Domicil

The domicil of the debtor in England and Wales at the date of the commencement of the proceedings suffices to confer jurisdiction.[8]

(ii) Presence

The court has jurisdiction if the debtor was personally present in England and Wales on the day on which the petition was presented.[9] This could work injustice in the case of a petition by a creditor where the debtor was merely a transitory visitor here; but that is now[10] a matter for the discretion of the court.[11]

(iii) Residence

If the debtor has either been ordinarily resident, or has had a place of residence, in England and Wales at any time in the three years immediately preceding the presentation of the petition, the court may assume jurisdiction.[12] The residence requirement does not have to be satisfied for the whole of the three years; it is sufficient if it existed at any time during that period. So the court would have jurisdiction over someone who never visited

4 A draft EEC Bankruptcy Convention has been under consideration in the EEC for some 20 years—see Hunter (1972) 21 ICLQ 682; (1976) 25 ICLQ 301; Report of the Advisory Committee on the EEC Bankruptcy Convention (1976), Cmnd 6602; Fletcher, *Conflict of Laws and European Community Law*, (1982) ch 6, and appendix C of this book which reproduces the latest (1980) published draft of the Convention. Agreement on a final Convention still seems remote. Activity has now moved to the Council of Europe; see the European Convention on Certain International Aspects of Bankruptcy (1990), 30 ILM 165 (1991) and see Graham [1989] CLP 217, 226–227.
5 This includes both the High Court and county courts: Insolvency Act 1986, s 373. Leave to serve the debtor out of the jurisdiction is governed by the Insolvency Rules, 1986, r 12.12.
6 Bankruptcy falls outside the Conventions appended to the Civil Jurisdiction and Judgments Acts 1982 and 1991, see Art 1(2), supra, p 289.
7 Under s 264(1)(a), (b) of the Insolvency Act 1986. For jurisdiction over other petitions, see infra, p 906. In all cases the exercise of jurisdiction is discretionary, see infra, p 906.
8 S 265(1)(a).
9 S 265(1)(b).
10 There was no jurisdiction in such circumstances under the Bankruptcy Act 1914, by reason of s 4(1)(d).
11 Infra, p 906.
12 S 265(1)(c)(i).

England in the three year period and sold his residence here two years before the proceedings began.

(iv) Carrying on business here

The English court has jurisdiction if the debtor has carried on business in England and Wales at any time in the three years preceding the presentation of the petition.[13] Furthermore, this extends to the case where the business was carried on by a firm or partnership of which the debtor was a member, or by an agent or manager for the debtor or such a firm or partnership.[14] As was the situation under the Bankruptcy Act 1914,[15] the court will have jurisdiction over a debtor on the basis of business carried on here, even though the debtor is not now here, nor has ever been here.[16]

(c) OTHER PETITIONS

It is possible for a bankruptcy petition to be presented either by any person (other than the debtor) who is bound by a voluntary arrangement proposed by the debtor and approved under Part VIII of the 1986 Act, or by the supervisor of such an arrangement.[17] A petition can also be presented after the making of a criminal bankruptcy order.[18] No jurisdictional rules are laid down by the 1986 Act in these cases, but it has been suggested[19] that in the case of a voluntary arrangement the debtor can be presumed to have submitted to the jurisdiction of the court. Furthermore, a creditor who is party to a voluntary arrangement may petition in this capacity even though no necessary jurisdictional link with the debtor exists.[20]

(d) DISCRETION

There seems little doubt that the jurisdiction of the courts under the Insolvency Act 1986 is discretionary, as it was under the Bankruptcy Act 1914.[21] Indeed, section 266(3) of the 1986 Act gives the court broad powers to dismiss or stay bankruptcy proceedings.

(e) CONCURRENT BANKRUPTCIES

A discretion to stay English bankruptcy proceedings may be very relevant in the case where, at the time of the English proceedings, there are, or have been, bankruptcy proceedings in a foreign country.[1] In some countries the doctrine of unity of bankruptcy prevails so that proceedings in the domicil of the debtor or of his place of business take precedence over all others.[2] This

---

13 S 265(1)(c)(ii).
14 S 265(2).
15 S 1(2).
16 See *Theophile v Solicitor-General* [1950] AC 186, [1950] 1 All ER 405; *Re Bird* [1962] 2 All ER 406, [1962] 1 WLR 686.
17 S 264(1)(c).
18 S 264(1)(d).
19 Dicey and Morris, p 1096.
20 S 266(1).
21 *Re McCulloch, ex p McCulloch* (1880) 14 ChD 716; *Re Artola Hermanos* (1890) 24 QBD 640; *Re A Debtor (No 737 of 1928)* [1929] 1 Ch 362.
1 See Smart [1989] JBL 126, who argues that greater general willingness to stay English proceedings on the basis of *forum non conveniens* (discussed supra, pp 221 et seq) should be extended to bankruptcy proceedings.
2 See *Re Artola Hermanos* (1890) 24 QBD 640 at 648–649.

doctrine has not been accepted in England, however theoretically convenient it may be.[3] There is no case where the court has stayed bankruptcy proceedings on this ground alone, rather than because, for example, there were no assets here. Similarly, the idea that the proceedings which are first in time should prevail has been rejected.[4] If there is to be one principal administration, a case can be made for it being in the place where the assets are chiefly situated or where the debtor, if a trader, had his main business headquarters; but neither of these facts may be true of the country in which proceedings are first started.

The principle that is adopted in English law is to accept that there will be separate independent bankruptcies in each jurisdiction. The English court will administer the assets situated in England, according to the rules set out in the Insolvency Act 1986, without regard to administrations that may be in progress in other countries, though it recognises the claims of all creditors, foreign as well as English. This does not mean, however, that the status of a foreign trustee in bankruptcy is disregarded. Though English law rejects the doctrine of unity it recognises the doctrine of universality, that is, as we shall see below,[5] it admits that the title of a foreign trustee extends to such movables of the debtor as are found in England, provided that no bankruptcy proceedings have been begun within the jurisdiction.

We have seen that the English court has a discretion to decline jurisdiction if an inequitable use is being made of the English statute,[6] but the existence of similar proceedings abroad is not of itself a valid reason for a refusal to exercise jurisdiction here. Jurisdiction, however, will be refused where an adjudication would be useless and embarrassing, as, for instance, where proceedings have been started abroad and there are no assets in England.[7] The principle that English jurisdiction is not ousted by the mere existence of foreign proceedings would seem to apply not only where the debtor himself has set the foreign court in motion but also where the creditors have started proceedings abroad.[8]

2. EFFECT OF AN ENGLISH ADJUDICATION IN BANKRUPTCY

(a) GENERAL

The Insolvency Act 1986 provides[9] that the estate of a bankrupt shall vest in his trustees. His estate is very widely defined[10] and extends essentially to all of his "property", which term, according to section 436, includes "money, goods, things in action, land and every description of property *wherever situated*."[11] It will be noticed that the 1986 Act expressly and deliberately attributes a very extensive effect to an English adjudication. Not only movables, but even immovables, belonging to the bankrupt "wherever situated",

---

3 Ibid, at 645.
4 Ibid, at 649.
5 Infra, pp 912–914.
6 Supra, p 906.
7 *Re Robinson, ex p Robinson* (1883) 22 ChD 816.
8 *Re a Debtor (No 199 of 1922)* [1922] 2 Ch 470.
9 S 306.
10 S 282.
11 Italics added.

ie whether in England or elsewhere, are to pass to the trustee.[12]

Whether the transfer of property abroad can actually be effected is another matter. Although there was a view that Commonwealth countries were obliged to give effect to similar provisions under the Bankruptcy Act 1914 and earlier legislation as "imperial statutes",[13] this view cannot be sustained in relation to the Insolvency Act 1986. It is clear that an English adjudication cannot of its own force have any effect on property situated in, say, Australia or France, and it has been suggested that it is unlikely that a court in a foreign country would permit property there to be used for the payment of United Kingdom taxes owed by the bankrupt.[14] Furthermore, if the English bankruptcy purports to act as an assignment of property abroad, it will only do so subject to any charges or liabilities attaching to the property under the law of the situs.[15]

(b) STATUTORY PROVISIONS ASSISTING THE TRUSTEE

The trustee is not, however, without steps which he can take to ensure that foreign property of the bankrupt vests in him. The powers of the trustees under English law are very wide-ranging in relation to the property of the bankrupt,[16] and it is provided specifically that nothing in the Insolvency Act 1986 is to be construed as restricting the capacity of the trustee to exercise his powers outside England and Wales.[17]

More important are the powers conferred by section 426 of the Insolvency Act 1986[18] in relation to the co-operation between courts and administrators both in the United Kingdom and elsewhere for ensuring that a trustee in bankruptcy in one country may secure property in another. These powers not only assist an English trustee in relation to property elsewhere, but apply also to a foreign trustee seeking to acquire property in England. They are discussed more fully below.[1]

(c) POSITION OF CREDITOR WHO RECOVERS DEBT ABROAD

There is one type of case in which the operation on foreign property of an English adjudication is of some practical importance, and in which the theory that the Insolvency Act 1986 embraces property wherever situated demands consideration. This is where a creditor recovers payment abroad from a debtor who has previously been made bankrupt in England. Can the English court make such a creditor disgorge what he has obtained? It is clear that the court is powerless if the creditor remains abroad; but what if he comes to England? Although the reported cases are old, they would still seem to be relevant to bankruptcies falling within the 1986 Act.

In this connection one rule is clearly established, namely, that a creditor, whether British or foreign, will not be allowed to claim in the English

---

12 The inclusion of immovables means that a wider effect is given to an English bankruptcy than an English court will, apart from statute, accord to a foreign bankruptcy, see infra, pp 912–914
13 Eg *Callender, Sykes & Co v Colonial Secretary of Lagos* [1891] AC 460 at 467; and see *Re Reilly* [1942] IR 416.
14 See *Re Gibbons, ex p Walter* [1960] Ir Jur Rep 60; cf *Ayres v Evans* (1981) 39 ALR 129.
15 Eg *Murphy's Trustee v Aitken* 1983 SLT 78.
16 Insolvency Act 1986, ss 306–314.
17 S 314(8).
18 See Woloniecki (1986) 35 ICLQ 644.
1 Infra, pp 915–916.

bankruptcy for any further debts unless he brings into hotchpot what he has already recovered abroad.[2]

So much is clear. The difficult question remains, however, whether a creditor who has obtained payment abroad, whether by action or not, and who does not seek to participate in the English bankruptcy, can be made to disgorge what he has recovered, on the ground that he has diminished the fund available for the general body of creditors. There are three cases, all decided between 1791 and 1795, in which the issue was raised. The first of these is *Sill v Worswick:*[3]

X, a domiciled Englishman, was adjudicated bankrupt at Lancaster, Sill being appointed trustee. Worswick, another domiciled Englishman, after and with full knowledge of the bankruptcy, made an affidavit before the Mayor of Lancaster of X's indebtedness to him, and on the strength of this brought an action in the British West Indies against a person who held certain moneys of X, and recovered in full the debt which was due to him from X.

It was held that the trustee could recover the amount in an action for money had and received.

The greater part of Lord LOUGHBOROUGH's judgment was occupied with showing that, since movable property is subject to the law of the owner's domicil, an adjudication made in the country of that domicil embraces property in any part of the world. This principle does not carry us far; for the problem is to discover the circumstances in which a creditor who has acted in disregard of it can be compelled to disgorge. On this, which is the sole issue of the case, the judge laid down a proposition which, he said, was too clear to require any discussion, namely, that a creditor, resident in England and therefore subject to the jurisdiction of the English court, cannot avail himself of a process which he has commenced in England so as to retain his debt against the trustee.

The facts which make it difficult to extract a general principle from this decision are that the diligent creditor started his proceedings for recovery in England, and also that the place of final recovery was within the dominions of the Crown. The crucial factor was the English residence of the creditor. Had he been resident in the West Indies, Lord LOUGHBOROUGH clearly intimated that the trustee would have had no right of action.[4]

The second decision is *Hunter v Potts:*[5]

The creditor and the bankrupt were both resident in England. After the bankruptcy and with knowledge of it, the creditor instructed his attorney in America to attach the effects of the bankrupt in Rhode Island. The attorney attached in the regular way certain money in the hands of X which was due to the bankrupt, and later obtained in the Court of Common Pleas at Rhode Island judgment against the bankrupt for £496 12s 9d, which sum he remitted to the creditor in England.

The King's Bench held that the trustee was entitled to recover this sum in an action for money had and received.

2 *Re Douglas, ex p Wilson* (1872) 7 Ch App 490; *Banco de Portugal v Waddell* (1880) 5 App Cas 161.
3 (1791) 1 Hy Bl 665.
4 Ibid, at 693. This seems to have been decided in *Waring v Knight*, see (1795) 2 Hy Bl 402 at 413.
5 (1791) 4 Term Rep 182.

Lord KENYON, in delivering the judgment of the court, was at pains to demonstrate why the English adjudication had to pass the property in Rhode Island to the trustee, but the true ground of the decision is indicated in the following sentence:

> For it must be remembered, that during the progress of this business all these parties resided in England; that the defendant, knowing of the commission and of the assignment, in order to gain a priority, transmitted an affidavit to Rhode Island to obtain an attachment of the bankrupt's property there, in violation of the rights of the rest of the creditors, which were then vested; but such an attempt cannot be sanctioned in a Court of Law.[6]

The third case is *Phillips v Hunter*[7] where the facts were as follows:

> A, B and C were trading partners in England. A and B were resident here, but C went to the USA to manage there the affairs of the partnership. D, who was also resident in England, contracted a debt here to A, B and C. However, D became insolvent and C, knowing that D had stopped payment of his debt and, after D had in England been declared bankrupt, took steps in the USA to protect the partners. In the name of all three of them, C attached a debt due to D in the USA and C obtained payment of the debt under the judgment of a court in Pennsylvania.

On these facts the Exchequer Chamber held by six judgments to one, there being a trenchant dissenting judgment by EYRE CJ, that the English trustee in bankruptcy was entitled to recover the money in an action against A, B and C for money had and received. The gist of the judgments of the majority is deducible from the following sentences:[8]

> It must be remembered that ... the bankrupts were English traders, that the defendants were partners in an English house, that the debt from the bankrupts to the defendants was contracted in England, that the bankrupts as well as the defendants were resident in England, and that [C], who ... must also be taken to be an English subject, went from this kingdom to America, for the special and temporary purpose of transacting business for the English house ... in which he continued to be a partner. ... All these facts appearing ... this case must be argued as arising between English subjects upon English property. When the debt therefore was contracted, all the parties were as much subject to the bankrupt laws, as to the other laws of England under which they lived.

In a later part of the judgment it is said that if a debtor's foreign property could be obtained by a creditor's *going from hence for that purpose*, the result would be damaging to the credit of the debtor in England.

It is submitted that the true principle deducible from these authorities is a very simple one, namely: Is the creditor subject to the English bankruptcy law or is he not? If he is subject to English bankruptcy jurisdiction, he is liable to refund what he has recovered abroad; if not subject to the jurisdiction he is immune from liability, unless, of course, he seeks to prove in the bankruptcy. But though the principle submitted is a simple one, its defect perhaps is the difficulty of defining with precision what is meant by subjection to the English bankruptcy jurisdiction. It would seem only equitable that the jurisdiction cannot be exercised against a *creditor* unless the same conditions are applicable to him at the time when he receives the payment as are

6 Ibid, at 194.
7 (1795) 2 Hy Bl 402.
8 Ibid, at 404–405.

applicable to jurisdiction over the debtor.[9] Logically, it is difficult to believe that the court possesses a wider jurisdiction over a creditor than over a debtor against whom an adjudication order is sought.[10]

3. CHOICE OF LAW

We have already noticed that a foreigner is entitled to prove in an English bankruptcy even though the debt which he claims was contracted abroad. He is, however, in exactly the same position as English creditors with regard to all matters that concern the administration of the estate. The duty of the trustee is to distribute the estate among all creditors, whether English or foreign, but all questions arising in connection with the distribution fall to be decided by English law as being the law of the forum. The law which distributes the assets must necessarily regulate the manner and course of distribution.

Thus, whether a debt is admissible of proof,[11] whether a creditor of a partnership can prove against the separate estate of an individual partner,[12] whether a foreign creditor who proves in the bankruptcy can be compelled to restore property that he has improperly obtained from the debtor,[13] and questions of priority of payment,[14] are all matters that must be governed by the law of the forum.[15] However, the issue as to what property may pass to the trustee and whether it is subject to charges or liabilities is a matter for the law of the situs.[16]

4. EFFECT IN ENGLAND OF A FOREIGN ADJUDICATION IN BANKRUPTCY

(a) ADJUDICATION IN SCOTLAND AND NORTHERN IRELAND

In considering the extent to which a foreign adjudication (or some analogous process) operates in England it is necessary to notice that adjudications in Scotland[17] and Northern Ireland[18] stand in a somewhat different position from those in other countries. The title of a trustee appointed in either one of these countries extends not only to the movables of the debtor but also to his immovables, no matter where they may be situated.[19] Thus, an English court would recognise that an adjudication in one of those jurisdictions had

9 Insolvency Act 1986, s 265, supra, pp 905–906.
10 Blom-Cooper, *Bankruptcy in Private International Law* (1954), pp 130 et seq; cf Dicey & Morris, pp 1110–1111, where it is suggested that the sole criterion is residence in England at the time of receipt of the payment; and see Nygh, p 487.
11 *Re Melbourn, ex p Melbourn* (1870) 6 Ch App 64.
12 *Brickwood v Miller* (1817) 3 Mer 279; cf *Re Doetsch* [1896] 2 Ch 836.
13 *Re Morton* (1875) LR 20 Eq 733.
14 *Thurburn v Steward* (1871) LR 3 PC 478; *Re Sefel Geophysical Ltd* (1988) 54 DLR (4th) 117.
15 As to the difficulty of distinguishing between administration, ie procedure, and substance see Blom-Cooper, op cit, pp 141 et seq.
16 *Murphy's Trustee v Aitken* 1983 SLT 78.
17 Bankruptcy (Scotland) Act 1985.
18 Bankruptcy and Insolvency (Ireland) Act 1857.
19 Anton, p 733; cf Dicey & Morris, pp 1118–1119.

passed to the trustee property situated in England and, probably, elsewhere.[20] However, any property in England will pass to the trustee in Scotland or Northern Ireland subject to any prior charges or liabilities.[21]

It seems clear that the English courts cannot question the jurisdiction of the courts in Scotland or Northern Ireland to make a bankruptcy order, because section 426(1) of the Insolvency Act 1986 provides that an order made in one part of the United Kingdom shall be enforced in the other part of the United Kingdom as if made there.[1] There is, however, a significant qualification to this provision which relates to the effectiveness of Scottish and Northern Ireland orders in England. The 1986 Act provides[2] that nothing in section 426(1) requires the *enforcement* of an order from another part of the United Kingdom in relation to property situated in England. So, although an English court may recognise that title has passed to the trustee under a Scottish bankruptcy, enforcement of his claim in England will still be a matter for the discretion of the English courts, but subject to the other provisions of section 426 relating to mutual judicial assistance in bankruptcy matters within the United Kingdom.[3]

(b) ADJUDICATION IN A FOREIGN COUNTRY

With regard to adjudications in countries outside the United Kingdom,[4] the question is whether the status of a foreign trustee is so far recognised by English law that he acquires a title to the bankrupt's property in England. Does the assignment of the bankrupt's property that has been made to the trustee by the foreign law under which he has been appointed entitle him to the English property, or is it necessary that there should be an independent adjudication in this country?

The English courts have consistently applied the doctrine of *universality*, according to which they hold that all *movable* property, no matter where it may be situated at the time of the assignment by the foreign law, passes to the trustee.[5] Thus the trustee can recover movables, including choses in action, found in England, and his title is not displaced if a creditor, after commencement of the bankruptcy, attaches property of the bankrupt by process of law in England. This doctrine is of ancient origin. In *Solomons v Ross*,[6] the facts were these:

X & Co, Dutch merchants, were declared bankrupt on 2 January 1794 and

---

20 The decision in *Galbraith v Grimshaw* [1910] AC 508 that, in the case of a Scottish bankruptcy, the Scottish trustee could neither rely on the English rule of relation-back because that only applied to English bankruptcies nor on the Scottish rules for equalising differences has been criticised by Anton, p 734.

21 Cf *Murphy's Trustee v Aitken* 1983 SLT 78.

1 Judgments given in bankruptcy or insolvency proceedings are excluded from the provisions in the Civil Jurisdiction and Judgments Act 1982 for the enforcement of other United Kingdom judgments; see s 18(3)(ba) (added by the Insolvency Act 1985, Sch 8, para 36 and amended by the Insolvency Act 1986, Sch 14) and s 18(3)(c)(i).

2 Insolvency Act 1986, s 426(2).

3 Infra, p 915.

4 For discussion of the undeveloped rules as to the jurisdictional circumstances in which English courts will recognise foreign bankruptcy decisions, see Dicey & Morris, pp 1115–1117; and see Smart (1989) 9 OJLS 557.

5 *Solomons v Ross* (1764) 1 Hy Bl 131n; *Jollett v Deponthieu* (1769) 1 Hy Bl 132n; *Alivon v Furnival* (1834) 1 Cr M & R 277.

6 (1764) 1 Hy Bl 131 n. For a full account and an evaluation of the case, see Nadelmann (1946) 9 MLR 154, who refers to another and a fuller report in Wallis's *Irish Chancery Reports* (1839) 59n.

Y was appointed curator of their property by the Chamber of Desolate Estates in Amsterdam. Previously, on 20 December 1793, Z, an English creditor of X & Co, had attached £1,200 in the hands of A which was due from A to X & Co. In March 1794 Z obtained judgment by default on the attachment, whereupon a writ of execution was issued against A. Being unable to pay, A gave Z a promissory note for the amount of the judgment. In proceedings brought by the curator, Y, it was held that A must pay the £1,200 to Y, and that the execution creditor, Z, must surrender the promissory note to A.

It was emphasised in the judgment, at least in one report of the case,[7] that Dutch law, in the event of a Dutch bankruptcy, permitted foreign creditors to share the assets equally with local creditors. It is not certain, therefore, that the English court would follow the decision if the trustee were appointed in a country where there is discrimination against foreign creditors.[8]

The courts, however, have not accepted the suggestion made in the decision that the title of the foreign trustee overrides encumbrances already acquired by third parties over property of the bankrupt situated in England. If, for instance, X obtains a garnishee order attaching a debt owed in England by A to B and B is *later* declared bankrupt abroad, the attachment ranks prior to the title of the foreign trustee.[9]

> In each case the question will be whether the bankrupt could have assigned to the trustee, at the date when the trustee's title accrued, the debt or assets in question situated in England.[10]

One difficult question is—What is meant by a "foreign trustee"? The original rule probably was that, for the doctrine of universality to apply, the trustee must be a person appointed by the law of the bankrupt's domicil. The very principle, indeed, upon which the doctrine was based found its justification in the conception of domicil. The argument was that movable property, having no locality, was subject to the law of the owner's domicil. Since a voluntary assignment valid according to the law of the owner's domicil was supposed to be effective everywhere, it was said that an involuntary assignment under the bankruptcy laws of that domicil must of necessity be equally effective. The modern cases, however, establish that a foreign trustee need not derive his title from the law of the bankrupt's domicil in order to substantiate his claim to English movables. Perhaps all that can be said positively is that it is sufficient if the bankrupt was "properly subject" to the jurisdiction of the courts of the country in which he has been made bankrupt, though it has been objected with some force that this is to beg the question.[11] It may be that the possession by the bankrupt of assets in the country of adjudication will entitle the trustee to claim movables in England.[12] What is certain is that he will be able to do so if the bankrupt was domiciled in that foreign country[13] or has been a party to the foreign proceedings in which the

7 The Irish report mentioned in the last note.
8 Nadelmann (1946) 9 MLR 154, 163 et seq.
9 *Galbraith v Grimshaw* [1910] AC 508; *Singer & Co v Fry* (1915) 84 LJKB 2025; *Anantapadmanabhaswami v Official Receiver of Secunderabad* [1933] AC 394; and see *Murphy's Trustee v Aitken* 1983 SLT 78.
10 *Galbraith v Grimshaw*, supra, at 510–511.
11 Blom-Cooper, op cit, p 91.
12 Ibid, p 92; cf *Re Artola Hermanos* (1890) 24 QBD 640 at 649.
13 *Re Blithman* (1866) LR 2 Eq 23. For the abandonment of the theory that bankruptcy in the debtor's domicil was essential, see Raeburn (1949) 26 BYBIL 177, 189 et seq.

adjudication order was made.[14] In the case of *Re Anderson*:[15]

A domiciled Englishman, who was entitled to a reversionary interest in English money, was adjudicated bankrupt in New Zealand in proceedings to which he was a party. By an oversight, the reversionary interest was not disclosed in the New Zealand proceedings. Six years later the debtor was declared bankrupt in England.

It was held that the New Zealand trustee, despite the fact that he was not appointed in the bankrupt's domicil, was entitled to the reversionary interest as against the English trustee.

Therefore, I think [said PHILLIMORE J] upon principle and authority, that the adjudication in New Zealand, being a valid adjudication according to the law of New Zealand, passed the right to movable property of the bankrupt in any country to his official assignee in bankruptcy in New Zealand. If he had not been a party to the adjudication, if it had been made against him in his absence, other considerations might very well have applied.[16]

The principle of universality does not apply to immovables situated in England;[17] but the English court may, in the exercise of its discretionary jurisdiction, make an order permitting a foreign curator or trustee to sell land situated in England for the benefit of the bankrupt owner's creditors.[18] The court may be assisted in so acting by the mutual support provisions of section 426 of the Insolvency Act 1986,[19] but it would seem able to make such an order in favour of a foreign trustee without having to rely on that section.[20]

(c) CONCURRENT BANKRUPTCIES

There may be concurrent bankruptcy proceedings in England and some foreign country. In such a case, where the adjudications in the two jurisdictions are almost simultaneous, the English court has a general jurisdiction to sanction an agreement between the English and foreign trustees in bankruptcy, providing for the pooling of all assets and for their rateable distribution between the English and foreign creditors.[1] If the two bankruptcy adjudications are successive and separated in time, a problem arises as to whether assets which are acquired, disclosed or discovered between the two adjudications shall be paid to the first or second trustee in bankruptcy. If both were English bankruptcies the assets would pass to the second trustee;[2] but if one is a foreign bankruptcy, whether it be the earlier or the later, the assets pass to the first trustee.[3]

---

14 *Re Davidson's Settlement Trusts* (1873) LR 15 Eq 383; *Re Lawson's Trusts* [1896] 1 Ch 175; *Re Anderson* [1911] 1 KB 896; *Re Craig* (1916) 86 LJ Ch 62; *Bergerem v Marsh* (1921) 125 LT 630.
15 [1911] 1 KB 896; see also *Re Temple* [1947] Ch 345; *Re C A Kennedy Co Ltd and Stibbe-Monk Ltd* (1977) 74 DLR (3d) 87.
16 [1911] 1 KB 896 at 902.
17 *Waite v Bingley* (1882) 21 Ch D 674 at 681–682; *Re Levy's Trusts* (1885) 30 ChD 119 at 123.
18 *Re Kooperman* [1928] WN 101; and *see Re Osborn* [1931–32] B & CR 189; *cf Schemmer v Property Resources Ltd* [1975] Ch 273, [1974] 3 All ER 451.
19 Infra, pp 915–916.
20 Cf *Re Kooperman* [1920] WN 101; Woloniecki (1986) 35 ICLQ 644, 647.
 1 *Re P Macfadyen & Co, ex p Vizianagaram* [1908] 1 KB 675.
 2 Insolvency Act 1986, ss 334–335.
 3 *Re Anderson, supra; Re Temple, supra;* but see Blom-Cooper, op cit, pp 111–116.

5. MUTUAL ASSISTANCE

Section 426 of the Insolvency Act 1986[4] provides a variety of ways in which courts and administrators in one country may provide assistance to a trustee in bankruptcy from another country who wishes to exercise control over property in the first country. It is convenient to examine these provisions first in relation to assistance within the United Kingdom and then in relation to foreign countries.

(a) ASSISTANCE WITHIN THE UNITED KINGDOM

Although a bankruptcy order made in one part of the United Kingdom must be recognised in another part of the United Kingdom as if made there,[5] this does not require a court in that other part to enforce the order in relation to property there.[6] However, an English court, for example, could seek assistance from a court in Scotland or Northern Ireland under section 426(4) of the Insolvency Act 1986 which provides that:

> The courts having jurisdiction in relation to insolvency law in any part of the United Kingdom shall assist the courts having the corresponding jurisdiction in any other part of the United Kingdom or any relevant country or territory.

If a request for assistance is made by an English court to one in Scotland or Northern Ireland, for example, to secure property there for the benefit of the English trustee, the Scottish or Northern Ireland court is given[7] a discretion to apply either its own, or English, insolvency law; but in exercising its discretion, that court "shall have regard in particular to the rules of private international law", whatever that may mean.[8] There seems little doubt that assistance under section 426(4) can include the claiming of property in Scotland or Northern Ireland.[9] Similarly an English court is obliged to provide assistance when requested by a Scottish or Northern Ireland court.

A further way in which assistance might be given in one part of the United Kingdom to a trustee appointed in another part is provided by section 426(3) of the 1986 Act under which the Secretary of State may by order make provision that a trustee under the insolvency law of one part of the United Kingdom has the same rights in regard to property in another part of the United Kingdom as if he were a trustee under the insolvency law[10] of that other part. So an English trustee could, under this reciprocal provision, have the same rights over property in Scotland as his Scottish counterpart,[11] and vice versa.

(b) ASSISTANCE BETWEEN THE UNITED KINGDOM AND OTHER COUNTRIES

The scheme for the provision of mutual assistance between United Kingdom courts under section 426(4) and (5)[12] also extends to assistance for and from

---

4 See Woloniecki (1986) 35 ICLQ 644; Smart (1990) 39 ICLQ 827, 844–853; Miller [1991] JBL 144.
5 Insolvency Act 1986, s 426(1).
6 Ibid, s 426(2).
7 Ibid, s 426(5).
8 Woloniecki (1986) 35 ICLQ 644, 654–661; Graham [1989] CLP 217, 225.
9 S 426(5).
10 See s 426(10).
11 If the English trustee submits a claim to the Scottish court, it is to be treated (by reason of s 426(5)) as if it was a request for assistance under s 426(4).
12 Supra.

courts in "any relevant country or territory". This means the Channel Islands, the Isle of Man and any foreign country or territory designated by the Secretary of State.[13] Section 426(4) and (5) may be rather more difficult to apply in relation to a foreign country than to a part of the United Kingdom, because it will be necessary to decide which aspects of the foreign insolvency law "correspond" to the equivalent provisions of the law of the relevant part of the United Kingdom.[14] Furthermore in the case, for example, of a request to the English court for assistance, the English court will have to decide how to exercise its discretion whether to apply English law or the foreign law and the only guidance provided is, again, to have regard to rules of private international law.[15]

6. DISCHARGE

Since the effect of a discharge in bankruptcy is to free the debtor from liabilities incurred prior to the order of discharge, it is important to know whether a discharge in one country is an effective plea in another. Where must the order of discharge be made in order to have universal effect? The answer that English law makes to this question depends on whether or not the order is made under the provisions of the English statute,[16] or the equivalent Scottish[17] or Northern Ireland[18] legislation or in a foreign bankruptcy.

(a) DISCHARGE UNDER AN ENGLISH BANKRUPTCY

If the bankruptcy occurs in England, any order of discharge that is made releases the debtor from all debts, whether or not governed by English law, which are provable in bankruptcy.[19] The discharge is effective, no matter what may be the proper law of the transaction under which the cause of action arose[20] for "an English certificate is usually a discharge as against all the world in the English courts".[1]

(b) DISCHARGE UNDER A SCOTTISH OR NORTHERN IRELAND BANKRUPTCY

A discharge under a Scottish[2] or Northern Ireland[3] bankruptcy will have effect as a discharge in England, whatever may be the proper law of the debt. The reason for this is that bankruptcy legislation in these two jurisdictions is legislation of the United Kingdom Parliament, effective in England.[4] Indeed, express provision is made in section 55 of the Bankruptcy (Scotland) Act

---

13 S 426(11).
14 S 426(10).
15 S 426(5).
16 Insolvency Act 1986.
17 Bankruptcy (Scotland) Act 1985.
18 Bankruptcy and Insolvency (Ireland) Act 1857.
19 Insolvency Act 1986, s 281(1).
20 Dicey & Morris, pp 1113–1115.
 1 *Armani v Castrique* (1844) 13 M & W 443 at 447; and see *Ellis v M'Henry* (1871) LR 6 CP 228 at 234–236; and see the authorities there cited.
 2 *Sidaway v Hay* (1824) 3 B & C 12; see Bankruptcy (Scotland) Act 1985.
 3 *Simpson v Mirabita* (1869) LR 4 QB 257; see Bankruptcy and Insolvency (Ireland) Act 1857.
 4 If any provisions of that legislation can be shown not to operate extra-territorially, then they will be ineffective in England: *Re Nelson, ex p Dare and Dolphin* [1918] 1 KB 459.

1985 to the effect that a discharge under that Act shall constitute a discharge throughout the United Kingdom.

(c) DISCHARGE UNDER A FOREIGN BANKRUPTCY

Where the discharge is not made under United Kingdom bankruptcy legislation but is made under the law of some foreign country, as, for example, where a debtor is discharged in France, the effect here of the discharge depends on the law that governs the obligation. If the order of discharge is made under the proper law of the debt or other liability in question, it is effective in England;[5] if made under any other law, it is ineffective in England.[6] A comparison between the effect in England of a discharge under a United Kingdom bankruptcy and a discharge under a foreign bankruptcy reveals the following situation. A discharge under an English bankruptcy is a discharge from a debt governed by French law; but a discharge under a French bankruptcy will not constitute a valid discharge in England unless it amounts to a valid discharge under the law governing the contract. The rule that a discharge by that law, and only by that law in the case of a discharge in a foreign country, is a discharge everywhere may be illustrated by *Gardiner v Houghton*:[7]

> It was pleaded to an action for money had and received that the debt was contracted in Victoria, Australia, while the defendant was resident there, and that he was subsequently discharged from the debt under the insolvency laws of Victoria. The response to the plea was that when the debt was contracted the *plaintiff* was resident at Liverpool; that the defendant was now resident in England; and that the debt ought to have been paid in England.

It was held that the response showed no answer, for it admitted that the contract was made in Victoria and it did not aver that the debt was payable only in England. In other words, it did not disprove that Victorian law was the proper law of the debt.

That a discharge under some law other than the law governing the contract is devoid of extra-territorial effect is well illustrated by *Gibbs & Son v Société Industrielle des Métaux*:[8]

> In that case the defendants, a French company, made a contract through their London broker for the purchase of copper from the plaintiffs, London dealers. The contract, besides being made in London, was expressed to be subject to the rules of the London Metal Exchange; delivery was to be at Liverpool; and payment was to be made in cash in London. It was therefore an English contract. In an action brought for non-acceptance of the copper, the defendants pleaded that by a judgment of a French court they had been pronounced to be in judicial liquidation. Assuming that by French law this pronouncement discharged the defendants from all liability under the contract, the question was whether it had the same effect in England so as to bar the plaintiffs' right to sue here.

The argument for the defendants was based on the French domicil of the

5 *Ellis v M'Henry*, supra, at 234, and authorities there cited.
6 *Gibbs & Son v Société Industrielle des Métaux* (1890) 25 QBD 399; and see *Smith v Buchanan* (1800) 1 East 6.
7 (1862) 2 B & S 743.
8 (1890) 25 QBD 399.

company. It was said that, when a debtor is domiciled in a foreign country and made bankrupt there, then any rule of the foreign bankruptcy law which prevents actions from being maintained against the debtor is recognised in England. This argument did not prevail and judgment was entered for the plaintiffs, as there had been no discharge under English law.

One problem resulting from the conclusion that the law governing the contract is to govern the effectiveness in England of a foreign discharge is this. Although a foreign discharge order, ineffective under the law applicable to the contract is regarded as ineffective in England and the debtor is still liable in England on his debt, nevertheless English law will recognise the foreign adjudication[9] as having passed the debtor's assets to his foreign trustee in bankruptcy. The debtor has lost his assets but not his liability. One solution is that the foreign discharge should be regarded as effective in England if recognised as effective by the country of the applicable law;[10] but the problem remains where such recognition is not possible.

---

9 At least where the jurisdiction of the foreign court is recognised in England; supra, pp 913–914.
10 Dicey & Morris, pp 1125–1126.

Index